PRESCHOOL PERIOD (3 to 6 years)	MIDDLE CHILDHOOD (6 to 12 years)
• Height and weight continue to increase rapidly. • The body becomes less rounded and more muscular. • The brain grows larger, neural interconnections continue to develop, and lateralization emerges. • Gross and fine motor skills advance quickly. Children can throw and catch balls, run, use forks and spoons, and tie shoelaces. • Children begin to develop handedness.	• Growth becomes slow and steady. Muscles develop, and "baby fat" is lost. • Gross motor skills (biking, swimming, skating, ball handling) and fine motor skills (writing, typing, fastening buttons) continue to improve.
• Children show egocentric thinking (viewing world from their own perspective) and "centration," a focus on only one aspect of a stimulus. • Memory, attention span, and symbolic thinking improve, and intuitive thought begins. • Language (sentence length, vocabulary, syntax, and grammar) improves rapidly.	• Children apply logical operations to problems. • Understanding of conservation (that changes in shape do not necessarily affect quantity) and transformation (that objects can go through many states without changing) emerge. • Children can "decenter"—take multiple perspectives into account. • Memory encoding, storage, and retrieval improve, and control strategies (meta-memory) develop. • Language pragmatics (social conventions) and metalinguistic awareness (self-monitoring) improve.
• Children develop self-concepts, which may be exaggerated. • A sense of gender and racial identity emerges. • Children begin to see peers as individuals and form friendships based on trust and shared interests. • Morality is rule-based and focused on rewards and punishments. • Play becomes more constructive and cooperative, and social skills become important.	• Children refer to psychological traits to define themselves. Sense of self becomes differentiated. • Social comparison is used to understand one's standing and identity. • Self-esteem grows differentiated, and a sense of self-efficacy (an appraisal of what one can and cannot do) develops. • Children approach moral problems intent on maintaining social respect and accepting what society defines as right. • Friendship patterns of boys and girls differ. Boys mostly interact with boys in groups, and girls tend to interact singly or in pairs with other girls.
Preoperational stage	Concrete operational stage
Initiative-versus-guilt stage	Industry-versus-inferiority stage
Phallic stage	Latency period
Preconventional morality level	Conventional morality level

		ADOLESCENCE (12 to 20 years)	EARLY ADULTHOOD (20 to 40 years)
PHYSICAL DEVELOPMENT		• Girls begin the adolescent growth spurt around age 10, boys around age 12. • Girls reach puberty around age 11 or 12, boys around age 13 or 14. • Primary sexual characteristics develop (affecting the reproductive organs), as do secondary sexual characteristics (pubic and underarm hair in both sexes, breasts in girls, deep voices in boys).	• Physical capabilities peak in the 20s, including strength, senses, coordination, and reaction time. • Growth is mostly complete, although some organs, including the brain, continue to grow. • For many young adults, obesity becomes a threat for the first time, as body fat increases. • Stress can become a significant health threat. • In the mid-30s, disease replaces accidents as the leading cause of death.
COGNITIVE DEVELOPMENT		• Abstract thought prevails. Adolescents use formal logic to consider problems in the abstract. • Relative, not absolute, thinking is typical. • Verbal, mathematical, and spatial skills improve. • Adolescents are able to think hypothetically, divide attention, and monitor thought through meta-cognition. • Egocentrism develops, with a sense that one is always being observed. Self-consciousness and introspection are typical. • A sense of invulnerability can lead adolescents to ignore danger.	• As world experience increases, thought becomes more flexible and subjective, geared to adept problem solving. • Intelligence is applied to long-term goals involving career, family, and society. • Significant life events of young adulthood may shape cognitive development.
SOCIAL/ PERSONALITY DEVELOPMENT		• Self-concept becomes organized and accurate and reflects others' perceptions. Self-esteem grows differentiated. • Defining identity is a key task. Peer relationships provide social comparison and help define acceptable roles. Popularity issues become acute; peer pressure can enforce conformity. • Adolescents' quest for autonomy can bring conflict with parents as family roles are renegotiated. • Sexuality assumes importance in identity formation. Dating begins.	• Forming intimate relationships becomes highly important. Commitment may be partly determined by the attachment style developed in infancy. • Marriage and children bring developmental changes, often stressful. Divorce may result, with new stresses. • Identity is largely defined in terms of work, as young adults consolidate their careers.
THEORIES & THEORISTS	Jean Piaget	Formal operations stage	
	Erik Erikson	Identity-versus-confusion stage	Intimacy-versus-isolation stage
	Sigmund Freud	Genital stage	
	Lawrence Kohlberg	Postconventional morality level may be reached	

MIDDLE ADULTHOOD
(40 to 65 years)

- Physical changes become evident. Vision declines noticeably, as does hearing, but less obviously.
- Height reaches a peak and declines slowly. Osteoporosis speeds this process in women. Weight increases, and strength decreases.
- Reaction time slows, but performance of complex tasks is mostly unchanged because of lifelong practice.
- Women experience menopause, with unpredictable effects. The male climacteric brings gradual changes in men's reproductive systems.

- Some loss of cognitive functioning may begin in middle adulthood, but overall cognitive competence holds steady because adults use life experience and effective strategies to compensate.
- Slight declines occur in the efficiency of retrieval from long-term memory.

- People in middle adulthood take stock, appraising accomplishments against a "social clock" and developing a consciousness of mortality.
- Middle adulthood, despite the supposed "midlife crisis," usually is tranquil and satisfying. Individuals' personality traits are generally stable over time.
- Although marital satisfaction is usually high, family relationships can present challenges.
- The view of one's career shifts from outward ambition to inner satisfaction or, in some cases, dissatisfaction. Career changes are increasingly common.

Generativity-versus-stagnation stage

LATE ADULTHOOD
(65 years to death)

- Wrinkles and gray or thinning hair are marks of late adulthood. Height declines as backbone disk cartilage thins. Women are especially susceptible to osteoporosis.
- The brain shrinks, and the heart pumps less blood through the body. Reactions slow, and the senses become less acute. Cataracts and glaucoma may affect the eyes, and hearing loss is common.
- Chronic diseases, especially heart disease, grow more common. Mental disorders, such as depression and Alzheimer's disease, may occur.

- Cognitive declines are minimal until the 80s. Cognitive abilities can be maintained with training and practice, and learning remains possible throughout the life span.
- Short-term memory and memory of specific life episodes may decline, but other types of memory are largely unaffected.

- Basic personality traits remain stable, but changes are possible. "Life review," a feature of this period, can bring either fulfillment or dissatisfaction.
- Retirement is a major event of late adulthood, causing adjustments to self-concept and self-esteem.
- A healthy lifestyle and continuing activity in areas of interest can bring satisfaction in late adulthood.
- Typical circumstances of late adulthood (reduced income, the aging or death of a spouse, a change in living arrangements) cause stress.

Ego-integrity-versus-despair stage

Discovering the Life Span

Fifth Edition

Robert S. Feldman
University of Massachusetts Amherst

 Pearson

To Alex, Miles, Naomi, Lilia, Rose, and Marina

Acknowledgments of third-party content appear on the appropriate page within the text.

Cover Image: Ihnatovich Maryia/Shutterstock; arbit/Shutterstock; A-Digit/DigitalVision Vectors/Getty Images; VasjaKoman/DigitalVision Vectors/Getty Images; A-Digit/DigitalVision Vectors/Getty Images

Library of Congress Cataloging-in-Publication Data

Names: Feldman, Robert S. (Robert Stephen).
Title: Discovering the life span/Robert S. Feldman, University of
   Massachusetts, Amherst.
Description: Fifth edition. | New York, NY : Pearson Education, Inc.,
   [2021] | Includes bibliographical references and index.
Identifiers: LCCN 2019021013 | ISBN 9780135710869 (paperback)
Subjects: LCSH: Developmental psychology. | Life cycle, Human. | Human
   growth.
Classification: LCC BF713 .F46 2021 | DDC 155—dc23
LC record available at https://lccn.loc.gov/2019021013

Revel Access Code Card

ISBN 10: 0-13-568537-0
ISBN 13: 978-0-13-568537-2

Rental Edition

ISBN 10: 0-13-571086-3
ISBN 13: 978-0-13-571086-9

Instructor's Review Copy

ISBN 10: 0-13-570677-7
ISBN 13: 978-0-13-570677-0

14 2022

Brief Contents

Contents

Preface

To the Student

Welcome to the field of lifespan development! It's a discipline that's about you, about your family and those who came before you, and about those who may follow in your footsteps. It's about your genetic heritage, and it's about the world in which you were raised.

Lifespan development is a field that will speak to you in a personal way. It covers the range of human existence from its beginnings at conception to its inevitable ending at death. It is a discipline that deals with ideas and concepts and theories, but one that above all has at its heart people—our fathers and mothers, our friends and acquaintances, and our very selves.

But before we jump into the world of lifespan development, let's spend a little time getting to know this book and the way it presents the material. Knowing how the book is constructed will pay off in big ways.

Getting to Know the Book

You've probably already read a fair number of textbooks over the course of your college career. This one is different.

Why? Because it's written from your perspective as a student. Every word, sentence, paragraph, and feature in this book is included because it's meant to explain the field of lifespan development in a way that excites you, engages you with the content, and facilitates the study of the material. And by doing that, it maximizes your chances for not only learning the material and getting a good grade in your class, but also applying the material in a way that will improve your life.

The organization of the book is based on what psychologists know about how students study most effectively. The text is divided into short modules, nestled within chapters, with each module having several clearly demarcated subsections. By focusing your study in short sections, you're much more likely to master the material.

Similarly, the material is organized into *learning objectives*, abbreviated as *LO*. At the start of every subsection, you'll find them in the form of statements. It makes sense to pay particular attention to the learning objectives because they indicate the material that instructors most want you to learn and that they use to develop test questions. The learning objectives are also listed at the beginning of each chapter.

The book also has a way of indicating which terms are most critical to your understanding of lifespan development. Key terms and concepts are printed in **boldface type**, and are defined in the margins. Less-critical terms and concepts are printed in *italics* and defined within the paragraph where they first appear, but not in the margin.

To further help you study, modules end with a "Review, Check, and Apply" section. The "Review" section includes a summary of the material in the module, organized by learning objective. Each module also includes four "Check Yourself" questions, which require that you recall and understand the material to answer correctly. Finally, there's a question that requires you to apply the material in the chapter to some real-world issue. By answering the "Applying Lifespan Development" question, you're demonstrating a higher-order understanding related to critical thinking.

You'll also find several recurring features in every chapter. There are opening vignettes designed to illustrate how lifespan development is relevant to everyday life. There are boxes, called "From Research to Practice," which include recent research that is applied to current social issues, and "Cultural Dimensions" sections that highlight multicultural issues related to lifespan development.

Ever wish you could apply the theoretical material you're reading about in a textbook to your own life? The section called "Development in Your Life" offers a variety of tips and guidelines, based on the chapter's theme, ranging from childrearing tips to choosing a career and planning your retirement. By applying these to your life, you'll learn the diversity of what the field of lifespan development has to offer.

Finally, there are several features illustrating how the material is relevant from the perspectives of people in different roles and professions, including parents, educators, healthcare providers, and social workers. "From the Perspective of . . ." asks you questions designed to help you think critically about how lifespan development applies to someone working in a specific field, and "Putting It All Together"—a summary at the end of each chapter—will help you integrate the material in the modules and learn how it applies across a variety of dimensions.

A Last Word . . .

I wrote this book for you. Not for your instructor, not for my colleagues, and not to see it sitting on my own bookshelf. I wrote this book as an opportunity to extend what I do in my own classes at the University of Massachusetts Amherst, and to reach a wider, and more diverse, set of students. For me, there's nothing more exciting as a college professor than to share my teaching and knowledge with as many students as possible.

I hope this book grabs your interest in lifespan development and shows you how it can apply to your own life and improve it. Let me know if it does, or anything else you'd like to convey to me. I'd love to hear from you, and you can easily reach me at feldman@chancellor.umass.edu. In the meantime, enjoy your introduction to lifespan development.

To the Instructor

I've never met an instructor of a lifespan development course who didn't feel that he or she was fortunate to teach the course. The subject matter is inherently fascinating, and there is a wealth of information to convey that is at once intriguing and practical. Students come to the course with anticipation, motivated to learn about a topic that, at base, is about their own lives and the lives of every other human being.

At the same time, the course presents unique challenges. For one thing, the breadth of lifespan development is so vast that it is difficult to cover the entire field within the confines of a traditional college term. In addition, many instructors find traditional lifespan development texts too long. Students are concerned about the length of the texts and have trouble completing the entire book. As a result, instructors are often reluctant to assign the complete text and are forced to drop material, often arbitrarily.

Finally, instructors often wish to incorporate into their classes computer-based electronic media that promote understanding of key concepts and take advantage of students' capabilities using electronic media. Yet traditional lifespan development textbooks do little to integrate the electronic media with the book. Consequently, in most courses, the book and accompanying electronic media stand largely in isolation to one another. This lack of integration diminishes the potential impact of both traditional and electronic media and the advantages that an integration of the two could produce in terms of helping students engage with and learn the subject matter.

Discovering the Life Span, **Fifth Edition**, directly addresses these challenges. The book, which is based on the highly popular *Development Across the Life Span*, is some 25 percent shorter than traditional lifespan books. At the same time, it maintains the student friendliness that has been the hallmark of the original. It is rich in examples and illustrates the applications that can be derived from the research and theory of lifespan developmentalists.

The book uses a modular approach to optimize student learning. Each chapter is divided into three modules, and in turn each module is divided into several smaller sections. Consequently, rather than facing long, potentially daunting chapters, students encounter material that is divided into smaller, more manageable chunks. Of course, presenting material in small chunks represents a structure that psychological research long ago found to be optimum for promoting learning.

The modular approach has another advantage: It allows instructors to customize instruction by assigning only those modules that fit their course. Each of the book's chapters focuses on a particular period of the life span, and within each chapter separate modules address the three main conceptual approaches to the period: physical development, cognitive development, and social and personality development. Because of the flexibility of this structure, instructors who wish to highlight a particular theoretical or topical approach to lifespan development can do so easily.

Finally, *Discovering the Life Span*, **Fifth Edition**, provides complete integration between the book and a huge array of media interactives and assessments in *Revel*, comprising videos, quizzes, and literally hundreds of activities that extend the text and make concepts come alive.

An Introduction to *Discovering the Life Span*, Fifth Edition

Discovering the Life Span, **Fifth Edition**—like its predecessor—provides a broad overview of the field of human development. It covers the entire range of the human life, from the moment of conception through death. The text furnishes a broad, comprehensive introduction to the field, covering basic theories and research findings, as well as highlighting current applications outside the laboratory. It covers the life span chronologically, encompassing the prenatal period, infancy and toddlerhood, the preschool years, middle childhood, adolescence, early and middle adulthood, and late adulthood. Within these periods, it focuses on physical, cognitive, and social and personality development.

In a unique departure from traditional lifespan development texts, each chapter integrates the physical, cognitive, and social and personality domains within each chronological period. Chapters begin with a compelling story about an individual representing the age period covered by the chapter, and the chapter ends by refocusing on that individual and integrating the three domains.

The book also blends and integrates theory, research, and applications, focusing on the breadth of human development. Furthermore, rather than attempting to provide a detailed historical record of the field, it focuses on the here and now, drawing on the past where appropriate, but with a view toward delineating the field as it now stands and the directions toward which it is evolving. Similarly, while providing descriptions of classic studies, the emphasis is more on current research findings and trends.

The book is designed to be user friendly. Written in a direct, conversational voice, it replicates as much as possible a dialogue between author and student. The text is meant to be understood and mastered on its own by students of every level of interest and motivation. To that end, it includes a variety of pedagogical features that promote mastery of the material and encourage critical thinking. These features include:

- **CHAPTER-OPENING PROLOGUES.** Each of the chapters starts with an attention-grabbing account of an individual who is at the developmental stage covered by the chapter. The material in the prologue sets the stage for the chapter, and the material is addressed in the end of the chapter when the physical, cognitive, and social and personality aspects are integrated.

- **MODULE-OPENING VIGNETTE.** Modules (which are nestled within chapters) begin with short vignettes, describing an individual or situation that is relevant to the basic developmental issues being addressed in the module.

- **LEARNING OBJECTIVES.** Every subsection begins with a learning objective, clearly specifying what students are expected to master after reading and studying the material. Learning objectives are listed at the beginning of each chapter.

- **FROM RESEARCH TO PRACTICE.** Each chapter includes a box that describes current developmental research or research issues, applied to everyday problems. Most of these boxes are new to the fifth edition.

- **CULTURAL DIMENSIONS.** Every chapter includes "Cultural Dimensions" sections incorporated into the text. These sections highlight issues relevant to today's multicultural society. Examples of these sections include discussions about preschools around the world, gay and lesbian relationships, the marketing of cigarettes to the less advantaged, and race, gender, and ethnic differences in life expectancy.

- **DEVELOPMENT IN YOUR LIFE.** Every chapter includes information on specific uses that can be derived from research conducted by developmental investigators. For instance, the text provides concrete information on how to encourage children to become more physically active, how to help troubled adolescents who might be contemplating suicide, and on planning and living a good retirement. In previous editions, this feature was titled "Becoming an Informed Consumer of Development."

- **REVIEW, CHECK, AND APPLY SECTIONS.** At the end of each module are short recaps of the chapters' main points, a series of questions on the chapter content, and a question oriented to apply the chapter content to the real world, keyed to the learning objectives.

- **"FROM THE PERSPECTIVE OF..." QUESTIONS.** Students will encounter frequent questions throughout the text designed to show the applicability of the material to a variety of professions, including education, nursing, social work, and healthcare.

- **THINKING ABOUT THE DATA.** Every chapter includes a "Thinking About the Data" figure, which invites students to apply critical thinking to a graph or diagram.

- **RUNNING GLOSSARY.** Key terms are defined in the margins of the page on which the term is presented.

- **END-OF-CHAPTER INTEGRATIVE MATERIAL.** At the end of each chapter, the chapter-opening prologue is recapped and addressed from the three domains of physical, cognitive, and social and personality development. In addition, questions address the prologue from the perspective of people such as parents, professional caregivers, nurses, and educators.

What's New in the Fifth Edition?

The fifth edition of *Discovering the Life Span* has been extensively revised in response to the comments of dozens of reviewers. Among the major changes are the following:

Additions of New and Updated Material. The revision incorporates a significant amount of new and updated information. For instance, advances in areas such as behavioral genetics, brain development, evolutionary perspectives, and cross-cultural approaches to development receive expanded and new coverage. Overall, hundreds of new citations have been added, with most of those from articles and books published in the last few years.

The fifth edition also includes the following improvements:

- THEORETICAL PERSPECTIVES. Each chapter includes a look at a topic through the lenses of various theoretical perspectives. For example, Chapter 1 discusses how various theorists would study the Ruiz family, profiled in the chapter opener.

- STRONGER EMPHASIS ON CULTURE. More so than in previous editions, *Discovering the Life Span*, Fifth Edition emphasizes the impact of culture on development.

- REDESIGNED CHAPTER SUMMARIES. "Putting It All Together" chapter summaries have been redesigned to more closely link to chapter content.

- CHAPTER-OPENING PHOTO. Every chapter opens with a photo representing the content to follow and tying into the Summary vignette.

New topics were added to every chapter. The following sample of new and revised topics featured in this edition provides a good indication of the currency of the revision:

Chapter 1: Introduction

- Revised prologue on Louise Brown and Elizabeth Carr, both born by *in vitro* fertilization
- Revised "perspective" prompt on cohort membership, emphasizing the cell phone generation
- Revised material on gender, culture, ethnicity, and race, including:
  - How roles played by men and women vary across cultures
  - Revised *Cultural Dimensions* box "How Culture, Ethnicity, and Race Influence Development" discusses cultural, ethnic, racial, socioeconomic, and gender considerations in the study of development
- Revised discussion of critical and sensitive periods
- Streamlined coverage of Freud's psychoanalytic perspective
- New examples in assessment of behavioral perspective
- New section on assessing cognitive neuroscience approaches
- New Figure 1-1 on brain differences in a person with autism
- Additional material on Vygotsky and scaffolding
- Theoretical perspectives: Discussion of how various theorists would study the Ruiz family, profiled in the chapter opener
- Updated Figure 1-5 on longitudinal vs. cross-sectional research
- New example of application of theories
- New Figure 1-2 on scientific method
- Additional coverage of ethnographic research and challenges
- Additional coverage of the importance of replication in psychological experiments
- New replication crisis discussion
- Revised *From Research to Practice* box on using lifespan development research for public policy
- Expanded meta-analysis discussion
- New coverage of informed consent and vulnerable populations

Chapter 2: The Start of Life

- New prologue on genetic testing
- New Figure 2-2 showing rise in number of triplet and higher-order births
- New *From Research to Practice* box on transgenerational epigenetic inheritance
- Updated Table 2-1 on the genetic basis of various disorders
- Updated Table 2-2 on fetal development monitoring techniques
- Updated Table 2-3 on DNA-based genetic tests
- Updated abortion statistics
- Marijuana use during pregnancy
- Opioid use during pregnancy
- Cultural myths of pregnancy
- New guidelines on drugs during delivery from the American College of Obstetricians and Gynecologists
- Importance of touch in newborns
- New research on immediate mother-child bonding
- Updated statistics on length of hospital stay
- New data on rates of infant mortality in the United States by race, including new Figure 2-17
- New Figure 2-14 on worldwide rates of infant mortality
- New Table 2-4 on risk factors for low-birthweight preterm infants
- New estimates of cost of caring for premature infants
- New material on risk factors for premature births
- Family and Medical Leave Act (FMLA) update
- Additional material on postpartum depression
- Updated statistics on IVF infants
- New coverage of circumcision rates

Chapter 3: Infancy

- Statistics on shaken baby syndrome, with new Figure 3-5 showing damage to the brain of a shaken baby
- Causes of cultural differences in infant sleep patterns
- Rates of poverty and hunger in the United States and worldwide
- Clarification of timing of breastfeeding and introduction of solid foods
- Change in key term from **scheme** to **schema**
- New *From Research to Practice* box on why formal education is lost on infants
- Theoretical perspectives: Comparing application of Piagetian and information processing theories
- Updated statistics on single-parent and no-parent families
- Updated statistics on teen pregnancy
- American Academy of Pediatrics guidelines on infant sleep location
- Mothers' sleep difficulties
- Efficacy of strategies to increase infant intelligence
- Suggestion to teach cause-and-effect in infants
- Newer critiques of Chomsky's nativist approach to language learning
- Imitative vocalization of infants
- Average size of families—changes

Chapter 4: The Preschool Years

- New opening vignette
- New definition of obesity in terms of BMI
- New statistics on obesity
- Obesity and overweight children in developing countries
- "Just-right phenomenon" eating rituals in children
- Updated statistics on parents' views of children's health
- Updated statistics on early childhood education
- Long-term benefits of preschool education
- Explaining the complementary nature of alternate theoretical perspectives
- Additional comparison of differing theoretical approaches
- Transgender preschoolers' challenges
- Mental health advantages of androgyny
- More symptoms of autism spectrum disorder
- New statistics of family life demographics
- Success of immigrant children despite different parenting styles
- New figure on child abuse
- Additional signs of child abuse
- Revised discussion of screen time
- Video deficit hypothesis
- Revised end-of-chapter summary to reflect new chapter opener

Chapter 5: Middle Childhood

- Revised obesity statistics
- New Figure 5-1 on obesity rates in childhood
- Obesity demographics
- Risk factors in asthma
- Prevalence of asthma
- Demographic differences in asthma
- Updated material on cyber-safety
- Prevalence of learning disabilities
- Theoretical perspectives: Explanatory theories of learning disabilities
- Incidence of ADHD
- New Figure 5-5 on bilingualism rates in the United States
- Cognitive advantages of bilingualism
- Revised section with new support for code-based reading instruction
- New edition of WISC-V
- Individuals with Disabilities Education Act (IDEA)
- Categories of bullying
- One-child policy in China and academic performance

- Updated material on family demographics
- Multigenerational families
- Self-care laws
- Free-range parenting

Chapter 6: Adolescence

- BMI definition of obesity
- Updated information on males with anorexia
- *From Research to Practice* box on brain development in adolescence
- Updated statistics on marijuana use and opioid abuse
- Figure 6-4 on marijuana use among teens
- Updated statistics on binge drinking and alcohol use among teens and its effect on the brain
- New Figure 6-5 on binge drinking
- Updated coverage of e-cigarettes
- New statistics on grade inflation
- New Figure 6-6 on child care choices
- New Figure 6-8 on how teens prefer to communicate with friends
- New statistics on social media use and video games
- Emerging adulthood
- Adolescent anxiety
- New statistics on suicide among adolescents
- New Figure 6-9 on behavioral problems of teens in terms of time spent with parents
- New *From Research to Practice* box on social comparison, self-esteem, and social media
- Cross-race friendships
- Transgender and gender-fluid persons
- New Figure 6-12 on teen pregnancy

Chapter 7: Early Adulthood

- New learning objective relating to emerging adulthood
- Brain development in early adulthood
- New recommendations for physical fitness
- New Figure 7-1 on connection between fitness and longevity
- New Figure 7-2 on obesity rates in the United States
- Updated statistics on obesity
- New Figure 7-3 on obesity rates worldwide
- More on cross-cultural differences in health beliefs
- Using mindfulness to reduce stress
- New section comparing theories of post-formal thinking in adulthood
- Additional creativity peaking examples
- Decline in flexibility in thinking relating to creativity

- Updated statistics on college attendance
- New Figure 7-6 on diversity increases in college attendance
- New Figure 7-7 on increase in students reporting problems with anxiety, depression, and relationships
- New statistics on support of gay marriage
- Mother's attachment style and parenting of infants
- New statistics on delay of marriage
- New Figure 7-9 on rates of cohabitation
- New Figure 7-10 on median age at first marriage
- New divorce statistics
- New fertility rate statistics
- Millennial generation views of work
- New material on emerging adulthood
- New Figure 7-14 on the gender gap in wages

Chapter 8: Middle Adulthood

- SES and health
- Cause of death statistics
- New data on hormone replacement therapy
- New Figure 8-5 on incidence of breast cancer
- Routine mammogram controversy
- Normative crises theories
- Life events theories
- Application of life events theories
- Updated divorce statistics
- Updated causes for divorce
- Remarriage failure statistics
- Stress from children returning compared to leaving during middle adulthood
- Rise in multigenerational families
- New statistics on life expectancy
- Update on intimate partner violence
- Honor killings and spousal abuse
- Revised leisure time statistics
- Burnout on the job
- Suicide and job loss

Chapter 9: Late Adulthood

- New *From Research to Practice* box on cognitive skills training in late adulthood
- New Figure 9-1 on growing size of the late adulthood population
- New data on leading causes of death in elderly people
- New data on Alzheimer rates
- New Figure 9-3, data on vehicular crashes involving older adults vs. teens

- Lengthening telomeres
- New drug therapies for extending life
- New Figure 9-6 on longer life spans
- New Figure 9-10 on technology adoption in late adulthood
- Socioemotional selectivity theory
- Cost of nursing home care
- New Figure 9-12 on living arrangements in late adulthood
- New Figure 9-13 on perceived benefits of growing older

Chapter 10: Death and Dying

- New prologue on a good death
- Theoretical perspectives: Alternative theories on dying to that of Kübler-Ross
- Four-component theory of grieving
- New *From Research to Practice* box on grief after spouse death
- Professional mourners in China
- Displays of grief in Egypt
- Additional ways of helping children deal with grief
- New statistics on assisted suicides and jurisdictions
- Treatment of dying across cultures
- Updated statistics on infant mortality in the United States and other countries
- New Figure 10-4 on predictions of life span versus reality
- Discussion of crisis intervention used for children who survived the Sandy Hook school shooting
- New Check Yourself question in module 10.3
- Revised Summary

A Final Note

I am excited about this new edition of *Discovering the Life Span*. I believe its length, structure, and media and text integration will help students learn the material in a highly effective way. Just as important, I hope it will nurture an interest in the field that will last a lifetime.

Teaching and Learning Resources

Discovering the Life Span is accompanied by a superb set of teaching and learning materials.

Revel ™

Revel is an interactive learning environment that deeply engages students and prepares them for class. Media and assessment integrated directly within the authors' narrative lets students read, explore interactive content, and practice in one continuous learning path. Thanks to the dynamic reading experience in Revel, students come to class prepared to discuss, apply, and learn from instructors and from each other.

Learn more about Revel

www.pearson.com/revel

The fifth edition includes integrated videos and media content throughout, allowing students to explore topics more deeply at the point of relevancy. Revel makes the content come alive as students respond to "Myth or Truth" and "Fun Facts and a Lie" interactives. Each chapter also includes at least one "Trending Topic" feature, which explores cutting-edge research or current events.

Highly engaging interactives encourage student participation. Interactive scenarios invite students into "choose your own path"–type activities. Other interactives lead them through how a health-care professional, counselor, teacher, or parent might react to a specific developmental situation or solve a problem. Students can also explore interactive figures using drag-and-drop and predictive graphing tools.

Each chapter includes a *Thinking About the Data* prompt, which encourages the student to think about what is behind the data they see in graphs and tables using a data-driven Social Explorer activity in Revel.

Finally, a set of carefully curated videos builds on text content, exploring developmental psychology from a variety of perspectives, including a deeper look at diversity and the latest in neuroscience.

Revel also offers the ability for students to assess their content mastery by taking multiple-choice quizzes that offer instant feedback and by participating in a variety of writing assignments, such as peer-reviewed questions and autograded assignments.

MyVirtualLife integration enables students to apply developmental concepts in a simulated environment within their Revel™ course. MyVirtualLife is an interactive simulation that allows students to parent a child from birth to age 18, making decisions on the child's behalf. Once the virtual child turns 18, the student user's perspective flips for the second half of the program, which enables students to live a simulated life and see the impact of their first-person decisions over the course of a lifetime.

Print and Media Supplements

- *Instructor's Resource Manual* (ISBN: 9780135871904). Designed to make your lectures more effective and save you preparation time, this extensive resource gathers together the most effective activities and strategies for teaching your course. The *Instructor's Resource Manual* includes learning objectives, key terms and concepts, self-contained lecture suggestions, and class activities for each chapter. Available for download via the Pearson Instructor's Resource Center (www.pearsonhighered.com).

- *PowerPoint Lecture Slides* (ISBN: 9780135872222). The PowerPoints provide an active format for presenting concepts from each chapter and feature prominent figures and tables from the text. The PowerPoint Lecture Slides are available for download via the Pearson Instructor's Resource Center (www.pearsonhighered.com).

- *Video Enhanced Lecture PowerPoint Slides* (ISBN: 9780135872253). The lecture PowerPoint slides have been embedded with video, enabling instructors to show videos within the context of their lecture. No Internet connection is required to play videos. Available for download on the Instructor's Resource Center (www.pearsonhighered.com).

- *PowerPoint Slides for Photos, Figures, and Tables* (ISBN: 9780135871881). These slides contain only the photos, figures, and line art from the textbook. Available for download on the Instructor's Resource Center (www.pearsonhighered.com).

- *Test Bank* (ISBN: 9780135871843). For the fifth edition, each question was checked to ensure that the correct answer was marked and the page reference was accurate. The test bank contains multiple-choice, true/false, and essay questions, each referenced to the relevant page in the book and correlated to chapter learning objectives. The test bank features the identification of each question as factual, conceptual, or applied and also makes use of Bloom's Taxonomy. Finally, each item is also identified in terms of difficulty level to allow professors to customize their tests and ensure a balance of question types. Each chapter of the test item file begins with the Total Assessment Guide: an easy to reference grid that makes creating tests easier by organizing the test questions by text section, question type, and whether it is factual, conceptual, or applied. The Test Bank is available for download via the Pearson Instructor's Resource Center (www.pearsonhighered.com).

- *MyTest* (ISBN: 9780135872178). The test bank comes with the Pearson MyTest, a powerful assessment generation program that helps instructors easily create and print quizzes and exams. Questions and tests can be authored online, allowing instructors ultimate flexibility and the ability to efficiently manage assessments anytime, anywhere. For more information, go to www.PearsonMyTest.com.

- *Pearson Teaching Films Lifespan Development Video* (ISBN: 0205656021). This video engages students and brings to life a wide range of topics spanning prenatal through the end of the life span. International videos shot on location allow students to observe similarities and differences in human development across various cultures.

- *Supplementary Texts.* Contact your Pearson representative to package any of these supplementary texts with *Discovering the Life Span*, Fifth Edition.
- *Current Directions in Developmental Psychology* (ISBN: 0205597505). Readings from the American Psychological Society. This exciting reader includes more than 20 articles that have been carefully selected for the undergraduate audience, and taken from the accessible *Current Directions in Psychological Science* journal. These timely, cutting-edge articles allow instructors to bring their students a real-world perspective about today's most current and pressing issues in psychology. The journal is discounted when packaged with this text for college adoptions.
- *Twenty Studies That Revolutionized Child Psychology* by Wallace E. Dixon Jr. (ISBN: 0130415723). Presenting the seminal research studies that have shaped modern developmental psychology, this brief text provides an overview of the environment that gave rise to each study, its experimental design, its findings, and its impact on current thinking in the discipline.
- *Human Development in Multicultural Contexts: A Book of Readings* (ISBN: 0130195235). Written by Michele A. Paludi, this compilation of readings highlights cultural influences in developmental psychology.
- *The Psychology Major: Careers and Strategies for Success* (ISBN: 0205684688). Written by Eric Landrum (Idaho State University), Stephen Davis (Emporia State University), and Terri Landrum (Idaho State University), this 160-page paperback provides valuable information on career options available to psychology majors, tips for improving academic performance, and a guide to the APA style of research reporting.

Acknowledgments

I am grateful to the following reviewers who provided a wealth of comments, constructive criticism, and encouragement:

Lola Aagaard, *Morehead State University*
Glen Adams, *Harding University*
Sharron Adams, *Wesleyan College*
Carolyn Adams-Price, *Mississippi State University*
Leslie Adams Lariviere, *Assumption College*
Judi Addelston, *Valencia Community College*
Bill Anderson, *Illinois State University*
Carrie Andreoletti, *Central Connecticut State University*
Harold Andrews, *Miami Dade College–Wolfson*
Ivan Applebaum, *Valencia Community College*

Sally Archer, *College of New Jersey*
Janet Arndt, *Gordon College*
Christine Bachman, *University of Houston–Downtown*
Harriet Bachner, *Pittsburg State University*
Nannette Bagstad, *Mayville State University*
Jolly Bailey, *Delaware Technical Community College*
Mary Ballard, *Appalachian State University*
Michelle Bannoura, *Hudson Valley Community College*
Daniel Barajas, *Community College of Denver*
Ted Barker, *Okaloosa-Walton College*
Catherine Barnard, *Kalamazoo Valley Community College*
Gena Barnhill, *Lynchburg College*
Sue Barrientos, *Butler Community College*
Sandra Barrueco, *The Catholic University of America*
Carolyn Barry, *Loyola College in Maryland*
Chris Barry, *University of Southern Mississippi*
Robin Bartlett, *Northern Kentucky University*
Shirley Bass-Wright, *St. Philip's College*
Kellie Bassell, *Palm Beach Community College*
Sherry Black, *Western Nevada College*
Bette Beane, *University of North Carolina at Greensboro*
Heidi Beattie, *Troy University*
Dan Bellack, *Trident Technical College*
Amy Bender, *University of Milwaukee*
Marshelle Bergstrom, *University of Wisconsin–Oshkosh*
Doreen Berman, *Queens College*
Debra Berrett, *Solano Community College*
Irene Bersola-Nguyen, *Sacramento State University*
Wendy Bianchini, *Montana State University*
John Bicknell, *Temple College*
Robert Birkey, *Goshen College*
Carol Bishop, *Solano Community College*
Sherry Black, *Western Nevada College*
Angela Blankenship, *Nash Community College*
Cheryl Bluestone, *Queensborough Community (CUNY)*
Judy Blumenthal, *Montgomery College*
Tracie Blumentritt, *University of Wisconsin–La Crosse*
Kathy Bobula, *Clark College*
Denise Ann Bodman, *Arizona State University*
Kathleen Bonnelle, *Lansing Community College*
Janet Boseovski, *The University of North Carolina at Greensboro*
Teri Bourdeau, *University of Tulsa*
Sarah Boysen, *Ohio State University*
Nicole Bragg, *Mt. Hood Community College*
Gregory Braswell, *Illinois State University*
Judith Breen, *College of DuPage*
Alaina Brenick, *University of Maryland*
Jennifer Brennom, *Kirkwood Community College*
Barbara Briscoe, *Kapiolani Community College*
Caralee Bromme, *San Joaquin Delta Community College*
Betty Cecile Brookover, *Xavier University of Louisiana*
Veda Brown, *Prairie View A&M University*

Janine Buckner, *Seton Hall University*
Sharon Burson, *Temple College*
Cathy Bush, *Carson-Newman College*
Jean Cahoon, *Pitt Community College*
Cheryl Camenzuli, *Molloy College*
Angela Campbell, *Harrisburg Area Community College*
Debb Campbell, *College of the Sequoias*
Lillian Campbell, *Humber College*
Diane Caulfield, *Honolulu Community College*
Rick Caulfield, *University of Hawaii at Manoa*
Lisa Caya, *University of Wisconsin–La Crosse*
Laura Chapin, *Colorado State University*
Jing Chen, *Grand Valley State University*
John Childers, *East Carolina University*
Saundra Ciccarelli, *Gulf Coast Community College*
Diana Ciesko, *Valencia Community College*
Cherie Clark, *Queens University of Charlotte*
Wanda Clark, *South Plains College*
J. B. Clement, *Daytona College*
Kimberly Cobb, *Edgecombe Community College*
Margaret Coberly, *University of Hawaii–Windward*
Lawrence Cohn, *University of Texas at El Paso*
Barbara Connolly, *University of Tennessee Health Sciences Center*
Deborah Copeland, *Palm Beach Community College*
Kristi Cordell-McNulty, *Angelo State University*
Pam Costa, *Tacoma Community College*
Ellen Cotter, *Georgia Southwestern State University*
Trina Cowan, *Northwest Vista College*
Jodi Crane, *Lindsey Wilson College*
Pat Crane, *Santa Ana College*
Amanda Creel, *Sowela Technical Community College*
Jeanne Cremeans, *Hillsborough Community College*
Don Crews, *Southwest Georgia Technical College*
Geraldine Curley, *Bunker Hill Community College*
Gregory Cutler, *Bay de Noc Community College*
Chris Daddis, *Ohio State University at Marion*
Anne Dailey, *Community College of Allegheny County*
Billy Daley, *Fort Hays State University*
Dianne Daniels, *University of North Carolina–Charlotte*
Karen Davis, *Southwest Georgia Technical College*
Minca Davis Brantley, *Miami Dade College*
Dora Davison, *Southern State Community College*
Paul Dawson, *Weber State University*
Barbara DeFilippo, *Lansing Community College*
Tara Dekkers, *Northwestern College*
J. DeSimone, *William Paterson University*
Michael Devoley, *Montgomery College*
David Devonis, *Graceland University*
Ginger Dickson, *University of Texas at El Paso*
Trina Diehl, *Northwest Vista College*
Darryl Dietrich, *The College of St. Scholastica*
Jennie Dilworth, *Georgia Southern University*
Stephanie Ding, *Del Mar College*

Betsy Diver, *Lake Superior College*
Delores Doench, *Southwestern Community College*
Margaret Dombrowski, *Harrisburg Area Community College–Lancaster*
Heather Dore, *Florida Community College at Jacksonville*
Jackie Driskill, *Texas Tech University*
Victor Duarte, *North Idaho College*
Susan Dubitsky, *Florida International University*
Shelley Dubkin-Lee, *Oregon State University*
Beryl Dunsmoir, *Concordia University at Austin*
Paula Dupuy, *University of Toledo*
Kathleen Dwinnells, *Kent State University–Trumbull Campus*
Darlene Earley-Hereford *Southern Union State Community College*
Y. van Ecke, *College of Marin*
David Edgerly, *Quincy University*
Jean Egan, *Asnuntuck Community College*
Trish Ellerson, *Miami University*
Kelley Eltzroth, *Mid-Michigan Community College*
Laurel End, *Mount Mary College*
Dale Epstein, *University of Maryland*
Diana Espinoza, *Laredo Community College*
Melissa Essman, *California State University, Fullerton*
Deborah Stipp, *Ivy Tech Community College*
Jenni Fauchier, *Metropolitan Community College*
Nancy Feehan, *University of San Francisco*
Jef Feldman, *Los Angeles Pierce College*
Pamela Fergus, *MCTC and IHCC*
Ric Ferraro, *University of North Dakota*
Donna Fletcher, *Florida State University*
Christine Floether, *Centenary College*
June Foley, *Clinton Community College*
Jeanene Ford, *Holmes Community College*
Lee Fournet, *Central Arizona College*
Jody Fournier, *Capital University*
Tony Fowler, *Florence-Darlington Technical College*
James Francis, *San Jacinto College*
Megan Fulcher, *Washington and Lee University*
Inoke Funaki, *Brigham Young University–Hawaii*
Sonia Gaiane, *Grossmont College*
Donna Gainer, *Mississippi State University*
Teresa Galyean, *Wytheville Community College*
Mary Garcia-Lemus, *California Polytechnic State University–San Luis Obispo*
Laura Garofoli, *Fitchburg State College*
Andy Gauler Florida, *Community College at Jacksonville*
C. Ray Gentry, *Lenior-Rhyne College*
Jarilyn Gess, *Minnesota State University Moorhead*
Sharon Ghazarian, *University of North Carolina at Greensboro*
Pam Gingold, *Merced College*
Shery Ginn, *Rowan Cabarrus Community College*
Drusilla Glascoe, *Salt Lake Community College*

Donna Goetz, *Elmhurst College*

Rob Goralewicz, *Dabney Lancaster Community College*

Christina Gotowka, *Tunxis Community College*

Thomas Grady, *Neosho County Community College*

Donna Gray, *Irvine Valley College*

Troianne Grayson, *Florida Community College at Jacksonville–South Campus*

Jo Greathouse, *Brazosport College*

Jerry Green, *Tarrant County College*

Janelle Grellner, *University of Central Oklahoma*

Kristi Guest, *University of Alabama–Birmingham*

James Guinee, *University of Central Arkansas*

Jill Haasch, *Glenville State College*

Sharon Habermann, *Providence Theological Seminary*

Helen Hagens, *Central Michigan University*

Lisa Hager, *Spring Hill College*

Carolyn Halliburton, *Dallas Baptist University*

Sam Hardy, *Brigham Young University*

Mark Harmon, *Reedley College–North Centers*

Dyan W. Harper, *University of Missouri–St. Louis*

Melody Harrington, *St. Gregory's University*

Nancy Hartshorne, *Central Michigan University*

Myra Harville, *Holmes Community College*

Loretta Hauxwell, *McCook Community College*

Christina Hawkey, *Arizona Western College*

Lora Haynes, *University of Louisville*

Sam Heastie, *Fayetteville State University*

Patti Heer, *Clarke College*

Jessica Hehman, *University of Redlands*

Steve Hendrix, *James Sprunt Community College*

Sarah Herald, *Arizona State University*

Mary Hetland, *Minnesota State Community*

Carolyn Hildebrandt, *University of Northern Iowa*

Pamela Hill, *San Antonio College*

Sharon Hogan, *Cuyahoga Community College*

Frank Holiwski, *South Georgia College*

Debra Hollister, *Valencia Community College*

Sachi Horback, *Baltimore City Community College*

Scott Horton, *Mitchell College*

Julie Howard, *Vanguard University*

Herman Huber, *College of Saint Elizabeth*

Martha Hubertz, *Florida Atlantic University*

Barbara Huff, *Chandler Gilbert Community College*

Heidi Humm, *Mercy College*

Bob Humphries, *Walsh University*

David Hurford, *Pittsburg State University*

MaryLu Hutchins, *West Liberty State College*

Cynthia Ingle, *Bluegrass Community and Technical College*

Nicolle Ionascu, *Queen's University*

Jessica Jablonski, *Richard Stockton College of New Jersey*

Sabra Jacobs, *Big Sandy Community and Technical College*

Alisha Janowsky, *University of Central Florida*

Debbra Jennings, *Richland College*

Sybillyn Jennings, *Russell Sage College*

Daphne Johnson, *Sam Houston State University*

Margaret Johnson, *Bridgewater State College*

Stephanie Johnson, *Southeast Community College*

Deborah Jones, *Florida Community College*

Katherine Jones, *Mississippi College*

James Jordan, *Lorain County Community College*

Linda G. Jordan, *Skagit Valley College*

Terri Joseph, *Kent State University East Liverpool*

Diana Joy, *Community College of Denver*

Carl Jylland-Halverson, *University of Saint Francis*

Louise Kahn, *University of New Mexico*

Susan Kamphaus, *Tulsa Community College West Campus*

Richard Kandus, *Mt. San Jacinto College*

Paul Kaplan, *SUNY at Stony Brook*

Michele Karpathian, *Waynesburg College*

Mark Kavanaugh, *Kennebec Valley Community College*

Henry Keith, *Delaware Technical & Community College*

Debbie Keller, *College of the Ozarks*

Jeffrey Kellogg, *Marian College*

Colleen Kennedy, *Roosevelt University*

Rosalie Kern, *Michigan Tech University*

Lisa Kiang, *Wake Forest University*

Tim Killian, *University of Arkansas*

William Kimberlin, *Lorain County Community College*

April Kindrick, *South Puget Sound Community College*

Michalene King, *Kent State University at Tuscarawas*

Jennifer King-Cooper, *Sinclair Community College*

Kenyon Knapp, *Troy University, Montgomery Campus*

Don Knox, *Midwestern State University*

Larry Kollman, *North Iowa Area Community College*

Leslee Koritzke, *Los Angeles Trade Tech College*

Nicole Korzetz, *Lee College*

Holly Krogh, *Mississippi University for Women*

August Lageman, *Virginia Intermont College*

Carol Laman, *Houston Community College*

Warren Lambert, *Somerset Community College*

Jonathan Lang, *Borough of Manhattan Community College*

Rich Lanthier, *George Washington University*

Leslie Lariviere, *Adams Assumption*

Kara Larkan-Skinner, *Amarillo College*

Yvonne Larrier, *Indiana University South Bend*

Constance Larson, *Northeast Community College*

Richard Lazere, *Portland Community College*

Jennifer Leaver, *Eastern Arizona College*

Maria LeBaron, *Randolph Community College*

Marilyn Lehmkuhl, *Alexandria Technical College*

Gary Leka, *University of Texas–Pan American*

Diane Lemay, *University of Maine at Augusta*

Elizabeth Lemerise, *Western Kentucky University*

Cynthia Lepley, *Thomas College*

Norma Lestikow, *Highland Community College*

Blue Levin, *Ridge Community College*
Lawrence Lewis, *Loyola University New Orleans*
Mary B. Eberly Lewis, *Oakland University*
Linda Liptok, *McIntosh Kent State University–Tuscarawas*
Nancey Lobb, *Alvin Community College*
R. Martin Lobdell, *Pierce College*
Janet Lohan, *Washington State University*
Don Lucas, *Northwest Vista College*
Joe Lund, *Taylor University*
Salvador Macias, *University of South Carolina–Sumter*
Grace Malonai, *Saint Mary's College of California*
Donna Mantooth, *Georgia Highlands College*
Deborah Marche, *Van Glendale Community College*
Rebecca Marcon, *University of North Florida*
T. Darin Matthews, *The Citadel*
Kelly McCabe, *University of Mary Hardin-Baylor*
William McCracken, *Delaware Technical & Community College*
Jason McCoy, *Cape Fear Community College*
Jim McDonald, *California State University–Fresno*
Cathy McElderry, *University of Alabama–Birmingham*
Jim McElhone, *University of Texas of the Permian Basin*
Cathy McEvoy, *University of South Florida*
Annie McManus, *Parkland College at Jacksonville*
Courtney McManus, *Colby Sawyer College*
Tai McMiller, *York Technical College*
Beth McNulty, *Lake Sumter Community College*
Marcia McQuitty, *Southwestern Theological Seminary*
Dixie Cranmer McReynolds, *St. Vincent's College*
Joan Means, *Solano Community College*
Omar Mendez, *William Paterson University of New Jersey*
K. Mentink, *Chippewa Valley Technical College*
Peter Metzner, *Vance Granville Community College*
LeeAnn Miner, *Mount Vernon Nazarene University*
Ellen Mink, *Elizabethtown Community and Technical College*
Michael Miranda, *Kingsborough Community College (CUNY)*
Steve Mitchell, *Somerset Community College*
Yvonne Montgomery, *Langston University*
Beverly Moore, *Sullivan County Community College*
Brad Morris, *Grand Valley State University*
Dolly Morris, *University Alaska Fairbanks, TVC Campus*
AudreyAnn C. Moses, *Hampton University*
Jean Mosley, *Oral Roberts University*
Carol Mulling, *Des Moines Area Community College*
Jeannette Murphey, *Meridian Community College*
Sylvia Murray, *University of South Carolina Upstate*
Ron Naramore, *Angelina College*
Sandra Naumann, *Delaware Technical Community College*
Lisa Newell, *Indiana University of Pennsylvania*
Glenda Nichols, *Tarrant County College–South*

David Nitzschke, *Western Iowa Tech Community College*
Harriett Nordstrom, *University of Michigan–Flint*
Meghan Novy, *Palomar College*
Elleen O'Brien, *University of Maryland, Baltimore County*
Valerie O'Krent, *California State University–Fullerton*
Shirley Ogletree, *Texas State–San Marcos*
Jennifer Oliver, *Rockhurst University*
Leanne Olson, *Wisconsin Lutheran College*
Rose Olver, *Amherst College*
Sharon Ota, *Honolulu Community College*
John Otey, *Southern Arkansas University*
Karl Oyster, *Tidewater Community College*
Gwynne Pacheco, *Hawaii Community College*
Roger Page, *Ohio State University–Lima*
Joseph Panza, *Southern Connecticut State University*
Jennifer Parker, *University of South Carolina Upstate*
Brian Parry, *San Juan College*
Joan Paterna, *Manchester Community College*
Julie Patrick, *West Virginia University*
Sue Pazynski, *Glen Oaks Community College*
Carola Pedreschi, *Miami Dade College*
Colleen Peltz, *Iowa Lakes Community College*
John Phelan, *Western Oklahoma State College*
Peter Phipps, *Dutchess Community College*
Michelle Pilati, *Rio Hondo College*
Laura Pirazzi, *San Jose State University*
Diane Pisacreta, *St. Louis Community College*
Deanna Pledge, *Stephens College*
Leslee Pollina, *Southeast Missouri State University*
Yuly Pomares, *Miami Dade College*
Jean Poppei, *The Sage Colleges/Russell Sage College*
Lydia Powell, *Vance-Granville Community College*
Sherri Restauri, *Jacksonville State University*
Kate Rhodes, *Dona Ana Community College*
Shannon Rich, *Texas Woman's University*
Cynthia Riedi, *Morrisville State College, Norwich Campus*
Laura Rieves, *Tidewater Community College*
Vicki Ritts, *St. Louis Community College–Meramec*
Jane Roda, *Penn State–Hazleton Campus*
Keith Rosenbaum, *Dallas Baptist University*
Karl Rosengren, *University of Illinois at Urbana–Champaign*
Renda Ross, *Capital University*
Willow Rossmiller, *Montana State University–Great Falls College of Technology*
Melinda Rouse, *Alamance Community College*
Marlo Rouse-Arnett, *Georgia Southern*
Lisa Routh, *Pikes Peak Community College*
Loretta Rudd, *Texas Tech University*
Robert Rycek, *University of Nebraska at Kearney*
Brooke Saathoff, *Labette Community College*
James Sapp, *Kentucky Christian University*
Marie Saracino, *Stephen F. Austin State University*
Al Sarno, *Hannibal-LaGrange College*

Patricia Sawyer, *Middlesex Community College*
Linda Schaefer, *Minot State University*
Troy Schiedenhelm, *Rowan Cabarrus Community College*
Celeste Schneider, *Saint Mary's College*
Pamela Schuetze, *Buffalo State College*
Joe Schuh, *Northern Kentucky University*
Candace Schulenburg, *Cape Cod Community College*
Eric Seemann, *University of Alabama–Huntsville*
Nancy Segal, *California State University–Fullerton*
Sandy Sego, *American International College*
Zewelanji Serpell, *James Madison University*
Nitya Sethuraman, *Indiana University*
Stacie Shaw, *Presentation College–Fairmont Campus*
Virginia Shipman, *University of New Mexico*
Beth Sigmon, *Robeson Community College*
Theresa Simantirakis, *Wilbur Wright College*
Denise Simonsen, *Fort Lewis College*
Julie Singer, *University of Nevada, Reno*
Peggy Skinner, *South Plains College*
Tara Smith, *Elizabethtown College*
Todd Smith, *Lake Superior State University*
Jerry Snead, *Coastal Carolina Community College*
James Snowden, *Midwestern State University*
Le'Ann Solmonson, *Stephen F. Austin State University*
Brooke Spatta, *Lynn University*
Tracy Spinrad, *School of Social and Family Dynamics*
Melinda Spohn, *Spokane Falls Community College*
Jeannine Stamatakis, *Lincoln University*
Richard States, *Allegany College of Maryland*
Jill Steinberg, *University of Wisconsin–Madison*
Robby Stewart, *Oakland University*
Nancy Stinnett, *University of Alabama*
Mary Hughes Stone, *San Francisco State University*
Terry Stone, *University of Nebraska–Omaha*
Julia Stork, *Jefferson State Community College*
Amy Strimling, *Sacramento City College*
Rose Suggett, *Southeast Community College*
Terre Sullivan, *Chippewa Valley Technical College*
Cyril Svoboda, *University of Maryland University College*
Peter Talty, *Keuka College*
Amber Tatnall, *SUNY Delhi*
Becky Taylor, *Texas Christian University*
Marianne Taylor, *Pacific Lutheran University*
Samuel Taylor, *Tacoma Community College*
Luis Terrazas, *California State University–San Marcos*
Thomas Thieman, *College of St. Catherine*
Linda EagleHeart Thomas, *The University of Montana–COT*
Mojisola Tiamiyu, *University of Toledo*
Vicki Tinsley, *Brescia University*
Ed Titus, *Troy University*
Ivonne Tjoefat, *Rochester Community & Technical College*
Adrian Tomer, *Shippensburg University*

Barbara Townsend, *Gannon University*
Jeannine Turner, *Florida State University*
Jeffrey Turner, *Mitchell College*
Dave Urso, *Lord Fairfax Community College*
Cecelia Valrie, *East Carolina University*
Michael Vandehey, *Midwestern State University*
Marina Vera, *Southwestern College*
Monica Vines, *Central Oregon Community College*
Steven Voss, *Moberly Area Community College*
John Wakefield, *University of North Alabama*
Rebecca Walker-Sands, *Central Oregon Community College*
James Wallace, *St. Lawrence University*
Todd Walter, *D'Youville College*
Mark Wasicsko, *Northern Kentucky University*
Debbie Watson, *Shawnee State University*
Sheree Watson, *University of Southern Mississippi*
Nancy Wedeen, *Los Angeles Valley College*
Glenn Weisfeld, *Wayne State University*
Orville Weiszhaar, *Minneapolis Community and Technical College*
Lori Werdenschlag, *Lyndon State College*
Laurie Westcott, *New Hampshire Community Technical College*
Linda Whitney, *Houston Community College Northwest*
Robert Wiater, *Bergen Community College*
Sharon Wiederstein, *Blinn College*
Vicki Will, *Brescia University*
Jacqueline Williams, *Moorpark College*
June Williams, *Southeastern Louisiana University*
Kay Williams, *Tidewater Community College*
Patti Williams, *Tidewater Community College*
Lois Willoughby, *Miami Dade College*
Stephen Wills, *Mercer University*
Cynthia Wilson, *University of South Alabama–Baldwin County*
Christy Wolfe, *University of Louisville*
Peter Wooldridge, *Durham Technical Community College*
Shelly Wooldridge, *University of Arkansas Community College at Batesville*
Bonnie Wright, *Gardner-Webb University*
Kent Yamauchi, *Pasadena City College*
Robin Yaure, *Penn State Mont Alto*
Ani Yazedjian, *Texas State University–San Marcos*
Mahbobeh Yektaparast, *Central Piedmont Community College*
Susan Zandrow, *Bridgewater State College*
Rowan Zeiss, *Blue Ridge Community College*
Laura Zettel-Watson, *California State University–Fullerton*
Elizabeth Zettler, *Rellinger Illinois College*
Ginny Zhan, *Kennesaw State University*
Ling-Yi Zhou, *University of St. Francis*
Renee Zucchero, *Xavier University*

Many others deserve a great deal of thanks. I am indebted to the numerous people who provided me with a superb education, first at Wesleyan University and later at the University of Wisconsin. Specifically, Karl Scheibe played a pivotal role in my undergraduate education, and the late Vernon Allen acted as mentor and guide through my graduate years. It was in graduate school that I learned about development, being exposed to such experts as Ross Parke, Joel Levin, Herb Klausmeier, and many others. My education continued when I became a professor. I am especially grateful to my colleagues at the University of Massachusetts, who make the university such a wonderful place in which to teach and do research.

Several people played central roles in the development of this book. The thoughtful and creative Stephen Hupp and Jeremy Jewell of Southern Illinois University–Edwardsville were partners in developing the Revel materials, and their input was critical. John Bickford of the University of Massachusetts Amherst provided important research and editorial support, and I am thankful for his help and superb writing skills. I am also grateful to Christopher Poirier of Stonehill College, who produced the wonderful Instructor Resource Manual and Test Bank that accompany *Development Across the Life Span*. Finally, Michelle Goncalves was essential in juggling and coordinating the multiple aspects of working on a project such as this, and I am very grateful for the substantial role they played.

I am also thankful to the superb Pearson team that was instrumental in the inception and development of this book. Jeff Marshall, the original Executive Editor, conceived of the format of this book. Now Kelli Strieby has taken over, and she has brought creativity and a wealth of good ideas to the project. Cathy Murphy, developmental editor on this edition, did a superb job of providing thoughtful advice and keeping on top of a myriad of details. On the production end of things, project manager Valerie Iglar-Mobley helped bring all aspects of the text together. Finally, I'd like to thank (in advance) marketing manager Christopher Brown, on whose skills I'm counting.

I also wish to acknowledge the members of my family, who play such an essential role in my life. My brother, Michael, my sisters-in-law and brother-in-law, my nieces and nephews, all make up an important part of my life. In addition, I am always indebted to the older generation of my family, who led the way in a manner I can only hope to emulate. I will always be obligated to Harry Brochstein, Mary Vorwerk, and Ethel Radler. Most of all, the list is headed by my father, Saul Feldman, and my mother, Leah Brochstein.

In the end, it is my immediate family who deserve the greatest thanks. My son, Jon, his wife, Leigh, and my grandsons Alex and Miles; my son, Josh, his wife, Julie, and my granddaughters Naomi and Marina; and my daughter, Sarah, her husband, Jeff, and my granddaughters Lilia and Rose, not only are nice, smart, and good-looking, but my pride and joy. And ultimately my wife, Katherine Vorwerk, provides the love and grounding that makes everything worthwhile. I thank them, with all my love.

Robert S. Feldman
University of Massachusetts Amherst

About the Author

Robert S. Feldman is Professor of Psychological and Brain Sciences and Senior Advisor to the Chancellor of the University of Massachusetts Amherst. He has also served as Dean of the College of Social and Behavioral Sciences, Interim Dean of the College of Education, and Deputy Chancellor of the University of Massachusetts.

A recipient of the College Distinguished Teacher Award, he teaches classes ranging in size from 10 to nearly 500 students. During the course of more than two decades as a college instructor, he has taught both undergraduate and graduate courses at Mount Holyoke College, Wesleyan University, and Virginia Commonwealth University in addition to the University of Massachusetts Amherst.

A Fellow of the American Psychological Association, American Association for the Advancement of Science, and the Association for Psychological Science, Professor Feldman received a B.A. with High Honors from Wesleyan University (and from which he received the Distinguished Alumni Award). He has an M.S. and Ph.D. from the University of Wisconsin–Madison. He is a winner of a Fulbright Senior Research Scholar and Lecturer award, and he has written more than 200 books, book chapters, and scientific articles. He has edited *Development of Nonverbal Behavior in Children* and *Applications of Nonverbal Behavioral Theory and Research* and co-edited *Fundamentals of Nonverbal Behavior*. He is also author of *Development Across the Life Span, Understanding Psychology*, and *P.O.W.E.R. Learning: Strategies for Success in College and Life*. His books have been translated into many languages, including Spanish, French, Portuguese, Dutch, Chinese, Korean, German, Arabic, Tagalog, and Japanese, and more than 2.5 million students have used his textbooks.

Professor Feldman's research interests include honesty and deception in everyday life, work that he described in *The Liar in Your Life,* a trade book. His research has been supported by grants from the National Institute of Mental Health and the National Institute on Disabilities and Rehabilitation Research. He is also past president of the Federation of Associations in the Behavioral and Brain Sciences Foundation, an organization that promotes the social sciences, a member of the Board of the Social Psychology Network, and is Chair of the Board and Executive Committee of New England Public Media.

Professor Feldman loves music, is an enthusiastic pianist, and enjoys cooking and traveling. He has three children and six grandchildren. He and his wife, a psychologist, live in western Massachusetts in a home overlooking the Holyoke Mountain Range.

Chapter 1
Introduction

Shutterstock

The Ruiz "Happy Birthday Family Reunion" was a big success. Marco Ruiz's grandfather, Geraldo, who would turn 90 the following day, was in his glory at the center of the festivities.

Marco's wife, Ellie, had hatched the reunion idea while planning next summer's wedding of their youngest daughter, Eva. Eva's fiancé, Peter, would be the first African American in the family, and Ellie's idea was to introduce him early so his ethnicity would be old news by the wedding day.

Ellie's brainstorm was apparently working, given the happy din of the crowd. Marco took a quiet census: his father, Damiano, and Ellie's mom and dad, plus a gaggle of uncles, aunts, siblings, and cousins from his and Ellie's families. One generation down, he counted his children and their families, and virtual busloads of nieces and nephews with their families, down to the youngest child, 4-year-old Alicia Wei-Li Saucedo, Geraldo's great-great-granddaughter, who had been adopted from China.

Marco watched as Grandpa Geraldo hugged and chatted happily with Alicia. There in one small picture frame was the story of the five generations of Grandpa's family, from 4 to 90.

Marco thought to himself: What is Grandpa making of all this? Is he wondering how he spawned all these different personalities? Is he speculating about their careers, their futures? Is he looking for traces of his stubbornness and short temper, his generosity and open-mindedness? Does he find in this gathering the vast ambitions that he had as a boy? Will any of them be—at last—the athlete that he never was, or will they be writers and thinkers like him and his children?

Marco smiled at Ellie's idea of "integrating" Peter into the family. Peter's skin color wasn't even an issue. The main stories were that Marco's nephew Ted was here with his fiancé, Tom, and his niece Clarissa had her girlfriend, Rosa, on her arm. Marco's smile grew broader. Let Grandpa wonder where this latest family trend came from.

1

Lifespan development is a diverse and growing field with a broad focus and wide applicability. It covers the entire life span of the individual from birth to death as it examines the ways in which people develop physically, intellectually, and socially. It asks and attempts to answer questions about the ways in which people change and remain the same over their years of life.

Many of the questions that developmentalists ask are, in essence, the scientist's version of the questions that parents ask about their children and themselves: how the genetic legacy of parents plays out in their children; how children learn; why they make the choices they make; whether personality characteristics are inherited and whether they change or remain stable over time; how a stimulating environment affects development; and many others. To pursue these answers, of course, developmentalists use the highly structured, formal scientific method, whereas parents mostly use the informal strategy of observing, engaging with, and loving their kids.

In this chapter, we will introduce the field of lifespan development. We first discuss the breadth of the field, both in the range of years it covers and in the topics it addresses, and we will look at the major theoretical perspectives that have examined those topics. We also describe the key features of the scientific method, the main approach that scientists take to answering questions of interest.

As you become acquainted with lifespan development, keep the chapter's learning objectives in mind. Not only do they offer a guide to what you will learn about the field, but they also provide a roadmap of the chapter's structure.

Module 1.1 *Beginnings*

LO 1.1 Describe the scope of the field of lifespan development.
LO 1.2 Describe cohorts, and explain how they influence development.
LO 1.3 Explain the differences between continuous change and discontinuous change.
LO 1.4 Distinguish between critical periods and sensitive periods.
LO 1.5 Describe how the study of lifespan development expanded.
LO 1.6 Summarize the influence of nature and nurture on development.

Module 1.2 *Theoretical Perspectives* on Lifespan Development

LO 1.7 Describe the fundamentals of the psychodynamic perspective.
LO 1.8 Describe the fundamentals of the behavioral perspective.
LO 1.9 Describe the fundamentals of the cognitive perspective.
LO 1.10 Describe the fundamentals of the humanistic perspective.
LO 1.11 Describe the fundamentals of the contextual perspective.
LO 1.12 Describe the fundamentals of the evolutionary perspective.
LO 1.13 Explain the value of using multiple perspectives to describe human development.

Module 1.3 *Research Methods*

LO 1.14 Explain the role theories and hypotheses play in the study of development.
LO 1.15 Contrast correlational and experimental research.
LO 1.16 Explain the types of studies and methods used in correlational research.
LO 1.17 Analyze how experiments can be used to determine cause and effect.
LO 1.18 Explain how theoretical and applied research complement each other.
LO 1.19 Compare longitudinal research, cross-sectional research, and sequential research.
LO 1.20 Describe some ethical issues that affect psychological research.

Module 1.1

Beginnings

New Conceptions

In many ways, the first meeting of Louise Brown and Elizabeth Carr was unremarkable: just two women, one in her thirties, the other in her fourties, chatting about their lives and their own children.

But in another sense, the meeting was extraordinary. Louise Brown was the world's first "test-tube baby," born by *in vitro fertilization (IVF)*, a procedure in which fertilization of a mother's egg by a father's sperm takes place outside of the mother's body. And Elizabeth Carr was the first baby born by IVF in the United States.

Louise was a preschooler when her parents told her how she was conceived, and throughout her childhood she was bombarded with questions. It became routine to explain to her classmates that she, in fact, was not born in a laboratory. At times, she felt completely alone. For Elizabeth, too, growing up was not easy, as she experienced bouts of insecurity.

Today, however, Louise and Elizabeth are hardly unique. They are among the more than 5 million babies that have been conceived using the procedure, one that has almost become routine. And both became mothers themselves, giving birth to babies who were conceived, incidentally, the old-fashioned way (Gagneux, 2016; Simpson, 2017; Moura-Ramos & Canavarro, 2018).

Louise Brown and Elizabeth Carr's conceptions may have been novel, but their development since then has followed a predictable pattern. Although the specifics of our development vary, the broad strokes set in motion more than three decades ago are remarkably similar for all of us. LeBron James, the Pope, and you—all are traversing the territory known as lifespan development.

Brown's conception is just one of the brave new worlds of the day. Issues that affect human development range from cloning to poverty to the prevention of AIDS. Underlying these are even more fundamental issues: How do we develop physically? How does our understanding of the world change throughout our lives? And how do our personalities and social relationships develop as we move through the life span?

These questions and many others are central to lifespan development. The field encompasses a broad span of time and a wide range of areas. Consider the range of interests that different specialists might focus on when considering Louise Brown and Elizabeth Carr:

- Lifespan development researchers who investigate behavior at the level of biological processes might determine if Louise and Elizabeth's functioning prior to birth was affected by their conception outside the womb.
- Specialists in lifespan development who study genetics might examine how the genetic endowment from their parents affects their later behavior.

- For lifespan development specialists who investigate the ways thinking changes over the course of life, their lives might be examined in terms of how each woman's understanding of the nature of her conception changed as she grew older.
- Researchers in lifespan development who focus on physical growth might consider whether their growth rates differed from children conceived more traditionally.
- Lifespan development experts who specialize in the social world and social relationships might look at the ways that Louise and Elizabeth interacted with others and the kinds of friendships they developed.

Although their interests take many forms, these specialists share one concern: understanding the growth and change that occur during life. Taking many different approaches, developmentalists study how both our biological inheritance from our parents and the environment in which we live jointly affect our future behavior, personality, and potential as human beings.

Whether they focus on heredity or environment, all developmental specialists acknowledge that neither one alone can account for the full range of human development. Instead, we must look at the interaction of heredity and environment, attempting to grasp how both underlie human behavior.

In this module, we orient ourselves to the field of lifespan development. We begin with a discussion of the scope of the discipline, illustrating the wide array of topics it covers and the full range of ages it examines. We also survey the main issues and controversies of the field and consider the broad perspectives that developmentalists take. Finally, we discuss the ways developmentalists use research to ask and answer questions.

Louise Brown, left, and Elizabeth Carr were both concieved by in vitro fertilization.

An Orientation to Lifespan Development

Have you ever wondered at the way an infant tightly grips your finger with tiny, perfectly formed hands? Or at the way an adolescent can make involved decisions about whom to invite to a party? Or what makes a grandfather at 80 so similar to the father he was at 40?

lifespan development
the field of study that examines patterns of growth, change, and stability in behavior that occur throughout the entire life span

If you've ever contemplated such things, you are asking the kinds of questions that scientists in the field of lifespan development pose. **Lifespan development** is the field of study that examines patterns of growth, change, and stability in behavior that occur throughout the life span.

In its study of growth, change, and stability, lifespan development takes a *scientific* approach. Like members of other scientific disciplines, researchers in lifespan development test their assumptions by applying scientific methods. They develop theories about development and use methodical, scientific techniques to validate the accuracy of their assumptions systematically.

Lifespan development focuses on *human* development. Although there are developmentalists who study nonhuman species, the vast majority study people. Some seek to understand universal principles of development, whereas others focus on how cultural, racial, and ethnic differences affect development. Still others aim to understand the traits and characteristics that differentiate one person from another. Regardless of approach, however, all developmentalists view development as a continuing process throughout the life span.

As developmental specialists focus on change during the life span, they also consider stability. They ask in which areas, and in what periods, people show change and growth, and when and how their behavior reveals consistency and continuity with prior behavior.

Finally, developmentalists assume that the process of development persists from the moment of conception to the day of death, with people changing in some ways right up to the end of their lives and in other ways exhibiting remarkable stability. They believe that no single period governs all development, but instead that people maintain the capacity for substantial growth and change throughout their lives.

Characterizing Lifespan Development: The Scope of the Field

LO 1.1   Describe the scope of the field of lifespan development.

Clearly, the definition of lifespan development is broad, and the scope of the field is extensive. Typically, lifespan development specialists cover several diverse areas, choosing to specialize in both a topical area and an age range.

physical development
development involving the body's physical makeup, including the brain, nervous system, muscles, and senses, and the need for food, drink, and sleep

TOPICAL AREAS IN LIFESPAN DEVELOPMENT   Some developmentalists focus on **physical development**, examining the ways in which the body's makeup—the brain, nervous system, muscles, and senses, and the need for food, drink, and sleep—helps determine behavior. For example, one specialist in physical development might examine the effects of malnutrition on the pace of growth in children, whereas another might look at how athletes' physical performance declines during adulthood (Fell & Williams, 2008; Muiños & Ballesteros, 2014).

cognitive development
development involving the ways that growth and change in intellectual capabilities influence a person's behavior

Other developmental specialists examine **cognitive development**, seeking to understand how growth and change in intellectual capabilities influence a person's behavior. Cognitive developmentalists examine learning, memory, problem solving, and intelligence. For example, specialists in cognitive development might want to see how problem-solving skills change over the course of life, or if cultural differences exist in the way people explain their academic successes and failures (Penido et al., 2012; Coates, 2016; St. Mary et al., 2018).

personality development
development involving the ways that the enduring characteristics that differentiate one person from another change over the life span

Finally, some developmental specialists focus on personality and social development. **Personality development** is the study of stability and change in the characteristics that differentiate one person from another over the life span. **Social development** is the way in which individuals' interactions and relationships with others grow, change, and remain stable over the course of life. A developmentalist interested in personality development might ask whether there are stable, enduring personality traits throughout the life span, whereas a specialist in social development might examine the effects

social development
the way in which individuals' interactions with others and their social relationships grow, change, and remain stable over the course of life

Table 1-1 Approaches to Lifespan Development

Orientation	Defining Characteristics	Examples of Questions Asked*
Physical development	Emphasizes how brain, nervous system, muscles, sensory capabilities, and needs for food, drink, and sleep affect behavior	• What determines the sex of a child? (2.1) • What are the long-term results of premature birth? (2.3) • What are the benefits of breast milk? (3.1) • What are the consequences of early or late sexual maturation? (6.1) • What leads to obesity in adulthood? (7.1) • How do adults cope with stress? (8.1) • What are the outward and internal signs of aging? (9.1) • How do we define death? (10.1)
Cognitive development	Emphasizes intellectual abilities, including learning, memory, problem solving, and intelligence	• What are the earliest memories that can be recalled from infancy? (3.2) • What are the intellectual consequences of watching television? (4.2) • Do spatial reasoning skills relate to music practice? (4.2) • Are there benefits related to bilingualism? (5.2) • How does an adolescent's egocentrism affect his or her view of the world? (6.2) • Are there ethnic and racial differences in intelligence? (5.2) • How does creativity relate to intelligence? (7.2) • Does intelligence decline in late adulthood? (9.2)
Personality and social development	Emphasizes enduring characteristics that differentiate one person from another, and how interactions with others and social relationships grow and change over the lifetime	• Do newborns respond differently to their mothers than to others? (2.3) • What is the best procedure for disciplining children? (4.3) • When does a sense of gender identity develop? (4.3) • How can we promote cross-race friendships? (5.3) • What are the causes of adolescent suicide? (6.3) • How do we choose a romantic partner? (7.3) • Do the effects of parental divorce last into old age? (9.3) • Do people withdraw from others in late adulthood? (9.3) • What are the emotions involved in confronting death? (10.1)

*Numbers in parentheses indicate in which chapter and module the question is addressed.

of racism or poverty or divorce on development (Lansford, 2009; Tine, 2014; Manning et al., 2017). These four major topic areas—physical, cognitive, social, and personality development—are summarized in Table 1-1.

AGE RANGES AND INDIVIDUAL DIFFERENCES In addition to choosing a particular topical area, developmentalists also typically look at a particular age range. The life span is usually divided into broad age ranges: the prenatal period (from conception to birth); infancy and toddlerhood (birth to age 3); the preschool period (ages 3 to 6); middle childhood (ages 6 to 12); adolescence (ages 12 to 20); young adulthood (ages 20 to 40); middle adulthood (ages 40 to 60); and late adulthood (ages 60 to death).

It's important to keep in mind that these periods are social constructions. A *social construction* is a shared notion of reality that is widely accepted but is a function of society and culture at a given time. Thus, the age ranges within a period—and even the periods themselves—are in many ways arbitrary and culturally derived. For example, the concept of childhood as a separate period did not exist in Western cultures before the 18th century—until then, children were seen simply as miniature adults. Furthermore, although some periods have a clear-cut boundary (infancy begins with birth, the preschool period ends with entry into public school, and adolescence starts with sexual maturity), others do not.

For instance, consider the period of young adulthood. Age 20 marks the end of the teenage period, but for many people the age change from 19 to 20 has little special significance, coming as it does in the middle of college. For them, more substantial changes are likely to occur when they leave college around age 22. Furthermore, in some cultures adulthood starts much earlier, as soon as a child can begin full-time work.

In fact, some developmentalists have proposed entirely new developmental periods. For instance, psychologist Jeffrey Arnett argues that adolescence extends into *emerging adulthood*, a period beginning in the late teenage years and continuing into the mid-20s. During emerging adulthood, people are no longer adolescents, but they haven't fully taken on the responsibilities of adulthood. Instead, they are still trying out different identities and engaging in self-focused exploration (de Dios, 2012; Syed & Seiffge-Krenke, 2013; Sumner, Burrow, & Hill, 2015; Arnett, 2016).

In short, there are substantial *individual differences* in the timing of events in people's lives. In part, this is a biological fact of life: People mature at different rates and

This wedding of two children in India is an example of how environmental factors can play a significant role in determining the age when a particular event is likely to occur.

reach developmental milestones at different points. However, environmental factors also play a significant role; for example, the typical age of marriage varies from one culture to another, depending in part on the functions that marriage plays in a given culture.

THE LINKS BETWEEN TOPICS AND AGES Each of the broad topic areas of lifespan development—physical, cognitive, social, and personality development—plays a role throughout the life span. Consequently, some developmental experts may focus on physical development during the prenatal period, and others during adolescence. Some might specialize in social development during the preschool years, whereas others look at social relationships in late adulthood. And still others might take a broader approach, looking at cognitive development through every period of life.

In this book, we'll take a comprehensive approach, proceeding chronologically from the prenatal period through late adulthood and death. Within each period, we'll look at physical, cognitive, social, and personality development.

Cohort and Other Influences on Development: Developing with Others in a Social World

LO 1.2 Describe cohorts, and explain how they influence development.

Bob, born in 1947, is a baby boomer; he was born soon after the end of World War II, when an enormous surge in the birth rate occurred as soldiers returned to the United States from overseas. He was an adolescent at the height of the civil rights movement and the beginning of protests against the Vietnam War. His mother, Leah, was born in 1922. She died at age 96, and she was part of the generation that passed its childhood and teenage years in the shadow of the Great Depression. Bob's son, Jon, was born in 1975. Now middle-aged and established in a career and raising his own family, he is a member of what has been called Generation X. Jon's younger sister, Sarah, who was born in 1982, is part of the next generation, which sociologists have called the Millennial Generation. She now is raising a preschooler of her own after finishing graduate school and starting her career. She sees post-Millennials, the generation that followed her, as being engrossed in social media and their iPhones.

These people are in part products of the social times and the cultures in which they live. Each belongs to a particular **cohort**, a group of people born at around the same time in the same place. Such major social events as wars, economic upturns and depressions, famines, and epidemics exert similar influences on members of a particular cohort (Mitchell, 2002; Dittman, 2005; Twenge, Gentile, & Campbell, 2015).

Cohort effects are an example of *history-graded influences*, biological and environmental influences associated with a particular historical moment. For instance, people who lived in New York City during the 9/11 terrorist attack on the World Trade Center experienced shared biological and environmental challenges as a result of the attack. Their development is going to be affected by this normative history-graded event (Laugharne, Janca, & Widiger, 2007; Park, Riley, & Snyder, 2012; Kim, Bushway, & Tsao, 2016).

cohort

a group of people born at around the same time in the same place

> **From an educator's perspective:** How would a student's cohort membership affect his or her readiness for school? For example, what would be the benefits and drawbacks of growing up in a cohort in which cell phone use was routine, compared with previous cohorts in which cell phone use was less common?

In contrast, *age-graded influences* are biological and environmental influences that are similar for individuals in a particular age group, regardless of when or where they are raised. For example, biological events such as puberty and menopause are universal events that occur at about the same time in all societies. Similarly, a sociocultural event such as entry into formal education can be considered an age-graded influence because it occurs in most cultures around age 6.

Development is also affected by *sociocultural-graded influences*, the social and cultural factors present at a particular time for a particular individual, depending on such variables as ethnicity, social class, and subcultural membership. For example, sociocultural-graded influences will be considerably different for white and nonwhite children, especially if one lives in poverty and the other in affluence. Similarly, children raised in remote and isolated areas of the African outback will experience significantly different upbringings from those raised in New York City (Rose et al., 2003; Hosokawa & Katsura, 2018). (See the *Cultural Dimensions* box.)

Finally, *non-normative life events* are specific, atypical events that occur in a particular person's life at a time when such events do not happen to most people. For example, a child whose parents die in an automobile accident when she is 6 has experienced a significant non-normative life event.

Cultural Dimensions
How Culture, Ethnicity, and Race Influence Development

In the United States, parents praise young children who ask a lot of questions for being "intelligent" and "inquisitive." The Dutch consider such children "too dependent on others." Italian parents judge inquisitiveness as a sign of social and emotional competence, not intelligence. Spanish parents praise character far more than intelligence, and Swedes value security and happiness above all.

What are we to make of the diverse parental expectations cited above? Is one way of looking at children's inquisitiveness right and the others wrong? Surely not, if we take into consideration the cultural contexts in which parents operate. In fact, different cultures and subcultures have their own views of appropriate and inappropriate methods and interpretations of childrearing, just as they have different developmental goals for children (Feldman & Masalha, 2007; Huijbregts et al., 2009; Chen, Chen, & Zheng, 2012).

Specialists in child development must take into consideration broad cultural factors. For example, as we'll discuss further in Chapter 4, children growing up in Asian societies tend to have a *collectivistic orientation*, focusing on the interdependence among members of society. In contrast, children in Western societies are more likely to have an *individualistic orientation*, in which they concentrate on the uniqueness of the individual.

Similarly, child developmentalists must also consider ethnic, racial, socioeconomic, and gender differences if they are to achieve an understanding of how people change and grow throughout the life span. If these specialists succeed in doing so, not only can they attain a better understanding of human development, but they may also be able to derive more precise applications for improving the human social condition.

To complicate the study of diverse populations, the terms *race* and *ethnic group* are often used inappropriately. *Race* originated as a biological concept, and it initially referred to classifications based on physical and structural characteristics of species. But such a definition has little validity in terms of humans, and research shows that it is not a meaningful way to differentiate people.

For example, depending on how race is defined, there are between 3 and 300 races, and no race is genetically distinct. The fact that 99.9 percent of humans' genetic makeup is identical in all humans makes the question of race seem insignificant. Thus, race today is generally thought of as a social construction, something defined by people and their beliefs (Smedley & Smedley, 2005; Alfred & Chlup, 2010; Kung et al., 2018).

In contrast, *ethnic group* and *ethnicity* are broader terms for which there is greater agreement. They relate to cultural background, nationality, religion, and language. Members of ethnic groups share a common cultural background and group history.

In addition, there is little agreement about which names best reflect different races and ethnic groups. Should the term *African American*—which has geographical and cultural implications—be preferred over *black*, which focuses primarily on race and skin color? Is *Native American* preferable to *Indian*? Is *Hispanic* more appropriate than *Latino*? And how can researchers accurately categorize people with multiracial backgrounds?

To fully understand development, then, we need to take the complex issues associated with human diversity into account. In fact, it is only by looking for similarities and differences among various ethnic, cultural, and racial groups that developmental researchers can distinguish principles of development that are universal from ones that are culturally determined. In the years ahead, then, it is likely that lifespan development will move from a discipline that primarily focuses on North American and European development to one that encompasses development around the globe (Matsumoto & Yoo, 2006; Kloep et al., 2009; Arnett, 2017).

Key Issues and Questions: Determining the Nature—and Nurture—of Lifespan Development

Lifespan development is a decades-long journey through shared milestones, with many individual routes along the way. For developmentalists, the variations in lifespan development raise many questions. What are the best ways to think about the enormous changes that a person undergoes from before birth to death? How important is chronological age? Is there a clear timetable for development? How can one begin to find common threads and patterns?

In this section we examine four of the most important—and continuously argued—issues in the field of lifespan development. We also consider the resolutions to which researchers have come regarding these issues.

Continuous Change Versus Discontinuous Change

LO 1.3   **Explain the differences between continuous change and discontinuous change.**

One of the primary issues challenging developmentalists is whether development proceeds in a continuous or discontinuous fashion. In **continuous change**, development is gradual, with achievements at one level building on those of previous levels. Continuous change is quantitative; the underlying developmental processes remain the same over the life span. In this view changes are a matter of degree, not of kind—like changes in a person's height. Some theorists suggest that changes in people's thinking abilities are also continuous, building on gradual improvements rather than developing entirely new processing capabilities.

In contrast, others see development as primarily a matter of **discontinuous change**, occurring in distinct stages. Each stage brings about behavior that is assumed to be qualitatively different from behavior at previous stages. Consider cognitive development again. Some cognitive developmentalists suggest that our thinking changes in fundamental ways as we develop, not just quantitatively but qualitatively.

Most developmentalists agree that it makes little sense to take an either–or position on this issue. Although many types of developmental change are continuous, others are clearly discontinuous (Heimann, 2003; Gumz et al., 2010; Burgers, 2016).

Critical and Sensitive Periods: Gauging the Impact of Environmental Events

LO 1.4   **Distinguish between critical periods and sensitive periods.**

If a woman comes down with a case of rubella (German measles) in the 11th week of pregnancy, the consequences for the child she is carrying—possible blindness, deafness, and heart defects—can be devastating. However, if she comes down with the same strain of rubella in the 30th week of pregnancy, damage to the child is unlikely.

The differing outcomes demonstrate the concept of critical periods. A **critical period** is a specific time during development when a particular event has its greatest consequences. Critical periods occur when the presence of certain kinds of environmental stimuli enable development to proceed normally, or when exposure to certain stimuli results in abnormal development. For example, mothers who take drugs at particular times during pregnancy may cause permanent harm to their developing child (Mølgaard-Nielsen, Pasternak, & Hviid, 2013; Nygaard et al., 2017).

Although early specialists in lifespan development placed great emphasis on critical periods, recent thinking suggests that individuals are more malleable, particularly in the domain of personality and social development. For instance, rather than suffering permanent damage from a lack of certain early social experiences, there is increasing evidence that people can use later experiences to help overcome previous deficits.

Consequently, developmentalists are now more likely to speak of **sensitive periods** rather than critical periods. In a sensitive period, organisms are particularly

continuous change
gradual development in which achievements at one level build on those of previous levels

discontinuous change
development that occurs in distinct steps or stages, with each stage bringing about behavior that is assumed to be qualitatively different from behavior at previous stages

critical period
a specific time during development when a particular event has its greatest consequences and the presence of certain kinds of environmental stimuli are necessary for development to proceed normally

sensitive period
a point in development when organisms are particularly susceptible to certain kinds of stimuli in their environments, but the absence of those stimuli does not always produce irreversible consequences

susceptible to certain kinds of stimuli in their environments. In contrast to a critical period, however, the absence of those stimuli during a sensitive period does not always produce irreversible consequences.

Although the absence of particular environmental influences during a sensitive period may hinder development, it is possible for later experiences to overcome the previous deficits. In other words, the concept of sensitive period recognizes the plasticity of developing humans (Hooks & Chen, 2008; Hartley & Lee, 2015; Piekarski et al., 2017).

Lifespan Approaches Versus a Focus on Particular Periods

LO 1.5   Describe how the study of lifespan development expanded.

Early developmentalists tended to focus their attention on infancy and adolescence, largely to the exclusion of other parts of the life span. Today, however, developmentalists believe the entire life span is important, largely because developmental growth and change continue during every part of life—as we'll discuss throughout this book.

Furthermore, to fully understand the social influences on a person of a given age, we need to understand the person's social environment—the people who in large measure provide those influences. For instance, to understand development in infants, we need to unravel the effects of their parents' ages on their social environments. A 15-year-old first-time mother and an experienced 37-year-old mother will provide parental influences of different sorts. Consequently, infant development is in part an outgrowth of adult development.

Additionally, as lifespan developmentalist Paul Baltes points out, development across the life span involves both gains and losses. With age, certain capabilities become more refined and sophisticated, whereas others decline. For example, vocabulary tends to grow throughout childhood and continue through most of adulthood, but certain physical abilities, like reaction time, improve until early and middle adulthood, and then begin to decline (Baltes, 2003; Ghisletta et al., 2010; Cid-Fernández, Lindín, & Díaz, 2016).

The Relative Influence of Nature and Nurture on Development

LO 1.6   Summarize the influence of nature and nurture on development.

One of the enduring questions of development involves how much of people's behavior is the result of genetics (nature) and how much is the result of the physical and social environment (nurture) (Wexler, 2006; Kong et al., 2018).

Nature refers to traits, abilities, and capacities that are inherited from one's parents. It encompasses any factor that is produced by the predetermined unfolding of genetic information—a process known as **maturation**. These genetic, inherited influences are at work as we move from the one-cell organism created at conception to the billions of cells that make up a fully formed human. Nature influences whether our eyes are blue or brown, whether we have thick hair throughout life or eventually go bald, and how good we are at athletics. Nature allows our brains to develop in such a way that we can read the words on this page.

maturation
the predetermined unfolding of genetic information

In contrast, *nurture* refers to the environmental influences that shape behavior. Some influences may be biological, such as the impact of a pregnant mother's use of cocaine on her unborn child or the amount and kind of food available to children. Other influences are more social, such as the ways parents discipline their children and the effects of peer pressure on an adolescent. Finally, some influences are a result of societal factors, such as the socioeconomic circumstances in which people find themselves.

Although developmentalists reject the notion that behavior is the sole result of either nature or nurture, the nature–nurture question can cause heated debate. Take, for instance, intelligence. If intelligence is primarily determined by heredity and is largely fixed at birth, then efforts to improve intellectual performance later in life may be doomed to failure. In contrast, if intelligence is primarily a result of environmental factors, such as the amount and quality of schooling and home stimulation, then an improvement in social conditions could cause intelligence to increase.

Clearly, neither nature nor nurture stands alone in most developmental matters. The interaction of genetic and environmental factors is complex, in part because certain genetically determined traits have not only a direct influence on children's behavior, but also an indirect influence in shaping children's *environments*. For example, children who cry a great deal—a trait that may be produced by genetic factors—may influence their environment by making their parents rush to comfort them whenever they cry. The parents' responsivity to their children's genetically determined behavior becomes an environmental influence on the children's subsequent development.

Similarly, although our genetic background orients us toward particular behaviors, those behaviors will not necessarily occur without an appropriate environment. People with similar genetic backgrounds (such as identical twins) may behave in different ways; and people with highly dissimilar genetic backgrounds can behave quite similarly to one another in certain areas (Segal et al., 2015; Sudharsanan, Behrman, & Kohler, 2016; Pfeifer & Hamann, 2018).

In sum, the nature–nurture question is challenging. Ultimately, we should consider the two sides of the issue as ends of a continuum, with particular behaviors falling somewhere between the ends. The same can be said of the other controversies that we have considered. For instance, continuous versus discontinuous development is not an either–or proposition; some forms of development fall toward the continuous end of the continuum, whereas others lie closer to the discontinuous end. In short, few statements about development involve either–or absolutes (Deater-Deckard & Cahill, 2006; Rutter, 2006; Selig & Lopez, 2016).

Review, Check, and Apply

Review

LO 1.1 Describe the scope of the field of lifespan development.

Lifespan development is a scientific approach to understanding human growth and change throughout life. The field covers a broad range of ages and topic areas. Its chief aim is to examine the links between human age groups and the areas of physical, cognitive, social, and personality development.

LO 1.2 Describe cohorts, and explain how they influence development.

Membership in a cohort, based on age and place of birth, subjects people to influences based on historical events (history-graded influences). People are also subject to age-graded influences, sociocultural-graded influences, and non-normative life events.

LO 1.3 Explain the differences between continuous change and discontinuous change.

In continuous change, development is gradual, with achievements at one level building on those of previous levels. Continuous change is quantitative; the underlying developmental processes remain the same over the life span. In contrast, in discontinuous change, development occurs in distinct stages. Each stage brings about behavior that is assumed to be qualitatively different from behavior at previous stages.

LO 1.4 Distinguish between critical periods and sensitive periods.

A critical period is a specific time during development when a particular event has its greatest consequences. In a sensitive period, organisms are particularly susceptible to certain kinds of stimuli in their environments. In contrast to a critical period, however, the absence of those stimuli during a sensitive period does not always produce irreversible consequences.

LO 1.5 Describe how the study of lifespan development expanded.

Early developmentalists tended to focus their attention on infancy and adolescence, largely to the exclusion of other parts of the life span. Today, however, developmentalists believe the entire life span is important, largely because developmental growth and change continue during every part of life.

LO 1.6 Summarize the influence of nature and nurture on development.

Nature refers to traits, abilities, and capacities that are inherited from one's parents. In contrast, *nurture* refers to the environmental influences that shape behavior.

Check Yourself

1. Three assumptions made by lifespan developmentalists are: (1) a focus on human development, (2) an understanding of stability in addition to growth and change, and (3) _____.

   a. the perception that development persists throughout our entire lives
   b. the perception that childhood developmental changes are the only changes worth studying
   c. the idea that some periods of the life span are more important than others
   d. the perception that development is a stagnant process

2. The time when children utter their first complete sentence is an example of _____.

   a. a history-graded influence
   b. an age-graded influence
   c. a sociocultural-graded influence
   d. a non-normative life event

3. Grady believes that human development occurs in small, measurable amounts. His sister Andrea disagrees and suggests that human development is more distinct and steplike. Their argument is most reflective of the _____ issue.

   a. critical and sensitive period
   b. nature and nurture
   c. continuous and discontinuous
   d. lifespan approach and particular period

4. A _____ is a specific time during development when a particular event has its greatest consequence.

   a. critical period
   b. sensitive period
   c. genetic period
   d. embryo period

Applying Lifespan Development

What are some examples of the ways culture (either broad culture or aspects of culture) affects human development?

Module 1.2

Theoretical Perspectives *on Lifespan Development*

In Europe, there was no concept of "childhood" until the 17th century. Instead, children were simply thought of as miniature adults. They were assumed to be subject to the same needs and desires as adults, to have the same vices and virtues, and to warrant no more privileges. They were dressed the same as adults, and their work hours were the same. Children also received the same punishments for misdeeds. If they stole, they were hanged; if they did well, they could achieve prosperity, at least so far as their station in life or social class would allow.

This view of childhood seems wrongheaded now, but at the time it was society's understanding of lifespan development. From this perspective, there were no differences because of age; except for size, people were assumed to be virtually unchanging, at least on a psychological level, throughout most of the life span (Aries, 1962; Acocella, 2003; Hutton, 2004; Wines, 2006).

It is easy to reject the medieval view but less clear how to formulate a contemporary substitute. Should our view of development focus on the biological aspects of change, growth, and stability over the life span? The cognitive or social aspects? Or some other factors?

In fact, people who study lifespan development approach the field from different perspectives. Each perspective encompasses one or more **theories**: broad, organized explanations and predictions concerning phenomena of interest. A theory provides a framework for understanding the relationships among a seemingly unorganized set of facts or principles.

We all develop theories about development, based on our experience, folklore, and stories in the media. However, theories in lifespan development are different. Whereas our own personal theories are haphazardly built on unverified observations, developmentalists' theories are more formal, based on a systematic integration of prior findings and theorizing. Theories allow developmentalists to summarize and organize prior observations, and they allow them to move beyond existing observations to draw deductions that may not be immediately apparent. In addition, theories are subject to rigorous testing through research. By contrast, the developmental theories of individuals are not subject to testing and may never be questioned at all (Thomas, 2001).

We'll consider the six major theoretical perspectives used in lifespan development—the psychodynamic, behavioral, cognitive, humanistic, contextual, and evolutionary perspectives—and discuss them in greater detail in later chapters. Each perspective emphasizes somewhat different aspects of development and steers developmentalists in particular directions. Furthermore, each continues to evolve, as befits a dynamic discipline.

Society's view of childhood, and what is appropriate to ask of children, has changed through the ages. These children worked full-time in mines in the early 1900s.

Everett Historical/Shutterstock

theories
broad explanations, and predictions about phenomena of interest

The Psychodynamic, Behavioral, and Cognitive Perspectives

Let's first examine the main characteristics of the psychodynamic, behavioral, and cognitive perspectives and how each explains lifespan development.

The Psychodynamic Perspective: Focusing on the Inner Person

LO 1.7 Describe the fundamentals of the psychodynamic perspective.

When Marisol was 6 months old, she was involved in a bloody automobile accident—or so her parents tell her because she has no recollection of it. Now, however, at age 24, she is having difficulty maintaining relationships, and her therapist is seeking to determine whether her current problems are a result of the accident.

psychodynamic perspective
the approach that states that behavior is motivated by inner forces, memories, and conflicts that are generally beyond people's awareness and control

Looking for such a link might seem a bit far-fetched, but not to proponents of the **psychodynamic perspective**. Advocates believe that much behavior is motivated by inner forces, memories, and conflicts of which a person has little awareness or control. These inner forces, which may stem from childhood, influence behavior throughout the life span.

FREUD'S PSYCHOANALYTIC THEORY The psychodynamic perspective is most closely associated with Sigmund Freud. Freud, who lived from 1856 to 1939, was a Viennese physician whose revolutionary ideas had a profound effect not only on psychology and psychiatry, but on Western thought in general (Greenberg, 2012; Roth, 2016; Mahalel, 2018).

psychoanalytic theory
the theory proposed by Freud that suggests that unconscious forces act to determine personality and behavior

Freud's **psychoanalytic theory** suggests that unconscious forces act to determine personality and behavior. To Freud, the *unconscious* is a part of the personality about which a person is unaware. It contains infantile wishes, desires, demands, and needs that are hidden from conscious awareness because of their disturbing nature. Freud suggested that the unconscious is responsible for a good part of our everyday behavior.

According to Freud, everyone's personality has three aspects: id, ego, and superego. The *id* is the raw, unorganized, inborn part of personality that is present at birth. It represents primitive drives related to hunger, sex, aggression, and irrational impulses. The *ego* is the part of personality that is rational and reasonable. The ego acts as a buffer between the external world and the primitive id.

psychosexual development
according to Freud, a series of stages that children pass through in which pleasure, or gratification, is focused on a particular biological function and body part

Finally, the *superego* represents a person's conscience, incorporating distinctions between right and wrong. It begins to develop from age 5 or 6 and is learned from an individual's parents, teachers, and other significant figures.

Freud also addressed personality development during childhood. He argued that **psychosexual development** occurs as children pass through distinct stages in which pleasure, or gratification, is focused on a particular biological function and body part. As illustrated in Table 1-2, he suggested that pleasure shifts from the mouth (the *oral stage*) to the anus (the *anal stage*) and eventually to the genitals (the *phallic stage* and the *genital stage*).

psychosocial development
according to Erik Erikson, development that encompasses changes in the understandings individuals have of themselves as members of society

According to Freud, if children are unable to gratify themselves sufficiently during a particular stage, or if they receive too much gratification, fixation may occur. *Fixation* is behavior reflecting a previous stage of development resulting from an unresolved conflict. For instance, fixation at the oral stage might produce an adult who is unusually absorbed in oral activities—eating, talking, or chewing gum.

ERIKSON'S PSYCHOSOCIAL THEORY Psychoanalyst Erik Erikson, who lived from 1902 to 1994, provided an alternative psychodynamic view, emphasizing our social interaction with other people. In Erikson's view, society and culture both challenge and shape us. **Psychosocial development** encompasses changes in our interactions with and understandings of one another, as well as in our knowledge and understanding of ourselves as members of society (Erikson, 1963; Malone et al., 2016; Knight, 2017).

Erikson's theory suggests that development proceeds throughout our lives in eight stages (see Table 1-2), which emerge in a fixed pattern and are similar for all people.

AISA - Everett/Shutterstock

Sigmund Freud

Table 1-2 Freud's and Erikson's Theories

Approximate Age	Freud's Stages of Psychosexual Development	Major Characteristics of Freud's Stages	Erikson's Stages of Psychosocial Development	Positive and Negative Outcomes of Erikson's Stages
Birth to 12–18 months	Oral	Interest in oral gratification from sucking, eating, mouthing, biting	Trust vs. mistrust	*Positive*: Feelings of trust from environmental support *Negative*: Fear and concern regarding others
12–18 months to 3 years	Anal	Gratification from expelling and withholding feces; coming to terms with society's controls relating to toilet training	Autonomy vs. shame and doubt	*Positive*: Self-sufficiency if exploration is encouraged *Negative*: Doubts about self, lack of independence
3 to 5–6 years	Phallic	Interest in the genitals; coming to terms with Oedipal conflict, leading to identification with same-sex parent	Initiative vs. guilt	*Positive*: Discovery of ways to initiate actions *Negative*: Guilt from actions and thoughts
5–6 years to adolescence	Latency	Sexual concerns largely unimportant	Industry vs. inferiority	*Positive*: Development of sense of competence *Negative*: Feelings of inferiority, no sense of mastery
Adolescence to adulthood (Freud) Adolescence (Erikson)	Genital	Reemergence of sexual interests and establishment of mature sexual relationships	Identity vs. role diffusion	*Positive*: Awareness of uniqueness of self, knowledge of role to be followed *Negative*: Inability to identify appropriate roles in life
Early adulthood (Erikson)			Intimacy vs. isolation	*Positive*: Development of loving, sexual relationships and close friendships *Negative*: Fear of relationships with others
Middle adulthood (Erikson)			Generativity vs. stagnation	*Positive*: Sense of contribution to continuity of life *Negative*: Trivialization of one's activities
Late adulthood (Erikson)			Ego-integrity vs. despair	*Positive*: Sense of unity in life's accomplishments *Negative*: Regret over lost opportunities of life

Each stage presents a crisis or conflict that the individual must resolve. Although no crisis is ever fully resolved, the individual must at least address the crisis of each stage sufficiently to deal with demands made during the next stage of development. Unlike Freud, who regarded development as relatively complete by adolescence, Erikson suggested that growth and change continue throughout the life span (de St. Aubin & McAdams, 2004).

ASSESSING THE PSYCHODYNAMIC PERSPECTIVE Freud's insight that unconscious influences affect behavior was a monumental accomplishment, and the fact that it seems at all reasonable to us shows how extensively the idea of the unconscious has pervaded thinking in Western cultures. In fact, work by contemporary researchers studying memory and learning suggests that we unconsciously carry with us memories that have a significant impact on our behavior.

However, many of the most basic principles of Freud's psychoanalytic theory have been questioned because they have not been validated by research. In particular, the notion that childhood stages determine adult personalities has little research support. In addition, because much of Freud's theory was based on a limited population of upper-middle-class Austrians living during a strict, puritanical era, its application to broad, multicultural populations is questionable. Finally, because Freud's theory focuses primarily on male development, it has been criticized as sexist and interpreted as devaluing women (Gillham, Law, & Hickey, 2010; O'Neil & Denke, 2016; Balsam, 2018).

Erikson's view that development continues throughout the life span is highly important—and has received considerable support. However, the theory also has its drawbacks. Like Freud's theory, it focuses more on men than women. Further, its vagueness makes it difficult to test rigorously. And, as with psychodynamic theories in general, it is difficult to make definitive predictions about a given individual's behavior using the theory (de St. Aubin & McAdams, 2004; Balsam, 2013).

Erik Erikson

The Behavioral Perspective: Focusing on Observable Behavior

LO 1.8   Describe the fundamentals of the behavioral perspective.

When Elissa Sheehan was 3, a large brown dog bit her, and she needed dozens of stitches and several operations. From the time she was bitten, she broke into a sweat whenever she saw a dog, and in fact never enjoyed being around any pet.

To a lifespan development specialist using the behavioral perspective, the explanation for Elissa's behavior is straightforward: She has a learned fear of dogs. Rather than looking inside the organism at unconscious processes, the **behavioral perspective** suggests that the keys to understanding development are observable behavior and environmental stimuli. If we know the stimuli, we can predict the behavior. In this respect, the behavioral perspective reflects the view that nurture is more important to development than nature.

Behavioral theories reject the notion that people universally pass through a series of stages. Instead, people are affected by the environmental stimuli to which they happen to be exposed. Developmental patterns, then, are personal, reflecting a particular set of environmental stimuli, and behavior is the result of continuing exposure to specific factors in the environment. Furthermore, developmental change is viewed in quantitative, rather than qualitative, terms. For instance, behavioral theories hold that advances in problem-solving capabilities as children age are largely a result of greater mental *capacities*, rather than changes in the *kind* of thinking that children can bring to bear on a problem.

CLASSICAL CONDITIONING: STIMULUS SUBSTITUTION

> Give me a dozen healthy infants, well-formed, and my own specified world to bring them up in and I'll guarantee to take any one at random and train him to become any type of specialist I might select—doctor, lawyer, artist, merchant-chief, and yes, even beggar-man and thief, regardless of his talents, penchants, tendencies, abilities. (Watson, 1925)

With these words, John B. Watson, one of the first American psychologists to advocate a behavioral approach, summed up the behavioral perspective. Watson, who lived from 1878 to 1958, believed strongly that we could gain a full understanding of development by carefully studying the stimuli that composed the environment. In fact, he argued that by effectively controlling—or *conditioning*—a person's environment, it was possible to produce virtually any behavior.

Classical conditioning occurs when an organism learns to respond in a particular way to a neutral stimulus. For instance, if the sound of a bell is paired with the arrival of meat, a dog will learn to react to the bell alone in the same way it reacts to the meat—by salivating and wagging its tail. The behavior is a result of conditioning, a form of learning in which the response associated with one stimulus (food) comes to be connected to another—in this case, the bell.

The same process of classical conditioning explains how we learn emotional responses. In the case of dog-bite victim Elissa Sheehan, for instance, Watson would say that one stimulus has been substituted for another: Elissa's unpleasant experience with a particular dog (the initial stimulus) has been transferred to other dogs and to pets in general.

OPERANT CONDITIONING   In addition to classical conditioning, the behavioral perspective accounts for other types of learning, especially what behavioralists call *operant conditioning*. **Operant conditioning** is a form of learning in which a voluntary response is strengthened or weakened by its association with positive or negative consequences. It differs from classical conditioning in that the response being conditioned is voluntary and purposeful rather than automatic (such as salivating). In operant conditioning, formulated and championed by psychologist B. F. Skinner (1904–1990), individuals learn to *operate* on their environments to bring about desired consequences (Skinner, 1975).

Whether or not children and adults will seek to repeat a behavior depends on whether it is followed by reinforcement. *Reinforcement* is the process by which a behavior is followed by a stimulus that increases the probability that the behavior will be repeated. Hence, a student is apt to work harder if he or she receives good grades;

behavioral perspective
the approach that suggests that the keys to understanding development are observable behavior and outside stimuli in the environment

classical conditioning
a type of learning in which an organism responds in a particular way to a neutral stimulus that normally does not bring about that type of response

operant conditioning
a form of learning in which a voluntary response is strengthened or weakened by its association with positive or negative consequences

John B. Watson

Hulton Archive/Archive Photos/Getty Images

workers are likely to labor harder if their efforts are tied to pay increases; and people are more apt to buy lottery tickets if they are reinforced by winning occasionally. In addition, *punishment*, the introduction of an unpleasant or painful stimulus or the removal of a desirable stimulus, will decrease the probability that a preceding behavior will occur in the future.

Behavior that is reinforced, then, is more likely to be repeated, whereas behavior that receives no reinforcement or is punished is likely to be *extinguished*, in the language of operant conditioning. Principles of operant conditioning are used in **behavior modification**, a formal technique for promoting the frequency of desirable behaviors and decreasing the incidence of unwanted ones. Behavior modification has been used in situations ranging from teaching people with severe intellectual disabilities basic language to helping people with self-control problems stick to diets (Wupperman et al., 2012; Wirth, Wabitsch, & Hauner, 2014; Miltenberger, 2016).

behavior modification
a formal technique for promoting the frequency of desirable behaviors and decreasing the incidence of unwanted ones

SOCIAL-COGNITIVE LEARNING THEORY: LEARNING THROUGH IMITATION A 5-year-old boy seriously injures his 22-month-old cousin while imitating a violent wrestling move he has seen on television. Although the baby sustained spinal cord injuries, he improved and was discharged 5 weeks after his hospital admission (Reuters Health eLine, 2002; Ray & Heyes, 2011).

Cause and effect? We can't know for sure, but it certainly seems possible, especially to social-cognitive learning theorists. According to developmental psychologist Albert Bandura and colleagues, a significant amount of learning is explained by **social-cognitive learning theory**, an approach that emphasizes learning by observing the behavior of another person, called a *model* (Bandura, 2002; 2018).

social-cognitive learning theory
learning by observing the behavior of another person, called a model

> **From a social worker's perspective:** How do the concepts of social learning and modeling relate to the mass media, and how might exposure to mass media influence a child's family life?

According to social-cognitive learning theory, behavior is learned primarily through observation and not through trial and error, as it is with operant conditioning. We don't need to experience the consequences of a behavior ourselves to learn it. Social-cognitive learning theory holds that when we see the behavior of a model being rewarded, we are likely to imitate that behavior. For instance, in one classic experiment, children who were afraid of dogs were exposed to a model, nicknamed the "Fearless Peer," who was seen playing happily with a dog (Bandura, Grusec, & Menlove, 1967). After exposure, the children who previously had been afraid were more likely to approach a strange dog than children who had not seen the model.

ASSESSING THE BEHAVIORAL PERSPECTIVE Research using the behavioral perspective has made significant contributions, ranging from employee training techniques to the development of procedures for curbing aggression in children with severe developmental disabilities. At the same time, the perspective has experienced internal disagreements. For example, although part of the same behavioral perspective, classical and operant conditioning and social learning theory disagree in some basic ways. Classical and operant conditioning consider learning in terms of external stimuli and responses, in which the only important factors are the observable features of the environment. People and other organisms are like inanimate "black boxes"; nothing that occurs inside the box is understood—nor much cared about, for that matter.

To social learning theorists, such an analysis is an oversimplification. They argue that what makes people different from rats and pigeons is the mental activity, in the form of thoughts and expectations. We cannot derive a full understanding of people's development without moving beyond external stimuli and responses.

In many ways, social learning theory has come to predominate in recent decades over classical and operant conditioning theories. In fact, another perspective that focuses explicitly on internal mental activity—the cognitive perspective—has become enormously influential.

The Cognitive Perspective: Examining the Roots of Understanding

LO 1.9 Describe the fundamentals of the cognitive perspective.

When 3-year-old Jake is asked why it sometimes rains, he answers "so the flowers can grow." When his 11-year-old sister Lila is asked the same question, she responds "because of evaporation from the surface of the earth." And when their cousin Ajima, who is studying meteorology in graduate school, considers the same question, her extended answer includes a discussion of cumulonimbus clouds, the Coriolis Effect, and synoptic charts.

cognitive perspective
the approach that focuses on the processes that allow people to know, understand, and think about the world

To a developmental theorist using the cognitive perspective, the difference in the sophistication of the answers is evidence of a different degree of knowledge and understanding, or cognition. The **cognitive perspective** focuses on the processes that allow people to know, understand, and think about the world.

The cognitive perspective emphasizes how people internally represent and think about the world. By using this perspective, developmental researchers hope to understand how children and adults process information and how their ways of thinking and understanding affect their behavior. They also seek to learn how cognitive abilities change as people develop, the degree to which cognitive development represents quantitative and qualitative growth in intellectual abilities, and how different cognitive abilities are related to one another.

PIAGET'S THEORY OF COGNITIVE DEVELOPMENT No one has had a greater impact on the study of cognitive development than Swiss psychologist Jean Piaget (1896–1980). Piaget proposed that all people pass through a fixed sequence of universal stages of cognitive development—and not only does the *quantity* of information increase in each stage, but the *quality* of knowledge and understanding also changes. His focus was on the change in cognition that occurs as children move from one stage to the next (Piaget, 1952, 1962, 1983). Broadly speaking, Piaget suggested that human thinking is arranged into *schemes*, organized mental patterns that represent behaviors and actions. In infants, schemes represent concrete behavior—a scheme for sucking, for reaching, and for each separate behavior. In older children, the schemes become more sophisticated and abstract, such as the skills involved in riding a bike or playing an interactive video game. Schemes are like intellectual computer software programs that direct and determine how data from the world are looked at and handled (Oura, 2014).

Piaget suggested that the growth in children's understanding of the world could be explained by two basic principles: assimilation and accommodation. *Assimilation* is the process in which people understand a new experience in terms of their current stage of cognitive development and existing ways of thinking. In contrast, *accommodation* refers to changes in existing ways of thinking in response to encounters with new stimuli or events. Assimilation and accommodation work in tandem to bring about cognitive development.

ASSESSING PIAGET'S THEORY Piaget has profoundly influenced our understanding of cognitive development and is one of the towering figures in lifespan development. He provided masterly descriptions of intellectual growth during childhood—descriptions that have stood the test of literally thousands of investigations. Broadly, then, Piaget's view of cognitive development is accurate.

However, the specifics of the theory have been questioned. For instance, some cognitive skills clearly emerge earlier than Piaget suggested. Furthermore, the universality of Piaget's stages has been disputed. Growing evidence suggests that particular cognitive skills emerge on a different timetable in non-Western cultures. And in every culture, some people never seem to reach Piaget's highest level of cognitive sophistication: formal, logical thought (De Jesus-Zayas, Buigas, & Denney, 2012; Müller, Burman, & Hutchison, 2013; Siegler, 2016).

Ultimately, the greatest criticism is that cognitive development is not necessarily as discontinuous as Piaget's stage theory suggests. Many developmental

On the reality show *Survivor*, contestants often must learn new survival skills to be successful. What form of learning is prevalent?

researchers argue that growth is considerably more continuous. These critics have suggested an alternative perspective, known as the *information processing approach*, that focuses on the processes that underlie learning, memory, and thinking throughout the life span.

INFORMATION PROCESSING APPROACHES Information processing approaches have become an important alternative to Piagetian approaches. **Information processing approaches** to cognitive development seek to identify the ways individuals take in, use, and store information.

information processing approaches
the model that seeks to identify the ways individuals take in, use, and store information

Information processing approaches grew out of developments in computers. They assume that even complex behavior such as learning, remembering, categorizing, and thinking can be broken down into a series of individual, specific steps.

Like computers, children are assumed by information processing approaches to have limited capacity for processing information. As they develop, though, they employ increasingly sophisticated strategies that allow them to process information more efficiently.

In stark contrast to Piaget's view, information processing approaches assume that development is marked more by quantitative advances than qualitative ones. Our capacity to handle information changes with age, as does our processing speed and efficiency. Furthermore, information processing approaches suggest that as we age, we are better able to control the nature of processing and the strategies we choose to process information.

An information processing approach that builds on Piaget's research is known as neo-Piagetian theory. In contrast to Piaget's original work, which viewed cognition as a single system of increasingly sophisticated general cognitive abilities, neo-Piagetian theory considers cognition as made up of different types of individual skills. Using the terminology of information processing approaches, neo-Piagetian theory suggests that cognitive development proceeds quickly in certain areas and more slowly in others. For example, reading ability and the skills needed to recall stories may progress sooner than the abstract computational abilities used in algebra or trigonometry. Furthermore, neo-Piagetian theorists believe that experience plays a greater role in advancing cognitive development than traditional Piagetian approaches claim (Loewen, 2006; LeFevre, 2016; Bisagno & Morra, 2018).

ASSESSING INFORMATION PROCESSING APPROACHES As we'll see in future chapters, information processing approaches have become a central part of our understanding of development. At the same time, they do not offer a complete explanation of behavior. For example, they have paid little attention to behavior such as creativity, in which the most profound ideas often are developed in a seemingly nonlogical, nonlinear manner. In addition, they do not take into account the social context in which development takes place—and theories that do this have become increasingly popular.

COGNITIVE NEUROSCIENCE APPROACHES One of the most recent additions to the array of approaches are **cognitive neuroscience approaches**, which look at cognitive development at the level of brain processes. Like other cognitive perspectives, cognitive neuroscience approaches consider internal mental processes, but they focus specifically on the neurological activity that underlies thinking, problem solving, and other cognitive behavior.

cognitive neuroscience approaches
approaches that examine cognitive development through the lens of brain processes

Cognitive neuroscientists seek to identify actual locations and functions within the brain that are related to different types of cognitive activities. For example, using sophisticated brain-scanning techniques, cognitive neuroscientists have demonstrated that thinking about the meaning of a word activates different areas of the brain than thinking about how the word sounds when spoken.

Cognitive neuroscientists are also providing clues to the cause of *autism spectrum disorder*, a major developmental disability that can produce profound language deficits and self-injurious behavior in young children. For example, neuroscientists have found that the brains of children with the disorder show explosive, dramatic growth in the first year of life, making their heads significantly larger than those of children

Figure 1-1 The Brain and Autism Spectrum Disorder

Researchers have found abnormalities in the temporal lobe of the brain in some children diagnosed with autism spectrum disorder. On the left is a brain scan of a child with autism spectrum disorder. At right is a brain scan of a child without it.

SOURCE: Boddaert, N. et al. [2009].

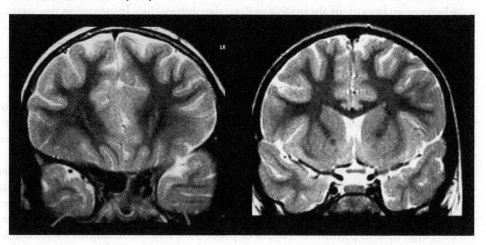

without the disorder (see Figure 1-1). By identifying children with the disorder early in their lives, health-care practitioners can provide crucial early intervention (Bal et al., 2010; Howard et al., 2014; Grant, 2017).

Cognitive neuroscience approaches are also on the forefront of cutting-edge research that has identified genes associated with disorders ranging from physical problems such as breast cancer to psychological disorders such as schizophrenia. Identifying the genes that make one vulnerable to such disorders is the first step in genetic engineering in which gene therapy can reduce the effects of a disorder or even prevent one from occurring (Strobel et al., 2007; Ranganath, Minzenberg, & Ragland, 2008; Rodnitzky, 2012).

ASSESSING COGNITIVE NEUROSCIENCE APPROACHES Cognitive neuroscience approaches represent a new frontier in child and adolescent development. Using sophisticated measurement techniques that many of them developed only in the past few years, cognitive neuroscientists are able to peer into the inner functioning of the brain. Advances in our understanding of genetics also have opened a new window into both normal and abnormal development and have suggested a variety of treatments for abnormalities.

Critics of the cognitive neuroscience approach have suggested that it sometimes provides a better *description* than *explanation* of developmental phenomena. For instance, the finding that children with autism have larger brains than those without the disorder does not explain why their brains became larger—that's a question that remains to be answered. Still, such work not only offers important clues to appropriate treatments but ultimately can also lead to a full understanding of a range of developmental phenomena.

The Humanistic, Contextual, and Evolutionary Perspectives

We now turn to the humanistic, contextual, and evolutionary perspectives to examine their main characteristics and how each one explains lifespan development.

The Humanistic Perspective: Concentrating on Uniquely Human Qualities

LO 1.10 Describe the fundamentals of the humanistic perspective.

The unique qualities of humans are the central focus of the humanistic perspective, the fourth of the major theories used by lifespan developmentalists. Rejecting the notion that behavior is largely determined by unconscious processes, the environment, or cognitive processing, the **humanistic perspective** contends that people have a natural capacity to make decisions about their lives and to control their behavior. According to this approach, each individual has the ability and motivation to reach more advanced levels of maturity, and people naturally seek to reach their full potential.

The humanistic perspective emphasizes *free will*, the ability of humans to make choices and come to decisions about their lives. Instead of relying on societal standards, then, people are assumed to be motivated to make their own decisions about what they do with their lives.

Carl Rogers, one of the major proponents of the humanistic perspective, suggests that people need positive regard, which results from an underlying wish to be loved and respected. Because positive regard comes from other people, we become dependent on them. Consequently, our view of ourselves and our self-worth is a reflection of how we think others view us (Rogers, 1971; Malchiodi, 2012; Kanat-Maymon et al., 2018).

Rogers, along with another key figure in the humanistic perspective, Abraham Maslow, suggests that self-actualization is a primary goal in life. *Self-actualization* is a state of self-fulfillment in which people achieve their highest potential in their own unique way (Maslow, 1970; Sheldon, Joiner, & Pettit, 2003; Malchiodi, 2012).

ASSESSING THE HUMANISTIC PERSPECTIVE   Despite its emphasis on important and unique human qualities, the humanistic perspective has not had a major impact on the field of lifespan development. This is primarily because of its inability to identify any sort of broad developmental change that is the result of increasing age or experience. Still, some of the concepts drawn from the humanistic perspective, such as self-actualization, have helped describe important aspects of human behavior and are widely discussed in areas ranging from health care to business (Elkins, 2009; Beitel et al., 2014; Hale et al., 2018).

The Contextual Perspective: Taking a Broad Approach to Development

LO 1.11   Describe the fundamentals of the contextual perspective.

Although lifespan developmentalists often consider physical, cognitive, personality, and social factors separately, such a categorization has one serious drawback: In the real world, none of these broad influences occurs in isolation from any other. Instead, there is a constant, ongoing interaction between the different types of influence.

The **contextual perspective** considers the relationship between individuals and their physical, cognitive, personality, and social worlds. It suggests that a person's unique development cannot be properly viewed without seeing how that person is enmeshed within a rich social and cultural context. We'll consider two major theories that fall under this category, Bronfenbrenner's bioecological approach and Vygotsky's sociocultural theory.

THE BIOECOLOGICAL APPROACH TO DEVELOPMENT   In acknowledging the problem with traditional approaches to lifespan development, psychologist Urie Bronfenbrenner (2000; 2002) has proposed an alternative perspective, the bioecological approach. The **bioecological approach** suggests that there are five levels of the environment that simultaneously influence individuals. Bronfenbrenner suggests that we cannot fully understand development without considering how a person is influenced by each of these levels.

- The *microsystem* is the everyday, immediate environment of children's daily lives. Homes, caregivers, friends, and teachers all are influences, but the child is not just a passive recipient. Instead, children actively help construct the microsystem, shaping their immediate world. The microsystem is the level to which most traditional work in child development has been directed.

- The *mesosystem* connects the various aspects of the microsystem. The mesosystem binds children to parents, students to teachers, employees to bosses, and friends to friends. It acknowledges the direct and indirect influences that bind us to one another, such as those that affect a mother who has a bad day at the office and then is short-tempered with her son or daughter at home.

humanistic perspective
the theory that contends that people have a natural capacity to make decisions about their lives and control their behavior

contextual perspective
the theory that considers the relationship between individuals and their physical, cognitive, personality, and social worlds

bioecological approach
the perspective suggesting that levels of the environment simultaneously influence individuals

- The *exosystem* represents broader influences: societal institutions such as local government, the community, schools, places of worship, and the local media. Each of these institutions can have an immediate and major impact on personal development, and each affects how the microsystem and mesosystem operate. For example, the quality of a school will affect a child's cognitive development and potentially can have long-term consequences.

- The *macrosystem* represents the larger cultural influences on an individual, including society in general, types of governments, religious and political value systems, and other broad, encompassing factors. For example, the value a culture places on education affects the values of the people who live in that culture. Children are part of both a broader culture (such as Western culture) and members of one or more subcultures (for instance, Mexican American subculture).

- Finally, the *chronosystem* underlies each of the previous systems. It involves the way the passage of time—including historical events (such as the terrorist attacks in September 2001) and more gradual historical changes (such as changes in the number of women who work outside the home)—affects children's development.

The bioecological approach emphasizes the *interconnectedness of the influences on development*. Because the various levels are related to one another, a change in one part of the system affects other parts. For instance, a parent's loss of a job (involving the mesosystem) has an impact on a child's microsystem.

Conversely, changes on one environmental level may make little difference if other levels are not also changed. For instance, improving the school environment may have a negligible effect on academic performance if children receive little support for academic success at home. Similarly, the influences among family members are multidirectional. Parents don't just influence their child's behavior; the child also influences the parents' behavior.

Finally, the bioecological approach stresses the importance of broad cultural factors that affect development. Consider, for instance, whether you agree that children should be taught that their classmates' assistance is essential to getting good grades in school, that they should plan to continue their fathers' businesses, or that they should take their parents' advice in choosing a career. If you have been raised in the most widespread North American culture, you would likely disagree with all three statements because they violate the premises of *individualism*, the dominant Western philosophy that emphasizes personal identity, uniqueness, freedom, and the worth of the individual.

By contrast, if you were raised in a traditional Asian culture, your agreement with the three statements is considerably more likely because the statements reflect the value orientation known as collectivism. *Collectivism* is the notion that the well-being of the group is more important than that of the individual. People raised in collectivistic cultures sometimes emphasize the welfare of the group at the expense of their own personal well-being.

The individualism–collectivism spectrum is one of several dimensions along which cultures differ. Similarly, the roles played by men and women also vary across cultures in significant ways. Such broad cultural values play an important role in shaping the ways people view the world and behave (Yu & Stiffman, 2007; Cheung et al., 2016; Sparrow, 2016).

ASSESSING THE BIOECOLOGICAL APPROACH Although Bronfenbrenner regards biological influences as an important component of the bioecological approach, ecological influences are central to the theory. In fact, some critics argue that the perspective pays insufficient attention to biological factors. Still, the bioecological approach is important because it suggests the multiple levels at which the environment affects children's development.

VYGOTSKY'S SOCIOCULTURAL THEORY To Russian developmentalist Lev Semenovich Vygotsky, a full understanding of development is impossible without taking into account the culture in which people develop. Vygotsky's **sociocultural theory** emphasizes how cognitive development proceeds as a result of social interactions between members of a culture (Vygotsky, 1926/1997; Fleer, Gonzalez, & Veresov, 2017; Newman, 2018).

sociocultural theory
the approach that emphasizes how cognitive development proceeds as a result of social interactions between members of a culture

Vygotsky, who lived a brief life from 1896 to 1934, argued that children's understanding of the world is acquired through their problem-solving interactions with adults and other children. As children play and cooperate with others, they learn what is important in their society and, at the same time, advance cognitively. Consequently, to understand development, we must consider what is meaningful to members of a given culture.

More than most other theories, sociocultural theory emphasizes that development is a *reciprocal transaction* between the people in a child's environment and the child. Vygotsky believed that people and settings influence the child, who in turn influences the people and settings. This pattern continues in an endless loop, with children being both recipients of socialization influences and sources of influence. For example, a child raised with his or her extended family nearby will grow up with a different sense of family life than a child whose relatives live far away. Those relatives, too, are affected by that situation and that child, depending on how close and frequent their contact is with the child.

According to Vygotsky, children can develop cognitively in their understanding of the world and learn what is important in society through play and cooperation with others.

Theorists who built on Vygotsky's work have used the example of "scaffolds," the temporary platforms used by construction workers when building a structure, to describe how children learn. *Scaffolding* is the temporary support that teachers, parents, and others provide children as they are learning a task. As children become increasingly competent and master a task, the scaffolding can be withdrawn, allowing children to carry out the task on their own (Lowe et al., 2013; Peralta et al., 2013; Dahl et al., 2017).

ASSESSING VYGOTSKY'S THEORY Sociocultural theory has become increasingly influential, despite Vygotsky's death almost eight decades ago. The reason is the growing acknowledgment of the central importance of cultural factors in development. Children do not develop in a cultural vacuum. Instead, their attention is directed by society to certain areas, and as a consequence, they develop particular kinds of skills. Vygotsky was one of the first developmentalists to recognize and acknowledge the importance of the cultural environment; sociocultural theory helps us to understand the rich and varied influences that shape development (Rogan, 2007; Frie, 2014; van der Veer & Yasnitsky, 2016).

Sociocultural theory is not without its critics, however. Some suggest that Vygotsky's strong emphasis on the role of culture and social experience led him to ignore the effects of biological factors on development. In addition, his perspective seems to minimize the role that individuals play in shaping their environment.

Evolutionary Perspectives: Our Ancestors' Contributions to Behavior

LO 1.12 Describe the fundamentals of the evolutionary perspective.

One increasingly influential approach is the evolutionary perspective, the sixth and final developmental perspective that we will consider. The **evolutionary perspective** seeks to identify behavior that is the result of our genetic inheritance from our ancestors (Goetz & Shackelford, 2006; Tomasello, 2011; Arístegui, Castro Solano, & Buunk, 2018).

Evolutionary approaches grow out of the groundbreaking work of Charles Darwin. In 1859, Darwin argued in *On the Origin of Species* that a process of natural selection creates traits in a species that are adaptive to its environment. Using Darwin's arguments, evolutionary approaches contend that our genetic inheritance not only determines such physical traits as skin and eye color, but also certain personality traits and social behaviors. For instance, some evolutionary developmentalists suggest that behaviors such as shyness and jealousy are produced in part by genetic causes, presumably because they helped in increasing survival rates of humans' ancient relatives (Buss, 2012; Easton, Schipper, & Shackelford, 2007; Geary & Berch, 2016).

evolutionary perspective
the theory that seeks to identify behavior that is a result of our genetic inheritance from our ancestors

Konrad Lorenz, seen here with geese who from their birth have followed him, considered the ways in which behavior reflects inborn genetic patterns.

The evolutionary perspective draws heavily on the field of *ethology*, which examines the ways in which our biological makeup influences our behavior. A primary proponent of ethology was Konrad Lorenz (1903–1989), who discovered that newborn geese are genetically preprogrammed to become attached to the first moving object they see after birth. His work, which demonstrated the importance of biological determinants in influencing behavior patterns, led developmentalists to consider the ways in which human behavior might reflect inborn genetic patterns.

The evolutionary perspective encompasses one of the fastest-growing areas within the field of lifespan development: behavioral genetics. *Behavioral genetics* studies the effects of heredity on behavior. Behavioral geneticists seek to understand how we might inherit certain behavioral traits and how the environment influences whether we actually display those traits. It also considers how genetic factors may produce psychological disorders such as schizophrenia (Rembis, 2009; Plomin et al., 2016; Mitra, Kavoor, & Mahintamani, 2018).

ASSESSING THE EVOLUTIONARY PERSPECTIVE There is little argument among lifespan developmentalists that Darwin's evolutionary theory provides an accurate description of basic genetic processes, and the evolutionary perspective is increasingly visible in the field of lifespan development. However, applications of the evolutionary perspective have been subjected to considerable criticism.

Some developmentalists are concerned that because of its focus on genetic and biological aspects of behavior, the evolutionary perspective pays insufficient attention to the environmental and social factors involved in producing children's and adults' behavior. Other critics argue that there is no good way to experimentally test theories derived from this approach because humans evolved so long ago. For example, it is one thing to say that jealousy helped individuals to survive more effectively and another thing to prove it. Still, the evolutionary approach has stimulated research on how our biological inheritance influences at least partially our traits and behaviors (Bjorklund, 2006; Baptista et al., 2008; Del Giudice, 2015).

Why "Which Approach Is Right?" Is the Wrong Question

LO 1.13 **Explain the value of using multiple perspectives to describe human development.**

We have considered the six major perspectives on development—psychodynamic, behavioral, cognitive, humanistic, contextual, and evolutionary—summarized in Table 1-3 and applied to a specific case. It would be natural to wonder which of the six provides the most accurate account of human development.

For several reasons, this is not an appropriate question. For one thing, each perspective emphasizes different aspects of development. For instance, the psychodynamic approach emphasizes unconscious determinants of behavior, whereas behavioral perspectives emphasize overt behavior. The cognitive and humanistic perspectives look more at what people *think* than at what they do. The contextual perspective examines social and cultural influences on development, and the evolutionary perspective focuses on how inherited biological factors underlie development.

Consider, for example, how a theorist from each of the major perspectives would study the Ruiz family described at the very beginning of this chapter. A psychodynamic theorist might focus on the ways in which early childhood experiences play out in the family members' adulthood, and even on the ways that the same psychological dysfunctions appear across different generations. In contrast, a behavioral theorist might concentrate on the ways in which patterns of behavior are learned and displayed in family members.

Table 1-3 Major Perspectives on Lifespan Development

Perspective	Key Ideas About Human Behavior and Development	Major Proponents	Example
Psychodynamic	Behavior throughout life is motivated by inner, unconscious forces, stemming from childhood, over which we have little control.	Sigmund Freud, Erik Erikson	This view might suggest that a young adult who is overweight has a fixation in the oral stage of development.
Behavioral	Development can be understood through studying observable behavior and environmental stimuli.	John B. Watson, B. F. Skinner, Albert Bandura	In this perspective, a young adult who is overweight might be seen as not being rewarded for good nutritional and exercise habits.
Cognitive	Emphasis on how changes or growth in the ways people know, understand, and think about the world affect behavior.	Jean Piaget	This view might suggest that a young adult who is overweight hasn't learned effective ways to stay at a healthy weight and doesn't value good nutrition.
Humanistic	Behavior is chosen through free will and motivated by our natural capacity to strive to reach our full potential.	Carl Rogers, Abraham Maslow	In this view, a young adult who is overweight may eventually choose to seek an optimal weight as part of an overall pattern of individual growth.
Contextual	Development should be viewed in terms of the interrelationship of a person's physical, cognitive, personality, and social worlds.	Urie Bronfenbrenner, Lev Vygotsky	In this perspective, being overweight is caused by a number of interrelated factors in that person's physical, cognitive, personality, and social worlds.
Evolutionary	Behavior is the result of genetic inheritance from our ancestors; traits and behaviors that are adaptive for promoting the survival of our species have been inherited through natural selection.	Influenced by early work of Charles Darwin, Konrad Lorenz	This view might suggest that a young adult might have a genetic tendency toward obesity because extra fat helped his or her ancestors to survive in times of famine.

Taking a different perspective, a cognitive theorist might look at the common thinking patterns shown by family members, while a humanistic theorist might focus on the life goals that individuals in the family share in common. Finally, a contextual theorist might be particularly interested in the ways in which the social and cultural environment in which they are living affects family members, while an evolutionary theorist might consider how genetic disorders have been passed through the family members' genes.

In short, each perspective focuses on different aspects of development and is based on its own premises. Consequently, the same developmental phenomenon can be looked at from a number of perspectives simultaneously. And in fact, some lifespan developmentalists use an *eclectic* approach, drawing on several perspectives simultaneously.

In the same way, the various theoretical perspectives provide different ways of looking at development. Considering them together paints a fuller portrait of the myriad ways human beings change and grow over the course of their lives.

Of course, the theories and explanations derived from the various perspectives in some cases provide alternate explanations for the same behavior. How do we choose among competing explanations? The answer can be found through *research*, which we consider in the final part of this chapter.

Review, Check, and Apply

Review

LO 1.7 Describe the fundamentals of the psychodynamic perspective.

The psychodynamic perspective suggests that behavior is motivated by inner forces, memories, and conflicts that are generally beyond people's awareness and control. It focuses on unconscious determinants of behavior. According to Freud's *psychoanalytic theory*, personality has three aspects: id, ego, and superego. In contrast, Erikson's *psychosocial* approach emphasizes our social interaction with others. He suggests that society and culture both challenge and shape us.

LO 1.8 Describe the fundamentals of the behavioral perspective.

The behavioral perspective suggests that the keys to understanding development are observable behavior and environmental stimuli. If we know the stimuli, we can predict the behavior. Behavioral theories reject the notion that people universally pass through a series of stages. Instead, people are affected by the environmental stimuli to which they happen to be exposed.

LO 1.9 Describe the fundamentals of the cognitive perspective.

Piaget proposed that all people pass through a fixed sequence of universal stages of cognitive development—and not only does the *quantity* of information increase in each stage, but also the *quality* of knowledge and understanding changes. His focus was on the change in cognition that occurs as children move from one stage to the next. Broadly speaking, Piaget suggested that human thinking is arranged into *schemes*, which are organized mental patterns that represent behaviors and actions.

LO 1.10 Describe the fundamentals of the humanistic perspective.

Despite its emphasis on important and unique human qualities, the humanistic perspective has not had a major impact on the field of lifespan development. This is primarily because of its inability to identify any sort of broad developmental change that is the result of increasing age or experience. Still, some of the concepts drawn from the humanistic perspective, such as self-actualization, have helped describe important aspects of human behavior and are widely discussed in areas ranging from health care to business.

LO 1.11 Describe the fundamentals of the contextual perspective.

The contextual perspective considers the relationship between individuals and their physical, cognitive, personality, and social worlds. It suggests that a person's unique development cannot be properly viewed without seeing how that person is enmeshed within a rich social and cultural context. Two major theories that fall under this category are Bronfenbrenner's bioecological approach and Vygotsky's sociocultural theory.

LO 1.12 Describe the fundamentals of the evolutionary perspective.

Charles Darwin argued that a process of natural selection creates traits in a species that are adaptive to its environment. Using Darwin's arguments, evolutionary approaches contend that our genetic inheritance not only determines such physical traits as skin and eye color, but also certain personality traits and social behaviors. For instance, some evolutionary developmentalists suggest that behaviors such as shyness and jealousy are produced in part by genetic causes, presumably because they helped in increasing survival rates of humans' ancient relatives.

LO 1.13 Explain the value of using multiple perspectives to describe human development.

Each perspective emphasizes different aspects of development. For instance, the psychodynamic approach emphasizes unconscious determinants of behavior, whereas behavioral perspectives emphasize overt behavior. The cognitive and humanistic perspectives look more at what people *think* than at what they do. The contextual perspective examines social and cultural influences on development, and the evolutionary perspective focuses on how inherited biological factors underlie development. Clearly, each perspective is based on its own premises and focuses on different aspects of development. Furthermore, the same developmental phenomenon can be looked at from a number of perspectives simultaneously.

Check Yourself

1. _____ are organized explanations and predictions concerning phenomena of interest and provide frameworks for understanding the relationships across variables.
   a. Evaluations
   b. Constitutions
   c. Intuitions
   d. Theories

2. The _____ perspective suggests that the key to understanding one's actions involves observation of those actions and the outside stimuli in the environment.
   a. psychodynamic
   b. cognitive
   c. behavioral
   d. operant conditioning

3. Bronfenbrenner's bioecological approach and Vygotsky's sociocultural theory fall under the category of the _____ perspective.
   a. humanistic
   b. ethnological
   c. contextual
   d. evolutionary

4. The researcher most closely associated with the evolutionary perspective is _____.
   a. Konrad Lorenz
   b. Jean Piaget
   c. Carl Rogers
   d. B. F. Skinner

Applying Lifespan Development

What examples of human behavior have you seen that seem to have been inherited from our ancestors because they helped individuals survive and adapt more effectively? Why do you think they are inherited?

Module 1.3

Research Methods

The Greek historian Herodotus wrote of an experiment conducted by Psamtik, the king of Egypt in the seventh century B.C. Psamtik was eager to prove the cherished Egyptian belief that his people were the oldest race on earth. To test this notion, he developed a hypothesis: If a child was never exposed to the language of his elders, he would instinctively adopt the primal language of humanity, the original language of the first people. Psamtik was certain this would be Egyptian.

For his experiment, Psamtik entrusted two Egyptian infants to the care of a herdsman in an isolated area. They were to be well looked after but not allowed to leave their cottage. And they were never to hear anyone speak a single word.

One day, when the children were 2 years old, they greeted the herdsman with the word "Becos!" The herdsman didn't know this word, but when the children continued to use it, he contacted Psamtik. The king sent for the children, who repeated the strange word to him. Psamtik did some research. Becos, it evolved, was "bread" in Phrygian. Because it was the first word the children spoke, Psamtik had to conclude the Phrygians had preceded the Egyptians.

With the perspective of several thousand years, we can easily see the shortcomings—both scientific and ethical—in Psamtik's approach (Hunt, 1993). Yet his procedure represents an improvement over mere speculation, and as such is sometimes looked on as the first developmental experiment in recorded history.

Theories, Hypotheses, and Correlational Studies

In the sections that follow, we examine how theories and hypotheses impact the study of development. We also consider the types of studies and methods that are used in research.

Theories and Hypotheses: Posing Developmental Questions

LO 1.14 Explain the role theories and hypotheses play in the study of development.

Questions such as those raised by Psamtik drive the study of development. In fact, developmentalists are still studying how children learn language. Others are working on such questions as: What are the effects of malnutrition on intellectual performance? How do infants form relationships with their parents, and does day care disrupt such relationships? Why are adolescents particularly susceptible to peer pressure? Can mentally challenging activities reduce the declines in intellectual abilities related to aging? Do any mental faculties improve with age?

To answer such questions, developmentalists, like all psychologists and other scientists, rely on the scientific method. The **scientific method** is the process of posing and answering questions using careful, controlled techniques that include systematic, orderly observation and the collection of data. The scientific method involves three major steps: (1) identifying questions of interest, (2) formulating an explanation, and (3) carrying out research that either lends support to the explanation or refutes it, as summarized in Figure 1-2.

The scientific method involves the formulation of *theories*, broad explanations and predictions about phenomena of interest that scientists create. For instance, many people theorize that a crucial bonding period between parent and child takes place immediately after birth and is a necessary ingredient in forming a lasting parent–child relationship. Without such a bonding period, they assume, the parent–child relationship will be forever compromised (Furnham & Weir, 1996).

Developmental researchers use theories to form hypotheses. A **hypothesis** is a prediction stated in a way that permits it to be tested. For instance, someone who subscribes to the general theory that bonding is crucial might derive the hypothesis that effective bonding occurs only if it lasts for a certain length of time.

scientific method
the process of posing and answering questions using careful, controlled techniques that include systematic, orderly observation and the collection of data

hypothesis
a prediction stated in a way that permits it to be tested

Figure 1-2 The Scientific Method

A cornerstone of research, the scientific method is used by psychologists as well as researchers from all other scientific disciplines.

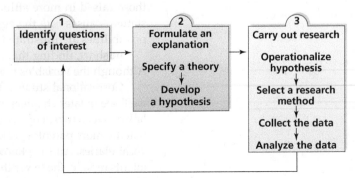

Choosing a Research Strategy: Answering Questions

LO 1.15 Contrast correlational and experimental research.

Once researchers have formed a hypothesis, they must develop a research strategy to test its validity. There are two major categories of research: correlational research and experimental research. Correlational research seeks to identify whether an association or relationship between two factors exists. As we'll see, **correlational research** cannot determine whether one factor *causes* changes in the other. For instance, correlational research could tell us if there is an association between the number of minutes a mother and her newborn child are together immediately after birth and the quality of the mother–child relationship when the child reaches age 2. Such correlational research indicates whether the two factors are *associated* or *related* to one another, but not whether the initial contact caused the relationship to develop in a particular way (Schutt, 2001).

In contrast, **experimental research** is designed to discover *causal* relationships between various factors. In experimental research, researchers deliberately introduce a change in a carefully structured situation to see the consequences of that change. For instance, a researcher conducting an experiment might vary the number of minutes that mothers and children interact immediately following birth, in an attempt to see whether the bonding time affects the mother–child relationship.

Because experimental research is able to answer questions of causality, it is fundamental to finding answers to various developmental hypotheses. However, some research questions cannot be answered through experiments, for either technical or ethical reasons (e.g., it would be unethical to design an experiment in which a group of infants was offered no chance to bond with a caregiver at all). In fact, a great deal of pioneering developmental research—such as that conducted by Piaget and Vygotsky—employed correlational techniques. Consequently, correlational research remains an important tool for developmental researchers.

Correlational Studies

LO 1.16 Explain the types of studies and methods used in correlational research.

As we've noted, correlational research examines the relationship between two variables to determine whether they are associated, or *correlated*. For instance, researchers interested in the relationship between televised aggression and subsequent behavior have found that children who watch a good deal of aggression on television—murders, crimes, shootings, and the like—tend to be more aggressive than those who watch only a little. In other words, viewing aggression and actual aggression are strongly associated, or correlated (Feshbach & Tangney, 2008; Qian, Zhang, & Wang, 2013; Coyne, 2016).

But can we conclude that the viewing of televised aggression *causes* the more aggressive behavior? Not at all. Consider some of the other possibilities: It might be that being aggressive in the first place makes children more likely to choose to watch violent programs. In this case, the aggressive tendency causes the viewing behavior, not the other way around.

Or consider that there may be a *third* factor operating on both the viewing and the aggression. Suppose, for example, that children of lower socioeconomic status are more likely to behave aggressively *and* to watch higher levels of aggressive television than those raised in more affluent settings. In this case, the third variable—socioeconomic status—causes *both* the aggressive behavior and the television viewing. (The various possibilities are illustrated in Figure 1-3.)

In short, finding that two variables are correlated proves nothing about causality. Although the variables may be linked causally, this is not necessarily the case.

Correlational studies do provide important information, however. For instance, as we'll see in later chapters, we know from correlational studies that the closer the genetic link between two people, the more highly associated is their intelligence. We have learned that the more parents speak to their young children, the more extensive are the children's vocabularies. And we know from correlational studies that the better the nutrition that infants receive, the fewer the cognitive and social problems they experience later (Colom, Lluis-Font, & Andrés-Pueyo, 2005; Robb, Richert, & Wartella, 2009; Deoni et al., 2018).

correlational research
research that seeks to identify whether an association or relationship between two factors exists

experimental research
research designed to discover causal relationships between various factors

Figure 1-3 Finding a Correlation

Finding a correlation between two factors does not imply that one factor *causes* the other factor to vary. For instance, suppose a study found that viewing television shows with high levels of aggression is correlated with actual aggression in children. The correlation may reflect at least three possibilities: (a) watching television programs containing high levels of aggression causes aggression in viewers; (b) children who behave aggressively choose to watch TV programs with high levels of aggression; or (c) some third factor, such as a child's socioeconomic status, leads both to high viewer aggression and to choosing to watch television programs with high aggression. What other factors, besides socioeconomic status, might be plausible third factors?

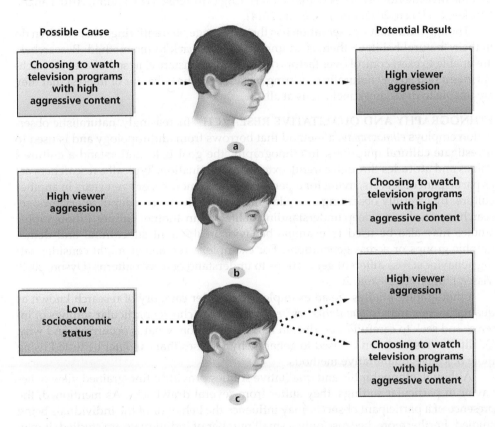

THE CORRELATION COEFFICIENT   The strength and direction of a relationship between two factors is represented by a mathematical score, called a *correlation coefficient*, that ranges from +1.0 to −1.0. A *positive* correlation indicates that as the value of one factor increases, it can be predicted that the value of the other will also increase. For instance, if we administer a job satisfaction survey and find that the more money people make in their first job, the higher their job satisfaction, and the less money they make, the lower their job satisfaction, we have found a positive correlation. The correlation coefficient would be indicated by a positive number, and the stronger the association between salary and job satisfaction, the closer the number would be to +1.0.

In contrast, a correlation coefficient with a *negative* value informs us that as the value of one factor increases, the value of the other factor declines. For example, suppose we found that the more time adolescents spend using instant messaging on their computers, the worse their academic performance is. This would produce a negative correlation, a number between 0 and −1.0. More instant messaging would be associated with lower performance, and less instant messaging with higher performance. The stronger the association between instant messaging and school performance, the closer the correlation coefficient will be to −1.0.

Finally, it may be that two factors are unrelated to one another. For example, it is unlikely that we would find a correlation between school performance and shoe size. In this case, the lack of a relationship would be indicated by a correlation coefficient close to 0.

It is important to repeat that, even if a correlation coefficient is strong, there is no way we can know whether one factor *causes* the other factor to vary. It simply means that the two factors are associated with one another in a predictable way.

naturalistic observation

a type of correlational study in which some naturally occurring behavior is observed without intervention in the situation

TYPES OF CORRELATIONAL STUDIES There are several types of correlational studies. **Naturalistic observation** is the observation of a naturally occurring behavior without intervention. For instance, an investigator who wishes to learn how often preschool children share toys might observe a classroom over a 3-week period, recording how often the preschoolers spontaneously share with one another. The key point is that the investigator observes without interfering (Mortensen & Cialdini, 2010; Fanger, Frankel, & Hazen, 2012; Graham et al., 2014).

Though naturalistic observation has the advantage of identifying what children do in their "natural habitat," there is an important drawback to the method: Researchers are unable to exert control over factors of interest. For instance, in some cases researchers might find so few naturally occurring instances of the behavior of interest that they are unable to draw any conclusions at all.

ETHNOGRAPHY AND QUALITATIVE RESEARCH Increasingly, naturalistic observation employs *ethnography*, a method that borrows from anthropology and is used to investigate cultural questions. In ethnography, the goal is to understand a culture's values and attitudes through careful, extended examination. Typically, researchers act as participant observers, living for a period of weeks, months, or even years in another culture. By carefully observing everyday life and conducting in-depth interviews, researchers can obtain a deep understanding of life within another culture. Ethnographic studies may also be used to examine behavior in different subcultural and demographic groups or across generations. For example, a researcher might consider eating behavior across different generations to understand obesity patterns (Dyson, 2003; Visser, Hutter, & Haisma, 2016).

Ethnographic studies are an example of a broader category of research known as qualitative research. In *qualitative research*, researchers choose particular settings of interest and seek to carefully describe, in narrative fashion, what is occurring, and why. Qualitative research can be used to generate hypotheses that can later be tested using more objective, quantitative methods.

Although ethnographic and qualitative studies provide a fine-grained view of behavior in particular settings, they suffer from several drawbacks. As mentioned, the presence of a participant observer may influence the behavior of the individuals being studied. Furthermore, because only a small number of individuals are studied, it may be hard to generalize the findings to other settings.

Finally, ethnographers carrying out cross-cultural research may misinterpret and misconceive what they are observing, particularly in cultures that are different from their own. For example, it may be difficult for an ethnographic researcher to understand completely the underlying meaning of a coming-of-age ritual in a given culture, such as the quinceañera, a celebration that occurs in many Hispanic cultures when a girl reaches the age of 15 (Polkinghorne, 2005; Hallett & Barber, 2014; Montemurro, 2014).

case studies

studies that involve extensive, in-depth interviews with a particular individual or small group of individuals

Case studies involve extensive, in-depth interviews with a particular individual or small group of individuals. They often are used not just to learn about the individual being interviewed, but also to derive broader principles or draw tentative conclusions that might apply to others. For example, case studies have been conducted on children who display unusual genius and on children who have spent their early years in the wild, apparently without human contact. These case studies have provided important information to researchers and have suggested hypotheses for future investigation (Wilson, 2003; Ng & Nicholas, 2010; Halkier, 2013).

Using *diaries*, participants are asked to keep a record of their behavior on a regular basis. For example, a group of adolescents may be asked to record each time they interact with friends for more than 5 minutes, thereby providing a way to track their social behavior.

survey research

a type of study where a group of people chosen to represent some larger population are asked questions about their attitudes, behavior, or thinking on a given topic

Surveys represent another sort of correlational research. In **survey research**, a group of people chosen to represent some larger population are asked questions about their attitudes, behavior, or thinking on a given topic. For instance, surveys have been conducted about parents' use of punishment on their children and on attitudes toward breastfeeding. From the responses, inferences are drawn regarding the larger population represented by the individuals being surveyed.

PSYCHOPHYSIOLOGICAL METHODS Some developmental researchers, particularly those using a cognitive neuroscience approach, make use of psychophysiological methods. **Psychophysiological methods** focus on the relationship between physiological processes and behavior. For instance, a researcher might examine the relationship between blood flow in the brain and problem-solving ability. Similarly, some studies use infants' heart rate as a measure of their interest in stimuli to which they are exposed (Field, Diego, & Hernandez-Reif, 2009; Mazoyer et al., 2009; Jones & Mize, 2016).

Among the most frequently used psychophysiological measures are:

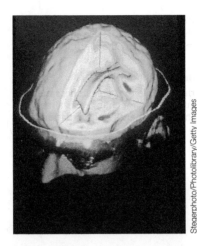

This fMRI shows activity in different regions of the brain.

psychophysiological methods
research that focuses on the relationship between physiological processes and behavior

- **Electroencephalogram (EEG).** The EEG uses electrodes placed on the skull to record electrical activity in the brain. The brain activity is transformed into a pictorial representation of brain wave patterns, permitting the diagnosis of disorders such as epilepsy and learning disabilities.

- **Computed tomography (CT) scan.** In a CT scan, a computer constructs an image of the brain by combining thousands of individual X-rays taken at slightly different angles. Although it does not show brain activity, it does illuminate the structure of the brain.

- **Functional magnetic resonance imaging (fMRI) scan.** An fMRI provides a detailed, three-dimensional computer-generated image of brain activity by aiming a powerful magnetic field at the brain. It offers one of the best ways of learning about the operation of the brain, down to the level of individual nerves.

Experiments: Determining Cause and Effect

Correlational research allows scientists to determine how two factors are associated with one another, but it tells us nothing about cause and effect. To determine whether changes in one factor cause changes in another factor, we need to conduct experiments.

The Basics of Experiments

LO 1.17 Analyze how experiments can be used to determine cause and effect.

In an **experiment**, an investigator or experimenter typically devises two different conditions (or *treatments*) and then compares how the behavior of the participants exposed to each condition is affected. One group, the *treatment* or *experimental group*, is exposed to the treatment variable being studied; the other, the *control group*, is not.

For instance, suppose you want to see if exposure to movie violence makes viewers more aggressive. You might show a group of adolescents a series of movies with a great deal of violent imagery. You would then measure their subsequent aggression. This group would constitute the treatment group. For the control group you might show a second group of adolescents movies that contain no violent imagery, and measure their subsequent aggression. By comparing the amount of aggression displayed by members of the treatment and control groups, you would be able to determine if exposure to violent imagery produces aggression in viewers. In fact, this describes an experiment conducted at the University of Louvain in Belgium. Psychologist Jacques-Philippe Leyens and colleagues found that the level of aggression rose significantly for the adolescents who had seen the movies containing violence (Leyens et al., 1975).

The central feature of this experiment—and all experiments—is the comparison of the consequences of different treatments. The use of both treatment and control groups allows researchers to rule out the possibility that something other than the experimental manipulation produced the results found in the experiment. For instance, if a control group was not used, experimenters could not be certain that some other factor, such as the time of day the movies were shown or even the mere passage of time, produced the observed changes. By using a control group, experimenters can draw accurate conclusions about causes and effects.

experiment
a process in which an investigator, called an *experimenter*, devises two different experiences for participants and then studies and compares the outcomes

independent variable
the variable that researchers manipulate in an experiment

dependent variable
the variable that researchers measure to see if it changes as a result of the experimental manipulation

INDEPENDENT AND DEPENDENT VARIABLES The **independent variable** is the variable that researchers manipulate in the experiment (in our example, it is the type of movie participants saw—violent or nonviolent). In contrast, the **dependent variable** is the variable that researchers measure to see if it changes as a result of the experimental manipulation. In our example, the degree of aggressive behavior shown by the participants after viewing violent or nonviolent films is the dependent variable. (One way to remember the difference: A hypothesis predicts how a dependent variable *depends* on the manipulation of the independent variable.) Every experiment has an independent and a dependent variable.

Experimenters must make sure their studies are not influenced by factors other than those they are manipulating. For this reason, they take great care to make sure that the participants in both the treatment and control groups are not aware of the purpose of the experiment (which could affect their responses or behavior) and that the experimenters do not influence who is chosen for the control and treatment groups. The procedure that is used for this is known as *random assignment*. In random assignment, participants are assigned to different experimental groups or "conditions" purely on the basis of chance. This way the laws of statistics ensure that personal characteristics that might affect the outcome of the experiment are divided proportionally among the participants in the different groups, making the groups equivalent. Equivalent groups achieved by random assignment allow an experimenter to draw conclusions with confidence.

Figure 1-4 illustrates the Belgian experiment on adolescents exposed to films containing violent or nonviolent imagery, and the effects of such imagery on subsequent aggressive behavior. As you can see, it contains each of the elements of an experiment:

- An independent variable (the assignment to a violent or nonviolent film condition)
- A dependent variable (measurement of the adolescents' aggressive behavior)

Figure 1-4 Elements of an Experiment

In this experiment, researchers randomly assigned a group of adolescents to one of two conditions: viewing a film that contained violent imagery or viewing a film that lacked violent imagery (manipulation of the independent variable). Then participants were observed later to determine how much aggression they showed (the dependent variable). Analysis of the findings showed that adolescents exposed to aggressive imagery showed more aggression later. **THINKING ABOUT THE DATA:** In this experiment and others like it, why is random assignment important?

SOURCE: Based on an experiment by Leyens et al., 1975.

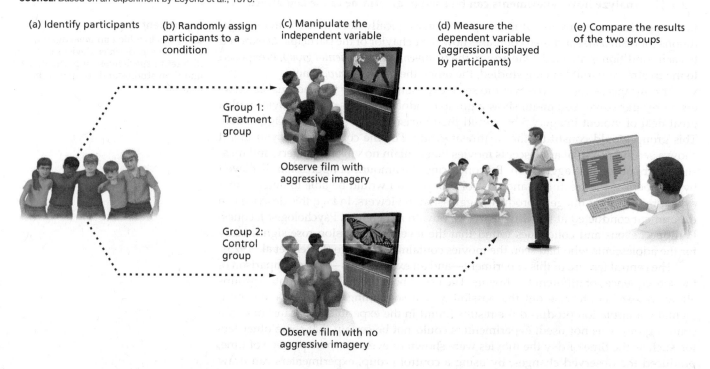

- Random assignment to condition (viewing a film with violent imagery versus a film with nonviolent imagery)
- A hypothesis that predicts the effect the independent variable will have on the dependent variable (that viewing a film with violent imagery will produce subsequent aggression)

Given the advantage of experiments—that they provide a means of determining causality—why aren't experiments always used? The answer is that there are some situations that a researcher, no matter how ingenious, simply cannot control. And there are some situations in which control would be unethical, even if it were possible. For instance, no researcher would be able to assign different groups of infants to parents of high and low socioeconomic status to learn the effects of such status on subsequent development. In situations in which experiments are logistically or ethically impossible, developmentalists employ correlational research.

Furthermore, keep in mind that a single experiment is insufficient to answer a research question definitively. Before complete confidence can be placed in a conclusion, research must be *replicated*, or repeated, sometimes using other procedures and techniques, with other types of participants. For example, researchers might want to replicate a study conducted with participants from rural locations in the United States using, instead, participants drawn from urban Asian settings before drawing universal principles from results. The importance of replication has grown in recent years as researchers have struggled, in some cases, to replicate findings from classic studies (Chopik et al., 2018; Shrout & Rodgers, 2018).

In order to summarize multiple findings and gain clarity across different studies, developmentalists increasingly turn to a procedure called meta-analysis. *Meta-analysis* is a statistical procedure that permits researchers to combine the results of many studies into one overall conclusion (Le et al., 2010; Krause, 2018; Kruschke & Liddell, 2018).

CHOOSING A RESEARCH SETTING   Deciding *where* to conduct a study may be as important as determining *what* to do. In the Belgian experiment on the influence of exposure to media aggression, the researchers used a real-world setting—a group home for boys who had been convicted of juvenile delinquency. They chose this **sample**, the group of participants chosen for the experiment, because it was useful to have adolescents whose normal level of aggression was relatively high, and because they could incorporate the films into the everyday life of the home with minimal disruption.

sample
the group of participants chosen for the experiment

Using a real-world setting (as in the aggression experiment) is the hallmark of a field study. A **field study** is a research investigation carried out in a naturally occurring setting. Field studies capture behavior in real-life settings, where research participants may behave more naturally than in a laboratory.

field study
a research investigation carried out in a naturally occurring setting

Field studies may be used in both correlational studies and experiments. They typically employ naturalistic observation, the technique in which researchers observe a naturally occurring behavior without intervening or changing the situation. A researcher might examine behavior in a child-care center, view the groupings of adolescents in high school corridors, or observe elderly adults in a senior center.

Because it is often difficult to control the situation and environment enough to run an experiment in a real-world setting, field studies are more typical of correlational designs than are experimental designs. Most developmental research experiments are conducted in laboratory settings. A **laboratory study** is a research investigation conducted in a controlled setting explicitly designed to hold events constant. The laboratory may be a room or building designed for research, as in a university psychology department. Their ability to control the settings in laboratory studies enables researchers to learn more clearly how their treatments affect participants.

laboratory study
a research investigation conducted in a controlled setting explicitly designed to hold events constant

Theoretical and Applied Research: Complementary Approaches

theoretical research
research designed specifically to test some developmental explanation and expand scientific knowledge

applied research
research meant to provide practical solutions to immediate problems

LO 1.18 Explain how theoretical and applied research complement each other.

Developmental researchers typically focus on either theoretical research or applied research. **Theoretical research** is designed to test some developmental explanation and expand scientific knowledge, whereas **applied research** is meant to provide practical solutions to immediate problems. For instance, if we were interested in the processes of cognitive change during childhood, we might carry out a study of how many digits children of various ages can remember after one exposure to multidigit

---

From Research to Practice

Using Lifespan Developmental Research to Improve Public Policy

Does the Head Start preschool program enhance children's cognitive and social development?

How does the use of social media affect the self-esteem of adolescents?

How are soldiers and their families affected when they return from war?

What are some effective ways to bolster schoolgirls' confidence in their math and science aptitude?

Should children with developmental disabilities be schooled in regular classrooms, or are they better off in special classrooms with other children who are similarly disabled?

How should society best address the opioid epidemic affecting adolescents and adults in the United States?

Each of these questions represents a significant policy issue that can be answered only by considering the results of relevant research studies. By conducting controlled studies, developmental researchers have made important contributions affecting education, family life, and health on a national scale. Consider, for instance, the variety of ways that public policy issues have been informed by various types of research findings (Cramer, Song, & Drent, 2016; Crupi & Brondolo, 2017; Kennedy-Hendricks et al., 2017):

- **Research findings can provide policymakers a means of determining what questions to ask in the first place.** For example, studies of children's caregivers (some of which we'll consider in Chapter 10) have led policymakers to question whether the benefits of infant day care are outweighed by possible deterioration in parent–child bonds. Research has also disconfirmed the widespread belief that childhood vaccinations are linked to autism spectrum disorder, contributing invaluable evidence to the controversy over the risks and benefits of mandatory child immunization (Price et al., 2010; Lester et al., 2013; Young, Elliston, & Ruble, 2016).

- **Research findings and the testimony of researchers are often part of the process by which laws are drafted.** A good deal of legislation has been passed

based on findings from developmental researchers. For example, research revealed that children with developmental disabilities benefit from exposure to children without special needs, ultimately leading to the passage of national legislation mandating that children with disabilities be placed in regular school classes as often as possible. Research showing that children raised by same-sex couples fare just as well as children raised by a mother and father has undermined an often-used but baseless argument that same-sex marriage is harmful to children (Gartrell & Bos, 2010; Bos et al., 2016).

- **Policymakers and other professionals use research findings to determine how best to implement programs.** Research has shaped programs designed to reduce the incidence of unsafe sex among teenagers, to increase the level of prenatal care for pregnant mothers, to encourage and support women in the pursuit of math and science studies, and to promote flu shots for older adults. The common thread among such programs is that many of the details of the programs are built on basic research findings.

- **Research techniques are used to evaluate the effectiveness of existing programs and policies.** Once a public policy has been implemented, it is necessary to determine whether it has been effective and successful in accomplishing its goals. To do this, researchers employ formal evaluation techniques, developed from basic research procedures. For instance, careful studies of DARE, a popular program meant to reduce children's use of drugs, began to find that it was ineffective. Using the research findings of developmentalists, DARE instigated new techniques, and preliminary findings suggest that the revised program is more effective (Phillips, Gormley, & Anderson, 2016; Barlett, Chamberlin, & Witkower, 2017; Cline & Edwards, 2017).

Shared Writing Prompt:

Despite the existence of research data that might inform policy about development, politicians rarely discuss such data in their speeches. Why do you think that is the case?

numbers—a theoretical approach. Alternatively, we might focus on the more practical question of how teachers can help children to remember information more easily. Such a study would represent applied research because the findings are applied to a particular setting and problem.

There is not always a clear distinction between theoretical and applied research. For instance, is a study that examines the consequences of ear infections in infancy on later hearing loss theoretical or applied? Because such a study may help illuminate the basic processes involved in hearing, it can be considered theoretical. But if it helps to prevent hearing loss, it may be considered applied (Lerner, Fisher, & Weinberg, 2000).

In fact, as we discuss in the accompanying *From Research to Practice* box, research of both a theoretical and an applied nature has played a significant role in shaping and resolving a variety of public policy questions.

Measuring Developmental Change

LO 1.19 Compare longitudinal research, cross-sectional research, and sequential research.

How people grow and change through the life span is central to the work of all developmental researchers. Consequently, one of the thorniest research issues they face concerns the measurement of change and differences over age and time. To solve this problem, researchers have developed three major research strategies: longitudinal research, cross-sectional research, and sequential research.

LONGITUDINAL STUDIES: MEASURING INDIVIDUAL CHANGE If you were interested in learning how a child develops morally between ages 3 and 5, the most direct approach would be to take a group of 3-year-olds and follow them until they were 5, testing them periodically.

This strategy illustrates longitudinal research. In **longitudinal research**, the behavior of one or more study participants is measured as they age. Longitudinal research measures change over time. By following many individuals over time, researchers can understand the general course of change across some period of life.

longitudinal research
research in which the behavior of one or more participants in a study is measured as they age

The granddaddy of longitudinal studies, which has become a classic, is a study of gifted children begun by Lewis Terman about 80 years ago. In the study—which has yet to be concluded—a group of 1,500 children with high IQs were tested about every 5 years. Now in their 80s, the participants—who call themselves "Termites"—have provided information on everything from intellectual accomplishment to personality and longevity (McCullough, Tsang, & Brion, 2003; Subotnik, 2006; Warne & Liu, 2017).

Longitudinal research has also provided insight into language development. For instance, by tracing how children's vocabularies increase on a day-by-day basis, researchers have been able to understand the processes that underlie the human ability to become competent in using language (Fagan, 2009; Kelloway & Francis, 2013; Dwyer et al., 2018).

Longitudinal studies can provide a wealth of information about change over time, but they have drawbacks. For one thing, they require a tremendous investment of time because researchers must wait for participants to become older. Furthermore, participants often drop out over the course of the research. Participants may drop out of a study, move away, or become ill or even die as the research proceeds.

Finally, participants who are observed or tested repeatedly may become "testwise" and perform better each time they are assessed as they become more familiar with the procedure. Even if the observations of participants in a study are not terribly intrusive (such as simply recording, over a lengthy period of time, vocabulary increases in infants and preschoolers), experimental participants may be affected by the repeated presence of an experimenter or observer.

Consequently, despite the benefits of longitudinal research, particularly its ability to look at change within individuals, developmental researchers often turn to other methods. The alternative they choose most often is the cross-sectional study.

CROSS-SECTIONAL STUDIES   Suppose again that you want to consider how children's moral development, their sense of right and wrong, changes from ages 3 to 5. Instead of following the same children over several years, we might look simultaneously at three groups of children: 3-year-olds, 4-year-olds, and 5-year-olds, perhaps presenting each group with the same problem and then seeing how they respond to it and explain their choices.

cross-sectional research
research in which people of different ages are compared at the same point in time

Such an approach typifies cross-sectional research. In **cross-sectional research**, people of different ages are compared at the same point in time. Cross-sectional studies provide information about differences in development between different age groups.

Cross-sectional research takes far less time than longitudinal research: Participants are tested at just one point in time. Terman's study might have been completed 75 years ago if Terman had simply looked at a group of gifted 15-year-olds, 20-year-olds, 25-year-olds, and so forth, up to 80-year-olds. Because the participants would not be periodically tested, there would be no chance that they would become test-wise, and problems of participant attrition would not occur. Why, then, would anyone choose to use a procedure other than cross-sectional research?

The answer is that cross-sectional research brings its own set of difficulties. Recall that every person belongs to a particular *cohort*, the group of people born at around the same time in the same place. If we find that people of different ages vary along some dimension, it may be because of differences in cohort membership, not age per se.

Consider a concrete example: If we find in a correlational study that people who are 25 perform better on a test of intelligence than those who are 75, there are several possible explanations other than that intelligence declines in old age. Instead, the finding may be attributable to cohort differences. The 75-year-olds may have had less formal education than the 15-year-olds because members of the older cohort were less likely to finish high school and attend college than members of the younger one. Or perhaps the older group received less adequate nutrition as infants than the younger group. In short, we cannot rule out the possibility that age-related differences in cross-sectional studies are actually cohort differences.

Cross-sectional studies may also suffer from *selective dropout*, in which participants in some age groups are more likely to stop participating than others. For example, suppose a study of cognitive development in preschoolers includes a long test of cognitive abilities, which young preschoolers find more difficult than older preschoolers. If more young children quit than older preschoolers and if it is the least competent young preschoolers who drop out, then the remaining sample of that age group will consist of the more competent young preschoolers—together with a broader and more representative sample of older preschoolers. The results of such a study would be questionable (Miller, 1998).

Finally, cross-sectional studies have an additional, and more basic, disadvantage: They are unable to inform us about changes in individuals or groups. If longitudinal studies are like videos taken of a person at various ages, cross-sectional studies are like snapshots of entirely different groups. Although we can establish differences related to age, we cannot fully determine whether such differences are related to change over time.

SEQUENTIAL STUDIES   Because both longitudinal and cross-sectional studies have drawbacks, researchers have turned to some compromise techniques. Among the most frequently employed are sequential studies, which are essentially a combination of longitudinal and cross-sectional studies.

sequential studies
research in which researchers examine a number of different age groups over several points in time

In **sequential studies**, researchers examine a number of different age groups at several points in time. For instance, an investigator interested in children's moral behavior might begin a sequential study by examining the behavior of three groups of children, who are either 3, 4, or 5 years old at the time the study begins.

The study continues for the next several years, with each participant tested annually. Thus, the 3-year-olds would be tested at ages 3, 4, and 5; the 4-year-olds at ages 4, 5, and 6; and the 5-year-olds at ages 5, 6, and 7. By combining the advantages of longitudinal and cross-sectional research, this approach permits developmental researchers to tease out the consequences of age *change* versus age *difference*. The major research techniques for studying development are summarized in Figure 1-5.

Ethics and Research

LO 1.20 Describe some ethical issues that affect psychological research.

In the "study" conducted by Egyptian King Psamtik, two children were removed from their mothers and held in isolation in an effort to learn about the roots of language. If you found yourself thinking this was extraordinarily cruel, you are in good company. Clearly, such an experiment raises blatant ethical concerns, and nothing like it would ever be done today.

But sometimes ethical issues are more subtle. For instance, U.S. government researchers proposed a conference to examine possible genetic roots of aggression. Some researchers had begun to raise the possibility that genetic markers might be found that would identify particularly violence-prone children. If so, it might be possible to track these children and provide interventions to reduce the likelihood of later violence.

Critics objected strenuously, however, arguing that identification might lead to a self-fulfilling prophecy. Children labeled as violence-prone might be treated in a way that would actually *cause* them to be more aggressive. Ultimately, under intense political pressure, the conference was canceled (Wright, 1995).

To help researchers deal with ethical problems, the major organizations of developmentalists, including the Society for Research in Child Development and the American Psychological Association, have developed ethical guidelines for researchers. Among the principles are those involving freedom from harm, informed consent, the use of deception, and maintenance of participants' privacy (American Psychological Association, 2002, 2017; Toporek, Kwan, & Williams, 2012; Joireman & Van Lange, 2015; see the *Development in Your Life* box):

- **Researchers must protect participants from physical and psychological harm.** Their welfare, interests, and rights come before those of researchers. In research, participants' rights always come first (Sieber, 2000; Fisher, 2004).

- **Researchers must obtain informed consent from participants before their involvement in a study.**   If they are older than age 7, participants must voluntarily agree to be in a study. If participants are younger than age 18, parents or guardians must also provide consent.

Obtaining informed consent is a requirement that raises significant ethical issues. Suppose, for instance, researchers want to study the psychological effects of abortion on adolescents. To obtain the consent of an adolescent minor who has had an abortion, the researchers would need to get her parents' permission as well. But if the adolescent hasn't told her parents about the abortion, the request for parental permission would violate her privacy—leading to a breach of ethics.

The importance of informed consent extends across a variety of populations. For example, young children may lack the cognitive abilities to provide truly informed consent, as well as participants with intellectual disabilities, psychological dysfunction, and those in late adulthood suffering cognitive declines. In addition, socioeconomic and cultural factors may impact the ability to obtain informed consent (Neyro et al., 2018; Read & Spar, 2018).

- **The use of deception in research must be justified and cause no harm.**   Although deception to disguise the true purpose of an experiment is permissible, any experiment that uses deception must undergo careful scrutiny by an independent panel before it is conducted. Suppose, for example, we want to know the reaction of participants to success and failure. It is ethical to tell participants that they will be playing a game when the true purpose is actually to observe how they respond to doing well or poorly on the task. However, this is ethical only if it causes no harm to

Figure 1-5 Research Techniques for Studying Development

In a *cross-sectional study*, 3-, 4-, and 5-year-olds are compared at a similar point in time (in 2020). In *longitudinal research*, a set of participants who are 3 years old in 2020 are studied when they are 4 years old (in 2021) and when they are 5 years old (in 2022). Finally, a *sequential study* combines cross-sectional and longitudinal techniques; here, a group of 3-year-olds would be compared initially in 2020 with 4- and 5-year-olds, but would also be studied 1 and 2 years later, when they themselves were 4 and 5 years old. Although the graph does not illustrate this, researchers carrying out this sequential study might also choose to retest the children who were 4 and 5 in 2020 for the next 2 years. What advantages do the three kinds of studies offer?

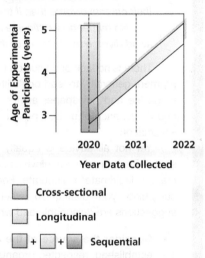

Cross-sectional

Longitudinal

+ + Sequential

participants, has been approved by a review panel, and includes a full explanation for participants when the study is over (Underwood, 2005).

- **Participants' privacy must be maintained.** If participants are videotaped during a study, for example, they must give their permission for the videotapes to be viewed. Furthermore, access to the tapes must be carefully restricted.

> **From the perspective of a health-care provider:** Do you think there are some special circumstances involving adolescents, who are not legally adults, that would justify allowing them to participate in a study without obtaining their parents' permission? What might such circumstances involve?

Development in Your Life

Thinking Critically About "Expert" Advice

Spanking is one of the best ways to discipline your child.
Never hit your child.

***

If a marriage is unhappy, children are better off if their parents divorce than if they stay together.
No matter how difficult a marriage is, parents should avoid divorce for the sake of their children.

There is no lack of advice on the best way to raise a child or, more generally, to lead one's life. From self-help books to magazine and newspaper advice columns, to social media and blogs, each of us is exposed to tremendous amounts of information.

Yet not all advice is equally valid. The mere fact that something is in print, on television, or on the Internet does not make it legitimate or accurate. Fortunately, some guidelines can help you distinguish when recommendations and suggestions are reasonable and when they are not:

- **Consider the source of the advice.** Information from established, respected organizations such as the American Medical Association, the American Psychological Association, and the American Academy of Pediatrics reflects years of study and is usually accurate. If you don't know the organization, investigate it further to find out more about its goals and philosophy.

- **Evaluate the credentials of the person providing advice.** Trustworthy information tends to come from established, acknowledged researchers and experts, not from people with obscure credentials. Consider where the author is employed and whether he or she has a particular political or personal agenda.

- **Understand the difference between *anecdotal evidence* and *scientific evidence*.** Anecdotal evidence is based on one or two instances of a phenomenon, haphazardly discovered or encountered; scientific evidence is based on careful, systematic procedures. If an aunt tells you that all her children slept through the night by 2 months of age and therefore your child will too, that is quite different from reading a report that 75 percent of children sleep through the night by 9 months. Of course, even with such a report, it would be a good idea to find out how large the study was or how this number was arrived at.

- **If advice is based on research findings, there should be a clear, transparent description of the studies on which the advice is based.** Who were the participants? What methods were used? What do the results show? Think critically about the way the findings were obtained before accepting them.

- **Don't overlook the cultural context of the information.** An assertion may be valid in some contexts but not in all. For example, it is typically assumed that providing infants the freedom to move about and exercise their limbs facilitates their muscular development and mobility. Yet in some cultures, infants spend most of their time closely bound to their mothers—with no apparent long-term damage (Kaplan & Dove, 1987; Tronick, 1995).

- **Don't assume that because many people believe something, it is necessarily true.** Scientific evaluation has often proved that some of the most basic presumptions about the effectiveness of various techniques are invalid.

In short, the key to evaluating information relating to human development is to maintain a healthy dose of skepticism. No source of information is invariably, unfailingly accurate. By keeping a critical eye on the statements you encounter, you'll be in a better position to determine the real contributions made by developmentalists to understanding how humans develop over the course of the life span.

Review, Check, and Apply

Review

LO 1.14 Explain the role theories and hypotheses play in the study of development.

Theories are systematically derived explanations of facts or phenomena. Theories suggest hypotheses, which are predictions that can be tested.

LO 1.15 Contrast correlational and experimental research.

Correlational research seeks to identify an association or relationship between two factors. Experimental research is designed to discover *causal* relationships between various factors. In experimental research, researchers deliberately introduce a change in a carefully structured situation to see the consequences of that change.

LO 1.16 Explain the types of studies and methods used in correlational research.

Correlational studies examine the relationship, or correlation, between two factors without demonstrating causality. Correlational methods include naturalistic observation, ethnography, case studies, survey research, and psychophysiological methods.

LO 1.17 Analyze how experiments can be used to determine cause and effect.

In an experiment, an investigator or experimenter typically devises two different conditions (or treatments) and then compares how the behavior of the participants exposed to each condition is affected. One group, the treatment or experimental group, is exposed to the treatment variable being studied; the other, the control group, is not.

LO 1.18 Explain how theoretical and applied research complement each other.

Theoretical research is designed to test some developmental explanation and expand scientific knowledge, whereas applied research is meant to provide practical solutions to immediate problems.

LO 1.19 Compare longitudinal research, cross-sectional research, and sequential research.

To measure change across human ages, researchers use longitudinal studies of the same participants over time, cross-sectional studies of different-age participants conducted at one time, and sequential studies of different-age participants at several points in time.

LO 1.20 Describe some ethical issues that affect psychological research.

Ethical issues that affect psychological research include the protection of participants from harm, informed consent of participants, limits on the use of deception, and the maintenance of privacy.

Check Yourself

1. To make a prediction in such a way that permits it to be tested, one must make a(n) _____.

   a. theory
   b. hypothesis
   c. analysis
   d. judgment

2. A researcher stands near an intersection and writes down the time it takes for the lead driver to start up after the light turns green. The researcher records the gender and approximate age of the driver. This researcher is most likely engaged in _____.

   a. a case study
   b. naturalistic observation
   c. an ethnography
   d. survey research

3. In a(n) _____, an investigator devises two conditions (treatment or control) and compares the outcomes of the participants exposed to those two different conditions to see how behavior is affected.

   a. experiment
   b. correlational study
   c. interview
   d. naturalistic observation

4. In a _____ research study, researchers are interested in measuring change in a single group of subjects over time.

   a. correlational
   b. cross-sectional
   c. longitudinal
   d. sequential

Applying Lifespan Development

Formulate a theory about one aspect of human development and a hypothesis that relates to it.

Chapter 1 Summary
Putting It All Together: Introduction

MARCO RUIZ, watching the large, multigenerational reunion we encountered in the chapter opener, found himself pondering many of the questions that developmentalists study formally. Putting himself into his grandpa's mind, he thought about how the traits for which his grandfather was noted might show up—or not—in the members of the generations at the reunion. He considered both inherited characteristics and personality traits and habits potentially acquired from social and environmental interactions. Marco's "thought experiment" on five generations of his grandfather's extended family gave him a lot to ponder, given the size and diversity of his experimental "sample."

MODULE 1.1
BEGINNINGS

- Marco's consideration of his five-generation household mirrors the work of developmentalists with a wide range of interests, including those who focus on genetic versus environmental influences, cognitive changes across the life span, and social and personality development. (pp. 4–10)

- The age range of Marco's family mirrors the full range that developmentalists cover, from before birth to old age. (p. 5)

- Each family member naturally experiences different cohort influences, which interact with their shared genetic heritage. (pp. 5–7)

- Key issues in development are reflected in Marco's thoughts, including the nature–nurture issue and continuity versus discontinuity. (pp. 7–10)

MODULE 1.2
THEORETICAL PERSPECTIVES ON LIFESPAN DEVELOPMENT

- Developmentalists with different perspectives might guide Marco's musings. Erik Erikson might help Marco interpret generational differences in his family in terms of stages along the life span; Piaget might illuminate little Alicia's developing thought processes; and Vygotsky might underscore the importance of social interactions in cognitive, social, and physical development. (pp. 12–22)

- Marco is likely to understand that it is best to avoid considering any particular theoretical perspective either all wrong or all right. (p. 22)

MODULE 1.3
RESEARCH METHODS

- Marco reveals an instinctive knack for constructing theories about development and considering informal hypotheses to test them. (pp. 25–33)

- Marco asks questions about the development of his family members and himself through a combination of a sort of "life experiment" and naturalistic observation. (p. 28)

- In a sense, Marco's curiosity about development contains elements of the case study (i.e., observing his family's life), longitudinal research (i.e., reflecting on and interpreting generational traits in his family), and the cross-sectional study (i.e., the family reunion) is a cross-section of development across the life span. (p. 33)

What would an EDUCATOR do?

How could you prepare Terri and Tony, Alicia's parents, for the changes in educational practice that may have occurred since they were in school? What might you tell them to look for in gauging young Alicia's cognitive, physical, and social readiness for school? What ideas could you give them to help Alicia prepare for school? Do you think Alicia's parents may need to be cautioned against taking Alicia's learning for granted, given their extended family's history of successful school experiences?

Mel Yates/Cultura/Getty Images

What would a PARENT do?

Marco is a parent and grandparent who is also a son and grandson. How would you suggest he balance his "upward" responsibilities toward his father and grandfather with his "downward" responsibilities toward his children and their children? Marco and Ellie's children themselves represent a range of developmental stages and ages. How would you help them deal differently with the needs and potential sources of support that such a variety of children offers?

Jim Esposito Photography L.L.C/ Photodisc/Getty Images

What would a HEALTH-CARE PROVIDER do?

How would you help Marco and Ellie understand the different stages of development, with all their varying states of physical, cognitive, and emotional health, represented in their family? How could you help them accept their power and limitations in perceiving and responding to their family's varied physical and emotional needs? How could you help Marco and Ellie prepare for a death in their family (e.g., grandparent, parent, spouse, children, grandchildren)?

Photodisc/Getty Images

What would YOU do?

How would you help Marco understand his varying roles as a father, son, grandson, and grandfather? What things would you suggest that Marco's father and grandfather could help him with or advise him about? Has the role of father and grandfather changed too much for cross-generational wisdom to be shared helpfully?

Asia Images Group/Getty Images

Chapter 2
The Start of Life

karen roach/Shutterstock

In every respect, Stephen Monaco seemed to be a healthy and normal 3-year-old. Yet one day, he developed a stomach virus that led to severe brain damage and the terrible diagnosis of a rare disease called isovaleric acidemia (IVA). IVA makes the body unable to metabolize a common amino acid found in protein. Unbeknownst to them, Stephen's parents were carriers of the disease, which struck Stephen without warning. Stephen became permanently disabled.

The case was different when Jana became pregnant again. Her daughter, Caroline, received prenatal testing before birth. Learning that she carried the mutation that led to Stephen's illness, doctors were able to give her medication the day she was born, and immediately put her on a special diet. Although Stephen will never be able to talk, walk, or feed himself, Caroline is an active, normal child. Genetic testing, says Jana, "gave Caroline the future that Stephen didn't get to have." (Kalb, 2006, p. 52; Spinelli, 2015)

A hidden genetic disorder robbed Jana and Tom Monaco's first child of a normal, healthy life. Their second child was spared the same fate by advances in genetic testing, which gave the Monacos a chance to intervene before the damage was done. They were able to stop Caroline's inherited disorder from doing the same damage by controlling aspects of her environment.

In this chapter, we start our voyage through the life span at its logical beginning: conception. We discuss genetics and the ways in which genetic information is transmitted from parents to child. We then introduce a topic that receives a great deal of attention from developmentalists: the comparative roles of heredity and environment (or nature versus nurture) in forming the individual.

Next, we proceed through the stages of the prenatal period, from fertilization to the fetal stage. We look at factors that can affect the health and development of the fetus before birth.

We finish the chapter with a discussion of the process of birth, including the ways women experience labor and the choices that parents have available for care before and during childbirth. We touch on some of the complications that can attend birth, including infants born significantly before or after their due date. We end with a discussion of the considerable abilities that newborns possess from the moment they enter the world.

Module 2.1 *Prenatal Development*

LO 2.1   Describe how genes and chromosomes provide our basic genetic endowment.

LO 2.2   Explain the mechanisms by which genes transmit information.

LO 2.3   Describe the role of genetic counselors and differentiate between different forms of prenatal testing.

LO 2.4   Explain how the environment and genetics work together to determine human characteristics.

LO 2.5   Explain how genetics and the environment jointly influence physical traits, intelligence, and personality.

LO 2.6   Describe ways in which genes influence the environment.

Module 2.2 *Prenatal Growth and Change*

LO 2.7   Explain the process of fertilization and the three stages of development.

LO 2.8   Describe some of the physical and ethical challenges that relate to pregnancy.

LO 2.9   Describe the threats to the fetal environment and what can be done about them.

Module 2.3 *Birth and the Newborn Infant*

LO 2.10   Describe the normal process of labor and the events that occur in the first few hours of a newborn's life.

LO 2.11   Describe the major current approaches to childbirth.

LO 2.12   Describe the causes of, consequences of, and treatments for preterm births and the risks that postmature babies face.

LO 2.13   Describe the process of cesarean delivery, and explain the reasons for its increase in use.

LO 2.14   Explain the factors that lead to stillbirth, infant mortality, and postpartum depression.

LO 2.15   Describe the physical capabilities of the newborn.

LO 2.16   Describe the sensory capabilities of the newborn.

LO 2.17   Describe the learning capabilities of the newborn.

LO 2.18   Describe the social competencies of newborns.

Module 2.1

Prenatal Development

Difficult Decisions

Leah and John Howard's joy at learning Leah was pregnant turned to anxiety when Leah's doctor discovered that her brother had died from Duchenne muscular dystrophy (DMD) at age 12. The disease, the doctor explained, was an X-linked inherited disorder. There was a chance Leah was a carrier. If so, there was a 50 percent chance that the baby would inherit the disease if it were a boy. The doctor advised them to have an ultrasound to determine the baby's sex. It turned out to be a boy.

The Howards faced new options. The doctor could take a chorion villus sampling now or wait a month and perform an amniocentesis. Both carried a very low risk for miscarriage. Leah chose amniocentesis, but the results were inconclusive. The doctor then suggested a fetal muscle biopsy to confirm the presence or lack of the muscle protein dystrophin. No dystrophin signaled DMD. The risk of miscarriage, however, was not inconsiderable.

Four months pregnant at this point and tired of the worries and tears, Leah and John decided to take their chances and look forward to their baby's birth.

The Howards' decision to forego a fetal muscle biopsy did not change the outcome. They did not wish to consider a late-term abortion, and DMD has no cure.

But their case illustrates the difficult decisions that parents sometimes face because of advances in the identification of inherited disorders and our understanding of genetics.

In this chapter, we'll examine what developmental researchers and other scientists have learned about the ways that heredity and the environment work in tandem to create and shape human beings, and how that knowledge is being used to improve people's lives. We begin with the basics of heredity, the genetic transmission of characteristics from biological parents to their children.

Earliest Development

We humans begin the course of our lives simply.

Like individuals from tens of thousands of other species, we start as a single tiny cell weighing no more than one 20-millionth of an ounce. But from this humble beginning, in a matter of a few months, a living, breathing individual infant is born. That first cell is created when a male reproductive cell, a *sperm*, pushes through the membrane of an *ovum*, a female reproductive cell. These *gametes*, as the male and female reproductive cells are also called, contain huge amounts of genetic information. About an hour or so after the sperm enters the ovum, the two gametes suddenly fuse, becoming one cell, a **zygote**. The resulting combination of their genetic instructions—more than 2 billion chemically coded messages—is sufficient to begin creating a whole person.

zygote

the new cell formed by the process of fertilization

Genes and Chromosomes: The Code of Life

LO 2.1 **Describe how genes and chromosomes provide our basic genetic endowment.**

genes

the basic unit of genetic information

The blueprints for creating a person are stored and communicated in our **genes**, the basic units of genetic information. The roughly 25,000 human genes are the biological equivalent of "software" that programs the future development of all parts of the body's "hardware."

DNA (deoxyribonucleic acid) molecules

the substance that genes are composed of that determines the nature of every cell in the body and how it will function

All genes are composed of specific sequences of **DNA (deoxyribonucleic acid) molecules**. The genes are arranged in specific locations and in a specific order along 46 **chromosomes**, rod-shaped portions of DNA that are organized in 23 pairs. Each of the sex cells—ovum and sperm—contains half this number, so that a child's mother and father each provide one of the two chromosomes in each of the 23 pairs. The 46 chromosomes (in 23 pairs) in the new zygote contain the genetic blueprint that will guide cell activity for the rest of the individual's life (see Figure 2-1). Through a process called *mitosis*, which accounts for the replication of most types of cells, nearly all the cells of the body will contain the same 46 chromosomes as the zygote.

chromosomes

rod-shaped portions of DNA that are organized in 23 pairs

Genes determine the nature and function of every cell in the body. For instance, they determine which cells will become part of the heart and which will become part of the muscles of the leg. Genes also establish how different parts of the body will function: how rapidly the heart will beat, or how much strength a muscle will have.

If each parent provides just 23 chromosomes, where does the vast diversity of human beings come from? The answer resides primarily in the processes that underlie the cell division of the gametes. When gametes—the sex cells, sperm and ova—are formed in the adult body in a process called *meiosis*, each gamete receives one of the two chromosomes that make up each of the 23 pairs. Because for each pair the chromosome that is chosen is largely a matter of chance, there are some 8 million different combinations possible. Furthermore, other processes, such as random transformations of particular genes, add to the variability of the genetic brew. The ultimate outcome: tens of *trillions* of possible genetic combinations.

With so many possible genetic mixtures, there is no likelihood that someday you'll bump into a genetic duplicate—with one exception: an identical twin.

MULTIPLE BIRTHS: TWO—OR MORE—FOR THE GENETIC PRICE OF ONE Although it is routine for dogs and cats to give birth to several offspring at one time, in humans multiple births are cause for comment. They should be: Less than 3 percent of all pregnancies produce twins, and the odds are even slimmer for triplets or higher-order multiples.

Why do multiple births occur? Some occur when a cluster of cells in the ovum splits off within the first 2 weeks after fertilization. The result is two genetically identical zygotes, which, because they come from the same original zygote, are called monozygotic. **Monozygotic twins** are twins who are genetically identical. Any differences in their future development can be attributed only to environmental factors.

However, multiple births are more commonly the result of two separate sperm fertilizing different ova, producing what are called dizygotic twins. **Dizygotic twins** are produced when two separate ova are fertilized by two separate sperm at roughly the same time. Because they are the result of two separate ovum–sperm combinations, they are no more genetically similar than two siblings born at different times.

Of course, not all multiple births produce only two babies. Triplets, quadruplets, and even higher-order multiples are produced by either (or both) of the mechanisms that yield twins. Thus, triplets may be some combination of monozygotic, dizygotic, or trizygotic.

Although the chances of having a multiple birth are typically slim, the odds rise considerably when fertility drugs are used before conception. Older women, too, are more likely to have multiple births, and multiple births are also more common in some families than in others. The increased use of fertility drugs and the rising average age of mothers giving birth led to a dramatic increase in multiple births in the 1980s and 1990s. However, that trend is declining, particularly in terms of multiple births (see Figure 2-2) (Parazzini et al., 2016; Adashi & Gutman, 2018; Martin et al., 2018).

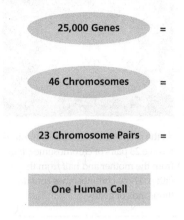

Figure 2-1 The Contents of a Single Human Cell

At the moment of conception, humans receive about 25,000 genes, contained in 46 chromosomes in 23 pairs.

monozygotic twins
twins who are genetically identical

dizygotic twins
twins who are produced when two separate ova are fertilized by two separate sperm at roughly the same time

Figure 2-2 Multiple Changes

The number and rate of multiple births rose considerably starting in the 1980s, but it leveled off and began to decline starting at the turn of the 21st century.

SOURCE: Martin, J. A., Hamilton, B. E., Osterman, M. J. K., Driscoll, A. K, & Drake, P. (2018). National Center for Health Statistics National Vital Statistics System Births: Final Data for 2016. 1. National Vital Statistics Reports, 67(1).

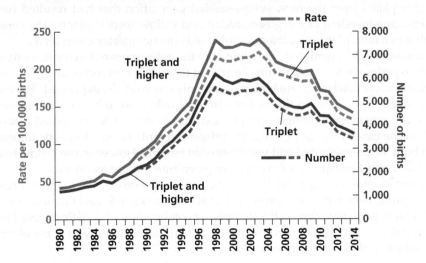

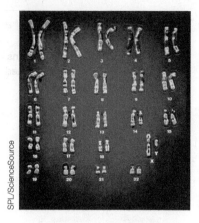

At the moment of conception, humans receive 23 pairs of chromosomes, half from the mother and half from the father. These chromosomes contain thousands of genes.

Figure 2-3 Determining Sex

When an ovum and sperm meet at the moment of fertilization, the ovum is certain to provide an X chromosome, whereas the sperm will provide either an X or a Y chromosome. If the sperm contributes its X chromosome, the child will have an XX pairing on the 23rd chromosome and will be a girl. If the sperm contributes a Y chromosome, the result will be an XY pairing—a boy. Does this mean that girls are more likely to be conceived than boys?

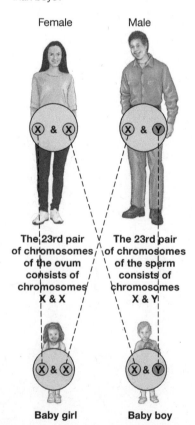

There are also racial, ethnic, and national differences in the rate of multiple births, probably as a result of inherited differences in the likelihood that more than one ovum will be released at a time. For example, 1 out of 70 African American couples have dizygotic twin births, compared with 1 out of 86 white American couples. Furthermore, in some areas of central Africa, the rate of dizygotic twin births is among the highest in the world (Choi, 2017).

BOY OR GIRL? ESTABLISHING THE SEX OF THE CHILD   In 22 of the 23 matched chromosome pairs, each chromosome is similar to the other member of its pair. The one exception is the 23rd pair—the one that determines the sex of the child. In females, the 23rd pair consists of two matching, relatively large X-shaped chromosomes, identified as XX. In males, by contrast, one member of the pair is an X-shaped chromosome, but the other is a shorter, smaller Y-shaped chromosome. This pair is identified as XY.

Because a female's 23rd pair of chromosomes are both X's, an ovum will always carry an X chromosome. A male's 23rd pair is XY, so each sperm could carry either an X or a Y chromosome. If the sperm contributes an X chromosome when it meets an ovum, the child will have an XX pairing on the 23rd chromosome—and will be a female. If the sperm contributes a Y chromosome, the result will be an XY pairing—a male (see Figure 2-3).

Because the father's sperm determines the gender of the child, new techniques are being developed to help specify in advance the gender of the child. In one new technique, lasers measure the DNA in sperm. Discarding sperm that harbor the unwanted sex chromosome dramatically increases the chances of having a child of the desired sex (Hayden, 1998; Belkin, 1999; Van Balen, 2005; Rai et al., 2018).

Sex selection raises ethical and practical issues. For example, in cultures that value one gender over the other, might there be a kind of gender discrimination before birth? And could there ultimately be a shortage of children of the less-preferred sex? Many questions of this type will have to be addressed before sex selection can ever become routine (Sleeboom-Faulkner, 2010; Bhagat, Laskar, & Sharma, 2012).

The Basics of Genetics: The Mixing and Matching of Traits

LO 2.2   Explain the mechanisms by which genes transmit information.

What determined the color of your hair? Why are you tall or short? What made you susceptible to hay fever? And why do you have so many freckles? To answer these questions, we need to consider the basic mechanisms through which the genes we inherit from our parents transmit information.

We can start by examining the discoveries of an Austrian monk, Gregor Mendel, in the mid-1800s. In a series of simple yet convincing experiments, Mendel cross-pollinated pea plants that always produced yellow seeds with pea plants that always produced green seeds. The result was not, as one might guess, a plant with a combination of yellow and green seeds. Instead, all of the resulting plants had yellow seeds. At first it appeared that the green-seeded plants had had no influence.

However, additional research on Mendel's part proved this was not true. He bred together plants from the new, yellow-seeded generation that had resulted from his original crossbreeding of the green-seeded and yellow-seeded plants. The consistent result was a ratio of three-quarters yellow seeds to one-quarter green seeds.

It was Mendel's genius to figure out why this ratio appeared so consistently. Based on his experiments with pea plants, he argued that when two competing traits, such as green or yellow coloring, were both present, only one could be expressed. The one that was expressed was called a **dominant trait**. Meanwhile, the other trait remained present in the organism, although unexpressed (displayed). This was called a **recessive trait**. In the case of the pea plants, the offspring plants received genetic information from both the green-seeded and yellow-seeded parents. However, the yellow trait was dominant, and consequently the recessive green trait did not assert itself.

Keep in mind, though, that genetic material from both parent plants is present in the offspring, even if it is unexpressed. The genetic information is known as the organism's genotype. A **genotype** is the underlying combination of genetic material present (but outwardly invisible) in an organism. In contrast, a **phenotype** is the observable trait—the trait that is actually seen.

Although the offspring of the yellow-seeded and green-seeded pea plants all have yellow seeds (i.e., they have a yellow-seeded phenotype), the genotype consists of genetic information relating to both parents.

And what is the nature of the information in the genotype? To answer that question, let's turn from peas to people. In fact, the principles are the same not just for plants and humans, but for the majority of species.

Recall that parents transmit genetic information to their offspring via the chromosomes they contribute through the gamete they provide during fertilization. Some of the genes form pairs called *alleles*, genes governing traits that may take alternate forms, such as hair or eye color. For example, brown eye color is a dominant trait (B); blue eyes are recessive (b). A child's allele may contain similar or dissimilar genes from each parent. If the child receives similar genes, he or she is said to be **homozygous** for the trait. In contrast, if the child receives different forms of the gene from its parents, he or she is said to be **heterozygous** for the trait. In the case of heterozygous alleles (Bb), the dominant characteristic (brown eyes) is expressed. However, if the child happens to receive a recessive allele from each of its parents, and therefore lacks a dominant characteristic (bb), he or she will display the recessive characteristic (in this case, blue eyes).

TRANSMISSION OF GENETIC INFORMATION One example of this process at work is the transmission of *phenylketonuria (PKU)*, an inherited disorder in which a child is unable to make use of phenylalanine, an essential amino acid present in proteins found in milk and other foods. If untreated, PKU allows phenylalanine to build to toxic levels, causing brain damage and intellectual disabilities (McCabe & Shaw, 2010; Waisbren & Antshel, 2013).

PKU is produced by a single allele, or pair of genes. As shown in Figure 2-4, we can label each gene of the pair with a *P* if it carries a dominant gene, which causes the normal production of phenylalanine, or a *p* if it carries the recessive gene that produces PKU. In cases in which neither parent is a PKU carrier, both the mother's and the father's pairs of genes are the dominant form, symbolized as *PP*, in which case the child's genes will be *PP*, and the child will not have PKU.

Consider what happens if one parent has the recessive p gene. In this case, symbolized as *Pp*, the parent will not have PKU, because the normal *P* gene is dominant. But the recessive gene can be passed down to the child. This is not so bad: If the child has only one recessive gene, it will not suffer from PKU. But what if both parents carry a recessive *p* gene? In this case, although neither parent has the disorder, it is possible for the child to receive a recessive gene from both parents. The child will have the *pp* genotype for PKU and will have the disorder.

Remember, though, that even children whose parents both have the recessive gene for PKU have only a 25 percent chance of inheriting the disorder. As a result of the laws of probability, 25 percent of children with *Pp* parents will receive the dominant gene from each parent (these children's genotype would be *PP*), and 50 percent will receive the dominant gene from one parent and the recessive gene from the other (their genotypes would be either *Pp* or *pP*). Only the unlucky 25 percent who receive the recessive gene from each parent and end up with the genotype *pp* will suffer from PKU.

POLYGENIC TRAITS PKU illustrates the basic principles of genetic transmission, although PKU transmission is simpler than most cases. Relatively few traits are governed by a single pair of genes. Instead, most traits are the result of polygenic inheritance. In **polygenic inheritance**, a combination of multiple gene pairs is responsible for the production of a particular trait.

Furthermore, some genes come in several alternate forms, and still others act to modify the way that particular genetic traits (produced by other alleles) are displayed. Genes also vary in terms of their *reaction range*, the potential degree of variability in the expression of a trait as a result of environmental conditions. And some traits, such as blood type, are produced by genes in which neither member of a pair of genes can be classified as purely dominant or recessive. Instead, the trait is expressed in terms of a combination of the two genes—such as type AB blood.

---

dominant trait
the one trait that is expressed when two competing traits are present

recessive trait
a trait within an organism that is present but is not expressed

genotype
the underlying combination of genetic material present (but not outwardly visible) in an organism

phenotype
an observable trait; the trait that is actually seen

homozygous
inheriting similar genes for a given trait from both parents

heterozygous
inheriting different forms of a gene for a given trait from each parent

polygenic inheritance
inheritance in which a combination of multiple gene pairs is responsible for the production of a particular trait

Figure 2-4 PKU Probabilities

Phenylketonuria (PKU), a disease that causes brain damage and intellectual disabilities, is produced by a single pair of genes inherited from one's mother and father. If neither parent carries a gene for the disease (a), a child cannot develop PKU. Even if one parent carries the recessive gene, but the other doesn't (b), the child cannot inherit the disease. However, if both parents carry the recessive gene (c), there is a one in four chance that the child will have PKU.

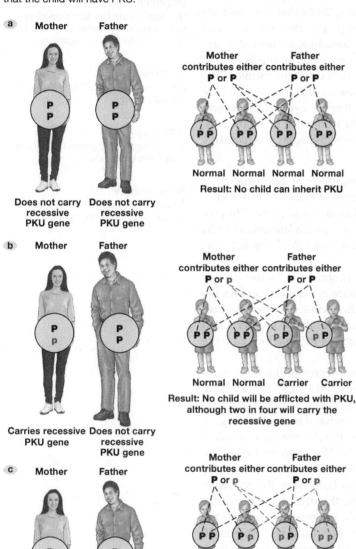

behavioral genetics
the study of the effects of heredity on behavior

X-linked genes
genes that are considered recessive and located only on the X chromosome

A number of recessive genes, called **X-linked genes**, are located only on the X chromosome. Recall that in females, the 23rd pair of chromosomes is an XX pair, whereas in males it is an XY pair. One result is that males have a higher risk for a variety of X-linked disorders—as the Howards' unborn son did in the story at the beginning of this module—because males lack a second X chromosome that can counteract the genetic information that produces the disorder. For example, males are significantly more apt to have red-green color blindness, a disorder produced by a set of genes on the X chromosome. Similarly, *hemophilia*, a blood disorder that is a recurrent problem in the royal families of Europe, is produced by X-linked genes.

THE HUMAN GENOME AND BEHAVIORAL GENETICS: CRACKING THE GENETIC CODE Mendel's trailblazing achievements mark only the beginning of our understanding of genetics. The most recent milestone was reached in early 2001, when molecular geneticists succeeded in mapping the sequence of genes on each chromosome. This is one of the most important accomplishments in the history of genetics (International Human Genome Sequencing Consortium, 2001; Oksenberg & Hauser, 2010; Maxson, 2013).

Already, the mapping of the gene sequence has significantly advanced our understanding of genetics. For instance, the number of human genes, long thought to be 100,000, has been revised downward to 25,000—not many more than organisms that are far less complex (see Figure 2-5). Furthermore, scientists have discovered that 99.9 percent of the gene sequence is shared by all humans—meaning that many of the differences that seemingly separate people—such as race—are, literally, only skin deep. Genome mapping will also help in the identification of disorders to which a given individual is susceptible (Serretti & Fabbri, 2013; Goldman & Domschke, 2014; Diez-Fairen et al., 2018).

The mapping of the human gene sequence is supporting the field of behavioral genetics. As the name implies, **behavioral genetics** studies the effects of heredity on behavior and psychological characteristics. Rather than simply examining stable, unchanging characteristics such as hair or eye color, behavioral genetics takes a broader approach, considering how our personality and behavioral habits are affected by genetic factors (McGue, 2010; Judge, Ilies, & Zhang, 2012; Krüger, Korsten, & Hoffman, 2017).

Personality traits such as shyness or sociability, moodiness, and assertiveness are among the areas being studied. Other behavioral geneticists study psychological disorders, such as depression, attention deficit hyperactivity disorder, and schizophrenia, looking for possible genetic links (Wang et al., 2012; Plomin et al., 2016; Holl et al., 2018; see Table 2-1).

INHERITED AND GENETIC DISORDERS: WHEN DEVELOPMENT DEVIATES FROM THE NORM As we saw with PKU, a recessive gene responsible for a disorder may be passed on unknowingly from one generation to the next, revealing itself only

Table 2-1 Current Understanding of the Genetic Basis of Selected Behavioral Disorders and Traits

Behavioral Trait	Current Beliefs About Genetic Basis
Huntington's disease	Mutations in HTT gene
Obsessive-compulsive disorder (OCD)	Several potentially relevant genes have been identified, but environment plays an important role
Fragile X intellectual disability	Mutations in the FMR gene
Early onset (familial) Alzheimer's disease	Three distinct genes have been identified; at least 11 mutations in the PSEN2 gene are related
Attention deficit hyperactivity disorder (ADHD)	Evidence in some studies has linked ADHD with dopamine-receptor D4 and D5 genes, but the complexity of the disease makes it difficult to identify a specific gene
Alcoholism	Research suggests that genes affecting the activity of the neurotransmitters serotonin and GABA likely are involved in risk for alcoholism
Schizophrenia spectrum disorder	There is no agreement, but deletions or duplications are related to the disorder; links to chromosomes 1, 5, 6, 10, 13, 15, and 22 have also been reported

SOURCE: Based on McGuffin, Riley, & Plomin, 2001; Genetics Home Reference, 2017.

Figure 2-5 Uniquely Human?

Humans have about 25,000 genes, making them not much more genetically complex than some primitive species.

SOURCE: Based on Macmillan Publishers Ltd.: "International Human Genome Sequencing Consortium, Initial Sequencing and Analysis of the Human Genome," Nature.

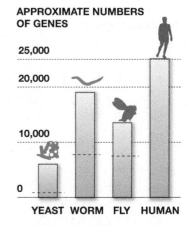

APPROXIMATE NUMBERS OF GENES

Estimated percentage of each creature's total genes found in humans are indicated by the dotted line.

when, by chance, it is paired with another recessive gene. When this happens, the gene will express itself and the unsuspected genetic disorder will be inherited.

Another way that genes are a source of concern is that they may become physically damaged. Genes may break down because of wear and tear or chance events occurring during the cell division processes of meiosis and mitosis. Sometimes genes, for no known reason, spontaneously change their form, a process called *spontaneous mutation*. Also, certain environmental factors, such as X-rays or even highly polluted air, may produce a malformation of genetic material. When damaged genes are passed on to a child, the results can be disastrous for physical and cognitive development (Barnes & Jacobs, 2013; Tucker-Drob & Briley, 2014).

In addition to PKU, which occurs once in 10,000 to 20,000 births, other inherited and genetic disorders include the following:

- **Down syndrome.** Instead of 46 chromosomes in 23 pairs, individuals with **Down syndrome** have an extra chromosome on the 21st pair. Once referred to as *mongolism*, Down syndrome is the most frequent cause of intellectual disabilities. It occurs in about 1 out of 500 births, although the risk is much greater in mothers who are unusually young or old (Channell et al., 2014; Glasson et al., 2016).

- **Fragile X syndrome.** **Fragile X syndrome** occurs when a particular gene is injured on the X chromosome. The result is mild to moderate intellectual disabilities (Cornish, Turk, & Hagerman, 2008; Hocking, Kogan, & Cornish, 2012; Shelton et al., 2017; Melancia & Trezza, 2018).

- **Sickle-cell anemia.** Around one-tenth of people of African descent carry genes that produce sickle-cell anemia, and 1 individual in 400 actually has the disease. **Sickle-cell anemia** is a blood disorder named for the shape of the red blood cells. Symptoms include poor appetite, stunted growth, swollen stomach, and yellowish eyes. People afflicted with the most severe form rarely live beyond childhood. However, for those with less severe cases, medical advances have produced significant increases in life expectancy (Ballas, 2010).

- **Tay-Sachs disease.** Occurring mainly in Jews of eastern European ancestry and in French-Canadians, **Tay-Sachs disease** usually causes death before its victims reach school age. There is no treatment for the disorder, which produces blindness and muscle degeneration before death.

- **Klinefelter's syndrome.** One male out of every 400 is born with **Klinefelter's syndrome**, the presence of an extra X chromosome. The resulting XXY complement produces underdeveloped genitals, extreme height, and enlarged breasts. Klinefelter's syndrome is one of a number of genetic abnormalities that result from receiving the improper number of sex chromosomes. For instance, there are

Down syndrome

a disorder produced by the presence of an extra chromosome on the 21st pair; once referred to as *mongolism*

fragile X syndrome

a disorder produced by injury to a gene on the X chromosome, producing mild to moderate intellectual disability

sickle-cell anemia

a blood disorder that gets its name from the shape of the red blood cells

Tay-Sachs disease

a disorder that produces blindness and muscle degeneration before death; there is no treatment

Klinefelter's syndrome

a disorder resulting from the presence of an extra X chromosome that produces underdeveloped genitals, extreme height, and enlarged breasts

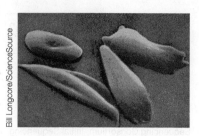

Sickle-cell anemia, named for the presence of misshapen red blood cells, is carried in the genes of 1 in 10 African Americans.

disorders produced by an extra Y chromosome (XYY), a missing second chromosome (X0, called *Turner's syndrome*), and three X chromosomes (XXX). Such disorders are typically characterized by problems relating to sexual characteristics and by intellectual deficits (Hong et al., 2014; Turriff et al., 2016).

It is important to keep in mind that the mere fact that a disorder has genetic roots does not mean that environmental factors do not also play a role. Consider sickle-cell anemia: Because the disease can be fatal in childhood, we'd expect that those who suffer from it would be unlikely to live long enough to pass it on. And this does seem to be true in the United States: Compared with parts of West Africa, the incidence in the United States is much lower.

But why the difference between the United States and West Africa? Ultimately, scientists determined that carrying the sickle-cell gene raises immunity to malaria, a common disease in West Africa. This heightened immunity meant that people with the sickle-cell gene had a genetic advantage (in terms of resistance to malaria) that offset, to some degree, the disadvantage of being a carrier of the gene.

Genetic Counseling: Predicting the Future from the Genes of the Present

LO 2.3   Describe the role of genetic counselors and differentiate between different forms of prenatal testing.

If you knew that your mother and grandmother had died of Huntington's disease—a devastating, always fatal inherited disorder marked by tremors and intellectual deterioration—how could you learn your own chances of getting the disease? The best way is a field that, just a few decades ago, was nonexistent: genetic counseling. **Genetic counseling** focuses on helping people deal with issues relating to inherited disorders.

genetic counseling
the discipline that focuses on helping people deal with issues relating to inherited disorders

Genetic counselors use a variety of data in their work. For instance, couples thinking about having a child may want to know the risks involved in a pregnancy. The counselor will take a thorough family history, looking for a familial incidence of birth defects that might indicate a pattern of recessive or X-linked genes. In addition, the counselor will take into account factors such as the age of the mother and father and any previous abnormalities in other children they may have already had (O'Doherty, 2014; Austin, 2016; Madlensky et al., 2017).

Typically, genetic counselors suggest a thorough physical examination to identify physical abnormalities that the potential parents may be unaware of. In addition, samples of blood, skin, and urine may be used to isolate and examine specific chromosomes. Possible genetic defects, such as the presence of an extra sex chromosome, can be identified by assembling a *karyotype*, a chart containing enlarged photos of each of the chromosomes.

PRENATAL TESTING   If the woman is already pregnant, there are a variety of techniques to assess the health of her unborn child (see Table 2-2 for a list of currently available tests). The earliest is a *first-trimester screen*, which combines a blood test and ultrasound sonography in the 11th to 13th week of pregnancy and can identify chromosomal abnormalities and other disorders, such as heart problems. In **ultrasound sonography**, high-frequency sound waves bombard the mother's womb, producing an image of the unborn baby, whose size and shape can then be assessed. Repeated use of ultrasound sonography can reveal developmental patterns.

ultrasound sonography
a process in which high-frequency sound waves scan the mother's womb to produce an image of the unborn baby, whose size and shape can then be assessed

A more invasive test, **chorionic villus sampling (CVS)**, can be employed in the 10th to 13th week of the first trimester, if blood tests and ultrasound have identified a potential problem or if there is a family history of inherited disorders. CVS involves inserting a thin needle into the placenta and taking small samples of hairlike material that surrounds the embryo. The test can be done between the 8th and 11th week of pregnancy. However, it produces a risk of miscarriage of 1 in 100 to 1 in 200. Because of the risk, its use is relatively infrequent.

chorionic villus sampling (CVS)
a test used to find genetic defects that involves taking samples of hairlike material that surrounds the embryo

In **amniocentesis**, a small sample of fetal cells is drawn by a tiny needle inserted into the amniotic fluid surrounding the unborn fetus. Carried out 15 to 20 weeks into the pregnancy, amniocentesis allows the analysis of the fetal cells that can identify a variety

amniocentesis
the process of identifying genetic defects by examining a small sample of fetal cells drawn by a needle inserted into the amniotic fluid surrounding the unborn fetus

Table 2-2 Fetal Development Monitoring Techniques

Technique	Description
Amniocentesis	Done between the 15th and 20th weeks of pregnancy, this procedure examines a sample of the amniotic fluid, which contains fetal cells. Recommended if either parent carries Tay-Sachs, spina bifida, sickle-cell, Down syndrome, muscular dystrophy, or Rh disease.
Chorionic villus sampling (CVS)	Done at 8 to 11 weeks, either transabdominally or transcervically, depending on where the placenta is located. Involves inserting a needle (abdominally) or a catheter (cervically) into the substance of the placenta but staying outside the amniotic sac and removing 10 to 15 milligrams of tissue. This tissue is manually cleaned of maternal uterine tissue and then grown in culture, and a karyotype is made, as with amniocentesis.
Embryoscopy	Examines the embryo or fetus during the first 12 weeks of pregnancy by means of a fiber-optic endoscope inserted through the cervix. Can be performed as early as week 5. Access to the fetal circulation may be obtained through the instrument, and direct visualization of the embryo permits the diagnosis of malformations.
Fetal blood sampling (FBS)	Performed after 18 weeks of pregnancy by collecting a small amount of blood from the umbilical cord for testing. Used to detect Down syndrome and most other chromosome abnormalities in the fetuses of couples who are at increased risk of having an affected child. Many other diseases can be diagnosed using this technique.
Sonoembryology	Used to detect abnormalities in the first trimester of pregnancy. Involves high-frequency transvaginal probes and digital-image processing. In combination with ultrasound, can detect more than 80 percent of all malformations during the second trimester.
Ultrasound (sonogram)	Uses very-high-frequency sound waves to detect structural abnormalities or multiple pregnancies, measure fetal growth, judge gestational age, and evaluate uterine abnormalities. Also used as an adjunct to other procedures such as amniocentesis.

of genetic defects with nearly 100 percent accuracy. In addition, the sex of the child can be determined. Although there is always a danger to the fetus in an invasive procedure such as amniocentesis, it is generally safe, with the risk of miscarriage 1 in 200 to 1 in 400.

After the various tests are complete, the couple will meet with the genetic counselor again. Typically, counselors avoid giving recommendations. Instead, they lay out the facts and present options for the parents, which typically range from doing nothing to taking more drastic steps, such as an abortion.

SCREENING FOR FUTURE PROBLEMS The newest role of genetic counselors involves testing people to identify whether they themselves, rather than their children, are susceptible to future disorders because of genetic abnormalities. For instance, Huntington's disease typically does not manifest until people reach their 40s. However, genetic testing can identify much earlier the flawed gene that produces Huntington's. Presumably, knowing that they carry the gene can help people prepare for the future (Tibben, 2007; Sánchez-Castañeda et al., 2015; Holman et al., 2018).

In addition to Huntington's disease, more than a thousand disorders, ranging from cystic fibrosis to ovarian cancer, can be predicted on the basis of genetic testing. Negative results can bring welcome relief, but positive results may produce just the opposite effect. In fact, genetic testing raises difficult practical and ethical questions (Wilfond & Ross, 2009; Klitzman, 2012; Zhao et al., 2018).

Suppose, for instance, a woman is tested in her 20s for Huntington's and finds that she does not carry the defective gene. Obviously, she would be relieved. But suppose she finds that she does carry the flawed gene and will therefore get the disease. In this case, she might well experience depression and remorse. In fact, some studies show that 10 percent of people who find they have the flawed gene that leads to

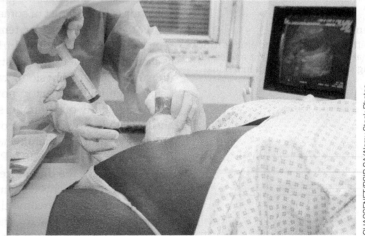

In amniocentesis, a sample of fetal cells is withdrawn from the amniotic sac and used to identify a number of genetic defects.

Huntington's disease never recover fully on an emotional level (Myers, 2004; Wahlin, 2007; Richmond-Rakerd, 2013).

Genetic testing is a complicated issue. It rarely provides a simple yes/no answer, typically presenting a range of probabilities instead. In some cases, the likelihood of becoming ill depends on the stressors in a person's environment. Personal differences also affect susceptibility to a disorder (Lucassen, 2012; Crozier, Robertson, & Dale, 2015; Djurdjinovic & Peters, 2017).

Today, many researchers and medical practitioners have moved beyond testing and counseling to actually modifying flawed genes. For example, in *germ line therapy*, cells with defective genes are taken from an embryo, repaired, and replaced.

> **From the perspective of a health-care provider:** What are some ethical and philosophical questions that surround the issue of genetic counseling? Might it sometimes be unwise to know ahead of time about possible disorders that might affect your child or yourself?

The Interaction of Heredity and Environment

> Like many other parents, Jared's mother, Leesha, and his father, Jamal, tried to figure out which of them their new baby resembled more. He seemed to have Leesha's big, wide eyes, and Jamal's generous smile. As Jared grew, they noticed that his hairline was just like Leesha's, and his teeth made his smile resemble Jamal's. He also seemed to act like his parents. For example, he was a charming little baby, always ready to smile at people who visited the house—just like his friendly, jovial dad. He seemed to sleep like his mom, which was lucky because Jamal was an extremely light sleeper who could do with as little as 4 hours a night, whereas Leesha liked a regular 7 or 8 hours.

Were Jared's ready smile and regular sleeping habits something he just luckily inherited from his parents? Or did Jamal and Leesha provide a happy and stable home that encouraged these welcome traits? What causes our behavior? Nature or nurture? Is behavior produced by genetic influences or factors in the environment?

The simple answer is: There is no simple answer.

The Role of the Environment in Determining the Expression of Genes: From Genotypes to Phenotypes

LO 2.4 **Explain how the environment and genetics work together to determine human characteristics.**

As developmental research accumulates, it is becoming increasingly clear that to view behavior as a result of *either* genetic *or* environmental factors is inappropriate because behavior is the product of some combination of the two.

For instance, consider **temperament**, patterns of arousal and emotionality that represent consistent and enduring characteristics in an individual. Suppose we found, as increasing evidence suggests, that a small percentage of children are born with an unusual degree of physiological reactivity—a tendency to shrink from anything unusual. Such infants react to novel stimuli with a rapid increase in heartbeat and unusual excitability of the limbic system of the brain. By age 4 or 5, children with heightened reactivity to stimuli are often considered shy by their parents and teachers. But not always: Some of them behave indistinguishably from their peers at the same age (De Pauw & Mervielde, 2011; Pickles et al., 2013; Smiley et al., 2016).

What makes the difference? The answer seems to be the children's environment. Children whose parents encourage them to be outgoing by arranging new opportunities for them may overcome their shyness. In contrast, children raised in a stressful environment marked by marital discord or a prolonged illness may be more likely to retain their shyness later in life (Kagan, 2010; Casalin et al., 2012; Merwin et al., 2017). Jared, described previously, may have been born with an easy temperament, which was easily reinforced by his caring parents.

temperament

patterns of arousal and emotionality that represent consistent and enduring characteristics in an individual

INTERACTION OF FACTORS   Such findings illustrate that many traits reflect **multifactorial transmission**, meaning that they are determined by a combination of both genetic and environmental factors. In multifactorial transmission, a genotype provides a range within which a phenotype may be expressed. For instance, people with a genotype that permits them to gain weight easily may vary in their actual body weight. They may be *relatively* slim, given their genetic heritage, but never able to get beyond a certain degree of thinness. In many cases, then, the environment determines how a particular genotype will be expressed as a phenotype (Plomin et al., 2016).

By contrast, certain genotypes are relatively unaffected by environmental factors. For instance, pregnant women who were severely malnourished during famines caused by World War II had children who were, on average, unaffected physically or intellectually as adults (Stein et al., 1975). Similarly, people will never grow beyond certain genetically imposed limitations in height, no matter how well or how much they eat. And the environment had little to do with Jared's hairline.

Although we can't attribute specific behaviors exclusively to nature or nurture, we can ask how much of a behavior is caused by genetic factors and how much by environmental factors. We'll turn to this question next.

multifactorial transmission
the determination of traits by a combination of both genetic and environmental factors in which a genotype provides a range within which a phenotype may be expressed

STUDYING DEVELOPMENT: HOW MUCH IS NATURE? HOW MUCH IS NURTURE?
Developmental researchers use several strategies to study the relative influence of genetic and environmental factors on traits, characteristics, and behavior. Their studies involve both nonhuman species and humans.

Nonhuman Animal Studies: Controlling Both Genetics and Environment   It is relatively simple to develop breeds of animals with genetically similar traits. The Butterball people do it all the time, producing Thanksgiving turkeys that grow especially rapidly so that they can be brought to market inexpensively. Similarly, strains of laboratory animals can be bred to share similar genetic backgrounds.

By observing genetically similar animals in different environments, scientists can determine, with reasonable precision, the effects of specific kinds of environmental stimulation. For example, to examine the effects of different environmental settings, researchers can raise some of the genetically similar animals in unusually stimulating environments, with lots of items to climb over or through, and others in relatively barren environments. Conversely, by exposing groups of genetically *dissimilar* animals to *identical* environments, researchers can examine in a different way the role that genetic background plays.

Animal research offers substantial opportunities, but the drawback is that we can't be sure how well our findings can be generalized to people. (Also see *From Research to Practice*.)

From Research to Practice

When Nurture Becomes Nature

A fundamental assumption about genetic inheritance has long been that environmental alterations of an organism's health cannot be passed down to future generations; if we cut off a mouse's tail, we do not expect its offspring to be tailless. Only genetic mutations—not lifestyle choices such as poor diet, nor environmental insults such as exposure to toxins—were thought to be heritable. But recent research finds that an individual's life experiences can be passed down to children, grandchildren, and subsequent generations.

It's a phenomenon called *transgenerational epigenetic inheritance*, and it works a bit differently from usual inheritance. Instead of changing the genetic code itself, life experiences change the parts of DNA that switch individual genes on or off.

Not every gene is active everywhere in the body; the DNA that is responsible for making insulin, for example, is only "switched on" in certain cells of the pancreas. When an event such as malnourishment or drug use affects the DNA "switches" in sperm or eggs, the alterations can be passed on to future generations (Daxinger & Whitelaw, 2012; Babenko, Kovaklchuk, & Metz, 2015; Nestler, 2016; Goldberg & Gould, 2018).

In one study, healthy male rats were fed a high-fat diet that caused them to put on weight and develop symptoms consistent with type 2 diabetes, such as insulin resistance. Although these rats did not have a preexisting genetic tendency to be diabetic, their daughters also developed symptoms of type 2 diabetes as adults—even though they ate normal diets.

Some researchers think that transgenerational epigenetic inheritance could partly explain the epidemic of childhood obesity: Our high-fat diets may not only put us at risk, but perhaps our children as well (Skinner, 2010; Crews et al., 2012).

Happily, it's not just harmful effects that can be passed on this way. One study showed that mice developed better memory after being exposed to an enriched and stimulating environment, as previous research showed would be the case, and that the mice's offspring also showed the beneficial memory effect even though they didn't experience the same enriched environment.

The implications of this research are astounding—it may well be the case that the poor life choices we make in our youth have consequences for our progeny as well as ourselves (Arai, Li, Hartley, & Feig, 2009; Nestler, 2011; Heard & Martienssen, 2014).

Shared Writing Prompt:

Why would the poor life choices we make in our youth, rather than those we might make later in life, have possible consequences for our children?

Contrasting Relatedness and Behavior: Adoption, Twin, and Family Studies   Clearly, researchers can't control either the genetic backgrounds or the environments of humans as they can with nonhumans. However, nature conveniently has provided ideal subjects for carrying out various kinds of "natural experiments"—twins.

Recall that monozygotic twins are *genetically* identical. Because their inherited backgrounds are precisely the same, any variations in their behavior must be entirely a result of environmental factors.

Theoretically, identical twins would make great subjects for experiments about the roles of nature and nurture. For instance, by separating identical twins at birth and placing them in totally different environments, researchers could assess the impact of environment unambiguously. Of course, ethical considerations make this impossible.

What researchers can—and do—study, however, are cases in which identical twins have been put up for adoption at birth and are raised in substantially different environments. Such instances allow us to draw fairly confident conclusions about the relative contributions of genetics and environment (Nikolas, Klump, & Burt, 2012; Strachan et al., 2017).

The data from such studies of identical twins raised in different environments are not always without bias. Adoption agencies typically take the characteristics (and wishes) of birth mothers into account when they place babies in adoptive homes. For instance, children tend to be placed with families of the same race and religion. Consequently, even when monozygotic twins are placed in different adoptive homes, there are often similarities between the two home environments. As a result, researchers can't always be certain that differences in behavior are the result of differences in the environment.

Monozygotic and dizygotic twins present opportunities to learn about the relative contributions of heredity and situational factors. What can psychologists learn from studying twins?

Studies of dizygotic twins also present opportunities to learn about nature and nurture. Recall that dizygotic twins are genetically no more similar than siblings in a family born at different times. By comparing the behavior of dizygotic twins with that of monozygotic twins (who are genetically identical) researchers can determine whether monozygotic twins tend to be more similar on a particular trait than dizygotic twins. If so, they can assume that genetics plays an important role in determining the expression of that trait.

Still another approach is to study people who are totally unrelated and therefore have dissimilar genetic backgrounds, but who share an environmental background. For instance, a family that adopts, at the same time, two young unrelated children probably will provide them with similar environments. In this case, similarities in the children's characteristics and behavior can be attributed with some confidence to environmental influences (Segal, 2000).

Finally, developmental researchers have examined groups of people in light of their degree of genetic similarity. For instance, on the one hand, if we find a high association on a particular trait between biological parents and their children but a weaker association between adoptive parents and their children, we have evidence for the importance of genetics in determining the expression of that trait. On the other hand, if there is a stronger association on a trait between adoptive parents and their children than between biological parents and their children, we have evidence for the importance of the environment in determining that trait. If a particular trait tends to occur at similar levels among genetically similar individuals, but at different levels among genetically distant individuals, genetics probably plays a major role in the development of that trait.

Developmental researchers using all these approaches, and more, for decades have come to a general conclusion: Virtually all traits, characteristics, and behaviors result from the combination and interaction of nature and nurture (Waterland & Jirtle, 2004; Jaworski & Accardo, 2010; Mathiesen, Sanson, & Karevold, 2018).

Genetics and the Environment: Working Together

LO 2.5 **Explain how genetics and the environment jointly influence physical traits, intelligence, and personality.**

Let's look at ways in which genetics and the environment influence our physical traits, intelligence, and personality.

PHYSICAL TRAITS: FAMILY RESEMBLANCES When patients entered the examining room of Dr. Cyril Marcus, they didn't realize that sometimes they were actually being treated by his identical twin brother, Dr. Stewart Marcus. So similar in appearance and manner were the twins that even long-time patients were fooled by this admittedly unethical behavior, which occurred in a bizarre case made famous in the film *Dead Ringers*.

Monozygotic twins are merely the most extreme example of the fact that the more genetically similar two people are, the more likely they are to share physical characteristics. Tall parents tend to have tall children, and short parents tend to have short children. Obesity also has a strong genetic component. For example, in one study, pairs of identical twins were put on diets that contained an extra 1,000 calories a day— and ordered not to exercise. Over a 3-month period, the twins gained almost identical amounts of weight. Moreover, different pairs of twins varied substantially in how much weight they gained, with some pairs gaining almost three times as much weight as other pairs (Bouchard et al., 1990).

Other, less obvious physical characteristics also show strong genetic influences. For instance, blood pressure, respiration rates, and even the age at which life ends are more similar in closely related individuals than in those who are less genetically alike (Melzer, Hurst, & Frayling, 2007; Wu, Treiber, & Snieder, 2013).

INTELLIGENCE: MORE RESEARCH, MORE CONTROVERSY No other nature– nurture issue has generated more research than intelligence. The reason is that intelligence, generally measured as an IQ score, is a central characteristic that differentiates humans from other species. In addition, intelligence is strongly related to scholastic success and, somewhat less strongly, to other types of achievement.

Genetics plays a significant role in intelligence. In studies of both overall or general intelligence and of specific subcomponents of intelligence (such as spatial skills, verbal skills, and memory), as can be seen in Figure 2-6, the closer the genetic link between two individuals, the greater the correspondence of their overall IQ scores.

Not only is genetics an important influence on intelligence, but the impact also increases with age. For instance, as fraternal (i.e., dizygotic) twins move from infancy to adolescence, their IQ scores become less similar. Not so with identical (monozygotic) twins, who become increasingly similar as they age (Silventoinen et al., 2012; Madison et al., 2016).

Figure 2-6 Genetics and IQ

The closer the genetic link between two individuals, the greater the correspondence between their IQ scores. **THINKING ABOUT THE DATA:** Why is there a difference in the median correlation of IQs between children reared together and siblings reared together? Alternatively, why is there a difference in the median correlation of IQs between children reared together and siblings reared apart? How would you characterize the influence of genetics and environment on IQ?

SOURCE: Based on Bouchard & McGue, 1981.

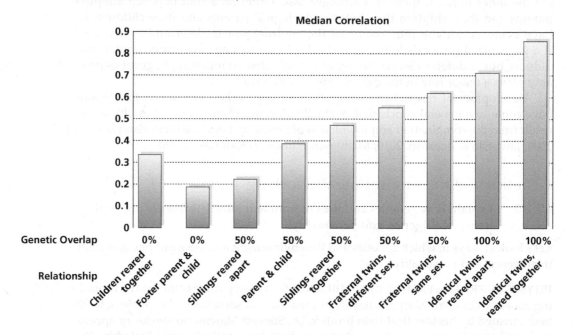

Although it is clear that heredity plays an important role in intelligence, investigators are much more divided on the question of the degree to which it is inherited. Perhaps the most extreme view is held by psychologist Arthur Jensen (2003), who argued that as much as 80 percent of intelligence is a result of heredity. Others have suggested more modest figures, ranging from 50 to 70 percent. It is critical to recall that such figures are averages across large groups of people, and any particular individual degree of inheritance cannot be predicted from these averages (Brouwer et al., 2014; Schmiedek, 2017).

It is important to keep in mind that, whatever role heredity plays, environmental factors such as exposure to books, good educational experiences, and intelligent peers are profoundly influential. Consequently, in terms of public policy, we need to focus on the environmental influences that are geared toward maximizing the intellectual development of each individual.

> **From an educator's perspective:** Some people have used the proven genetic basis of intelligence to argue against strenuous educational efforts on behalf of individuals with below-average IQs. Does this viewpoint make sense based on what you have learned about heredity and environment? Why or why not?

GENETIC AND ENVIRONMENTAL INFLUENCES ON PERSONALITY: DO WE INHERIT OUR PERSONALITY? We do, at least in part. Evidence suggests that some of our most basic personality traits have genetic roots. For example, two of the "Big Five" personality traits, neuroticism and extroversion, have been linked to genetic factors. *Neuroticism*, as used by personality researchers, is the degree of emotional stability an individual characteristically displays. *Extroversion* is the degree to which a person seeks to be with others, to behave in an outgoing manner, and generally to be sociable. For instance, Jared, the baby described previously, may have inherited an outgoing personality from his extroverted father, Jamal (Horwitz, Luong, & Charles, 2008; Zyphur et al., 2013; Briley & Tucker-Drob, 2017).

How do we know which personality traits reflect genetics? Some evidence comes from direct examination of genes themselves. For instance, it appears that a specific gene is influential in determining risk-taking behavior. This novelty-seeking gene affects the production of the brain chemical dopamine, making some people more prone than others to seek out novel situations and to take risks (Ray et al., 2009; Veselka et al., 2012; Muda et al., 2018).

Other evidence comes from studies of twins. In one major study, researchers looked at the personality traits of hundreds of pairs of twins. Because a good number of the twins were genetically identical but had been raised apart, it was possible to determine with some confidence the influence of genetic factors (Tellegen et al., 1988). The researchers found that certain traits reflected the contribution of genetics considerably more than others. As you can see in Figure 2-7, social potency (the tendency to be a masterful, forceful leader who enjoys being the center of attention) and traditionalism (strict endorsement of rules and authority) are strongly associated with genetic factors (Harris, Vernon, & Jang, 2007; South et al., 2015).

Are some children born to be outgoing and extroverted? The answer seems to be "yes."

Even less basic personality traits are linked to genetics. For example, political attitudes, religious interests and values, and even attitudes toward human sexuality have genetic components (Koenig et al., 2005; Bradshaw & Ellison, 2008; Kandler, Bleidorn, & Riemann, 2012).

Clearly, genetic factors play a role in determining personality—but so does the environment in which a child is raised. For example, some parents encourage high activity levels as a manifestation of independence and intelligence. Other parents may encourage lower levels of activity, feeling that more passive children will get along better in society. In part, these parental attitudes are culturally determined: U.S. parents may encourage higher activity levels, whereas parents in Asian cultures may encourage

Figure 2-7 Inheriting Traits

These traits are among the personality factors that are related most closely to genetic factors. The higher the percentage, the greater the degree to which the trait reflects the influence of heredity. Do these figures mean that "leaders are born, not made"? Why or why not?

SOURCE: Based on Tellegen, A., Lykken, D. T., Bouchard, T. J., Jr., Wil-cox, K. J., Segal, N. L., & Rich, S. (1988). Personal-ity similarity in twins reared apart and together. Journal of Personality and Social Psychology, 54, 1031–1039.

Trait	%
Social potency	61%
A person high in this trait is masterful, a forceful leader who likes to be the center of attention.

Traditionalism	60%
Follows rules and authority, endorses high moral standards and strict discipline.

Stress reaction	55%
Feels vulnerable and sensitive and is given to worries and is easily upset.

Absorption	55%
Has a vivid imagination readily captured by rich experience; relinquishes sense of reality.

Alienation	55%
Feels mistreated and used, that "the world is out to get me."

Well-being	54%
Has a cheerful disposition, feels confident and optimistic.

Harm avoidance	50%
Shuns the excitement of risk and danger, prefers the safe route even if it is tedious.

Aggression	48%
Is physically aggressive and vindictive, has taste for violence and is "out to get the world."

Achievement	46%
Works hard, strives for mastery, and puts work and accomplishment ahead of other things.

Control	43%
Is cautious and plodding, rational and sensible, likes carefully planned events.

Social closeness	33%
Prefers emotional intimacy and close ties, turns to others for comfort and help.

greater passivity. In both cases, children's personalities will be shaped in part by their parents' attitudes (Cauce, 2008; Luo et al., 2017).

Because both genetic and environmental factors have consequences for a child's personality, personality development is a perfect example of the interplay between nature and nurture. Furthermore, it is not only individuals who reflect the interaction of nature and nurture, but even entire cultures, as we see in the *Cultural Dimensions* box.

Cultural Dimensions

Cultural Differences in Physical Arousal: Might a Culture's Philosophical Outlook Be Determined by Genetics?

The Buddhist philosophy of many Asian cultures emphasizes harmony and peace. In contrast, many Western philosophies accentuate the control of anxiety, fear, and guilt, which are assumed to be basic parts of the human condition.

Could such philosophical approaches reflect, in part, genetic factors? That is the controversial suggestion made by developmental psychologist Jerome Kagan and his colleagues. They speculate that the underlying temperament of a given society, determined genetically, may predispose people in that society toward a particular philosophy (Kagan, 2003, 2010).

Kagan bases his admittedly speculative suggestion on well-confirmed findings that show clear differences in temperament between Caucasian and Asian children. For instance, one study that compared 4-month-old infants in China, Ireland, and the United States found several relevant differences. In comparison to the Caucasian American babies and the Irish babies, the Chinese babies had significantly lower motor activity, irritability, and vocalization.

Kagan suggests that the Chinese, who enter the world temperamentally calmer, may find Buddhist notions of serenity more in tune with their nature. In contrast, Westerners, who are emotionally more volatile, tense, and prone to guilt, may be attracted to philosophies that focus on the control of unpleasant feelings, which are usual features of everyday experience (Kagan, 2003, 2010).

Of course, neither philosophical approach is better or worse than the other; that's a matter of personal values. Also, any individual within a culture can be more or less temperamentally volatile, and the range of temperaments even within a single culture is vast. Finally, environmental conditions can have a significant effect on the portion of a person's temperament that is not genetically determined. But what this speculation does reflect is the complex interaction between culture and temperament. Religion may help mold temperament; temperament may make certain religious ideals more attractive.

To validate this intriguing notion would require additional research to determine just how the unique interaction of heredity and environment within a given culture may produce a framework for viewing and understanding the world.

The Buddhist philosophy emphasizes harmony and peacefulness. Could this decidedly non-Western philosophy be a reflection, in part, of genetic causes?

PSYCHOLOGICAL DISORDERS: THE ROLE OF GENETICS AND ENVIRONMENT

When Elani Dimitrios turned 13, her cat, Mefisto, began to give her orders. At first the orders were harmless: "Wear two different socks to school" or "Eat out of a bowl on the floor." Her parents dismissed these events as signs of a vivid imagination, but when Elani approached her little brother with a hammer, her mother intervened forcibly. Elani later recalled, "I heard the order very clearly: Kill him, kill him. It was as if I was possessed."

In a sense, she *was* possessed: possessed with *schizophrenia spectrum disorder*, one of the most severe types of psychological disorders (typically referred to more simply as *schizophrenia*). Normal and happy through childhood, Elani increasingly lost her hold

Figure 2-8 The Genetics of Schizophrenia

The psychological disorder of schizophrenia has clear genetic components. The closer the genetic links between someone with schizophrenia and another family member, the more likely it is that the other person will also develop schizophrenia.

SOURCE: Based on Gottesman, 1991.

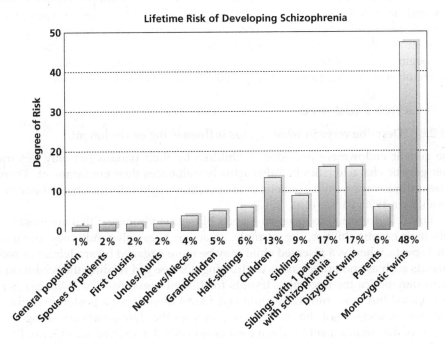

on reality as she entered adolescence. For the next two decades, she would be in and out of institutions, struggling to ward off the ravages of the disorder.

What was the cause of Elani's mental disorder? Evidence suggests that schizophrenia is brought about by genetic factors and runs in families. Moreover, the closer the genetic links between family members, the more likely it is that if one person develops schizophrenia, the other will too. For instance, a monozygotic twin has close to a 50 percent risk of developing schizophrenia when the other twin develops the disorder (see Figure 2-8). By contrast, a niece or nephew of a person with schizophrenia has less than a 5 percent chance of developing the disorder (van Haren et al., 2012; Kläning et al., 2016; So et al., 2018).

These data also illustrate that genetics alone does not influence the development of the disorder. If genetics were the sole cause, the risk for an identical twin would be 100 percent. Consequently, other factors account for the disorder, ranging from structural abnormalities in the brain to a biochemical imbalance (Hietala, Cannon, & van Erp, 2003; Howes & Kapur, 2009; Wada et al., 2012).

It also seems that even if individuals harbor a genetic predisposition toward schizophrenia, they are not destined to develop the disorder. Instead, they may inherit an unusual sensitivity to stress in the environment. If stress is low, schizophrenia will not occur. But if stress is sufficiently strong, schizophrenia will result. However, for someone with a strong genetic predisposition toward the disorder, even relatively weak environmental stressors may lead to schizophrenia (Francis et al., 2013; Walder et al., 2014; Smulevich et al., 2018).

Several other psychological disorders have been shown to be related, at least in part, to genetic factors. For instance, major depression, alcoholism, autism spectrum disorder, and attention-deficit hyperactivity disorder have significant inherited components (Monastra, 2008; Burbach & van der Zwaag, 2009; Cho et al., 2017).

The example of schizophrenia spectrum disorder and other genetically related psychological disorders also illustrates a fundamental principle regarding the relationship between heredity and environment, a principle that underlies much of our previous discussion. Specifically, the role of genetics is often to produce a tendency toward a future course of development. When and whether a certain behavioral characteristic will actually be displayed depends on the nature of the environment. Thus, although a predisposition for schizophrenia may be present at birth, typically people do not show the disorder until adolescence—if at all.

Similarly, certain other kinds of traits are more likely to be displayed as the influence of parents and other socializing factors declines. For example, adopted children may, early in their lives, display traits that are relatively similar to their adoptive parents' traits, given the overwhelming influence of the environment on young children. As they get older and their parents' day-to-day influence declines, genetically influenced traits may begin to manifest themselves as unseen genetic factors begin to play a greater role (Arsenault et al., 2003; Poulton & Caspi, 2005; Tucker-Drob & Briley, 2014).

Can Genes Influence the Environment?

LO 2.6   Describe ways in which genes influence the environment.

The genetic endowment provided to children by their parents not only determines their genetic characteristics but also actively influences their environment. There are at least three ways a child's genetic predisposition might influence his or her environment (Scarr, 1998; Barker et al., 2018).

First, children tend to focus on aspects of their environment that are most in tune with their genetic abilities. For example, an active, aggressive child may gravitate toward sports, whereas a reserved child may be more engaged by academics or solitary pursuits such as computer games or drawing. Or one girl reading the school bulletin board may notice the upcoming tryouts for Little League baseball, whereas her less coordinated but more musically endowed friend might spot a poster recruiting students for an after-school chorus. In these examples the children are attending to those aspects of the environment in which their genetically determined abilities can flourish.

Second, the gene–environment influence may be more passive and less direct. For example, a particularly sports-oriented parent, who has genes that promote good physical coordination, may provide many opportunities for a child to play sports.

Finally, the genetically driven temperament of a child may *evoke* certain environmental influences. For instance, an infant's demanding behavior may cause parents to be more attentive to the infant's needs than they would be otherwise. Or a child who is genetically well coordinated may play ball with anything in the house so often that her parents notice and decide to give her some sports equipment.

In sum, determining whether behavior is primarily attributable to nature or nurture is like shooting at a moving target. Not only are behaviors and traits a joint outcome of genetic and environmental factors, but the relative influence of genes and environment for specific characteristics shifts over the life span. Although the genes we inherit at birth set the stage for our future development, the constantly shifting scenery and the other characters in our lives determine just how our development eventually plays out. The environment both influences our experiences and is molded by the choices we are temperamentally inclined to make.

Review, Check, and Apply

Review

LO 2.1   Describe how genes and chromosomes provide our basic genetic endowment.

A child receives 23 chromosomes from each parent. These 46 chromosomes provide the genetic blueprint that will guide cell activity for the rest of the individual's life.

LO 2.2   Explain the mechanisms by which genes transmit information.

A genotype is the underlying combination of genetic material present in an organism but invisible; a phenotype is the visible trait, the expression of the genotype. For example, PKU, a disease that causes brain damage and intellectual disabilities, is produced by a single pair of genes inherited from one's mother and father. If neither parent carries a gene for the disease, a child cannot develop PKU. Even if one parent carries the recessive gene, but the other doesn't, the child cannot inherit the disease. However, if both parents carry the recessive gene, there is a one in four chance that the child will have PKU.

LO 2.3 Describe the role of genetic counselors and differentiate between different forms of prenatal testing.

Genetic counselors use a variety of data and techniques to advise future parents of possible genetic risks to their unborn children. A variety of techniques can be used to assess the health of an unborn child if a woman is already pregnant, including ultrasound, CVS, and amniocentesis.

LO 2.4 Explain how the environment and genetics work together to determine human characteristics.

Behavioral characteristics are often determined by a combination of genetics and environment. Genetically based traits represent a potential, called the *genotype*, which may be affected by the environment and is ultimately expressed in the phenotype.

LO 2.5 Explain how genetics and the environment jointly influence physical traits, intelligence, and personality.

Virtually all human traits, characteristics, and behaviors are the result of the combination and interaction of nature and nurture. For example, intelligence contains a strong genetic component but can be significantly influenced by environmental factors. Some personality traits, including neuroticism and extroversion, have been linked to genetic factors, and even attitudes, values, and interests have a genetic component.

LO 2.6 Describe ways in which genes influence the environment.

Children may influence their environment through genetic traits that cause them to construct—or influence their parents to construct—an environment that matches their inherited dispositions and preferences.

Check Yourself

1. Sex cells (the ova and the sperm) are different from other cells because they:
   a. have twice the 46 chromosomes necessary, so that when the cells combine and material is "spilled," the appropriate number of chromosomes will still be there.
   b. have half of the 46 chromosomes so that when they combine, the new zygote will have all the genetic information necessary.
   c. are younger than all other cells in the developing human body.
   d. are the only cells with chromosomal information.

2. According to Gregor Mendel, when competing traits are both present, only one trait, also known as the _____ trait, can be expressed.
   a. homozygous   c. polygenic
   b. recessive   d. dominant

3. Most behavioral traits are a product of genetic influence and environmental factors. This is also known as _____.
   a. systematic desensitization
   b. creative orientation
   c. genetic predetermination
   d. multifactorial transmission

4. According to psychologist Jerome Kagan, differences in temperament between Chinese and American children suggest a culture's philosophical outlook may be related to _____ factors.
   a. environmental   c. cultural
   b. genetic   d. social

Applying Lifespan Development

How might an environment different from the one you experienced have affected the development of personality characteristics that you believe you inherited from one or both of your parents?

Module 2.2

Prenatal Growth and Change

Jill and Casey Adams own a small New York advertising firm. When Jill found out she was pregnant, the couple knew they'd need to make radical changes in their lifestyle. Donut breakfasts and fast-food lunches would have to give way to healthier meals with lots of protein and veggies. Gone too were late night parties and clubbing with clients. "No alcohol," their midwife stressed. They would also need to give up smoking. Near her due date now, Jill says the changes were tough but good. "And we use our new lifestyle to connect with health-conscious companies. Instead of clubbing until dawn with clients, we now go jogging at dawn with them."

From the moment of conception, development proceeds relentlessly. Much of it is guided by the complex set of genetic guidelines inherited from the parents, but much is also influenced from the start by environmental factors (Leavitt & Goldson, 1996). And both parents, like Jill and Casey Adams, will have the chance to provide a good prenatal environment.

In this module, we trace the first stirrings of life, when the father's sperm meets the mother's egg. We consider the stages of prenatal development, as the fertilized egg rapidly grows and differentiates into the vast variety of cells that make up the human body. We also look at how pregnancy can go awry and conclude with a discussion of the factors that present threats to normal development.

The Prenatal Period

When most of us think about the facts of life, we tend to focus on the events that cause a male's sperm cells to begin their journey toward a female's ovum. Yet the act of sex that brings about the potential for conception is both the consequence and the start of a long string of events that precede and follow conception.

The Moment of Conception and the Onset of Development

LO 2.7 **Explain the process of fertilization and the three stages of development.**

fertilization
the process by which a sperm and an ovum—the male and female gametes, respectively—join to form a single new cell

Fertilization, or conception, is the joining of sperm and ovum to create the single-celled zygote from which all of us began our lives. Both the male's sperm and the female's ovum come with a history of their own. Females are born with around 400,000 ova located in the two ovaries (see Figure 2-9 for the basic anatomy of the female reproductive organs).

However, the ova do not mature until the female reaches puberty. From that point until she reaches menopause, the female will ovulate about every 28 days. During ovulation, an egg is released from one of the ovaries and pushed by minute hair cells through the fallopian tube toward the uterus. If the ovum meets a sperm in the fallopian tube, fertilization takes place.

Sperm, which look a little like microscopic tadpoles, have a shorter life span. They are created by the testicles at a rapid rate: An adult male typically produces several hundred million sperm a day. Consequently, the sperm ejaculated during sexual intercourse are of considerably more recent origin than the ovum to which they are heading.

When sperm enter the vagina, they begin a winding journey through the cervix—the opening into the uterus—and into the fallopian tube, where fertilization may take place. However, only a tiny fraction of the 300 million sperm that are typically ejaculated during sexual intercourse ultimately survive the arduous journey. That's usually okay, though: It takes only one sperm to fertilize an ovum, and each sperm and ovum contains all the genetic data necessary to produce a new human.

At that point, the onset of development occurs. The prenatal period consists of three phases: the germinal, embryonic, and fetal stages.

Figure 2-9 Anatomy of the Female Reproductive Organs

The basic anatomy of the female reproductive organs is illustrated in this cutaway view.

SOURCE: Based on Moore & Persaud, 2003.

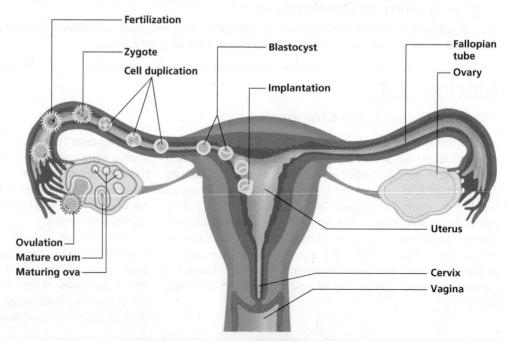

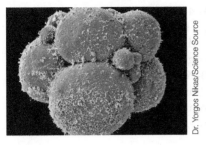

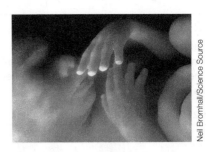

(a) Germinal stage: fertilization to 2 weeks   (b) Embryonic stage: 2 weeks to 8 weeks   (c) Fetal stage: 8 weeks to birth

THE GERMINAL STAGE: FERTILIZATION TO 2 WEEKS   During the **germinal stage**, the first—and shortest—stage of the prenatal period, the zygote begins to divide and grow in complexity. The fertilized egg (now called a *blastocyst*) travels toward the *uterus*, where it becomes implanted in the uterus's wall, which is rich in nutrients. The germinal stage is characterized by methodical cell division, which gets off to a quick start: Three days after fertilization, the organism consists of some 32 cells, and by the next day the number doubles. Within a week, it comprises 100 to 150 cells, and the number rises with increasing rapidity.

In addition to increasing in number, the cells of the organism become increasingly specialized. For instance, some cells form a protective layer around the mass of cells, while others begin to establish the rudiments of a placenta and umbilical cord. When fully developed, the **placenta** serves as a conduit between the mother and fetus, providing nourishment and oxygen via the *umbilical cord*, which also removes waste materials from the developing child. The placenta also plays a role in fetal brain development (Kalb, 2012).

THE EMBRYONIC STAGE: 2 TO 8 WEEKS   By the end of the germinal period—just 2 weeks after conception—the organism is firmly secured to the wall of the mother's uterus. At this point, the child is called an *embryo*. The **embryonic stage** is the period from 2 to 8 weeks following fertilization. One of the highlights of this stage is the development of the major organs and basic anatomy.

At the beginning of this stage, the developing child has three distinct layers, each of which will form a different set of structures that eventually make up every part of the body. The outer layer of the embryo, the *ectoderm*, will form skin, hair, teeth, sense organs, and the brain and spinal cord. The *endoderm*, the inner layer, produces the digestive system, liver, pancreas, and respiratory system. Sandwiched between the ectoderm and endoderm is the *mesoderm*, from which the muscles, bones, blood, and circulatory system are forged.

If you were looking at an embryo at the end of the embryonic stage, you might be hard-pressed to identify it as human. Only an inch long, an 8-week-old embryo has what appear to be gills and a tail-like structure. However, a closer look reveals several familiar features. Rudimentary eyes, nose, lips, and even teeth can be recognized, and the embryo has stubby bulges that will form arms and legs.

The head and brain undergo rapid growth during the embryonic period. The head begins to represent a significant proportion of the embryo's size, encompassing about 50 percent of its total length. The growth of nerve cells, called *neurons*, is astonishing: During pregnancy, an average of 250,000 neurons are produced every minute! The nervous system begins to function around the 5th week, emitting weak brain waves (Nelson & Bosquet, 2000; Stiles & Jernigan, 2010).

THE FETAL STAGE: 8 WEEKS TO BIRTH   It is not until the final period of prenatal development, the fetal stage, that the developing child becomes easily recognizable. The **fetal stage** starts about 8 weeks after conception and continues until birth. The fetal stage formally starts when the major organs have differentiated.

Now called a **fetus**, the developing child undergoes astoundingly rapid change. It increases in length some 20 times, and its proportions change dramatically. At 2 months, around half the fetus is what will ultimately be its head; by 5 months, the head accounts for just over a quarter of its total size (see Figure 2-10). The fetus also

germinal stage
the first—and shortest—stage of the prenatal period, which takes place during the first 2 weeks following conception

placenta
a conduit between the mother and fetus, providing nourishment and oxygen via the umbilical cord

embryonic stage
the period from 2 to 8 weeks following fertilization during which significant growth occurs in the major organs and body systems

fetal stage
the stage that begins at about 8 weeks after conception and continues until birth

fetus
a developing child, from 8 weeks after conception until birth

Figure 2-10 Body Proportions

During the fetal period, the proportions of the body change dramatically. At 2 months, the head represents about half the fetus, but by the time of birth, it is one-quarter of its total size.

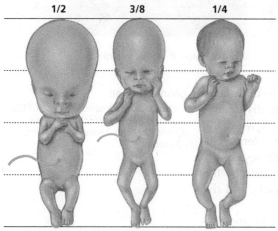

1/2	3/8	1/4

2 months after conception	5 months after conception	Newborn

substantially increases in weight. At 4 months, the fetus weighs an average of about 4 ounces; at 7 months, it weighs about 3 pounds; and at the time of birth, the average child weighs slightly more than 7 pounds.

At the same time, the developing child is rapidly becoming more complex. Organs become more differentiated and start to work. By 3 months, for example, the fetus swallows and urinates. In addition, the interconnections between the different parts of the body become more complex and integrated. For example, arms develop hands; hands develop fingers; fingers develop nails.

As this is happening, the fetus makes itself known to the outside world. By 4 months, a mother can feel the movement of her child, and several months later others can feel the baby's kicks through the mother's skin. In addition, the fetus can turn, do somersaults, cry, hiccup, clench its fist, open and close its eyes, and suck its thumb.

The brain, too, becomes increasingly sophisticated. The symmetrical left and right halves of the brain, known as *hemispheres*, grow rapidly, and the interconnections between neurons become more complex. The neurons become coated with an insulating material called *myelin*, which helps speed the transmission of messages from the brain to the rest of the body.

By the end of the fetal period, brain waves indicate that the fetus passes through different stages of sleep and wakefulness. The fetus is able to hear (and feel the vibrations of) sounds to which it is exposed. Researchers Anthony DeCasper and Melanie Spence (1986) asked a group of pregnant mothers to read aloud the Dr. Seuss story *The Cat in the Hat* two times a day during the latter months of pregnancy. Three days after the babies were born, they appeared to recognize the story, responding more to it than to another story with a different rhythm.

In weeks 8 to 24 following conception, hormones are released that lead to the increasing differentiation of male and female fetuses. For example, high levels of androgen are produced in males that affect the size of brain cells and the growth of neural connections. Some scientists speculate that this may ultimately lead to differences in male and female brain structure and even to later variations in gender-related behavior (Burton et al., 2009; Jordan-Young, 2012; Adhya et al., 2018).

Just as no two adults are alike, no two fetuses are the same. Some fetuses are exceedingly active (a trait that will probably remain with them after birth), whereas others are more sedentary. Some have relatively quick heart rates, and others have slower rates. Such differences are in part a result of genetic characteristics inherited at the moment of fertilization. Other differences, though, are caused by the nature of the environment in which the child spends its first 9 months. The prenatal environment can affect infants' development in many ways—for good or ill (Tongsong et al., 2005; Monk, Georgieff, & Osterholm, 2013; Haabrekke et al., 2018).

Pregnancy Problems

LO 2.8 **Describe some of the physical and ethical challenges that relate to pregnancy.**

For some couples, conception presents challenges—both physical and ethical—that relate to pregnancy.

infertility

the inability to conceive after 12 to 18 months of trying to become pregnant

INFERTILITY Some 15 percent of couples suffer from **infertility**, the inability to conceive after 12 to 18 months of trying. Infertility is correlated with age: The older the parents, the more likely infertility will occur (see Figure 2-11). Regardless of when it occurs in the life span, the inability to conceive is a difficult problem for couples, who may feel a combination of sadness, frustration, and even guilt, particularly on the part of the individual who is infertile (Sexton, Byrd, & von Kluge, 2010; Gremigni et al., 2018; Casu et al., 2018).

In men, infertility most often results from producing too few sperm. Use of illicit drugs or cigarettes and previous bouts of sexually transmitted infections (STIs) also

Figure 2-11 Older Women and Risks of Pregnancy

Not only does the rate of infertility increase as women get older, but the risk of chromosomal abnormality also increases.

SOURCE: Based on Reproductive Medicine Associates of New Jersey(2002), Age and rate of infertility in women.

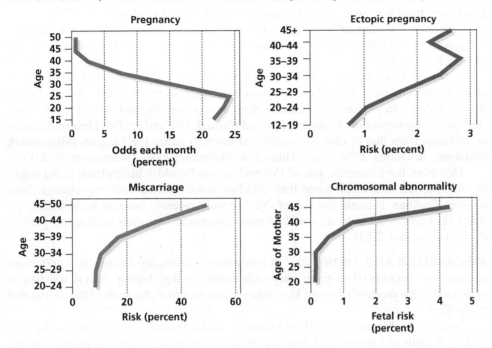

increase infertility. For women, the most common cause is failure to release an egg through ovulation. This may occur because of a hormone imbalance, a damaged fallopian tube or uterus, stress, or abuse of alcohol or drugs (Kelly-Weeder & Cox, 2007; Wilkes et al., 2009; Galst, 2018).

Several treatments for infertility exist. Some difficulties can be corrected through the use of drugs or surgery. Another option may be **artificial insemination**, a procedure in which a man's sperm is placed directly into a woman's reproductive tract by a physician. In some situations, the woman's husband provides the sperm, and in others, the source is an anonymous donor from a sperm bank.

In other cases, fertilization takes place outside the mother's body. **In vitro fertilization (IVF)** is a procedure in which a woman's ova are removed from her ovaries, and a man's sperm is used to fertilize the ova in a laboratory. The fertilized egg is then implanted in the uterus. Similarly, *gamete intrafallopian transfer (GIFT)* and *zygote intrafallopian transfer (ZIFT)* are procedures involving the implantation of an egg and sperm or a fertilized egg in a woman's fallopian tubes. In IVF, GIFT, and ZIFT, implantation is usually done in the woman who provided the donor eggs. More rarely, a *surrogate mother* is used. The surrogate mother is artificially inseminated by the biological father or some other male, brings the baby to term, and gives up rights to it (Aydiner, Yetkin, & Seli, 2010; Hertz & Nelson, 2015).

IVF is increasingly successful, with pregnancy rates as high as 48 percent for women younger than age 35 (but with lower rates for older women). (Actual live birth rates are lower because not all pregnancies ultimately result in birth.) It is also becoming more commonplace. Worldwide, more than 8 million babies have been created through IVF (Neiderberger et al., 2018).

Furthermore, reproductive technologies are becoming increasingly sophisticated, permitting parents to choose the sex of their baby. One technique is to separate sperm carrying the X and Y chromosome and implant the desired type into a woman's uterus. In another technique, eggs are removed from a woman and fertilized with sperm through IVF. Three days after fertilization, the embryos are tested to determine their sex. If they are the desired gender, they are then implanted into the mother (Duenwald, 2004; Kalb, 2004; Whittaker, 2015).

artificial insemination

a process of fertilization in which a man's sperm is placed directly into a woman's reproductive tract by a physician

in vitro fertilization (IVF)

a procedure in which a woman's ova are removed from her ovaries, and a man's sperm are used to fertilize the ova in a laboratory

The use of surrogate mothers, IVF, and sex selection techniques presents a web of ethical and legal issues, as well as many emotional concerns. In some instances, surrogate mothers have refused to give up the child after its birth, and in others, the surrogate mother has sought to have a role in the child's life. In such cases, the rights of the mother, the father, the surrogate mother, and ultimately the baby are in conflict. Even more troubling are concerns raised by sex selection techniques.

Although these ethical and legal questions are difficult to resolve, we can answer one question: How do children conceived through emerging reproductive technologies such as IVF fare?

Research shows that they do quite well. In fact, some studies find that the quality of life for the children of families who have used such techniques may be superior to that of children in families who used natural conception. Furthermore, the later psychological adjustment of children conceived through IVF and artificial insemination is no different from that of children conceived through natural techniques (Hjelmstedt, Widström, & Collins, 2006; Siegel, Dittrich, & Vollmann, 2008; Anderson et al., 2015).

However, the increasing use of IVF techniques by older individuals (who might be well into late adulthood when their children reach adolescence) may change these positive findings. Because the use of IVF has only recently become widespread, we don't yet know what outcomes will be most common in families with aging parents (Colpin & Soenen, 2004).

MISCARRIAGE AND ABORTION   A *miscarriage*—medically known as a spontaneous abortion—occurs when pregnancy ends before the developing child is able to survive outside the mother's womb. The embryo detaches from the wall of the uterus and is expelled.

Some 15 to 20 percent of all pregnancies end in miscarriage, usually in the first several months of pregnancy. Many occur so early that the mother is not even aware she was pregnant and may not even know she has suffered a miscarriage. Typically, miscarriages are attributable to some sort of genetic abnormality. Whatever the cause, women who suffer miscarriage frequently experience anxiety, depression, and grief. Even after subsequently having a healthy child, women who have had a miscarriage in the past still have a higher risk for depression and may have difficulty caring for their healthy child (Murphy, Lipp, & Powles, 2012; Sawicka, 2016; Mutiso, Murage, & Mukaindo, 2018).

Each year, over 56 million pregnancies worldwide end in *abortion*, in which a mother voluntarily chooses to terminate pregnancy. Women in developing countries are more likely to have abortions than women in more developed countries, and the number of abortions in developed countries has declined significantly over the past several decades (Guttmacher Institute, 2017).

Involving a complex set of physical, psychological, legal, and ethical issues, abortion is a difficult choice for every woman. A task force of the American Psychological Association, which looked at the aftereffects of abortion, found that, following an abortion, most women experienced a combination of relief over terminating an unwanted pregnancy and regret and guilt. However, in most cases, the negative psychological aftereffects did not last, except for a small proportion of women who already had serious emotional problems (APA Reproductive Choice Working Group, 2000; Sedgh et al., 2012).

Other research finds that abortion may be associated with an increased risk of future psychological problems; however, the findings are mixed, and there are significant individual differences in how women respond to the experience of abortion. What is clear is that in all cases, abortion is a difficult decision (Cockrill & Gould, 2012; van Ditzhuijzen et al., 2013; Guttmacher Institute, 2017).

The Prenatal Environment: Threats to Development

LO 2.9   Describe the threats to the fetal environment and what can be done about them.

According to the Siriono people of South America, a pregnant woman who eats the meat of certain animals risks having a child who acts and looks like those animals. In other cultures, mothers should avoid stepping over ropes, because doing so might lead to the umbilical cord wrapping around the child's neck. Other cultures advise pregnant mothers to avoid cutting their hair while pregnant in order to prevent vision problems in their infant (Cole, 1992; Rogers, 2018).

Although these views are the stuff of folklore, there is some evidence that a mother's feelings and emotions may have an effect on her fetus. For example, a mother's anxiety during pregnancy may affect the sleeping patterns of the fetus before birth. There are even aspects of a mother's and father's behavior, both before and after conception, that can produce lifelong consequences for the child. Some effects show up immediately, but others don't appear until years later (Couzin, 2002; Tiesler & Heinrich, 2014).

Among the most profound negative effects are those caused by teratogenic agents. A **teratogen** is an environmental agent such as a drug, chemical, virus, or other factor that produces a birth defect. Although the placenta is responsible for keeping teratogens from the fetus, it is not 100 percent successful, and probably every fetus is exposed to some teratogens.

teratogen
a factor that produces a birth defect

The timing and quantity of exposure to a teratogen are crucial. At some phases of prenatal development, a certain teratogen may have only a minimal impact, and at others, the consequences may be significant. Generally, teratogens have their largest effects during periods of especially rapid prenatal development. Sensitivity to specific teratogens is also related to racial and cultural background. For example, Native American fetuses are more susceptible to the effects of alcohol than European American fetuses (Kinney et al., 2003; Winger & Woods, 2004; Rentner, Dixon, & Lengel, 2012; Winiarski et al., 2018).

Furthermore, different organ systems are vulnerable to teratogens at different times. For example, the brain is most susceptible 15 to 25 days after conception, whereas the heart is most vulnerable 20 to 40 days after conception (Pajkrt et al., 2004; see Figure 2-12).

MOTHER'S DIET A mother's diet clearly plays an important role in fetal development. A mother who eats a varied diet high in nutrients is apt to have fewer complications during pregnancy, an easier labor, and a generally healthier baby than a mother whose diet is restricted in nutrients (Guerrini, Thomson, & Gurling, 2007; Marques et al., 2014).

With 800 million hungry people in the world, the problem of diet is of immense global concern. Even worse, the number of people vulnerable to hunger is close to 1 *billion*. Clearly, restrictions in diet that bring about hunger on such a massive scale affect millions of children born to women living in those conditions (World Food Programme, 2016).

Fortunately, there are ways to counteract maternal malnutrition. Dietary supplements for mothers can reverse some of the problems produced by a poor diet. Furthermore, research shows that babies who were malnourished as fetuses, but who are subsequently raised in enriched environments, can overcome some of the effects of early malnutrition. However, the reality is that few of the world's children whose mothers were malnourished *before* their birth are apt to find themselves in enriched environments after birth (Kramer et al., 2008; Olness, 2003).

MOTHER'S AGE More women are giving birth later in life than was true just 2 or 3 decades ago. This change is largely a result of transformations in society as more women seek advanced degrees and defer childrearing until they have started careers.

Women older than age 30 who give birth are at greater risk for a variety of pregnancy and birth complications than younger women. They are more apt to give birth prematurely and to have children with low birthweights. This occurs in part because of a decline in the condition of a woman's eggs. By the time women reach age 42, 90 percent of their eggs are no longer normal (Gibbs, 2002; Moore & de Costa, 2006).

Older mothers are also considerably more likely to give birth to children with Down syndrome, a form of intellectual disability. About 1 in 100 babies born to mothers older than age 40 has Down syndrome; for mothers older than age 50, the incidence increases to 1 in 4. However, some research shows that older mothers are not automatically at risk. For instance, one study found that when women in their 40s who have not experienced

Figure 2-12 Teratogen Sensitivity

Depending on their state of development, some parts of the body vary in their sensitivity to teratogens.

SOURCE: Moore, 1974.

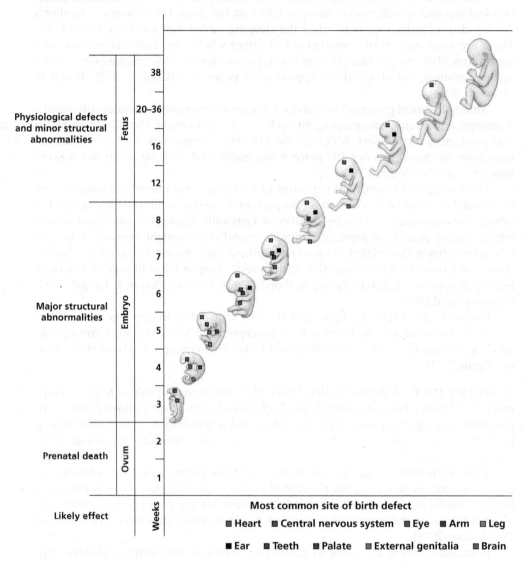

Likely effect		Most common site of birth defect

■ Heart ■ Central nervous system ■ Eye ■ Arm ■ Leg

■ Ear ■ Teeth ■ Palate ■ External genitalia ■ Brain

health difficulties are considered, they are no more likely to have prenatal problems than those in their 20s (Gaulden, 1992; Kirchengast & Hartmann, 2003; Carson et al., 2016).

The risks involved in pregnancy are greater not only for older mothers, but for atypically young women as well. Women who become pregnant during adolescence are more likely to have premature deliveries. Furthermore, the mortality rate of infants born to adolescent mothers is double that for mothers in their 20s (Kirchengast & Hartmann, 2003; Sedgh et al., 2015).

Keep in mind that the higher mortality rate for babies of adolescent mothers reflects more than just physiological problems related to the mothers' young age. Young mothers often face adverse social and economic factors that can affect infant health. Many teenage mothers do not have adequate financial or social support, a situation that prevents them from getting good prenatal care and parenting support after the baby is born. Poverty or social circumstances, such as a lack of parental involvement or supervision, may even have set the stage for the adolescent to become pregnant in the first place (Langille, 2007; Meade, Kershaw, & Ickovics, 2008).

MOTHER'S HEALTH Mothers who eat the right foods, maintain an appropriate weight, and exercise appropriately maximize the chances of having a healthy baby. Furthermore, they can reduce the lifetime risk of obesity, high blood pressure, and heart disease in their children by maintaining a healthy lifestyle (Walker & Humphries, 2005, 2007).

Depending on when it strikes, an illness in a pregnant woman can have devastating consequences. For instance, the onset of *rubella* (German measles) before the 11th week of pregnancy can cause blindness, deafness, heart defects, or brain damage in the baby. In later stages of a pregnancy, however, rubella has less serious effects.

Several other diseases may affect a developing fetus, depending on when they are contracted. For instance, *chicken pox* may produce birth defects, and *mumps* may increase the risk of miscarriage.

Some STIs such as *syphilis* can be transmitted directly to the fetus, who will be born with the disease. Other STIs such as *gonorrhea* are transmitted to the child as it passes through the birth canal at birth.

AIDS (acquired immune deficiency syndrome) is the newest of the diseases to affect a newborn. Mothers who have the disease or who merely are carriers of the virus may pass it on to their fetuses through the blood that reaches the placenta. However, if mothers with AIDS are treated with antiviral drugs such as AZT during pregnancy, less than 5 percent of infants are born with the disease. Those infants who are born with AIDS must remain on antiviral drugs their entire lives (Nesheim et al., 2004).

A mother's mental health status can also affect her children. For example, if the mother suffers from clinical depression while she is pregnant, the development of her children may be negatively affected.

MOTHER'S DRUG USE   The use of many kinds of drugs—both legal and illegal—poses serious risks to the unborn child. Even over-the-counter remedies for common ailments can have surprisingly injurious consequences. For instance, aspirin taken for a headache can lead to fetal bleeding and growth impairments.

Some drugs taken by mothers cause problems for their children decades after they are taken. As recently as the 1970s, the artificial hormone *DES (diethylstilbestrol)* was frequently prescribed to prevent miscarriage. Only later was it found that the daughters of mothers who took DES stood a much higher than normal chance of developing a rare form of vaginal or cervical cancer and had more difficulties during and after their pregnancies. Sons of the mothers who had taken DES had their own problems, including a higher than average rate of reproductive difficulties (Schecter, Finkelstein, & Koren, 2005; Verdoux et al., 2017).

Birth control or fertility pills taken by pregnant women before they are aware of their pregnancy can also cause fetal damage. Such medicines contain sex hormones that, when produced naturally, are related to sexual differentiation in the fetus and gender differences after birth. These medicines can cause significant damage to developing brain structures (Brown, Hines, & Fane, 2002).

Illicit drugs may pose equally great, and sometimes even greater, risks for the environments of prenatal children. For one thing, the purity of drugs purchased illegally varies significantly, so drug users can never be quite sure what specifically they are ingesting. Furthermore, the effects of some commonly used illicit drugs can be particularly devastating.

Consider, for instance, the use of *marijuana*. Marijuana is one of the most commonly used drugs; millions of people in the United States have admitted trying it, and its use is now legal in many jurisdictions. However, marijuana used during pregnancy can restrict the oxygen that reaches the fetus. Its use can lead to infants who are irritable, nervous, and easily disturbed. Children exposed to marijuana prenatally show learning and memory deficits at the age of 10 (Goldschmidt et al., 2008; Willford, Richardson, & Day, 2012; Richardson, Hester, & McLemore, 2016; Massey et al., 2018).

The most recent drug problem involving pregnant mothers is the opioid epidemic in the United States. Opioids are highly addictive, and some are relatively inexpensive to obtain. Many pregnant women who are addicted to opioids such as heroin or oxycodone face barriers when they seek treatment, because the kinds of drug treatments that would normally be used to help recovery may be dangerous to the unborn child. In fact, some drug treatment facilities turn pregnant mothers away. It is a health crisis of growing proportions (Ockerman, 2017).

Fotolia

Pregnant women who drink alcohol place their unborn children at significant risk.

fetal alcohol spectrum disorder (FASD)

a disorder caused by the pregnant mother consuming substantial quantities of alcohol during pregnancy, potentially resulting in intellectual disability and delayed growth in the child

fetal alcohol effects (FAE)

a condition in which children display some, but not all, of the problems of FAS as a result of the mother's consumption of alcohol during pregnancy

MOTHER'S USE OF ALCOHOL AND TOBACCO A pregnant woman who reasons that having a drink every once in a while or smoking an occasional cigarette has no appreciable effect on her unborn child is kidding herself; increasing evidence suggests that even small amounts of alcohol and nicotine can disrupt the development of the fetus.

Mothers' use of alcohol can have profound consequences for the unborn child. The children of alcoholics who consume substantial quantities of alcohol during pregnancy, are at the greatest risk. Approximately 1 out of every 750 infants is born with **fetal alcohol spectrum disorder (FASD)**, a disorder that may include below-average intelligence and sometimes intellectual disability, delayed growth, and facial deformities. FASD is now the primary preventable cause of intellectual disability (Calhoun & Warren, 2007; Bakoyiannis et al., 2014; Wilhoit, Scott & Simecka, 2017).

Even mothers who use smaller amounts of alcohol during pregnancy place their children at risk. **Fetal alcohol effects (FAE)** is a condition in which children display some, although not all, of the problems of FASD due to their mother's consumption of alcohol during pregnancy (Baer, Sampson, & Barr, 2003; Molina et al., 2007).

Children who do not have FAE may still be affected by their mothers' use of alcohol. Studies have found that maternal consumption of an average of just two alcoholic drinks a day during pregnancy is associated with lower intelligence in their offspring at age 7. Other research concurs, suggesting that relatively small quantities of alcohol taken during pregnancy can have future adverse effects on children's behavior and psychological functioning. Furthermore, the consequences of alcohol ingestion during pregnancy are long lasting. For example, one study found that the success of 14-year-olds on a test involving spatial and visual reasoning was related to their mothers' alcohol consumption during pregnancy. The more the mothers reported drinking, the less accurately their children responded (Streissguth, 2007; Chiodo et al., 2012; Domeij, 2018).

Because of these risks, physicians today counsel pregnant women and women who are trying to become pregnant to stop drinking alcohol entirely. They also caution against another practice proven to have an adverse effect on an unborn child: smoking.

Like alcohol consumption, smoking has many consequences, none of which are good. For starters, it reduces the oxygen content and increases the carbon monoxide of the mother's blood, which quickly restricts the oxygen available to the fetus. In addition, the nicotine and other toxins in cigarettes slow the respiration rate of the fetus and speed up its heart rate.

The ultimate result is an increased possibility of miscarriage and a higher likelihood of death during infancy. In fact, estimates suggest that smoking by pregnant women leads to more than 100,000 miscarriages and the deaths of 5,600 babies in the United States alone each year (Triche & Hossain, 2007; Geller, Nelson, & Bonacquisti, 2013).

Smokers are two times as likely as nonsmokers to have babies with an abnormally low birthweight, and smokers' babies are shorter, on average, than those of nonsmokers. Furthermore, women who smoke during pregnancy are 50 percent more likely to have children with intellectual disabilities. Finally, mothers who smoke are more likely to have children who exhibit disruptive behavior during childhood (McCowan et al., 2009; Alshaarawy & Anthony, 2014).

DO FATHERS AFFECT THE PRENATAL ENVIRONMENT? It would be easy to believe that fathers, having done their part to cause conception, have no further effect on the *prenatal* environment of the fetus, but it turns out that a father's behavior may well have an influence. In fact, health practitioners are applying new research to suggest ways fathers can support healthy prenatal development (Martin et al., 2007; Vreeswijk et al., 2013).

For instance, fathers-to-be should avoid smoking. Secondhand smoke may affect the health of the mother and her unborn child. The more the father smokes, the lower the birthweight of his children (Khader et al., 2011).

Similarly, alcohol and drug use by a father can have significant effects on the fetus. Alcohol and drugs impair sperm and may lead to chromosomal damage, which may affect the fetus at conception. Alcohol and drug use may also create stress in the mother and generally produce an unhealthy environment. In addition, workplace toxins such as lead or mercury may bind to sperm and cause birth defects (Choy et al., 2002; Dare et al., 2002; Guttmannova et al., 2016).

Finally, fathers who are physically or emotionally abusive to their pregnant wives can harm their unborn children by increasing maternal stress or causing actual physical damage. In fact, around 5 percent of women face physical abuse during pregnancy (Bacchus, Mezey, & Bewley, 2006; Martin et al., 2006; Kingston et al., 2016).

Development in Your Life

Optimizing the Prenatal Environment

If you are contemplating ever having a child, you may be overwhelmed, at this point in the chapter, by the number of things that can go wrong. Don't be. Although both genetics and the environment pose their share of risks, in the vast majority of cases, pregnancy and birth proceed without mishap. Moreover, there are several things that women can do—both before and during pregnancy—to optimize the probability that pregnancy will progress smoothly (Centers for Disease Control and Prevention, 2017).

- **For women who are planning to become pregnant, several precautions are in order.** First, schedule any necessary nonemergency X-rays only during the first 2 weeks after your menstrual periods. Second, be sure you are vaccinated against rubella (German measles) at least 3 months—preferably 6 months—before getting pregnant. Finally, discontinue birth control pills, which disrupt hormone production, at least 3 months before trying to conceive.

- **Eat well before and during pregnancy.** As the saying goes, pregnant mothers are eating for two. It is more essential than ever to eat regular, well-balanced meals. In addition, take prenatal vitamins, including folic acid, which can decrease the likelihood of birth defects (Amitai et al., 2004; Stephenson et al., 2018).

- **Don't use alcohol or other drugs.** The evidence is clear that many drugs pass directly to the fetus

and may cause birth defects. It is also clear that the more one drinks, the greater the risk to the fetus. The best advice: Don't use *any* drug unless directed by a physician. If you are planning to get pregnant, encourage your partner to avoid using alcohol or other drugs too (O'Connor & Whaley, 2006; Coleman-Cowger et al., 2018).

- **Monitor caffeine intake.** Although it is not clear that caffeine produces birth defects, it is known that the caffeine in coffee, tea, and chocolate can pass to the fetus, acting as a stimulant. Because of this, you probably shouldn't drink more than a few cups of coffee a day (Diego et al., 2007; Galéra et al., 2016; Hvolgaard Mikkelsen et al., 2017).

- **Whether you are pregnant or not, don't smoke.** This holds true for mothers, fathers, and anyone else in the vicinity of the pregnant mother because research suggests that smoke in the fetal environment can affect birthweight. Smoking is the single most preventable cause of illness and death among infants and their mothers.

- **Exercise regularly.** In most cases, pregnant women can continue with low-impact exercise but should avoid extreme exercise, especially on very hot or cold days. (Evenson, 2011; DiNallo, Downs, & Le-Masurier, 2012; Centers for Disease Control and Prevention, 2017).

From the perspective of a health-care provider: In addition to avoiding smoking, what other sorts of things might fathers-to-be do to help their unborn children develop normally in the womb?

Review, Check, and Apply

Review

LO 2.7   Explain the process of fertilization and the three stages of development.

When sperm enter the vagina, they begin a journey that takes them through the cervix, the opening into the uterus, and into the fallopian tube, where fertilization may take

place. Fertilization takes place when the sperm and ovum join to start prenatal development. The germinal stage (fertilization to 2 weeks) is marked by rapid cell division and specialization, and the attachment of the zygote to the wall of the uterus. During the embryonic stage (2 to 8 weeks), the ectoderm, the mesoderm, and the endoderm begin to grow and specialize. The fetal stage (8 weeks to birth) is characterized by a rapid increase in complexity and differentiation of the organs. The fetus becomes active, and most of its systems become operational.

LO 2.8 **Describe some of the physical and ethical challenges that relate to pregnancy.**

Some couples need medical aid to help them conceive. Among the alternate routes to conception are artificial insemination and in vitro fertilization (IVF). Some women may also experience miscarriage or opt for an abortion.

Check Yourself

1. The fertility treatment in which fertilization is induced inside the mother's body is known as _____.

   a. artificial insemination
   b. intracervical insemination
   c. intrauterine insemination
   d. in vitro fertilization

2. Fertilization that occurs outside the mother's body is called _____.

   a. artificial insemination
   b. infertility
   c. in vitro fertilization (IVF)
   d. intracervical insemination

3. Match the following descriptions of prenatal development to their appropriate labels: germinal, embryonic, and fetal.

LO 2.9 **Describe the threats to the fetal environment and what can be done about them.**

A teratogen is an environmental agent such as a drug, chemical, virus, or other factor that produces a birth defect. Factors in the mother that may affect the unborn child include diet, age, illnesses, and drug, alcohol, and tobacco use. The behaviors of fathers and others in the environment may also affect the health and development of the unborn child.

   a. This stage lasts from 8 weeks until birth and involves the differentiation of major organs. _____
   b. From 2 to 8 weeks following fertilization, when the major organs and basic anatomy begin developing. _____
   c. The first and shortest stage, where the zygote begins to divide and grow in complexity during the first 2 weeks following conception. _____

4. A _____ is an environmental agent such as a drug, chemical, virus, or other factor that produces a birth defect.

   a. terminal button
   b. teratogen
   c. terrapin
   d. chromosome

Applying Lifespan Development

Studies show that "crack babies" (babies born to mothers who used cocaine during pregnancy) who are starting school have significant difficulty dealing with multiple stimuli and forming close attachments. How might both genetic and environmental influences have combined to produce these results?

Module 2.3

Birth and the Newborn Infant

Tania and Lou Kerry hadn't planned to have a second child so soon, but 3 months after their son Caleb was born, Tania became pregnant again. Tania's midwife referred her to an obstetrician for the second birth. The reason? Women who become pregnant within months of giving birth are more likely to deliver prematurely. The midwife wanted a doctor on board in case Tania went into labor early.

Despite help from both her mother and Lou, Tania was exhausted most of the pregnancy and worried the new baby would come too soon. "Take it one day at a time," her doctor advised. "Every day that baby stays in the womb, its chances of survival increase."

Tania was almost in the home stretch at 35 weeks when her water broke. Because the baby was early, she came very fast. Tania gave birth in the ambulance on the way to the hospital, but the medics knew what to do for her daughter, who weighed less

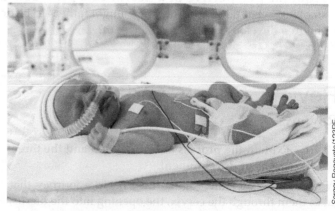

Sergey Rogovets/123RF

than 5 pounds. *After a month in an incubator, Gemma Kerry is home with her family. "We were lucky," Tania says. "Not every preemie survives."*

Infants were not meant to be born as early as Gemma. Yet, for a variety of reasons, more than 10 percent of all babies today are born early, and the odds of their leading a normal life are improving dramatically.

All births, even those that reach full term, are a combination of excitement and anxiety. In the vast majority of cases delivery goes smoothly, and it is an amazing and joyous moment when a new being enters the world. The excitement of birth is soon replaced by wonder at the extraordinary nature of newborns themselves. Babies enter the world with a surprising array of abilities, ready from the first moments of life outside the womb to respond to the world and the people in it.

In this module we'll examine the events that lead to the delivery and birth of a child, and take an initial look at the newborn. We first consider labor and delivery, exploring how the process usually proceeds, as well as several alternative approaches.

We next examine some of the possible complications of birth. Problems that can occur range from premature births to infant mortality. Finally, we consider the extraordinary range of capabilities of newborns. We'll look not only at their physical and perceptual abilities, but at the way they enter the world with the ability to learn and with skills that help form the foundations of their future relationships with others.

Birth

> I wasn't completely naïve. I mean, I knew that it was only in movies that babies come out of the womb all pink, dry, and beautiful. But still, I was initially taken aback by my son's appearance. Because of his passage through the birth canal, his head was cone-shaped, a bit like a wet, partly deflated football. The nurse must have noticed my reaction because she hastened to assure me that this would change in a matter of days. She then moved quickly to wipe off the whitish sticky substance all over his body, informing me as she did so that the fuzzy hair on his ears was only temporary. I leaned in and put my finger into my boy's hand. He rewarded me by closing his hand around it. I interrupted the nurse's assurances. "Don't worry," I stammered, tears suddenly filling my eyes. "He's absolutely the most beautiful thing I've ever seen."

For those of us accustomed to thinking of newborns in the images of baby food commercials, this portrait of a typical newborn may be surprising. Yet most **neonates**—the term used for newborns—resemble this one. Make no mistake, however: Babies are a welcome sight to their parents from the moment of birth.

The neonate's outward appearance is caused by a variety of factors during its journey from the uterus, down the birth canal, and into the world. We can trace this journey, beginning with the release of the chemicals that initiate labor.

neonates
the term used for newborns

From Labor to Delivery

LO 2.10   Describe the normal process of labor and the events that occur in the first few hours of a newborn's life.

About 266 days after conception, a protein called *corticotropin-releasing hormone (CRH)* triggers the release of various hormones, and the process that leads to birth begins. One critical hormone is *oxytocin*, from the mother's pituitary gland. When the concentration of oxytocin becomes high enough, the uterus begins periodic contractions (Terzidou, 2007; Tattersall et al., 2012; Gordon et al., 2017).

LABOR: THE PROCESS OF BIRTH BEGINS   During the prenatal period, the uterus, which is composed of muscle tissue, slowly expands as the fetus grows. For most of the pregnancy it is inactive, but after the fourth month it occasionally contracts to ready itself for the delivery. These *Braxton-Hicks contractions* are sometimes called "false labor" because they can fool eager and anxious parents.

When birth is imminent, the uterus begins to contract intermittently. The increasingly intense contractions force the head of the fetus against the *cervix*, the neck of the uterus that separates it from the vagina. Eventually, the contractions become strong enough to propel the fetus slowly down the birth canal until it enters the world

Figure 2-13 The Three Stages of Labor

Stage 1	Stage 2	Stage 3

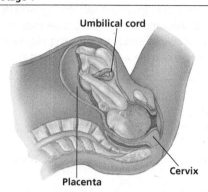

Umbilical cord
Cervix
Placenta

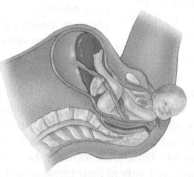

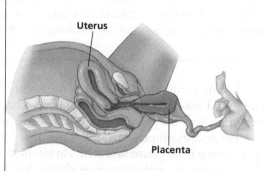

Uterus
Placenta

Uterine contractions initially occur every 8 to 10 minutes and last 30 seconds. Toward the end of labor, contractions may occur every 2 minutes and last as long as 2 minutes. As the contractions increase, the cervix, which separates the uterus from the vagina, becomes wider, eventually expanding to allow the baby's head to pass through.

The baby's head starts to move through the cervix and birth canal. Typically lasting around 90 minutes, the second stage ends when the baby has completely left the mother's body.

The child's umbilical cord (still attached to the neonate) and the placenta are expelled from the mother. This stage is the quickest and easiest, taking just a few minutes.

episiotomy
an incision sometimes made to increase the size of the opening of the vagina to allow the baby to pass

(Mittendorf et al., 1990). This exertion and the narrow birth passageway often give newborns a battered, conehead appearance.

Labor proceeds in three stages (see Figure 2-13). In the *first stage of labor*, the uterine contractions initially occur around every 8 to 10 minutes and last about 30 seconds. As labor proceeds, the contractions occur more frequently and last longer. Toward the end of labor, the contractions may occur every 2 minutes and last almost 2 minutes. As the first stage of labor ends, the contractions reach their greatest intensity, a period known as *transition*. The mother's cervix fully opens, eventually expanding enough (usually to around 10 centimeters) to allow the baby's head to pass through.

During the *second stage of labor*, which typically lasts around 90 minutes, the baby's head proceeds further with each contraction, increasing the size of the vaginal opening. Because the area between the vagina and rectum must stretch, an incision called an **episiotomy** is sometimes made to increase the size of the opening of the vagina. However, this practice is now seen as potentially harmful, and the number of episiotomies has fallen drastically in the past decade (Manzanares et al., 2013; Ballesteros-Meseguer et al., 2016; Gebuza et al., 2018).

The second stage of labor ends when the baby has completely left the mother's body. Finally, in the *third stage of labor* the child's umbilical cord (still attached to the neonate) and the placenta are expelled from the mother. This stage is the quickest and easiest, taking just a few minutes.

The nature of a woman's reactions to labor reflects, in part, cultural factors. Although there is no evidence that the physiological aspects of labor differ among women of different cultures, expectations about labor and interpretations of its pain do vary significantly from one culture to another (Callister et al., 2003; Fisher, Hauck, & Fenwick, 2006; Steel et al., 2014). For instance, there is a kernel of truth to popular stories of women in some societies putting down their tools, giving birth, and immediately returning to work with their neonates on their backs. Accounts of the !Kung people in Africa describe women giving birth without much ado—or assistance—and quickly recovering. In contrast, many societies regard childbirth as dangerous or even as essentially an illness.

BIRTH: FROM FETUS TO NEONATE Birth occurs when the fetus emerges fully from its mother's body. In most cases, babies automatically make the transition for their oxygen needs from the placenta to their lungs. Consequently, most newborns spontaneously cry, which helps them clear their lungs and breathe on their own.

Table 2-3 Apgar Scale

A score is given for each sign at 1 minute and 5 minutes after the birth. If there are problems with the baby, an additional score is given at 10 minutes. A score of 7–10 is considered normal, whereas 4–7 might require some resuscitative measures, and a baby with an Apgar score less than 4 requires immediate resuscitation.

SOURCE: Apgar, 1953; Rozance & Rosenberg, 2012.

	Sign	0 Points	1 Point	2 Points
A	Appearance (skin color)	Blue-gray, pale all over	Normal, except for extremities	Normal over entire body
P	Pulse	Absent	Below 100 bpm	Above 100 bpm
G	Grimace (reflex irritability)	No response	Grimace	Sneezes, coughs, pulls away
A	Activity (muscle tone)	Absent	Arms and legs flexed	Active movement
R	Respiration	Absent	Slow, irregular	Good, crying

What happens next varies from situation to situation and from culture to culture. In Western cultures, health-care workers are almost always on hand to assist with the birth. In the United States, 99 percent of births are attended by professional health-care workers, but in many less-developed countries less than half of births have professional health-care workers in attendance (United Nations Statistics Division, 2012).

The Apgar Scale In most cases, the newborn undergoes a quick visual inspection. While parents lovingly count fingers and toes, health-care workers use the **Apgar scale**, a standard measurement system that looks for a variety of indications of good health (see Table 2-3). Developed by physician Virginia Apgar, the scale directs attention to five basic qualities, recalled most easily by using Apgar's name as a guide: *a*ppearance (color), *p*ulse (heart rate), *g*rimace (reflex irritability), *a*ctivity (muscle tone), and *r*espiration (respiratory effort).

The newborn receives a score ranging from 0 to 2 on each of the five qualities, for an overall score between 0 and 10. Most score 7 or above; the 10 percent who score less than 7 require help to start breathing. Newborns who score 4 or less need immediate, lifesaving intervention.

In addition to problems or defects already present in the fetus, the process of birth itself may sometimes cause difficulties. Oxygen deprivation is one of the most profound. At times during labor, the umbilical cord may get wrapped around the neck or pinched during a prolonged contraction, thereby cutting off the supply of oxygen. Lack of oxygen for a few seconds is not harmful, but if it lasts longer it may cause serious harm. A restriction of oxygen, or **anoxia**, lasting a few minutes can produce cognitive deficits such as language delays and even intellectual disabilities due to brain cell death (Hynes, Fish, & Manly, 2014; Tazopoulou et al., 2016).

Newborn Medical Screening Just after birth, newborns typically are tested for a variety of diseases and genetic conditions. The American College of Medical Genetics recommends that all newborns be screened for 29 disorders, ranging from hearing difficulties and sickle-cell anemia to extremely rare conditions such as isovaleric acidemia (IVA), a disorder that interferes with the normal metabolism of leucine, an important amino acid. IVA and other disorders can be detected from a tiny quantity of blood drawn from an infant's heel (American College of Medical Genetics, 2006).

The advantage of newborn screening is that it permits early treatment of problems that might go undetected for years. In some cases, devastating conditions can be prevented through early treatment of the disorder, such as the implementation of a particular kind of diet (Kayton, 2007; Timmermans & Buchbinder, 2012; Rentmeester, Pringle, & Hogue, 2017).

The exact number of tests that a newborn experiences varies drastically from state to state. In some states, only three tests are mandated, and in others more than 30 are required. In jurisdictions with only a few tests, many disorders go undiagnosed. In fact, each year around 1,000 infants in the United States suffer from disorders that could

Apgar scale
a standard measurement system that looks for a variety of indications of good health in newborns

anoxia
a restriction of oxygen to the baby, lasting a few minutes during the birth process, which can produce cognitive defects

have been detected at birth if appropriate screening had been conducted (American Academy of Pediatrics, 2008; Sudia-Robinson, 2011; McClain & Cokley, 2017).

As advances in medical science give rise to newer and better screening procedures, the question of how many and which diseases to screen for in newborn infants will continue to be a matter for debate. Clearly, more research is needed in order to determine the need for early testing (Hertzberg et al., 2011).

Physical Appearance and Initial Encounters   After assessing the newborn's health, health-care workers deal with the remnants of the child's passage through the birth canal. They clean away the *vernix*, the thick, greasy substance (like cottage cheese) that covers the newborn and smooths the passage through the birth canal. The fine, dark fuzz known as *lanugo* that covers the newborn's body soon disappears. The newborn's eyelids may be puffy from fluids that accumulated during labor, and blood or other fluids may remain on parts of his or her body.

The clean newborn is then handed to the parent or parents for their first, miraculous encounter with their child. The importance of this initial encounter has become a matter of controversy. Some psychologists and physicians have argued that **bonding**, the close physical and emotional contact between parent and child during the period immediately following birth, is crucial for lasting parent–child relationships. More recent research suggests otherwise, however. Although it does appear that mothers who have early physical contact with their babies are more responsive to them than those who don't have such contact, the difference lasts only a few days (Miles et al., 2006; Bigelow & Power, 2012; Stikes & Barbier, 2013; Ropars et al., 2018).

Although immediate mother–child bonding does not seem critical to the relationship between mother and child, it *is* important for newborns to be gently touched and massaged soon after birth. The physical stimulation they receive leads to the production of chemicals in the brain that instigate growth. Ultimately, infant massage is related to weight gain, better sleep–waking patterns, better neuromotor development, and reduced rates of infant mortality (Kulkarni et al., 2011; van Reenen & van Rensburg, 2013; Álvarez, et al., 2017).

bonding

close physical and emotional contact between parent and child during the period immediately following birth

Approaches to Childbirth: Where Medicine and Attitudes Meet

LO 2.11   Describe the major current approaches to childbirth.

Carrie Blackstone had her first baby under the supervision of medical doctors and found the experience impersonal and artificial. So for her second baby, she and her husband, Sami McClough, decided on an African method of birthing that she had read about.

"The African way is more natural. You sit on a birthing stool, which has a hole in the middle. The baby comes through the hole, no fuss, no muss. And no doctors unless they're needed."

Carrie and Sami found a nurse-midwife program at Manhattan's Maternity Center that would permit her to use the stool. When the time came, Carrie and Sami were together through the whole process. With the first contractions, Sami helped her to stand up and they began rocking, "like a slow, comfortable dance," she says. "The rocking helped me through the worst contractions.

"Then I sat on the stool and when the midwife said 'Push!' out came my Dara's head." The midwife placed Dara on Carrie's breast and examined her then and there.

Parents in the Western world have developed a variety of strategies—and some strong opinions—to help them deal with something as natural as giving birth, which occurs apparently without much thought throughout the nonhuman animal world. Today parents need to decide: Should the birth take place in a hospital or in the home? Should a physician, a nurse, or a midwife assist? Is the father's presence desirable? Should siblings and other family members be on hand to participate in the birth?

Most of these questions, of course, are matters not of fact but of values and opinions. No single approach will be effective for everyone, and no conclusive research indicates that one procedure is significantly more effective than another. And not only are personal preferences involved, but culture also plays a role in the choice of birthing procedures.

The abundance of choices is largely a result of a reaction to traditional medical practices that had been common in the United States until the early 1970s. Before that time, the typical birth went something like this: A woman in labor was placed in a room with many other women, all of whom were in various stages of childbirth, and some of whom were screaming in pain. Fathers and other family members were not allowed to be present. Just before delivery, the woman was rolled into a delivery room, where the birth took place. Often she was so drugged that she was not aware of the birth at all.

ALTERNATIVE BIRTHING PROCEDURES Now not all mothers give birth in hospitals, and not all births follow the traditional course. Among the alternatives:

- **Lamaze Method.** Based on the writings of Dr. Fernand Lamaze, this method uses breathing techniques and relaxation training (Lamaze, 1970). Typically, mothers-to-be attend weekly training sessions to learn to relax various parts of the body on command. A "coach," usually the father, is trained at the same time. Through the training, women learn how to deal positively with pain and to relax at the onset of a contraction. Part of the method is to build self-confidence in parents-to-be, demystifying the process of birth, and providing mothers with a number of coping techniques to increase their self-confidence.

  Does it work? Most mothers, as well as fathers, report that a Lamaze birth is a positive experience. However, we can't be sure that parents who choose the Lamaze method aren't already more highly motivated about the experience of childbirth than parents who do not choose the technique. Furthermore, there is a lack of definitive research on the benefits of Lamaze techniques. Still, Lamaze remains one of the most popular childbirth methods in the United States (Larsen et al., 2001; Zwelling, 2006).

Although observation of nonhuman animals highlights the importance of contact between mother and offspring following birth, research on humans suggests that immediate physical contact is less critical.

- **Bradley Method.** The Bradley Method, which is sometimes known as "husband-coached childbirth," is based on the principle that childbirth should be natural, without medication or medical interventions. To prepare for childbirth, mothers-to-be are taught muscle relaxation, breathing techniques, techniques for "trusting their bodies," and practices to promote good nutrition and exercise. Parents are urged to take responsibility for childbirth, and the use of physicians is viewed as unnecessary and sometimes even dangerous. As you might expect, the discouragement of traditional medical interventions is highly controversial (Reed, 2005).

- **Hypnobirthing.** Hypnobirthing is a relatively new technique involving a form of self-hypnosis during delivery that produces a sense of peace and calm, thereby reducing pain. The basic concept is to produce a state of focused concentration in which a mother relaxes her body while focusing inward. Increasing research evidence shows the technique can be effective in reducing pain (White, 2007; Alexander, Turnball, & Cyna, 2009; Wright, & Geraghty, 2017).

- **Water Birthing.** Still relatively uncommon in the United States, water birthing is a practice in which a woman enters a pool of warm water to give birth. The theory is that the warmth and buoyancy of the water is soothing, easing the length and pain of labor and childbirth, and the entry into the world is soothed for the infant, who moves from the watery environment of the womb to the birthing pool. Although there is some evidence that water birthing reduces pain and the length of labor, there is a risk of infection from the unsterile water (Thöni, Mussner, & Ploner, 2010; Jones et al., 2012; Lathrop, Bonsack, & Haas, 2018).

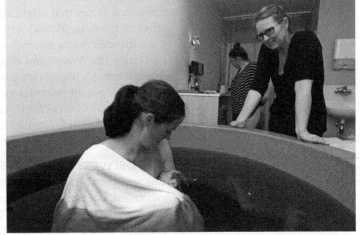

With water birthing, the woman enters a pool of warm water to give birth.

CHILDBIRTH ATTENDANTS: WHO DELIVERS? Traditionally, *obstetricians*, physicians who specialize in delivering babies, have been the childbirth attendants of choice. In the past few decades, more mothers have instead chosen to use a *midwife*, a childbirth attendant who stays with the mother throughout labor and delivery. Midwives—most often nurses specializing in childbirth—are used primarily for pregnancies in which no complications are expected. The use of midwives has increased steadily in the United States—there are now 7,000 of them—and they are employed in 10 percent of births. Midwives help deliver some 80 percent of babies in other parts of the world, often at home. Home birth is common in countries at all levels of economic development. For instance, a third of all births in the Netherlands occur at home (Ayoub, 2005; Klein, 2012; Sandall, 2014).

The newest trend is also one of the oldest: the doula (pronounced *doo-lah*). A *doula* provides emotional, psychological, and educational support during birth. A doula does not replace an obstetrician or midwife and does not do medical examinations. Instead, doulas provide the mother with support and suggest consideration of birthing alternatives. This represents a return to a centuries-old tradition in which supportive, experienced older women serve as birthing assistants and guides. A growing body of research indicates that the presence of a doula is beneficial to the birth process, speeding deliveries and reducing reliance on drugs. Yet concerns remain about their use. Unlike certified midwives, who are nurses and receive an additional year or two of training, doulas do not need to be certified or have any particular level of education (Humphries & Korfmacher, 2012; Simkin, 2014; Darwin et al., 2017).

> **From the perspective of a health-care provider:** Although 99 percent of U.S. births are attended by professional medical workers or birthing attendants, this is the case in only about half of births worldwide. What do you think are some reasons for this, and what are the implications of this statistic?

USE OF ANESTHESIA AND PAIN-REDUCING DRUGS Certainly the ongoing discovery of pain-reducing drugs is one of the greatest advances of modern medicine, but the use of medication during childbirth has both benefits and pitfalls. About half of women who give birth receive *epidural anesthesia*, which produces numbness from the waist down. Traditional epidurals immobilize women and can prevent them from helping to push the baby. A newer form—a *walking epidural* or *dual spinal-epidural*—uses smaller needles and administers doses continuously. This permits women to move more freely and has fewer side effects (Simmons et al., 2007; Osterman & Martin, 2011).

It is important to remember that pain reduction comes at a cost. Drugs reach not just the mother but the fetus as well, and the stronger the drug, the greater its effects on the fetus and neonate. For example, anesthetics may temporarily depress the flow of oxygen to the fetus and slow labor. In addition, newborns whose mothers have been anesthetized are less physiologically responsive, show poorer motor control during the first days after birth, cry more, and may have more difficulty breastfeeding. Further, because of the size difference, doses that might have a minimal effect on the mother can have a magnified effect on the fetus (Ransjö-Arvidson et al., 2001; Torvaldsen et al., 2006; Irland, 2010).

However, most research suggests that drugs as currently used produce only minimal risks. The American College of Obstetricians and Gynecologists (ACOG) suggests that a woman's request for pain relief at any stage of labor should be honored, and that the proper use of minimal amounts of drugs for pain relief is reasonable and has no significant effect on a child's later well-being (Alberts, Elkind, & Ginsberg, 2007; Costa-Martins et al., 2014; American College of Obstetricians and Gynecologists, 2017). (See the *Development in Your Life* box.)

POSTDELIVERY HOSPITAL STAY: DELIVER, THEN DEPART? When Diane Mensch was sent home from the hospital just a day after the birth of her third child, she still felt exhausted. But her insurance company insisted that 24 hours was sufficient time to recover, and it refused to pay for more. Three days later, her newborn was back in the hospital with jaundice. Mensch is convinced the problem would have been discovered and treated sooner had she and her newborn been allowed to remain in the hospital longer (Begley, 2018).

Development in Your Life

Dealing with Labor

Every woman who is soon to give birth has some fear of labor. Most have heard gripping tales of extended, 48-hour labors. Still, few mothers would deny that the rewards of giving birth are worth the effort.

There is no right or wrong way to deal with labor. However, several strategies can help make the process as positive as possible:

- **Be flexible.** Although you may have carefully planned your labor, don't feel obliged to follow through exactly. If one strategy is ineffective, try another.

- **Communicate with your health-care providers.** Let them know what you are experiencing and ask for help and information. They should be able to give you an indication of how much longer you will be in labor, which may help you feel you can handle it.

- **Remember that labor is... laborious.** Expect to become fatigued, but realize that toward the end you may well get a second wind.

- **Accept your partner's support.** If a spouse or other partner is present, allow that person to make you comfortable and provide support. Research has shown that women who are supported by a spouse or partner have a more comfortable birth experience (Kennell, 2002).

- **Be realistic and honest about your reactions to pain.** Even if you had planned an unmedicated delivery, realize that you may find the pain hard to bear. At that point, consider drugs. Asking for pain medication is not a sign of failure.

- **Focus on the big picture.** Keep in mind that labor is part of a process that leads to an event unmatched in the joy it can bring.

Mensch's experience is not unusual. In the 1970s the average hospital stay for a normal birth was 3.9 days. By the 1990s, it was 2 days. The change was prompted in large part by medical insurance companies focused on reducing costs.

Medical providers acknowledge that there are definite risks involved, both for mothers and their newborns, for too fast a departure from hospitals. For instance, mothers may experience bleeding from tissues torn during childbirth, and newborns may require the intensive medical care that hospitals uniquely provide. Furthermore, mothers are better rested and more satisfied with their care when they stay longer (Campbell et al., 2016).

In accordance with these views, the U.S. Congress has passed legislation mandating a minimum insurance coverage of 48 hours for childbirth. Furthermore, the American Academy of Pediatrics has issued comprehensive guidelines detailing how long women (and their infants) should stay in the hospital based on various health criteria relating to the infant and mother (Bentz, 2015).

Birth Complications

When Ivy Brown's son was born dead, a nurse told her that sad as it was, she was not alone: A surprisingly high number of births in her city, Washington, D.C., ended with the death of the child. That fact spurred Brown to become a grief counselor, specializing in infant mortality. She formed a committee of physicians and city officials to study the capital's high infant mortality rate and find solutions to lower it. "If I can spare one mother this terrible grief, my loss will not be in vain," Brown says.

The overall infant mortality rate in Washington, D.C., the capital of the richest country in the world, is 7.1 per 1,000 live births in 2016—a number that has actually declined from a high of 13.1 in 2007. For non-Hispanic black mothers, the number is far worse, registering at 11.5 per 1,000 live births (Lloyd, 2018).

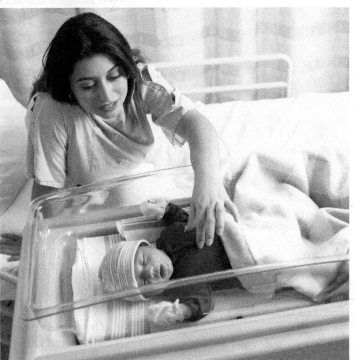

Mothers who spend more time in the hospital following the birth of a child do better than those discharged after a shorter period.

Air Images/Shutterstock

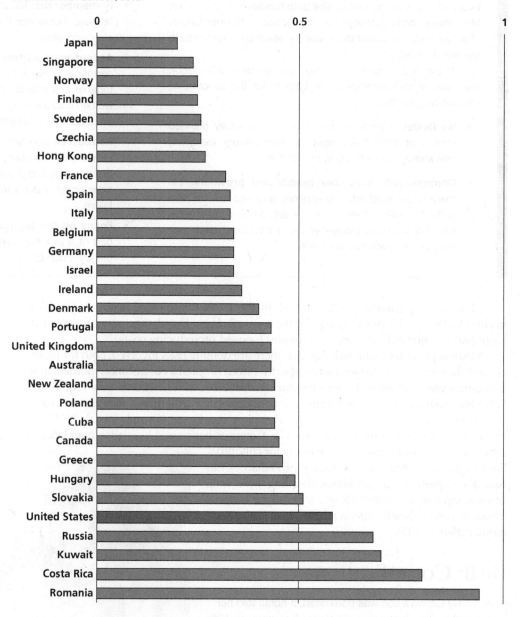

Figure 2-14 International Infant Mortality

Infant mortality rates in selected countries. Although the United States has greatly reduced its infant mortality rate in the past 25 years, it still ranks behind numerous other industrialized countries. What are some of the reasons for this?

SOURCE: *World Factbook*, 2018.

Overall, more than 50 countries have better infant mortality rates than the United States, which has 5.8 deaths for every 1,000 live births. This rate is worse than countries such as Hungary, Cuba, and Slovenia (World Factbook, 2018; see Figure 2-14).

Why do infants have less chance of survival in the United States than in other, less-developed countries? To answer this question, we need to consider the problems that can occur during labor and delivery.

Preterm Infants and Postmature Babies

LO 2.12   Describe the causes of, consequences of, and treatments for preterm births and the risks that postmature babies face.

preterm infants
infants who are born prior to 38 weeks after conception (also known as *premature infants*)

Around 1 out of 10 infants are born earlier than normal. **Preterm infants**, or premature infants, are born before 38 weeks after conception. Because they have not had time to develop fully as fetuses, preterm infants are at high risk for illness and death.

The extent of danger faced by preterm babies largely depends on the child's weight at birth, which has great significance as an indicator of the extent of the baby's development. Although the average newborn weighs around 3,400 grams (about 7.5 pounds), **low-birthweight infants** weigh less than 2,500 grams (around 5.5 pounds). Only 7 percent of U.S. newborns are in the low-birthweight category, but they account for most newborn deaths (DeVader et al., 2007).

Although most low-birthweight infants are preterm, some are small-for-gestational-age babies. **Small-for-gestational-age infants** are infants who, because of delayed fetal growth, weigh 90 percent (or less) of the average weight of infants of the same gestational age. Small-for-gestational-age infants are sometimes also preterm but may not be. The syndrome may be caused by inadequate nutrition during pregnancy (Bergmann, Bergmann, & Dudenhausen, 2008; Karagianni et al., 2010).

If the baby is not very premature and the weight at birth is not extremely low, the threat is relatively minor. In such cases, the best treatment may be to keep the baby in the hospital to gain weight. Additional weight is critical because fat layers help prevent chilling in neonates, who are not efficient at regulating body temperature.

Research also shows that preterm infants who receive more responsive, stimulating, and organized care are apt to show more positive outcomes than those children whose care is not as good. Some of these interventions are quite simple. For example, "kangaroo care," in which infants are held skin-to-skin against their parents' chests, appears to be effective in helping preterm infants develop. Massaging preterm infants several times a day triggers the release of hormones that promote weight gain, muscle development, and abilities to cope with stress (Kaffashi et al., 2013; Athanasopoulou & Fox, 2014; Nobre et al., 2017).

Newborns who are born more prematurely and who have birthweights significantly below average face a tougher road. They are highly vulnerable to infection, and because their lungs are not fully developed, they have problems taking in oxygen. As a consequence, they may experience *respiratory distress syndrome (RDS)*, with potentially fatal consequences.

To deal with RDS, low-birthweight infants are often placed in incubators, enclosures in which temperature and oxygen content are carefully monitored. Too low a concentration of oxygen will not provide relief, and too high a concentration can damage the delicate retinas of the eyes, leading to permanent blindness.

Preterm neonates are unusually sensitive to the sights, sounds, and sensations they experience, and their breathing may be interrupted or their heart rates may slow. They are often unable to move smoothly, with uncoordinated arm and leg movements that can be disconcerting to parents (Miles et al., 2006; Valeri et al., 2015).

Despite the difficulties they experience at birth, the majority of preterm infants eventually develop normally in the long run. However, the tempo of development often proceeds more slowly for preterm children compared to children born at full term, and subtler problems sometimes emerge later. For example, by the end of their first year, only 10 percent of prematurely born infants display significant problems, and only 5 percent are seriously disabled. By age 6, however, approximately 38 percent have mild problems that call for special educational interventions. For instance, some preterm children show learning disabilities, behavior disorders, or lower-than-average IQ scores. They may also be at greater risk for mental illness. Others have difficulties with physical coordination. Still, around 60 percent of preterm infants are free of even minor problems (Hall et al., 2008; Nosarti et al., 2012; El Ayoubi et al., 2016).

VERY-LOW-BIRTHWEIGHT INFANTS: THE SMALLEST OF THE SMALL The story is less positive for the most extreme cases of prematurity. **Very-low-birthweight infants** weigh less than 1,250 grams (around 2.25 pounds) or, regardless of weight, have been in the womb less than 30 weeks.

low-birthweight infants
infants who weigh less than 2,500 grams (around 5.5 pounds) at birth

small-for-gestational-age infants
infants who, because of delayed fetal growth, weigh 90 percent (or less) of the average weight of infants of the same gestational age

very-low-birthweight infants
infants who weigh less than 1,250 grams (around 2.25 pounds) or, regardless of weight, have been in the womb less than 30 weeks

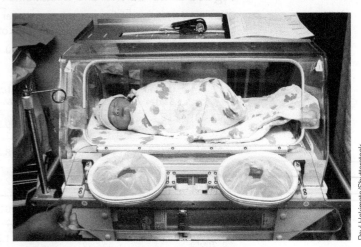

Preterm infants stand a much greater chance of survival today than they did even a decade ago.

Paul Hakimata/Shutterstock

Very-low-birthweight infants not only are tiny—some fitting easily in the palm of the hand at birth—they hardly seem to belong to the same species as full-term newborns. Their eyes may be fused shut, and their earlobes may look like flaps of skin on the sides of their heads. Their skin is a darkened red color, whatever their race.

Very-low-birthweight babies are in grave danger from the moment they are born because their organ systems are immature. Before the mid-1980s, these babies would not have survived; recent medical advances have pushed the *age of viability*, the point at which an infant can survive prematurely, to about 22 weeks—some 4 months earlier than the normal term. Of course, the longer the baby develops after conception, the higher the chance of survival. A baby born earlier than 25 weeks has less than a 50–50 chance of survival (see Figure 2-15) (Seaton et al., 2012).

If a very-low-birthweight preterm infant survives, the medical costs can be astonishing—between 3 and 50 times higher than the medical costs for a full-term child during the first 3 years of life. This fact has engendered ethical debates about the expenditure of substantial financial and human resources in cases in which a positive outcome may be unlikely (Prince, 2000; Doyle, 2004a; Petrou, 2006; Cavallo et al., 2015).

Still, emerging evidence suggests that high-quality care can provide protection from some of the risks of prematurity, and that by the time they reach adulthood, premature babies may be little different from other adults. Still, the costs of caring for preterm infants are enormous: Estimates put the cost of caring for premature infants at $6 billion a year (Grosse et al., 2017).

WHAT CAUSES PRETERM AND LOW-BIRTHWEIGHT DELIVERIES?   About half of preterm and low-birthweight births are unexplained, but several known causes account for the remainder. In some cases, the cause arises from difficulties in the mother's reproductive system. For instance, twins place unusual stress on their mothers, which can lead to early labor. In fact, most multiple births are preterm to some degree (Tan et al., 2004; Luke & Brown, 2008).

In other cases, preterm and low-birthweight babies are a result of the immaturity of the mother's reproductive system. Young mothers—younger than age 15—are more prone to deliver prematurely than older ones. In addition, a woman who becomes pregnant within 6 months of her previous delivery is more likely to have a preterm or low-birthweight infant than a woman whose reproductive system has had a chance to recover. The father's age matters, too: Pregnant women with older male partners are more likely to have preterm deliveries (Branum, 2006; Blumenshine et al., 2011; Teoli, Zullig, & Hendryx, 2015).

Finally, factors that affect the general health of the mother, such as nutrition, level of medical care, amount of stress in the environment, and economic support, are all related to prematurity and low birthweight. Rates of preterm births differ between

Figure 2-15 Survival and Gestational Age

Chances of a fetus surviving greatly improve after 28 to 32 weeks. Rates shown are the number per 1,000 babies born in the United States after specified lengths of gestation who do not survive the first year of life.

SOURCE: Based on MacDorman, M. F., & Matthews, T. J. (2009). Behind international rankings of infant mortality: How the United States compares with Europe. NCHS Data Brief, # 2.

	United States	Austria	Denmark	England and Wales[2]	Finland	Northern Ireland	Norway	Poland	Scotland	Sweden
22–23 weeks[1]	707.7	888.9	947.4	880.5	900.0	1,000.0	555.6	921.1	1,000.0	515.2
24–27 weeks	236.9	319.6	301.2	298.2	315.8	268.3	220.2	530.6	377.0	197.7
28–31 weeks	45.0	43.8	42.2	52.2	58.5	54.5	56.4	147.7	60.8	41.3
32–36 weeks	8.6	5.8	10.3	10.6	9.7	13.1	7.2	23.1	8.8	12.8
37 weeks or more	2.4	1.5	2.3	1.8	1.4	1.6	1.5	2.3	1.7	1.5

1 Infant mortality rates at 22–23 weeks of gestation may be unreliable due to reporting differences.
2 England and Wales provided 2005 data.

Table 2-4 Risk Factors for Low-Birthweight Preterm Infants

- Women who have delivered preterm before, or who have experienced preterm labor
- Being pregnant with twins, triplets, or higher-order multiples
- The use of assisted reproductive technologies
- Certain medical conditions, including:
  - Urinary tract infections
  - Sexually transmitted infections
  - Certain vaginal infections
  - High blood pressure
  - Bleeding from the vagina
  - Certain developmental abnormalities in the fetus
  - Being underweight or obese before pregnancy
  - Short time period between pregnancies (less than 6 months between a birth and the beginning of the next pregnancy)
  - Placenta previa, a condition in which the placenta grows in the lowest part of the uterus and covers all or part of the opening to the cervix
  - Being at risk for rupture of the uterus
  - Diabetes
  - Blood clotting problems

Other factors that may increase risk for preterm labor and premature birth include:

- Ethnicity—preterm labor and birth occur more often among certain racial and ethnic groups
- Age of the mother—younger than 18 and older than 35
- Certain lifestyle and environmental factors, including:
  - Late or no health care during pregnancy
  - Smoking
  - Drinking alcohol
  - Using illegal drugs
  - Domestic violence, including physical, sexual, or emotional abuse
  - Lack of social support
  - Stress
  - Long working hours with long periods of standing
  - Exposure to certain environmental pollutants

SOURCE: U.S. Department of Health and Human Services, National Institutes of Health, Eunice Kennedy Shriver Institute of Child Health and Human Development, 2017.

racial groups, not because of race per se, but because members of racial minorities have disproportionately lower incomes and higher stress as a result. For instance, the percentage of low-birthweight infants born to African American mothers is double that for Caucasian American mothers. (A summary of the factors associated with increased risk of low birthweight is shown in Table 2-4; Field et al., 2008; Butler, Wilson, & Johnson, 2012; Teoli, Zullig, & Hendryx, 2015.)

POSTMATURE BABIES: LATER, LARGER One might imagine that a baby who spends extra time in the womb might have some advantages, given the opportunity to continue growth undisturbed by the outside world. Yet **postmature infants**—those still unborn 2 weeks after the mother's due date—face several risks.

For example, the blood supply from the placenta may become insufficient to nourish the still-growing fetus. A decrease in blood to the brain may lead to brain damage. Similarly, labor is riskier (for both mother and child) if a fetus nearly the size of a 1-month-old infant has to make its way through the birth canal (Fok & Tsang, 2006).

Postmature infants are less of a problem than preterm babies because medical practitioners can induce labor artificially through drugs or a cesarean delivery.

postmature infants
infants still unborn 2 weeks after the mother's due date

Cesarean Delivery: Intervening in the Process of Birth

LO 2.13 **Describe the process of cesarean delivery, and explain the reasons for its increase in use.**

> As Elena entered her 18th hour of labor, her obstetrician began to look concerned. She told Elena and her husband, Pablo, that the fetus's heart rate had begun to fall after each contraction. After trying some simple remedies, such as repositioning Elena on her side, the obstetrician came to the conclusion that the fetus was in distress. She told them that the baby should be delivered immediately by cesarean delivery.

cesarean delivery
a birth in which the baby is surgically removed from the uterus, rather than traveling through the birth canal

Elena became one of the more than 1 million mothers in the United States who have a cesarean delivery each year. In a **cesarean delivery** (sometimes known as a *c-section*), the baby is surgically removed from the uterus, rather than traveling through the birth canal.

Cesarean deliveries occur most frequently when the fetus shows distress of some sort. For instance, if the fetus appears to be in danger, as indicated by a sudden rise in its heart rate, or if blood is seen coming from the mother's vagina during labor, a cesarean may be performed. In addition, mothers older than 40 are more likely to have cesarean deliveries than younger mothers. Overall, cesarean deliveries in the United States now make up 32 percent of all deliveries (Tang et al., 2006; Romero, Coulson, & Galvin, 2012; Centers for Disease Control and Prevention, 2017).

Cesarean deliveries are sometimes used when the baby is in *breech position*, feet first in the birth canal. Breech position births, which occur in about 1 of 25 births, place the baby at risk because the umbilical cord is more likely to be compressed, depriving the baby of oxygen. Cesarean deliveries are also more likely in *transverse position* births, in which the baby lies crosswise in the uterus, or when the baby's head is so large it has trouble moving through the birth canal.

fetal monitor
a device that measures the baby's heartbeat during labor

The routine use of **fetal monitors**, which measure the baby's heartbeat during labor, has contributed to a soaring rate of cesarean deliveries. Some 25 percent of children in the United States are born in this way, up about 500 percent from the early 1970s (Hamilton, Martin, & Ventura, 2011; Paterno et al., 2016).

Are cesareans an effective medical intervention? Other countries have substantially lower rates of cesarean deliveries (see Figure 2-16), and there is no association between successful birth consequences and the rate of cesarean deliveries. In addition, cesarean deliveries are major surgeries that carry dangers. The mother's recovery can be relatively lengthy, particularly when compared to a normal delivery. Further, the risk of maternal infection is higher with cesarean deliveries (Miesnik & Reale, 2007; Ryding et al., 2015; Salahuddin et al., 2018).

Finally, a cesarean delivery presents some risks for the baby. Because cesarean babies are spared the stresses of passing through the birth canal, their relatively easy passage into the world may deter the normal release of certain stress-related hormones, such as catecholamines, into the newborn's bloodstream. These hormones help prepare the neonate to deal with the stress of the world outside the womb, and their absence may be detrimental to the newborn child. In fact, research indicates that babies born by cesarean delivery who have not experienced labor are more likely to experience breathing problems upon birth than those who experience at least some labor before being born via a cesarean delivery. Finally, mothers who deliver by cesarean are less satisfied with the birth experience, although their dissatisfaction does not influence the quality of mother–child interactions (Janevic et al., 2014; Xie et al., 2015; Kjerulff & Brubaker, 2017).

Because the increase in cesarean deliveries is, as we have said, connected to the use of fetal monitors, medical authorities now recommend that they not be used routinely. There is evidence that outcomes are no better for newborns who have been monitored

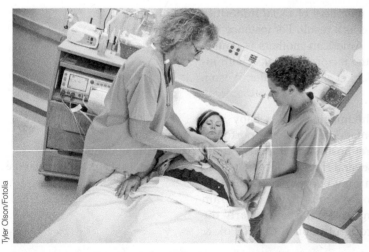

Tyler Olson/Fotolia

The use of fetal monitors has contributed to a sharp increase of cesarean deliveries in spite of evidence showing few benefits from the procedure.

Figure 2-16 Cesarean Deliveries

The rate at which cesarean deliveries are performed varies substantially from one country to another. Why do you think the United States has such a high rate?

SOURCE: Based on Organization for Economic Cooperation and Development (OECD). (2015). OECD Health Statistics 2015. Downloaded from http://dx.doi.org/10.1787/health-data-en.

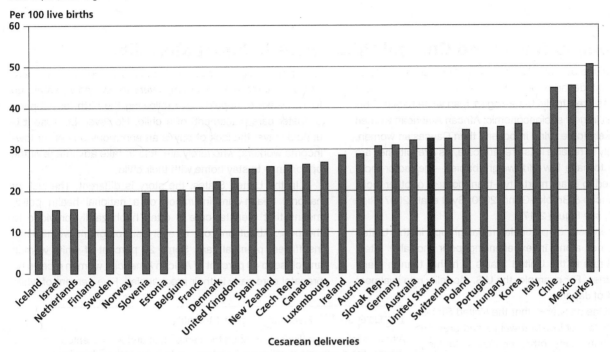

Cesarean deliveries

than for those who have not been monitored. In addition, monitors tend to indicate fetal distress when there is none—false alarms—with disquieting regularity. Monitors do, however, play a critical role in high-risk pregnancies and in cases of preterm and postmature babies (Freeman, 2007).

Stillbirth, Infant Mortality, and Postpartum Depression

LO 2.14 Explain the factors that lead to stillbirth, infant mortality, and postpartum depression.

There are many problems associated with the end of pregnancy. Among the most difficult to deal with are the death of a child and depression following the birth of a child. We'll consider them next.

STILLBIRTH AND INFANT MORTALITY: THE TRAGEDY OF PREMATURE DEATH Sometimes a child does not live to pass through the birth canal. **Stillbirth,** the delivery of a child who is not alive, occurs in less than 1 delivery out of 100. If the death is detected before labor begins, labor is typically induced, or physicians may perform a cesarean to remove the body as soon as possible. In other cases of stillbirth, the baby dies during its journey through the birth canal.

The overall rate of **infant mortality** (defined as death within the first year of life) in the United States is 5.8 deaths per 1,000 live births. Infant mortality generally has been declining since the 1960s, and declined 12 percent from 2005 to 2011 (Loggins & Andrade, 2014; Prince et al., 2016; World Factbook, 2018).

Whether the death is a stillbirth or occurs after the child is born, the loss of a baby is tragic, and the impact on parents is enormous. The loss and grief parents feel, and their passage through it, is similar to that experienced when an older loved one dies (discussed in Chapter 10). In fact, the juxtaposition of the first dawning of life and an unnaturally early death may make the death particularly difficult to accept and deal with. Depression is common, and it is often intensified because of a lack of support. Some parents even experience posttraumatic stress disorder (Badenhorst et al., 2006; Cacciatore & Bushfield, 2007; Turton, Evans, & Hughes, 2009).

stillbirth
the delivery of a child who is not alive, occurring in fewer than 1 delivery in 100

infant mortality
death within the first year of life

There are also differences related to race, socioeconomic status, and culture in infant mortality, as we discuss in the *Cultural Dimensions* box.

Cultural Dimensions

Overcoming Racial and Cultural Differences in Infant Mortality

Even though the overall U.S. infant mortality rate has declined over the past decades, African American babies are more than twice as likely to die before age 1 than white babies. This difference is largely socioeconomic: African American women are more likely to be living in poverty than Caucasian women, and are likely to receive less prenatal care. As a result, they are more likely to have low-birthweight babies—the factor most closely linked to infant mortality—than mothers of other racial groups (Duncan & Brooks-Gunn, 2000; Byrd et al., 2007; Rice et al., 2017; see Figure 2-17).

But members of particular racial groups in the United States are not alone in experiencing poor mortality rates. The overall rate in the United States is higher than in many other countries. For example, the U.S. mortality rate is almost double that of Japan.

Why? One answer is that the United States has a higher rate of low-birthweight and preterm deliveries than many other countries. In fact, when U.S. infants are compared to infants of the same weight who are born in other countries, the mortality rate differences disappear (MacDorman et al., 2005; Davis & Hofferth, 2012).

Another reason relates to economic diversity. Compared to many other countries, the United States has a higher proportion of people living in poverty, who are less likely to have adequate medical care and to be healthy. This has an impact on the overall mortality rate (Bremner & Fogel, 2004; MacDorman et al., 2005; Close et al., 2013).

Also, many countries do a much better job in providing prenatal care. For instance, low-cost and even free care, both before and after delivery, is often available. Paid maternity leave is frequently provided, lasting in some cases as long as 51 weeks. The opportunity to take an extended maternity leave can lead to better mental health for mothers and higher-quality interactions with their infants (Waldfogel, 2001; Ayoola et al., 2010; Mandal, 2018).

Better health care is only part of the story. In certain European countries, pregnant women receive many additional privileges, such as transportation benefits for medical visits. In Norway, pregnant women may be given living expenses for up to 10 days so they can be close to a hospital when it is time to give birth. And when their babies are born, new mothers receive, for just a small payment, the assistance of trained home helpers (DeVries, 2005).

In the United States, the U.S. *Family and Medical Leave Act (FMLA)* requires most employers to give new parents up to 12 weeks of unpaid leave following the birth (or adoption or foster care placement) of a child. However, because it is unpaid leave, the lack of pay is an enormous barrier for low-income workers, who rarely are able to take advantage of the opportunity to stay home with their child.

In the United States, the story is different. The lack of national health-care insurance or a national health policy means that prenatal care is often haphazardly provided to the poor. About one out of every six pregnant women has insufficient prenatal care. Some 20 percent of white women and close to 40 percent of African American women receive no prenatal care early in their pregnancies. Five percent of white

Figure 2-17 Race and Infant Mortality

Although infant mortality has dropped for members of underrepresented groups, the death rate is still more than twice as high for African American children as for white children. These figures show the number of deaths in the first year of life for every 1,000 live births.

SOURCE: Child Health USA, 2009.

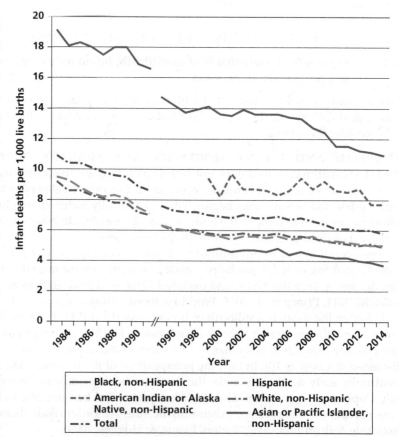

mothers and 11 percent of African American mothers do not see a health-care provider until the last 3 months of pregnancy; some never see a health-care provider at all (Hueston, Geesey, & Diaz, 2008; Friedman, Heneghan, & Rosenthal, 2009; Cogan et al., 2012).

Ultimately, the lack of prenatal services results in a higher mortality rate. Yet this situation can be changed if greater support is provided. A start would be to ensure that all economically disadvantaged pregnant women have access to free or inexpensive high-quality medical care from the beginning of pregnancy. Furthermore, barriers that prevent poor women from receiving such care should be reduced. For instance, programs can be developed that help pay for transportation to a health facility or for the care of older children while the mother is making a health-care visit. The cost of these programs is likely to be offset by the savings they make possible: Healthy babies cost less than infants who have chronic problems as a result of poor nutrition and prenatal care (Edgerley et al., 2007; Barber & Gertler, 2009; Hanson, 2012).

From an educator's perspective: Why do you think the United States has for so long lacked national educational and health-care policies that could reduce infant mortality rates overall and particularly among poorer people? What arguments would you make to change this situation?

POSTPARTUM DEPRESSION: MOVING FROM THE HEIGHTS OF JOY TO THE DEPTHS OF DESPAIR Consider this situation:

Renata was overjoyed when she found out that she was pregnant and spent the months of her pregnancy happily preparing for her baby's arrival. The birth was routine, the baby a healthy, pink-cheeked boy. But a few days after her son's birth, she sank into the depths of depression. Constantly crying, confused, feeling incapable of caring for her child, she was experiencing unshakable despair.

The diagnosis: postpartum depression. *Postpartum depression*, a period of deep depression following the birth of a child, affects some 10 percent of new mothers. The deep sadness that is its main symptom may last for months or even years. Mothers experiencing postpartum depression may withdraw from their family and friends, experience overwhelming fatigue or loss of energy, or feel intense irritability and anger. Furthermore, mothers may feel stigmatized by others (Mickelson et al., 2017).

In about 1 in 500 cases, the symptoms evolve into a total break with reality. In extremely rare instances, postpartum depression may turn deadly. For example, Andrea Yates, a mother in Texas who was charged with drowning all five of her children in a bathtub, said that postpartum depression led to her actions (Yardley, 2001; Oretti, Harris, & Lazarus, 2003; Misri, 2007).

The onset of depression usually comes as a complete surprise. Certain mothers seem more likely to become depressed, such as those who have been clinically depressed at some point in the past or who have depressed family members. Furthermore, women who are unprepared for the range of emotions that follow birth—some positive, some negative—may be more prone to depression (LaCoursiere, Hirst, & Barrett-Connor, 2012; Pawluski, Lonstein, & Fleming, 2017).

Postpartum depression may be triggered by the pronounced swings in hormone production that occur after birth. During pregnancy, the production of estrogen and progesterone increases significantly. However, 24 hours after birth they plunge to normal levels. This rapid change may result in depression (Yim et al., 2009; Engineer et al., 2013; Glynn & Sandman, 2014).

The Highly Competent Newborn

Relatives gather around the infant car seat and its occupant, Kaita Castro, born just 2 days ago. This is Kaita's first day home from the hospital. Kaita's nearest cousin, 4-year-old Tabor, seems uninterested in the new arrival. "Babies can't do anything fun. They can't even do anything at all," he says.

Kaita's cousin, Tabor, is partly right. There are many things babies cannot do. Neonates arrive in the world quite incapable of successfully caring for themselves, for example. Why are human infants born so dependent, whereas members of other species seem to arrive much better equipped for their lives?

One reason is that, in a sense, humans are born too soon. The brain of the average newborn is just one-quarter what it will be at adulthood. In comparison, the brain of the macaque monkey, which is born after just 24 weeks of gestation, is 65 percent of its adult size. Because of the relative puniness of the infant human brain, some have suggested that we emerge from the womb 6 to 12 months early.

In reality, evolution knew what it was doing: If we stayed inside our mothers' bodies an additional half-year to a year, our heads would be so large that we'd never manage to get through the birth canal.

The relatively underdeveloped brain of the human newborn helps explain the infant's apparent helplessness. But developmental researchers are coming to realize that infants enter this world with an astounding array of capabilities. In fact, in many ways, they are highly competent across all domains of development: physical, cognitive, and social.

Physical Competence: Meeting the Demands of a New Environment

LO 2.15   Describe the physical capabilities of the newborn.

The world the neonate faces is markedly different from the "womb world." Consider, for instance, the significant changes that Kaita encountered as she began the first moments of life in her new environment.

Kaita's first task was to bring air into her body. Inside her mother, the umbilical cord delivered air and removed carbon dioxide. The outside world was different: Once the umbilical cord was cut, Kaita's respiratory system had to start its lifetime's work.

For Kaita, the task was automatic. Most newborn babies begin to breathe on their own as soon as they are exposed to air. The ability to breathe immediately indicates that the respiratory system is reasonably well developed, despite its lack of rehearsal in the womb.

reflexes
unlearned, organized involuntary responses that occur automatically in the presence of certain stimuli

Neonates emerge from the uterus more practiced in other types of physical activities. For example, newborns such as Kaita have **reflexes**—unlearned, organized involuntary responses that occur automatically in the presence of certain stimuli. Some reflexes have been rehearsed for several months before birth. The *sucking reflex* and the *swallowing reflex* permit Kaita to ingest food right away. The *rooting reflex*, which involves turning in the direction of a stimulus (such as a light touch) near the mouth, is also related to eating. It guides Kaita toward nearby sources of food, such as a mother's nipple.

Other reflexes that present themselves at birth—such as coughing, sneezing, and blinking—help the infant avoid stimuli that are potentially bothersome or hazardous. Kaita's sucking and swallowing reflexes, which help her to consume her mother's milk, are coupled with the newfound ability to digest nutriments. The newborn's digestive system initially produces feces in the form of *meconium*, a greenish-black material that is a remnant of the neonate's days as a fetus.

Because the liver, a critical component of the digestive system, does not always work effectively at first, almost half of newborns develop a yellowish tinge to their bodies and eyes. This *neonatal jaundice* is most prevalent in preterm and low-weight neonates and is typically not dangerous. Treatment involves placing the baby under fluorescent lights or administering medicine.

Sensory Capabilities: Experiencing the World

LO 2.16   Describe the sensory capabilities of the newborn.

Just after Kaita was born, her father was certain that she looked directly at him. Did she, in fact, see him?

This is a hard question to answer. When sensory experts talk of "seeing," they mean both a sensory reaction to stimulation and an interpretation of that stimulation (the distinction between sensation and perception). Furthermore, it is tricky to pinpoint the specific sensory skills of newborns who can't explain what they are experiencing.

Still, it is clear that neonates such as Kaita can see to some extent. Although their visual acuity is not fully developed, they actively pay attention to certain types of information in their environment.

For instance, newborns attend to high-information elements in their field of vision, such as objects that sharply contrast with the rest of the environment. Furthermore, they can discriminate levels of brightness. There is even evidence that they may have a sense of size constancy—the awareness that objects stay the same size even though the size of the image on the retina varies with distance (Chien et al., 2006; Frankenhuis, Barrett, & Johnson, 2013; Wilkinson et al., 2014).

In addition, not only can newborn babies distinguish different colors, but they also seem to prefer particular ones. For example, they can distinguish among red, green, yellow, and blue, and they take more time staring at blue and green objects (Dobson, 2000; Alexander & Hines, 2002; Zemach, Chang, & Teller, 2007).

Newborns can also hear. They react to certain sounds, showing startle reactions to loud, sudden noises, for instance. They also recognize sounds. For example, a crying newborn, hearing other newborns crying, will continue to cry. But on hearing a recording of its own crying, the newborn is more likely to stop crying, as if recognizing a familiar sound (Dondi, Simion, & Caltran, 1999; Fernald, 2001).

Starting at birth, infants are able to distinguish colors and even show preferences for particular ones.

The auditory system is not completely developed, however, and auditory acuity is not as great as it will be. Moreover, amniotic fluid, which is initially trapped in the middle ear, must drain before the newborn can fully hear.

In addition to sight and hearing, the other senses also function quite adequately in the newborn. It is obvious that newborns are sensitive to touch. For instance, they respond to stimuli such as the hairs of a brush, and they are aware of puffs of air so weak that adults cannot notice them.

The senses of smell and taste are also well developed. Newborns suck and increase other physical activity when the odor of peppermint is placed near the nose. They also pucker their lips when a sour taste is placed on them, and respond with suitable facial expressions to other tastes as well. Such findings clearly indicate that the senses of touch, smell, and taste are not only present at birth, but are reasonably sophisticated (Cohen & Cashon, 2003; Armstrong et al., 2007).

In one sense, the sophistication of the sensory systems of newborns such as Kaita is not surprising. After all, the typical neonate has had 9 months to prepare for his or her encounter with the outside world. Human sensory systems begin their development well before birth. Furthermore, the passage through the birth canal may place babies in a state of heightened sensory awareness, preparing them for the world that they are about to encounter for the first time.

CIRCUMCISION OF NEWBORN MALE INFANTS   *Circumcision* is the surgical removal of part or all of the foreskin from the penis. It is most commonly performed shortly after birth. An estimated 58 percent of newborn males in the United States are circumcised, and worldwide the prevalence is around 33 percent. For overall prevalence across all age groups, 81 percent of males in the United States are circumcised (Owings, Uddin, & Williams, 2013; Morris, Bailis, & Wiswell, 2014).

Parents usually choose circumcision for a combination of health, religious, cultural, and traditional reasons. But although it is one of the most common surgical procedures in the United States, a number of medical associations have, in the past, argued that it was medically unnecessary (American Academy of Pediatrics, 1999; American Academy of Family Physicians, 2002).

However, new research has added a twist: We now know that circumcision provides protection against sexually transmitted diseases. Furthermore, the risk of urinary tract infections is reduced in circumcised males, especially during the first year of life, and the risk of penile cancer is about three times higher in uncircumcised men than in men who were circumcised at birth. Consequently, the U.S. Centers for Disease Control and Prevention (CDC) has released policy recommendations affirming male circumcision as an important public health measure. This recommendation is consistent with the newest policy statement of the American Academy of Pediatrics, which suggests that the health benefits of male circumcision outweigh the risks, although that the benefits are not so great to recommend circumcision for all newborn males (American Academy of Pediatrics, 2012); Morris, Krieger, & Klausner, 2017; Centers for Disease Control and Prevention, 2018).

In any case, circumcision is a surgical procedure that is not without complications. The most common are bleeding and infection, both of which are easily treated. The procedure is also painful and stressful to the infant because it is typically done without general anesthesia. Further, some experts believe that circumcision reduces sensation and sexual pleasure later in life, while others argue that it is unethical to remove a healthy body part without a person's consent when there is no medical need to do so. One thing is clear: Circumcision is highly controversial and evokes strong emotions. The decision ultimately comes down to the parents' personal preferences and values (Goldman, 2004).

Early Learning Capabilities

LO 2.17   Describe the learning capabilities of the newborn.

One-month-old Michael Samedi was on a car ride with his family when a violent thunderstorm suddenly began. Flashes of lightning were quickly followed by loud thunderclaps. Michael, clearly disturbed, began to cry. With each new thunderclap, the fervor of his crying increased, although he calmed when his mother soothingly held him closely and sang softly to him. Still, in the months that followed, Michael reacted with great anxiety in thunderstorms. Before long it wasn't just the thunder that would upset him; the lightning alone was enough to make him cry out. In fact, even as an adult, Michael feels his chest tighten and his stomach churn at the mere sight of lightning.

classical conditioning
a type of learning in which an organism responds in a particular way to a neutral stimulus that normally does not bring about that type of response

CLASSICAL CONDITIONING   The source of Michael's fear is classical conditioning, a type of learning first identified by Ivan Pavlov, a Russian scientist. In **classical conditioning**, an organism learns to respond in a particular way to a neutral stimulus that normally does not bring about that type of response. Classical conditioning is one of several theories that explain learning.

Pavlov discovered that by repeatedly pairing two stimuli, such as the sound of a bell and the arrival of meat, he could make hungry dogs learn to respond (in this case by salivating) not only when the meat was presented, but also even when the bell was sounded without the meat (Pavlov, 1927).

The key feature of classical conditioning is stimulus substitution, in which a stimulus that doesn't naturally bring about a particular response is paired with a stimulus that does evoke that response. Repeatedly presenting the two stimuli together results in the second stimulus taking on the properties of the first. In effect, the second stimulus is substituted for the first. Thus, in the earlier example with the infant Michael, the lightning and thunder provoked similar responses—fear—and ultimately lightning alone evoked a fear response.

One of the earliest examples of classical conditioning shaping human emotions was the case of 11-month-old "Little Albert" (Watson & Rayner, 1920; Fridlund et al., 2012). Although he initially adored furry animals and showed no fear of rats, Little Albert learned to fear them when, during a laboratory demonstration, a loud noise was sounded every time he played with a cute and harmless white rat. In fact, the fear generalized to other furry objects, including rabbits and even a Santa Claus mask. (By the way, this demonstration would be considered unethical today and would never be conducted.)

Clearly, classical conditioning is in operation from the time of birth. One- and 2-day-old newborns who are stroked on the head just before receiving a drop of sweet-tasting liquid soon learn to turn their heads and suck at the head-stroking alone (Herbert et al., 2004; Welch, 2016).

OPERANT CONDITIONING Infants also respond to operant conditioning, another learning theory. **Operant conditioning** is a form of learning in which a *voluntary* response is strengthened or weakened, depending on its association with positive or negative consequences. In operant conditioning, infants learn to act deliberately on their environments to bring about a desired consequence. An infant who learns that crying in a certain way attracts her parents' attention is displaying operant conditioning.

Like classical conditioning, operant conditioning functions from the earliest days of life. For instance, researchers have found that even newborns readily learn through operant conditioning to keep sucking on a nipple when it permits them to continue hearing their mothers read a story or to listen to music. Similarly, in the vignette earlier about baby Michael, who grew frightened in thunderstorms, operant conditioning explains how Michael may have learned that his mother's comforting presence could reduce his anxiety (DeCasper & Fifer, 1980; Lipsitt, 1986; Welch, & Ludwig, 2017).

HABITUATION Probably the most primitive form of learning is habituation. **Habituation** is the decrease in the response to a stimulus that occurs after repeated presentations of the same stimulus.

Habituation in infants relies on the fact that when newborns are presented with a new stimulus, they produce an *orienting response*, in which they become quiet and attentive and experience a slowed heart rate as they take in the novel stimulus. When the novelty wears off, the infant no longer reacts. If a new and different stimulus is presented, the infant once again reacts with an orienting response. When this happens, we can say that the infant recognizes the original stimulus and can distinguish it from others.

Habituation occurs in every sensory system, and researchers have studied it in several ways. One is to examine changes in sucking, which stops temporarily when a new stimulus is presented. This reaction is not unlike that of adults who temporarily put down their knife and fork when a dinner companion makes an interesting statement to which they wish to pay particular attention. Other measures of habituation include changes in heart rate, respiration rate, and the length of time an infant looks at a particular stimulus (Macchi et al., 2012; Rosburg, Weigl, & Sörös, 2014; Dumont et al., 2017).

The development of habituation is linked to physical and cognitive maturation. It is present at birth and becomes more pronounced over the first 12 weeks of infancy. Difficulties involving habituation may be a sign of developmental problems such as intellectual disabilities (Moon, 2002).

The three basic processes of learning that we've considered—classical conditioning, operant conditioning, and habituation—are summarized in Table 2-5.

operant conditioning
a form of learning in which a voluntary response is strengthened or weakened, depending on its association with positive or negative consequences

habituation
the decrease in the response to a stimulus that occurs after repeated presentations of the same stimulus

Table 2-5 Three Basic Processes of Learning

Type	Description	Example
Classical conditioning	A situation in which an organism learns to respond in a particular way to a neutral stimulus that normally does not bring about that type of response	A hungry baby stops crying when her mother picks her up because she has learned to associate being picked up with subsequent feeding.
Operant conditioning	A form of learning in which a voluntary response is strengthened or weakened, depending on its positive or negative consequences	An infant who learns that smiling at his or her parents brings positive attention may smile more often.
Habituation	The decrease in the response to a stimulus that occurs after repeated presentations of the same stimulus	A baby who showed interest and surprise at first seeing a novel toy may show no interest after seeing the same toy several times.

Social Competence: Responding to Others

LO 2.18   Describe the social competencies of newborns.

Soon after Kaita was born, her older brother looked into her crib and opened his mouth wide, pretending to be surprised. Kaita's mother was amazed when Kaita imitated his expression, opening her mouth as if *she* were surprised.

Researchers registered surprise of their own when they found that newborns could apparently imitate others' behavior. Although infants have all the facial muscles needed to express basic emotions, the appearance of such expressions was assumed to be random.

However, research beginning in the late 1970s began to suggest a different conclusion. For instance, developmental researchers found that, when exposed to an adult modeling a behavior that the infant already performed spontaneously, such as opening the mouth or sticking out the tongue, the newborn appeared to imitate the behavior (Meltzoff & Moore, 1977, 2002; Nagy, 2006).

Even more exciting were findings from studies conducted by developmental psychologist Tiffany Field and her colleagues. They first showed that infants could discriminate between such basic facial expressions as happiness, sadness, and surprise. They then exposed newborns to an adult model with a happy, sad, or surprised facial expression. The results suggested that newborns produced a reasonably accurate imitation of the adult's expression (Field et al., 2010).

This result was questioned, however, when subsequent research found consistent evidence for only one movement: sticking out the tongue. And even that seemed to disappear around the age of 2 months. Because it seems unlikely that imitation would be limited to a single gesture of only a few months' duration, researchers began to question the previous findings. In fact, some researchers suggested that sticking out the tongue was not imitation but merely an exploratory behavior (Jones, 2006, 2007; Tissaw, 2007; Huang, 2012).

The jury is still out on exactly when true imitation begins, although it seems clear that some forms of imitation begin early. Imitative skills are important because effective social interactions rely in part on the ability to react to other people in an appropriate way and to understand the meaning of others' emotional states. Consequently, newborns' ability to imitate provides them with an important foundation for social interaction later in life (Zeedyk & Heimann, 2006; Legerstee & Markova, 2008; Beisert et al., 2012).

Several other aspects of newborns' behavior also act as forerunners for more formal types of social interaction that develop later. As shown in Table 2-6, certain characteristics of neonates mesh with parental behavior to help produce a social relationship between child and parent, as well as relationships with others (Eckerman & Oehler, 1992).

For example, newborns cycle through various **states of arousal**, different degrees of sleep and wakefulness, that range from deep sleep to great agitation. Caregivers become involved in easing the baby through transitions from one state to another. For instance, a father who rhythmically rocks his crying daughter to

states of arousal
different degrees of sleep and wakefulness through which newborns cycle, ranging from deep sleep to great agitation

Table 2-6 What Encourages Social Interaction Between Newborns and Their Parents?

Full-Term Newborns	Parents
Show a preference for certain stimuli	Offer preferred stimuli more than others
Begin to show a predictable cycle of arousal states	Build on their cycles to achieve more regulated states
Show some consistency in time patterns	Conform to and shape the newborn's patterns
Show awareness of parent's actions	Help newborn grasp what meaning the actions have
React and adapt to actions of parent	Act in predictable, consistent ways
Show evidence of a desire to communicate	Work to understand their newborn's communicative efforts

SOURCE: Based on Eckerman & Oehler, 1992; LeMoine, Mayoral, & Dean, 2015.

calm her is engaged with her in a joint activity that is a prelude to future social interactions of different sorts. Similarly, newborns pay particular attention to their mothers' voices, in part because they have become familiar with them after months in the womb. In turn, parents and others modify their speech when talking to infants to gain their attention and encourage interaction, using a different pitch and tempo than they use with older children and adults (Smith & Trainor, 2008; Waters et al., 2017).

The ultimate outcome of the social interactive capabilities of the newborn infant, and the responses from parents, is a paved path for future social interactions. In sum, then, neonates display remarkable physical, perceptual, *and* social capabilities.

> **From a child-care worker's perspective:** Developmental researchers no longer view the neonate as a helpless, incompetent creature, but rather as a remarkably competent, developing human being. What do you think are some implications of this change in viewpoint for methods of childrearing and child care?

This infant is imitating the happy expressions of the adult. Why is this important?

Review, Check, and Apply

Review

LO 2.10 **Describe the normal process of labor and the events that occur in the first few hours of a newborn's life.**

In the first stage of labor, contractions occur about every 8 to 10 minutes, increasing in frequency, duration, and intensity until the mother's cervix expands. In the second stage of labor, which lasts about 90 minutes, the baby begins to move through the cervix and birth canal and ultimately leaves the mother's body. In the third stage of labor, which lasts only a few minutes, the umbilical cord and placenta are expelled from the mother. After it emerges, the newborn, or neonate, is usually inspected for irregularities, cleaned, and returned to its mother and father. It also undergoes newborn screening tests.

LO 2.11 **Describe the major current approaches to childbirth.**

Parents-to-be have a variety of choices regarding the setting for the birth, medical attendants, and whether to use pain-reducing medication. Sometimes, medical intervention, such as cesarean birth, becomes necessary.

LO 2.12 **Describe the causes of, consequences of, and treatments for preterm births and the risks that postmature babies face.**

Preterm, or premature, infants, born less than 38 weeks following conception, generally have low birthweight, which can cause chilling, vulnerability to infection, respiratory distress syndrome, and hypersensitivity to environmental stimuli. They may even show adverse effects later in life, including slowed development, learning disabilities, behavior disorders, below-average IQ scores, and problems with physical coordination. Very-low-birthweight infants are in special danger because of the immaturity of their organ systems. However, medical advances have pushed the age of viability of the infant back to about 24 weeks following conception. Postmature babies, who spend extra time in their mothers' wombs, are also at risk.

LO 2.13 **Describe the process of cesarean delivery, and explain the reasons for its increase in use.**

Cesarean deliveries are performed when the fetus is in distress, in the wrong position, or unable to progress through the birth canal. The routine use of a fetal monitor has contributed to a soaring rate of cesarean deliveries.

LO 2.14 **Explain the factors that lead to stillbirth, infant mortality, and postpartum depression.**

The infant mortality rate in the United States is higher than the rate in many other countries, and is higher for low-income families than for higher-income families. Postpartum depression, an enduring, deep feeling of sadness, affects about 10 percent of new mothers. In severe cases, its effects can be harmful to the mother and the child, and aggressive treatment may be employed.

LO 2.15 Describe the physical capabilities of the newborn.

Human newborns quickly master breathing through the lungs, and they are equipped with reflexes to help them eat, swallow, find food, and avoid unpleasant stimuli.

LO 2.16 Describe the sensory capabilities of the newborn.

Newborns' sensory competence includes the ability to distinguish objects in the visual field and to see color differences, the ability to hear and to discern familiar sounds, and sensitivity to touch, odors, and tastes.

LO 2.17 Describe the learning capabilities of the newborn.

From birth, infants learn through habituation, classical conditioning, and operant conditioning.

LO 2.18 Describe the social competencies of newborns.

Infants develop the foundations of social competence early in life. Newborns are able to imitate the behavior of others, a capability that helps them form social relationships and facilitates the development of social competence.

Check Yourself

1. Labor proceeds in three stages. The longest stage of labor is _____.
   a. the first stage
   b. the second stage
   c. the third stage
   d. hard to determine

2. The _____ scale measures infant health by assessing appearance (color), pulse (heart rate), grimace (reflex irritability), activity (muscle tone), and respiration (respiratory effort).
   a. Bronfenbrenner
   b. Brazelton
   c. Anoxia
   d. Apgar

3. Which of the following factors influence a woman's delivery?
   a. Her preparation for childbirth
   b. The support she has before and during delivery
   c. Her culture's view of pregnancy and delivery
   d. All of the above

4. To survive the first few minutes or even days, infants are born with _____, or unlearned, organized, involuntary responses that occur automatically in the presence of certain stimuli.
   a. sensory capabilities
   b. acute hearing
   c. narrow vision
   d. reflexes

Applying Lifespan Development

Can you think of examples of the use of classical conditioning on adults in everyday life, in such areas as entertainment, advertising, or politics?

Chapter 2 Summary
Putting It All Together: The Start of Life

JANA AND TOM MONACO, the parents we met in the chapter opener, averted tragedy because of the availability of genetic testing. After their first child was diagnosed with a rare disease, they used prenatal genetic testing to determine if their next child carried the mutation that produced the disease. When the testing revealed their daughter carried the mutation, they were able to provide treatment to prevent the onset of the disease, and she would go on to lead a normal life.

karen roach/Shutterstock

MODULE 2.1
PRENATAL DEVELOPMENT

- Like all parents, Jana and Tom contributed 23 chromosomes to each child at conception. Their babies' sex was determined from the particular mix of one pair of chromosomes. (pp. 42–43)
- Even before their babies' birth, Jana and Tom had a range of options for checking for gender, possible genetic defects, and fetal growth. Measures available to them included procedures such as ultrasound sonography, amniocentesis, and fetal blood sampling. (pp. 48–49)
- Many of their daughter's characteristics will have a strong genetic component, but virtually all will represent some combination of genetics and environment. (pp. 50–58)

MODULE 2.2
PRENATAL GROWTH AND CHANGE

- In the prenatal period, Jana's babies showed a multistage pattern of development, starting with the germinal stage, progressing to the embryonic stage, and completing the prenatal period in the fetal stage. (pp. 60–62)
- Jana was comparatively young, watched her diet, exercised regularly, and relied on her husband Tom's strong support. Consequently, aside from the genetic mutation she carried, there were few other potential threats to her babies' health and development. (pp. 64–69)
- Because Jana ate a nutritious diet, exercised, and abstained from alcohol during the pregnancy, she had relatively few worries about teratogenic agents harming the fetuses. (pp. 64–69)

MODULE 2.3
BIRTH AND THE NEWBORN INFANT

- Jana's labor for both her births was relatively easy, but women experience labor in different ways because of individual and cultural differences. (pp. 71–74)
- Jana chose to use a midwife, one of several alternative birthing methods. (pp. 74–77)
- Like the vast majority of births, Jana's was completely normal and successful. (p. 77)
- Although the infants seemed utterly helpless and dependent when born, they actually possessed from birth an array of useful capabilities and skills. (pp. 85–91)

What would a PARENT do?

What strategies would you use to prepare yourself for the birth of a child you suspected might carry a genetic mutation? How would you evaluate the different options for prenatal care and delivery? How would you prepare an older child for the birth of a new baby?

Photodisc/
Getty Images

What would a HEALTH-CARE PROVIDER do?

How would you prepare Jana and Tom for the birth of their daughter? How would you respond to their concerns and anxieties? What would you tell them about the different options they have for giving birth?

Mark Andersen/
Rubberball/
Getty Images

What would an EDUCATOR do?

What strategies might you use to teach Jana and Tom about the stages of pregnancy and the process of birth? What might you tell them about infancy to prepare them for caring for their children?

Tom Baker/123RF

What would YOU do?

What would you say to Jana and Tom about the impending birth of their daughter? What advice would you give to Jana and Tom about prenatal care and their decision to use a genetic testing?

Odua Images/
Shutterstock

Chapter 3
Infancy

Syda Productions/Shutterstock

Although they welcomed their adopted daughter Jenna to their family when she was 4 months old, she was still an infant and, to new parents Malia and Tom Turin, a complete mystery. They had by then read what they felt was every baby book ever published, listened intently to tons of advice from experienced friends, and attended a series of training sessions designed, it seemed, to bewilder rather than clarify.

They felt like total amateurs as they drove Jenna home from the airport. Every movement or sound she made was greeted with a diaper change and a bottle in the mouth. Although weary after the long drive home, they barely slept that night because they were listening for sounds from her crib, which might signal distress.

But they soon understood that Jenna was a healthy, cheerful baby. They learned when she needed feeding and changing, and they responded to her nighttime crying by rocking and soothing her until she quieted. They learned to talk to and play with her and to be comfortable around her. They learned, in short, to be parents.

It took a while, but they had arrived. Still, they knew not to be too relaxed, for theirs would be a long journey of many uncertain steps.

All infants, whether they have basically good dispositions like Jenna or are fussy and demanding, are engaging, energetic, and challenging. And they are constantly changing as they develop physically, cognitively, socially, and in terms of developing their own unique personality.

In this chapter, we examine infancy, the period of the life span that starts at birth and continues through the first 2 years of life. We'll first discuss the ways in which infants grow physically, examining their remarkably rapid progress from largely instinctual beings to individuals with a range of complex physical abilities.

Turning to infants' cognitive development, we'll discuss the notion of stages of development, as well as some alternative views. We'll consider the amazing growth in learning, memory, and language that infants experience—and adults witness with awe.

Finally, we will examine social and personality development. We will look at personality and temperament and observe how gender differences are a matter of both genes and environment. We'll see how infants begin to develop as social beings, moving from interactions with their parents to relations with other adults and children.

Above all, we'll marvel at the rate of infants' progress, and we will get a preview of the ways in which characteristics that date from infancy continue to influence the individual into adulthood. As we proceed, keep in mind how the seeds of our futures appear in our earliest beginnings.

Module 3.1 *Physical Development* in Infancy

LO 3.1 Describe how the human body develops in the first 2 years of life, including the four principles that govern its growth.

LO 3.2 Describe how the nervous system and brain develop in the first 2 years of life, and explain how the environment affects such development.

LO 3.3 Explain the body rhythms and states that govern an infant's behavior.

LO 3.4 Explain how the reflexes that infants are born with both protect them and help them adapt to their surroundings.

LO 3.5 Identify the milestones of gross motor and fine motor skill development in infancy.

LO 3.6 Summarize the role of nutrition in the physical development of infants, including the benefits of breastfeeding.

LO 3.7 Describe the sensory capabilities of infants.

LO 3.8 Summarize the multimodal approach to perception.

Module 3.2 *Cognitive Development* in Infancy

LO 3.9 Summarize the fundamental features of Piaget's theory of cognitive development, and describe the sensorimotor stage.

LO 3.10 Summarize the arguments both in support of and critical of Piaget's theory of cognitive development.

LO 3.11 Describe how information processing approaches explain cognitive development in infants, and summarize the memory capabilities of infants in the first 2 years of life.

LO 3.12 Explain how infant intelligence is measured using information processing approaches.

LO 3.13 Outline the processes by which children learn to use language.

LO 3.14 Differentiate the major theories of language development, and describe how children influence adults' language.

Module 3.3 *Social and Personality Development* in Infancy

LO 3.15 Discuss how children express and experience emotions in the first 2 years of life, and summarize the development of social referencing.

LO 3.16 Describe the sense of self that children possess in the first 2 years of life, including the development of a theory of mind.

LO 3.17 Explain attachment in infancy, how it affects a person's future social competence, and the roles that caregivers play in infants' social development.

LO 3.18 Discuss the development of peer relationships in infancy.

LO 3.19 Describe individual differences that distinguish an infant's personality and the roles that temperament and gender play.

LO 3.20 Describe 21st-century families and their consequences for children, including the impact of nonparental child care on infants.

Module 3.1

Physical Development in Infancy

Dreaming of Sleep

Liz and Seth Kaufman are so exhausted they have a hard time staying awake through dinner. The problem? Their 3-month-old son, Evan, who showed no signs of adopting normal patterns of eating and sleeping any time soon. "I thought babies were these big sleep fanatics, but Evan takes little cat naps of an hour throughout the night, and then stays awake all day," Liz says. "I'm running out of ways to entertain him because all I want to do is sleep."

Evan's feeding schedule is hard on Liz, too. "He wants to nurse every hour for 5 hours in a row, which makes it hard to keep up my milk supply. Then he goes another 5 hours not wanting to nurse, and I'm positively, painfully engorged." Seth tries to help out, walking at night with Evan when he won't sleep, offering him a bottle of Liz's expressed milk at 3 a.m. "But sometimes he just refuses the bottle," Seth says. "Only Mommy will do."

The pediatrician has assured the Kaufmans that their son is healthy and blossoming. "We're pretty sure Evan will come out of this just fine," Liz says. "It's us we're wondering about."

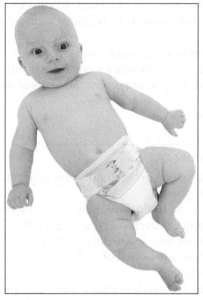

BananaStock/Getty Images

Evan's parents can relax. Their son will settle down. Modern parents frequently scrutinize their children's behavior, worrying over what they see as potential abnormalities (for the record, the range of ages at which developmentally healthy children sleep through the night is sizeable) and celebrating important milestones. In this module, we consider the nature of the astonishing physical development that occurs during infancy, a period that starts at birth and continues until the second birthday. We begin by discussing the pace of growth during infancy, noting obvious changes in height and weight as well as less apparent changes in the nervous system. We also consider how infants quickly develop increasingly stable patterns in such basic activities as sleeping, eating, and attending to the world.

Our discussion then turns to infants' thrilling gains in motor development as skills emerge that eventually will allow an infant to roll over, take the first step, and pick up a cookie crumb from the floor—skills that ultimately form the basis of later, even more complex behaviors. We start with basic, genetically determined reflexes and consider how even these may be modified through experience. We also discuss the nature and timing of the development of particular physical skills, look at whether their emergence can be sped up, and consider the importance of early nutrition to their development.

Finally, we explore how infants' senses develop. We investigate how sensory systems like hearing and vision operate, and how infants sort through the raw data from their sense organs and transform it into meaningful information.

Figure 3-1 Height and Weight Growth

Although the greatest increase in height and weight occurs during the first year of life, children continue to grow throughout infancy and toddlerhood.

SOURCE: Based on Cratty, B. (1979). Perceptual and motor development in infants and children (2nd ed.). Englewood Cliffs, NJ: Prentice-Hall.

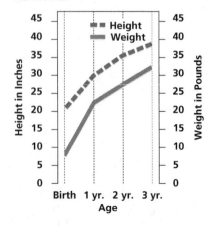

Growth and Stability

The average newborn weighs slightly more than 7 pounds, which is less than the weight of the average Thanksgiving turkey. Its length is about 20 inches, shorter than a loaf of French bread. It is helpless; if left to fend for itself, it could not survive.

Yet after just a few years, the story is different. Babies grow much larger, they become mobile, and they become increasingly independent. How does this growth happen? We can answer this question first by describing the changes in weight and height that occur over the first 2 years of life, and then by examining some of the principles that underlie and direct that growth.

Physical Growth: The Rapid Advances of Infancy

LO 3.1 **Describe how the human body develops in the first 2 years of life, including the four principles that govern its growth.**

Infants grow at a rapid pace over the first 2 years of their lives (see Figure 3-1). By the age of 5 months, the average infant's birthweight has doubled to around 15 pounds. By the first birthday, the baby's weight has tripled to about 22 pounds. Although the pace of weight gain slows during the second year, it still continues to increase. By the end of his or her second year, the average child weighs around four times as much as he or she did at birth. Of course, there is a good deal of variation among infants. Height and weight measurements, which are taken regularly during physical examinations in a baby's first year, provide a way to spot problems in development.

The weight gains of infancy are matched by increased length. By the end of the first year, the typical baby grows almost a foot and is about 30 inches tall. By their second birthdays, children average a height of 3 feet.

Not all parts of an infant's body grow at the same rate. For instance, at birth the head accounts for one-quarter of the newborn's entire body size. During the first 2 years of life, the rest of the body begins to catch up. By age 2, the baby's head is only one-fifth of its body length, and by adulthood it is only one-eighth (see Figure 3-2).

There also are gender and ethnic differences in weight and length. Girls generally are slightly shorter and weigh slightly less than boys, and these differences remain throughout childhood (and, as we will see later in the book, the disparities become considerably greater during adolescence). Furthermore, Asian infants tend to be slightly smaller than North American Caucasian infants, and African American infants tend to be slightly bigger than North American Caucasian infants.

The disproportionately large size of infants' heads at birth is an example of one of four major principles (summarized in Table 3-1) that govern growth.

Figure 3-2 Decreasing Proportions

At birth, the head represents one-quarter of the neonate's body. By adulthood, the head is only one-eighth the size of the body. Why is the neonate's head so large?

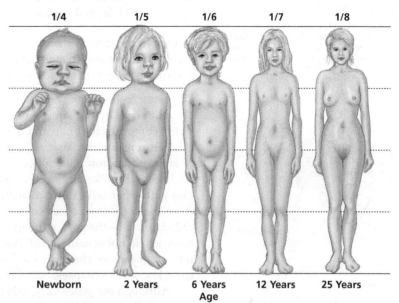

| 1/4 | 1/5 | 1/6 | 1/7 | 1/8 |

| Newborn | 2 Years | 6 Years Age | 12 Years | 25 Years |

- The **cephalocaudal principle** states that growth follows a direction and pattern that begins with the head and upper body parts and then proceeds to the rest of the body. The cephalocaudal growth principle means that we develop visual abilities (located in the head) well before we master the ability to walk (closer to the end of the body).

- The **proximodistal principle** states that development proceeds from the center of the body outward. The proximodistal principle means that the trunk of the body grows before the extremities of the arms and legs. Furthermore, the development of the ability to use various parts of the body also follows the proximodistal principle. For instance, effective use of the arms precedes the ability to use the hands.

- The **principle of hierarchical integration** states that simple skills typically develop separately and independently, but that these simple skills are integrated into more complex ones. Thus, the relatively complex skill of grasping something in the hand cannot be mastered until the developing infant learns how to control—and integrate—the movements of the individual fingers.

- Finally, the **principle of the independence of systems** suggests that different body systems grow at different rates. For instance, the patterns of growth for body size, the nervous system, and sexual maturation are quite different.

cephalocaudal principle

the principle that growth follows a pattern that begins with the head and upper body parts and then proceeds down to the rest of the body

proximodistal principle

the principle that development proceeds from the center of the body outward

principle of hierarchical integration

the principle that simple skills typically develop separately and independently but are later integrated into more complex skills

principle of the independence of systems

the principle that different body systems grow at different rates

Table 3-1 The Major Principles Governing Growth

Cephalocaudal Principle	Proximodistal Principle	Principle of Hierarchical Integration	Principle of the Independence of Systems
Growth follows a pattern that begins with the head and upper body parts and then proceeds to the rest of the body. Based on Greek and Latin roots meaning "head-to-tail."	Development proceeds from the center of the body outward. Based on the Latin words for "near" and "far."	Simple skills typically develop separately and independently. Later they are integrated into more complex skills.	Different body systems grow at different rates.

Figure 3-3 The Neuron

The basic element of the nervous system, the neuron has a number of components.

SOURCE: Based on Van der Graaff, J., Branje, S., De Wied, M., Hawk, S., Van Lier, P., & Meeus, W. (2014). Perspective taking and empathic concern in adolescence: Gender differences in developmental changes. Developmental Psychology, 50, 881–888.

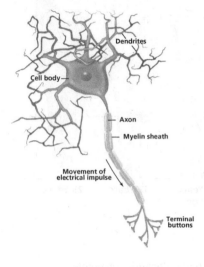

neuron

the basic nerve cell of the nervous system

synapse

the gap at the connection between neurons, through which neurons chemically communicate with one another

The Nervous System and Brain: The Foundations of Development

LO 3.2   Describe how the nervous system and brain develop in the first 2 years of life, and explain how the environment affects such development.

When Rina was born, she was the first baby among her parents' circle of friends. These young adults marveled at the infant, oohing and aahing at every sneeze and smile and whimper, trying to guess at their meaning.

Whatever feelings, movements, and thoughts Rina was experiencing, they were all brought about by the same complex network: the infant's nervous system. The *nervous system* comprises the brain and the nerves that extend throughout the body.

Neurons are the basic cells of the nervous system. Figure 3-3 shows the structure of an adult neuron. Like all cells in the body, neurons have a cell body containing a nucleus. But unlike other cells, neurons have a distinctive ability: They can communicate with other cells, using a cluster of fibers called *dendrites* at one end. Dendrites receive messages from other cells. At their opposite end, neurons have a long extension called an *axon*—the part of the neuron that carries messages destined for other neurons. Neurons do not actually touch one another. Rather, they communicate with other neurons by means of chemical messengers, *neurotransmitters*, that travel across the small gaps, known as **synapses**, between neurons.

Although estimates vary, infants are born with between 100 billion and 200 billion neurons. To reach this number, neurons multiply at an amazing rate before birth. In fact, at some points in prenatal development, cell division creates some 250,000 additional neurons every minute.

At birth, most neurons in an infant's brain have relatively few connections to other neurons. During the first 2 years of life, however, a baby's brain will establish billions of new connections between neurons. Furthermore, the network of neurons becomes increasingly complex, as illustrated in Figure 3-4. The intricacy of neural connections continues to increase throughout life. In fact, in adulthood a single neuron is likely to have a minimum of 5,000 connections to other neurons or other body parts.

SYNAPTIC PRUNING Babies are actually born with many more neurons than they need. In addition, although synapses are formed throughout life, based on our

Figure 3-4 Neuron Networks

Over the first 2 years of life, networks of neurons become increasingly complex and interconnected. Why are these connections important?

SOURCE: Based on Conel, J. L. (1939, 1975). The postnatal development of the human cerebral cortex (Vols. I–VIII). Cambridge, MA: Harvard University Press.

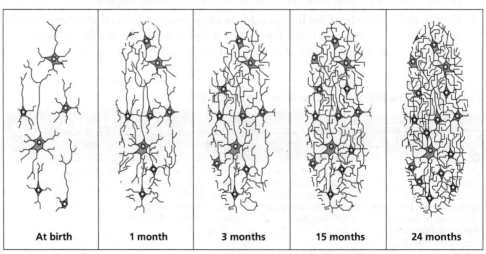

| At birth | 1 month | 3 months | 15 months | 24 months |

changing experiences, the billions of new synapses infants form during the first 2 years are more numerous than necessary. What happens to the extra neurons and synaptic connections?

Like a farmer who, to strengthen the vitality of a fruit tree, prunes away unnecessary branches, brain development enhances certain capabilities in part by a "pruning down" of unnecessary neurons. As infants' experience of the world increases, neurons that do not become interconnected with other neurons become unnecessary. They eventually die out, increasing the efficiency of the nervous system.

As unnecessary neurons are being reduced, connections between remaining neurons are expanded or eliminated as a result of their use or disuse during the baby's experiences. If a baby's experiences do not stimulate certain nerve connections, these, like unused neurons, are eliminated—a process called **synaptic pruning**. The result of synaptic pruning is to allow established neurons to build more elaborate communication networks with other neurons. Unlike most other aspects of growth, then, the development of the nervous system proceeds most effectively through the loss of cells (Schafer & Stevens, 2013; Zong et al., 2015; Athanasiu et al., 2017).

After birth, neurons continue to increase in size. In addition to growth in dendrites, the axons of neurons become coated with **myelin**, a fatty substance that, like the insulation on an electric wire, provides protection and speeds the transmission of nerve impulses. So, even though many neurons are lost, the increasing size and complexity of the remaining ones contribute to impressive brain growth. A baby's brain triples its weight during his or her first 2 years of life, and it reaches more than three-quarters of its adult weight and size by age 2.

As the neurons grow, they also reposition themselves, becoming arranged by function. Some move into the **cerebral cortex**, the upper layer of the brain, whereas others move to *subcortical levels*, which are below the cerebral cortex. The subcortical levels, which regulate such fundamental activities as breathing and heart rate, are the most fully developed at birth. As time passes, however, the cells in the cerebral cortex, which are responsible for higher-order processes such as thinking and reasoning, become more developed and interconnected.

Although the brain is protected by the bones of the skull, it is highly sensitive to some forms of injury. One particularly devastating injury comes from a form of child abuse called *shaken baby syndrome*, in which an infant is shaken by a caretaker, usually out of frustration or anger because of a baby's crying. Shaking can lead the brain to rotate within the skull, causing blood vessels to tear and destroying the intricate connections between neurons, producing severe medical problems, long-term physical and learning disabilities, and often death.

Estimates of the incidence of shaken baby syndrome range from 1,000 to 3,000 cases a year in the United States. One-quarter of babies who are shaken ultimately die, and 80 percent of survivors have permanent brain damage (Narang & Clarke, 2014; Grinkevičiūtė et al., 2016; Centers for Disease Control and Prevention, 2017a; also see Figure 3-5).

ENVIRONMENTAL INFLUENCES ON BRAIN DEVELOPMENT   Brain development, much of which unfolds automatically because of genetically predetermined patterns, is also strongly susceptible to environmental influences. In fact, the brain's **plasticity**, the degree to which a developing structure or behavior is modifiable as a result of experience, is relatively great.

The brain's plasticity is greatest during the first several years of life. Because many areas of the brain are not yet devoted to specific tasks, if one area is injured, other areas can take over for the injured area. For example, preterm infants who suffer damage due to bleeding in the brain can recover almost entirely by age 2. In addition, even when particular parts of infants' brains are injured due to accidents, other parts of the brain can compensate, aiding in recovery (Guzzetta et al., 2013; Rocha-Ferreira & Hristova, 2016).

Similarly, infants who suffer mild to moderate brain injuries typically are less affected and recover more fully than adults who have experienced similar types of brain

synaptic pruning
the elimination of neurons as the result of nonuse or lack of stimulation

myelin
protective insulation that surrounds parts of neurons—which speeds the transmission of electrical impulses along brain cells

cerebral cortex
the upper layer of the brain

plasticity
the degree to which a developing structure or behavior is modifiable as a result of experience

Figure 3-5 Shaken Baby
This computed tomography (CT) scan shows severe brain injury in an infant suspected of being abused by caretaker shaking.
SOURCE: Matlung et al., 2011.

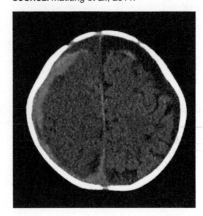

injuries. Infants' brains thus show a high degree of plasticity (Stiles, 2012; Inguaggiato, Sgandurra, & Cionci, 2017; Damashek et al., 2018).

Infants' sensory experiences affect both the size of individual neurons and the structure of their interconnections. Consequently, compared with those brought up in more enriched environments, infants raised in severely restricted settings are likely to show differences in brain structure and weight (Cirulli, Berry, & Alleva, 2003; Couperus & Nelson, 2006; Glaser, 2012).

Furthermore, researchers have found that there are certain sensitive periods during the course of development. A **sensitive period** is a specific but limited time, usually early in children's lives, during which they are particularly susceptible to environmental influences or stimulation. A sensitive period may be associated with a behavior—such as the development of vision—or with the development of a structure of the body, such as the configuration of the brain (Uylings, 2006; Hartley & Lee, 2015).

The existence of sensitive periods raises several important issues. For one thing, it suggests that unless an infant receives a certain level of early environmental stimulation during a sensitive period, the infant may suffer damage or fail to develop capabilities that can never be fully remedied. If this is true, providing successful later intervention for such children may prove to be particularly challenging (Zeanah, 2009; Steele et al., 2013).

The opposite question also arises: Does an unusually high level of stimulation during sensitive periods produce developmental gains beyond what a more commonplace level of stimulation would provide?

Such questions have no simple answers. Determining how unusually impoverished or enriched environments affect later development is one of the major questions addressed by developmental researchers as they try to find ways to maximize opportunities for developing children.

In the meantime, developmentalists suggest that there are many simple ways parents and caregivers can provide a stimulating environment that will encourage healthy brain growth. Cuddling, talking and singing to, and playing with babies all help enrich their environment (Garlick, 2003).

sensitive period
a point in development when organisms are particularly susceptible to certain kinds of stimuli in their environments, but the absence of those stimuli does not always produce irreversible consequences

---

> **From a social worker's perspective:** What are some cultural or subcultural influences that might affect parents' childrearing practices?

Integrating the Bodily Systems: The Life Cycles of Infancy

LO 3.3   **Explain the body rhythms and states that govern an infant's behavior.**

If you happen to overhear new parents discuss their newborns, chances are one or several bodily functions will be the subject. In the first days of life, infants' body rhythms—waking, eating, sleeping, and eliminating waste—govern infants' behavior, often at seemingly random times.

These most basic activities are controlled by a variety of bodily systems. Although each of these individual behavioral patterns probably is functioning quite effectively, it takes some time and effort for infants to integrate the separate behaviors. In fact, one of the neonate's major missions is to make its individual behaviors work in harmony, helping it, for example, to sleep through the night (Waterhouse & DeCoursey, 2004).

rhythms
repetitive, cyclical patterns of behavior

RHYTHMS AND STATES   One of the most important ways that behavior becomes integrated is through the development of various **rhythms**, which are repetitive, cyclical patterns of behavior. Some rhythms are immediately obvious, such as the change from wakefulness to sleep. Others are subtler, but still easily noticeable, such as breathing and sucking patterns. Still other rhythms may require careful observation to be noticed. For instance, newborns may go through periods in which they jerk their legs in a regular pattern every minute or so. Although some of these rhythms are apparent

Table 3-2 Primary Behavioral States

States	Characteristics	Percentage of Time When Alone in State
Awake States		
Alert	Attentive or scanning, infants' eyes are open, bright, and shining.	6.7
Nonalert waking	Eyes are usually open, but dull and unfocused. Varied, but typically high motor activity.	2.8
Fuss	Fussing is continuous or intermittent, at low levels.	1.8
Cry	Intense vocalizations occurring singly or in succession.	1.7
Transition States Between Sleep and Waking		
Drowse	Infant's eyes are heavy lidded, but opening and closing slowly. Low level of motor activity.	4.4
Daze	Open, but glassy and immobile eyes. State occurs between episodes of alert and drowse. Low level of activity.	1.0
Sleep–wake transition	Behaviors of both wakefulness and sleep are evident. Generalized motor activity; eyes may be closed, or they open and close rapidly. State occurs when baby is awakening.	1.3
Sleep States		
Active sleep	Eyes closed; uneven respiration; intermittent rapid eye movements. Other behaviors: smiles, frowns, grimaces, mouthing, sucking, sighs, and sigh sobs.	50.3
Quiet sleep	Eyes are closed, and respiration is slow and regular. Motor activity limited to occasional startles, sighs, sobs, or rhythmic mouthing.	28.1
Transitional Sleep States		
Active-quiet transition sleep	During this state, which occurs between periods of active sleep and quiet sleep, the eyes are closed, and there is little motor activity. Infant shows mixed behavioral signs of active sleep and quiet sleep.	1.9

SOURCE: Based on Thoman & Whitney, 1990.

just after birth, others emerge slowly over the first year as the neurons of the nervous system become increasingly integrated (Thelen & Bates, 2003).

One of the major body rhythms is that of an infant's **state**, the degree of awareness he or she displays to both internal and external stimulation. As can be seen in Table 3-2, such states include various levels of wakeful behaviors, such as alertness, fussing, and crying, as well as different levels of sleep. Each change in state brings about an alteration in the amount of stimulation required to get infants' attention (Diambra & Menna-Barreto, 2004; Anzman-Frasca et al., 2013).

state

the degree of awareness an infant displays to both internal and external stimulation

SLEEP: PERCHANCE TO DREAM?   At the beginning of infancy, the major state that occupies a baby's time is sleep—much to the relief of exhausted parents, who often regard sleep as a welcome respite from caregiving responsibilities. On average, newborn infants sleep some 16 to 17 hours a day. However, there are wide variations. Some sleep more than 20 hours, and others sleep as little as 10 hours a day (Tikotzky & Sadeh, 2009; de Graag et al., 2012; Korotchikov et al., 2016; Hanafin, 2018).

Infants sleep a lot, but you shouldn't wish to "sleep like a baby." The sleep of infants comes in fits and starts. Rather than covering one long stretch, sleep initially comes in spurts of around 2 hours, followed by periods of wakefulness. Because of this, infants—and their sleep-deprived parents—are "out of sync" with the rest of the world, for whom sleep comes at night and wakefulness during the day (Burnham et al., 2002; Blomqvist et al., 2017).

Infants sleep in spurts, often making them out of sync with the rest of the world.

Most babies do not sleep through the night for several months. Parents' sleep is interrupted, sometimes several times a night, by infants' cries for food and physical contact.

Luckily for their parents, infants gradually settle into a more adultlike pattern. After a week, babies sleep a bit more at night and are awake for slightly longer periods during the day. Typically, by the age of 16 weeks, infants begin to sleep as much as 6 continuous hours at night, and daytime sleep falls into regular naplike patterns. Most infants sleep through the night by the end of the first year, and the total amount of sleep they need each day is down to about 15 hours (Mao et al., 2004; Magee, Gordon, & Caputi, 2014).

Hidden beneath the supposedly tranquil sleep of infants is another cyclic pattern. During periods of sleep, infants' heart rates increase and become irregular, their blood pressure rises, and they begin to breathe more rapidly. Sometimes, although not always, their closed eyes begin to move in a back-and-forth pattern, as if they were viewing an action-packed scene. This period of active sleep is similar, although not identical, to the **rapid eye movement (REM) sleep** that is found in older children and adults and is associated with dreaming (Blumberg et al., 2013; Spiess et al., 2018).

At first, this active, REM-like sleep takes up around one-half of an infant's sleep, compared with just 20 percent of an adult's sleep (see Figure 3-6). However, the quantity of active sleep quickly declines, and by the age of 6 months, amounts to just one-third of total sleep time (Burnham et al., 2002; Staunton, 2005; Ferri, Novelli, & Bruni, 2017).

The appearance of active sleep periods that are similar to REM sleep in adults raises the intriguing question of whether infants dream during those periods. No one knows the answer, although it seems unlikely. First of all, young infants do not have much to dream about, given their relatively limited experiences. Furthermore, the brain waves of sleeping infants appear to be qualitatively different from those of adults who are dreaming. It is not until the baby reaches 3 or 4 months of age that the wave patterns become similar to those of dreaming adults, suggesting that young infants are not dreaming during active sleep—or at least are not doing so in the same way as adults do (Zampi et al., 2002).

rapid eye movement (REM) sleep
the period of sleep that is found in older children and adults and is associated with dreaming

Figure 3-6 REM Sleep Through the Life Span

As we age, the proportion of REM sleep increases as the proportion of non-REM sleep declines. In addition, the total amount of sleep falls as we get older.

SOURCE: Based on Roffwarg, Muzio, & Dement, 1966.

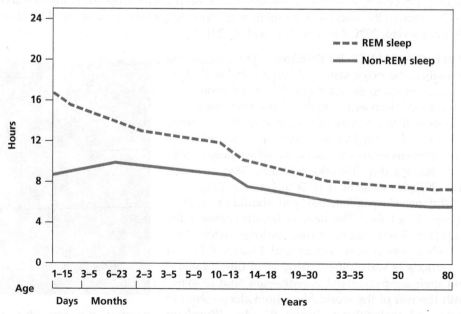

Then what is the function of REM sleep in infants? Although we don't know for certain, some researchers think it provides a means for the brain to stimulate itself—a process called *autostimulation* (Roffwarg, Muzio, & Dement, 1966). Stimulation of the nervous system would be particularly important in infants, who spend so much time sleeping and relatively little in alert states.

Infants' sleep cycles seem largely preprogrammed by genetic factors, but environmental influences also play a part. For instance, cultural practices affect infants' sleep patterns. For example, among the Kipsigis of Africa, infants sleep with their mothers at night, a practice known as *co-sleeping* that is typical in most non-Western cultures (Super & Harkness, 1982). Infants are allowed to nurse whenever they wake. In the daytime, they accompany their mothers during daily chores, often napping while strapped to their mothers' backs. Because they are often out and on the go, Kipsigis infants do not sleep through the night until much later than babies in Western societies, and for the first 8 months of life, they seldom sleep longer than 3 hours at a stretch.

In comparison, 8-month-old infants in the United States may sleep as long as 8 hours at a time. One reason for these cultural differences may relate to the use of artificial light and shades used to manage natural light that varies across cultures. (Gerard, Harris, & Thach, 2002; Sundnes & Andenaes, 2016; Sauvet et al., 2018).

Wherever their infants sleep, one fact is clear: Across a variety of cultures, mothers report experiencing a variety of sleep disturbances. Clearly, caring for an infant may be inconsistent with getting a good night's rest (Mindell et al., 2013; Mindell, Leichman, & Walters, 2017).

Where infants sleep has been a source of controversy. While earlier views held that it was better for infants to sleep in a room separate from their parents, at least in Western cultures, the American Academy of Pediatrics issued new guidelines in 2016 stating that children should sleep in the same room—but *not* the same bed—as their parents for the first 6 months of their lives, and preferably for a full year. As we consider next, these guidelines were designed to decrease the number of infants who experience SIDS, sudden infant death syndrome (Moon, 2016).

SIDS: THE UNANTICIPATED KILLER For a tiny percentage of infants, the rhythm of sleep is interrupted by a deadly affliction: sudden infant death syndrome, or SIDS. **Sudden infant death syndrome (SIDS)** is a disorder in which seemingly healthy infants die in their sleep. Put to bed for a nap or for the night, an infant simply never wakes up.

sudden infant death syndrome (SIDS)
the unexplained death of a seemingly healthy baby

SIDS strikes about 2,500 infants in the United States each year. Although it seems to occur when the normal patterns of breathing during sleep are interrupted, scientists have been unable to discover why that might happen. It is clear that infants don't smother or choke; they die a peaceful death, simply ceasing to breathe.

Although no reliable means for preventing the syndrome has been found, the American Academy of Pediatrics now suggests that babies sleep on their backs rather than on their sides or stomachs—called the *back-to-sleep* guideline. In addition, they suggest that parents consider giving their babies a pacifier during naps and bedtime. Also, as we discussed earlier, they suggest that infants should sleep in their parents' room for at least the first 6 months after birth (Task Force on Sudden Infant Death Syndrome, 2011; Ball & Volpe, 2013; Jonas, 2016; Moon, 2016).

The number of deaths from SIDS has decreased significantly since these guidelines were developed (see Figure 3-7). Still, SIDS is the leading cause of death in children under the age of 1 year (Daley, 2004; Blair et al., 2006).

Many hypotheses have been suggested to explain why infants die from SIDS. These include problems such as undiagnosed sleep disorders, suffocation, nutritional deficiencies, problems with reflexes, brainstem abnormalities, and undiagnosed illness. Still, the actual cause of SIDS remains elusive (Mitchell, 2009; Duncan et al., 2010; Lavezzi, Corna, & Matturri, 2013; Freyne et al., 2014; Macchione et al., 2018).

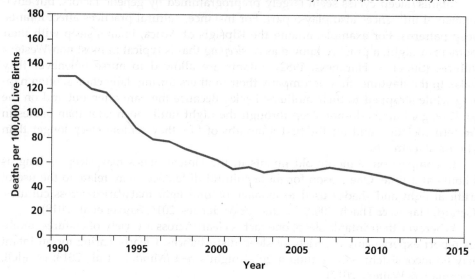

Figure 3-7 Declining Rates of SIDS

In the United States, SIDS rates have dropped dramatically as parents have become more informed and put babies to sleep on their backs instead of their stomachs.

SOURCE: American SIDS Institute, based on data from the Centers for Disease Control and Prevention and the National Center for Health Statistics, 2019, National Vital Statistics System, Compressed Mortality File.

Motor Development

Suppose you were hired by a genetic engineering firm to redesign newborns and were charged with replacing the current version with a new, more mobile one. The first change you'd probably consider in carrying out this (luckily fictitious) job would be in the conformation and composition of the baby's body.

The shape and proportions of newborn babies are simply not conducive to easy mobility. Their heads are so large and heavy that young infants lack the strength to raise them. Because their limbs are short in relation to the rest of the body, their movements are further impeded. Furthermore, their bodies are mainly fat, with a limited amount of muscle; the result is that they lack strength.

Fortunately, it doesn't take too long before infants begin to develop a remarkable amount of mobility. In fact, even at birth they have an extensive repertoire of behavioral possibilities brought about by innate reflexes, and their range of motor skills grows rapidly during the first 2 years of life.

Reflexes: Our Inborn Physical Skills

LO 3.4 **Explain how the reflexes that infants are born with both protect them and help them adapt to their surroundings.**

> When her father pressed 3-day-old Christina's palm with his finger, she responded by tightly winding her small fist around his finger and grasping it. When he moved his finger upward, she held on so tightly that it seemed he might be able to lift her completely off her crib floor.

THE BASIC REFLEXES In fact, her father was right: Christina probably could have been lifted in this way. The reason for her resolute grip was activation of one of the dozens of reflexes with which infants are born. **Reflexes** are unlearned, organized, involuntary responses that occur automatically in the presence of certain stimuli. Newborns enter the world with a collection of reflexive behavioral patterns that help them adapt to their new surroundings and serve to protect them.

As we can see from the list of reflexes in Table 3-3, many reflexes clearly represent behavior that has survival value, helping to ensure the well-being of infants. For instance, the *swimming reflex* makes a baby who is lying face down in a body of water

reflexes
unlearned, organized involuntary responses that occur automatically in the presence of certain stimuli

Table 3-3 Some Basic Reflexes in Infants

Reflex	Approximate Age of Disappearance	Description	Possible Function
Rooting reflex	3 weeks	Neonate's tendency to turn its head toward things that touch its cheek.	Food intake
Stepping reflex	2 months	Movement of legs when held upright with feet touching the floor.	Prepares infants for independent locomotion
Swimming reflex	4–6 months	Infant's tendency to paddle and kick in a sort of swimming motion when lying face down in a body of water.	Avoidance of danger
Moro reflex	6 months	Activated when support for the neck and head is suddenly removed. The arms of the infant are thrust outward and then appear to grasp onto something.	Similar to primate's protection from falling
Babinski reflex	8–12 months	An infant fans out its toes in response to a stroke on the outside of its foot.	Unknown
Startle reflex	Remains in different form	An infant, in response to a sudden noise, flings out its arms, arches its back, and spreads its fingers.	Protection
Eye-blink reflex	Remains	Rapid shutting and opening of eye on exposure to direct light.	Protection of eye from direct light
Sucking reflex	Remains	Infant's tendency to suck at things that touch its lips.	Food intake
Gag reflex	Remains	An infant's reflex to clear its throat.	Prevents choking

paddle and kick in a sort of swimming motion. The obvious consequence of such behavior is to help the baby move from danger and survive until a caregiver can come to its rescue. Similarly, the *eye-blink reflex* seems designed to protect the eye from too much direct light, which might damage the retina.

Given the protective value of many reflexes, it might seem beneficial for them to remain with us for our entire lives. In fact, some do: The eye-blink reflex remains functional throughout the full life span. In contrast, quite a few reflexes, such as the swimming reflex, disappear after a few months. Why should this be the case?

Researchers who focus on evolutionary explanations of development attribute the gradual disappearance of reflexes to the increase in voluntary control over behavior that occurs as infants become more able to control their muscles. In addition, it may be that reflexes form the foundation for future, more complex behaviors. As these more intricate behaviors become well learned, they encompass the previous reflexes. Finally, it is possible that reflexes stimulate parts of the brain responsible for more complex behaviors, helping them develop (Lipsitt, 2003).

ETHNIC AND CULTURAL DIFFERENCES AND SIMILARITIES IN REFLEXES
Although reflexes are, by definition, genetically determined and universal throughout all infants, there are actually some cultural variations in the ways they are displayed. For instance, consider the *Moro reflex* that is activated when support for the neck and head is suddenly removed. The Moro reflex consists of an infant's arms thrusting outward and then appearing to seek to grasp onto something. Most scientists feel that the Moro reflex represents a leftover response that we humans have inherited from our nonhuman ancestors. The Moro reflex is an extremely useful behavior for monkey babies, who travel about by clinging to their mothers' backs. If they lose their grip, they fall down unless they are able to grasp quickly onto their mother's fur—using a Moro-like reflex (Zafeiriou, 2004; Rousseau et al., 2017).

The Moro reflex is found in all humans, but it appears with significantly different vigor in different children. Some differences reflect cultural and ethnic variations (Freedman, 1979). For instance, Caucasian infants show a pronounced response to situations that produce the Moro reflex. Not only do they fling out their arms, but

(a)

(b)

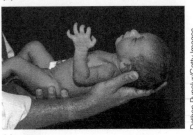

(c)

Infants showing (a) the grasping reflex, (b) the startle reflex, and (c) the Moro reflex.

they also cry and respond in a generally agitated manner. In contrast, Navajo babies react to the same situation much more calmly. Their arms do not flail out as much, and they cry only rarely.

Motor Development in Infancy: Landmarks of Physical Achievement

LO 3.5 **Identify the milestones of gross motor and fine motor skill development in infancy.**

Probably no physical changes are more obvious—and more eagerly anticipated—than the increasing array of motor skills that babies acquire during infancy. Most parents can remember their child's first steps with a sense of pride and awe at how quickly she or he changed from a helpless infant, unable even to roll over, into a person who could navigate quite effectively in the world.

GROSS MOTOR SKILLS Even though the motor skills of newborn infants are not terribly sophisticated, at least compared with attainments that will soon appear, young infants still are able to accomplish some kinds of movement. For instance, when placed on their stomachs, they wiggle their arms and legs and may try to lift their heavy heads. As their strength increases, they are able to push hard enough against the surface on which they are resting to propel their bodies in different directions. They often end up moving backward rather than forward, but by the age of 6 months they become rather accomplished at moving themselves in particular directions. These initial efforts are the forerunners of crawling, in which babies coordinate the motions of their arms and legs and propel themselves forward. Crawling appears typically between 8 and 10 months. (Figure 3-8 provides a summary of some of the milestones of normal motor development.)

Walking comes later. At around the age of 9 months, most infants are able to walk by supporting themselves on furniture, and half of all infants can walk well by the end of their first year of life.

Figure 3-8 Milestones of Motor Development

Fifty percent of children are able to perform each skill at the month indicated in the figure. However, the specific timing at which each skill appears varies widely. For example, one-quarter of children are able to walk well at 11.1 months; by 14.9 months, 90 percent of children are walking well. Is knowledge of such average benchmarks helpful or harmful to parents?

SOURCE: Based on Frankenburg, W. K., Dodds, J., Archer, P., Shapiro, H., & Bresnick, B. (1992). The Denver II: A major revision and restandardization of the Denver Developmental Screening Test. Pediatrics, 89, 91–97.

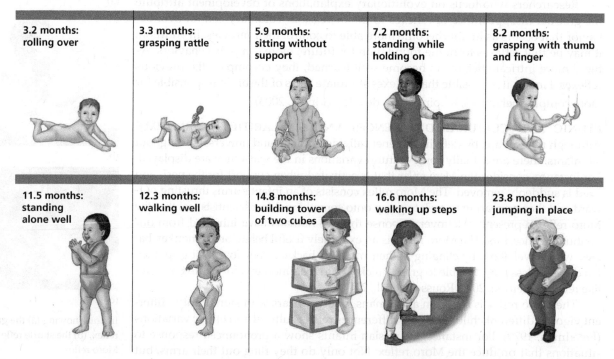

| 3.2 months: rolling over | 3.3 months: grasping rattle | 5.9 months: sitting without support | 7.2 months: standing while holding on | 8.2 months: grasping with thumb and finger |

| 11.5 months: standing alone well | 12.3 months: walking well | 14.8 months: building tower of two cubes | 16.6 months: walking up steps | 23.8 months: jumping in place |

Table 3-4 Milestones of Fine Motor Development

Age (months)	Skill
3	Opens hand
3	Holds rattle
8	Grasps with thumb and finger
11	Holds crayon
14	Builds a tower with two square objects
16	Places pegs into a board
24	Imitates lines on a piece of paper
33	Imitates a circle

At the same time infants are learning to move around, they are perfecting the ability to remain in a stationary sitting position. At first, babies cannot remain seated upright without support. But they quickly master this ability, and most are able to sit without support by the age of 6 months.

FINE MOTOR SKILLS As infants are perfecting their gross motor skills, such as sitting upright and walking, they are also making advances in their fine motor skills (see Table 3-4). For instance, by the age of 3 months, infants show some ability to coordinate the movements of their limbs.

Furthermore, although infants are born with a rudimentary ability to reach toward an object, this ability is neither sophisticated nor accurate, and it disappears around the age of 4 weeks. A different, more precise, form of reaching reappears at 4 months. It takes some time for infants to coordinate successful grasping after they reach out, but in fairly short order they are able to reach out and hold onto an object of interest (Foroud & Whishaw, 2012; Libertus, Joh, & Needham, 2016; Karl et al., 2018).

The sophistication of fine motor skills continues to grow. By the age of 11 months, infants are able to pick up off the ground objects as small as marbles—something caregivers need to be concerned about because the next place such objects often go is in the mouth. By the time they are 2 years old, children can carefully hold a cup, bring it to their lips, and take a drink without spilling a drop.

Grasping, like other motor advances, follows a sequential developmental pattern in which simple skills are combined into more sophisticated ones. For example, infants first begin picking things up with their whole hand. As they get older, they use a *pincer grasp*, where thumb and index finger meet to form a circle. The pincer grasp allows for considerably more precise motor control (Thoermer et al., 2013; Dionísio et al., 2015; Senna et al., 2017).

DEVELOPMENTAL NORMS: COMPARING THE INDIVIDUAL TO THE GROUP
Keep in mind that the timing of the milestones in motor development that we have been discussing is based on norms. **Norms** represent the average performance of a large sample of children of a given age. They permit comparisons between a particular child's performance on a particular behavior and the average performance of the children in the norm sample.

For instance, one of the most widely used techniques to determine infants' normative standing is the **Brazelton Neonatal Behavioral Assessment Scale (NBAS)**, a measure designed to determine infants' neurological and behavioral responses to their environment.

The NBAS provides a supplement to the traditional Apgar test that is given immediately following birth. Taking about 30 minutes to administer, the NBAS includes 27 separate categories of responses that constitute four general aspects of infants' behavior: interactions with others (such as alertness and cuddliness), motor behavior, physiological control (such as the ability to be soothed after being upset), and responses to stress (Canals et al., 2003; Ohta & Ohgi, 2013).

Although the norms provided by scales such as the NBAS are useful in making broad generalizations about the timing of various behaviors and skills, they must be

norms
the average performance of a large sample of children of a given age

Brazelton Neonatal Behavioral Assessment Scale (NBAS)
a measure designed to determine infants' neurological and behavioral responses to their environment

interpreted with caution. Because norms are averages, they mask substantial individual differences in the times when children attain various achievements.

Norms are useful only to the extent that they are based on data from a large, heterogeneous, culturally diverse sample of children. Unfortunately, many of the norms on which developmental researchers have traditionally relied have been based on groups of infants who are predominantly Caucasian and from the middle and upper socioeconomic strata (e.g., Gesell, 1946). The reason: Much of the research was conducted on college campuses, using the children of graduate students and faculty.

This limitation would not be critical if no differences existed in the timing of development in children from different cultural, racial, and social groups. But they do. For example, as a group, African American babies show more rapid motor development than Caucasian babies throughout infancy. Moreover, there are significant variations related to cultural factors, as we discuss in the *Cultural Dimensions* box (de Onis et al., 2007; Wu et al., 2008; Mendonça, Sargent, & Fetters, 2016).

Nutrition in Infancy: Fueling Motor Development

LO 3.6   Summarize the role of nutrition in the physical development of infants, including the benefits of breastfeeding.

> Rosa sighed as she sat down to nurse the baby—again. She had fed 4-week-old Juan about every hour today, and he still seemed hungry. Some days, it seemed like all she did was breastfeed her baby. "Well, he must be going through a growth spurt," she decided, as she settled into her favorite rocking chair and put the baby to her nipple.

The rapid physical growth that occurs during infancy is fueled by the nutrients that infants receive. Without proper nutrition, infants cannot reach their physical potential, and they may suffer cognitive and social consequences as well.

Although there are vast individual differences in what constitutes appropriate nutrition—infants differ in terms of growth rates, body composition, metabolism, and activity levels—some broad guidelines do hold. In general, infants should consume about 50 calories per day for each pound they weigh—an allotment that is twice the suggested caloric intake for adults (Skinner et al., 2004).

Typically, though, it's not necessary to count calories for infants. Most infants regulate their caloric intake quite effectively on their own. If they are allowed to consume as much as they seem to want, and are not pressured to eat more, they will do fine.

MALNUTRITION   *Malnutrition*, the condition of having an improper amount and balance of nutrients, produces several results, none of which are good. For instance, malnutrition is more common among children living in many developing countries than among children who live in more industrialized, affluent countries. Malnourished children in these countries begin to show a slower growth rate by the age of 6 months. By the time they reach the age of 2 years, their height and weight are only 95 percent the height and weight of children in more industrialized countries.

Children who have been chronically malnourished during infancy later score lower on IQ tests and tend to do less well in school. These effects may linger even after the children's diet has improved substantially (Ratanachu-Ek, 2003; Waber et al., 2014).

The problem of malnutrition is greatest in underdeveloped countries, where overall 10 percent of infants are severely malnourished. Undernutrition is a problem across the globe, and is particularly widespread in Asia and Africa. In some countries the problem is especially severe. For example, 25 percent of North Korean children are stunted from chronic malnutrition, and 4 percent are acutely malnourished (United Nations Children's Fund, World Health Organization, & World Bank Group, 2018).

Problems of malnourishment are not restricted to developing countries, however. In the United States, around 20 percent of children live in poverty, which puts them at risk for malnutrition. Overall, some 26 percent of families who have children 3 years old and younger live in poverty, and 6 percent of Americans live in extreme poverty, meaning their income is $10,000 a year or less. The poverty rates are even higher for black, Hispanic, and American Indian families (National Center for Children in Poverty, 2013; Koball & Jiang, 2018).

Cultural Dimensions

Motor Development Across Cultures

Among the Ache people, who live in the rain forest of South America, infants face an early life of physical restriction. Because the Ache lead a nomadic existence, living in a series of tiny camps in the rain forest, open space is at a premium. Consequently, for the first few years of life, infants spend nearly all their time in direct physical contact with their mothers. Even when they are not physically touching their mothers, they are permitted to venture no more than a few feet away.

Infants among the Kipsigis people, who live in a more open environment in rural Kenya, Africa, lead quite a different existence. Their lives are filled with activity and exercise. Parents seek to teach their children to sit up, stand, and walk from the earliest days of infancy. For example, young infants are placed in shallow holes in the ground designed to keep them in an upright position. Parents begin to teach their children to walk starting at the 8th week of life. Infants are held with their feet touching the ground, and they are pushed forward.

Clearly, infants in these two societies lead different lives (Super, 1976; Kaplan & Dove, 1987). But do the relative lack of early motor stimulation for Ache infants and the efforts of the Kipsigis to encourage motor development really make a difference?

The answer is both yes and no. It's yes, in that Ache infants tend to show delayed motor development, relative both to Kipsigis infants and to children raised in Western societies. Although their social abilities are no different, Ache children tend to begin walking at around 23 months, about a year later than the typical child in the United States. In contrast, Kipsigis children, who are encouraged in their motor development, learn to sit up and walk several weeks earlier, on average, than U.S. children.

In the long run, however, the differences between Ache, Kipsigis, and Western children disappear. By late childhood, about age 6, there is no evidence of differences in general, overall motor skills among Ache, Kipsigis, and Western children.

As we see with the Ache and Kipsigis babies, variations in the timing of motor skills seem to depend in part on parental expectations of what is the "appropriate" schedule for the emergence of specific skills. For instance, one study examined the motor skills of infants who lived in a single city in England, but whose mothers varied in ethnic origin. In the research, English, Jamaican, and Indian mothers' expectations were first assessed regarding several markers of their infants' motor skills. The Jamaican mothers expected their infants to sit and walk significantly earlier than did the English and Indian mothers, and the actual emergence of these activities was in line with their expectations. The source of the Jamaican infants' earlier mastery seemed to lie in the treatment of the children by their parents. For instance, Jamaican mothers gave their children practice in stepping quite early in infancy (Hopkins & Westra, 1990; Bornstein, 2012).

In sum, cultural factors help determine the time at which specific motor skills appear. Activities that are an intrinsic part of a culture are more apt to be purposely taught to infants in that culture, leading to the potential of their earlier emergence.

Cultural influences affect the rate of the development of motor skills.

Severe malnutrition during infancy may lead to several disorders. Malnutrition during the first year can produce *marasmus*, a disease in which infants stop growing. Marasmus, attributable to a severe deficiency in proteins and calories, causes the body to waste away and ultimately results in death. Older children are susceptible to *kwashiorkor*, a disease in which a child's stomach, limbs, and face swell with water. To a casual observer, it appears that a child with kwashiorkor is actually chubby. However, this is an illusion: The child's body is in fact struggling to make use of the few nutrients that are available (Douglass & McGadney-Douglass, 2008; Galler et al., 2010).

From an educator's perspective: Think of reasons why malnourishment, which slows physical growth, also harms IQ scores and school performance. How might malnourishment affect education in developing countries?

In some cases, infants who receive sufficient nutrition act as though they have been deprived of food. Looking as though they suffer from marasmus, they are underdeveloped, listless, and apathetic. The real cause, though, is emotional: They lack sufficient love

nonorganic failure to thrive
a disorder in which infants stop growing due to a lack of stimulation and attention as the result of inadequate parenting

and emotional support. In such cases, known as **nonorganic failure to thrive**, children stop growing not for biological reasons but because of a lack of stimulation and attention from their parents. Usually occurring by the age of 18 months, nonorganic failure to thrive can be reversed through intensive parent training or by placing children in a foster home where they can receive emotional support.

OBESITY It is clear that malnourishment during infancy has potentially disastrous consequences for an infant. Less clear, however, are the effects of *infant obesity*, defined as weight greater than 20 percent above the average for infants of a particular length. Although there is no clear association between obesity during infancy and obesity at age 16, some research suggests that overfeeding during infancy may lead to the creation of an excess of fat cells, which remain in the body throughout life and may predispose a person to be overweight. In fact, weight gains during infancy are associated with weight at age 6. Other research shows an association between obesity after age 6 and adult obesity, suggesting that obesity in babies ultimately may be found to be associated with adult weight problems. A clear link between overweight babies and overweight adults, however, has not yet been found (Murasko, 2015; Mallan et al., 2016; Munthali et al., 2017).

Although the evidence linking infant obesity to adult obesity is inconclusive, it's plain that the societal view that "a fat baby is a healthy baby" is not necessarily correct. Indeed, cultural myths about food clearly lead to overfeeding. But other factors are related to obesity in infants. For example, infants delivered via cesarean section are twice as likely to become obese as are infants born vaginally (Huh et al., 2011).

Parents should concentrate, then, on providing appropriate nutrition. But just what constitutes proper nutrition? Probably the biggest question revolves around whether infants should be breastfed or given a formula of commercially processed cow's milk with vitamin additives, as we consider next.

BREAST OR BOTTLE? Fifty years ago, if a mother asked her pediatrician whether breastfeeding or bottlefeeding was better, she would have received a simple and clear-cut answer: Bottle-feeding was the preferred method. Starting around the 1940s, the general belief among child-care experts was that breastfeeding was an obsolete method that put children unnecessarily at risk.

With bottle-feeding, the argument went, parents could keep track of the amount of milk their baby was receiving and could thereby ensure that the child was taking in sufficient nutrients. In contrast, mothers who breastfed their babies could never be certain just how much milk their infants were getting. Use of the bottle was also supposed to help mothers keep their feedings to a rigid schedule of one bottle every 4 hours, the recommended procedure at that time.

Today, however, a mother would get a different answer to the same question. Child-care authorities agree: For the first 12 months of life, there is no better food for an infant than breast milk. Breast milk not only contains all the nutrients necessary for growth, but it also seems to offer some degree of immunity to a variety of childhood diseases, such as respiratory illnesses, ear infections, diarrhea, and allergies. Breast milk is more easily digested than cow's milk or formula, and it is sterile, warm, and convenient for the mother to dispense. There is even some evidence that breast milk may enhance cognitive growth, leading to high adult intelligence (Duijts et al., 2010; Julvez et al., 2014; Rogers & Blissett, 2017).

Breastfeeding is not a cure-all for infant nutrition and health, and the millions of mothers who must use formula (either because they are physically unable to produce milk or because of social factors such as work schedules) should not be concerned that their children are suffering significant harm. (In fact, recent research suggests that infants fed enriched formula show better cognitive development than those using traditional formula.) But it does continue to be clear that the popular slogan used by groups advocating the use of breastfeeding is right on target: "Breast Is Best" (Sloan, Stewart, & Dunne, 2010; Ludlow et al., 2012; Luby et al., 2016).

INTRODUCING SOLID FOODS: WHEN AND WHAT? Although pediatricians agree that breast milk is the ideal initial food, at some point infants require more nutrients than breast milk alone can provide. Although the American Academy of Pediatrics and the American Academy of Family Physicians recommends exclusive breastfeeding for about 6 months, followed by continued breastfeeding for 1 year or longer, solid foods can begin to be introduced after 6 months (American Academy of Pediatrics, 2013).

Solid foods are introduced into an infant's diet gradually, one at a time, so the parent can become aware of preferences and allergies. Most often cereal comes first, followed by strained fruits. Vegetables and other foods typically are introduced next, although the order varies significantly from one infant to another.

The timing of *weaning*, the gradual cessation of breast- or bottle-feeding, varies greatly. In developed countries such as the United States, weaning frequently occurs as early as 3 or 4 months. However, some mothers continue breastfeeding for 2 or 3 years or beyond. The American Academy of Pediatrics recommends that infants be fed breast milk for the first 12 months, and longer if mutually desired by mother and infant (American Academy of Pediatrics, 2013; Lee, 2017).

The Development of the Senses

William James, one of the founding fathers of psychology, believed the world of infants is a "blooming, buzzing confusion" (James, 1890/1950). Was he right?

In this case, James's wisdom failed him. The newborn's sensory world does lack the clarity and stability that we can distinguish as adults, but day by day the world grows increasingly comprehensible as an infant's ability to sense and perceive the environment develops. In fact, babies appear to thrive in an environment enriched by pleasing sensations.

The processes that underlie infants' understanding of the world around them are sensation and perception. **Sensation** is the physical stimulation of the sense organs, and **perception** is the mental process of sorting out, interpreting, analyzing, and integrating stimuli from the sense organs and brain.

The study of infants' capabilities in the realm of sensation and perception challenges the ingenuity of investigators. As we'll see, researchers have developed a number of procedures for understanding sensation and perception in different realms.

sensation
the physical stimulation of the sense organs

perception
the sorting out, interpretation, analysis, and integration of stimuli involving the sense organs and brain

Experiencing the World: The Sensory Capabilities of Infants

LO 3.7   **Describe the sensory capabilities of infants.**

From the time of Lee Eng's birth, everyone who met him felt that he gazed at them intently. His eyes seemed to meet those of visitors. They seemed to bore deeply and knowingly into the faces of people who looked at him.

How good, in fact, was Lee's vision, and what, precisely, could he make out of his environment? Quite a bit, at least up close. And sight is just one of the senses through which Lee experienced the world in his first days after birth. As we'll see, newborns also have the ability to perceive sounds, smells, and tastes, and are sensitive to pain and touch.

VISUAL PERCEPTION   According to some estimates, a newborn's distance vision ranges from 20/200 to 20/600, which means that an infant can only see with accuracy visual material up to 20 feet that an adult with normal vision is able to see with similar accuracy from a distance of between 200 and 600 feet (Leat, Yadav, & Irving, 2009).

These figures indicate that an infant's distance vision is one-tenth to one-third that of the average adult's. This isn't so bad, actually: The vision of newborns provides the same degree of distance acuity as the uncorrected vision of many adults who wear eyeglasses or contact lenses. Furthermore, infants' distance vision grows increasingly acute. By 6 months of age, the average infant's vision is already 20/20—in other words, identical to that of adults (Cavallini et al., 2002; Corrow et al., 2012; Braun & Kavšek, 2018).

Although an infant's distant vision is 10 to 30 times poorer than the average adult's, the vision of newborns provides the same degree of distance acuity as the uncorrected vision of many adults who wear eyeglasses or contact lenses.

Figure 3-9 Visual Cliff

The "visual cliff" experiment examines the depth perception of infants. Most infants in the age range of 6 to 14 months cannot be coaxed to cross the cliff, apparently responding to the fact that the patterned area drops several feet.

Mark Richard/PhotoEdit

Figure 3-10 Preferring Complexity

In a classic experiment, researcher Robert Fantz found that 2- and 3-month-old infants preferred to look at more complex stimuli than simple ones.

SOURCE: Based on Fantz, 1961.

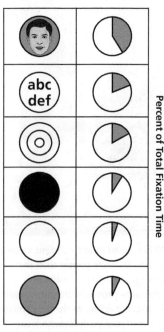

Percent of Total Fixation Time

Depth perception is a particularly useful ability, helping babies acknowledge heights and avoid falls. In a classic study, developmental psychologists Eleanor Gibson and Richard Walk (1960) placed infants on a sheet of heavy glass. A checkered pattern appeared under one-half of the glass sheet, making it seem that the infant was on a stable floor. However, in the middle of the glass sheet, the pattern dropped down several feet, forming an apparent "visual cliff." The question Gibson and Walk asked was whether infants would willingly crawl across the cliff when called by their mothers (see Figure 3-9).

The results were clear: Most of the infants in the study, who ranged in age from 6 to 14 months, could not be coaxed over the apparent cliff. Clearly most of them had already developed the ability to perceive depth by that age (Campos, Langer, & Krowitz, 1970; Kretch & Adolph, 2013; Adolph, Kretch, & LoBue, 2014).

Infants also show clear visual preferences—preferences that are present from birth. Given a choice, infants reliably prefer to look at stimuli that include patterns than to look at simpler stimuli (see Figure 3-10). How do we know? Developmental psychologist Robert Fantz (1963) created a classic test. He built a chamber in which babies could lie on their backs and see pairs of visual stimuli above them. Fantz could determine which of the stimuli the infants were looking at by observing the reflections of the stimuli in their eyes.

Fantz's work was the impetus for a great deal of research on the preferences of infants, most of which points to a critical conclusion: Infants are genetically preprogrammed to prefer particular kinds of stimuli. For instance, just minutes after birth they show preferences for certain colors, shapes, and configurations of various stimuli. They prefer curved over straight lines, three-dimensional figures to two-dimensional ones, and human faces to nonfaces. Such capabilities may be a reflection of the existence of highly specialized cells in the brain that react to stimuli of a particular pattern, orientation, shape, and direction of movement (Hubel & Wiesel, 2004; Gliga et al., 2009; Soska, Adolph, & Johnson, 2010).

However, genetics is not the sole determinant of infant visual preferences. Just a few hours after birth, infants have already learned to prefer their own mother's face to other faces. Similarly, between the ages of 6 and 9 months, infants become more adept at distinguishing between the faces of humans, while they become less able to distinguish faces of members of other species. They also distinguish between male and female faces. Such findings provide another clear piece of evidence of how heredity and environmental experiences are woven together to determine an infant's capabilities (Quinn et al., 2008; Otsuka et al., 2012; Bahrick et al., 2016).

AUDITORY PERCEPTION: THE WORLD OF SOUND What is it about a mother's lullaby that helps soothe crying babies, like Jenna, whom we discussed in the chapter opener? Some clues emerge when we look at the capabilities of infants in the realm of auditory sensation and perception.

Infants hear from the time of birth—and even before, as the ability to hear begins prenatally. Even in the womb, the fetus responds to sounds outside of its mother. Furthermore, infants are born with preferences for particular sound combinations (Trehub, 2003; Pundir et al., 2012; Missana, Altvater-Mackensen, & Grossmann, 2017).

Because they have had some practice in hearing before birth, it is not surprising that infants have reasonably good auditory perception after they are born. In fact, infants actually are more sensitive to certain very high and very low frequencies than adults—a sensitivity that seems to increase during the first 2 years of life. In contrast, infants are initially less sensitive than adults to middle-range frequencies. Eventually, however, their capabilities within the middle range improve (Fernald, 2001; Lee & Kisilevsky, 2014; Zhang et al., 2017).

In addition to the ability to detect sound, infants need several other abilities to hear effectively. For instance, *sound localization* permits us to pinpoint the direction from which a sound is emanating. Compared to adults, infants have a slight handicap in this task because effective sound localization requires the use of the slight difference in the times at which a sound reaches our two ears. Sound that we hear first in the right ear tells us that the source of the sound is to our right. Because infants' heads are smaller than those of adults, the difference in timing of the arrival of sound at the two ears is less than it is in adults, so they have difficulty determining from which direction sound is coming (Winkler et al., 2016; Thomas et al., 2018).

Despite the potential limitation brought about by their smaller heads, infants' sound localization abilities are actually fairly good even at birth, and they reach adult levels of success by the age of 1 year. Furthermore, young infants are capable of making the fine discriminations that their future understanding of language will require (van Heugten, & Johnson, 2010; Purdy et al., 2013; Slugocki & Trainor, 2014).

By the age of 4 months, infants are able to discriminate their own names from other, similar sounding words. How do you think infants are able to develop this capability?

SMELL AND TASTE   What do infants do when they smell a rotten egg? Pretty much what adults do—crinkle their noses and generally look unhappy. In contrast, the scents of bananas and butter produce a pleasant reaction on the part of infants (Pomares, Schirrer, & Abadie, 2002; Godard et al., 2016).

The sense of smell is so well developed, even among young infants, that at least some 12- to 18-day-old babies can distinguish their mothers on the basis of smell alone. For instance, in one experiment infants were exposed to the smell of gauze pads worn under the arms of adults the previous evening. Infants who were being breastfed were able to distinguish their mothers' scent from those of other adults. However, not all infants could do this: Those who were being bottle-fed were unable to make the distinction. Moreover, both breastfed and bottle-fed infants were unable to distinguish their fathers on the basis of odor (Allam, Marlier, & Schaal, 2006; Lipsitt & Rovee-Collier, 2012).

Infants seem to have an innate sweet tooth (even before they have teeth!), and they show facial expressions of disgust when they taste something bitter. Very young infants smile when a sweet-tasting liquid is placed on their tongues. They also suck harder at a bottle if it is sweetened. Because breast milk has a sweet taste, it is possible that this preference may be part of our evolutionary heritage, retained because it offered a survival advantage (Blass & Camp, 2015).

SENSITIVITY TO PAIN   Infants are born with the capacity to experience pain. Obviously, no one can be sure if the experience of pain in children is identical to that in adults, any more than we can tell if an adult friend who complains of a headache is experiencing pain that is more or less severe than our own pain when we have a headache.

What we do know is that pain produces distress in infants. Their heartbeat increases, and they sweat, show facial expressions of discomfort, and change the intensity and tone of crying when they are hurt (Kohut & Riddell, 2009; Rodkey & Riddell, 2013; Pölkki et al., 2015).

There appears to be a developmental progression in reactions to pain. For example, a newborn infant who has her heel pricked for a blood test responds with distress, but it takes her several seconds to show the response. In contrast, only a few months later, the same procedure brings a much more immediate response. It is possible that the delayed reaction in infants is produced by the relatively slower transmission of information within the newborn's less-developed nervous system (Puchalski & Hummel, 2002).

Infants' sense of smell is so well developed that they can distinguish their mothers on the basis of smell alone.

RESPONDING TO TOUCH   Touch is one of the most highly developed sensory systems in a newborn. It is also one of the first to develop; there is evidence that

Touch is one of the most highly developed sensory systems in a newborn.

by 32 weeks after conception, the entire body is sensitive to touch. Furthermore, several of the basic reflexes present at birth, such as the rooting reflex, require touch sensitivity to operate: An infant must sense a touch near the mouth to automatically seek a nipple to suck (Field, 2014).

Infants' abilities in the realm of touch are particularly helpful in their efforts to explore the world. Several theorists have suggested that one of the ways children gain information about the world is through touching. As mentioned previously, at the age of 6 months, infants are apt to place almost any object in their mouths, apparently taking in data about its configuration from their sensory responses to the feel of it in their mouths (Ruff, 1989).

Touch also plays an important role in an organism's future development because it triggers a complex chemical reaction that assists infants in their efforts to survive. For example, gentle massage stimulates the production of certain chemicals in an infant's brain that instigate growth (Gordon et al., 2013; Ludwig & Field, 2014; Guzzetta & Cion, 2016).

Multimodal Perception: Combining Individual Sensory Inputs

LO 3.8   Summarize the multimodal approach to perception.

> When Eric Pettigrew was 7 months old, his grandparents presented him with a squeaky rubber doll. As soon as he saw it, he reached out for it, grasped it in his hand, and listened as it squeaked. He seemed delighted with the gift.

One way of considering Eric's sensory reaction to the doll is to focus on each of the senses individually: what the doll looked like to Eric, how it felt in his hand, and what it sounded like. In fact, this approach has dominated the study of sensation and perception in infancy.

However, let's consider another approach: We might examine how the various sensory responses are integrated with one another. Instead of looking at each individual sensory response, we could consider how the responses work together and are combined to produce Eric's ultimate reaction. The **multimodal approach to perception** considers how information that is collected by various individual sensory systems is integrated and coordinated (Farzin, Charles, & Rivera, 2009).

multimodal approach to perception
the approach that considers how information that is collected by various individual sensory systems is integrated and coordinated

> **From a health-care worker's perspective:** People who are born without the use of one sense often develop unusual abilities in one or more other senses. What can health-care professionals do to help infants who are lacking in a particular sense?

Although the multimodal approach is a relatively recent innovation in the study of how infants understand their sensory world, it raises some fundamental issues about the development of sensation and perception. For instance, some researchers argue that sensations are initially integrated with one another in infants, whereas others maintain that infants' sensory systems are initially separate and that brain development leads to increasing integration (Lickliter & Bahrick, 2000; Lewkowicz, 2002; Flom & Bahrick, 2007).

We do not know yet which view is correct. However, it does appear that by an early age, infants are able to relate what they have learned about an object through one sensory channel to what they have learned about it through another. For instance, even 1-month-old infants are able to recognize by sight objects that they have previously held in their mouths but never seen (Meltzoff, 1981; Steri & Spelke, 1988). Clearly, some cross-talk between various sensory channels is already possible a month after birth.

Infants' abilities in multimodal perception showcase their sophisticated perceptual abilities, which continue to grow throughout the period of infancy. Such perceptual growth is aided by infants' discovery of **affordances**, the options that a given situation or stimulus provides. For example, infants learn that they might potentially fall when walking down a steep ramp—that is, the ramp *affords* the possibility of falling. Such knowledge is crucial as infants make the transition from crawling to walking. Similarly, infants learn that an object shaped in a certain way can slip out of their hands if not grasped correctly. For example, Eric is learning that his toy has several affordances: He can grab it and squeeze it, listen to it squeak, and even chew comfortably on it if he is teething (Huang, 2012; Walker-Andrews et al., 2013; Oudeyer & Smith, 2016; also see the *Development in Your Life* box).

affordances
the action possibilities that a given situation or stimulus provides

Development in Your Life

Exercising Your Infant's Body and Senses

Recall how cultural expectations and environments affect the age at which various physical milestones, such as the first step, occur. Although most experts feel attempts to accelerate physical and sensory-perceptual development yield little advantage, parents should ensure that their infants receive sufficient physical and sensory stimulation. There are several specific ways to accomplish this goal:

- Carry a baby in different positions—switching among a backpack, a frontpack, or a football hold with the infant's head in the palm of your hand and its feet lying on your arm lets infants view the world from several perspectives.

- Let infants explore their environment. Don't contain them too long in a barren environment. Let them crawl

or wander around—after first making the environment "childproof" by removing dangerous objects.

- Engage in "rough-and-tumble" play. Wrestling, dancing, and rolling around on the floor—if not violent—are activities that are fun and that stimulate older infants' motor and sensory systems.

- Let babies touch their food and even play with it. Infancy is too early to start teaching table manners.

- Provide toys that stimulate the senses. Provide toys that can stimulate more than one sense at a time. For example, brightly colored, textured toys with movable parts are enjoyable and help sharpen infants' senses.

Review, Check, and Apply

Review

LO 3.1 Describe how the human body develops in the first 2 years of life, including the four principles that govern its growth.

Human babies grow rapidly in height and weight, especially during the first 2 years of life. Major principles that govern human growth include the cephalocaudal principle, the proximodistal principle, the principle of hierarchical integration, and the principle of the independence of systems.

LO 3.2 Describe how the nervous system and brain develop in the first 2 years of life, and explain how the environment affects such development.

The nervous system contains a huge number of neurons, more than will be needed as an adult. "Extra" connections and neurons that are not used are eliminated as an infant develops. Brain development, largely predetermined genetically, also contains a strong element of plasticity—a susceptibility to environmental influences. Many aspects of development occur during sensitive periods when the organism is particularly susceptible to environmental influences.

LO 3.3 Explain the body rhythms and states that govern an infant's behavior.

One of the primary tasks of infants is the development of rhythms—cyclical patterns that integrate individual behaviors. An important rhythm pertains to infants' state—the degree of awareness of stimulation it displays.

LO 3.4 Explain how the reflexes that infants are born with both protect them and help them adapt to their surroundings.

Reflexes are unlearned, automatic responses to stimuli that help newborns survive and protect themselves. Some reflexes also have value as the foundation for future, more conscious behaviors.

LO 3.5 Identify the milestones of gross motor and fine motor skill development in infancy.

The development of gross motor and fine motor skills proceeds along a generally consistent timetable in normal children, with substantial individual and cultural variations. In the first year, advances in gross motor skills allow children to roll over, sit upright without support, stand while holding onto something, and then stand alone. A child who grasps an object with thumb and finger at 8 months may hold a crayon adaptively at 11 months, and imitate strokes on paper by age 2.

LO 3.6   Summarize the role of nutrition in the physical development of infants, including the benefits of breastfeeding.

Adequate nutrition is essential for physical development. Malnutrition and undernutrition affect physical aspects of growth and may also affect IQ and school performance. Breastfeeding has distinct advantages over bottle-feeding, including the nutritional completeness of breast milk, its provision of a degree of immunity to certain childhood diseases, and its easy digestibility. In addition, breastfeeding offers significant physical and emotional benefits to both child and mother.

LO 3.7   Describe the sensory capabilities of infants.

Very early on, infants can see depth and motion, distinguish colors and patterns, show clear visual preferences, localize and discriminate sounds, and recognize the sound and smell of their mothers. Infants are also sensitive to pain and touch, the latter of which plays an important role in the child's future development.

LO 3.8   Summarize the multimodal approach to perception.

The multimodal approach to perception considers how information that is collected by various individual sensory systems is integrated and coordinated.

Check Yourself

1. The process that allows established neurons to build stronger networks and reduces unnecessary neurons during the first 2 years of life is called _____.
   a. hierarchical integration
   b. independent plasticity
   c. cephalocaudal modification
   d. synaptic pruning

2. Behavior becomes integrated through the development of _____, which are repetitive, cyclical patterns of behavior.
   a. states
   b. rhythms
   c. REM sleep
   d. reflexes

3. Which of the following *is not* one of the consequences of malnutrition during infancy?
   a. Malnourished children are more likely to become obese in adolescence and develop diabetes.
   b. Malnourished children show a slower growth rate by the age of 6 months.
   c. Malnourished children score lower on IQ tests later in life.
   d. Malnourished children have a lower height and weight by age 2 than nonmalnourished children.

4. _____ is the physical stimulation of the sense organs.
   a. Perception
   b. Crying
   c. Crawling
   d. Sensation

Applying Lifespan Development

If you were selecting a mobile as a gift for a young infant, what features would you look for to make the mobile as interesting as possible to the baby?

Module 3.2

Cognitive Development in Infancy

Making Things Happen

Nine-month-old Raisa Novak has just begun to crawl. "I've had to baby-proof everything," her mother Bela says. One of the first things Raisa discovered as she began moving about the living room was the radio/CD player. At first, she pushed all the buttons in random order. But after just 1 week, she knows the red button makes the radio come on. "She has always loved music," Bela says. "She is clearly thrilled that she can make it happen whenever she wants." Raisa now crawls around the house looking for buttons to push, and cries when she gets to the dishwasher or the DVD player or the television because she can't reach their buttons—yet. "I will really have my hands full when she begins to walk," Bela says.

Alain Schroeder/ONOKY/Getty Images

How much of the world do infants understand? How do they begin to make meaning of it all? Does intellectual stimulation accelerate an infant's cognitive development? We address these questions in this module as we consider cognitive development during the first years of life, focusing on how infants develop their knowledge and understanding of the world. We first discuss the work of Swiss psychologist Jean Piaget, whose theory of developmental stages served as a highly influential impetus for a considerable amount of work on cognitive development.

We then cover more contemporary views of cognitive development, examining information processing approaches that seek to explain how cognitive growth occurs. We also examine memory in infants and address individual differences in intelligence.

Finally, we consider language, the cognitive skill that permits infants to communicate with others. We look at the roots of language in prelinguistic speech and trace the milestones indicating the development of language skills in the progression from the baby's first words to phrases and sentences.

Piaget's Approach to Cognitive Development

Olivia's dad is wiping up the mess around the base of her high chair—for the third time today! It seems to him that 14-month-old Olivia takes great delight in dropping food from the high chair. She also drops toys, spoons—anything, it seems—just to watch how they hit the floor. She almost appears to be experimenting to see what kind of noise or what size of splatter is created by each different thing she drops.

Swiss psychologist Jean Piaget (1896–1980) probably would have said that Olivia's dad is right in theorizing that Olivia is conducting her own series of experiments to learn more about the workings of her world. Piaget's views of the ways infants learn could be summed in a simple equation: *Action = Knowledge*.

Piaget argued that infants do not acquire knowledge from facts communicated by others, nor through sensation and perception. Instead, Piaget suggested that knowledge is the product of direct motor behavior. Although many of his basic explanations and propositions have been challenged by subsequent research, as we'll discuss later, the view that in significant ways infants learn by doing remains unquestioned (Piaget, 1962, 1983; Zuccarini et al., 2016).

Key Elements of Piaget's Theory

LO 3.9   Summarize the fundamental features of Piaget's theory of cognitive development, and describe the sensorimotor stage.

As we first noted in Chapter 1, Piaget's theory is based on a stage approach to development. He assumed that all children pass through a series of four universal stages in a fixed order from birth through adolescence: sensorimotor, preoperational, concrete operational, and formal operational. He also suggested that movement from one stage to the next occurs when a child reaches an appropriate level of physical maturation *and* is exposed to relevant experiences. Without such experience, children are assumed to be incapable of reaching their cognitive potential. Some approaches to cognition focus on changes in the *content* of children's knowledge about the world, but Piaget argued that it was critical to also consider the changes in the *quality* of children's knowledge and understanding as they move from one stage to another.

For instance, as they develop cognitively, infants experience changes in their understanding about what can and cannot occur in the world. Consider a baby who participates in an experiment during which she is exposed to three identical versions of her mother all at the same time, thanks to some well-placed mirrors. A 3-month-old infant will interact happily with each of these images of her mother. However, by 5 months of age, the child becomes quite agitated at the sight of multiple mothers. Apparently, by this time the child has figured out that he or she has but one mother, and viewing three at a time is thoroughly alarming (Bower, 1977). To Piaget, such reactions indicate that a baby is beginning to master principles regarding the way the world operates, indicating that he or she has begun to construct a mental sense of the world that he or she didn't have 2 months previously.

Piaget believed that the basic building blocks of the way we understand the world are mental structures called **schema**, organized patterns of functioning that adapt and change with mental development. At first, schema are related to physical, or sensorimotor, activity, such as picking up or reaching for toys. As children develop, their schema move to a mental level, reflecting thought. Schema are similar to computer

schema
organized patterns of functioning that adapt and change with mental functioning

Swiss psychologist Jean Piaget.

assimilation

the process in which people understand an experience in terms of their current stage of cognitive development and way of thinking

accommodation

changes in existing ways of thinking that occur in response to encounters with new stimuli or events

sensorimotor stage (of cognitive development)

Piaget's initial major stage of cognitive development, which can be broken down into six substages

software: They direct and determine how data from the world, such as new events or objects, are considered and dealt with (Rakison & Oakes, 2003; Rakison & Krogh, 2012; Di Paolo, Buhrmann, & Barandiaran, 2017).

If you give a baby a new cloth book, for example, he or she will touch it, mouth it, perhaps try to tear it or bang it on the floor. To Piaget, each of these actions represents a schema, and they are the infants' way of gaining knowledge and understanding of this new object.

Piaget suggested that two principles underlie the growth in children's schema: assimilation and accommodation. **Assimilation** is the process by which people understand an experience in terms of their current stage of cognitive development and way of thinking. Assimilation occurs, then, when a stimulus or event is acted upon, perceived, and understood in accordance with existing patterns of thought. For example, an infant who tries to suck on any toy in the same way is assimilating the objects to her existing sucking schema. Similarly, a child who encounters a flying squirrel at a zoo and calls it a "bird" is assimilating the squirrel to his or her existing schema of bird.

In contrast, when we change our existing ways of thinking, understanding, or behaving in response to encounters with new stimuli or events, **accommodation** takes place. For instance, when a child sees a flying squirrel and calls it "a bird with a tail," he or she is beginning to *accommodate* new knowledge, modifying his or her schema of bird.

Piaget believed that the earliest schema are primarily limited to the reflexes with which we are all born, such as sucking and rooting. Infants start to modify these simple early schema almost immediately, through the processes of assimilation and accommodation, in response to their exploration of the environment. Schema quickly become more sophisticated as infants become more advanced in their motor capabilities—to Piaget, a signal of the potential for more advanced cognitive development. Because Piaget's sensorimotor stage of development begins at birth and continues until the child is about 2 years old, we consider it here in detail.

Piaget suggests that the **sensorimotor stage**, the initial major stage of cognitive development, can be broken down into six substages. These are summarized in Table 3-5. It is important to keep in mind that although the specific substages of the sensorimotor period may at first appear to unfold with great regularity, as though infants reach a particular age and smoothly proceed into the next substage, the reality of cognitive development is somewhat different. First, the ages at which infants actually reach a particular stage vary a good deal among different children. The exact timing of a stage reflects an interaction between infants' level of physical maturation and the nature of the social environment in which they are being raised. Consequently, although Piaget contended that the order of the substages does not change from one child to the next, he admitted that the timing can and does vary to some degree.

Piaget viewed development as a more gradual process than the notion of different stages might seem to imply. Infants do not go to sleep one night in one substage and wake up the next morning in the next one. Instead, there is a rather steady shifting of behavior as a child moves toward the next stage of cognitive development. Infants also pass through periods of transition, in which some aspects of their behavior reflect the next higher stage, and other aspects indicate their current stage (see Figure 3-11).

SUBSTAGE 1: SIMPLE REFLEXES The first substage of the sensorimotor period is *Substage 1: Simple reflexes*, encompassing the first month of life. During this time, the various inborn reflexes, described in Module 3.1, are at the center of a baby's physical and cognitive life, determining the nature of his or her interactions with the world. At the same time, some of the reflexes begin to accommodate the infant's experience with the nature of the world. For instance, an infant who is being breastfed but who also receives supplemental bottles may start to change the way he or she sucks, depending on whether a nipple is on a breast or a bottle.

SUBSTAGE 2: FIRST HABITS AND PRIMARY CIRCULAR REACTIONS *Substage 2: First habits and primary circular reactions*, the second substage of the sensorimotor period, occurs from 1 to 4 months of age. In this period, infants begin to coordinate what were separate actions into single, integrated activities. For instance, an infant might combine grasping an object with sucking on it, or staring at something while touching it.

Table 3-5 Piaget's Six Substages of the Sensorimotor Stage

Substage	Age	Description	Example
Substage 1: Simple reflexes	First month of life	During this period, the various reflexes that determine infants' interactions with the world are at the center of its cognitive life.	The sucking reflex causes infants to suck at anything placed in his or her lips.
Substage 2: First habits and primary circular reactions	From 1 to 4 months	At this age infants begin to coordinate what were separate actions into single, integrated activities.	An infant might combine grasping an object with sucking on it, or staring at something with touching it.
Substage 3: Secondary circular reactions	From 4 to 8 months	During this period, infants take major strides in shifting their cognitive horizons beyond themselves and begin to act on the outside world.	A child who repeatedly picks up a rattle in her crib and shakes it in different ways to see how the sound changes is demonstrating her ability to modify her cognitive schema about shaking rattles.
Substage 4: Coordination of secondary circular reactions	From 8 to 12 months	In this stage infants begin to use more calculated approaches to producing events, coordinating several schema to generate a single act. They achieve object permanence during this stage.	An infant will push one toy out of the way to reach another toy that is lying, partially exposed, under it.
Substage 5: Tertiary circular reactions	From 12 to 18 months	At this age, infants develop what Piaget regards as the deliberate variation of actions that bring desirable consequences. Rather than just repeating enjoyable activities, infants appear to carry out miniature experiments to observe the consequences.	A child will drop a toy repeatedly, varying the position from which he drops it, carefully observing each time to see where it falls.
Substage 6: Beginnings of thought	From 18 months to 2 years	The major achievement of Substage 6 is the capacity for mental representation or symbolic thought. Piaget argued that only at this stage can infants imagine where objects that they cannot see might be.	Children can even plot in their heads unseen trajectories of objects, so that if a ball rolls under a piece of furniture, they can figure out where it is likely to emerge on the other side.

Figure 3-11 Transitions

Infants do not suddenly shift from one stage of cognitive development to the next. Instead, Piaget argues that there is a period of transition in which some behavior reflects one stage, while other behavior reflects the more advanced stage. Does this gradualism argue against Piaget's interpretation of stages?

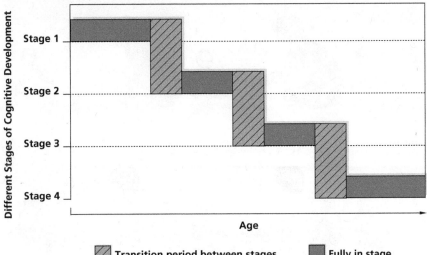

If an activity engages a baby's interests, he or she may repeat it over and over, simply for the sake of continuing to experience it. This repetition of a chance motor event helps the baby start building cognitive schema through a process known as a *circular reaction*. *Primary circular reactions* are schema reflecting an infant's repetition of interesting or enjoyable actions, just for the enjoyment of doing them, which focus on an infant's own body.

SUBSTAGE 3: SECONDARY CIRCULAR REACTIONS *Substage 3: Secondary circular reactions* are more purposeful. According to Piaget, this third stage of cognitive development in infancy occurs from 4 to 8 months of age. During this period, a child begins to act on the outside world. For instance, infants now seek to repeat enjoyable events in their environments if they happen to produce them through chance activities. A child who repeatedly picks up a rattle in her crib and shakes it in different ways to see how the sound changes is demonstrating her ability to modify her cognitive schema about shaking rattles. She is engaging in what Piaget calls *secondary circular reactions*, which are schema regarding repeated actions that bring about a desirable consequence.

SUBSTAGE 4: COORDINATION OF SECONDARY CIRCULAR REACTIONS Some major leaps forward occur in *Substage 4: Coordination of secondary circular reactions*, which lasts from 8 months to 12 months. In Substage 4, infants begin to employ *goal-directed behavior*, in which several schema are combined and coordinated to generate a single act to solve a problem. For instance, infants will push one toy out of the way to reach another toy that is lying, partially exposed, under it.

Infants' newfound purposefulness, their ability to use means to attain particular ends, and their skill in anticipating future circumstances owe their appearance in part to the developmental achievement of object permanence that emerges in Substage 4. **Object permanence** is the realization that people and objects exist even when they cannot be seen. It is a simple principle, but its mastery has profound consequences.

Consider, for instance, 7-month-old Chu, who has yet to learn the idea of object permanence. Chu's mother shakes a rattle in front of him, then takes the rattle and places it under a blanket. To Chu, who has not mastered the concept of object permanence, the rattle no longer exists. He will make no effort to look for it.

Several months later, when he reaches Substage 4, the story is quite different (see Figure 3-12). This time, as soon as his mother places the rattle under the blanket, Chu tries to toss the cover aside, eagerly searching for the rattle. Chu clearly has learned

object permanence
the realization that people and objects exist even when they cannot be seen

---

Figure 3-12 Object Permanence

Before infants understand the idea of object permanence, they will not search for an object that has been hidden right before their eyes. But several months later, they will search for it, illustrating that they have attained object permanence. Why is the concept of object permanence important?

Before Object Permanence

After Object Permanence

that the object continues to exist even when it cannot be seen. For infants who achieve an understanding of object permanence, then, out of sight is decidedly not out of mind.

The attainment of object permanence extends not only to inanimate objects, but to people, too. It gives Chu the security that his father and mother still exist even when they have left the room.

SUBSTAGE 5: TERTIARY CIRCULAR REACTIONS   *Substage 5: Tertiary circular reactions* is reached at around the age of 12 months and extends to 18 months. As the name of the stage indicates, during this period infants develop these reactions, which are schema regarding the deliberate variation of actions that bring desirable consequences. Rather than just repeating enjoyable activities, as they do with secondary circular reactions, infants appear to carry out miniature experiments to observe the consequences.

For example, Piaget observed his son Laurent dropping a toy swan repeatedly, varying the position from which he dropped it, carefully observing each time to see where it fell. Instead of just repeating the action each time, Laurent made modifications in the situation to learn about their consequences. As you may recall from our discussion of research methods in Chapter 1, this behavior represents the essence of the scientific method: An experimenter varies a situation in a laboratory to learn the effects of the variation. To infants in Substage 5, the world is their laboratory, and they spend their days leisurely carrying out one miniature experiment after another.

SUBSTAGE 6: BEGINNINGS OF THOUGHT   The final stage of the sensorimotor period is *Substage 6: Beginnings of thought*, which lasts from 18 months to 2 years. The major achievement of Substage 6 is the capacity for mental representation, or symbolic thought. A *mental representation* is an internal image of a past event or object. Piaget argued that by this stage infants can imagine where objects might be that they cannot see. They can even plot in their heads unseen trajectories of objects, so if a ball rolls under a piece of furniture, they can figure out where it is likely to emerge on the other side.

> **From a caregiver's perspective:** What are some implications for childrearing practices of Piaget's observations about the ways children gain an understanding of the world? Would you use the same approaches in childrearing for a child growing up in a non-Western culture?

Appraising Piaget: Support and Challenges

LO 3.10   **Summarize the arguments both in support of and critical of Piaget's theory of cognitive development.**

Most developmental researchers would probably agree that in many significant ways, Piaget's descriptions of how cognitive development proceeds during infancy are quite accurate. Yet, there is substantial disagreement over the validity of the theory and many of its specific predictions. (Müller, Ten Eycke, & Baker, 2015; Barrouillet, 2015; Bjorklund, 2018).

Let's start with what is clearly accurate about the Piagetian approach. Piaget was a masterful reporter of children's behavior, and his descriptions of growth during infancy remain a monument to his powers of observation. Furthermore, literally thousands of studies have supported Piaget's view that children learn much about the world by acting on objects in their environment. Finally, the broad outlines sketched out by Piaget of the sequence of cognitive development and the increasing cognitive accomplishments that occur during infancy are generally accurate (Müller et al., 2013; Müller, Ten Eycke, & Baker, 2015; Fowler, 2017).

However, specific aspects of the theory have come under increasing scrutiny—and criticism—in the decades since Piaget carried out his pioneering work. For example, some researchers question the stage conception that forms the basis of Piaget's theory. Although, as we noted previously, even Piaget acknowledged that children's transitions between

Piaget's theory suggests that infants develop schemas that represent their understanding of cause-and-effect, as when a child pushes a key on a keyboard and sees the image on the screen change.

Research on babies in non-Western cultures suggests that Piaget's stages are not universal but are to some degree culturally derived.

stages are gradual, critics contend that development proceeds in a much more continuous fashion. Rather than showing major leaps of competence at the end of one stage and the beginning of the next, improvement comes in more gradual increments, growing step-by-step in a skill-by-skill manner.

For instance, developmental researcher Robert Siegler suggests that cognitive development proceeds not in stages but in "waves." According to Siegler, children don't one day drop a mode of thinking and the next take up a new form. Instead, there is an ebb and flow of cognitive approaches that children use to understand the world (Siegler, 2012; Siegler & Lortie-Forgues, 2014; Siegler, 2016; Lemaire, 2018).

Other critics dispute Piaget's notion that cognitive development is grounded in motor activities. They charge that Piaget overlooked the importance of the sensory and perceptual systems that are present from a very early age in infancy—systems about which Piaget knew little.

To bolster their views, Piaget's critics also point to more recent studies that cast doubt on Piaget's view that infants are incapable of mastering the concept of object permanence until they are close to a year old. For instance, some work suggests that younger infants did not appear to understand object permanence because the techniques used to test their abilities were not sensitive enough to their true capabilities (Bremner, Slater, & Johnson, 2015; Baillargeon & Dejong, 2017).

It may be that a 4-month-old doesn't search for a rattle hidden under a blanket because she hasn't learned the motor skills necessary to do the searching—not because she doesn't understand that the rattle still exists. Similarly, the apparent inability of young infants to comprehend object permanence may reflect more about their memory deficits than their lack of understanding of the concept: The memories of young infants may be poor enough that they simply do not recall the previous concealment of the toy. In fact, when more age-appropriate tasks are employed, some researchers have found indications of object permanence in children as young as 3½ months (Scott & Baillargeon, 2013; Baillargeon et al., 2015; Sim & Zu, 2017).

Piaget's work also seems to describe children from developed Western countries better than those in non-Western cultures. For instance, some evidence suggests that cognitive skills emerge on a different timetable for children in non-Western cultures than for children living in Europe and the United States. Infants raised in the Ivory Coast of Africa, for example, reach the various substages of the sensorimotor period at an earlier age than infants reared in France (Dasen et al., 1978; Mistry & Saraswathi, 2003; Tamis-LeMonda et al., 2012).

However, even Piaget's most passionate critics concede that he has provided us with a masterful description of the broad outlines of cognitive development during infancy. His failings seem to be in underestimating the capabilities of younger infants and in his claims that sensorimotor skills develop in a consistent, fixed pattern. Still, his influence has been enormous and, although the focus of many contemporary developmental researchers has shifted to newer information processing approaches that we discuss next, Piaget remains a towering and pioneering figure in the field of development (Kail, 2004; Maynard, 2008; Fowler, 2017).

Information Processing Approaches to Cognitive Development

> Amber Nordstrom, 3 months old, breaks into a smile as her brother Marcus stands over her crib, picks up a doll, and makes a whistling noise through his teeth. In fact, Amber never seems to tire of Marcus's efforts at making her smile, and, soon, whenever Marcus appears and simply picks up the doll, her lips begin to curl into a smile.

Clearly, Amber remembers Marcus and his humorous ways. But how does she remember him? And how much else can Amber remember?

To answer questions such as these, we need to diverge from the road that Piaget laid out for us. Rather than seeking to identify the universal, broad milestones in cognitive development through which all infants pass, as Piaget tried to do, we must consider the specific processes by which individual babies acquire and use the information to which they are exposed. We need, then, to focus less on the qualitative changes in infants' mental lives and consider more closely their quantitative capabilities.

Information processing approaches to cognitive development seek to identify the way that individuals take in, use, and store information. According to this approach, the quantitative changes in infants' abilities to organize and manipulate information represent the hallmarks of cognitive development.

Taking this perspective, cognitive growth is characterized by increasing sophistication, speed, and capacity in information processing. Previously, we compared Piaget's idea of schema to computer software, which directs the computer in how to deal with data from the world. We might compare the information processing perspective on cognitive growth to the improvements that come from the use of more efficient programs that lead to increased speed and sophistication in the processing of information. Information processing approaches, then, focus on the types of "mental programs" that people use when they seek to solve problems (Hugdahl & Westerhausen, 2010; Fagan & Ployhart, 2015).

information processing approaches
the model that seeks to identify the way that individuals take in, use, and store information

The Foundations of Information Processing: Encoding, Storage, and Retrieval

LO 3.11 Describe how information processing approaches explain cognitive development in infants, and summarize the memory capabilities of infants in the first 2 years of life.

Information processing has three basic aspects: encoding, storage, and retrieval (see Figure 3-13). *Encoding* is the process by which information is initially recorded in a form usable to memory. Infants and children—indeed, all people—are exposed to a massive amount of information; if they tried to process it all, they would be overwhelmed. Consequently, they encode selectively, picking and choosing the information to which they will pay attention.

Even if someone has been exposed to the information initially and has encoded it in an appropriate way, there is still no guarantee that he or she will be able to use it in the future. Information must also have been stored in memory adequately. *Storage* refers to the placement of material into memory. Finally, success in using the material in the future depends on retrieval processes. *Retrieval* is the process by which material in memory storage is located, brought into awareness, and used.

We can use our comparison to computers again here. Information processing approaches suggest that the processes of encoding, storage, and retrieval are analogous to different parts of a computer. Encoding can be thought of as a computer's keyboard, through which one inputs information; storage is the computer's hard drive, where information is stored; and retrieval is analogous to software that accesses the information for display on the screen. Only when all three processes are operating—encoding, storage, and retrieval—can information be processed.

AUTOMATIZATION In some cases, encoding, storage, and retrieval are relatively automatic, and in other cases they are deliberate. *Automatization* is the degree to which an activity requires attention. Processes that require relatively little attention are automatic; processes that require relatively large amounts of attention are controlled. For example, some activities such as walking, eating with a fork, or reading may be automatic for you, but at first they required your full attention.

Figure 3-13 Information Processing

The process by which information is encoded, stored, and retrieved.

Automatic mental processes help children in their initial encounters with the world by enabling them to easily and "automatically" process information in particular ways. For instance, by age 5, children automatically encode information in terms of frequency. Without a lot of attention to counting or tallying, they become aware, for example, of how often they have encountered various people, permitting them to differentiate familiar from unfamiliar people (Homae et al., 2012; Seyfarth & Cheney, 2013).

Some of the things we learn automatically are unexpectedly complex. For example, infants have the ability to learn subtle statistical patterns and relationships. The existence of basic mathematical skills in infants has been supported by findings that nonhumans are born with some basic numeric proficiency. Even newly hatched chicks show some counting abilities. And it is not too long into infancy that children demonstrate an understanding of such basic physics as movement trajectories and gravity (Gopnik, 2010; van Marle & Wynn, 2011; Hespos & van Marle, 2012; Christodoulou, Lac, & Moore, 2017).

The result of this growing body of research suggests that infants have an innate grasp of certain basic mathematical functions and statistical patterns. This inborn proficiency is likely to form the basis for learning more complex mathematics and statistical relationships later in life (McCrink & Wynn, 2009; Posid & Cordes, 2015; Edwards et al., 2015).

MEMORY CAPABILITIES IN INFANCY

> Arif Terzić was born during the war in Bosnia. He spent his first 2 years hiding in a basement with his mother. The only light he saw came from a kerosene lamp. The only sounds he heard were his mother's hushed lullabies and the explosion of shells. Someone he never saw left food for them. There was a tap, but sometimes the water was too filthy to drink. At one point, his mother suffered a kind of breakdown. She fed him when she remembered. But she didn't speak. Or sing.

> Arif was lucky. His family emigrated to the United States when he was 2. His father found work. They rented a little house. Arif went to preschool and then kindergarten. Today, he has friends, toys, a dog, and loves soccer. "He doesn't remember Bosnia," his mother says. "It's like it never happened."

How likely is it that Arif truly remembers nothing of his infancy? And if he ever does recall his first 2 years of life, how accurate will his memories be? To answer these questions, we need to consider the qualities of memory that exist during infancy.

memory
the process by which information is initially recorded, stored, and retrieved

Certainly, infants have **memory** capabilities, defined as the process by which information is initially recorded, stored, and retrieved. As we've seen, infants can distinguish new stimuli from old, and this implies that some memory of the old must be present. Unless infants have some memory of an original stimulus, it would be impossible for them to recognize that a new stimulus differed from the previous one.

Infants' capability to recognize new stimuli from old tells us little about how age brings about changes in the capacities of memory and in its fundamental nature. Do infants' memory capabilities increase as they get older? The answer is clearly affirmative. In one study, infants were taught that they could move a mobile hanging over the crib by kicking their legs. It took only a few days for 2-month-old infants to forget their training, but 6-month-old infants still remembered for as long as 3 weeks (Rovee-Collier, 1999; Haley et al., 2010).

Furthermore, infants who were later prompted to recall the association between kicking and moving the mobile showed evidence that the memory continued to exist even longer. Infants who had received just two training sessions lasting 9 minutes each still recalled about a week later, as illustrated by the fact that they began to kick when placed in the crib with the mobile. Two weeks later, however, they made no effort to kick, suggesting that they had forgotten entirely.

But they hadn't forgotten: When the babies saw a reminder—a moving mobile—their memories were apparently reactivated. In fact, infants could remember the association, following prompting, for as long as an additional month. Other evidence confirms these results, suggesting that hints can reactivate memories that at first seem lost, and that the older the infant, the more effective such prompting is (DeFrancisco & Rovee-Collier, 2008; Brito & Barr, 2014; Fisher-Thompson, 2017).

The Duration of Memories Although the processes that underlie memory retention and recall seem similar throughout the life span, the quantity of information stored and recalled does differ markedly as infants develop. Older infants can retrieve information more rapidly and they can remember it longer. But just how long? Can memories from infancy be recalled, for example, after babies grow up?

Researchers disagree on the age from which memories can be retrieved. Although early research supported the notion of **infantile amnesia**, the lack of memory for experiences occurring before 3 years of age, more recent research shows that infants do retain memories. For example, in one study, 6-month-old infants were shown a series of unusual events, such as intermittent periods of light and dark and strange sounds. When the children were later tested at the age of 1½ years or 2½ years, they demonstrated that they recalled the experience. Other research indicates that infants show memory for behavior and situations that they have seen only once (Callaghan, Li, & Richardson, 2014; Madsen & Kim, 2016; Bucci & Stanton, 2017).

infantile amnesia
the lack of memory for experiences that occurred before 3 years of age

Still, although it is at least theoretically possible for memories to remain intact from a very young age—if subsequent experiences do not interfere with their recollection—in most cases memories of personal experiences in infancy do not last into adulthood. Memories of personal experience seem not to become accurate before age 18 to 24 months (Howe, 2003; Howe, Courage, & Edison, 2004; Bauer, 2007).

The Cognitive Neuroscience of Memory Some of the most exciting research on the development of memory is coming from studies of the neurological basis of memory. Advances in brain scan technology, as well as studies of adults with brain damage, suggest that there are two separate systems involved with long-term memory. These two systems, called *explicit memory* and *implicit memory*, retain different sorts of information.

Explicit memory is memory that is conscious and that can be recalled intentionally. When we try to recall a name or phone number, we're using explicit memory. In comparison, implicit memory consists of memories of which we are not consciously aware, but that affect performance and behavior. Implicit memory consists of motor skills, habits, and activities that can be remembered without conscious cognitive effort, such as how to ride a bike or climb a stairway.

Explicit and implicit memories emerge at different rates and involve different parts of the brain. The earliest memories seem to be implicit, and they involve the cerebellum and brain stem. The forerunner of explicit memory involves the hippocampus, but true explicit memory doesn't emerge until the second half of the first year. When explicit memory does emerge, it involves an increasing number of areas of the cortex of the brain (Bauer, 2007; Low & Perner, 2012).

Individual Differences in Intelligence: Is One Infant Smarter Than Another?

LO 3.12 Explain how infant intelligence is measured using information processing approaches.

Maddy Rodriguez is a bundle of curiosity and energy. At 6 months of age, she cries heartily if she can't reach a toy, and when she sees a reflection of herself in a mirror, she gurgles and seems, in general, to find the situation quite amusing.

Jared Lynch, at 6 months, is a good deal more inhibited than Maddy. He doesn't seem to care much when a ball rolls out of his reach, losing interest in it rapidly. And, unlike Maddy, when he sees himself in a mirror, he pretty much ignores the reflection.

As anyone who has spent any time at all observing more than one baby can tell you, not all infants are alike. Some are full of energy and life, apparently displaying a natural-born curiosity, whereas

Infant intelligence is difficult to define and measure. Is this child displaying intelligent behavior?

Table 3-6 Approaches Used to Detect Differences in Intelligence During Infancy

Developmental quotient	Formulated by Arnold Gesell, the developmental quotient is an overall development score that relates to performance in four domains: motor skills (balance and sitting), language use, adaptive behavior (alertness and exploration), and personal–social behavior.
Bayley Scales of Infant Development	Developed by Nancy Bayley, the Bayley Scales of Infant Development evaluate an infant's development from 2 to 42 months. The Bayley Scales focus on two areas: mental (senses, perception, memory, learning, problem solving, and language) and motor abilities (fine and gross motor skills).
Visual-recognition memory measurement	Measures of visual-recognition memory, the memory of and recognition of a stimulus that has been previously seen, also relate to intelligence. The more quickly an infant can retrieve a representation of a stimulus from memory, the more efficient, presumably, is that infant's information processing.

---

others seem, by comparison, somewhat less interested in the world around them. Does this mean that such infants differ in intelligence?

Answering questions about how and to what degree infants vary in their underlying intelligence is not easy. Although it is clear that different infants show significant variations in their behavior, the issue of just what types of behavior may be related to cognitive ability is complicated. Interestingly, the examination of individual differences between infants was the initial approach taken by developmental specialists to understand cognitive development, and such issues still represent an important focus within the field.

What is infant intelligence? Developmental specialists have devised several approaches (summarized in Table 3-6) to illuminate the nature of individual differences in intelligence during infancy.

DEVELOPMENTAL SCALES Developmental psychologist Arnold Gesell formulated the earliest measure of infant development, which was designed to distinguish between normally developing and atypically developing babies (Gesell, 1946). Gesell based his scale on examinations of hundreds of babies. He compared their performance at different ages to learn what behaviors were most common at a particular age. If an infant varied significantly from the norms of a given age, he or she was considered to be developmentally delayed or advanced.

Following the lead of researchers who sought to quantify intelligence through a specific score (known as an intelligence quotient, or IQ, score), Gesell developed a developmental quotient (DQ). The **developmental quotient** is an overall developmental score that relates to performance in four domains: motor skills (e.g., balance and sitting), language use, adaptive behavior (such as alertness and exploration), and personal–social (e.g., adequately feeding and dressing oneself).

Later researchers have created other developmental scales. For instance, Nancy Bayley developed one of the most widely used measures for infants. The **Bayley Scales of Infant Development** evaluate an infant's development from 2 to 42 months. The Bayley Scales focus on two areas: mental and motor abilities. The mental scale focuses on the senses, perception, memory, learning, problem solving, and language, and the motor scale evaluates fine and gross motor skills (see Table 3-7). Like Gesell's

developmental quotient
an overall developmental score that relates to performance in four domains: motor skills, language use, adaptive behavior, and personal–social

Bayley Scales of Infant Development
a measure that evaluates an infant's development from 2 to 42 months

---

Table 3-7 Sample Items from the Bayley Scales of Infant Development

Age	2 months	6 months	12 months	17–19 months	23–25 months	38-42 months
Mental Scale	Turns head to locate origin of sound; visibly responds to disappearance of face	Picks up cup by handle; notices illustrations in a book	Constructs tower of two cubes; can turn pages in a book	Mimics crayon stroke; labels objects in photo	Pairs up pictures; repeats a two-word sentence	Can identify four colors; past tense evident in speech; distinguishes gender
Motor Scale	Can hold head steady and erect for 15 seconds; sits with assistance	Sits up without aid for 30 seconds; grasps foot with hands	Walks when holding onto someone's hand or furniture; holds pencil in fist	Stands on right foot without help; remains upright climbing stairs with assistance	Strings three beads; jumps length of 4 inches	Can reproduce drawing of a circle; hops two times on one foot; descends stairs, alternating feet

SOURCE: Based on Bayley, 1993.

approach, the Bayley approach yields a DQ. A child who scores at an average level—meaning average performance for other children at the same age—receives a score of 100 (Bos, 2013; Greene et al., 2013).

The virtue of approaches such as those taken by Gesell and Bayley is that they provide a good snapshot of an infant's current developmental level. Using these scales, we can tell in an objective manner whether a particular infant falls behind or is ahead of his or her same-age peers. They are particularly useful in identifying infants who are substantially behind their peers, and who therefore need immediate special attention (Aylward & Verhulst, 2000; Sonne, 2012).

What such scales are *not* useful for is predicting a child's future course of development. A child whose development is identified by these measures as relatively slow at the age of 1 year will not necessarily display slow development at age 5, or 12, or 25. The association between most measures of behavior during infancy and adult intelligence, then, is minimal (Murray et al., 2007; Burakevych et al., 2017).

> **From a nurse's perspective:** In what ways is the use of developmental scales for infants (such as the Gesell and Bayley scales) helpful? In what ways is it dangerous? How would you minimize the danger if you were advising a parent?

INFORMATION PROCESSING APPROACHES TO INDIVIDUAL DIFFERENCES IN INTELLIGENCE Contemporary approaches to infant intelligence suggest that the speed with which infants process information may correlate most strongly with later intelligence, as measured by IQ tests administered during adulthood.

How can we tell if a baby is processing information quickly or not? Most researchers use habituation tests. Infants who process information efficiently ought to be able to learn about stimuli more quickly. Consequently, we would expect that they would turn their attention away from a given stimulus more rapidly than those who are less efficient at information processing, leading to the phenomenon of habituation. Similarly, measures of *visual-recognition memory*, the memory and recognition of a stimulus that has been previously seen, as well as attention and representational competence, also relate to IQ. The more quickly an infant can retrieve a representation of a stimulus from memory, the more efficient, presumably, is that infant's information processing (Robinson & Pascalis, 2005; Karmiloff-Smith et al., 2010; Trainor, 2012).

Research using an information processing framework clearly suggests a relationship between information processing efficiency and cognitive abilities: Measures of how quickly infants lose interest in stimuli that they have previously seen, as well as their responsiveness to new stimuli, correlate moderately well with later measures of intelligence. Infants who are more efficient information processors during the 6 months following birth tend to have higher intelligence scores between 2 and 12 years of age, as well as higher scores on other measures of cognitive competence (Rose et al., 2009; Otsuka et al., 2014).

Although information processing efficiency during infancy relates moderately well to later IQ scores, we need to keep in mind two qualifications. Even though there is an association between early information processing capabilities and later measures of IQ, the correlation is only moderate in strength. Consequently, we should not assume that intelligence is somehow permanently fixed in infancy. (Also see the *From Research to Practice* feature regarding ways of promoting infants' cognitive development.)

ASSESSING INFORMATION PROCESSING APPROACHES The information processing perspective on cognitive development during infancy is different from Piaget's. Rather than focusing on broad explanations of the *qualitative* changes that occur in infants' capabilities, as Piaget does, information processing looks at *quantitative* change. Piaget sees cognitive growth occurring in fairly sudden spurts; information processing sees more gradual, step-by-step growth. (Think of the difference between a track-and-field runner leaping hurdles and a slow-but-steady marathon racer.)

From Research to Practice

Why Formal Education Is Lost on Infants

Can you make babies smarter?

Apparently, a lot of parents think so, because collectively they're spending millions of dollars exposing infants to educational toys and media that they hope will be beneficial to their infants' cognitive growth. Parents who want to give their infant children a leg up on learning quickly find that there is no shortage of products and services that claim to do exactly that. Educational videos such as "Baby Einstein" and "Brainy Baby" promise to stimulate young minds. A wide variety of infant toys are marketed with claims that they can enhance cognitive development. And parents sometimes try implementing structured learning activities of their own design, such as flash cards, to make their babies smarter.

But do any of these strategies really work? Most evidence suggests that they don't work very well, and that in some cases their use may even backfire and impede learning. The problem stems from the faulty assumption that infants learn the way older children do—that they can benefit from structured activities that have specific learning goals. Research suggests that this approach is at odds with the way that infants actually try to make sense of their world. Whereas older children and adults take in information in a goal-directed way, looking for solutions to defined problems, infants merely explore their surroundings in an unplanned way. Structured learning experiences fail to account for this unique infant perspective (Zimmerman, Christakis, & Meltzoff, 2007; Berger et al., 2015; Anderson, 2016).

Moreover, some research shows that educational media not only are ineffective in promoting cognitive development, but they may actually harm it. For example, one study showed that children who watched educational videos and DVDs between the ages of 7 and 16 months actually showed poorer language development, knowing fewer words and phrases, than those who did not watch such media. However, the results have not received consistent support (Zimmerman, Christakis, & Meltzoff, 2007; Ferguson & Donnellon, 2014).

In short, research does not consistently support the usefulness of strategies that seek to advance infants' cognitive development. For the moment, parents and other caretakers should follow the advice of the American Academy of Pediatrics, that media exposure prior to the age of 2 should be limited, particularly during meals and an hour before bedtime. Instead, it suggests using strategies that have consistently be shown to be beneficial to infant cognitive development: talking, playing, reading, and singing to infants and encouraging hands-on exploration and social interaction (AAP Council on Communications and the Media, 2016).

Shared Writing Prompt:

Do you think that purchasing educational toys and media for infants is worth a try, despite the lack of scientific research supporting its use? Why? Under what conditions might its use actually have undesirable consequences?

For example, consider how researchers using Piagetian and information processing approaches would explain the cognitive advances displayed by Raisa Novak (described at the beginning of this module), who began to learn the rudiments of cause-and-effect through the experience of pushing buttons to turn on devices. Piagetian theorists would focus on the naturally enfolding cognitive advances following a set pattern, considering the qualitative changes that occur in her thinking. In contrast, an information processing theorist would focus on the quantitative advances brought about by Raisa's experience.

Because information processing researchers consider cognitive development in terms of a collection of individual skills, they are often able to use more precise measures of cognitive ability, such as processing speed and memory recall, than proponents of Piaget's approach. Still, the precision of these individual measures makes it harder to get an overall sense of the nature of cognitive development, something at which Piaget was a master. It's as if information processing approaches focus more on the individual pieces of the puzzle of cognitive development, whereas Piagetian approaches focus more on the whole puzzle (Kagan, 2008; Quinn, 2008).

Ultimately, both Piagetian and information processing approaches provide an account of cognitive development in infancy. Coupled with advances in understanding the biochemistry of the brain and theories that consider the effects of social factors on learning and cognition, the two help us paint a full picture of cognitive development. (Also see the *Development in Your Life* box, which considers some effective strategies for promoting infants' cognitive development.)

Development in Your Life

What Can You Do to Promote Infants' Cognitive Development?

Although no formal programs for promoting infants' cognitive development have been proven to be scientifically valid, there are certain things can be done to support their cognitive development. The following suggestions, based on findings of developmental researchers, offer a starting point:

- **Provide infants the opportunity to explore the world.** As Piaget suggests, children learn by doing, and they need the opportunity to explore and probe their environment.

- **Be responsive to infants on both a verbal and a non-verbal level.** Try to speak *with* babies, as opposed to *at* them. Ask questions, listen to their responses, and provide further communication (Merlo, Bowman, & Barnett, 2007).

- **Read to your infants.** Although they may not understand the meaning of your words, they will respond to

your tone of voice and the intimacy provided by the activity. Reading together also is associated with later literacy skills and begins to create a lifelong reading habit.

- **Play cause-and-effect games.** Provide opportunities to learn cause-and-effect through games such as repeatedly filling a container with objects or water and then dumping them out.

- **Don't push infants, and don't expect too much too soon.** Your goal should not be to create a genius; it should be to provide a warm, nurturing environment that will allow an infant to reach his or her potential.

- **Finally, keep in mind that you don't have to be with an infant 24 hours a day.** Just as infants need time to explore their world on their own, parents and other caregivers need time off from child-care activities.

The Roots of Language

Vicki and Dominic were engaged in a friendly competition over whose name would be the first word their baby, Maura, said. "Say 'mama,'" Vicki would coo before handing Maura over to Dominic for a diaper change. Grinning, he would take her and coax, "No, say 'daddy.'" Both parents ended up losing—and winning—when Maura's first word sounded more like "baba," and seemed to refer to her bottle.

Mama. No. Cookie. Dad. Jo. Most parents can remember their baby's first word, and no wonder. It's an exciting moment, this emergence of a skill that is, arguably, unique to human beings.

But those initial words are just the first and most obvious manifestations of language. Many months previously, infants began to understand the language used by others to make sense of the world around them. How does this linguistic ability develop? What is the pattern and sequence of language development? And how does the use of language transform the cognitive world of infants and their parents? We consider these questions, and others, as we address the development of language during the first years of life.

The Fundamentals of Language: From Sounds to Symbols

LO 3.13 Outline the processes by which children learn to use language.

Language, the systematic, meaningful arrangement of symbols, provides the basis for communication. But it does more than this: It is closely tied to the way we think about and understand the world. It enables us to reflect on people and objects and to convey our thoughts to others.

Language has several formal characteristics that must be mastered as linguistic competence is developed. They include the following:

- **Phonology.** Phonology refers to the basic sounds of language, called *phonemes*, that can be combined to produce words and sentences. For instance, the "a" in "mat" and the "a" in "mate" represent two different phonemes in English. Although English employs just 40 phonemes to create every word in the language, other languages have as many as 85 phonemes—and some have as few as 15 (Swingley, 2017).

- **Morphemes.** A morpheme is the smallest language unit that has meaning. Some morphemes are complete words, whereas others add information necessary for interpreting a word, such as the endings "-s" for plural and "-ed" for past tense.

language
the systematic, meaningful arrangement of symbols, which provides the basis for communication

- **Semantics.** Semantics are the rules that govern the meaning of words and sentences. As their knowledge of semantics develops, children are able to understand the subtle distinction between "Ellie was hit by a ball" (an answer to the question of why Ellie doesn't want to play catch) and "A ball hit Ellie" (used to announce the current situation).

In considering the development of language, we need to distinguish between linguistic *comprehension*, the understanding of speech, and linguistic *production*, the use of language to communicate. One principle underlies the relationship between the two: Comprehension precedes production. An 18-month-old may be able to understand a complex series of directions ("Pick up your coat from the floor and put it on the chair by the fireplace") but may not yet have strung more than two words together when speaking for himself or herself. Throughout infancy, comprehension also outpaces production. For example, during infancy, comprehension of words expands at a rate of 22 new words a month, while production of words increases at a rate of about nine new words a month, once talking begins (Phung, Milojevich, & Lukowski, 2014; Kim, 2016; Swingley, 2017; Stahl & Feigenson, 2018; see Figure 3-14).

EARLY SOUNDS AND COMMUNICATION Spend 24 hours with even a very young infant and you will hear a variety of sounds: cooing, crying, gurgling, murmuring, and assorted types of other noises. These sounds, although not meaningful in themselves, play an important role in linguistic development, paving the way for true language (O'Grady & Aitchison, 2005; Martin, Onishi, & Vouloumanos, 2012; Kalashnikova & Burnham, 2018).

Prelinguistic communication is communication through sounds, facial expressions, gestures, imitation, and other nonlinguistic means. When a father responds to his daughter's "ah" with an "ah" of his own, and then the daughter repeats the sound, and the father responds once again, they are engaged in prelinguistic communication. Clearly, the "ah" sound has no particular meaning. However, its repetition, which mimics the give-and-take of conversation, teaches infants something about turn-taking and the back-and-forth of communication (Reddy, 1999; Orr, 2018).

Figure 3-14 Comprehension Precedes Production

Throughout infancy, the comprehension of speech precedes the production of speech.

SOURCE: Based on Bornstein & Lamb, 1992.

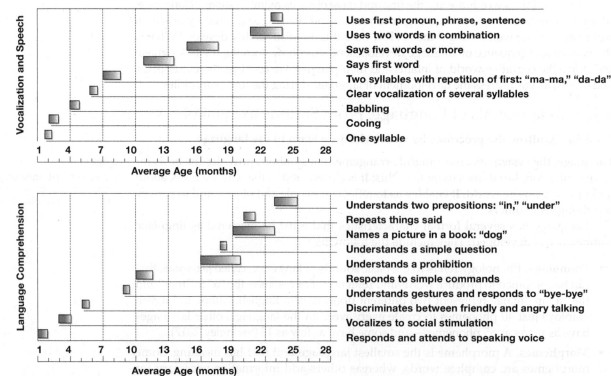

The most obvious manifestation of prelinguistic communication is babbling. **Babbling**, making speechlike but meaningless sounds, starts at the age of 2 or 3 months and continues until around the age of 1 year. When they babble, infants repeat the same vowel sound over and over, changing the pitch from high to low (as in "ee-ee-ee," repeated at different pitches). After the age of 5 months, the sounds of babbling begin to expand, reflecting the addition of consonants (such as "bee-bee-bee-bee").

babbling
making speechlike but meaningless sounds

Babbling is a universal phenomenon, accomplished in the same way throughout all cultures. While they are babbling, infants spontaneously produce all of the sounds found in every language, not just the language they hear people around them speaking.

Babbling, which follows a prelinguistic stage of cooing, typically follows a progression from simple to more complex sounds. Although exposure to the sounds of a particular language does not seem to influence babbling initially, eventually experience does make a difference. By the age of 6 months, babbling reflects the sounds of the language to which infants are exposed. The difference between cultures is so noticeable that even untrained listeners can distinguish between babbling infants who have been raised in cultures in which French, Arabic, or Cantonese languages are spoken. Furthermore, the speed at which infants begin homing in on their own language is related to the speed of later language development (Depaolis, Vihman, & Nakai, 2013; Masapollo, Polka, & Ménard, 2015; Antovich & Graf Estes, 2018; Lee et al., 2018).

FIRST WORDS When a mother and father first hear their child say "Mama" or "Dada," or even "baba," as in the case of Maura, the baby described previously in this section, it is hard to be anything but delighted. But their initial enthusiasm may be dampened a bit when they find that the same sound is used to ask for a cookie, a doll, and a ratty old blanket.

First words generally are spoken somewhere around the age of 10 to 14 months, but may occur as early as 9 months. Once an infant starts to produce words, vocabulary increases at a rapid rate. By the age of 15 months, the average child has a vocabulary of 10 words and methodically expands that vocabulary until the one-word stage of language development ends at around 18 months. Once that happens, a sudden spurt in vocabulary occurs. In just a short period—a few weeks somewhere between 16 and 24 months of age—there is an explosion of language, in which a child's vocabulary typically increases from 50 to 400 words (Nazzi & Bertoncini, 2003; McMurray, Aslin, & Toscano, 2009).

The first words in children's early vocabularies typically regard objects and things, both animate and inanimate. Most often they refer to people or objects who constantly appear and disappear ("Mama"), to animals ("kitty"), or to temporary states ("wet"). These first words are often **holophrases**, one-word utterances that stand for a whole phrase, whose meaning depends on the particular context in which they are used. For instance, a youngster may use the phrase "ma" to mean, depending on the context, "I want to be picked up by Mom" or "I want something to eat, Mom" or "Where's Mom?" (O'Grady & Aitchison, 2005).

holophrases
one-word utterances that stand for a whole phrase, the meaning of which depends on the particular context in which they are used

Culture has an effect on the type of first words spoken. For example, unlike North American English-speaking infants, who are more apt to use nouns initially, Chinese Mandarin-speaking infants use more verbs than nouns. However, by the age of 20 months, there are remarkable cross-cultural similarities in the types of words spoken. For example, a comparison of 20-month-olds in Argentina, Belgium, France, Israel, Italy, and the Republic of Korea found that children's vocabularies in every culture contained greater proportions of nouns than other classes of words (Tardif, 1996; Bornstein, Cote, & Maital, 2004; Andruski, Casielles, & Nathan, 2014).

FIRST SENTENCES

When Aaron was 19 months old, he heard his mother coming up the back steps, as she did every day just before dinner. Aaron turned to his father and distinctly said, "Ma come."

In stringing those two words together, Aaron took a giant step in his language development.

The explosive increase in vocabulary that comes at around 18 months is accompanied by another accomplishment: the linking together of individual words into sentences that convey a single thought. Although there is a good deal of variability in the time at which children first create two-word phrases, it is generally around 8 to 12 months after they say their first word.

The linguistic advance represented by two-word combinations is important because the linkage not only provides labels for things in the world but also indicates the relations between them. For instance, the combination may declare something about possession ("Mama key") or recurrent events ("Dog bark"). Interestingly, most early sentences don't represent demands or even necessarily require a response. Instead, they are often merely comments and observations about events occurring in the child's world (O'Grady & Aitchison, 2005; Rossi et al., 2012).

Two-year-olds using two-word combinations tend to employ particular sequences that are similar to the ways in which adult sentences are constructed. For instance, sentences in English typically follow a pattern in which the subject of the sentence comes first, followed by the verb, and then the object ("Josh threw the ball"). Children's speech most often uses a similar order, although not all the words are initially included. Consequently, a child might say "Josh threw" or "Josh ball" to indicate the same thought. What is significant is that the order is typically not "threw Josh" or "ball Josh," but rather the usual order of English, which makes the utterance much easier for an English speaker to comprehend (Hirsh-Pasek & Michnick-Golinkoff, 1995; Masataka, 2003).

Although the creation of two-word sentences represents an advance, the language used by children still is by no means adultlike. As we've just seen, 2-year-olds tend to leave out words that aren't critical to the message, similar to the way we might write a telegram for which we were paying by the word. For that reason, their talk is often called **telegraphic speech**. Rather than saying, "I showed you the book," a child using telegraphic speech might say, "I show book." "I am drawing a dog" might become "Drawing dog" (see Table 3-8).

Early language has other characteristics that differentiate it from the language used by adults. For instance, consider Sarah, who refers to the blanket she sleeps with as "blankie." When her Aunt Ethel gives her a new blanket, Sarah refuses to call the new one a "blankie," restricting the word to her original blanket.

Sarah's inability to generalize the label of "blankie" to blankets in general is an example of **underextension**, using words too restrictively, which is common among children just mastering spoken language. Underextension occurs when language novices think that a word refers to a specific instance of a concept, instead of to all examples of the concept (Masataka, 2003).

As infants like Sarah grow more adept with language, the opposite phenomenon sometimes occurs. In **overextension**, words are used too broadly, overgeneralizing their meaning. For example, when Sarah refers to buses, trucks, and tractors as "cars," she is demonstrating overextension, making the assumption that any object with wheels must be a car. Although overextension reflects speech errors, it also shows that advances are occurring in the child's thought processes: The child is beginning to develop general mental categories and concepts (McDonough, 2002; Wałaszewska, 2011).

telegraphic speech
speech in which words not critical to the message are left out

underextension
the overly restrictive use of words, common among children just mastering spoken language

overextension
the overly broad use of words, overgeneralizing their meaning

Table 3-8 Children's Imitation of Sentences Showing Decline of Telegraphic Speech

Sample Sentences	Speakers	26 months	29 months	32 months	35 months
I put on my shoes	Kim Darden	Shoes Shoes on	My shoes My shoes on	I put on shoes Put on shoes	A Put on my shoes
I will not go to bed	Kim Darden	No bed Not go bed	Not go bed I not go bed	I not go bed I not go to bed	I not go to bed I will not go bed
I want to ride the pony	Kim Darden	Pony, pony Want pony	Want ride pony I want pony	I want ride pony I want the pony	I want to ride pony A

A = accurate imitation.

SOURCE: Based on Brown & Fraser, 1963.

Infants also show individual differences in the style of language they use. For example, some use a **referential style**, in which language is used primarily to label objects. Others tend to use an **expressive style**, in which language is used primarily to express feelings and needs about oneself and others (Owens, 2016).

Language styles reflect, in part, cultural factors. For example, mothers in the United States label objects more frequently than do Japanese mothers, encouraging a more referential style of speech. In contrast, mothers in Japan are more apt to speak about social interactions, encouraging a more expressive style of speech (Fernald & Morikawa, 1993; Farran et al., 2016).

The Origins of Language Development

LO 3.14   Differentiate the major theories of language development, and describe how children influence adults' language.

The immense strides in language development during the preschool years raise a fundamental question: How does proficiency in language come about? Linguists are deeply divided on how to answer this question.

LEARNING THEORY APPROACHES: LANGUAGE AS A LEARNED SKILL   One view of language development emphasizes the basic principles of learning. According to the **learning theory approach**, language acquisition follows the basic laws of reinforcement and conditioning discussed in Chapter 1 (Skinner, 1957). For instance, a child who articulates the word "da" may be hugged and praised by her father, who jumps to the conclusion that he or she is referring to him. This reaction reinforces the child, who is more likely to repeat the word. In sum, the learning theory perspective on language acquisition suggests that children learn to speak by being rewarded for making sounds that approximate speech. Through the process of *shaping*, language becomes more and more similar to adult speech.

There's a problem, though, with the learning theory approach. It doesn't seem to adequately explain how children acquire the rules of language as readily as they do. For instance, young children are reinforced when they make errors. Parents are apt to be just as responsive if their child says, "Why the dog won't eat?" as they are if the child phrases the question more correctly ("Why won't the dog eat?"). Both forms of the question are understood correctly, and both elicit the same response; reinforcement is provided for both correct and incorrect language usage. Under such circumstances, learning theory is hard put to explain how children learn to speak properly.

Children are also able to move beyond specific utterances they have heard, and produce novel phrases, sentences, and constructions—an ability that also cannot be explained by learning theory. Furthermore, children can apply linguistic rules to nonsense words. In one study, 4-year-old children heard the nonsense verb "to pilk" in the sentence "the bear is pilking the horse." Later, when asked what was happening to the horse, they responded by placing the nonsense verb in the correct tense and voice: "He's getting pilked by the bear."

NATIVIST APPROACHES: LANGUAGE AS AN INNATE SKILL   Such conceptual difficulties with the learning theory approach have led to the development of an alternative, championed by linguist Noam Chomsky and known as the nativist approach (Chomsky, 1999, 2005). The **nativist approach** argues that there is a genetically determined, innate mechanism that directs the development of language. According to Chomsky, people are born with an innate capacity to use language, which emerges, more or less automatically, as a result of maturation.

Chomsky's analysis of different languages suggests that all the world's languages share a similar underlying structure, which he calls **universal grammar**. In this view, the human brain is wired with a neural system called the **language-acquisition device (LAD)** that both permits the understanding of language structure and provides a set of strategies and techniques for learning the particular characteristics of the language to which a child is exposed. In this view, language is uniquely human, made possible by a genetic predisposition to both comprehend and produce words and sentences (Bolhuis et al., 2014; Newmeyer, 2016; Yang et al., 2017).

referential style
a style of language use in which language is used primarily to label objects

expressive style
a style of language use in which language is used primarily to express feelings and needs about oneself and others

learning theory approach
the theory that language acquisition follows the basic laws of reinforcement and conditioning

nativist approach
the theory that a genetically determined, innate mechanism directs language development

universal grammar
Noam Chomsky's theory that all the world's languages share a similar underlying structure

language-acquisition device (LAD)
a neural system of the brain hypothesized to permit understanding of language

Support for Chomsky's nativist approach comes from recent findings identifying a specific gene related to speech production. Further support comes from research showing that language processing in infants involves brain structures similar to those in adult speech processing, suggesting an evolutionary basis to language (Dehaene-Lambertz, Hertz-Pannier, & Dubois, 2006; Clark & Lappin, 2013; Onnis, Truzzi, & Ma, 2018).

The view that language is an innate ability unique to humans also has its critics. For instance, some researchers argue that certain primates are able to learn at least the basics of language, an ability that calls into question the uniqueness of the human linguistic capacity. Furthermore, some critics believe that infants' use of general cognitive abilities underlies their language learning. Still others point out that although humans may be genetically primed to use language, its use still requires significant social experience for it to be used effectively (Goldberg, 2004; Ibbotson & Tomasello, 2016; Smith, 2018).

THE INTERACTIONIST APPROACHES Neither the learning theory nor the nativist perspective fully explains language acquisition. As a result, some theorists have turned to a theory that combines both schools of thought. The *interactionist perspective* suggests that language development is produced through a combination of genetically determined predispositions and environmental circumstances that help teach language.

The interactionist perspective accepts that innate factors shape the broad outlines of language development. However, interactionists also argue that the specific course of language development is determined by the language to which children are exposed and the reinforcement they receive for using language in particular ways. Social factors are considered to be key to development, because the motivation provided by one's membership in a society and culture and one's interactions with others leads to the use of language and the growth of language skills (Dixon, 2004; Yang, 2006; Graf Estes, 2014).

Just as there is support for some aspects of learning theory and nativist positions, the interactionist perspective has also received some support. We don't know, at the moment, which of these positions will ultimately provide the best explanation. More likely, different factors play different roles at different times during childhood.

INFANT-DIRECTED SPEECH Say the following sentence aloud: Do you like the applesauce?

Now pretend that you are going to ask the same question of an infant, and speak it as you would for a young child's ears.

Chances are several things happened when you translated the phrase for the infant. First of all, the wording probably changed, and you may have said something like, "Does baby like the applesauce?" At the same time, the pitch of your voice probably rose, your general intonation most likely had a singsong quality, and you probably separated your words carefully.

infant-directed speech

a type of speech directed toward infants, characterized by short, simple sentences

The shift in your language was as a result of your use of **infant-directed speech**, a style of speech that characterizes much of the verbal communication directed toward infants. This type of speech pattern used to be called *motherese* because it was assumed that it applied only to mothers. However, that assumption was wrong, and the gender-neutral term *infant-directed speech* is now used more frequently.

Infant-directed speech is characterized by short, simple sentences. Pitch becomes higher, the range of frequencies increases, and intonation is more varied. There is also repetition of words, and topics are restricted to items that are assumed to be comprehensible to infants, such as concrete objects in the baby's environment (Soderstrom, 2007; Matsuda et al., 2011; Hartman, Ratner, & Newman, 2017).

Sometimes infant-directed speech includes amusing sounds that are not even words, imitating the prelinguistic speech of infants. In other cases, it has little formal structure, but it is similar to the kind of telegraphic speech that infants use as they develop their own language skills.

Infant-directed speech changes as children become older. Around the end of the first year, infant-directed speech takes on more adultlike qualities. Sentences become

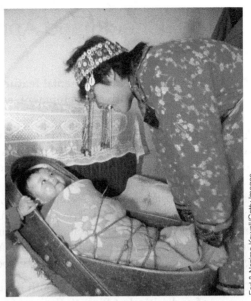

Infant-directed speech, which is common across cultures, includes the use of short, simple sentences and is spoken in a pitch that is higher than that used with older children and adults.

longer and more complex, although individual words are still spoken slowly and deliberately. Pitch is also used to focus attention on particularly important words (Soderstrom et al., 2008; Kitamura & Lam, 2009; Yamamoto & Haryu, 2018).

Infant-directed speech plays an important role in infants' acquisition of language. As discussed in the *Cultural Dimensions* box, infant-directed speech occurs all over the world, though there are cultural variations. Newborns prefer such speech to regular language, a fact that suggests that they may be particularly receptive to it. Furthermore, some research suggests that babies who are exposed to a great deal of infant-directed speech early in life seem to begin to use words and exhibit other forms of linguistic competence earlier (Bergelson & Swingley, 2012; Frank, Tenenbaum, & Fernald, 2013; Eaves et al., 2016).

Cultural Dimensions

Is Infant-Directed Speech Similar Across All Cultures?

Do mothers in the United States, Sweden, and Russia speak the same way to their infants?

In some respects, they clearly do. Although the words themselves differ across languages, the way the words are spoken to infants is quite similar. According to a growing body of research, there are basic similarities across cultures in the nature of infant-directed speech (Werker et al., 2007; Fais et al., 2010; Broesch & Bryant, 2015).

For example, 6 of the 10 most frequent major characteristics of speech directed at infants used by native speakers of English and Spanish are common to both languages: exaggerated intonation, high pitch, lengthened vowels, repetition, lower volume, and heavy stress on certain key words (such as emphasizing the word "ball" in the sentence, "No, that's a *ball*") (Blount, 1982). Similarly, mothers in the United States, Sweden, and Russia all exaggerate and elongate the pronunciation of the three vowel sounds of "ee," "ah," and "oh" when speaking to infants in similar ways, despite differences in the languages in which the sounds are used (Kuhl et al., 1997).

Even deaf mothers use a form of infant-directed speech: When communicating with their infants, deaf mothers use sign language at a significantly slower tempo than when communicating with adults, and they frequently repeat the signs (Swanson, Leonard, & Gandour, 1992; Masataka, 2000).

From an educator's perspective: How do you think the use of infant-directed speech helps infants learn language?

Review, Check, and Apply

Review

LO 3.9 Summarize the fundamental features of Piaget's theory of cognitive development, and describe the sensorimotor stage.

Piaget's theory of human development involves a succession of stages through which children progress from birth to adolescence. As infants move from one stage to another, the way they understand the world changes. The sensorimotor stage has six substages. The sensorimotor stage, from birth to about 2 years, involves a gradual progression through simple reflexes, single coordinated activities, interest in the outside world, purposeful combinations of activities, manipulation of actions to produce desired outcomes, and symbolic thought.

LO 3.10 Summarize the arguments both in support of and critical of Piaget's theory of cognitive development.

Although Piaget's theory accurately describes cognitive development in the broad sense, many specifics of the theory, particularly the age at which various skills develop, has been challenged.

LO 3.11 Describe how information processing approaches explain cognitive development in infants, and summarize the memory capabilities of infants in the first 2 years of life.

Information processing approaches to the study of cognitive development seek to learn how individuals receive, organize, store, and retrieve information. Such approaches differ from Piaget's theory by considering quantitative changes in children's ability to process information. Infants have memory capabilities from their earliest days, although the accuracy of infant memories is a matter of debate.

LO 3.12 Explain how infant intelligence is measured using information processing approaches.

Traditional measures of infant intelligence, such as Gesell's developmental quotient and the Bayley Scales of Infant Development, focus on average behavior observed at particular ages in large numbers of children. Information processing approaches to assessing intelligence rely on variations in the speed and quality with which infants process information.

LO 3.13 Outline the processes by which children learn to use language.

Prelinguistic communication involves the use of sounds, gestures, facial expressions, imitation, and other nonlinguistic means to express thoughts and states. Prelinguistic communication prepares infants for speech. Infants typically produce their first words between the ages of 10 and 14 months. At around 18 months, children typically begin to link words together into primitive sentences that express single thoughts. Beginning speech is characterized by the use of holophrases, telegraphic speech, underextension, and overextension.

LO 3.14 Differentiate the major theories of language development, and describe how children influence adults' language.

Learning theorists believe that basic learning processes account for language development, whereas nativists like Noam Chomsky and his followers argue that humans have an innate language capacity. The interactionists suggest that language is a consequence of both environmental and innate factors. In using infant-directed speech, adults shift their use of language to a higher pitch and a style of speech using, short, simple sentences.

Check Yourself

1. According to Piaget, children can move from one cognitive stage to another only when a child _____ and is exposed to relevant experiences.
   a. is adequately nourished
   b. is born with a genetic predisposition for learning
   c. has constructed a mental sense of the world
   d. reaches an appropriate level of physical maturation

2. Unlike Piaget's approach to cognitive development, which stresses the _____ changes that occur in infants' capabilities, the information processing approach to cognitive development emphasizes the _____ changes.
   a. gross motor; fine motor
   b. qualitative; quantitative
   c. sensory; perceptual
   d. explicit; implicit

3. Like other 2-year-olds, Mason can say "Doggie bye, bye" and "Milk gone." These two-word phrases are examples of _____ speech.
   a. holophrastic
   b. telegraphic
   c. interpretive
   d. active

4. One theory, the _____ approach, suggests that a genetically determined, innate mechanism directs language development.
   a. nativist
   b. universal
   c. learning theory
   d. evolutionary

Applying Lifespan Development

What are some ways in which children's linguistic development reflects their acquisition of new ways of interpreting and dealing with their world?

Module 3.3

Social and Personality Development in Infancy

Emotional Rollercoaster

Chantelle Evans has always been a happy baby. That's why her mother Michelle was so surprised to find her 10-month-old daughter in tears when she returned to pick her up from a neighbor after having lunch with friends. "Chantelle knows Janine," Michelle says. "She sees her regularly out in the yard. I don't understand why she was so unhappy. I was only away for 2 hours." Janine told Michelle she had tried everything—rocking Chantelle, singing to her—but nothing helped. It wasn't until Chantelle, red-faced, tears streaming, saw her mother again that she smiled.

Michelle Evans will someday be able to have lunch with friends without worrying that her daughter is miserable, but Chantelle's reaction is perfectly normal for a 10-month-old baby. In this module we consider social and personality development in infancy. We begin by examining the emotional lives of infants, considering which emotions they feel and how well they can read others' emotions. We look at how babies view their own and others' mental lives.

We then turn to infants' social relationships. We look at how they forge bonds of attachment and the ways they interact with family members and peers. Finally, we cover the characteristics that differentiate one infant from another and discuss differences in the

way children are treated depending on their gender. We'll consider the nature of family life and look at the advantages and disadvantages of infant child care outside the home, a child-care option that today's families increasingly employ.

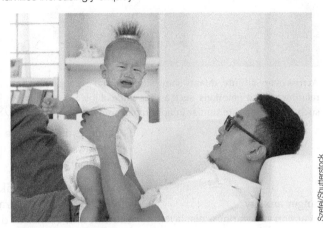

Typically, infants begin to display stranger anxiety near the end of the first year of life.

Developing the Roots of Sociability

> Germaine smiles when he catches a glimpse of his mother. Tawanda looks angry when her mother takes away the spoon that she is playing with. Sydney scowls when a loud plane flies overhead.

A smile. A look of anger. A scowl. The emotions of infancy are written all over a baby's face. Yet do infants experience emotions in the same way that adults do? When do they become capable of understanding what others are experiencing emotionally? And how do they use others' emotional states to make sense of their environment? We consider some of these questions as we seek to understand how infants develop emotionally and socially.

Emotions in Infancy: Do Infants Experience Emotional Highs and Lows?

LO 3.15 Discuss how children express and experience emotions in the first 2 years of life, and summarize the development of social referencing.

Anyone who spends any time at all around infants knows they display facial expressions that seem indicative of their emotional states. In situations in which we expect them to be happy, they seem to smile; when we might assume they are frustrated, they show anger; and when we might expect them to be unhappy, they look sad.

In fact, these basic facial expressions are remarkably similar across the most diverse cultures. Whether we look at babies in India, the United States, or the jungles of New Guinea, the expression of basic emotions is the same. Furthermore, the nonverbal expression of emotion, called *nonverbal encoding*, is fairly consistent among people of all ages. These consistencies have led researchers to conclude that we are born with the capacity to display basic emotions (Ackerman & Izard, 2004; Bornstein, Suwalsky, & Breakstone, 2012; Rajhans et al., 2016).

Infants display a fairly wide range of emotional expressions. Almost all mothers report that by the age of 1 month their babies have nonverbally expressed interest and joy. Careful coding of infants' nonverbal expressions shows that interest, distress, and disgust are present at birth, and that other emotions emerge over the next few months. Such findings are

Across every culture, infants show similar facial expressions relating to basic emotions, such as this smile of joy. Do you think such expressions are similar in nonhuman animals?

consistent with the work of the famous naturalist Charles Darwin, whose 1872 book *The Expression of the Emotions in Man and Animals* argued that humans and primates have an inborn, universal set of emotional expressions—a view consistent with today's evolutionary approach to development (Benson, 2003; MacLean et al., 2014; Smith & Weiss, 2017; Webb, Ayers, & Andress, 2018).

Although infants display similar *kinds* of emotions, the *degree* of emotional expressivity varies among infants. Children in different cultures show reliable differences in emotional expressiveness, even during infancy. For example, by the age of 11 months, Chinese infants are generally less expressive than European, American, and Japanese infants (Camras et al., 2007; Izard, Woodburn, & Finlon, 2010; Easterbrooks et al., 2013).

STRANGER ANXIETY AND SEPARATION ANXIETY

"She used to be such a friendly baby," thought Erika's mother. "No matter whom she encountered, she had a big smile. But almost the day she turned 7 months old, she began to react to strangers as if she were seeing a ghost. Her face crinkles up with a frown, and she either turns away or stares at them with suspicion. It's as if she has undergone a personality transplant."

stranger anxiety
the caution and wariness displayed by infants when encountering an unfamiliar person

What happened to Erika is, in fact, quite typical. By the end of the first year, infants often develop both stranger anxiety and separation anxiety. **Stranger anxiety** is the caution and wariness displayed by infants when encountering an unfamiliar person. Such anxiety typically appears in the second half of the first year.

What brings on stranger anxiety? Brain development and the increased cognitive abilities of infants play a role. As infants' memory develops, they are able to separate the people they know from the people they don't. The same cognitive advances that allow them to respond so positively to those people with whom they are familiar also give them the ability to recognize people who are unfamiliar. Furthermore, between 6 and 9 months, infants begin trying to make sense of their world, trying to anticipate and predict events. When something happens that they don't expect—such as the appearance of an unknown person—they experience fear. It's as if an infant has a question but is unable to answer it (Volker, 2007; Mash, Bornstein, & Arterberry, 2013).

separation anxiety
the distress displayed by infants when a customary care provider departs

Separation anxiety is the distress displayed by infants when a customary care provider departs. Separation anxiety, which is also universal across cultures, usually begins at about 7 or 8 months (see Figure 3-15). It peaks around 14 months, and then

Figure 3-15 Separation Anxiety

Separation anxiety, the distress displayed by infants when their usual care provider leaves their presence, is a universal phenomenon beginning at around the age of 7 or 8 months. It peaks at around the age of 14 months and then begins to decline. Does separation anxiety have survival value for humans?

SOURCE: Based on Kagan, J., Kearsley, R., & Zelazo, P. R. (1978). Infancy: Its place in human development. Cambridge, MA: Harvard University Press.

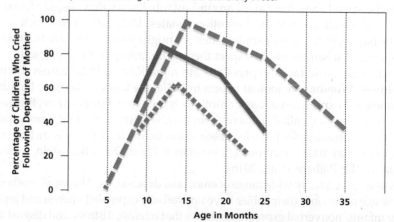

decreases. Separation anxiety is largely attributable to the same reasons as stranger anxiety. Infants' growing cognitive skills allow them to ask reasonable questions, but they may be questions that they are too young to understand the answer to: "Why is my mother leaving?" "Where is she going?" and "Will she come back?"

Stranger anxiety and separation anxiety represent important social progress. They reflect both cognitive advances and the growing emotional and social bonds between infants and their caregivers—bonds that we'll consider later in the module when we discuss infants' social relationships.

SMILING

> As Luz lay sleeping in her crib, her mother and father caught a glimpse of the most beautiful smile crossing her face. Her parents were sure that Luz was having a pleasant dream. Were they right?

Probably not. The earliest smiles expressed during sleep probably have little meaning, although no one can be absolutely sure. By 6 to 9 weeks of age, babies begin to smile reliably at the sight of stimuli that please them, including toys, mobiles, and—to the delight of parents—people. The first smiles tend to be relatively indiscriminate because infants first begin to smile at the sight of almost anything they find amusing. However, as they get older, they become more selective in their smiles.

A baby's smile in response to another person, rather than to nonhuman stimuli, is considered a *social smile*. As babies get older, their social smiles become directed toward particular individuals, not just anyone. By the age of 18 months, social smiling, directed more toward mothers and other caregivers, becomes more frequent than smiling directed toward nonhuman objects. Moreover, if an adult is unresponsive to a child, the amount of smiling decreases. In short, by the end of the second year children are quite purposefully using smiling to communicate their positive emotions, and they are sensitive to the emotional expressions of others (Reissland & Cohen, 2012; Wörmann et al., 2014; Bai, Repetti, & Sperling, 2016).

DECODING OTHERS' FACIAL EXPRESSIONS   In Chapter 2, we discussed the possibility that neonates can imitate adults' facial expressions even minutes after birth. Although their imitative abilities certainly do not imply that they can understand the meaning of others' facial expressions, such imitation does pave the way for *nonverbal decoding* abilities, which begin to emerge fairly soon. Using these abilities, infants can interpret others' facial and vocal expressions that carry emotional meaning. For example, they can tell when a caregiver is happy to see them and pick up on worry or fear in the faces of others (Hernandez-Reif et al., 2006; Striano & Vaish, 2006; Hoehl et al., 2012).

In the first 6 to 8 weeks, infants' visual precision is sufficiently limited that they cannot pay much attention to others' facial expressions. But they soon begin to discriminate among different facial expressions of emotion and even seem to be able to respond to differences in emotional intensity conveyed by facial expressions. By the time they reach the age of 4 months, infants already have begun to understand the emotions that lie behind the facial and vocal expressions of others (Farroni et al., 2007; Kim & Johnson, 2013; Cong et al., 2018).

SOCIAL REFERENCING: FEELING WHAT OTHERS FEEL

> Twenty-three-month-old Stephania watches as her older brother Eric and his friend Chen argue loudly with each other and begin to wrestle. Uncertain of what is happening, Stephania glances at her mother. Her mother, though, wears a smile, knowing that Eric and Chen are just playing. On seeing her mother's reaction, Stephania smiles too, mimicking her mother's facial expression.

Like Stephania, most of us have been in situations in which we feel uncertain. In such cases, we sometimes turn to others to see how they are reacting. This reliance on others, known as social referencing, helps us decide what an appropriate response ought to be.

Social referencing is the intentional search for information about others' feelings to help explain the meaning of uncertain circumstances and events. Like Stephania, we use social referencing to clarify the meaning of a situation and so to reduce our uncertainty about what is occurring.

social referencing
the intentional search for information about others' feelings to help explain the meaning of uncertain circumstances and events

Social referencing first occurs around the age of 8 or 9 months. It is a fairly sophisticated social ability: Infants need it not only to understand the significance of others' behavior, by using such cues as their facial expressions, but also to understand the meaning of those behaviors within the context of a specific situation (Hepach & Westermann, 2013; Mireault et al., 2014; Walle, Reschke, & Knothe, 2017).

> **From a social worker's perspective:** In what situations do adults rely on social referencing to work out appropriate responses? How might social referencing be used to influence parents' behavior toward their children?

The Development of Self

LO 3.16 Describe the sense of self that children possess in the first 2 years of life, including the development of a theory of mind.

Do infants know who they are? And what are their thoughts about thinking? We consider the following questions next.

SELF-AWARENESS

Elysa, 8 months old, crawls past the full-length mirror that hangs on a door in her parents' bedroom. She barely pays any attention to her reflection as she moves by. On the other hand, her cousin Brianna, who is almost 2 years old, stares at herself in the mirror as she passes and laughs as she notices, and then rubs off a smear of jelly on her forehead.

Perhaps you have had the experience of catching a glimpse of yourself in a mirror and noticing a hair out of place. You probably reacted by attempting to push the unruly hair back into place. Your reaction shows more than that you care about how you look. It implies that you have a sense of yourself, the awareness and knowledge that you are an independent social entity to which others react, and which you attempt to present to the world in ways that reflect favorably upon you.

However, we are not born with the knowledge that we exist independently from others and the larger world. Very young infants do not have a sense of themselves as individuals; they do not recognize themselves in photos or mirrors. However, the roots of **self-awareness**, knowledge of oneself, begin to grow after the age of 12 months.

We know this from a simple but ingenious experimental technique in which an infant's nose is secretly colored with a dab of red powder. Then the infant is seated in front of a mirror. If infants touch their noses or attempt to wipe off the rouge, we have evidence that they have at least some knowledge of their physical characteristics. Although some infants as young as 12 months seem startled on seeing the rouge spot, for most a reaction does not occur until between 17 and 24 months of age. This awareness is one step in infants' understanding of themselves as independent objects (Rochat, 2004; Brownell et al., 2010; Rochat, Broesch, & Jayne, 2012).

self-awareness
knowledge of oneself

theory of mind
knowledge and beliefs about how the mind works and how it affects behavior

THEORY OF MIND: INFANTS' PERSPECTIVES ON THE MENTAL LIVES OF OTHERS AND THEMSELVES Infants begin to understand certain things about their own and others' mental processes at quite an early age, starting to develop a **theory of mind**, their knowledge and beliefs about how the mind works and how it influences behavior. Theories of mind are the explanations that children use to explain how others think.

For instance, cognitive advances during infancy that we discussed earlier in this chapter permit older infants to see people in a different way from other objects. They learn to see other people as *compliant agents*, beings similar to themselves who behave under their own power and who have the capacity to respond to infants' requests (Rochat, 2004; Slaughter & Peterson, 2012).

In addition, children's capacity to understand intentionality and causality grows during infancy. For example, 10- and 13-month-olds are able to mentally represent social dominance,

Research suggests that this 18-month-old baby is exhibiting a clearly developing sense of self.

believing that larger size is related to the ability to dominate other, smaller sized individuals and objects. Furthermore, infants have a kind of innate morality, in which they show a preference for helpfulness (Sloane, Baillargeon, & Premack, 2012; Ruffman, 2014; Yott & Poulin-Dubois, 2016).

Furthermore, as early as 18 months, they begin to understand that others' behaviors have meaning and that the behaviors they see people enacting are designed to accomplish particular goals, in contrast to the "behaviors" of inanimate objects. For example, a child comes to understand that his father has a specific goal when he is in the kitchen making sandwiches. In contrast, his father's car is simply parked in the driveway, having no mental life or goal (Ahn, Gelman, & Amsterlaw, 2000; Wellman et al., 2008; Senju et al., 2011).

Another piece of evidence for infants' growing sense of mental activity is that by the age of 2, infants begin to demonstrate the rudiments of empathy. **Empathy** is an emotional response that corresponds to the feelings of another person. At 24 months of age, infants sometimes comfort others or show concern for them. To do this, they need to be aware of the emotional states of others. For example, 1-year-olds are able to pick up emotional cues by observing the behavior of an actress on television (Legerstee, 2014; Xu, Saether, & Sommerville, 2016; Peltola, Yrttiaho, & Leppänen, 2018).

empathy
an emotional response that corresponds to the feelings of another person

Furthermore, during their second year, infants begin to use deception, both in games of "pretend" and in outright attempts to fool others. A child who plays "pretend" and who uses falsehoods must be aware that others hold beliefs about the world—beliefs that can be manipulated.

In short, by the end of infancy children have developed the rudiments of their own personal theory of mind. It helps them understand the actions of others and it affects their own behavior. Still, theory of mind is not fully developed during infancy and grows in sophistication as children continue to age (Caron, 2009).

Forming Relationships

Luis Camacho, now 38, clearly remembers the feelings that haunted him on the way to the hospital to meet his new sister Katy. Though he was only 4 at the time, that day of infamy is still vivid to him today. Luis would no longer be the only kid in the house; he would have to share his life with a baby sister. She would play with his toys, read his books, and be with him in the back seat of the car.

What really bothered him, of course, was that he would have to share his parents' love and attention with a new person. And not just any new person—a girl, who would automatically have a lot of advantages. Katy would be cuter, needier, more demanding, more interesting—more everything—than he. He would be underfoot at best, neglected at worst.

Luis also knew that he was expected to be cheerful and welcoming. So he put on a brave face at the hospital and walked without hesitation to the room where his mother and Katy were waiting.

The arrival of a newborn brings a dramatic change to a family's dynamics. No matter how welcome a baby's birth, it causes a fundamental shift in the roles that people play within the family. Mothers and fathers must start to build a relationship with their infant, and older children must adjust to the presence of a new member of the family and build their own alliance with their infant brother or sister.

Although the process of social development during infancy is neither simple nor automatic, it is crucial: The bonds that grow between infants and their parents, siblings, family, and others provide the foundation for a lifetime's worth of social relationships.

Attachment: Forming Social Bonds

LO 3.17   **Explain attachment in infancy, how it affects a person's future social competence, and the roles that caregivers play in infants' social development.**

The most important aspect of social development that takes place during infancy is the formation of attachment. **Attachment** is the positive emotional bond that develops between a child and a particular, special individual. When children experience

attachment
the positive emotional bond that develops between a child and a particular individual

attachment to a given person, they feel pleasure when they are with them and feel comforted by their presence at times of distress. The nature of our attachment during infancy affects how we relate to others throughout the rest of our lives (Bergman et al., 2015; Kim et al., 2017; Zajac et al., 2018).

To understand attachment, the earliest researchers turned to the bonds that form between parents and children in the nonhuman animal kingdom. For instance, ethologist Konrad Lorenz (1965) observed newborn goslings, who have an innate tendency to follow their mother, the first moving object to which they typically are exposed after birth. Lorenz found that goslings hatched from an incubator, who viewed him just after hatching, would follow his every movement, as if he were their mother. As we discussed in Chapter 1, he labeled this process *imprinting*: behavior that takes place during a critical period and involves attachment to the first moving object that is observed.

Lorenz's findings suggested that attachment was based on biologically determined factors, and other theorists agreed. For instance, Freud suggested that attachment grew out of a mother's ability to satisfy a child's oral needs. Similarly, British psychiatrist John Bowlby (1951) argued that attachment is based primarily on infants' needs for safety and security. As they develop, infants come to learn that their safety is best provided by a particular individual, typically the mother, and they develop a relationship with the primary caregiver that is qualitatively different from the bonds formed with others. In his view, attachment provides a type of home base. As children become more independent, they can progressively roam further away from their secure base.

THE AINSWORTH STRANGE SITUATION AND PATTERNS OF ATTACHMENT

Ainsworth Strange Situation

a sequence of staged episodes that illustrate the strength of attachment between a child and (typically) his or her mother

Developmental psychologist Mary Ainsworth built on Bowlby's theorizing to develop a widely used experimental technique to measure attachment (Ainsworth et al., 1978). The **Ainsworth Strange Situation** consists of a sequence of staged episodes that illustrate the strength of attachment between a child and (typically) his or her mother.

The "strange situation" follows this general eight-step pattern: (1) The mother and baby enter an unfamiliar room; (2) the mother sits down, leaving the baby free to explore; (3) an adult stranger enters the room and converses first with the mother and then with the baby; (4) the mother exits the room, leaving the baby alone with the stranger; (5) the mother returns, greeting and comforting the baby, and the stranger leaves; (6) the mother departs again, leaving the baby alone; (7) the stranger returns; and (8) the mother returns and the stranger leaves.

secure attachment pattern

a style of attachment in which children use the mother as a kind of home base and are at ease when she is present; when she leaves, they become upset and go to her as soon as she returns

Infants' reactions to the various aspects of the Strange Situation vary considerably, depending on the nature of their attachment to their mothers. One-year-olds typically show one of four major patterns—secure, avoidant, ambivalent, and disorganized–disoriented (summarized in Table 3-9). Children who have a **secure attachment pattern** use the mother as the type of home base that Bowlby described. These children seem at ease in the Strange Situation as long as their mothers are present. They explore independently, returning to her occasionally. Although they may or may not appear upset when she leaves, securely attached children immediately go to her when she returns and seek contact. Most North American children—about two-thirds—fall into the securely attached category.

Table 3-9 Classifications of Infant Attachment

| Label | Classification Criteria | | | |
	Seeking Proximity with Caregiver	Maintaining Contact with Caregiver	Avoiding Proximity with Caregiver	Resisting Contact with Caregiver
Avoidant	Low	Low	High	Low
Secure	High	High (if distressed)	Low	Low
Ambivalent	High	High (often preseparation)	Low	High
Disorganized–disoriented	Inconsistent	Inconsistent	Inconsistent	Inconsistent

In contrast, children with an **avoidant attachment pattern** do not seek proximity to the mother, and after she has left, they typically do not seem distressed. Furthermore, they seem to avoid her when she returns. It is as if they are indifferent to her behavior. Some 20 percent of 1-year-old children are in the avoidant category.

Children with an **ambivalent attachment pattern** display a combination of positive and negative reactions to their mothers. Initially, ambivalent children are in such close contact with the mother that they hardly explore their environment. They appear anxious even before the mother leaves, and when she does leave, they show great distress. But upon her return, they show ambivalent reactions, seeking to be close to her but also hitting and kicking, apparently in anger. About 10 to 15 percent of 1-year-olds fall into the ambivalent classification (Cassidy & Berlin, 1994; Meins, 2016).

Although Ainsworth identified only three categories, a more recent expansion of her work finds that there is a fourth category: disorganized–disoriented. Children who have a **disorganized–disoriented attachment pattern** show inconsistent, contradictory, and confused behavior. They may run to the mother when she returns but not look at her, or seem initially calm and then suddenly break into angry weeping. Their confusion suggests that they may be the least securely attached children of all. About 5 to 10 percent of all children fall into this category (Cole, 2005; Bernier & Meins, 2008; Reijman, Foster, & Duschinsky, 2018).

The quality of attachment between infants and their mothers has significant consequences for relationships at later stages of life. For example, boys who are securely attached at the age of 1 year show fewer psychological difficulties at older ages than do avoidant or ambivalent children. Similarly, children who are securely attached as infants tend to be more socially and emotionally competent later, and others view them more positively (Simpson et al., 2007; MacDonald et al., 2008; Bergman, Blom, & Polyak, 2012).

In cases in which the development of attachment has been severely disrupted, children may suffer from *reactive attachment disorder*, a psychological problem characterized by extreme problems in forming attachments to others. In young children, it results in feeding difficulties, unresponsiveness to social overtures from others, and a general failure to thrive. Reactive attachment disorder is rare and typically the result of abuse or neglect (Hornor, 2008; Schechter & Willheim, 2009; Puckering et al., 2011).

PRODUCING ATTACHMENT: THE ROLES OF MOTHER AND FATHER

> As 5-month-old Annie cries passionately, her mother comes into the room and gently lifts her from her crib. After just a few moments, as her mother rocks Annie and speaks softly, Annie's cries cease, and she cuddles in her mother's arms. But the moment her mother places her back in the crib, Annie begins to wail again, leading her mother to pick her up once again.

The pattern is familiar to most parents. Infants cry, the parent reacts, and the infant responds in turn. Such seemingly insignificant sequences as these, repeatedly occurring in the lives of infants and parents, help pave the way for the development of relationships between children, their parents, and the rest of the social world. We'll consider how each of the major caregivers and infants play a role in the development of attachment.

> **From a social worker's perspective:** What might a social worker seeking to find a good home for a foster child look for when evaluating potential foster parents?

Mothers and Attachment Sensitivity to their infants' needs and desires is the hallmark of mothers of securely attached infants. Such a mother tends to be aware of her child's moods, and she takes into account her child's feelings as they interact. She is also responsive during face-to-face interactions, provides feeding "on demand," and is warm and affectionate to her infant (McElwain & Booth-LaForce, 2006; Priddis & Howieson, 2009; Evans, Whittingham, & Boyd, 2012).

avoidant attachment pattern
a style of attachment in which children do not seek proximity to the mother; after the mother has left, they seem to avoid her when she returns as if they are angered by her behavior

ambivalent attachment pattern
a style of attachment in which children display a combination of positive and negative reactions to their mothers

disorganized–disoriented attachment pattern
a style of attachment in which children show inconsistent, often contradictory behavior, such as approaching the mother when she returns but not looking at her

A growing body of research highlights the importance of a father's demonstration of love for his children. In fact, certain disorders such as depression and substance abuse have been found to be more related to fathers' than to mothers' behavior.

Japanese parents seek to avoid separation and stress during infancy and do not foster independence. As a result, Japanese children often have the appearance of being less securely attached according to the Strange Situation, but using other measurement techniques they may well score higher in attachment.

It is not only a matter of responding in *any* fashion to their infants' signals that separates mothers of securely attached and insecurely attached children. Mothers of secure infants tend to provide the appropriate level of response. In fact, overly responsive mothers are just as likely to have insecurely attached children as underresponsive mothers. In contrast, mothers whose communication involves *interactional synchrony*—in which caregivers respond to infants appropriately and both caregiver and child match emotional states—are more likely to produce secure attachment (Hane, Feldstein, & Dernetz, 2003; Ambrose & Menna, 2013).

Fathers and Attachment   Up to now, we've barely touched on one of the key players involved in the upbringing of a child: the father. In fact, if you looked at the early theorizing and research on attachment, you'd find little mention of the father and his potential contributions to the life of infants (Freeman, Newland, & Coyl, 2010; Palm, 2014).

However, it has become increasingly clear that—despite societal norms that sometimes relegate fathers to secondary childrearing roles—infants can form their primary initial relationship with their fathers. Indeed, much of what we have said about mothers' attachment also applies to fathers. For example, fathers' expressions of nurturance, warmth, affection, support, and concern are extremely important to their children's emotional and social well-being. Furthermore, some psychological disorders, such as substance abuse and depression, have been found to be related more to fathers' than mothers' behavior (Roelofs et al., 2006; Condon et al., 2013; Braungart-Rieker et al., 2015).

Infants' social bonds extend beyond their parents, especially as they grow older. For example, one study found that although most infants formed their first primary relationship with one person, around one-third had multiple relationships, and it was often difficult to determine which attachment was primary. Furthermore, by the time the infants were 18 months old, most had formed multiple relationships. In sum, infants may develop attachments not only to their mothers, but also to a variety of others (Booth, Kelly, & Spieker, 2003; Seibert & Kerns, 2009; Dagan & Sagi, 2018; see also the *Cultural Dimensions* box).

Cultural Dimensions

Does Attachment Differ Across Cultures?

John Bowlby's observations of the biologically motivated efforts of the young of other species to seek safety and security were the basis for his views on attachment and his reason for suggesting that seeking attachment was biologically universal, an effort that we should find not only in other species, but also among humans of all cultures.

Research has shown that human attachment is not as culturally universal as Bowlby predicted. Certain attachment patterns seem more likely among infants of particular cultures. For example, one study of German infants showed that most fell into the avoidant category. Other studies, conducted in Israel and Japan, have found a smaller proportion of infants who were securely attached than in the United States. Finally, comparisons of Chinese and Canadian children show that Chinese children are more inhibited than Canadians in the Strange Situation (Rothbaum et al., 2000; Tomlinson, Murray, & Cooper, 2010; Kieffer, 2012).

Do such findings suggest that we should abandon the notion that attachment is a universal biological tendency? Not necessarily. Most of the data on attachment have been obtained by using the Ainsworth Strange Situation, which may not be the most appropriate measure in non-Western cultures. For example, Japanese parents seek to avoid separation and stress during infancy, and they don't strive to foster independence to the same degree as parents in many Western societies. Because of their relative lack of prior experience in separation, infants placed in the Strange Situation may experience unusual stress—producing the appearance of less secure attachment in Japanese children. If a different measure of attachment were used, one that might be administered later in infancy, more Japanese infants could likely be classified as secure. In short, attachment is affected by cultural norms and expectations (Vereijken, Riksen-Walraven, & Kondo-Ikemura, 1997; Dennis, Cole, & Zahn-Waxler, 2002; Archer et al., 2015).

Infants' Sociability With Their Peers: Infant–Infant Interaction

LO 3.18 Discuss the development of peer relationships in infancy.

Although it is clear that they do not form "friendships" in the traditional sense, babies do react positively to the presence of peers from early in life, and they engage in rudimentary forms of social interaction.

Infants' sociability is expressed in several ways. From the earliest months of life, they smile, laugh, and vocalize while looking at their peers. They show more interest in peers than in inanimate objects and pay greater attention to other infants than they do to a mirror image of themselves. They also begin to show preferences for peers with whom they are familiar compared with those they do not know. For example, studies of identical twins show that twins exhibit a higher level of social behavior toward each other than toward an unfamiliar infant (Eid et al., 2003; Legerstee, 2014; Kawakami, 2014).

Infants' level of sociability rises with age. Nine- to 12-month-olds mutually present and accept toys, particularly if they know each other. They also play social games, such as peekaboo or crawl-and-chase. Such behavior is important because it serves as a foundation for future social exchanges in which children will try to elicit responses from others and then offer reactions to those responses. These kinds of exchanges are important to learn, because they continue even into adulthood. For example, someone who says, "Hi, what's up?" may be trying to elicit a response to which he or she can then reply (Endo, 1992; Eckerman & Peterman, 2001).

Finally, as infants age, they begin to imitate each other. For instance, 3-month-old infants who are familiar with one another sometimes reproduce each other's behavior and vocalizations. Such imitation serves a social function and can also be a powerful teaching tool (Ray & Heyes, 2011; Brownell, 2016; Pelaez, Borroto, & Carrow, 2018).

To some developmentalists, the capacity of young children to engage in imitation suggests that imitation may be inborn. In support of this view, research has identified a class of neurons in the brain that seems related to an innate ability to imitate. *Mirror neurons* are neurons that fire not only when an individual enacts a particular behavior, but also when the individual simply observes *another* organism carrying out the same behavior (Falck-Ytter et al., 2006; Paulus, 2014).

For example, research on brain functioning shows activation of the inferior frontal gyrus both when an individual carries out a particular task and when observing another individual carrying out the same task. Mirror neurons may help infants understand others' actions, to develop a theory of mind, and to show goal-directed behavior from the time of birth. Dysfunction of mirror neurons may be related to the development of disorders involving children's theory of mind as well as autism spectrum disorder, a psychological disorder involving significant emotional and linguistic problems (Welsh et al., 2009; von Hofsten & Rosander, 2015; Hanawa et al., 2016).

Differences Among Infants

Lincoln was a difficult baby; his parents both agreed. For one thing, it seemed like they could never get him to sleep at night. He cried at the slightest noise—a problem because his crib was near the windows facing a busy street. Worse yet, once he started crying, it seemed to take forever to calm him down again. One day his mother, Aisha, was telling her mother-in-law, Mary, about the challenges of being Lincoln's mom. Mary recalled that her own son, Lincoln's father, Malcom, had been much the same way. "He was my first child, and I thought this was how all babies acted. So, we just kept trying different ways until we found out how he worked. I remember, we put his crib all over the apartment until we finally found out where he could sleep, and it ended up being in the hallway for a long time. Then his sister, Maleah, came along, and she was so quiet and easy, I didn't know what to do with my extra time!"

As the story of Lincoln's family shows, babies are not all alike, and neither are their families. In fact, as we'll see, some of the differences among people seem to be present from the moment we are born. The differences among infants include overall personality and temperament, and differences in the lives they lead—differences based on their gender, the nature of their families, and the ways in which they are cared for.

Personality Development: The Characteristics That Make Infants Unique

LO 3.19   Describe individual differences that distinguish an infant's personality and the roles that temperament and gender play.

personality
the sum total of the enduring characteristics that differentiate one individual from another

The origins of **personality**, the sum total of the enduring characteristics that differentiate one individual from another, stem from infancy. From birth onward, infants begin to show unique, stable traits and behaviors that ultimately lead to their development as distinct, special individuals (Caspi, 2000; Kagan, 2000; Shiner, Masten, & Roberts, 2003).

According to psychologist Erik Erikson, whose approach to personality development we first discussed in Module 1.2, infants' early experiences are responsible for shaping one of the key aspects of their personalities: whether they will be basically trusting or mistrustful.

Erikson's theory of psychosocial development
the theory that considers how individuals come to understand themselves and the meaning of others'—and their own—behavior

Erikson's theory of psychosocial development considers how individuals come to understand themselves and the meaning of others'—and their own—behavior (Erikson, 1963). The theory suggests that developmental change occurs throughout people's lives in eight distinct stages, the first of which occurs in infancy.

trust-versus-mistrust stage
according to Erik Erikson, the period during which infants develop a sense of trust or mistrust, largely depending on how well their needs are met by their caregivers

According to Erikson, during the first 18 months of life, we pass through the **trust-versus-mistrust stage**. During this period, infants develop a sense of trust or mistrust, largely depending on how well their needs are met by their caregivers. Mary's attention to Malcom's needs, in the previous example, probably helped him develop a basic sense of trust in the world. Erikson suggests that if infants are able to develop trust, they experience a sense of hope, which permits them to feel as if they can fulfill their needs successfully. On the other hand, feelings of mistrust lead infants to see the world as harsh and unfriendly, and they may have later difficulties in forming close bonds with others.

autonomy-versus-shame-and-doubt stage
the period during which, according to Erik Erikson, toddlers (age 18 months to 3 years) develop independence and autonomy if they are allowed the freedom to explore, or shame and self-doubt if they are restricted and overprotected

During the end of infancy, children enter the **autonomy-versus-shame-and-doubt stage**, which lasts from 18 months to 3 years. During this period, children develop independence and autonomy if parents encourage exploration and freedom within safe boundaries. However, if children are restricted and overly protected, they feel shame, self-doubt, and unhappiness.

Erikson argues that personality is primarily shaped by infants' experiences. However, as we discuss next, other developmentalists concentrate on consistencies of behavior that are present at birth, even before the experiences of infancy. These consistencies are viewed as largely genetically determined and as providing the raw material of personality.

TEMPERAMENT: STABILITIES IN INFANT BEHAVIOR

> Sarah's parents thought there must be something wrong. Unlike her older brother Josh, who had been so active as an infant that he seemed never to be still, Sarah was much more placid. She took long naps and was easily soothed on those relatively rare occasions when she became agitated. What could be producing her extreme calmness?

temperament
patterns of arousal and emotionality that represent consistent and enduring characteristics of an individual

The most likely answer: The difference between Sarah and Josh reflected differences in temperament. As we first discussed in Chapter 2, **temperament** encompasses patterns of arousal and emotionality that are consistent and enduring characteristics of an individual (Kochanska & Aksan, 2004; Rothbart, 2007; Gartstein et al., 2017).

Temperament refers to *how* children behave, as opposed to *what* they do or *why* they do it. Infants show temperamental differences in general disposition from the time of birth, largely as a result initially of genetic factors, and temperament tends to be fairly stable well into adolescence. On the other hand, temperament is not fixed and unchangeable: Childrearing practices can modify temperament significantly. In fact, some children show little consistency in temperament from one age to another (Werner et al., 2007; de Lauzon-Guillain et al., 2012; Kusangi, Nakano, & Kondo-Ikemura, 2014).

Temperament is reflected in several dimensions of behavior. One central dimension is *activity level*, which reflects the degree of overall movement. Some babies (like

Sarah and Maleah, in the previous examples) are relatively placid, and their movements are slow and almost leisurely. In contrast, the activity level of other infants (like Josh) is quite high, with strong, restless movements of the arms and legs.

Another important dimension of temperament is the nature and quality of an infant's mood, and in particular a child's *irritability*. Some infants are relatively easygoing, and others are less so. For example, irritable infants fuss a great deal, and they are easily upset. They are also difficult to soothe when they do begin to cry. (Other aspects of temperament are listed in Table 3-10.)

Categorizing Temperament: Easy, Difficult, and Slow-to-Warm Babies   Because temperament can be viewed along so many dimensions, some researchers have asked whether there are broader categories that can be used to describe children's overall behavior. According to Alexander Thomas and Stella Chess, who carried out a large-scale study of a group of infants that has come to be known as the *New York Longitudinal Study* (Thomas & Chess, 1980), babies can be described according to one of several profiles:

- Easy babies. **Easy babies** have a positive disposition. Their body functions operate regularly, and they are adaptable. They are generally positive, showing curiosity about new situations, and their emotions are moderate or low in intensity. This category applies to about 40 percent (the largest number) of infants.

- Difficult babies. **Difficult babies** have more negative moods and are slow to adapt to new situations. When confronted with a new situation, they tend to withdraw. About 10 percent of infants belong in this category.

- Slow-to-warm babies. **Slow-to-warm babies** are inactive, showing relatively calm reactions to their environment. Their moods are generally negative, and they withdraw from new situations, adapting slowly. Approximately 15 percent of infants are slow-to-warm.

As for the remaining 35 percent, they cannot be consistently categorized. These children show a variety of combinations of characteristics. For instance, one infant may have relatively sunny moods, but react negatively to new situations, or another may show little stability of any sort in terms of general temperament.

The Consequences of Temperament: Does Temperament Matter?   One obvious question to emerge from the findings of the relative stability of temperament is whether a particular kind of temperament is beneficial. The answer seems to be that no single type of temperament is invariably good or bad. Instead, children's long-term adjustment depends on the **goodness-of-fit** of their particular temperament to the nature and demands of the environment in which they find themselves. For instance, children with a low activity level and low irritability may do particularly well in an environment in which they are left to explore on their own and are allowed largely to direct their own behavior. In contrast, high-activity-level, highly irritable children may do best with greater direction, which permits them to channel their energy in particular directions (Thomas & Chess, 1980; Schoppe-Sullivan et al., 2007; Yu et al., 2012).

easy babies
babies who have a positive disposition; their body functions operate regularly, and they are adaptable

difficult babies
babies who have negative moods and are slow to adapt to new situations; when confronted with a new situation, they tend to withdraw

slow-to-warm babies
babies who are inactive, showing relatively calm reactions to their environment; their moods are generally negative, and they withdraw from new situations, adapting slowly

goodness-of-fit
the notion that development is dependent on the degree of match between children's temperament and the nature and demands of the environment in which they are being raised

Table 3-10 Some Dimensions of Temperament in Infants, With Behavioral Indicators

Dimension	Behavioral Indicators
Activity level	High: wriggles while diaper is changed Low: lies still while being dressed
Approach/withdrawal	Approach orientation: accepts novel foods and toys easily Withdrawal orientation: cries when a stranger comes near
Quality of mood	Negative: cries when carriage is rocked Positive: smiles or smacks lips when tasting new food
Distractibility	Low: continues crying even when diaper is changed High: stops fussing when held and rocked
Rhythmicity	Regular: has consistent feeding schedule Irregular: has varying sleep and waking schedule
Threshold of responsiveness	High: not startled by sudden noises or bright lights Low: pauses sucking on bottle at approach of parent or slight noise

For instance, Mary, the grandmother in the earlier example, found ways to adjust the environment for her son, Malcom. Malcom and Aisha may need to do the same for their own son, Lincoln.

Some research does suggest that certain temperaments are, in general, more adaptive than others. For instance, difficult children, in general, are more likely to show behavior problems by school age than those classified in infancy as easy children. But not all difficult children experience problems. The key determinant seems to be the way parents react to their infants' difficult behavior. If they react by showing anger and inconsistency—responses that their child's difficult, demanding behavior readily evokes—then the child is ultimately more likely to experience behavior problems. On the other hand, parents who display more warmth and consistency in their responses are more likely to have children who avoid later problems (Thomas, Chess, & Birch, 1968; Salley, Miller, & Bell, 2013; Sayal et al., 2014).

GENDER: BOYS IN BLUE, GIRLS IN PINK   "It's a boy." "It's a girl." One of these two statements, or some variant, is probably the first announcement made after the birth of a child. From the moment of birth, girls and boys are treated differently. Their parents send out different kinds of birth announcements. They are dressed in different clothes and wrapped in different-colored blankets. They are given different toys (Coltrane & Adams, 1997; Serbin, Poulin-Dubois, & Colburne, 2001; Halim et al., 2018).

Parents play with boy and girl babies differently: From birth on, fathers tend to interact more with sons than daughters, whereas mothers interact more with daughters. Because, as we noted previously in the module, mothers and fathers play in different ways (with fathers typically engaging in more physical, rough-and-tumble activities and mothers in traditional games such as peekaboo), male and female infants are clearly exposed to different styles of activity and interaction from their parents (Clearfield & Nelson, 2006; Bouchard et al., 2007; Zosuls, Ruble, & Tamis-LeMonda, 2014).

The behavior exhibited by girls and boys is interpreted in different ways by adults. For instance, when researchers showed adults a video of an infant whose name was given as either "John" or "Mary," adults perceived "John" as adventurous and inquisitive, whereas "Mary" was fearful and anxious, although it was the same baby performing a single set of behaviors (Condry & Condry, 1976). Clearly, adults view the behavior of children through the lens of gender. **Gender** refers to the sense of being male or female. The term *gender* is often used to mean the same thing as *sex*, but they are not actually the same. *Sex* typically refers to sexual anatomy and sexual behavior, whereas *gender* refers to the social perceptions of maleness or femaleness.

There is a considerable amount of disagreement over both the extent and causes of such gender differences, even though most agree that boys and girls do experience at least partially different worlds based on gender. Some gender differences are fairly clear from the time of birth. For example, male infants tend to be more active and fussier than female infants. Boys' sleep tends to be more disturbed than that of girls. Boys grimace more, although no gender difference exists in the overall amount of crying. There is also some evidence that male newborns are more irritable than female newborns, although the findings are inconsistent. Differences between male and female infants, however, are generally minor (Crawford & Unger, 2004; Losonczy-Marshall, 2008).

Gender differences emerge more clearly as children age—and become increasingly influenced by the gender roles that society sets out for them. For instance, by the age of 1 year, infants are able to distinguish between males and females. Girls at this age prefer to play with dolls or stuffed animals, and boys seek out blocks and trucks. Often, of course, these are the only options available to them, because of the choices their parents and other adults have made in the toys they provide (Cherney, Kelly-Vance, & Glover, 2003; Alexander, Wilcox, & Woods, 2009; Gansen, 2018).

By the time they reach the age of 2, boys behave more independently and less compliantly than girls. Much of this behavior can be traced to parental reactions to previous behavior. For instance, when a child takes his or her first steps, parents tend

gender
the sense of being male or female

to react differently, depending on the child's gender: Boys are encouraged more to go off and explore the world, whereas girls are hugged and kept close. It is hardly surprising, then, that by the age of 2, girls tend to show less independence and greater compliance (Poulin-Dubois, Serbin, & Eichstedt, 2002).

Societal encouragement and reinforcement do not, however, completely explain differences in behavior between boys and girls. For example, one study examined girls who were exposed before birth to abnormally high levels of *androgen*, a male hormone, because their mothers unwittingly took a drug containing the hormone while pregnant. Later, these girls were more likely to play with toys stereotypically preferred by boys (such as cars) and less likely to play with toys stereotypically associated with girls (such as dolls). Although there are many alternative explanations for these results—you can probably think of several yourself—one possibility is that exposure to male hormones affected the brain development of the girls, leading them to favor toys that involve certain kinds of preferred skills (Mealey, 2000; Servin et al., 2003; Kahlenberg & Hein, 2010).

In sum, differences in behavior between boys and girls begin in infancy and—as we will see in future modules—continue throughout childhood (and beyond). Although gender differences have complex causes, representing some combination of innate, biologically related factors and environmental factors, they play a profound role in the social and emotional development of infants.

Family Life in the 21st Century

LO 3.20 Describe 21st-century families and their consequences for children, including the impact of nonparental child care on infants.

Family life today is different from the way it was even a few decades ago. A quick review tells the story:

- The number of single-parent families has increased significantly in the last three decades, as the number of two-parent households has declined. As of 2017, 64 percent of children ages 0 to 17 live with two married parents, down from 77 percent in 1980. Nearly a quarter of children live with only their mothers, 4 percent live with only their fathers, and 4 percent live with neither of their parents. Three-quarters of white-alone, non-Hispanic children lived with two married parents in 2016, compared with 60 percent of Hispanic and only 34 percent of black-alone children (Childstats.gov, 2017).

- The average size of families is shrinking. As of 2017, on average, there are 2.5 people per household, compared to 3.1 in 1970. The number of people living in nonfamily households (without any relatives) is more than 41 million (U.S. Bureau of the Census, 2017).

- Although the number of adolescents giving birth has declined substantially over the last 5 years, nearly 10 in 1,000 births are to adolescent women aged 15 to 17, the vast majority of whom are unmarried (Childstats.gov, 2017).

- Fifty-seven percent of mothers of infants work outside the home (U.S. Bureau of Labor Statistics, 2013).

- Forty-three percent of children younger than the age of 18 live in low-income households, up from 40 percent in 2006. Sixty-nine percent of black children and 63 percent of Hispanic children live in low-income families (Jiang, Granja, & Koball, 2017).

At the very least, these statistics suggest that many infants are being raised in environments in which substantial stressors are present. Such stress makes it an unusually difficult task to raise children—never easy even under the best circumstances.

The number of single-parent families has increased dramatically over the past 20 years. If the current trend continues, 60 percent of all children will live at some time with a single parent.

> **From a social worker's perspective:** Imagine you are a social worker visiting a foster home. It is 11 AM. You find the breakfast dishes in the sink and books and toys all over the floor. The infant you have placed in the home is happily pounding on pots and pans as his foster mother claps time. The kitchen floor is gooey under the baby's high chair. What is your professional assessment?

On the other hand, society is adapting to the new realities of family life in the 21st century. Several kinds of social support exist for the parents of infants, and society is evolving new institutions to help in their care. One example is the growing array of child-care arrangements available to help working parents.

How does infant child care affect later development? Consider the following:

> For most of the years my two kids were in child care, I worried about it. Did that weird day-care home where my daughter stayed briefly as a toddler do irreparable harm? Was my son irretrievably damaged by that child-care center he disliked? (Shellenbarger, 2003, p. D1)

Every day, parents ask themselves questions like these. The issue of how infant child care affects later development is a pressing one for many parents, who, because of economic, family, or career demands, leave their children to the care of others for a portion of the day. In fact, almost two-thirds of all children between 4 months and 3 years of age spend time in nonparental child care. Overall, more than 80 percent of infants are cared for by people other than their mothers at some point during their first year of life. The majority of these infants begin child care outside the home before the age of 4 months and are enrolled for almost 30 hours per week (NICHD Early Child Care Research Network, 2006; also see Figure 3-16). What effects do such arrangements have on later development?

Although the answer is largely reassuring, the newest research to come from the massive, long-term Study of Early Child Care and Youth Development, the longest-running examination of child care ever conducted, suggests that long-term participation in day care may have unanticipated consequences.

First the good news. According to most of the evidence, high-quality child care outside the home produces only minor differences from home care in most respects and may even enhance certain aspects of development. For example, research finds little or no difference in the strength or nature of parental attachment bonds of infants who have been in high-quality child care compared with infants raised solely by their parents (Vandell et al., 2005; Sosinsky & Kim, 2013; Ruzek et al., 2014).

Figure 3-16 Where Are Children Cared For?

According to a major study by the National Institute of Child Health and Human Development, children spend more time in some kind of child care outside the home or family as they get older.

SOURCE: NICHD Early Child Care Research Network, 2006.

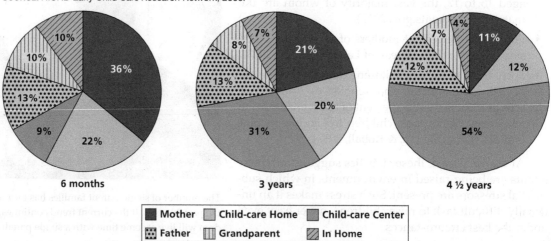

In addition to the direct benefits from involvement in child care outside the home, there are indirect benefits. For example, children in lower-income households and those whose mothers are single may benefit from the educational and social experiences in child care, as well as from the higher income produced by parental employment. Furthermore, children may experience improvements in nutrition and eating habits (NICHD Early Child Care Research Network, 2003a; Dearing, McCartney, & Taylor, 2009; Dev et al., 2017).

Furthermore, children who participate in Early Head Start—a program that serves at-risk infants and toddlers in high-quality child-care centers—can solve problems better, pay greater attention to others, and use language more effectively than poor children who do not participate in the program. In addition, their parents (who are also involved in the program) benefit from their participation. Participating parents talk and read more to their children, and they are less likely to spank them. Likewise, children who receive good, responsive child care are more likely to play well with other children (Maccoby & Lewis, 2003; Loeb et al., 2004; Raikes et al., 2014).

High-quality infant child care seems to produce only minor differences from home care in most respects, and some aspects of development may even be enhanced. What aspects of development might be enhanced by participation in infant child care outside the home?

However, some of the findings on participation in child care outside the home are less positive. Infants may be somewhat less secure when they are placed in low-quality child care or if they are placed in multiple child-care arrangements. In addition, children who spend long hours in outside the home child-care situations have a lower ability to work independently and have less effective time management skills (Vandell et al., 2005).

Development in Your Life

Choosing the Right Infant Care Provider

One finding that emerges with absolute clarity from research conducted on the consequences of infant child-care programs is that the benefits of child care—peer learning, greater social skills, greater independence—occur only when child care is of high quality. But what distinguishes high-quality child care from low-caliber programs? Parents should consider these questions in choosing a program (American Academy of Pediatrics HealthyChildren.org, 2015):

- Are there enough providers? A desirable ratio is one adult for every three infants, although one to four can be adequate.

- Are group sizes manageable? Even with several providers, a group of infants should not be larger than eight.

- Has the center complied with all governmental regulations, and is it licensed?

- What are the hours?

- Do the people providing the care seem to like what they are doing? What are their educational qualifications? Are they experienced? Do they seem happy in the job, or is offering child care just a way to earn money?

- What do the caregivers do during the day? Do they spend their time playing with, listening and talking to,

and paying attention to the children? Do they seem genuinely interested in the children? Is there a television constantly on?

- Are the children safe and clean? Does the environment allow infants to move around safely? Is the equipment and furniture in good repair? Do the providers adhere to the highest levels of cleanliness? After changing a baby's diaper, do providers wash their hands?

- What training do the providers have in caring for children? Do they demonstrate a knowledge of the basics of infant development and an understanding of how normal children develop? Do they seem alert to signs that development may depart from normal patterns?

- Finally, is the environment happy and cheerful? Child care is not just a babysitting service: For the time an infant is there, it is the child's whole world. You should feel fully comfortable and confident that the child-care center is a place where your infant will be treated as an individual.

In addition to following these guidelines, contact the National Association for the Education of Young Children (NAEYC), from which you can get the name of a resource and referral agency in your area. Go to the NAEYC Web site at www.naeyc.org.

The newest research, which focuses on preschoolers, finds that children who spend 10 or more hours a week in group child care for a year or more have an increased probability of being disruptive in class, and that the effect continues through the sixth grade. Although the increase in the likelihood of acting disruptive is not substantial—every year spent in a child-care center resulted in a 1 percent higher score on a standardized measure of problem behavior completed by teachers—the results were quite reliable (Belsky et al., 2007).

In sum, the ballooning body of research finds that the effects of participation in group child care are neither unambiguously positive nor unambiguously negative. What is clear, though, is that the *quality* of child care is critical. Ultimately, more research is needed on just who makes use of child care and how it is used by members of different segments of society to fully understand its consequences (NICHD Early Child Care Research Network, 2005; Belsky, 2006, 2009; Schipper et al., 2006; also see the *Development in Your Life* feature on choosing the right infant care provider).

Review, Check, and Apply

Review

LO 3.15 Discuss how children express and experience emotions in the first 2 years of life, and summarize the development of social referencing.

Infants display a variety of facial expressions, which are similar across cultures and appear to reflect basic emotional states. Early in life, infants develop the capability of nonverbal decoding: determining the emotional states of others based on their facial and vocal expressions. Through social referencing, infants from the age of 8 or 9 months use the expressions of others to clarify ambiguous situations and learn appropriate reactions to them.

LO 3.16 Describe the sense of self that children possess in the first 2 years of life, including the development of a theory of mind.

Infants begin to develop self-awareness at about the age of 12 months. They also begin to develop a theory of mind at this time: knowledge and beliefs about how they and others think.

LO 3.17 Explain attachment in infancy, how it affects a person's future social competence, and the roles that caregivers play in infants' social development.

Attachment, a strong, positive emotional bond that forms between an infant and one or more significant people, is a crucial factor in enabling individuals to develop social relationships. Infants display one of four major attachment patterns: securely attached, avoidant, ambivalent, and disorganized-disoriented. Research suggests an association between an infant's attachment pattern and his or her social and emotional competence as an adult. Mothers' interactions with their babies are particularly important for social development. Mothers who respond effectively to their babies' social overtures appear to contribute to the babies' ability to become securely attached. Through a process of reciprocal socialization, infants and caregivers interact and affect one another's behavior, which strengthens their mutual relationship.

LO 3.18 Discuss the development of peer relationships in infancy.

From an early age, infants engage in rudimentary forms of social interaction with other children, and their level of sociability rises as they age.

LO 3.19 Describe individual differences that distinguish an infant's personality and the roles that temperament and gender play.

The origins of personality, the sum total of the enduring characteristics that differentiate one individual from another, arise during infancy. Temperament encompasses enduring levels of arousal and emotionality that are characteristic of an individual. Temperamental differences underlie the broad classification of infants into easy, difficult, and slow-to-warm categories. As infants age, gender differences become more pronounced, mostly as a result of environmental influences. Differences are accentuated by parental expectations and behavior.

LO 3.20 Describe 21st-century families and their consequences for children, including the impact of nonparental child care on infants.

The varieties of families, ranging from traditional two-parent to blended to same-sex couples, mirrors the complexity of modern-day society. Child care, a societal response to the changing nature of the family, can be beneficial to the social development of children, fostering social interaction and cooperation, if it is of high quality.

Check Yourself

1. When Darius bumped his knee on the table, he gazed at his mother to look at her reaction. When he saw that she was alarmed, he began crying. This is an example of _____.
   a. fear
   b. anxiety
   c. social referencing
   d. self-awareness

2. One way mothers can improve the likelihood of secure attachment in their children is to respond to their needs appropriately. Another name for this communication in which mothers and children match emotional states is _____.
   a. emotional matching
   b. goodness of fit
   c. interactional synchrony
   d. environmental assessment

3. Patterns of arousal and emotionality that are consistent and enduring in an individual are known as an individual's _____.
   a. goodness-of-fit
   b. temperament
   c. personality
   d. mood

4. Research finds that high-quality child care outside the home may _____.
   a. change a child's temperament
   b. alter the strength and nature of parental attachments
   c. eliminate gender differences
   d. enhance certain aspects of development

Applying Lifespan Development

If you were introducing a bill in Congress regarding the minimum licensing requirements for child-care centers, what would you emphasize?

Chapter 3 Summary
Putting It All Together: Infancy

Syda Productions/Shutterstock

FOUR-MONTH-OLD JENNA (whom we met in this chapter's opener) was a model infant in almost every respect. However, there was one aspect of her behavior that posed a dilemma: how to respond when she woke up in the middle of the night and cried despondently. It usually was not a matter of being hungry because typically she had been fed recently. And it was not caused by her diaper being soiled because usually that had been changed recently. Instead, it seemed that Jenna just wanted to be held and entertained, and when she wasn't, she cried dramatically until someone came to her.

MODULE 3.1
PHYSICAL DEVELOPMENT IN INFANCY

- Jenna's body is developing various rhythms (repetitive, cyclical patterns of behavior) that are responsible for the change from sleep to wakefulness. (p. 100)
- Jenna will sleep in spurts of around 2 hours, followed by periods of wakefulness, until about 16 weeks, when she will begin to sleep as long as 6 continuous hours. (p. 102)
- Because Jenna's sense of touch is one of her most highly developed senses (and one of the earliest developed), she will respond to gentle touches, such as a soothing caress, which can calm a crying, fussy infant. (pp. 113–114)

MODULE 3.2
COGNITIVE DEVELOPMENT IN INFANCY

- Jenna has learned that her behavior (crying) can produce a desired effect (someone holding and entertaining her). (pp. 119–121)
- As Jenna's brain develops, she is able to separate people she knows from people she doesn't; this is why she responds so positively when someone she knows comes to comfort her during the night. (pp. 138–139)

MODULE 3.3
SOCIAL AND PERSONALITY DEVELOPMENT IN INFANCY

- Jenna has developed attachment (the positive emotional bond between her and particular individuals) to those who care for her. (pp. 141–144)
- To feel secure, Jenna needs to know that her caregivers will provide an appropriate response to the signals she is sending. (pp. 141–144)
- Part of Jenna's temperament is that she is irritable. Irritable infants can be fussy and are difficult to soothe when they do begin to cry. (pp. 146–147)
- Because irritability is relatively stable, Jenna will continue to display this temperament at age 1 and even age 2. (pp. 146–147)

What would a PARENT do?

What strategies would you use in dealing with Jenna? Would you go to her every time she cried? Or, would you try to wait her out, perhaps setting a time limit before going to her?

Photodisc/Getty Images

What would a HEALTH-CARE PROVIDER do?

How would you recommend that Jenna's caregivers deal with the situation? Are there any dangers that the caregivers should be aware of?

Mark Andersen/Rubberball/Getty Images

What would an EDUCATOR do?

Suppose Jenna spends a few hours every weekday afternoon in day care. If you were a child-care provider, how would you deal with Jenna if she wakes up from naps soon after falling asleep?

Tom Baker/123RF

What would YOU do?

How would you deal with Jenna? What factors would affect your decision? Based on your reading, how do you think Jenna will respond?

Asia Images Group/Getty Images

Chapter 4
The Preschool Years

Chen, a wildly energetic preschooler who just turned 3, was trying to stretch far enough to reach the cookie jar that he spied sitting on the kitchen counter. Because the jar was just beyond his grasp, he pushed a chair from the kitchen table over to the counter and climbed up.

Because he still couldn't reach the cookies from the chair, Chen climbed onto the kitchen counter and crawled over to the cookie bowl. He pried the lid off the jar, thrust his hand in, pulled out a cookie, and began to munch on it.

But not for long. His curiosity getting the better of him, he grabbed another cookie and began to work his body along the counter toward the sink. He climbed in, twisted the cold water faucet to the "on" position, and happily splashed in the cold water.

Chen's father, who had left the room for only a moment, returned to find Chen sitting in the sink, soaked, with a contented smile on his face.

In this chapter, we focus on the physical, cognitive, and social and personality growth that occur during the preschool years. We begin by considering the physical changes children undergo during those years. We discuss weight and height, nutrition, and health and wellness. The brain and its neural pathways change too, and we will touch on some intriguing findings relating to gender differences in the way the brain functions. We also look at how both gross and fine motor skills change over the preschool years.

Intellectual development is the focus of the next section of the chapter. We examine the major approaches to cognitive development, including Piaget's stage theory, information processing approaches, and an emerging view of cognitive development that gives great weight to the influence of culture. We also consider the important advances in language development that occur during the preschool years, and we discuss several factors that influence cognitive development, including exposure to television and participation in child-care and preschool programs.

Finally, we look at social and personality development in these years, focusing first on how children figure out who they are and develop a sense of racial and gender identity. We discuss the nature of their friendships and the significance of the ways they play together. We next look at parents, considering the different styles of parenting that are common today as well as their implications for their children's future development and personalities. We conclude with a look at the ways in which preschool-age children begin to develop a moral sense and learn how to control aggression.

Module 4.1 *Physical Development* in the Preschool Years

LO 4.1   Describe the state of children's bodies during the preschool years.
LO 4.2   Describe the state of children's overall health during the preschool years.
LO 4.3   Explain how children's brains change and develop during the preschool years.
LO 4.4   Explain the relationship between brain growth and cognitive development.
LO 4.5   Describe the process of gross motor development in preschool-age children.
LO 4.6   Describe the process of fine motor development in preschool-age children.

Module 4.2 *Cognitive Development* in the Preschool Years

LO 4.7   Analyze Piaget's explanation of cognitive development during the preschool years.
LO 4.8   Evaluate how Piaget's approach stands up to the test of time.
LO 4.9   Analyze information processing approaches to cognitive development in the preschool years.
LO 4.10 Describe Vygotsky's view of cognitive development in the preschool years.
LO 4.11 Explain how children's language develops in the preschool years.
LO 4.12 Describe the effects of informal and formal learning resources on preschoolers.

Module 4.3 *Social and Personality Development* in the Preschool Years

LO 4.13 Explain how preschool-age children develop a concept of themselves.
LO 4.14 Analyze how preschool-age children develop a sense of gender.
LO 4.15 Describe the sorts of social relationships that are typical of preschool-age children.
LO 4.16 Analyze how children's theory of mind changes during the preschool years.
LO 4.17 Describe the changing nature of families and the diversity of parenting styles preschoolers experience.
LO 4.18 Analyze the factors that contribute to child abuse and neglect, and describe personal characteristics that may protect children.
LO 4.19 Explain how preschool-age children develop a moral sense.
LO 4.20 Analyze theoretical perspectives on the ways in which aggression develops in preschool-age children.

Module 4.1

Physical Development in the Preschool Years

The children in Corinne Green's preschool class are going on a field trip to a farm. It's all Green can do to keep the more excitable members of her class from running up and down the aisle of the bus or jumping on the seats. To focus the group, she leads them in a series of familiar classroom games. First, she claps out various rhythms, and the children try to copy each one. When they tire of this, she engages them in a round of "I spy," choosing objects everyone can see. Then she leads them in songs that include hand motions, such as "The Itsy Bitsy Spider."

Not all of Green's young charges need to be settled. Four-year-old Danny Brock is busy drawing cows, horses, and pigs. His sketches are simple, but they are easily recognizable as the animals he expects to see on the farm. Su-Yun Davis is telling the girl next to her about barns, tractors, and henhouses. Su-Yun is using what she remembers from a farm she visited with her parents 4 months previously. Megan Haas is quietly eating the lunch she brought, one potato chip at a time, a good 2 hours before her teacher will announce lunchtime. "There's never a dull moment with preschoolers," Green says. "They're always doing something. And in a class of 20, it's often 20 different somethings."

The children in Green's preschool class, running and clapping their hands in imitative rhythms, were infants not so long ago. But the physical development that children undergo at this age results in more than leaping and climbing. It also enables Danny to produce recognizable objects in his drawings and Su-Yun to remember the details of moments that occurred months before.

The Growing Body

During the preschool years, children experience rapid advances in their physical abilities that are nothing short of astounding. Just how far they develop is apparent when we look at the changes they undergo in their size, shape, and physical abilities.

By age 2, the average child in the United States weighs around 25 to 30 pounds and is close to 36 inches tall. By the time they are 6 years old, they weigh about 46 pounds and stand 46 inches tall (see Figure 4-1).

These averages mask significant individual differences. For instance, 10 percent of 6-year-olds weigh 55 pounds or more, and 10 percent weigh 36 pounds or less. Furthermore, average differences between boys and girls increase during the preschool years. Although at age 2 the differences are relatively small, during the preschool years boys start becoming taller and heavier, on average, than girls.

Economics also affects these averages. The better nutrition and health care typically received by children in developed countries translates into differences in growth. For instance, the average Swedish 4-year-old is as tall as the average 6-year-old in Bangladesh. Even within the United States, children in families with incomes below the poverty level are more likely to be short than children raised in more affluent homes (Petrou & Kupek, 2010; Mendoza et al., 2017).

Changes in Body Shape and Nutrition

LO 4.1   Describe the state of children's bodies during the preschool years.

The bodies of a 2-year-old and a 6-year-old vary not only in height and weight but also in shape. During the preschool years, boys and girls become less round and more slender. Moreover, their arms and legs lengthen, and the size relationship between the head and the rest of the body becomes more adultlike. In fact, by the time children reach age 6, their proportions are similar to those of adults.

Other physical changes occur internally. Muscle size increases, and children grow stronger. Bones become sturdier, and the sense organs continue to develop. For instance, the *eustachian tube* in the ear changes its orientation so radically that it may cause the earaches that are so typical of the preschool years.

Figure 4-1 Gaining Height and Weight

The preschool years are marked by steady increases in height and weight. The figures show the median point for boys and girls at each age, in which 50 percent of children in each category are above this height or weight level and 50 percent are below.

SOURCE: National Center for Health Statistics in collaboration with the National Center for Chronic Disease Prevention and Health Promotion, 2000.

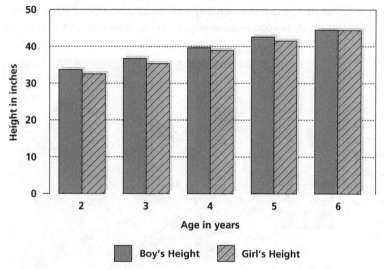

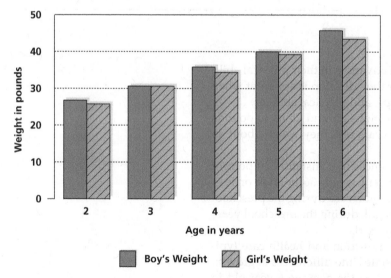

obesity

body weight more than 20 percent higher than the average weight for a person of a given age and height

Because the rate of growth is slower than during infancy, preschoolers need less food, which may cause parents to worry. However, children tend to be adept at eating enough if they are provided with nutritious meals.

In fact, anxiously encouraging children to eat more than they want may lead them to become overweight or even obese. *Overweight* is defined as *a body mass index (BMI)* between the 85th and 95th percentiles of children of the same age and sex. (BMI is calculated by dividing a child's weight in kilograms by the square of their height in meters.) If the BMI is even greater, then children are considered obese. **Obesity** is defined as a BMI at or above the 95th percentile for children of the same age and sex.

The prevalence of obesity among older preschoolers increased significantly through the 1980s and 1990s. However, research released in 2014 found that the incidence of obesity in the United States declined over the prior 10 years from nearly 14 percent to just over 8 percent—a significant breakthrough in children's health (Tavernise, 2014; Miller & Brooks-Gunn, 2015).

Still, obese and overweight young children remain a significant concern across the globe, particularly in developing countries. The large majority of obese and overweight young children live in developing countries in which good nutrition is less prevalent. If current trends continue, there will be 70 million overweight and obese infants and young children by 2025 (Commission on Ending Childhood Obesity, 2018).

The best strategy for parents is to make sure that they make a variety of low-fat, high-nutrition foods available. Foods that have a relatively high iron content are particularly important: Iron-deficiency anemia, which causes constant fatigue, is one of the prevalent nutritional problems in developed countries such as the United States. High-iron foods include dark green vegetables (such as broccoli), whole grains, and some kinds of meat, such as lean hamburger. It is also important to avoid foods with high sodium content and to include foods with low fat content (Brotanek et al., 2007; Grant et al., 2007; Jalonick, 2011).

Preschoolers also need vitamin A, which promotes growth. It is found in milk and eggs, as well as yellow and orange vegetables such as squash and carrots. Also important are vitamin C, found in fruit, which supports healthy tissue and skin, and calcium, found in dairy products, which helps promote bone and tooth formation.

Ultimately, children should be given the opportunity to develop their own food preferences. Exposing children to new foods by encouraging them to take just one bite is a relatively low-stress way of expanding children's diets (Hamel & Robins, 2013; Struempler et al., 2014, Johnson et al., 2018).

In behavior called the *just-right phenomenon,* some preschool children develop strong rituals and routines about the kinds of foods they will eat. They may only eat certain foods that are prepared in a particular way and presented to them in a particular manner on a plate. In adults, such rigidity would be a sign of a psychological disorder, but it is normal in young children. Almost all preschoolers eventually outgrow it (Evans et al., 1997; Evans et al., 2006).

Encouraging children to eat more than they seem to want naturally may lead them to increase their food intake beyond an appropriate level.

> **From a health-care worker's perspective:** How might biology and environment combine to affect the physical growth of a child adopted as an infant from a developing country and reared in a more industrialized one?

Health and Illness

LO 4.2   Describe the state of children's overall health during the preschool years.

The average preschooler has 7 to 10 colds and other minor respiratory illnesses in each of the years from age 3 to 5. In the United States, a runny nose as a result of the common cold is the most frequent—and happily, the least severe—kind of health problem during the preschool years. In fact, the majority of children in the United States are reasonably healthy during this period, and 88 percent of parents of children 4 or younger report their children are in excellent or very good health (Kalb, 1997; National Health Interview Survey, 2015).

Although the sniffles and coughs that are the symptoms of such illnesses are certainly distressing to children, the unpleasantness is usually not too severe and the illnesses usually last only a few days. (For more on keeping preschoolers healthy, see the *Development in Your Life* box.)

The greatest risk that preschoolers face comes from neither illness nor nutritional problems but from accidents: Before the age of 10, children are twice as likely to die from an injury as from an illness. In fact, U.S. children have a one in three chance every year of receiving an injury that requires medical attention (Field & Behrman, 2003; Granié, 2010; National Safety Council, 2013).

The danger of injuries during the preschool years is in part a result of high levels of physical activity. Combine the physical activity, curiosity, and lack of judgment that characterize this age group, and it is no wonder that preschoolers are accident prone.

Furthermore, some children are more apt than others to take risks and consequently to be injured. Boys, who typically are more active than girls and tend to take more risks, have a higher rate of injuries. Economic factors also play a role. Children raised under conditions of poverty in urban areas, whose inner-city neighborhoods may contain more hazards than more affluent areas, are two times more likely to die of injuries than children living in affluence (Morrongiello, Klemencic, & Corbett, 2008; Steinbach et al., 2016; Titi, van Niekerk, & Ahmed, 2018).

Parents and caregivers can take precautions to prevent injuries, starting by "childproofing" homes and classrooms with electrical outlet covers and child locks on cabinets. Car seats and bike helmets can help prevent injuries from accidents. Parents and teachers also need to be aware of the dangers from long-term hazards (Morrongiello, Corbett, & Bellissimo, 2008; Morrongiello et al., 2009; Sengoelge et al., 2014).

For example, lead poisoning is a significant danger for many children. Some 14 million children are at risk for lead poisoning resulting from exposure to lead, according to the Centers for Disease Control and Prevention. Despite stringent legal restrictions on the amount of lead in paint and gasoline, lead is still found on painted walls and window frames—particularly in older homes—and in gasoline, ceramics, lead-soldered pipes, automobile and truck exhaust, and even dust and water (Dozor & Amler, 2013; Herendeen & MacDonald, 2014; Bogar et al, 2017).

Furthermore, even tiny amounts of lead in the water drunk by children can lead to permanent health and developmental problems. This point was made apparent,

Even tiny amounts of lead in the water drunk by children can lead to permanent health and developmental problems, as we saw in the case of the water crisis in Flint, Michigan.

tragically, in the case of Flint, Michigan, where the city water supply became contaminated with lead when water was rerouted through water pipes that allowed lead to leak into the water supply starting in 2014. Residents had to use bottled water until the situation could be remedied (Goodnough & Atkinson, 2016).

Because even tiny amounts of lead can permanently harm children, the U.S. Department of Health and Human Services has called lead poisoning the most severe health threat to children younger than age 6. Exposure to lead has been linked to lower intelligence, problems in verbal and auditory processing, and hyperactivity and distractibility. High lead levels have also been linked to higher levels of antisocial behavior, including aggression and delinquency in school-age children. At yet higher levels of exposure, lead poisoning results in illness and death (Nigg et al., 2008; Marcus, Fulton, & Clarke, 2010; Lewis et al., 2018).

The Growing Brain

The brain grows at a faster rate than any other part of the body. Two-year-olds have brains that are about three-quarters the size and weight of an adult brain. By age 5, children's brains weigh 90 percent of average adult brain weight. In comparison, the average 5-year-old's total body weight is just 30 percent of average adult body weight (Nihart, 1993; House, 2007).

Why does the brain grow so rapidly? One reason is an increase in the number of interconnections among cells, which supports more complex communication between neurons and permits the rapid growth of cognitive skills. In addition, the amount of **myelin**—the protective insulation that surrounds parts of neurons—increases, which speeds the transmission of electrical impulses along brain cells (Dalton & Bergenn, 2007; Klingberg & Betteridge, 2013; Dean et al., 2014).

myelin
protective insulation that surrounds parts of neurons and speeds the transmission of electrical impulses along brain cells

Development in Your Life

Keeping Preschoolers Healthy

There is no way around it: Even the healthiest preschooler occasionally gets sick. Social interaction with others ensures that illnesses will be passed from one child to another. However, some diseases are preventable, and others can be minimized if simple precautions are taken:

- Preschoolers should eat a well-balanced diet containing the proper nutrients, particularly foods containing sufficient protein. Keep offering healthy foods; even if children initially reject them, they may grow to like them.

- Encourage preschoolers to exercise.

- Children should get as much sleep as they wish. Being fatigued makes children more susceptible to illness.

- Children should avoid contact with others who are ill. If

they play with kids who are sick, parents should make sure they wash their hands thoroughly.

- Be sure that children follow an appropriate schedule of immunizations. Despite the beliefs of some parents, there is absolutely *no* scientific basis for believing that common vaccinations should be avoided because they can increase the risk of autism spectrum disorder. The American Academy of Pediatrics and the U.S. Centers for Disease Control and Prevention affirm that *children should* receive *all recommended vaccinations*, unless otherwise told not to by a reputable medical professional (Daley & Glanz, 2011; Krishna, 2018).

- Finally, if a child does get ill, remember this: Minor illnesses during childhood sometimes provide immunity to more serious illnesses later on.

Brain Lateralization

LO 4.3 **Explain how children's brains change and develop during the preschool years.**

By the end of the preschool period, the *corpus callosum*, a bundle of nerve fibers that connects the two hemispheres of the brain, becomes considerably thicker, developing as many as 800 million individual fibers that help coordinate brain functioning between the two hemispheres. At the same time, the two halves of the brain become increasingly differentiated and specialized. **Lateralization**, the process in which certain functions are located more in one hemisphere than the other, becomes more pronounced during the preschool years.

For most people, the left hemisphere is primarily involved with tasks that necessitate verbal competence, such as speaking, reading, thinking, and reasoning. The right hemisphere develops its own strengths, especially in nonverbal areas such as comprehension of spatial relationships, recognition of patterns and drawings, music, and emotional expression (Pollak, Holt, & Wismer Fries, 2004; Watling & Bourne, 2007; Dundas, Plaut, & Behrmann, 2013; see Figure 4-2).

Each hemisphere also begins to process information in a slightly different manner. The left hemisphere processes data sequentially, one piece at a time. The right hemisphere processes information in a more global manner, reflecting on it as a whole (Holowaka & Petitto, 2002; Barber et al., 2012).

Although there is some specialization, in most respects the two hemispheres act in tandem and are interdependent. In fact, each hemisphere can perform most of the tasks of the other. For example, the right hemisphere does some language processing and plays an important role in language comprehension (Corballis, 2003; Hutchinson, Whitman, & Abeare, 2003; Hall, Neal, & Dean, 2008; Segal & Gollan, 2018).

There are also individual differences in lateralization. For example, many of the 10 percent of people who are left-handed or ambidextrous (able to use both hands interchangeably) have language centered in the right hemisphere or have no specific language center (Compton & Weissman, 2002; Isaacs et al., 2006; Szaflarski et al., 2012; Porac, 2016).

Even more intriguing are differences in lateralization related to gender. For instance, starting during the first year and continuing in the preschool years, boys and girls show some hemispheric differences associated with lower-body reflexes and the processing of auditory information. Boys also clearly tend to show greater lateralization of language in the left hemisphere; among females, language is more evenly divided between the hemispheres. Such differences may help explain why girls' language development proceeds more rapidly during the preschool years than boys' (Castro-Schilo & Kee, 2010; Filippi et al., 2013; Agcaoglu et al., 2015).

Figure 4-2 Looking into the Brain

This series of brain scans using positron emission tomography (PET) illustrates that activity in the right or left hemisphere of the brain differs according to the task in which a person is engaged. How might educators use this finding in their approach to teaching?

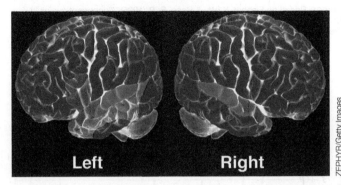

Left   Right

ZEPHYR/Getty Images

lateralization

the process in which certain cognitive functions are located more in one hemisphere of the brain than in the other

The Links Between Brain Growth and Cognitive Development

LO 4.4 **Explain the relationship between brain growth and cognitive development.**

Neuroscientists are beginning to understand the ways in which brain growth is related to cognitive development. Although we do not yet know the direction of causality (i.e., does brain development produce cognitive advances, or vice versa?), we can clearly see the relationship.

For example, there are periods during childhood when the brain shows unusual growth spurts, and these periods are linked to advances in cognitive abilities. One study that measured electrical activity in the brain found unusual spurts at between 1½ and 2 years, a time when language abilities increase rapidly.

Figure 4-3 Brain Growth Spurt

Electrical activity in the brain has been linked to advances in cognitive abilities at various stages across the life span. In this graph, activity increases dramatically between 1½ and 2 years, a period during which language rapidly develops.

SOURCE: Based on Fischer, K. W., & Rose, S. P. (1995). Concurrent cycles in the dynamic development of brain and behavior. Newsletter of the Society for Research in Child Development, p. 16.

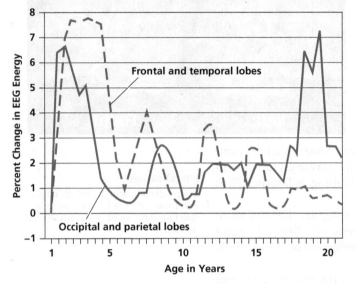

Other spurts occurred around other ages when cognitive advances are particularly intense (Mabbott et al., 2006; Westermann et al., 2007; Sadeghi et al., 2013; see Figure 4-3).

Other research has suggested that the increases in myelin in the brain may be related to preschoolers' growing cognitive capabilities. For example, myelination of the *reticular formation*, an area of the brain associated with attention and concentration, is completed by the time children are about 5 years old. This may be associated with children's growing attention spans, as they approach school age. The improvement in memory that occurs during the preschool years may also be associated with myelination: During the preschool years, myelination is completed in the hippocampus, an area associated with memory (Rolls, 2000).

In addition, there is significant growth in the nerves connecting the *cerebellum*, a part of the brain that controls balance and movement, to the *cerebral cortex*, the structure responsible for sophisticated information processing. The growth in these nerve fibers is related to the significant advances in motor skills and cognitive processing during the preschool years (Carson, 2006; Gordon, 2007).

Motor Development

> Anya sat in the sandbox at the park, chatting with the other parents and playing with her two children, 5-year-old Nicholai and 13-month-old Smetna. While she chatted, she kept a close eye on Smetna, who would still put sand in her mouth sometimes if she wasn't stopped. Today, however, Smetna seemed content to run the sand through her hands and try to put it into a bucket. Nicholai, meanwhile, was busy with two other boys, rapidly filling and emptying the other sand buckets to build an elaborate sand city, which they would then destroy with toy trucks.

When children of different ages gather at a playground, it's easy to see that preschool children have come a long way in their motor development. Both their gross and fine motor skills have become increasingly fine-tuned. Smetna, for example, is still mastering putting sand into a bucket, whereas her older brother Nicholai uses that skill easily as part of his larger goal of building a sand city.

Gross Motor Skills

LO 4.5   Describe the process of gross motor development in preschool-age children.

By the time they are 3 years old, children have mastered a variety of skills: jumping, hopping on one foot, skipping, and running. By ages 4 and 5, their skills have become more refined as they have gained increasing control over their muscles. For instance, at age 4 they can throw a ball with enough accuracy that a friend can catch it, and by age 5 they can toss a ring and have it land on a peg 5 feet away. Five-year-olds can learn to ride bikes, climb ladders, and ski downhill—activities that all require considerable coordination (Clark & Humphrey, 1985; Osorio-Valencia et al., 2018). (Figure 4-4 summarizes major gross motor skills that emerge during the preschool years.)

These achievements may be related to brain development and myelination of neurons in areas of the brain related to balance and coordination. Another likely reason is that children spend a great deal of time practicing these skills. During this period, the general level of activity is extraordinarily high. In fact, the activity level is higher at age 3 than at any other point in the entire life span (Miller, Church, & Poole, 2018).

Figure 4-4 Significant Gross Motor Skills in Early Childhood.

Age 3

Able to walk up stairs, alternating feet

Unable to stop or turn suddenly

Able to jump a length of 15–24 inches

Age 4

Able to walk down a long staircase, alternating feet, with assistance

Have some control in starting, stopping, and turning

Length of jump increases to 24–33 inches

Age 5

Able to walk down a long staircase, alternating feet

Capable of starting, stopping, and turning in games

Able to make a running jump of 28–36 inches

Girls and boys differ in certain aspects of gross motor coordination, in part because of differences in muscle strength, which is usually somewhat greater in boys than in girls. For instance, boys can typically throw a ball better and jump higher, and a boy's overall activity level tends to be greater than a girl's. In contrast, girls generally surpass boys in tasks that involve limb coordination. For instance, at age 5, girls are better than boys at jumping jacks and balancing on one foot (Largo, Fischer, & Rousson, 2003; Spessato et al., 2013).

Another aspect of muscular skills—one that parents often find most problematic—is bowel and bladder control. When—and how—should children be toilet trained? Few child-care issues raise so much concern among parents as toilet training. Current guidelines of the American Academy of Pediatrics suggest that there is no single time to begin toilet training and that training should begin only when children are ready (American Academy of Pediatrics, 2009; Lundblad, Hellström, & Berg, 2010).

When are children "ready"? The signs of readiness include staying dry at least 2 hours at a time during the day or waking up dry after naps; having regular and predictable bowel movements; giving an indication, through facial expressions or words, that urination or a bowel movement is about to occur; having the ability to follow simple directions; having the ability to get to the bathroom and undress alone; experiencing discomfort with soiled diapers; asking to use the toilet or potty chair; and expressing the desire to wear underwear.

Furthermore, children must be ready not only physically, but emotionally, and if they show strong signs of resistance to toilet training, toilet training should be put off. Similarly, it may be reasonable to delay toilet training if there is a major change in the home environment, such as the birth of a new baby or a major illness. Although some children show signs of readiness for toilet training between 18 and 24 months, some are not ready until 30 months or older (Fritz & Rockney, 2004; Connell-Carrick, 2006; Greer, Neidert, & Dozier, 2016).

Partially in response to the American Academy of Pediatrics guidelines, toilet training has begun later over the last few decades. For example, in 1957, 92 percent of children were toilet trained by 18 months. Today, the average age of toilet training is around 30 months (van Nunen et al., 2015; Rouse et al., 2017).

During the preschool years, children grow in both fine and gross motor skills.

Fine Motor Skills

LO 4.6 **Describe the process of fine motor development in preschool-age children.**

At the same time that their gross motor abilities are increasing, children are progressing in their ability to use fine motor skills, which involve more delicate, smaller body movements such as using a fork and spoon, cutting with scissors, tying shoelaces, and playing the piano.

The skills involved in fine motor movements require practice. The emergence of fine motor skills shows clear developmental patterns. At age 3, children can draw a circle and square with a crayon, and they can undo their clothes when they go to the bathroom. They can put a simple jigsaw puzzle together, and they can fit blocks of different shapes into matching holes. However, they do not show much precision and polish in these tasks, often, for example, forcing puzzle pieces into place.

By age 4, their fine motor skills are better. They can draw a person that looks like a person, and they can fold paper into triangular designs. And by the time they are 5, they can hold and manipulate a thin pencil properly.

How do preschoolers decide which hand to hold the pencil in as they work on their fine motor skills? For many, their choice was made soon after birth.

Beginning in early infancy, many children show signs of a preference for the use of one hand over the other—the development of **handedness**. By 7 months, some infants seem to favor one hand by grabbing more with it (Marschik et al., 2008; Morange-Majoux, Lemoine, & Dellatolas, 2013; Garcia & Teixeira, 2017).

Most children display a clear tendency by the end of the preschool years. Some 90 percent are right-handed and 10 percent are left-handed, and more boys than girls are left-handed.

handedness
the preference of using one hand over another

Review, Check, and Apply

Review

LO 4.1 **Describe the state of children's bodies during the preschool years.**

The preschool period is marked by steady physical growth and rapid advances in physical ability. Preschoolers tend to eat less than they did as babies, but generally regulate their food intake appropriately, given nutritious options and the freedom to develop their own choices and controls.

LO 4.2 **Describe the state of children's overall health during the preschool years.**

The preschool period is generally the healthiest time of life, with only minor illnesses threatening children.

Accidents and environmental hazards are the greatest threats.

LO 4.3 **Explain how children's brains change and develop during the preschool years.**

In addition to physical growth, the preschool period is marked by rapid brain growth. The increase in myelin in the brain is particularly important for intellectual development. Among other changes, the brain develops lateralization, a tendency of the two hemispheres to adopt specialized tasks.

LO 4.4 Explain the relationship between brain growth and cognitive development.

There are periods during childhood when the brain shows unusual growth spurts, and these periods are linked to advances in cognitive abilities.

LO 4.5 Describe the process of gross motor development in preschool-age children.

Gross motor developments advance rapidly during the preschool years. Boys' and girls' gross motor skills begin to diverge, with boys typically doing better at tasks requiring strength and girls doing better at tasks requiring

coordination. To be toilet trained effectively, children must be ready both physically and emotionally. Although some children show signs of readiness between 18 and 24 months, some are not ready until 30 months or older.

LO 4.6 Describe the process of fine motor development in preschool-age children.

Fine motor skills, which develop concurrently with gross motor skills, involve delicate, small body movements. Fine motor skills require considerable practice to develop. Preschoolers are also developing handedness—a decided preference for one hand over the other.

Check Yourself

1. Which of the following suggestions *is not* recommended for preventing obesity in children?

   a. Provide food that is high in nutritional value.
   b. Make sure meals are low in fat.
   c. Ensure a consistent diet with little variety.
   d. Allow children to develop their own food preferences.

2. During the preschool years, the two halves of the brain become more specialized in a process called _____.

   a. homogeneity
   b. myelination
   c. brain fusion
   d. lateralization

3. A major reason that motor skills develop so rapidly during the preschool years is that myelination of neurons increases in areas of the brain related to _____.

   a. balance and coordination
   b. sensory perception
   c. strength and endurance
   d. cognitive growth

4. One example of a fine motor skill is _____.

   a. hopping on one foot
   b. cutting with scissors
   c. throwing a ball accurately
   d. climbing a ladder

Applying Lifespan Development

What are some ways that increased understanding of issues relating to the physical development of preschoolers might help parents and caregivers in their care of children?

Module 4.2

Cognitive Development in the Preschool Years

Jesse and the Three Bears

Three-year-old Jesse is acting out his favorite story—The Three Bears. From the next room, his mother hears him playing each of the characters. "Someone's been eating my porridge," Jesse growls in a deep Papa Bear voice. "Someone's been sitting in my chair," he says moments later in the exact tones of his mother. Jesse then uses his own voice for Baby Bear. "Someone's been sleeping in my bed, and she's still here!" This is followed by the high-pitched squealing his mother knows is Jesse's Goldilocks waking to see the three bears.

In some ways, the intellectual sophistication of 3-year-olds is astounding. Their creativity and imagination leap to new heights; their language is increasingly sophisticated; and they reason and think about the world in ways that would have been impossible even a few months previously. But what underlies the dramatic advances in intellectual development of the preschool years? In this module, we will consider a number of approaches to understanding children's thinking and the development of cognitive abilities in the preschool years.

Piaget's Approach to Cognitive Development

Psychologist Jean Piaget, whose stage approach to cognitive development we discussed in Module 3.2, saw the preschool years as a time of both stability and change. He placed the preschool years into a single stage of cognitive development, the preoperational stage, which lasts from age 2 until around age 7.

Piaget's Stage of Preoperational Thinking

LO 4.7 Analyze Piaget's explanation of cognitive development during the preschool years.

preoperational stage

according to Piaget, the stage from approximately age 2 to age 7 in which children's use of symbolic thinking grows, mental reasoning emerges, and the use of concepts increases

operations

organized, formal, logical mental processes

During the **preoperational stage**, children's use of symbolic thinking grows, mental reasoning emerges, and the use of concepts increases. Seeing Mom's car keys may prompt a question, "Go to store?" as the child comes to see the keys as a symbol of a car ride. In this way, children become better at representing events internally and less dependent on sensorimotor activity to understand the world around them. Yet they are still not capable of **operations**, which are organized, formal, logical mental processes.

According to Piaget, a key aspect of preoperational thought is *symbolic function*, the ability to use a mental symbol, a word, or an object to stand for or represent something that is not physically present. For example, preschoolers can use a mental symbol for a car (the word *car*), and they understand that a small toy car is representative of the real thing. They have no need to get behind the wheel of an actual car to understand its basic purpose and use.

THE RELATION BETWEEN LANGUAGE AND THOUGHT Symbolic function is at the heart of one of the major advances of the preoperational period: the increasingly sophisticated use of language. Piaget suggests that the advances in language during the preschool years reflect improvements over the type of thinking that is possible during the previous sensorimotor period. Instead of slow, sensorimotor-based thinking, symbolic thought, which relies on improved linguistic ability, allows preschoolers to represent actions virtually, at much greater speed.

Even more important, language allows children to think beyond the present to the future. Rather than being grounded in the here and now, preschoolers can imagine future possibilities through language in the form of fantasies and daydreams.

CENTRATION: WHAT YOU SEE IS WHAT YOU THINK Place a dog mask on a cat and what do you get? According to 3- and 4-year-old preschoolers, a dog. To them, a cat with a dog mask ought to bark like a dog, wag its tail like a dog, and eat dog food. In every respect, the cat has been transformed into a dog.

centration

the process of concentrating on one limited aspect of a stimulus and ignoring other aspects

To Piaget, the root of this belief is centration, a key element, and limitation, of thinking in the preoperational period. **Centration** is the process of concentrating on one limited aspect of a stimulus—typically its superficial elements—and ignoring others. These elements come to dominate preschoolers' thinking, leading to inaccuracy.

Centration is the cause of the error illustrated in Figure 4-5. Asked which row contains more buttons, children who are 4 or 5 usually choose the row that looks longer, rather than the one that actually contains more buttons. This occurs even though children this age know quite well that 10 is more than 8. Rather than taking into account their understanding of quantity, they focus on appearance.

Preschoolers' focus on appearances might be related to another aspect of preoperational thought, the lack of conservation.

Figure 4-5 Which Row Contains More Buttons?

When preschoolers are shown these two rows and asked which row has more buttons, they usually respond that the lower row of buttons contains more, because it looks longer. They answer in this way even though they know quite well that 10 is greater than 8. Do you think preschoolers can be *taught* to answer correctly?

CONSERVATION: LEARNING THAT APPEARANCES ARE DECEIVING   Consider the following scenario:

Four-year-old Jaime is shown two drinking glasses. One is short and broad; the other, tall and thin. A teacher half-fills the short, broad glass with apple juice. The teacher then pours the juice into the tall, thin glass. The juice fills the tall glass almost to the brim. The teacher asks Jaime a question: Is there more juice in the second glass than there was in the first?

If you view this as an easy task, so do children like Jaime. The problem is that they almost always get it wrong.

Most 4-year-olds say that there is more apple juice in the tall, thin glass than there was in the short, broad one. In fact, if the juice is poured back into the shorter glass, they are quick to say that there is now less juice than there was in the taller glass.

The reason is that children of this age have not mastered conservation. **Conservation** is the knowledge that quantity is unrelated to the arrangement and physical appearance of objects. Some other conservation tasks are shown in Figure 4-6.

conservation
the knowledge that quantity is unrelated to the arrangement and physical appearance of objects

Figure 4-6 Common Tests of Children's Understanding of the Principle of Conservation

Why is a sense of conservation important?

Type of Conservation	Modality	Change in Physical Appearance	Average Age Invariance Is Grasped
Number	Number of elements in a collection 	Rearranging or dislocating elements 	6–7 years
Substance (mass)	Amount of a malleable substance (e.g., clay or liquid) 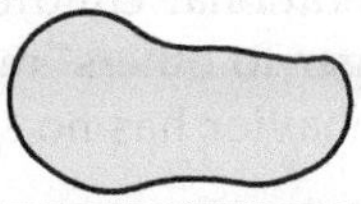	Altering shape 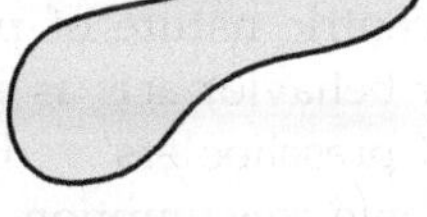	7–8 years
Length	Length of a line or object 	Altering shape or configuration 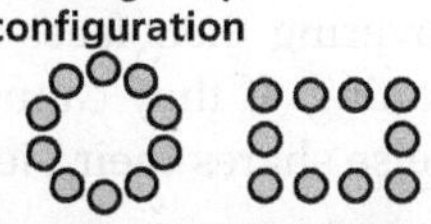	7–8 years
Area	Amount of surface covered by a set of plane figures 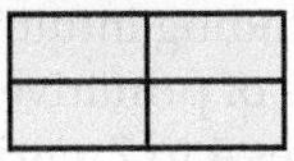	Rearranging the figures 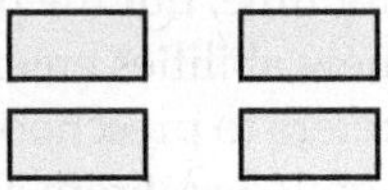	8–9 years
Weight	Weight of an object 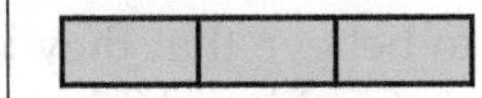	Altering shape 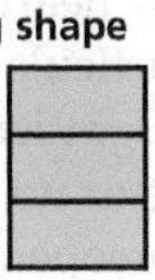	9–10 years
Volume	Volume of an object (in terms of water displacement) 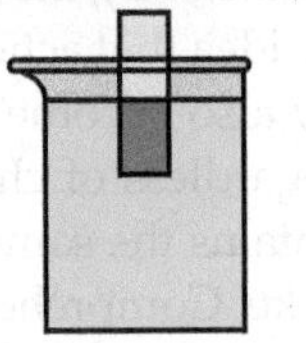	Altering shape 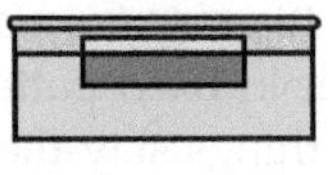	14–15 years

Why do children in the preoperational stage make conservation errors? Piaget suggests that the main reason is that their tendency toward centration prevents them from focusing on the relevant features of the situation. Furthermore, they cannot follow the sequence of transformations that accompanies changes in the appearance of a situation.

INCOMPLETE UNDERSTANDING OF TRANSFORMATION Preoperational, preschool children who see several worms during a walk in the woods may believe that they are all the same worm. The reason: The children view each sighting in isolation, unable to understand that a transformation would be necessary for a worm to move quickly from one location to the next.

transformation
the process in which one state is changed into another

As Piaget used the term, **transformation** is the process in which one state is changed into another. For instance, adults know that if a pencil that is held upright is allowed to fall down, it passes through a series of successive stages until it reaches its final, horizontal resting spot. In contrast, children in the preoperational period are unable to envision or recall the successive transformations that the pencil followed in moving from the upright to the horizontal position.

EGOCENTRISM: THE INABILITY TO TAKE OTHERS' PERSPECTIVES Another hallmark of the preoperational period is egocentric thinking. **Egocentric thought** is thinking that does not take into account the viewpoints of others. Preschoolers do not understand that others have different perspectives. Egocentric thought takes two forms: lack of awareness that others see things from a different physical perspective and failure to realize that others may hold thoughts, feelings, and points of view that differ from theirs. (Note that egocentric thought does *not* imply intentional selfishness or a lack of consideration.)

egocentric thought
thinking that does not take into account the viewpoints of others

Egocentric thinking lies behind children's lack of concern over their nonverbal behavior and the impact it has on others. For instance, 4-year-olds who receive a gift of socks may frown as they open the package, unaware that their face can be seen by others and reveals their true feelings.

Egocentrism largely explains why many preschoolers talk to themselves, even in the presence of others, and often ignore what others are telling them. This behavior illustrates the egocentric nature of preoperational children's thinking: the lack of awareness that their behavior acts as a trigger to others' reactions and responses. Consequently, much of preschoolers' verbal behavior has no social motivation but is meant purely for their own consumption.

Similarly, egocentrism can also be seen in hiding games. In hide-and-seek, 3-year-olds may "hide" by covering their faces with a pillow—even though they remain in plain view. Their reasoning: If they cannot see others, others cannot see them. They assume that everyone else shares their view.

THE EMERGENCE OF INTUITIVE THOUGHT Because Piaget labeled this the "*pre*operational period" and focused on cognitive deficiencies, it is easy to assume that preschoolers are marking time, but the period is far from idle. Cognitive development proceeds steadily, and new abilities emerge, including intuitive thought.

intuitive thought
thinking that reflects preschoolers' use of primitive reasoning and their avid acquisition of knowledge about the world

Intuitive thought refers to preschoolers' use of primitive reasoning and their avid acquisition of world knowledge. From about ages 4 to 7, curiosity blossoms. Children ask "Why?" questions about nearly everything. At the same time, they may act as if they are authorities on particular topics, certain that they have the final word on an issue. Their intuitive thought leads them to believe that they know answers to all kinds of questions, with little or no logical basis for this confidence.

In the late stages of the preoperational period, children's intuitive thinking prepares them for more sophisticated reasoning. For instance, preschoolers come to understand that pushing harder on the pedals makes a bicycle move faster or that pressing a button on a remote control makes the television change channels. By the end of the preoperational stage, preschoolers begin to grasp *functionality*, the idea that actions, events, and outcomes are related to one another in fixed patterns. They also become aware of *identity*, the understanding that certain things stay the same, regardless of changes in shape, size, and appearance—for instance, that a lump of clay contains the same amount of clay whether it is clumped into a ball or stretched out like a snake. Comprehension of identity is necessary for children to develop an understanding of conservation (the understanding, as we discussed previously, that quantity is not related to physical appearances). Piaget regarded the development of conservation as the transition from the preoperational period to the next stage, concrete operations, which we will discuss in Chapter 5.

Evaluating Piaget's Approach to Cognitive Development

LO 4.8   Evaluate how Piaget's approach stands up to the test of time.

Piaget, a masterly observer of children's behavior, provided a detailed portrait of preschoolers' cognitive abilities. The broad outlines of his approach have given us a useful way of thinking about the progressive advances in cognitive ability during the preschool years (Siegal, 1997).

However, it is important to consider Piaget's approach to cognitive development within the appropriate historical context and in light of more recent research findings. As we discussed previously, Piaget's theory is based on extensive observations of relatively few children. Despite his insightful and groundbreaking observations, recent experimental investigations suggest that in certain regards, Piaget underestimated children's capabilities.

Take, for instance, Piaget's views of how children in the preoperational period understand numbers. He contended that preschoolers' thinking is seriously handicapped, as evidenced by their performance on tasks involving conservation and reversibility, the understanding that a transformation can be reversed to return something to its original state. Yet more recent experimental work suggests otherwise.

For instance, developmental psychologist Rochel Gelman has found that children as young as 3 can easily tell the difference between rows of two and three toy animals, regardless of the animals' spacing. Older children are able to note differences in number, performing tasks such as identifying which of two numbers is larger and indicating that they understand some rudiments of addition and subtraction problems (Brandone et al., 2012; Gelman, 2015; Dietrich et al., 2016).

Gelman concludes that children have an innate ability to count, akin to the ability to use language that some theorists see as universal and genetically determined. This is clearly at odds with Piagetian notions, which suggest that children's numerical abilities do not blossom until after the preoperational period.

Some developmentalists (particularly those who favor the information processing approach) also believe that cognitive skills develop in a more continuous manner than Piaget's theory implies. They believe that rather than thought changing in quality, as Piaget argues, the changes in thinking ability are more quantitative, improving gradually (Gelman & Baillargeon, 1983; Case, 1991).

There are further difficulties with Piaget's view. His contention that conservation does not emerge until the end of the preoperational period has not stood up to experimental scrutiny. Children can learn to answer correctly on conservation tasks if they are given certain training and experiences. The fact that one can improve children's performance argues against the Piagetian view that children in the preoperational period have not reached a level of cognitive maturity to understand conservation (Ping & Goldin-Meadow, 2008).

In sum, Piaget tended to concentrate on preschoolers' *deficiencies* in logical thought. By focusing more on children's competence, recent theorists have found evidence for a surprising degree of capability in preschoolers.

Alternative Approaches: Information Processing Theory and Vygotsky

Even as an adult, Paco has clear recollections of his first trip to a farm, which he took when he was 3 years old. He was visiting his godfather, who lived in Puerto Rico, and the two of them went to a nearby farm. Paco recounts seeing what seemed like hundreds of chickens, and he clearly recalls his fear of the pigs, who seemed huge, smelly, and frightening. Most of all, he recalls the thrill of riding on a horse with his godfather.

The fact that Paco has a clear memory of his farm trip is not surprising: Most people have unambiguous, and seemingly accurate, memories dating as far back as age 3.

This preschooler may recall this ride in 6 months, but by the time she is 12, it will probably be forgotten. Can you explain why?

autobiographical memory

memory of particular events from one's own life

scripts

broad representations in memory of events and the order in which they occur

Forensic developmental psychologists focus on the reliability of children's memories in a legal context.

But are the processes used to form memories at that age similar to those that operate later in life? More broadly, what general changes in the processing of information occur during the preschool years?

Information Processing Approaches to Cognitive Development

LO 4.9   Analyze information processing approaches to cognitive development in the preschool years.

Information processing approaches to cognitive development focus on changes in the kinds of "mental programs" that children use when approaching problems. They compare the changes in children's cognitive abilities during the preschool years to the way a computer program becomes more sophisticated as a programmer modifies it based on experience. For many child developmentalists, information processing approaches represent the dominant, most comprehensive, and most accurate explanation of how children develop cognitively (Siegler, 1994; Lacerda, von Hofsten, & Heimann, 2001).

We'll focus on two areas that highlight the approach taken by information processing theorists: understanding of numbers and memory development.

PRESCHOOLERS' UNDERSTANDING OF NUMBERS   As we saw previously, preschoolers have a greater understanding of numbers than Piaget thought. Researchers using information processing approaches have found increasing evidence for the sophistication of preschoolers' numerical understanding. The average preschooler is not only able to count, but also to do so in a fairly systematic, consistent manner (Siegler, 1998; Milburn et al., 2018).

For instance, developmental psychologist Rochel Gelman suggests that preschoolers follow set principles in their counting. Shown a group of items, they know they should assign just one number to each item and count each item only once. Moreover, even when they get the *names* of numbers wrong, they are consistent in their usage. For instance, a 4-year-old who counts three items as "1, 3, 7" will say "1, 3, 7" when counting another group of different items. And if asked, he or she will probably say that there are seven items in the group (Slusser, Ditta, & Sarnecka, 2013; Xu & LeFevre, 2016; Brueggemann & Gable, 2018).

By the age of 4, most children are able to carry out simple addition and subtraction problems by counting, and they are able to compare different quantities quite successfully (Donlan, 1998; Gilmore & Spelke, 2008).

MEMORY: RECALLING THE PAST   Think back to your own earliest memory. If you are like Paco, described previously, and most other people too, it probably is of an event that occurred after age 3. **Autobiographical memory**, memory of particular events from one's own life, achieves little accuracy until then and increases gradually throughout the preschool years. The accuracy of preschoolers' memories is partly determined by when the memories are assessed. Not all autobiographical memories last into later life. For instance, a child may remember the first day of kindergarten 6 months or a year later, but later in life might not remember it at all. Further, unless an event is particularly vivid or meaningful, it is not likely to be remembered (Valentino et al., 2014; McDonnell et al., 2016; Valentino et al., 2018).

Preschoolers' autobiographical memories not only fade, but may also not be wholly accurate. For example, if an event happens often, it may be hard to remember one specific time it happened. Preschoolers' memories of familiar events are often organized into **scripts**, broad representations in memory of events and the order in which they occur. For example, a young preschooler might represent eating in a restaurant in terms of a few steps: talking to a server, getting the food, and eating. With age, the scripts become more elaborate: getting in the car, being seated at the restaurant, choosing food, ordering, waiting for the meal to come, eating, ordering dessert, and paying for the food. Particular instances of such scripted events are recalled with less accuracy than events that are unscripted (Sutherland, Pipe, & Schick, 2003; Yanaoka & Saito, 2017).

CHILDREN'S EYEWITNESS TESTIMONY: MEMORY ON TRIAL Preschoolers' memories have another important characteristic: They are susceptible to suggestion. This is a special concern when children testify in legal situations, such as when abuse is suspected. Consider the following.

> I saw the crayons. They were all the colors of the rainbow. And gold, too. I was wanting to color with them all day. But then a big man, a giant, came and he stole all the crayons. It happened while we were napping.

Despite the detailed account by this 4-year-old boy of his witnessing the theft of a carton of crayons, there's a problem: The incident didn't happen this way. The memory is entirely false.

The 4-year-old's explicit recounting of a theft that had not actually occurred evolved over a week of questioning about a classroom incident. A sealed carton of crayons disappeared. The children were questioned but none of them knew the carton contained crayons or where it went. The boy quoted here then overheard the teacher tell the principal that the last time she'd seen the crayons was just before nap time. Several days later, she read a fairy tale in class, "Jack and the Beanstalk," which featured a giant. These details became part of his narrative.

This incident has implications for research in a new and rapidly growing field: forensic developmental psychology.

Forensic developmental psychology focuses on the reliability of children's autobiographical memories in the context of the legal system, when they may be witnesses or victims (Goodman, 2006; Bruck & Ceci, 2012).

Children's memories are susceptible to the suggestions of adults asking them questions. This is particularly true of preschoolers, who are considerably more vulnerable to suggestion than either adults or school-age children. The error rate is heightened when the same question is asked repeatedly. False memories—of the "stolen crayon" type just reported—in fact may be more persistent than actual memories. In addition, when questions are highly suggestive (i.e., when questioners attempt to lead a person to particular conclusions), children are more apt to make mistakes (Lowenstein, Blank, & Sauer, 2010; Stolzenberg & Pezdek, 2013; Otgaar et al., 2018).

INFORMATION PROCESSING IN PERSPECTIVE According to information processing approaches, cognitive development consists of gradual improvements in the ways people perceive, understand, and remember information. With age and practice, preschoolers process information more efficiently and with greater sophistication, and they are able to handle increasingly complex problems. In this view, it is these quantitative advances in information processing—and not the qualitative changes suggested by Piaget—that constitute cognitive development (Zhe & Siegler, 2000; Rose, Feldman, & Jankowski, 2009; Bernstein et al., 2017).

For supporters of information processing, the reliance on well-defined processes that can be tested by research is one of the perspective's most important features. Rather than relying on somewhat vague concepts, such as Piaget's notions of assimilation and accommodation, information processing approaches provide a comprehensive, logical set of concepts.

For instance, as preschoolers grow older, they have longer attention spans, can monitor and plan what they are attending to more effectively, and become increasingly aware of their cognitive limitations. This places some of Piaget's findings in a different light. For instance, increased attention allows older children, as distinct from preschoolers, to attend to both the height *and* width of tall and short glasses and to understand that the amount of liquid in the glasses stays the same when it is poured back and forth—that is, to grasp conservation.

Yet information processing approaches have their detractors. One important criticism is that information processing approaches "lose the forest for the trees" by paying so much attention to the detailed, individual sequence of mental processes that they never adequately paint a comprehensive picture of cognitive development—which Piaget clearly did quite well.

Consequently, theorists using both Piagetian and information processing approaches can be considered to take complementary approaches to explaining behavior. For example, consider the chapter opening scenario, about the very active preschooler named Chen who found a way to climb across the kitchen counter to reach a cookie jar. A Piagetian approach might focus on the development of schemas that permitted Chen to understand the concept of goal-focused behavior. In contrast, information processing approaches might concentrate on the memory improvements that allowed Chen to recall where the cookies were stored.

Hence, information processing accounts of behavior provide a different, but complementary view, of behavior. In any case, information processing approaches have been highly influential over the past several decades. They have inspired a tremendous amount of research that has helped us gain some insights into how children develop cognitively.

Vygotsky's View of Cognitive Development: Taking Culture into Account

LO 4.10 Describe Vygotsky's view of cognitive development in the preschool years.

> As her daughter watches, a member of the Chilcotin Indian tribe prepares a salmon for dinner. When the daughter asks a question about a small detail of the process, the mother takes out another salmon and repeats the entire process. According to the tribal view of learning, understanding and comprehension can come only from grasping the total procedure, and not from learning about the individual subcomponents of the task (Tharp, 1989).

The Chilcotin view of how children learn about the world contrasts with the prevalent view of Western society, which assumes that only by mastering the separate parts of a problem can one fully comprehend it. Do differences in the ways particular cultures and societies approach problems influence cognitive development? According to Russian developmental psychologist Lev Vygotsky, who lived from 1896 to 1934, the answer is a clear yes.

Vygotsky viewed cognitive development as the product of social interactions. Instead of concentrating on individual performance, Vygotsky's increasingly influential view focuses on the social aspects of development and learning.

Vygotsky saw children as apprentices, learning cognitive strategies and other skills from adult and peer mentors who not only present new ways of doing things, but also provide assistance, instruction, and motivation. Consequently, he focused on the child's social and cultural world as the source of cognitive development. According to Vygotsky, children gradually grow intellectually and begin to function on their own because of the assistance that adult and peer partners provide (Vygotsky, 1926/1997; Tudge & Scrimsher, 2003).

Vygotsky contends that culture and society establish the institutions, such as preschools and play groups, that promote development by providing opportunities for cognitive growth. Furthermore, by emphasizing particular tasks, culture and society shape the nature of specific cognitive advances. Unless we look at what is important and meaningful to members of a given society, we may seriously underestimate the nature and level of cognitive abilities that ultimately will be attained. For example, children's toys reflect what is important and meaningful in a particular society. In Western societies, preschoolers commonly play with toy wagons, automobiles, and other vehicles, in part reflecting the mobile nature of the culture (Veraksa et al., 2016; Yeniasir, Gökbulut, & Yaraşir, 2017; Esteban-Guitart, 2018).

Vygotsky's approach is therefore quite different from Piaget's. Where Piaget looked at children and saw junior scientists, working by themselves to develop an independent understanding of the world, Vygotsky saw cognitive apprentices, learning from master teachers the skills valued in the child's culture (Mahn & John-Steiner, 2013; Neal Kimball & Turner, 2018).

Sovfoto/Eastfoto

Russian developmental psychologist Lev Vygotsky proposed that the focus of cognitive development should be on a child's social and cultural world, as opposed to the Piagetian approach concentrating on individual performance.

THE ZONE OF PROXIMAL DEVELOPMENT AND SCAFFOLDING: FOUNDATIONS OF COGNITIVE DEVELOPMENT Vygotsky proposed that children's cognitive abilities increase through exposure to information that is new enough to be intriguing, but not too difficult to contend with. He called this the **zone of proximal development (ZPD)**, the level at which a child can *almost*, but not fully, perform a task independently, but can do so with the assistance of someone more competent. For cognitive development to occur, new information must be presented—by parents, teachers, or more skilled peers—within the ZPD. For example, preschoolers might not be able to figure out by themselves how to stick a handle on the clay pot they're making, but they can do it with advice from their child-care teacher (Zuckerman & Shenfield, 2007; Norton & D'Ambrosio, 2008; Warford, 2011).

The concept of the ZPD suggests that even though two children might be able to achieve the same amount without help, if one child receives aid, he or she may improve substantially more than the other. The greater the improvement that comes with help, the larger the ZPD.

The assistance or structuring provided by others has been termed *scaffolding* after the temporary scaffolds that aid in building construction. **Scaffolding** is the support for learning and problem solving that encourages independence and growth (Puntambekar & Hübscher, 2005; Blewitt et al., 2009). As in construction, the scaffolding that older people provide, which facilitates the completion of identified tasks, is removed once children can solve a problem on their own (Taynieoeaym & Ruffman, 2008; Ankrum, Genest, & Belcastro, 2013; Leonard & Higson, 2014).

To Vygotsky, scaffolding not only helps children solve specific problems, but it also aids in the development of their overall cognitive abilities. In education, scaffolding involves, first of all, helping children think about and frame a task appropriately. In addition, a parent or teacher is likely to provide clues to task completion that fit the child's level of development and to model behavior that can lead to task completion.

> **From an educator's perspective:** If children's cognitive development is dependent on interactions with others, what obligations does society have regarding such social settings as preschools and neighborhoods?

One key aspect of the aid that more accomplished individuals provide to learners comes in the form of cultural tools. *Cultural tools* are actual, physical items (e.g., pencils, paper, calculators, computers, and so forth), as well as an intellectual and conceptual framework for solving problems. The framework includes the language that is used within a culture, its alphabetical and numbering schemes, its mathematical and scientific systems, and even its religious systems. These cultural tools provide a structure that can be used to help children define and solve specific problems, as well as an intellectual point of view that encourages cognitive development.

For example, consider the cultural differences in how people talk about distance. In cities, distance is usually measured in blocks ("the store is about 15 blocks away"). To a child from a rural background, more culturally meaningful terms are needed, such as yards, miles, practical rules of thumb such as "a stone's throw," or references to known distances and landmarks ("about half the distance to town").

To make matters more complicated, "how far" questions are sometimes answered in terms not of distance, but of time ("it's about 15 minutes to the store"), which will be understood variously to refer to walking or riding time, depending on context—and, if riding time, to different forms of riding—by ox cart, bicycle, bus, canoe, or automobile, again depending on cultural context. The nature of the tools available to children to solve problems and perform tasks is highly dependent on the culture in which they live.

EVALUATING VYGOTSKY'S CONTRIBUTIONS Vygotsky's view has become increasingly influential, which is surprising given that he died more than 75 years ago at the age of 37 (Winsler, 2003; Gredler & Shields, 2008). His influence has grown because

zone of proximal development (ZPD)
according to Vygotsky, the level at which a child can *almost*, but not fully, perform a task independently, but can do so with the assistance of someone more competent

scaffolding
the support for learning and problem solving that encourages independence and growth

his ideas help explain a growing body of research on the importance of social interaction in promoting cognitive development. The idea that children's comprehension of the world flows from their interactions with their parents, peers, and other members of society is increasingly well supported. It is also consistent with a growing body of multicultural and cross-cultural research that finds evidence that cognitive development is shaped, in part, by cultural factors (Hedegaard & Fleer, 2013; Friedrich, 2014; Yasnitsky & van der Veer, 2016).

Of course, not every aspect of Vygotsky's theorizing has been supported, and he can be criticized for a lack of precision in his conceptualization of cognitive growth. For instance, such broad concepts as the ZPD are not terribly precise, and they do not always lend themselves to experimental tests (Daniels, 2006).

Furthermore, Vygotsky was largely silent on how basic cognitive processes such as attention and memory develop and how children's natural cognitive capabilities unfold. Because of his emphasis on broad cultural influences, he did not focus on how individual bits of information are processed and synthesized. These processes, essential to a complete understanding of cognitive development, are more directly addressed by information processing theories. Still, Vygotsky's melding of the cognitive and social worlds of children has been an important advance in our understanding of cognitive development.

The Growth of Language and Learning

I tried it out and it was very great!
This is a picture of when I was running through the water with Mommy.
Where are you going when I go to the fireworks with Mommy and Daddy?
I didn't know creatures went on floats in pools.
We can always pretend we have another one.
And the teacher put it up on the counter so no one could reach it.
I really want to keep it while we're at the park.
You need to get your own ball if you want to play "hit the tree."
When I grow up and I'm a baseball player, I'll have my baseball hat, and I'll put it on, and I'll play baseball. (Schatz, 1994, p. 179)

Listen to Ricky, at age 3. In addition to recognizing most letters of the alphabet, printing the first letter of his name, and writing the word "HI," he is capable of producing these complex sentences.

During the preschool years, children's language skills reach new heights of sophistication. They begin the period with reasonable linguistic capabilities, but with significant gaps in both comprehension and production. In fact, no one would mistake a 3-year-old's language for an adult's. However, by the end of the preschool years, they can hold their own with adults, comprehending and producing language with many of the qualities of adults' language. How does this transformation occur?

Language Development

LO 4.11   Explain how children's language develops in the preschool years.

Language blooms so rapidly between the ages of the late 2s and the mid-3s that researchers have yet to understand the exact pattern. What is clear is that sentence length increases steadily, and the number of ways children combine words and phrases to form sentences—known as **syntax**—doubles each month. By the time a preschooler is 3, the various combinations reach into the thousands.

There are also enormous leaps in the number of words children use. By age 6, the average child has a vocabulary of around 14,000 words—acquired at a rate of nearly one new word every 2 hours, 24 hours a day. They manage this feat through a process known as **fast mapping**, in which new words are associated with their meaning after only a brief encounter (Marinellie & Kneile, 2012; Venker, Kover, & Weismer, 2016; Aravind, et al., 2018).

syntax
the way in which an individual combines words and phrases to form sentences

fast mapping
instances in which new words are associated with their meaning after only a brief encounter

By the age of 3, preschoolers routinely use plurals and possessive forms of nouns (such as "boys" and "boy's"), the past tense (adding "-ed" at the end of words), and articles ("the" and "a"). They can ask, and answer, complex questions ("Where did you say my book is?" and "Those are trucks, aren't they?").

Preschoolers' skills extend to the appropriate formation of words that they have never before encountered. For example, in one classic experiment (Berko, 1958), the experimenter told the children that a figure was a "wug," and then showed them a card with two of the cartoon figures. "Now there are two of them," the children were told, and they were then asked to supply the missing word in the sentence, "There are two _____" (the answer to which, of course, is "wugs"). (See Figure 4-7.)

Not only did children show that they knew rules about the plural forms of nouns, but they also understood possessive forms of nouns and the third-person singular and past-tense forms of verbs—all for words that they had never encountered, because they were nonsense words with no real meaning (O'Grady & Aitchison, 2005).

Preschoolers also learn what *cannot* be said as they acquire the principles of grammar. **Grammar** is the system of rules that determine how our thoughts can be expressed. For instance, preschoolers come to learn that "I am sitting" is correct, whereas the similarly structured "I am knowing [that]" is incorrect. Although they still make frequent mistakes of one sort or another, 3-year-olds follow the principles of grammar most of the time. Some errors are noticeable—such as the use of *mens* and *catched*—but these errors are actually quite rare. In fact, young preschoolers are correct in their grammatical constructions more than 90 percent of the time (Guasti, 2002; Abbot-Smith & Tomasello, 2010; Normand et al., 2013).

PRIVATE SPEECH In even a short visit to a preschool, you're likely to notice some children talking to themselves during play periods. A child might be reminding a doll about a trip to the grocery store later, or, while playing with a toy racing car, might speak of an upcoming race. In some cases, the talk is sustained, as when a child, working on a puzzle, says things like, "This piece goes here.... Uh-oh, this one doesn't fit.... Where can I put this piece?... This can't be right."

Some developmentalists suggest that **private speech**, speech by children that is spoken and directed to themselves, performs an important function. For instance, Vygotsky suggested that it is used as a guide to behavior and thought. By communicating with themselves through private speech, children are able to try out ideas, acting as their own sounding boards. In this way, private speech facilitates children's thinking and helps them control their behavior—much as you might say "Take it easy" or "Calm down" when trying to control your anger over some situation. In Vygotsky's view, then, private speech serves as an important social function and is also a forerunner to the internal dialogues that we use when we reason with ourselves during thinking (Winsler et al., 2006; Al-Namlah, Meins, & Fernyhough, 2012; McGonigle-Chalmers, Slater, & Smith, 2014; Sawyer, 2017).

In addition, private speech may be a way for children to practice the practical skills required in conversation, known as *pragmatics*. **Pragmatics** is the aspect of language relating to communicating effectively and appropriately with others. The development of pragmatic abilities permits children to understand the basics of conversations—turn-taking, sticking to a topic, and what should and should not be said, according to the conventions of society. When children are taught that the appropriate response to receiving a gift is "thank you," or that they should use different language in various settings (on the playground versus in the classroom), they are learning the pragmatics of language.

SOCIAL SPEECH The preschool years also mark the growth of social speech. **Social speech** is speech directed toward another person and meant to be understood by that person. Before age 3, children seem to be speaking only for their own entertainment, apparently uncaring whether anyone else can understand. However, during the preschool years, children begin to direct their speech to others, wanting others to listen and becoming frustrated when they cannot make themselves understood. As a result, they begin to adapt their speech to others through pragmatics, as discussed previously.

Figure 4-7 Appropriate Formation of Words

Even though no preschooler—like the rest of us—is likely to have ever before encountered a wug, they are able to produce the appropriate word to fill in the blank (which, for the record, is *wugs*).

SOURCE: Based on Berko, J. (1958). The child's learning of English morphology. Word, 14, 150–177.

This animal is called a wug.

We added another wug. Now there are two _____.

grammar
the system of rules that determine how our thoughts can be expressed

private speech
speech by children that is spoken and directed to themselves

pragmatics
the aspect of language that relates to communicating effectively and appropriately with others

social speech
speech directed toward another person and meant to be understood by that person

Informal and Formal Learning

LO 4.12 Describe the effects of informal and formal learning resources on preschoolers.

Children are notorious sponges for information, whether it comes from an informal source, such as television or the Web, or a more formal educational program established for the explicit purpose of teaching. The result can be more or less beneficial, depending on the quality and dependability of the "teacher." We will take a look at both informal sources of information and learning, available through the media, and more formal sources, offered typically by early education programs.

MEDIA AND SCREEN TIME IN THE LIVES OF PRESCHOOLERS   One of the most vexing problems parents of preschoolers face is determining what, and how much, media their children should be allowed to view. Are preschoolers learning from the time they spend viewing media, or are there downsides to exposure to media?

The answer is complicated, and evolving. It is certainly true that left to their own devices, preschoolers would likely put in quite a bit of time viewing various kinds of media. Indeed, they already do: The average preschooler is exposed to over 4 hours per day of screen time, which includes watching media on handheld devices, television, and computers. Furthermore, more than a third of households with children 2 to 7 years of age say that the television is on "most of the time" in their homes (Gutnick et al., 2010; Tandon et al., 2011).

Additionally, 70 percent of preschoolers between the ages of 4 and 6 have used a computer, and a quarter of them use one every day. Those who use a computer spend an average of an hour a day, and the majority use it by themselves. With help from their parents, almost one-fifth of older preschoolers have sent an e-mail (Rideout, Vandewater, & Wartella, 2003; McPake, Plowman, & Stephen, 2013).

THE UP- AND DOWNSIDES OF MEDIA VIEWING   It is unclear what, exactly, children are learning from media exposure they experience. When they do watch television or online videos, preschool children often do not fully understand the plots of the stories they are viewing, particularly in longer programs. They are unable to recall significant story details after viewing a program, and the inferences they make about the motivations of characters are limited and often erroneous. Moreover, preschool children may have difficulty separating fantasy from reality in programming, with some believing, for example, that there is a real Big Bird living on *Sesame Street* (Richert & Schlesinger, 2017).

Preschool-age children exposed to advertising are not able to critically understand and evaluate the messages to which they are exposed. Consequently, they are likely to fully accept advertisers' claims about their product. The likelihood of children believing advertising messages is so high that the American Psychological Association has recommended that television advertising targeting children under the age of 8 be restricted (Nash, Pine, & Messer, 2009; Nicklas et al., 2011; Harris & Kalnova, 2018).

One further concern about preschoolers' use of media relates to the inactivity it produces. Preschoolers who watch more than 2 hours per day of television and videos or use computers for significant amounts of time have a higher risk of obesity than those who watch less (Jordan & Robinson, 2008; Strasburger, 2009; Cox et al, 2012).

In short, the world to which preschoolers are exposed is imperfectly understood and unrealistic. However, as they get older and their information processing capabilities improve, preschoolers' understanding of the material they see on television and on the computer improves. They remember things more accurately, and they become better able to focus on the central message of what they're watching. This improvement suggests that the powers of media may be harnessed to bring about cognitive gains—exactly what the producers of *Sesame Street* set out to do (Berry, 2003; Uchikoshi, 2006; Njoroge et al., 2016).

To address the concern of children putting in too much screen time, the American Academy of Pediatrics recommended in 2016 that children younger than 18 months be discouraged from using screen media other than video chats. For preschoolers older than 2 years of age, they suggest limiting media to 1 hour or less of high-quality programming per day. They also recommend that no screens should be used during meals and for 1 hour before bedtime (American Academy of Pediatrics, 2016; also see the *From Research to Practice* box).

From Research to Practice

Screen Time and the Video Deficit

In a world that is increasingly saturated with technology designed to entertain us or keep us connected to each other, it is not surprising that mobile devices are being used by very young children. For example, in restaurants it's commonplace to see toddlers seated with their parents at a table, wearing earbuds and watching their favorite show on their parent's smartphone or playing a video game on a tablet. Many parents expect that using this technology will provide some sort of educational benefit for their child. But do young children learn as well from a screen as they would from interacting directly with an adult?

No, they do not, because of what has been termed the *video deficit*. Research has consistently found that for many learning tasks such as word-learning and imitation, young children learn much more quickly when interacting with an adult in person than they do watching instruction on a screen. For example, one study found that 12- to 18-month-olds learned many more new words when taught through live parent interaction compared to children who watched

a popular DVD that attempted to teach the same words (DeLoache et al., 2010).

We don't yet fully understand what causes the video deficit in young children. However, a recent study looked at how toddlers' eye movements differ when they are being taught where to find a hidden object that was presented either on a screen or by a person. Researchers found that the toddlers interacting with a screen actually looked *more* at the place where the object was hidden and yet were *less likely* to find the object than were the toddlers interacting with a real person. This study and many like it underscore the importance of in-person interactions for young children and perhaps caution us not to rely on technology for education (Kirkorian et al., 2016).

Shared Writing Prompt:

How might awareness of the video deficit influence strategies that parents and teachers use to educate young children?

EARLY CHILDHOOD EDUCATION: TAKING THE "PRE" OUT OF THE PRESCHOOL PERIOD The term *preschool period* is something of a misnomer: Almost three-quarters of children in the United States are enrolled in some form of care outside the home, much of it designed either explicitly or implicitly to teach skills that will enhance intellectual and social abilities (see Figure 4-8). There are several reasons for this, but one major factor is the rise in the number of families in which both parents work outside the home. For instance, a high proportion of fathers work outside the home, and around 65 percent of women with children younger than age 6 are employed, most of them full-time (Bureau of Labor Statistics, 2018).

However, there is another reason that preschools are popular: Developmental psychologists have found evidence that children can benefit substantially from involvement in some form of educational activity before they enroll in formal schooling, which

Figure 4-8 Care Outside the Home

Approximately 60 percent of children under 6 in the United States are enrolled in some form of care outside the home—a trend that is the result of more parents employed full-time. Evidence suggests that children can benefit from early childhood education.

SOURCE: Child Welfare Information Gateway, 2018.

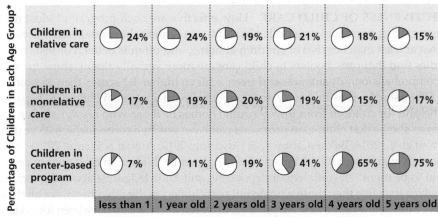

*Columns do not add up to 100 because some children participated in more than one type of day care.

typically takes place at age 5 or 6 in the United States. When compared to children who stay at home and have no formal educational involvement, most children enrolled in good preschools experience clear cognitive and social benefits (National Association for the Education of Young Children, 2005; Bakken, Brown, & Downing, 2017).

THE VARIETIES OF EARLY EDUCATION   The variety of early education alternatives is vast. Some outside-the-home care for children is little more than babysitting, whereas other options are designed to promote intellectual and social advances. Among the major choices are the following:

- *Child-care centers* typically provide care for children outside the home, while their parents are at work. Although many child-care centers aim to provide some form of intellectual stimulation, their primary purpose tends to be more social and emotional than cognitive.

- Some child care is provided in *family child-care centers*, small operations run in private homes. Because centers in some areas are unlicensed, the quality of care can be uneven. Because teachers in licensed child-care programs are more often trained professionals than those who provide family child care, the quality of care is often higher.

- *Preschools* are explicitly designed to provide intellectual and social experiences for children. They tend to be more limited in their schedules than family care centers, typically providing care for only 3 to 5 hours per day. Because of this limitation, preschools serve children mainly from middle and higher socioeconomic levels, in cases where parents don't need to work full-time.

  Like child-care centers, preschools vary enormously in the activities they provide. Some emphasize social skills, whereas others focus on intellectual development. Some do both. For instance, Montessori preschools, which use a method developed by Italian educator Maria Montessori, employ a carefully designed set of materials to create an environment that fosters sensory, motor, and language development. Children are provided with a variety of activities to choose from, with the option of moving from one to another (Gutek, 2003).

  Similarly, in the Reggio Emilia preschool approach—another Italian import—children participate in what is called a *negotiated curriculum* that emphasizes the joint participation of children and teachers. The curriculum builds on the interests of children, promoting their cognitive development through the integration of the arts and participation in weeklong projects (Hong & Trepanier-Street, 2004; Rankin, 2004; Paolella, 2013).

  Preschool readiness programs appear to be cost effective. According to a comprehensive cost-benefit analysis of the long-term economic benefits of preschool participation, every dollar spent results in returns of $3 to $4 in long-term benefits (Gormley et al., 2005; Nakajima et al., 2016; Karoly, 2018).

- *School child care* is provided by some local school systems in the United States. Almost half the states fund prekindergarten programs for 4-year-olds, often aimed at disadvantaged children. Because they typically are staffed by better-trained teachers than less-regulated child-care centers, school child-care programs are often of higher quality than other early education alternatives.

THE EFFECTIVENESS OF CHILD CARE   How effective are such programs? Most research suggests that preschoolers enrolled in child-care centers show intellectual development that at least matches that of children at home, and often is better. For instance, some studies find that preschoolers in child care are more verbally fluent, show memory and comprehension advantages, and even achieve higher IQ scores than at-home children. Other studies find that early and long-term participation in child care is particularly helpful for children from lower-income homes or those who are at risk. Some research even shows that child-care programs can have positive consequences 25 years later (Vivanti et al., 2014; Bakken, Brown, & Downing, 2017; Ansari & Pianta, 2018).

Similar advantages are found for social development. Children in high-quality programs tend to be more self-confident, independent, and knowledgeable about the social world in which they live than those who do not participate. On the other hand, not all the outcomes of outside-the-home care are positive: Children in child care have been found to be less polite, less compliant, less respectful of adults, and sometimes more competitive and aggressive than their peers. Furthermore, children who spend more than 10 hours a week in preschools have a slightly higher likelihood of being disruptive in class (NICHD Early Child Care Research Network, 2003a; Douglass & Klerman, 2012; Vivanti et al., 2014).

It is important to keep in mind that not all early childhood care programs are equally effective. High-quality care provides intellectual and social benefits, whereas low-quality care not only is unlikely to furnish benefits, but also actually may harm children (NICHD Early Child Care Research Network, 2006; Dearing, McCartney, & Taylor, 2009).

THE QUALITY OF CHILD CARE   How can we define "high quality"? The major characteristics of high-quality care include the following (Leach et al., 2008; Rudd, Cain, & Saxon, 2008; Lloyd, 2012):

- The care providers are well trained, preferably with bachelor's degrees.
- The child-care center has an appropriate overall size and ratio of care providers to children. Single groups should not have many more than 14 to 20 children, and there should be no more than 5 to 10 three-year-olds per caregiver, or 7 to 10 four- or five-year-olds per caregiver.
- The child-to-teacher ratio should be 10:1 or better.
- The curriculum of a child-care facility is carefully planned out and coordinated among the teachers.
- The language environment is rich, with a great deal of conversation.
- The caregivers are sensitive to children's emotional and social needs, and they know when and when not to intervene.
- Materials and activities are age appropriate.
- Basic health and safety standards are followed.
- Children should be screened for vision, hearing, and health problems.
- At least one meal a day should be served.
- The facility should provide at least one family support service.

No one knows how many programs in the United States can be considered "high quality," but there are many fewer than desirable. In fact, the United States lags behind almost every other industrialized country in the quality of its child care as well as in its quantity and affordability (Muenchow & Marsland, 2007; Pianta et al., 2009; OECD, 2107; also see the *Cultural Dimensions* box).

Cultural Dimensions

Preschools Around the World: Why Does the United States Lag Behind?

In France and Belgium, access to preschool is a legal right. Sweden and Finland provide child care for preschoolers whose parents want it. Russia has an extensive system of state-run *yasli-sads*, nursery schools and kindergartens, attended by 75 percent of children age 3 to 7 in urban areas.

In contrast, the United States has no coordinated national policy on preschool education—or on the care of children in general. There are several reasons for this. For one, decisions about education have traditionally been left to the states and to local school districts. For another, the United States, unlike many other countries, has no tradition of teaching preschoolers. Finally, the status of preschools in the United States has been traditionally low. Consider, for instance, that preschool and nursery school teachers are the lowest paid of all teachers. (Teacher salaries increase as the age of students rises. Thus,

college and high school teachers are paid most, whereas preschool and elementary school teachers are paid least.)

Different societies view the purpose of early childhood education differently (Lamb et al., 1992). For instance, in a cross-country comparison of China, Japan, and the United States, researchers found that parents in the three countries view the purpose of preschools differently. Although parents in China tend to see preschools primarily as a way of giving children a good start academically, Japanese parents view them mostly as a way of giving children the opportunity to be members of a group. In the United States, in comparison, parents regard the primary purpose of preschools as making children more independent and self-reliant, although obtaining a good academic start and having group experiences are also important (Huntsinger et al., 1997; Johnson et al., 2003).

> **From an educator's perspective:** What do you think might be some implications for a preschool teacher who has children from China, Japan, and the United States in the classroom?

Review, Check, and Apply

Review

LO 4.7 **Analyze Piaget's explanation of cognitive development during the preschool years.**

According to Piaget, children in the preoperational stage develop symbolic function, a change in their thinking that is the foundation of further cognitive advances. Preoperational children are hampered by a tendency toward egocentric thought.

LO 4.8 **Evaluate how Piaget's approach stands up to the test of time.**

Recent developmentalists, although acknowledging Piaget's gifts and contributions, take issue with his underestimation of preschoolers' capabilities.

LO 4.9 **Analyze information processing approaches to cognitive development in the preschool years.**

A different approach to cognitive development is taken by proponents of information processing theories, who focus on preschoolers' storage and recall of information and on quantitative changes in information processing abilities (such as attention). Children's memories are susceptible to the suggestions of adults asking them questions. This is particularly true of preschoolers, who are considerably more vulnerable to suggestion than either adults or school-age children. With age and practice, preschoolers process information more efficiently and with greater sophistication, and they are able to handle increasingly complex problems.

LO 4.10 **Describe Vygotsky's view of cognitive development in the preschool years.**

Lev Vygotsky proposed that the nature and progress of children's cognitive development are dependent on the children's social and cultural context. Vygotsky developed two theoretical frameworks that have proven to have practical value in education: the zone of proximal development and scaffolding.

LO 4.11 **Explain how children's language develops in the preschool years.**

Children rapidly progress from two-word utterances to longer, more sophisticated expressions that reflect their growing vocabularies and emerging grasp of grammar.

LO 4.12 **Describe the effects of informal and formal learning resources on preschoolers.**

The effects of television are mixed. Preschoolers' sustained exposure to emotions and situations that are not representative of the real world have raised concerns. However, preschoolers can derive meaning from such targeted programs as *Sesame Street*, which are designed to bring about cognitive gains. Early childhood educational programs, offered as center-based or school-based child care or as preschool, can lead to cognitive and social advances. The United States lacks a coordinated national policy on preschool education.

Check Yourself

1. According to Piaget, although preschool-age children begin to use symbolic thinking, they are not capable of _____, or organized, logical mental processes that characterize schoolchildren.

   a. operations
   b. transcendence
   c. egocentric thought
   d. social interaction

2. According to the information processing approach, memories of particular events occurring in one's own life are known as _____.

   a. personal memory
   b. explicit memory
   c. autobiographical memory
   d. cultural memory

3. Preschoolers are able to learn the meaning of words after only a brief encounter. This is known as _____.

   a. grammar
   b. fast mapping
   c. syntax
   d. social speech

4. Montessori preschools are designed to create an environment that promotes _____ development.

   a. social and cultural
   b. cognitive and memory
   c. artistic and creative
   d. sensory, motor, and language

Applying Lifespan Development

In your view, how do thought and language development relate to one another in preschoolers' development? Is it possible to think without understanding a language?

Module 4.3

Social and Personality Development in the Preschool Years

"I don't think I would have caught it on my own," says Marcia Mueller, a preschool teacher in Lincoln, Illinois. "Like any teacher, I'm alert for issues that our children may have, but David Hansen was an easy 4-year-old, always seeking to please, always empathizing with other kids when they cried. Still, when his parents mentioned their concerns, I looked more closely.

"I noticed that David never seemed 'fun-loving'—never running around or climbing the slide or swinging on the swings. One time he threw a LEGO block against the wall. When I approached, he said 'I'm no good at LEGOs. I'll never be good at them. I shouldn't play with them.'

"I began to notice that David quickly turned learning frustrations into personal sources of guilt. For instance, he would never even try to say the days of the week in Circle Time until he was sure he would get them right. In fact, he never tried anything—the alphabet, counting to 10—until he was certain he had mastered it. When I noticed David sometimes staring off into space, generally a normal

behavior, I began to wonder if he wasn't just distracted but truly bothered by something.

"I talked to our director, and we met with David's parents. They decided to take him to a child psychologist, who eventually determined that David had childhood depression."

In this module, we address social and personality development during the preschool period. We begin by examining how children continue to form a sense of self, focusing on how they develop their self-concepts, including their concept of gender. Next we focus on preschoolers' social lives, especially how they play with one another, and we consider how parents and other authority figures use discipline to shape children's behavior.

Finally, we examine two key aspects of social behavior: moral development and aggression. We consider how children develop a notion of right and wrong, and we look at factors that lead preschool-age children to behave aggressively.

Forming a Sense of Self

Although the question "Who am I?" is not explicitly posed by most preschool-age children, it underlies much of their development during the preschool years, and the answer may affect them for the rest of their lives.

Self-Concept in the Preschool Years

LO 4.13 Explain how preschool-age children develop a concept of themselves.

> Mary-Alice's preschool teacher raised her eyebrows slightly when the 4-year-old took off her coat. Mary-Alice, usually dressed in well-matched play suits, was a medley of prints. She had on a pair of flowered pants, along with a completely clashing plaid top. The outfit was accessorized with a striped headband, socks in an animal print, and Mary-Alice's polka-dotted rain boots. Mary-Alice's mom gave a slightly embarrassed shrug. "Mary-Alice got dressed all by herself this morning," she explained as she handed over a bag containing spare shoes, just in case the rain boots became uncomfortable during the day.

PSYCHOSOCIAL DEVELOPMENT: RESOLVING THE CONFLICTS Psychoanalyst Erik Erikson may well have praised Mary-Alice's mother for helping Mary-Alice develop a sense of initiative (if not of fashion), and thereby promoting her psychosocial development. **Psychosocial development** encompasses changes in individuals' understanding of themselves and of others' behavior. According to Erikson, society and culture present a series of challenges that shift as people age. Erikson believed that people pass through eight distinct stages, each characterized by a crisis or conflict that the person must resolve. Our experiences as we try to resolve these conflicts lead us to develop ideas about ourselves that can last for the rest of our lives.

In the early part of the preschool period, children are ending the autonomy-versus-shame-and-doubt stage and entering what Erikson called the **initiative-versus-guilt stage**, which lasts from around age 3 to 6. During this period, children face conflicts between the desire to act independently of their parents and the guilt that comes if they don't succeed. They come to see themselves as persons in their own right, and they begin to make decisions on their own.

Parents (like Mary-Alice's mother) who react positively can help their children resolve these opposing feelings. By providing their children with opportunities to act self-reliantly, while still giving them direction and guidance, parents can support their

psychosocial development
according to Erik Erikson, development that encompasses changes in the understandings individuals have of themselves as members of society and in their comprehension of the meaning of others' behavior

initiative-versus-guilt stage
according to Erik Erikson, the period during which children age 3 to 6 years experience conflict between independence of action and the sometimes negative results of that action

Psychosocial development relates to changes in an understanding of one's own and others' behavior.

children's initiative. By contrast, parents who discourage their children's independence may contribute to a sense of guilt that persists throughout their lives and affects their self-concept, which begins to develop during this period.

SELF-CONCEPT: THINKING ABOUT THE SELF If you ask preschool-age children to specify what makes them different from other kids, they readily respond with answers like, "I'm a good runner" or "I'm a big girl." Such answers relate to **self-concept**—their identity, or their set of beliefs about what they are like as individuals (Marsh, Ellis, & Craven, 2002; Bhargava, 2014; Crampton & Hall, 2017).

Children's self-concepts are not necessarily accurate. In fact, preschool children typically overestimate their skills and knowledge across all domains of expertise. Consequently, their view of the future is quite rosy: They expect to win the next game they play, to beat all opponents in an upcoming race, to write great stories when they grow up. Even when they have just experienced failure at a task, they are likely to expect to do well in the future. This optimistic view arises because they do not yet compare themselves and their performance against others, thereby gaining the freedom to take chances and try new activities (Verschueren, Doumen, & Buyse, 2012; Ehm, Lindberg, & Hasselhorn, 2013; Jia, Lang, & Schoppe-Sullivan, 2016).

Preschool-age children's view of themselves reflects their culture. For example, many Asian societies tend to have a **collectivistic orientation**, in which individuals tend to regard themselves as parts of a larger social network in which they are interconnected with and responsible to others. In contrast, children in Western cultures are more likely to develop an **individualistic orientation** that emphasizes personal identity and the uniqueness of the individual, seeing themselves as self-contained and autonomous, in competition with others for scarce resources (Lehman, Chiu, & Schaller, 2004; Wang, 2006; Huppert et al., 2018).

Preschoolers' developing self-concepts can also be affected by their culture's attitudes toward various racial and ethnic groups. Preschoolers' awareness of their ethnic or racial identity is subtly influenced by the attitudes of the people, schools, and other cultural institutions with which they come into contact (see the *Cultural Dimensions* box).

self-concept
a person's identity, or set of beliefs about what one is like as an individual

collectivistic orientation
a philosophy that promotes the notion of interdependence

individualistic orientation
a philosophy that emphasizes personal identity and the uniqueness of the individual

race dissonance
the phenomenon in which minority children indicate preferences for majority values or people

Cultural Dimensions

Developing Racial and Ethnic Awareness

The preschool years mark an important turning point for children. Their answer to the question of who they are begins to take into account their racial and ethnic identity.

For most preschool-age children, racial awareness comes relatively early. Certainly, even infants are able to distinguish different skin colors, but it is only later that children begin to attribute meaning to different racial characteristics.

By the time they are 3 or 4 years of age, preschool-age children notice differences among people based on skin color, and they begin to identify themselves as a member of a particular group, such as "Hispanic" or "black." Although at first they do not realize that ethnicity and race are enduring features of who they are, later they begin to understand the significance that society places on ethnic and racial membership (Quintana et al., 2008; Guerrero et al., 2010; Setoh et al., 2017).

Some preschoolers have mixed feelings about their racial and ethnic identity. In fact, some experience **race dissonance**, the phenomenon in which minority children indicate preferences for majority values or people. For instance, some studies find that as many as 90 percent of African American children, when asked about their reactions to drawings of black and white children, react more negatively to those depicting black children than white children. However, this reaction does not translate into lower self-esteem; rather, the white preference appears to be a result of the powerful influence of the dominant culture, rather than a disparagement of their own race (Holland, 1994; Quintana, 2007).

Gender Identity: Developing Femaleness and Maleness

LO 4.14   Analyze how preschool-age children develop a sense of gender.

Boys' awards: Very Best Thinker, Most Eager Learner, Most Imaginative, Most Enthusiastic, Most Scientific, Best Friend, Mr. Personality, Hardest Worker, Best Sense of Humor.

Girls' awards: All-Around Sweetheart, Sweetest Personality, Cutest Personality, Best Sharer, Best Artist, Biggest Heart, Best Manners, Best Helper, Most Creative.

What's wrong with this picture? Quite a bit to one parent, whose daughter received one of the girls' awards during a kindergarten graduation ceremony (Deveny, 1994). Whereas the girls were getting pats on the back for their pleasing personalities, the boys were receiving awards for their intellectual and analytic skills.

This situation is not rare: Girls and boys often live in different worlds beginning at birth and continuing into the preschool years and beyond (Bornstein et al., 2008; Conry-Murray, 2013; Brinkman et al., 2014).

Gender, the sense of being male or female, is well established by the time children reach the preschool years. By age 2, children consistently label people as male or female (Campbell, Shirley, & Candy, 2004; Dinella, Weisgram, & Fulcher, 2017).

One way gender shows up is in play. Preschool boys spend more time than girls in rough-and-tumble play, whereas preschool girls spend more time in organized games and role-playing. During this time boys begin to play more with boys, and girls with girls, a trend that increases during middle childhood. Girls begin to prefer same-sex play-mates a little earlier than boys. They first have a clear preference for interacting with other girls at age 2, while boys don't show much preference for same-sex playmates until age 3 (Boyatzis, Mallis, & Leon, 1999; Martin & Fabes, 2001; Raag, 2003; Martin et al., 2013).

Preschool-age children often have strict ideas about how boys and girls are supposed to act. In fact, their expectations about gender-appropriate behavior are even more gender-stereotyped than those of adults. Beliefs in gender stereotypes become increasingly pronounced up to age 5, and although they become somewhat less rigid by age 7, they do not disappear. In fact, the gender stereotypes held by preschoolers resemble those held by traditional adults in society (Halim et al., 2014; Emilson, Folkesson, & Lindberg, 2016; Paz-Albo Prieto et al., 2017).

Like adults, preschoolers expect that males are more apt to have traits involving competence, independence, forcefulness, and competitiveness. In contrast, females are viewed as more likely to have traits such as warmth, expressiveness, nurturance, and submissiveness. Although these are *expectations*, and say nothing about the way that men and women actually behave, such expectations provide the lens through which preschool-age children view the world and affect their behavior as well as the way they interact with peers and adults (Blakemore, 2003; Gelman, Taylor, & Nguyen, 2004; Martin & Dinella, 2012).

During the preschool period, differences in play according to gender become more pronounced. In addition, boys tend to play with boys, and girls with girls.

> **From a child-care provider's perspective:** If a girl in a preschool child-care setting loudly tells a boy that he can't play with the dolls in the play area because he's a boy, what is the best way to handle the situation?

Why should gender play such a powerful role during the preschool years (as well as during the rest of the life span)? Developmentalists have proposed several explanations.

BIOLOGICAL PERSPECTIVES It is hardly surprising that the biological characteristics associated with sex lead to gender differences. Hormones, for example, have been found to affect gender-based behaviors. Girls exposed to unusually high levels of *androgens* (male hormones) prenatally are more likely to display "typically male" behaviors than their sisters who were not exposed to androgens (Knickmeyer & Baron-Cohen, 2006; Burton et al., 2009; Mathews et al., 2009).

Androgen-exposed girls preferred boys as playmates and spent more time than other girls playing with toys associated with the male role, such as cars and trucks. Similarly, boys exposed prenatally to atypically high levels of female hormones are apt to display more behaviors that are stereotypically female than is usual (Servin et al., 2003; Knickmeyer & Baron-Cohen, 2006).

Some developmentalists see gender differences as serving the biological goal of survival of the species. Using an evolutionary approach, these theorists suggest that males with stereotypically masculine qualities, such as forcefulness and competitiveness, may have been able to attract females who could give them hardy offspring. Females who excelled at stereotypically feminine tasks, such as nurturing, may have been valued because they could help their children survive the dangers of childhood (Browne, 2006; Ellis, 2006).

Of course, it is difficult to attribute behavioral characteristics unambiguously to biological factors. Because of this, we must consider other explanations for gender differences.

SOCIAL LEARNING APPROACHES According to social learning approaches, children learn gender-related behavior and expectations by observing others, including parents, teachers, siblings, and even peers. A boy might admire a Major League Baseball player and become interested in sports. A girl might watch her babysitter practicing cheerleading moves and begin to try them herself. Observing the praise and honor that gender-appropriate behavior earns leads the child to mimic that behavior (Rust et al., 2000).

Books and the media, and in particular television and video games, also play a role in perpetuating traditional views of gender-related behavior. Analyses of the most popular television shows find that male characters outnumber female characters by two to one. Furthermore, females are more apt to appear with males, whereas female–female relationships are relatively uncommon (Calvert et al., 2003; Chapman, 2016).

Television and other media also present men and women in traditional gender roles, often defining female characters in terms of their relationships with males. Furthermore, females are more likely to appear as victims than males. They are less likely to be presented as productive or as decision makers, and more likely to be portrayed as characters interested in romance, their homes, and their families. Such models, according to social learning theory, have a powerful influence on preschoolers' definitions of appropriate behavior (Nassif & Gunter, 2008; Prieler et al., 2011; Matthes, Prieler & Adam, 2016).

In some cases, preschoolers learn social roles directly, not through models. For example, preschool-age children may be told by their parents to act like a "little girl" or "little man." What this generally means is that girls should behave politely and boys should be tough. Such direct training sends a clear message about expected behavior for the different genders (Leaper, 2002).

COGNITIVE APPROACHES In the view of some theorists, one aspect of forming a clear sense of identity is the desire to establish a **gender identity**, a perception of oneself as male or female. To do this, children develop a **gender schema**, a cognitive

gender identity
the perception of oneself as male or female

gender schema
a cognitive framework that organizes information relevant to gender

framework that organizes information relevant to gender (Barberá, 2003; Martin & Ruble, 2004; Signorella & Frieze, 2008).

Gender schemas are developed early in life and serve as a lens through which preschoolers view the world, encompassing "rules" about what is appropriate and inappropriate for males and females. Some girls may decide that wearing pants is what boys do and apply the rule so rigidly that they refuse to wear anything but dresses. Or a preschool boy may reason that it is inappropriate for him to wear makeup for a school play because makeup is worn by girls—even though all the other boys and girls are wearing it (Frawley, 2008).

According to *cognitive-developmental theory*, proposed by Lawrence Kohlberg, this rigidity is in part a reflection of preschoolers' understanding of gender (Kohlberg, 1966). Specifically, young preschoolers erroneously believe that sex differences are based not on biological factors but on differences in appearance or behavior. Employing this view of the world, a boy may think he could turn into a girl if he put on a dress and tied his hair in a ponytail. However, by age 4 or 5, children develop an understanding of **gender constancy**, the awareness that people are permanently males or females, depending on fixed, unchangeable biological factors.

gender constancy
the belief that people are permanently males or females, depending on fixed, unchangeable biological factors

For some children, gender identification is particularly challenging. *Transgender children* believe that they are trapped in the body of the other gender. There are some reports of transgender children expressing to their parents that they believe their gender identity is different from that assigned at birth as early as they learn to talk, starting at 18 to 24 months. But there is relatively little research on the issue, and little guidance exists for parents about how to deal with preschoolers who express the conviction that they identify with the other gender (Prince-Embury & Saklofaske, 2014; Fast & Olson, 2017).

Interestingly, gender schemas appear well before children understand gender constancy. Even young preschool-age children assume that certain behaviors are appropriate—and others are not—on the basis of stereotypic views of gender (Ruble et al., 2007; Karniol, 2009; Halim et al., 2014).

Is it possible to avoid viewing the world in terms of gender schemas? According to some experts, one way is to encourage children to be **androgynous**, a state in which gender roles encompass characteristics thought typical of both sexes. For instance, parents and caregivers can encourage preschool children to see males as assertive but at the same time warm and tender. Similarly, girls might be encouraged to see the female role as both empathetic and tender and competitive, assertive, and independent. Some research finds that children who think of themselves as having the characteristics of both sexes have some mental health advantages as they grow older (Bem, 1987; Pauletti et al., 2017).

androgynous
a state in which gender roles encompass characteristics thought typical of both sexes

Like the other approaches to gender development, the cognitive perspective does not imply that differences between the two sexes are in any way improper or inappropriate. Instead, it suggests that preschoolers should be taught to treat others as individuals. Furthermore, preschoolers need to learn the importance of fulfilling their own talents, acting as individuals and not as representatives of a gender.

Friends and Family: Preschoolers' Social Lives

When Juan was 3, he had his first best friend, Emilio. Juan and Emilio, who lived in the same apartment building in San Jose, were inseparable. They played incessantly with toy cars, racing them up and down the apartment hallways until some of the neighbors began to complain about the noise. They pretended to read to one another, and sometimes they slept over at each other's home—a big step for a 3-year-old. Neither boy seemed more joyful than when he was with his "best friend"—the term each used for the other.

An infant's family can provide nearly all the social contact he or she needs. As preschoolers, however, many children, like Juan and Emilio, begin to discover the joys of peer friendships. Let's take a look at both sides of preschoolers' social development: friends and family.

Jamie Grill/Blend Images/Age Fotostock

As preschoolers get older, their conception of friendship evolves and the quality of their interactions changes.

functional play

play that involves simple, repetitive activities typical of 3-year-olds

constructive play

play in which children manipulate objects to produce or build something

parallel play

action in which children play with similar toys, in a similar manner, but do not interact with each other

onlooker play

action in which children simply watch others at play, but do not actually participate themselves

associative play

play in which two or more children actually interact with one another by sharing or borrowing toys or materials, although they do not do the same thing

cooperative play

play in which children genuinely interact with one another, taking turns, playing games, or devising contests

The Development of Friendships

LO 4.15   Describe the sorts of social relationships that are typical of preschool-age children.

Before age 3, most social activity involves simply being in the same place at the same time, without real social interaction. However, at around the age of 3, children begin to develop real friendships as peers are seen as individuals who hold special qualities and rewards. Although preschoolers' relations with adults reflect children's needs for care, protection, and direction, their relations with peers are based more on the desire for companionship, play, and fun. Gradually, they come to view friendship as a continuing state that offers not just immediate pleasure, but the promise of future activity (Proulx & Poulin, 2013; Paulus & Moore, 2014; Paulus, 2016).

Interactions with friends change during the preschool period. For 3-year-olds, the focus of friendship is the enjoyment of doing things together and playing jointly. Older preschoolers pay more attention to trust, support, and shared interests. Throughout the entire period, however, play remains an important part of all friendships (Shin et al., 2014; Daniel, et al., 2016).

PLAYING BY THE RULES: THE WORK AND CATEGORIZATION OF PLAY   In Rosie Graiff's class of 3-year-olds, Minnie bounces her doll's feet on the table as she sings softly to herself. Ben pushes his toy car across the floor, making motor noises. Sarah chases Abdul around and around the perimeter of the room.

Play is more than what children of preschool age do to pass the time. Instead, play helps preschoolers develop socially, cognitively, and physically (Hughett, Kohler, & Raschke, 2013; Fleer, 2017).

At the beginning of the preschool years, children engage in **functional play**—simple, repetitive activities typical of 3-year-olds, such as pushing cars on the floor, skipping, and jumping. Functional play involves doing something to be active rather than to create something (Bober, Humphry, & Carswell, 2001; Kantrowitz & Evans, 2004).

By age 4, children become involved in a more sophisticated form of play. In **constructive play** children manipulate objects to produce or build something. A child who builds a house out of LEGOs or puts a puzzle together is involved in constructive play: He or she has an ultimate goal—to produce something. The creation need not be novel, because children may repeatedly build a house of blocks, let it fall, and then rebuild it.

Constructive play gives children a chance to practice their physical and cognitive skills and fine muscle movements. They gain experience in solving problems about the ways and the sequences in which things fit together. They also learn to cooperate with others as the social nature of play becomes more important to them (Love & Burns, 2006; Oostermeijer, Boonen, & Jolles, 2014).

THE SOCIAL ASPECTS OF PLAY   If two preschoolers sit side by side at a table, each assembling a different puzzle, are they engaged jointly in play?

According to pioneering work done by Mildred Parten (1932), the answer is yes. She suggests that these preschoolers are engaged in **parallel play**, in which children play with similar toys, in a similar manner, but do not interact with each other. Preschoolers also engage in another form of play, a highly passive one: onlooker play. In **onlooker play**, children simply watch others at play, but do not actually participate themselves.

As they get older, however, preschool-age children engage in more sophisticated forms of social play that involve greater interaction. In **associative play**, two or more children interact with one another by sharing or borrowing toys or materials, although they do not do the same thing. In **cooperative play**, children genuinely play with one another, taking turns, playing games, or devising contests.

Solitary and onlooker play continue in the later stages of the preschool period. There are simply times when children prefer to play by themselves. And when newcomers join a group, one strategy for becoming part of the group—often successful—is to engage in onlooker play, waiting for an opportunity to join the play more actively (Lindsey & Colwell, 2003).

The nature of pretend, or make-believe, play also changes during the period, becoming in some ways more *un*realistic—and imaginative—as preschoolers shift from using only realistic objects to using less concrete ones. Thus, at the start of the preschool period, children may pretend to listen to a radio only if they have a plastic radio on hand. Later, they may use an entirely different object, such as a large cardboard box, as a pretend radio (Parsons & Howe, 2013; Russ, 2014; Thibodeau et al., 2016).

Vygotsky (1926/1997) argued that pretend play, particularly if it involves social play, is an important means for expanding preschool-age children's cognitive skills. Through make-believe play, children are able to "practice" activities (such as pretending to use a computer or read a book) that are a part of their particular culture and broaden their understanding of the way the world functions.

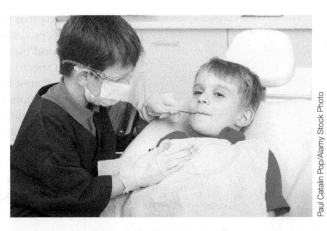

According to developmentalist Lev Vygotsky, children are able, through make-believe play, to practice activities that are part of their particular culture and broaden their understanding of the way the world functions.

> **From an educator's perspective:** How might a preschool school teacher encourage a shy child to join a group of preschoolers who are playing?

Preschoolers' Theory of Mind: Understanding What Others Are Thinking

LO 4.16   Analyze how children's theory of mind changes during the preschool years.

One reason that children's play changes is the continuing development of preschoolers' theory of mind—their knowledge and beliefs about how the mind operates. Using their theory of mind, preschool children increasingly see the world from others' perspectives. Even children as young as 2 are able to understand that others have emotions. By age 3 or 4, preschoolers know that they can imagine something that is not physically present, such as a zebra, and that others can do the same. They can also pretend that something has happened and react as if it really had occurred, a skill that becomes part of their imaginative play (Wellman, 2012; Lane et al., 2013; Wu & Su, 2014).

Preschool-age children also become more insightful regarding the motives and reasons behind people's behavior. They begin to understand that their mother is angry because she was late for an appointment, even if they themselves haven't seen her be late. Furthermore, by age 4, children's understanding that people can be fooled by physical reality (such as magic tricks involving sleight-of-hand) becomes surprisingly sophisticated. This increase in understanding helps children become more socially skilled as they gain insight into what others are thinking (Fitzgerald & White, 2002; Eisbach, 2004; Fernández, 2013).

There are limits, however, to 3-year-olds' theory of mind. For instance, their understanding of "belief" is incomplete, as illustrated by their performance on the *false belief* task. In the false belief task, preschoolers are shown a doll named Maxi who places chocolate in a cabinet and then leaves. After Maxi is gone, his mother moves the chocolate somewhere else.

Preschoolers are then asked where Maxi will look for the chocolate when he returns. Three-year-olds answer (erroneously) that Maxi will look for it in the new location. In contrast, 4-year-olds correctly realize that Maxi has the false belief that the chocolate is still in the cabinet, and that's where he will look for it (Amsterlaw & Wellman, 2006; Brown & Bull, 2007; Lecce et al., 2014; Ornaghi, Pepe, & Grazzini, 2016).

By the end of the preschool years, most children easily solve false belief problems. But one group has difficulty with it throughout their lifetimes: children with autism spectrum disorder. (*Autism spectrum disorder* is the psychological disorder that produces significant language and emotional difficulties.)

Children with autism spectrum disorder find it particularly difficult to relate to others, in part because they find it difficult to understand what others are thinking. According to the Centers for Disease Control and Prevention, about 1 in 68 children (primarily males) have autism spectrum disorder. The disorder is characterized by a lack of connection to other people, even parents, and an avoidance of interpersonal situations. Furthermore, preschoolers with autism spectrum disorder may not want to be picked up or cuddled, and they may find eye contact unpleasant and seek to avoid it. Individuals with autism spectrum disorder are bewildered by false belief problems no matter how old they are (Carey, 2012; Miller, 2012; Peterson, 2014).

Cultural factors also play an important role in the development of theory of mind and the interpretations that children bring to bear on others' actions. For example, children in more industrialized Western cultures may be more likely to see others' behavior as a result of the kind of people they are, a function of the people's personal traits and characteristics ("She won the race because she is really fast"). In contrast, children in non-Western cultures may see others' behavior as produced by forces that are less under their personal control ("She won the race because she was lucky") (Tardif, Wellman, & Cheung, 2004; Wellman et al., 2006; Liu et al., 2008).

Preschoolers' Family Lives

LO 4.17   Describe the changing nature of families and the diversity of parenting styles preschoolers experience.

> Four-year-old Benjamin was watching TV while his mom cleaned up after dinner. After a while, he wandered in and grabbed a towel, saying, "Mommy, let me help you do the dishes." Surprised by this unprecedented behavior, she asked him, "Where did you learn to do dishes?"
>
> "I saw it on a video," he replied, "Only it was the dad helping. Since we don't have a dad, I figured I'd do it."

CHANGES IN FAMILY LIFE   For many preschool-age children, life does not mirror what we see in reruns of old sitcoms. Many face the realities of an increasingly complicated world. For instance, in 1960, less than 10 percent of children younger than age 18 lived with one parent. Three decades later, a single parent heads more than a quarter of all families. There are also large racial disparities: 52 percent of all African American children and 29 percent of Hispanic children live with a single parent, compared with 22 percent of white children (Grall, 2009; U.S. Census, 2017).

Still, for most children the preschool years are not a time of turmoil. Instead, the period is characterized by growing interactions with the world at large. Preschoolers form genuine friendships and develop close ties with other children—a circumstance facilitated by a warm, supportive home environment. Research finds that strong, positive relationships between parents and children encourage children's relationships with others (Vu, 2015).

EFFECTIVE PARENTING: TEACHING DESIRED BEHAVIOR   The key element in most families is the parent; the parent is usually the person with whom the child interacts most often and most consistently, and it is up to the parent to teach the child how to behave. Parents, generally working with little direct guidance, tend to develop distinctive styles when dealing with their preschool-age children, and their styles can be classified into a few broad categories. Consider the following hypothetical situation.

> While she thinks no one is looking, Maria goes into her brother Alejandro's bedroom, where he has been saving the last of his Halloween candy. Just as she takes his last peanut butter cup, the children's mother walks into the room and immediately takes in the situation.

If you were Maria's mother, which of the following reactions seems most reasonable?

1. Tell Maria to go to her room and stay there for the rest of the day, and take away access to her favorite blanket, the one she sleeps with every night and during naps.
2. Mildly tell Maria that what she did was not such a good idea, and she shouldn't do it in the future.
3. Explain why her action would upset her brother, and tell her to go to her room for an hour as punishment.
4. Forget about it, and let the children sort it out themselves.

Each of these responses represents one of the major parenting styles identified by Diana Baumrind (1971, 1980) and updated by Eleanor Maccoby and colleagues (Baumrind, 1971, 1980; Maccoby & Martin, 1983).

1. **Authoritarian parents** are controlling, punitive, rigid, and cold. Their word is law, and they value strict, unquestioning obedience. They do not tolerate expressions of disagreement.

2. **Permissive parents** provide lax and inconsistent feedback. They require little of their children and don't see themselves as holding much responsibility for how their children turn out. They place little or no limits or control on their children's behavior.

3. **Authoritative parents** are firm, setting clear and consistent limits. Although they tend to be relatively strict, like authoritarian parents, they are loving and emotionally supportive. They also try to reason with their children, explaining why they should behave in a particular way ("Alejandro is going to be upset"), and communicating the rationale for any punishment they may impose. Authoritative parents encourage their children to be independent.

4. **Uninvolved parents** show virtually no interest in their children, displaying indifferent, rejecting behavior. They are detached emotionally and see their role as no more than feeding, clothing, and providing shelter. In its most extreme form, uninvolved parenting results in *neglect*, a form of child abuse. (The four patterns are summarized in Table 4-1.)

Parents' disciplinary styles usually produce differences in children's behavior—although there are many exceptions (Cheah et al., 2009; Lin, Chiu, & Yeh, 2012; Flouri & Midouhas, 2017; also see the *Development in Your Life* box):

- Children of authoritarian parents tend to be withdrawn, show little sociability, are not friendly, and often behave uneasily around their peers. Girls are especially dependent on their parents, whereas boys are unusually hostile.

- Children of permissive parents tend to be dependent and moody and are low in social skills and self-control. They share many characteristics of children of authoritarian parents.

- Children of authoritative parents fare best. They generally are independent, friendly, self-assertive, and cooperative. They have strong motivation to achieve and are typically successful and likable. They regulate their own behavior effectively, in terms of both their relationships with others and their emotional self-regulation.

- Children of uninvolved parents are the worst off, showing disrupted emotional development. They feel unloved and emotionally detached, and their physical and cognitive development may be impeded as well.

authoritarian parents
parents who are controlling, punitive, rigid, and cold, and whose word is law. They value strict, unquestioning obedience from their children and do not tolerate expressions of disagreement

permissive parents
parents who provide lax and inconsistent feedback and require little of their children

authoritative parents
parents who are firm, setting clear and consistent limits, but who try to reason with their children, giving explanations for why they should behave in a particular way

uninvolved parents
parents who show almost no interest in their children and indifferent, rejecting behavior

Children with authoritarian parents are often uneasy with peers and are not well adjusted. What are the consequences of parents who are too permissive? Too uninvolved?

Paul Catalin Pop/Alamy Stock Photo

Table 4-1 Parenting Styles

How Demanding Parents Are of Children	Demanding	Undemanding
How Responsive Parents Are to a Child	**Authoritative**	**Permissive**
Highly Responsive	**Characteristics:** firm, setting clear and consistent limits **Relationship with Children:** Although they tend to be relatively strict, like authoritarian parents, they are loving and emotionally supportive and encourage their children to be independent. They also try to reason with their children, giving explanations for why they should behave in a particular way, and communicating the rationale for any punishment they may impose.	**Characteristics:** lax and inconsistent feedback **Relationship with Children:** They require little of their children, and they don't see themselves as holding much responsibility for how their children turn out. They place little or no limits or control on their children's behavior.
	Authoritarian	**Uninvolved**
Low Responsive	**Characteristics:** controlling, punitive, rigid, cold **Relationship with Children:** Their word is law, and they value strict, unquestioning obedience from their children. They also do not tolerate expressions of disagreement.	**Characteristics:** displaying indifferent, rejecting behavior **Relationship with Children:** They are detached emotionally and see their role as only providing food, clothing, and shelter. In its extreme form, this parenting style results in neglect, a form of child abuse.

Development in Your Life

Disciplining Children

The question of how to discipline children has been raised for generations. Answers from developmentalists today include the following (O'Leary, 1995; Brazelton & Sparrow, 2003; Flouri, 2005):

- **For most children in Western cultures, authoritative parenting works best.** Parents should be firm and consistent, providing clear direction and rules, but explaining why the rules make sense, using language that children can understand.

- **Spanking is *never* an appropriate discipline technique, according to the American Academy of Pediatrics.** Not only is spanking less effective than other techniques in curbing undesirable behavior, but it also leads to additional, unwanted outcomes, such as the potential for more aggressive behavior. Even though most Americans were spanked as

children, the research is totally clear in demonstrating that spanking is inappropriate (Bell & Romano, 2012; American Academy of Pediatrics, 2012b; Afifi et al., 2017).

- **Use time-out for punishment.** It is best to remove children from a situation in which they have misbehaved and take away enjoyable activities for a set period.

- **Tailor parental discipline to the characteristics of the child and the situation.** Try to keep the child's personality in mind, and adapt discipline to it.

- **Use routines (such as a bath routine or a bedtime routine) to avoid conflict.** To avoid a nightly struggle, make the potential conflict situation predictably enjoyable. For instance, routinely reading a bedtime story or engaging in a nightly "wrestling" match with the child can defuse potential battles.

Of course, no classification system is an infallible predictor of how children will fare. In a significant number of cases the children of authoritarian and permissive parents develop successfully.

Furthermore, most parents are inconsistent, switching from their dominant mode to one of the others. For instance, when a child darts into the street, an authoritarian style is generally the most effective (Eisenberg & Valiente, 2002; Gershoff, 2002).

CULTURAL DIFFERENCES IN CHILDREARING PRACTICES It's important to keep in mind that the findings regarding childrearing styles we have been discussing are chiefly applicable to Western societies. The style of parenting that is most successful may depend quite heavily on the norms of a particular culture—and what parents in a particular culture are taught regarding appropriate childrearing practices (Keller et al., 2008; Yagmurlu & Sanson, 2009; Yaman et al., 2010; Calzada et al., 2012; Dotti Sani & Treas, 2016).

For example, the Chinese concept of *chiao shun* suggests that parents should learn to be strict, firm, and in tight control of their children's behavior. They accept that they have a duty to train their children to adhere to socially and culturally desirable standards of behavior, particularly in their school performance. Children's acceptance of this style is seen as a sign of parental respect (Russell, Crockett, & Chao, 2010; Lui & Rollock, 2013; Frewen et al., 2015; Chuang et al., 2018).

In short, childrearing practices reflect cultural perspectives on the nature of children as well as on the appropriate role of parents. No single parenting pattern or style is universally appropriate. For example, parents who are immigrants often hold different views of appropriate childrearing practices than natives in a country, and yet raise children who are quite successful (Pomerantz & Wang, 2011; Chen, Sun, & Yu, 2017; Kuppens & Ceulemans, 2018).

Child Abuse, Neglect, and Resilience: The Hidden Side of Family Life

LO 4.18 **Analyze the factors that contribute to child abuse and neglect, and describe personal characteristics that may protect children.**

The figures are disheartening: At least 500 children are killed by their parents or caretakers every year, and 140,000 others are physically injured every year. Around 3 million children are abused or neglected in the United States each year. The abuse takes several forms, ranging from actual physical abuse to psychological mistreatment (National Clearinghouse on Child Abuse and Neglect Information, 2004; U.S. Department of Health and Human Services, 2007; Criss, 2017; see Figure 4-9).

CHILDHOOD SEXUAL ABUSE   In some cases, the abuse children suffer is sexual in nature. Childhood sexual abuse is surprisingly common. Although it is hard to obtain accurate statistics about its prevalence (many, if not most, cases go unreported), estimates are that some 500,000 cases of childhood sexual abuse occur each year in the United States. As many as one in six boys and one in four girls are sexually abused before the age of 18, and worldwide 73 million boys and 150 million girls younger than age 18 have experienced sexual abuse (Sedlak et al., 2010; American Psychological Association, 2014).

Figure 4-9 Types of Child Abuse

Neglect is the most frequent form of abuse. How can educators and health-care providers help identify cases of child abuse?

SOURCE: Child Welfare Information Gateway, 2018

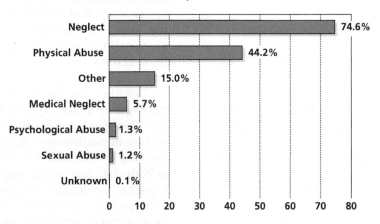

In the majority of cases, a relative or acquaintance of the child carries out sexual abuse, and most typically the perpetrators of child sexual abuse are male heterosexuals. Although most victims know their abusers, older children and adolescents may first come in contact with their abusers online (Finkelhor et al., 2005; Sklenarova et al., 2018).

THE WARNING SIGNS OF ABUSE   Child abuse can occur in any household, regardless of economic well-being or social status. It is most prevalent in families living in stressful environments. Poverty, single parenthood, and higher-than-average levels of marital conflict help create such environments. Stepfathers are more likely to abuse stepchildren than genetic fathers are to abuse their own offspring. Child abuse is also more likely when there is a history of violence between spouses (Osofsky, 2003; Evans, 2004; Ezzo & Young, 2012). (Table 4-2 lists some of the warning signs of abuse.)

Abused children are more likely to be fussy, resistant to control, and not readily adaptable to new situations. They have more headaches and stomachaches, experience more bedwetting, are generally more anxious, and may show developmental delays. Children in certain age groups are also more likely to be the targets of abuse: Three- and 4-year-olds and 15- to 17-year-olds are somewhat more likely to be abused than children of other ages (Straus & Gelles, 1990; Ammerman & Patz, 1996; Haugaard, 2000; Carmody et al., 2014).

Table 4-2   What are the Warning Signs of Child Abuse?

Because child abuse is typically a secret crime, identifying the victims of abuse is particularly difficult. Still, there are several signs in a child that indicate that he or she is the victim of violence (Robbins, 1990):

- visible, serious injuries that have no reasonable explanation
- bite or choke marks
- burns from cigarettes or immersion in hot water
- feelings of pain for no apparent reason
- fear of adults or care providers
- inappropriate attire in warm weather (long sleeves, long pants, high-necked garments)—possibly to conceal injuries to the neck, arms, and legs
- extreme behavior—highly aggressive, extremely passive, extremely withdrawn
- fear of physical contact
- in cases of sexual abuse: the use of new words for private body parts, mimicking sexual acts with toys or stuffed animals, or resistance at removing clothes

If you suspect a child is a victim of aggression, it is your responsibility to act. Call your local police or the department of social services in your city or state, or call Childhelp U.S.A. at 1-800-422-4453.

Talk to a teacher or a member of the clergy. Remember, by acting decisively you can literally save someone's life.

REASONS FOR PHYSICAL ABUSE Why does physical abuse occur? Most parents do not intend to hurt their children. In fact, most parents who abuse their children later express bewilderment and regret about their behavior.

One reason for child abuse is the vague demarcation between permissible and impermissible forms of physical violence. U.S. folklore says that spanking is not merely acceptable, but often necessary. Almost half of mothers with children younger than 4 have spanked their child in the previous week, and close to 20 percent believe it is appropriate to spank a child younger than 1 year of age. In some other cultures, physical discipline is even more common (Lansford et al., 2005; Deb & Adak, 2006; Shor, 2006).

Unfortunately, the line between "spanking" and "beating" is fuzzy, and spankings begun in anger can escalate into abuse. In fact, increasing scientific evidence suggests that spanking should be avoided entirely. Although physical punishment may produce immediate compliance, there are serious long-term side effects. For example, spanking is associated with inferior parent–child relationships, poorer mental health for both child and parent, higher levels of delinquency, and more antisocial behavior. Spanking also teaches children that violence is an acceptable solution to problems. Consequently, the American Academy of Pediatrics strongly recommends *against* the use of physical punishment of any sort (Afifi et al., 2006; Zolotor et al., 2008; Gershoff et al., 2012; Gershoff et al., 2018).

Another factor that leads to high rates of abuse in Western countries is privacy. In most Western cultures children are raised in private, isolated households. In many other cultures, childrearing is the joint responsibility of several people and even society as a whole, and other people are available to help out when a parent's patience is tested (Chaffin, 2006; Elliott & Urquiza, 2006).

THE CYCLE OF VIOLENCE HYPOTHESIS Many people who abuse children were themselves abused as children. According to the **cycle of violence hypothesis**, the abuse and neglect that children suffer predispose them as adults to abuse and neglect their own children (Heyman & Slep, 2002; Henschel, de Bruin, & Möhler, 2014; Bland, Lambie, & Beset, 2018).

cycle of violence hypothesis
the theory that the abuse and neglect that children suffer predispose them as adults to abuse and neglect their own children

According to this hypothesis, victims of abuse have learned from their childhood experiences that violence is an appropriate and acceptable form of discipline, and they have failed to learn the skills needed to solve problems and instill discipline without violence (Blumenthal, 2000; Ethier, Couture, & Lacharite, 2004; Ehrensaft et al., 2015).

Of course, being abused as a child does not inevitably lead to abuse of one's own children. In fact, statistics show that only about one-third of people who were abused or neglected as children abuse their own children (Straus & McCord, 1998; Spatz Widom, Czaja, & DuMont, 2015; Anderson et al., 2018).

Increasingly, spanking and other forms of physical violence are being seen as a human rights violation. The United Nations Committee on the Rights of the Child has called physical punishment "legalized violence against children," and it has called for its elimination. A treaty supporting this view has been ratified by 192 countries, with the exception of the United States and Somalia (Smith, 2012).

psychological maltreatment
abuse that occurs when parents or other caregivers harm children's behavioral, cognitive, emotional, or physical functioning

PSYCHOLOGICAL MALTREATMENT Children may also be the victims of more subtle forms of mistreatment. **Psychological maltreatment** occurs when parents or other caregivers harm children's behavioral, cognitive, emotional, or physical functioning. It may be the result of overt behavior or neglect (Higgins & McCabe, 2003; Garbarino, 2013).

For example, abusive parents may frighten, belittle, or humiliate their children, who may be made to feel like disappointments or failures. Parents may say that they wish that their children had never been born. Children may be threatened with abandonment or even death. In other instances, older children may be exploited. They may be forced to seek employment and then to give their earnings to their parents.

This infant was abandoned in a field and may have been severely neglected.

In other cases of psychological maltreatment, the abuse takes the form of neglect. Parents may ignore their children or act emotionally unresponsive. The children may be given unrealistic responsibilities or may be left to fend for themselves.

Although some children are sufficiently resilient to survive psychological maltreatment, lasting damage often results. Psychological maltreatment has been associated with low self-esteem, lying, misbehavior, and underachievement in school. In extreme cases, it can lead to criminal behavior, aggression, and murder. In other instances, children who have been psychologically maltreated become depressed and even commit suicide (Allen, 2008; Palusci & Ondersma, 2012; Gray & Rarick, 2018).

One reason that psychological maltreatment—as well as physical abuse—produces so many negative consequences is that the brains of victims undergo permanent changes as a result of the abuse (see Figure 4-10). For example, childhood maltreatment can lead to reductions in the size of the amygdala and hippocampus in adulthood. The stress, fear, and terror accompanying abuse may also produce permanent changes in the brain resulting from overstimulation of the limbic system. Because the limbic system is involved in the regulation of memory and emotion, the result can be antisocial behavior during adulthood (Twardosz & Lutzker, 2009; Thielen et al., 2016; Presseau et al., 2017).

Abusive parents may frighten, belittle, or humiliate their children, who may be made to feel like disappointments or failures. Although some children are sufficiently resilient to survive psychological maltreatment, lasting damage often results.

RESILIENCE: OVERCOMING THE ODDS Given the seriousness of child abuse and the damage it can cause, it's remarkable that not all children who have been abused are permanently scarred. In fact, some do surprisingly well. What enables some children to overcome stress and trauma that in most cases haunts others for life?

The answer appears to be resilience. **Resilience** is the ability to overcome high-risk circumstances that place a child at high risk for psychological or physical damage, such as extremes of poverty, prenatal stress, or violence in the home. Several factors seem to reduce and, in certain cases, eliminate some children's reactions to difficult circumstances (Collishaw et al., 2007; Monahan, Beeber, & Harden, 2012; Sciaraffa, Zeanah, & Zeanah, 2017).

resilience
the ability to overcome circumstances that place a child at high risk for psychological or physical damage

According to developmental psychologist Emmy Werner, resilient children tend to have temperaments that evoke positive responses. They tend to be affectionate, easygoing, and good-natured. They are easily soothed as infants, and elicit care from the most nurturant people in any given environment. In a sense, resilient children make their own environments by drawing out behavior in others that they need for their own development. As they grow to school age, they are socially pleasant, outgoing, and have good communication skills. They tend to be intelligent and independent, feeling that they can shape their own fate without depending on others or luck (Martinez-Torteya et al., 2009; Naglieri, Goldstein, & LeBuffe, 2010; Newland, 2014).

These characteristics suggest ways to help children who are at risk. Programs that have been successful in helping especially vulnerable children provide competent and caring adult models who teach the children problem-solving skills and help them to communicate their needs to those who are in a position to help (Maton et al., 2004; Condly, 2006; Goldstein & Brooks, 2013).

Figure 4-10 Abuse Alters the Brain

The limbic system, composed of the hippocampus and amygdala, can be permanently altered as a result of childhood abuse.

SOURCE: Based on Scientific American. (2002, March 1). Scars that won't heal: The neurobiology of child abuse. Scientific American, p. 71.

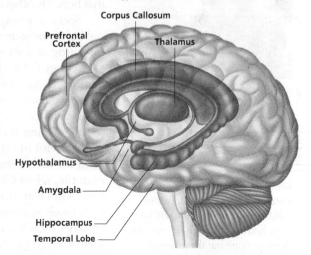

Moral Development and Aggression

Lena and Carrie were part of a group of preschoolers who wanted to act out *Cinderella*. The teacher began assigning parts. "Lena, you can be Cinderella. And Carrie, you'll be her Fairy Godmother." Tears welled up in Carrie's eyes. "I don't want to be a Fairy Godmother," she sobbed. Lena put her arms around Carrie. "You can be Cinderella, too. We'll be twin Cinderellas." Carrie cheered up at once, grateful that Lena had understood her feelings and responded with kindness.

In this short scenario we see many of the key elements of morality, preschool style. Changes in children's views of the right way to behave are an important element of growth during the preschool years.

At the same time, the kind of aggression displayed by preschoolers is also changing. We can consider the development of morality and aggression as two sides of the coin of human conduct, and both involve a growing awareness of others.

Developing Morality: Following Society's Rights and Wrongs

LO 4.19　Explain how preschool-age children develop a moral sense.

moral development
the changes in people's sense of justice and of what is right and wrong, and in their behavior related to moral issues

Moral development refers to changes in people's sense of justice and of what is right and wrong, and in their behavior related to moral issues. Developmentalists have considered moral development in terms of children's reasoning about morality, attitudes toward moral lapses, and behavior when faced with moral issues. In the process of studying moral development, several approaches have evolved.

PIAGET'S VIEW OF MORAL DEVELOPMENT　Child psychologist Jean Piaget was one of the first to study moral development. He suggested that moral development, like cognitive development, proceeds in stages (Piaget, 1932). He called the earliest stage *heteronomous morality*, in which rules are seen as invariant and unchangeable. During this stage, which lasts from about age 4 to age 7, children play games rigidly, assuming that there is one, and only one, way to play. At the same time, though, they may not even fully grasp game rules. Consequently, a group of children may be playing together, with each child playing according to a slightly different set of rules. Nevertheless, they enjoy playing with each other. Piaget suggests that every child may "win" such a game, because winning means having a good time, as opposed to competing.

Heteronomous morality is ultimately replaced by two later stages of morality: incipient cooperation and autonomous cooperation. In the *incipient cooperation stage*, which lasts from around age 7 to age 10, children's games become more clearly social. Children learn the actual rules and play according to this shared knowledge. Rules are still seen as largely unchangeable, and there is a "right" way to play the game.

It is not until the *autonomous cooperation stage*, which begins at about age 10, that children become fully aware that formal game rules can be modified if the players agree. This is the beginning of the understanding that rules of law are created by people and are subject to change according to the will of people.

prosocial behavior
helping behavior that benefits others

SOCIAL LEARNING APPROACHES TO MORALITY　Whereas Piaget emphasizes how limitations in preschoolers' cognitive development lead to particular forms of moral *reasoning*, social learning approaches focus more on how the environment in which preschoolers operate produces **prosocial behavior**, which is helping behavior that benefits others (Caputi et al., 2012; Schulz et al., 2013; Buon, Habib, & Frey, 2017).

Social learning approaches acknowledge that some instances of children's prosocial behavior stem from situations in which they have received positive reinforcement for acting in a moral way. For instance, when Claire's mother tells her she has been a "good girl" for sharing a box of candy with her brother, Claire's behavior has been reinforced. As a consequence, she is more likely to engage in sharing behavior in the future (Ramaswamy & Bergin, 2009).

However, not all prosocial behavior has to be directly reinforced. According to social learning theorists, children also learn moral behavior indirectly by observing the behavior of others, called *models*. Children imitate models who receive reinforcement for their behavior and ultimately learn to perform the behavior themselves. For example, when Claire's friend Jake watches Claire share her candy with her brother, and Claire is praised for her behavior, Jake is more likely to engage in sharing behavior himself at some later point. Unfortunately, the opposite also holds true: If a model behaves selfishly, children who observe such behavior tend to behave more selfishly themselves (Hastings et al., 2007; Bandura, 2018).

Steve Hix/Corbis/Getty Images

Because of their increasing understanding of moral development, children may worry they will be punished even though no one sees them carrying out the misdeed.

Children do more than simply mimic behavior that they see rewarded in others. When they observe moral conduct, they are reminded of society's norms about the importance of moral behavior as conveyed by parents, teachers, and other authority figures. They notice the connections between particular situations and certain kinds of behavior. This increases the likelihood that similar situations will elicit similar behavior in the observer.

Consequently, modeling paves the way for the development of more general rules and principles in a process called **abstract modeling**. Rather than always modeling the particular behavior of others, older preschoolers begin to develop generalized principles that underlie the behavior they observe. After observing repeated instances in which a model is rewarded for acting in a morally desirable way, children begin the process of inferring and learning the general principles of moral conduct (Bandura, 2016).

abstract modeling
the process in which modeling paves the way for the development of more general rules and principles

GENETIC APPROACHES TO MORALITY The newest, and highly controversial, approach to morality suggests that particular genes may underlie some aspects of moral behavior. According to this view, preschoolers have a genetic predisposition to behave generously or selfishly.

In one study designed to illustrate this approach, researchers gave preschoolers the opportunity to behave generously by sharing stickers. Those who were more selfish and less generous were more likely to have a variation in a gene called AVPR1A, which regulates a hormone in the brain that is related to social behavior (Avinun et al., 2011).

It is unlikely that the gene mutation fully accounts for the preschoolers' lack of generosity. The environment in which the children were raised also is likely to play a significant, and perhaps predominant, role in determining moral behavior. Still, the findings are provocative in showing that generosity may have genetic roots.

EMPATHY AND MORAL BEHAVIOR According to some developmentalists, **empathy**—the understanding of what another individual feels—lies at the heart of some kinds of moral behavior.

empathy
the understanding of what another individual feels

The roots of empathy grow early. One-year-old infants cry when they hear other infants crying. By ages 2 and 3, toddlers will offer gifts and spontaneously share toys with other children and adults, even strangers (Ruffman, Lorimer, & Scarf, 2017). During the preschool years, empathy continues to grow as children's ability to monitor and regulate their emotional and cognitive responses increases.

Some theorists believe that increasing empathy (along with other positive emotions, such as sympathy and admiration) leads children to behave morally. In addition, some negative emotions—such as anger at an unfair situation or shame over previous transgressions—also may promote moral behavior (Rieffe, Ketelaar, & Wiefferink, 2010; Bischof-Köhler, 2012; Eisenberg, Spinrad, & Morris, 2014).

Aggression and Violence in Preschoolers: Sources and Consequences

LO 4.20 **Analyze theoretical perspectives on the ways in which aggression develops in preschool-age children.**

Four-year-old Duane could not contain his anger and frustration any more. Although he usually was mild-mannered, when Eshu began to tease him about the split in his pants and kept it up for several minutes, Duane finally snapped. Rushing over to Eshu, Duane pushed him to the ground and began to hit him with his small, closed fists. Because he was so distraught, Duane's punches were not terribly effective, but they were severe enough to hurt Eshu and bring him to tears before the preschool teachers could intervene.

Aggression among preschoolers is common, though attacks such as this are not. Verbal hostility, shoving matches, kicking, and other forms of aggression may occur throughout the preschool period, although the degree to which aggression is acted out changes as children become older.

Eshu's taunting is also a form of aggression. **Aggression** is intentional injury or harm to another person. Infants don't act aggressively; it is hard to contend that their behavior is *intended* to hurt others, even if they inadvertently manage to do so. In contrast, by the time they reach preschool age, children demonstrate true aggression.

aggression
intentional injury or harm to another person

Aggression, both physical and verbal, is present throughout the preschool period.

emotional self-regulation

the capability to adjust emotions to a desired state and level of intensity

instrumental aggression

aggression motivated by the desire to obtain a concrete goal

relational aggression

nonphysical aggression that is intended to hurt another person's psychological well-being

During the early preschool years, some of the aggression is addressed at attaining a desired goal, such as getting a toy away from another person or using a particular space occupied by another person. Consequently, in some ways the aggression is inadvertent, and minor scuffles may in fact be a typical part of early preschool life. It is the rare child who does not demonstrate at least an occasional act of aggression.

However, extreme and sustained aggression is a cause of concern. In most children, the amount of aggression declines as they move through the preschool years, as does the frequency and average length of episodes of aggressive behavior (Persson, 2005).

A child's personality and social development contribute to this decline in aggression. Throughout the preschool years, children become better at controlling the emotions that they are experiencing. **Emotional self-regulation** is the capability to adjust emotions to a desired state and level of intensity. Starting at age 2, children are able to talk about their feelings, and they engage in strategies to regulate them. As they get older, they develop more effective strategies, learning to better cope with negative emotions. In addition to their increasing self-control, children are also developing sophisticated social skills. Most learn to use language to express their wishes and to negotiate with others (Philippot & Feldman, 2005; Helmsen, Koglin, & Petermann, 2012; Rose et al., 2016).

Despite these typical declines in aggression, some children remain aggressive throughout the preschool period. Furthermore, aggression is a relatively stable characteristic: The most aggressive preschoolers tend to be the most aggressive children during the school-age years (Schaeffer, Petras, & Ialongo, 2003; Davenport & Bourgeois, 2008).

Boys typically show higher levels of physical, instrumental aggression than girls. **Instrumental aggression** is aggression motivated by the desire to obtain a concrete goal, such as playing with a desirable toy that another child is playing with.

In contrast, although girls show lower levels of instrumental aggression, they may be just as aggressive, but in different ways from boys. Girls are more likely to practice **relational aggression**, which is nonphysical aggression that is intended to hurt another person's feelings. Such aggression may manifest as name-calling, withholding friendship, or simply saying mean, hurtful things that make the recipient feel bad (Murray-Close, Ostrov, & Crick, 2007; Valles & Knutson, 2008; Ambrose & Menna, 2013).

THE ROOTS OF AGGRESSION   How can we explain the aggression of preschoolers? Some theoreticians suggest that aggression is an instinct, part and parcel of the human condition. For instance, Freud's psychoanalytic theory suggests that we all are motivated by sexual and aggressive instincts (Freud, 1920). And ethologist Konrad Lorenz, an expert in animal behavior, argues that animals—including humans—share a fighting instinct that stems from primitive urges to preserve territory, maintain a steady supply of food, and weed out weaker animals (Lorenz, 1974).

Similar arguments are made by evolutionary theorists and *sociobiologists*, scientists who consider the biological roots of social behavior. They argue that aggression leads to increased opportunities to mate, improving the likelihood that one's genes will be passed on to future generations. In addition, aggression may help to strengthen the species and its gene pool as a whole, because the strongest survive. Ultimately, then, aggressive instincts promote the survival of one's genes to pass on to future generations (Archer, 2009).

Although instinctual explanations are logical, they have relatively little experimental support. They also fail to take into account the increasingly sophisticated cognitive abilities that humans develop as they get older. Moreover, they provide little guidance in determining when and how children, as well as adults, will behave aggressively, other than noting that aggression is an inevitable part of the human condition. Consequently, developmentalists have turned to other approaches.

SOCIAL LEARNING APPROACHES TO AGGRESSION   The day after Duane lashed out at Eshu, Lynn, who had watched the entire scene, got into an argument with Ilya. They verbally bickered for a while, and suddenly Lynn balled her hand into a fist and tried to punch Ilya. The preschool teachers were stunned: It was rare for Lynn to get upset, and she had never displayed aggression before.

Is there a connection between the two events? Social learning theorists would answer yes, because to them aggression is largely a learned behavior based on children's observation and prior learning. To understand the causes of aggressive behavior, then, we should look at the system of rewards and punishments in a child's environment.

Social learning approaches emphasize how social and environmental conditions teach individuals to be aggressive. Using a behavioral perspective, they argue that aggressive behavior is learned through direct reinforcement. For instance, preschool-age children may learn that they can continue to play with the most desirable toys by aggressively refusing their classmates' requests for sharing. In the parlance of traditional learning theory, they have been reinforced for acting aggressively, and they are more likely to behave aggressively in the future.

But as we saw when discussing morality, social learning approaches suggest that reinforcement also comes indirectly. Research suggests that exposure to aggressive models leads to increased aggression, particularly if the observers are themselves angered, insulted, or frustrated. For example, Albert Bandura and his colleagues illustrated the power of models in a classic study of preschool-age children (Bandura, Ross, & Ross, 1963). One group of children watched a film of an adult playing aggressively and violently with a Bobo doll (a large, inflated plastic clown designed as a punching bag for children that always returns to an upright position after being knocked over). In comparison, children in another condition watched a film of an adult playing sedately with a set of Tinkertoys (see Figure 4-11). Later, the preschool-age children were allowed to play with a number of toys, which included both the Bobo doll and the Tinkertoys. But first, the children were led to feel frustration by being refused the opportunity to play with a favorite toy.

As predicted by social learning approaches, the preschool-age children modeled the behavior of the adult. Those who had seen the aggressive model playing with the Bobo doll were considerably more aggressive than those who had watched the calm, unaggressive model playing with the Tinkertoys.

VIEWING VIOLENCE ON TV: DOES IT MATTER?   The majority of preschool-age children are exposed to aggression via television. Children's television programs contain higher levels of violence (69 percent) than other types of programs (57 percent). In an average hour, children's programs contain more than twice as many violent incidents as other types of programs (Wilson et al., 2002).

This high level of televised violence, viewed in light of research findings on modeling aggression, raises a significant question: Does viewing aggression increase the likelihood that children (and later adults) will perform aggressive acts?

Figure 4-11 Modeling Aggression

This series of photos is from Albert Bandura's classic Bobo doll experiment, designed to illustrate social learning of aggression. The photos clearly show how the adult model's aggressive behavior (in the first row) is imitated by children who had viewed the aggressive behavior (second and third rows).

Courtesy of Albert Bandura

The overwhelming weight of evidence suggests that observation of televised aggression does lead to subsequent aggression. Longitudinal studies have found that children's preferences for violent television shows at age 8 are correlated with the seriousness of criminal convictions by age 30. Other evidence supports the notion that observation of media violence can lead to bullying, a greater readiness to act aggressively, and insensitivity to the suffering of victims of violence (Christakis & Zimmerman, 2007; Kirsh, 2012; Merritt et al., 2016).

> **From an educator's perspective:** How might a preschool teacher or parent help children notice the violence in the programs they watch and protect them from its effects?

Television is not the only source of media violence. Many video games contain highly aggressive behavior, and many children play such games. For example, 14 percent of children age 3 and younger and around 50 percent of those ages 4 to 6 play video games. Because research conducted with adults shows that playing violent video games is associated with behaving aggressively, children who play video games containing violence may likewise be at risk for behaving aggressively (Hasan et al., 2013; Bushman, Gollwitzer, & Cruz, 2014; Greitemeyer, 2018).

Fortunately, social learning principles suggest not only the problem but also the solution. Children can be explicitly taught to view violence with a critical eye. If they learn that violence is not representative of the real world, that viewing violence can affect them negatively, and that they should avoid imitating the behavior they see on television, they may interpret the programs differently and be less influenced by them (Persson & Musher-Eizenman, 2003; Donnerstein, 2005).

Furthermore, just as exposure to aggressive models leads to aggression, observation of *non-aggressive* models can *reduce* aggression. Preschoolers don't just learn from others how to be aggressive; they can also learn how to avoid confrontation and to control their aggression, as we'll discuss later.

COGNITIVE APPROACHES TO AGGRESSION: THE THOUGHTS BEHIND VIOLENCE Two children, waiting for their turn in a game of kickball, inadvertently knock into one another. One child's reaction is to apologize; the other's is to shove, saying angrily, "Cut it out."

Despite the fact that each child bears the same responsibility for the minor event, they have different reactions. What the first child sees as an accident, the second child sees as a provocation.

The cognitive approach to aggression suggests that to understand preschoolers' moral development it is necessary to examine their interpretations of others' behavior and of the environmental context of the behavior. According to developmental psychologist Kenneth Dodge and his colleagues, some children are more prone than others to assume that actions are aggressively motivated. They are unable to pay attention to the appropriate cues in a situation and interpret the behaviors in the situation erroneously, assuming that what is happening is hostile. Subsequently, in deciding how to respond, they base their behavior on their inaccurate interpretation, behaving aggressively in response to a situation that never in fact existed (Dodge & Petit, 2003).

Although the cognitive approach describes the process that leads some children to behave aggressively, it fails to explain why they perceive situations inaccurately and why they so readily respond with aggression. However, the cognitive approach is useful in pointing out a means to reduce aggression: By teaching preschool-age children to interpret situations more accurately, we can induce them to be less prone to view others' behavior as motivated by hostility and less likely to respond with aggression themselves. (See the *Development in Your Life* box.)

Social learning explanations of aggression suggest that children's observation of aggression on television and video games can result in actual aggression.

Jonathan Nourok/PhotoEdit, Inc.

Development in Your Life

Increasing Moral Behavior and Reducing Aggression in Preschool-Age Children

Here are some practical and readily accomplished strategies for encouraging moral conduct and reducing aggression, based on ideas from the many approaches we have discussed (Bor & Bor, 2004; Eisenberg, 2012):

- **Provide opportunities for preschool-age children to observe others acting in a cooperative, helpful, prosocial manner.** Encourage them to interact with peers in joint activities in which they share a common goal. Such cooperative activities can teach the importance and desirability of working with—and helping—others.

- **Do not ignore aggressive behavior.** Parents and teachers should intervene when they see aggression in preschoolers, sending a clear message that aggression is an unacceptable way to resolve conflicts.

- **Help preschoolers devise alternative explanations for others' behavior.** With children who are prone to aggression and apt to view others' conduct as more hostile than it actually is, parents and teachers should

help them see that the behavior of their peers has several possible interpretations.

- **Monitor preschoolers' media viewing and overall screen time, particularly the violence that they view.** Discourage preschoolers from watching shows depicting aggression and encourage them to watch particular shows that are designed, in part, to foster moral conduct, such as *Sesame Street* and *Harry the Bunny*.

- **Help preschoolers understand their feelings.** When children become angry—and all children do—they must learn to deal with their feelings constructively. Tell them *specific* things they can do to improve the situation. ("I see you're really angry with Jake for not giving you a turn. Don't hit him, but tell him you want a chance to play with the game.")

- **Explicitly teach reasoning and self-control.** Preschoolers can understand the rudiments of moral reasoning, and they should be reminded why certain behaviors are desirable. For instance, explicitly saying "If you take all the cookies, others will have no dessert" is preferable to saying, "Good children don't eat all the cookies."

Review, Check, and Apply

Review

LO 4.13 Explain how preschool-age children develop a concept of themselves.

According to Erikson's psychosocial development theory, preschool-age children move from the autonomy-versus-shame-and-doubt stage (18 months to 3 years) to the initiative-versus-guilt stage (ages 3 to 6). Preschoolers' self-concepts are formed partly from their own perceptions and estimations of their characteristics, partly from their parents' behavior toward them, and partly from cultural influences.

LO 4.14 Analyze how preschool-age children develop a sense of gender.

Gender differences emerge early and conform to social stereotypes about what is appropriate and inappropriate for each sex. The strong gender expectations held by preschoolers are explained in different ways by different theorists. Some point to genetic factors as evidence for a biological explanation of gender expectations. Social learning theorists focus on environmental influences, whereas cognitive theorists propose that children form gender schemas, which are cognitive frameworks that organize information that the children gather about gender.

LO 4.15 Describe the sorts of social relationships that are typical of preschool-age children.

Play among preschoolers is an important form of social learning. Children generally move from parallel play, to onlooker play, to associative play, and ultimately to cooperative play. In the preschool period, social relationships begin to encompass genuine friendships, which involve trust and endure over time.

LO 4.16 Analyze how children's theory of mind changes during the preschool years.

Children's theory of mind continues to develop during the preschool period, enabling them to see the world increasingly from others' perspectives. Preschoolers begin to understand how others think and why they do the things they do, and through imaginative play, they begin to grasp the difference between reality and imagination.

LO 4.17 Describe the changing nature of families and the diversity of parenting styles preschoolers experience.

Families change in nature and structure over the years, but a strong and positive home environment is essential to children's healthy development. Parental disciplinary styles differ both individually and culturally. In the United States and other Western societies, parents' styles tend to be mostly authoritarian, permissive, uninvolved, or authoritative. The authoritative style is regarded as the most effective.

LO 4.18 Analyze the factors that contribute to child abuse and neglect, and describe personal characteristics that may protect children.

Child abuse, which may be either physical or psychological, occurs especially in stressful home environments. Firmly held notions regarding family privacy and the use of physical punishment in childrearing contribute to the high rate of abuse in the United States. Moreover, the cycle of violence hypothesis points to the likelihood that people who were abused as children may turn into abusers as adults. Children who have been abused often survive their backgrounds by relying on the temperamental quality of resilience.

LO 4.19 Explain how preschool-age children develop a moral sense.

Piaget believed that preschool-age children are in the heteronomous morality stage of moral development,

characterized by a belief in external, unchangeable rules of conduct and sure, immediate punishment for all misdeeds. In contrast, social learning approaches to morality emphasize interactions between environment and behavior in moral development, in which models of behavior play an important role. Some developmentalists believe that moral behavior is rooted in a child's development of empathy. Other emotions, including the negative emotions of anger and shame, may also promote moral behavior.

LO 4.20 Analyze theoretical perspectives on the ways in which aggression develops in preschool-age children.

Aggression, which involves intentional harm to another person, begins to emerge in the preschool years. Some ethologists, such as Konrad Lorenz, believe that aggression is simply a biological fact of human life. Social learning theorists focus on the role of the environment, including the influence of models and social reinforcement, as factors influencing aggressive behavior. The cognitive approach to aggression emphasizes the role of interpretations of the behaviors of others in determining aggressive or nonaggressive responses.

Check Yourself

1. According to Erikson, during the preschool years children face a key conflict relating to psychosocial development that involves the development of _____.
   a. morality
   b. identity
   c. initiative
   d. trust

2. Five-year-old Kayla has been practicing her jump-roping skills for the past 6 weeks so she can enter a contest at her school. After one afternoon of practice she tells her mother, "I am a terrific jump roper." This statement is an example of Kayla's increasing development of her _____.
   a. independence
   b. self-concept

   c. competitiveness
   d. narcissism

3. Which of the following characteristics is typical of a child who has permissive parents?
   a. low self-control
   b. independence
   c. amiability
   d. cooperativeness

4. According to _____ theory, the factor that increases the likelihood that a preschooler will engage in prosocial behavior is his or her environment.
   a. cognitive-behavioral
   b. social learning
   c. psychoanalytic
   d. humanistic

Applying Lifespan Development

If high-prestige models of behavior are particularly effective in influencing moral attitudes and actions, are there implications for individuals in industries such as sports, advertising, and entertainment?

Chapter 4 Summary
Putting It All Together: The Preschool Years

B. Christopher/Alamy Stock Photo

CHEN, the enthusiastic 3-year-old who crawled across the kitchen counter to reach a cookie jar in the chapter opener, was probably born curious and prone to explore. Chen was testing the limits of his physical abilities and pushing against the barriers that confined him. Chen used his developing skills to help him find answers to the questions that were formulating in his mind as he encountered the world. His adventurous personality seemingly enabled him to explore his environment without a thought for the consequences. Throughout every waking moment, Chen was putting together all of his emerging developmental tools to exercise control over his world.

MODULE 4.1

***PHYSICAL DEVELOPMENT* IN THE PRESCHOOL YEARS**

- Chen grew physically in the preschool years, learning to exercise with ease and developing abilities such as walking, climbing, and swimming. (p. 157)
- Chen also learned to use and control his gross and fine motor skills, showing considerable physical dexterity. (pp. 162–164)
- Chen's brain grew, and with it his cognitive abilities, such as the ability to observe phenomena and formulate questions about what he sees. (p. 162)

MODULE 4.2

***COGNITIVE DEVELOPMENT* IN THE PRESCHOOL YEARS**

- Chen's memory capacity increased, which enabled him to recall what he would find in the cookie jar. (p. 170)
- Chen observed others and learned how to perform challenging tasks. (p. 173)
- Chen's language skills continued to develop, permitting him to express himself increasingly effectively. (p. 174)
- Chen developed the cognitive skills to formulate questions about phenomena he observed and to plan for ways to find the answers to his questions. (p. 169)

MODULE 4.3

***SOCIAL AND PERSONALITY DEVELOPMENT* IN THE PRESCHOOL YEARS**

- Chen's self-concept includes seeing himself as a proficient climber, a view that he may overestimate, putting him at risk for accidents. (p. 181)
- Chen has reached the age at which his friendships will likely form around shared interests like hiking and swimming. (p. 186)
- Chen's parents appear to have an authoritative parenting style, which supports his sense of independence and self-assertiveness. (p. 189)

What would a PARENT do?

How would you help Chen to consider the possible consequences of his behavior? How would you assess his readiness to consider consequences? What would you say to Chen about considering the effects of his actions on his physical safety?

Jim Esposito Photography L.L.C./Getty Images

What would a HEALTH-CARE WORKER do?

What would you tell Chen's caregivers about risks to which he is especially prone as he develops physically and cognitively? How would you advise Chen's parents to focus their child-proofing efforts in their home as Chen grows?

Photodisc/Getty Images

What would YOU do?

What would you do to promote Chen's development? How would you advise Chen's caregivers in helping Chen to channel his adventurous nature and curiosity in appropriate directions? How would you advise Chen's caregivers to deal with Chen's apparent fearlessness? Should it be discouraged?

Asia Images Group/Getty Images

What would an EDUCATOR do?

What strategies would you use to promote Chen's social development? How would you help Chen to forge relationships with his peers? How would you deal with Chen's potential leadership qualities? What would you do to help him avoid taking foolhardy risks? What would you say to Chen's teachers about steps to take in monitoring the actions of children like Chen?

Mel Yates/Getty Images

Chapter 5
Middle Childhood

It was 9-year-old Jan Vega's first Little League baseball game. With strong encouragement from her parents, she had tried out for the local team—the only girl to do so—and now she was a Yankee. But she still worried about her teammates. They didn't seem too thrilled to have a girl in the lineup.

The coach assigned Jan to second base. She kept her eyes on the ball and her glove ready at all times, but play after play, the ball went to the shortstop, who threw it to first base for the out. Jan was disappointed. The boys were never going to give her a chance. "Baseball is more than batting and catching," her coach reminded her at the seventh inning. "To play well, you have to use your head." Jan returned to the field, determined and alert.

Now it was the last inning. The Yankees had a one-run lead, but the Orioles had the final at-bats and their best batter was standing at the plate, with only one out and a runner on first base. The game was on the line.

Later, Jan would say that she saw the ball coming straight toward the plate as the batter swung. That she knew it would meet the bat squarely and head right up the middle. That the shortstop was in no position to field it. That it was her ball.

As the ball hit the bat she ran to her right, stretched to snare the bouncing ball, tagged second base to get the runner out, and slung the ball to first to complete the double play. Game over. "Go Vega!" her teammates shouted. Jan smiled as they clapped her on the back.

In middle childhood, children enter school eager to learn all they can about the world. Often the regular classroom setting serves them well and contributes to their physical, intellectual, and social development; sometimes, however, children display needs or deficits that require special interventions to make the most of their abilities and keep their self-esteem intact.

In this chapter, we follow children taking the crucial step into formal schooling. We look at the physical changes that prepare them for new challenges. We discuss the patterns of growth—and excess—that are typical of this period and the new levels of motor skills that enable them to perform actions as diverse as throwing a ball and playing the violin. We also discuss threats to their well-being and consider the special needs that can impinge on children's school lives.

Next, we consider the growing intellectual and conceptual skills and the increasingly sophisticated use of language that are hallmarks of this period. We visit the place where they spend most of their time: school. We consider reading and the policy dispute over the best way to teach it. We also address the surprisingly controversial topic of intelligence.

Finally, we consider school-age children as members of society, including their membership in school and family. We look at the ways school-age children understand themselves and develop self-esteem. We consider how they relate to one another, including members of the opposite sex. We then examine the many shapes and configurations that families take, finishing with a further discussion of schooling.

Module 5.1 *Physical Development* in Middle Childhood

LO 5.1 Summarize the ways in which children grow during the school years, and discuss the factors that influence their growth.

LO 5.2 Explain how nutrition affects children's growth and functioning, and identify the risks posed by obesity.

LO 5.3 Identify the advances in motor skills during middle childhood.

LO 5.4 Summarize the main health and safety concerns of school-age children.

LO 5.5 Explain how sensory impairments and learning disabilities may impact children's school performance and social relationships.

LO 5.6 Identify the behaviors associated with ADHD, and discuss how it impacts children's school performance.

Module 5.2 *Cognitive Development* in Middle Childhood

LO 5.7 Identify and summarize the major theoretical approaches to cognitive development in middle childhood.

LO 5.8 Summarize the development of language during middle childhood, and explain the cognitive advantages bilingualism offers.

LO 5.9 Describe the five stages of reading, and compare teaching approaches.

LO 5.10 Summarize the various trends in U.S. education.

LO 5.11 Compare and contrast the different methods of assessing intelligence.

LO 5.12 Summarize the approaches to educating children with intellectual disabilities and children who are intellectually gifted in middle childhood.

Module 5.3 *Social and Personality Development* in Middle Childhood

LO 5.13 Summarize how children's view of themselves changes in middle childhood, and explain how this shift affects their self-esteem.

LO 5.14 Identify the six stages in Kohlberg's theory of moral development, and compare and contrast them with Gilligan's sequence of stages.

LO 5.15 Identify Damon's stages of friendship, and explain the factors that determine popularity in middle childhood.

LO 5.16 Explain how gender and race affect friendships at this age.

LO 5.17 Identify the variety of family constellations, and assess their impact on children.

LO 5.18 Describe the challenges to family life posed by work, divorce, and poverty.

Module 5.1

Physical Development in Middle Childhood

Eleven-year-old Tommy Rinaldo hates gym. Today the game he's being forced to play is basketball. Three times he's dribbled the ball off his foot, and twice other kids have taken it away. Tommy has decided that the best strategy is to avoid the ball entirely.

Now, however, a loose ball has come his way. Instinctively picking it up, he dribbles toward the basket, somehow making it all the way down court. With a pretty good motion, he turns and heaves up the ball. It doesn't go in, but after it hits the rim, one of his classmates grabs the rebound and makes the shot.

The other kid says "Good assist" to Tommy. Maybe basketball isn't so bad after all.

Fuse/Corbis/Getty Images

Tommy Rinaldo has come a long way since the preschool years, when quick, coordinated running, dribbling, and shooting were not possible.

Such moments characterize middle childhood because children's physical, cognitive, and social skills reach new heights. Beginning at age 6 and continuing to about age 12, this period is often called the "school years." Physical growth is remarkable. Motor skills soar.

We begin by examining physical and motor development in middle childhood. We discuss how children's bodies change and the twin problems of malnutrition and obesity. We examine the

development of gross motor skills (like dribbling a basketball) and fine motor skills (like playing scales on a piano). We discuss the health of children during this period, including their psychological health.

We finish the module by considering the sensory and learning difficulties of children with special needs. We also discuss a disorder that has grown in importance in recent decades, attention deficit hyperactivity disorder.

The Growing Body

> Cinderella, dressed in yella,
> Went upstairs to kiss her fellah.
> But she made a mistake and she kissed a snake.
> How many doctors did it take?
> One, two,...

> While the other girls chanted this jump-rope rhyme, Kat proudly displayed her new ability to jump backward. In second grade, Kat was becoming quite good at jumping rope. In first grade, she simply had not been able to master it. But over the summer, she had spent many hours practicing, and now that practice was paying off.

As Kat is gleefully experiencing, children make great physical strides in middle childhood, mastering many new skills. How does this progress occur? We'll first consider typical physical growth during this period, then turn our attention to exceptional children.

Slow but steady. These words characterize the nature of growth during middle childhood. In contrast to the swift growth from birth to age 5 and the remarkable growth spurt of adolescence, middle childhood is relatively tranquil. The body has not shifted into neutral; physical growth continues, but at a more stately pace than in the preschool years.

Height and Weight Changes

LO 5.1   Summarize the ways in which children grow during the school years, and discuss the factors that influence their growth.

In elementary school, children in the United States grow, on average, 2 to 3 inches a year. By age 11, the average height for girls is 4 feet, 10 inches, and boys average 4 feet, 9½ inches. This is the only period in life when girls tend to be taller than boys.

This reflects the slightly more rapid physical development of girls, who start their adolescent growth spurt around age 10.

Weight gain in middle childhood follows a similar pattern; boys and girls both gain around 5 to 7 pounds a year. Weight is also redistributed. As "baby fat" disappears, children's bodies become more muscular and their strength increases.

These average height and weight increases disguise significant individual differences. Children of the same age can be 6 or 7 inches apart in height. Culture may also influence growth.

Most children in North America receive sufficient nutrients to grow to their full potential. In other parts of the world, however, inadequate nutrition and disease take their toll, producing children who are shorter and weigh less. The discrepancies can be dramatic: Poor children in cities such as Kolkata, Hong Kong, and Rio de Janeiro are smaller than affluent children in the same cities.

In the United States, most variations in height and weight are the result of people's unique genetic inheritance, including genetic factors relating to racial and ethnic background. Asian and Oceanic Pacific children tend to be shorter than those of northern and central European ancestry. In addition, the rate of growth is generally more rapid for black children than for white children (Deurenberg, Deurenberg-Yap, & Guricci, 2002; Deurenberg et al., 2003).

Even within racial and ethnic groups, individuals vary significantly. We cannot attribute racial and ethnic differences solely to genetic factors because dietary customs as well as variations in levels of affluence also may contribute to differences. In addition, severe stress—brought on by factors such as parental conflict or alcoholism—can affect the pituitary gland, thereby affecting growth (Koska et al., 2002; Lai, 2006).

Nutrition and Obesity

LO 5.2 Explain how nutrition affects children's growth and functioning, and identify the risks posed by obesity.

There is a relationship between size and nutrition. But size isn't the only area affected by diet. For instance, nutrition is related to social and emotional functioning at school age. Children who receive more nutrients are more involved with their peers, show more positive emotion, and have less anxiety than children with less adequate nutrition. Nutrition is also linked to cognitive performance. For example, in one study, children in Kenya who were well nourished performed better on a test of verbal abilities and on other cognitive measures than those who had mild to moderate undernutrition. Malnutrition may influence cognitive development by dampening children's curiosity, responsiveness, and motivation to learn (Yousafzai, Yakoob, & Bhutta, 2013; Jackson, 2015; Tooley, Makhoul, & Fisher, 2016).

Although undernutrition and malnutrition clearly lead to physical, social, and cognitive difficulties, in some cases *over*nutrition—the intake of too many calories—and weight concerns lead to problems of their own.

Weight concerns can border on obsession, particularly in girls. Many 6-year-old girls worry about becoming "fat," and some 40 percent of girls ages 9 to 10 are trying to lose weight. Their concern with weight often reflects the U.S. preoccupation with slimness, which permeates the entire society (Greenwood & Pietromonaco, 2004; Liechty, 2010).

For example, when her mother asks if she would like bread with her meal, Ruthellen replies that she better not because she thinks she may be getting fat. Ruthellen, who is of normal weight and height, is 6 years old.

Despite the prevalent view that thinness is a virtue, childhood obesity is rising. *Obesity* is defined as a BMI at or above the 95th percentile for children of the same age and sex. (BMI is calculated by dividing a child's weight in kilograms by the square of their height in meters). By this definition, 18.5 percent of U.S. children are

Variations of 6 inches in height between children of the same age are not unusual and are well within normal ranges.

Inadequate nutrition and disease affect growth significantly. Children in poorer areas of cities such as Kolkata, Hong Kong, and Rio de Janeiro are smaller than their counterparts in affluent areas of the same cities.

Figure 5-1 Obesity on the Rise

The percentage of children and adolescents age 2 to 19 years who are overweight has increased dramatically in the past two decades.

SOURCE: Hales et al., 2017.

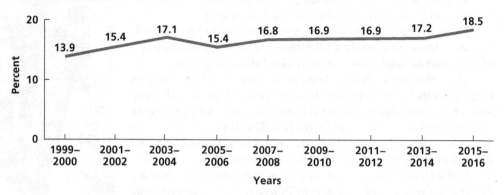

obese—a proportion that has more than tripled since the 1970s. And it's not only a problem in the U.S.; the number of children ages 5 to 19 who are obese has increased 1,000 percent from 1975 to 2016 (Ogden et al., 2015; Hales et al., 2017; NCD Risk Factor Collaboration, 2017; also see Figure 5-1).

Obesity is found more often in children in low-income families. In addition, the prevalence of obesity is related to ethnicity in the United States: Hispanic and American Indian/Alaska Native younger children show greater levels of obesity than whites and blacks (Ogden et al., 2015; Bodell et al., 2018).

The costs of childhood obesity last a lifetime. Obese children are more likely to be overweight as adults and have a greater risk of heart disease, diabetes, and other diseases. Some scientists believe an epidemic of obesity may be leading to a decline in life span in the United States (Park, 2008; Keel et al., 2010; Mehlenbeck, Farmer, & Ward, 2014).

Obesity is caused by a combination of genetic and social characteristics as well as diet. Particular inherited genes are related to obesity and predispose certain children to be overweight. For example, adopted children tend to have weights that are more similar to those of their birth parents than to those of their adoptive parents (Bray, 2008; Skledar et al., 2012; Maggi et al., 2015).

Social factors also affect children's weight problems. Children need to control their own eating. Parents who are controlling and directive about their children's eating may produce children who lack internal controls to regulate their own food intake (Wardle, Guthrie, & Sanderson, 2001; Doub, Small, & Brich, 2016; Gomes, Barros, & Pereira, 2017).

Poor diets also contribute to obesity. Despite their knowledge that certain foods are necessary for a balanced, nutritious diet, many parents provide their children with too few fruits and vegetables and more fats and sweets than recommended. School lunch programs have sometimes contributed to the problem by failing to provide nutritious options (Story, Nanney, & Schwartz, 2009; Janicke, 2013).

Given how energetic children this age can be, it is surprising that a major factor in childhood obesity is a lack of exercise. School-age children tend to engage in relatively little exercise and are not particularly fit. Around 40 percent of boys age 6 to 12 are unable to do more than one pull-up, and a quarter can't do any. Furthermore, children have shown little or no improvement in the amount of exercise they get, despite national efforts to increase the fitness of school-age children, in part because many schools have reduced the time available for recess and gym classes. From ages 6 to 18, boys decrease their physical activity by 24 percent and girls by 36 percent (Sallis & Glanz, 2006; Weiss & Raz, 2006; Ige, DeLeon, & Nabors, 2017).

Why is the level of exercise relatively low? One answer is that many kids are watching television and playing computer or video games. Such sedentary activities not only prevent exercise, but children also often snack while viewing TV or surfing the Web (Goldfield et al., 2012; Chahal et al., 2013; Lambrick et al., 2016; Falbe et al., 2017; see the *Development in Your Life* box).

Development in Your Life

Keeping Children Fit

Matías sits at a desk five days a week for most of the day, usually getting no exercise. On weekends, he spends the majority of his time watching videos and playing video games, often drinking soda and eating snack foods. When he goes out to eat, it's often at places like McDonald's, eating foods that are high in calories and fats.

Although this sketch fits many adults, Matías is just 6. Many school-age children in the United States, like Matías, get little or no regular exercise and consequently are physically unfit and at risk for obesity and other health problems.

To encourage children to be more physically active (Tyre & Scelfo, 2003; Okie, 2005):

- **Make exercise fun.** Children repeat what they enjoy. Overly competitive activities or those that sideline children with inferior skills, though, may create a lifelong distaste for exercise.

- **Be an exercise role model.** Children who see their parents, teachers, or adult friends exercising regularly may view fitness as a regular part of their lives, too.

- **Gear activities to the child's physical level and motor skills.** Use child-size equipment to make children feel successful.

- **Encourage the child to find a partner.** Roller skating, hiking, and many other activities are more fun when shared with a friend, a sibling, or a parent.

- **Start slowly.** Ease sedentary children into regular physical activity. Try 5 minutes of exercise daily. Over 10 weeks, aim for 30 minutes, three to five times a week.

- **Urge participation in organized sports activities, but do not push too hard.** Not every child is athletically inclined. Make participation and enjoyment—not winning—the goal.

- **Don't use physical activity as a punishment.** Encourage children to join organized activities they enjoy.

- **Provide a healthy diet. Good nutrition gives children energy.** Soda and sugary, fatty snack foods do not.

Motor Development and Safety

The fact that the fitness level of school-age children is not as high as we would desire does not mean that such children are physically incapable. In fact, even without regular exercise, children's gross and fine motor skills develop substantially over the course of the school years.

Leaps and Bounds: The Rapid Growth of Motor Skills

LO 5.3   Identify the advances in motor skills during middle childhood.

In middle childhood, muscular coordination and manipulative skills advance to near-adult levels, making it possible for children of this age to engage in a wide range of new activities.

GROSS MOTOR SKILLS One important improvement in gross motor skills is in muscle coordination. Watching a softball player pitch a ball past a batter to her catcher, or Kat, the jump-roper described previously in the module, we are struck by the many skills children have mastered since their awkward preschool days. Most can readily learn to ride a bike, ice skate, swim, and skip rope (see Figure 5-2).

Years ago, developmentalists concluded that gender differences in gross motor skills became increasingly pronounced during middle childhood years, with boys outperforming girls. However, when comparing boys and girls who regularly take part in similar activities—such as softball—gender variations are minimal (Jurimae & Saar, 2003; Gentier et al., 2013).

Why the change? Expectations probably played a role. Society did not expect girls to be highly active and told girls they would do worse than boys in sports. The girls' performance reflected that message.

Today, society's message has changed, at least officially. For instance, the American Academy of Pediatrics suggests that boys and girls should engage in the same sports and games, and that they can do so in mixed-gender groups. There is no reason to separate the sexes in physical exercise and sports until puberty, when the smaller size of

Figure 5-2 Gross Motor Skills Developed from 6 to 12 Years

SOURCE: Adapted from Cratty, 1986.

6 Years	7 Years	8 Years	9 Years	10 Years	11 Years	12 Years
Girls superior in accuracy of movement; boys superior in more forceful, less complex acts.

Can throw with the proper weight, shift, and step.

Acquire the ability to skip. | Can balance on one foot with eyes closed.

Can walk on a 2-inch-wide balance beam without falling off.

Can hop and jump accurately into small squares (hopscotch).

Can correctly execute a jumping-jack exercise. | Can grip objects with 12 pounds of pressure.

Can engage in alternate rhythmical hopping in a 2–2, 2–3, or 3–3 pattern.

Girls can throw a small ball 33 feet; boys can throw a small ball 59 feet.

The number of games participated in by both sexes is the greatest at this age. | Girls can jump vertically 8.5 inches over their standing height plus reach; boys can jump vertically 10 inches.

Boys can run 16.6 feet per second; girls can run 16 feet per second. | Can judge and intercept directions of small balls thrown from a distance.

Both girls and boys can run 17 feet per second. | Boys can achieve standing broad jump of 5 feet; girls can achieve standing broad jump of 4.5 feet. | Can achieve high jump of 3 feet. |

females makes them more susceptible to injury in contact sports (American Academy of Pediatrics, 2004; Daniels & Lavoi, 2013; Deaner, Balish, & Lombardo, 2016).

FINE MOTOR SKILLS   Typing at a computer keyboard. Writing in cursive with pen and pencil. Drawing detailed pictures. These are some of the accomplishments that depend on the improved fine motor coordination of early and middle childhood. Six- and 7-year-olds are able to tie their shoes and fasten buttons; by age 8, they can use each hand independently; and by 11 and 12, they can manipulate objects with almost as much capability as they will show in adulthood.

One reason for advances in fine motor skills is that the amount of myelin in the brain increases significantly between the ages of 6 and 8. *Myelin* provides protective insulation that surrounds parts of nerve cells. Because increased levels of myelin raise the speed at which electrical impulses travel between neurons, messages can reach muscles more rapidly and control them better (Lakhani et al., 2016).

Health and Safety During Middle Childhood

LO 5.4   Summarize the main health and safety concerns of school-age children.

> Imani was miserable. Her nose was running, her lips were chapped, and her throat was sore. Although she had stayed home from school and watched old reruns on TV, she still felt that she was suffering mightily.

Despite her misery, Imani's situation is not so bad. She'll get over the cold in a few days and be none the worse for it. In fact, she may be a little *better* off because she is now immune to the specific cold germs that made her ill.

Imani's cold may end up being the most serious illness she gets during middle childhood. This is generally a period of robust health, and most ailments children do contract tend to be mild and brief. Routine immunizations have produced a considerably lower incidence of the life-threatening illnesses that 50 years ago claimed a significant number of children. However, illness is not uncommon. More than 90 percent of children are likely to have at least one serious medical condition over the 6-year period of middle childhood, according to one large survey. And though most children have short-term illnesses, about one in nine has a chronic, persistent condition, such as repeated migraine headaches. And some illnesses are actually becoming more prevalent (Dey & Bloom, 2005; Siniatchkin et al., 2010; Celano, Holsey, & Kobrynski, 2012).

Safety issues also pose a risk to health in middle childhood. Although accidents remain the greatest threat to children's safety, the Internet is a new and growing concern to many parents with children in this age group.

ASTHMA   Asthma is among the diseases that have shown a significant increase in prevalence over the past several decades. *Asthma* is a chronic condition characterized by periodic attacks of wheezing, coughing, and shortness of breath. More than 8 percent of U.S. children suffer from the disorder, and worldwide more than 150 million children suffer from the disease (Bowen, 2013; Gandhi et al., 2016; Centers for Disease Control and Prevention, 2017).

During middle childhood, children master many types of skills that they could not previously perform well, such as those that depend on fine motor coordination.

Asthma attacks occur when the airways leading to the lungs constrict, making breathing more difficult and causing wheezing. Attacks are triggered by a variety of factors. Among the most common are respiratory infections (such as colds or flu), allergic reactions to airborne irritants (such as pollution, cigarette smoke, dust mites, and animal dander and excretions), stress, and exercise (Noonan & Ward, 2007; Marin et al., 2009; Ross et al., 2012).

Racial and ethnic minorities are particularly at risk for the disease, because they are more at risk for exposure to environmental factors due to higher rates of poverty. Because they may live in poorer areas, they are more at risk for exposure to poor air quality and chemicals, factors that increase the risk of asthma. But genetic factors also seem to be at work (Forno & Celedon, 2009; Fedele et al., 2016).

ACCIDENTS   The increasing independence of school-age children leads to new safety issues. Between the ages of 5 and 14, the rate of injury for children increases. Boys are more apt to be injured than girls, probably because their overall level of physical activity is greater. Some ethnic and racial groups are at greater risk than others: Injury death rates are highest for American Indian and Alaska Natives, and lowest for Asians and Pacific Islanders. Whites and African Americans have approximately the same death rates from injuries (Noonan, 2003; Borse et al., 2008).

The increased mobility of this age is a source of several kinds of accidents. Children who regularly walk to school, many traveling such a distance alone for the first time, face being hit by cars and trucks. Because of lack of experience, they may misjudge how far they are from an oncoming vehicle. Bicycle accidents pose an increasing risk, particularly as children venture out onto busier roads (Schnitzer, 2006).

The most frequent injury to children is automobile accidents. Auto crashes annually kill 5 out of every 100,000 children between the ages of 5 and 9. Fires and burns, drowning, and gun-related deaths follow in frequency (Schiller & Bernadel, 2004; Centers for Disease Control and Prevention, 2012).

Two ways to reduce auto and bicycle injuries are to use seat belts consistently and to wear appropriate protective cycling gear. Bicycle helmets have significantly reduced head injuries, and in many localities their use is mandatory. Knee and elbow pads have proven to reduce injuries for roller-blading and skateboarding (Blake et al., 2008; Lachapelle, Noland, & Von Hagen, 2013).

SAFETY IN CYBERSPACE   One contemporary threat to the safety of school-age children comes from the Internet. Cyberspace makes available material that many parents find objectionable.

Although certain programs can be used to automatically block known sites that are dangerous to children or that contain objectionable material, most experts feel that the most reliable safeguard is close supervision by parents. According to the National Center for Missing and Exploited Children, a nonprofit organization that works with

Children's access to computers and the Internet needs to be monitored.

the U.S. Department of Justice, parents should warn their children never to provide personal information, such as home addresses or telephone numbers, to people on public computer "bulletin boards" or in chat rooms. In addition, children should not be allowed to hold face-to-face meetings with people they meet via computer, at least not without a parent present.

There are no reliable statistics that provide a true sense of the risk presented by exposure to cyberspace. But certainly a potential hazard exists, and parents must offer their children guidance. It is wrong to assume that just because children are in the supposed safety of their own bedrooms, logged on to home computers, they are truly safe (Mitchell et al., 2011; Reio & Ortega, 2016).

> **From an educator's perspective:** Do you think using blocking software or computer chips to screen offensive Internet content is a practical idea? Are such controls the best way to keep children safe in cyberspace?

PSYCHOLOGICAL DISORDERS

> Ben Cramer, 8, loves baseball and mystery stories. He has a dog, Frankie, and a blue racing bike.
>
> Ben also has bipolar disorder, a serious psychological disorder. Engaged in his schoolwork one minute, he'll refuse to even look at his teacher the next. Often a good friend, he'll suddenly lash out at the other children in the class. Sometimes, he believes he can do anything: touch fire and not get burned or jump off the roof and fly. Other times, he feels so sad and small, and he writes poems about dying.

Bipolar disorder such as Ben's is diagnosed when a person cycles back and forth between two extreme emotional states: unrealistically high spirits and energy, and depression. For years, most people neglected the symptoms of such psychological disorders in children, and even today they may be overlooked. Yet it is a common problem: One in five children and adolescents has a psychological disorder that produces at least some impairment. For example, about 5 percent of preteens suffer from childhood depression, and 13 percent of children between ages 9 and 17 experience an anxiety disorder. The estimated cost of treatment of children's psychological disorders is $250 billion per year (Cicchetti & Cohen, 2006; Kluger, 2010; Holly et al., 2015).

Advocates for the use of antidepressants such as Prozac, Zoloft, Paxil, and Wellbutrin for children suggest that drug therapies can successfully treat their depression and other psychological disorders. Drugs may provide the only relief in cases where traditional therapies that use verbal methods are ineffective. At least one clinical test shows that the drugs are effective with children (Hirschtritt et al., 2012; Lawrence et al., 2017; Zhang et al., 2018).

Critics, however, question the long-term effectiveness of antidepressants for children. No one knows the consequences of their use on the developing brain, nor their overall long-term effects. Little is known about the correct dosage for age or size, and some observers suggest that children's versions of the drugs, in orange- or mint-flavored syrups, might lead to overdoses or eventually encourage the use of illegal drugs (Rothenberger & Rothenberger, 2013; Seedat, 2014).

Finally, some evidence links antidepressants with an increased risk of suicide. The possible link prompted the U.S. Food and Drug Administration to issue a warning about a class of antidepressants known as selective serotonin reuptake inhibitors (SSRIs). Some experts have urged completely banning their use for children and adolescents (Gören, 2008; Sammons, 2009; Ghaemi, Vohringer, & Whitham, 2013).

Although the use of antidepressants to treat children is controversial, it is clear that childhood depression and other psychological disorders remain a significant problem at other points in the life span. Not only are they disruptive during childhood, but they also put children at risk for future disorders (Franic et al., 2010; Sapyla & March, 2012; Palanca-Maresca et al., 2017).

Children with Special Needs

Karen Avery was a happy-go-lucky child — until she got to first grade. A reading assessment put Karen in the lowest reading group. Despite lots of one-on-one time with her teacher, Karen's reading did not improve. She couldn't recognize words she'd seen the day before, or the day before that. Her retention problems soon became apparent across the curriculum. Karen's parents agreed to let the school give her some diagnostic tests. The results suggested Karen's brain had problems transferring information from her short-term (working) memory to her long-term memory. She was labeled as a child with a learning disability. By law, she could now get the help she really needed.

Karen joined millions of children who are classified as learning disabled, one of several special needs children can have. Although every child has different capabilities, children with *special needs* differ significantly in physical attributes or learning abilities. Their needs present major challenges for care providers and teachers.

Sensory Difficulties and Learning Disabilities

LO 5.5   Explain how sensory impairments and learning disabilities may impact children's school performance and social relationships.

Anyone who has lost his or her eyeglasses or a contact lens has a sense of how difficult even basic, everyday tasks must be for the sensory impaired. To function without adequate vision, hearing, or speech poses a tremendous challenge.

VISUAL PROBLEMS   Visual impairment has both a legal and an educational meaning. Legal impairment is defined precisely: *Blindness* is visual acuity below 20/200 after correction (meaning the inability to see at 20 feet what is typically seen at 200 feet), whereas *partial sightedness* is visual acuity of less than 20/70 after correction.

Even if a child is not legally blind, visual problems may seriously affect schoolwork. For one thing, the legal criterion pertains solely to distance vision, while most school tasks require close-up vision. The legal definition also does not consider abilities in the perception of color, depth, and light—all of which might influence a student's success. About 1 student in 1,000 requires special education services because of visual impairment.

Most severe visual problems are identified fairly early, but an impairment can go undetected. Visual problems can also emerge gradually, because development brings changes in the apparatus of the eye.

AUDITORY PROBLEMS   Auditory impairments can cause social as well as academic problems because much peer interaction involves informal conversation. Hearing loss, affecting 1 to 2 percent of the school-age population, goes beyond not hearing enough, varying on a number of dimensions (Yoshinaga-Itano, 2003; Smith, Bale, & White, 2005; Martin-Prudent et al., 2016).

In some cases, hearing is impaired only at certain frequencies, or pitches. For example, the loss may be great at pitches in the normal speech range, yet minimal in other frequencies, such as those of very high or low sounds. Different levels of amplification at different frequencies may be required; a hearing aid that amplifies all frequencies equally may be ineffective, amplifying sounds the child can hear to an uncomfortable degree.

How a child adapts depends on when the hearing loss begins. The effects will likely be more severe in a child with little or no exposure to the sound of language,

visual impairment
a difficulty in seeing that may include blindness or partial sightedness

auditory impairment
a special need that involves the loss of hearing or some aspect of hearing

Auditory can produce both academic and social difficulties, and they may lead to speech difficulties.

producing an inability to understand or produce speech. For a child who has learned language, hearing loss will not seriously affect subsequent linguistic development.

Severe and early loss of hearing can impair abstract thinking. Concrete concepts can be visually illustrated but abstract concepts depend on language for meaning. For example, it is difficult to explain the concept of "freedom" or "soul" without use of language (Meinzen-Derr et al., 2014; Fitzpatrick et al., 2017).

SPEECH PROBLEMS   Auditory difficulties may be accompanied by **speech impairments**, one of the most public types of exceptionality: Speech that deviates from the norm is obvious whenever the child speaks. It also interferes with communication, and may produce maladjustment in the speaker. Speech impairments occur in around 5 percent of the school-age population (Bishop & Leonard, 2001; National Institute on Deafness and Other Communication Disorders, 2016).

Childhood-onset fluency disorder (stuttering) involves a substantial disruption in the rhythm and fluency of speech and is the most common speech impairment. Despite a great deal of research, no specific cause has been identified. Occasional stuttering is not unusual in young children—and occasionally occurs in normal adults—but chronic stuttering can be a severe problem. Not only does stuttering hinder communication, but it can also produce embarrassment and stress in children, who may become inhibited from conversing with others and speaking aloud in class (Choi et al., 2013; Sasisekaran, 2014; Connally, 2018).

Parents and teachers can help children who stutter by not drawing attention to the issue and by giving them sufficient time to finish what they are saying, no matter how protracted the statement becomes. It does not help stutterers to finish their sentences for them or otherwise correct their speech (Ryan, 2001; Howell, Bailey, & Kothari, 2010; Beilby, Byrnes, & Young, 2012).

LEARNING DISABILITIES: DISCREPANCIES BETWEEN ACHIEVEMENT AND CAPACITY TO LEARN   Like Karen Avery, described previously, 1 in 5 children has a learning disability or attentional issues, according to the National Center for Learning Disabilities. **Learning disabilities** interfere with children's ability to listen, speak, read, write, reason, or do math. An ill-defined category, learning disabilities are diagnosed when children's academic performance differs from their potential to learn (Bos & Vaughn, 2005; Bonifacci et al., 2016; National Center for Learning Disabilities, 2018).

Such a broad definition includes a wide and varied range of difficulties. For instance, *dyslexia*, a reading disability, can result in the visual misperception of letters, unusual difficulty in spelling or sounding out letters, and left-right confusion. Dyslexia is not fully understood, but the problem may lie in the part of the brain that breaks words into the sound elements that make up language (McGough, 2003; Lachmann et al., 2005; Sumner, Connelly, & Barnett, 2014).

What is the cause of learning disabilities? Some theories look to neuroscientific explanations based on genetic factors. Using that approach, researchers have found that the brains of children with dyslexia show structural and functional differences from those of typical children. Other theorists focus on environmental causes, such as poor early nutrition or allergies, drug use by mothers during pregnancy, or exposure to diseases such as meningitis (Shaywitz, 2004; Richards et al., 2015).

Attention Deficit Hyperactivity Disorder

LO 5.6   Identify the behaviors associated with ADHD, and discuss how it impacts children's school performance.

Troy Dalton, age 7, exhausted his teacher. Unable to sit still, he roamed the classroom all day, distracting the other children. In reading group, he jumped up and down in his seat, dropping his book and knocking over the whiteboard. During read aloud, he ran around the room, humming noisily and shouting, "I'm a jet plane!" Once, he flung himself through the air, landing on another boy and breaking his arm. "He's the definition of perpetual motion," the teacher told Troy's mother (who looked pretty exhausted herself). The school finally decided to split Troy's day between the three second-grade classrooms. It was not a perfect solution, but it did allow his primary teacher to do some actual teaching.

---

speech impairment
speech that deviates so much from the speech of others that it calls attention to itself, interferes with communication, or produces maladjustment in the speaker

childhood-onset fluency disorder (stuttering)
substantial disruption in the rhythm and fluency of speech; the most common speech impairment

learning disabilities
difficulties in the acquisition and use of listening, speaking, reading, writing, reasoning, or mathematical abilities

Seven-year-old Troy Dalton's high energy and low attention span are a result of attention deficit hyperactivity disorder, which occurs in 3 to 5 percent of the school-age population. **Attention deficit hyperactivity disorder (ADHD)** is marked by inattention, impulsiveness, a low tolerance for frustration, and generally a great deal of inappropriate activity. All children show such traits some of the time, but for those diagnosed with ADHD, such behavior is common and interferes with their home and school functioning (Whalen et al., 2002; Sciberras et al., 2013; Van Neste et al., 2015).

Figure 5-3 The Brains of Children with ADHD

The brains of children with ADHD (in the top row) show less thickening of the cortex compared to the brains of typical children at the same age.

SOURCE: Shaw et al., 2007.

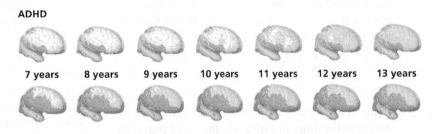

ADHD

7 years   8 years   9 years   10 years   11 years   12 years   13 years

Typically developing controls

It is often difficult to distinguish between children who are highly active and those with ADHD. Common symptoms of ADHD include:

- persistent difficulty in finishing tasks, following instructions, and organizing work
- fidgeting, squirming, inability to watch an entire television program
- frequent interruption of others or excessive talking
- a tendency to jump into a task before hearing all the instructions
- difficulty in waiting or remaining seated

Lacking a simple test to identify ADHD, it is hard to know for sure how many children have the disorder. The Centers for Disease Control and Prevention put the proportion of children 3 to 17 years of age with ADHD at 9.4 percent, with boys being twice as likely as girls to be diagnosed with the disorder. Other estimates are lower. Only a trained clinician can make an accurate diagnosis, following an extensive evaluation of the child and interviews with parents and teachers (Danielson et al., 2018).

The causes of ADHD are not clear, although some research finds that it is related to a delay in neural development. Specifically, it may be that the thickening of the brain's cortex, which lags in children with ADHD 3 years behind that of children without the disorder (see Figure 5-3).

Considerable controversy surrounds the treatment of ADHD. Because it has been found that doses of Ritalin or Dexedrine (which, paradoxically, are stimulants) reduce activity levels in hyperactive children, many physicians routinely prescribe drug treatment (Arnsten, Berridge, & McCracken, 2009; Weissman et al., 2012; Pelham et al., 2016).

Although in many cases such drugs are effective in increasing attention span and compliance, in some cases the side effects (such as irritability, reduced appetite, and depression) are considerable, and the long-term health consequences of this treatment are unclear. Consequently, other treatments, such as behavioral therapy, are also used (Rose, 2008; Cortese et al., 2013; Thapar & Cooper, 2016).

In addition to drugs, behavior therapy is often used to treat ADHD. Parents and teachers learn techniques that primarily use rewards (such as verbal praise) to improve behavior. Teachers can increase the structure of classroom activities, among other management techniques, because ADHD children find unstructured tasks difficult (Chronis, Jones, & Raggi, 2006; DuPaul & Weyandt, 2006).

Finally, because some research has shown links between ADHD and children's diet, particularly in terms of fatty acids or food additives, dietary treatments have sometimes been prescribed. However, dietary treatments are usually insufficient by themselves (Cruz & Bahna, 2006; Stevenson, 2006). (Parents and teachers can receive support from the Children and Adults with Attention-Deficit/Hyperactivity Disorder organization at www.chadd.org.)

attention deficit hyperactivity disorder (ADHD)

a learning disorder marked by inattention, impulsiveness, a low tolerance for frustration, and generally a great deal of inappropriate activity

Review, Check, and Apply

Review

LO 5.1 Summarize the ways in which children grow during the school years, and discuss the factors that influence their growth.

In middle childhood, height and weight increase gradually. Differences in height and weight are influenced by both genetic and social factors.

LO 5.2 Explain how nutrition affects children's growth and functioning, and identify the risks posed by obesity.

Adequate nutrition promotes physical, social, and cognitive development, whereas overnutrition and a sedentary lifestyle may lead to obesity. Obesity affects 15 percent of U.S. children and leads to greater risk of heart disease, diabetes, and other diseases.

LO 5.3 Identify the advances in motor skills during middle childhood.

Gross motor skills continue to improve during the school years. Muscular coordination and manipulative skills advance to near-adult levels.

LO 5.4 Summarize the main health and safety concerns of school-age children.

Although middle childhood is generally a time of robust health, one study found that more than 90 percent of children in this age group will experience at least one serious medical condition. Threats to safety include accidents, a result of increased independence and mobility, and unsupervised access to cyberspace. One in five children and adolescents has a psychological disorder.

LO 5.5 Explain how sensory impairments and learning disabilities may impact children's school performance and social relationships.

Children who have special needs relating to vision, hearing, and speech may find the school environment especially challenging. Those with visual impairments may struggle with close-up vision, and perception of color and depth, which can impact their school performance. Auditory impairment affects both academic performance and peer interaction. Understanding abstract concepts depends on language for meaning and cannot be visually illustrated. Speech impairments make communication difficult and may make a child fearful of speaking. Learning disabilities include difficulties in acquiring and using listening, speaking, reading, writing, reasoning, or mathematical abilities. Dyslexia, for example, makes it particularly difficult for children to learn to read, which in turn affects every area of their academic performance.

LO 5.6 Identify the behaviors associated with ADHD, and discuss how it impacts children's school performance.

Children with ADHD have difficulty following instructions and finishing tasks. They are often fidgety and unable to sit still. They tend to talk excessively and frequently interrupt others. Attention deficit hyperactivity disorder poses attention, organization, and activity problems for 3 to 5 percent of school-age children.

Check Yourself

1. Which of the following is a long-term outcome associated with childhood obesity?

   a. Stunted growth
   b. Being overweight as an adult
   c. Greater risk of accidents
   d. Development of learning disabilities

2. One explanation for the advances in fine motor skills during middle school involves the increase in the amount of _____ in the brain.

   a. myelin
   b. neurons
   c. genes
   d. gray matter

3. When it comes to school-age children and injuries associated with accidents, which of the following statements is true?

   a. The number of accidents occurring in the school-age years is significantly fewer than in earlier years.
   b. There is no relationship between gender and the prevalence of injuries associated with accidents.
   c. Drowning is the most frequent cause of accidental death.
   d. Boys are significantly more likely than girls to be injured.

4. _____, the most common speech impairment, involves a substantial disruption in the rhythm and fluency of speech.

   a. Telegraphic speech   c. Protracted speech
   b. Stuttering   d. Slow mapping

Applying Lifespan Development

If hearing is associated with abstract thinking, how do people who were born deaf think?

Module 5.2

Cognitive Development in Middle Childhood

Jen Draper stops washing the dishes and comes to the living room. Her 8-year-old daughter Raylene has asked her to listen as she reads from A Single Shard *by Linda Sue Park.*

The book is a novel about a boy in 12th-century Korea. As Raylene reads, tears come to Jen's eyes, not because of the events in the story, but because her daughter has found a way to grow beyond her small apartment and move confidently into the wider world.

Raylene formed a love of books on her own, taught herself to read them, and takes complete responsibility for finding good books at the local library. Her teachers have told Jen—never much of a reader herself—that her daughter is reading well above her third-grade level.

To support her daughter's habit, Jen has bought Raylene a few books recommended by her teachers. She now looks proudly at the bookcase one of the teachers gave her recently, which is beginning to look occupied.

It was a proud moment for Jen Draper, and a significant accomplishment for her daughter, who has progressed beyond the first-grade books that she had initially chosen to a challenging book written at the fifth-grade level.

Middle childhood is often referred to as the "school years" because it marks the beginning of formal education for most children. Sometimes the physical and cognitive growth that occurs during middle childhood is gradual; other times it is sudden; but always it is remarkable.

During middle childhood, children blossom with ideas and plans—and the language to express them orally and in writing. And it is during this period that much of their future development is charted.

FatCamera/E+/Getty Images

We begin our discussion by examining several approaches to describe and explain cognitive development, including Piagetian and information processing theories and the important ideas of Vygotsky. We look at language development and the questions surrounding bilingualism—an increasingly pressing social policy issue in the United States.

Next we consider several issues involving schooling. After discussing the scope of education throughout the world, we examine the critical skill of reading and the nature of multicultural education. The module ends with a discussion of intelligence, a characteristic closely tied to school success. We look at the nature of IQ tests and at the education of children who are either significantly below or above the intellectual norm.

Intellectual and Language Development

> Jared's parents were delighted when he came home from kindergarten one day and announced he had learned why the sky was blue. He talked about the earth's atmosphere— although he mispronounced the word—and how tiny bits of moisture in the air reflected the sunlight. His explanation had rough edges (he couldn't quite grasp what "atmosphere" was), but he had the general idea. His parents felt it was quite an achievement for their 5-year-old.
>
> Fast-forward 6 years. Jared, now 11, has already invested an hour in his homework. Having completed a two-page worksheet on multiplying and dividing fractions, he is working on his U.S. Constitution project. He is taking notes for his report, which explains what political factions were involved in creating the document and how the Constitution had been amended over time.

Jared's vast intellectual advances are not uncommon. During middle childhood, cognitive abilities broaden, and children increasingly understand and master complex skills. But their thinking is not yet fully mature.

Perspectives on Cognitive Development in Middle Childhood

LO 5.7   Identify and summarize the major theoretical approaches to cognitive development in middle childhood.

Several perspectives explain the cognitive advances and limitations of middle childhood.

Cognitive development makes substantial advances in middle childhood.

concrete operational stage

the period of cognitive development between 7 and 12 years of age, which is characterized by the active, and appropriate, use of logic

decentering

the ability to take multiple aspects of a situation into account

PIAGETIAN APPROACHES TO COGNITIVE DEVELOPMENT Let's return to Jean Piaget's view of the preschooler considered in Module 4.2. From Piaget's perspective, preschoolers think *preoperationally*. They are largely egocentric and lack the ability to use *operations*—organized, formal, logical mental processes.

The Rise of Concrete Operational Thought All of this changes during the school years in what Piaget calls the **concrete operational stage**. Occurring between ages 7 and 12, this stage is characterized by the active, and appropriate, use of logic. Concrete operational thought applies *logical operations* to concrete problems. For instance, when children in this stage confront a conservation problem (such as determining whether the amount of liquid poured from one container to another of a different shape stays the same), they use cognitive and logical processes to answer, no longer judging solely by appearance. They are able to reason correctly that because none of the liquid has been lost, the amount stays the same. Being less egocentric, they can consider multiple aspects of a situation, an ability known as **decentering**. Jared, the sixth grader described previously, used decentering to consider the views of the various factions behind the U.S. Constitution.

The shift from preoperational to concrete operational thought takes time. Children shift between these modes of thought before concrete operations take a firm hold; they are able to answer conservation problems but unable to explain why. When asked for their reasoning, they may simply respond, "Because."

However, once concrete operations take hold, children make several cognitive leaps, such as understanding the concept of *reversibility*—the notion that transformations to a stimulus can be reversed. Grasping this, children realize that a ball of clay squeezed into a long, thin rope can become a ball again. More abstractly, this concept allows children to understand that if 3 + 5 equals 8, then 5 + 3 also equals 8—and, later, that 8 − 3 equals 5.

Concrete operational thinking also permits children to grasp such concepts as the relationship between time and speed. For instance, consider the problem in which two cars traveling different-length routes start and finish at the same points in the same amount of time. Children entering the concrete operational period reason that the cars' speed is the same. However, between ages 8 and 10, children begin to understand that for both cars to arrive simultaneously at the finish point, the car traveling the longer route must be moving faster.

Despite the advances that occur during the concrete operational stage, children still experience one critical limitation in their thinking. They remain tied to concrete, physical reality. Furthermore, they are unable to understand truly abstract or hypothetical questions, or ones that involve formal logic.

Piaget in Perspective: Right and Wrong As we learned previously, researchers who followed Piaget have found much to applaud—and much to criticize.

Piaget was a virtuoso observer of children. His many books contain brilliant, careful observations of children at work and play. His theories have had powerful educational implications, and many schools use his principles to guide instruction (Brainerd, 2003; Hebe, 2017).

In some ways, Piaget's approach succeeded in describing cognitive development. At the same time, critics have raised compelling and reasonable grievances. As noted previously, many researchers argue that Piaget underestimated children's capabilities, in part because of the limitations of the mini-experiments he conducted. When a broader array of experimental tasks is used, children show less consistency within stages than Piaget predicted (Bibace, 2013; Siegler, 2016).

In short, increasing evidence suggests that children's cognitive abilities emerge earlier than Piaget envisioned. Some children demonstrate concrete operational thinking before age 7, when Piaget suggested these abilities first appear.

Still, we cannot dismiss Piaget. Although some early cross-cultural research implied that children in certain cultures remain preoperational, failing to master conservation and develop concrete operations, more recent research suggests otherwise. For instance, with proper training in conservation, children in non-Western cultures who do not conserve learn to do so. In one study, urban Australian children—who develop concrete operations on Piaget's timetable—were compared to rural Aborigine children, who typically do not conserve, at the age of 14 (Dasen et al., 1979). With training, the rural Aborigine children showed conservation skills similar to those of their urban counterparts, although about 3 years later (see Figure 5-4).

When children are interviewed by researchers from their own culture, who share their language and customs, and whose reasoning tasks relate to important cultural domains, the children are much more likely to display concrete operational thinking (Jahoda, 1983). Such research suggests that Piaget was right in arguing that concrete operations are universally achieved during middle childhood. Performance differences between Western and some non-Western children on Piagetian measures of conservation and concrete operations probably reflect a difference in experiences. The progress of cognitive development cannot be understood without considering a child's culture (Mishra & Dasen, 2013; Wang et al., 2016; Knight, Safa, & White, 2018).

INFORMATION PROCESSING IN MIDDLE CHILDHOOD   It is a significant achievement for first graders to learn basic math tasks, such as single-digit addition and subtraction, as well as the spelling of simple words like *dog*. But by sixth grade, children are able to work with fractions and decimals, completing a worksheet like the one done by Jared, the boy cited previously. They can spell words such as *exhibit* and *residence*.

According to *information processing approaches*, children handle information with increasing sophistication. Like computers, they process more data as the size of their memories increases and the "programs" they use to do this become more complex (Kuhn et al., 1995; Kail, 2003; Zelazo et al., 2003; McCormick & Scherer, 2018).

Memory   As noted, **memory** in the information processing model is the ability to record, store, and retrieve information. For a child to remember a piece of information, the three processes must all function properly. Through *encoding*, the child records the information in a form usable to memory. Children who never learned that 5 + 6 = 11, or who didn't heed this fact when it was taught, will never be able to recall it. They never encoded the information in the first place.

But exposure to a fact is not enough; the information also has to be *stored*. In our example, the information 5 + 6 = 11 must be placed and maintained in the memory system. Finally, proper memory functioning requires that stored material must be *retrieved*. Through retrieval, material in storage is located, made conscious, and used.

During middle childhood, short-term memory (also referred to as *working memory*) capacity greatly improves. Children are increasingly able to hear a string of digits ("1-5-6-3-4") and then repeat them in reverse order ("4-3-6-5-1"). At the start of the preschool period, they can remember and reverse only about two digits; by the beginning of adolescence, they can perform the task with as many as six digits. In addition, they use more sophisticated strategies for recalling information, which can be improved with training (Jack, Simcock, & Hayne, 2012; Jarrold & Hall, 2013; Resing et al., 2017).

Figure 5-4 Conservation Training

Rural Australian Aborigine children trail their urban counterparts in the development of their understanding of conservation; with training, they later catch up. Without training, around half of 14-year-old Aborigines do not have an understanding of conservation. What can be concluded from the fact that training influences the understanding of conservation?

SOURCE: Based on Dasen et al., 1979.

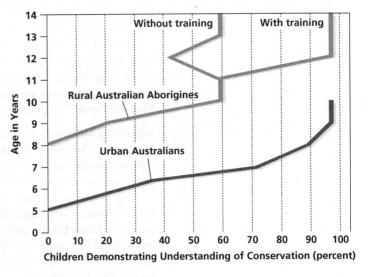

memory
the process by which information is initially recorded, stored, and retrieved

metamemory
an understanding about the processes that underlie memory, which emerges and improves during middle childhood

Memory capacity may shed light on another issue in cognitive development. Some developmental psychologists suggest that preschool children may have difficulty solving conservation problems because of memory limitations. They argue that young children simply may not be able to recall all the necessary information to solve such problems.

Metamemory, a grasp of the processes that underlie memory, also emerges and improves during middle childhood. By the start of first grade, when their theory of mind becomes more sophisticated, children have a general notion of what memory is. They understand that some people have better memories than others (Ghetti & Angelini, 2008; Jaswal & Dodson, 2009; Cottini et al., 2018).

School-age children understand memory in more sophisticated ways as they increasingly engage in *control strategies*—intentionally used tactics to improve cognitive processing. For instance, school-age children know that rehearsal, the repetition of information, improves memory, and they increasingly make use of this strategy (Sang, Miao, & Deng, 2002; Coffman et al., 2018).

Improving Memory Can children be trained to be more effective in the use of control strategies? Definitely. School-age children can be taught to use particular strategies, although such teaching is not a simple matter. For instance, children need to know not only how to use a memory strategy, but also when and where to use it most effectively.

For example, an innovative technique called the *keyword strategy* can help students learn a foreign language, the state capitals, or any information that pairs two sets of words or labels that sound alike (Wyra, Lawson, & Hungi, 2007). For instance, in learning foreign language vocabulary, a foreign word such as the Spanish word for duck (*pato*, pronounced *pot-o*) is paired with a common English word—in this case it might be *pot*. The English word is the keyword. Once the keyword is chosen, children then form a mental image of the two words interacting with one another. For instance, a student might use an image of a duck taking a bath in a pot to remember the word *pato*.

VYGOTSKY'S APPROACH TO COGNITIVE DEVELOPMENT AND CLASSROOM INSTRUCTION Learning environments can encourage children to adopt these strategies as well. Recall that Russian developmentalist Lev Vygotsky proposed that cognitive advances occur through exposure to information within a child's *zone of proximal development*, or ZPD. In the ZPD, a child can almost, but not quite, understand or perform a task.

Vygotsky's approach has particularly encouraged the development of classroom practices that promote children's active participation in their learning. Consequently, classrooms are seen as places where children should experiment and try out new activities (Vygotsky, 1926/1997; Gredler & Shields, 2008; Gredler, 2012).

According to Vygotsky, education should focus on activities that involve interaction with others. Both child–adult and child–child interactions can promote cognitive growth. The interactions must be carefully structured to fall within each child's ZPD.

Vygotsky's work has influenced several current and noteworthy innovations. For example, *cooperative learning*, where children work in groups to achieve a common goal, uses several aspects of Vygotsky's theory. Students working in cooperative groups benefit from the insights of others. A wrong turn by one child may be corrected by others in the group. On the other hand, not every group member is equally helpful: As Vygotsky's approach would imply, individual children benefit most when some of the group members are more competent at the task and can act as experts (DeLisi, 2006; Slavin, 2013; Gillies, 2014).

> **From an educator's perspective:** Suggest how a teacher might use Vygotsky's approach to teach 10-year-olds about colonial America.

Reciprocal teaching is another educational practice that reflects Vygotsky's approach to cognitive development. *Reciprocal teaching* is a technique used to teach reading comprehension strategies. Students are taught to skim the content of a passage, raise questions about its central point, summarize the passage, and finally predict what will happen next. A key to this technique is its reciprocal nature, its emphasis on giving students a chance to take on the role of teacher. In the beginning, teachers lead students through the comprehension strategies. Gradually, students progress through their zones of proximal development, taking more and more control over use of the strategies, until the students are able to take on a teaching role. The method has shown impressive success in raising reading comprehension levels, particularly for students experiencing reading difficulties (Spörer, Brunstein, & Kieschke, 2009; Lundberg & Reichenberg, 2013; Davis & Voirin, 2016).

Language Development: What Words Mean

LO 5.8 **Summarize the development of language during middle childhood, and explain the cognitive advantages bilingualism offers.**

If you listen to school-age children, their speech sounds similar to that of adults. However, the apparent similarity is deceiving. The linguistic sophistication of children—particularly early in the school-age period—still needs refining to reach adult levels.

MASTERING THE MECHANICS OF LANGUAGE   Vocabulary continues to increase rapidly during the school years. The average 6-year-old has a vocabulary of from 8,000 to 14,000 words, whereas another 5,000 words appear from ages 9 to 11.

Children's mastery of grammar also improves. For instance, the passive voice is seldom used during the early school-age years (as in "The dog was walked by Jon," compared with the active voice, "Jon walked the dog"). Six- and 7-year-olds rarely use conditional sentences, such as "If Sarah will set the table, I will wash the dishes." During middle childhood, however, the use of passive voice and conditional sentences increases. In addition, children's understanding of *syntax*, the rules governing how words and phrases can be combined to form sentences, grows.

By first grade, most children pronounce words quite accurately. However, certain *phonemes*, units of sound, remain troublesome. For instance, the ability to pronounce *j*, *v*, *th*, and *zh* sounds develops later.

School-age children may also have difficulty decoding sentences when the meaning depends on *intonation*, or tone of voice. For example, consider the sentence, "George gave a book to David and he gave one to Bill." If the word "he" is emphasized, the meaning is "George gave a book to David and David gave a different book to Bill." But if the intonation emphasizes the word *and*, then the meaning changes to "George gave a book to David and George also gave a book to Bill." School-age children cannot easily sort out subtleties such as these (Wells, Peppé, & Goulandris, 2004; Thornton, 2010; Bosco et al., 2013).

Conversational skills also develop as children become more competent in using *pragmatics*, the rules governing the use of language to communicate in social settings.

For example, although children in early childhood are aware of the rules of conversational turn-taking, their use is sometimes primitive. Consider the following conversation between 6-year-olds Yonnie and Max:

YONNIE: My dad drives a FedEx truck.
MAX: My sister's name is Molly.
YONNIE: He gets up really early in the morning.
MAX: She wet her bed last night.

Later, however, conversations show more give-and-take, with children responding to each other's comments. For instance, this conversation between 11-year-olds Mia and Josh reflects a greater mastery of pragmatics:

MIA: I don't know what to get Claire for her birthday.
JOSH: I'm getting her earrings.
MIA: She already has a lot of jewelry.
JOSH: I don't think she has that much.

Students working in cooperative groups benefit from the insights of others.

METALINGUISTIC AWARENESS   A significant development in middle childhood is children's increasing understanding of their own use of language, or **metalinguistic awareness**. By age 5 or 6, they understand that a set of rules governs language. In the early years they learn and comprehend these rules implicitly, but during middle childhood they understand them more explicitly (Benelli et al., 2006; Saiegh-Haddad, 2007; Tighe et al., 2018).

Metalinguistic awareness helps children's comprehension when information is fuzzy or incomplete. For instance, when preschoolers receive ambiguous or unclear information, such as directions for a complicated game, they rarely ask for clarification, and tend to blame themselves for any confusion. By the age of 7 or 8, children realize that miscommunication may be a result of the person communicating with them as well. Consequently, school-age children are more likely to ask for clarifications (Apperly & Robinson, 2002; van den Herik, 2017).

HOW LANGUAGE PROMOTES SELF-CONTROL   Their growing sophistication with language helps children control and regulate their behavior. In one experiment, children were told they could have one marshmallow treat if they chose to eat it immediately, but two treats if they waited. Most of the children, who ranged in age from 4 to 8, chose to wait, but the strategies they used differed significantly.

The 4-year-olds often chose to look at the marshmallows while waiting, a strategy that was not terribly effective. In contrast, 6- and 8-year-olds used language to help overcome temptation, although in different ways. The 6-year-olds spoke and sang to themselves, reminding themselves they would get more treats if they waited. The 8-year-olds focused on aspects of the marshmallows unrelated to taste, such as appearance, which helped them to wait. In short, children increasingly use "self-talk" to regulate their behavior. Their self-control grows as their linguistic capabilities increase.

BILINGUALISM: SPEAKING IN MANY TONGUES

John Dewey Elementary is a school known for its progressive and democratic attitudes. On the campus of a large university, it boasts a staff of classroom aides who in sum speak 15 different languages, including Hindi and Hausa. The challenge is that there are more than 30 languages spoken by the students.

Across America, the voices with which children speak are changing. Nearly one in five people in the United States—some 62 million—speak a language other than English at home, a percentage that is growing. **Bilingualism**—the use of more than one language—is increasingly common (Shin & Bruno, 2003; Graddol, 2004; Hoff & Core, 2013; see Figure 5-5).

Children with little or no English proficiency must learn both the standard school curriculum and the language in which it is taught. One approach to achieving this is *bilingual education*, in which children are initially taught in their native language, while they learn English. This enables students to develop a strong foundation in basic subject areas using their native language. The goal of most bilingual programs is to gradually shift instruction into English.

An alternative approach is to immerse students in English, teaching solely in that language. To proponents of this approach, initially teaching students in another language hinders their efforts to learn English and slows their integration into society. These two quite different, highly politicized approaches have some politicians arguing for "English-only" laws, whereas others urge schools to respect the challenges nonnative speakers face by offering some instruction in their native language.

Still, the psychological research does seem clear that being bilingual is associated with certain cognitive advantages. With a wider range of linguistic possibilities to choose from in assessing a situation, speakers of two languages show greater cognitive flexibility, and their executive functioning (involved in the cognitive control of behavior) may be superior. They solve problems with greater creativity and versatility. Furthermore, learning in one's native tongue is also associated with higher self-esteem in minority students (Hermanto, Moreno, & Bialystok, 2012; Yang, Hartanto, & Yang, 2016; Hsin & Snow, 2017).

Figure 5-5 Percentage of People 5 Years and Over Who Spoke a Language Other Than English at Home

SOURCE: U.S. Census Bureau, 2017, American Community Survey.

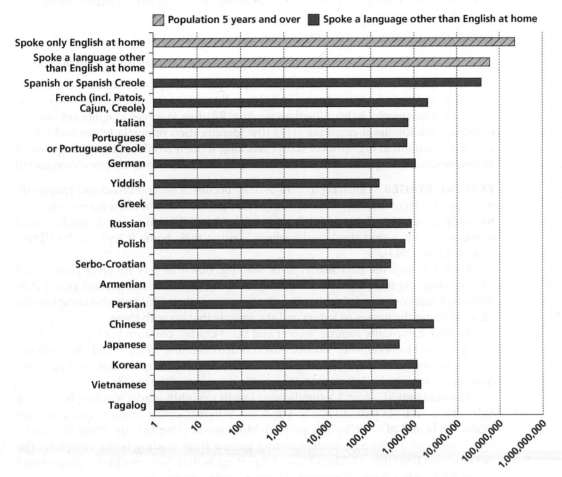

Bilingual students often have greater metalinguistic awareness, understand the rules of language more explicitly, and show great cognitive sophistication. They may even score higher on tests of intelligence, according to some research. Furthermore, brain scans comparing bilingual individuals with those who speak only one language find differences suggesting different types of brain activation (Piller, 2010; Burgaleta et al., 2013; Sierpowska et al., 2018).

Finally, because many linguists contend that universal processes underlie language acquisition, as we noted in Chapter 3, instruction in a native language may enhance instruction in a second language. In fact, some educators believe that second-language learning should be a regular part of elementary schooling for *all* children (McCardle & Hoff, 2006; Frumkes, 2018).

Schooling: The Three Rs (and More) of Middle Childhood

As the six other children in his reading group turned to him, Glenn shifted uneasily in his chair. Reading was hard for him, and he always felt anxious when asked to read aloud. But with his teacher's encouraging nod, he plunged in, hesitant at first, then gaining momentum as he read the story of a mother's first day on a new job. He was happy and proud to find that he could read the passage quite nicely. He broke into a broad smile when his teacher said, "Well done, Glenn."

Such moments, repeated over and over, make—or break—a child's educational experience. School is society's formal attempt to transfer its accumulated knowledge, beliefs, values, and wisdom to new generations. The success of this transfer determines, in a real sense, the future fortunes of the world, as well as the success of each student.

Reading: Learning to Decipher the Meaning Behind Words

LO 5.9   Describe the five stages of reading, and compare teaching approaches.

The accomplishments of both Glenn (described previously) and Raylene Draper (described in the prologue) in advancing their reading are important because there is no task more fundamental to learning than reading. Reading involves a significant number of skills, from low-level cognitive skills (the identification of single letters and letter–sound association) to higher-level skills (matching written words with meanings stored in memory, and using context and prior knowledge to determine a sentence's meaning).

READING STAGES   Learning to read usually occurs in several broad and frequently overlapping stages. In *Stage 0*, from birth to first grade, children learn the prerequisites for reading, including letter identification, recognition of familiar words (such as their name or *stop* on a stop sign), and perhaps writing their name (Chall, 1992; Oakhill, Cain, & Elbro, 2014).

Stage 1 brings the first real type of reading, but it largely involves *phonological recoding* skills. At this stage, which usually encompasses first and second grade, children can sound out words by blending the letters together. Children also complete the job of learning the names of letters and the sounds that go with them.

In *Stage 2*, typically around second and third grades, children learn to read aloud with fluency. However, they do not attach much meaning to the words because the effort involved in simply sounding out words is usually so great that relatively few cognitive resources are left over to process the meaning of the words.

The next period, *Stage 3*, extends from fourth to eighth grade. Reading becomes a means to an end—in particular, a way to learn. Whereas earlier reading was an accomplishment in and of itself, by this point children use reading to learn about the world. However, even at this age, understanding gained from reading is not complete. For instance, one limitation children have at this stage is that they are able to comprehend information only when it is presented from a single perspective.

In the final period, *Stage 4*, children are able to read and process information that reflects multiple points of view. This ability, which begins during the transition into high school, permits children to develop a far more sophisticated understanding of material. This explains why great works of literature are not read at an earlier stage of education. It is not so much that younger children do not have the vocabulary to understand such works (although this is partially true); it is that they lack the ability to understand the multiple points of view that sophisticated literature invariably presents.

HOW SHOULD WE TEACH READING?   Educators have long been engaged in a debate over the most effective means of teaching reading. This debate centers on a disagreement about how information is processed during reading. According to proponents of *code-based approaches to reading*, teachers should focus on the basic skills that underlie reading. Code-based approaches emphasize the components of reading, such as letter sounds and combinations—phonics—and how letters and sounds combine to make words. They suggest that reading consists of processing the components of words, combining them into words, and using these to derive the meaning of sentences and passages (Dickinson, Golinkoff, & Hirsh-Pasek, 2010; Hagan-Burke et al., 2013; Cohen et al., 2016).

In contrast, some educators argue that the most successful approach is *whole language*, which regards reading as a natural process, similar to the acquisition of oral language. According to this view, children learn to read through authentic writing, such as sentences, stories, poems, lists, and charts. Rather than sounding out words, children make guesses about the meaning of words based on the context. Children become proficient readers, learning whole words and phrases through such a trial-and-error approach (Sousa, 2005; Donat, 2006).

A growing body of research suggests the code-based approach is superior to the whole-language approach. One study found that children tutored in phonics for a year improved their reading substantially, compared to a group of good readers, and that the neural pathways involved in reading became closer to those of good readers. Consequently, based on an accumulation of evidence, most reading experts now support reading instruction using code-based approaches (Brady, 2011; Vaish, 2014; Castles, Rastle, & Nation, 2018).

Whatever approach is used to teach reading, reading produces significant changes in the wiring of the brain. It boosts the organization of the visual cortex of the brain, and it improves the processing of spoken language (see Figure 5-6).

Educational Trends: Beyond the Three Rs

LO 5.10   Summarize the various trends in U.S. education.

Schooling has changed significantly in the past few decades, with U.S. schools returning to the traditional three Rs (reading, writing, and arithmetic). The focus on these fundamentals departs from prior trends that emphasized children's social well-being and allowing students to choose their own study topics instead of following a set curriculum (Merrow, 2012; Hudley, 2016; VanWheelden, 2016).

Elementary schools today also stress individual accountability. Teachers may be held responsible for their students' learning, and both students and teachers may be required to take state or national tests to assess their competence (McDonnell, 2004).

As the U.S. population becomes more diverse, elementary schools are paying increased attention to student diversity issues and multiculturalism. And with good reason: Cultural, as well as language, differences affect students socially and educationally. The demographic makeup of students in the United States is undergoing an extraordinary shift. The proportion of Hispanics is likely to more than double in the next 50 years. By the year 2050, non-Hispanic Caucasians will likely be a minority of the United States' total population (Colby & Ortman, 2015; see Figure 5-7).

Consequently, educators are increasingly concerned about multicultural issues. The accompanying *Cultural Dimensions* feature on multicultural education discusses how the goals for educating students from different cultures have changed significantly and are still being debated.

CULTURAL ASSIMILATION OR PLURALISTIC SOCIETY?   Multicultural education, in part, is a response to a **cultural assimilation model** in which the goal was to assimilate individual cultural identities into a unique, unified American culture. In practice this meant that non-English speakers were discouraged from using their native language and were totally immersed in English.

Figure 5-6 Reading and the Brain

The act of reading involves activation of significant areas of the brain, as these scans illustrate. In the top scan, an individual is reading aloud; in the bottom scan, the person is reading silently.

SOURCE: SPL/Science Source.

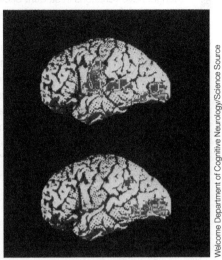

Welcome Department of Cognitive Neurology/Science Source

cultural assimilation model
the model in which the goal was to assimilate individual cultural identities into a unique, unified American culture

Figure 5-7 The Changing Face of America

Current projections of the population makeup of the United States show that by the year 2050, the proportion of non-Hispanic whites will decline as the proportion of minority group members increases. What will be some of the impacts on social workers as the result of changing demographics?

SOURCE: U.S. Bureau of the Census, 2010a.

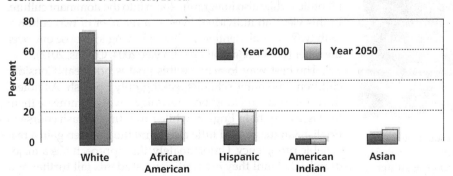

Cultural Dimensions

Multicultural Education

Classrooms in the United States have always been populated by students with diverse backgrounds and experiences. Only recently, though, have variations in student backgrounds been viewed as a major challenge—and opportunity—that educators face.

In fact, this diversity in the classroom relates to a fundamental objective of education, which is to transmit the information a society deems important. As the famous anthropologist Margaret Mead (1942) once said, "In its broadest sense, education is the cultural process, the way in which each newborn human infant, born with a potentiality for learning greater than that of any other mammal, is transformed into a full member of a specific human society, sharing with the other members of a specific human culture" (p. 633).

Culture, then, can be seen as a set of behaviors, beliefs, values, and expectations shared by the members of a society. But culture is not simply "Western culture" or "Asian culture." It is also made up of *subcultural* groups. Membership in a cultural or subcultural group might be of minor concern to educators if it didn't substantially impact the way students experience school. In recent years, considerable thought has gone into providing **multicultural education**, with the goal of helping minority students develop competence in the majority culture while maintaining positive group identities built on their original cultures (Nieto, 2005; Ngo, 2010; Matriano & Swee-Hin, 2013; Gharaei, Thijs, & Verkuyten, 2018).

multicultural education
a form of education in which the goal is to help minority students develop confidence in the culture of the majority group while maintaining positive group identities that build on their original cultures

> **From an educator's perspective:** Should one goal of society be to foster cultural assimilation in children from other cultures? Why or why not?

pluralistic society model
the concept that American society is made up of diverse, coequal cultural groups that should preserve their individual cultural features

In the early 1970s, however, educators and minority groups suggested that cultural assimilation should be replaced by a **pluralistic society model**. In this model, American society is made up of diverse, coequal cultural groups that preserve their unique cultural features.

The pluralistic model grew, in part, from the belief that teachers who emphasized the dominant culture and discouraged nonnative English speakers from using their native tongues in effect devalued subcultural heritages and lowered those students' self-esteem. Instructional materials inevitably feature culture-specific events and understandings. Thus, minority children might never be exposed to important aspects of their culture. For example, English-language texts rarely present the great themes in Spanish literature and history (such as the search for the Fountain of Youth and the Don Juan legend). Thus, Hispanic students risked missing important components of their heritage.

bicultural identity
Maintaining one's original cultural identity while integrating oneself into the dominant culture

Ultimately, educators began to argue that the presence of students representing diverse cultures enriched and broadened the educational experience of all students. Pupils and teachers exposed to people from different backgrounds could better understand the world and gain greater sensitivity to the values and needs of others (Levin et al., 2012; Thijs & Verkuyten, 2013; Theodosiou-Zipiti & Lamprianou, 2016).

FOSTERING A BICULTURAL IDENTITY Most educators now agree that minority children should develop a **bicultural identity**, where schools support children's original cultural identities while also integrating them into the dominant culture. In this view, an individual lives as a member of two cultures, with two cultural identities, without having to choose one over the other (Oyserman et al., 2003; Vyas, 2004; Collins, 2012).

The best way to achieve this goal is not clear. Consider children who enter school speaking only Spanish. As noted, the traditional "melting-pot" technique would immerse them in classes taught in English while providing a crash course in English language (and little else) until the children gain a reasonable proficiency. Unfortunately, this approach has a major drawback: Until they are proficient, students fall further and further behind their peers (First & Cardenas, 1986).

E.D. Torial/Alamy Stock Photo

Pupils and teachers exposed to a diverse group could better understand the world and gain a greater sensitivity to the values and needs of others. What are some ways of developing greater sensitivity in the classroom?

More contemporary bicultural approaches encourage children to maintain membership in more than one culture. For a Spanish-speaking child, instruction would begin in Spanish and shift rapidly to include English. The school would also conduct a multicultural program for all children, where material on the cultures of all students is presented. Such instruction is meant to enhance the self-image of every student (Fowers & Davidov, 2006; Mok & Morris, 2012; Lourie, 2016).

Although most educational experts favor bicultural approaches, the general public does not always agree. For instance, the "English-only" movement mentioned previously seeks to prohibit school instruction in any non-English language. Which view will prevail remains to be seen.

SCHOOLING AROUND THE WORLD AND ACROSS GENDERS: WHO GETS EDUCATED? In the United States, as in most developed countries, a primary school education is both a universal right and a legal requirement. Virtually all children enjoy a free education through the 12th grade.

Children in other parts of the world are not always so fortunate. More than 160 million of the world's children do not even receive a primary education. An additional 100 million children are educated only to a level comparable to our elementary school, and close to a billion individuals (two-thirds of them women) are illiterate throughout their lives.

In almost all developing countries, fewer females than males receive formal education, a discrepancy found at every level of schooling. Even in developed countries, women lag behind men in their exposure to science and technological topics. These differences reflect widespread, deeply held cultural and parental biases that favor males over females. Educational levels in the United States are more nearly equal between men and women. Especially in the early years, boys and girls share equal access to opportunities.

Intelligence: Determining Individual Strengths

> "Why should you tell the truth?" "How far is Los Angeles from New York?" "A table is made of wood; a window of _____."
>
> As 10-year-old Hyacinth sat hunched over her desk, faced with a series of questions like these, she tried to guess the point of the test she was taking. Clearly, the test covered material not discussed by her fifth-grade teacher, Ms. White-Johnston.
>
> "What number comes next in this series: 1, 3, 7, 15, 31, _____?"
>
> As she worked through the test, she gave up trying to guess its rationale. She'd leave that to her teacher and simply try to figure out the correct answers.

Hyacinth was taking an intelligence test. It might surprise her to learn that others also questioned the meaning and importance of the test. Intelligence test items are painstakingly prepared, and the tests are designed to predict academic success (for reasons we'll soon discuss). Many developmentalists, however, harbor doubts that such tests are entirely appropriate for assessing intelligence.

Understanding just what intelligence means has proven a major challenge for researchers in defining what separates intelligent from unintelligent behavior. Although nonexperts have their own definitions (one survey found that laypersons view intelligence as three components: problem-solving ability, verbal ability, and social competence), it has been more difficult for experts to concur (Sternberg et al., 1981; Howe, 1997). Still, a general definition of intelligence is possible: **Intelligence** is the capacity to understand the world, think with rationality, and use resources effectively when faced with challenges (Wechsler, 1975).

intelligence
the capacity to understand the world, think with rationality, and use resources effectively when faced with challenges

To understand how researchers have variously approached the task of defining intelligence and devising *intelligence tests*, we need to consider some of the historical milestones in this area.

Intelligence Benchmarks: Differentiating the Intelligent from the Unintelligent

LO 5.11   Compare and contrast the different methods of assessing intelligence.

The Paris schools faced a problem as the 20th century began: Regular instruction was failing many students. These children—many of whom were mentally retarded—were seldom identified early enough to shift them to special classes. The French minister of instruction asked psychologist Alfred Binet to devise a method for identifying students who might benefit from special instruction.

BINET'S TEST Binet took a practical approach. Years of observation suggested that prior tests for intelligence—some based on reaction time or eyesight—were ineffectual. Binet, using a trial-and-error approach, administered items and tasks to students identified as either "bright" or "dull." He retained the tasks that the bright students completed correctly and the dull students failed. Tasks that did not discriminate were discarded. The end result was a test that reliably distinguished fast and slow learners.

Binet's pioneering efforts left three important legacies. The first was his pragmatic approach to constructing intelligence tests. Binet did not have theoretical preconceptions about what intelligence was. Instead, he used a trial-and-error approach to psychological measurement that continues to be the predominant approach to test construction. His definition of intelligence as *that which his test measured* has been adopted by many modern researchers, and it is particularly popular among test developers who wish to avoid arguments about the underlying nature of intelligence.

Binet's legacy links intelligence and school success. His approach to constructing a test ensured that intelligence—defined as performance on the test—and school success would be virtually identical. Thus, Binet's intelligence test, and today's tests that use his methods, are reasonable predictors of school performance. They do not, however, provide useful information for other attributes, such as social skills or personality traits, that are largely unrelated to academic proficiency.

Finally, Binet developed a method to link each intelligence test score with a **mental age**, the age of the children who, on average, achieved that score. If a 6-year-old girl scored 30 on the test, and this was the average score for 10-year-olds, her mental age would be 10. Similarly, a 15-year-old boy who scored a 90—matching the mean score for 15-year-olds—would have a mental age of 15 (Wasserman & Tulsky, 2005).

Although mental age indicates how students are performing relative to their peers, it does not permit adequate comparisons between students of different **chronological (or physical) ages**. By using mental age alone, for example, it would be assumed that a 15-year-old whose mental age is 17 would be as bright as a 6-year-old whose mental age is 8, when actually the 6-year-old shows a much greater *relative* intelligence.

The **intelligence quotient (IQ)**, a score that accounts for a student's mental *and* chronological age, provides a solution. The traditional method of calculating an IQ score uses the following formula, in which MA equals mental age and CA equals chronological age:

$$\text{IQ score} = \frac{\text{MA}}{\text{CA}} \times 100$$

As this formula demonstrates, people whose MA is equal to their CA will always have an IQ of 100. If the CA exceeds the MA—implying below-average intelligence—the score will be below 100, and if the CA is lower than the MA—suggesting above-average intelligence—the score will be above 100.

Using this formula, consider our example of a 15-year-old who scores a MA of 17. This student's IQ is $17/15 \times 100$, or 113. In comparison, the IQ of a 6-year-old scoring a mental age of 8 is $8/6 \times 100$, or 133—a higher IQ score.

IQ scores today are calculated in a more sophisticated manner and are known as *deviation IQ scores*. The average deviation IQ score remains at 100, but now, by the degree of deviation from this score, the proportion of people with similar scores can be calculated. For instance, about two-thirds of all people fall within 15 points of 100, scoring between 85 and 115. Beyond this range, the percentage of people in the same score category drops significantly.

MEASURING IQ: PRESENT-DAY APPROACHES TO INTELLIGENCE Since Binet, intelligence tests have become increasingly accurate measures of IQ, though most remain rooted in his original work. For example, one of the most widely used tests—the **Stanford-Binet Intelligence Scales, Fifth Edition (SB5)**—began as an American revision of Binet's original test. The test consists of age-appropriate items—for example, young children are asked about everyday activities or given complex figures to copy.

mental age
the typical intelligence level found for people at a given chronological age

chronological (or physical) age
the actual age of the child taking the intelligence test

intelligence quotient (IQ)
a score that accounts for a student's mental *and* chronological age

Stanford-Binet Intelligence Scales, Fifth Edition (SB5)
a test that consists of a series of items that vary according to the age of the person being tested

Older people are asked to explain proverbs, solve analogies, and describe similarities between word groups. Test-takers are given progressively more difficult problems until they are unable to proceed.

The **Wechsler Intelligence Scale for Children, Fifth Edition (WISC-V)** is another widely used test. The test (an offshoot of the Wechsler Adult Intelligence Scale) breaks the total score into measures of verbal and performance (or nonverbal) skills. As you can see from Figure 5-8, word problems are used to test skills such as comprehension,

Wechsler Intelligence Scale for Children, Fifth Edition (WISC-V)
a test for children that provides separate measures of verbal and performance (or nonverbal) skills, as well as a total score

Figure 5-8 Measuring Intelligence

The Wechsler Intelligence Scale for Children, Fifth Edition (WISC-V), includes items such as these. What do such items cover? What do they miss?

Name	Goal of Item	Example
Verbal Scale		
Information	Assess general information	How many nickels make a dime?
Comprehension	Assess understanding and evaluation of social norms and past experience	What is the advantage of keeping money in the bank?
Arithmetic	Assess math reasoning through verbal problems	If two buttons cost 15 cents, what will be the cost of a dozen buttons?
Similarities	Test understanding of how objects or concepts are alike, tapping abstract reasoning	In what way are an hour and a week alike?
Performance Scale		
Digit symbol	Assess speed of learning	Match symbols to numbers using key. 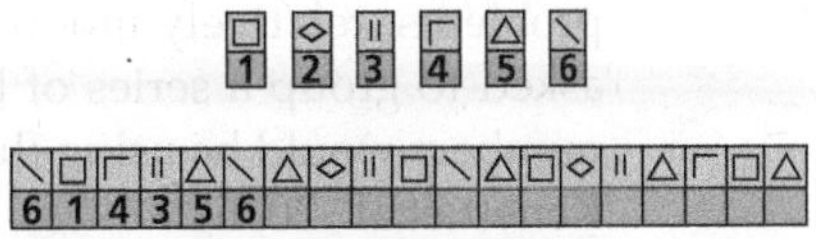
Picture completion	Visual memory and attention	Identify what is missing. 
Object assembly	Test understanding of relationship of parts to wholes	Put pieces together to form a whole. 

Kaufman Assessment Battery for Children, Second Edition (KABC-II)
an intelligence test that measures children's ability to integrate different stimuli simultaneously and to use sequential thinking

whereas typical nonverbal tasks are copying a complex design, sequencing pictures, and assembling objects. The test's separate portions make it easier to identify specific problems a test-taker may have. For example, significantly higher scores on the performance part than on the verbal part may indicate linguistic development difficulties (Zhu & Weiss, 2005; Wahlstrom et al., 2018).

The **Kaufman Assessment Battery for Children, Second Edition (KABC-II)** takes a different approach. It tests children's ability to integrate different kinds of stimuli simultaneously and to use sequential thinking. The KABC-II's special virtue is its flexibility. It allows the test-giver to use alternative wording or gestures, or even to pose questions in a different language, to maximize performance. This makes testing more valid and equitable for children to whom English is a second language (Kaufman et al., 2005; Drozdick et al., 2018).

What do the IQ scores mean? For most children, they are reasonable predictors of school performance. That's not surprising, given that intelligence tests were developed to identify students who were having difficulties (Sternberg & Grigorenko, 2002).

But the story differs for performance outside of school; for example, although people with higher scores tend to finish more years of schooling, once this is statistically controlled for, IQ scores do not closely relate to income and later success in life. Two people with different scores may both earn bachelor's degrees at the same college, but the person with a lower IQ might have a higher income and a more successful career. These difficulties with traditional IQ scores have led researchers to consider alternative approaches (McClelland, 1993).

WHAT IQ TESTS DON'T TELL: ALTERNATIVE CONCEPTIONS OF INTELLIGENCE

The intelligence tests schools use most today regard intelligence as a single factor, a unitary mental ability. This attribute is commonly called *g* (Spearman, 1927; Lubinski, 2004). Assumed to underlie performance on every aspect of intelligence, the *g* factor is what IQ tests presumably measure.

However, many theorists disagree that intelligence is unidimensional. Some developmentalists suggest that two kinds of intelligence exist: fluid and crystallized (Catell, 1987). **Fluid intelligence** reflects the ability to solve and reason about novel problems, relatively independent of past specific knowledge; for example, a student asked to group a series of letters according to some criterion or to remember a set of numbers would be using fluid intelligence (Shangguan & Shi, 2009; Ziegler et al., 2012; Kenett et al., 2016).

fluid intelligence
reflects the ability to solve and reason about novel problems

crystallized intelligence
the accumulation of information, skills, and strategies that people have learned through experience and that they can apply in problem-solving situations

In contrast, **crystallized intelligence** is the information, skills, and strategies that people have accumulated through experience. People solving a crossword puzzle are using crystallized intelligence because they are recalling specific words they have learned in the past (Hill et al., 2013; Thorsen, Gustafsson, & Cliffordson, 2014; Hülür et al., 2017).

Other theorists divide intelligence into even more parts. Psychologist Howard Gardner suggests that we have at least eight distinct intelligences, each relatively independent (see Figure 5-9). Gardner suggests that these intelligences operate together, depending on the activity we engage in (Chen & Gardner, 2005; Gardner & Moran, 2006; Roberts & Lipnevich, 2012).

> **From an educator's perspective:** Does Howard Gardner's theory of multiple intelligences suggest that classroom instruction should be modified from an emphasis on the traditional three Rs of reading, writing, and arithmetic?

Vygotsky, whose cognitive development approach we discussed previously, took a different approach to intelligence. He suggested we assess intelligence by looking not only at fully developed cognitive processes, but at those in current development as well. To do this, he contended that assessment tasks should involve cooperative interaction between the assessed individual and the assessor—a process called *dynamic assessment*. In short, intelligence is reflected both in how children perform on their own and how they perform when helped by adults (Vygotsky, 1926/1997; Lohman, 2005).

Psychologist Robert Sternberg (2003a, 2005), taking another approach, suggests intelligence is best viewed as information processing. In this view, how people store

Figure 5-9 Gardner's Eight Intelligences

Howard Gardner has theorized that there are eight distinct intelligences, each relatively independent.

SOURCE: Based on Walters & Gardner, 1986.

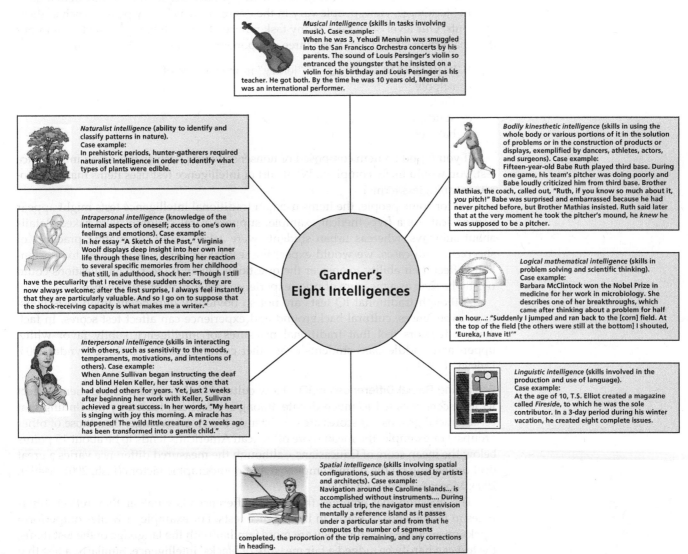

material in memory and later use it to solve intellectual tasks provides the most precise concept of intelligence. Rather than focusing on the subcomponents that make up the *structure* of intelligence, information-processing approaches examine the *processes* underlying intelligent behavior (Floyd, 2005).

Studies of the nature and speed of problem-solving processes show that people with higher intelligence levels differ from others in the number of problems they solve and the methods they use. People with high IQ scores spend more time on the initial stages of problem solving, retrieving relevant information from memory. In contrast, those who score lower tend to skip ahead and make less informed guesses. The processes used in solving problems may reflect important differences in intelligence (Sternberg, 2005).

Sternberg's work on information processing approaches led him to develop the **triarchic theory of intelligence**. In this model, three aspects of information processing denote intelligence: the componential, the experiential, and the contextual. The *componential* aspect reflects how efficiently people process and analyze information. Efficiency in these areas allows people to infer relationships among different parts of a problem, solve the problem, and then evaluate their solution. People with a strong componential element score highest on traditional tests of intelligence (Sternberg, 2005; Ekinci, 2014; Sternberg, 2016).

triarchic theory of intelligence
Sternberg's theory that intelligence is made up of three major components: componential, experiential, and contextual

The *experiential* element is the insightful component of intelligence. People with a strong experiential element can easily compare new material with what they know and can combine and relate known facts in novel and creative ways. Finally, the *contextual* element concerns practical intelligence, or ways of dealing with everyday demands.

In Sternberg's view, people vary in the degree to which they possess each of these elements. Our level of success at any task reflects the match between the task and our own pattern of strength on these three components (Sternberg, 2003b, 2008).

GROUP DIFFERENCES IN IQ   A "jontry" is an example of a

a. rulpow
b. flink
c. spudge
d. bakwoe

If you found an item composed of nonsense words such as this on an intelligence test, you would likely complain. What sort of intelligence test uses items that incorporate meaningless terms?

Yet for some people, the items used on traditional intelligence tests might appear nonsensical. As a hypothetical example, suppose rural children were asked details about subways, whereas urban students were asked about the mating practices of sheep. In both cases, we would expect the test-takers' prior experiences to substantially affect their ability to answer the questions. On an IQ test, such questions could rightly be seen as a measure of prior experience rather than of intelligence.

Although traditional IQ tests are not so obviously dependent upon test-takers' prior experiences, cultural background and experience can affect test scores. In fact, many educators feel that traditional measures of intelligence subtly favor white, upper- and middle-class students over other cultural groups (Ortiz & Dynda, 2005; Dale et al., 2014).

Explaining Racial Differences in IQ   How cultural background and experience affect IQ test scores has led to much debate among researchers, fueled by the finding that certain racial groups' IQ scores are consistently lower, on average, than those of other groups. For example, the mean score of African Americans tends to be about 15 points below the mean score of Caucasians—although the measured difference varies a great deal depending on the IQ test employed and demographic factors (Fish, 2001; Maller, 2003; Morin & Midlarsky, 2017).

The question that emerges from such differences is whether they reflect differences in intelligence or biases in intelligence tests. For example, if whites outperform blacks on an IQ test because they are more familiar with the language of the test items, the test can hardly be judged a fair measure of blacks' intelligence. Similarly, a test that solely used African American vernacular English would not be an impartial measure of intelligence for Caucasians.

How to interpret differences between the IQ test scores of different cultural groups is a major controversy in child development: To what degree is intelligence determined by heredity, and to what degree by environment? The social implications make this issue important. If intelligence is mostly hereditary and therefore largely fixed at birth, attempts to alter cognitive abilities, such as schooling, will have limited success. If intelligence is largely environmentally determined, modifying social and educational conditions is a more promising strategy to increase cognitive functioning (Weiss, 2003; Nisbett et al., 2012).

The *Bell Curve* Controversy   Although the relative contributions of heredity and environment to intelligence have been investigated for decades, the smoldering debate became a raging fire with the publication of a book by Richard J. Herrnstein and Charles Murray (1994), *The Bell Curve*. Herrnstein and Murray argue that the average 15-point IQ difference between whites and blacks is primarily a result of heredity. They also argue that this difference accounts for the higher rates of poverty, lower employment, and higher use of welfare among minority groups.

These conclusions met with outrage, and many researchers who examined the data used in the book came to quite different conclusions. Most developmentalists and psychologists argued that racial differences in measured IQ can be explained by environmental differences. In fact, mean IQ scores of black and white children are quite similar when various economic and social factors are statistically taken into account simultaneously. For instance, children from similar middle-class backgrounds, whether African American or Caucasian, tend to have similar IQ scores (Alderfer, 2003; Nisbett, 2005).

Critics also maintained there is little evidence that IQ causes poverty and other social ills. In fact, some critics suggested, as mentioned previously, that IQ scores were unrelated to later success in life (e.g., Reifman, 2000; Nisbett, 2005; Sternberg, 2005).

Finally, members of cultural and social minority groups may score lower than those in the majority group because of the biases of the tests. Traditional IQ tests may discriminate against minority groups who lack exposure to the environment majority group members have experienced (Fagan & Holland, 2007; Razani et al., 2007).

The issue of whether racial differences in IQ exist is highly controversial and ultimately relates to questions of the genetic and environmental determinants of intelligence.

Most traditional IQ tests are constructed using white, English-speaking, middle-class populations as their test subjects. Thus, children from different backgrounds may perform poorly on them—not because they are less intelligent, but because the questions are culturally biased in favor of the majority group. A classic study found that in one California school district, Mexican American students were 10 times more likely than whites to be placed in special education classes (Mercer, 1973; Hatton, 2002; U.S. Department of Education, 2016).

More recent findings show that nationally, twice as many black students as white students are classified as having mild intellectual disabilities, a difference attributed primarily to cultural bias and poverty. Although certain IQ tests (such as the System of Multicultural Pluralistic Assessment [SOMPA]) are designed to be valid regardless of cultural background, no test can be completely unbiased (Hatton, 2002; Hagmann-von Arx, Lemola, & Grob, 2018).

In short, most experts were not convinced by *The Bell Curve*'s contention that genetic factors largely determine differences in group IQ scores. Still, we cannot put the issue to rest because it is impossible to design a definitive experiment to determine the cause of these differences. (One cannot ethically assign children to different living conditions to find the effects of environment, nor genetically control or alter intelligence levels in unborn children.)

Today, IQ is seen as the product of *both* nature and nurture interacting in a complex manner. Genes are seen to affect experiences, and experiences are viewed as influencing the expression of genes. Psychologist Eric Turkheimer found evidence that although environmental factors play a larger role in the IQ of poor children, genes are more influential for affluent children (Harden, Turkheimer, & Loehlin, 2007; Turkheimer et al., 2017).

Ultimately, determining the absolute degree to which intelligence is influenced by genetic and environmental factors may be less important than improving children's living conditions and educational experiences. Enriching the quality of children's environments will better permit all children to reach their full potential and to maximize their contributions to society (Posthuma & de Geus, 2006; Nisbett et al., 2012).

Below and Above Intelligence Norms: Intellectual Disabilities and Intellectual Giftedness

LO 5.12 **Summarize the approaches to educating children with intellectual disabilities and children who are intellectually gifted in middle childhood.**

Although Connie kept pace with her peers in kindergarten, by first grade, she was academically the slowest in almost every subject. She tried hard but it took her longer than the others to absorb new material, and she regularly required special attention to keep up with the class.

In some areas, though, she excelled: When asked to draw or produce something with her hands, her performance exceeded her classmates'. She produced beautiful work that was much admired. The other students in the class felt that there was something different about Connie, but they couldn't identify the source of the difference and spent little time pondering the issue.

Connie's parents and teacher, though, knew what made her special. Extensive testing in kindergarten had shown that Connie's intelligence was well below normal, and she was officially classified as a special needs student.

If Connie had been attending school before 1975, she would most likely have been placed in a special needs classroom as soon as her low IQ was identified. Such classes, consisting of students with a range of afflictions, including emotional difficulties, severe reading problems, and physical disabilities such as multiple sclerosis, as well as those with lower IQs, were usually kept separate from the regular educational process.

All that changed in 1975 when Congress passed Public Law 94–142, the Education for All Handicapped Children Act, which was followed up by the Individuals with Disabilities Education Act (IDEA) in 2004. The intent of the laws—an intent largely realized—was to ensure that children with special needs were educated in the **least restrictive environment**, that is, the setting most similar to that of children without special needs (Rozalski, Stewart, & Miller, 2010; IDEA, 2018).

In practice, the law has integrated children with special needs into regular classrooms and activities to the greatest extent possible, as long as doing so is educationally beneficial. Children are to be removed from the regular classroom only for those subjects specifically affected by their exceptionality; for all other subjects, they are to be taught in regular classrooms. Of course, some children with severe handicaps still need a mostly or entirely separate education. But the law integrates exceptional children and typical children to the fullest extent possible (Yell, 2019).

This approach to special education, designed to minimize the segregation of exceptional students, is called mainstreaming. In **mainstreaming**, exceptional children are integrated as much as possible into the regular education system and are provided with a broad range of alternatives (Belkin, 2004; Crosland & Dunlap, 2012).

The benefits of mainstreaming have led some professionals to promote an alternative educational model known as full inclusion. *Full inclusion* is the integration of all students, even those with the most severe disabilities, into regular classes. In such a system, separate special education programs would cease to operate. Full inclusion is controversial, and it remains to be seen how widespread such a practice will become (Mangiatordi, 2012; Greenstein, 2016; Bešić et al., 2017).

Regardless of whether they are educated using mainstreaming or full inclusion, children whose intelligence is significantly beyond the typical range represent a challenge for educators. We will consider both those who are below and those who are above the norms.

BELOW THE NORM: INTELLECTUAL DISABILITY Approximately 1 to 3 percent of the school-age population is considered to be intellectually disabled. Estimates vary so widely because the most commonly accepted definition of intellectual disability, which was previously referred to professionally as *mental retardation*—a term that is still used frequently—is one that leaves a great deal of room for interpretation. According to the American Association on Intellectual and Developmental Disabilities, **intellectual disability** is characterized by significant limitations both in intellectual functioning and in adaptive behavior, which covers many everyday social and practical skills (American Association on Intellectual and Developmental Disabilities, 2012).

Most cases of intellectual disability are classified as *familial intellectual disability*, in which no cause is apparent beyond a history of retardation in the family. In other cases, there is a clear biological cause. The most common such causes are *fetal alcohol syndrome*, resulting from the mother's use of alcohol while pregnant, and *Down syndrome*, caused by the presence of an extra chromosome. Birth complications, such as a temporary lack of oxygen, may also produce retardation (Plomin, 2005; Manning & Hoyme, 2007).

---

least restrictive environment
the setting that is most similar to that of children without special needs

mainstreaming
an educational approach in which exceptional children are integrated to the extent possible into the traditional educational system and are provided with a broad range of educational alternatives

intellectual disability
a disability characterized by significant limitations both in intellectual functioning and in adaptive behavior, which covers many everyday social and practical skills

Although limitations in intellectual functioning can be measured in a relatively straightforward manner—using standard IQ tests—it is more difficult to determine how to gauge limitations in other areas. Ultimately, this imprecision leads to a lack of uniformity in the ways experts apply the label of "intellectual disability." Furthermore, it has resulted in significant variation in the abilities of people who are categorized as experiencing intellectual disability. Accordingly, intellectually disabled people range from those who can be taught to work and function with little special attention to those who are virtually untrainable and who never develop speech or such basic motor skills as crawling or walking.

This girl with Down syndrome is mainstreamed into this class.

The vast majority of the intellectually disabled—some 90 percent—have relatively low levels of deficits. Classified with **mild intellectual disability**, they score in the range of 50 or 55 to 70 on IQ tests. Typically, their retardation is not even identified before they reach school, although their early development often is slower than average. Once they enter elementary school, their retardation and their need for special attention usually become apparent, as it did with Connie, the first grader profiled at the beginning of this discussion. With appropriate training, these students can reach a third- to sixth-grade educational level, and although they cannot carry out complex intellectual tasks, they are able to hold jobs and function quite independently and successfully.

mild intellectual disability
intellectual disability in which IQ scores fall in the range of 50 or 55 to 70

Intellectual and adaptive limitations become more apparent, however, at higher levels of mental retardation. People whose IQ scores range from 35 or 40 to 50 or 55 are classified with **moderate intellectual disability**. Composing between 5 and 10 percent of those classified as intellectually disabled, those who are moderately intellectually disabled display distinctive behavior early in their lives. They are slow to develop language skills, and their motor development is also affected. Regular schooling is usually not effective in training people with moderate intellectual disability to acquire academic skills because generally they are unable to progress beyond the second-grade level. Still, they are capable of learning occupational and social skills, and they can learn to travel independently to familiar places. Typically, they require moderate levels of supervision.

moderate intellectual disability
intellectual disability in which IQ scores range from 35 or 40 to 50 or 55

At the most significant levels of intellectual disability—those who are classified with **severe intellectual disability** (IQs ranging from 20 or 25 to 35 or 40) and **profound intellectual disability** (IQs below 20 or 25)—the ability to function is severely limited. Usually, such people have little or no speech, have poor motor control, and may need 24-hour nursing care. At the same time, however, some people with severe intellectual disability are capable of learning basic self-care skills, such as dressing and eating, and they may even develop the potential to become partially independent as adults. Still, the need for relatively high levels of care continues throughout the life span, and most severely and profoundly intellectually disabled people are institutionalized for the majority of their lives.

severe intellectual disability
intellectual disability in which IQ scores range from 20 or 25 to 35 or 40

profound intellectual disability
intellectual disability in which IQ scores fall below 20 or 25

ABOVE THE NORM: THE GIFTED AND TALENTED

Amy Leibowitz picked up reading at age 3. By 5, she was writing her own books. First grade bored her within a week. As her school had no program for gifted children, it was suggested she skip to second grade. From there, she went to fifth grade. Her parents were proud but concerned. When they asked the fifth-grade teacher where she felt Amy really belonged, the teacher said she was ready, academically, for high school.

It sometimes surprises people that the gifted and talented are considered to have a form of exceptionality. Yet 3 to 5 percent of such children present special challenges of their own.

There is no formal definition of **gifted and talented** students. However, the federal government considers the term *gifted* to include "children who give evidence of high performance capability in areas such as intellectual, creative, artistic, leadership capacity, or specific academic fields, and who require services or activities not ordinarily

gifted and talented
children who show evidence of high performance capability in areas such as intellectual, creative, artistic, leadership capacity, or specific academic fields

provided by the school in order to fully develop such capabilities" (Ninety-Seventh Congress, 1981). In addition to intellectual exceptionality, unusual potential in non-academic areas is also included in the concept. Gifted and talented children, no less than students with low IQs, warrant special concern—although programs for them are often the first to be dropped when schools face budgetary problems (Schemo, 2004; Mendoza, 2006; Olszewski-Kubilius & Thomson, 2013).

Despite the stereotype that the gifted are "unsociable," "poorly adjusted," and "neurotic," research suggests that highly intelligent people tend to be outgoing, well adjusted, and popular (Bracken & Brown, 2006; Shaunessy et al., 2006; Cross et al., 2008).

For instance, one landmark, long-term study of 1,500 gifted students, which began in the 1920s, found that the gifted were healthier, better coordinated, and psychologically better adjusted than their less intelligent classmates. Furthermore, they received more awards and distinctions, earned more money, and made many more contributions in art and literature than the average person. By the time they had reached age 40, they had collectively produced more than 90 books, 375 plays and short stories, and 2,000 articles, and they had registered more than 200 patents. Perhaps not surprisingly, they reported greater satisfaction with their lives than the nongifted (Reis & Renzulli, 2004; Duggan & Friedman, 2014).

Yet being gifted and talented is no guarantee of school success. The verbal abilities that allow the expression of ideas and feelings can equally voice glib and persuasive statements that happen to be inaccurate. Furthermore, teachers sometimes misinterpret the humor, novelty, and creativity of unusually gifted children and regard their intellectual fervor as disruptive or inappropriate. And peers may be unsympathetic: Some very bright children try to hide their intelligence in an effort to fit in (Swiatek, 2002).

Educators have devised two approaches to teaching the gifted and talented: acceleration and enrichment. **Acceleration** allows gifted students to move ahead at their own pace, even if this means skipping grade levels. The materials in acceleration programs are not always different; they may simply be provided at a faster pace than for the average student (Wells, Lohman, & Marron, 2009; Wood et al., 2010; Lee, Olszewski-Kubilius, & Thomson, 2012).

An alternative approach is **enrichment**, through which students are kept at grade level but are enrolled in special programs and given individual activities to allow greater depth of study. In enrichment, the material differs not only in the timing of its presentation, but in its sophistication as well. Thus, enrichment materials are designed to provide an intellectual challenge to the gifted student, encouraging higher-order thinking (Worrell, Szarko, & Gabelko, 2001; Rotigel, 2003).

acceleration

special programs that allow gifted students to move ahead at their own pace, even if this means skipping to higher grade levels

enrichment

an approach through which students are kept at grade level but are enrolled in special programs and given individual activities to allow greater depth of study on a given topic

---

Review, Check, and Apply

Review

LO 5.7 Identify and summarize the major theoretical approaches to cognitive development in middle childhood.

Piaget believed school-age children are in the concrete operational stage, whereas information-processing approaches focus on quantitative improvements in memory and in the sophistication of the mental programs children use. Vygotsky suggested school-age children should have the opportunity to experiment and participate actively with their peers in their learning.

LO 5.8 Summarize the development of language during middle childhood, and explain the cognitive advantages bilingualism offers.

As language develops, vocabulary, syntax, and pragmatics improve; metalinguistic awareness grows; and language is used as a self-control device. Bilingual students tend to show greater metalinguistic awareness, grasp the rules of language more explicitly, and demonstrate great cognitive sophistication.

LO 5.9 Describe the five stages of reading, and compare teaching approaches.

The five stages of reading include Stage 0 (from birth to first grade) during which children may learn letter names and recognize a few familiar words. Stage 1, the first real type of reading, largely involves children completing the job of learning letter names and the sounds that go with them. In Stage 2, children learn to read aloud with fluency. Reading becomes a means to an end, a way to learn, in Stage 3. And by Stage 4, children are able to read and process information that reflects multiple viewpoints. There is growing evidence that code-based approaches to teaching reading are more successful than the whole language approach.

LO 5.10 Summarize the various trends in U.S. education.

U.S. schools have returned in recent decades to a focus on traditional academic skills. Most educators agree that schools should help minority children develop a bicultural identity, where children's original cultural identities are supported while also integrating them into the dominant culture. Schooling is considered a legal right in the United States and many other countries, but millions of the world's children do not receive even a primary education.

LO 5.11 Compare and contrast the different methods of assessing intelligence.

Measuring intelligence has traditionally been a matter of testing skills that promote academic success. Among tests used to measure intelligence are the Wechsler Intelligence Scale for Children, Fifth Edition, (WISC-V) and the Kaufman Assessment Battery for Children, Second Edition (KABC-II). Recent theories of intelligence suggest there may be several distinct intelligences or several components of intelligence that reflect different ways of processing information.

LO 5.12 Summarize the approaches to educating children with intellectual disabilities and children who are intellectually gifted in middle childhood.

By law, children with special needs must be educated in the least restrictive environment. This has led to mainstreaming, which integrates such children into the regular education system as much as possible. The needs of gifted and talented children are sometimes addressed through acceleration and enrichment programs.

Check Yourself

1. Vygotsky proposed that cognitive advances take place when children are exposed to information within their _____.

   a. sphere of logic
   b. zone of proximal development
   c. region of metamemory
   d. domain of control strategies

2. According to the _____ approach to reading, reading should be taught by presenting the basic skills underlying reading. Examples include phonics and how letters and words are combined to make words.

   a. whole-language
   b. linguistic
   c. code-based
   d. dynamic

3. According to Steinberg's triarchic theory of intelligence, the three aspects of information processing are _____.

   a. contextual, referential, and crystallization
   b. developmental, componential, and structural
   c. experiential, experimental, and judgmental
   d. componential, experiential, and contextual

4. For children whose intelligence falls below the normal range, the recommendation from the Education for All Handicapped Children Act is that they be educated in _____ environment.

   a. a separate but equal
   b. the most restrictive
   c. the least restrictive
   d. a needs-oriented

Applying Lifespan Development

How do fluid and crystallized intelligence interact? Which of the two is likely to be more influenced by genetics and which by environment? Why?

Module 5.3

Social and Personality Development in Middle Childhood

When 9-year-old Matt Donner's family relocated from Topeka, Kansas, to Providence, Rhode Island, after his father was promoted, Matt was both excited and fearful. Moving to a new part of the country was exciting. But Matt had been a quiet and unassuming fourth grader in his old hometown with a small circle of friends. How well would he make the adjustment to fifth grade in his new home?

Not well, it turns out. His shy manner got in the way of making new friends. Instead of sitting with other kids at lunchtime, Matt sat alone with a book. "They all knew each other already. That made it really hard," Matt lamented. "I just didn't fit in."

Matt's regional accent and small stature didn't help matters. It wasn't long before classmates were mocking his speech and tripping him in the halls. His locker was broken into so many times that Matt gave up using it and just carried his books with him. Teachers either didn't care, or more likely didn't notice—the bullying rarely happened in front of them. Matt's greatest fear was that his parents would find out and be disappointed in him. He didn't want them to know that he had let himself become a victim.

The Developing Self

> Karla Holler sits comfortably in the treehouse she built in a tall apple tree growing in her suburban home's backyard. At age 9, she's just finished the latest addition, nailing pieces of wood together, expertly wielding a hammer. She and her father started building the treehouse when she was 5 years old, and she has been making small additions to it ever since. By this point, she has developed a clear sense of pride regarding the treehouse, and she spends hours in it, savoring the privacy it provides.

Karla's growing sense of competence is reflected in this passage. Conveying what psychologist Erik Erikson calls "industriousness," Karla's quiet pride in her accomplishment illustrates one of the ways in which children's views of themselves evolve.

A Different Mirror: The Changing Ways Children View Themselves

LO 5.13   Summarize how children's view of themselves changes in middle childhood, and explain how this shift affects their self-esteem.

In the preschool years, a child might answer the question "Who are you?" by saying, "I'm tall for my age and I can run fast." Thanks to the rapid cognitive advances of middle childhood, that same child at age 10 might reply, "I'm funny, kind, and very good at piano." Children also begin to reflect on their traits and abilities: to judge themselves and make self-evaluations.

industry-versus-inferiority stage
according to Erik Erikson, the period from age 6 to 12 characterized by a focus on efforts to attain competence in meeting the challenges presented by parents, peers, school, and the other complexities of the modern world

PSYCHOSOCIAL DEVELOPMENT IN MIDDLE CHILDHOOD: INDUSTRY VERSUS INFERIORITY   According to Erikson, middle childhood is largely about competence. Lasting roughly from ages 6 to 12, the **industry-versus-inferiority stage** is characterized by efforts to meet the challenges presented by parents, peers, school, and the complex modern world.

During this period, children direct their energies to mastering the enormous body of information presented in school and making a place for themselves in their social worlds. Success in this stage brings feelings of mastery and a growing sense of competence, like those expressed by Karla regarding her building experience. On the other hand, difficulties in this stage lead to feelings of failure and inadequacy. As a result, children may withdraw from academic pursuits, showing less interest and motivation to excel, and from interactions with peers.

The sense of industry that children such as Karla attain at this stage has lasting effects. One study examined how childhood industriousness and hard work were related to adult behavior by following a group of 450 men over a 35-year period, starting in early childhood (Vaillant & Vaillant, 1981). The men who were most industrious and hardworking as children were most successful as adults, both professionally and personally. In fact, childhood industriousness was more closely associated with adult success than was intelligence or family background.

UNDERSTANDING ONE'S SELF: A NEW RESPONSE TO "WHO AM I?"   During middle childhood, children seek to answer the question "Who am I?" Although the question will assume greater urgency in adolescence, elementary-age children still try to find their place in the world.

The cognitive advances discussed in the previous module aid children in their quest for self-understanding. They begin to view themselves less in terms of external, physical attributes and more in terms of psychological traits (Aronson & Bialostok, 2016; Thomaes, Brummelman & Sedikides, 2017).

According to Erik Erikson, middle childhood encompasses the industry-versus-inferiority stage, characterized by a focus on meeting the challenges presented by the world.

Rob Marmion/Shutterstock

For instance, 6-year-old Carey describes herself as "a fast runner and good at drawing"—characteristics dependent on motor skills in external activities. In contrast, 11-year-old Meiping characterizes herself as "pretty smart, friendly, and helpful to my friends." Because of her increasing cognitive skills, Meiping's view of herself is based on psychological characteristics, inner traits that are more abstract.

Children's views of who they are also become more complex. In Erikson's view, children are seeking endeavors where they can be successfully industrious. As they get older, children discover their strengths and weaknesses. Ten-year-old Ginny, for instance, comes to understand she is good at arithmetic but not good at spelling; 11-year-old Alberto decides he is good at softball but lacks the stamina to play soccer well.

Children's self-concepts become divided into personal and academic spheres. They evaluate themselves in four major areas, each of which can be broken down further; for example, the nonacademic self-concept includes physical appearance, peer relations, and physical ability, whereas the academic self-concept is similarly divided. Research on students' self-concepts in English, mathematics, and nonacademic realms shows that the separate realms do not always correlate, although overlap exists. For example, a child who sees herself as a star math student will not necessarily feel she is great at English (Marsh & Hau, 2003; Ehm et al., 2013; Lohbeck, Tietjens, & Bund, 2016).

SELF-ESTEEM: DEVELOPING A POSITIVE—OR NEGATIVE—VIEW OF ONESELF

Children don't dispassionately view themselves as just a list of physical and psychological traits. Instead, they judge themselves as being good or bad in particular ways. **Self-esteem** is an individual's overall and specific self-evaluation. Whereas self-concept reflects beliefs and cognitions about the self (*I am good at trumpet; I am not so good at social studies*), self-esteem is more emotionally oriented (*Everybody thinks I'm a nerd*) (Bracken & Lamprecht, 2003; Mruk, 2013).

self-esteem
an individual's overall and specific positive and negative self-evaluation

Self-esteem develops in important ways during middle childhood. As noted, children increasingly compare themselves to others, assessing how they measure up to society's standards. They also increasingly develop their own internal standards of success, and measure how well they compare to those. One advance that occurs in this period is that, like self-concept, self-esteem becomes increasingly differentiated. At age 7, most children have self-esteem that reflects a global, fairly simple view of themselves. Overall positive self-esteem makes them believe they are relatively good at all things. If their overall self-esteem is negative, they feel inadequate at most things (Lerner et al., 2005; Coelho, Marchante & Jimerson, 2016).

As children move into middle childhood, however, their self-esteem is higher in some areas and lower in others; for example, a boy's overall self-esteem may be positive in some areas (such as artistic ability) and negative in others (such as athletic skills).

Change and Stability in Self-Esteem Overall self-esteem is generally high during middle childhood, but begins to decline around age 12, affected mainly by the change of schools: Students leaving elementary school and entering either middle school or junior high school show a decline in self-esteem, which then gradually rises again (Robins & Trzesniewski, 2005; Poorthuis et al., 2014).

In contrast, some children have chronically low self-esteem. Children with low self-esteem face a tough road, in part because their self-esteem becomes enmeshed in a cycle of failure that grows increasingly difficult to break. Assume, for instance, that Harry, a student with chronically low self-esteem, is facing an important test. Because of his low self-esteem, he expects to do poorly. As a consequence, he is quite anxious—so anxious that he is unable to concentrate well and study effectively. Furthermore, he may decide not to study much because he figures that if he's going to do badly anyway, why bother studying?

Of course, Harry's anxiety and lack of effort bring the result he expected: He does poorly on the test. This failure confirms Harry's expectation, reinforces his low self-esteem, and the cycle of failure continues.

Students with high self-esteem fall into a cycle of success. Higher expectations lead to more effort and less anxiety, increasing the odds of success. In turn, success affirms the high self-esteem that began the cycle.

> **From an educator's perspective:** What can teachers do to help children whose low self-esteem is causing them to fail? How can this cycle of failure be broken?

Parents can help break the cycle of failure by promoting their children's self-esteem. The best way to do this is through the use of the *authoritative* childrearing style that we discussed in Chapter 4. Authoritative parents are warm and emotionally supportive, while still setting clear limits for their children's behavior. In contrast, other parenting styles have less positive effects on self-esteem. Parents who are highly punitive and controlling send a message to their children that they are untrustworthy and unable to make good decisions—a message that can undermine children's sense of adequacy. Highly indulgent parents, who indiscriminately praise and reinforce their children regardless of their actual performance, can create a false sense of self-esteem in their children, which ultimately may be just as damaging to children (Taylor et al., 2012; Raboteg-Saric & Sakic, 2013; Harris et al., 2015).

Race and Self-Esteem   If you were a member of a racial group that routinely experienced prejudice and discrimination, your self-esteem would likely be affected. Early research confirmed that hypothesis and found that African Americans had lower self-esteem than Caucasians. A set of pioneering studies a generation ago found that African American children shown black and white dolls preferred the white dolls over the black ones (Clark & Clark, 1947). The interpretation drawn from the study: The self-esteem of the African American children was low.

However, more recent research has shown these assumptions to be overstated. The picture is more complex. For example, although white children initially show higher self-esteem, black children begin to show slightly higher self-esteem than white children around age 11. This shift occurs as African American children become more identified with their racial group, develop more complex views of racial identity, and increasingly view the positive aspects of their group membership (Zeiders, Umaña-Taylor, & Derlan, 2013; Sprecher, Brooks, & Avogo, 2013; Davis et al., 2017).

Hispanic children also show an increase in self-esteem toward the end of middle childhood, although even in adolescence their self-esteem still trails that of whites. In contrast, Asian American children show the opposite pattern: Their self-esteem in elementary school is higher than that of whites and blacks, but by the end of childhood, it is lower than that of whites (Verkuyten, 2008; Kapke, Gerdis, & Lawton, 2017).

One explanation for the complex relationship between self-esteem and minority group status comes from *social identity theory*. According to the theory, minority group members are likely to accept the majority group's negative views only if they perceive that there is little possibility of changing the power and status differences between the groups. If minority group members feel that prejudice and discrimination can be reduced, and they blame society for the prejudice and not themselves, self-esteem should not differ between majority and minority groups (Tajfel & Turner, 2004; Thompson, Briggs-King, & LaTouche-Howard, 2012).

In fact, as group pride and ethnic awareness on the part of minority group members has grown, differences in self-esteem between members of different ethnic groups have narrowed. This trend has been supported by increased sensitivity to the importance of multiculturalism (Lee, 2005; Tatum, 2017). (For another look at aspects of multiculturalism, see the *Cultural Dimensions* box.)

Knape/Getty Images

In pioneering research conducted several decades ago, African American girls' preference for white dolls was viewed as an indication of low self-esteem. More recent evidence, however, suggests that whites and African American children show little difference in self-esteem.

Cultural Dimensions

Are Children of Immigrant Families Well Adjusted?

Immigration to the United States has risen significantly in the past 30 years. Children in immigrant families account for almost 25 percent of children in the United States. Children of immigrant families are the fastest-growing segment of children in the country (Hernandez et al., 2008).

In many ways, children of immigrants fare quite well. In fact, in some ways they are better off than their nonimmigrant peers. For example, they tend to have equal or better grades in school than children whose parents were born in the United States. Psychologically, they also do quite well, showing similar levels of self-esteem as nonimmigrant children, although they do report feeling less popular and less in control of their lives (Kao, 2000; Driscoll, Russell, & Crockett, 2008; Jung & Zhang, 2016).

On the other hand, many children of immigrants face challenges. Their parents often have limited education, and they work at jobs that pay poorly. Unemployment rates are often higher for immigrants than the general population. In addition, parental English proficiency may be lower. Many children of immigrants lack good health insurance (Hernandez et al., 2008; Turney & Kao, 2009).

However, even the immigrant children who are not financially well off are often more highly motivated to succeed and place greater value on education than do children in nonimmigrant families. In addition, many immigrant children come from societies that emphasize collectivism, and consequently they may feel more obligation and duty toward their family to succeed. Finally, their country of origin may give some immigrant children a strong enough cultural identity to prevent them from adopting undesirable "American" behaviors—such

as materialism or selfishness (Fuligni & Yoshikawa, 2003; Suárez-Orozco, Suárez-Orozco, & Todorova, 2008).

During the middle childhood years, it thus appears that children in immigrant families often do quite well in the United States. The story is less clear, however, when immigrant children reach adolescence and adulthood. For instance, some research shows higher rates of obesity (a key indicator of physical health) in adolescents. Research is just beginning to clarify how effectively immigrants cope over the course of the life span (Fuligni & Fuligni, 2008; Perreira & Ornelas, 2011; Fuligni, 2012).

Ira Berger/Alamy Stock Photo

Immigrant children tend to fare quite well in the United States, partly because many come from societies that emphasize collectivism, and consequently they may feel more obligation and duty to their family to succeed. What are some other cultural differences that can lead to the success of immigrant children?

Moral Development

LO 5.14   Identify the six stages in Kohlberg's theory of moral development, and compare and contrast them with Gilligan's sequence of stages.

> Your wife is near death from an unusual kind of cancer. One drug exists that the physicians think might save her—a form of radium that a scientist in a nearby city has recently developed. The drug, though, is expensive to manufacture, and the scientist is charging 10 times what the drug costs him to make. He pays $1,000 for the radium and charges $10,000 for a small dose. You have gone to everyone you know to borrow money, but you can only get $2,500—one-quarter of what you need. You've told the scientist that your wife is dying and asked him to sell it more cheaply or let you pay later. But the scientist has said, "No, I discovered the drug and I'm going to make money from it." In desperation, you consider breaking into the scientist's laboratory to steal the drug for your wife. Should you do it?

According to developmental psychologist Lawrence Kohlberg and his colleagues, the answer that children give to this question reveals central aspects of their sense of morality and justice. He suggests that people's responses to moral dilemmas such as this one reveal their stage of moral development—as well as information about their level of cognitive development (Colby & Kohlberg, 1987; Buon, Habib & Frey, 2017).

Kohlberg contends that people pass through stages as their sense of justice evolves and the reasoning they use to make moral judgments changes. Younger school-age children tend to think in terms of either concrete, unvarying rules ("It is always wrong to steal" or "I'll be punished if I steal") or the rules of society ("Good people don't steal" or "What if everyone stole?").

By adolescence, however, individuals can reason on a higher plane, typically having reached Piaget's stage of formal operations. They are capable of comprehending abstract, formal principles of morality, and they consider broader issues of morality and of right and wrong in cases like the one just presented. ("Stealing may be acceptable if you are following your own conscience and doing the right thing.")

Kohlberg suggests that moral development emerges in a three-level sequence, further subdivided into six stages (see Table 5-1). At the lowest level, *preconventional*

Table 5-1 Kohlberg's Sequence of Moral Reasoning

Level	Stage	In Favor of Stealing	Against Stealing
LEVEL 1	**STAGE 1**		
Preconventional morality The main considerations are the avoidance of punishment and the desire for rewards.	Obedience and punishment orientation: People obey rules to avoid being punished. Obedience is its own reward.	"You shouldn't just let your wife die. People will blame you for not doing enough, and they'll blame the scientist for not selling you the drug for less money."	"You can't steal the drug because you'll be arrested and go to jail. Even if you aren't caught, you'll feel guilty and you'll always worry that the police may figure out what you did."
	STAGE 2		
	Reward orientation: People obey rules to earn rewards for their own benefit.	"Even if you get caught, the jury will understand and give you a short sentence. Meanwhile, your wife is alive. And if you're stopped before you get the drug to your wife, you could probably just return the drug without penalty."	"You shouldn't steal the drug because you're not responsible for your wife's cancer. If you get caught, your wife will still die and you'll be in jail."
LEVEL 2	**STAGE 3**		
Conventional morality Membership in society becomes important. People behave in ways that will win the approval of others.	"Good boy" morality: People want to be respected by others and try to do what they're supposed to do.	"Who will blame you if you steal a life-saving drug? But if you just let your wife die, you won't be able to hold your head up in front of your family or your neighbors."	"If you steal the drug, everyone will treat you like a criminal. They will wonder why you couldn't have found some other way to save your wife."
	STAGE 4		
	Authority and social-order-maintaining morality: People believe that only society, not individuals, can determine what is right. Obeying society's rules is right in itself.	"A husband has certain responsibilities toward his wife. If you want to live an honorable life, you can't let fear of the consequences get in the way of saving her. If you ever want to sleep again, you have to save her."	"You shouldn't let your concern for your wife cloud your judgment. Stealing the drug may feel right at the moment, but you'll live to regret breaking the law."
LEVEL 3	**STAGE 5**		
Postconventional morality People accept that there are certain ideals and principles of morality that must govern our actions. These ideals are more important than any particular society's rules.	Morality of contract, individual rights, and democratically accepted law: People rightly feel obligated to follow the agreed rules of society. But as societies develop over time, rules have to be updated to make societal changes reflect underlying social principles.	"If you simply follow the law, you will violate the underlying principle of saving your wife's life. If you do take the drug, society will understand your actions and respect them. You can't let an outdated law prevent you from doing the right thing."	"Rules represent society's thinking on the morality of actions. You can't let your short-term emotions interfere with the more permanent rules of society. If you do, society will judge you negatively, and in the end you will lose self-respect."
	STAGE 6		
	Morality of individual principles and conscience: People accept that laws are attempts to write down specific applications of universal moral principles. Individuals must test these laws against their consciences, which tend to express an inborn sense of those principles.	"If you allow your wife to die, you will have obeyed the letter of the law, but you will have violated the universal principle of life preservation that resides within your conscience. You will blame yourself forever if your wife dies because you obeyed an imperfect law."	"If you become a thief, your conscience will blame you for putting your own interpretation of moral issues above the legitimate rule of law. You will have betrayed your own standards of morality."

SOURCE: Based on Kohlberg, 1969.

morality (stages 1 and 2), people follow rigid rules based on punishments or rewards (e.g., a student might evaluate the moral dilemma in the story by saying it was not worth stealing the drug because you could go to jail.)

In the next level, *conventional morality* (stages 3 and 4), people approach moral problems as good, responsible members of society. Some would decide *against* stealing the drug because they would feel guilty or dishonest for violating social norms. Others would decide *in favor* of stealing the drug because they would be unable to face others if they did nothing. All of these people would be reasoning at the conventional level of morality.

Finally, individuals using *postconventional morality* (stages 5 and 6) invoke universal moral principles that are considered broader than the rules of their particular society. People who would condemn themselves if they did not steal the drug because they would be violating their own moral principles are reasoning at the postconventional level.

Kohlberg's theory proposes that people move through the stages in a fixed order and are unable to reach the highest stage until adolescence because of deficits in cognitive development before then (Kurtines & Gewirtz, 1987). However, not everyone is presumed to reach the highest stages; Kohlberg found that postconventional reasoning is relatively rare.

Although Kohlberg's theory provides a good account of the development of moral *judgments*, the links with moral *behavior* are less strong. Still, students at higher stages are less likely to engage in antisocial behavior at school and in the community. One experiment found that 15 percent of students who reasoned at the postconventional level cheated when given the opportunity, compared to more than half of students at lower levels. Though those at higher levels cheated less, they still cheated. Clearly, knowing what is right is not the same as acting that way (Semerci, 2006; Prohaska, 2012; Wu & Liu, 2014).

Kohlberg's theory has also been criticized because it is based solely on observations of Western cultures. In fact, cross-cultural research finds that those in more industrialized, technologically advanced cultures move through the stages more rapidly than members of nonindustrialized countries. One explanation is that Kohlberg's higher stages are based on moral reasoning involving governmental and societal institutions such as the police and court system. In less industrialized areas, morality may be based more on relationships between people. In short, the nature of morality may differ in diverse cultures, and Kohlberg's theory is more suited for Western cultures (Fu et al., 2007).

In addition, developmental psychologist Elliot Turiel has argued that Kohlberg did not sufficiently distinguish moral reasoning from other sorts of reasoning. In Turiel's view, called *moral domain theory*, he argues that children distinguish between the domains of social conventional reasoning and moral reasoning. In social conventional reasoning, the focus is on rules that have been established by society such as eating mashed potatoes with a fork or asking to be excused after eating. Such rules are largely arbitrary (does it really matter if a child uses a spoon to eat mashed potatoes?). In contrast, moral reasoning focuses on issues of fairness, justice, the rights of others, and avoidance of harm to others. In comparison to social conventional rules, whose purpose is to ensure the smooth functioning of society, moral rules are based on more abstract concepts of justice (Turiel, 2010).

Finally, an additional problematic aspect of Kohlberg's theory is the difficulty it has explaining *girls'* moral judgments. Because Kohlberg's theory was based largely on data from males, some researchers have argued that it better describes boys' moral development than girls'. This would explain the surprising finding that women typically score at a lower level than men on tests of moral judgments using Kohlberg's stages. This result has led to an alternative account of moral development for girls.

Psychologist Carol Gilligan has suggested that differences in the ways boys and girls are raised in our society lead to basic distinctions in how men and women view moral behavior. According to her, boys view morality primarily in terms of broad principles such as justice or fairness, whereas girls see it in terms of responsibility toward individuals and willingness to sacrifice themselves to help specific individuals within the context of particular relationships. Compassion for individuals, then, is a greater factor in moral behavior for women than it is for men (Gilligan, 2015).

Table 5-2 Gilligan's Three Stages of Moral Development in Women

Stage	Characteristics	Example
Stage 1 Orientation toward individual survival	Initial concentration is on what is practical and best for self. Gradual transition from selfishness to responsibility, which includes thinking about what would be best for others.	A first grader may insist on playing only games of her own choosing when playing with a friend.
Stage 2 Goodness as self-sacrifice	Initial view is that a woman must sacrifice her own wishes to what other people want. Gradual transition from "goodness" to "truth," which takes into account needs of both self and others.	Now older, the same girl may believe that to be a good friend, she must play the games her friend chooses, even if she herself doesn't like them.
Stage 3 Morality of nonviolence	A moral equivalence is established between self and others. Hurting anyone—including oneself—is seen as immoral. Most sophisticated form of reasoning, according to Gilligan.	The same girl may realize that both friends must enjoy their time together and look for activities that both she and her friend can enjoy.

SOURCE: Gilligan, 1982.

Gilligan views morality as developing among females in a three-stage process (summarized in Table 5-2). In the first stage, called "orientation toward individual survival," females first concentrate on what is practical and best for them, gradually making a transition from selfishness to responsibility, that is, thinking about what would be best for others. In the second stage, termed "goodness as self-sacrifice," females begin to think they must sacrifice their own wishes to those of others.

Ideally, women make a transition from "goodness" to "truth," in which they take into account their own needs, too. This transition leads to the third stage, "morality of nonviolence," in which women decide that hurting anyone is immoral—including themselves. This realization establishes a moral equivalence between themselves and others and represents, according to Gilligan, the most sophisticated level of moral reasoning.

It is obvious that Gilligan's sequence of stages is quite different from Kohlberg's, and some developmentalists have suggested that her rejection of Kohlberg's work is too sweeping and that gender differences are not as pronounced as first thought. For instance, some researchers argue that both males and females use similar "justice" and "care" orientations in making moral judgments. Clearly, the question of how boys and girls differ in their moral orientations, as well as the nature of moral development in general, is far from settled (Tappan, 2006; Donleavy, 2008; Lapsley, 2016).

Relationships: Building Friendship in Middle Childhood

In Lunch Room Number Two, Jamillah and her new classmates chew slowly on sandwiches and sip quietly on straws from cartons of milk.... Boys and girls look timidly at the strange faces across the table from them, looking for someone who might play with them in the schoolyard, someone who might become a friend.

For these children, what happens in the schoolyard will be just as important as what happens in the school. And when they're out on the playground, there will be no one to protect them. No child will hold back to keep from beating them at a game, humiliating them in a test of skill, or harming them in a fight. No one will run interference or guarantee membership in a group. Out on the playground, it's sink or swim. No one automatically becomes your friend. (Kotre & Hall, 1990, pp. 112–113)

As Jamillah and her classmates demonstrate, friendship plays an increasingly important role in middle childhood. Building and maintaining friendships become a large part of social life.

Friends influence development in several ways. Friendships provide children with information about the world as well as themselves. Friends provide emotional support that allows children to respond more effectively to stress. Having friends makes a child a less likely target of aggression. It can teach them how to manage their emotions and help them interpret their own emotional experiences. Friendships teach children how to communicate and interact with others. They also foster intellectual growth by increasing children's range of experiences (Gifford-Smith & Brownell, 2003; Majors, 2012; Lundby, 2013).

Friends and other peers become increasingly influential at this stage but parents and other family members remain significant. Most developmentalists believe that children's psychological functioning and their general development are the product of multiple factors, including peers and parents (Parke, Simpkins, & McDowell, 2002; Laghi et al., 2014). (We'll talk more about the family's influence later in this module.)

Stages of Friendship: Changing Views of Friends

LO 5.15   **Identify Damon's stages of friendship, and explain the factors that determine popularity in middle childhood.**

At this stage, a child's concept of friendship passes through three distinct stages, according to developmental psychologist William Damon (Damon & Hart, 1988).

STAGE 1: BASING FRIENDSHIP ON OTHERS' BEHAVIOR   In this stage, from ages 4 to 7, children see friends as others who like them and with whom they share toys and other activities. They view the children they spend the most time with as their friends. A kindergartner who is asked, "How do you know that someone is your best friend?" may say that his best friend is someone who plays games with him and who likes him back (Damon, 1983; Erdley & Day, 2017).

What children in this stage seldom do, however, is consider others' personal qualities as the basis of friendships. Instead, they use a concrete approach, primarily choosing friends for their behavior. They like those who share, shunning those who don't share, who hit, or who don't play with them. In the first stage, friends are viewed largely as presenting opportunities for pleasant interactions.

STAGE 2: BASING FRIENDSHIP ON TRUST   In the next stage, children's view of friendship becomes complicated. Lasting around ages 8 to 10, this stage involves taking others' personal qualities and traits as well as the rewards they provide into consideration. But the centerpiece of friendship in this second stage is mutual trust. Friends are seen as those one can count on to help out when needed. Violations of trust are taken seriously, and friends cannot make amends just by engaging in positive play, as they might at previous ages. Instead, the expectation is that formal explanations and apologies must be provided before a friendship can be reestablished.

STAGE 3: BASING FRIENDSHIP ON PSYCHOLOGICAL CLOSENESS   The third stage of friendship begins toward the end of middle childhood, from ages 11 to 15, when children develop the view of friendship they will hold in adolescence. Although we'll discuss this perspective in detail later, the main criteria for friendship shift toward intimacy and loyalty. Friendship becomes characterized by feelings of closeness, usually brought on by sharing personal thoughts and feelings. Friendships are also somewhat exclusive. By the end of middle childhood, children seek friends who will be loyal, and they view friendship less in terms of shared activities than in terms of the psychological benefits it brings.

Mutual trust is considered to be the centerpiece of friendship during middle childhood.

Children also develop clear ideas about which behaviors they like and dislike in friends, preferring others who invite them to share in activities and who are helpful, both physically and psychologically. They dislike behaviors such as physical or verbal aggression.

INDIVIDUAL DIFFERENCES IN FRIENDSHIP: WHAT MAKES A CHILD POPULAR? Why is it that some children are the schoolyard equivalent of the life of the party, whereas others are social isolates whose overtures toward peers are dismissed or disdained? Developmentalists have attempted to answer this question by examining individual differences in popularity.

Status Among School-Age Children: Establishing One's Position Children's friendships exhibit clear status hierarchies. **Status** is the evaluation of a role or person by other relevant members of a group. Children who have high status have greater access to resources such as games, toys, books, and information. Lower-status children are more likely to follow their lead. Status can be measured in several ways. Often, children are asked directly how much they like or dislike particular classmates. They also may be asked whom they would most (and least) like to play or work with.

Status is an important determinant of friendships. High-status children tend to befriend those of a higher status, whereas lower-status children are likely to have friends of lower status. Status is also related to the number of friends a child has: Higher-status children tend to have more friends than those of lower status.

A variety of factors lead some children to be unpopular and socially isolated from their peers.

But it is not only the quantity of social interactions that separates high-status children from low-status children; the nature of their interactions also differs. Higher-status children are more likely to be viewed as friends by other children. They are more likely to form cliques—groups viewed as exclusive and desirable—and to interact with a greater number of children. Lower-status children tend to play with younger or less-popular children (McQuade et al., 2014; van den Berg et al., 2017).

Popularity is a reflection of children's status. Mid- to high-status children are more likely to initiate and coordinate social interaction, making their general level of social activity higher than children of low status (Erwin, 1993; Shutts, 2015).

What Personal Characteristics Lead to Popularity? Popular children share several personality traits. They are usually helpful, cooperating with others on joint projects. They also tend to be funny and to appreciate others' attempts at humor. Compared with less-popular children, they are better at reading nonverbal behavior and understanding the emotional experiences of others. They also control their nonverbal behavior more effectively, presenting themselves well. In short, popular children are high in **social competence**, the collection of social skills that permits individuals to perform successfully in social settings (Feldman, Tomasian, & Coats, 1999; McQuade et al., 2016; Erdley & Day, 2017).

Although generally popular children are friendly, open, and cooperative, one subset of popular boys (but not popular girls) displays an array of negative behaviors, including being aggressive, disruptive, and causing trouble. Despite these behaviors, these boys are often remarkably popular, being viewed as cool and tough by their peers. This popularity may occur because they are seen as boldly breaking rules that others feel constrained to follow (Woods, 2009; Schonert-Reichl et al., 2012; Scharf, 2014).

Social Problem-Solving Abilities Another factor in popularity is children's skill at social problem-solving. **Social problem-solving** is the use of strategies for solving social conflicts in mutually satisfactory ways. Because social conflicts are frequent—even

status
the evaluation of a role or person by other relevant members of a group

social competence
the collection of social skills that permit individuals to perform successfully in social settings

social problem-solving
the use of strategies for solving social conflicts in ways that are satisfactory both to oneself and to others

Fotolia

among best friends—successful strategies for dealing with them are an important element of social success (Murphy & Eisenberg, 2002; Siu & Shek, 2010; Dereli-Iman, 2013).

According to developmental psychologist Kenneth Dodge, successful social problem-solving proceeds through a series of steps that correspond to children's information-processing strategies (see Figure 5-10). Dodge argues that the ways children solve social problems are a result of the decisions they make at each point in the sequence (Dodge & Price, 1994; Dodge et al., 2003; Lansford et al., 2014).

By carefully delineating each of the stages, Dodge provides a means to target interventions toward a specific child's deficits. For instance, some children routinely misinterpret the meaning of others' behavior (step 2), and then respond according to their misinterpretation.

Generally, popular children are better at interpreting others' behavior. They also possess a wider inventory of techniques for dealing with social problems. In contrast, less-popular children tend to show less understanding of others' behavior, and thus their reactions may be inappropriate. Their strategies for dealing with social problems are more limited; they sometimes simply don't know how to apologize or help someone who is unhappy feel better (Rose & Asher, 1999; Rinaldi, 2002; Lahat et al., 2014).

Unpopular children may become victims of a phenomenon known as *learned helplessness*. Because they don't understand the root causes of their unpopularity, children may feel that they have little or no ability to improve their situation. As a result, they may simply give up and don't even try to become more involved with their peers. In turn, their learned helplessness becomes a self-fulfilling prophecy, reducing the chances that they will become more popular in the future (Seligman, 2007; Aujoulat, Luminet, & Deccache, 2007; Altermatt & Broady, 2009; Sorrenti et al., 2018).

Figure 5-10 Problem-Solving Steps

Children's problem-solving proceeds through several steps involving different information processing strategies.

SOURCE: Based on Dodge, 1985.

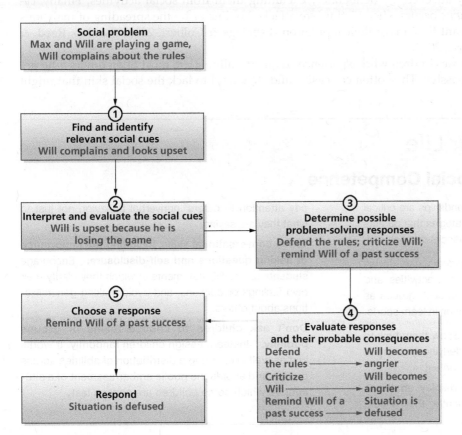

Teaching Social Competence   Happily, unpopular children can learn social competence. Several programs aim to teach children the skills that seem to underlie general social competence. In one experimental program, a group of unpopular fifth and sixth graders were taught how to converse with friends. They were taught ways to disclose material about themselves, to learn about others by asking questions, and to offer help and suggestions in a nonthreatening way.

Compared with a group who did not receive training, the children in the experiment interacted more with their peers, held more conversations, developed higher self-esteem, and—most critically—were more accepted by their peers than before training (Asher & Rose, 1997; Bierman, 2004; Fransson et al., 2016). (For more on increasing children's social competence, see the *Development in Your Life* feature.)

BULLYING: SCHOOLYARD AND ONLINE VICTIMIZATION

> Austin Rodriguez, an Ohio teen, attempted suicide after classmates bullied him for being gay. They reportedly hid his gym clothes and tried to prevent him from entering the locker room or the lunchroom. They made nasty remarks on the Internet.

> Rachel Ehmke, a Minnesota seventh grader, hung herself when the bullying got too awful to live with. The 13-year-old had been hounded for months by a group of girls who called her "prostitute," scrawled "slut" all over her notebook, and harassed her online.

Austin and Rachel are not alone in facing the torment of bullying, whether it comes at school or on the Internet. Almost 85 percent of girls and 80 percent of boys report experiencing some form of harassment in school at least once, and 160,000 U.S. schoolchildren stay home from school each day because they are afraid of being bullied. Others encounter bullying on the Internet, which may be even more painful because often the bullying is done anonymously or may involve public postings (Mishna, Saini, & Solomon, 2009; Law et al., 2012; Barlett, Chamberlin, & Witkower, 2017).

There are four general types of bullying. In *verbal bullying*, victims are called names, threatened, or made fun of because of physical or other attributes. *Physical bullying* represents actual aggression, in which children may be hit, pushed, or touched inappropriately. *Relational bullying* may be more subtle; it occurs when children are socially attacked, by deliberately excluding them from social activities. Finally, *cyberbullying* occurs when victims are attacked online or by the spreading of malicious lies meant to damage their reputation (Espelage & Colbert, 2016; Osanloo, Reed, & Schwartz, 2017).

Those children who experience frequent bullying are most often loners who are fairly passive. They often cry easily, and they tend to lack the social skill that might

Development in Your Life

Increasing Children's Social Competence

It is clear that building and maintaining friendships are critical in children's lives. Fortunately, there are strategies that parents and teachers can use to increase children's social competence.

- **Encourage social interaction.** Teachers can devise ways to get children to take part in group activities, and parents can encourage membership in such groups as Brownies and Cub Scouts or participation in team sports.

- **Teach listening skills to children.** Show them how to listen carefully and respond to the underlying meaning of a communication as well as its overt content.

- **Make children aware that people display emotions and moods nonverbally.** Consequently, they should pay attention to others' nonverbal behavior, not just to what they are saying.

- **Teach conversational skills, including the importance of asking questions and self-disclosure.** Encourage students to use "I" statements in which they clarify their own feelings or opinions, and avoid making generalizations about others.

- **Don't ask children to choose teams or groups publicly.** Instead, assign children randomly: It works just as well in ensuring a distribution of abilities across groups and avoids the public embarrassment of a situation in which some children are chosen last.

otherwise defuse a bullying situation. For example, they are unable to think of humorous comebacks to bullies' taunts. But though children such as these are more likely to be bullied, even children without these characteristics occasionally are bullied during their school careers: Some 90 percent of middle-school students report being bullied at some point in their time at school, beginning as early as the preschool years (Katzer, Fetchenhauer, & Belschak, 2009; Lapidot-Lefler & Dolev-Cohen, 2014; Jansen et al., 2016).

About 10 to 15 percent of students bully others at one time or another. About half of all bullies come from abusive homes—meaning, of course, that half don't. They tend to watch more television containing violence, and they misbehave more at home and at school than do nonbullies. When their bullying gets them in trouble, they may try to lie their way out of the situation, and they show little remorse for their victimization of others. Furthermore, bullies, compared with their peers, are more likely to break the law as adults. Although bullies are sometimes popular among their peers, some ironically become victims of bullies themselves (Barboza et al., 2009; Peeters, Cillessen, & Scholte, 2010; Dupper, 2013).

One of the most effective ways to reduce the incidence of bullying is through school programs that enlist and involve students. For example, schools can train students to intervene when they see an instance of bullying, rather than watching passively. Empowering students to stand up for victims has been shown to reduce bullying significantly (Storey et al., 2008; Munsey, 2012; Juvonen et al., 2016; Menolascino & Jenkins, 2018).

Gender, Race, and Friendships

LO 5.16 Explain how gender and race affect friendships at this age.

Just as friendships in middle childhood are often determined by status, they are also influenced by gender and race. In preschool, children generally choose friends among those who enjoy the same activities. By middle childhood, children have a more sophisticated sense of self. That self includes both a gender and a racial or ethnic identity. Although such growing awareness may cement some friendships, it can cause others to cool.

GENDER AND FRIENDSHIPS: THE SEX SEGREGATION OF MIDDLE CHILDHOOD

Girls rule; boys drool.
Boys are idiots. Girls have cooties.
Boys go to college to get more knowledge; girls go to Jupiter to get more stupider.

Those are some of the views of elementary school boys and girls regarding members of the other sex. Avoidance of the other sex becomes quite pronounced at this age, with social networks often consisting almost entirely of same-sex groupings (Rancourt et al., 2013; Zosuls et al., 2014; Braun & Davidson, 2016).

Interestingly, this segregation of friendships occurs in almost all societies. In nonindustrialized societies, same-gender segregation may result from the types of activities children engage in. For instance, in many cultures, boys are assigned one type of chore and girls another. Participation in different activities may not wholly explain sex segregation, however: Children in more developed countries, who attend the same schools and participate in many of the same activities, still tend to avoid members of the other gender (Steinmetz et al., 2014; Kottak, 2019).

The lack of cross-gender interaction in middle childhood means that boys' and girls' friendships are restricted to their own sex. The nature of friendships within these two groups is quite different.

Boys typically have larger networks of friends, and they tend to play in groups rather than pairing off. Differences in status within the group are usually pronounced, with an acknowledged leader and a hierarchy of members. Because of the fairly rigid rankings that represent the relative social power of those in the group, known as the **dominance hierarchy**, members of higher status can safely question and oppose those lower in the hierarchy (Pedersen et al., 2007; Pun, Birch & Baron, 2017).

dominance hierarchy
rankings that represent the relative social power of those in a group

Boys tend to be concerned with their place in the dominance hierarchy, and they attempt to maintain and improve their status. This makes for a style of play known as *restrictive*. In restrictive play, interactions are interrupted when a boy feels his status is challenged. A boy who feels that he is unjustly challenged by a lower-status peer may attempt to end the interaction by scuffling over a toy or otherwise behaving assertively. Consequently, boys tend to play in bursts, rather than in more extended, tranquil episodes (Benenson & Apostoleris, 1993; Estell et al., 2008; Cheng et al., 2016).

The language of friendship used among boys reflects their concern over status and challenge. Consider this conversation between two boys who are good friends:

Child 1: Get out of my space! You're too close to me.
Child 2: Make me.
Child 1: You know I can.
Child 2: Ha! You're just a wuss.
Child 1: Don't force me.
Child 2: You loser. You can't do a thing.

Friendship patterns among girls are quite different. Rather than a wide network of friends, girls focus on one or two "best friends." In contrast to boys, who seek out status differences, girls avoid differences, preferring to maintain equal-status friendships.

Conflicts among girls are usually solved through compromise, by ignoring the situation, or by giving in, rather than by seeking to make one's point of view prevail. The goal is to smooth over disagreements, making social interaction easy and nonconfrontational (Noakes & Rinaldi, 2006).

The language used by girls tends to reflect their view of relationships. Rather than blatant demands ("Give me the pencil"), girls are more apt to use less confrontational and directive language. Girls tend to use indirect forms of verbs, such as "Let's go to the movies" or "Would you want to trade books with me?" rather than "I want to go to the movies" or "Let me have these books" (Goodwin, 1990; Besage, 2006).

CROSS-RACE FRIENDSHIPS: INTEGRATION IN AND OUT OF THE CLASSROOM For the most part, friendships among children are *not* color-blind. Children's closest friendships tend to be with others of the same race. In fact, as children age there is a decline in the number and depth of friendships outside their own racial group. By age 11 or 12, it appears that African American children become particularly aware of and sensitive to the prejudice and discrimination directed toward members of their race. At that point, they are likely to make distinctions between members of ingroups (groups to which people feel they belong) and members of outgroups (groups to which they feel they do not belong) (Rowley et al., 2008; Bagci et al., 2014).

When third graders from one long-integrated school were asked to name a best friend, around one-quarter of white children and two-thirds of black children chose a child of the other race. In contrast, by 10th grade, less than 10 percent of whites and 5 percent of blacks named a different-race best friend (McGlothlin & Killen, 2005; Rodkin & Ryan, 2012; Munniksma et al., 2017).

> **From a social worker's perspective:** How might it be possible to decrease the segregation of friendships along racial lines? What factors would have to change in individuals or in society?

As children age, there is a decline in the number of and depth of friendships outside their own racial group. What are some ways in which schools can foster mutual acceptance?

Peter Byron/PhotoEdit

However, although they may not choose each other as best friends, whites and blacks—as well as members of other minority groups—can show a high degree of mutual acceptance. This pattern is particularly true in schools with on-going integration efforts. This makes sense: A good deal of research supports the notion that contact between majority and minority group members can reduce prejudice and discrimination (Hewstone, 2003; Quintana & McKown, 2008; Korol, Fietzer, & Ponterotto, 2018).

Family Life in Middle Childhood

Jared's mom works the day shift as a nurse at the hospital, so Jared's grandmother picks him up from school. When they get home, his grandfather takes him out to the field behind their apartment house to practice batting and catching because Jared, age 10, dreams of someday playing first base for the San Francisco Giants. Often, four or five other children show up and join the fun, which lasts until Jared's grandmother calls him in to help her make dinner for the family. His mom will be home at six and she'll be hungry. "My family is like a team," Jared says. "My mom, my grandparents, me—we all pitch in and help make it work." Jared is a member of a multigenerational family. His parents divorced when he was 3, and the next year his grandparents moved in.

As we've noted in previous chapters, the structure of the family has changed over the past few decades. With an unprecedented variety of family constellations, a soaring divorce rate, and an increase in the number of parents who both work outside the home, the environment faced by children passing through middle childhood in the 21st century is different from the one faced by prior generations.

One of the biggest challenges of middle childhood is the increasing independence that characterizes children's behavior. Children move from being controlled to increasingly controlling their own destinies—or at least conducting them. Middle childhood, then, is a period of **coregulation** in which children and parents jointly control behavior. Increasingly, parents provide broad guidelines for conduct, and children control their everyday behavior. For instance, parents may urge their daughter to buy a nutritious school lunch, but the daughter's decision to buy pizza and two desserts is her own.

coregulation
a period in which parents and children jointly control children's behavior

Families Today: A Variety of Constellations

LO 5.17   Identify the variety of family constellations, and assess their impact on children.

What makes a family? In the past century, that question would likely have been met with the reply, "Two parents and two or more children." And the parents would rarely have been of the same sex. Today, families come in many sizes and types. A child's family may be the one parent he or she lives with, or it may include siblings, stepparents, stepsiblings, grandparents, and other relatives.

FAMILY LIFE: THE INFLUENCE OF PARENTS AND SIBLINGS During middle childhood, children spend less time with their parents. Still, parents remain their major influence, providing essential assistance, advice, and direction (Parke, 2004).

Siblings also have an important influence, for good and for bad. Although brothers and sisters can provide support, companionship, and security, they can also be a source of strife. *Sibling rivalry* can occur, especially when the siblings are the same sex and similar in age. Parents may intensify sibling rivalry by seeming to favor one child over another—a perception that may or may not be accurate. A decision as straightforward as granting older siblings more freedom may be interpreted as favoritism. In some cases, perceived favoritism may damage the self-esteem of the younger sibling. But sibling rivalry is not inevitable (McHale, Kim, & Whiteman, 2006; Caspi, 2012; Skrzypek, Maciejewska-Sobczak, & Stadnicka-Dmitriew, 2014; O'Connor & Evans, 2018).

Cultural differences are linked to sibling experiences. For example, in Mexican American families, which have particularly strong values regarding the importance of family, siblings are less likely to respond negatively when younger siblings receive preferential treatment (McHale et al., 2005; McGuire & Shanahan, 2010).

What about children who have no siblings? Disproving the stereotype that only children are spoiled and self-centered, they are as well-adjusted as children with brothers and sisters. In fact, in some ways, only children are better adjusted, with higher self-esteem and stronger motivation to achieve. This had been particularly good news for parents in the People's Republic of China, where until fairly recently a strict one-child policy was in effect. Studies there show that Chinese only-children often academically outperform children with siblings (Miao & Wang, 2003; Liu et al., 2017).

SINGLE-PARENT FAMILIES Although the majority of children in the United States (69 percent) live with two parents, the remaining 31 percent live in some other arrangement, such as living with a single parent or grandparents. There are also some significant racial disparities: Seventy-four percent of white children live with two married parents, compared with 60 percent of Hispanic and 34 percent of black children (ChildStats.gov, 2017).

In rare cases, death is the reason for single parenthood. More frequently, either no spouse was ever present, the spouses have divorced, or the spouse is absent. In the vast majority of cases, the single parent who is present is the mother.

What consequences are there for children in one-parent homes? Much depends on whether a second parent was present before and the nature of the parents' relationship at that time. Furthermore, the economic status of the single-parent family plays a role. Single-parent families are often less well-off financially than two-parent families, and living in relative poverty has a negative impact on children (Davis, 2003; Harvey & Fine, 2004; Nicholson et al., 2014).

MULTIGENERATIONAL FAMILIES In some households children, parents, and grandparents live together. The number of multigenerational families is growing; some 19 percent of the U.S. population lived in households with multiple generations in 2014, up from 17 percent just 5 years earlier. The number of multigenerational families grew in part because of the economic downturn in 2008, as well as increases in the cost of housing (Carrns, 2016).

Multigenerational families can make for a rich living experience for children, but there is also the potential for conflict if "layers" of adults act as disciplinarians without coordinating what they do.

The prevalence of three-generation families who live together is greater among African Americans than among Caucasians. In addition, African American families, which are more likely than Caucasian families to be headed by single parents, often rely substantially on the help of grandparents in everyday child care, and cultural norms tend to be highly supportive of grandparents taking an active role (Oberlander, Black, & Starr, 2007; Pittman & Boswell, 2007; Kelch-Oliver, 2008).

LIVING IN BLENDED FAMILIES For many children, the aftermath of divorce includes a remarriage. In more than 10 million households in the United States, at least one spouse has remarried. More than 5 million remarried couples have at least one stepchild with them in what have come to be called **blended families**. Overall, 16 percent of all children in the United States live in blended families (U.S. Bureau of the Census, 2001; Bengtson et al., 2004; PEW Research Center, 2015).

blended families
remarried couples who have at least one stepchild living with them

Children in a blended family face challenges. They often have to deal with *role ambiguity*, in which roles and expectations are unclear. They may be uncertain about their responsibilities, how to behave toward stepparents and stepsiblings, and how to make a host of tough everyday decisions. For instance, they may have to choose which parent to spend holidays and vacations with, or decide between conflicting advice from biological parent and stepparent. Some find the disruption of routine and of established family relationships difficult. For instance, a child used to her mother's complete attention may find it hard to see her mother showing interest and affection to a stepchild (Belcher, 2003; Guadalupe & Welkley, 2012; Mundy & Wofsy, 2017).

Still, school-age children in blended families often adjust relatively smoothly—especially compared with adolescents—for several reasons. For one thing, the family's financial situation is often improved after a

Denise Hager/Catchlight Visual Services/Alamy Stock Photo

Blended families occur when previously married husbands and wives with children remarry.

parent remarries. In addition, there are usually more people to share the burden of household chores. Finally, the higher "population" of the family increases opportunities for social interaction (Greene, Anderson, & Hetherington, 2003; Hetherington & Elmore, 2003).

Families blend most successfully when the parents create an environment that supports self-esteem and a climate of family togetherness. Generally, the younger the children, the easier the transition (Kirby, 2006; Jeynes, 2007).

FAMILIES WITH GAY, LESBIAN, AND TRANSGENDER PARENTS   An increasing number of children have two mothers or two fathers. Estimates suggest that between 1 million and 5 million families are headed by two lesbian or two gay parents in the United States, and some 6 million children have lesbian or gay parents (Patterson 2007, 2009; Gates, 2013).

In the past, gays, lesbians, transgender and other non-heterosexual individuals have faced significant barriers to adopting children. Many adoption agencies had explicit rules prohibiting adoptions by non-heterosexual parents, and in some states such adoptions were illegal. However, with the legalization of gay and lesbian marriage, these barriers are falling. Furthermore, researchers have begun to look at children raised in homes by gay and lesbian parents and, as we discuss in the *From Research to Practice* box, the consequences are largely positive.

RACE AND FAMILY LIFE   Although there are as many types of families as there are individuals, research finds some consistencies related to race. For example, African American families often have a particularly strong sense of family, offering welcome and support to extended family members in their homes. Because there is a relatively

From Research to Practice

Two Moms, Two Dads: How Do Children Fare with Gay, Lesbian, and Transgender Parents?

How do children in lesbian, gay, and transgender households fare? Although there is little data on the effects of a transgender parent on children, a growing body of research on the effects of same-sex parenting on children shows that children develop similarly to the children of heterosexual families. Their sexual orientation is unrelated to that of their parents, their behavior is no more or less gender-typed, and they seem equally well adjusted (Fulcher, Sutfin, & Patterson, 2008; Patterson, 2009; Goldberg, 2010a). One large-scale analysis examined 33 studies of the effects of parental gender and sexual identity on their children's outcomes. No overall effects were found for children's sexual orientation cognitive abilities or gender identity. There were some differences in terms of parent–child relationships, in which the relationship between parent and child was perceived to *better* among same-gender parents, compared with different-gender parents. The research also found that children of same-gender parents showed more typical gender play and behavior than children of different-gender parents. Finally, children with lesbian or gay parents had higher levels of psychological adjustment than children with heterosexual parents (Fedewa, Black, & Ahn, 2015).

Other research shows that children of lesbian and gay parents have similar relationships with their peers as children of heterosexual parents. They also relate to adults—both those who are gay and those who are straight—no differently from children whose parents are heterosexual. And when they reach adolescence, their romantic relationships and sexual behavior are no different from those of adolescents living with opposite-sex parents (Patterson, 2009; Golombok et al., 2003; Wainright, Russell, & Patterson, 2004; Wainright & Patterson, 2008).

In short, research shows that there is little developmental difference between children whose parents are gay and lesbian and those who have heterosexual parents. There is insufficient research to make the same statement about transgender parenting; more studies need to be conducted before conclusions can be drawn. What is clearly different for children with same-sex parents is the possibility of discrimination and prejudice due to their parents' sexual orientation, although U.S. society has become considerably more tolerant of such unions. In fact, the 2015 U.S. Supreme Court ruling legalizing same-sex marriages should accelerate the trend of acceptance of such unions (Davis, Saltzburg, & Locke, 2009; Biblarz & Stacey, 2010; Kantor, 2015; Miller, Kors, & Macfie, 2017).

Shared Writing Prompt:

How might gay and lesbian parents prepare their children to deal with the prejudice and discrimination that they potentially may face?

high level of female-headed households among African Americans, extended families often lend crucial social and economic support. In addition, there is a relatively high proportion of families headed by older adults, such as grandparents, and some studies find that children in grandmother-headed households are particularly well adjusted (Taylor, 2002; Parke, 2004).

Hispanic families tend to regard family life and community and religious organizations highly. Children are taught to value their family ties and to see themselves as a central part of an extended family. Ultimately, their sense of self stems from the family. Hispanic families also tend to be larger, with an average size of 3.70, compared to 3.08 for Caucasian families and 3.32 for African American families (Cauce & Domenech-Rodriguez, 2002; Halgunseth, Ispa, & Rudy, 2006; U.S. Bureau of the Census, 2017).

Although relatively little research has been conducted on Asian American families, emerging findings suggest that fathers are apt to be powerful figures who maintain discipline. In keeping with the collectivist orientation of Asian cultures, children tend to believe that family needs have a higher priority than personal needs, and males, in particular, are expected to care for their parents throughout their lifetimes (Ishi-Kuntz).

Challenges to Family Life

LO 5.18   Describe the challenges to family life posed by work, divorce, and poverty.

Tamara's mother, Brenda, waited outside her daughter's second-grade classroom for the end of the school day. Tamara came over to greet her mother as soon as she spotted her. "Mom, can Anna come over to play today?" Tamara demanded. Brenda had been looking forward to spending some time alone with Tamara, who had spent the last 3 days at her dad's house. But, Brenda reflected, Tamara hardly ever got to ask kids over after school, so she agreed to the request. Unfortunately, it turned out today wouldn't work for Anna's family, so they tried to find an alternate date. "How about Thursday?" Anna's mother suggested. Before Tamara could reply, her mother reminded her, "You'll have to ask your dad. You're at his house that night." Tamara's face fell. "OK," she mumbled.

How will Tamara's adjustment be affected from dividing her time between the two homes where she lives with her divorced parents? What about the adjustment of her friend, Anna, who lives with both her parents, both of whom work outside the home? These are just a few of the questions we need to consider as we look at the ways that children's home life affects their lives during middle childhood.

HOME AND ALONE: WHAT DO CHILDREN DO?

When 10-year-old Johnetta Colvin comes home after a day at Martin Luther King Elementary School, the first thing she does is grab a few cookies and turn to her phone. She spends some time texting with her friends and then typically spends an hour watching television. During commercials, she looks at her homework.

What she doesn't do is chat with her parents. She's home alone.

self-care children
children who let themselves into their homes after school and wait alone until their caretakers return from work; previously known as *latchkey children*

Johnetta is a **self-care child**, the term for children who let themselves into their homes after school and wait alone until their parents return from work. Some 12 to 14 percent of children in the United States between the ages of 5 and 12 spend some time alone after school, without adult supervision Moreover, three states have a minimum age for leaving a child home alone. Illinois law requires children to be 14 years old; in Maryland the minimum age is 8, while in Oregon, children must be 10 before being left home alone (Berger, 2000; Child Welfare Information Gateway, 2013).

In the past, such children were called *latchkey children*, a term connoting sadness, loneliness, and neglect. Today a new view is emerging. According to sociologist Sandra Hofferth, given the hectic schedule of many children's lives, a few hours alone may provide a helpful period of decompression. Furthermore, it may give children an opportunity to develop autonomy (Hofferth & Sandberg, 2001).

Research has identified few differences between self-care children and others. Although some children report negative experiences (such as loneliness), they do not seem emotionally damaged by the experience. In addition, if they stay by themselves rather than "hanging out" unsupervised with friends, they may avoid activities that can lead to difficulties (Goyette-Ewing, 2000; Klein, 2017).

The time alone also gives children a chance to focus on homework and school or personal projects. In fact, children with employed parents may have higher self-esteem because they feel they are contributing to the household (Goyette-Ewing, 2000; Ruiz-Casares & Heymann, 2009).

Some parents have taken the concept of self-care one step further, arguing that children should have the opportunity to explore their neighborhoods on their own. *Free-range parenting* is a parenting style that seeks to foster children's independence by allowing them to travel unsupervised to areas in their neighborhood. Caregivers practicing free-range parenting have sometimes run afoul of child neglect laws, and there have been some well-publicized instances of parents being arrested for allowing their school-age children to play by themselves or walk to a neighborhood store. The legal issues have yet to be sorted out, and it remains a controversial topic (Vota, 2017).

Self-care children spend time after school alone while their parents are at work.

DIVORCE Having divorced parents is no longer distinctive. Only around half the children in the United States spend their entire childhood in the same household with both parents. The rest will live in single-parent homes or with stepparents, grandparents, or other nonparental relatives; and some end up in foster care (Harvey & Fine, 2004; Nicholson et al., 2014).

How do children react to divorce? The answer is complex. For 6 months to 2 years following a divorce, children and parents may show signs of psychological maladjustment such as anxiety, depression, sleep disturbances, and phobias. Even though most children stay with their mothers, the quality of the mother–child relationship mostly declines, often because children feel caught in the middle between their mothers and fathers (Lansford, 2009; Maes, De Mol, & Buysse, 2012; Weaver & Schofield, 2015).

During the early stage of middle childhood, children often blame themselves for the breakup. By age 10, they feel pressure to choose sides and experience some degree of divided loyalty (Hipke, Wolchik, & Sandler, 2010).

The longer-term consequences of divorce are less clear. Some studies have found that 18 months to 2 years later, most children begin to return to their predivorce state of adjustment. For many children, long-term consequences are minimal (Guttmann & Rosenberg, 2003; Harvey & Fine, 2004; Schaan & Vögele, 2016).

Other evidence suggests that the fallout from divorce lingers. For example, compared with children from intact families, twice as many children of divorced parents enter psychological counseling (although sometimes counseling is mandated by a judge as part of the divorce). In addition, people who have experienced parental divorce are more at risk for experiencing divorce themselves later in life (Uphold-Carrier & Utz, 2012; South, 2013; Mahrer & Wolchik, 2017).

How children react to divorce depends on several factors. One is the economic standing of the family the child is living with. In many cases, divorce brings a decline in both parents' standards of living. When this occurs, children may be thrown into poverty (Ozawa & Yoon, 2003; Fischer, 2007; Seijo et al., 2016).

In other cases, the negative consequences of divorce are less severe because the divorce reduces the hostility and anger in the home. If the household before the divorce was overwhelmed by parental strife—as is the case in around 30 percent of divorces—the greater calm of a postdivorce household may be beneficial to children. This is particularly true for children who maintain a close, positive relationship with the parent with whom they do not live. Still, in the 70 percent of divorces where the predivorce level of conflict is not high, children may have a more difficult time adjusting (Faber & Wittenborn, 2010; Finley & Schwartz, 2010; Lansford, 2009; Amato & Afifi, 2006).

From a health-care provider's perspective: How might the development of self-esteem in middle childhood be affected by a divorce? Can constant hostility and tension between parents lead to a child's health problems?

POVERTY AND FAMILY LIFE Regardless of race, children in economically disadvantaged families face hardships. Poor families have fewer everyday resources, and there are more disruptions in children's lives. For example, parents may be forced to look for less expensive housing or a different job. As a result, parents may be less responsive to their children's needs and provide less social support (Evans, 2004; Duncan, Magnuson, & Votruba-Drzal, 2014).

The stress of difficult family environments, along with other stress in the lives of poor children—such as living in unsafe neighborhoods with high rates of violence and attending inferior schools—ultimately takes its toll. Economically disadvantaged children are at risk for poorer academic performance, higher rates of aggression, and conduct problems. In addition, declines in economic well-being are linked to physical and mental health problems. Specifically, the chronic stress associated with poverty makes children more susceptible to cardiovascular disease, depression, and diabetes (Morales & Guerra, 2006; Tracy et al., 2008; Duncan, Magnuson, & Votruba-Drzal, 2014).

Although orphanages of the early 1900s were crowded and institutional (*top*), today the equivalent, called *group homes* or *residential treatment centers* (*bottom*), are much more pleasant.

GROUP CARE: ORPHANAGES IN THE 21ST CENTURY The term *orphanage* evokes stereotypical images of grim institutional life. The reality today is different. *Group homes* or *residential treatment centers* (the word *orphanage* is rarely used) typically house a relatively small number of children whose parents are no longer able to care for them adequately. They are usually funded by a combination of federal, state, and local aid. Nearly a half million children in the United States live in foster care (Jones-Harden, 2004; Bruskas, 2008; Child Welfare Information Gateway, 2017).

About three-quarters of children in group care have suffered neglect and abuse prior to being placed in group care. Each year, 300,000 are removed from their homes, most of whom can be returned to their homes after social service agencies intervene with their families. But the remaining one-quarter are so psychologically damaged that they are likely to remain in group care throughout childhood. Adoption (or even temporary foster care) is not an option for most of these children, who have developed severe emotional and behavior problems, such as high levels of aggression or anger (Bass, Shields, & Behrman, 2004; Chamberlain et al., 2006; Leloux-Opmeer, 2016).

Group care is neither inherently good nor bad. The outcome depends on the staff of the group home and whether child- and youth-care workers know how to develop an effective, stable, and strong emotional bond with a child. If a child is unable to form a meaningful relationship with a worker in a group home, the setting may well be harmful (Hawkins-Rodgers, 2007; Knorth et al., 2008; McCall et al., 2018).

Review, Check, and Apply

Review

LO 5.13 Summarize how children's view of themselves changes in middle childhood, and explain how this shift affects their self-esteem.

According to Erikson, children at this time are in the industry-versus-inferiority stage. In middle childhood, children begin to use social comparison, and self-concepts are based on psychological rather than physical characteristics. Children increasingly develop their own internal standards of success and measure how well they compare to those standards.

LO 5.14 Identify the six stages in Kohlberg's theory of moral development, and compare and contrast them with Gilligan's sequence of stages.

According to Kohlberg, moral development proceeds from a concern with rewards and punishments, through a focus on social conventions and rules, toward a sense of universal moral principles. Gilligan has suggested, however, that girls may follow a different progression of moral development, one based on responsibility toward individuals and compassion rather than broad principles.

LO 5.15 Identify Damon's stages of friendship, and explain the factors that determine popularity in middle childhood.

Children's understanding of friendship changes from the sharing of enjoyable activities, through the consideration of personal traits that can meet their needs, to a focus on intimacy and loyalty. Friendships in childhood display status hierarchies. Improvements in social problem-solving and social information processing can lead to better interpersonal skills and greater popularity.

LO 5.16 Explain how gender and race affect friendships at this age.

Boys and girls engage increasingly in same-sex friendships, with boys' friendships involving group relationships and girls' friendships characterized by pairings of girls with equal status. As children age there is a decline in the number and depth of friendships outside their own racial group.

LO 5.17 Identify the variety of family constellations, and assess their impact on children.

Children may grow up in traditional two-parent, mom-and-dad families, but many children today are part of single-parent families, multigenerational families, blended families, and gay- and lesbian-parented families. The impact on children's well-being in such nontraditional families depends on the economic status of the household, society's acceptance, and the absence or presence of tension in the adult(s).

LO 5.18 Describe the challenges to family life posed by work, divorce, and poverty.

In two parent or single-parent households where all the adults work full-time, many children spend time alone after school, without adult supervision. These self-care children may experience loneliness at times but many also develop independence and enhanced self-esteem from their experience. How divorce affects children depends on such factors as financial circumstances and the comparative levels of tension in the family before and after the divorce. Poverty increases the disruptions in a child's life, and parents are often too consumed with the basics of survival to devote much time to their children's other needs. Children of poverty are at risk for poorer academic performance and higher rates of aggression.

Check Yourself

1. As children develop a better self-understanding in middle childhood, they begin to view themselves less in terms of physical attributes and more in terms of their _____.
   a. familial relationships
   b. psychological traits
   c. environmental characteristics
   d. motor skills

2. According to _____, people pass through a series of six stages as their sense of justice and their level of reasoning evolves with age and cognitive development.
   a. Freud   c. Kohlberg
   b. Piaget   d. Skinner

3. _____ is the evaluation of the role or person by other relevant members of the group and is usually discussed in reference to children and their peer groups.
   a. Dominance hierarchy
   b. Social competence
   c. Friendship
   d. Status

4. A child's response to divorce many include _____.
   a. schizophrenia, violent outbursts, and academic failure
   b. increased anxiety, sleep disturbances, and depression
   c. phobias, schizophrenia, and gender confusion
   d. violent outbursts, depression, and self-mutilation

Applying Lifespan Development

Politicians often speak of "family values." How does this term relate to diverse family situations such as divorced parents, single parents, blended families, working parents, self-care children, and children in group care?

Chapter 5 Summary
Putting It All Together: Middle Childhood

JAN (the student we met in the chapter prologue) successfully tried out for her local Little League team, the Yankees. She was excited to play the sport she loved, but her teammates—all boys—let her know in subtle and not-so-subtle ways that they weren't thrilled about having a girl in the lineup. At Jan's first game, the shortstop and first-base player seemed to collude to freeze her out of the action. She was unhappy about it, but she stayed in the game, and used both her skills and intelligence to make a great play that won the game for her team. As a result, she gained her teammates' approval and acceptance. It was a much-deserved happy moment.

MODULE 5.1
PHYSICAL DEVELOPMENT IN MIDDLE CHILDHOOD

- Steady growth and increased abilities characterized Jan's physical development in these years. (pp. 204–205)
- Jan's gross and fine motor skills developed as her muscle coordination improved and she practiced new skills. Her abilities were very similar to the boys on the team. (pp. 207–208)
- Good eating habits and the regular exercise Jan got from playing ball helped to keep her at a healthy weight. (pp. 205–206)

MODULE 5.2
COGNITIVE DEVELOPMENT IN MIDDLE CHILDHOOD

- Jan's ability to grasp the relationship between speed and direction on the ball field showed that she had entered the stage of concrete operational thought. (p. 216)
- Jan's growing sophistication with language helped her to regulate her behavior during the ballgame. Instead of running off the field when her teammates seemed to exclude her, she was able to remind herself that she had earned a spot on the team and could play the game well if she got the opportunity. (pp. 219–220)
- Jan displayed both fluid and crystallized intelligence on the field, and the development of her intellectual skills was aided by participation in Little League. (p. 229)

MODULE 5.3
SOCIAL AND PERSONALITY DEVELOPMENT IN MIDDLE CHILDHOOD

- In this period, characterized by Erikson as the industry-versus-inferiority stage, Jan showed a readiness to take on the challenges presented by her peers and their biased view of girls in sports. (p. 236)
- That Jan tried out for Little League shows a healthy level of self-esteem. Although she was disappointed at her teammates' initial reaction to having a girl in the lineup, she stayed in the game and gave it her best. (p. 237)
- The acceptance and approval of her teammates helped provide emotional support for Jan. Sticking it out in Little League and making the winning play improved her social status. (pp. 244–245)

What would a PARENT do?

What strategies would you use to help Jan retain her self-esteem in the face of her teammates' skepticism about a girl ballplayer? How would you encourage her? How would you deal with her frustration?

What would a HEALTH-CARE WORKER do?

What suggestions would you make to Jan regarding diet and exercise to keep her healthy and improve muscular strength?

What would YOU do?

How would you deal with a situation in which your daughter was confronted by prejudice against her gender? How would you encourage her to act when people suggest she is not qualified to do something because she is a girl?

What would an EDUCATOR do?

How would you promote gender equality in the classroom? How would you deal with the fact that it is normal for boys and girls in middle childhood to socialize in same-sex groupings, and to avoid or poke fun at each other? What activities could you design to increase mutual respect between boys and girls?

Chapter 6
Adolescence

Olena Zaskochenko/123RF

In middle school, Julie Jacobs had one goal: to be popular. She ditched her "nerdy" grade school friends, bought a new wardrobe from the trendiest stores at the mall, and started shadowing the kids from the in crowd. She laughed at their jokes and boosted their egos at every opportunity. Soon, she began getting friended on Facebook by some of the girls. Then she was invited to a cool party where one of the boys on the football team asked her to dance.

Julie felt she was on her way. But then, she started drinking. It was just something the cool kids did. By ninth grade, she was drinking a lot. "I felt carefree and funny when I was drinking," she recalls. "I felt like nothing really mattered." Her grades began dropping from As to Bs, then down to Cs and worse. She fought with her parents constantly. They grounded her when she came home late. They checked her room for liquor. "The more they pried, the crazier I got," she recalls. It took failing her junior year to wake up. "I realized I wasn't going to graduate with my class, wasn't going to get into college," Julie says. "I'd treated high school like a joke because that was the cool attitude, but I'd always thought of myself as smart. Having to repeat my junior year was devastating."

Julie signed up with a substance abuse counselor and a therapist. She changed schools, opting for one that specializes in the arts. She'd always been a good writer so she joined a fiction writing club. "I saw kids my age doing amazing work and it made me want to do my best," Julie says. The next summer, she attended a month-long workshop for teen writers. The director was impressed with her work. He introduced her to a New York agent. Julie's first book earned 52 rejections, but her next book scored a contract. It will be out at the end of her second year of college. "I finally figured out that I have to define what's cool for me," she says, "because if I fail, I'm the one who takes the rap."

In this chapter we study adolescence, the transitional stage between childhood and adulthood. Adolescents face many challenges in all aspects of their life. Physically, their bodies are maturing quickly—sometimes distressingly quickly. Adolescents become sexually interested, and many of them face worries about their bodies. We will look at some of the issues that sometimes plague adolescents like Julie, including those relating to obesity and nutrition, harmful substances, and sexually transmitted infections (STIs).

Beyond the physical aspects of development, adolescents grow cognitively as well. The most notable change we will discuss is adolescents' growing awareness of their own thought processes. We also consider how adolescents deal with the institution that occupies a great deal of their waking time—school—and discuss the growing impact of the Internet on adolescents' lives, learning, and relationships.

Finally, we turn to the changes that adolescents undergo in their relationships with others. We begin with a consideration of the ways in which they create their concepts of themselves and how they form and protect their self-esteem and identity. We discuss their relationships with parents as adolescents redefine their place within the family. Finally, we discuss dating and sex, which achieve central importance during this period and which encompass issues of intimacy.

Module 6.1 *Physical Development* in Adolescence

LO 6.1 Describe the physical changes that adolescents experience.
LO 6.2 Analyze the nutritional needs and concerns of adolescents.
LO 6.3 Explain the relationship between brain development and cognitive growth in adolescents.
LO 6.4 Describe major threats to adolescents from substance use and abuse.
LO 6.5 Describe the dangers that adolescent sexual practices can present.

Module 6.2 *Cognitive Development* in Adolescence

LO 6.6 Analyze Piaget's account of adolescent cognitive development.
LO 6.7 Explain the information processing view of adolescent cognitive development.
LO 6.8 Describe major factors that affect adolescent school performance.
LO 6.9 Explain the nature and consequences of the use of media by adolescents.

Module 6.3 *Social and Personality Development* in Adolescence

LO 6.10 Describe how adolescents develop their self-concept and self-esteem.
LO 6.11 Analyze diverse theoretical approaches to understanding identity formation.
LO 6.12 Explain why anxiety, depression, and suicide are important issues in adolescence.
LO 6.13 Analyze how the parent–child relationship changes during adolescence.
LO 6.14 Analyze the nature and importance of peer relationships during adolescence.
LO 6.15 Describe the functions and characteristics of dating during adolescence.
LO 6.16 Explain how sexuality develops in the adolescent years.

Module 6.1

Physical Development in Adolescence

Changing Circumstances

Gavin Wyman is locked in an argument with his dad. Though it's not their first battle, it's the biggest one to date. Fifteen-year-old Gavin is set on traveling to Puerto Rico next month at the end of the school year to help with disaster relief after a recent hurricane. His dad is equally set against the idea. "Grandpa was a Freedom Rider," Gavin argues. "And you went to Guatemala with Habitat for Humanity."

"Grandpa was 18 when he went south to fight for civil rights," Gavin's father reminds him, "and I was 20 when I went to Guatemala." "But I'm almost 16," Gavin cries, his voice cracking. "Besides, kids grow up a lot faster today." Gavin's dad looks at his son, who now towers several inches over him, and sees a boy just one year out of middle school asking to travel far from home on his own. Gavin looks at

his dad and sees a jailer bent on limiting Gavin's life and treating him like a child. The argument is once again in stalemate, but Gavin is determined. He falls asleep that night, imagining himself doing heroic deeds in Puerto Rico: helping people to build a new and better life, maybe even saving lives. In Puerto Rico, he thinks, people will appreciate him, look up to him.

Like Gavin, many adolescents crave independence and feel that their parents fail to see how much they've matured. They are keenly aware of their changing bodies and their increasingly complex cognitive abilities. Every day, they deal with careening emotions, social networks that are in constant flux, and the temptations of sex, alcohol, and drugs. In this period of life that evokes excitement, anxiety, glee, and despair, they—like Gavin—are eager to prove they can handle whatever challenges come their way.

Adolescence is the developmental stage between childhood and adulthood. It is generally said to start just before the teenage years, and end just after them. Considered neither children nor adults, adolescents are in a transitional stage marked by considerable growth.

This module focuses on physical growth during adolescence. We first consider the extraordinary physical maturation that occurs during adolescence, triggered by the onset of puberty. We then discuss the consequences of early and late maturation and how they differ for males and females. We also consider nutrition. After examining the causes—and consequences—of obesity, we discuss eating disorders, which are surprisingly common at this stage.

The module concludes with a discussion of several major threats to adolescents' well-being—drugs, alcohol, tobacco, and STIs.

adolescence
the developmental stage that lies between childhood and adulthood

Physical Maturation

For young males of the Awa tribe, adolescence begins with an elaborate and—to Western eyes—gruesome ceremony to mark the passage from childhood to adulthood. The boys are whipped for 2 or 3 days with sticks and prickly branches. Through the whipping, the boys atone for their previous infractions and honor tribesmen who were killed in warfare.

Most of us probably feel gratitude that we did not have to endure such physical trials when we entered adolescence. But members of Western cultures have their own rites of passage, admittedly less fearsome, such as bar mitzvahs and bat mitzvahs at age 13 for Jewish boys and girls, and confirmation ceremonies in many Christian denominations (Eccles, Templeton, & Barber, 2003; Hoffman, 2003; Pankalla & Kośnik, 2018).

> **From an educator's perspective:** Why do you think many cultures regard the passage to adolescence as a significant transition that calls for unique ceremonies?

Regardless of their nature, the underlying purpose of these ceremonies tends to be the same across cultures: symbolically celebrating the physical changes that transform a child's body into an adult body capable of reproduction.

Growth During Adolescence: The Rapid Pace of Physical and Sexual Maturation

LO 6.1 Describe the physical changes that adolescents experience.

In only a few months, adolescents can grow several inches as they are transformed, at least physically, from children to young adults. During such a growth spurt—a period of very rapid growth in height and weight—boys, on average, grow 4.1 inches a year and girls 3.5 inches. Some adolescents grow as much as 5 inches in a single year (Tanner, 1972; Caino et al., 2004).

Boys' and girls' growth spurts begin at different ages. As you can see in Figure 6-1, girls' spurts begin around age 10, and boys start around age 12. At age 11, girls tend to be taller than boys. But by 13, boys, on average, are taller than girls—a state that persists for the remainder of the life span.

Puberty, the period when the sexual organs mature, begins when the pituitary gland in the brain signals other glands to begin producing the sex hormones, *androgens* (male hormones) or *estrogens* (female hormones), at adult levels. (Males and females produce both types of sex hormones, but males have higher levels of androgens and females have higher levels of estrogens.) The pituitary gland also signals the body to

puberty
the period during which the sexual organs mature

Figure 6-1 Growth Patterns

Patterns of growth are depicted in two ways. The first figure shows height at a given age, and the second shows the height increase that occurs from birth through the end of adolescence. Notice that girls begin their growth spurt around age 10, whereas boys begin their growth spurt at about age 12. However, by age 13, boys tend to be taller than girls. What are the social consequences of being taller or shorter than average for boys and girls?

SOURCE: Adapted from Cratty, 1986.

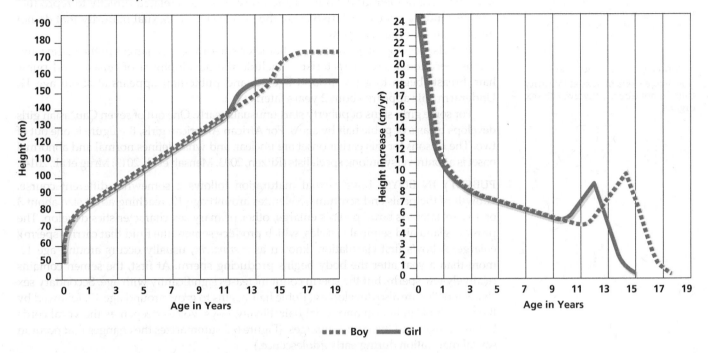

produce more growth hormones. These interact with the sex hormones to cause the growth spurt and puberty. The hormone *leptin* also appears to play a role in the onset of puberty.

Like the growth spurt, puberty begins earlier for girls, starting at around age 11 or 12, whereas boys begin at about age 13 or 14. However, this varies widely. Some girls begin puberty as early as 7 or 8 or as late as age 16.

PUBERTY IN GIRLS Although it is not clear why puberty begins when it does, environmental and cultural factors play a role. For example, **menarche**, the onset of menstruation and probably the most obvious sign of puberty in girls, varies greatly around the world. In poorer, developing countries, menstruation begins later than in more economically advantaged countries. Even within wealthier countries, more affluent girls begin to menstruate earlier than less affluent girls.

It appears that girls who are better nourished and healthier tend to start menstruation earlier than those suffering from malnutrition or chronic disease. Some studies have suggested that weight or the proportion of fat to muscle in the body play a key role in the onset of menarche. For example, in the United States, athletes with a low percentage of body fat may start menstruating later than less active girls. Conversely, obesity—which increases the secretion of leptin, a hormone related to the onset of menstruation—leads to earlier puberty (Sanchez-Garrido & Tena-Sempere, 2013; Shen et al., 2016; Kyweluk et al., 2018).

Other factors can affect the timing of menarche. For example, environmental stress from parental divorce or intense family conflict can result in an early onset (Ellis, 2004; Belsky et al., 2007; Allison & Hyde, 2013).

Over the past century or so, girls in the United States and other cultures have been entering puberty at earlier ages. In the late 19th century, menstruation began, on average, around age 14 or 15, compared with today's 11 or 12. The average age for other indicators of puberty, such as the attaining of adult height and sexual maturity, has also dropped, probably as a result of reduced disease and improved nutrition (Harris, Prior, & Koehoorn, 2008; James et al., 2012; Sun et al., 2017).

menarche
the onset of menstruation

secular trend
a pattern of change occurring over several generations

primary sex characteristics
characteristics associated with the development of the organs and structures of the body that directly relate to reproduction

secondary sex characteristics
the visible signs of sexual maturity that do not directly involve the sex organs

The earlier start of puberty is an example of a significant **secular trend**. Secular trends occur when a physical characteristic changes over the course of several generations, such as earlier onset of menstruation or increased height resulting from better nutrition over the centuries.

Menstruation is one of several changes in puberty related to the development of primary and secondary sex characteristics. **Primary sex characteristics** are associated with the development of the organs and body structures related directly to reproduction. **Secondary sex characteristics** are the visible signs of sexual maturity that do not involve the sex organs directly.

In girls, developing primary sex characteristics involves changes in the vagina and uterus. Secondary sex characteristics include the development of breasts and pubic hair. Breasts begin to grow around age 10, and pubic hair appears at about age 11. Underarm hair appears about 2 years later.

For some girls, signs of puberty start unusually early. One out of seven Caucasian girls develops breasts or pubic hair by age 8. For African American girls, the figure is one out of two. The reasons for this earlier onset are unclear, and what defines normal and abnormal onset is a controversy among specialists (Ritzen, 2003; Mensah et al., 2013; Mrug et al., 2014).

PUBERTY IN BOYS Boys' sexual maturation follows a somewhat different course. Growth of the penis and scrotum accelerates around age 12, reaching adult size about 3 or 4 years later. As boys' penises enlarge, other primary sex characteristics develop. The prostate gland and seminal vesicles, which produce semen (the fluid that carries sperm), enlarge. A boy's first ejaculation, known as *spermarche*, usually occurs around age 13, more than a year after the body begins producing sperm. At first, the semen contains relatively few sperm, but the sperm count increases significantly with age. Secondary sex characteristics are also developing. Pubic hair begins to grow around age 12, followed by the growth of underarm and facial hair. Finally, boys' voices deepen as the vocal cords become longer and the larynx enlarges. (Figure 6-2 summarizes the changes that occur in sexual maturation during early adolescence.)

Figure 6-2 Sexual Maturation

The changes in sexual maturation that occur for males and females during early adolescence.

SOURCE: Based on Patton & Viner, 2007.

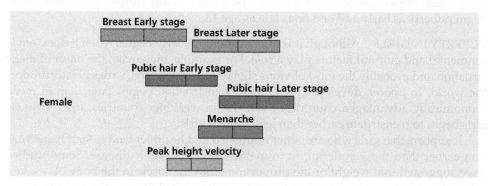

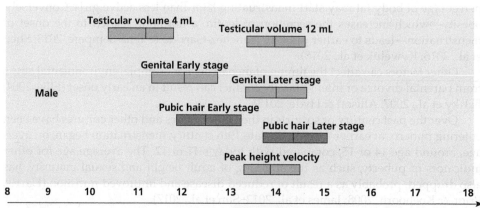

The surge in hormones that triggers puberty also may lead to rapid mood swings. Boys may have feelings of anger and annoyance associated with higher hormone levels. In girls, higher levels of hormones are associated with depression as well as anger (Fujisawa & Shinohara, 2011; Sun et al., 2016).

BODY IMAGE: REACTIONS TO PHYSICAL CHANGES IN ADOLESCENCE Unlike infants, who also undergo rapid growth, adolescents are aware of what is happening to their bodies, and they may react with horror or joy. Few, though, are neutral about the changes they are witnessing.

Some of the changes of adolescence carry psychological weight. In the past, girls tended to view menarche with anxiety because Western society emphasized the negative aspects of menstruation, including its cramps and messiness. Today, however, society views menstruation more positively, in part because more open discussion has demystified it; for example, television commercials for tampons are commonplace. As a result, menarche now typically increases self-esteem, enhances status, and provides greater self-awareness because girls see themselves as young adults (Matlin, 2003; Yuan, 2012; Chakraborty & De, 2014).

Note the changes that have occurred in just a few years in these pre- and post-puberty photos of the same boy.

Photos left and right: Lewis, Sherry

A boy's first ejaculation is roughly equivalent to menarche. However, although girls generally tell their mothers about the onset of menstruation, boys rarely mention their first ejaculation to their parents or even their friends. Why? One reason is that mothers provide the tampons or sanitary napkins girls need. For boys, the first ejaculation may be seen as a sign of their budding sexuality, an area they feel both uncertain about and reluctant to discuss with others (Janssen, 2007).

Menstruation and ejaculations occur privately, but changes in body shape and size are quite public. Teenagers frequently are embarrassed by these changes. Girls, in particular, are often unhappy with their new bodies. Western ideals of beauty call for an extreme thinness at odds with the actual shape of most women. Puberty considerably increases the amount of fatty tissue, and enlarges the hips and buttocks—a far cry from the pencil-thin body society seems to demand (Kretsch et al., 2016; Senín-Calderón et al., 2017; de Haan et al., 2018).

How children react to the onset of puberty depends in part on when it happens. Girls and boys who mature either much earlier or later than most of their peers are especially affected.

THE TIMING OF PUBERTY: THE CONSEQUENCES OF EARLY AND LATE MATURATION There are social consequences for early or late maturation. And these social consequences are important to adolescents.

Early Maturation For boys, early maturation is largely a plus. Early maturing boys tend to be more successful athletes, presumably because of their larger size. They also tend to be more popular and to have a more positive self-concept.

Early maturation in boys, though, does have a downside. Boys who mature early are more apt to have difficulties in school and to become involved in delinquency and substance abuse. Being larger in size, they are more likely to seek the company of older boys and become involved in age-inappropriate activities. Early maturers are also more conforming and lacking in humor, although they are more responsible and cooperative in adulthood. Overall, though, early maturation is positive for boys (Lynne et al., 2007; Mensah et al., 2013; Beltz et al., 2014).

The story is a bit different for early maturing girls. For them, the obvious changes in their bodies—such as the development of breasts—may lead them to feel uncomfortable and different from their peers. Moreover, because girls, in general, mature earlier than boys, early maturation tends to come at a young age in the girl's life. Early maturing girls may have to endure ridicule from their less mature classmates (Hubley & Arim, 2012; Skoog & Özdemir, 2016; Su et al., 2018).

Early maturation, though, is not a completely negative experience for girls. Those who mature earlier are more often sought as dates, and their popularity may enhance their self-concept. This can be psychologically challenging, however. Early maturers may not be socially ready for the kind of one-on-one dating situations that most girls deal with at a later age. Moreover, their obvious deviance from their later-maturing peers may produce anxiety, unhappiness, and depression (Kaltiala-Heino, Kosunen, & Rimpela, 2003; Galvao et al., 2013).

Consequently, unless a young girl who has developed secondary sex characteristics early can handle the disapproval she may encounter when she conspicuously displays her growing sexuality, the outcome of early maturation may be negative. In countries in which attitudes about sexuality are more liberal, the results of early maturation may be more positive. For example, in Germany, which has a more open view of sex, early maturing girls have higher self-esteem than such girls in the United States. Furthermore, the consequences of early maturation vary even within the United States, depending on the views of girls' peer groups and on prevailing community standards regarding sex (Petersen, 2000; Güre, Uçanok, & Sayil, 2006).

Late Maturation   As with early maturers, the situation for late maturers is mixed, although here boys fare worse than girls. Boys who are smaller and lighter tend to be considered less attractive. Being small, they are at a disadvantage in sports activities. They may also suffer socially because boys are expected to be taller than their dates. If these difficulties diminish a boy's self-concept, the disadvantages of late maturation could extend well into adulthood. Coping with the challenges of late maturation may actually help males, however. Late-maturing boys grow up to be assertive and insightful, and are more creatively playful than early maturers (Kaltiala-Heino, Kosunen, & Rimpela, 2003; Skoog, 2013; Benoit, Lacourse, & Claes, 2014).

The picture for late-maturing girls is generally positive even though they may be overlooked in dating and other mixed-sex activities during junior high and middle school and may have relatively low social status. In fact, late-maturing girls may suffer fewer emotional problems. Before they reach 10th grade and have begun to mature visibly, they are more apt to fit the slender, "leggy" body type society idealizes than their early maturing peers, who tend to look heavier in comparison (Kaminaga, 2007; Leen-Feldmer et al., 2008).

The reactions to early and late maturation paint a complex picture. As we have seen, an individual's development is affected by a constellation of factors. Some developmentalists suggest that changes in peer groups, family dynamics, and particularly schools and other societal institutions may determine an adolescent's behavior more than age of maturation and the effects of puberty in general (Mendle et al., 2007; Spear, 2010; Hubley & Arim, 2012).

Nutrition, Food, and Eating Disorders: Fueling the Growth of Adolescence

LO 6.2   Analyze the nutritional needs and concerns of adolescents.

At 16, Ariel Porter was pretty, outgoing, and popular. But when a boy she liked kidded her about having thighs like "tree trunks," she took it seriously. She began to obsess about food, using her mom's food scale to weigh everything that went into her mouth. She kept charts to portion sizes and calories, cutting her food into tiny morsels and then leaving most of it on her plate.

In a few months, Ariel went from 110 pounds to 90. Her hips and ribs became clearly visible, and her fingers and knees ached constantly. She stopped menstruating, and her fingernails broke easily. Still, Ariel insisted she was overweight. It wasn't until her older sister returned from college that Ariel believed she had a problem. Her sister took one look at her, gasped audibly, and broke down crying.

Ariel's problem was a severe eating disorder, anorexia nervosa. As we have seen, the cultural ideal of slim and fit favors late-developing girls. But when development does occur, how do girls, and increasingly, boys, cope with an image in the mirror that deviates from the popular media ideal?

The rapid physical growth of adolescence is fueled by an increase in food consumption. Particularly during the growth spurt, adolescents eat substantial quantities of food, increasing their intake of calories rather dramatically. During the teenage years, the average girl requires some 2,200 calories a day, and the average boy requires 2,800. Of course, not just any calories nourish this growth. Several nutrients are essential, particularly calcium and iron. Milk and certain vegetables provide calcium for bone growth, and calcium may prevent osteoporosis—the thinning of bones—that affects 25 percent of women in later life. Iron is also necessary because iron-deficiency anemia is not uncommon among teenagers.

Obesity has become the most common nutritional concern during adolescence. In addition to issues of health, what are some psychological concerns about obesity in adolescence?

For most adolescents, the major issue is eating a sufficient balance of nutritious foods. Two extremes of nutrition concern a substantial minority and can create real threats to health: obesity and eating disorders like the one afflicting Ariel Porter.

OBESITY The most common nutritional concern in adolescence is obesity. One in five adolescents is overweight (having a body mass index—BMI—between the 85th and 95th percentile of adolescents of the same age and sex, and 1 in 20 can be classified as obese (a BMI at or above the 95th percentile for adolescents of the same age and sex). The proportion of females who are classified as obese increases over the course of adolescence (Kimm et al., 2003; Mikulovic et al., 2011; U.S. Preventive Services Task Force, 2017).

Adolescents are obese for the same reasons as younger children, but special concerns with body image may have severe psychological consequences at this age. The potential health consequences of obesity during adolescence are also problematic. Obesity taxes the circulatory system, increasing the risk of high blood pressure and diabetes. Obese adolescents also have an 80 percent chance of becoming obese adults (Huang et al., 2013; Morrison et al., 2015; Gowey et al., 2016).

Lack of exercise is a major culprit. One survey found that by the end of the teenage years, few females get much exercise outside of school physical education classes. In fact, the older they get, the less they exercise. This is especially true for older black female adolescents, more than half of whom report *no* physical exercise outside of school, compared with about a third of white adolescents (Nicholson & Browning, 2012; Puterman et al., 2016; Kornides et al., 2018).

Additional reasons for the high rate of obesity during adolescence include the easy availability of fast foods, which deliver large portions of high-calorie, high-fat cuisine at prices adolescents can afford. Furthermore, many adolescents spend a significant proportion of their leisure time inside their homes watching television, playing video games, and surfing the Web. Such sedentary activities not only keep adolescents from exercising, but they often are accompanied by snacks of junk foods (Thivel et al., 2011; Laska et al., 2012; Bailey-Davis et al., 2017).

ANOREXIA NERVOSA AND BULIMIA NERVOSA Fear of fat and of growing obese can create its own problems—for example, Ariel Porter suffered from **anorexia nervosa**, a severe eating disorder in which individuals refuse to eat. A troubled body image leads some adolescents to deny that their behavior and appearance, which may become skeletal, are out of the ordinary.

Anorexia is a dangerous psychological disorder; some 15 to 20 percent of its victims starve themselves to death. It primarily afflicts women between the ages of 12 and 40; intelligent, successful, and attractive white adolescent girls from affluent homes are the most susceptible. Anorexia is also becoming a problem for boys; about 10 percent of victims are male. This percentage is rising and is often associated with the use of steroids. Because of cultural expectations, males are less likely to seek

anorexia nervosa

a severe eating disorder in which individuals refuse to eat, while denying that their behavior and appearance, which may become skeletal, are out of the ordinary

This young woman suffers from anorexia nervosa, a severe eating disorder in which people refuse to eat, while denying that their behavior and appearance are out of the ordinary.

bulimia nervosa
an eating disorder characterized by binges on large quantities of food, followed by purges of the food through vomiting or the use of laxatives

treatment for eating disorders (Schecklmann et al., 2012; Herpertz-Dahlmann, 2015; Austen & Griffiths, 2018).

Though they eat little, anorexics tend to focus their lives on food. They may shop often, collect cookbooks, talk about food, or cook huge meals for others. They may be incredibly thin but their body images are so distorted that they see themselves as disgustingly fat and try to lose more weight. Even when they grow skeletal, they cannot see what they have become.

Bulimia nervosa, another eating disorder, is characterized by *binge eating*, consuming large amounts of food, followed by *purging* through vomiting or the use of laxatives. Bulimics may eat an entire gallon of ice cream or a whole package of tortilla chips, but then feel such powerful guilt and depression that they intentionally rid themselves of the food. The disorder poses real risks. Though a bulimia nervosa sufferer's weight remains fairly normal, the constant vomiting and diarrhea of the binge-and-purge cycles may produce a chemical imbalance that triggers heart failure.

Why eating disorders occur is not clear, but several factors may be at work. Dieting often precedes the onset of eating disorders because society exhorts even normal-weight individuals to be ever thinner. Losing weight may lead to feelings of control and success that encourage more dieting. Girls who mature early and have a higher level of body fat are more susceptible to eating disorders in later adolescence as they try to trim their mature bodies to fit the cultural ideal of a thin, boyish physique. Adolescents who are clinically depressed are also prone to develop eating disorders later (Wade & Watson, 2012; Schvey, Eddy, & Tanofsky-Kraff, 2016; Paans et al., 2018).

Some experts suggest that a biological cause may underlie both anorexia nervosa and bulimia nervosa. Twin studies suggest genetic components are involved. In addition, hormonal imbalances sometimes occur in sufferers (Baker et al., 2009; Keski-Rahkonen et al., 2013; Xu et al., 2017).

Other attempts to explain eating disorders emphasize psychological and social factors. For instance, some experts suggest that the disorders are a result of perfectionistic, overdemanding parents or by-products of other family difficulties. Culture also plays a role. Anorexia nervosa, for instance, is found primarily in cultures that idealize slender female bodies. Because in most places such a standard does not hold, anorexia is not prevalent outside the United States (Bennett, 2008; Bodell, Joiner, & Ialongo, 2012; Lewis et al., 2018).

For example, anorexia is relatively rare in Asia, with the exceptions of areas in which Western influence is greatest. Furthermore, anorexia nervosa is a fairly recent disorder. It was not seen in the 17th and 18th centuries, when the ideal of the female body was a plump corpulence. The increasing number of boys with anorexia in the United States may be related to a growing emphasis on a muscular male physique that features little body fat (Mangweth, Hausmann, & Walch, 2004; Greenberg, Cwikel, & Mirsky, 2007; Pearson, Combs, & Smith, 2010).

Brain Development and Thought: Paving the Way for Cognitive Growth

LO 6.3 Explain the relationship between brain development and cognitive growth in adolescents.

Teenagers tend to assert themselves more as they gain greater independence. This independence is, in part, the result of changes in the brain that bring significant advances in cognitive abilities. As the number of neurons (the cells of the nervous system) continues to grow, and their interconnections become richer and more complex, adolescent thinking becomes more sophisticated (Toga & Thompson, 2003; Petanjek et al., 2008; Blakemore, 2012).

The brain produces an oversupply of gray matter during adolescence, which is later pruned back by 1 to 2 percent each year (see Figure 6-3). Myelination—the process

Figure 6-3 Pruning Gray Matter

As children grow into adulthood, gray matter is pruned from the brain. These composite scans show changes in gray matter and other physical changes in the cortex from age 4 through 21.

SOURCE: Gogtay et al., 2004.

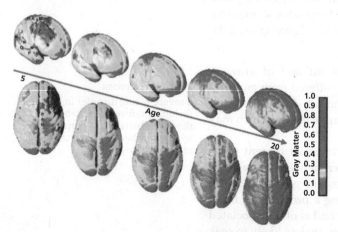

of insulating nerve cells with fat cells—increases, making the transmission of neural messages more efficient. Both pruning and increased myelination contribute to the growing cognitive abilities of adolescents (Sowell et al., 2003; Mychasluk & Metz, 2016; Oyefiade et al., 2018).

The prefrontal cortex of the brain, which is not fully developed until the early 20s, undergoes considerable development during adolescence. The *prefrontal cortex* allows people to think, evaluate, and make complex judgments in a uniquely human way. It underlies the increasingly complex intellectual achievements that are possible during adolescence.

At this stage, the prefrontal cortex becomes increasingly efficient in communicating with other parts of the brain, creating a communication system that is more distributed and sophisticated, which permits the different areas of the brain to process information more effectively (Scherf, Sweeney, & Luna, 2006; Hare et al., 2008; Wiggins et al., 2014).

The prefrontal cortex also provides impulse control. An individual with a fully developed prefrontal cortex is able to inhibit the desire to act on such emotions as anger or rage. In adolescence, however, the prefrontal cortex is biologically immature; the ability to inhibit impulses is not fully developed (Weinberger, 2001; Steinberg & Scott, 2003; Eshel et al., 2007; Cao et al., 2018).

Ayush Garg

The prefrontal cortex, the area of the brain responsible for impulse control, is biologically immature during adolescence, leading to some of the risky and impulsive behavior associated with the age group.

This brain immaturity may lead to some of the risky and impulsive behaviors that are characteristic of adolescence. Furthermore, some researchers theorize that not only do adolescents underestimate the risks of risky behavior, but they also overestimate the rewards that will come from the behavior. A number of areas of the brain in developing adolescents make them more sensitive to social stimuli, which in turn makes risky behavior more rewarding, as well as making them more susceptible to the influence of their peers. It is not until they reach adulthood that adolescents learn to demonstrate greater self-regulation (Albert, Chein, & Steinberg, 2013; Smith, Chein, & Steinberg, 2013; Blankenstein et al., 2018).

SLEEP DEPRIVATION With increasing academic and social demands, adolescents go to bed later and get up earlier, leaving them sleep deprived. This deprivation coincides with a shift in their internal clocks. Older adolescents have a need to go to bed later and to sleep later in the morning, requiring 9 hours of sleep to feel rested. Yet half of adolescents sleep 7 hours or less each night, and almost one in five gets less than 6 hours. Because they typically have early morning classes but don't feel sleepy until late at night, they end up getting far less sleep than their bodies crave (Wolfson & Richards, 2011; Dagys et al., 2012; Cohen-Zion et al., 2016).

Sleep-deprived teens have lower grades, are more depressed, and have greater difficulty controlling their moods. They are also at great risk for auto accidents (Roberts, Roberts, & Duong, 2009; Luo, Zhang, & Pan, 2013; de Bruin et al., 2017).

Threats to Adolescents' Well-Being

It took a car crash to wake Tom Jansen up—literally and figuratively. The police called at 12:30 a.m. and told him to pick up his 13-year-old daughter at the hospital. The accident wasn't serious, but what Tom learned that night might have saved Roni's life. The police found alcohol on her breath and on that of every other occupant of the car, including the driver.

> Tom always knew that someday he'd have to have the "alcohol and drug talk" with Roni, but he had hoped it would be in high school, not middle school. Thinking back, he now saw that he had been wrong to chalk up the classic signs of a drug or alcohol problem—school absences, declining grades, general listlessness—to "adolescent angst." It was time to face facts.
>
> He and Roni met with a counselor weekly for several months. At first Roni was hostile, but one evening she started sobbing while they were doing the dishes. Tom simply held her, never saying a word. But from that moment, he knew his Roni was back.

Tom Jansen learned that alcohol was not the only drug Roni was using. As her friends later admitted, Roni had all the signs of becoming what they called a "garbage head"—someone who would try anything. Had the accident never happened, Roni might have gotten into serious trouble or even lost her life.

Drugs, Alcohol, and Tobacco

LO 6.4 **Describe major threats to adolescents from substance use and abuse.**

Few cases of adolescent alcohol use produce such extreme results as mentioned in Roni's story, but the use of alcohol, as well as other kinds of substance use and abuse, is one of several health threats in adolescence, usually one of the healthiest periods of life. Although the extent of risky behavior is unknown, drugs, alcohol, and tobacco pose serious threats to adolescents' health and well-being.

DRUG ABUSE How commonly do adolescents use drugs during adolescence? Very. For example, 1 in 15 high school seniors smokes marijuana on a daily or near-daily basis. Furthermore, marijuana usage has remained at fairly high levels over the past decade, and attitudes about its use have become more positive as marijuana has been legalized in a number of states for adult usage (Johnston et al., 2016; Lipperman-Kreda & Grube, 2018; also see Figure 6-4).

Adolescents use drugs for many reasons. Some seek to get high and elevate their mood. Others hope to escape the pressures of everyday life, however temporarily. Some adolescents try drugs simply for the thrill of doing something illegal.

Other adolescents get hooked on drugs after being prescribed painkillers by physicians to treat a medical condition, and then find it difficult to stop. The drug use of well-known role models, such as movie stars and athletes, may also be enticing. And peer pressure plays a role: Adolescents are especially influenced by their peer groups (Nation & Heflinger, 2006; Young et al., 2006; Pandina, Johnson, & White, 2010).

Sometimes drugs are used illegally in an effort to enhance academic performance. A growing number of high school students are using drugs such as Adderall,

Figure 6-4 Marijuana Use Remains Steady

According to an annual survey, the proportion of students reporting marijuana use over the past 12 months has remained steady at fairly high levels.

SOURCE: Schulenberg et al., 2017.

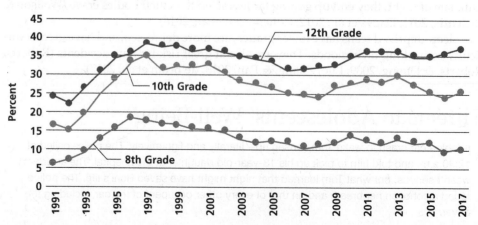

---

an amphetamine prescribed for attention deficit hyperactivity disorder. Adderall users assume it increases focus, and they think it increases the ability to study and allows them to study for long hours (Schwarz, 2012; Munro et al., 2017).

The use of drugs poses several dangers. Some drugs are addictive. **Addictive drugs** produce a biological or psychological dependence, leading users to increasingly crave them.

With a biological addiction, the drug's presence becomes so common that the body cannot function in its absence. Addiction causes actual physical—and potentially lingering—changes in the nervous system. The drug may no longer provide a "high," but may be necessary to maintain the perception of normalcy (Hauser et al., 2017).

Drugs also can produce psychological addiction. People grow to depend on drugs to cope with everyday stress. If used as an escape, drugs may prevent adolescents from confronting—and solving—the problems that led to drug use in the first place. Even casual use of less hazardous drugs can escalate to dangerous forms of substance abuse.

Adolescent drug use makes up a large part of the current opioid epidemic that is affecting the United States. As we will discuss later in the book, the rate of overdoses due to opioid use has increased dramatically in the past decade. (Opioids include both legally prescribed drugs such as codeine, fentanyl, and OxyContin, and illegal drugs such as heroin.) Almost 100 Americans die every day from an opioid overdose, and the number of drug overdose deaths among 15- to 19-year-olds increased 15 percent for males from 2014 to 2015, and 35 percent for females from 2013 to 2015 (Katz, 2017).

Whatever the reason for using drugs in the first place, drug addiction is among the most difficult of all behaviors to modify. Even with extensive treatment, addictive cravings are hard to suppress.

ALCOHOL: USE AND ABUSE Sixty-two percent of college students have something in common: They've consumed at least one alcoholic drink during the past 30 days. One third say they've had five or more drinks within the past 2 weeks, while 1 in 25 report having 15 or more. High school students, too, are drinkers: More than 60 percent of high school seniors report having consumed alcohol by the end of high school, and 42 percent have done so by 8th grade. About 45 percent of 12th graders and quarter of 8th graders say that they have been drunk at least once in their lives (Ford, 2007; Johnston et al., 2016; Schulenberg et al., 2017).

Binge drinking is a particular problem on college campuses. Binge drinking is defined for men as drinking five or more drinks in one sitting; for women, who tend to weigh less and whose bodies absorb alcohol less efficiently, binge drinking is defined as four drinks in one sitting. Surveys find that almost 40 percent of male college students and 35 percent of female college students say they participated in binge drinking during the previous 2 weeks (see Figure 6-5) (Cheng & Anthony, 2018; National Institute on Alcohol Abuse and Alcoholism, 2018; Johnston et al., 2018).

Binge drinking affects even those who don't drink or drink very little. Two-thirds of lighter drinkers reported that they have been disturbed by drunken students while sleeping

Figure 6-5 Binge Drinking Among College Students

Although binge drinking has declined slightly since figures first began to be collected in the 1980s (at least among males), the overall percentage of 19- to 22-year-old college students who report having engaged in binge drinking in the past 2 weeks remains high. Why is binge drinking so common?

SOURCE: Johnston et al., 2018.

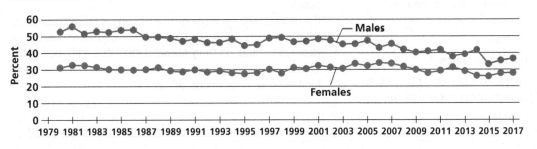

or studying. Around a third have been insulted or humiliated by a drunken student, and 25 percent of women between the ages of 18 and 24 report experiencing alcohol-related sexual assault or date rape (Squeglia et al., 2012; Herman-Kinney & Kinney, 2013; Spear et al., 2013; National Institute on Alcohol Abuse and Alcoholism, 2018).

Furthermore, brain scans show damaged tissue in teenage binge drinkers compared to non-binge drinkers. They have thinner and lower-volume regions in the prefrontal cortex and cerebellar regions, and their white matter is reduced. Such findings suggest that that alcohol has toxic effects on the brain during a period in which the brain is particularly susceptible to damage, and it may lead to permanent damage to the structure of neurons in the brain (Cservenka & Brumback, 2017; Kaarre et al., 2018).

There are many reasons adolescents drink. For some—especially male athletes, who tend to drink more than their peers—drinking is a way to prove their prowess. As with drug use, others drink to release inhibitions and tension, and to reduce stress. Many begin because they believe everyone else is drinking heavily, something known as the *false consensus effect* (Dunn et al., 2012; Archimi & Kuntsche, 2014; Drane, Modecki, & Barber, 2017).

alcoholics

people with alcohol problems who have learned to depend on alcohol and are unable to control their drinking

Some adolescents cannot control their alcohol use. **Alcoholics** learn to depend on alcohol and are unable to stop drinking. They develop an increasing tolerance for it, and they need to drink ever-larger amounts to get the positive effects they crave. Some drink throughout the day, and others go on binges.

Why some adolescents become alcoholics is not fully understood. Genetics plays a role: Alcoholism runs in families, though not all alcoholics have family members with alcohol problems. For adolescents with an alcoholic parent or family member, alcoholism may be triggered by efforts to deal with the stress (Berenson, 2005; Clarke et al., 2008; Kendler et al., 2018).

Of course, the origins of an adolescent's alcohol or drug problems matter less than getting help. Parents, teachers, and friends can help a teen—if they realize there is a problem. Some of the telltale signs are described in the *Development in Your Life* box.

Development in Your Life

Hooked on Drugs or Alcohol?

It is not always easy to know if an adolescent is abusing drugs or alcohol, but there are signals. Among them are the following:

Identification with the drug culture

- Drug-related magazines or slogans on clothing
- Conversation and jokes that involve drugs
- Hostility when discussing drugs
- Collection of beer cans

Signs of physical deterioration

- Memory lapses, short attention span, difficulty concentrating
- Poor physical coordination, slurred or incoherent speech
- Unhealthy appearance, indifference to hygiene and grooming
- Bloodshot eyes, dilated pupils

Dramatic changes in school performance

- Marked downturn in grades—not just from Cs to Fs, but from As to Bs and Cs; assignments not completed
- Increased absenteeism or tardiness

Changes in behavior

- Chronic dishonesty (lying, stealing, cheating); trouble with the police
- Changes in friends; evasiveness in talking about new friends
- Possession of large amounts of money
- Increasing and inappropriate anger, hostility, irritability, secretiveness
- Reduced motivation, energy, self-discipline, self-esteem
- Diminished interest in extracurricular activities and hobbies

(Adapted from Franck & Brownstone, 1991; Johnston et al., 2007)

If an adolescent—or anyone else—fits any of these descriptors, help is probably needed. Call the national hotline run by the National Institute on Drug Abuse at (800) 662-4357 or visit the Web site at www.nida.nih.gov. You can also find a local listing for Alcoholics Anonymous online.

TOBACCO: THE DANGERS OF SMOKING   Despite an awareness of the dangers of smoking, many adolescents indulge in it. Recent figures show that, overall, smoking is declining among adolescents, but the numbers remain substantial, and within certain groups, the numbers are increasing. Smoking is on the rise among girls, and in several countries, including Austria, Norway, and Sweden, more girls than boys are smoking. There are racial differences, too: White children and those of lower socioeconomic status are more likely to experiment with cigarettes and to start smoking earlier than black children and those of higher socioeconomic status. Also, significantly more white males of high school age smoke than do their black male peers, although the difference is narrowing (Baker, Brandon, & Chassin, 2004; Fergusson et al., 2007; Proctor, Barnett, & Muilenburg, 2012).

Smoking is becoming a habit that is harder to maintain because there are growing social sanctions against it. It's becoming more difficult to find a comfortable place to smoke: More places, including schools and places of business, have become "smoke-free." Even so, a good number of adolescents still smoke, despite knowing the dangers of smoking and of secondhand smoke. Why, then, do adolescents begin to smoke and maintain the habit?

One reason is that for some adolescents, smoking is seen as a rite of passage, a sign of growing up. In addition, seeing influential models, such as film stars, parents, and peers, smoking increases the chances that an adolescent will take up the habit. Cigarettes are also addictive. Nicotine, the active chemical ingredient of cigarettes, can produce biological and psychological dependency quickly. Although one or two cigarettes do not usually produce a lifetime smoker, it takes only a little more to start the habit. In fact, people who smoke as few as 10 cigarettes early in their lives stand an 80 percent chance of becoming habitual smokers (Wills et al., 2008; Holliday & Gould, 2016; Azagba, 2018).

One of the newest trends in smoking is the use of e-cigarettes, known as *vaping*. E-cigarettes are battery-powered cigarette-shaped devices that deliver nicotine that is vaporized to form a mist. Vaping has become quite prevalent among adolescents; around one-fifth of 12th graders report vaping in the past year (Johnston et al., 2018).

Vaping appears to be less harmful than traditional cigarettes. However the health effects of vaping are unclear, although some research suggests that vaping during adolescence increases the likelihood of smoking tobacco later in life, and the U.S. government has sought to regulate the sale of e-cigarettes (Lanza, Russell, & Braymiller, 2017; Dunbar et al., 2018; Lee et al., 2018).

Sexually Transmitted Infections

LO 6.5   Describe the dangers that adolescent sexual practices can present.

One out of four adolescents contracts a **sexually transmitted infection (STI)** before graduating from high school. Four in 10 sexually active teenage girls have had an STI that has the potential for causing infertility. Overall, around 2.5 million teenagers contract an STI each year (Forhan et al., 2009; Centers for Disease Control and Prevention, 2017; also see Figure 6-6).

sexually transmitted infection (STI)
an infection that is spread through sexual contact

The most common STI is *human papilloma virus (HPV)*. HPV can be transmitted through genital contact without intercourse. Most infections do not have symptoms, but HPV can produce genital warts and, in some cases, can lead to cervical cancer. A vaccine that protects against some kinds of HPV is now available. The U.S. Centers for Disease Control and Prevention recommends it be routinely administered to girls and boys 11 to 12 years of age—a recommendation that has provoked considerable political reaction (Schwarz et al., 2012; Wilson et al., 2017).

Another common STI is *trichomoniasis*, an infection in the vagina or penis, which is caused by a parasite. Initially without symptoms, it can eventually cause a painful discharge. *Chlamydia*, a bacterial infection, starts with few symptoms, but later causes burning urination and a discharge from the penis or vagina. It can lead to pelvic inflammation and even to sterility. Chlamydia can be treated with antibiotics (Nockels & Oakshott, 1999; Fayers et al., 2003).

Figure 6-6 Sexually Transmitted Infections (STIs) Among Adolescents

Most new cases of sexually transmitted infections occur in youth and young adults.

SOURCE: Henry J. Kaiser Family Foundation, 2014.

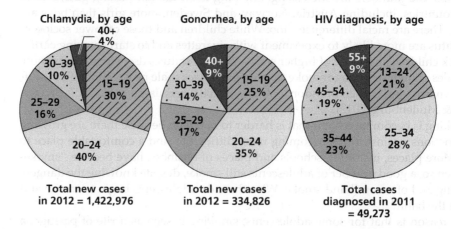

Genital herpes is a virus not unlike the cold sores that appear around the mouth. Its first symptoms are often small blisters or sores around the genitals, which may break open and become quite painful. Although the sores may heal after a few weeks, the infection often recurs and the cycle repeats itself. When the sores reappear, this incurable infection is contagious.

Gonorrhea and *syphilis* are the oldest known STIs, with cases recorded by ancient historians. Both infections were deadly before antibiotics, but they can now be treated effectively. *Acquired immunodeficiency syndrome*, or *AIDS*, is the deadliest of sexually transmitted diseases and a leading cause of death among young people. AIDS has no permanent cure, but treatments have improved greatly in recent years, and AIDS is no longer the sure death sentence that it used to be. Although it began as a problem that primarily affected homosexuals, it has spread to other populations, including heterosexuals and intravenous drug users. Minorities have been particularly hard hit: African Americans and Hispanics account for 70 percent of new AIDS cases, and African American males have almost eight times the prevalence of AIDS as Caucasian males. Already, more than 35 million people have died from AIDS worldwide, and people living with the disease number 36 million worldwide (UNAIDS, 2018).

> **From a health-care provider's perspective:** Why do adolescents' increased cognitive abilities, including the ability to reason and to think experimentally, fail to deter them from abusing drugs and alcohol, using tobacco, and contracting STIs? How might you use these abilities to design a program to prevent these problems?

Short of abstinence, there is no certain way to avoid STIs. However, there are ways to make sex safer; these are listed in Table 6-1.

Even with substantial sex education, the use of safer sex practices is far from universal. Teenagers believe their chances of contracting STIs are minimal. This is particularly true when they view their partner as "safe"—someone they know well and with whom they have had a relatively long-term relationship (Widman et al., 2014; Doull et al., 2017).

Unfortunately, unless one knows a partner's complete sexual history and STI status, unprotected sex remains a risk. And that information is difficult to get. Not only is it embarrassing to ask, partners may not be accurate reporters, whether from ignorance of their own exposure, embarrassment, forgetfulness, or a desire for privacy. As a result, STIs remain a significant problem.

Table 6-1 Safer Sex Practices

The only foolproof method of avoiding a sexually transmitted infection (STI) is abstinence. However, by following the "safer sex" practices listed, one can significantly reduce the risk of contracting an STI:

- **Know your sexual partner—well.** Before having sex with someone, learn about his or her sexual history.
- **Use condoms.** For those in sexual relationships, condoms are the most reliable means of preventing transmission of STIs. In addition, dental dams (also called *vaginal dams*) can provide a precautionary barrier during oral sex.
- **Avoid the exchange of bodily fluids, particularly semen.** In particular, avoid anal intercourse. The AIDS virus in particular can spread through small tears in the rectum, making anal intercourse without condoms particularly dangerous. Oral sex, once thought relatively safe, is now viewed as potentially dangerous for contracting the AIDS virus.
- **Stay sober.** Using alcohol and drugs impairs judgment and can lead to poor decisions—and it makes using a condom correctly more difficult.
- **Consider the benefits of monogamy.** People in long-term, monogamous relationships with partners who have been faithful are at a lower risk of contracting STIs.

Review, Check, and Apply

Review

LO 6.1 Describe the physical changes that adolescents experience.

Adolescence is a period of rapid physical growth, including the changes puberty brings. Adolescents' responses to puberty range widely—from confusion to increased self-esteem. Both boys and girls face positive as well as negative consequences regarding early and late maturation.

LO 6.2 Analyze the nutritional needs and concerns of adolescents.

Adequate nutrition is essential to fuel adolescents' physical growth. Changing physical needs and environmental pressures can cause obesity or eating disorders.

LO 6.3 Explain the relationship between brain development and cognitive growth in adolescents.

Changes in the brain during adolescence, including the ongoing development of the prefrontal cortex, bring significant advances in cognitive abilities. For all its growth, though, the adolescent brain is not yet fully mature, leading to the conclusion that people younger than age 18 should not be subject to the death penalty.

LO 6.4 Describe major threats to adolescents from substance use and abuse.

The use of illegal drugs and alcohol is prevalent among adolescents as a way to find pleasure, avoid pressure, or gain the approval of peers. Some drugs popular among adolescents are addictive, producing either a physical or a psychological dependence. Binge drinking is a problem for drinkers and those around them, causing brain damage in the drinker and irresponsible or dangerous behavior toward others. The negative health effects of tobacco use are well-established. Despite this, adolescents often smoke to enhance their image or to emulate adults.

LO 6.5 Describe the dangers that adolescent sexual practices can present.

One out of four adolescents contracts an STI before graduating from high school. AIDS is the most serious of the STIs. Safe sex practices or abstinence can prevent AIDS, but adolescents often ignore these strategies.

Check Yourself

1. Which of the following is an example of a primary sex characteristic?
   a. Growth of pubic hair
   b. Development of breasts
   c. Changes in the uterus
   d. Sudden increase in height

2. The most common nutritional concern in adolescence is _____.
   a. anorexia nervosa
   b. sleep deprivation
   c. bulimia nervosa
   d. obesity

3. Adolescents may grow to depend on drugs to cope with the stresses they encounter every day. This is known as _____.
   a. binge drinking
   b. biological dependence
   c. compensatory drug use
   d. psychological dependence

4. _____ is the most common sexually transmitted infection.
   a. Syphilis
   b. Human papilloma virus (HPV)
   c. Chlamydia
   d. Acquired immunodeficiency syndrome (AIDS)

Applying Lifespan Development
How might adolescents' concerns about self-image contribute to smoking and alcohol use?

Module 6.2

Cognitive Development in Adolescence

She grew up to be a lawyer, district attorney, and ultimately a Justice of the Supreme Court, but Sonia Sotomayor did not start life at the top. Born in New York City to Puerto Rican parents, Sotomayor lost her father when she was 9. Although she was raised in poverty, she excelled academically and graduated from Princeton University and Yale Law School. After a distinguished legal career, she was appointed to the Supreme Court, becoming the first Hispanic Justice.

WDC Photos/Alamy Stock Photo

The extraordinary success of Sonia Sotomayor is but one example of the impressive intellectual growth that occurs during adolescence. In fact, by the end of this stage, adolescents match adults in cognitive abilities in major respects.

In this module, we examine adolescents' cognitive development. We first consider the Piagetian approach, discussing how adolescents use formal operations to solve problems. We then look at a different viewpoint: the increasingly influential information processing perspectives. We consider the growth of metacognitive abilities, through which adolescents gain awareness of their own thinking processes. We also look at the ways in which metacognition leads to egocentrism and the invention of personal fables.

The module then examines school performance. After discussing the profound impact that socioeconomic status has on school achievement, we consider school performance and ethnicity. We then look at the impact cyberspace has on education, the skills students must learn to use the Internet effectively, and the dangers posed by the Internet. We close with a discussion of the role socioeconomic status plays in high school dropout rates.

Cognitive Development

Ms. Mejia smiled as she read a highly creative paper. As part of her eighth-grade American Government class, she asked students to write about what their lives would be like if America had not won its war for independence from Britain. She had tried a similar task with her sixth graders, but many of them were unable to imagine anything other than what they knew. Her eighth graders, however, were inventing some interesting scenarios. One boy imagined himself as Lord Lucas; a girl imagined that she would serve a rich land-owner; another that she would plot to overthrow the government.

What is it that sets adolescents' thinking apart from that of younger children? One of the major changes is the ability to think beyond the concrete, current situation to what *might* or *could* be. Adolescents are able to keep in their heads a variety of abstract possibilities, and they can see issues in relative, as opposed to absolute, terms. Instead of viewing problems as having black-and-white solutions, they are capable of perceiving shades of gray.

Once again we can use several alternate approaches, based on different theories, to explain adolescents' cognitive development. We'll begin by returning to Piaget's theory, which has had a significant influence on how developmentalists think about thinking during adolescence.

Piagetian Approaches to Cognitive Development: Using Formal Operations

LO 6.6   Analyze Piaget's account of adolescent cognitive development.

Leigh, age 14, is asked to solve a problem: What determines the speed at which a pendulum moves back and forth? Leigh is given a weight hanging from a string and told that she can vary several things: the length of the string, the weight of the object, the amount of force used to push the string, and the height to which the weight is raised in an arc before it is released.

Leigh doesn't remember, but she was asked to solve the same problem at age 8 as part of a longitudinal research study. She was then in the concrete operational period, and her efforts were not successful. Her haphazard approach showed no systematic plan of action. For instance, she simultaneously tried to push the pendulum harder *and* shorten the length of the string *and* increase the weight on the string. Because she varied so many factors at once, when the pendulum's speed changed, she had no way of knowing what had made the difference.

Now, Leigh is more systematic. Rather than immediately pushing and pulling at the pendulum, she stops to think about which factors to consider. She ponders how she might test which factor is important, forming a hypothesis. Then, just as a scientist conducts an experiment, she varies only one factor at a time. By examining each variable separately and systematically, she comes to the correct solution: The length of the string determines the speed of the pendulum.

USING FORMAL OPERATIONS TO SOLVE PROBLEMS   Leigh's approach to the pendulum question, a problem devised by psychologist Jean Piaget, shows she has moved into the formal operational period of cognitive development (Piaget & Inhelder, 1958). In the **formal operational stage** people develop the ability to think abstractly. Piaget suggested that people reach it at the start of adolescence, around age 12.

formal operational stage
the period at which people develop the ability to think abstractly

Adolescents can consider problems in abstract rather than concrete terms by using formal principles of logic. They can test their understanding by systematically conducting rudimentary experiments and observing the results. Thus, the adolescent Leigh could think about the pendulum problem abstractly, and she understood how to test her hypotheses.

Adolescents are able to use formal reasoning, starting with a general theory about what causes a certain outcome and then deducing explanations for the situations in which that outcome occurs. Like scientists who form hypotheses, discussed in Chapter 1, they can test their theories. What distinguishes this kind of thinking from previous stages is the ability to start with the abstract and move to the concrete; in previous stages, children are tied to the concrete present. At age 8, Leigh just moved things around to see what would happen in the pendulum problem, a concrete approach. At age 12, she began with the abstract idea that each variable should be tested separately.

Adolescents also can use propositional thought during this stage. *Propositional thought* is reasoning that uses abstract logic in the absence of concrete examples. Such thinking allows adolescents to understand that if certain premises are true, then a conclusion must also be true. For example:

All men are mortal.   *[premise]*
Socrates is a man.   *[premise]*
Therefore, Socrates is mortal.   *[conclusion]*

Adolescents understand that if both premises are true, then so is the conclusion. They are capable of using similar reasoning when premises and conclusions are stated more abstractly, as follows:

All As are B.   *[premise]*
C is an A.   *[premise]*
Therefore, C is a B.   *[conclusion]*

Although Piaget proposed that the formal operational stage begins at the onset of adolescence, he also hypothesized that—as with all the stages—full cognitive

Like scientists who form hypotheses, adolescents in the formal operational stage use systematic reasoning. They start with a general theory about what produces a particular outcome and then deduce explanations for specific situations in which they see that particular outcome.

capabilities emerge gradually through a combination of physical maturation and environmental experiences. It is not until around age 15, Piaget says, that adolescents fully settle into the formal operational stage.

In fact, evidence suggests that many people hone these skills at a later age, and some never fully employ them at all. Most studies show that only 40 to 60 percent of college students and adults achieve formal operational thinking completely, with some estimates as low as 25 percent. But many adults who do not use formal operational thought in every domain are fully competent in *some* respects (Sugarman, 1988; Keating, 2004).

The culture in which they are raised affects how adolescents use formal operations. People with little formal education, who live in isolated, technologically unsophisticated societies, are less likely to use formal operations than formally educated people in more sophisticated societies (Segall et al., 1990; Commons, Galaz-Fontes, & Morse, 2006; Asadi, Amiri, & Molavi, 2014).

It is not that adolescents (and adults) from cultures using few formal operations are incapable of attaining them. It is more likely that what characterizes formal operations—scientific reasoning—is not equally valued in all societies. If everyday life does not require or promote a certain type of reasoning, it is not likely that people will use such reasoning when confronting a problem (Gauvain, 1998).

THE CONSEQUENCES OF ADOLESCENTS' USE OF FORMAL OPERATIONS The ability to reason abstractly, to use formal operations, changes adolescents' everyday behavior. Whereas before they may have blindly accepted rules and explanations, their increased abstract reasoning abilities may lead to strenuous questioning of their parents and other authority figures.

In general, adolescents become more argumentative. They enjoy using abstract reasoning to poke holes in others' explanations, and their increased critical thinking abilities zero in on parents' and teachers' perceived shortcomings. For instance, they may see their parents' arguments against using drugs as inconsistent if their parents used drugs in adolescence without consequence. But adolescents can be indecisive, too, because they are able to see the merits of multiple sides to issues (Elkind, 1996; Alberts et al., 2007; Knoll et al., 2017).

Coping with these new critical abilities can be challenging for parents, teachers, and other adults who deal with adolescents. But it makes adolescents more interesting because they actively seek to understand the values and justifications they encounter.

EVALUATING PIAGET'S APPROACH Each time we've considered Piaget's theory, several concerns have arisen. Let's summarize some of them here:

- Piaget suggests that cognitive development proceeds in universal, step-like stages. Yet significant differences exist in cognitive abilities from one person to the next, especially when we compare individuals from different cultures. We also find inconsistencies within the same individual. People indicate they have reached a certain level of thinking in some tasks but not others. If Piaget were correct, a person ought to perform uniformly well on reaching a given stage (Siegler, 2007).

- The Piagetian notion of stages suggests that cognitive growth occurs in relatively rapid shifts from one stage to the next. Many developmentalists, however, argue that cognitive development is more continuous—increasing in quantitative accumulations rather than qualitative leaps forward. They also contend that Piaget's theory better *describes* behavior at a given stage than *explains* why the shift to a new stage occurs (Case, 1999; Birney & Sternberg, 2006).

- Citing the nature of the tasks Piaget used to measure cognitive abilities, critics suggest that he underestimated the age at which certain abilities emerge. It is now widely accepted that infants and children are more sophisticated than Piaget asserted (Siegler, 2007; Siegler & Lin, 2010).

- Some developmentalists argue that formal operations are not the epitome of thinking and that more sophisticated forms do not emerge until early adulthood. Developmental psychologist Giesela Labouvie-Vief (2006) argues that a complex society requires thought not necessarily based on pure logic. Instead, thinking must be flexible, allow for interpretive processes, and reflect the subtlety of cause and effect in real world events—something that Labouvie-Vief calls *postformal thinking* (Labouvie-Vief, 2006; Hamer & Van Rossum, 2016).

These criticisms regarding Piaget's approach to cognitive development have genuine merit. Yet Piaget's theory has inspired countless studies on the development of thinking capacities and processes, and it also has spurred much classroom reform. His bold statements about the nature of cognitive development sparked opposition that brought forth new approaches, such as the information processing perspective we examine next (Taylor & Rosenbach, 2005; Kuhn, 2008; Bibace, 2013).

Information Processing Perspectives: Gradual Transformations in Abilities

LO 6.7   Explain the information processing view of adolescent cognitive development.

From an information processing perspective, adolescents' cognitive abilities grow gradually and continuously. Unlike Piaget's view that increasing cognitive sophistication is a reflection of stagelike spurts, the **information processing approach** sees changes in adolescents' cognitive abilities as gradual transformations in the capacity to take in, use, and store information. Multiple progressive changes occur in the ways people organize their thinking, develop strategies to deal with new situations, sort facts, and advance in memory capacity and perceptual abilities (Pressley & Schneider, 1997; Wyer, 2004).

information processing approach
the model that seeks to identify the way that individuals take in, use, and store information

METACOGNITION: THINKING ABOUT THINKING   Adolescents' general intelligence—as measured by traditional IQ tests—remains stable, but dramatic improvements occur in the specific abilities that underlie intelligence. Verbal, mathematical, and spatial abilities increase. Memory capacity grows, and adolescents become adept at handling more than one stimulus at a time—as when they study for a biology test while streaming music.

As Piaget noted, adolescents grow increasingly sophisticated in understanding problems, grasping abstract concepts and hypothetical thinking, and comprehending the possibilities inherent in situations. This permits them, for instance, to endlessly dissect the course their relationships might hypothetically take.

Adolescents know more about the world, too. Their store of knowledge increases as the amount of material they are exposed to grows and their memory capacity enlarges. In sum, mental abilities markedly improve during adolescence (Kail, 2004; Kail & Miller, 2006; Atkins et al., 2012).

According to information processing theories of cognitive development, one of the main reasons for adolescents' advances in mental abilities is the growth of metacognition. **Metacognition** is the knowledge of one's own thinking processes and the ability to monitor one's own cognition. Although younger children can use some metacognitive strategies, adolescents are much more adept at understanding their own mental processes.

metacognition
the knowledge that people have about their own thinking processes and their ability to monitor their cognition

For example, as their understanding of their memory capacity improves, adolescents can better gauge how long they need to memorize given material for a test. They also can judge when the material is fully memorized much more accurately than in younger days. Their improved metacognition permits adolescents to comprehend and master school material more effectively (Rahko et al., 2016; Zakrzewski, Johnson, & Smith, 2017; Shute et al., 2018).

These new abilities also can make adolescents deeply introspective and self-conscious—two characteristics which, as we see next, may produce a high degree of egocentrism.

EGOCENTRISM IN THINKING: ADOLESCENTS' SELF-ABSORPTION   Carlos thinks his parents are "control freaks"; he cannot figure out why they insist he call and let them know where he is when he borrows the car. Jeri views Molly's purchase of earrings just like hers as the ultimate compliment, even though Molly may have been unaware Jeri had a similar pair when she bought them. Lu is upset with his biology teacher for giving a long, difficult midterm exam on which he did poorly.

Adolescents' newly sophisticated metacognitive abilities make them readily imagine that others are focused on them, and they may create elaborate scenarios about others' thoughts. This is the source of the egocentrism that can dominate adolescents' thinking. **Adolescent egocentrism** is a state of self-absorption in which the world is seen as focused on oneself. This egocentrism makes adolescents highly critical of authority figures, hostile to criticism, and quick to find fault with others' behavior (Schwartz, Maynard, & Uzelac, 2008; Inagaki, 2013; Rai et al., 2014; Lin, 2016).

Adolescents may develop an **imaginary audience**, fictitious observers who pay as much attention to their behavior as they do themselves. Unfortunately, these scenarios suffer from the same kind of egocentrism as the rest of their thinking. For instance, a student sitting in a class may be sure a teacher is focusing on her, and a teenager at a basketball game may be convinced that everyone is staring at the pimple on his chin.

Egocentrism leads to a second distortion in thinking: that one's experiences are unique. Adolescents develop **personal fables**, the view that what happens to them is unique, exceptional, and shared by no other. Teenagers whose romantic relationships have ended may feel that no one has ever hurt the way they do, that no one was ever treated so badly, and that no one can understand their pain (Alberts et al., 2007; Rai et al., 2016).

> **From a social worker's perspective:** In what ways does egocentrism complicate adolescents' social and family relationships? Do adults entirely outgrow egocentrism and personal fables?

Personal fables may make adolescents feel invulnerable to the risks that threaten others. They may see no need to use condoms during sex because, in the personal fables they construct, pregnancy and STIs only happen to other kinds of people, not to them. They may drink and drive because in their personal fables they are careful drivers, always in control (Greene et al., 2000; Vartanian, 2000; Reyna & Farley, 2006).

adolescent egocentrism
a state of self-absorption in which the world is viewed from one's own point of view

imaginary audience
an adolescent's belief that his or her own behavior is a primary focus of others' attention and concerns

personal fables
the view held by some adolescents that what happens to them is unique, exceptional, and shared by no one else

School Performance

Jared Camber is annoyed. His iPhone has stopped synching to the Web and now he has to pull out his earbuds, put his calculus textbook down, and pause the game he's playing on his PlayStation 4. He fiddles with the iPhone and finally gets it working. As he puts his earbuds back in and returns to his calculus book and video game, he shouts to his father to find out the score of the basketball game he hears playing in the next room. To his surprise, his father answers that he doesn't know because he's been reading a book instead of paying attention. Jared rolls his eyes and silently judges his dad a bit dimwitted for being unable to do both things at the same time.

Adolescents' personal fables may lead them to feel invulnerable and to engage in risky behavior, like these Brazilian boys (known as "surfistas") riding on the roof of a high-speed train.

H. John Maier Jr./The LIFE Images Collection/Getty Images

Adolescent School Performance: A Complex Picture

LO 6.8   Describe major factors that affect adolescent school performance.

Jared's ability at age 17 to listen to music, do his homework, and play a video game all at the same time may or may not signal some kind of advance over his father's limited focus on one thing at a time. In part, Jared's talent for multitasking is surely as a result of the different eras in which he and his father were raised, but it may also be partly attributable to the cognitive changes that accompanied his advance into adolescence. Think of it this way: It is *possible* that Jared actually can perform more mental tasks simultaneously than his father, but it is *certain* that he can do more tasks *well* than he could do just a few years earlier.

Do the advances in adolescents' metacognition, reasoning, and other cognitive abilities lead to improved school performance? If we use grades as the measure of performance, the answer is yes. High school students' grades have risen in the past decade. The mean high school grade point average went up from 3.27 to 3.38 from 1998 to 2016. And the greatest amount of grade inflation occurred in high schools with students who are wealthier, and where most students are white (College Board, 2005; Buckley, Letukas, & Wildavsky, 2018).

At the same time, independent measures of achievement, such as SAT scores, have not risen. A more likely explanation for the higher grades is the phenomenon of grade inflation: Students have not changed; instead, instructors are awarding higher grades for the same performance (Cardman, 2004).

Further evidence for grade inflation comes from the relatively poor achievement of students in the United States when compared to students in other countries. For instance, students in the United States score lower on standardized math and science tests when compared to students in other industrialized countries (Organization for Economic Cooperation and Development [OECD], 2014; Desilver, 2017; see Figure 6-7).

There is no single reason for this achievement gap, but a combination of factors, such as less class time and less intensive instruction, is at work. The broad diversity of the U.S. school population also may affect performance relative to other countries in which the school population is more homogeneous and affluent (Stedman, 1997; Schemo, 2001).

Figure 6-7 U.S. Math Performance Compared with Other Countries

When compared to the math performance of students across the world, U.S. students perform at below-average levels.

SOURCE: Based on Organization for Economic Cooperation and Development [OECD], 2014.

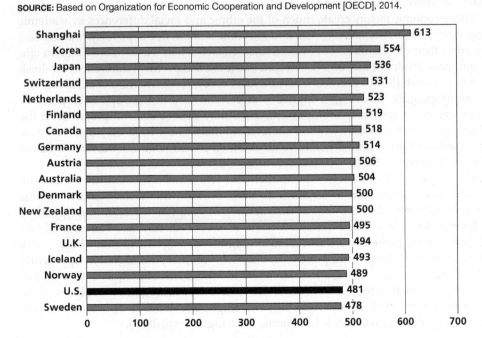

The poorer accomplishments of U.S. students is also reflected in high school graduation rates. Although the United States once stood first in the percentage of the population graduating from high school, it has dropped to 24th among industrialized countries. Only 79 percent of U.S. high school students graduate—a rate considerably lower than those of other developed countries. Certainly, as we discuss next, differences in socioeconomic status are reflected in school performance within the United States (Organization for Economic Cooperation and Development [OECD], 1998, 2001, 2014).

SOCIOECONOMIC STATUS AND SCHOOL PERFORMANCE: INDIVIDUAL DIFFERENCES IN ACHIEVEMENT All students are entitled to an equal education, but some groups enjoy more advantages than others, as the relationship between educational achievement and socioeconomic status (SES) clearly indicates.

Middle- and high-SES students, on average, earn higher grades, score higher on standardized achievement tests, and complete more years of school than students from lower-SES homes. This disparity does not start in adolescence; the same findings hold for children in lower grades. However, by high school, the effects of socioeconomic status are more pronounced (Tucker-Drob & Harden, 2012; Roy & Raver, 2014; Li, Allen, & Casillas, 2017).

Why do children from middle- and high-SES homes show greater academic success? Children living in poverty lack many of the advantages of their more affluent peers. Moreover, their nutrition and health may be poorer. If they live in crowded conditions or attend inadequate schools, they may have few places to study. Their homes may lack the books and computers common in more affluent households (Chiu & McBride-Chang, 2006; Wamba, 2010; Cross et al., 2018).

For these reasons, impoverished students may be disadvantaged from their first day of school. As they grow up, their school performance may continue to lag and, in fact, the difference may snowball. High school success builds heavily on basic skills presumably learned previously. Children who experience early problems may find themselves falling ever further behind (Biddle, 2001; Hoff, 2012; Duncan, Magnuson, & Votruba-Drzal, 2017).

ETHNIC AND RACIAL DIFFERENCES IN SCHOOL ACHIEVEMENT Significant achievement differences between ethnic and racial groups paint a troubling picture of American education. School achievement data indicate that, on average, African American and Hispanic students perform at lower levels, receive lower grades, and score lower on standardized achievement tests than Caucasian students. In contrast, Asian American students tend to earn higher grades than Caucasian students (Frederickson & Petrides, 2008; Shernoff & Schmidt, 2008; Byun & Park, 2012; Kurtz-Costes, Swinton, & Skinner, 2014).

Socioeconomic factors create much of the ethnic and racial differences in academic achievement. More African American and Hispanic families live in poverty, and this fact may affect their children's school performance. In fact, when we compare different ethnic and racial groups at the same socioeconomic level, achievement differences diminish but do not vanish (Meece & Kurtz-Costes, 2001; Cokley, 2003; Guerrero et al., 2006).

Anthropologist John Ogbu argues that certain minority groups may perceive school success as relatively unimportant. They may believe societal prejudice in the workplace dictates that they will not succeed, no matter how hard they try. They may conclude that effort in school will have no eventual payoff (Ogbu, 1992; Archer-Banks & Behar-Horenstein, 2012).

Ogbu suggests that minority group members who enter a new culture voluntarily are more likely to succeed in school than those brought into a new culture against their will. He notes that the sons and daughters of voluntary Korean immigrants to the United States tend to be quite successful in school. In contrast, Korean children in Japan, whose parents were forced to immigrate during World War II and work as forced laborers, tend to do poorly in school. Involuntary immigration apparently leaves lasting scars, reducing the motivation to succeed in subsequent generations. Ogbu suggests that in the United States, the involuntary immigration as slaves of the ancestors of many African American students might be related to their motivation to succeed (Ogbu, 1992; Toldson & Lemmons, 2013; Ogunyemi, 2017).

From an educator's perspective: Why might descendants of people who were forced to immigrate to a country be less successful academically than those who came voluntarily? What approaches might be used to overcome this obstacle?

Another factor has to do with attributions for academic success. As we discussed previously, students from many Asian cultures tend to relate achievement to situational factors such as their effort. In contrast, African American students are apt to attribute success to external causes beyond their control, such as luck or societal biases. Students who believe effort leads to success, and expend that effort, are likely to do better in school than students who do not believe effort matters (Saunders, Davis, & Williams, 2004; Hannover et al., 2013).

Adolescents' beliefs about the consequences of poor school performance may also contribute to racial and ethnic differences. Specifically, African American and Hispanic students may believe they can succeed *despite* poor performance. This belief can cause them to expend less effort. In contrast, Asian American students may believe that they must do well in school to get a good job and be successful. Asian Americans, then, are motivated to work hard for fear of the consequences (Murphy et al., 2010).

DROPPING OUT OF SCHOOL   Most students complete high school, but some half a million students each year drop out before graduating. The consequences are severe. High school dropouts earn 42 percent less than graduates, and their unemployment rate is 50 percent.

Adolescents leave school for a variety of reasons. Some leave because of pregnancy or problems with the English language. Some must leave for economic reasons, needing to support themselves or their families.

Dropout rates differ according to gender and ethnicity. Males are more likely to drop out than females. Although the dropout rate for all ethnicities has been declining in recent decades, Hispanic and black students still are less likely to finish high school than non-Hispanic white students. However, not all minority groups show higher dropout rates; for example, Asians drop out at a lower rate than Caucasians (Bowers, Sprott, & Taff, 2013; U.S. Department of Education, 2015; National Center for Educational Statistics, 2016a).

Poverty largely determines whether a student completes high school. Students from lower-income households are three times more likely to drop out than those from middle- and upper-income households. Because economic success is so dependent on education, dropping out often perpetuates a cycle of poverty (National Center for Education Statistics, 2016b).

Adolescents' Media Use: Screen Time in the Digital Age

LO 6.9   Explain the nature and consequences of the use of media by adolescents.

Most adolescents make use of social media and other technologies to a staggering degree. According to a comprehensive survey using a sample of boys and girls 8 to 18 years old conducted by the Kaiser Family Foundation (a well-respected think tank), young people spend an average of 6.5 hours a day with media. Furthermore, because around a quarter of the time they are using more than one form of medium simultaneously, they are actually being exposed to the equivalent of 8.5 hours per day (Rideout, Foehr, & Roberts, 2010; Twenge, Martin, & Spitzberg, 2018).

The amount of media use can be extraordinary. For example, some teenagers send nearly 30,000 texts a month, often carrying on multiple conversations simultaneously. The use of texting often supplants other forms of social interaction, such as telephone calls or even face-to-face interactions. In fact, one recent survey found that two-thirds of teenagers report preferring to communicate with their friends via a text than in person (Lenhart, 2010; Richtel, 2010; Rideout & Robb, 2018; see Figure 6-8).

Figure 6-8 Don't Talk to Me, Text Me Instead

In 2018, more teenagers say they would rather text a friend than talk with them in person, a significant change from 2012.

SOURCE: Rideout & Robb, 2018.

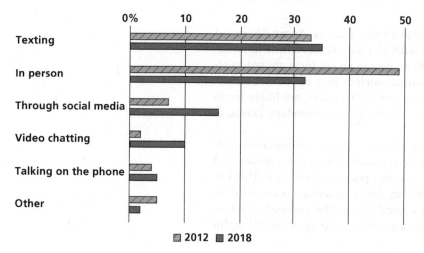

Adolescents are also likely to use multiple social platforms, with Facebook, Instagram, and Snapchat being most popular. There are also gender differences; boys are more likely to use Facebook, while girls are more likely to use visually oriented platforms such as Tumblr, Pinterest, and Instagram. Both boys and girls have few privacy concerns: Surveys show that nearly all share their names, birthdates, and photos of themselves. Finally, adolescents use social media to advance their romantic interests (Lenhart, Smith, & Anderson, 2015; Office of Adolescent Health, 2016).

For many adolescents, another form of social media involves engagement in online video games. In addition to their gaming aspects, video games provide a means to communicate with peers. Furthermore, some research suggests that video games provide cognitive stimulation. For example, even violent types of action or "shooter" video games produce improvements in attention, visual processing, spatial skills, and mental rotation abilities (Green & Bavelier, 2012; Uttal et al., 2013; Kowal et al., 2018).

There are clear downsides to the social media use of adolescents. For example, some developmentalists suggest that the high frequency of social media use is related to a decline in face-to-face social competence. In this view, online involvement reduces the opportunities to learn social skills. However, some aspects of social media use may actually help adolescents learn certain types of social skills and thereby enhance their overall social competence (Yang & Brown 2015; Reich, 2017).

Furthermore, some forms of online activities can be mean-spirited. For example, some teenagers make use of the Web to bully others—a process in which victims are repeatedly texted or e-mailed hurtful messages. The source of such *cyberbullying* can remain anonymous, and the messages may be particularly abusive. Although they do not inflict physical harm, they can be psychologically damaging (Best, Manktelow, & Taylor, 2014; Bartlett et al., 2017; Hood & Duffy, 2018).

The omnipresence of the Web allows adolescents to tap into a vast array of information. However, it is not yet obvious how Web access will change education or whether the impact will be uniformly positive. For instance, schools have had to change their curricula to include specific instruction in a key skill for deriving value from the Web: learning to sort through huge bodies of information to identify what is most useful and discard what is not. To obtain the full benefits of the Web, then, students must obtain the ability to search, choose, and integrate information in order to create new knowledge (Trotter, 2004; Guilamo-Ramos et al., 2015).

Despite the substantial benefits of the Web, its use also has a downside. The Web makes material available that many parents and other adults find highly objectionable. In addition, there is a growing problem of Internet gambling. High school and college students can easily bet on sports events and participate in games such as poker on the Web using credit cards (King, Delfabbro, & Griffiths, 2010; Derevensky, Shek, & Merrick, 2010; Giralt et al., 2018).

The use of computers also presents a challenge involving socioeconomic status, race, and ethnicity. Poorer adolescents and members of minority groups have less access to computers than more affluent adolescents and members of socially advantaged groups—a phenomenon known as the *digital divide* (Olsen, 2009; Broadbent & Papadopoulos, 2013; Gonzales, 2016).

Review, Check, and Apply

Review

LO 6.6 Analyze Piaget's account of adolescent cognitive development.

Adolescence corresponds to Piaget's formal operations period, a stage characterized by abstract reasoning and an experimental approach to problems. Because of their ability to reason abstractly, adolescents begin to question authority and often become argumentative.

LO 6.7 Explain the information processing view of adolescent cognitive development.

According to the information processing perspective, cognitive advances in adolescence are quantitative and gradual because many aspects of thinking and memory improve. Growth in metacognition enables the monitoring of thought processes and mental capacities. Adolescents are susceptible to egocentrism and the perception that their behavior is constantly observed by an imaginary audience. They are likely to construct personal fables about their uniqueness and immunity to harm.

LO 6.8 Describe major factors that affect adolescent school performance.

Academic performance is linked in complex ways to socioeconomic status, race, and ethnicity. Poorer performance by some groups of students is linked to lower socioeconomic status, which often leads to a lack of resources essential to learning. Both gender and ethnicity affect the incidence of dropping out, which is at a surprisingly high level in the United States.

LO 6.9 Explain the nature and consequences of the use of media by adolescents.

Adolescents spend a large amount of time using digital media. There are both benefits and risks in this phenomenon. Benefits include increased access to information and culture; risks include access to inappropriate and harmful materials and behaviors. A key problem with the growing importance of media in schools is the inequality of access to computers and the Internet. Poorer adolescents and members of minority groups usually have less access than more affluent adolescents and members of more advantaged groups.

Check Yourself

1. Fifteen-year-old Wyatt is able to solve the physics problem from class in abstract rather than in concrete terms. According to Piaget, Wyatt is now capable of _____.

   a. preoperational thought
   b. formal operational thought
   c. egocentrism
   d. sensorimotor thought

2. _____ is the knowledge that people have about their own thinking processes and their ability to monitor their cognition.

   a. Metacognition
   b. Postformal thinking
   c. Egocentrism
   d. Sensorimotor thought

3. Because of the unfavorable comparison of U.S. standardized test scores to the scores of other countries, the gradual shift upward of adolescents' grades in the past decade has been attributed to _____.

   a. increased immigration
   b. grade inflation
   c. achievement deflation
   d. decreased motivation

4. The unequal access that adolescents have to educational computers and technology, depending on their socioeconomic status, race, and ethnicity, has been termed _____.

   a. the achievement gap
   b. cyberbullying
   c. the opportunity trap
   d. the digital divide

Applying Lifespan Development

What sorts of *external* factors (i.e., not attributable to the students) might negatively affect the performance of U.S. students on international achievement tests?

Module 6.3

Social and Personality Development in Adolescence

Could satellites in space help the visually impaired navigate through daily life?

That's what Ameen Abdulrasool, when he was an 18-year-old high school student, figured when he invented a system that promises independence for the visually impaired. Ameen, who attended high school in Chicago, was inspired by automobile navigation systems that use Global Positioning System satellites to help car drivers avoid getting lost.

Ameen, whose father and several other relatives are blind, wanted to devise a system that would let the visually impaired know where they were and how to reach particular destinations. To do this, he put together an iPod-size instrument that would receive the satellite signals, bracelets to be worn on each arm, and earphones. After users program in a destination, they receive voice commands telling them what direction to turn. At the same time, the bracelets vibrate to indicate the right direction.

It took 3 years of trial and error, but the system has proven highly effective. It promises to expand the world of the visually impaired, who now may be able to plot a course through the world as never before (Kemker, 2017).

What drove Ameen to invent his device? What was it about his personality and identity that led him to try to want to help his blind relatives? What inspired him to act in a selfless and even heroic way?

In this module, we discuss personality and social development during adolescence.

We begin by considering how adolescents form their views of themselves. We look at self-concept, self-esteem, and identity development. We also examine three major psychological difficulties: anxiety, depression, and suicide.

Next, we discuss relationships. We consider how adolescents reposition themselves within the family and how the influence of family members declines in some spheres as peers take on new importance. We also examine the ways in which adolescents interact with their friends, and the ways in which popularity is determined.

Finally, the module considers dating and sexual behavior. We look at the role of dating and close relationships in adolescents' lives, and we consider sexual behavior and the standards that govern adolescents' sex lives. We conclude by looking at teenage pregnancy and at programs that seek to prevent unwanted pregnancy.

Identity: Asking "Who Am I?"

> "You have no idea how much pressure a 13-year-old has to deal with. You've got to look cool, act cool, wear the right clothes, wear your hair a certain way—and your friends have different ideas about all these things than your parents, know what I mean? And you've got to have friends or you're nobody. And then some of your friends say you're not cool if you don't drink or do drugs, but what if you don't want that?" —Anton Merced

The thoughts of 13-year-old Anton Merced demonstrate a clear awareness—and self-consciousness—regarding his new place in society. During adolescence, questions like "Who am I?" and "Where do I belong in the world?" begin to take a front seat.

Self-Concept and Self-Esteem

LO 6.10   Describe how adolescents develop their self-concept and self-esteem.

One reason issues of identity become so important is that adolescents' intellectual capacities become more adult-like. They see how they stack up to others and realize they are individuals, separate from everyone else. The dramatic physical changes of puberty make adolescents acutely aware of their own bodies and aware that others are reacting to them in new ways. Whatever the cause, adolescence brings major changes in teenagers' self-concepts and self-esteem—in sum, their views of their own identity.

SELF-CONCEPT: WHAT AM I LIKE?   Valerie describes herself this way: "Others look at me as laid-back, relaxed, and not worrying too much. But really, I'm often nervous and emotional."

The fact that Valerie distinguishes others' views from her own represents a developmental advance. In childhood, she would have characterized herself by traits that would not differentiate her view from others'. However, when adolescents describe who they are, they take into account both their own and others' views (Preckel et al., 2013; McLean & Syed, 2015; Griffin, Adams, & Little, 2017).

This broader view of themselves is one aspect of adolescents' increasing sense of identity. They can see various aspects of the self simultaneously, and this view becomes more organized and coherent. They look at the self from a psychological perspective, viewing traits not as concrete entities but as abstractions (Adams, Montemayor, & Gullotta, 1996). For example, teenagers are more likely than younger children to define themselves by their ideology (e.g., "I'm an environmentalist") than by physical characteristics (e.g., "I'm the fastest runner in my class").

In some ways, this broader, multifaceted self-concept can be a mixed blessing, especially during early adolescence. At that time, adolescents may be troubled by the complexity of their personalities. Younger adolescents may want to view themselves in a certain way ("I'm a sociable person and love to be with people"), and they may become concerned when their behavior contradicts that view ("Even though I want to be sociable, sometimes I can't stand being around my friends and just want to be alone"). By the end of adolescence, however, teenagers find it easier to accept that behaviors and feelings change with the situation (Trzesniewski, Donnellan, & Robins, 2003; Hitlin, Brown, & Elder, 2006).

SELF-ESTEEM: HOW DO I LIKE MYSELF? Although adolescents increasingly perceive who they are (their self-concept), this does not mean they like themselves (their self-esteem). Their increasingly accurate self-concept permits them to see themselves fully—warts and all. It's what they do with these perceptions that determines their self-esteem.

Adolescents' sense of who they are takes their own and others' views into account.

The same cognitive sophistication that differentiates various aspects of the self also leads adolescents to evaluate those aspects in different ways (Chan, 1997; Cohen, 1999). An adolescent may have high self-esteem regarding academic performance, but lower self-esteem in relationships. Or the opposite may apply, as this adolescent notes:

"Do I *like* myself? What a question! Well, let's see. I like some of what I am, like I'm a good listener and a good friend, but I don't like other things, like my jealous side. I'm no genius at schoolwork—my parents would like me to do better—but if you're too smart you don't have a lot of friends. I'm pretty good at sports, especially swimming. But the best thing about me is that I'm a good friend, you know, loyal. I'm pretty well known for that, and pretty popular."

GENDER DIFFERENCES IN SELF-ESTEEM Several factors determine an adolescent's self-esteem, among them gender. Notably in early adolescence, girls' self-esteem tends to be lower and more vulnerable than boys' (Mäkinen et al., 2012; Ayres & Leaper, 2013; Jenkins & Demaray, 2015).

Compared to boys, girls tend to worry more about physical appearance and social success—as well as academic achievement. Although boys care about these things, their attitudes are often more casual. Stereotypical societal messages suggesting brains and popularity do not mix pose a difficult bind for girls: If girls do well academically, they jeopardize their social success. No wonder their self-esteem is more fragile than boys' (Ayres & Leaper, 2013; Jenkins & Demaray, 2015; Ra & Cho, 2017).

Although self-esteem tends to be higher in boys, they have their vulnerabilities too. Gender stereotypes may lead boys to believe they should always be confident, tough, and fearless. Boys facing difficulties (e.g., not making a sports team or being rejected for a date) may feel incompetent as males as well as miserable about their defeat (Pollack, Shuster, & Trelease, 2001; Witt, Donnellan, & Trzesniewski, 2011; Levant et al., 2016).

A strong sense of racial identity during adolescence is tied to higher levels of self-esteem.

SES AND RACE DIFFERENCES IN SELF-ESTEEM Socio-economic status (SES) and race also influence self-esteem. Adolescents of higher SES tend to have higher self-esteem than those of lower SES, especially in middle and later adolescence.

Social status factors that enhance one's standing and self-esteem, such as having more expensive clothes or a car, may become more conspicuous at this time (Dai et al., 2012; Cuperman, Robinson, & Ickes, 2014).

Race and ethnicity also influence self-esteem, but their impact has declined as prejudicial treatment of minorities has eased. Early studies found that minority status led to lower self-esteem. African Americans and Hispanics, researchers explained, had lower self-esteem than Caucasians because society's prejudice made them feel disliked and rejected, and this was incorporated into their self-concepts. Subsequent research, however, suggests that black adolescents differ little from whites in their levels of self-esteem. One explanation is that social movements within the African American community to bolster racial pride have helped. Research finds that a stronger sense of racial identity is related to higher self-esteem in African Americans and Hispanics (Phinney, 2008; Kogan et al., 2014; Benner et al., 2018).

Another reason for a similarity in self-esteem between adolescents of different racial groups is that teenagers tend to focus their preferences and priorities on what they excel at. Consequently, African American youths may concentrate on what they most enjoy and gain self-esteem from their successes in that domain (Yang & Blodgett, 2000; Phinney, 2005; Aoyagi, Santos, & Updegraff 2017).

Self-esteem may be influenced not by race alone, but by a complex combination of factors. Some developmentalists have considered race and gender simultaneously, coining the term *ethgender* to refer to their joint influence. One study that took both race and gender into account found that African American and Hispanic males had the highest levels of self-esteem, whereas Asian and Native American females had the lowest levels (Biro et al., 2006; Adams, 2010; Guo et al., 2012).

Perspectives on Identity Formation

LO 6.11   Analyze diverse theoretical approaches to understanding identity formation.

Developmental psychologists agree that the adolescent quest for identity is a serious issue that must be resolved before further development is possible. There is general consensus that religion and spirituality often play a role in defining one's identity and that the racial and ethnic background of the individual make a significant difference. We look at these issues in the following sections.

ERIK ERIKSON: RESOLVING THE IDENTITY CRISIS   According to Erik Erikson, the search for identity inevitably leads some adolescents to an identity crisis involving substantial psychological turmoil (Erikson, 1963). Erikson's theory of this stage, which is summarized with his other stages in Table 6-2, suggests teenagers try to figure out what is unique and distinctive about themselves—a task they manage with increasing sophistication because of the cognitive gains of adolescence.

Erikson argues that adolescents strive to discover their strengths and weaknesses and the roles that best suit their future lives. This often involves "trying on" different roles or choices to see if they fit their capabilities and views about themselves. In this process, adolescents seek to understand who they are by narrowing and making choices about their personal, occupational, sexual, and political commitments. Erikson calls this the **identity-versus-identity-confusion stage**.

identity-versus-identity-confusion stage
the period during which teenagers seek to determine what is unique and distinctive about themselves

In Erikson's view, adolescents who do not find a suitable identity may go off course in several ways. They may adopt socially unacceptable roles to express what they do *not* want to be. Forming and maintaining lasting, close relationships may elude them. In general, their sense of self becomes "diffuse," failing to organize around a unified core identity.

In contrast, those who forge an appropriate identity set a foundation for future psychosocial development. They learn their unique capabilities and believe in them, and they develop an accurate sense of self. They are prepared to take full advantage of their unique strengths (Allison & Schultz, 2001).

Societal Pressures and Reliance on Friends and Peers   Societal pressures are also high during the identity-versus-identity-confusion stage. Adolescents feel pressure

Table 6-2 A Summary of Erikson's Stages

Stage	Approximate Age	Positive Outcomes	Negative Outcomes
Trust versus mistrust	Birth–1.5 years	Feelings of trust from others' support	Fear and concern regarding others
Autonomy versus shame and doubt	1.5–3 years	Self-sufficiency if exploration is encouraged	Doubts about self; lack of independence
Initiative versus guilt	3–6 years	Discovery of ways to initiate actions	Guilt from actions and thoughts
Industry versus inferiority	6–12 years	Development of sense of competence	Feelings of inferiority; little sense of mastery
Identity versus identity confusion	Adolescence	Awareness of uniqueness of self; knowledge of roles	Inability to identify appropriate roles in life
Intimacy versus isolation	Early adulthood	Development of loving, sexual relationships and close friendships	Fear of relationships with others
Generativity versus stagnation	Middle adulthood	Sense of contribution to continuity of life	Trivialization of one's activities
Ego-integrity versus despair	Late adulthood	Sense of unity in life's accomplishments	Regret over lost opportunities of life

SOURCE: Erikson, 1963.

from parents and friends to decide whether their post–high school plans include work or college and, if the former, which occupation to follow. Up to this point, their educational lives have followed a universal track, laid out by U.S. society. However, the track ends at high school, leaving adolescents with difficult choices about which path to follow.

During this period, friends and peers are increasingly sought as sources of information. Dependence on adults declines. As we discuss later, this increasing dependence on peers enables adolescents to forge close relationships. Comparing themselves to others helps to clarify their own identities.

This reliance on peers in defining their own identities and learning to form relationships links this stage of psychosocial development and the next stage Erikson proposed, known as *intimacy versus isolation*. It also relates to gender differences in identity formation. Erikson suggested that males and females move through the identity-versus-identity-confusion period differently. He argued that males are more likely to experience the social development stages in the order shown in Table 6-2, developing a stable identity before committing to an intimate relationship. In contrast, he suggested that females reverse the order, seeking intimate relationships and then defining their identities through these relationships. These ideas largely reflect the social conditions at the time he was writing, when women were less likely to go to college or establish their own careers and instead often married early. Today, the experiences of boys and girls seem relatively similar during the identity-versus-identity-confusion period.

Psychological Moratorium   Because of the pressures of the identity-versus-identity-confusion period, Erikson suggested that many adolescents pursue a *psychological moratorium*, a period during which they take time off from the upcoming responsibilities of adulthood to explore various roles and possibilities. For example, many college students take a semester or year off to travel, work, or find another way to examine their priorities.

Many adolescents, for practical reasons, cannot pursue a psychological moratorium to leisurely explore various identities. For economic reasons, some must work part-time after school and then take jobs immediately after high school, leaving them little time to experiment. Such adolescents need by no means be psychologically damaged. Successfully holding a part-time job while attending school may offer a psychological reward that outweighs the lack of opportunity to try out various roles.

Limitations of Erikson's Theory   Erikson has been criticized for using male identity development as the standard against which to compare female identity. He saw males

Table 6-3 Marcia's Four Categories of Adolescent Development

		Commitment	
		Present	Absent
CRISIS/EXPLORATION	PRESENT	**Identity achievement** "I enjoyed working at an advertising company the last two summers, so I plan to go into advertising."	**Moratorium** "I'm taking a job at my mom's bookstore until I figure out what I really want to do."
	ABSENT	**Identity foreclosure** "My dad says I'm good with kids and would be a good teacher, so I guess that's what I'll do."	**Identity diffusion** "Frankly, I have no idea what I'm going to do."

SOURCE: Based on Marcia, 1980.

as developing intimacy only after achieving a stable identity, which is viewed as the norm. To critics, Erikson's view is based on male-oriented concepts of individuality and competitiveness. Alternatively, psychologist Carol Gilligan suggests that women develop identity while establishing relationships. In this view, the building of caring networks between herself and others is key to a woman's identity (Gilligan, Brown, & Rogers, 1990; Gilligan, 2004; Kroger, 2006).

MARCIA'S APPROACH: UPDATING ERIKSON Using Erikson's theory as a springboard, psychologist James Marcia suggests that identity can be seen in terms of which of two characteristics—crisis or commitment—is present or absent. *Crisis* is a period in which an adolescent consciously chooses between various alternatives and makes decisions. *Commitment* is psychological investment in a course of action or an ideology. One adolescent might career from one activity to another, with nothing lasting beyond a few weeks, whereas another becomes totally absorbed in volunteering at a homeless shelter (Peterson, Marcia, & Carpendale, 2004; Marcia, 2007; Crocetti, 2017).

After conducting lengthy interviews with adolescents, Marcia proposed four categories of identity (see Table 6-3).

identity achievement

the status of adolescents who commit to a particular identity following a period of crisis during which they consider various alternatives

1. **Identity achievement**. Teenagers in this category have successfully explored and thought through who they are and what they want to do. Following a period of crisis during which they considered various alternatives, these adolescents have committed to a particular identity. Teens who have reached this identity status tend to be psychologically healthier, and higher in achievement motivation and moral reasoning than adolescents of any other status.

identity foreclosure

the status of adolescents who prematurely commit to an identity without adequately exploring alternatives

2. **Identity foreclosure**. These are adolescents who have committed to an identity without passing through a period of crisis in which they explored alternatives. Instead, they accepted others' decisions about what was best for them. Typical of this category is a son who enters the family business because it is expected, or a daughter who becomes a physician because her mother is one. Foreclosers are not necessarily unhappy, but they tend to have something called "rigid strength": Happy and self-satisfied, they have a high need for social approval and tend to be authoritarian.

moratorium

the status of adolescents who may have explored various identity alternatives to some degree, but have not yet committed themselves

3. **Moratorium**. Adolescents in this category have explored some alternatives but made no commitments. As a result, Marcia suggests, they show relatively high anxiety and experience psychological conflict, though they are often lively and appealing, seeking intimacy with others. Such adolescents typically settle on an identity, but only after a struggle.

identity diffusion

the status of adolescents who consider various identity alternatives, but never commit to one or never even consider identity options in any conscious way

4. **Identity diffusion**. These adolescents neither explore nor commit to various alternatives. They tend to shift from one thing to the next. While appearing carefree, according to Marcia, their lack of commitment impairs their ability to form close relationships. They are often socially withdrawn.

Some adolescents shift among the four categories; for example, moving between moratorium and identity achievement in what is called a "MAMA" cycle (moratorium—identity achievement—moratorium—identity achievement). Or, a forecloser who selected a career path without much thought in early adolescence may reassess and make a more active choice later. For some individuals, identity formation takes place beyond adolescence. However, for most people, identity gels in the late teens and early 20s (Al-Owidha, Green, & Kroger, 2009; Duriez et al., 2012; Mrazek, Harada, & Chiao, 2015).

According to Marcia's approach, psychologically healthy identity development can be seen in adolescents who choose to commit to a course of action or ideology.

Max Whittaker/Getty Images News/Getty Images

> **From a social worker's perspective:** Do you believe that all four of Marcia's identity statuses can lead to reassessment and different choices later in life? Are there stages in Marcia's theory that may be difficult to achieve for adolescents who live in poverty? Why?

In some ways, Marcia's identity status perspective foreshadows what other researchers have called emerging adulthood. **Emerging adulthood** is the period beginning in the late teenage years and extending into the mid-20s. It is a transitional stage between adolescence and adulthood that spans the third decade of life (Arnett, 2011; 2016).

As we will discuss in greater detail when we consider early adulthood in the next chapter, emerging adulthood is a period in which teenagers have left adolescence, although brain growth continues and neural circuits become more complex. But it is typically a period of uncertainty, in which post-adolescents are working to determine who they are and their path forward (Verschueren et al., 2017).

emerging adulthood
the period from the late teenage years extending to the mid-20s in which people are still sorting out their options for the future

RELIGION AND SPIRITUALITY IN IDENTITY FORMATION Consider the following:

> Ever wonder why God made mosquitoes? How about why God gave Adam and Eve the ability to rebel if He knew how much of a mess it would cause? Can someone be saved and later lose their salvation? Do pets go to heaven?

As exemplified in this blog post, questions of religion and spirituality begin to be asked during adolescence. Religion is important to many people because it offers a formal means of satisfying spirituality needs. *Spirituality* is a sense of attachment to some higher power such as God, nature, or something sacred. Although spirituality needs are typically tied to religious beliefs, they may be independent. Many people who consider themselves to be spiritual individuals do not participate in formal religious practices or are not tied to any particular religion. Because their cognitive abilities increase during adolescence, teenagers are able to think more abstractly about religious matters. Furthermore, as they grapple with general questions of identity, religious identity may be questioned. After having accepted their religious identity in an unquestioning manner during childhood, adolescents may view religion more critically and seek to distance themselves from formal religion. In other cases, they may be drawn more closely to their religious affiliation because it offers answers to such abstract questions as "Why am I here on this earth?" and "What is the meaning of life?" Religion provides a way of viewing the world and universe as having intentional design—a place that was created by something or someone (Yonker, Schnabelrauch, & DeHaan, 2012; Levenson, Aldwin, & Igarashi, 2013; Longo, Bray, & Kim-Spoon, 2017).

According to James Fowler, our understanding and practice of faith and spirituality proceeds through a series of stages that extend throughout the life span. During childhood, individuals hold a fairly literal view of God and Biblical figures. For example, children may think of God as living at the top of the earth and being able to see what everyone is doing (Fowler & Dell, 2006; Boyatzis, 2013).

In adolescence, the view of spirituality becomes more abstract. As they build their identity, adolescents typically develop a core set of beliefs and values. On the other hand, in many cases, adolescents do not consider their views either in depth or systematically, and it is not until later that they become more reflective.

As they leave adolescence, people typically move into the *individuative-reflective stage* of faith in which they reflect on their beliefs and values. They understand that their view is one of many, and that multiple views of God are possible. Ultimately, the final stage of faith development is the *conjunctive stage*, in which individuals develop a broad, inclusive view of religion and all humanity. They see humanity as a whole, and they may work to promote a common good. In this stage, they may move beyond formal religion and hold a unified view of people across the globe.

THE ROLE OF RACE AND ETHNICITY IN IDENTITY FORMATION Forming an identity is often difficult for adolescents, but it is especially challenging for members of racial and ethnic groups that face discrimination. Society's contradictory values tell adolescents that society should be color blind, that race and ethnic background should not affect opportunities and achievement, and that if they do achieve, society will accept them. Based on a traditional *cultural assimilation model*, this view says individual cultural identities should be assimilated into a unified culture in the United States—the melting-pot model.

In contrast, the *pluralistic society model* suggests that U.S. society is made up of diverse, coequal cultural groups that should preserve their individual features. This model grew from the belief that cultural assimilation denigrates the heritage of minorities and lowers their self-esteem.

According to this view, then, racial and ethnic factors become a central part of adolescents' identity and are not submerged in an attempt to assimilate into the majority culture. From this perspective, identity development includes development of *racial and ethnic identity*—the sense of membership in a racial or ethnic group and the feelings that are associated with that membership. It includes a sense of commitment and ties with a particular racial or ethnic group (Phinney, 2008; Umaña-Taylor et al., 2014; Wang, Douglass, & Yip, 2017).

The middle ground says minority group members can form a *bicultural identity*, drawing from their own culture while integrating themselves into the dominant culture. This view suggests that an individual can hold two cultural identities, without having to prefer one over the other (Shi & Lu, 2007; Hayes & Endale, 2018).

The choice of a bicultural identity is increasingly common. In fact, the number of people who identified themselves as belonging to more than one race is considerable and increased 134 percent from 2000 to 2010 (U.S. Bureau of the Census, 2011).

The process of identity formation is always complex and may be doubly so for minority group members. Racial and ethnic identity takes time to form. For some, it may require a prolonged period, but the result can be a rich, multifaceted identity (Jensen, 2008; Klimstra et al., 2012; Yoon et al., 2017).

Anxiety, Depression, and Suicide: Psychological Difficulties in Adolescence

LO 6.12 Explain why anxiety, depression, and suicide are important issues in adolescence.

One day in ninth grade it struck Leanne Taunton that she was stuck without hope inside a dreadful world. "It was like the air was a big weight pressing in on me from all sides. I couldn't shake the feeling, and I couldn't ignore it. There was nothing I could do."

A friend listened to her sympathetically and invited her to her basement. "We started doing drugs, using whatever was in the medicine cabinet," her friend recalls. "At first it seemed to offer some relief, but in the end we both had to go home again, if you know what I mean."

For Leanne, the relief also proved short. Too short. One day she grabbed her father's razor, filled up the tub, and slashed her wrists. At the ripe age of 15 she had had enough.

Although the vast majority of teenagers weather the search for identity—as well as other challenges of the age—without major psychological difficulties, some find adolescence particularly stressful, and some develop severe psychological problems. Three of the most serious are adolescent anxiety, depression, and suicide.

ADOLESCENT ANXIETY All adolescents occasionally experience anxiety, a feeling of apprehension or tension in reaction to stressful situations; it is a totally normal reaction to stress.

In some cases, though, adolescents develop anxiety disorders, which are the most prevalent psychological disorder in the age group, striking around 8 percent of the population. *Anxiety disorders* occur when anxiety occurs without external justification, and it impacts normal, everyday functioning. Sometimes anxiety occurs as a result of exposure to a specific stimulus, such as fear of a specific animal or insect, or a fear of crowded places or heights. In other cases, though, anxiety is less specific and may be caused, for instance, by a fear of social situations in general (Merikangas, Nakamura, & Kessler, 2009; Stopa et al., 2013).

Adolescents with anxiety disorders can be hypervigilant, worried that their anxiety will be triggered by something in their environment and seeking to avoid situations that can produce anxiety. Moreover, if they cannot avoid anxiety-producing circumstances, they may become overwhelmed and experience physical symptoms such as panic attacks that produce a range of symptoms, including sweating, faintness, or gastric distress (Carleton et al., 2014).

ADOLESCENT DEPRESSION No one is immune to sadness and bad moods, including adolescents. The end of a relationship, failure at an important task, the death of a loved one—all may produce profound feelings of sadness, loss, and grief. In such situations, depression is a typical reaction.

More than a quarter of adolescents report feeling so sad or hopeless for 2 or more weeks in a row that they stopped doing their normal activities. Almost two-thirds of teenagers say they have experienced such feelings at some point. In contrast, only a small minority of adolescents—some 3 percent—experience *major depression*, a full-blown psychological disorder that is severe and lingers for long periods (Grunbaum, Lowry, & Kahn, 2001; Galambos, Leadbeater, & Barker, 2004; Thapar et al., 2012).

Gender, ethnic, and racial differences also affect depression rates. As is true for adults, adolescent girls experience depression more often than boys. Some studies show black adolescents having a higher rate of depression than white adolescents, though not all research supports this conclusion. Native Americans, too, have higher rates of depression (Verhoeven, Sawyer, & Spence, 2013; English, Lambert, & Ialongo, 2014; Blom et al., 2016).

In cases of severe, long-term depression, biological factors are often involved. Some adolescents do seem genetically predisposed to experience depression, but environmental and social factors related to the extraordinary changes in their social lives also have an impact. An adolescent who loses a loved one to death, for example, or who grows up with an alcoholic or depressed parent is at a higher risk of depression. Being unpopular, having few close friends, and experiencing rejection are also associated with adolescent depression (Eley, Liang, & Plomin, 2004; Zalsman et al., 2006; Herberman Mash et al., 2014).

Why the depression rate is higher for girls than boys is puzzling. There is little evidence of a link to hormone differences or a particular gene. Some psychologists speculate that stress is greater for girls in adolescence because of the many, often conflicting, demands of the traditional female role. Recall the girl, quoted in our discussion of self-esteem, who feared academic achievement would endanger her popularity. Such conflict may make her feel helpless. Add to this the fact that traditional gender roles still give higher status to men than women (Gilbert, 2004; Hyde, Mezulis, & Abramson, 2008; Chaplin, Gillham, & Seligman, 2009).

Girls' higher levels of depression in adolescence may reflect gender differences in coping with stress, rather than differences in mood. Girls may be more likely to react to stress by turning inward, resulting in a sense of helplessness and hopelessness. In contrast, boys more often externalize the stress and act more impulsively or aggressively, or turn to drugs and alcohol (Wu et al., 2007; Brown et al., 2012; Anyan & Hjemdal, 2016).

Between 25 and 40 percent of girls and 20 to 35 percent of boys experience occasional episodes of depression during adolescence, although the incidence of major depression is far lower.

ADOLESCENT SUICIDE   Adolescent suicide in the United States has tripled in the past 30 years. Overall, one teenage suicide occurs every 90 minutes, for an annual rate of 12.2 suicides per 100,000 adolescents. Of the 21 million college students in the United States, 2.2 million have had serious thoughts of suicide, 336,000 have attempted suicide, and 1,400 have actually died of suicide in the previous year (American College Health Association, 2018).

The reported rate of suicide may actually understate the true number; parents and medical personnel often prefer to report a death as an accident rather than suicide. Even so, suicide is the second-most common cause of death for 15- to 24-year-olds, after accidents. For white children and teenagers between 10 and 17, the rate of suicide was up 70 percent between 2006 and 2016. And although black children in the same age group kill themselves at lower rates, the rate of increase was higher, at 77 percent (Conner & Goldston, 2007; Healthychildren.org, 2016; *Morbidity Mortality Weekly Report*, 2017).

The rate of adolescent suicide is higher for boys, although girls *attempt* suicide more frequently. Attempts among males are more likely to be fatal because boys tend to use more violent means, such as guns, whereas girls tend to choose less violent means, such as drug overdose. Some estimates suggest there are as many as 200 attempted suicides by both sexes for every successful one (Dervic et al., 2006; Pompili et al., 2009; Payá-González et al., 2015).

The reasons for the increase in adolescent suicide are unclear. The most obvious explanation is that adolescent stress has increased. But why should stress have increased particularly for teenagers? The suicide rate for other age groups has remained fairly stable over the same period.

Several theories in addition to stress have sought to explain the increase in suicide. One theory suggests that depression is a root cause. Depressed teenagers who feel profound hopelessness are at greater risk for suicide (although most depressed individuals do not commit suicide). Social inhibition, perfectionism, and high levels of stress and anxiety are also related to an increased risk. Another theory is that the easy availability of guns—more prevalent in the United States than in other industrialized nations—as well as relatively easy access to illegal drugs contributes to the suicide rate as well (Arnautovska & Grad, 2010; Hetrick et al., 2012; Wiederhold, 2014).

In addition, teenage brains are more prone to risk-taking, potentially accounting for some suicides. Also, some suicide cases are associated with family conflicts and relationship or school difficulties. Some stem from a history of abuse and neglect. The rate of suicide among drug and alcohol abusers is also relatively high (Wilcox, Conner, & Caine, 2004; Xing et al., 2010; Jacobson et al., 2013).

Some suicides appear to be caused by exposure to the suicide of others. In *cluster suicide*, one suicide leads to attempts by others to kill themselves. For instance, some high schools have experienced a series of suicides following a well-publicized case. As a result, many schools have established crisis intervention teams to counsel students when one student commits suicide (Daniel & Goldston, 2009; Abrutyn & Mueller, 2014; Milner, Too, & Spittal, 2018).

There are several warning signs of potential suicide. Among them are the following (also see the *Development in Your Life* box):

- Direct or indirect talk about suicide, such as "I wish I were dead" or "You won't have me to worry about any longer"
- School difficulties, such as missed classes or a decline in grades

Lee Young Ho/Sipa USA/Newscom

The rate of adolescent suicide has tripled in the past 30 years. These individuals mourn following the suicide of a family member.

Development in Your Life

Preventing Adolescent Suicide

If you suspect an adolescent, or anyone else, is contemplating suicide, act! Here are several suggestions:

- Talk to the person. Listen with understanding and without judging.

- Talk specifically about suicidal thoughts; ask questions such as: Do you have a plan? Have you bought a gun? Where is it? Have you stockpiled pills? Where are they? The Public Health Service notes that, "contrary to popular belief, such candor will not give a person dangerous ideas or encourage a suicidal act."

- Try to distinguish between general upset and more serious danger, as when suicide plans *have* been made. If the crisis is acute, *do not leave the person alone.*

- Be supportive, let the person know you care, and try to break down his or her feelings of isolation.

- Take charge of finding help. Do not fear invading the person's privacy. Do not try to handle the problem alone. Get professional help immediately.

- Make the environment safe, removing (not just hiding) weapons such as guns, razors, scissors, medication, and other potentially dangerous items.

- Do not keep suicide talk or threats secret; these are calls for help and call for immediate action.

- Do not challenge, dare, or use verbal shock treatment on the person to correct his or her thinking.

- Make a contract with the person, getting a promise or commitment, preferably in writing, not to attempt suicide until you have talked further.

- Don't be overly reassured by a sudden improvement of mood. Such quick "recoveries" may be merely the relief of deciding to commit suicide or the temporary release of talking to someone; most likely, the underlying problems have not been resolved.

For immediate help with a suicide-related problem, call (800) 273-8255 (the National Suicide Prevention Lifeline) or text them at 741741. You will reach trained counselors. You can also contact the Lifeline Crisis chat line at http://chat. suicidepreventionlifeline.org/GetHelp/LifelineChat.aspx.

- Making arrangements as if preparing for a long trip, such as giving away prized possessions or arranging for the care of a pet
- Writing a will
- Loss of appetite or excessive eating
- General depression, including a change in sleeping patterns, slowness and lethargy, and uncommunicativeness
- Dramatic changes in behavior, such as a shy person suddenly acting outgoing
- Preoccupation with death in music, art, or literature

Relationships: Family and Friends

When Paco Lizzagara entered junior high school, his good relationship with his parents changed drastically. Paco felt his parents were always "on his case." Instead of giving him the freedom he felt he deserved at age 13, they seemed to be more restrictive. Paco's parents saw things differently. They felt that they were not the source of tension in the house—he was. In their eyes, Paco, with whom they'd always enjoyed a stable, loving relationship, suddenly seemed transformed. They saw him shutting them out, and when he did speak with them, he criticized their politics, their dress, and their preferences in TV shows. To his parents, Paco's behavior was upsetting and bewildering.

Family Ties: Changing Relations with Relations

LO 6.13   Analyze how the parent–child relationship changes during adolescence.

The social world of adolescents is far wider than that of younger children. As relationships outside the home grow in significance, interactions with family evolve, taking on a new, and sometimes difficult, character (Collins & Andrew, 2004).

THE QUEST FOR AUTONOMY Parents are sometimes angered, and more frequently puzzled, by adolescents' conduct. Children who previously accepted their parents' judgments, declarations, and guidelines begin to question—and sometimes rebel against—their parents' views.

One cause of these clashes is the shifting roles children and parents confront during adolescence. Adolescents seek **autonomy**, independence and a sense of control over their lives. Most parents intellectually view this shift as a normal part of adolescence—a primary developmental task of the period—and in many ways they welcome it as a sign of growth (Hare et al., 2015; Campione-Barr et al., 2015).

However, the day-to-day realities of adolescents' increasing autonomy may prove difficult for parents to deal with. Intellectually appreciating this growing independence and allowing a teen to attend an unsupervised party are two different things. To the adolescent, her parents' refusal indicates a lack of trust or confidence. To the parents, it's simply good sense: "I trust you," they may say. "It's the others who will be there that I worry about."

In most families, teenagers' autonomy grows gradually over the adolescent years. One study of adolescents' changing views of their parents found that as autonomy increases, parents are seen more realistically as people in their own right. For example, rather than seeing their parents as authoritarian disciplinarians mindlessly reminding them to do their homework, adolescents may come to see their parents' emphasis on excelling in school as evidence of parental regrets about their own lack of education and a wish to see their children have more options in life. At the same time, adolescents come to depend more on themselves and to feel more like separate individuals.

The increase in adolescent autonomy changes the parent–child relationship, which tends to be asymmetrical in early adolescence, when parents hold most of the power and influence. By the end of adolescence, power and influence are more balanced; the relationship is more egalitarian, although parents typically retain the upper hand (Goede, Branje, & Meeus, 2009; Inguglia et al., 2014; Kiang & Bhattacharjee, 2018).

CULTURE AND AUTONOMY The degree of autonomy achieved varies from one family to the next. Cultural factors play a role. In Western societies, which value individualism, adolescents seek autonomy at a relatively early stage. In contrast, Asian societies are more collectivistic, believing the welfare of the group is above that of the individual. In such societies, adolescents' aspirations to autonomy are less pronounced (Supple et al., 2009; Perez-Brena, Updegraff, & Umaña-Taylor, 2012; Czerwińska-Jasiewicz, 2017).

autonomy
having independence and a sense of control over one's life

Compared with adolescents from more individualistic societies, adolescents from more collectivistic cultures tend to feel greater obligation to their families.

> **From a social worker's perspective:** In what ways do you think parents with different styles—authoritarian, authoritative, permissive, and uninvolved—react to attempts to establish autonomy during adolescence? Are the styles of parenting different for a single parent? Are there cultural differences?

A sense of obligation to family also varies among cultures. In collectivistic cultures, adolescents tend to feel a greater obligation to fulfill their family's expectations—to provide assistance, show respect, and offer financial support. In such societies, the push for autonomy is weaker and its development is slower (Leung, Pe-Pua, Karnilowicz, 2006; Chan & Chan, 2013; Hou, Kim, & Wang, 2016).

The extended timetable for autonomy in collectivistic cultures appears to have no negative consequences for adolescents. What matters is the match between cultural expectations and developmental patterns, not the specific timetable (Zimmer-Gembeck, & Collins, 2003; Updegraff et al., 2006).

Gender also plays a role. In general, male adolescents are permitted more autonomy at an earlier age than females. This is consistent with traditional gender stereotypes, in which males are seen as more independent and females as more dependent on others. In fact, parents who hold traditional views on gender are less likely to encourage their daughters' autonomy (Bumpus, Crouter, & McHale, 2001; Fousiani et al., 2014).

THE MYTH OF THE GENERATION GAP Teen movies often depict adolescents and their parents in total opposition, victims of a **generation gap**, a deep divide in attitudes, values, aspirations, and worldviews. For example, the parent of an environmentalist might turn out to own a polluting factory. These exaggerations are funny because they contain a truth—parents and teenagers often see things differently.

generation gap
a divide between parents and adolescents in attitudes, values, aspirations, and worldviews

The reality, however, is another matter. The generation gap, when it exists, is really quite narrow. Adolescents and their parents tend to agree on many things. Republican parents generally have Republican children; members of the Christian right have children with similar views; parents who advocate for abortion rights have children who are pro-choice. On social, political, and religious issues, parents and adolescents tend to be in sync, and children's worries mirror those of their parents. Adolescents' concerns about society's problems reflect those of many adults (Knafo & Schwartz, 2003; Smetana, 2005; Grønhøj & Thøgersen, 2012).

Most adolescents and their parents get along quite well. Despite their quest for autonomy and independence, most teenagers have deep love, affection, and respect for their parents—as their parents do for them. Although some parent–adolescent relationships are seriously troubled, the majority are positive and help adolescents avoid the kind of peer pressure discussed later in the module (Black, 2002; Riesch et al., 2010; Coleman, 2014).

Even though teenagers spend less time with their families in general, the amount of time they spend alone with each parent remains remarkably stable across adolescence. There is no evidence that suggests family problems are worse in adolescence than at other stages of development, and in fact, the more time spent with parents, the fewer the adolescents' behavioral problems (Granic, Hollenstein, & Dishion, 2003; Milkie et al., 2015; see Figure 6-9).

CONFLICTS WITH PARENTS Of course, if most adolescents get along with their parents most of the time, that means sometimes they don't. No relationship is always smooth. Parents and teens may agree about social and political issues, but they often differ on matters of personal taste, such as music and clothing. Also, parents and children may disagree when children act on their autonomy and independence sooner than parents feel is right. Consequently, parent–child conflicts are more likely to occur during adolescence, particularly in the early stages, although not every family is affected to the same degree (Arnett, 2000; Smetana, Daddis, & Chuang, 2003; García-Ruiz et al., 2013).

According to developmental psychologist Judith Smetana, conflict is greater in early adolescence because of differing definitions of, and rationales for, appropriate and inappropriate conduct. Parents may frown on multiple ear piercings because society traditionally deems it inappropriate, whereas adolescents may view the issue as one of personal choice (Smetana, 2005, 2006; Rote et al., 2012).

The newly sophisticated reasoning of adolescents (discussed in the previous module) leads them to regard parental rules in more complex ways. Arguments that might convince a school-age child ("Do it because I tell you to do it.") are less compelling to an adolescent.

Figure 6-9 Time Spent with Parents and Magnitude of Behavioral Problems

The more time adolescents are involved with activities with both their parents, the less likely they are to exhibit behavioral problems.

SOURCE: Milkie et al., 2015.

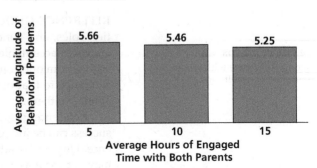

The argumentativeness and assertiveness of early adolescence may at first increase conflict, but they play a key role in the evolution of parent–child relationships. Although parents may initially react defensively to their children's challenges and grow inflexible and rigid, in most cases they come to realize their children *are* growing up and they want to support them in that process.

As parents realize that their children's arguments are often compelling and fairly reasonable, and that they can be trusted with more freedom, they become more yielding, allowing and perhaps even encouraging independence. As this process occurs in mid-adolescence, the conflict of the early years declines.

This does not hold true for all adolescents. The majority of teenagers maintain stable relations with their parents, but as many as 20 percent pass through a fairly rough time (Dmitrieva et al., 2004; Branje, 2018).

CULTURAL DIFFERENCES IN PARENT–CHILD CONFLICTS DURING ADOLESCENCE
Parent–child conflicts are found in every culture, but there does seem to be less conflict between parents and teenagers in "traditional," preindustrial cultures. Teens in such cultures experience fewer mood swings and instances of risky behavior than teens in industrialized countries (Eichelsheim et al., 2010; Jensen & Dost-Gözkan, 2014; Shah et al., 2016).

The reason may be the degree of independence that adolescents expect and adults permit. In more industrialized societies, with an emphasis on individualism, independence is expected of adolescents. Consequently, adolescents and their parents must negotiate the amount and timing of that independence—a process that often leads to strife. In more traditional societies, individualism is less valued; therefore, adolescents are less inclined to seek independence. The result is less parent–child conflict (Dasen, 2000, Dasen & Mishra, 2002; Griffith & Grolnick, 2014).

Relationships with Peers: The Importance of Belonging

LO 6.14 **Analyze the nature and significance of peer relationships during adolescence.**

For many parents, the most fitting symbol of adolescence is the cell phone, on which incessant texting occurs. For their children, communicating with friends is an indispensable lifeline, a compulsive need that underscores their significance at this stage. Continuing the trend from middle childhood, adolescents spend increasing hours with their peers as these relationships grow in importance. In fact, there is probably no period of life in which peer relationships matter as much as in adolescence (Bukowski, Laursen, & Rubin, 2018).

SOCIAL COMPARISON Peers become more important for many reasons. They enable adolescents to compare and evaluate opinions, abilities, and even physical changes—a process called *social comparison*. Because the physical and cognitive changes of this age are so unique and so pronounced, especially in early puberty, adolescents turn to others who share and can shed light on their own experiences. Parents, being well beyond these changes, cannot provide social comparison. Adolescents' questioning of adult authority and their desire for autonomy also render parents—and adults in general—inadequate sources of knowledge (Li & Wright, 2013; Schaefer & Salafia, 2014; Tian, Yu, & Huebner, 2017).

REFERENCE GROUPS As noted, adolescence is a time of trying out new identities, roles, and conduct. Peers provide information about what roles and behavior are most acceptable by serving as a reference group. **Reference groups** are people with whom one compares oneself. Just as a professional ballplayer compares his performance to that of other pro players, so do teenagers compare themselves to peers similar to them.

Reference groups offer a set of *norms*, or standards, by which abilities and social success can be judged. A teenager need not belong to a group for it to serve as a reference. Unpopular adolescents, belittled and rejected by members of a popular group, may yet use it as a reference group.

reference groups
groups of people with whom one compares oneself

CLIQUES AND CROWDS: BELONGING TO A GROUP   Increased cognitive sophistication allows adolescents to group others in more discriminating ways. Even if others do not belong to the teen's reference group, they typically are part of some identifiable group. Rather than defining people in concrete terms by what they do ("football players" or "musicians") as a younger child might, adolescents use more abstract terms ("jocks" or "skaters" or "stoners") (Brown, 2004).

Adolescents form two types of groups: cliques and crowds. **Cliques** are groups of from 2 to 12 people whose members have frequent social interactions with one another. **Crowds** are larger, comprising individuals who share certain characteristics but do not necessarily interact. "Jocks" and "nerds" represent crowds found in many high schools.

Membership in a clique or a crowd is determined by the degree of similarity with other members. One key similarity is substance use; adolescents tend to choose friends whose alcohol and drug use matches their own. Their friends often mirror their academic success and general behavior patterns, although this is not always true. For instance, in early adolescence, peers who are aggressive may be more attractive than those who are well behaved (Kupersmidt & Dodge, 2004; Hutchinson & Rapee, 2007; Kiuru et al., 2009).

The emergence of distinct cliques and crowds at this stage reflects adolescents' increased cognitive capabilities. Group labels are abstractions, requiring teens to judge people they may seldom interact with and have little direct knowledge about. It is not until mid-adolescence that teenagers are cognitively able to make the subtle judgments that distinguish between different cliques and crowds (Brown & Klute, 2003; Witvliet et al., 2010; also see the *From Research to Practice* box).

GENDER RELATIONS   As children enter adolescence, their social groups are composed almost universally of same-sex friends. Boys hang out with boys; girls hang out with girls. This sex segregation is called the **sex cleavage**.

cliques
groups of from 2 to 12 people whose members have frequent social interactions with one another

crowds
larger groups than cliques, composed of individuals who share particular characteristics but who may not interact with one another

sex cleavage
sex segregation in which boys interact primarily with boys and girls primarily with girls

From Research to Practice

Is Anyone "Liking" Me? Social Comparison and Self-Esteem in the Digital Age

Social networking sites like Facebook have become a part of daily life. In fact, it's likely that you are reading this chapter on your laptop or smartphone while also checking your social media feed as well as those of your friends. But the quick pace of technology has left researchers racing to study how these social networking sites affect us. And not all of the news is good, as research has uncovered a "dark side" to social media use. For example, a recent review of 23 different studies of frequent and consistent Facebook users found a significant association with increased psychological distress. Similarly, one longitudinal study found that Facebook use over time led to lower self-ratings of life satisfaction and well-being (Kross et al., 2013; Marino et al., 2018).

But what could be the cause of the relationship between our use of social networking sites and our psychological well-being? One group of researchers gathered data from college students to find out how social comparison might affect self-esteem. In their study, participants were asked to view a fictitious social media profile of another student at their university. One group viewed a social media profile that consisted of photos of the person during a recent vacation. This profile showed "high activity," with a high number of "likes" and comments. The other group viewed a "low activity" version of the same profile and photos with many fewer "likes" and comments (Vogel et al., 2014).

The researchers hypothesized that self-esteem would be lower in those participants who made an upward social comparison to the high-activity profile than in those participants who made a downward social comparison to the low-activity profile. In fact, this was the case: Participant self-esteem was lower in those who had viewed the fictitious high-activity profile with more "likes" and comments. So as our personal relationships become reflected in the digital world of social networking sites, it seems that a symbolic thumbs-up is a key ingredient to one's self-esteem—for better or worse.

The practical implications of this research are many. For example, counselors working with teens or adults with depression should assess their client's social media use and how it might be negatively affecting their mood. And in turn, counselors could educate their clients regarding more adaptive social networking site practices. This research is also important to parents, teachers, counselors, and school psychologists, as they teach kids adaptive ways to use social networking sites and how to appropriately cope with online bullying or rejection.

Shared Writing Prompt:

How do you think that receiving more "likes" and comments on one's social media posts affects people's relationships with others as well as their feelings about themselves?

The situation changes with the onset of puberty. Boys and girls experience the hormonal surge that causes the sex organs to mature. At the same time, society suggests it is time for romantic involvement. These developments change the ways the opposite sex is viewed. Where a 10-year-old is likely to see every member of the other sex as "annoying" and "a pain," heterosexual teenage boys and girls regard each other's personality and sexuality with greater interest. (For gays and lesbians, pairing off holds other complexities, as we will see when we discuss adolescent dating.)

In early puberty, boys' and girls' cliques, previously on parallel but separate tracks, begin to converge. Adolescents attend boy–girl dances or parties, although the boys still tend to socialize with boys, and the girls with girls. Soon, adolescents spend more time with the other sex. New cliques emerge, composed of both genders. Not everyone participates initially: Early on, the leaders of the same-sex cliques and those with the highest status lead the way. Eventually, however, most teenagers belong to mixed-gender cliques. At the end of adolescence, cliques and crowds become less influential. Many dissolve as pairing off occurs (Manning et al., 2014). Furthermore, they are affected by diversity issues, as we discuss in the *Cultural Dimensions* feature.

Cultural Dimensions

Race Segregation: The Great Divide of Adolescence

When Robert Corker, a student at Tufts University, first stepped into the gym, he was immediately pulled into a pick-up basketball game. "The guys thought I'd be good at basketball just because I'm tall and black. Actually, I stink at sports and quickly changed their minds. Fortunately we all laughed about it later," Robert says.

* * *

When Sandra Cantú, a Puerto Rican nursing student at the University of Alabama, entered the cafeteria wearing her hospital whites, two female students assumed she was a cafeteria worker and asked her to clear off their table.

* * *

Race relations are no easier for white students to manage. Ted Connors, a white senior at Southern Methodist, recalls the day he asked a student in his dorm for help with his Spanish homework. "He laughed in my face," Ted recalls, "I assumed he spoke Spanish just because his name was Hector Gonzalez. Actually, he had grown up in Michigan and spoke only English. It took quite a while to live that one down."

* * *

The pattern of racial misunderstanding experienced by these students is repeated over and over in schools and colleges throughout the United States. Even when they attend desegregated schools with significant diversity, people of different ethnicities and races interact very little. Moreover, even if they have a friend of a different ethnicity within the confines of a school, most adolescents don't interact with that friend outside of school (Hamm, Brown, & Heck, 2005; Benner & Wang, 2017).

It doesn't start out this way. During elementary school and early adolescence, integration is common among students of differing ethnicities. However, by middle and late adolescence, students segregate (Knifsend & Juvonen, 2014; Tatum, 2017).

Why is racial and ethnic segregation the rule, even in schools that have long been desegregated? One reason is that minority students may seek support from others who share their status (where "minority," used in its sociological sense, indicates a subordinate group lacking power compared to a dominant group). By associating with others of their own group, members of minority groups are able to affirm their own identity.

Members of different racial and ethnic groups may be segregated in the classroom as well. As discussed previously, members of groups that have experienced discrimination tend to be less successful in school. Thus, ethnic and racial segregation in high school may be based on academic achievement rather than ethnicity.

Lower academic performance may place minority students in classes with fewer majority students, and vice versa. Such class assignment practices may maintain and promote racial and ethnic segregation, especially in schools where rigid academic tracking assigns students to "low," "medium," and "high" tracks depending on their prior achievement (Lucas & Berends, 2002).

Segregation in school may also reflect prejudice, both perceived and real, toward members of other groups. Students of color may feel that the white majority is discriminatory and hostile, and thus prefer to stick to same-race groups. White students may assume that minority students are antagonistic and unfriendly. Such mutually destructive attitudes make meaningful interaction difficult (Phinney, Ferguson, & Tate, 1997; Tropp, 2003).

Is this voluntary racial and ethnic segregation inevitable? No. Adolescents who have interacted regularly and extensively with other races in childhood are more likely to have friends of different races. Schools that actively promote integration in classes create an environment that fosters cross-race friendships. Furthermore, having friends of another race helps minority group members deal with discrimination they may encounter (Hewstone, 2003; Davies et al., 2011; Benner & Wang, 2017).

Figure 6-10 The Social World of Adolescence

An adolescent's popularity can fall into one of four categories, depending on the opinions of his or her peers. Popularity is related to differences in status, behavior, and adjustment.

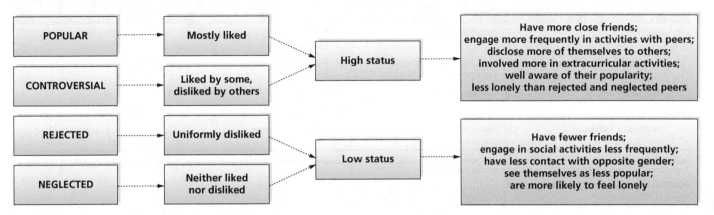

POPULAR ---> **Mostly liked** ---> **High status**

CONTROVERSIAL ---> **Liked by some, disliked by others**

High status ---> Have more close friends; engage more frequently in activities with peers; disclose more of themselves to others; involved more in extracurricular activities; well aware of their popularity; less lonely than rejected and neglected peers

REJECTED ---> **Uniformly disliked** ---> **Low status**

NEGLECTED ---> **Neither liked nor disliked**

Low status ---> Have fewer friends; engage in social activities less frequently; have less contact with opposite gender; see themselves as less popular; are more likely to feel lonely

POPULARITY AND REJECTION   Most adolescents are highly tuned in to who is popular and who is not. In fact, for some, popularity—or lack of it—is the central focus of their lives.

The social world of adolescents is more complex than who is popular or unpopular. Some adolescents are controversial. In contrast to *popular* adolescents, who are mostly liked, **controversial adolescents** are liked by some and disliked by others. A controversial adolescent may be highly popular within a particular group, such as the string orchestra, but less so among other classmates. There are also **rejected adolescents**, who are uniformly disliked, and **neglected adolescents**, who are neither liked nor disliked (see Figure 6-10)—whose status is so low everyone overlooks them.

In most cases, popular and controversial adolescents tend to enjoy a higher status, and rejected and neglected teenagers share a lower status. Popular and controversial adolescents have more close friends, engage in more activities with their peers, and disclose more about themselves than less popular students. They participate in more extracurricular school activities. Well aware of their own popularity, they are less lonely than their less popular classmates (Becker & Luthar, 2007; Closson, 2009; Estévez et al., 2014).

The social world of rejected and neglected adolescents is far less pleasant. They have fewer friends, engage in fewer social activities, and have less contact with the opposite sex. They see themselves—accurately—as less popular, and they are more likely to feel lonely (McElhaney, Antonishak, & Allen, 2008; Woodhouse, Dykas, & Cassidy, 2012).

controversial adolescents
children who are liked by some peers and disliked by others

rejected adolescents
children who are actively disliked and whose peers may react to them in an obviously negative manner

neglected adolescents
children who receive relatively little attention from their peers in the form of either positive or negative interactions

The sex segregation of childhood continues during the early stages of adolescence. However, by the time of middle adolescence, this segregation decreases, and boys' and girls' cliques begin to converge.

Unpopular adolescents fall into several categories. Controversial adolescents are liked by some and disliked by others; rejected adolescents are uniformly disliked; and neglected adolescents are neither liked nor disliked.

Table 6-4 High School Status

According to College Men		According to College Women	
High-status high school girls:	**High-status high school boys:**	**High-status high school girls:**	**High-status high school boys:**
1. Are good-looking	1. Take part in sports	1. Have high grades and are intelligent	1. Take part in sports
2. Have high grades and are intelligent	2. Have high grades and are intelligent	2. Participate in sports	2. Have high grades and are intelligent
3. Take part in sports	3. Are popular with girls	3. Are sociable	3. Are sociable
4. Are sociable	4. Are sociable	4. Are good-looking	4. Are good-looking
5. Are popular with boys	5. Have nice cars	5. Have nice clothes	5. Participate in school clubs or government

Note: Results are based on responses from students at Louisiana State University, Southeastern Louisiana University, State University of New York at Albany, State University of New York at Stony Brook, University of Georgia, and the University of New Hampshire.
SOURCE: Based on Suitor, Minyard, & Carter, 2001.

As illustrated in Table 6-4, men and women differ in their ideas of what determines status in high school. College men suggest that appearance is what most determines a girl's status, whereas college women believe it is her grades and intelligence (Suitor, Minyard, & Carter, 2001).

CONFORMITY: PEER PRESSURE IN ADOLESCENCE Whenever Aldos Henry said he wanted a particular brand of sneakers or a certain style of shirt, his parents blamed it on peer pressure and told him to think for himself.

In arguing with Aldos, his parents were taking a view prevalent in U.S. society: that teenagers are highly susceptible to **peer pressure**, the pressure to conform to the behavior and attitudes of one's peers. Were his parents correct?

Adolescents *are* highly susceptible to the influence of their peers when considering what to wear, whom to date, and what movies to see. Wearing the right clothes, down to the right brand, can be a ticket to popularity. It shows you know what's what. But when it comes to nonsocial matters, such as choosing a career path or trying to solve a problem, they are more likely to consult an adult (Closson, Hart, & Hogg, 2017).

Especially in middle and late adolescence, teenagers look to those they see as experts. For social concerns, they turn to the experts—their peers. For arenas where adults hold the knowledge, teenagers tend to ask their advice and accept their opinions (Perrine & Aloise-Young, 2004; Choo & Shek, 2013).

Overall, susceptibility to peer pressure does not suddenly soar in adolescence. Instead, adolescence changes the source of influence. Whereas children conform fairly consistently to their parents, pressures to conform to peers increase in adolescence as teens establish an identity apart from their parents'.

Ultimately, adolescents conform less to both peers *and* adults as their autonomy increases. As their confidence grows and they are able to make their own decisions, adolescents are apt to act independently and to reject pressures from others. Before they learn to resist peer pressure, however, teenagers may get into trouble, often along with their friends (Cook, Buehler, & Henson, 2009; Monahan, Steinberg, & Cauffman, 2009; Meldrum, Miller, & Flexon, 2013).

JUVENILE DELINQUENCY: THE CRIMES OF ADOLESCENCE Adolescents, along with young adults, commit more crimes than any other age group. This is a somewhat misleading statistic: Because certain behaviors (such as drinking) are illegal for adolescents, it is easy for them to break the law. But even disregarding such crimes, adolescents are disproportionately responsible for violent crimes, such as murder, assaults, and rape, as well as property crimes involving theft, robbery, and arson.

What steers adolescents toward criminal activity? Some offenders, known as **undersocialized delinquents**, were raised with little discipline or by harsh, uncaring parents. Although they are influenced by peers, their parents did not teach them appropriate social behavior or how to regulate their own conduct. Undersocialized

peer pressure
the influence of one's peers to conform to their behavior and attitudes

undersocialized delinquents
adolescent delinquents who are raised with little discipline or with harsh, uncaring parental supervision

delinquents typically begin criminal activities well before the onset of adolescence (Hoeve et al., 2008; Barrett & Katsiyannis, 2017).

Undersocialized delinquents share several characteristics. They tend to be aggressive and violent early in life, leading to peer rejection and academic failure. They are more likely to have been diagnosed with attention deficit hyperactivity disorder as children, and they tend to be less intelligent than average (Silverthorn & Frick, 1999; Rutter, 2003; Peach & Gaultney, 2013).

Undersocialized delinquents often suffer from psychological problems, and as adults they fit a pattern called *antisocial personality disorder*. They are unlikely to be successfully rehabilitated, and many undersocialized delinquents live on the margins of society their entire lives (Frick et al., 2003; Peach & Gaultney, 2013).

A larger group of adolescent offenders are socialized delinquents. **Socialized delinquents** know and subscribe to the norms of society; they are fairly normal psychologically. For them, offenses committed in adolescence do not lead to a life of crime. Instead, most socialized delinquents engage in some petty crimes (such as shoplifting) during adolescence, but do not continue into adulthood.

Socialized delinquents are typically highly peer influenced, their delinquency often occurring in groups. Some research also suggests that their parents supervise their behavior less than other parents. But these minor delinquencies are often a result of giving in to group pressure or seeking to establish one's identity as an adult (Fletcher et al., 1995; Thornberry & Krohn, 1997).

Undersocialized delinquents are raised with little discipline or by harsh, uncaring parents, and they begin antisocial activities at a relatively early age. In contrast, socialized delinquents know and usually follow the norms of society, and they are highly influenced by their peers.

socialized delinquents adolescent delinquents who know and subscribe to the norms of society and who are fairly normal psychologically

Dating, Sexual Behavior, and Teenage Pregnancy

It took him almost a month, but Sylvester Chiu finally got up the courage to ask Jackie Durbin, via a carefully crafted text, to the movies. It was hardly a surprise to Jackie, though. Sylvester had first told his friend Erik about his plans, and Erik had told Jackie's friend Cynthia, who had in turn told Jackie, who was primed to say "yes" when Sylvester finally texted.

Welcome to the complex world of adolescent dating, an important ritual in the liturgy of adolescent relationships.

Dating: Close Relationships in the 21st Century

LO 6.15 Describe the functions and characteristics of dating during adolescence.

Changing cultural factors largely determine when and how adolescents begin to date. Until recently, exclusive dating was a cultural ideal, viewed in the context of romance. Society encouraged dating as a way for adolescents to explore relationships that might lead to marriage. Today, some adolescents believe that dating is outmoded and limiting, and in some places *hooking up*—a vague term that covers everything from kissing to sexual intercourse—is regarded as more appropriate. Still, despite changing cultural norms, dating remains the dominant form of social interaction that leads to intimacy among adolescents (Denizet-Lewis, 2004; Manning, Giordano, & Longmore, 2006; Bogle, 2008; Rice, McGill, & Adler-Baeder, 2017).

THE FUNCTIONS OF DATING Dating is a way to learn how to establish intimacy with another individual. It can provide entertainment and, depending on the status of the person one is dating, prestige. It even can be used to develop a sense of one's own identity (Friedlander et al., 2007; Paludi, 2012; Kreager et al., 2016).

Unfortunately, dating, at least in early and middle adolescence, does not serve the function of developing intimacy very well. On the contrary, it is often a superficial activity in which the participants rarely let down their guards and never expose themselves emotionally. Psychological intimacy may be lacking even when sex is part of the relationship (Collins, 2003; Furman & Shaffer, 2003; Tuggle, Kerpelman, & Pittman, 2014).

True intimacy becomes more common during later adolescence. At that point, both participants may take dating more seriously as a way to select a possible mate for marriage.

For adolescents who identify as LGBTQ (lesbian, gay, bisexual, transgender, and queer or questioning), dating presents special challenges. In some cases, blatant homophobic prejudice expressed by classmates may lead gays and lesbians to date members of the other sex in an effort to fit in. If they do seek relationships with others with similar identities, they may find it difficult to find partners, because others may not openly express their sexual orientation. LGBTQ couples who do openly date face possible harassment, making the development of a relationship all the more difficult (Savin-Williams, 2003, 2006; Dentato, Argüello, & Smith, 2018).

DATING, RACE, AND ETHNICITY   Culture influences dating patterns among adolescents of different racial and ethnic groups, particularly those whose parents have immigrated from other countries. Foreign-born parents may try to control dating behavior to preserve traditional values or confine dating to their own racial or ethnic group.

Some immigrant parents may hold especially conservative attitudes because they themselves may be living in an arranged marriage and may never have experienced dating. They may insist that there will be no dating without chaperones, a position that will inevitably lead to conflict with their children (Hoelter, Axinn, & Ghimire, 2004; Lau et al., 2009; Shenhav, Campos, & Goldberg, 2017).

Sexual Relationships

LO 6.16   Explain how sexuality develops in the adolescent years.

The hormonal changes of puberty trigger not only the maturation of the sexual organs, but also a new range of feelings. Sexual behavior and thoughts are among the central concerns of adolescents, occupying the minds of almost all adolescents a good deal of the time (Kelly, 2001; Ponton, 2001).

masturbation
sexual self-stimulation

MASTURBATION   Often the first sex act in which adolescents engage is solitary sexual self-stimulation, or masturbation. By age 15, 80 percent of teenage boys and 20 percent of teenage girls report that they have masturbated. In males, frequency is high in the early teens and then begins to decline, whereas in females, frequency is lower initially and increases throughout adolescence. There are also racial differences. For example, black men and women masturbate less than whites (Schwartz, 1999; Hyde & DeLamater, 2004).

Although masturbation is widespread, it still may produce feelings of shame and guilt. There are several reasons for this. One is that adolescents may believe that masturbation signifies the inability to find a sexual partner—an erroneous assumption, since statistics show that three-quarters of married men and two-thirds of married women report masturbating between 10 and 24 times a year. For some, the sense of shame about masturbation is the result of a lingering legacy of misguided views of masturbation, in part based on religious prohibitions, cultural and social norms, and bad science (Das, 2007; Gerressu et al., 2008; Colarusso, 2012).

Today, experts on sexual behavior view masturbation as a normal, healthy, and harmless activity. In fact, some suggest that it provides a useful way to learn about one's own sexuality (Levin, 2007; Hyde & Delamater, 2013).

SEXUAL INTERCOURSE   Although it may be preceded by many different types of sexual intimacy, including deep kissing, massaging, petting, and oral sex, sexual intercourse remains a major milestone in the perceptions of most heterosexual adolescents. Consequently, the main focus of researchers investigating sexual behavior has been on the act of heterosexual intercourse.

The average age at which adolescents first have heterosexual intercourse has been steadily declining over the past 50 years, and about one in five adolescents have had sex before the age of 15. Overall, the average age of first sexual intercourse is 17, and around three-quarters of adolescents have had sex before the age of 20 (see Figure 6-11). At the same time, though, many teenagers are postponing sex, and the number of adolescents who say they have never had sexual intercourse increased by 13 percent from 1991 to 2007 (*Morbidity and Mortality Weekly Report*, 2008; Guttmacher Institute, 2012).

There also are racial and ethnic differences in timing of initial sexual intercourse: blacks generally have sex for the first time earlier than do Puerto Ricans, who have sex earlier than do whites. These racial and ethnic differences likely reflect differences in socioeconomic conditions, cultural values, and family structure (Singh & Darroch, 2000; Hyde & DeLamater, 2008).

Strong societal norms govern sexual conduct. A few decades ago the prevailing norm was the *double standard*: Premarital sex was permissible for males but not females, and men should be sure to marry virgins. Today the double standard has begun to give way to *permissiveness with affection*. Under this standard, premarital intercourse is permissible for both men and women in the context of a long-term, committed, or loving relationship (Hyde & Delamater, 2004; Earle et al., 2007).

Figure 6-11 Adolescents and Sexual Activity

The age at which adolescents have sexual intercourse for the first time is declining, and about three-quarters have had sex before the age of 20.

SOURCE: Finer & Philbin, 2013.

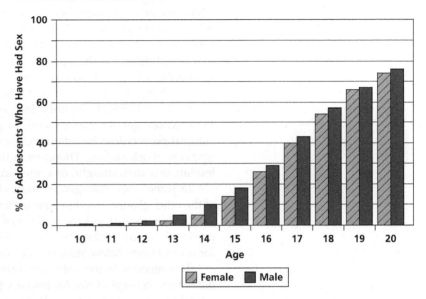

> **From the perspective of a health-care provider:** A parent asks you how to prevent her 14-year-old son from engaging in sexual activity until he is older. What would you tell her?

The demise of the double standard is far from complete. Attitudes toward sexual conduct are still typically more lenient for males than for females, even in socially liberal cultures. And in some cultures, the standards for men and women are quite distinct. For example, in North Africa, the Middle East, and the majority of Asian countries, women are expected to abstain from sexual intercourse until they are married. In Mexico, males are considerably more likely than females to have premarital sex. In contrast, in sub-Saharan Africa, women are more likely to have sexual intercourse before marriage, and intercourse is common among unmarried teenage women (Wellings et al., 2006; Ghule, Balaiah, & Joshi, 2007; Riyani & Parker, 2018).

SEXUAL ORIENTATION AND IDENTITY: LGBTQ AND MORE When we consider adolescents' sexual development, the most frequent pattern is *heterosexuality*, sexual attraction and behavior directed to the other sex. Yet some teenagers are *homosexual*, in which their sexual attraction and behavior is oriented to members of their own sex. (Most male homosexuals prefer the term *gay* and female homosexuals the label *lesbian* because they refer to a broader array of attitudes and lifestyles than the term *homosexual*, which focuses on the sexual act.) Other people find they are *bisexual*, sexually attracted to people of both sexes. And others see their sexual identity as fluid, or are questioning their identities.

Many teens experiment with homosexuality and other sexual identities. For example, around 20 to 25 percent of adolescent boys and 10 percent of adolescent girls have at least one same-sex sexual encounter. In fact, homosexuality and heterosexuality are not completely distinct sexual orientations. Alfred Kinsey, a pioneering sex researcher, argued that sexual orientation should be viewed as a continuum in which "exclusively homosexual" is at one end and "exclusively heterosexual" is at the other. In between are people who show both homosexual and heterosexual behavior. Although accurate figures are difficult to obtain, most experts believe that between 4 percent and 10 percent of both men and women are exclusively homosexual during extended periods of their lives (Kinsey, Pomeroy, & Martin, 1948; Diamond, 2003a, 2003b; Russell & Consolacion, 2003).

Sexuality is further complicated by the distinction between sexual orientation, which refers to a person's sexual interests, and gender identity—the gender a person believes he or she is psychologically. Sexual orientation and gender identity are not necessarily related to one another: A man with a strong masculine gender identity may be attracted to other men, and traditional "masculine" or "feminine" behavior is not necessarily related to a person's sexual orientation or gender identity (Hunter & Mallon, 2000; Greydanus & Pratt, 2016).

Some individuals identify as transgender. *Transgender* is an umbrella term for those whose gender identity and/or gender expression is different from the typical cultural expectations based on their sex assignment at birth. It does not imply a particular sexual orientation. Therefore, a transgender individual may also identify as gay, lesbian, bisexual, straight, or something else.

In some cases, transgender individuals may feel that they are trapped in the body of the other gender, and they may seek sex-change operations in which their genitals are surgically removed and the genitals of the desired sex are created. It is a difficult path, one involving counseling, hormone injections, and living as a member of the desired sex for several years before surgery. Ultimately, though, the outcome can be quite positive.

Transgender individuals are different from those who are called *intersex* or the older term *hermaphrodite*. An intersex person is born with an atypical combination of sexual organs or chromosomal or gene patterns. For instance, they may be born with both male and female sex organs, or with ambiguous organs. Only one in 4,500 births are intersex infants (Diamond, 2013).

WHAT DETERMINES SEXUAL ORIENTATION?   The factors that induce people to develop a particular sexual orientation and identity are not well understood. Evidence suggests that genetic and biological factors play a central role. Identical twins are more likely to both be homosexual than pairs of siblings who don't share their genetic makeup. Other research finds that various structures of the brain are different according to sexual orientation, and hormone production also seems to be linked to sexual orientation (Ellis et al., 2008; Fitzgerald, 2008; Santtila et al., 2008).

In the past, some theoreticians suggested that family or peer environmental factors play a role. For example, Freud argued that homosexuality was the result of inappropriate identification with the opposite-sex parent (Freud, 1922/1959). The difficulty with Freud's theoretical perspective and other, similar perspectives that followed is that there simply is no research evidence to suggest that any particular family dynamic or childrearing practice is consistently related to sexual orientation. Similarly, explanations based on learning theory, which suggest that homosexuality arises because of rewarding, pleasant homosexual experiences and unsatisfying heterosexual ones, are not supported by research (Bell & Weinberg, 1978; Isay, 1990; Golombok & Tasker, 1996).

In short, there is no accepted explanation of why some adolescents develop a heterosexual orientation and others a homosexual orientation. Most experts believe that sexual orientation develops out of a complex interplay of genetic, physiological, and environmental factors (LeVay & Valente, 2003; Mustanski, Kuper, & Greene, 2014).

CHALLENGES FACING ADOLESCENTS WITH LGBTQ SEXUAL ORIENTATIONS AND IDENTITIES   Adolescents who have nontraditional sexual orientations and identities face a more difficult time than other teens. For example, U.S. society still harbors ignorance and prejudice about homosexuality, insisting that people have a choice in the matter—which they do not. Gay, lesbian, and transgender teens may be rejected by their family or peers and harassed or even assaulted by others. As a result, adolescents who have nontraditional sexual orientations are at greater risk for depression, with suicide rates significantly higher than for heterosexual adolescents. Gays and lesbians who do not conform to gender stereotypes are particularly susceptible to victimization, and they have lower rates of adjustment (Toomey et al., 2010; Madsen & Green, 2012; Mitchell, Ybarra, & Korchmaros, 2014).

Most people ultimately come to grips with their sexual orientation and become comfortable with it. Although lesbian, gay, bisexual, and transgender adolescents may experience mental health difficulties as a result of the stress, prejudice, and discrimination they face, homosexuality is not considered a psychological disorder by any major psychological or medical association. All of them endorse efforts to reduce discrimination against homosexuals. Furthermore, society's attitudes toward homosexuality are changing, particularly among younger individuals. For example, a majority of U.S. citizens support gay marriage, which became legal in the United States in 2015 (Baker & Sussman, 2012; Patterson, 2013; Hu, Xu, & Tornello, 2016; Platt, Wolf, & Scheitle, 2018).

TEENAGE PREGNANCY Feedings at 3:00 am, diaper changes, and visits to the pediatrician are not part of most people's vision of adolescence. Yet, every year, tens of thousands of adolescents in the United States give birth. The good news, though, is that the number of teenage pregnancies has decreased significantly in the past two decades. In fact, in 2014, the birth rate for U.S. teenagers was the lowest level ever reported in the seven decades that the government has been tracking pregnancies (see Figure 6-12). Birth rates declined to historic lows in all racial and ethnic groups, but disparities remain, with the rate of births higher for non-Hispanic black and Hispanic teens than for whites. Overall, the rate of teen births is 20.3 per 1,000 births (Colen, Geronimus, & Phipps, 2006; Hamilton, Martin, & Ventura, 2009; Hamilton & Ventura, 2012; Centers for Disease Control and Prevention, 2018).

Several factors explain the drop in teenage pregnancies:

- New initiatives have raised awareness of the risks of unprotected sex. For example, about two-thirds of U.S. high schools have comprehensive sex education programs (Villarosa, 2003; Corcoran & Pillai, 2007).

- The rates of sexual intercourse among teenagers have declined. The percentage of teenage girls who have ever had sexual intercourse dropped from 51 percent in 1988 to 43 percent in 2006–2010 (Martinez, Copen, & Abma, 2011; Centers for Disease Control and Prevention, 2018; Kann et al., 2018).

- The use of condoms and other forms of contraception has increased. For example, virtually all sexually experienced girls ages 15–19 have used some method of contraception. Among sexually active adolescents, 54 percent report that either they or their partner had used a condom during their last sexual intercourse (Martinez, Copen, & Abma, 2011; Centers for Disease Control and Prevention, 2018; Kann et al., 2018).

Figure 6-12 U.S. Teen Pregnancy Rates

The rate of teenage pregnancies has dropped dramatically since the early 1990s.

SOURCE: Hamilton, Rossen, & Chong, 2018.

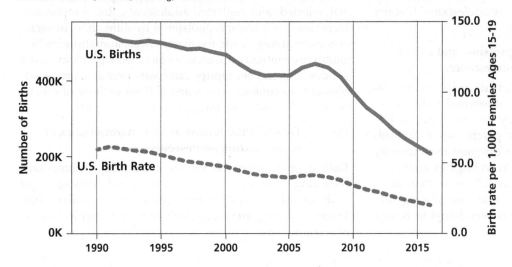

This 16-year-old mother and her child are representative of a major social problem: teenage pregnancy. Why is teenage pregnancy a greater problem in the United States than in other countries?

- Substitutes for sexual intercourse may be more prevalent. For example, data from the 1995 National Survey of Adolescent Males found that about half of 15- to 19-year-old boys reported having received oral sex, an increase of 44 percent since the late 1980s. It is possible that oral sex, which many teenagers do not even consider "sex," may increasingly be viewed as an alternative to sexual intercourse (Bernstein, 2004; Chandra, et al., 2011).

One thing that apparently hasn't led to a reduction in teenage pregnancies is asking adolescents to take a virginity pledge. These public pledges—a centerpiece of some forms of sex education—apparently are ineffective. In one study of 12,000 teenagers who had taken the pledge, 88 percent reported eventually having premarital sexual intercourse. However, pledges did delay the start of sex an average of 18 months (Bearman & Bruckner, 2004).

An unintended pregnancy can be devastating to mother and child. Teenage mothers today are much less likely than in previous years to be married. In many cases, mothers care for their children without the help of the father. Lacking financial and emotional support, the mother may have to abandon her own education and be relegated to unskilled, poorly paying jobs for the rest of her life. In some cases, she may develop long-term dependency on welfare. Furthermore, her physical and mental health may suffer as she faces unrelenting stress from the continual demands on her time (Gillmore et al., 2006; Oxford et al., 2006; Pirog, Jung, & Lee, 2018).

Review, Check, and Apply

Review

LO 6.10 Describe how adolescents develop their self-concept and self-esteem.

Self-concept grows more differentiated as the view of the self becomes more organized, broader, and more abstract, and takes account of the views of others. During this period, adolescents develop both their self-concept and their self-esteem. Both gender and socioeconomic status affect the assessment of self-esteem.

LO 6.11 Analyze diverse theoretical approaches to understanding identity formation.

Both Erikson's identity-versus-identity-confusion stage and Marcia's four identity statuses focus on the adolescent's struggle to determine an identity and a role in society. Spirituality plays a role in many adolescents' identity definition, as do race and ethnicity.

LO 6.12 Explain why anxiety, depression, and suicide are important issues in adolescence.

Some adolescents experience anxiety disorders, which develop when anxiety occurs without external justification, and it impacts normal, everyday functioning. Anxiety disorders are the most prevalent psychological problem in adolescence. Other adolescents question their identity and self-worth, which can lead to feelings of confusion and depression. Depression affects girls more than boys. Although reasons for increased suicide rates among adolescents are unclear, depression has been found to be one risk factor.

LO 6.13 Analyze how the parent–child relationship changes during adolescence.

The search for autonomy may change relations between teenagers and their parents, temporarily creating conflict in some cases, but the generation gap is narrower than is generally thought.

LO 6.14 Analyze the nature and importance of peer relationships during adolescence.

Peers, by providing social comparison and reference groups, enable adolescents to gauge appropriate behavior and attitudes. Cliques and crowds are particularly important in this regard. Adolescents generally sort themselves into degrees of popularity, including popular, controversial, rejected, and neglected adolescents. Racial separation increases in adolescence, bolstered by differences in socioeconomic status, academic experiences, and attitudes. Sex cleavage eventually dissolves as most teenagers join mixed gender cliques. Peer groups can create pressure among adolescents to conform views and actions to those of others. Some adolescents may engage in criminal activity.

LO 6.15 Describe the functions and characteristics of dating during adolescence.

Dating in adolescence serves a number of functions, including intimacy, entertainment, and prestige. For LGBTQ adolescents, dating presents particular challenges as dating practices clash with stereotypical views of relationships.

LO 6.16 **Explain how sexuality develops in the adolescent years.**

Sexual intercourse among heterosexual adolescents is a major milestone that most people reach during this period. The age of first intercourse reflects cultural differences and has been declining over the past 50 years. Sexual orientation, which is most accurately viewed as a continuum rather than categorically, develops as the result of a complex combination of factors.

Check Yourself

1. Andrew plans to become a lawyer and is now studying hard to earn good grades so he can eventually enter law school. He has pursued this course largely because his father and mother are both prominent attorneys who always expected him to follow in their footsteps. According to James Marcia, Andrew is an example of _____.
   a. identity achievement
   b. identity foreclosure
   c. moratorium
   d. identity diffusion

2. The people with whom adolescents compare themselves are referred to as _____.
   a. cliques
   b. in-groups
   c. crowds
   d. reference groups

3. Which of the following is *not* typically a function of dating in the early adolescent years?
   a. Selecting a marriage partner
   b. Earning prestige
   c. Providing entertainment
   d. Understanding one's identity

4. People who feel they are trapped in the body of a person of the other gender are referred to as _____.
   a. homosexual
   b. bisexual
   c. transgender
   d. intersexual

Applying Lifespan Development

What aspects of the social world of adolescents work against the achievement of true intimacy in dating?

Chapter 6 Summary
Putting It All Together: Adolescence

FROM AGES 13 TO 18, Julie, the young woman we met in the chapter opener, evolved from a young adolescent consumed with her social status to a mature teenager capable of defining her own "cool." In mid-adolescence, she abused alcohol and let her grades go down in order to be popular, but she got a wake-up call when she failed her junior year. She knew she was smart, so she began making smart choices. She left her old school for one that specialized in the arts and joined a club dedicated to something she was good at—fiction writing. She enrolled in a summer workshop for teen writers, where she connected with adults who could help her. She completed a novel. When it was rejected, she wrote another and started college. Her second book won a contract. Julie had weathered adolescence successfully.

MODULE 6.1
PHYSICAL DEVELOPMENT IN ADOLESCENCE

- Adolescents have many physical issues to deal with. (pp. 260–264)
- Julie's concern about her appearance is typical in adolescence, especially for girls, when the body changes and the normal weight gain puberty brings can cause anxiety. (pp. 260–264)
- Adolescent brain development, including the growth of the prefrontal cortex of the brain, permitted Julie to think about and evaluate the behavior of her old friends in comparison to the new identity she wished to have. Such complex thinking, emerging in adolescence, can sometimes lead to confusion. (pp. 266–268)
- The pressure to be popular led Julie to abuse alcohol—a major threat to the well-being of adolescents. (p. 268–271)

MODULE 6.2
COGNITIVE DEVELOPMENT IN ADOLESCENCE

- Adolescents' personal fables can make them feel invulnerable to risk, as Julie felt when she started drinking to be cool. (p. 278)
- Julie's awareness of what she values in herself and her ability to reflect on what gives her the most joy exemplify adolescents' advanced mental abilities. (pp. 276–279)

MODULE 6.3
SOCIAL AND PERSONALITY DEVELOPMENT IN ADOLESCENCE

- Julie's devotion to connecting with the in crowd typifies the great importance of peer relationships in adolescence. (pp. 296–297)
- Though Julie knows her parents love her, she was annoyed when they checked her room for alcohol and fought with her about her dropping grades in school. Such conflicts often occur in early adolescence when teens are struggling for autonomy and independence. (pp. 293–296)
- For Julie, being smart and making independent choices became positive, key aspects of her identity, answering the question, "Who am I?" (pp. 284–293)
- Julie thinks she has to be part of the in crowd to have high self-esteem, but her social status is not the only factor that affects her feelings about herself. (pp. 285–286)
- Julie's enrollment in a fiction writing workshop and her subsequent decision to publish a novel is an example of Marcia's identity achievement. (pp. 288–289)

What would a PARENT do?

Was Julie's parents' anger at their daughter's late hours and drinking the best response to the problem? In what ways did they show their love for Julie? In what ways might they have been more supportive?

Photodisc/GettyImages

What would a HEALTH-CARE WORKER do?

Julie's concern with popularity drove her to make poor decisions about using alcohol. How could a health-care provider help Julie to understand the risks she was taking? Should suggestions include advice about how to socialize without drinking when alcohol is readily available?

Photodisc/Getty Images

What would YOU do?

If you were Julie's friend, how would you offer encouragement and support for the independent decisions she's making? Do you think your friendship would survive her choosing a path different from yours?

Asia Images Group/Getty Images

What would an EDUCATOR do?

If you were Julie's writing instructor, how would you help her prepare for a career in fiction writing? Would you advise her to develop other interests and experiment more before choosing a career path?

Tom Baker/123RF

Chapter 7
Early Adulthood

Javier Sanchez Mingorance/123RF

Petra Tarkif, 27, and Mo Wright, 28, work as sales associates for an office supply chain. They've been living together for 4 years. Both of them are college graduates with degrees that, as Mo says, "have absolutely no relationship with what we're doing."

Says Petra, "We're almost 30 with nothing to show for it but a couple of low-level jobs. We should be doing something better with our lives."

"Right," Mo chimes in. "We want to get married and have kids, but before that we'd really like to buy a house, which we can't afford. We could move to a bigger city and look for better jobs, but houses are even more expensive in big cities."

"Meanwhile the clock is ticking," says Petra. "We want to be parents while we're still young-ish." She looks at Mo. "You've talked about business school, and I'd like to learn computer coding, but going back to school would take more time and money than we can afford."

Mo pulls out some papers. "Maybe there's a way. I talked to Doug, our manager. He says the company offers career training for management and technical jobs. He thinks we're good candidates for the program and he'll recommend both of us, if we want. That would be a step in the right direction."

Early adulthood, the period from approximately age 20 to 40, is a time of continued development. In fact, young adults like Petra and Mo face some of the most pressing questions they will ever face and experience considerable stress as they answer them.

At their physical peak in their 20s, they are on the threshold of the worrisome 30s, when the body begins to send messages of decline and to exact a price for excess and inattention. Cognitively, most people have stopped their formal learning, but some want to take it up again either in college or in some other setting. Socially, young adults are often settling into a career, and sometimes they have to consider whether the path they are on is right for them after all. And they still have to answer the really big questions about marriage and children. Staring so many weighty decisions in the face can cause a great deal of stress in young adults.

In fact, some psychologists believe that the beginning of early adulthood can be characterized as a special stage of development known as *emerging adulthood*. Emerging adulthood is the period beginning in the late teenage years and extending into the mid-20s. Although they are no longer adolescents, people in their early 20s are not fully adults because they haven't fully taken on the responsibilities of adulthood. Instead, they are still seeking to identify who they are and what course their life will follow (Tanner, Arnett, & Leis, 2009; Arnett, 2016).

In this chapter, we'll look at the physical, cognitive, and social and personality changes that accompany young adulthood. This period of life, in which people are too often considered "developed" rather than "developing," in fact harbors many changes. Like Petra and Mo, young adults continue to develop throughout the period.

Module 7.1 *Physical Development* in Early Adulthood

LO 7.1 Describe the physical changes that occur in early adulthood, and identify the barriers people with physical disabilities face.

LO 7.2 Summarize the impact of fitness and diet on general health in early adulthood, and identify other health hazards for this age group.

LO 7.3 Identify the origins of stress, and explain its consequences.

LO 7.4 Identify strategies for coping with stress.

Module 7.2 *Cognitive Development* in Early Adulthood

LO 7.5 Identify and summarize the various approaches to postformal thinking.

LO 7.6 Discuss the different types of intelligence, and explain how each affects the career success of young adults.

LO 7.7 Summarize the demographic makeup of college students in the United States, and describe how that population is changing.

LO 7.8 Discuss how gender bias and stereotypes affect the college performance of women and students of color.

Module 7.3 *Social and Personality Development* in Early Adulthood

LO 7.9 Discuss the concept of emerging adulthood.

LO 7.10 Explain how young adults respond to the need for intimacy and friendship and how liking turns to loving.

LO 7.11 Differentiate the different kinds of love.

LO 7.12 Identify the factors that influence young adults' choice of partner, and give examples of how these are affected by gender and culture.

LO 7.13 Summarize the sorts of relationships people enter into in early adulthood, and identify the characteristics of a successful marriage.

LO 7.14 Identify the factors that influence a couple's decision to have children, and summarize the impact children have on a marriage.

LO 7.15 Explain Vaillant's stage of career consolidation, and identify the motivations—other than money—people have for seeking a job.

LO 7.16 Summarize Ginzberg's career choice theory, Holland's personality type theory, and how gender affects work choices.

Module 7.1

Physical Development in Early Adulthood

Kaneesha Davis graduated near the top of her class with a degree in economics. Her dream was to find work helping poor and struggling middle-class people achieve their dreams—starting a business, buying a home, and eventually having a family. But Kaneesha graduated from college $90,000 in debt. She felt forced to take a job in the loan department of a Chicago bank that she really didn't want, but which paid well. "I think they hired me because they could tick off two boxes on their 'diversity' chart: Black and female," Kaneesha says. "It certainly wasn't because we share goals."

Kaneesha's difficulty in finding a job that matches her talents and her dreams is not at all unusual for young people today. People in early adulthood are at the height of their physical abilities, and generally enjoy good health, but they also can experience tremendous stress as they launch themselves into the adult world. Significant changes—and challenges—occur as new opportunities arise and people choose to take on (or to forgo) a new set of roles as spouse, parent, and worker.

This module focuses on physical development during this period. It begins with a look at the physical changes that extend into early adulthood. Though more subtle than the physical changes of adolescence, growth continues and various motor skills change as well. We also look at physical disabilities and the ways people deal with them. Next, we look at diet and weight, examining the prevalence of obesity in this age group. We consider what other health risks young adults face. Finally, we discuss stress and coping during the early years of adulthood.

Physical Development and Health

> Grady McKinnon grinned as his mountain bike left the ground briefly. The 27-year-old financial auditor was delighted to be out for a camping and biking weekend with four of his college buddies. Grady had been worried that an upcoming deadline at work would make him miss this trip. When they were still in school, Grady and his friends used to go biking nearly every weekend. But jobs and marriage—and even a child for one of the guys—started taking up a lot of their attention. This was their only trip this summer. He was sure glad he hadn't missed it.

Grady and his friends were probably in the best physical condition of their lives when they began mountain biking regularly in college. Even now, as Grady's life becomes more complicated and sports start to take a back seat to work and other personal demands, he is enjoying one of the healthiest periods of his life. Still, Grady has to cope with the stress produced by the challenges of adult life.

Physical Changes and Challenges

LO 7.1 **Describe the physical changes that occur in early adulthood, and identify the barriers people with physical disabilities face.**

In most respects, physical development and maturation are complete at early adulthood. Most people have attained their full height, with limbs proportional to their size, rendering the gangliness of adolescence a memory. People in their early 20s tend to be healthy, vigorous, and energetic. Although **senescence**, the natural physical decline brought about by increasing age, has begun, age-related changes are not usually obvious until later in life. At the same time, some growth continues; for example, some people, particularly late maturers, continue to gain height in their early 20s.

senescence
the natural physical decline brought about by aging

Other parts of the body also reach full maturity. The brain grows in both size and weight, reaching its maximum during early adulthood (and then contracting later in life). The gray matter continues to be pruned back, and myelination (the process in which nerve cells are insulated by a covering of fat cells) continues to increase. These brain changes help support the cognitive advances of early adulthood. Furthermore, the changes in the brain means that young adults' minds are still malleable and adaptive to new experiences. For example, learning a new language, musical instrument, or job skill is easier for young adults than it is for older adults (Li, 2012; Schwarz & Bilbo, 2014; Knežević & Marinković, 2017).

THE SENSES: SUBTLE SHIFTS The senses are as sharp as they will ever be. Although there are changes in the elasticity of the eye—a process that may begin as early as

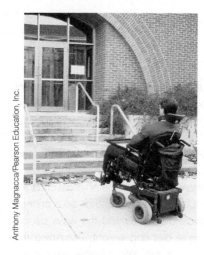

Despite the passage of the Americans with Disabilities Act (ADA), people with physical disabilities still cannot gain access to many older buildings.

age 10—they are so minor that they produce no deterioration in vision. Hearing, too, is at its peak, although women can detect higher tones more readily than men (McGuinness, 1972). Under quiet conditions, the average young adult can hear the ticking of a watch 20 feet away. The other senses, including taste, smell, and sensitivity to touch and pain, maintain their acuity throughout early adulthood.

MOTOR FUNCTIONING   If you are a professional athlete, you are generally considered over the hill by the end of your 20s. Although there are notable exceptions, even athletes who train constantly tend to lose their physical edge once they reach their 30s. In some sports, the peak passes even sooner. Swimmers are at their best in their late teens and gymnasts even younger (Schultz & Curnow, 1988).

Our psychomotor abilities also peak during early adulthood. Reaction time is quicker, muscle strength greater, and eye–hand coordination better than at any other period (Mella, Fagot, & Ribaupierre, 2016).

PHYSICAL DISABILITIES: COPING WITH PHYSICAL CHALLENGE   Beyond these physical changes, more than 50 million people in the United States are physically or mentally challenged, according to the official definition of *disability*—a condition that substantially limits a major life activity such as walking or vision. People with disabilities are in large part an undereducated and underemployed minority group. Fewer than 10 percent of people with major handicaps have finished high school, fewer than 25 percent of disabled men and 15 percent of disabled women work full-time, and unemployment rates are high. In addition, the jobs that people with disabilities find are often routine and low-paying positions (Albrecht, 2005; Power & Green, 2010; Foote, 2013).

Some barriers to a full life are physical. Despite passage in 1990 of the landmark Americans with Disabilities Act (ADA), which mandates full access to public establishments such as stores, office buildings, hotels, and theaters, people in wheelchairs still cannot gain access to many older buildings.

> **From a social worker's perspective:**   What sorts of interpersonal barriers do people with disabilities face? How can those barriers be removed?

Another barrier is prejudice. People with disabilities sometimes face pity or avoidance as nondisabled people focus so much on the disability that they overlook other characteristics. Others treat people with disabilities as if they were children. This can take its toll on the way people with disabilities think about themselves.

Fitness, Diet, and Health

LO 7.2   **Summarize the impact of fitness and diet on general health in early adulthood, and identify other health hazards for this age group.**

Aidan Tindell, accustomed to the shaving mirror in his own apartment, got a shock when he glimpsed his image in a friend's full-length mirror. It was not a pretty sight. Aidan had somehow developed a belly—and a pretty good-sized one. As if in a vision, he conjured up the long evenings he spent in a local sports bar with his friends, downing beers and burgers. Aidan knew something had to give, and he was afraid it was going to be his lifestyle.

The fitness of early adulthood doesn't come naturally or to everyone. To reach their physical potential, people must exercise and maintain a proper diet.

PHYSICAL FITNESS   Only a small time commitment is needed to yield significant health benefits. According to the American College of Sports Medicine and the Centers for Disease Control and Prevention, people should accumulate at least 150 minutes of moderate-intensity physical activity per week. Exercise time can be continuous or in bouts of at least 10 minutes, as long as the daily total reaches 30 minutes. Moderate-intensity activity includes walking briskly at 3 to 4 mph, biking at speeds up to 10 mph, golfing while carrying or pulling clubs, fishing by casting from shore, playing ping-pong, or canoeing at 2 to 4 mph. Even common household chores, such as weeding, vacuuming, and mowing with a power mower, provide moderate exercise (American College of Sports Medicine, 2011; DeBlois & Lefferts, 2017).

> **From an educator's perspective:** Can people be taught the lifelong advantages of regular exercise? Should school-based physical education programs be changed to foster a lifelong commitment to exercise?

The advantages of exercise are many. Exercise increases cardiovascular fitness, meaning that the heart and circulatory system operate more efficiently. Furthermore, lung capacity increases, raising endurance. Muscles become stronger, and the body is more flexible. The range of movement is greater, and the muscles, tendons, and ligaments are more elastic. Moreover, exercise during this period helps reduce *osteoporosis*, the thinning of the bones, in later life.

Exercise also may optimize the immune response of the body, helping it fight off disease. It may even decrease stress and anxiety and reduce depression. It can provide a sense of control over the body and a feeling of accomplishment. Regular exercise offers the possibility of another, ultimately more important, reward: It is associated with increased longevity (Jung & Brawley, 2010; Treat-Jacobson, Bronäs, & Salisbury, 2014; see Figure 7-1).

GOOD NUTRITION: NO SUCH THING AS A FREE LUNCH? According to guidelines provided by the U.S. Department of Agriculture, people can achieve good nutrition by eating foods that are low in fat, including vegetables, fruits, whole-grain foods, fish, poultry, lean meats, and low-fat dairy products. In addition, whole-grain foods and cereal products, vegetables (including dried beans and peas), and fruits are beneficial in another way: They help people raise the amount of complex carbohydrates and fiber they ingest. Milk and other sources of calcium are also needed to prevent osteoporosis. Finally, people should reduce salt intake (U.S. Department of Agriculture, 2006; Jones et al., 2012; Tyler et al., 2014; Allison, 2018).

Adolescents don't suffer too much from a diet high in junk foods and fat because they are undergoing tremendous growth. The body is less forgiving to young adults, who must reduce their caloric intake to maintain their health.

OBESITY The adult population of the United States is growing—in more ways than one. Obesity, defined is defined as a BMI at or above the 95th percentile for adults of the same age and sex, is on the rise in the United States. Just over 36 percent of adults are obese, a percentage that has nearly tripled since the 1960s. Furthermore, as age increases, more and more people are classified as obese. Approximately 70 percent of adults age 20 and over are overweight (National Health and Nutrition Examination Survey, 2014 Ogden et al., 2015; Chapuis-de-Andrade, de Araujo, & Lara, 2017; see Figure 7-2).

Although obesity is an issue for countries around the world, the United States stands out. The world average weight for adults is 137 pounds; in the United States, the average is 180 (Walpole, 2012; see Figure 7-3).

HEALTH Health risks in general are slight during early adulthood. People are less susceptible to colds and other minor illnesses than they were as children, and they recover quickly from those that they do catch.

Adults in their 20s and 30s stand a higher risk of dying from accidents, primarily car accidents, than from most other causes. But there are other killers: Among the leading

Figure 7-1 The Result of Fitness: Longevity

The greater the fitness level, as measured by adherence to the Health and Human Services (HHS) guidelines, the higher the gains in life expectancy due to physical activity.

SOURCE: National Cancer Institute, 2012.

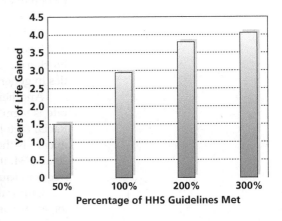

Figure 7-2 Rising Obesity

Despite greater awareness of the importance of good nutrition, the percentage of adults with weight problems in the United States has risen dramatically over the past few decades. Why do you think this rise has occurred?

SOURCE: National Health and Nutrition Examination Survey, 2014.

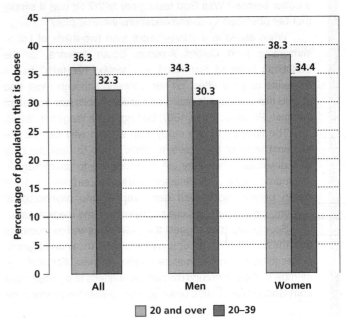

sources of death for people 25 to 34 are AIDS, cancer, heart disease, and suicide. Amid the grim statistics of mortality, the age 35 represents a significant milestone. It is at that point that illness and disease overtake accidents as the leading cause of death—the first time this is true since infancy.

Not all people fare equally well during early adulthood. Lifestyle decisions, such as the use—or abuse—of alcohol, tobacco, or drugs, or engaging in unprotected sex, can hasten *secondary aging*, physical declines brought about by environmental factors or behavioral choices. These substances can also increase the mortality risk from the causes just mentioned.

Cultural factors, including gender and race, are related to the risk of dying. For instance, men are more apt to die than women, primarily in automobile accidents. Furthermore, African Americans have twice the death rate of Caucasians, and minorities in general have a higher likelihood of dying than their Caucasian peers.

Another major cause of death for men in this age group is violence. The murder rate is significantly higher in the United States than in any other developed country. Racial factors are also related to the homicide rate in the United States. Although homicide is the third most frequent cause of death for white males between the ages of 20 and 34, it is *the* most frequent cause of death for black males and the second most frequent cause of death for Hispanic males in the same age range.

Cultural factors also influence young adults' lifestyles and health-related behavior, as discussed in the *Cultural Dimensions* feature.

Cultural Dimensions

How Cultural Beliefs Influence Health and Health Care

Gisella recently had a mild stroke. Although she recovered from it, she was advised by her physician to change her diet and to exercise more, or else she would be at an increased risk for another stroke. Gisella followed the advice, but she also spent more time at church, praying for good health. She found that she never felt better, and her physician commented on her good health at a routine visit 6 months later.

Why do you think Gisella's health improved? Was it because she changed her eating and exercise habits? Did she become a better person? Was God testing her faith? Or was it simply that her physician's recommendations were helpful?

When asked in a survey, more than two-thirds of Latino immigrants from Central America, South America, or the Caribbean believed that "God was testing her faith" had a moderate or great effect on her recovery, although most also agreed that a change in eating and activity habits was important (Murguia, Peterson, & Zea, 1997; Gurung, 2010; Yang et al., 2016).

The findings of this study help explain why Latinos are the least likely of any Western ethnic group to seek the help of a physician when they are ill. According to psychologists Alejandro Murguia, Rolf Peterson, and Maria Zea (1997), cultural health beliefs, along with demographic and psychological barriers, reduce people's use of physicians and medical care.

Specifically, they suggest that Latinos, as well as members of some non-Western groups, are more likely than non-Hispanic whites to believe in supernatural causes of illness. For instance, members of these groups may attribute illness to a punishment from God, a lack of faith, or a hex. Such beliefs may reduce the motivation to seek medical care from a physician (Landrine & Klonoff, 1994; Yang et al., 2016; Srivastava, 2017).

Finances also play a role. Lower socioeconomic status reduces the ability to pay for traditional medical care, which is expensive and may indirectly encourage the continued reliance on less traditional and less expensive methods. In addition, the lower level of involvement in the mainstream culture that is characteristic of recent immigrants to the United States is associated with a lower likelihood of visiting a physician and obtaining mainstream medical care (Antshel & Antshel, 2002; Abe et al., 2018).

Furthermore, cultural differences play a role in how psychological disorders are viewed and experienced. For example, members of some Plains Indians tribes commonly hear the voices of the dead calling to them from the afterlife, and that is seen as normal in their culture. Similarly, anorexia nervosa—an eating disorder in which people become obsessed with their weight and body image and sometimes may starve themselves—is seen primarily in cultures that hold strict societal standards relating to weight and slimness. In cultures in which body standards are different, anorexia nervosa is not seen (Jacob, 2014; Munro, Randell, & Lawrie, 2017).

Health-care providers need to take cultural beliefs into account when treating members of different cultural groups. For example, if a patient believes that the source of his or her illness is a spell cast by a jealous romantic rival, the patient may not comply with medical regimens that ignore that perceived source. To provide effective health care, then, health-care providers must be sensitive to such cultural health beliefs.

Stress and Coping: Dealing with Life's Challenges

It's 5 p.m. and Rosa Convoy, a 25-year-old single mother, has just finished her work as a receptionist at a dentist's office and is on her way home. She has exactly 2 hours to pick up her daughter Zoe from child care, get home, make and eat dinner, pick up and return with a babysitter from down the street, say goodbye to Zoe, and get to her 7 p.m. programming class at a local community college. It's a marathon she runs every Tuesday and Thursday night, and she knows she doesn't have a second to spare if she wants to reach the class on time.

Rosa Convoy is experiencing **stress**, the physical and emotional response to events that threaten or challenge us. Our lives are crowded with events and circumstances, known as *stressors*, that threaten our equilibrium. Stressors need not be unpleasant events: Even the happiest events—starting a long-sought job or planning a wedding—can produce stress (Shimizu & Pelham, 2004; Aschbacher et al., 2013).

Researchers in the field of **psychoneuroimmunology (PNI)**—the study of the relationship among the brain, the immune system, and psychological factors—have examined the outcomes of stress. The most immediate is a biological reaction, as hormones secreted by the adrenal glands cause a rise in heart rate, blood pressure, respiration rate, and sweating. In some situations, these immediate effects are beneficial because the "emergency reaction" they produce in the sympathetic nervous system enables people to defend themselves from a sudden, threatening situation (Janusek, Cooper, & Mathews, 2012; Irwin, 2015; Moraes et al., 2018).

At the same time, long-term, continuous exposure to stressors may result in a reduction of the body's ability to deal with stress. As stress-related hormones are constantly secreted, the heart, blood vessels, and other body tissues may deteriorate. As a consequence, people become more susceptible to diseases as their ability to fight off germs declines. In short, both *acute stressors* (sudden, one-time events) and *chronic stressors* (long-term, continuing events) have the potential to produce significant physiological consequences (Wheaton & Montazer, 2010; Rohleder, 2012; Maimari, 2017).

stress
the physical and emotional response to events that threaten or challenge us

psychoneuroimmunology (PNI)
the study of the relationship among the brain, the immune system, and psychological factors

The Origins and Consequences of Stress

LO 7.3   Identify the origins of stress, and explain its consequences.

Experienced job interviewers, college counselors, and owners of bridal shops all know that not everyone reacts the same way to a potentially stressful event. Researchers agree: They have found that people move through two stages as they determine whether (and how) they experience stress (Lazarus, 1991; Folkman, 2010).

Although we commonly think of negative events, such as car mishaps, as leading to stress, even welcome events, like getting married, can be stressful.

primary appraisal
the assessment of an event to determine whether its implications are positive, negative, or neutral

Primary appraisal—the individual's assessment of an event to determine whether its implications are positive, negative, or neutral—is the first step. If a person sees the event as primarily negative, he or she appraises it in terms of the harm that it has caused in the past, how threatening it is likely to be, and how likely it is that the challenge can be resisted successfully. For example, you are likely to feel differently about an upcoming French test if you passed the last one with flying colors than you would if you did poorly.

secondary appraisal
the assessment of whether one's coping abilities and resources are adequate to overcome the harm, threat, or challenge posed by the potential stressor

The second step is secondary appraisal. **Secondary appraisal** is the person's answer to the question, "Can I handle it?"—an assessment of whether the coping abilities and resources on hand are adequate. If resources are lacking and the threat is great, the person will feel stress. A traffic ticket is always upsetting, but if you can't afford the fine, the stress is greater.

Stress varies with the person's appraisal, and that appraisal varies with the person's circumstances. For example, events and circumstances that produce negative emotions produce more stress. Similarly, situations that are uncontrollable or unpredictable produce more stress than those that are more predictable (Taylor, 2014).

> **From the perspective of a health-care provider:** Are there periods of life that are relatively stress free, or do people of all ages experience stress? Do stressors differ from age to age?

Over the long run, the constant wear and tear of fighting off stress can have formidable costs. Headaches, backaches, skin rashes, indigestion, chronic fatigue, and even the common cold are stress-related illnesses (Kalynchuk, 2010; Andreotti et al., 2014; Wisse & Sleebos, 2016).

In addition, *the immune system*—the organs, glands, and cells that are the body's line of defense against disease—may be damaged by stress. Stress can interfere with the immune system's ability to stop germs from reproducing or cancer cells from spreading (Caserta et al., 2008; Liu et al., 2012; Ménard et al., 2017).

To get a sense of how much stress you have in your own life, complete the questionnaire in Table 7-1.

Table 7-1 How Stressed Are You?

The statements below will help you determine your level of stress. Mark the appropriate number in each box, then add up those numbers to find your score. Your answers should reflect your experiences in the last month only. To help you rate the extent of your stress, use the key at the bottom.

1. I become upset when something happens unexpectedly.
   0 = never, 1 = almost never, 2 = sometimes, 3 = fairly often, 4 = very often

2. I feel I'm unable to control the things that are most important in my life.
   0 = never, 1 = almost never, 2 = sometimes, 3 = fairly often, 4 = very often

3. I feel nervous and "stressed."
   0 = never, 1 = almost never, 2 = sometimes, 3 = fairly often, 4 = very often

4. I feel confident about my ability to handle my personal problems.
   4 = never, 3 = almost never, 2 = sometimes, 1 = fairly often, 0 = very often

5. In general, I feel things are going my way.
   4 = never, 3 = almost never, 2 = sometimes, 1 = fairly often, 0 = very often

6. I'm able to control irritations in my life.
   4 = never, 3 = almost never, 2 = sometimes, 1 = fairly often, 0 = very often

7. I feel I cannot cope with all the things I need to do.
   0 = never, 1 = almost never, 2 = sometimes, 3 = fairly often, 4 = very often

8. Generally, I feel on top of things.
   4 = never, 3 = almost never, 2 = sometimes, 1 = fairly often, 0 = very often

9. I get angry at things that are beyond my control.
   0 = never, 1 = almost never, 2 = sometimes, 3 = fairly often, 4 = very often

10. I feel problems pile up to such an extent that I cannot overcome them.
   0 = never, 1 = almost never, 2 = sometimes, 3 = fairly often, 4 = very often

How Do You Measure Up?

Stress levels vary from person to person, but you can compare your total score to the averages below:

Age		Gender		Marital Status	
18–29	14.2	Men	12.1	Widowed	12.6
30–44	13.0	Women	13.7	Married or living with	12.4
45–54	2.6			Single or never wed	14.1
55–64	11.9			Divorced	14.7
65 & over	12.0			Separated	16.6

SOURCE: Based on Sheldon Cohen, Dept. of Psychology, Carnegie Mellon University.

Coping with Stress

LO 7.4   Identify strategies for coping with stress.

Stress is a normal part of every life. But some young adults are better than others at **coping**, the effort to control, reduce, or learn to tolerate the threats that lead to stress (Kam, Pérez Torres, & Steuber Fazio, 2018; Farrell, Ollendick, & Muris, 2019). What's the secret to coping? It turns out that people use a variety of strategies.

Some people use *problem-focused coping*—managing a threatening situation by directly changing it to make it less stressful. For example, a man having difficulties on the job may ask his boss to change his responsibilities, or he may look for another job.

Other people employ *emotion-focused coping*—the conscious regulation of emotion. For instance, a mother having trouble finding appropriate care for her child while she is at work may tell herself that she should look at the bright side: At least she has a job (Master et al., 2009; Gruszczyńska, 2013; Pow & Cashwell, 2017).

Sometimes, people acknowledge that they are in a stressful situation that cannot be changed, but they cope by managing their reactions. For example, they may take up meditation or exercise to reduce their physical reactions.

Coping is also aided by the presence of *social support*, assistance and comfort supplied by others. Turning to others can provide both emotional support (in the form of a shoulder to cry on) and practical, tangible support (such as a temporary loan). In addition, others can provide information, offering specific advice on how to deal with stressful situations (Green, DeCourville, & Sadava, 2012; Seçkin, 2013; Vallejo-Sánchez & Pérez-García, 2015; Falgares et al., 2018).

Finally, even if people do not consciously cope with stress, some psychologists suggest that they may unconsciously use defensive coping mechanisms. **Defensive coping** involves unconscious strategies that distort or deny the true nature of a situation. For instance, people may trivialize a life-threatening illness or tell themselves that failing a major test is unimportant.

coping
the effort to control, reduce, or learn to tolerate the threats that lead to stress

defensive coping
coping that involves unconscious strategies that distort or deny the true nature of a situation

---

Development in Your Life

Coping with Stress

Some general guidelines can help people cope with stress, including the following (Bionna, 2006; Taylor, 2014):

- **Seek control over the situation.**   Taking charge of a situation that is producing stress can take you a long way toward coping with it. For example, if you are feeling stress about a test, do something about it—such as starting to study.

- **Redefine "threat" as "challenge."**   Changing the definition can make a situation seem less threatening. "Look for the silver lining" is not bad advice. For example, if you're fired, look at it as an opportunity to get a new and better job.

- **Use mindfulness.**   Mindfulness stress reduction techniques involve learning to become aware of one's surroundings, making every moment count, and observing one's thoughts and feelings without judging them. Research has demonstrated that getting into a mindful state helps people manage and reduce stress responses (Meland et al., 2015; Ramasubramanian, 2017).

- **Find social support.**   Almost any difficulty can be faced more easily with the help of others. Friends, family members, and even telephone hotlines staffed by trained counselors can provide significant support.

- **Use relaxation techniques.**   Reducing the physiological arousal brought about by stress can be effective in coping with stress. Techniques that produce relaxation, such as transcendental meditation, Zen and yoga, progressive muscle relaxation, and hypnosis, have been shown to be effective. One that works particularly well was devised by physician Herbert Benson and is illustrated in Table 7-2 (Benson & Proctor 2011).

- **Maintain a healthy lifestyle that will reinforce your body's natural coping mechanisms.**   Exercise, eat nutritiously, get enough sleep, and avoid or reduce the use of alcohol, tobacco, or other drugs.

- **Take a break.**   It can be useful to even temporarily remove yourself from a situation that's causing stress.

- **If all else fails, keep in mind that a life without stress would be dull.**   Stress is natural, and successfully coping with it can be gratifying.

Table 7-2 How to Elicit the Relaxation Response

Some general advice on regular practice of the relaxation response:

- Try to find 10 to 20 minutes in your daily routine; before breakfast is a good time.
- Sit comfortably.
- For the period you will practice, try to arrange your life so you won't have distractions. Put on the answering machine, and ask someone else to watch the kids.
- Time yourself by glancing periodically at a clock or watch (but don't set an alarm). Commit yourself to a specific length of practice, and try to stick to it.

There are several approaches to eliciting the relaxation response. Here is one standard set of instructions:

Step 1.	Pick a focus word or short phrase that's firmly rooted in your personal belief system. For example, a nonreligious individual might choose a neutral word like *one* or *peace* or *love*. A Christian person desiring to use a prayer could pick the opening words of Psalm 23, *The Lord is my shepherd;* a Jewish person could choose *Shalom*.
Step 2.	Sit quietly in a comfortable position.
Step 3.	Close your eyes.
Step 4.	Relax your muscles.
Step 5.	Breathe slowly and naturally, repeating your focus word or phrase silently as you exhale.
Step 6.	Throughout, assume a passive attitude. Don't worry about how well you're doing. When other thoughts come to mind, simply say to yourself, "Oh, well," and gently return to the repetition.
Step 7.	Continue for 10 to 20 minutes. You may open your eyes to check the time, but do not use an alarm. When you finish, sit quietly for a minute or so, at first with your eyes closed and later with your eyes open. Then do not stand for 1 or 2 minutes.
Step 8.	Practice the technique once or twice a day.

SOURCE: Benson and Scribner, 2011.

In some cases, people use drugs or alcohol to escape from stressful situations. Like defensive coping, drinking and drug use do not help address the situation causing the stress, and they can increase a person's difficulties. For example, people may become addicted to the substances that initially provided them with a pleasurable sense of escape. (See the *Development in Your Life* box on how to cope with stress.)

Review, Check, and Apply

Review

LO 7.1 Describe the physical changes that occur in early adulthood, and identify the barriers people with physical disabilities face.

By young adulthood, the body and the senses are at their peak, but growth still proceeds, particularly in the brain. People with physical disabilities face not only physical barriers but also psychological barriers caused by prejudice.

LO 7.2 Summarize the impact of fitness and diet on general health in early adulthood, and identify other health hazards for this age group.

Exercise and diet become important in young adulthood; even short time commitments to exercise and improved nutrition yield significant health benefits. Obesity is increasingly a problem for this age group. Accidents present the greatest risk of death. In the United States, violence is also a significant risk during young adulthood, particularly for non-white males.

LO 7.3 Identify the origins of stress, and explain its consequences.

Our appraisal of the level of stress caused by an event or situation varies by individual temperament and circumstances. Origins of stress include: events that produce negative emotions; unexpected or uncontrollable situations; ambiguous or confusing events; and having to accomplish too many tasks simultaneously. Stress, which is healthy in small doses, can be harmful to the body and mind if it is frequent or long lasting. Long-term exposure to stressors may cause deterioration in the heart, blood vessels, and other body tissues. Stress is linked to many common ailments.

LO 7.4 Identify strategies for coping with stress.

Strategies for coping with stress include problem-focused coping, emotion-focused coping, and the use of social support. Using the relaxation technique can also be helpful. Another strategy, defensive coping, which relies on avoidance, can prevent a person from dealing with the reality of the situation.

Check Yourself

1. _____ is the natural physical decline brought about by aging.
   a. Maturation
   b. Plasticity
   c. Senescence
   d. Lateralization

2. At the age of _____, illness and disease overtake accidents as the leading cause of death.
   a. 25
   b. 35
   c. 40
   d. 45

3. Researchers in the field of _____ study the relationship among the brain, the immune system, and psychological factors, and have found that stress can produce several outcomes.

   a. psychoanalysis
   b. chronic disease management
   c. resilience analysis
   d. psychoneuroimmunology

4. Avoiding thinking about a stressful situation by drinking, taking drugs, or just denying the true nature of a situation are all examples of _____ coping.

   a. defensive
   b. problem-focused
   c. secondary
   d. somatic

Applying Lifespan Development

In what circumstances can stress be an adaptive, helpful response? In what circumstances is it maladaptive?

Module 7.2

Cognitive Development in Early Adulthood

Paul Galesko was an "A-list" student in high school—popular, a member of the drama society and the marching band, and at the top of his class. Paul had been a driven student since his first year, challenging himself each semester with a strict diet of advanced and honors classes. Paul's parents had instilled in him the value of education as a way to a better life; their lives had been difficult because they lacked a college education and had decided to have children while they were still young and not yet financially established.

Paul was excited when he got into his first-choice college, but things didn't go as he expected that first year. Actually, he hadn't known what to expect at all. Because no one in his family had gone to college, he was exploring new territory. He tried to do it all—tough classes, weekend parties, a job at the student union, writing for the campus newspaper, and more. Finally, the pressure wore him down and he showed up at the campus infirmary with signs of exhaustion.

Although Paul was, in his own words, "exploring new territory" by going to college, he and his parents shared a belief in the value of higher education. The different paths taken by Paul and his parents represent the increasing diversity in family background, socioeconomic status, race, and ethnicity that characterizes college populations today.

This module focuses on cognitive development during early adulthood. Although traditional approaches to cognitive development

regarded adulthood as an inconsequential plateau, we will examine some new theories that suggest that significant cognitive growth occurs during the period. We also consider the impact of life events on cognitive development and the nature of adult intelligence.

The last part of the module examines college, an institution that shapes intellectual growth. We consider who goes to college, and how gender and race can influence achievement. We end by examining some of the adjustment problems that college students face.

Cognitive Development and Intelligence

Ben is known to be a heavy drinker, especially when he goes to parties. Tyra, Ben's wife, warns him that if he comes home drunk one more time, she will leave him and take the children. Tonight Ben is out late at an office party. He comes home drunk. Does Tyra leave Ben?

To the typical adolescent this case (drawn from research by Adams and Labouvie-Vief, 1986) is open and shut: Tyra leaves Ben. But in early adulthood, the answer is less clear. People become less concerned with sheer logic and instead take into account real-life concerns that may influence and temper behavior.

Intellectual Growth and Postformal Thought

LO 7.5 Identify and summarize the various approaches to postformal thinking.

If we subscribed to the traditional view of cognitive development, we would expect to find little intellectual growth in early adulthood. Piaget argued that by the time

From Research to Practice

How Long Do Young Adult Brains Continue to Develop?

Once you have reached young adulthood, you're free to explore a variety of new experiences from which society shields children and adolescents because their so-called impressionable minds are still developing. Parental guidance, consent, and supervision are no longer required. Your access to very violent movies, bars and nightclubs, and all kinds of other adult-only situations is increasingly unfettered. But is your brain really done developing?

Research indicates that it actually isn't, and it won't be until later in your 20s. Rather than being fully grown, the young adult brain continues to grow new neural connections and to prune away unused pathways. This is generally a good thing—it means that young adults' minds are still malleable and adaptive to new experiences. For example, learning a new language, musical instrument, or job skill is easier for young adults than it is for older adults (Whiting, Chenery, & Copland, 2011).

One part of the brain in particular, the prefrontal cortex, doesn't mature until well into young adulthood. This region is responsible for such higher-order mental functions as planning, decision making, and impulse control. It's little

wonder, then, that the greatest risks to health and well-being in this stage of life mainly involve poor judgment—motor vehicle accidents, violence, drug abuse, and excessive drinking chief among them. But it's also a time of opportunity when young adults can instill such highly beneficial traits as resilience, self-control, and self-regulation (Raznahan et al., 2011; Giedd, 2012; Steinberg, 2014).

What you do with this time can have important implications going forward. For example, some research has found that the more that young adults used Facebook, the worse they felt at the time and the more their satisfaction with life declined over time. This fits with a broader concern expressed by scientists who study young adult brain development: The choice of activities in young adulthood can have lasting consequences, for better or worse (Beck, 2012; Giedd, 2012; Kross et al., 2013).

Shared Writing Prompt:

What could young adults do to optimize their ongoing brain development?

---

people left adolescence, their thinking, at least qualitatively, had largely become what it would be for the rest of their lives. They might gather more information, but the ways in which they thought about it would not change.

Was Piaget's view correct? Increasing evidence suggests that he was mistaken.

postformal thought
thinking that acknowledges that adult predicaments must sometimes be solved in relativistic terms

POSTFORMAL THOUGHT Developmental psychologist Gisela Labouvie-Vief suggests that the nature of thinking changes during early adulthood. She asserts that thinking based solely on formal operations (Piaget's final stage, reached during adolescence) is insufficient to meet the demands placed on young adults. The complexity of society, which requires specialization, and the challenge of finding one's way through that complexity require thought that transcends logic to include practical experience, moral judgments, and values (Labouvie-Vief, 2006; 2009; Lemieux, 2013; Hamer & van Rossum, 2017).

Young adults exhibit what is called postformal thinking. **Postformal thought** is thinking that goes beyond Piaget's formal operations. Rather than being based on purely logical processes, with absolutely right and wrong answers to problems, postformal thought acknowledges that adult predicaments must sometimes be solved in relativistic terms.

The nature of thought changes qualitatively during early adulthood.

PERRY'S APPROACH TO POSTFORMAL THINKING To psychologist William Perry (Perry, 1981), the developmental growth of early adulthood involves mastering new ways of understanding the world. In examining intellectual and moral growth during college, Perry found that students entering college tended to use *dualistic thinking* in their views of the world: Something was either right or wrong; people were either good or bad; others were either for them or against them.

However, as these students encountered new ideas and points of view from other students and their professors, their dualistic thinking declined. Consistent with postformal thinking, students began to accept that issues can have more than one plausible side. Furthermore, they understood that it is possible to hold multiple perspectives on an issue. Their attitude toward authorities also changed: Instead of assuming that experts had all the answers, they began to realize that their own thinking had validity if their position was well thought out and rational.

In fact, according to Perry, they had reached a stage in which knowledge and values were regarded as *relativistic*. Rather than seeing the world as having absolute standards and values, they argued that different societies, cultures, and individuals could have different standards and values, and all of them could be equally valid.

> **From an educator's perspective:** Do you think it is possible for adolescent students to learn postformal thinking (e.g., by direct instruction on breaking the habit of dualistic thinking)? Why or why not?

SCHAIE'S STAGES OF DEVELOPMENT Developmental psychologist K. Warner Schaie offers another perspective on postformal thought. Taking up where Piaget left off, Schaie suggests that adults' thinking follows a set pattern of stages (illustrated in Figure 7-3). But Schaie focuses on the ways in which information is *used* during adulthood, rather than on changes in the acquisition and understanding of new information, as in Piaget's approach (Schaie & Willis, 1993; Schaie & Zanjani, 2006; Schaie, 2016).

Schaie suggests that before adulthood, the main cognitive developmental task is acquisition of information. Consequently, he labels the first stage of cognitive development, which encompasses all of childhood and adolescence, the **acquisitive stage**. Information gathered before we grow up is largely squirreled away for future use. In fact, much of the rationale for education during childhood and adolescence is to prepare people for future activities.

The situation changes considerably in early adulthood when the focus shifts from the future to the here and now. According to Schaie, young adults are in the achieving stage, applying their intelligence to attain long-term goals regarding their careers, family, and contributions to society. During the **achieving stage**, young adults must confront and resolve several major issues, and the decisions they make—such as what job to take and whom to marry—have implications for the rest of their lives.

During the late stages of early adulthood and in middle adulthood, people move into the responsible and executive stages. In the **responsible stage**, middle-aged adults are mainly concerned with protecting and nourishing their spouses, families, and careers.

Sometime later, further into middle adulthood, many people (but not all) enter the **executive stage** in which they take a broader perspective, becoming more concerned about the larger world. People in the executive stage put energy into nourishing and sustaining societal institutions. They may become involved in town government, religious congregations, service clubs, charitable groups, and factory unions—organizations that have a larger purpose in society.

acquisitive stage
according to Schaie, the first stage of cognitive development, encompassing all of childhood and adolescence

achieving stage
the point reached by young adults in which intelligence is applied to specific situations involving the attainment of long-term goals regarding careers, family, and societal contributions

responsible stage
the stage where the major concerns of middle-aged adults relate to their personal situations, including protecting and nourishing their spouses, families, and careers

executive stage
the period in middle adulthood when people take a broader perspective than previously, including concerns about the world

Figure 7-3 Schaie's Stages of Adult Development

SOURCE: Based on Schaie, 1977–1978.

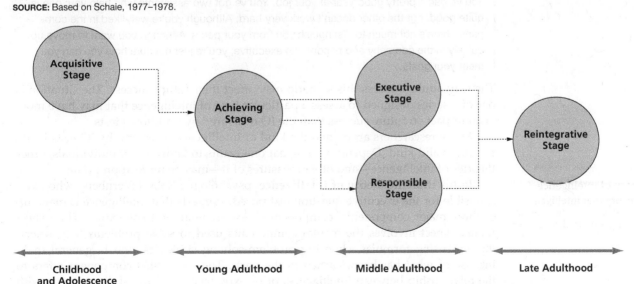

Profound events such as the birth of a child or the death of a loved one can stimulate cognitive development by offering an opportunity to reevaluate our place in the world. What are some other profound events that might stimulate cognitive development?

reintegrative stage
the period of late adulthood during which the focus is on tasks that have personal meaning

Finally, the **reintegrative stage** is the period of late adulthood during which people focus on tasks that have personal meaning. They no longer focus on acquiring knowledge to solve potential problems that they may encounter. Instead, they acquire information about issues that specifically interest them. Furthermore, they have less interest in—and patience for—things that they do not see as having some immediate application to their lives.

LIFE EVENTS AND COGNITIVE DEVELOPMENT Marriage. The death of a parent. Starting a first job. The birth of a child. Buying a house.

Milestones such as these, whether welcome or unwanted, can cause stress. But do they also cause cognitive growth? Some research evidence—spotty and largely based on case studies—suggests that the answer may be yes. For instance, the birth of a child may trigger fresh insights into the nature of relationships—one's place in the world and one's role in perpetuating humanity. Similarly, the death of a loved one may cause a reevaluation of what is important and a new look at the way life should be led (Kandler et al., 2012; Andersson & Conley, 2013; Karatzias, Yan, & Jowett, 2015). Experiencing the ups and downs of life may lead young adults to think about the world in novel, more complex and sophisticated, less rigid ways. They are now capable of using postformal thought to see and grasp trends and patterns, personalities, and choices. This allows them to deal effectively with the complex social worlds of which they are a part.

COMPARING THE THEORIES OF POSTFORMAL THOUGHT We've considered a number of theoretical approaches to postformal thought. Is there one particular theory that is most accurate in describing the way people's thinking changes during adulthood? Not really, because it turns out that the theories are not mutually exclusive. Instead, Labouvie-Vief's focus on postformal thinking, Perry's views on dualistic and relativistic thinking, and Schaie's focus on the stages of adult thought are concerned with different aspects of the changes we see in adult thinking.

However, there is one exception to the generalization that the theories looking at adult thought are not mutually exclusive, and that relates to Piaget's theory. In contrast to the theories that see thinking developing throughout adulthood, Piaget believed that the qualitative changes in adult thought were minimal once we reached adolescence. Based on decades of research, it seems clear that Piaget underestimated the changes that occur post-adolescence, and that thinking continues to advance in both qualitative and quantitative ways throughout adulthood.

Intelligence: What Matters in Early Adulthood?

LO 7.6 **Discuss the different types of intelligence, and explain how each affects the career success of young adults.**

You've had a pretty good year at your job. You've got two assistants who help you; one is quite good, but the other doesn't work very hard. Although you're well-liked in the company, there's not much to distinguish you from your peers. Although you want to move up quickly in the company and become an executive, you're just not sure how you can you meet your goals.

The way adults address this scenario may affect their future success. The situation is one of a series designed to assess a particular type of intelligence that may have more of an impact on future success than the IQ measured by traditional tests.

Many researchers argue that the kind of intelligence measured by IQ tests is not the only valid kind. Depending on what one wants to know about individuals, other theories of intelligence—and other measures of it—may be more appropriate.

triarchic theory of intelligence
Sternberg's theory that intelligence is made up of three major components: componential, experiential, and contextual

In his **triarchic theory of intelligence**, psychologist Robert Sternberg, who is responsible for the executive question just posed, suggests that intelligence is made up of three major components: componential, experiential, and contextual. The *componential* aspect involves the mental components used to solve problems (e.g., selecting and using formulas, choosing problem-solving strategies, and in general making use of what has been learned in the past). The *experiential* component refers to the relationship between intelligence, prior experience, and the ability to cope with new situations. This is the insightful aspect of intelligence, which allows people to relate what they already know to a new situation and facts never before encountered. Finally, the *contextual* component of intelligence takes account of the demands of everyday, real-world environments. For instance, the contextual component is involved in adapting to on-the-job professional demands (Sternberg, 2005, 2015).

Traditional IQ tests tend to focus on the componential aspect. Yet increasing evidence suggests that a more useful measure, particularly when comparing and predicting adult success, is the contextual component—the aspect of intelligence that has come to be called *practical intelligence.*

PRACTICAL AND EMOTIONAL INTELLIGENCE According to Sternberg, traditional IQ scores relate quite well to academic success but not to other types of achievement, such as career success. Although it is clear that success in business requires some level of the IQ sort of intelligence, the rate of career advancement and the ultimate success of business executives is only marginally related to IQ scores (Sternberg, 2006; Grigorenko et al., 2009; Ekinci, 2014).

Sternberg contends that success in a career necessitates practical intelligence. Whereas academic success is based on knowledge obtained largely from reading and listening, **practical intelligence** is learned primarily by observing others and modeling their behavior. People with practical intelligence have good "social radar." They understand and handle even new situations effectively, reading people and circumstances insightfully based on their previous experiences.

practical intelligence
according to Sternberg, intelligence that is learned primarily by observing others and modeling their behavior

There is another, related type of intelligence. **Emotional intelligence** is the set of skills that underlies the accurate assessment, evaluation, expression, and regulation of emotions. Emotional intelligence is what enables people to get along well with others, to understand what they are feeling and experiencing, and to respond appropriately to their needs. Emotional intelligence is of obvious value to career and personal success as a young adult (Kross & Grossmann, 2012; Crowne, 2013; Wong, 2016; Szczygieł & Mikolajczak, 2017).

emotional intelligence
the set of skills that underlie the accurate assessment, evaluation, expression, and regulation of emotions

From an educator's perspective: Do you think educators can teach people to be more intelligent? Are there components or varieties of intelligence that might be more "teachable" than others? If so, which: componential, experiential, contextual, practical, or emotional?

CREATIVITY: NOVEL THOUGHT The hundreds of musical compositions of Wolfgang Amadeus Mozart, who died at the age of 35, were largely written during early adulthood. This pattern—major works produced during early adulthood—is true of many other creative individuals. Many mathematicians and physicists produce their major works during early adulthood. Overall, creative productivity seems to peak in the late 30s and early 40s, and then slowly decline. But there are many exceptions, and the most creative people maintain their creativity throughout their life span (Simonton, 2017; Nikolaidis & Barbey, 2018; see Figure 7-4).

One reason for the higher creative output of early adulthood may be that after this period creativity can be stifled by the fact that the more people know about a subject, the less likely they are to be creative. Early adulthood may be the peak of creativity because many problems encountered professionally are novel. In addition, as we age we become less flexible in our thinking, and we are less likely to adopt unfamiliar hypotheses and assumptions (Gopnik et al., 2017).

On the other hand, many people do not reach their pinnacle of creativity until much later in life. For instance, Frank Lloyd Wright designed the Guggenheim Museum in New York at age 70. Charles Darwin was still writing influential works well into his 70s, and Pablo Picasso was painting in his 90s. Furthermore, overall productivity, as opposed to the period of a person's most important output, remains fairly steady throughout adulthood, particularly in the humanities (Simonton, 2009; Hanna, 2016).

Overall, the study of creativity reveals few consistent developmental patterns. One reason is the difficulty of determining just what constitutes **creativity**, which is

creativity
the combination of responses or ideas in novel ways

Figure 7-4 Creativity and Age

The period of maximum creativity differs depending on the particular field. The percentages refer to the total lifetime major works produced during the particular age period. Why do poets peak earlier than novelists?

SOURCE: Based on Dennis, 1966.

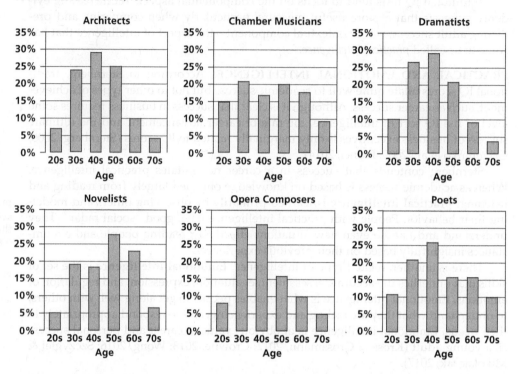

defined as combining responses or ideas in novel ways. Because definitions of what is "novel" may vary from one person to the next, it is hard to identify a particular behavior unambiguously as creative.

This hasn't stopped psychologists from trying. One suggested component of creativity is a person's willingness to take risks that may yield high payoffs. Creative people are like successful stock market investors who follow the "buy low, sell high" rule. Creative people develop and endorse ideas that are unfashionable or regarded as wrong ("buying low"), assuming that eventually others will see their value and embrace them ("selling high"). According to this theory, creative adults take a fresh look at ideas that were initially discarded, particularly if the problem is a familiar one. They are flexible enough to move away from tried-and-true ways of doing things and to consider new approaches (Sternberg, Kaufman, & Pretez, 2002; Sternberg, 2009; Sawyer, 2012).

College: Pursuing Higher Education

As soon as the class ends at 3:30, Laura Twombly, restarting college at age 30, packs her books and rushes to her car. She speeds to reach her job by 4 p.m., anxious to avoid another warning from her supervisor. After her shift, she picks up her son, Derek, from her mother's house and hurries home.

From 8:30 to 9:30 Laura spends time with Derek before putting him to bed. At 10, she starts studying for her business ethics test. She gives up at 11, setting the alarm for 5 a.m. so she can finish studying before Derek wakes around 7. Then she dresses and feeds him and herself and hurries to drop Derek off at her mother's house and start another round of classes, work, study, and mothering.

Laura Twombly, one of the one-third of college students who are older than 24, faces unusual challenges as she pursues her college degree. Older students like her represent just one aspect of the increasing diversity—in family background, socioeconomic status, race, and ethnicity—that characterizes college campuses today.

For any student, though, attending college is a significant accomplishment. College attendance is not commonplace: Nationwide, high school graduates who enter college are in the minority.

The Demographics of Higher Education: Who Attends College?

LO 7.7 Summarize the demographic makeup of college students in the United States, and describe how that population is changing.

What types of students enter college? As in the U.S. population as a whole, U.S. college students are primarily white and middle class. About 51 percent of the college population is white, compared with 18 percent Hispanic, 13 percent black, 6 percent Asian, and 12 percent other races or ethnicities. Furthermore, as total enrollment in college increased by 12 percent during the 10-year period from 2006 to 2016, minority enrollment increased by almost 40 percent (see Figure 7-5; U.S. Department of Education, 2016; Diversity in Academe, 2018).

For students who do not attend or complete college, the consequences can be significant. Higher education is an important way for people to improve their economic well-being. Just 3 percent of adults who have a college education live below the poverty line. Compare that with high school dropouts: They are 10 times more likely to be living in poverty.

THE GENDER GAP IN COLLEGE ATTENDANCE A higher proportion of women attend college than men. Seventy-one percent of female high school graduates enrolled in college the fall following graduation, compared with only 61 percent of males. The gender gap is even greater for minority students, with 69 percent of black women enrolled compared to 57 percent of black men, and 76 percent of Hispanic women enrolled compared to 62 percent of Hispanic men. Furthermore, projections show that the gap between women and men is expected to grow over the next decade (Adebayo, 2008; Lopez & Gonzalez-Barrera, 2014).

Figure 7-5 Change in Enrollment by Race and Ethnicity

Diversity in college student enrollment increased significantly between 2006 and 2016.

SOURCE: U.S. Department of Education, 2016.

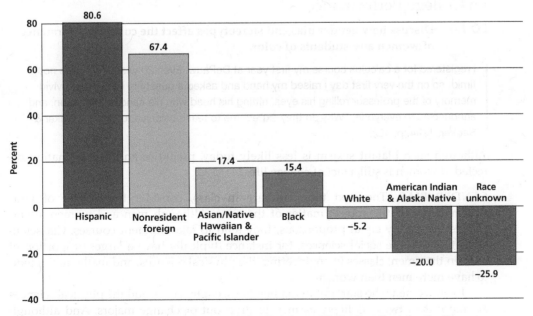

Note: Education Department data for 2006 does not classify Asian and Native Hawaiian/other Pacific Islander separately as they do for 2016; therefore, these two 2016 catgories are added together here. The "two or more" category is not included in this calculation because the 2006 Education Department data do not include it.

The number of older students starting or returning to college continues to grow. More than a third of college students are 24 years old or older. Why are so many older, nontraditional students taking college courses?

Why the gender gap? It may be that men have more job opportunities when they graduate from high school. For instance, the military, trade unions, and jobs that require physical strength may be both more available and more attractive to men. Furthermore, women often have better high school academic records than men, and they may be admitted to college at greater rates (Buchmann & DiPrete, 2006; England & Li, 2006; Rocheleau, 2016).

THE CHANGING COLLEGE STUDENT: NEVER TOO LATE TO GO TO COLLEGE? If the phrase "average college student" brings to mind an image of an 18- or 19-year-old, you should begin to rethink your view. Increasingly, students are older. In fact, from 2000 to 2016, the enrollment of students 25 years and older, like Laura Twombly, the 30-year-old student profiled previously, increased 27 percent. Almost half of all community college students are age 22 or older, and of those, 10 percent are older than 40 years old. (American Association of Community Colleges, 2018; Snyder, 2018).

Why are so many older, nontraditional students taking college courses? One reason is economic. A college degree is becoming increasingly important for obtaining a job. Many employers encourage or require workers to undergo college-based training to learn new skills or update old ones.

In addition, as young adults age, they begin to feel the need to settle down with a family. This change in attitude can reduce their risk-taking behavior and make them focus more on acquiring the ability to support their family—a phenomenon that has been labeled *maturation reform*.

> **From an educator's perspective:** How does the growing number of older, nontraditional students affect the college classroom, given what you know about human development? Why?

The Effects of Gender Bias and Negative Stereotypes on College Performance

LO 7.8   Discuss how gender bias and stereotypes affect the college performance of women and students of color.

> I registered for a calculus course my first year at DePauw. Even 20 years ago I was not timid, so on the very first day I raised my hand and asked a question. I still have a vivid memory of the professor rolling his eyes, hitting his head with his hand in frustration, and announcing to everyone, "Why do they expect me to teach calculus to girls?" (Sadker & Sadker, 1994, p. 162)

Although such blatant sexism is less likely today, prejudice and discrimination directed at women is still a fact of college life.

GENDER BIAS The next time you are in class, consider the gender of your classmates—and the subject matter of the class. Although men and women attend college in roughly equal proportions, they tend to take different courses. Classes in education and the social sciences, for instance, typically have a larger proportion of women than men; classes in engineering, the physical sciences, and mathematics tend to have more men than women.

Even women who start out in mathematics, engineering, and the physical sciences are more than twice as likely as men to drop out or change majors. And although the number of women seeking graduate degrees in science and engineering has been increasing, women still lag behind men (National Science Foundation, Division of Resource Statistics, 2002; York, 2008; Halpern, 2014).

The differences in gender distribution and attrition rates across subject areas are no accident. They reflect the powerful influence of gender stereotypes that operate throughout the world of education—and beyond. For instance, when women in their first year of college are asked to name a likely career choice, they are much less apt to choose careers that have traditionally been dominated by men, such as engineering or computer programming, and more likely to choose professions that have traditionally been populated by women, such as nursing and social work. Furthermore, even when they do choose to enter math- and science-related fields, they may face sex discrimination (Ceci & Williams, 2010; Lane, Goh, & Driver-Linn, 2012; Heilbronner, 2013).

Both male and female college professors treat men and women differently, even though the different treatment is largely unintentional and the professors are unaware of their actions. Professors call on men more frequently than women and make more eye contact with men than with women. Furthermore, male students are more likely to receive extra help. Finally, the quality of the responses received by male and female students differs, with male students receiving more positive reinforcement for their comments than female students (Sadker & Silber, 2007; Riley, 2014).

As a result of the powerful influence of gender stereotypes in the world of education, women are underrepresented in the areas of physical science, math, and engineering. What can be done to reverse this trend?

Although some cases of unequal treatment represent *hostile sexism* in which people treat women in a way that is overtly harmful, in other cases women are the victims of benevolent sexism. In *benevolent sexism*, women are placed in stereotyped and restrictive roles that appear, on the surface, to be positive.

For instance, a male college professor may compliment a female student on her good looks or offer to give her an easier research project so she won't have to work so hard. Although the professor may feel that he is merely being thoughtful, in fact he may be making the woman feel that she is not being taken seriously, and he may be undermining her view of her competence. Benevolent sexism can be just as harmful as hostile sexism (Glick & Fiske, 2012; Rudman & Fetterolf, 2014; Chonody, 2016).

STEREOTYPE THREAT AND DISIDENTIFICATION WITH SCHOOL *African Americans don't do well in academic pursuits. Women lack ability in math and science.*

These erroneous and damaging stereotypes about African Americans and women still persist, and they play out in vicious ways. For instance, when African Americans start elementary school, their standardized test scores are only slightly lower than those of Caucasian students, and yet a 2-year gap emerges by the sixth grade. And even though more African American high-school graduates are enrolling in college, the eventual undergraduate graduation rate for blacks is far lower at 41 percent than for whites at 63 percent (U.S. Department of Education, National Center for Education Statistics, 2017).

Analogously, even though boys and girls perform virtually identically on standardized math tests in elementary and middle school, this changes when they reach high school. At that level, and even more so in college, males tend to do better in math than females. In fact, when women take college math, science, and engineering courses, they are more likely to do poorly than men who enter college with the same level of preparation and identical SAT scores (Dennehy, 2018).

According to psychologist Claude Steele, the reason behind the declining levels of performance for both women and African Americans is the same: *academic disidentification*, a lack of personal identification with an academic domain. For women, disidentification is specific to math and science; for African Americans, it is more generalized across academic domains. In both cases, negative societal stereotypes produce a state of **stereotype threat**, obstacles to performance that come from awareness of the stereotypes held by society about academic abilities (Carr & Steele, 2009; Ganley et al., 2013; Shapiro, Aronson, & McGlone, 2016).

stereotype threat
obstacles to performance that come from awareness of the stereotypes held by society about academic abilities

For instance, women seeking to achieve in fields that rely on math and science may worry about the failure that society predicts for them. They may decide, paradoxically, that failure in a male-dominated field, because it would confirm societal stereotypes, presents such great risks that the struggle to succeed is not worth the effort, and they may not try very hard (Inzlicht & Ben-Zeev, 2000; Johnson et al., 2012; Pietri et al., 2018).

Similarly, African Americans may work under the pressure of feeling that they must disconfirm the negative stereotype regarding their academic performance. The pressure can be anxiety provoking and threatening and can reduce their performance below their true ability level. Ironically, stereotype threat may be most severe for better, more confident students, who have not internalized the negative stereotype to the extent of questioning their own abilities (Carr & Steele, 2009; Steele, 2012).

Rather than ignoring negative stereotypes, women and African Americans may perform less well and, ultimately, disidentify with schooling and academic pursuits relevant to the stereotype. This is exactly what a recent longitudinal study of African Americans found (O'Hara et al., 2012).

first-year adjustment reaction

a cluster of psychological symptoms, including loneliness, anxiety, withdrawal, and depression, relating to the college experience suffered by first-year college students

COLLEGE ADJUSTMENT: REACTING TO THE DEMANDS OF COLLEGE LIFE It's not only members of underrepresented groups who face challenges in college. Many students, particularly recent high school graduates living away from home for the first time, have problems adjusting during their college years.

The first year of college is particularly difficult for some. The **first-year adjustment reaction** is a cluster of psychological symptoms, including loneliness, anxiety, and depression, relating to the college experience. Although any first-year student may experience this reaction, it is particularly prevalent among students who were unusually successful, either academically or socially, in high school. When they begin college, their sudden change in status may cause distress.

First-generation college students, who are the first in their families to attend college, are particularly susceptible to difficulties during their first year of college. They may arrive at college without a clear understanding of how the demands of college differ from those of high school, and the social support they have from their families may be inadequate. In addition, they may be less well-prepared for college work (Barry et al., 2009; Credé & Niehorster, 2012; Glover, Jenkins, & Troutman, 2019).

Most often, the first-year adjustment reaction passes as students make friends, experience academic success, and integrate themselves into campus life. In other cases, though, the problems remain and may fester, leading to more serious psychological difficulties (see the *Development in Your Life* box).

Students who have been successful and popular in high school are particularly vulnerable to the first-year adjustment reaction in college. Counseling, as well as increasing familiarity with campus life, can help a student adjust.

Development in Your Life

When Do College Students Need Professional Help with Their Problems?

How can you tell if a student who is feeling depressed and unhappy may need professional help? Although there are no hard-and-fast rules, there are signals that indicate that professional help is warranted. Among them:

- psychological distress that lingers and interferes with a person's sense of well-being and ability to function
- feelings that one is unable to cope effectively with the stress
- hopeless or depressed feelings, with no apparent reason
- the inability to build close relationships
- physical symptoms—such as headaches, stomach cramps, or skin rashes—that have no apparent underlying cause

If some of these signals are present, it would be helpful to discuss them with a help provider, such as a counseling psychologist, clinical psychologist, or other mental health worker. The best place to start is the campus medical center. A personal physician, neighborhood clinic, or local board of health can also provide a referral.

How prevalent are psychological problems? Surveys find that almost half of college students report having at least one significant psychological issue. Other research finds that almost a third of students reported being depressed (see Figure 7-6; Benton et al., 2003; Gruttadaro & Crudo, 2012).

Figure 7-6 College Problems

The percentage of students reporting psychological difficulties at a campus counseling center.

SOURCE: Novotney, 2014.

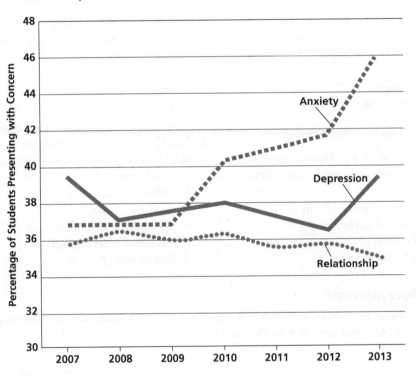

Review, Check, and Apply

Review

LO 7.5 Identify and summarize the various approaches to postformal thinking.

Cognitive development continues in young adulthood with the emergence of postformal thought, which goes beyond logic to encompass interpretive and subjective thinking. Labouvie-Vief suggests that young adults' thinking must develop to handle ambiguous situations. Perry suggests that people move from dualistic thinking to relativistic thought during early adulthood. According to Schaie, people pass through five stages in the way they use information: acquisitive, achieving, responsible, executive, and reintegrative. Major life events contribute to cognitive growth by providing opportunities and incentives to re-think one's self and one's world.

LO 7.6 Discuss the different types of intelligence, and explain how each affects the career success of young adults.

New views of intelligence encompass the triarchic the-ory, practical intelligence, and emotional intelligence. People who score high on all three components of the triarchic theory of intelligence will be able to solve prob-lems, use prior experience to cope with new situations, and adapt to the demands of the real world. People with practical intelligence learn by observing others and mod-eling their behavior. Like people with emotional intelli-gence, they have good social radar and read people well. Creativity seems to peak during early adulthood, with young adults viewing even long-standing problems as novel situations.

LO 7.7 Summarize the demographic makeup of college students in the United States, and describe how that population is changing.

Rates of college enrollment differ across gender, racial, and ethnic lines. The majority of college students are white and middle class. Although the absolute number of minority students attending college has increased, the overall pro-portion of the minority population entering college has decreased. The average age of college students is steadily increasing as more adults return to college.

LO 7.8 Discuss how gender bias and stereotypes affect the college performance of women and students of color.

The phenomena of academic disidentification and stereo-type threat help explain the lower performance of women and African Americans in certain academic domains. First-generation college students may lack a clear understanding of the demands of college and may be less prepared for the work. First-year students may experience first-year adjust-ment reaction, characterized by a cluster of psychological symptoms, including loneliness, anxiety, and depression.

Check Yourself

1. The idea that problem solving in adulthood has to con-sider previous experiences, logical thinking, and the relative benefits and costs to a decision is also known as _____.

   a. formal operational thought
   b. concrete operational thought
   c. postformal thought
   d. dualistic thinking

2. Sternberg's triarchic theory of intelligence suggests that intelligence is made up of three major compo-nents: _____.

   a. componential, experiential, and contextual
   b. emotional, practical, and experiential
   c. practical, social, and creative
   d. creative, intuitive, and executive

3. High school dropouts are _____ times more likely to live below the poverty line as adults who have a col-lege education.

   a. 3
   b. 5
   c. 10
   d. 20

4. Failing to identify oneself as successful in a certain academic domain such as math and science for women and academics in general for African Americans is known as _____.

   a. stereotype threat
   b. academic disidentification
   c. inadequate orientation
   d. bias stereotype

Applying Lifespan Development

How would you educate college professors who behave differently toward male and female students? What factors contribute to this phenomenon? Can this situation be changed?

Module 7.3

Social and Personality Development in Early Adulthood

Grace Kennedy is an exuberant 26-year-old who shares an apartment with three other young adults in Brooklyn, New York. When not work-ing at the local food co-op, Grace plays rock violin in two area bands and composes on the piano. Her apartment is often full of musicians, some of them composers like Grace, and the conversation is always lively, alternating between the serious and the humorous with ease.

Grace's siblings are all married, including her younger sister, but Grace has had a string of lovers. Her current boyfriend, Jones, *plays bass in her retro art-rock band. "Jones and I really connect, but who knows if that will last, and I don't see why it needs to," says Grace. When her sister Kate, who is married with three chil-dren, asks her if she ever longs for a home of her own and a fam-ily, Grace replies, "I find the idea of shutting myself away in my own little home depressing. I like living, loving, and working with a variety of people. Society should realize that happiness comes in many shapes."*

Is Grace an example of a young woman who has difficulties with intimacy, or is she part of a larger trend in how women and men in their 20s are approaching the complexities of adulthood?

In either case, early adulthood is a period that poses a variety of developmental tasks (see Table 7-3). We come to grips with the notion that we are no longer simply other people's children, and we begin to perceive ourselves as adults, full members of society with significant responsibilities (Tanner, Arnett, & Leis, 2009; Arnett, 2010).

This module examines those challenges, concentrating on relationships with others. First, we consider the concept of emerging adulthood, which some developmentalists consider a separate stage of the life span. Next, we look at love in its many varieties, including gay and lesbian relationships. We consider how people choose partners, influenced by societal and cultural factors.

Then we examine marriage, including the choice of whether to marry and the factors that influence the success of marriage. We consider how children affect marital happiness, and we look at the roles children play in a marriage for heterosexual, gay, and lesbian couples. Also, we discuss the factors that influence family size today, which reflect the complexity of issues young adults face in relationships.

Finally, we move to careers, another major preoccupation of young adults. We see how identity during early adulthood is often tied to one's job and how people decide on the kind of work they do. The module ends with a discussion of the reasons people work and ways to choose a career.

Pressmaster/Fotolia

Table 7-3 The Developmental Tasks of Adulthood

Adulthood (Ages 20–40)	Middle Adulthood (Ages 40–60)	Late Adulthood (Ages 60+)
• Taking responsibility for yourself • Understanding that you have a unique history and that it is not permanent • Managing the separation from your parents • Redefining the relationship with your parents • Gaining and interpreting your sexual experiences • Becoming capable of intimacy with another (non-family) person • Managing money • Developing skills that can lead to a career • Considering career possibilities • Considering parenthood and possibly becoming a parent • Defining your values • Finding a place in society	• Understanding that time is passing and accepting it • Accepting that you are aging • Accepting changes in your body, including appearance and health • Developing an acceptable work identity • Becoming a member of society • Understanding that society is constantly changing • Keeping old friends and making new ones • Coping with changes in your sexuality • Continuously reworking your spousal or partner relationship • Altering your relationship with your children as they age • Passing on knowledge, skills, and values to the next generation • Managing money effectively for short- and long-term goals • Experiencing the illness and death of persons close to you, especially parents • Finding a place in society	• Spending time well • Remaining social rather than isolated • Making friends and new connections • Adjusting to changing sexuality • Staying healthy • Managing physical pain, ailments, and limitations • Making life without work a comfortable lifestyle • Using time wisely for engaging work and recreation • Managing finances effectively for yourself and your dependents • Focusing on the present and future, not dwelling on the past • Adjusting to ongoing losses of close connections • Accepting care from children and grandchildren

SOURCE: Based on Colarusso & Nemiroff, 1981.

Forging Relationships: Intimacy, Liking, and Loving During Emerging and Early Adulthood

> Dianne Maher swept Thad Ramon off his feet—literally. "I was setting up the cafeteria for a dance and she was sweeping the floor. Next thing I knew a push broom was under my heels and down I went. I didn't hurt myself or anything, and my pride wasn't injured, but you could say my heart took a beating. There she was, sly grin on her face, and all I could do was stare and laugh. We started talking and laughing some more and soon we discovered we had a lot more than silliness in common. We've been together ever since."

Thad followed his heart and in his senior year of college publicly proposed to Dianne in that same cafeteria. They plan to get married beside the college duck pond and at the end of the ceremony march beneath crossed push brooms held by their ushers and bridesmaids.

Not everyone falls in love quite as easily as Thad and Dianne. For some, it is tortuous, meandering through soured relationships and fallen dreams; for others, it is a road never taken. For some, love leads to marriage and the storybook picture of home, children, and long years together. For many, it leads to a less happy ending, to divorce and custody battles.

Emerging Adulthood

LO 7.9   Discuss the concept of emerging adulthood.

emerging adulthood
the period from the late teenage years extending to the mid–20s in which people are still sorting out their options for the future

Do you feel as though you're not really an "adult," despite having reached an age where you are legally an adult? Are you still unsure of who you are and what you want to do with your life, and feeling unready to go out in the world on your own? If so, what you're experiencing is a developmental period known as **emerging adulthood**—a transitional stage between adolescence and adulthood that spans the third decade of life. Researchers are increasingly considering emerging adulthood to be a distinct developmental period during which the brain is still growing and modifying its neural pathways. It's typically a time of uncertainty and self-discovery during which the emerging adult is still figuring out the world and his or her place in it (Arnett, 2014a, 2016).

Emerging adulthood is marked by five features. *Identity exploration* entails learning to make important decisions about love, work, and one's core beliefs and values. In one comprehensive survey of over 1,000 diverse emerging adults age 18 to 29 throughout the United States, 77 percent agreed with the statement "This is a time of life for finding out who I really am." Another feature of emerging adulthood is *instability*, which can be represented as changes in life plans or goals, fluctuating career and educational paths, rocky relationships, and even shifts in ideologies. In the survey, 83 percent of respondents agreed that "This time of my life is full of changes" (Arnett, 2014b).

A third feature of emerging adulthood is *self-focus*: It's a time of life that comes between parental control and the obligations of child-raising and career. With fewer people to answer to, emerging adults enjoy the luxury of focusing on themselves for a while before making any serious commitments. "This is a time of my life for focusing on myself" was a statement with which 71 percent of respondents to the survey agreed. Given all this, it's probably not surprising that a fourth feature of emerging adulthood is *feeling in-between*, a sense of being no longer an adolescent but not yet really an adult either. For some emerging adults the feeling is enhanced by remaining dependent in some ways on their parents, and for others it's more a sense of uncertainty and hesitation in accepting full adulthood just yet. Half of the respondents to the survey were unwilling to agree completely that they had reached adulthood (Arnett, 2014b).

Finally, despite the stress and anxiety that are associated with the uncertainties of emerging adulthood, it is also a time of *optimism*. Nearly 90 percent of survey respondents agreed that "I am confident that someday I will get what I want out of life" and 83 percent agreed "At this time of my life, anything is possible." Part of the reason for this optimism is the tendency for young adults today to be better educated than their parents were, such that their optimism has a basis in reality. And happily, by the time they are 30, most emerging adults have found their way and have settled more comfortably into their adult roles (Arnett, 2014b, 2015; Ozmen, Brelsford, & Danieu, 2017).

The existence of the period of emerging adulthood is driven by the nature of economic changes in industrialized countries in the last several decades. As these economies have shifted toward technology and information, an increasing time has to be spent becoming educated. Furthermore, the age of marriage has risen, as has the timing of the birth of children (Arnett, 2016).

Furthermore, both men and women have increasing ambivalence about becoming adults. Surveys show that people in their late teens and early 20s respond with "yes and no" most frequently when asked if they have reached adulthood (Arnett, 2006, 2016; Verschueren et al., 2017).

Intimacy, Friendship, and Love

LO 7.10   Explain how young adults respond to the need for intimacy and friendship and how liking turns to loving.

Intimacy and relationships are major considerations during emerging and early adulthood. Relationships are the core of young adults' happiness, and many worry whether they are developing serious relationships "on time." Even those who are not interested in forming long-term relationships typically are focused, to some extent, on connecting with others.

SEEKING INTIMACY: ERIKSON'S VIEW OF YOUNG ADULTHOOD   Erik Erikson regarded young adulthood as the time of the **intimacy-versus-isolation stage**, which spans the period of postadolescence into the early 30s. During this period, the focus is on developing close, intimate relationships with others.

Erikson's idea of intimacy comprises several aspects. One is selflessness, the sacrifice of one's own needs to those of another. Another is sexuality, the experience of joint pleasure from focusing not just on one's own gratification but also on that of one's partner. Finally, there is deep devotion, marked by efforts to fuse one's identity with the identity of a partner.

According to Erikson, those who experience difficulties during this stage are often lonely, isolated, and fearful of relationships. Their difficulties may stem from a previous failure to develop a strong identity. In contrast, young adults who are able to form intimate relationships on a physical, intellectual, and emotional level successfully resolve the crisis of this stage of development.

Although Erikson's approach has been influential, it's troubling today because he limited healthy intimacy to heterosexuality. Same-sex partnerships, couples who are childless by choice, and other relationships different from Erikson's ideal were regarded as less than satisfactory. Furthermore, Erikson focused more on men than women and did not consider racial and ethnic identity, greatly limiting the applicability of his theory (Yip, Sellers, & Seaton, 2006; Kimmel, 2015).

Still, Erikson's work has been influential historically because of its emphasis on examining the continued growth and development of personality throughout the life span. Furthermore, it inspired other developmentalists to consider psychosocial growth during young adulthood and the range of intimate relationships we develop, from friendship to mates for life (Whitbourne, Sneed, & Sayer, 2009).

FRIENDSHIP   Most of our relationships are friendships, and maintaining them is an important part of adult life. Why? One reason is that people have a basic *need for belonging* that leads them in early adulthood to establish and maintain at least a minimum number of relationships that foster a sense of belonging with others (Wrzus et al., 2017).

But how do particular people end up becoming our friends? One of the most important factors is proximity—people form friendships with others who live nearby and with whom they have frequent contact. People who are nearby can obtain the rewards of friendship, such as companionship, social approval, and the occasional helping hand, at relatively little cost.

Similarity also plays an important role in friendship formation. Birds of a feather *do* flock together: People are more attracted to others who hold attitudes and values similar to their own (Preciado et al., 2012; Mikulincer et al., 2015; Ilmarinen, Lönnqvist, & Paunonen, 2016).

The importance of similarity becomes evident when we consider cross-race friendships. As we noted in our discussion of adolescence, the number of cross-race close friendships dwindles throughout the life span. In fact, although most adults claim to have a close friend of a different race, when they are queried regarding the names of close friends, few include a person of a different race.

We also choose friends for their personal qualities. What's most important? According to results of surveys, people are most attracted to others who keep confidences and are loyal, warm, and affectionate. In addition, people like those who are supportive, frank, and have a good sense of humor (You & Bellmore, 2012).

intimacy-versus-isolation stage according to Erikson, the period of postadolescence into the early 30s that focuses on developing close, intimate relationships with others

People are most attracted to those who can keep confidences and are loyal, warm, and affectionate.

FALLING IN LOVE: WHEN LIKING TURNS TO LOVING

> After a few chance encounters at the laundromat where they wash their clothes each week, Rebecca and Jerry begin talking. They find they have a lot in common, and they begin to look forward to what are now semiplanned meetings. After several weeks, they go out on their first official date and discover that they are well suited to each other.

If such a pattern seems predictable, it is: Most relationships develop by following a surprisingly regular progression (Burgess & Huston, 1979; Berscheid, 1985):

- Two people interact more often and for longer periods, and the range of settings increases.
- They increasingly seek each other's company.
- They open up more and more, disclosing more intimate information. They begin to share physical intimacies.
- They are more willing to share both positive and negative feelings, and they may offer criticism in addition to praise.
- They begin to agree on their goals for the relationship.
- Their reactions to situations become more similar.
- They begin to feel that their own psychological well-being is tied to the success of the relationship, viewing it as unique, irreplaceable, and cherished.
- Finally, their definition of themselves and their behavior changes: They begin to see themselves and act as a couple, rather than as two separate individuals.

The Faces of Love

LO 7.11 Differentiate the different kinds of love.

Is "love" just a lot of "liking"? Most developmental psychologists would say no; love not only differs quantitatively from liking, it represents a qualitatively different state. For example, love, at least in its early stages, involves relatively intense physiological arousal, all-encompassing interest, recurrent fantasies, and rapid swings of emotion. Furthermore, compared to liking, love includes closeness, passion, and exclusivity (Ramsay, 2010; Barsade & O'Neill, 2014; Silton & Ferris, 2017).

Not all love is the same. We don't love our mothers the same way we love girl-friends or boyfriends, brothers or sisters, or lifelong friends. What distinguishes these different types of love? Some psychologists suggest that our love relationships can fall into two different categories: passionate or companionate.

passionate (or romantic) love
a state of powerful absorption in someone

companionate love
the strong affection for those with whom our lives are deeply involved

labeling theory of passionate love
the theory that individuals experience romantic love when two events occur together: intense physiological arousal and situational cues suggesting that the arousal is as a result of love

PASSIONATE AND COMPANIONATE LOVE: THE TWO FACES OF LOVE **Passionate (or romantic) love** is a state of powerful absorption in someone. It includes intense physiological interest and arousal, and caring for another's needs. In comparison, **companionate love** is the strong affection that we have for those with whom our lives are deeply involved (Hendrick & Hendrick, 2003; Acevedo, 2018).

What is it that fuels the fires of passionate love? According to one theory, strong emotions—even negative ones such as jealousy, anger, or fear of rejection—may be the source of deepening passionate love.

In psychologists Elaine Hatfield and Ellen Berscheid's **labeling theory of passionate love**, individuals experience romantic love when two events occur together: intense physiological arousal and situational cues that indicate that "love" is the appropriate label for the feelings being experienced (Berscheid & Walster, 1974). The physiological arousal can be produced by sexual arousal, excitement, or even negative emotions such as jealousy. If that arousal is subsequently labeled as "I must be falling in love" or "he really turns me on," the experience is attributed to passionate love.

The theory helps to explain why people may feel deepened love even in the face of rejection or hurt. If negative emotions produce strong physiological arousal and this arousal is interpreted as "love," then people may decide that they are even more in love than they were before they experienced the negative emotions.

But why should people label an emotional experience "love" when there are so many alternative explanations? One answer is that in Western cultures, romantic love is seen as possible, acceptable, and desirable. The virtues of passion are extolled in songs, commercials, TV shows, and films. Young adults are primed and ready to experience love in their lives (Florsheim, 2003; Karandashev, 2017).

This is not universal across cultures; in many cultures, passionate, romantic love is a foreign concept. Marriages are arranged on the basis of economic and status considerations. Even in Western cultures, the concept of romantic love was not "invented" until the Middle Ages, when social philosophers first suggested that love ought to be a requirement for marriage. Their goal was to provide an alternative to the raw sexual desire that had served as the primary basis for marriage before (Haslett, 2004; Moore & Wei, 2012).

STERNBERG'S TRIANGULAR THEORY: THE THREE FACES OF LOVE   To psychologist Robert Sternberg, love is more complex than a simple division into passionate and companionate types. He suggests instead that love is made up of three components: intimacy, passion, and decision/commitment. The **intimacy component** encompasses feelings of closeness, affection, and connectedness. The **passion component** comprises the motivational drives relating to sex, physical closeness, and romance. The **decision/commitment component** embodies both the initial cognition that one loves another person and the longer-term determination to maintain that love (Sternberg, 2006; Sternberg, 2014).

These components can be combined to form eight different types of love depending on which of the three components is either present or missing from a relationship (see Table 7-4). For instance, *nonlove* refers to people who have only the most casual of relationships; it consists of the absence of the three components of intimacy, passion, and decision/commitment. *Liking* develops when only intimacy is present; *infatuated love* exists when only passion is felt; and *empty love* exists when only decision/commitment is present.

Other types of love involve a mix of two or more components. For instance, *romantic love* occurs when intimacy and passion are present, and *companionate love* when intimacy and decision/commitment occur jointly. When two people experience romantic love, they are drawn together physically and emotionally, but they do not necessarily view the relationship as lasting. Companionate love, on the other hand, may occur in long-lasting relationships in which physical passion has taken a backseat.

Fatuous love exists when passion and decision/commitment, without intimacy, are present. Fatuous love is a kind of mindless loving in which there is no emotional bond between the partners.

Finally, the eighth kind of love is *consummate love*. In consummate love, all three components of love are present. But don't assume that consummate love is the "ideal" love.

intimacy component
according to Sternberg, the component of love that encompasses feelings of closeness, affection, and connectedness

passion component
according to Sternberg, the component of love that comprises the motivational drives relating to sex, physical closeness, and romance

decision/commitment component
according to Sternberg, the third aspect of love that embodies both the initial cognition that one loves another person and the longer-term determination to maintain that love

Table 7-4 The Combinations of Love

| | Component | | | |
Type of Love	Intimacy	Passion	Decision/Commitment	Example
Nonlove	Absent	Absent	Absent	The way you might feel about the person who takes your ticket at the movies.
Liking	Present	Absent	Absent	Good friends who have lunch together at least once or twice a week.
Infatuated love	Absent	Present	Absent	A "fling" or short-term relationship based only on sexual attraction.
Empty love	Absent	Absent	Present	An arranged marriage or a couple who have decided to stay married "for the sake of the children."
Romantic love	Present	Present	Absent	A couple who have been happily dating a few months, but have not made any plans for a future together.
Companionate love	Present	Absent	Present	A couple who enjoy each other's company and their relationship, although they no longer feel much sexual interest in each other.
Fatuous love	Absent	Present	Present	A couple who decides to move in together after knowing each other for only 2 weeks.
Consummate love	Present	Present	Present	A loving, sexually vibrant, long-term relationship.

Many long-lasting and entirely satisfactory relationships are based on other types of love. Furthermore, the type of love that predominates in a relationship varies over time. In strong, loving relationships the level of decision/commitment peaks and remains fairly stable. By contrast, passion tends to peak early in a relationship, but then declines and levels off. Intimacy also increases fairly rapidly but can continue to grow over time.

Sternberg's triangular theory of love emphasizes both the complexity of love and its dynamic, evolving quality. As people and relationships develop, so does their love.

Choosing a Partner: Recognizing Mr. or Ms. Right

LO 7.12   **Identify the factors that influence young adults' choice of partner, and give examples of how these are affected by gender and culture.**

For many young adults, the search for a partner is a major pursuit during early adulthood. Society offers a wealth of advice, as a glance at the magazines at supermarket check-out counters confirms. Still, the road to identifying a life partner is not always easy.

SEEKING A SPOUSE: IS LOVE THE ONLY THING THAT MATTERS?   Most people have no hesitation in declaring that the major factor in choosing a spouse is love. Most people in the United States, that is: If we ask people in other societies, love becomes a secondary consideration. For instance, in some cultures, love is seen as a possible positive outcome of a good marriage, but not as a necessary precondition for getting married in the first place. Furthermore, one survey of college students asked if they would marry someone they did not love. Hardly anyone in the United States, Japan, or Brazil would consider it. On the other hand, a high proportion of college students in Pakistan and India would find it acceptable to marry without love (Levine, 1993; Bruckner, 2013; Kottak, 2019).

What else matters? The characteristics differ considerably from one culture to another. For instance, a survey of nearly 10,000 people from around the world found that in China, men ranked good health most important and women rated emotional stability and maturity most critical. In South Africa, men from a Zulu background rated emotional stability first, and Zulu women rated dependable character the greatest concern (Buss et al., 1990; Buss, 2003).

Yet there are commonalities across cultures. For instance, love and mutual attraction, even if not at the top of a specific culture's list, were relatively highly desired across all cultures. Furthermore, traits such as dependability, emotional stability, pleasing disposition, and intelligence were highly valued almost universally.

Certain gender differences were similar across cultures (Sprecher, Sullivan, & Hatfield, 1994). Men, more than women, prefer a potential marriage partner who is physically attractive. In contrast, women, more than men, prefer a potential spouse who is ambitious and industrious.

One explanation for cross-cultural similarities in gender differences rests on evolutionary theory. According to psychologist David Buss (2006), human beings, as a species, seek out certain characteristics in their mates that are likely to maximize the availability of beneficial genes. He argues that males in particular are genetically programmed to seek out mates with traits that indicate they have high reproductive capacity. Consequently, physically attractive, younger women might be more desirable because they are more capable of having children over a longer time period.

In contrast, women are genetically programmed to seek out men who have the potential to provide scarce resources to increase the likelihood that their offspring will survive. Consequently, they are attracted to mates who offer the highest potential of providing economic well-being (Li et al., 2002; Fletcher et al., 2017).

The evolutionary explanation for gender differences has come under heavy fire. Not only is the explanation untestable, but the similarities across cultures relating to different gender preferences may also simply reflect similar patterns of gender stereotyping that have nothing to do with evolution. In addition, although some of the gender differences in what men and women prefer are consistent across cultures, there are numerous inconsistencies as well.

Finally, some critics of the evolutionary approach suggest that the finding that women prefer a partner who has good earning potential may have nothing to do with evolution and everything to do with the fact that men generally hold more power, status, and other resources fairly consistently across different cultures. Consequently, it is a rational choice for women to prefer a high-earning-potential spouse. On the other hand, because men don't need to take economic considerations into account, they can use more inconsequential criteria—like physical attractiveness—in choosing a spouse. In short, the consistencies that are found across cultures may be the result of the realities of economic life that are similar throughout different cultures (Eagly & Wood, 2003; Wood & Eagly, 2010).

FILTERING MODELS: SIFTING OUT A SPOUSE Although surveys help to identify valued characteristics, they are less helpful in illuminating how individual partners are chosen. According to the *filter explanation*, people seeking a mate screen potential candidates through successively finer-grained filters. The explanation assumes that people first filter for factors relating to broad determinants of attractiveness. Once these early screens have done their work, more sophisticated types of screening are used (see Figure 7-7). The end result is a choice based on compatibility between the two individuals (Janda & Klenke-Hamel, 1980; Lauer & Lauer, 2019).

What determines compatibility? People often marry according to the principle of homogamy. **Homogamy** is the tendency to marry someone who is similar in age, race, education, religion, and other basic demographic characteristics. Homogamy, long the dominant standard for U.S. marriages, has been declining recently, particularly among certain ethnic groups. For example, the rate of marriage between African American men and women of other races increased significantly. Still, for other groups—such as Hispanic and Asian immigrants—the principle of homogamy still has considerable influence (Fu & Heaton, 2008; Mu & Xie, 2014; Horwitz et al., 2016).

Another important societal standard is the *marriage gradient*, the tendency for men to marry women who are slightly younger, smaller, and lower in status, and women to marry men who are slightly older, larger, and higher in status (Pyke & Adams, 2010; Olson, DeFrain, & Skogrand, 2019).

Figure 7-7 Filtering Potential Marriage Partners

According to one approach, we screen potential mates through successively finer-grained filters to settle on an appropriate spouse.

SOURCE: Based on Janda & Klenke-Hamel, 1980.

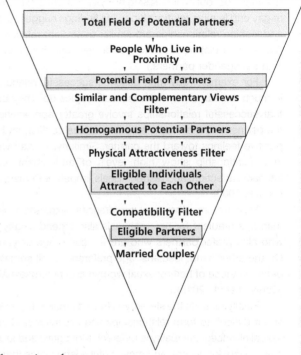

homogamy
the tendency to marry someone who is similar in age, race, education, religion, and other basic demographic characteristics

From a social worker's perspective: How do the principles of homogamy and the marriage gradient work to limit options for high-status women? How do they affect men's options?

The marriage gradient has important, and unfortunate, effects on partner choice. For one thing, it limits the number of potential mates for women, especially as they age, while allowing men a wider choice of partners throughout life. But it is unfortunate for low-status men, who do not marry because they cannot find women of low enough status or cannot find women of the same or higher status who are willing to accept them as mates. Consequently, they are, in the words of sociologist Jessie Bernard (1982), "bottom of the barrel" men. On the other hand, some women will be unable to marry because they are higher in status or seek someone of higher status than anyone in the available pool of men—"cream of the crop" women, in Bernard's words.

The marriage gradient makes finding a spouse particularly difficult for well-educated African American women who would prefer to marry an African American man. Fewer African American men attend college than African American women, making the potential pool of men who are suitable—as defined by society and the marriage gradient—relatively small. The pool of men is further limited because of the relatively higher rate of incarceration of black males (which is six times greater

Cultural Dimensions

Gay and Lesbian Relationships: Men with Men and Women with Women

Most developmental research has examined heterosexual relationships, but an increasing number of studies have looked at gay and lesbian relationships. The findings suggest that gay and lesbian relationships are similar to straight relationships. (There is almost no research yet on relationships of couples with transgender partners.)

For example, gay men describe successful relationships in much the same way heterosexual couples do. They believe that successful relationships involve greater appreciation for the partner and the couple as a whole, less conflict, and more positive feelings toward the partner. Similarly, lesbian women in a relationship show high levels of attachment, caring, intimacy, affection, and respect (Beals, Impett, & Peplau, 2002; Kurdek, 2006).

Furthermore, the age preferences expressed in the marriage gradient for heterosexuals also extend to gay men, who also prefer partners who are the same age or younger. On the other hand, lesbians' age preferences fall somewhere between those of heterosexual women and heterosexual men (Conway et al., 2015).

Finally, despite the stereotype that gay males, in particular, find it difficult to form relationships and are interested in only sexual alliances, the reality is different. Most gays and lesbians seek loving, long-term, and meaningful relationships that differ little qualitatively from those desired by heterosexuals. Although some research suggests that homosexual relationships are less long-lasting than heterosexual relationships, the factors that lead to relationship stability—partners' personality traits, support for the relationship from others, and dependence on the relationship—are similar for homosexual and heterosexual

couples (Diamond & Savin-Williams, 2003; Kurdek, 2008; Savin-Williams, 2016).

Opinions on very few social issues have changed as much as attitudes toward same-sex marriage, which the Supreme Court ruled legal in the United States in 2015. Just over 60 percent of Americans say same-sex couples should be able to marry legally, a significant shift in sentiment over the past 20 years. Furthermore, there are significant generational differences: whereas two-thirds of people younger than 30 support same-sex marriage, only 38 percent of those older than 65 support the legalization of gay marriage (Pew Research Center, 2014b; Vandermaas-Peeler et al., 2018).

Research finds that the quality of lesbian and gay relationships differs little from that of heterosexual relationships.

than that of whites). Consequently, relative to women of other races, African American women are more apt to marry men who are less educated than they are—or not marry at all (Willie & Reddick, 2003; Johnson, 2011; Olson, DeFrain, & Skogrand, 2019; also see the *Cultural Dimensions* box).

ATTACHMENT STYLES AND ROMANTIC RELATIONSHIPS: DO ADULT LOVING STYLES REFLECT ATTACHMENT IN INFANCY? "I want a girl just like the girl that married dear old Dad." So go the lyrics of an old song, suggesting that the songwriter would like to find someone who loves him as much as his mother did. Is there a kernel of truth in this sentiment? Put more broadly, is the kind of attachment that people experience during infancy reflected in their adult romantic relationships?

Increasing evidence suggests that it very well may be. As we discussed previously, attachment refers to the positive emotional bond that develops between a child and a particular individual. Most infants fall into one of three attachment categories: securely attached infants, who have healthy, positive, trusting relationships with their caregivers; avoidant infants, who are relatively indifferent to caregivers and avoid interactions with them; and ambivalent infants, who show great distress when separated from a caregiver but appear angry on the caregiver's return.

Some psychologists believe that our attachment style as infants is repeated in the quality of our intimate relationships as adults.

According to psychologist Phillip Shaver and his colleagues, attachment styles continue into adulthood and affect the nature of romantic relationships (Dinero et al., 2008; Frías, Shaver, & Mikulincer, 2015; Shaver et al., 2017). For instance, consider the following statements:

1. I find it relatively easy to get close to others and am comfortable depending on them and having them depend on me. I don't often worry about being abandoned or about someone getting too close to me.
2. I am somewhat uncomfortable being close to others; I find it difficult to trust them completely, difficult to allow myself to depend on them. I am nervous when anyone gets too close, and often love partners want me to be more intimate than I feel comfortable being.
3. I find that others are reluctant to get as close as I would like. I often worry that my partner doesn't really love me or won't want to stay with me. I want to merge completely with another person, and this desire sometimes scares people away (Shaver, Hazan, & Bradshaw, 1988).

Agreement with the first statement reflects a *secure attachment style*. Adults who agree with this statement readily enter into relationships and feel happy and confident about the future success of their relationships. Most young adults—slightly more than half—display the secure style of attachment (Luke, Sedikides, & Carnelley, 2012; Molero et al., 2016).

In contrast, adults who agree with the second statement typically display an *avoidant attachment style*. These individuals, who make up about a quarter of the population, tend to be less invested in relationships, have higher break-up rates, and often feel lonely.

Finally, agreement with the third category is reflective of an *ambivalent attachment style*. Adults with an ambivalent style have a tendency to become overly invested in relationships, have repeated break-ups with the same partner, and have relatively low self-esteem. Around 20 percent of adults fall into this category (Li & Darius, 2012).

Attachment style is also related to the care that adults give their romantic partners when they need assistance. Secure adults tend to provide more sensitive and supportive care, responding to their partner's psychological needs. In contrast, anxious adults are more likely to provide compulsive, intrusive (and ultimately less helpful) assistance. Attachment style is also related to parenting: Mothers' relationships with their infants reflect the mother's attachment style (Mikulincer & Shaver, 2009; Shaver et al., 2017; Stern et al., 2018).

In short, there are similarities between infants' attachment styles and their behavior as adults. People who are having difficulty in relationships might look back to their infancy as a root of their problems (Berlin, Cassidy, & Appleyard, 2008; Draper et al., 2008; Simpson & Rholes, 2015).

The Course of Relationships

Relationships are especially challenging in early adulthood. One of the primary questions young adults face is whether and when to marry.

Cohabitation, Marriage, and Other Relationship Choices: Sorting Out the Options of Early Adulthood

LO 7.13   Summarize the sorts of relationships people enter into in early adulthood, and identify the characteristics of a successful marriage.

For some people, the primary issue is not *whom* to marry, but *whether* to marry. Although surveys show that most heterosexuals (and a growing number of homosexuals) say they want to get married, a significant number choose some other route. For instance, the past three decades have seen both a decline in the number of married couples and a significant rise in couples living together without being married, a

Figure 7-8 Cohabitation

The number of unmarried couples living together has increased significantly in every adult age group.

SOURCE: U.S. Bureau of the Census, 2010; Pew Research Center, 2017.

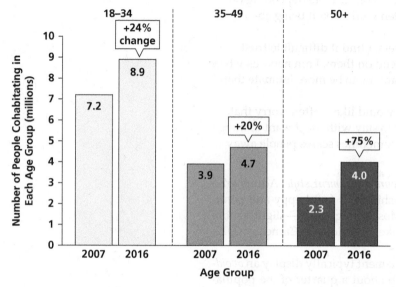

cohabitation
couples living together without being married

status known as **cohabitation** (see Figure 7-8). In fact, today, some 7.5 million people are cohabiting in the United States. Married couples now make up a minority of households: 48 percent of all U.S. households contained a married couple, a historically low figure. In comparison, in 1950, 78 percent of households were occupied by a married couple (Roberts, 2006; Jay, 2012).

Most young adults will live with a romantic partner for at least one period of time during their 20s. Furthermore, most marriages today occur after a period in which the couple has cohabited.

Why do so many couples choose to cohabit rather than to marry? Some feel they are not ready to make a lifelong commitment. Others feel that cohabitation provides "practice" for marriage. (This is more likely for women than men. Women tend to see cohabitation as a step toward marriage; men are more likely to view it as a way to test a relationship (Jay, 2012; Perelli-Harris & Styrc, 2017).)

Some couples reject marriage altogether. They believe that marriage is outmoded and that it is unrealistic to expect a couple to spend a lifetime together (Miller, Sassler, & Kus-Appough, 2011; Pope & Cashwell, 2013).

Those who feel that cohabiting increases their chances of a happy marriage are incorrect. In fact, the chances of divorce are higher for those who have previously cohabited, according to data collected in both the United States and western Europe (Rhoades, Stanley, & Markman, 2009; Tang, Curran, & Arroyo, 2014; Perelli-Harris et al., 2017).

MARRIAGE Despite the prevalence of cohabitation, most people view marriage as the preferred option during early adulthood. Many see marriage as the appropriate culmination of a loving relationship, whereas others feel it is the "right" thing to do after reaching a particular age. Others seek marriage because spouses fill many roles, including economic, sexual, therapeutic, and recreational. Marriage is also the only fully accepted way to have children. Finally, marriage offers legal benefits and protections.

Although marriage remains important, it is not a static institution. For example, fewer U.S. citizens are now married than at any time since the late 1890s. Part of this decline in marriage is attributable to higher divorce rates, but the decision of people to marry later in life is also a contributing factor. The median age of first marriage in the United States is now 29.5 years for men and 27.4 years for women—the oldest ages for both genders since national statistics were first collected more than a century ago (see Figure 7-9; U.S. Bureau of the Census, 2017).

Many European countries offer legal alternatives to marriage. For instance, France offers "Civil Solidarity Pacts," in which couples receive many of the same legal rights as married couples. What differs is the lack of a legal lifetime commitment; Civil Solidarity Pacts can be dissolved more easily than marriages (Lyall, 2004; Fitzpatrick, 2018).

Does this mean that marriage is losing its viability as a social institution? Probably not. Some 90 percent of people eventually marry, and on national polls almost everyone agrees that a good family life is important. In fact, about 60 percent of never-married men and women say they would like to get married (Strong & Cohen, 2013).

From a social worker's perspective: Why do you think society has established such a powerful norm in favor of marriage? What effects might such a norm have on a person who prefers to remain single?

WHAT MAKES MARRIAGE WORK? Successful marriages share several characteristics. The partners visibly show affection and communicate relatively little negativity.

Figure 7-9 Postponing Marriage

Median age at first marriage: 1890–2017. The age of first marriage is the highest since national statistics were first collected in the late 1800s. What factors account for this?

SOURCE: U.S. Bureau of the Census, 2017.

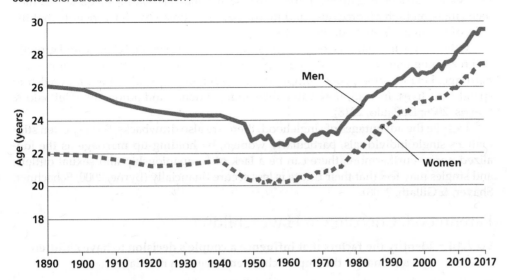

They tend to perceive themselves as an interdependent couple rather than as two independent individuals. They experience social homogamy, having similar interests and agreeing on role distribution—such as who takes out the garbage and who takes care of the children (Huston et al., 2001; Stutzer & Frey, 2006; Cordova, 2014).

The increasing understanding of the components of successful marriages has not prevented an epidemic of divorce. The statistics are grim: Only about half of U.S. marriages remain intact. More than 800,000 U.S. marriages end in divorce each year, and there are 43.2 divorces for every 1,000 individuals. This is a decline from the mid-1970s peak of 5.3 divorces per 1,000 people, and most experts think that the rate is leveling off (National Center for Health Statistics, 2017; see Figure 7-10).

EARLY MARITAL CONFLICT Conflict in marriage is not unusual. According to some statistics, nearly half of newly married couples experience a significant degree of conflict. One of the major reasons is that partners may initially idealize one another, but as reality sets in they become more aware of flaws. In fact, spousal perceptions of marital quality over the first 10 years of marriage decline in the early years, followed by a period of stabilization, and then additional decline (Karney & Bradbury, 2005; Kilmann & Vendemia, 2013).

Common sources of marital conflict include difficulty making the transition from adolescence to adulthood; trouble developing a separate identity; and the challenge of allocating time across spouse, friends, and family members (Murray, Bellavia, & Rose, 2003; Madigan, Plamondon, & Jenkins, 2017).

Still, most married couples view the early years of marriage as deeply satisfying. In negotiating changes in their relationship and learning more about each other, many couples find themselves more deeply in love than before. In fact, the newlywed period is for many couples one of the happiest of their married lives, despite the challenges they may face (McNulty & Karney, 2004; McNulty et al., 2013; Lavner et al., 2018).

STAYING SINGLE: I WANT TO BE ALONE For some people, living alone is the right path, consciously chosen, through life. In fact, *singlehood*, living

Figure 7-10 Divorce Around the World

Countries around the world have substantial divorce rates, although in some places the rate is declining.

SOURCE: Adapted from Population Council Report, 2009.

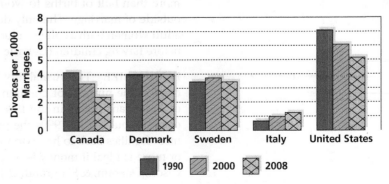

alone without an intimate partner, has increased significantly in the past several decades, encompassing around 20 percent of women and 30 percent of men. Almost 20 percent will probably spend their entire lives in singlehood (U.S. Bureau of the Census, 2012).

People who choose singlehood give several reasons for their decision. One is that they view marriage negatively. Rather than seeing marriage in idealized terms, they focus more on high divorce rates and marital strife. Ultimately, they conclude that the risks of forming a lifetime union are too high.

Others view marriage as too restrictive, valuing their personal change and growth, and reasoning that growth would be impeded by the stable, long-term commitment of marriage. Finally, some people simply do not meet anyone with whom they wish to spend their lives. Instead, they value their independence and autonomy (DePaulo & Morris, 2006; DePaulo, 2018).

Despite the advantages of singlehood, there are also drawbacks. Society often stigmatizes single individuals, particularly women, by holding up marriage as the idealized norm. Furthermore, there can be a lack of companionship and sexual outlets, and singles may feel that their future is less secure financially (Byrne, 2000; Schachner, Shaver, & Gillath, 2008).

Parenthood: Choosing to Have Children

LO 7.14 **Identify the factors that influence a couple's decision to have children, and summarize the impact children have on a marriage.**

What makes a couple decide to have children? Certainly not economics: According to the U.S. government, a middle-class family with two children spends around $233,000 for each child by the time the child reaches the age of 18. Add in the costs of college, and the figure comes to more than $300,000 per child. And if you take into account the cost of care provided by families for their children, the total costs of caring for children are at least twice as high as the government estimates (Folbre, 2012; Lino et al., 2017).

The most commonly cited reasons for having children are psychological. Parents expect to derive pleasure from helping their children grow, fulfillment from their children's accomplishments, satisfaction from seeing them become successful, and enjoyment from forging a close bond with them. For some there may also be a self-serving element in the decision, focusing on the hope that their children will provide for them in their old age, maintain a family business or farm, or offer companionship. Others have children because of a strong societal norm: More than 90 percent of married couples have at least one child.

In some cases children are unplanned, the result of the failure or absence of birth control. If the couple had planned to have children in the future, the pregnancy may be welcome. But in families that had actively not wanted children, or already had "enough" children, the pregnancy can be problematic (Leathers & Kelley, 2000; Pajulo, Helenius, & MaYes, 2006).

The couples most likely to have unwanted pregnancies are often the most vulnerable—younger, poorer, and less educated couples. Fortunately, there has been a dramatic rise in the use and effectiveness of contraceptives, and the incidence of undesired pregnancies has declined in recent decades (Centers for Disease Control and Prevention [CDC], 2005; Villarosa, 2003).

For many young adults, the decision to have children is independent of marriage. Although overall most women (59 percent) are married when they have children, more than half of births to women in the United States younger than 30 now occur outside of marriage. The only demographic group for which this is not true is young adult women with a college education; they overwhelmingly still choose to be married before having children (DeParle & Tavernise, 2012).

FAMILY SIZE The availability of effective contraceptives has also dramatically decreased the number of children in the average American family. Almost 70 percent of Americans polled in the 1930s agreed that the ideal number of children was three or more, but by the 1990s the percentage had shrunk to less than 40 percent. Today, most families seek to have no more than two children—although most say that three or more is ideal if money is no object (see Figure 7-11) (Gallup Poll, 2004; Saad, 2011; Olson, DeFrain, & Skogrand, 2019).

Figure 7-11 Smaller Is Better

Continuing trends over the past 75 years, U.S. parents continue to prefer families with fewer children. What do you think is the ideal number of children for a family to have?

SOURCE: Based on Saad, L. (2011, June 30). Americans' preference for smaller families edges higher. Princeton, NJ: Gallup Poll.

Americans' Ideal Number of Children for a Family, 1936–2011

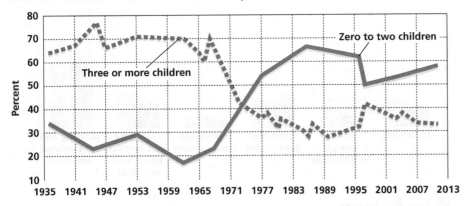

These preferences have been translated into changes in the actual birth rate. In 1957, the fertility rate reached a post–World War II peak in the United States of 3.7 children per woman and then began to decline. Today, the rate is at 1.9 children per woman, which is less than the replacement level, the number of children that one generation must produce to be able to replenish its numbers. In contrast, in some underdeveloped countries, the fertility rate is much higher—as high as 6.5 in Niger (World Bank, 2017).

What has produced this decline in the fertility rate? In addition to the availability of birth control, increasing numbers of women have joined the workforce. The pressures of simultaneously holding a job and raising children have convinced many women to have fewer children.

Furthermore, many women who are developing their careers choose to have children later. In fact, women between 30 and 34 are the only ones whose rate of births has actually increased over previous decades. Still, women who have their first child in their 30s do not have as many children as women who begin earlier. Also, research suggesting that there are health benefits for mothers who space their children apart may lead families to have fewer children (Marcus, 2004).

Financial considerations, particularly the increasing cost of college, may also act as a disincentive for bearing larger numbers of children. Finally, some couples doubt they will be good parents or simply don't want the work and responsibility involved in childrearing.

DUAL-EARNER COUPLES One of the major historical shifts affecting young adults began in the last half of the 20th century: a marked increase in the number of families in which both parents work. Close to three-quarters of married women with school-aged children are employed outside the home, and more than half of mothers with children younger than age 6 are working. In the mid-1960s, only 17 percent of mothers of 1-year-olds worked full-time; now, more than 50 percent do. In the majority of families, both husband and wife work (Barnett & Hyde, 2001; Matias et al., 2017).

For married couples who both work and have no children, the combined total of paid work (in the office) and unpaid work (the chores at home) is nearly identical, at 8 hours 11 minutes for men, and 8 hours 3 minutes for women. And even for those families who have children younger than 18, women who are employed full-time do only 20 minutes more of combined paid and unpaid work (Konigsberg, 2011).

On the other hand, the nature of husbands' contributions to the household often differs from that of wives. For instance, husbands tend to carry out chores such as mowing the lawn or doing house repairs that are more easily scheduled in advance (or sometimes postponed), and often can be carried out on the weekend. In contrast, women's household chores tend to be devoted to things that need immediate attention,

As increasing numbers of women have joined the workforce, more are choosing to have fewer children and to have them later.

Figure 7-12 Division of Labor

Although husbands and wives generally work at their paying jobs a similar number of hours each week, wives are apt to spend more time than their husbands doing home chores and in child-care activities. Why do you think this pattern exists?

SOURCE: U.S. Bureau of Labor Statistics, 2012.

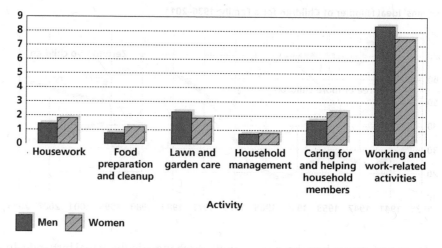

Note: Figures refer to average hours per day for persons who engaged in the activity.

such as child care and meal preparation, and often can't be scheduled on the weekend or put off. As a result, wives experience greater levels of anxiety and stress (U.S. Bureau of Labor Statistics, 2012; Ogolsky, Dennison, & Monk, 2014; see Figure 7-12).

THE TRANSITION TO PARENTHOOD: TWO'S A COUPLE, THREE'S A CROWD? Consider this quote from a spouse who just became a parent:

> We had no idea what we were getting into when our first child was born. We certainly prepared for the event, reading magazine articles and books and even attending a class on child care. But when Sheanna was actually born, the sheer enormity of the task of taking care of her, her presence at every moment of the day, and the awesome responsibility of raising another human being weighed on us like nothing we'd ever faced. Not that it was a burden. But it did make us look at the world with an entirely different perspective.

The arrival of a child alters virtually every aspect of family life. Spouses are suddenly placed in new roles—"mother" and "father"—which may overwhelm their older, continuing roles of "wife" and "husband." In addition, new parents face significant physical and psychological demands, including near-constant fatigue, new financial responsibilities, and an increase in household chores (Meijer & van den Wittenboer, 2007).

Furthermore, in contrast with cultures in which childrearing is regarded as a communal task, Western culture's emphasis on individualism leaves parents to forge their own paths after the birth of a child, often without community support (Rubin & Chung, 2006; Lamm & Keller, 2007).

The consequence is that many couples experience the lowest level of marital satisfaction of any point in their marriage. This is particularly true for women, who tend to be more dissatisfied than men with their marriages after the arrival of children. The most likely reason is that women often bear the brunt of childrearing, even if both parents seek to share these responsibilities (Laflamme, Pomerleau, & Malcuit, 2002; Lu, 2006).

Marital satisfaction does not decrease for all couples upon the birth of a child. According to work by John Gottman and colleagues, satisfaction can stay steady or even rise (Shapiro, Gottman, & Carrère, 2000; Gottman & Gottman, 2018).

Three factors permit couples to successfully weather the stress that follows the birth of a child:

- Working to build fondness and affection toward each other
- Remaining aware of events in each other's life, and responding to those events
- Considering problems as controllable and solvable

In addition, couples who are well satisfied with their marriages as newlyweds are more likely to be satisfied as they raise their children. Couples who harbor realistic expectations regarding the effort involved in childrearing also tend to be more satisfied after they become parents. Furthermore, parents who work together as a *coparenting team*, thoughtfully adopting common childrearing goals and strategies, are more apt to be satisfied with their parenting roles (Schoppe-Sullivan et al., 2006; McHale & Rotman, 2007).

In short, having children can lead to greater marital satisfaction for couples already satisfied with their marriage. For dissatisfied couples, having children may make a bad situation worse (Driver, Tabares, & Shapiro, 2003; Lawrence et al., 2008; Holland & McElwain, 2013).

GAY AND LESBIAN PARENTS   In increasing numbers, children are being raised in families with two moms or two dads. Some 20 percent of gay men and lesbian women are parents.

How do lesbian and gay households compare to heterosexual households? Studies of couples before children arrive show that, compared to heterosexual households, homosexual partners tend to divide labor more evenly and to more strongly hold the ideal of an egalitarian allocation of household work (Kurdek, 2003; Patterson, 2018).

However, the arrival of a child (usually through adoption or artificial insemination) changes the dynamics of household life considerably. As in heterosexual unions, role specialization develops. For instance, childrearing tends to fall more to one member of the couple, whereas the other spends more time in paid employment. Although both partners usually say they share household tasks and decision making equally, biological mothers are often more involved in child care (Fulcher et al., 2006; Goldberg, 2010b).

The evolution of homosexual couples when children arrive appears to be more similar to that of heterosexual couples than dissimilar, particularly in the increased role specialization occasioned by the requirements of child care. The experience for children of being in a household with two parents of the same sex is also similar. Most research suggests that children raised in households in which the parents are homosexual show no differences in terms of eventual adjustment from those raised in heterosexual households. Although they may face greater challenges from a society in which the roots of prejudice against homosexuality are deep, children who have two moms or two dads ultimately seem to fare well (Goldberg, 2010b; Weiner & Zinner, 2015; Farr, 2017).

Work: Choosing and Embarking on a Career

Why did I decide that I wanted to be a lawyer? The answer is embarrassing. When I got to my senior year of college, I began to worry about what I was going to do when I graduated. My parents kept asking what kind of work I was thinking about, and I felt the pressure rising with each call from home. At the time, there was some big trial in the news, and it got me thinking about what it might be like to be an attorney. I had always been fascinated by *Law and Order* when it had been on television. For these reasons, and just about none other, I decided to take the law boards and apply to law school.

Early adulthood is a period of decisions with lifelong implications. One of the most critical is the choice of a career path. This decision influences financial prosperity, of course, but also status, the sense of self-worth, and the contribution that a person will make in life. Decisions about work go to the core of a young adult's identity.

The Role of Work

LO 7.15   Explain Vaillant's stage of career consolidation, and identify the motivations—other than money—people have for seeking a job.

According to psychiatrist George Vaillant, the stage of development that young adults reach is called *career consolidation*. During **career consolidation**, which begins between the ages of 20 and 40, young adults become centered on their careers.

career consolidation
a stage that is entered between the ages of 20 and 40, when young adults become centered on their careers

IDENTITY DURING YOUNG ADULTHOOD Vaillant based his conclusion on a comprehensive longitudinal study of male graduates of Harvard, begun when they were freshmen in the 1930s (Vaillant & Vaillant, 1990; Vaillant, 2003).

In their early 20s, the men tended to be influenced by their parents' authority. But in their late 20s and early 30s, they started to act with greater autonomy. They married, had children, and began to focus on their careers—the period of career consolidation.

Vaillant draws a relatively uninspiring portrait of people in this stage. His participants worked hard as they climbed the corporate ladder. They tended to be rule followers conforming to the norms of their professions. Rather than showing the independence and questioning that they had displayed in college, they threw themselves unquestioningly into their work.

Vaillant argues that work plays such an important role that the career consolidation stage should be seen as an addition to Erikson's intimacy-versus-isolation stage of psychosocial identity. In Vaillant's view, career concerns supplant the focus on intimacy, and the career consolidation stage marks a bridge between intimacy-versus-isolation and generativity-versus-stagnation. (Generativity refers to an individual's contribution to society, as we discuss later.)

Reactions to Vaillant's viewpoint are mixed. Critics point out that Vaillant's sample, although relatively large, comprised a highly restricted, unusually bright group of men. Furthermore, societal norms have changed considerably since the 1930s, and people's views of the importance of work may have shifted. In addition, the lack of women in the sample and the fact that there have been major changes in the role of work in *women's* lives make Vaillant's conclusions even less generalizable.

Furthermore, research on what has been called the *millennial generation*—those born after 1980 and who entered young adulthood around the millennium in 2000—seem to have different views of work than earlier generations. They are much more likely to expect to change jobs multiple times; the idea of working for life for a single company is less attractive than to previous generations. They also have high (and sometimes unrealistic) expectations about how successful they will be, but don't necessarily feel that they will need to work hard to achieve that success. In fact, work-life balance is of considerable importance to millennials, who see employment as just one facet of a well-rounded life (Kuron et al., 2015; Deal & Levenson, 2016).

Still, whatever their attitudes about work, it is clear that employment plays an important role in young adults' lives and that it makes up a significant part of both men's and women's identity—if for no other reason than that many people spend more time working than they do on any other activity. We turn now to how people decide what careers to follow—and the implications of that decision.

extrinsic motivation
motivation that drives people to obtain tangible rewards, such as money and prestige

intrinsic motivation
motivation that causes people to work for their own enjoyment, for personal rewards

Extrinsic motivation drives people as a way of obtaining tangible rewards, such as money, prestige, or an expensive automobile. How might extrinsic motivation be illustrated in a less developed, non-Western culture?

WHY DO PEOPLE WORK? MORE THAN EARNING A LIVING Beyond forming an identity through work, young adults express many reasons—well outside of earning money—for seeking a job.

Intrinsic and Extrinsic Motivation Certainly, people work to obtain concrete rewards, or out of extrinsic motivation. **Extrinsic motivation** drives people to obtain tangible rewards, such as money and prestige (Becker et al., 2018).

But people also work for their own enjoyment, for personal rewards. This is known as **intrinsic motivation**. People in many Western societies tend to subscribe to the Puritan work ethic, the notion that work is important in and of itself. According to this view, working is a meaningful act that brings psychological well-being and satisfaction.

Work contributes to personal identity, as noted previously. Consider what people, at least in Western society, say about themselves when they first meet someone. After their name and where they live, they typically tell what they do for a living. What they do is a large part of who they are.

Work may also be central to people's social lives as a source of friends and activities. Work relationships can easily become personal friendships. In addition, work brings social obligations, such as dinner with the boss or the annual year-end party.

Finally, the kind of work people do helps to determine **status**, the evaluation by society of the role a person plays. Many jobs are associated with a particular status. For instance, traditionally physicians and college teachers are near the top of the status hierarchy, whereas ushers and shoe shiners occupy the bottom.

status
the evaluation of a role or person by other relevant members of a group or society

Satisfaction on the Job   Status affects job satisfaction: The higher the status of the job, the more satisfied people tend to be. Furthermore, the status of the job of the major wage-earner can affect the status of the other members of the family (Schieman, McBrier, & van Gundy, 2003).

Of course, status isn't everything: Worker satisfaction depends on a number of factors, not the least of which is the nature of the job itself. For example, some people who work at computers are monitored on a minute-by-minute basis; supervisors can consistently see how many keystrokes they are entering. In some firms in which workers use the telephone for sales or to take customer orders, conversations are monitored by supervisors. Workers' Web use and e-mail are also monitored or restricted by a large number of employers. Not surprisingly, such forms of job stress produce worker dissatisfaction (MacDonald, 2003).

Job satisfaction is higher when workers have input into the nature of their jobs and feel their ideas and opinions are valued. People also prefer jobs that offer variety over those that require only a few repeated skills. Finally, the more influence employees have over others, either directly as supervisors or more informally, the greater their job satisfaction (Peterson & Wilson, 2004; Thompson & Prottas, 2006; Carton & Aiello, 2009).

Picking an Occupation: Choosing Life's Work

LO 7.16   **Summarize Ginzberg's career choice theory, Holland's personality type theory, and how gender affects work choices.**

Some people know from childhood what they want to do for a living; for others, the choice of a career is a matter of chance. Many of us fall somewhere in the middle.

GINZBERG'S CAREER CHOICE THEORY   According to Eli Ginzberg (1972), people typically move through stages in choosing a career. The first stage is the **fantasy period**, which lasts until around age 11. During the fantasy period, people make and discard career choices without regard to skills, abilities, or available job opportunities. A child may decide she wants to be a rock star—despite being unable to carry a tune (Ginzberg, 1972; Multon, 2000).

During the **tentative period**, which spans adolescence, people begin to think more practically about the requirements of various jobs and their own abilities and interests. They also consider how well a particular occupation might satisfy their personal values and goals.

Finally, in early adulthood, people enter the **realistic period**, in which they explore specific career options either through actual experience on the job or through training for a profession. After initially exploring what they might do, people begin to narrow their choices and eventually commit to a particular career.

Critics have charged that Ginzberg's theory oversimplifies the process of choosing a career. Because it was based on subjects from middle socioeconomic levels, his theory may overstate the choices available to people in lower socioeconomic levels. Furthermore, the ages associated with the various stages may be too rigid. For instance, a person who begins to work immediately after high school most likely makes serious career decisions earlier than a person who attends college. In addition, economic factors cause many people to change careers at different points in their adult lives.

HOLLAND'S PERSONALITY TYPE THEORY   Other theories of career choice emphasize how personality affects career decisions. According to John Holland, certain

fantasy period
according to Ginzberg, the period, lasting until about age 11, when career choices are made, and discarded, without regard to skills, abilities, or available job opportunities

tentative period
the second stage of Ginzberg's theory, which spans adolescence, when people begin to think more practically about the requirements of various jobs and how their own abilities might fit with them

realistic period
the third stage of Ginzberg's theory, which occurs in early adulthood, when people begin to explore specific career options, either through actual experience on the job or through training for a profession, and then narrow their choices and make a commitment

According to one theory, people move through a series of life stages in choosing a career. The first stage is the fantasy period, which lasts until a person is around 11 years old.

personality types match particularly well with certain careers. If the correspondence between personality and career is good, people will enjoy their careers more and be more likely to stay in them; but if the match is poor, they will be unhappy and more likely to shift to other careers (Holland, 1997; Wilson & Hutchison, 2014).

According to Holland, six personality types are important in career choice:

- **Realistic.** These are down-to-earth, practical problem solvers, physically strong but with mediocre social skills. They make good farmers, laborers, and truck drivers.

- **Intellectual.** Intellectual types are oriented toward the theoretical and abstract. Although not particularly good with people, they are well suited to careers in math and science.

- **Social.** People with this personality type have strong verbal skills and are good with people. They make good salespersons, teachers, and counselors.

- **Conventional.** Conventional types prefer highly structured tasks. They make good clerks, secretaries, and bank tellers.

- **Enterprising.** These are risk-takers and take-charge types. They are good leaders and may be particularly effective as managers or politicians.

- **Artistic.** These individuals use art to express themselves and often prefer the world of art to interactions with people. They are best suited to occupations involving the arts.

Holland's theory suffers from a central flaw: Not everyone fits neatly into personality types. Furthermore, there are clear exceptions, with people holding jobs that are "wrong" for their personality type. Still, the basics of the theory have been validated, and they form the foundation of several of the "job quizzes" that people take to see what occupations they might be right for (Deng, Armstrong, & Rounds, 2007; Armstrong, Rounds, & Hubert, 2008; also see the *Development in Your Life* box.)

GENDER AND CAREER CHOICES: WOMEN'S WORK A generation ago, many women entering early adulthood assumed that they would become housewives. Even women who sought work outside the home were relegated to certain professions. Until the 1960s, employment ads in U.S. newspapers were almost always divided into two sections: "Help Wanted: Male" and "Help Wanted: Female." The men's ads included professions such as police officer, construction worker, and legal counsel; the women's ads were for secretaries, teachers, cashiers, and librarians.

Development in Your Life

Choosing a Career

One of the greatest challenges of early adulthood is making a decision that will have lifelong implications: the choice of a career. Although most people can be happy in a variety of jobs, choosing among the options can be daunting. Here are some guidelines for facing the career question.

- Systematically evaluate your choices. Online sites such as LinkedIn.com and monster.com contain a wealth of career information, and most colleges and universities have helpful career centers.

- Know yourself. Evaluate your strengths and weaknesses, perhaps by completing a questionnaire on your interests, skills, and values at a college career center.

- Create a "balance sheet" listing the gains and losses from a particular profession. First, list gains and losses for yourself and then for others, such as family members. Next, write down your projected self-approval

or self-disapproval from the potential career—and the projected social approval or disapproval you are likely to receive from others.

- "Try out" different careers through internships. By seeing a job firsthand, interns get a sense of what an occupation is truly like.

- Remember that there are no permanent mistakes. People today increasingly change careers in early adulthood and even beyond. No one should feel locked into a decision made previously in life. As we have seen throughout this book, people develop substantially over the course of their lives.

- It is reasonable to expect that shifting values, interests, abilities, and life circumstances might make a different career more appropriate later in life than the one chosen during early adulthood.

The breakdown of jobs reflected society's view of what the two genders were best suited for. Traditionally, women were considered most appropriate for **communal professions**, occupations associated with relationships, such as nursing. In contrast, men were perceived as best suited for agentic professions. **Agentic professions** are associated with getting things accomplished, such as carpentry. It is probably no coincidence that communal professions typically have lower status and pay than agentic professions (Trapnell & Paulhus, 2012; Wood & Eagly, 2015; Locke & Heller, 2017).

communal professions
occupations that are associated with relationships, such as nursing

agentic professions
occupations that are associated with getting things accomplished, such as carpentry

> **From a social worker's perspective:** How does the division of jobs into communal and agentic relate to traditional views of male–female differences?

Although discrimination based on gender is far less blatant today than it was several decades ago—it is now illegal, for instance, to advertise a position specifically for one gender—remnants of gender prejudice persist. Women are less likely to be found in traditionally male-dominated professions such as engineering and computer programming. In addition, as shown in Figure 7-13, despite significant progress in the past 40 years, women's earnings still lag behind those of men. Women earn an average of 82 cents for every dollar that men earn. Women who are members of certain minority groups are even worse off: Black women earn 63 cents for every dollar that white men earn. And women in many professions earn significantly less than men in identical jobs (Frome et al., 2006; U.S. Bureau of Labor Statistics, 2014, 2017).

More women are working outside the home than ever before. Between 1950 and 2010, the percentage of the female population (age 16 and older) in the U.S. labor force increased from 35 percent to close to 60 percent, and women today make up around 47 percent of the labor force. Almost all women expect to earn a living, and almost all do at some point in their lives. Furthermore, in 24 percent of U.S. households, women earn more than their husbands (U.S. Bureau of Labor Statistics, 2013; DeWolf, 2017).

Figure 7-13 The Gender-Wage Gap

Women's weekly earnings as a percentage of men's have increased since 1979 but are still only a bit more than 79 percent and have remained steady over the past three years.

SOURCE: U.S. Bureau of Labor Statistics, 2017.

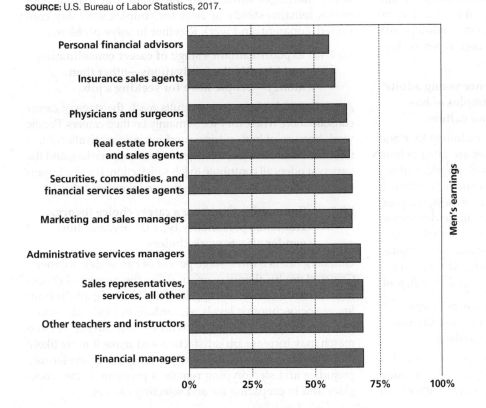

Opportunities for women have improved considerably. Women are more likely to be physicians, lawyers, insurance agents, and bus drivers than in the past. However, within job categories gender differences persist. For example, female bus drivers are more apt to have part-time school bus routes, whereas men hold better-paying, full-time routes in cities. Female pharmacists are more likely to work in hospitals, and men work in higher-paying jobs in retail stores (Paludi, Paludi, & DeSouza, 2011; Colella & King, 2018).

Women and minorities in high-status, visible professional roles often hit what has come to be called the *glass ceiling*. The glass ceiling is an invisible barrier in an organization that prevents individuals from being promoted beyond a certain level. It operates subtly, and often the people responsible for keeping the glass ceiling in place are unaware of how their actions perpetuate discrimination against women and minorities (Dobele, Rundle-Thiele, Kopanidis, 2014; Ben-Noam, 2018).

Review, Check, and Apply

Review

LO 7.9 Discuss the concept of emerging adulthood.

Emerging adulthood is a period between adolescence and adulthood that spans the third decade of life. Researchers and theorists increasingly believe that emerging adulthood is a distinct period.

LO 7.10 Explain how young adults respond to the need for intimacy and friendship and how liking turns to loving.

Young adults face Erikson's intimacy-versus-isolation stage, with those who resolve this conflict being able to develop intimate relationships with others.

LO 7.11 Differentiate the different kinds of love.

Passionate love is characterized by intense physiological arousal, intimacy, and caring, whereas companionate love is characterized by respect, admiration, and affection. Sternberg's triangular theory identifies three basic components (intimacy, passion, and decision/commitment), which can be combined to form different types of love through which a relationship can evolve.

LO 7.12 Identify the factors that influence young adults' choice of partner, and give examples of how these are affected by gender and culture.

Many factors go into choosing a spouse, including love and mutual attraction, which in some cultures are rated behind good health and maturity. Men tend to rate physical attractiveness in a partner more highly than women do. Women give high marks to ambition and industriousness in a partner. Evolutionary theories to account for these differences have been criticized. It may be that cross-cultural gender preferences reflect similar patterns of gender stereotyping. In general, the values applied to relationships by heterosexual, gay, and lesbian couples are more similar than different.

LO 7.13 Summarize the sorts of relationships people enter into in early adulthood, and identify the characteristics of a successful marriage.

Although most young adults say they plan to marry, a significant number of young couples today are choosing cohabitation, and others prefer living alone without an intimate partner. Success in marriage includes partners who visibly show affection and communicate relatively little negativity, perceive themselves as an interdependent couple instead of two independent individuals, share similar interests, and agree on role distribution.

LO 7.14 Identify the factors that influence a couple's decision to have children, and summarize the impact children have on a marriage.

The most common reasons for having children are psychological. Parents derive pleasure from helping their children grow, fulfillment from their accomplishments, and enjoyment from forging a close bond with them. The birth of a child alters almost every aspect of family life. Spouses find themselves in new roles, faced with increased physical and psychological demands, and new financial responsibilities. Many marriages suffer from the strain, but marital happiness remains steady or rises for couples who stay connected, coparent, and work together to solve problems.

LO 7.15 Explain Vaillant's stage of career consolidation, and identify the motivations—other than money—people have for seeking a job.

According to Vaillant, young adults reach the stage of career consolidation, where they focus mainly on their careers. People work because of both extrinsic and intrinsic motivational factors. The nature of a job, the degree of status it confers, and the variety it offers all contribute to job satisfaction. It's also important to workers to feel their ideas and opinions are valued.

LO 7.16 Summarize Ginzberg's career choice theory, Holland's personality type theory, and how gender affects work choices.

Ginzberg offers a three-stage period of career development. Critics claim his theory oversimplifies the process of choosing a career and may lack applicability to young adults from lower socioeconomic levels. According to Holland, certain personality types match well with certain careers. A close match may increase job satisfaction and make it more likely that a person will remain in the job long term. Gender-role prejudice and stereotyping remain a problem in the workplace and in preparing for and selecting careers.

Check Yourself

1. According to Erikson, adults spend their early adult years _____.
   a. consolidating careers
   b. developing their identities
   c. being industrious
   d. developing relationships with others

2. _____ love is the strong affection we have for those individuals with whom our lives are deeply involved.
   a. Passionate
   b. Consummate
   c. Intimate
   d. Companionate

3. When asked why they want to have children, most young adults cite _____ reasons.
   a. personal
   b. psychological
   c. financial
   d. societal

4. According to Vaillant, during young adulthood, individuals become centered on their careers. This stage is known as _____.
   a. career consolidation
   b. life comprehension
   c. professional attainment
   d. career comprehension

Applying Lifespan Development

If Vaillant's study were performed today on women, in what ways do you think the results would be similar to or different from those of the original study?

Chapter 7 Summary
Putting It All Together: Early Adulthood

PETRA TARKIF AND MO WRIGHT face many developmental issues typical of young adults. They have to consider the questions of health and aging, and the uncomfortable admission that they do not have all the time in the world. They have to look at their relationship and decide whether to marry. They have to face the questions they have about children and career. They have to reevaluate their wish to continue their education. Fortunately they have each other—and a considerable developmental arsenal of useful skills and abilities.

Javier Sanchez Mingorance/123RF

MODULE 7.1
PHYSICAL DEVELOPMENT IN EARLY ADULTHOOD

- Petra and Mo's bodies and senses are at their peak, with their physical development nearly complete. (p. 311)
- During this period, the couple will increasingly need to pay attention to diet and exercise. (pp. 312–313)
- Because they face so many important decisions, Petra and Mo are prime candidates for stress. (pp. 315-318)

MODULE 7.2
COGNITIVE DEVELOPMENT IN EARLY ADULTHOOD

- Petra and Mo are in Schaie's achieving stage, confronting major life issues, including career and marriage. (p. 321)
- They are able to apply postformal thought to the complex issues they face. (p. 320)
- Dealing with major life events, although causing stress, may also foster cognitive growth in both of them. (p. 322)
- Petra and Mo's idea about returning to college is not unusual today, when colleges are serving a diversity of students, including many older students. (pp. 324–326)

MODULE 7.3
SOCIAL AND PERSONALITY DEVELOPMENT IN EARLY ADULTHOOD

- Petra and Mo are at a time when love relationships and friendship are of major importance. (pp. 331–333)
- The couple are likely to be experiencing a combination of intimacy, passion, and decision/commitment. (pp. 334–336)
- Petra and Mo have been cohabiting and are now exploring marriage as a relationship option. (pp. 339–342)
- Petra and Mo are not unusual in deciding about marriage and children— decisions with major implications for the relationship. (pp. 342–345)
- The couple must also decide how to handle the possible shift from two jobs to one, at least temporarily— a decision that is far more than financial. (pp. 342–344)

What would a HEALTH-CARE PROVIDER do?

Given that Petra and Mo are young, in good health, and physically fit, what strategies would you advise them to pursue to stay that way?

Photodisc/Getty Images

What would YOU do?

If you were a friend of Petra and Mo, what factors would you advise them to consider as they contemplate moving from cohabitation to marriage? Would your advice be the same if only Petra or Mo asked you?

Laurence Mouton/PhotoAlto Agency RF Collections/Getty Images

What would a CAREER COUNSELOR do?

Assuming Petra and Mo decide to have children, what advice would you give them about handling the major expenses they face and the impact of children on their careers? Would you advise one of them to put his or her career on hold and pursue childrearing full-time? If so, how would you counsel them to decide which career should be put on hold?

Sheer Photo, Inc/ Stockbyte/Getty Images

What would an EDUCATOR do?

A friend of Mo's has told him that he might "feel like an old man" if he pursues management training or business school such a long time after getting his undergraduate degree. Do you agree? Would you advise Mo to pursue his studies right away, before he gets too old, or to wait until his life settles down?

Mel Yates/Cultura/Getty Images

Chapter 8
Middle Adulthood

Aleksandar Tomic/123RF

Terri Donovan, 50, raised five kids while working full-time as an urban planner for the city of New York. "It was not a cushy job," Terri says. "I raced about the city all day, and there were meetings almost every night. Zoning Board. Planning Board." Terri did her share of parenting, too. "I never missed a school play or band concert. I read the bedtime stories most nights. And we did everything together on the weekends, even the laundry." Sometimes she felt she would "go nuts." Yet, when her youngest child left home last year, she wandered around for 3 months, thinking, "What next?"

It was Brian who helped her figure out the answer. He booked a trip to Italy, their first real vacation in more than a decade. "We went sightseeing and ate fabulous leisurely meals, but most of all we focused on being together." Back home, she and Brian scheduled a weekly date night. "We finally have time for sex and long walks," she says. Terri also started helping out one night a week at the local soup kitchen.

The biggest change came when Terri decided to quit her job. "I wanted to help the people in my community," she says. Now, she's running for a seat in the state legislature. And her oldest daughter is pregnant. "When my kids left home, I realized they'd been the center of my life," Terri says. "So I'm looking forward to my grandchild—as long as my daughter and her family don't move in."

Middle adulthood is a time of significant transitions. Grown children leave home. People change the way they view their career. Sometimes, they change careers entirely as Terri did. Marriages undergo reevaluation. Often, couples find this a period of strengthened ties, as the "empty nest" leaves them free for uninterrupted intimacy. But sometimes they divorce. Middle age is also a period of deepening roots. Family and friends ascend in importance as career ambitions begin to take a backseat. And there is more time for leisure activities.

In this chapter, we first look at the physical changes of middle adulthood and how people cope with them. Then, we consider sexuality and menopause and debate the use of hormone replacement drugs for women. We also look at health issues that become of increasing concern in midlife.

Next, we consider the changing intellectual abilities of middle-aged adults, and ask the question: Does intelligence decline over time? We investigate various types of intelligence and look at how each is affected by the aging process. We also look at memory. Finally, we look at social development and examine what changes and what remains stable over time in an adult's personality. We consider the evidence for the so-called midlife crisis and discuss how family relationships change. We end by examining how people are spending their increased leisure time in middle age.

Module 8.1 *Physical Development* in Middle Adulthood

LO 8.1   Describe the physical changes that affect people in middle adulthood.
LO 8.2   Analyze the changing nature of sexuality in middle adulthood.
LO 8.3   Describe the health of the average person in middle adulthood.
LO 8.4   Describe risk factors and preventive measures for heart disease and cancer in middle adulthood.

Module 8.2 *Cognitive Development* in Middle Adulthood

LO 8.5   Analyze changes in the nature and use of intelligence in middle adulthood.
LO 8.6   Describe how aging affects memory and how memory can be improved.

Module 8.3 *Social and Personality Development* in Middle Adulthood

LO 8.7   Explain varied perspectives on personality development during middle adulthood.
LO 8.8   Analyze whether personality is stable or changes over the life span.
LO 8.9   Describe typical patterns of marriage and divorce in middle adulthood.
LO 8.10 Analyze the effects and significance of changes in family patterns in middle adulthood.
LO 8.11 Describe causes and characteristics of family violence in the United States.
LO 8.12 Describe the benefits and challenges of work life in middle adulthood.
LO 8.13 Describe how people experience leisure time in middle adulthood.

Module 8.1

Physical Development in Middle Adulthood

Fighting Against Time

Since she began racing 4 years ago, Deborah Thelonius has won around a dozen long-distance competitions, including a 26-mile marathon. Her specialty is high-altitude running, and she holds the record at the Pike's Peak Marathon, where she had to climb 20 miles to a height of more than 14,000 feet above sea level.

Thelonius is 48.

But her running hasn't come without a price. She trains 6 days a week, and the arthritis in her knees create a lot of pain. But she's *not about to give up running. As she says, "It brings me a kind of satisfaction that I can't get from anything else. I'm going to keep at it as long as my body holds out."*

Thelonius's success at high-altitude running is indicative of a revolution that is occurring in terms of the physical activity of people in middle adulthood. People reaching the midcentury mark are joining health clubs in record numbers, seeking to maintain their health and agility as they age.

It is in middle adulthood, roughly the period from age 40 to 65, that people often first notice and feel the effects of aging. Their bodies and, to some extent, their cognitive abilities begin to change in unwelcome ways. Looking at the physical, cognitive, and social changes of midlife, however, we see this is also a time when many people reach the height of their capabilities, when they are engaged in shaping their lives as never before.

We begin the module by considering physical development. We consider changes in height, weight, and strength, and discuss the subtle declines in various senses.

We also look at sexuality in middle adulthood. We examine the effects of change in hormone production for both men and women—particularly, menopause—and the various therapies available to ease this transition. We consider, too, the role attitude plays.

We then examine both health and illness in midlife. We consider the impact of stress and pay special attention to two major health problems—heart disease and cancer.

Physical Development and Sexuality

Soon after turning 40, Sharon Boker-Tov noticed that it took longer to bounce back from minor illnesses such as colds and the flu. Then she noticed changes in her eyesight: She needed more light to read fine print, and she had to adjust how far she held newspapers from her face to read them easily. Finally, she couldn't deny that the gray strands in her hair, which had first appeared in her late 20s, were becoming a virtual forest.

Physical Transitions: The Gradual Change in the Body's Capabilities

LO 8.1 Describe the physical changes that affect people in middle adulthood.

In middle adulthood, people become aware of the gradual changes in their bodies that aging brings. Some of these changes are the result of senescence, or naturally occurring declines. Other changes, however, are related to lifestyle choices, such as diet, exercise, smoking, and alcohol or drug use. As we'll see, lifestyle choices can have a major impact on people's physical, and even cognitive, fitness in midlife.

Although physical changes occur throughout life, these changes take on new significance in midlife, particularly in Western cultures that highly value a youthful appearance. The psychological significance of aging may far exceed the relatively minor and gradual changes a person experiences. Sharon Boker-Tov had gray hairs in her 20s, but in her 40s they multiplied to an extent she could not ignore. She was no longer young.

People's emotional reactions to midlife's physical changes depend in part on their self-concepts. When self-image is tied closely to one's physical attributes—as it often is for those who are athletic or are physically quite attractive—middle adulthood can be particularly difficult. The changes the mirror reveals signal aging and mortality as well as a loss of physical attractiveness. Those middle-aged adults, however, whose views of themselves are not so closely tied to physical attributes generally report no less satisfaction with their body images than younger adults (Hillman, 2012; Murray & Lewis, 2014).

Physical appearance often plays an especially significant role in how women see themselves. This is particularly true in Western cultures, where women face strong societal pressures to retain a youthful look. Society applies a double standard to men and women regarding appearance: Older women tend to be viewed in unflattering terms, whereas older men are frequently seen as attractively "mature" (Andreoni & Petrie, 2008; Pruis & Janowsky, 2010; Hofmeier et al., 2017).

HEIGHT, WEIGHT, AND STRENGTH: THE BENCHMARKS OF CHANGE Most people reach their maximum height in their 20s and remain close to that height until around age 55. People then begin a "settling" process in which the bones attached to the spinal column become less dense. Although the loss of height is slow, women average a 2-inch decline and men a 1-inch decline over the rest of the life span (Bennani et al., 2009).

Women are more prone to this decline because they are at greater risk of osteoporosis. **Osteoporosis**, a condition in which the bones become brittle, fragile, and thin, is often caused by a lack of calcium in the diet. Although it has a genetic component,

osteoporosis
a condition in which the bones become brittle, fragile, and thin, often brought about by a lack of calcium in the diet

osteoporosis is one aspect of aging that can be affected by lifestyle choices. Women—and men—can reduce the risk of osteoporosis by eating a calcium-rich diet (calcium is found in milk, yogurt, cheese, and some leafy greens) and by exercising regularly (Rizzoli, Abraham, & Brandi, 2014; Peng et al., 2016; Migliaccio et al., 2018).

Body fat tends to increase in middle adulthood. Even those who have always been slim may begin to gain weight. Because height is not increasing, and actually may be declining, these gains increase the incidence of obesity. This weight gain can often be avoided. Lifestyle choices play a major role. People who exercise regularly tend to avoid obesity, as do those who live in cultures where life is more active than it is in many Western cultures.

Declines in strength accompany height and weight changes. Strength gradually decreases, particularly in the back and leg muscles. By age 60, people average a 10 percent loss of their maximum strength. Still, such a loss is relatively minor, and most people are easily able to compensate for it. Again, lifestyle choices matter. Regular exercise tends to make people feel stronger and more able to compensate for any losses.

THE SENSES: THE SIGHTS AND SOUNDS OF MIDDLE AGE The vision changes Sharon Boker-Tov experienced are so common that reading glasses and bifocals have become a stereotypical emblem of middle age. Like Sharon, most people notice changes in the sensitivity not only of their eyes but also of other sense organs. All the organs seem to shift at about the same rate, but the changes are particularly marked in vision and hearing.

Vision Starting at around age 40, *visual acuity*—the ability to discern fine spatial detail in both close and distant objects—begins to decline. The shape of the eye's lens changes and its elasticity deteriorates, which makes it harder to focus images sharply onto the retina. The lens becomes less transparent, so less light passes through the eye (Yan, Li, & Liao, 2010).

A nearly universal change in midlife is the loss of near vision, called **presbyopia**. Even people who have never needed glasses or contact lenses find themselves holding print at an increasing distance to bring it into focus. Eventually, they need reading glasses. For those who were already nearsighted, presbyopia may require bifocals or two sets of glasses (Koopmans & Kooijman, 2006; Kemper, 2012; Donaldson et al., 2017).

Midlife brings other vision changes. Depth perception, distance perception, and the ability to see in three dimensions all decline. The loss of rods (a kind of receptor cell in the eye) and a decrease in lens transparency also impairs people's ability to adapt to darkness, making it more difficult to navigate a dark room and to drive at night (Andrews, d'Avossa, & Sapir, 2017).

Although normal aging brings changes in vision, in some cases disease is involved. One of the most frequent eye problems is glaucoma, which may, if left untreated, lead to blindness. **Glaucoma** occurs when pressure in the fluid of the eye increases, either because the fluid cannot drain properly or because too much is produced. Around 1 to 2 percent of people older than age 40 are afflicted, and African Americans are particularly susceptible.

Initially, the increased pressure may constrict the neurons involved in peripheral vision and lead to tunnel vision. Ultimately, the pressure can become so high that all nerve cells are constricted, which causes complete blindness. Fortunately, with early detection, glaucoma can be treated. Medication can reduce the pressure, as can surgery to restore normal drainage of eye fluid (Lambiase et al., 2009; Jindal, 2013; Sentis et al., 2016).

Hearing Hearing declines in acuity in midlife, though the changes tend to be less evident than those affecting vision.

Environmental factors cause some of the hearing losses. People who work near loud noises—such as airplane mechanics and construction workers—are more apt to suffer debilitating and permanent hearing loss.

Many changes are simply related to aging. Age brings a loss of *cilia*, or hair cells, in the inner ear, which transmit neural messages to the brain when vibrations bend them. Like the lens of the eye, the eardrum becomes less elastic with age, reducing sensitivity to sound (Wiley et al., 2005; Knight, Wigham, & Nigam, 2017; National Institute on Deafness and Other Communication Disorders, 2018).

presbyopia
a nearly universal change in eyesight during middle adulthood that results in some loss of near vision

glaucoma
a condition in which pressure in the fluid of the eye increases, either because the fluid cannot drain properly or because too much fluid is produced

Beginning around age 40, visual acuity, the ability to discern fine spatial detail, begins to drop. Most people begin to suffer from presbyopia, a decline in near vision.

Fuse/Corbis/Getty Images

The ability to hear high-pitched, high-frequency sounds usually declines first, a problem called **presbycusis**. Men are more prone to hearing loss than women, starting at around age 55 (Veras & Mattos, 2007; Gopinath et al., 2012; Koike, 2014).

Declines in hearing do not markedly affect most people in middle age. Many compensate for any losses relatively easily—by asking people to speak up, turning up the volume of a television set, or paying closer attention to what others are saying.

Reaction Time   One common concern is that people slow down once they reach middle adulthood. Such a worry is not valid in most cases. Reaction time does increase (i.e., it takes longer to react to a stimulus), but usually the increase is mild and hardly noticeable. For instance, reaction time in responding to a loud noise increases by about 20 percent from age 20 to 60. Tasks requiring the coordination of various skills—such as driving a car—show less of an increase. Still, it takes more time to move the foot from the gas pedal to the brake when a driver faces an emergency situation. Changes in the speed at which the nervous system processes nerve impulses increase reaction time (Roggeveen, Prime, & Ward, 2007; Godefroy et al., 2010).

Despite increased reaction time, middle-aged drivers have fewer accidents than younger ones, partly because they tend to be more careful and take fewer risks. Moreover, older drivers' greater experience benefits them. The minor slowing of reaction time is compensated by their expertise (Cantin et al., 2009; Endrass, Schreiber, & Kathmann, 2012; Meador, Boyd, & Loring, 2017).

Lifestyle choices can retard the slowing down process. An active exercise program counteracts the effects of aging, improving health, muscle strength, and endurance (see Figure 8-1).

presbycusis
loss of the ability to hear sounds of high frequency

Figure 8-1 The Benefits of Exercise

There are many benefits from maintaining a high level of physical activity throughout life.

SOURCE: DiGiovanna, 1994.

The Advantages of Exercise

Muscle System

Slower decline in energy molecules, muscle cell thickness, number of muscle cells, muscle thickness, muscle mass, muscle strength, blood supply, speed of movement, stamina

Slower increase in fat and fibers, reaction time, recovery time, development of muscle soreness

Nervous System

Slower decline in processing impulses by the central nervous system

Slower increase in variations in speed of motor neuron impulses

Circulatory System

Maintenance of lower levels of LDLs and higher HDL/cholesterol and HDL/LDL ratios

Decreased risk of high blood pressure, atherosclerosis, heart attack, stroke

Skeletal System

Slower decline in bone minerals

Decreased risk of fractures and osteoporosis

Psychological Benefits

Enhanced mood

Feelings of well-being

Reduces stress

Sexuality in Middle Adulthood: The True, the False, and the Controversial

LO 8.2 **Analyze the changing nature of sexuality in middle adulthood.**

> At age 51, Elaine was really looking forward to her postmenopausal life. Her youngest child had just left home to study art, and she had recently reduced her work schedule to a comfortable 30 hours a week. She envisioned the year to come as an opportunity for a "second honeymoon" with her husband, Greg, with no need for contraceptives or fears of becoming pregnant.

> Her imagined honeymoon quickly evaporated in a heat wave of hot flashes and night sweats. Though Elaine recognized these as normal symptoms of menopause, she was having to change her clothing three or more times a day. And she was having more headaches. Her doctor prescribed hormone therapy to replace the estrogen she was losing through menopause. The drugs eased her symptoms. Four months later, she and Greg booked a month's getaway in Greece.

Although interest in sex remains high for many people in middle adulthood, as Elaine's story illustrates, the physical changes associated with aging, such as menopause for women, can throw a curve ball at romance. We will look at some of the factors that affect men's and women's sexuality in midlife and the roles both attitude and prescription drugs can play in alleviating some of the problems commonly associated with this life stage.

THE ONGOING SEXUALITY OF MIDDLE AGE The frequency of sexual intercourse declines with age (see Figure 8-2), but sexual pleasure remains a vital part of most middle-aged adults' lives. About half of men and women age 45 to 59 report having sexual intercourse once a week or more. Close to three-quarters of men and more than half of women age 50 to 59 report masturbating. Half of men age 50 to 59 and a third of women in that age group have received oral sex from a different-sex partner in the past year. Similarly, sex remains an important activity for gay and lesbian couples during middle adulthood (Herbenick et al., 2010; Koh & Sewell, 2015; Paine, Umberson, & Reczek, 2018).

For many, midlife brings a sexual enjoyment and freedom that were missing previously. With their children grown and away from home, married couples have more time for uninterrupted sex. Women who have gone through menopause no longer fear pregnancy or need to use birth control (DeLamater, 2012).

Both men and women may face challenges to their sexuality in midlife. A man often needs more time to achieve an erection, and it takes longer after an orgasm to have another. The volume of fluid that is ejaculated declines, as does the production of *testosterone*, the male sex hormone (Hyde & Delameter, 2017; Yarber & Sayad, 2019).

For women, the vaginal walls thin and grow less elastic. The vagina begins to shrink and its entrance becomes compressed, which can make intercourse painful. For most women, though, the changes do not reduce sexual pleasure. Those women who do find intercourse less enjoyable can seek help from an increasing array of drugs, such as topical creams and testosterone patches, that are designed to increase sexual pleasure (Freedman & Ellison, 2004; Nappi & Polatti, 2009; Spring, 2015).

THE FEMALE CLIMACTERIC AND MENOPAUSE Women enter a period, around age 45, known as the climacteric that lasts for 15 to 20 years. The **female climacteric** marks the transition that ends the childbearing years.

The most notable sign of this transition is menopause. **Menopause** is the cessation of menstruation. Menstrual periods begin to occur irregularly and less frequently during a 2-year period starting at around age 47 or 48, although this may begin as

female climacteric
the period that marks the transition from being able to bear children to being unable to do so

menopause
the cessation of menstruation

Sexuality continues to be a vital part of most couples' lives in middle adulthood.

early as age 40 or as late as age 60. Menopause is completed when a woman passes a year without a menstrual period.

Menopause is important because it marks the end of a woman's natural fertility (although eggs implanted in a postmenopausal woman can produce a pregnancy). In addition, estrogen and progesterone levels—the female sex hormones—begin to drop (Schwenkhagen, 2007).

These changes in hormone production may produce a variety of symptoms, although this varies significantly for individuals. One of the most prevalent symptoms is "hot flashes," in which women experience a surge of heat above the waist. A woman may get red and begin to sweat when a hot flash occurs. Afterward, she may feel chilled. Some women have hot flashes several times a day; others, not at all.

During menopause, headaches, feelings of dizziness, heart palpitations, and aching joints are relatively common, though not universal. In one survey, only half of the women reported having hot flashes, and only about one-tenth of all women experience severe distress during menopause. Many women—perhaps as many as half—have no significant symptoms at all (Ishizuka, Kudo, & Tango, 2008; Strauss, 2013; Guérin, Goldfield, & Prud'homme, 2017).

For many women, menopause symptoms may begin a decade before menopause actually occurs. *Perimenopause* describes this period before menopause when hormone production begins to change. It is marked by sometimes radical fluctuations in hormone levels, resulting in some of the same symptoms found in menopause (Winterich, 2003; Shea, 2006; Shuster et al., 2010).

For some women, the symptoms of perimenopause and menopause are considerable. Treating these problems, though, can be challenging, as we consider next.

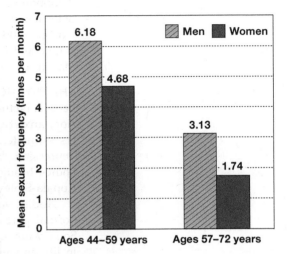

Figure 8-2 Frequency of Heterosexual Sexual Intercourse in Middle and Late Adulthood

SOURCE: Karraker, DeLamater, & Schwartz, 2011.

THE DILEMMA OF HORMONE THERAPY: NO EASY ANSWER

Sandra Kendrick was certain she was having a heart attack. She had been weeding her garden when suddenly she couldn't get enough air into her lungs. She felt as if she were on fire, becoming lightheaded and dizzy. A feeling of nausea came over her. She made it to the kitchen to call 911 and then fell to the floor. When the emergency team examined her, she was both relieved and embarrassed to learn that her symptoms indicated not a heart attack but her first hot flash.

A decade ago, physicians would have had a straightforward remedy for hot flashes and other uncomfortable symptoms caused by the onset of menopause: They would have prescribed regular doses of a hormone replacement drug.

For millions of women who experienced similar difficulties, it was a solution that worked. In *hormone therapy (HT)*, estrogen and progesterone are administered to alleviate the worst of the symptoms experienced by menopausal women. HT clearly reduces a variety of problems, such as hot flashes and loss of skin elasticity. In addition, HT may reduce coronary heart disease by changing the ratio of "good" cholesterol to "bad" cholesterol. HT also decreases the thinning of the bones related to osteoporosis, which, as we discussed, becomes a problem for many people in late adulthood (Lisabeth & Bushnell, 2012; Engler-Chiurazzi, Singh, & Simpkins, 2016; Braden et al., 2017).

Furthermore, some studies show that HT is associated with reduced risks of stroke and colon cancer. Estrogen may improve memory and cognitive performance in healthy women and reduce depression. Finally, increased estrogen may lead to a greater sex drive (Cumming et al., 2009; Garcia-Portilla, 2009; Lambrinoudaki & Pérez-López, 2013).

Although HT may sound like a cure-all, there are risks involved. For instance, it increases the risk of breast cancer and blood clots. Furthermore, some women taking a combination of estrogen and progesterone have been found to be at higher risk for stroke, pulmonary embolism, and heart disease. Increased risk of stroke and pulmonary embolism also has been found to be associated with estrogen-alone therapy. Consequently, some health-care providers believe that the risks of HT outweigh the benefits (Lobo, 2009; LaCroix et al., 2011).

The most recent thinking among medical experts is that it's not a simple all-or-nothing proposition; some women are simply better candidates for HT than others. Although HT seems to be less appropriate for older, postmenopausal women because of the increased risk of coronary heart disease and other health complications, younger women at the onset of menopause and who are experiencing severe symptoms might still benefit from the therapy, at least on a short-term basis (Lewis, 2009; Beck, 2012; Martin & Barbieri, 2018).

THE PSYCHOLOGICAL CONSEQUENCES OF MENOPAUSE Traditionally, many people, including experts, believed that menopause was linked directly to depression, anxiety, crying spells, lack of concentration, and irritability. Some researchers estimated that as many as 10 percent of menopausal women suffered severe depression. It was assumed that physiological changes in menopausal women's bodies brought about such disagreeable outcomes (Soares & Frey, 2010; Mauas, Kopala-Sibley, & Zuroff, 2014).

Today, most researchers take a different view, regarding menopause as a normal part of aging that does not, by itself, produce psychological symptoms. Some women do experience psychological difficulties, but they do so at other times in life as well (Freeman, Sammel, & Liu, 2004; Somerset et al., 2006; Wroolie & Holcomb, 2010).

Research shows that a woman's expectations can significantly affect her experience of menopause. Women who expect to have difficulties are more likely to attribute every physical symptom and emotional swing to menopause, whereas those with more positive attitudes are less apt to do so. A woman's attribution of physical symptoms, then, may affect her perception of menopause—and thus her actual experience of the period (Breheny & Stephens, 2003; Bauld & Brown, 2009; Strauss, 2011).

> **From the perspective of a health-care provider:** What cultural factors in the United States might contribute to a woman's negative experience of menopause? How?

THE MALE CLIMACTERIC Do men experience the equivalent of menopause? Not really. Lacking anything akin to menstruation, they cannot experience its discontinuation. But men do experience changes in midlife that are referred to as the male climacteric. The **male climacteric** is the period of physical changes in the reproductive system (which may be accompanied by psychological changes) that occurs late in midlife, typically in a man's 50s.

Because the changes are gradual, it is hard to pinpoint the exact period of the male climacteric. For instance, despite declines in testosterone levels and sperm count, men are able to father children throughout middle age. And it is no easier in men than in women to attribute psychological symptoms to subtle physiological changes.

One physical change that occurs frequently is enlargement of the *prostate gland*. By age 40, about 10 percent of men have enlarged prostates, and the percentage increases to half of all men by the age of 80. Enlargement of the prostate produces problems with urination, including difficulty starting urination or a need to urinate frequently at night.

Sexual problems also increase as men age. In particular, *erectile dysfunction*, in which men are unable to achieve or maintain an erection, becomes more common. Drugs such as Viagra®, Levitra®, and Cialis® often prove an effective treatment (Shamloul & Ghanem, 2013; Glina, Cohen, & Vieira, 2014; Wentzell, 2017).

male climacteric
the period of physical and psychological change relating to the male reproductive system that occurs during late middle age

Health

> It was a normal exercise session for Jerome Yanger. Up at 5:30 a.m., he climbed onto his exercise bike and began vigorously pedaling, hoping to meet, and exceed, his average speed of 14 miles per hour. Stationed in front of the television, he used the remote control to tune to the morning business news. Occasionally glancing up at the television, he began reading a report he had begun the night before, silently cursing at some of the poor sales figures he was seeing. By the time his half-hour of exercise was over, he had finished the report, signed a few letters his administrative assistant had typed for him, and left two voicemails for some colleagues.

Most of us would be ready for a nap after such a packed half hour. For Jerome Yanger, however, it was routine: He always tried to multitask, thinking it more efficient. Developmentalists might see it as symptomatic of a behavior style that puts Jerome at risk for coronary heart disease.

Although most people are healthy in middle adulthood, they also grow increasingly susceptible to many health problems. We will look at some typical midlife health issues, focusing on coronary heart disease and cancer.

Wellness and Illness: The Ups and Downs of Middle Adulthood

LO 8.3 Describe the health of the average person in middle adulthood.

Health concerns become increasingly important to people in middle age. Surveys asking what worries adults show health—as well as safety and money—to be an issue of concern. More than half of adults say they are either "afraid" or "very afraid" of having cancer (see Figure 8-3).

For most people, however, midlife is a period of health. According to census figures, the vast majority of middle-aged adults report no chronic health difficulties and face no limitations on their activities.

Figure 8-3 Worries of Adulthood

As people enter middle adulthood, financial, work, family, and health and safety concerns become increasingly important.

SOURCE: American Psychological Association, 2015, reprinted by permission.

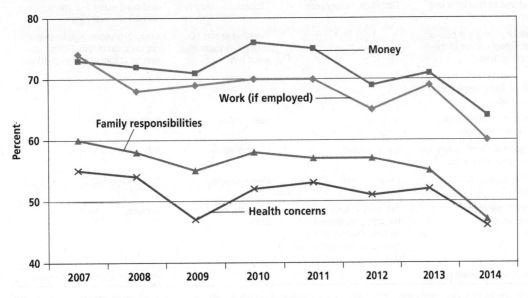

In fact, in some ways health is better in middle adulthood than in previous periods of life. People ages 45 to 65 are less likely than younger adults to experience infections, allergies, respiratory diseases, and digestive problems. They may contract fewer of these diseases now because they have already experienced them and built up immunities.

Certain chronic diseases do begin to appear in middle adulthood. Arthritis typically begins after age 40, and diabetes is most likely to occur between ages 50 and 60, particularly in those who are overweight. Hypertension (high blood pressure) is one of the most frequent chronic disorders. Often called the "silent killer" because it is symptomless, hypertension, if left untreated, greatly increases the risk of strokes and heart disease. For such reasons, health providers recommend that adults have a variety of preventive and diagnostic medical tests during middle adulthood (see Table 8-1).

The onset of chronic diseases in middle age boosts the death rate above that of prior periods. Still, death remains rare: Only 2 women and 3 men out of every 100 40-year-olds are expected to die before age 50, and 5 women and 7 men out of every 100 50-year-olds are expected to die before age 60. And the death rate for people between 40 and 60 has declined dramatically over the past 50 years. There also are cultural variations in health, as we consider in the *Cultural Dimensions* box (Social Security Administration, 2018).

Stress continues to have a significant impact on health, as it did in young adulthood, although the stressors may have changed. For example, parents may worry about their adolescent child's potential illicit drug use rather than whether their toddler is ready to give up his pacifier.

No matter what events trigger stress, the results are similar. *Psychoneuroimmunologists*, who study the relationship between the brain, the immune system, and psychological

Table 8-1 Adult Preventive Health-Care Screening Recommendations

These are general guidelines for healthy adults who have no symptoms of disease.

Screening	Description	Ages 40–49	Ages 50–59	Age 60+
Blood Pressure	Used to detect hypertension, which can lead to heart attack, stroke, or kidney disease.	Every 2 years.	Every 2 years.	Every 2 years; every year if family history of hypertension.
Cholesterol— Total/HDL	Used to detect high cholesterol levels, which increase risk of heart disease.	All adults should receive total cholesterol screening, HDL cholesterol, LDL cholesterol, and triglycerides AT LEAST ONCE. Cardiac risk factors and lipoprotein results will determine frequency of follow-up by your health-care provider.		
Eye Examination	Used to determine if glasses are required and to check for eye disease.	Every 2–4 years. Diabetics—every year.	Every 2–4 years. Diabetics—every year.	Every 2–4 years. At age 65 and over, every 1–2 years. Diabetics—every year.
Flexible Sigmoidoscopy or Double Contrast Barium Enema or Colonoscopy	A procedure using a scope or X-ray to detect cancer of the colon and rectum.	—	Baseline at age 50. Every 3–5 years after initial test.	Every 3–5 years. Age to stop depends on health. Follow-up normal colonoscopy in 8–10 yrs.
Fecal Occult Blood Screening	Detects unseen blood in stool, which is an early warning sign for colon cancer.	—	Every year.	Every year.
Rectal Exam (Digital)	Examination of prostate or ovaries to detect cancer.	—	Every year.	Every year.
Urinalysis Screening	Examination to detect presence of excess protein in urine.	Every 5 years.	Every 5 years.	Every 3–5 years.
Immunizations (Shots) Tetanus	Protection against infection after injury.	Every 10 years.	Every 10 years.	Every 10 years.
Influenza (Flu)	Protection against the influenza virus.	Any person with chronic medical conditions such as heart disease, lung diseases, kidney disease, diabetes.	Annually, age 50 and older.	Annually, age 65 and older.
Pneumococcal	Protection against pneumonia.			At age 65, then every 6 years.

Note: Additional guidelines specific to women include breast exams, mammograms, pap smears, and pelvic exams; additional guidelines for men include prostate- specific antigen tests and testicular self-exams.

Cultural Dimensions

Individual Variation in Health: Socioeconomic Status and Gender Differences

Overall figures for the health of middle-aged adults mask vast individual differences. Although most people are healthy, some are beset by a variety of ailments. Genetics play a role. For instance, hypertension often runs in families.

Social and environmental factors also affect health. For example, the death rate for middle-aged African Americans in the United States is twice the rate for Caucasians. Why should this be true?

Socioeconomic status (SES) is a significant factor. For whites and blacks of the same SES level, the death rate for blacks is actually lower than for whites. Members of lower-income families, however, are more likely to experience a disabling illness, and at an earlier age. In fact, one study found that the gap in life expectancy between the richest 1 percent and poorest 1 percent was 14.6 years. As can be seen in Figure 8-4, the higher the income level, the longer the life expectancy for both men and women (Chetty et al., 2016; Link et al., 2017).

There are many reasons for this. People in lower-SES households are more apt to work in dangerous occupations, such as mining or construction work. Lower-income people also often have inferior health-care coverage. The crime rates and environmental pollutants are generally higher in lower-income neighborhoods. A higher incidence of accidents and health hazards, and thus a higher death rate, is linked to lower levels of income (Hendren, Humiston, & Fiscella, 2012; Börsch-supan et al., 2019).

Gender also makes a difference. Women's overall mortality rate is lower than men's—a trend that holds true from birth—but the incidence of illness among midlife women is higher than for men.

Women are more susceptible to minor, short-term illness and chronic but non-life-threatening diseases such as migraine headaches, whereas men are more susceptible to serious illnesses such as heart disease. Fewer women smoke than men, which reduces their risk for cancer and heart disease; women drink less alcohol than men, which lowers the incidence of cirrhosis of the liver and auto accidents; and they work at less dangerous jobs.

Another reason for the higher rate of illness in women may be that more medical research targets men and the disorders they suffer. The vast majority of medical research money goes to preventing life-threatening diseases faced mostly by men, rather than to chronic conditions such as heart disease that may cause disability and suffering, but not necessarily death. Typically, research on diseases that strike both men and women focuses on men as subjects rather than women. This bias is now being addressed in initiatives by the U.S. National Institutes of Health, but the historical pattern has been one of gender discrimination by a male-dominated research community (Vidaver et al., 2000; Liu & Dipietro-Mager, 2016).

Figure 8-4 Life Expectancy and Income

For both men and women, the higher the income level, the longer the life span.

SOURCE: Adapted from Chetty et al., 2016.

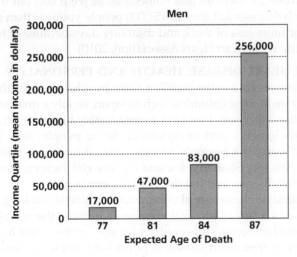

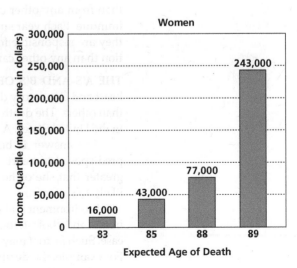

Figure 8-5 The Consequences of Stress

Stress produces three major consequences: direct physiological effects, harmful behaviors, and indirect health-related behaviors.

SOURCE: Adapted from Baum, 1994.

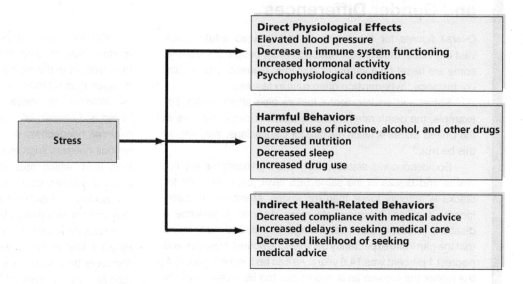

Direct Physiological Effects
Elevated blood pressure
Decrease in immune system functioning
Increased hormonal activity
Psychophysiological conditions

Harmful Behaviors
Increased use of nicotine, alcohol, and other drugs
Decreased nutrition
Decreased sleep
Increased drug use

Indirect Health-Related Behaviors
Decreased compliance with medical advice
Increased delays in seeking medical care
Decreased likelihood of seeking medical advice

factors, report that stress has three main consequences, summarized in Figure 8-5. First, stress has direct physiological effects, ranging from increased blood pressure and hormonal activity to decreased immune system response. Second, stress leads people to engage in unhealthy behaviors, such as cutting back on sleep, smoking, drinking, or taking other drugs. Finally, stress has indirect effects on health-related behavior. People under a lot of stress may be less likely to seek out good medical care, to exercise, or to comply with medical advice. All of these can lead to or affect serious health conditions, including heart disease (Emery, Anderson, & Goodwin, 2013; de Frias & Whyne, 2015; Whittaker, 2018).

Heart Disease and Cancer: The Big Worries of Middle Adulthood

LO 8.4   Describe risk factors and preventive measures for heart disease and cancer in middle adulthood.

More men die in middle age from diseases relating to the heart and circulatory system than from any other cause. Women are less vulnerable, as we'll see, but they are not immune. Each year such diseases kill around 151,000 people younger than age 65, and they are responsible for more loss of work and disability days because of hospitalization than any other cause (American Heart Association, 2010).

THE A'S AND B'S OF HEART DISEASE: HEALTH AND PERSONALITY   Although heart and circulatory diseases are a major problem, some people have a much lower risk than others. The death rate in some countries, such as Japan, is only a quarter of the rate in the United States. A few other countries have a considerably higher death rate. Why?

The answer is both genetics and environment. Some people seem genetically predisposed to heart disease. If a person's parents suffered from it, the likelihood is greater that she or he will too. Similarly, sex and age are risk factors: Men are more likely to suffer from heart disease, and the risk rises as people age.

Environment and lifestyle choices are also important. Cigarette smoking, a diet high in fats and cholesterol, and a lack of physical exercise all increase the risk of heart disease. Such factors may explain country-to-country variations in the rate of heart disease. For example, the death rate from heart disease in Japan is relatively low and may be as a result of differences in diet: The typical Japanese diet is much lower in fat than it is in the United States (Scarborough et al., 2012; Platt et al., 2014; Hirsch & Morlière, 2017).

Diet is not the only factor. Psychological factors—particularly how stress is perceived and experienced—appear to be related to heart disease. For instance, a set of personality characteristics, known as *Type A behavior pattern*, appears to be a factor in the development of coronary heart disease.

The Type A behavior pattern is characterized by competitiveness, impatience, and a tendency toward frustration and hostility. Type A people are extremely ambitious, and they engage in *polyphasic activities*—multiple activities carried out simultaneously. They are the true multitaskers whom you see talking on their phones while working on their laptop computers while riding the commuter train—and eating breakfast. Easily angered, they become both verbally and nonverbally hostile if prevented from reaching their goals.

In contrast, many people have virtually the opposite characteristics in what is known as the *Type B behavior pattern*. The Type B behavior pattern is characterized by noncompetitiveness, patience, and a lack of aggression. In contrast to Type A personalities, Type B personalities experience little sense of time urgency, and they are rarely hostile.

Type A and Type B behavior is significant because the distinction is related to the risk of coronary heart disease. Type A men have twice the rate of coronary heart disease, a greater number of fatal heart attacks, and five times as many heart problems as Type B men (Wielgosz & Nolan, 2000; Mohan & Singh, 2016).

In addition to being characterized as competitive, people with Type A personalities also tend to engage in polyphasic activities, or doing a number of things at once. Does a Type A personality deal with stress differently from a Type B personality?

It's important to note that some critics believe that the evidence for the existence of Type A and Type B behavior patterns is questionable. Moreover, some evidence suggests that only certain components of Type A behavior are most involved in producing disease and not the entire constellation of behaviors associated with the pattern. Specifically, it seems as if the hostility and anger components of Type A behavior are the central link to coronary heart disease (Eaker et al., 2004; Kahn, 2004; Myrtek, 2007).

Although the relationship between at least some Type A behaviors and heart disease is relatively clear, this does not mean that all middle-aged adults who can be characterized as Type A are destined to suffer from coronary heart disease. Other types of negative emotions besides the hostility found in Type A behavior have been linked to heart disease. For example, psychologist Johan Denollet has identified behavior he calls *Type D*—for "distressed"—that is linked to coronary heart disease. He believes that insecurity, anxiety, and having a negative outlook put people at risk for heart attacks (van den Tooren & Rutte, 2016; Lin et al., 2017; Bekendam et al., 2018).

THE THREAT OF CANCER Few diseases are as frightening as cancer, and many middle-aged adults view a cancer diagnosis as a death sentence. Although the reality is different—many forms of cancer respond well to medical treatment, and 40 percent of those diagnosed are still alive 5 years later—the disease raises many fears. And there is no denying that cancer is the second-leading cause of death in the United States (Xu et al., 2018).

The precise trigger for cancer is still not known, but the process by which it spreads is clear. Certain cells in the body begin to multiply rapidly and uncontrollably. As they increase in number, these cells form tumors. Unimpeded, they draw nutrients from healthy cells and body tissue. Eventually, they destroy the body's ability to function.

Like heart disease, cancer is associated with a variety of genetic and environmental risk factors. Some cancers have clear genetic components. For example, a family history of breast cancer—the most common cause of cancer death among women—raises the risk for a woman.

Several environmental and behavioral factors are also related to the risk of cancer. Poor nutrition, smoking, alcohol use, excessive exposure to sunlight, exposure to radiation, and particular occupational hazards (such as exposure to certain chemicals or asbestos) are all known to increase the chances of developing cancer.

After a diagnosis, several forms of treatment are possible, depending on the type of cancer. One treatment is *radiation therapy*, in which radiation targets the tumor in an attempt to destroy it. Patients undergoing *chemotherapy* ingest controlled doses of toxic substances meant to poison the tumor. Finally, surgery is used to remove the tumor (and often the surrounding tissue). The form of treatment is determined by how far the cancer has spread when it is first identified.

Because early detection improves a patient's chances, diagnostic techniques that help identify the first signs of cancer are of great importance. This is especially true in middle adulthood, when the risk of certain cancers increases.

Physicians urge women to do routine breast exams and men to regularly check their testicles for signs of cancer. Cancer of the prostate gland, the most common type of cancer in men, can be detected by routine rectal exams and by a blood test that identifies prostate-specific antigen (PSA).

Mammograms provide internal scans of women's breasts to help identify early-stage cancer. However, at what age women should begin to routinely have the procedure has been controversial, as we will see in the *From Research to Practice* box.)

From Research to Practice

Routine Mammograms: At What Age Should Women Start?

Statistically, the earlier breast cancer is diagnosed, the better a woman's chances of survival. But just how to accomplish early identification has produced some degree of contention in the medical field. In particular, controversy surrounds the age at which *mammograms*, a kind of weak X-ray used to examine breast tissue, should be routinely administered to women.

Mammograms are among the best means of detecting breast cancer in its earliest stages. The technique allows physicians to identify tumors while they are still very small. Patients have time for treatment before the tumor grows and spreads to other parts of the body. Mammograms have the potential for saving many lives, and nearly all medical professionals suggest that at some point during middle adulthood women should routinely obtain them.

But at what age should women start having annual mammograms? The risk of breast cancer begins to grow at around age 30, and then cancer becomes increasingly more likely. Ninety-five percent of new cases occur in women age 40 and older (Howlader et al., 2017).

———

———

The American Cancer Society guidelines suggest that women ages 40 to 44 should have the choice to start annual breast cancer mammogram screenings if they wish to do so. Between ages 45 and 54, it is recommended that they

have an annual mammogram. Women age 55 and older should switch to mammograms every 2 years, or they can have annual screenings if they wish. Finally, women should continue to have mammograms as long as they are in good health and expected to live 10 more years or longer (American Cancer Society, 2017; see Figure 8-6).

The American Cancer Society recommendation is controversial. For example, the American College of Radiology argues that women age 40 and above should receive annual screenings. They note that the 10-year risk of a 40-year-old woman is 1 in 69, and that 1 in 6 breast cancers occur in women 40 to 49 years of age (Kopans, 2017).

Ultimately, the determination of the timing of screenings is a highly personal one. Women should consult their health-care providers and discuss the latest research regarding the frequency of mammograms. For women who have a history of breast cancer in their families or a mutation in a gene called BRCA, the evidence is clear that mammograms starting at age 40 are beneficial (Grady, 2009; Winters et al., 2017).

Shared Writing Prompt:

Would your advice regarding the frequency of screening for breast cancer to a 40-year-old who was a family member differ from advice to a stranger? Why and how?

Figure 8-6

Age and the Risk of Breast Cancer. Starting around age 30, the risk of breast cancer increases, as these annual incidence figures show.

SOURCE: SEER, 2014.

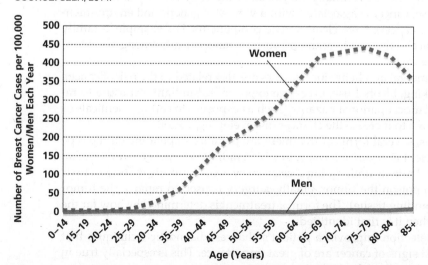

Review, Check, and Apply

Review

LO 8.1 **Describe the physical changes that affect people in middle adulthood.**

People in middle adulthood experience gradual changes in physical characteristics and appearance. Weight gain can be controlled through regular exercise and a healthy diet. The acuity of the senses, particularly vision, hearing, and speed of reaction, decline slightly during middle age.

LO 8.2 **Analyze the changing nature of sexuality in middle adulthood.**

Sexuality in middle adulthood changes slightly, but couples, freed from childbearing and parenting, can enjoy a new level of intimacy and pleasure. Physical changes affecting sexuality occur in both genders. Both the female climacteric, which includes menopause, and the male climacteric seem to have physical and perhaps psychological symptoms.

LO 8.3 **Describe the health of the average person in middle adulthood.**

In general, middle adulthood is a period of good health, although susceptibility to chronic diseases, such as arthritis, diabetes, and hypertension, increases. Stress continues to have a significant impact on health in middle adulthood, causing direct physiological effects, unhealthy lifestyle choices, and indirect effects on health-related behavior.

LO 8.4 **Describe risk factors and preventive measures for heart disease and cancer in middle adulthood.**

Heart disease is a risk for middle-aged adults. Both genetic and environmental factors contribute to heart disease, including the Type A behavior pattern. The precise causes of cancer are still unknown, but the process by which it spreads is clear. Therapies such as radiation therapy, chemotherapy, and surgery can successfully treat cancer.

Check Yourself

1. A decline in the ability to hear high-pitched, high-frequency sounds is known as _____.

   a. glaucoma
   b. presbycusis
   c. osteoporosis
   d. presbyopia

2. The period of time that marks a woman's transition from being able to bear children to not being able to do so is known as the _____.

   a. midlife transition
   b. perimenopausal period
   c. female climacteric
   d. postpartum period

3. Which of the following is a direct physiological consequence of stress in middle adulthood?

   a. Drug use or abuse
   b. Failure to comply with medical advice
   c. Cutting back on sleep
   d. Decreased immune system response

4. Insecurity, extreme ambition, anxiety, and hostility put people at risk for heart attacks. This behavior is referred to as the _____ behavior pattern.

   a. Type A
   b. Jekyll and Hyde
   c. Type B
   d. hypertensive stress

Applying Lifespan Development

What social policies might be developed to lower the incidence of disabling illness among members of lower socioeconomic groups?

Module 8.2

Cognitive Development in Middle Adulthood

Taking the Challenge

Gina Madison has always loved a challenge. That's why she applied to be a contestant on the game show Jeopardy! *"Why should young people have all the fun?" she asks, laughing. I figure at age 46, I know a thing or two."* Jeopardy! *requires quick thinking and quick response time. Was Gina worried that despite her world experience and accumulated knowledge, she would be bested by contestants half her age? "Not really," she says. "My husband and I do crossword puzzles every morning at breakfast." Gina also reads a great deal. "Books about brain research are my favorites," she says. "They're discovering that you really can teach an 'old dog' new tricks."*

Gina, like many people in midlife, enjoys challenging her mind and keeping it sharp. She feels confident enough to take on people half her age in a contest of wits and quick response time. She knows she has something that younger contestants do not: decades of life experience and knowledge.

The second module of the chapter focuses on cognitive development in middle age. We look at the tricky question of whether intelligence declines during the period, and we consider the difficulty of answering the question fully. We also examine memory and how its capabilities change in middle adulthood.

Intelligence and Memory

> It began innocently enough. Forty-five-year-old Bina Clingman couldn't remember whether she had mailed the letter that her husband had given her, and she wondered, briefly, whether this was a sign of aging. The next day, the question recurred when she spent 20 minutes looking for a phone number she knew she had written down on a piece of paper—somewhere. By the time she found it, she was surprised and even a little anxious. "Am I losing my memory?" she asked herself, feeling both annoyance and a degree of concern.

Many people in their 40s feel more absentminded than they did 20 years previously, and they have some concern about becoming less mentally able as they age. Common wisdom suggests that people lose some mental sharpness in midlife. But how accurate is this notion?

Does Intelligence Decline in Adulthood?

LO 8.5   Analyze changes in the nature and use of intelligence in middle adulthood.

For years, experts provided an unwavering response when asked whether intelligence declined in adulthood: Intelligence peaks at age 18, stays fairly steady until the mid-20s, and then gradually declines until the end of life.

Today, developmentalists view questions about changes in intelligence across the life span as more complicated, and they have come to different, and more complex, conclusions.

THE DIFFICULTIES IN ANSWERING THE QUESTION   The conclusion that intelligence starts to diminish in the mid-20s was based on extensive research. *Cross-sectional studies*—which test people of different ages at the same point in time—clearly showed that older subjects were less likely to score well than younger subjects on traditional intelligence tests of the sort we discussed previously.

But consider the drawbacks of cross-sectional research—in particular, the possibility that it may suffer from *cohort effects*. Recall that cohort effects are influences associated with growing up at a particular historical time that affect persons of a particular age. For instance, suppose that compared to younger subjects, the older people in a cross-sectional study had had less adequate educations, less stimulating jobs, or were less healthy. In that case, the lower IQ scores of the older group could not be attributed solely, or perhaps even partially, to differences in intelligence based on age. Because they do not control for cohort effects, cross-sectional studies may well *underestimate* intelligence in older subjects.

To overcome the cohort problems of cross-sectional studies, developmentalists began to use *longitudinal studies*, in which the same people are studied periodically over a span of time. These studies revealed a different developmental pattern for intelligence: Adults tended to show stable and even increasing intelligence test scores until their mid-30s, and in some cases up to their 50s. Then the scores began to decline (Bayley & Oden, 1955).

But let's consider the drawbacks of longitudinal studies, too. People taking an intelligence test repeatedly may perform better because they become familiar—and comfortable—with the testing situation. Similarly, through repeated exposure to the same test, they may begin to remember some of the test items. Consequently, practice effects may account for the superior performance of people on longitudinal measures of intelligence as opposed to cross-sectional measures (Salthouse, 2009).

It is also difficult for researchers using longitudinal studies to keep their samples intact. Participants may move away, decide they no longer want to participate, or become ill and die. Over time, the participants who remain may represent a healthier, more stable, and more psychologically positive group of people than those who are no longer part of the sample. If this is the case, longitudinal studies may *overestimate* intelligence in older subjects.

CRYSTALLIZED AND FLUID INTELLIGENCE Drawing conclusions about age-related changes in intelligence is challenging. For instance, many IQ tests include sections based on physical performance, such as arranging a group of blocks. These sections are timed and scored on the basis of how quickly an item is completed. If older people take longer on physical tasks—recall that reaction time slows with age—then their poorer performance on IQ tests may result from physical rather than cognitive changes.

To complicate the issue further, many developmental theorists believe there are two kinds of intelligence: fluid intelligence and crystallized intelligence. As we noted previously, **fluid intelligence** reflects the ability to solve and reason about novel problems, relatively independent of past specific knowledge. A detective solving a crime uses fluid intelligence by pulling together separate clues and figuring out the motive. **Crystallized intelligence** is the information, skills, and strategies that people have accumulated through experience. It reflects the facts that we have learned. People solving a crossword puzzle are using crystallized intelligence because they are recalling specific words they have learned in the past.

The distinction between fluid and crystallized intelligence is important in answering the question of whether intelligence declines with age: Research has found that fluid intelligence declines with age, whereas crystallized intelligence holds steady and can actually improve (Deary, 2010; Ghisletta et al., 2012; Manard et al., 2015; see Figure 8-7).

If we look at more specific types of intelligence, other age-related differences and developments begin to show up. According to developmental psychologist K. Warner Schaie, who has conducted extensive longitudinal research on adult intellectual development, we should consider many types of ability, such as spatial orientation, numeric ability, verbal ability, and so on, rather than the broad divisions of crystallized and fluid intelligence (Schaie, Willis, & Pennak, 2005).

Examined this way, the question of how intelligence changes in adulthood yields yet another, more specific, answer. Schaie has found that certain abilities, such as inductive reasoning, spatial orientation, perceptual speed, and verbal memory, begin to decline

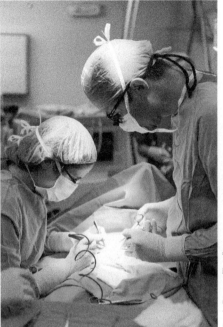

It is difficult to evaluate cognitive abilities in middle adulthood. Although some types of mental abilities may begin to decline, crystallized intelligence holds steady and actually may increase.

Frank Boston/Fotolia

fluid intelligence
reflects the ability to solve and reason about novel problems

crystallized intelligence
the accumulation of information, skills, and strategies that people have learned through experience and that they can apply in problem-solving situations

Figure 8-7 Changes in Crystalized and Fluid Intelligence

Although crystallized intelligence increases with age, fluid intelligence begins to decline in middle age. What are the implications for general competence in middle adulthood?

SOURCE: Schaie, 1994.

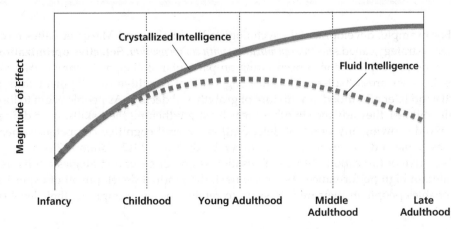

gradually at around age 25 and continue to do so through old age. Numeric and verbal abilities show a different pattern. Numeric ability tends to increase until the mid-40s, is lower at age 60, and then remains steady. Verbal ability rises until the start of middle adulthood, around age 40, then stays fairly steady (Schaie, Willis, & Pennak, 2005).

Why do these changes occur? One reason is that brain functioning begins to change in middle adulthood. For example, researchers have found that 20 genes that are vital to learning, memory, and mental flexibility begin to function less efficiently as early as age 40. Furthermore, as people age, the specific areas of their brains used to accomplish particular tasks change. For instance, older adults use both brain hemispheres for tasks that in younger people involve just one hemisphere (Fling et al., 2011; Phillips, 2011; Bielak et al., 2013).

REFRAMING THE ISSUE: WHAT IS THE SOURCE OF COMPETENCE DURING MIDDLE ADULTHOOD?   It is during midlife that people come to hold some of the most important and powerful positions in society, despite gradual declines in certain cognitive abilities. How do we explain such continuing, even growing, competence?

Psychologist Timothy Salthouse (1994, 2010) suggests there are four reasons why this discrepancy exists. First, it is possible that typical measures of cognitive skills tap a different type of cognition than what is required to be successful in certain occupations. Recall the discussion of practical intelligence, in which we found that traditional IQ tests fail to measure cognitive abilities that are related to occupational success. Perhaps we would find no discrepancy between intelligence and cognitive abilities in midlife if we used measures of practical intelligence rather than traditional IQ tests to assess intelligence.

A second factor also relates to the measurement of IQ and occupational success. It is possible that the most successful middle-aged adults are not representative of midlife adults in general. It may be that only a small proportion of people are highly successful, and the rest, who experience only moderate or little success, have changed occupations, retired, or become sick and died. Highly successful people, then, may be an unrepresentative sample.

Also, the degree of cognitive ability required for professional success may simply not be that high. According to this argument, people can succeed professionally and still be on the decline in certain cognitive abilities. In other words, they have brains to spare.

Finally, it may be that older people are successful because they have developed specific kinds of expertise and particular competencies. Whereas IQ tests measure reactions to novel situations, occupational success may be influenced by specific, well-practiced abilities. Consequently, middle-aged individuals may maintain and even expand the distinctive talents they need for professional accomplishment, despite a decline in overall intellectual skills. This explanation has generated research on expertise.

> **From the perspective of an educator:** How do you think the apparent discrepancy between declining IQ scores and continuing cognitive competence in middle adulthood would affect the learning ability of middle-aged adults who return to school?

selective optimization
the process by which people concentrate on particular skill areas to compensate for losses in other areas

For example, developmental psychologists Paul Baltes and Margaret Baltes have studied a strategy called *selective optimization with compensation.* **Selective optimization** is the process people use in concentrating on particular skill areas to compensate for losses in other areas. Baltes and Baltes suggest that cognitive development during middle and later adulthood is a mixture of growth and decline. As people begin to lose certain abilities, they advance in other areas by strengthening their skills. In so doing, they avoid showing any practical deterioration. Overall cognitive competence, then, remains stable and may even improve (Erber, 2010; Deary, 2012; Palmore, 2017).

Selective optimization with compensation is one of several strategies adults use to maintain high performance. As we see next, the gradual development of expertise also enables people in their middle years to retain, and even improve, their level of competence.

THE DEVELOPMENT OF EXPERTISE: SEPARATING EXPERTS FROM NOVICES If you were ill and needed a diagnosis, would you rather visit a young physician fresh out of medical school, or a more experienced, middle-aged physician?

If you chose the older physician, you probably assumed that he or she would have more expertise. **Expertise** is the skill or knowledge acquired in a particular area. More focused than broad intelligence, expertise develops as people devote attention and practice to a subject or skill and, in so doing, gain experience. For example, physicians become better at diagnosing the symptoms of a medical problem as they gain experience. A person who does a lot of cooking comes to know how a recipe will taste if certain modifications are made (Morita et al., 2008; Reuter et al., 2012, 2014).

What separates the experts from the less skilled? Whereas beginners use formal procedures and rules, often following them strictly, experts rely on experience and intuition, and they often bend the rules. Their experience allows them to process information automatically. Experts often have trouble articulating how they draw conclusions; their solutions just seem right to them—and *are* likely to be right. Brain imaging studies show that experts use different neural pathways than novices to solve problems (Grabner, Neubauer, & Stern, 2006).

Finally, experts develop better problem-solving strategies than non-experts, and they're more flexible in their approach. Experience provides them with alternative solutions to the same problem, increasing the probability of success (Arts, Gijselaers, & Boshuizen, 2006; McGugin & Tanaka, 2010; Hülür et al., 2018).

Not everyone develops an area of expertise in middle adulthood. Professional responsibilities, amount of leisure time, educational level, income, and marital status all affect the development of expertise.

Cognitive development during middle and later adulthood is a mixture of growth and decline. As people begin to lose certain abilities as a result of biological deterioration, they also advance in other areas by strengthening their skills.

expertise
the acquisition of skill or knowledge in a particular area

How Does Aging Affect Memory?

LO 8.6 **Describe how aging affects memory and how memory can be improved.**

Whenever Mary Donovan can't find her car keys, she mutters to herself that she is "losing her memory." Like Bina Clingman, who was worried about forgetting letters and phone numbers, Mary probably believes that memory loss is common in middle age. However, if she is a typical midlife adult, her assessment may not be accurate. Research shows that most people exhibit minimal or no memory loss. Because of societal stereotypes, however, people may attribute their absentmindedness to aging, even though they have been that way all their lives. It is the meaning they give to their forgetfulness that changes, rather than their actual ability to remember (Chasteen et al., 2005; Hoessler & Chasteen, 2008; Hess, Hinson, & Hodges, 2009).

TYPES OF MEMORY To understand the nature of memory changes, we must consider that memory is traditionally viewed as three sequential components: sensory memory, short-term memory (also called *working memory*), and long-term memory. *Sensory memory* is an initial, momentary storage of information. Information is recorded by the sensory system as a raw, meaningless stimulus. Next, information moves into *short-term memory*, which holds it for 15 to 25 seconds. If the information is rehearsed, it then moves into *long-term memory*, where it is stored on a relatively permanent basis.

Both sensory memory and short-term memory show virtually no weakening in middle age. Long-term memory, however, declines for some people. It appears this decline is not a fading or a complete loss of memory, but rather a less efficient registering and storing of information. Age also makes people less efficient at retrieving information. Even if the information was adequately stored in long-term memory, it may become more difficult to locate or isolate it (Salthouse, 2010, 2014).

Memory declines in middle age are relatively minor, and most can be compensated for by various cognitive strategies. Paying greater attention to material when it is first encountered can aid in its later recall. Your lost car keys may have more to do with your inattentiveness when you put them down than with a decline in memory.

Many middle adults find it hard to pay attention to certain things for some of the same reasons expertise develops. They are used to using memory shortcuts, *schemas*, to ease the burden of remembering the many things they experience each day.

schemas
organized bodies of information stored in memory

MEMORY SCHEMAS   To recall information, people often use **schemas**, organized bodies of information stored in memory. Schemas represent the way the world is organized, allowing people to categorize and interpret new information. For example, if we have a schema for eating in a restaurant, we don't regard a meal in a new restaurant as a completely new experience. We know we will be seated at a table or counter and offered a menu from which to select food. Our schema for eating out tells us how to treat the server, what sorts of food to eat first, and that we should leave a tip (Hebscher & Gilboa, 2016).

People hold schemas for individuals (such as the particular behavior patterns of one's mother, wife, or child) as well as for categories of people (mail carriers, lawyers, or professors) and behaviors or events (dining in a restaurant or visiting the dentist). People's schemas organize their behavior and help them to interpret social events. A person who knows the schema for visiting the doctor will not be surprised when he is asked to undress.

Schemas also convey cultural information. Consider an old Native American folktale in which the hero participates with several companions in a battle and is shot by an arrow. He feels no pain. When he returns home and tells the story, something black emerges from his mouth, and he dies the next morning.

This tale puzzles most Westerners. They are unschooled in the particular Native American culture the story comes from. However, to someone familiar with that culture, the story makes perfect sense: The hero feels no pain because his companions are ghosts, and the "black thing" coming from his mouth is his departing soul.

For a Native American, it may be easy to recall the story, because it makes sense in a way that it doesn't to members of other cultures. Material that fits into existing schemas is easier to recall than material that doesn't fit. For example, a person who usually puts her keys in her purse may lose them because she doesn't recall putting them on the counter. It's not the "usual place" (Fiske & Taylor, 1991; Tse & Altarriba, 2007; also see *Development in Your Life*).

mnemonics
formal strategies for organizing material in ways that make it more likely to be remembered

Development in Your Life

Effective Strategies for Remembering

We are all forgetful at times. However, there are techniques for more effective recall. **Mnemonics** (pronounced "nee-MON-iks") are formal strategies for organizing material in ways that make it easier to remember. Among the mnemonics that work are the following (Bloom & Lamkin, 2006; Morris & Fritz, 2006):

- **Get organized.** For people who have trouble recalling where they left their keys or remembering appointments, the simplest approach is to become more organized. Using a date book, hanging keys on a hook, or using Post-It notes can aid recall.

- **Pay attention.** You can improve your recall by paying close attention to new information, and purposefully thinking that you will need to recall it. For example, when you park your car at the mall, pay attention at the moment you park, and remind yourself that you really want to remember the location.

- **Use the encoding specificity phenomenon.** According to the encoding specificity phenomenon, people are most likely to recall information in environments that are similar to those in which they initially learned ("encoded") it. For instance, people are best able to recall information on a test if the test is held in the room in which they studied (Tulving, 2016).

- **Visualize.** Making mental images of ideas can help you recall them later. For example, if you want to remember that global warming may lead to rising oceans, think of yourself on a beach on a hot day, with the waves coming closer and closer to where you're sitting.

- **Rehearse.** Practice makes memory perfect, or if not perfect, at least better. By practicing or rehearsing what you wish to recall, you can substantially improve your memory.

Review, Check, and Apply

Review

LO 8.5   **Analyze changes in the nature and use of intelligence in middle adulthood.**

The question of whether intelligence declines in middle adulthood is complicated by limitations in cross-sectional studies and longitudinal studies. Intelligence appears to be divided into components, some of which decline, whereas others hold steady or even improve. In general, cognitive competence in middle adulthood holds fairly steady despite declines in some areas of intellectual functioning. Many people develop strategies to optimize their intellectual performance as they age, often concentrating on particular skill areas to make up for declines in other areas, a process called *selective optimization with compensation*. Expertise—the skill or knowledge acquired in a particular area—develops as people devote attention and practice to a subject or skill and, in so doing, gain experience.

LO 8.6   **Describe how aging affects memory and how memory can be improved.**

Memory may appear to decline in middle age, but, in fact, long-term memory deficits are probably as a result of ineffective strategies of storage and retrieval. People categorize and interpret new information according to the schemas they have developed about how the world is organized and operates. Mnemonics help people organize material in ways that improve recall. These formal strategies include getting organized, visualizing, rehearsing, paying attention, and using the encoding specificity phenomenon.

Check Yourself

1. According to _____ studies that test people of different ages at the same time, older subjects scored lower than younger subjects on traditional intelligence tests.

   a. longitudinal
   b. objective
   c. cross-sectional
   d. observational

2. Over the years, one of the types of intelligence that increases with age is _____ intelligence, or the accumulation of information, skills, and strategies that people have learned through experience.

   a. emotional
   b. crystallized
   c. intrapersonal
   d. naturalist

3. Middle-aged individuals find it hard to pay attention to everything that is going on around them and often rely on _____, or mental shortcuts, to reduce the stress of remembering so many things.

   a. schemas
   b. theory of mind
   c. naturalistic observation
   d. memory

4. _____ are formal strategies for organizing material in ways that make it more likely to be remembered.

   a. Mnemonics
   b. Schemas
   c. Perceptions
   d. Heuristics

Applying Lifespan Development

In what ways do schemas give midlife adults an edge over younger adults?

Module 8.3

Social and Personality Development in Middle Adulthood

All in the Family

Geoff Kelvin lives with his spouse, Juan; their adopted 6-year-old son, Paul; and Geoff's dad. When asked how midlife is treating him, Geoff, 48, laughs. "I'm in the middle, all right," he says. "The middle of a big, noisy, rich life I could not have imagined at 20." Geoff teaches fifth grade and loves it. "Working with kids, being a parent, it keeps you on your toes." Adopting Paul has also opened up his personality. "Growing up gay, I kept a bit of distance around me," he admits. "But having a kid puts you smack in the center of a social scene where everyone shares this big job called parenting. Now, I swap stories and share concerns with the other moms and dads."

Two years ago, Geoff's dad suffered a stroke that left him partly paralyzed. "We never got along that well. He wasn't too keen on his only son being gay," Geoff says. "But I said, 'You have to move in. There's no place else to go.'" The first months were bumpy, but then Juan quit his job at a drug research company—he was sick of office politics—to stay home and write articles about environmental issues.

The decision worked out well. "Juan was happier, and he had the patience to deal with my dad," Geoff says. "In fact, he changed my dad's views about gays and gay marriage. Now, we all get along, and my dad loves to joke that he lives in a 'real man cave.'"

The complex and changing patterns of Geoff and Juan's family life are not unusual: Few lives follow a set, predictable pattern through middle adulthood. In fact, one of the remarkable characteristics of middle age is its variety, as the paths that different people travel continue to diverge. In this module we focus on the personality and social development that occurs in midlife. We begin by examining the changes that typify this period. We also explore some of the controversies in developmental psychologists' understandings of midlife, including whether the midlife crisis, a phenomenon popularized in the media, is fact or fiction.

Next we consider the various familial ties that bind people together (or come unglued) in middle adulthood, including marriage, divorce, the empty nest, and grandparenting. We also look at a bleak, but prevalent, side of family relations: family violence.

Finally, the module examines work and leisure in midlife. We consider the changing role of work in people's lives and look at work-related problems, such as burnout and unemployment. The module concludes with a discussion of leisure time, which becomes more important during middle age.

Personality Development

> My 40th birthday was not an easy one. I did not wake up feeling different—that's never been the case. But during my 40th year, I did come to realize the finiteness of life. The die was cast. I understood that I probably wasn't going to be president of the United States—a secret ambition—or CEO of a major corporation. Time had become more of an adversary than an ally. But it was curious: My usual pattern of focusing on the future, planning each step, began to shift. I started appreciating what I had. I looked at my life and was pretty satisfied with some of my accomplishments. I began focusing on what was going right, not on what I was lacking. This didn't happen in a day; it took several years after turning 40 before I felt this way. Even now, it is hard to fully accept that I am middle-aged.

As this 47-year-old man suggests, realizing that one has reached midlife can be difficult. In many Western societies, age 40 undeniably marks one as middle-aged—at least in the public eye—and suggests that one is on the threshold of a "midlife crisis." How true this view is, as we'll see, depends on your perspective.

Perspectives on Adult Personality Development

LO 8.7 Explain varied perspectives on personality development during middle adulthood.

normative-crisis theories
the approach to personality development that is based on fairly universal stages tied to a sequence of age-related changes or crises

> Taryn Binder was 45 when she had her first child. She never had expected to have a child so late in life, but that's the way things worked out. When her child was born, she stopped working, intending to return to her job in a few weeks. But she enjoyed motherhood so much, she ended up taking a full 6 months off before she returned to work. Even then, she questioned whether she should stay full-time with her child longer.

Traditional views of adult personality development have suggested that people move through a fixed series of stages, each tied closely to age. These stages are related to specific crises in which an individual undergoes an intense period of questioning and psychological change. This perspective is a feature of the normative-crisis models of personality development. **Normative-crisis theorists** see personality development as universal stages of sequential, age-related changes or crises. For example, Erik Erikson's psychosocial theory predicts that people move through a series of stages and crises throughout their life span which are tied to particular ages.

Some critics suggest that normative-crisis approaches may be outmoded. They arose at a time when society had fairly rigid and uniform roles for people. Traditionally, men were expected to work and support a family; women were expected to stay at home and take care of the children. These roles played out at relatively uniform ages.

Today, there is considerable variety in both the roles and the timing. For people like Taryn Binder, having children came later than average. Others never marry and live with a partner of the same or other sex and perhaps adopt a child or forgo children altogether. In sum, social changes have called into question normative-crisis perspectives closely tied to age (Barnett & Hyde, 2001; Fraenkel, 2003).

> **From a social worker's perspective:** In what ways might normative-crisis models of personality development be specific to Western culture?

Because of this variation, some theorists, such as Ravenna Helson, focus on **life events theories**, which suggest that particular events, rather than age per se, determine how personality develops. For instance, a woman who has her first child at age 21 may experience similar psychological forces as a woman who has her first child at age 39. These two women, despite their very different ages, share certain commonalities of personality development (Luhmann et al., 2013; Arnarson et al., 2016; Hentschel, Eid & Kutscher, 2017).

It is not clear whether the normative-crisis view or the life events perspective more accurately depicts personality development and change in adulthood. What is clear is that developmental theorists all agree that midlife is a time of continuing, significant psychological growth.

ERIKSON'S STAGE OF GENERATIVITY VERSUS STAGNATION   As we discussed previously, psychoanalyst Erikson characterized midlife as a period of **generativity-versus-stagnation**. One's middle adulthood, according to Erikson, is either spent in generativity—making a contribution to family, community, work, and society—or in stagnation. Generative people strive to guide and encourage future generations. Often, people find generativity through parenting, but other roles can fill this need, such as working directly with young people, acting as mentors. Or the need for generativity may be satisfied through creative and artistic output, seeking to leave a lasting contribution. The focus of generativity, then, is beyond the self, as one looks toward the continuation of one's own life through others (Schoklitsch & Baumann, 2012; Wink & Staudinger, 2016; Serrat et al., 2017).

A lack of psychological growth in this period results in stagnation. Focusing on their own trivial activities, people may feel they have contributed little to the world, that their presence has counted for little. Some people find themselves floundering, still seeking new, potentially more fulfilling careers. Others become frustrated and bored.

Erikson provides a broad overview, but some psychologists suggest that we need a more precise look at midlife changes in personality. We'll consider three alternative approaches.

BUILDING ON ERIKSON'S VIEWS: VAILLANT, GOULD, AND LEVINSON
Developmentalist George Vaillant argues that an important period between ages 45 and 55 centers on "keeping the meaning" versus rigidity. Seeking to extract meaning from their lives, adults also seek to "keep the meaning" by accepting the strengths and weaknesses of others. Although they realize it is not perfect, they strive to safeguard their world, and they are relatively content. The man quoted at the beginning of this section, for example, appears content with the meaning he has found in his life. People who are unable to achieve this contentment risk becoming rigid and increasingly isolated from others (Malone et al., 2016).

Psychiatrist Roger Gould (Gould 1978) offers an alternative to Erikson's and Vaillant's views. He agrees that people move through a series of stages and potential crises, but he suggests that adults pass through seven stages associated with specific age periods (see Table 8-2). According to Gould, people in their late 30s and early 40s begin to feel a sense of urgency about attaining life's goals as they realize that their life is finite. Coming to grips with this reality can propel people toward maturity.

life events theories
the approach to personality development that is based on the timing of particular events in an adult's life rather than on age per se

generativity-versus-stagnation
according to Erikson, the stage during middle adulthood in which people consider their contributions to family and society

Table 8-2 Summary of Gould's Transformations in Adult Development

Stage	Approximate Age	Development(s)
1	16 to 18	Plan to leave home and terminate parental control
2	18 to 22	Leave the family and begin to reorient toward peers
3	22 to 28	Become independent and commit to career and (often) spouse and children
4	29 to 34	Question themselves and experience confusion; they may become dissatisfied with marriage and career
5	35 to 43	Feel an urgent need to achieve life goals, becoming increasingly aware of the passage and limits of time; they often realign life goals
6	43 to 53	Settle down at last, with acceptance of their lives
7	53 to 60	Grow more tolerant, accepting their past; they become less negative and generally more mellow

SOURCE: Based Gould, 1978.

Gould based his model of development on a small sample and relied heavily on his own clinical judgments. Little research has supported his description of the various stages, which was heavily influenced by the psychoanalytic perspective.

Another alternative to Erikson's work is psychologist Daniel Levinson's *seasons of life* theory. According to Levinson (1986, 1992), who intensively interviewed men, the early 40s are a period of transition and crisis. He suggests that adult men pass through a series of stages beginning with early adulthood, around age 20, and continuing into midlife. The beginning stages center on leaving one's family and entering the adult world.

However, at around age 40 or 45, people move to what Levinson calls the midlife transition. The *midlife transition* is a time of questioning, a focus on the finite nature of life. People begin to question some of their fundamental assumptions. They experience the first signs of aging, and they confront the fact that they will not accomplish all their aims before they die.

midlife crisis

a stage of uncertainty and indecision brought about by the realization that life is finite

In Levinson's view, this assessment may lead to a **midlife crisis**, a stage of uncertainty and indecision. Facing signs of physical aging, men may also discover that even the accomplishments of which they are proudest have brought them less satisfaction than they expected. They may try to define what went wrong and seek ways to correct past mistakes. The midlife crisis is a painful and tumultuous period of questioning.

Levinson's view is that most people are susceptible to a fairly profound midlife crisis. Before accepting his perspective, we need to consider some critical drawbacks in his research. First, his initial theory was based on 40 men, and his work with women was conducted years later and, again, on a small sample. Levinson also overstated the consistency and generality of the patterns he found. In fact, the notion of a universal midlife crisis has come under considerable criticism (Cousins, 2013; Thorpe et al., 2014; Etaugh, 2018).

THE MIDLIFE CRISIS: REALITY OR MYTH? Central to Levinson's model is the concept of midlife crisis, a period in the early 40s presumed to be marked by intense psychological turmoil. The notion has taken on a life of its own: There is a general expectation in U.S. society that age 40 is an important psychological juncture.

Such a view is problematic: The evidence is simply lacking. In fact, most research suggests that most people pass into middle age with relative ease. The majority regard midlife as a particularly rewarding time. If they are parents, the physically demanding period of childrearing is usually over, and in some cases children have left the home, allowing parents the opportunity to rekindle their intimacy. Many people find that their careers have blossomed, and they feel quite content with their lives. Focusing on the present, they seek to maximize their involvement with family, friends, and other social groups. Those who regret the course of their lives may be motivated to change directions, and those who do change end up better off psychologically (Willis, Martin, & Rocke, 2010; Robinson, Demetre, & Litman, 2017).

Furthermore, how one feels about one's age is actually associated with health outcomes. People who feel younger than their chronological age are more likely to avoid death than those who feel older than their chronological age. In other words, the younger people felt, the less likely they were to die within an 8-year period following being asked the question of how old they felt (see Figure 8-8; Miche et al., 2014; Rippon & Steptoe, 2015).

In short, the evidence for a midlife crisis experienced by most people is no more compelling than the evidence for a stormy adolescence. Yet, like that notion, the idea that the midlife crisis is nearly universal seems unusually well entrenched in "common wisdom." Why is this the case?

One reason may be that turmoil in middle age is both obvious and easily remembered by observers. A 40-year-old man who divorces his wife, trades his Toyota Sienna for a red Porsche 911 convertible, and marries a much younger woman makes a greater impression than a happily married man who remains with his spouse (and Toyota) through middle adulthood. We are more likely to notice and recall marital difficulties than the lack of them. In this way the myth of a blustery and universal midlife crisis is perpetuated. For most people, though, a midlife crisis is more the stuff of fiction than of reality. In fact, for some people midlife brings few, if any, changes. As we consider in the *Cultural Dimensions* segment, in some cultures, middle age is not even considered a separate period of life.

Figure 8-8 Feeling Younger and Age of Death

People who said they felt younger than their chronological age were more likely to live longer than those who felt older than their chronological age.

SOURCE: Rippon & Steptoe, 2015.

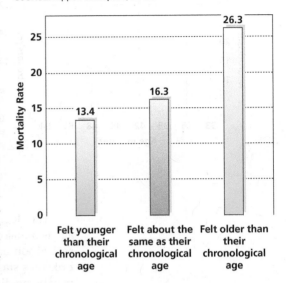

Stability Versus Change in Personality

LO 8.8 **Analyze whether personality is stable or changes over the life span.**

Jane Hennesey, age 53 and a vice president of an investment banking firm, says she still feels like a kid. Many middle-aged adults would agree. Although most people say they have changed a good deal since adolescence—and mostly for the better—many also perceive important similarities in basic personality traits between their present and younger selves.

Cultural Dimensions
Middle Age: In Some Cultures It Doesn't Exist

There's no such thing as middle age.

One could draw that conclusion by looking at the women living in the Oriya culture in Orissa, India. According to research by developmental anthropologist Richard Shweder, who studied how high-caste Hindu women view aging, a distinct period of middle age does not exist. These women view their life course not by chronological age, but by the nature of one's social responsibility, family management issues, and moral sense at a given time (Shweder, 2003).

The model of aging of the Oriyan women encompasses two phases of life: life in her father's house (*bapa gharo*), followed by life in her husband's mother's house (*sasu gharo*). These two segments fit the context of Oriyan family life, which consists of multigenerational households in which marriages are arranged. After they are married, husbands remain with their parents, and wives are expected to move in with their in-laws. Upon marriage, a wife changes social status from a child (someone's daughter) to a sexually active female (a daughter-in-law).

The shift from child to daughter-in-law typically occurs around the ages 18 to 20. However, chronological age, per se, does not mark significant boundaries in life for Oriyan women, nor do physical changes, such as the onset of menstruation or its cessation at menopause. It is the change from daughter to daughter-in-law that significantly alters social responsibility. Women must shift their focus from their own parents to the parents of their husband, and they must become sexually active to perpetuate the husband's family line.

To a Western eye, the life course of these women might seem restricted, because they rarely have careers outside the home, but Oriyan women do not see themselves in this light. In fact, in the Oriya culture, domestic work is highly respected and valued. Oriyan women also view themselves as more cultured and civilized than men, who must work outside the home.

The notion of a separate middle age is clearly a cultural construction. The significance of a particular age range differs widely, depending on the culture in which one lives.

Figure 8-9 The Stability of Personality

According to Paul Costa and Robert McCrae, basic personality traits such as neuroticism, extroversion, and openness are stable and consistent throughout adulthood.

SOURCE: Based on Costa & McCrae, 1992.

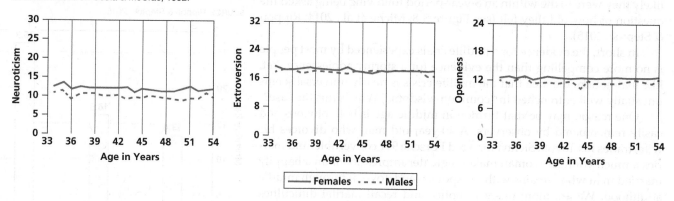

The degree to which personality is stable across the life span or changes as we age is a major issue of personality development in middle adulthood. Theorists such as Erikson and Levinson clearly suggest that substantial change occurs over time. Erikson's stages and Levinson's seasons describe set patterns of change. The change may be predictable and age related, but it is substantial.

An impressive body of research, however, suggests that for individual traits, personality is quite stable and continuous over the life span. Developmental psychologists Paul Costa and Robert McCrae find remarkable stability in particular traits. Even-tempered 20-year-olds are even-tempered at age 75; affectionate 25-year-olds become affectionate 50-year-olds; and disorganized 26-year-olds are still disorganized at age 60. Similarly, self-concept at age 30 is a good indication of self-concept at age 80. In fact, traits may become more ingrained as people age (Curtis, Windsor, & Soubelet, 2015; Debast et al., 2014; Mõttus et al., 2017; also see Figure 8-9).

STABILITY AND CHANGE IN THE "BIG FIVE" PERSONALITY TRAITS Quite a bit of research has centered on the personality traits known as the "Big Five"—because they represent the five major clusters of personality characteristics. These are:

- Neuroticism, the degree to which a person is moody, anxious, and self-critical
- Extraversion, how outgoing or shy a person is
- Openness, a person's level of curiosity and interest in new experiences
- Agreeableness, how easygoing and helpful a person tends to be
- Conscientiousness, a person's tendencies to be organized and responsible

The majority of studies find that the Big Five traits are relatively stable past the age of 30, although variations exist for specific traits. In particular, neuroticism, extraversion, and openness tend to experience decline somewhat from early adulthood, whereas agreeableness and conscientiousness tend to increase—findings that are consistent across cultures. The basic pattern, however, is one of stability through adulthood (Hahn, Gottschling, & Spinath, 2012; Curtis, Windsor, & Soubelet, 2015; Wettstein et al., 2017).

Does evidence for the stability of traits contradict the theories of personality change championed by Erikson, Gould, and Levinson? Not necessarily, for the contradictions may be more apparent than real.

People's basic traits do show continuity over the course of their adult lives. But, people are also susceptible to changes, and adulthood is packed with major changes in family status, career, and even the economy. The physical changes of aging, illness, the death of a loved one, and an increased awareness of life's finite span also can spur changes in how people view themselves and the world at large (Roberts, Walton, & Viechtbauer, 2006).

HAPPINESS ACROSS THE LIFE SPAN Suppose you hit it big winning the Powerball lottery. Would you be a happier person? For most people, the answer would be no. A growing body of research shows that adults' *subjective well-being* or general happiness remains stable over their lives. Even winning the lottery increases subjective well-being only temporarily; 1 year later, people's happiness tends to return to pre-lottery levels (Diener, 2000; Stone et al., 2010; Diener et al., 2018).

The steadiness of subjective well-being suggests that most people have a general "set point" for happiness, a level of happiness that is relatively consistent despite the day-to-day ups and downs of life. Although specific events may temporarily elevate or depress a person's mood (e.g., a surprisingly high job evaluation or being laid off from work), people eventually return to their general level of happiness.

In contrast, happiness set points are not completely fixed. Under some conditions, set points can change as a result of particular life events, such as divorce, death of a spouse, unemployment, and disability. Furthermore, people differ in the extent to which they can adapt to events (Lucas, 2007; Diener, Lucas, & Scollon, 2009; Moor & Graaf, 2016).

Most people's happiness set points seem to be fairly high. Some 30 percent of people in the United States rate themselves as "very happy," whereas only 10 percent rate themselves as "not too happy." Most people say they are "pretty happy." These findings are similar across different social groups. Men and women rate themselves as equally happy, and blacks rate themselves as "very happy" at only slightly lower rates than whites. Regardless of their economic situation, residents of countries across the world have similar levels of happiness (Kahneman et al., 2006; Della Fave et al., 2013; Diener et al., 2018). The conclusion: Money doesn't buy happiness.

Relationships: Family in Middle Age

> For Kathy and Bob, going to their son Jon's college orientation was a shockingly new experience in the life of their family. It hadn't really registered that he would be leaving home when he was accepted at a college on the other side of the country. It didn't hit them just how much this would change their family until they said good-bye and left him on his new campus. It was a wrenching experience. Kathy and Bob worried about their son in the ways that parents always do, but they also felt a profound loss—their job of raising their son, basically, was done. Now he was largely on his own. This thought filled them with pride and anticipation for his future, but with great sadness, too. They would miss him.

For members of many non-Western cultures who live in extended families in which multiple generations spend their lives in the same household or village, middle adulthood is nothing special. But in Western cultures, family dynamics change significantly in midlife. For most parents, there are major shifts in their relationships with their children, and with other family members as well. It is a period of changing roles that, in 21st-century Western cultures, encompasses an increasing number of combinations and permutations. We'll start by looking at how marriage develops and changes over this period, and then consider some of the many alternative forms of family life today (Kaslow, 2001).

Marriage and Divorce

LO 8.9 Describe typical patterns of marriage and divorce in middle adulthood.

Fifty years ago, midlife was similar for most people. Men and women, married since early adulthood, were still married to each other. One hundred years ago, when life expectancy was much shorter, people in their 40s were usually married—but not necessarily to the people they had first married. Spouses often died; people might be well into their second marriage by middle age.

Today, the story is different and more varied. More people are single at midlife, having never married. Single people may live alone or with a partner. Some have divorced, lived alone, and then remarried. Many people's marriages end in divorce, and many families "blend" together into new households, containing children and stepchildren from previous marriages. Some couples still spend 40 to 50 years together, the bulk of those years during middle adulthood. Many experience the peak of marital satisfaction during middle age.

THE UPS AND DOWNS OF MARRIAGE   Even happily married couples have their ups and downs, with satisfaction rising and falling over the course of the marriage. In the past, most research has suggested that marital satisfaction follows a U-shaped configuration. Specifically, marital satisfaction seemed to decline soon after the marriage began, falling until it reached its lowest point following the births of the couple's children. At that point, satisfaction seemed to increase, eventually returning to the same level as at the start of the marriage (VanLaningham, Johnson, & Amato, 2001; Medina, Lederhos, & Lillis, 2009; Stroope, McFarland, & Uecker, 2015).

On the other hand, newer research has called the U-shaped pattern into question. This research suggests that marital satisfaction begins to decline after the start of a marriage and continues to decline across the course of the life span (Umberson et al., 2006; Liu, Elliott, & Umberson, 2010; Olson, DeFrain, & Skogrand, 2019).

The discrepancy in research findings regarding the course of marital satisfaction may be due to factors specific to the type of marriages studied. For example, age discrepancy between spouses, personality of the husband and wife, or the presence or absence of children may account for the discrepancy in findings.

What is clear is that middle-aged couples cite several sources of marital satisfaction. For instance, both men and women typically state that their spouse is "their best friend" and that they like their spouses as people. They also view marriage as a long-term commitment and agree on their aims and goals. Finally, most also feel that their spouses have grown more interesting over the course of the marriage (Schmitt, Kliegel, & Shapiro, 2007; Landis et al., 2013; Baker, McNulty, & VanderDrift, 2017).

Sexual satisfaction is related to general marital satisfaction. What matters is not how often couples have sex. Instead, satisfaction is related to *agreeing* about their sex lives (Litzinger & Gordon, 2005; Butzer & Campbell, 2008; Schoenfeld et al., 2017).

Are there "secrets" to successful marriages? Not really. However, there are proven coping mechanisms that allow couples to remain together happily. Among them (Orbuch, 2009; Bernstein, 2010; Williams, 2016):

- **Holding realistic expectations.** Successful couples understand that there are some things about your partner that you may not like all that much. They accept that their partner will do things that they don't like some of the time.

- **Focusing on the positive.** Thinking about the things that they like about their partner helps them to accept the things that bother them.

- **Compromising.** Partners in successful marriages understand that they are not going to win every argument, and they don't keep score.

- **Avoiding suffering in silence.** If something does bother them, they let their partner know about it. But they don't bring it up in an accusatory way. Instead, they talk about it at a time when they are both calm.

DIVORCE

Louise knew after a year that the marriage was doomed. Tom never listened to a word she said, never asked her how her day had been, and never lifted a hand to help around the house. He was completely self-centered and seemingly unaware of her existence. Still, it took 23 years before she got up the nerve to tell him she wanted a divorce. His response was casual: "Do what you want. Makes no difference to me." After her initial relief that there would be no resistance, she felt betrayed and foolish. All the anguish, all the trying to make a go of it, all the pain of a bad marriage—and they both knew all along that there was no point.

Divorce among midlife couples is actually rising, despite a decline in divorces overall in recent decades. One in eight women who is in her first marriage will get divorced after the age of 40. The divorce rate for people 50 and over has doubled since 1990. And for those over 65, the divorce rate has roughly tripled since 1990 (Enright, 2004; Brown & Lin, 2012; Thomas, 2012; Stepler, 2017; also see Figure 8-10).

Why do marriages unravel in middle adulthood? There are many causes. One is that the decision to divorce is cumulative, and people may simply have increasingly grown apart or are dissatisfied with their marriage (Hawkins, Willoughby, & Doherty, 2012).

Furthermore, people spend less time together in middle adulthood than in earlier years. In individualistic Western cultures, people are concerned with their personal happiness. If their marriage is not satisfying, they feel that divorce may increase their happiness. Divorce is also more socially acceptable than in the past, and there are fewer legal impediments to it. In some cases—but certainly not all—the financial costs are not high. In fact, as more women enter the workforce, the economic reasons that would have otherwise kept women from divorcing their husbands are no longer strong enough to keep the marriage together. Consequently, as opportunities for women grow, wives may feel less dependent on their husbands, both emotionally and economically (Brown & Lin, 2012; Canham et al., 2014; Crowley, 2018).

Another reason for divorce is that romantic, passionate feelings may fade over time. Because Western culture emphasizes the importance of romance and passion, members of marriages in which passion has declined may feel that that is a sufficient reason to divorce. In some marriages, it is a lack of excitement and boredom that leads to marital dissatisfaction. In addition, there is a great deal of stress in households in which both parents work, and this stress puts a strain on marriages. Much of the energy directed toward families and maintaining relationships in the past is now directed toward work and other institutions outside the home (Macionis, 2001; Tsapelas, Aron, & Orbuch, 2009).

Finally, some marriages end because of *infidelity*, in which a spouse engages in sexual activity with a person outside of the marriage. Although statistics are highly suspect—if you lie to your spouse, why would you be honest to a pollster?—one survey found that 20 percent of men and 15 percent of women younger than the age of 35 say they have been unfaithful. In a given year, about 12 percent of men and 7 percent of women say they have had sex outside their marriage (Atkins & Furrow, 2008; Steiner et al., 2015).

Whatever the causes, divorce can be especially difficult in midlife. It can be particularly hard for women who have played the traditional role of mother and never performed substantial work outside the home. They may face age discrimination, finding that younger people are preferred, even in jobs with minimal requirements. Without a good deal of training and support, these divorced women, lacking recognized job skills, may remain virtually unemployable (Williams & Dunne-Bryant, 2006; Hilton & Anderson, 2009; Bowen & Jensen, 2017).

Many people who divorce in midlife, though, end up happy. Women, in particular, are apt to find that developing a new, independent self-identity is a positive outcome. Both men and women who divorce in midlife are also likely to form new relationships, and they typically remarry (Enright, 2004; Langlais, Anderson, & Greene, 2017).

REMARRIAGE Many of the people who divorce—some 75 to 80 percent—end up marrying again, usually within 2 to 5 years. In fact, 4 in 10 new marriages involve remarriage. Previously married people are most likely to marry people who have also been divorced, partly because divorced people tend to be the ones in the available pool, but also because those who have gone through divorce share similar experiences (Pew Research Center, 2014a; Lamdi & Cruz, 2014).

Although the rate of remarriage is high, it is far higher in some groups than in others. For instance, it is harder for women—particularly older women—to remarry than it is for men. Whereas 64 percent of men remarry after divorce or the death of a spouse, only 52 percent of women remarry (Livingston, 2014).

This age difference stems from the *marriage gradient* we discussed previously: Societal norms push men to marry women who are younger, smaller, and lower in status than themselves. The older a woman is, the fewer socially acceptable men she has available to her because those men her age are likely to be looking for younger women.

Figure 8-10 Rising Divorces in Middle Adulthood

Among people 50 and older, both the divorce rate and the number of people who experience divorce have risen significantly, and the increases are projected to continue in the future.

SOURCE: Stepler, Pew Research Center, 2017.

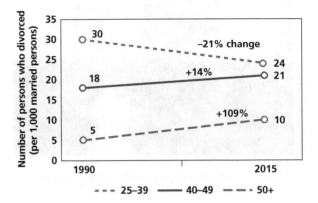

Around three-quarters of people who divorce remarry again, usually within 2 to 5 years.

As we discussed, women are also disadvantaged by double standards regarding physical attractiveness. Older women may be perceived as unattractive, whereas older men may be seen as "distinguished" and "mature" (Buss, 2003; Doyle, 2004; Khodarahimi & Fathi, 2017).

There are several reasons marrying again may be more appealing than remaining single. A person who remarries avoids the social consequences of divorce. Even in the 21st century, when divorce is common, it carries with it a certain stigma. In addition, divorced people overall report less satisfaction with life than married people (Lucas, 2005).

Divorced people miss the companionship that marriage provides. Men in particular report feeling lonely and experience more physical and mental health problems following divorce. Marriage also provides clear economic benefits, such as sharing the cost of a house and medical benefits reserved for spouses (Olson, DeFrain & Skogrand, 2019).

Second marriages differ from first marriages. Older couples tend to be more mature and realistic in their expectations. They often view marriage in less romantic terms than younger couples, and they are more cautious. They are also likely to be more flexible about roles and duties; they share household chores and decision making more equitably (Mirecki et al., 2013).

Unfortunately, this doesn't guarantee that second marriages will last. The divorce rate is higher than for first marriages; 67 percent of second marriages fail, and 75 percent of third marriages fail. One factor that explains this is that second and third marriages may include stresses not present in first marriages, such as the blending of different families. Another reason is that having experienced and survived one divorce, partners may be less committed and more ready to walk away from an unhappy second or third marriage. Finally, one or both partners may have personality and emotional characteristics that don't make them easy to live with (Coleman, Ganong, & Weaver, 2001; Olson, DeFrain, & Skogrand, 2019).

Despite the high divorce rate for second marriages, many people remarry quite successfully. In such cases, couples report as great a degree of satisfaction as those who are in successful first marriages (Michaels, 2006; Ayalon & Koren, 2015).

Family Evolutions

LO 8.10 **Analyze the effects and significance of changes in family patterns in middle adulthood.**

For many parents, a major midlife transition is the departure of children who are going to college, getting married, joining the military, or taking a job far from home. Even people who become parents at relatively late ages are likely to face this transition, because middle adulthood spans nearly a quarter-century. As we saw in Kathy and Bob's story, a child's departure can be wrenching—so much so, in fact, that it has been labeled the "empty nest syndrome." The **empty nest syndrome** refers to the unhappiness, worry, loneliness, and depression some parents feel when their children leave home (Erickson, Martinengo, & Hill, 2010).

Many parents report that major adjustments are required. For women who were stay-at-home mothers, the loss can be quite pronounced. Traditional homemakers, who focus significant time and energy on their children, face a challenging time.

Although the loss can be difficult, parents also find that some aspects of this transition are quite positive. Even mothers who have stayed at home find they have time for other interests, such as community or recreational activities, when the children leave. They may also enjoy the opportunity to get a job or return to school. Finally, many women find that motherhood is not easy; surveys show that most people regard motherhood as harder than it used to be. Such women may now feel liberated from a difficult set of responsibilities (Morfei et al., 2004; Chen, Yang, & Dale Aagard, 2012).

empty nest syndrome
the experience that relates to parents' feelings of unhappiness, worry, loneliness, and depression resulting from their children's departure from home

Though feelings of loss are common for most people, there is little, if any, evidence that the departure of children produces anything more than temporary feelings of sadness and distress. This is especially true for women who have worked outside the home (Crowley, Hayslip, & Hobdy, 2003; Kadam, 2014).

In fact, there are discernible benefits when children leave home. Spouses have more time for one another. Married or unmarried people can attend to their own work without having to worry about helping the kids with homework, carpools, and the like. It is not surprising that parents often find it more stressful to have their children return home to live with them than it was to have the children depart (Tosi & Grundy, 2018).

Some parents react to the departure of their children by becoming what are known as *helicopter parents*, parents who intrusively intervene in their children's lives. Helicopter parenting first became apparent when parents micro-managed their children's college careers, complaining to instructors and administrators about poor grades that their children received or seeking to get them into certain classes. In some cases, the phenomenon extends to the workplace; some employers complain that parents call human relations departments to extoll the virtues of their children as potential employees.

Although statistics about the prevalence of helicopter parenting are hard to come by, it is clear that the phenomenon is real. One survey of 799 employers found that nearly one-third said that parents had submitted resumes for their child, sometimes not even informing their son or daughter. One-quarter said that parents had contacted them, urging them to hire their son or daughter. And 4 percent said that a parent had accompanied the child on a job interview. Some parents even help their children complete work assignments once they get a job (Gardner, 2007; Ludden, 2012; Frey & Tatum, 2016).

In most cases, though, parents permit their children to develop independently once they leave home. However, children may not always leave home for good, and the empty nest sometimes becomes replenished with what have been called "boomerang children," as we discuss next.

BOOMERANG CHILDREN: REFILLING THE EMPTY NEST

Carole Olis doesn't know what to make of her 23-year-old son, Rob. He has been living at home since his graduation from college more than 2 years ago. Her six older children returned to the nest for just a few months and then bolted.

"I ask him, 'Why don't you move out with your friends?'" says Mrs. Olis. Rob has a ready answer: "They all live at home, too."

Carole Olis is not alone in being surprised by the return of her son. In the United States, a significant number of young adults are coming back to live with their middle-aged parents.

Known as **boomerang children**, these returning offspring typically cite economic issues as the main reason for coming back home. Because of a difficult economy, many young adults cannot find jobs after college, or the positions they do find pay so little that they have difficulty making ends meet. Others return home after the breakup of a marriage. Overall, close to one-third of young adults ages 25 to 34 are living with their parents. In some European countries, the proportion is even higher (Roberts, 2009; Parker, 2012).

Because about half of boomerang children pay rent to their parents, parental finances may benefit. The arrangement doesn't seem to affect social relationships within the family: half say it makes no difference or is a plus. Only a quarter of boomerang children find the arrangement has been bad for their relationship with their parents (Parker, 2012; see Figure 8-11).

boomerang children
young adults who return, after leaving home for some period, to live in the homes of their middle-aged parents

Figure 8-11 Boomerang Children's Views of Their Situation

The percentage of those saying that living with their parents at this stage of life has been bad, good, or no different in terms of their relationship.

SOURCE: Pew Research Center, 2012.

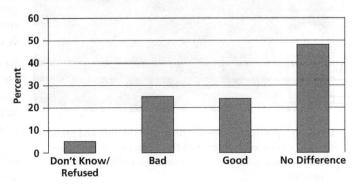

sandwich generation
couples who in middle adulthood must fulfill the needs of both their children and their aging parents

THE SANDWICH GENERATION: BETWEEN CHILDREN AND PARENTS At the same time children are leaving the nest, or returning as boomerang children, many middle-aged adults face another challenge: the care of their own aging parents. The term **sandwich generation** refers to these middle-aged adults who are squeezed between the needs of their children and those of their parents (Grundy & Henretta, 2006; Chassin et al., 2009; Steiner & Fletcher, 2017).

The sandwich generation is a relatively new phenomenon, produced by several converging trends. First, people are marrying later and having children at an older age. At the same time, people are living longer. Thus, it is not unlikely that midlife adults will have parents who are alive and require care while they still have children who need a significant amount of nurturing.

The care of aging parents can be psychologically tricky. There is a degree of role reversal, with children becoming more parental and parents becoming more dependent. As we'll discuss later, elderly people, used to being independent, may resent and resist their children's help. They do not want to be burdens. Most elderly people who live alone say they do not wish to live with their children.

Middle-aged adults provide a range of care for their parents. They may provide financial support to supplement a parent's meager pension. They might also help manage a household, doing tasks such as removing storm windows in the spring or shoveling snow in the winter.

In some cases, elderly parents may be invited to live in their child's home. Census data reveal that multigenerational households—three or more generations—are the fastest growing of all household arrangements. Almost 20 percent of the U.S. population lives with multiple generations under the same roof—almost 61 million people. The number of multigenerational households has increased by more than 50 percent since 1980 (Carrns, 2016).

Multigenerational families present a tricky situation because roles are renegotiated. Typically, the adult children—who are no longer children—are in charge of the household. Both they and their parents must make adjustments and find some common ground in making decisions. Elderly parents may find their new dependence difficult, and this can be wrenching for their adult child as well. The youngest generation may resist including the oldest generation.

In many cases, the burden of care is not shared equally, with the larger share most often assumed by women. Even when both husband and wife are in the labor force, women tend to be more involved in the day-to-day care, even when the parent or parents are their in-laws (Putney & Bengtson, 2001; Corry et al., 2015).

Culture also influences how caregivers view their roles. Members of Asian cultures, which are more collectivistic, are more likely to view caregiving as a traditional and ordinary duty. In contrast, members of more individualistic cultures may feel familial ties are less central, and caring for the older generation may be seen as a burden (Kim & Lee, 2003; Ron, 2014; Kiilo, Kasearu, & Kutsar, 2016).

Despite the burden of being sandwiched in between two generations, which can stretch the caregiving child's resources, there are significant rewards. The psychological attachment between middle-aged children and their elderly parents can continue to grow. Both sides can see each other more realistically. They may grow closer, more accepting of each other's weaknesses and more appreciative of each other's strengths (Vincent, Phillipson, & Downs, 2006; Aazami, Shamsuddin, & Akamal, 2018).

BECOMING A GRANDPARENT: WHO, ME? When her eldest son and daughter-in-law had their first child, Leah couldn't believe it. At age 54, she was a grandmother! She kept telling herself she felt far too young to be anybody's grandparent.

Middle adulthood often brings one of the unmistakable symbols of aging: becoming a grandparent. For some people, the new role has been eagerly awaited. They may miss the

Living in a multigenerational setting with children and grandchildren can be rewarding for all three generations. Are there any disadvantages to this type of situation for the sandwich generation?

energy and excitement and even the demands of young children, and they may see grandparenthood as the next stage in the natural progression of life. Others are less pleased with the prospect, seeing it as a clear signpost of aging.

Grandparenting tends to fall into different styles. *Involved* grandparents are actively engaged in and have influence over their grandchildren's lives. They hold clear expectations about the ways their grandchildren should behave. A retired grandparent who takes care of a grandchild while his or her parents work is an example of an involved grandparent (Mueller, Wilhelm, & Elder, 2002; Fergusson, Maughan, & Golding, 2008; Mansson, 2013).

In contrast, *companionate* grandparents are more relaxed. Rather than taking responsibility for their grandchildren, they act as supporters and buddies to them. Grandparents who visit and call frequently, and perhaps occasionally take their grandchildren on vacations or invite them to visit without their parents, are companionate grandparents.

Finally, the most aloof type of grandparents are *remote*. They are detached and distant, showing little interest in their grandchildren. Remote grandparents, for example, would rarely make visits to see their grandchildren and might complain about their childish behavior when they did see them.

There are marked gender differences in the extent to which people enjoy grandparenthood. Generally, grandmothers are more interested and experience greater satisfaction than grandfathers, particularly when they have a high level of interaction with younger grandchildren (Smith & Drew, 2002).

Black grandparents are more apt to be involved than are white grandparents. The most reasonable explanation for this is the greater prevalence of multigenerational households among African Americans than among Caucasians. In addition, African American families are more likely to be headed by single parents. Thus, they often rely substantially on the help of grandparents in everyday child care, and cultural norms tend to be highly supportive of grandparents taking an active role (Keene, Prokos, & Held, 2012; Bertera & Crewe, 2013; Cox & Miner, 2014).

Family Violence: The Hidden Epidemic

LO 8.11 Describe causes and characteristics of family violence in the United States.

Domestic violence is at epidemic levels in the United States. One in four women and one in seven men have been the victims of severe physical violence by an intimate partner during their lifetimes. More than half the women who were murdered in one recent 10-year period were murdered by a partner. Between 21 percent and 34 percent of women will be slapped, kicked, beaten, choked, or threatened or attacked with a weapon at least once by an intimate partner. In fact, continuing, severe violence characterizes close to 15 percent of all marriages in the United States. In addition, many women are victims of psychological abuse, such as verbal or emotional abuse. Domestic violence is also a worldwide problem. Estimates suggest that one in three women around the globe experience violent victimization during their lives (Garcia-Moreno et al., 2005; Smith et al., 2017; also see Figure 8-12).

In the United States, no segment of society is immune from spousal abuse. Violence occurs across social strata, races, ethnic groups, and religions. Both gay and straight partnerships can be abusive. It also occurs across genders: Although in most instances, the husband is the abuser, in about 8 percent of the cases wives physically abuse their husbands (Dixon & Browne, 2003; Smith et al., 2017; Rolle et al., 2018).

Certain factors increase the likelihood of abuse. Spousal abuse is more apt to occur in large families for whom both financial strain and verbal aggression are common. Those husbands and wives who grew up in families where violence was present are also more likely to be violent themselves (Ehrensaft, Cohen, & Brown, 2003; Lackey, 2003; Paulino, 2016).

Figure 8-12 Violent Victimization by Victim–Offender Relationship

SOURCE: Truman & Morgan, 2014.

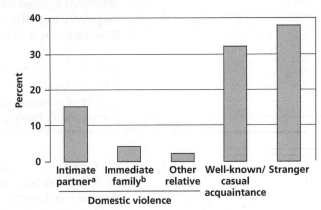

[a]Includes current or former spouses, boyfriends, and girlfriends.
[b]Includes parents, children, and siblings.

Figure 8-13 The Stages of Violence

SOURCE: Adapted from Walker, 1979; Gondolf, 1985.

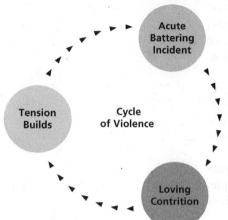

The factors that put a family at risk are similar to those associated with child abuse, another form of family violence. Child abuse occurs most frequently in stressful environments, at lower socioeconomic levels, in single-parent families, and in situations of intense marital conflict. Families with four or more children have higher abuse rates, and those with low incomes have seven times the rate of families with higher incomes. But not all types of abuse are higher in poorer families: Incest is more likely to occur in affluent families (Cox, Kotch, & Everson, 2003; Ybarra & Thompson, 2017).

THE STAGES OF SPOUSAL ABUSE   Marital aggression by a husband typically occurs in three stages (Walker, 1999; see Figure 8-13). In the initial *tension-building* stage, a batterer becomes upset and shows dissatisfaction through verbal abuse. He may also use some physical aggression, such as shoving or grabbing. The wife may desperately try to avoid the impending violence, attempting to calm her spouse or withdraw from the situation. Such behavior may only enrage the husband, who senses his wife's vulnerability. Her efforts to escape may escalate his anger.

In the next stage—an *acute battering incident*—the physical abuse actually occurs, lasting from several minutes to hours. Wives may be shoved against walls, choked, slapped, punched, kicked, and stepped on. Their arms may be twisted or broken, they may be shaken severely, thrown down a flight of stairs, or burned with cigarettes or scalding liquids. About a quarter of wives are forced to engage in sexual activity, which takes the form of aggressive sexual acts and rape.

Finally, in some—but not all—cases, the episode ends with the *loving contrition* stage. At this point, the husband feels remorse and apologizes for his actions. He may provide first aid and sympathy, assuring his wife that he will never act violently again. Because wives may feel they were somehow partly at fault, they may accept the apology and forgive their husbands. They want to believe that the aggression will never occur again.

The loving contrition stage helps explain why many wives remain with abusive husbands and continue to be victims. Wishing desperately to keep their marriages intact, and believing that they have no good alternatives, some wives remain out of a vague sense that they are responsible for the abuse. In other cases, wives fear their husbands may come after them if they leave.

THE CYCLE OF VIOLENCE   Still other wives stay with batterers because they, like their husbands, learned in childhood that violence is an acceptable means of settling disputes.

Individuals who abuse their spouses and children were often the victims of abuse themselves. According to the **cycle of violence hypothesis**, abuse and neglect of children predisposes them to abusiveness as adults. In line with social learning theory, the cycle of violence hypothesis suggests that family aggression is perpetuated from one generation to another. It is a fact that individuals who abuse their wives often witnessed spousal abuse at home as children, just as parents who abuse their children frequently were the victims of abuse as children (Renner & Slack, 2006; Whiting et al., 2009; Eriksson & Mazerolle, 2015).

cycle of violence hypothesis
the theory that the abuse and neglect that children suffer predispose them as adults to abuse and neglect their own children

> **From health-care provider's perspective:** What can be done to end the cycle of violence, in which people who were abused as children grow up to be abusers of others?

Growing up in an abusive home does not invariably lead to abusiveness as an adult. Only about one-third of people who were abused or neglected as children abuse their own children as adults, and two-thirds of abusers were not themselves abused as children. The cycle of violence, then, does not tell the full story of abuse.

Whatever the causes of abuse, there are ways to deal with it, as we consider next.

SPOUSAL ABUSE AND SOCIETY: THE CULTURAL ROOTS OF VIOLENCE

Although marital violence and aggression is often seen as a particularly North American phenomenon, other cultures have traditions that regard violence as acceptable. In some cultures, the idea of "honor killings" still persists, in which it is deemed acceptable to kill a woman if she has brought dishonor to the family or community. Wife battering and honor killings often occur in cultures that view women as inferior to men and treat them as property (Ahmed, 2018).

In Western societies, too, wife beating was once acceptable. According to English common law—the foundation of the legal system in the United States—husbands could beat their wives. In the 1800s, this law was modified to permit only certain kinds of beating. Specifically, a husband could not beat his wife with a stick or rod that was thicker

Parents who abuse their own spouses and children were often victims of abuse themselves as children, reflecting a cycle of violence.

than his thumb—the origin of the phrase "rule of thumb." It was not until the late 19th century that spousal abuse was made illegal in the United States.

Some experts on abuse suggest that its root cause is the traditional power structure in which women and men function. They argue that the more a society differentiates between men's and women's status, the more likely it is that abuse will occur.

They cite research examining the legal, political, educational, and economic roles of women and men. For example, some research has compared battering statistics across the various states in the United States. Abuse is more likely to occur in states where women are of particularly low or high status compared with women in other states. Apparently, relatively low status makes women easy targets of violence, whereas unusually high status may make husbands feel threatened and thus more likely to behave abusively (Vandello & Cohen, 2003; Banks, 2016; also see the *Development in Your Life* box).

Development in Your Life

Dealing with Spousal and Intimate Partner Abuse

Spousal abuse occurs in some 25 percent of all marriages and in other forms of intimate relationships, but efforts to deal with victims of abuse are underfunded and inadequate to meet current needs. In fact, some psychologists argue that the same factors that led society to underestimate the magnitude of the problem for many years now hinder the development of effective interventions. Still, there are several measures to help the victims of spousal abuse:

- **Teach both wives and husbands a basic premise:** Violence is *never*, under *any* circumstances, an acceptable means of resolving disagreements.

- **Call the police.** Assault, including spousal assault, is against the law. It may be difficult to involve law enforcement officers, but this is a realistic way of handling the problem. Judges can also issue restraining orders requiring abusive husbands to stay away from their wives.

- **Understand that the remorse shown by a spouse, no matter how heartfelt, may have no bearing on possible future violence.** Even if a husband shows loving regret and vows that he will never be violent again, such a promise is no guarantee against future abuse.

- **If you are the victim of abuse, seek a safe haven.** Many communities have shelters for the victims of domestic violence that can house women and their children. Because addresses of shelters are kept confidential, an abusive spouse will not be able to find you. Telephone numbers are listed in the yellow or blue pages of phone books, and local police should also have the numbers.

- **If you feel in danger from an abusive partner, seek a restraining order** from a judge in court. A restraining order forbids a spouse to come near you, under penalty of law.

- **Call the National Domestic Violence Hotline at 1-800-799-7233** for immediate help or advice.

Work and Leisure

> Enjoying a weekly game of golf... starting a neighborhood watch program... coaching a Little League baseball team... joining an investment club... traveling... taking a cooking class... attending a theater series... running for the local town council... going to the movies with friends... hearing lectures on Buddhism... fixing up a porch in the back of the house... chaperoning a high school class on an out-of-state trip... lying on a beach, reading a book during an annual vacation...

Adults in their middle years actually enjoy a rich variety of activities. Although middle adulthood often represents the peak of career success and earning power, it is also a time when people throw themselves into leisure and recreational activities. In fact, midlife may be the period when work and leisure activities are balanced most easily. No longer feeling a need to prove themselves on the job, and increasingly valuing their contributions to family, community, and—more broadly—society, middle-aged adults may find that work and leisure complement one another in ways that enhance overall happiness.

Work in Middle Adulthood: The Good and the Bad

LO 8.12 Describe the benefits and challenges of work life in middle adulthood.

For many, productivity, success, and earning power are greatest in middle age, but occupational success may become far less alluring than it once was. This is particularly true for those who have not achieved the career success they had hoped for. In such cases, family and other off-the-job interests become more important than work.

WORK AND CAREERS: JOBS AT MIDLIFE The factors that make a job satisfying change during middle age. Younger adults focus on abstract and future-oriented concerns, such as the opportunity for advancement or the possibility of recognition and approval. Middle-aged employees care more about the here-and-now qualities of work. They are more concerned with pay, working conditions, and specific policies, such as how vacation time is calculated. As at previous stages of life, changes in overall job quality are associated with changes in stress levels for both men and women (Cohrs, Abele, & Dette, 2006; Rantanen et al., 2012; Hamlet & Herrick, 2014).

In general, though, the relationship between age and work is positive: The older workers are, the more overall job satisfaction they experience. This is not altogether surprising, because younger adults who are dissatisfied with their jobs will quit them and find new positions that they like better. Also, because older workers have fewer opportunities to change jobs, they may learn to live with what they have and accept that it is the best they are likely to get. Such acceptance may ultimately translate into satisfaction (Tangri, Thomas, & Mednick, 2003).

CHALLENGES OF WORK: ON-THE-JOB SATISFACTION Job satisfaction is not universal in middle adulthood. For some people, dissatisfaction with working conditions or with the nature of the job increases their stress. Conditions may become so bad that the result is burnout or a decision to change jobs, as in the following case.

> For 44-year-old Peggy Augarten, her early-morning shifts in the intensive care unit of a suburban hospital were becoming increasingly difficult. It had always been hard to lose a patient, but recently she found herself crying over patients at the strangest moments: while she was doing the laundry, washing the dishes, or watching TV. When she began to dread going to work, she knew that her feelings about her job were undergoing a fundamental change.

burnout
a situation that occurs when workers experience dissatisfaction, disillusionment, frustration, and weariness from their jobs

Augarten's response probably reflects the phenomenon of burnout. **Burnout** occurs when workers experience dissatisfaction, disillusionment, frustration, and weariness from their jobs. It occurs most often in jobs that involve helping others, and it often strikes those professionals who once were the most idealistic and driven. In some ways, such workers may be overcommitted to their jobs. Realizing that they can make only minor dents in huge social problems such as poverty and medical care can be disappointing and demoralizing. Furthermore, many such professions require long hours, and it is hard to achieve work-life balance (Dunford et al., 2012; Rössler et al., 2015; Miyasaki et al., 2017; see Table 8-3).

Burnout is often characterized by cynicism about one's work. An employee might say to himself, "What am I working so hard for? No one is going to notice that I've come in on budget for the last 2 years." Workers also may feel indifferent about their job performance. The idealism a worker felt entering a profession may give way to pessimism and the attitude that it is impossible to provide any kind of meaningful solution to a problem.

Burnout occurs when a worker experiences dissatisfaction, disillusionment, frustration, or weariness from his or her job.

People can combat burnout, even those in professions with high demands and seemingly insurmountable burdens. For example, the nurse who despairs of not having enough time for every patient can be helped to realize that a more feasible goal—such as giving patients a quick backrub—can be equally important.

In addition, jobs can also be structured so that workers (and their supervisors) pay attention to small victories in their daily work, such as the pleasure of a client's gratitude, even though the "big picture" of disease, poverty, racism, and an inadequate educational system may look gloomy. Furthermore, engaging in "best practices" on the job, and knowing that one is doing one's best, can decrease burnout. Finally, mentally disengaging from work during leisure time is helpful in reducing the consequences of burnout (Bährer-Kohler, 2013; Crowe, 2016; Wilkinson, Infantolino, & Wacha-Montes, 2017).

UNEMPLOYMENT: THE DASHING OF THE DREAM For many workers, unemployment is a hard reality, affecting them psychologically and economically. For those who have been fired, laid off by corporate downsizing, or forced out of jobs by technological advances, being out of work can be psychologically and even physically devastating.

Unemployment can leave people feeling anxious, depressed, and irritable. Their self-confidence may plummet, and they may be unable to concentrate. In addition, higher unemployment rates are related to the risk of suicide (Inoue et al., 2006; Paul & Moser, 2009; Nordt et al., 2015).

Table 8-3 High-Burnout Careers

1. Physician
2. Nurse
3. Social Worker
4. Teacher
5. School Principal
6. Attorney
7. Police Officer
8. Public Accountant
9. Fast Food Worker
10. Retail Worker

SOURCE: White, 2017.

Becoming unemployed in midlife can be a shattering experience that may taint your view of the world.

Even seemingly positive aspects of unemployment, such as having more time, can affect people negatively. Unemployed people may feel depressed and at loose ends, making them less apt to take part in community activities, use libraries, and read than employed people. They are more likely to be late for appointments and even for meals (Ball & Orford, 2002; Tyre & McGinn, 2003; Zuelke et al., 2018).

And these problems may linger. Middle-aged adults tend to stay unemployed longer than younger workers, and they have fewer opportunities for gratifying work as they age. Employers may discriminate against older applicants, making it more difficult to find a new job. Such discrimination is both illegal and based on misguided assumptions: Research finds that older workers miss fewer work days, hold their jobs longer, are more reliable, and are more willing to learn new skills (Wickrama et al., 2018).

Midlife unemployment is a shattering experience. For some people, especially those who never find meaningful work again, it taints their view of life. Such involuntary—and premature—retirement can lead to pessimism, cynicism, and despondency. Accepting the new situation takes time and a good deal of psychological adjustment. And there are challenges for those who *do* find a new career, too (Waters & Moore, 2002; Pelzer, Schaffrath, & Vernaleken, 2014).

SWITCHING—AND STARTING—CAREERS AT MIDLIFE For some people, midlife brings a hunger for change. For those who are dissatisfied with their jobs, who switch careers after a period of unemployment, or who return to a job market they left years ago, development leads to new careers.

People change careers in middle adulthood for several reasons. Their job may offer little challenge, or they have achieved mastery, making the once difficult, routine. Other people switch because their jobs have changed in ways they do not like, or they may have lost their job. They may be asked to accomplish more with fewer resources, or technology may have drastically changed their daily activities and they no longer enjoy what they do.

Still others are unhappy with their status and wish to make a fresh start. Some are burned out or feel that they are on a treadmill. And some people simply want something new. They view middle age as the last chance to make a meaningful occupational change.

Finally, a significant number of people, most of them women, return to the job market after raising children. Some need to find paying work after a divorce. Since the mid-1980s, the number of women in the workforce who are in their 50s has grown significantly. Around half of women between the ages of 55 and 64—and an even larger percentage of those who graduated from college—are now in the workforce.

People may enter new professions with unrealistically high expectations and then be disappointed by the realities. Middle-aged people, starting new careers, may also be placed in entry-level positions. Thus, their peers on the job may be considerably younger than they are. Still, in the long run, starting a new career in midlife can be invigorating. (Otto, Dette-Hagenmeyer, & Dalbert, 2010; Feldman & Ng, 2013).

Some forecasters suggest that career changes will become the rule, not the exception. According to this view, technological advances will occur so rapidly that people will be forced periodically to change their profession, often dramatically. People will have not one, but several, careers during their lifetimes. As the *Cultural Dimensions* segment shows, this is especially true for those who make the major life and career change: immigrating to another country as adults.

> **From a social worker's perspective:** Why do you think immigrants' ambition and achievements are widely underestimated? Do conspicuous negative examples play a role (as they do in perceptions of the midlife crisis and stormy adolescence)?

Cultural Dimensions

Immigrants on the Job: Making It in America

If we rely solely on much of what we hear from certain anti-immigrant politicians in the United States, we would probably view immigrants to the United States as straining the educational, prison, welfare, and health-care systems while contributing little to U.S. society. But the assumptions that underlie anti-immigrant sentiment are in fact quite wrong.

Some 43 million people in the United States were born outside the country, representing close to around 14 percent of the population, nearly three times the percentage in 1970. First- and second-generation immigrants comprise almost a quarter of the population of the United States (see Figure 8-14; Congressional Budget Office, 2013).

Today's immigrants are somewhat different from those of the earlier waves at the beginning of the 20th century. Only a third are white, compared with almost 90 percent of immigrants who arrived before 1960. Critics argue that many new immigrants lack the skills that will allow them to make a contribution to the high-tech economy of the 21st century.

The critics are wrong in many fundamental respects. For instance, consider the following data (Flanigan, 2005; Gorman, 2010; Camarota & Zeigler 2015):

- Most legal and illegal immigrants ultimately succeed financially. For example, although they initially experience higher rates of poverty than native-born Americans, immigrants who arrived in the United States prior to 1980

and have had a chance to establish themselves actually have a higher family income than native-born Americans. Immigrants are twice as likely to start businesses as citizens born in the U.S. Furthermore, companies owned by immigrants are more likely to hire employees than companies owned by native-born citizens (ADL, 2017).

- Most of the projected increase in immigration comes from increases in legal immigrants, not illegal immigration.

- Few immigrants come to the United States to get on welfare. Instead, most say they come because of opportunities to work and prosper in the United States. Non-refugee immigrants who are old enough to work are less likely to be on welfare than native-born U.S. citizens.

- Given time, immigrants contribute more to the economy than they take away. Although initially costly to the government, often because they hold low-paying jobs and therefore pay no income taxes, immigrants become more productive as they get older.

Why are immigrants often ultimately financially successful? One explanation is that immigrants who voluntarily choose to leave their native countries are particularly motivated and driven to be successful, whereas those who choose *not* to immigrate may be relatively less motivated.

Figure 8-14 Immigrants in the United States.

Since 1970 the number of immigrants in the United States has steadily climbed and, barring changes in immigration policy, immigrants who arrive in the future plus their descendants will account for roughly three-fourths of future U.S. population increases.

SOURCE: Camarota & Zeigler, 2015.

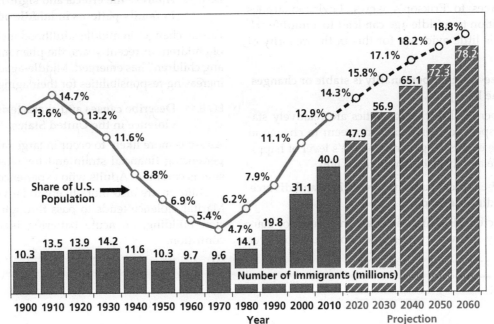

Leisure Time: Life Beyond Work

LO 8.13 Describe how people experience leisure time in middle adulthood.

With the typical work week hovering between 35 and 40 hours—and becoming shorter for most people—most middle-aged adults have some 28 waking hours per week of leisure time (Bureau of Labor Statistics, 2018). What do they do with it?

For one thing, they watch television. Middle-aged people average around 15 hours of television each week. But adults do much more with their leisure time. For many people, midlife offers a renewed opportunity to take up activities outside the home. As children leave, parents have substantial time to participate in leisure activities like sports or to participate in town committees. In fact, middle-aged adults in the United States spend about 5 hours a day in social and leisure activities (Lindstrom et al., 2005; Bureau of Labor Statistics, 2018).

A significant number of people find leisure so alluring that they take early retirement. For early retirees who have adequate financial resources to last the remainder of their years, life can be quite gratifying. Early retirees tend to be in good health, and they may take up a variety of new activities (Jopp & Hertzog, 2010).

Although midlife offers the opportunity for more leisure, most people report that the pace of their lives does not seem slower. Much of their free time is scattered throughout the week in 15- and 30-minute chunks as they pursue a variety of activities. Thus, despite a documented increase of leisure time over the past few decades, many people feel they have no more free time than they did previously (Weller, 2017).

Review, Check, and Apply

Review

LO 8.7 Explain varied perspectives on personality development during middle adulthood.

In normative-crisis models, people pass through age-related stages of development; life events models focus on how people change in response to various life events. Erikson characterizes midlife as a time spent either in generativity or stagnation. Vaillant, Gould, and Levinson offer alternatives to Erikson's views. Levinson argues that the transition to middle age can lead to a midlife crisis, but there is little evidence for this in the majority of people.

LO 8.8 Analyze whether personality is stable or changes over the life span.

Broad, basic personality characteristics are relatively stable. Specific aspects of personality do seem to change in response to life events. In general, people's level of happiness remains relatively stable throughout life.

LO 8.9 Describe typical patterns of marriage and divorce in middle adulthood.

Marital satisfaction rises and falls over the course of marriage, generally following a U-shaped configuration over the years. In happy marriages, most people also feel that their spouses have grown more interesting over the years. There are many reasons why marriages end in divorce, including lack of satisfaction, less time spent together, and infidelity. Divorce may increase happiness, and the process of divorce is more socially acceptable.

LO 8.10 Analyze the effects and significance of changes in family patterns in middle adulthood.

Family changes in middle adulthood include the departure of children. In recent years, the phenomenon of "boomerang children" has emerged. Middle-aged adults often have increasing responsibilities for their aging parents.

LO 8.11 Describe causes and characteristics of family violence in the United States.

Abuse is more likely to occur in large families who are experiencing financial strain and for whom verbal aggression is common. Adults who experienced family violence as children are also more likely to be violent themselves. Marital violence tends to pass through three stages: tension building, an acute battering incident, and loving contrition.

LO 8.12 Describe the benefits and challenges of work life in middle adulthood.

People in middle age view their jobs differently than before, placing more emphasis on specific job factors, such as pay and working conditions, and less on career striving and ambition. Midlife career changes are becoming more prevalent, motivated usually by dissatisfaction, the need for more challenge or status, or the desire to return to the workforce after childrearing.

LO 8.13 Describe how people experience leisure time in middle adulthood.

People in midlife usually have increased leisure time. Often they use it to become more involved outside the home in recreational and community activities.

Check Yourself

1. According to the _____ model of personality development, individuals at different ages can experience the same emotional and personality changes because they have shared common occurrences in their lives.
   a. normative-crisis
   b. psychosexual
   c. life events
   d. self-understanding

2. Couples who, in middle adulthood, need to take care of their aging parents and their children are often referred to by psychologists as the _____ generation.
   a. boomer
   b. betweener
   c. sandwich
   d. boomerang

3. The stage of marital aggression in which the batterer expresses remorse and apologizes for the violence is known as the _____ stage.
   a. cycle of violence
   b. acute battering
   c. tension-building
   d. loving contrition

4. Compared to younger adults, middle-aged adults who lose their jobs _____.
   a. tend to stay unemployed longer and have fewer opportunities for gratifying work as they age
   b. tend to find jobs quickly because of their skills but find it difficult to stay employed
   c. find it difficult to get new jobs, but once employed have a stable work history
   d. are less likely to become depressed, which facilitates their search for new employment

Applying Lifespan Development

Why might striving for occupational success be less appealing in middle age than before? What cognitive and personality changes might contribute to this phenomenon?

Chapter 8 Summary
Putting It All Together: Middle Adulthood

TERRI DONOVAN, at 50, found the free time that had eluded her for several decades as she raised her family while working full-time. Chronologically and developmentally right in the middle of middle adulthood, she sent her youngest child to college, reignited her romance with her husband, took up volunteer work, and ran for the state legislature. Though Terri was certainly in a midlife transition, she did not experience a "midlife crisis." She realized she still had half a life ahead of her if all went well, and she was determined to forge strong connections with the people around her.

Aleksandar Tomic/123RF

MODULE 8.1
PHYSICAL DEVELOPMENT IN MIDDLE ADULTHOOD

- Although certain chronic diseases, like arthritis and hypertension, do begin to appear in midlife, like most middle-aged adults, Terri is in good health. (p. 355)
- If Terri makes walking a regular exercise, it will compensate for the gradual loss of strength that occurs in middle adulthood. (p. 356)
- With an easing of obligations to her children, Terri has more time and energy to enjoy sex with her husband. However, if she hasn't gone through menopause, she will still need to use contraception. (pp. 358–360)

MODULE 8.2
COGNITIVE DEVELOPMENT IN MIDDLE ADULTHOOD

- Terri has developed expertise and a high competency in her work as an urban planner, which brings her continued success even though midlife brings an overall decline in intellectual skills. (pp. 370–371)
- Her understanding of what is involved in urban planning allows Terri to quickly evaluate a potential project, see what's involved, and decide if it interests her. (pp. 368–371)
- It is likely that Terri has a great deal of practical intelligence in addition to the more traditional kind. (p. 369)

MODULE 8.3
SOCIAL AND PERSONALITY DEVELOPMENT IN MIDDLE ADULTHOOD

- Though Terri is in midlife transition, the actions she takes to find more connected relationships, and to change her career in a way that's truly satisfying to her, result in growth rather than stagnation. (pp. 374–377)
- Terri's openness to new experiences, her extraversion, and her talent for organization are personality traits that have remained stable throughout her life. (p. 377)
- Volunteering in her local soup kitchen, and rekindling her romance with her husband eased sadness Terri experienced when her youngest child left for college. (p. 382)

What would YOU do?

Would you advise Terri to slow up on the transitions in her life, to consolidate her changes? Why or why not?

Asia Images Group/ Getty Images

What would a MARRIAGE COUNSELOR do?

Would you advise Terri to focus on rekindling her romance with Brian and put off running for the legislature for a year or two? If Terri wins the election, what suggestions would you give her to keep her marriage in focus as she starts a challenging new career?

Sheer Photo, Inc/ Stockbyte/Getty Images

What would a HEALTH-CARE PROVIDER do?

Considering her age and the physical changes her body is going through, what dietary and exercise guidelines would you recommend Terri observe to prevent fatigue and combat stress in a demanding public service job?

Mark Andersen/ Rubberball/Getty Images

What would a CAREER COUNSELOR do?

Would you advise Terri to set aside her political aspirations and take up work as a consultant in urban planning for New York City, a position for which she is exceptionally qualified and that would allow her to control her own schedule?

Jeffery Titcomb/Stock Connection Blue/Alamy Stock Photo

Chapter 9
Late Adulthood

Dmitriy Shironosov/123RF

Peter Sarnov, 79, and his sister Ella Malone, 73, live together in a house they purchased 5 years ago after both their spouses died in the same year. "We lived together as kids back in Newark," says Peter, "and we always got along well despite the 6-year age difference. When we were suddenly alone, we talked to each other at my wife's wake and basically said, 'Why not?' And it's been working out great, so far. At least I think so."

At this, Ella takes up the thread. "Great is right. We fit like a couple of matched spoons. No conflict, no hassle, and exactly as much togetherness as we want. And you know what? That 6-year age difference doesn't seem so big anymore."

Asked if their compatibility stems from their sibling similarity, they both laugh out loud. "What similarity?" asks Peter. "It would be hard to find two people more different. Look, I'm a homebody. I like sitting around the house and reading. I'm a movie buff with millions of movies on DVD. I'm a gardener and I love cooking. My greatest pleasure is to have a couple of old friends over for dinner and a movie. I even like keeping the house reasonably clean and doing the laundry."

"And I'm always on the go," adds Ella. "I'm in a sewing circle and two book clubs, I play golf as often as I can, and I work in the hospital gift shop. I'm taking Spanish at the community college, I'm learning to play chess, and I often take trips out west or abroad with or without Peter."

"Basically we're two sides of a coin," says Peter. "I'm neat, she's not. She goes out, I stay home. She's competitive, I'm laid back. I cook, she eats. But neither of us is ever bored."

"And though we're both a little forgetful," Ella says with a smile, "we seem to forget different things. If I forget an appointment, Peter reminds me, and if he's trying to recall a name, I always know it. The absolute best thing is that we never get on each other's nerves. I know we couldn't say that about our marriages," she laughs.

And Peter laughs with her.

The period of late adulthood, which starts around age 65, is characterized by great changes—and ongoing personal development. Older adults face profound physical, cognitive, and social changes, and by and large they figure out strategies for adjusting to them. No two strategies are exactly alike, as illustrated by the quite different paths chosen by Peter Sarnov and Ella Malone, but most older adults manage this stage successfully.

In late adulthood, people begin the decline that will be part of their lives until death. But we will see that all aspects of this period—physical, cognitive, and social—are largely misrepresented in popular stereotypes. Older people can maintain physical and mental strength virtually until the day they die, and their social worlds can also remain as vital and active as they want.

Physically, people older than 65 certainly begin a gradual transition from full strength and health to an increasing concern about illness, pain, and disease. But this is not the only thing going on in their lives. They can stay healthy for quite a long time and can continue most if not all of the activities that they enjoyed when younger. Cognitively, we find that older people adjust quite well to the changes that seem designed to impede them by adopting new strategies for solving problems and compensating for lost abilities. And socially, many of them become adept at coping with the changes in their lives, such as the death of a spouse and retirement from work.

Peter and Ella are typical only in being atypical. Through their unique approaches to aging, they make the point that old age can be what people want it to be—not what society thinks it ought to be.

Module 9.1 *Physical Development* in Late Adulthood

LO 9.1 Describe the myths and realities of aging.

LO 9.2 Summarize the physical changes that occur in old age.

LO 9.3 Explain how aging affects the senses.

LO 9.4 Summarize the health problems elderly people experience, and list the factors that influence the state of a person's health.

LO 9.5 Discuss the different theories of aging, and summarize the research to increase life expectancy.

Module 9.2 *Cognitive Development* in Late Adulthood

LO 9.6 Describe the challenges of determining the cause of age changes in intelligence.

LO 9.7 Summarize the effects of aging on cognitive functioning, and identify the factors that may affect it.

LO 9.8 Explain how memory capability changes in late adulthood.

LO 9.9 Identify the learning opportunities available to older adults, and describe their value to cognitive functioning.

Module 9.3 *Social and Personality Development* in Late Adulthood

LO 9.10 Identify and describe the various theories of personality development in late adulthood.

LO 9.11 Explain how age relates to the distribution of resources, power, and privilege.

LO 9.12 Define wisdom, and describe how it is associated with age.

LO 9.13 Differentiate the theories of aging, and explain how culture shapes the way older people are treated.

LO 9.14 Describe the living arrangements available to older adults, and explain how each affects the quality of their lives.

LO 9.15 Discuss the financial security of older people and the social and economic ramifications of work and retirement in later adulthood.

LO 9.16 Identify the issues couples face in late adulthood, and describe the challenges presented by the death of a spouse or partner.

LO 9.17 Identify the relationships that are important to older adults, and explain why they matter.

LO 9.18 Discuss what causes elder abuse and how it can be prevented.

Module 9.1

Physical Development in Late Adulthood

To Live Forever

John Benjamin thinks it's a snap to be 74. "Compared to all that hustling to make a career and raise a family, life is much easier now," he says. He admits there have been changes. "I used to run every day, but my knees started giving me trouble about 10 years ago and I switched to biking. Much easier on the joints." Another change is his sense of smell. "People say 'stop and smell the roses,' but I can't smell the roses anymore," he jokes. Still, there's plenty about life John does enjoy. "I was a lawyer for 40 years, and when I retired, I started blogging about Supreme Court decisions. My daughter helped me set up the blog. Now, I'm writing a book on the Supreme Court over the last 50 years." John also plays viola in a string quartet, a group he formed 10 years ago, and he goes swing dancing with his partner, Maddie. "I call her my girlfriend because though she's got a year on me, she's so young and sassy in her attitude. We went to Paris last spring, and café-hopped on the Left Bank until the wee hours." Asked if he has any other big ambitions besides finishing his book, John considers for a moment. "I guess I just want to live forever. That's my major goal now."

John Benjamin is not alone when it comes to showing renewed vitality in late adulthood. Increasingly, older people are pioneering new fields, achieving new endeavors, and generally reshaping how we perceive the later stages of life. For a growing number of people in late adulthood, vigorous mental and physical activity remains an important part of daily life.

Old age used to be equated with loss: loss of brain cells, intellectual capabilities, energy, and sex drive. That view is being displaced as **gerontologists**, specialists who study aging, paint a different picture. Rather than a period of decline, late adulthood is seen as a stage in which people continue to change—to grow in some areas and, yes, to decline in others.

Even the definition of *old* is changing. Many people in late adulthood, which begins around age 65 and continues to death, are as vigorous and involved with life as people several decades younger. We can no longer define old age by chronological years alone; we must also take into account people's physical and psychological well-being, their *functional ages*. Some researchers divide people into three groups according to functional ages: the *young old* are healthy and active; the *old old* have some health problems and difficulties with daily activities; and the *oldest old* are frail and need care.

Gerontologists have found that people in late adulthood can be as vigorous and active as those many years younger.

According to functional age, an active, healthy 100-year-old would be considered young old, whereas a 65-year-old in the late stages of emphysema would be among the oldest old.

We begin this module with a discussion of the myths and realities of aging, examining some stereotypes that color our understanding of late adulthood. We look at the outward and inward signs of aging and the ways the nervous system and senses change with age.

Next, we consider health and well-being. After examining some of the major disorders that affect older people, we look at what determines wellness and why old people are susceptible to disease. We then consider sexuality in late adulthood. We also focus on theories that seek to explain the aging process, as well as on gender, race, and ethnic differences in life expectancy.

Physical Development in Late Adulthood

Astronaut-turned-senator John Glenn was 77 years old when he returned to space on a 10-day mission to help NASA study how the elderly adjust to space travel. Although sheer altitude sets Glenn apart from others, many people lead active, vigorous lives during late adulthood, fully engaged with life.

gerontologists
specialists who study aging

Aging: Myth and Reality

LO 9.1   Describe the myths and realities of aging.

Late adulthood holds a unique distinction among life's stages: Because people are living longer, late adulthood is getting longer. Whether we start counting at 65 or 70, there is

Figure 9-1 The Flourishing Elderly

The number of people in the United States over age 65 is projected to double by 2060 from the number in 2014. What are the factors that contribute to this increase?

SOURCE: Adapted from Mather, Jacobsen, & Pollard, 2015.

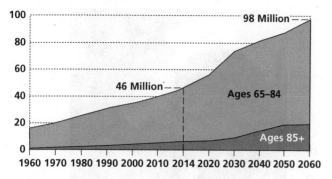

today a greater proportion of people alive in late adulthood than at any time in world history. In fact, demographers have divided the period using the same terms—but with different meanings—as researchers of functional aging. For demographers, the terms are purely chronological. The *young old* are 65 to 74 years old. The *old old* are between 75 and 84, and the *oldest old* are 85 and older.

THE DEMOGRAPHICS OF LATE ADULTHOOD One out of every eight Americans is 65 or older, and projections suggest that by 2050 nearly one-quarter of the population will be 65 and older. The number of people over the age of 85 is projected to increase from the current 6 million to 20 million by 2060 (see Figure 9-1; Mather, Jacobsen, & Pollard, 2015).

The fastest-growing segment of the population is the oldest old—people 85 or older. In the past two decades, the size of this group has nearly doubled. The population explosion among older people is not limited to the United States. As can be seen in Figure 9-2, the number of elderly is increasing substantially in countries around the globe. By 2050, the number of adults worldwide older than 60 will exceed the number of people younger than 15 for the first time in history (Sandis, 2000; United Nations, Department of Economic and Social Affairs, Population Division, 2013).

AGEISM: CONFRONTING THE STEREOTYPES OF LATE ADULTHOOD Crotchety. Old codger. Old coot. Senile. Geezer. Old hag.

Such are the labels of late adulthood. They don't draw a pretty picture: These words are demeaning and biased, representing both overt and subtle ageism. **Ageism** is prejudice and discrimination directed at older people.

Ageism suggests that older people are in less than full command of their mental faculties. Many attitude studies find that older adults are viewed more negatively than younger ones on a variety of traits, particularly those relating to general competence and attractiveness (Jesmin, 2014; Nelson, 2016; Ayalon & Tesch-Römer, 2017; Zhang et al., 2018).

Furthermore, many Western societies revere youth and admire a youthful appearance. It is the rare advertisement that includes an elderly person, unless it is for a

ageism
prejudice and discrimination directed at older people

Figure 9-2 The Elderly Population Worldwide

Longer life is transforming population profiles worldwide, with the proportion of those older than 60 predicted to increase substantially by 2050.

SOURCE: Based on United Nations, Department of Economic and Social Affairs, Population Division, 2013.

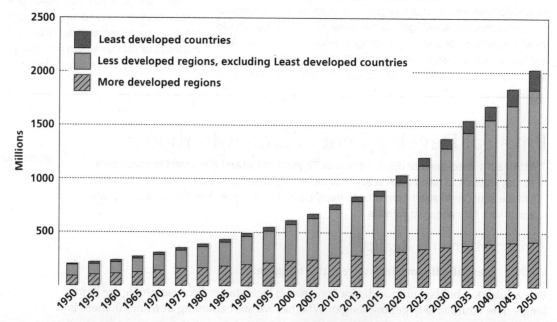

product specifically designed for older adults. And in media depictions, older persons are often presented as someone's parents or grandparents rather than as individuals in their own right (Ferguson & Brohaugh, 2010; Swift et al., 2017).

Today's ageism is, in some ways, a peculiarly modern and Western cultural phenomenon. In the American colonial period, a long life was an indication of a virtuous life, and older people were held in high esteem. Similarly, elders are venerated in most Asian societies because they have attained special wisdom by living so long, and many Native American societies have traditionally viewed older people as storehouses of information about the past (Bodner, Bergman, & Cohen-Fridel, 2012; Maxmen, 2012; Vauclair et al., 2017).

Today, however, negative views of older people prevail in U.S. society, and they are based on misinformation. Test your knowledge about aging by answering the questions in Table 9-1. Most people score no higher than chance on the items, getting about 50 percent correct (Palmore, 1992).

Given the prevalence of ageist stereotypes, it is reasonable to ask if there is a kernel of truth in them.

The answer is largely no. Aging produces consequences that vary greatly from one person to the next. Although some elderly people are in fact physically frail, have cognitive difficulties, and require constant care, others are vigorous and independent. Furthermore, some problems that at first glance seem attributable to old age are actually a result of illness, improper diet, or insufficient nutrition. As we will see, late adulthood can bring change and growth on a par with—and sometimes even greater than—previous periods of the life span (Whitbourne, 2007; Ridgway, 2018).

What do you see when you look at this woman? Ageism is found in widespread negative attitudes toward older people, suggesting that they are in less than full command of their faculties.

> **From a social worker's perspective:** When older people win praise and attention for being "vigorous," "active," and "youthful," is this a message that combats or supports ageism?

Table 9-1 The Myths of Aging

1. The majority of old people (age 65 and older) have defective memory, are disoriented, or are demented. T or F?
2. The five senses (sight, hearing, taste, touch, and smell) all tend to weaken in old age. T or F?
3. The majority of old people have no interest in, nor capacity for, sexual relations. T or F?
4. Lung capacity tends to decline in old age. T or F?
5. The majority of old people are sick most of the time. T or F?
6. Physical strength tends to decline in old age. T or F?
7. At least one-tenth of the aged are living in long-stay institutions (such as nursing homes, mental hospitals, and homes for the aged). T or F?
8. Many older adults maintain large social networks of friends. T or F?
9. Older workers usually cannot work as effectively as younger workers. T or F?
10. Over three-fourths of the aged are healthy enough to carry out their normal activities. T or F?
11. The majority of old people are unable to adapt to change. T or F?
12. Old people usually take longer to learn something new. T or F?
13. It is almost impossible for the average old person to learn something new. T or F?
14. Older people tend to react slower than do younger people. T or F?
15. In general, old people tend to be pretty much alike. T or F?
16. The majority of old people say they are seldom bored. T or F?
17. The majority of old people are socially isolated. T or F?
18. Older workers have fewer accidents than do younger workers. T or F?

Scoring

All odd-numbered statements are false; all even-numbered statements are true. Most college students miss about six, and high school students miss about nine. Even college instructors miss an average of about three.

SOURCE: Adapted from Palmore, 1992; Kahn & Rowe, 1999.

Physical Transitions in Older People

LO 9.2 Summarize the physical changes that occur in old age.

> "Feel the burn." That's what the teacher says, and many of the 14 women in the class are doing just that. As the teacher continues through a variety of exercises, the women participate to varying degrees. Some stretch and reach vigorously, and others mostly just sway to the music. It's not much different from thousands of exercise classes across the United States, yet to the youthful observer, there is one surprise: The youngest woman in this class is 66 years old, and the oldest, dressed in a sleek Spandex leotard, is 81.

The surprise registered by this observer reflects the stereotype that people older than 65 are sedentary, incapable of vigorous exercise. The reality is different. Although their physical capabilities are likely to have changed, many older people remain agile and fit long into old age. Still, the outer and inner changes that began subtly during middle adulthood become unmistakable during old age (Sargent-Cox, Anstey, & Luszcz, 2012; Fontes & Oliveira, 2013).

As we discuss aging, we should take note of the distinction between primary and secondary aging. **Primary aging**, or *senescence*, involves universal and irreversible changes resulting from genetic programming. In contrast, **secondary aging** encompasses changes that are the result of illness, health habits, and other individual factors, which are not inevitable. Although the physical and cognitive changes of secondary aging are common, they are potentially avoidable and can sometimes be reversed.

OUTWARD SIGNS OF AGING One of the most obvious indicators of aging is the hair, which usually becomes distinctly gray and eventually white, and may thin out. The face and other parts of the body become wrinkled as the skin loses elasticity and *collagen*, the protein that forms the basic fibers of body tissue.

People may become shorter by as much as 4 inches, partially because of changes in posture, but mostly because the cartilage in the disks of the backbone becomes thinner. This is particularly true for women, who are more susceptible than men to **osteoporosis**, or thinning of the bones, largely a result of reduced estrogen production.

Osteoporosis, which affects 25 percent of women older than 60, is a primary cause of broken bones among older people. It is largely preventable if exercise is adequate and calcium and protein intake were sufficient previously in life. Osteoporosis can be treated and even prevented with drugs such as Fosamax (alendronate) (Wang et al., 2013; Hansen et al., 2014; Braun et al., 2017).

Although negative stereotypes against appearing old affect both genders, they are particularly potent for women. In fact, in Western cultures there is a *double standard* for appearance, by which women are judged more harshly than men. For instance, gray hair in men is often viewed as "distinguished"; in women it is a sign of being "over the hill" (Krekula, 2016; Chrisler & Johnston-Robledo, 2018).

As a consequence, women may feel more pressure than men to hide the signs of aging by dyeing their hair, undergoing cosmetic surgery, and using age-concealing cosmetics. The double standard is diminishing, however, as more men grow interested in looking younger and fall prey to a new wave of male-oriented cosmetic products, such as wrinkle creams. Ironically, as the double standard eases, ageism is becoming more of a concern for both sexes (Crawford & Unger, 2004; Ojala, Pietilä, & Nikander, 2016).

INTERNAL AGING As the outward signs become more apparent, there are also changes in the internal functioning of the organ systems. The brain becomes smaller and lighter. As it shrinks, it pulls away from the skull; the space between the brain and skull doubles from age 20 to age 70. The brain uses less oxygen and glucose, and blood flow is reduced. The number of neurons, or brain cells, declines in some parts of the brain, although not as much as was once thought. Research suggests that the number of cells in the cortex may drop only minimally or not at all. In fact, some evidence suggests that certain types of neuronal growth may continue throughout the life span (Gattringer et al., 2012; Jäncke et al., 2015; Hamasaki et al., 2018).

The reduced flow of blood in the brain is due in part to the heart's reduced ability to pump blood through hardening and shrinking blood vessels. A 75-year-old man

primary aging
aging that involves universal and irreversible changes that, because of genetic programming, occur as people get older

secondary aging
changes in physical and cognitive functioning that are as a result of illness, health habits, and other individual differences, but are not the result of increased age itself and are not inevitable

osteoporosis
a condition in which the bones become brittle, fragile, and thin, often brought about by a lack of calcium in the diet

pumps less than three-quarters of the blood that he could pump during early adulthood (Yildiz, 2007; Wu et al., 2016).

Other bodily systems also work at lower capacity. The respiratory system is less efficient, and the digestive system produces less digestive juice and is less efficient in pushing food through the system—thereby increasing the incidence of constipation. Some hormones are produced at lower levels. Muscle fibers decrease both in size and in amount, and they become less efficient at using oxygen from the bloodstream and storing nutrients (Deruelle et al., 2008; Suetta & Kjaer, 2010; Morley, 2012).

Although these changes are normal, they often occur earlier in people who have less healthy lifestyles. For example, smoking accelerates declines in cardiovascular capacity at any age.

Lifestyle factors can also slow the changes associated with aging. For instance, people whose exercise program includes weightlifting may lose muscle fiber at a slower rate than those who are sedentary. Similarly, physical fitness is related to better performance on mental tests, may prevent a loss of brain tissue, and may even aid in the development of new neurons. In fact, studies suggest that sedentary older adults who begin aerobic fitness training ultimately show cognitive benefits (Solberg et al., 2013; Lin et al., 2014; Bonavita & Tedeschi, 2017).

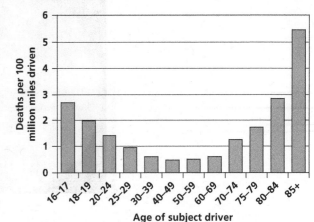

Even in late adulthood, exercise is possible—and beneficial.

SLOWING REACTION TIME

> Carlos winced as the "game over" message came up on his grandsons' video game system. He enjoyed trying out their games, but he just couldn't shoot down those bad guys as quickly as his grandkids could.

As people get older, they take longer: longer to put on a tie, reach a ringing phone, press the buttons in a video game. One reason is a lengthening of reaction time, which begins to increase in middle age and by late adulthood may rise significantly (Benjuya, Melzer, & Kaplanski, 2004; Der & Deary, 2006; van Schooten, et al., 2018).

It is not clear why people slow down. One explanation, known as the **peripheral slowing hypothesis**, suggests that the peripheral nervous system, which encompasses the nerves that branch from the spinal cord and brain to the extremities of the body, becomes less efficient with age. Because of this, it takes longer for information from the environment to reach the brain and for commands from the brain to be transmitted to the muscles (Salthouse, 2006, 2017; Kimura, Yasunaga, & Wang, 2013).

According to the **generalized slowing hypothesis**, on the other hand, processing in all parts of the nervous system, including the brain, is less efficient. As a consequence, slowing occurs throughout the body, including the processing of both simple and complex stimuli, and the transmission of commands to the muscles (Harada, Love, & Triebel, 2013).

Although we don't know which explanation is more accurate, it is clear that the slowing of reaction time and general processing results in a higher incidence of accidents for elderly people. Slowed reaction and processing time means they can't efficiently receive information from the environment that may indicate a dangerous situation. Slowed decision-making processes impair their ability to remove themselves from harm's way. Still, drivers older than 70 have fewer auto accidents per mile driven than teenagers when accidents are figured in terms of miles of driving (Tefft, 2012; Leversen, Hopkins, & Sigmundsson, 2013; see Figure 9-3).

The Senses: Sight, Sound, Taste, and Smell

LO 9.3 Explain how aging affects the senses.

Old age brings declines in the sense organs, which has major psychological consequences because the senses are people's link with the world.

peripheral slowing hypothesis
the theory that suggests that overall processing speed declines in the peripheral nervous system with increasing age

generalized slowing hypothesis
the theory that processing in all parts of the nervous system, including the brain, is less efficient as we age

Figure 9-3 Vehicle Fatalities Across the Life Span
Drivers over age 70 have a superior crash record to drivers 19 and younger when crashes are calculated per mile of driving. Why is this the case? **THINKING ABOUT THE DATA:** At what age do fatalities begin to approach those of 16-year-olds? What factors lead to this increase?

SOURCE: Tefft, 2012.

VISION Changes in the physical apparatus of the eye—the cornea, lens, retina, and optic nerve—diminish visual abilities. The lens becomes less transparent, allowing only a third as much light to reach the retina at 60 as at 20. The optic nerve also becomes less efficient in transmitting nerve impulses. As a result, vision declines along several dimensions. We see distant objects less well, need more light to see clearly, and take longer to adjust from dark to light and vice versa (Gawande, 2007; Owsley, Ghate, & Kedar, 2018).

These changes cause everyday problems. Driving, particularly at night, becomes more challenging. Reading requires more light, and eye strain comes more easily. Of course, eyeglasses and contact lenses can correct many of these problems, and the majority of older people see reasonably well (Owsley, Stalvey, & Phillips, 2003; Boerner et al., 2010).

Several eye diseases become more common during late adulthood. For instance, *cataracts*—cloudy or opaque areas on the lens of the eye that interfere with the passage of light—frequently develop. Cataracts bring blurred vision and glare in bright light. If cataracts are left untreated, the lens becomes milky white and blindness results. However, cataracts can be surgically removed, and eyesight can be restored with eyeglasses, contact lenses, or *intraocular lens implants*, in which a plastic lens is permanently placed in the eye (Walker, Anstey, & Lord, 2006; Miyata et al., 2018).

Another serious problem among elderly individuals is glaucoma. *Glaucoma* occurs when pressure in the fluid of the eye increases, either because the fluid cannot drain properly or because too much fluid is produced. Glaucoma can be treated with drugs or surgery if it is detected early enough.

The most common cause of blindness in people older than 60 is *age-related macular degeneration* (AMD), which affects the *macula*, a yellowish area near the retina at which visual perception is most acute. When a portion of the macula thins and degenerates, the eyesight gradually deteriorates (see Figure 9-4). If diagnosed early, macular degeneration can sometimes be treated with medication or lasers. There is also some evidence that a diet rich in antioxidant vitamins (C, E, and A) can reduce the risk of AMD (Jager, Mieler, & Miller, 2008; Vingolo, Salvatore, & Limoli, 2013; Bainbridge & Wallhagen, 2014).

HEARING Around 30 percent of adults between 65 and 74 have some hearing loss, and the figure rises to 50 percent among people older than 75. Overall, more than 10 million elderly people in the United States have hearing impairments of one kind or another (Chisolm, Willott, & Lister, 2003; Pacala & Yueh, 2012; National Institute on Deafness and Other Communication Disorders, 2018).

Figure 9-4 The World Through Macular Degeneration

(a) Age-related macular degeneration affects the macula, a yellowish area of the eye located near the retina. Eyesight gradually deteriorates once the portion of the macula thins and degenerates.
(b) Macular degeneration leads to a gradual deterioration of the center of the retina, leaving only peripheral vision. This is an example of what a person with macular degeneration might see.
SOURCE: AARP, 2005.

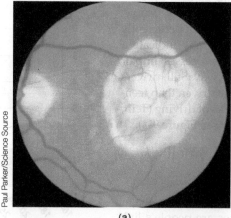

(a)   (b)

Paul Parker/Science Source   Pearson Education

Aging particularly affects the ability to hear higher frequencies. This makes it hard to hear conversations amid background noise or when several people are speaking simultaneously. Some elderly people actually find loud noises painful.

Although hearing aids would probably be helpful around 75 percent of the time, only 20 percent of elderly people wear them. One reason is that hearing aids are far from perfect. They amplify background noises as much as conversations, making it difficult for wearers to separate what they want to hear from other sounds. Furthermore, many people feel that hearing aids make them appear even older and encourage others to treat them as if they were disabled (Lesner, 2003; Meister & von Wedel, 2003; Weinstein, 2018).

Hearing loss can be deadly to one's social life. Unable to hear conversations fully, some elderly people with hearing problems withdraw from others, unwilling to respond because they are unsure what was said to them. They can easily feel left out and lonely. Hearing loss can also lead to feelings of paranoia as conversational blanks are filled according to fear rather than reality. If someone hears "I hate going to Maude's" instead of "I hate going to the mall," a bland opinion about shopping can be interpreted as an expression of personal animosity (Myers, 2000; Goorabi, Hoseinabadi, & Share, 2008; Ozmeral et al., 2016).

Hearing loss may hasten cognitive decline. The struggle to understand what is being said can shunt mental resources away from processing information, causing difficulties in remembering and understanding information (Wingfield, Tun, & McCoy, 2005; Mikkola et al., 2015; Moser, Luxenberger & Freidl, 2017).

TASTE AND SMELL Elderly people who have always enjoyed eating may experience a real decline in the quality of life because of changes in sensitivity to taste and smell. Both senses become less discriminating, causing food to be less appetizing than it was previously (Nordin, Razani, & Markison, 2003; Murphy, 2008).

The decrease in taste and smell sensitivity has a physical cause. The tongue loses taste buds over time, making food less tasty. The problem is compounded as the olfactory bulbs in the brain begin to shrivel. Because taste depends on smell, this makes food taste even blander.

The loss of taste and smell sensitivity has an unfortunate side effect: Because food does not taste as good, people eat less and open the door to malnutrition. They may also oversalt their food, thereby increasing their risk of *hypertension*, or high blood pressure, one of the most common health problems of old age. Furthermore, alterations in taste and smell have been associated with major depression (Smith et al., 2006; Yoshikawa et al., 2018; Hur et al., 2018).

The Impact of Aging on Health

Sandra Frye passes around a photo of her father. "He was 75 when this was taken. He looks great and he could still sail back then, but he was already forgetting things like what he'd done yesterday or what he'd eaten for breakfast."

Frye takes part in a support group for family members of Alzheimer's patients. The second picture she shares shows her father 10 years later. "It was sad. He'd start talking to me and his words would jumble. Then he'd forget who I was. He forgot he had a younger brother or that he'd been a pilot in World War II. A year after this photo, he was bedridden. Six months later, he died."

When Sandra Frye's father was diagnosed, he joined the 4.5 million Americans with Alzheimer's disease, a debilitating condition that saps both physical and mental powers. In some ways, Alzheimer's feeds the stereotypical view of elderly people as more apt to be ill than healthy.

However, the reality is different: Most elderly people are in relatively good health for most of old age. According to surveys conducted in the United States, almost three-quarters of people 65 years old and older rate their health as good, very good, or excellent.

Still, to be old is in fact to be susceptible to diseases, and maintaining their physical and mental health is a major concern of older adults. Let's consider some of the major physical and psychological disorders of older people.

Health Problems and Wellness in Older People

LO 9.4   Summarize the health problems elderly people experience, and list the factors that influence the state of a person's health.

Most of the illnesses and diseases of late adulthood are not peculiar to old age; people of all ages suffer from cancer and heart disease, for instance. However, the incidence of these diseases rises with age, raising the odds that a person will be ill during old age. Moreover, older people bounce back more slowly from illnesses than younger people, and a full recovery may be impossible.

COMMON PHYSICAL DISORDERS   The leading causes of death in elderly people are heart disease, cancer, and chronic respiratory problems, which claim close to three-quarters of people in late adulthood. Because aging weakens the immune system, older adults are also more susceptible to infectious diseases (National Council on Aging, 2015; National Center for Health Statistics, 2017).

In addition, most older people have at least one chronic, long-term condition, and three-quarters have at least two. For instance, *arthritis*, an inflammation of one or more joints, afflicts roughly half of older people. Arthritis can cause painful swelling, and it can be disabling, preventing people from performing the simplest of everyday tasks, such as unscrewing a jar of food or turning a key in a lock. Although aspirin and other drugs can relieve some of the swelling and reduce the pain, arthritis cannot be cured (Leverone & Epstein, 2010; National Council on Aging, 2016).

Around one-third of older people have *hypertension*, or high blood pressure. Many people who have high blood pressure are unaware of their condition because it has no symptoms, which makes it more dangerous. Left untreated, hypertension can weaken and damage blood vessels and the heart and may raise the risk of strokes (Hermida et al., 2013; Oliveira, de Menezes, & de Olinda, 2017; Reddy, Ganguly, & Sharma, 2018).

PSYCHOLOGICAL AND MENTAL DISORDERS   Some 15 to 25 percent of people older than 65 are thought to show some symptoms of psychological disorder, a lower percentage than in younger adults. The behavioral symptoms related to these disorders are sometimes different in older and younger adults (National Council on Aging, 2016).

One of the more prevalent problems is major depression, which is characterized by feelings of intense sadness, pessimism, and hopelessness. Among the reasons cited for depression are the experience of cumulative losses of their spouses, partners, and friends, and their own declining health and physical capabilities (Vink et al., 2009; Taylor, 2014; Förster et al., 2018).

Some elderly people suffer from psychological disorders induced by the combinations of drugs they may be taking for various medical conditions. They may also be taking inappropriate doses of some medications because the metabolism of a 75-year-old and that of a 25-year-old differ, and the doses appropriate for them may differ too. Because of these possibilities, older people who take medications must be careful to inform their physicians and pharmacists of every drug—with dosage information—that they take. They should also avoid medicating themselves with over-the-counter drugs, because a combination of nonprescription and prescription drugs may be dangerous.

major neurocognitive disorder
the most common mental disorder of the elderly, it covers several diseases, each of which includes serious memory loss accompanied by declines in other mental functioning

The most common mental disorder of elderly people is **major neurocognitive disorder**, previously referred to as *dementia*, a broad category of diseases encompassing serious memory loss accompanied by declines in other mental functioning. Although major neurocognitive disorder has many causes, the symptoms are similar: declining memory, lessened intellectual abilities, and impaired judgment. The chances of experiencing major neurocognitive disorder increase with age. Less than 2 percent of people between 60 and 65 are diagnosed with the disorder, but the percentages double for every 5-year period past 65. There are some ethnic differences, too, with African Americans and Hispanics showing higher levels of major neurocognitive disorder than Caucasians (Alzheimer's Association & Centers for Disease Control and Prevention, 2018).

Alzheimer's disease
a progressive brain disorder that produces loss of memory and confusion

ALZHEIMER'S DISEASE   **Alzheimer's disease**, a progressive brain disorder that produces loss of memory and confusion, leads to the deaths of 100,000 people in the United States each year. One in 10 people age 65 and older has Alzheimer's; 19 percent of those age 75 to 84 have the disease, and nearly half of people over the age of 85 are affected by the disease. In fact, unless a cure is found, some 14 million people will be victims of Alzheimer's by 2050—triple the current number (Park et al., 2014; Alzheimer's Association, 2017).

The first sign of Alzheimer's is usually forgetfulness. A person may have trouble recalling words during a conversation or may return to the grocery store several times after having already done the shopping. At first, recent memories are affected, and then older ones. Eventually, people with the disease are totally confused, unable to speak intelligibly or to recognize even their closest family and friends. In the final stages, they lose voluntary control of their muscles and are bedridden. Because victims of the disorder are initially aware of the future course of the disease, they may understandably suffer from anxiety, fear, and depression.

Biologically, Alzheimer's occurs when production of *beta amyloid precursor protein*—which normally promotes the production and growth of neurons—goes awry, creating large clumps of cells called plaque that trigger inflammation and deterioration of nerve cells. The brain shrinks, and several areas of the hippocampus and frontal and temporal lobes show deterioration. Furthermore, certain neurons die, which leads to a shortage of various neurotransmitters, such as acetylcholine (Medeiros et al., 2007; Bredesen, 2009; Callahan et al., 2013; National Institute on Aging, 2017).

Although the physical changes that produce Alzheimer's are clear, what is not known is the trigger. Genetics clearly plays a role, with some families showing a much higher incidence of Alzheimer's than others. In fact, in certain families half the children appear to inherit the disease from their parents. Furthermore, years before Alzheimer's symptoms emerge, people who are genetically at high risk for the disease show differences in brain functioning when they are trying to recall information, as illustrated in the brain scans in Figure 9-5 (Baulac et al., 2009; Désiréa et al., 2013; Broce et al., 2018).

Most evidence suggests that Alzheimer's is an inherited disorder, but nongenetic factors such as high blood pressure or diet may increase susceptibility. In one cross-cultural study, poor black residents in a Nigerian town were less likely to develop Alzheimer's than a comparable sample of African Americans living in the United States. The researchers speculate that variations in diet between the two groups—the residents of Nigeria ate mainly vegetables—might account for the differences in the Alzheimer's rates (Hendrie et al., 2001; Chen et al., 2010; Fuso et al., 2012; Roussotte et al., 2014).

Scientists are also studying certain viruses, dysfunctions of the immune system, and hormone imbalances that may produce the disease. Other studies have found that lower levels of linguistic ability in the early 20s are associated with declines in cognitive capabilities resulting from Alzheimer's much later in life (Alisky, 2007; Carbone et al., 2014; Balin et al., 2018).

At present, there is no cure for Alzheimer's, only treatments for the symptoms. The most promising drugs are related to the loss of the neurotransmitter acetylcholine (Ach) that occurs in some forms of the disease. Donepezil (Aricept), galantamine (Razadyne), rivastigmine (Exelon), and tacrine (Cognex) are among the most common drugs prescribed, but they are effective in only half of Alzheimer's patients, and only temporarily (de Jesus Moreno, 2003; Gauthier & Scheltens, 2009; Alzheimer's Association, 2017a).

Other drugs being studied include anti-inflammatory drugs, which may reduce the brain inflammation that occurs in Alzheimer's. In addition, the chemicals in vitamins C and E are being tested, because some evidence suggests that people who take such vitamins are at lower risk for developing the disorder (Alzheimer's Association, 2004; Mohajeri & Leuba, 2009; Sabbagh, 2009; Wang et al., 2015).

As victims lose the ability to feed and clothe themselves, or even to control bladder and bowel functions, they must be cared for 24 hours a day. Because of this, most

Figure 9-5 A Different Brain?

Brain scans show differences between the brains of those with Alzheimer's disease and those who do not suffer from it.

SOURCE: Bookheimer et al., 2000.

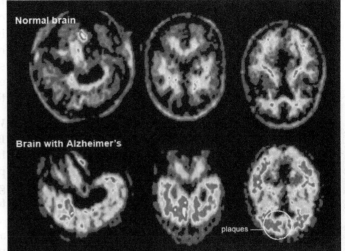

Before her death at age 64, legendary basketball coach Pat Summitt lived with Alzheimer's disease for 5 years.

people with Alzheimer's live out their lives in nursing homes, accounting for some two-thirds of the residents of nursing homes (Prigerson, 2003; Sparks, 2008; Gaugler et al., 2014).

Caregivers often become secondary victims of the disease. It is easy to become frustrated, angry, and exhausted by the demands of Alzheimer's patients, whose needs may be overpowering. In addition to the physical chore of providing total care, caregivers face the loss of a loved one, who not only is visibly deteriorating but can act emotionally unstable and even fly into rages (Sanders et al., 2008; Iavarone et al., 2014; Pudelewicz, Talarska, & Bączyk, 2018; also see the *Development in Your Life* feature.)

WELLNESS IN LATE ADULTHOOD: THE RELATIONSHIP BETWEEN AGING AND ILLNESS Sickness is not inevitable in old age. Whether an older person is ill or well depends less on age than on a variety of factors, including genetic predisposition, past and present environmental factors, and psychological factors.

Certain diseases, such as cancer and heart disease, have a clear genetic component, but a genetic predisposition does not automatically mean that a person will get a particular illness. People's lifestyles—smoking, diet, and exposure to cancer-causing agents such as sunlight or asbestos—may raise or lower their chances of coming down with such a disease.

Furthermore, economic well-being also plays a role. For instance, as it does at all stages of life, living in poverty restricts access to medical care. Even relatively well-off people may have difficulties finding affordable health care. For example, the average 65-year-old couple retiring in 2018 is estimated to need $280,000 to pay for medical costs through their retirement. Furthermore, older people spend almost 13 percent of their total expenditures on health care, more than two times what younger individuals spend (Federal Interagency Forum on Aging-Related Statistics, 2010; Wild et al., 2014; O'Brien, 2018).

Finally, psychological factors play an important role in determining susceptibility to illness. For example, a sense of control over one's environment, such as making choices involving everyday matters, leads to a better psychological state and superior health outcomes (Levy, Slade, & Kasl, 2002; Taylor, 2014).

People can enhance their physical well-being—and longevity—simply by doing what people of all ages should do: Eat wisely, exercise, and avoid obvious threats to health, such as smoking. The goal of medical and social service professionals is now to extend people's *active life spans*, the amount of time they remain healthy and able to enjoy their lives (Sawatzky & Naimark, 2002; Gavin & Myers, 2003; Katz & Marshall, 2003; Malhotra et al., 2016).

Sometimes, older people have trouble following even these simple guidelines. For instance, estimates suggest that between 15 percent and 50 percent of elderly people do not have adequate nutrition, and several million experience hunger every day (Strohl, Bednar, & Longley, 2012; Giacalone et al., 2016).

The reasons are varied. Some elderly people have too little money to purchase adequate food, and some are too frail to shop or cook for themselves. Others feel little motivation to prepare and eat proper meals, particularly if they live alone or are depressed. For those with decreased taste and smell sensitivity, eating may no longer be enjoyable. And some older people may never have eaten well-balanced meals in previous periods of their lives (Vandenberghe-Descamps et al., 2017; Horning et al., 2018).

Obtaining sufficient exercise may also prove problematic for older people. Illness may interfere with exercise, and inclement weather may confine an older person to the house. Furthermore, problems can combine: A person who is poor with insufficient

Development in Your Life

Caring for People with Alzheimer's Disease

Alzheimer's disease is one of the most difficult illnesses to deal with, but several steps can be taken to help both patient and caregiver deal with Alzheimer's.

- Make patients feel secure in their home environments by keeping them occupied in everyday tasks of living as long as possible.

- Label everyday objects, furnish calendars and detailed but simple lists, and give oral reminders of time and place.

- Keep clothing simple: Provide clothes with few zippers and buttons, and lay them out in the order in which they should be put on.

- Put bathing on a schedule. People with Alzheimer's may be afraid of falling and of hot water, and may therefore avoid needed bathing.

- Prevent driving. Although patients often want to continue driving, their accident rate is high—some 20 times higher than average.

- Monitor telephone use. Patients with Alzheimer's who answer the phone may agree to offers from telephone salespeople and investment counselors.

- Provide opportunities for exercise, such as a daily walk. This prevents muscle deterioration and stiffness.

- Caregivers should remember to take time off and lead their own lives. Seek out support from community service organizations.

- Call or write to the Alzheimer's Association, which can provide support and information. The Association can be reached at 225 N. Michigan Ave. Fl. 17, Chicago, IL 60601-7633; Tel. 1-800-272-3900; http://www.alz.org.

---

funds to eat properly may have little energy to put into physical activity (Kelley et al., 2009; Logsdon et al., 2009; Pargman & Dobersek, 2018).

SEXUALITY IN OLD AGE: USE IT OR LOSE IT   Do your grandparents have sex?

Probably. Increasing evidence suggests that people are sexually active well into their 80s and 90s, despite societal stereotypes prevalent in the United States, suggesting that it is somehow improper for two 75-year-olds to have sexual intercourse, and even worse for a 75-year-old to masturbate. In many other cultures, elderly people are expected to remain sexually active, and in some societies, people are expected to become less inhibited as they age (Lindau et al., 2007; De Conto, 2017).

Two major factors determine whether an elderly person will engage in sexual activity. One is good physical and mental health. The other is previous regular sexual activity. "Use it or lose it" seems an accurate description of sexual functioning in older people. Sexual activity can and often does continue throughout the life span. Furthermore, there's some intriguing evidence that having sex may have some unexpected side benefits: Some research shows that having sex regularly is associated with an increased life span (Huang et al., 2009; Hillman, 2012; McCarthy & Pierpaoli, 2015)!

Surveys show that almost half of men and a third of women older than age 70 masturbate. The average frequency for those who masturbated was once a week. Around two-thirds of married men and women had sex with their spouses, again averaging around once a week. In addition, the percentage of people who view their sexual partners as physically attractive actually increases with age (Araujo, Mohr, & McKinlay, 2004; Ravanipour, Gharibi, & Gharibi, 2013).

Of course, there are some changes in sexual functioning. Testosterone declines during adulthood by approximately 30 to 40 percent from the late 40s to the early 70s. It takes a longer time, and more stimulation, for men to get a full erection. The refractory period—the time following an orgasm before a man can become aroused again—may last one or more days. To improve sexual functioning, many men take drugs such as Viagra or Cialis (Gökçe & Yaman, 2017).

Diet is an important factor in the relationship between aging and illness.

Photo_DDD/Shutterstock

Women's vaginas become thin and inelastic, and they produce less natural lubrication, making intercourse more difficult. It is important to realize that older adults—like younger ones—are susceptible to sexually transmitted diseases. In fact, 10 percent of people diagnosed with AIDS are older than 50, and the rate of new cases of other sexually transmitted infections is among the highest for any age group. In some nursing homes, sexually transmitted diseases represent a major health issue (Seidman, 2003; National Institute of Aging, 2004; Ducharme, 2018).

Approaches to Aging: Why Is Death Inevitable?

LO 9.5 Discuss the different theories of aging, and summarize the research to increase life expectancy.

Hovering over late adulthood is the specter of death. At some point, no matter how healthy we have been throughout life, we know that we will experience physical declines and that life will end. But why?

There are two major approaches to explaining why we undergo physical deterioration and death: genetic programming theories and wear-and-tear theories.

genetic programming theories of aging

theories that suggest that our body's DNA genetic code contains a built-in time limit for the reproduction of human cells

wear-and-tear theories of aging

the theory that the mechanical functions of the body simply wear out with age

Genetic programming theories of aging suggest that our body's DNA contains a built-in time limit for the reproduction of human cells. After a genetically determined period, the cells can no longer divide, and the individual begins to deteriorate (Rattan, Kristensen, & Clark, 2006).

The theory comes in several variants. One is that the genetic material contains a "death gene" programmed to tell the body to deteriorate and die. Researchers who take an evolutionary viewpoint suggest that a long life span after the reproductive years is unnecessary for the survival of the species. According to this view, genetic diseases that strike later in life continue to exist because they allow people time to have children, thus passing along genes that are "programmed" to cause diseases and death.

Another variant is that the cells can duplicate only a certain number of times. Throughout our lives, new cells are produced through cell duplication to repair and replenish our various tissues and organs. According to this view, the genetic instructions for running the body can be read only a certain number of times before they become illegible and cells stop reproducing. Because the body is not being renewed at the same rate, bodily deterioration and death ensue (Thoms, Kuschal, & Emmert, 2007).

Evidence for the genetic programming theory comes from research showing that human cells permitted to divide in the laboratory can do so successfully only around 50 times. Each time they divide, *telomeres*, which are tiny, protective areas of DNA at the tip of chromosomes, grow shorter. When a cell's telomere has just about disappeared, the cell stops replicating, making it susceptible to damage and producing signs of aging (Epel, 2009; Kolyada et al., 2016; Murdock et al., 2017).

In contrast, **wear-and-tear theories of aging** argue that the mechanical functions of the body simply wear out—the way cars and washing machines do. In addition, some wear-and-tear theorists suggest that the body's constant manufacture of energy to fuel its activities creates by-products. These by-products, combined with the toxins and threats of everyday life (such as radiation, chemical exposure, accidents, and disease), eventually reach such high levels that they impair the body's normal functioning. The ultimate result is deterioration and death.

One specific category of by-products that has been related to aging includes free radicals, electrically charged molecules or atoms that are produced by the cells of the body. Because of their electrical charge, free radicals may cause negative effects on other cells of the body. A great deal of research suggests that oxygen-free radicals may be implicated in a number of age-related problems, including cancer, heart disease, and diabetes (Sierra, 2006; Hayflick, 2007; Sonnen et al., 2009; Lustgarten, Muller, & Van Remmen, 2011).

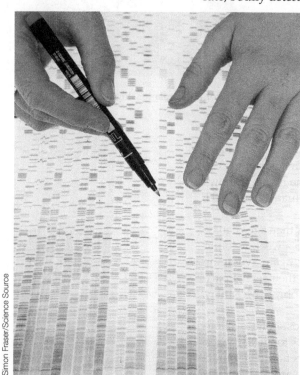

Simon Fraser/Science Source

According to genetic programming theories of aging, our DNA genetic code contains a built-in limit on the length of life.

RECONCILING THE THEORIES OF AGING Genetic programming theories and wear-and-tear theories make different suggestions about the inevitability of death. Genetic programming theories suggest that there is a built-in time limit to life—it's programmed in the genes, after all. On the other hand, wear-and-tear theories, particularly those that focus on the toxins that are built up during the course of life, paint a somewhat more optimistic view. They suggest that if a means can be found to eliminate the toxins produced by the body and by exposure to the environment, aging might well be slowed. For example, certain genes seem to slow aging and increase their ability to withstand age-related diseases (Ghazi, Henis-Korenblit, & Kenyon, 2009). We don't know which class of theories provides the more accurate account. Each is supported by some research, and each seems to explain certain aspects of aging. Ultimately, though, the mystery remains (Horiuchi, Finch, & Mesle, 2003; Friedman & Janssen, 2010; Aldwin & Igarashi, 2015).

LIFE EXPECTANCY: HOW LONG HAVE I GOT? Although why we die is not fully understood, we do know how to calculate our average life expectancy: Most of us can expect to live into old age. The **life expectancy**—the average age of death for members of a population—of a baby born in 2018, for instance, is 77 years for a male and 81 years for a female born in North America.

Average life expectancy is on the rise. In 1776, average U.S. life expectancy was 35. By the early 1900s, it had risen to 47. And in only four decades, from 1950 to 1990, it increased from 68 to older than 75. Predictions are that it will continue to rise steadily, possibly reaching into the 80s by 2050 (see Figure 9-6).

There are several reasons for this. Health and sanitation are generally better, with many diseases, such as smallpox, wiped out entirely. There are now vaccines and preventive measures for many diseases that used to kill young people, such as measles and mumps. Working conditions are better and products are safer. Many people are making healthful lifestyle choices such as keeping their weight down, eating fresh fruit and vegetables, and exercising—all of which can extend their active life spans, the years they spend in health and enjoyment of life.

Just how much can the life span be increased? The most common answer is around 120 years, the age reached by Jeanne Calment, the oldest person in the world until she died in 1997 at 122. Living longer would probably require major genetic alterations that are both technically and ethically improbable. Still, recent scientific and technological advances suggest that significantly extending the life span is not an impossibility.

POSTPONING AGING: CAN SCIENTISTS FIND THE FOUNTAIN OF YOUTH? Are researchers close to finding the scientific equivalent of the fountain of youth?

Not yet, but they're getting closer, at least in nonhuman species. For instance, researchers have extended the lives of nematodes (microscopic, transparent worms that typically live for just 9 days) to 50 days—the equivalent of extending human life to 420 years. Researchers have also doubled fruit flies' lives (Libert et al., 2007; Ocorr et al., 2007; Fedichev 2018).

The most promising avenues for increasing the length of life are these:

- **Telomere therapy.** Telomeres are the tiny areas at the tips of chromosomes that grow shorter each time a cell divides and eventually disappear, ending cell replication. Some scientists believe that if telomeres could be lengthened, aging could be slowed. Researchers are now looking for genes that control the production of telomerase, an enzyme that seems to regulate the length of telomeres. Furthermore, some researchers believe that one can lengthen telomeres, and hence lengthen life, by following good health practices (Chung et al., 2007; Reynolds, 2016; Blackburn & Epel, 2017).

- **Drug therapy.** Scientists have discovered that the drug *rapamycin* could extend life in mice by 14 percent by interfering with the activity of a protein *mTOR*. This finding suggests the drug may have an effect on expanding the life span and improving memory. Another substance, *GDF11*, appears to restore muscles strength

Figure 9-6 Living to Age 100

If increases in life expectancy continue, it may be a common occurrence for people to live to be 100 by the end of this century. What implications does this have for society?

SOURCE: United Nations, Department of Economic and Social Affairs, "World Population Prospects, 2015," cited in Stepler, 2016.

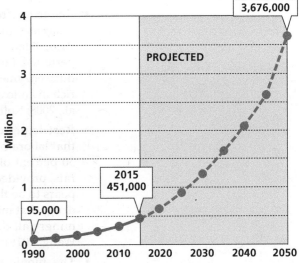

life expectancy
the average age of death for members of a population

and slow deterioration of neurons, at least in mice (Santos et al., 2011; Stipp, 2012; Katsimpardi et al., 2014; Zhang et al., 2014).

- **Unlocking longevity genes.** Certain genes control the body's ability to cope with environmental challenges and physical adversity. If harnessed, those genes may provide a way to increase the life span. One particularly promising family of genes are *sirtuins*, which may promote longer life (Sinclair & Guarente, 2006; Glatt et al., 2007; Fujitsuka et al., 2016).

- **Reducing free radicals through antioxidant drugs.** Free radicals—unstable molecules that drift through the body—damage other cells and lead to aging. Antioxidant drugs that can reduce the number of free radicals may eventually be perfected. Furthermore, it may be possible to insert in human cells genes that produce enzymes that act as antioxidants. In the meantime, nutritionists urge a diet rich in antioxidant vitamins, which are found in fruits and vegetables (Haleem et al., 2008; Kolling & Knopf, 2014; Pomatto & Davies, 2018).

- **Restricting calories.** For at least the past decade, researchers have known that laboratory rats who are fed an extremely low-calorie diet, providing 30 to 50 percent of their normal intake, often live 30 percent longer than better-fed rats, provided they get all the vitamins and minerals they need. The reason appears to be that they produce fewer free radicals. Researchers hope to develop drugs that mimic the effects of calorie restriction without forcing people to feel hungry all the time (Ingram, Young, & Mattison, 2007; Cuervo, 2008; Liang & Wang, 2018).

- **The bionic solution: replacing worn-out organs.** Heart transplants ... liver transplants ... lung transplants. We live in an age when replacing damaged or diseased organs seems nearly routine.

One major problem remains: Transplants often fail because the body rejects the foreign tissue. To overcome this problem, some researchers advocate growing replacement organs from the person's own cloned cells, which will not be rejected. Even more radically, genetically engineered cells from nonhumans that do not evoke rejection could be cloned, harvested, and transplanted into humans. Finally, it may be possible to create artificial organs that can completely replace diseased or damaged ones (Kwant et al., 2007; Li & Zhu, 2007; Forni, Darmon, & Schetz, 2017).

Sci-fi ideas for extending human life are exciting, but society must work to solve a more immediate problem: the significant disparity in life expectancies between members of different racial and ethnic groups. We discuss this important issue in the accompanying *Cultural Dimensions* feature.

> **From a health-care professional's perspective:** Given what you've learned about explanations of life expectancy, how might you try to extend your own life?

Cultural Dimensions

Racial and Ethnic Differences in Life Expectancy

- The average white child born in the United States is likely to live 79.1 years. The average black child is likely to live 3.5 years less.

- A child born in Japan has a life expectancy of more than 85 years; for a child born in Afghanistan, life expectancy is just over 52 years (*World Factbook*, 2018).

There are several reasons for these troubling discrepancies. Consider, for example, the gender gap in life expectancy, which is particularly pronounced. Across the industrialized world, women live longer than men by some 4 to 10 years. This female advantage begins just after conception: Although slightly more males are conceived, males are more likely to die during the prenatal period, infancy, and childhood. Consequently, by the age of 30 there are roughly equal numbers of men and women. But by the age of 65, 84 percent of females and only 70 percent of males are still alive. For those older than 85, the gender gap widens: For every male, 2.57 women are still alive (United Nations World Population Prospects, 2006; Central Intelligence Agency, 2018).

There are several explanations for the gender gap. One is that the naturally higher levels of the hormones estrogen and progesterone in women provide some protection from diseases such as heart attacks. It is also possible that women engage in healthier behavior during their lives, such as eating well. However, no conclusive evidence supports any of these explanations fully (Emslie & Hunt, 2008; Aichele, Rabbitt & Ghisletta, 2016).

Whatever its cause, the gender gap has continued to increase. During the early part of the 20th century, there was only a 2-year difference in favor of women, but in the 1980s this gap grew to 7 years. The size of the gap now seems to have leveled off, largely because men are more likely than previously to engage in positive health behaviors (such as smoking less, eating better, and exercising more).

Racial and ethnic differences are more troubling because they underline socioeconomic disparities in the United States. Life expectancy is almost 10 percent greater for Caucasians than for African Americans (see Figure 9-7). Furthermore, in contrast to Caucasians, whose life expectancy keeps edging up, African Americans have actually experienced slight declines in life expectancy in recent years.

Figure 9-7 Life Expectancy of African Americans and Caucasians

Male African Americans have a shorter life expectancy than male Caucasians, just as female African Americans have a shorter life expectancy than female Caucasians.

SOURCE: National Center for Health Statistics, 2016.

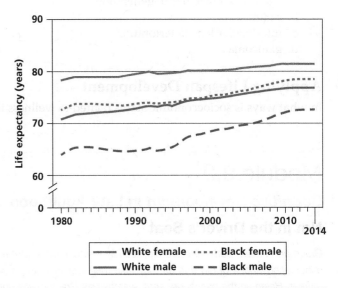

Review, Check, and Apply

Review

LO 9.1   Describe the myths and realities of aging.

Older people are often subject to ageism—prejudice and discrimination against people based on their age. Not all cultures view aging negatively. Elderly people are revered in Asian and Native American societies.

LO 9.2   Summarize the physical changes that occur in old age.

Old age brings many physical transitions and internal changes. Outwardly, the hair may gray and thin. People may lose a few inches of height as the cartilage in the disks of the spine grows thinner. Internally, the respiratory and digestive systems grow less efficient. The brain shrinks and uses less oxygen, but the number of cells in the cortex may only drop minimally if at all. Reaction time slows with aging. Although their physical capabilities are likely to have changed, many older people remain agile and fit.

LO 9.3   Explain how aging affects the senses.

Old age brings declines in vision, hearing, taste, and smell. The declines in the senses can have major psychological consequences.

LO 9.4   Summarize the health problems elderly people experience, and list the factors that influence the state of a person's health.

Most illnesses and diseases of late adulthood are not peculiar to old age; however, incidents of cancer and heart disease rise with age. People in late adulthood are also more prone to develop arthritis, hypertension, major neurocognitive disorder, and Alzheimer's disease. The state of health in late adulthood is influenced by a variety of factors, including genetic predisposition, environmental factors, and psychological factors. Proper diet, exercise, and avoidance of health risks can lead to prolonged wellness during old age, and sexuality can continue throughout the life span in healthy adults.

LO 9.5   Discuss the different theories of aging, and summarize the research to increase life expectancy.

Whether death is caused by genetic programming or by general physical wear and tear is an unresolved question. Life expectancy, which has risen for centuries, varies with gender, race, and ethnicity. New approaches to increasing life expectancy include telomere therapy, reducing free radicals through antioxidant drugs, restricting caloric intake, and replacing worn-out organs.

Check Yourself

1. _____ aging involves universal and irreversible changes that, as a result of genetic programming, occur as people get older.

   a. Secondary
   b. Internal
   c. Inactive
   d. Primary

2. The most common cause of blindness in people older than 60 is _____.

   a. age-related macular degeneration
   b. cataracts
   c. interlocular lens deterioration
   d. glaucoma

3. Alzheimer's disease, _____, leads to the deaths of 100,000 people every year in the United States and affects nearly half of all people older than age 85.

   a. a degenerative cell disorder
   b. a chronic hypertension condition
   c. a progressive brain disorder
   d. a neurocognitive immune condition

4. _____ theories of aging suggest that our DNA contains a built-in time limit for reproduction of human cells.

   a. Wear-and-tear
   b. Life expectancy
   c. Genetic programming
   d. Chemical exposure

Applying Lifespan Development

In what ways is socioeconomic status related to wellness in old age and to life expectancy?

Module 9.2

Cognitive Development in Late Adulthood

Not in the Driver's Seat

Grace and Helen, both 80 years old, are idly complaining about the minor annoyances of old age as they take their weekly drive to the market. Helen, in the passenger seat, watches as Grace drives right through a red light. Knowing her eyes aren't what they used to be, Helen says nothing. But when the same thing happens again at the next two intersections, Helen knows she can't blame her eyesight and speaks up.

"Grace, are you all right? You just drove through three straight red lights. Didn't you see them?"

"Good heavens!" Grace exclaims. "I thought you were driving."

The old joke at the start of this module sums up the stereotypic view of older people as befuddled and forgetful. Today the view is different. Researchers have come to discount the view that the cognitive abilities of older people inevitably decline. Overall intellectual ability and specific cognitive skills, such as memory and problem solving, are more likely to remain strong. In fact, with appropriate practice and environmental stimuli, cognitive skills can actually improve.

Yellow Dog Productions/DigitalVision/Getty Images

This module discusses intellectual development during late adulthood. We look at the nature of intelligence in older people and the various ways cognitive abilities change. We also assess how different types of memory fare during late adulthood, and we consider ways to reverse intellectual declines in older people.

Intelligence

> When CNN didn't renew Daniel Schorr's reporting contract in 1985, he was 69 and no one was surprised to see him retiring.
>
> Except Daniel Schorr.
>
> Instead of hanging up his typewriter, Schorr quickly found work at National Public Radio (NPR). Until 2 weeks before his death at the age of 93, he continued to deliver regular analysis and commentary on NPR's *Weekend Edition, All Things Considered*, and other news programs.

Daniel Schorr's story of durable intellectual activity is unusual but not unique. A growing number of people who depend on their wits for a livelihood, or just to keep going, have reached ages that would have been considered unthinkable when they started out—and have remained intellectually active. In the world of entertainment alone, comedians Bob Hope and George Burns and composer Irving Berlin all lived to see their hundredth birthdays.

Cognitive Functioning in Older People

LO 9.6   Describe the challenges of determining the cause of age changes in intelligence.

The notion that older people become less cognitively adept initially arose from misinterpretations of research evidence comparing younger and older people's performance on the same IQ test, using traditional cross-sectional experimental methods. For example, a group of 30-year-olds and 70-year-olds might have taken the same test and had their performance compared.

However, cross-sectional methods do not take into account *cohort effects*—influences attributable to growing up in a particular era. If the younger group—because of when they grew up—has more education, on average, they will probably do better on the test for that reason alone. Furthermore, older people might do worse on any intelligence test with a timed portion simply because of their slower reaction time.

Longitudinal studies, which follow the same individuals for many years, are not much better. As we discussed previously, repeated exposure to the same test may cause overfamiliarity, and participants may become unavailable over time, leaving a smaller and possibly more cognitively skilled group of subjects.

Recent Conclusions About the Nature of Intelligence in Late Adulthood

LO 9.7   Summarize the effects of aging on cognitive functioning, and identify the factors that may affect it.

More recent research has attempted to address these drawbacks. In an ambitious—and ongoing—study of intelligence in older people, developmental psychologist K. Warner Schaie uses sequential methods, which combine cross-sectional and longitudinal methods by examining several different age groups at a number of points in time.

In Schaie's massive study, carried out in Seattle, Washington, 500 randomly chosen individuals took a battery of tests of cognitive ability. The people belonged to different age groups, starting at age 20 and extending at 5-year intervals to age 70. The participants were tested, and continue to be tested, every 7 years, and more people are recruited every year. At this point, more than 5,000 participants have been tested (Schaie, Willis & Pennack, 2005; Schaie & Willis, 2011).

The study, along with other research, supports several generalizations (Craik & Salthouse, 2008; Xue et al., 2018):

- Some abilities gradually decline starting at around age 25, whereas others stay relatively steady (see Figure 9-8). There is no uniform pattern of age-related intellectual changes. For example, fluid intelligence (the ability to deal with new problems and situations) declines with age, and crystallized intelligence (the store of information, skills, and strategies that people have acquired) remains steady and in some cases improves (Schaie, 1993; Deary, 2014).

- On average, some cognitive declines are found in all abilities by age 67, but they are minimal until the 80s. Even at age 81, less than half of the people tested showed consistent declines over the previous 7 years.

- There are also significant individual differences. Some people begin to show declines in their 30s, whereas others show no declines until their 70s. In fact, around a third of people in their 70s score higher than the average young adult.

- Environmental and cultural factors play a role. People with no chronic disease, higher socioeconomic status (SES), involvement in an intellectually stimulating environment, a flexible personality style, a bright spouse or partner, good perceptual processing speed, and satisfaction with their accomplishments in midlife or early old age showed less decline.

Figure 9-8 Changes in Intellectual Functioning

Although some intellectual abilities decline across adulthood, others stay relatively steady.

SOURCE: Changes in Intellectual Functioning from Schaie, K. W. (1994). "The course of adult intellectual development." p. 307. *American Psychologist, 49*, 304–313. Copyright © 1994 by the American Psychological Association.

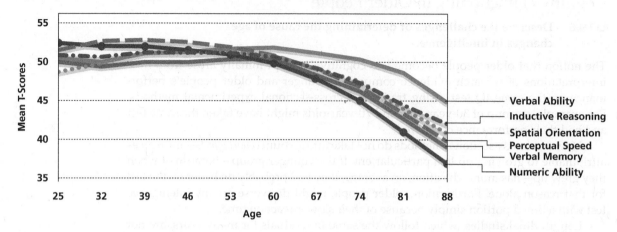

The relationship between environmental factors and intellectual skills suggests that with stimulation, practice, and motivation, older people can maintain their mental abilities. Such *plasticity* illustrates that the changes that occur in intellectual abilities during late adulthood are not fixed. In mental life, as in so many other areas of human development, the motto "use it or lose it" fits. This suggests that there may be interventions to help older adults maintain their information processing skills.

However, not all developmentalists accept the "use it or lose it" hypothesis. Developmental psychologist Timothy Salthouse suggests that the rate of true, underlying cognitive decline in late adulthood is unaffected by mental exercise. Instead, he argues that some people—the kind who have consistently engaged in high levels of mental activity such as completing crossword puzzles—enter late adulthood with a "cognitive reserve." This allows them to continue to perform at relatively high mental levels, despite underlying declines. Still, most developmentalists accept the hypothesis that mental exercise is beneficial (Salthouse, 2012, 2017).

Memory and Learning

> I have no trouble remembering everything that happened 40 or 50 years ago—dates, places, faces, music. But I'm going to be 90 my next birthday, November 14, and I find I can't remember what happened yesterday. (*Time*, 1980, p. 57)

This is the way composer Aaron Copland described his memory in old age. Our confidence in the accuracy of Copland's analysis is strengthened by an error in his statement: On his next birthday, he would be only 80 years old!

Memory

LO 9.8 Explain how memory capability changes in late adulthood.

Is memory loss inevitable? Not necessarily. Cross-cultural research reveals that in societies that hold older people in relatively high esteem, such as in China, people are less likely to show memory losses. In such cultures, positive expectations may lead people to think more positively about their own capabilities (Levy & Langer, 1994; Hess, Auman, & Colcombe, 2003).

Even those memory declines that do occur are limited primarily to *episodic memories*, which relate to specific life experiences, such as when you first visited New York City. Other types of memory, such as *semantic memories* (general knowledge and facts, such as the capital of North Dakota) and *implicit memories* (memories about which people are not consciously aware, such as how to ride a bike), are largely unaffected by age (Dixon & Cohen, 2003; Nilsson, 2003).

Memory capacity changes during old age. For instance, *short-term memory* slips gradually until age 70, when the decline becomes more pronounced. The largest drop is for information that is presented quickly and orally, such as when someone at a computer helpline rattles off a series of complicated steps for fixing a computer problem. In addition, older people find it harder to recall information about unfamiliar things, such as prose passages, names and faces of people, and the directions on a medicine label, possibly because new information is not registered and processed effectively when initially encountered. Still, these changes are minor, and most elderly people automatically learn to compensate for them (Rentz et al., 2010; Carmichael et al., 2012; Klaming et al., 2017).

Memory loss is not as common among Chinese elderly as it is in the West. What are some factors that contribute to cultural differences in memory loss of the elderly?

AUTOBIOGRAPHICAL MEMORY: RECALLING THE DAYS OF OUR LIVES When it comes to **autobiographical memory**, memories about one's own life, older people are as subject to lapses as younger individuals. For instance, recall frequently follows the *Pollyanna principle*, in which pleasant memories are more likely to be recalled than unpleasant memories. Similarly, people tend to forget information that is not congruent with the way they currently see themselves. Thus, a strict parent who forgets that she got drunk at her high school prom is making her memories "fit" her current conception of herself (Loftus, 2004; Skowronski, Walker, & Betz, 2003; Martinelli et al., 2013).

autobiographical memory
memories about one's own life

Everyone tends to recall particular periods of life better than others. As can be seen in Figure 9-9, 70-year-olds tend to recall autobiographical details from their 20s and 30s best, whereas 50-year-olds are likely to have more memories of their teenage years and their 20s. In both cases, recall is better for earlier years than for more recent decades, but not as complete as for recent events (Rubin, 2000).

People in late adulthood also use information that they recall in different ways from younger individuals when they make decisions. For example, they process information more slowly and may make poorer judgments when complex rules are involved, and they focus more on emotional content than younger people. On the other hand, the accumulated knowledge and experience of people in late adulthood can compensate for their deficits, particularly if they are highly motivated to make good decisions (Peters et al., 2007).

EXPLAINING MEMORY CHANGES IN OLD AGE Explanations for memory changes in older people focus on three main categories: environmental factors, information processing deficits, and biological factors.

- **Environmental factors.** Certain environmental factors common to many older people may cause declines in memory. For example, older people often take prescription drugs that hinder memory, and this, rather than age per se, may account for their lower performance on memory tasks.

  In addition, retirees, no longer facing job challenges, may use memory less. Further, their motivation to recall information may be lower than before, and they may be less motivated than younger people to do their best in experimental testing situations.

- **Information processing deficits.** Memory declines may also be linked to changes in information processing capabilities. The ability to inhibit irrelevant information and thoughts that interfere with problem solving may decrease, and the

Figure 9-9 Remembrances of Things Past

Recall of autobiographical memories varies with age, with 70-year-olds recalling details from their 20s and 30s best, and 50-year-olds recalling memories from their teenage years and 20s. People of both ages also recall more recent memories best of all.

SOURCE: Rubin, 1986.

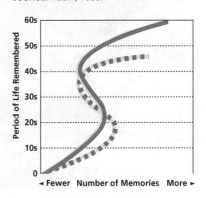

Period of Life Remembered

◄ Fewer   Number of Memories   More ►

▬▬ Recollection at Age 70
▪▪▪ Recollection at Age 50

Figure 9-10 Technology Use and Age

Older individuals in the United States are far less likely to use the Internet than those who are younger.

SOURCE: Anderson & Perrin, 2017.

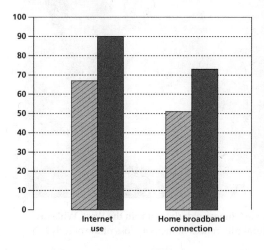

Adults 65 and older   Total population

speed of information processing may decline (Palfai, Halperin, & Hoyer, 2003; Salthouse, Atkinson, & Berish, 2003; Ising et al., 2014; Fortenbaugh et al., 2015).

Another information processing view suggests that older adults lose the ability to concentrate on new material and have difficulty paying attention to appropriate stimuli and organizing material in memory. According to this information-processing-deficit approach, which has substantial research support, older people use less efficient processes to retrieve information from memory. This leads to declines in recall abilities (Castel & Craik, 2003; Luo & Craik, 2008, 2009; Huntley et al., 2017).

- **Biological factors.** The last of the major approaches concentrates on biological factors. According to this view, memory changes are a result of brain and body deterioration. For instance, declines in episodic memory may be related to the deterioration of the frontal lobes of the brain or a reduction in estrogen. Some studies also show a loss of cells in the hippocampus, which is critical to memory. However, some memory deficits occur without any evidence of underlying biological deterioration (Eberling et al., 2004; Lye et al., 2004; Bird & Burgess, 2008; Stevens et al., 2008; Sandrini et al., 2016).

Never Too Late to Learn

LO 9.9   **Identify the learning opportunities available to older adults, and describe their value to cognitive functioning.**

Martha Tilden and Jim Hertz, both 71, loved the Metropolitan Opera House tour, the talk by the famous tenor, the ballet, and the lectures they attended during the "Lincoln Center Festival" trip they are just finishing.

Martha and Jim are veterans of Road Scholar (formerly Elderhostel), which has updated itself by scrapping any suggestion of "elderness" or cheap student housing. All the educational programs that Martha and Jim have taken have featured comfortable hotel or dorm rooms and mixed-age events. Now Martha and Jim are discussing their next program, trying to decide between a wildlife trip to Ontario and a "Building Bridges to Islam" program in Virginia.

Road Scholar is one of the largest educational programs for people in late adulthood, offering travel and learning classes worldwide. Represented on campuses across the world, Road Scholar is further evidence that intellectual growth and change continue throughout people's lives. As we saw previously, exercising cognitive skills may help older adults maintain their intellectual functioning (Simson, Wilson, & Harlow-Rosentraub, 2006; Spiers, 2012).

In addition, many public colleges encourage senior citizens to enroll in classes by offering free tuition. Some retirement communities are even located at or near college campuses (Powell, 2004).

Although some elderly people are doubtful about their intellectual capabilities and consequently hesitate to compete with younger students in regular classes, their concern is largely misplaced. Older adults often have no trouble maintaining their standing in rigorous college classes. Furthermore, professors and other students generally find the presence of older people, with their varied and substantial life experiences, a real educational benefit (Simson, Wilson, & Harlow-Rosentraub, 2006; Hannon, 2015).

One of the biggest generational divides involves the use of technology. People 65 and older are less likely to use technology than younger individuals, although the gap is not as large as it once was. Around 40 percent of older adults use smartphones, up from 18 percent in 2013 (see Figure 9-10).

Still, many older adults are not participating in the digital revolution. A third of adults above the age of 65 never use the Internet, and about half don't have home broadband. Moreover, the proportion of those who own smartphones is 42 percentage points lower than younger Americans (Anderson & Perrin, 2017).

Why are older people less likely to use technology? One reason is that they are less interested and motivated, in part because they are less likely to be working and therefore less in need of learning new technology skills.

An increasing number of people in late adulthood are using technology.

But another barrier is cognitive. For example, because fluid intelligence (the ability to deal with new problems and situations) shows some declines with age, this may impact the ability to learn technology (Charness & Boot, 2009; Erickson & Johnson, 2011).

This hardly means that people in late adulthood are unable to learn to use technology. In fact, an increasing number of individuals are using e-mail and social networking sites such as Facebook. It is likely that the lag in the adoption of technology between younger and older adults will continue to decline as technology use becomes even more widespread in the general society (Costa & Veloso, 2016; also see the *From Research to Practice* box.).

From Research to Practice

Can We Train the Brain? Interventions to Improve Cognitive Functioning

Can we improve cognitive functioning through training? Well-designed research suggests that the answer is yes, although many questions remain to be answered.

In a 10-year groundbreaking, federally sponsored study of nearly 3,000 adults, called the Advance Cognitive Training for Independent and Vital Elderly (ACTIVE), researchers looked at nearly 3,000 participants with a mean age of 74 at the start of the study. Participants received 10 cognitive training sessions lasting about an hour each, with each successive session becoming increasingly challenging. Three groups of participants received memory training (such as mnemonic strategies for memorizing word lists), reasoning training (such as finding the pattern in a series of numbers), or processing speed training (such as identifying objects that flashed briefly on a computer screen). Some participants also received "booster" training 1 year later and again 3 years later, each time consisting of four more sessions (Willis et al., 2006).

Remarkably, cognitive benefits were evident 5 years after the original training sessions. Compared to a control group that received no training, participants who received reasoning training performed 40 percent better on reasoning tasks at the 5-year mark, those who received memory training performed 75 percent better on memory tasks, and those who received speed training performed a staggering 300 percent better on speed tasks (Vedantam, 2006; Willis et al., 2006).

Even more surprising, some of the improvements were evident 10 years after the initial treatment. The improvements persisted for those who received the reasoning and processing speed training. Furthermore, participants who received training reported that it was easier for them to manage their daily activities, such as handling their finances and medications,

although standardized tests did not show a difference among groups (Rebok et al., 2013; Rebok et al., 2014; Parisi et al., 2017).

Overall, the findings are quite promising. Yet some caveats are in order. First, the results are from a single study, and much more research needs to be conducted. Second, the findings do not suggest that the use of commercially available apps that purport to improve memory and cognitive functioning, such as those sold by Lumosity or Clockwork Brain, are effective. In fact, the U.S. Federal Trade Commission rebuked Lumosity and ordered that rebates be sent to customers who were duped by exaggerated advertising claims. There is yet to be definitive evidence that apps actually produce greater cognitive ability in older adults—or younger ones, for that matter (Robbins, 2016; Katz & Marshall, 2018).

It is also important to note that not all developmentalists believe the "use it or lose it" hypothesis. For example, developmental psychologist Timothy Salthouse suggests that the rate of true, underlying cognitive decline in late adulthood is unaffected by mental exercise. Instead, he argues that some people—the kind who have consistently engaged throughout their lives in high levels of mental activity, such as completing crossword puzzles—enter late adulthood with a "cognitive reserve." This cognitive reserve allows them to continue to perform at relatively high mental levels, even though underlying declines are actually happening. His hypothesis is controversial, though, and most developmentalists accept the hypothesis that mental exercise is beneficial (Salthouse, 2012, 2017).

Shared Writing Prompt:

What advice would you give people in late adulthood about the steps they should take to avoid loss of cognitive skills?

Review, Check, and Apply

Review

LO 9.6 **Describe the challenges of determining the cause of age changes in intelligence.**

Because of cohort effects and other challenges, it is difficult to draw conclusions about the reasons for age changes in intelligence using cross-sectional and longitudinal studies.

LO 9.7 **Summarize the effects of aging on cognitive functioning, and identify the factors that may affect it.**

Although some intellectual abilities gradually decline throughout adulthood, starting at around age 25, others stay relatively steady. For example, research shows that although fluid intelligence declines with age, crystallized intelligence remains steady, and may even improve, in late adulthood. There is no uniform pattern of age-related intellectual changes. Environmental and cultural factors may affect cognitive functioning.

LO 9.8 **Explain how memory capability changes in late adulthood.**

Declines in memory affect mainly episodic memories and short-term memory. Explanations of memory changes in

old age have focused on environmental factors, information processing declines, and biological factors.

LO 9.9 **Identify the learning opportunities available to older adults, and describe their value to cognitive functioning.**

Educational programs like Road Scholar offer learning opportunities for older adults. Many public colleges also encourage senior citizens to enroll in classes. Exercising cognitive skills may help people keep their intellectual functioning sharp in late adulthood.

Check Yourself

1. One problem with conducting cross-sectional research on aging and cognition is that this method does not take into consideration _____, the influences attributable to growing up in a particular era.
   a. genetic effects
   b. environmental effects
   c. cohort effects
   d. religious effects

2. The relationship between environmental factors and intellectual skills suggests that with _____, older people can maintain their mental abilities.
   a. stimulation, practice, and motivation
   b. exercise, a kind spouse, and a flexible personality style
   c. autobiographical memory, motivation, and prescription drugs
   d. increased estrogen, exercise, and a cohort group

3. When it comes to autobiographical memories, older individuals, like younger individuals, follow the _____, in that they are more likely to remember pleasant memories.
   a. saliency principle
   b. semantic l effect
   c. Pollyanna principle
   d. positive effect

4. It is likely that the gap in technology skills between younger and older adults will decrease as _____.
   a. young adults get jobs, have families, and are too busy for social media
   b. technology use continues to expand in the general society
   c. technology creates simpler machines and special apps for the elderly
   d. older adults are treated with more respect online

Applying Lifespan Development

How might cultural factors, such as the esteem in which a society holds its older members, work to affect an older person's memory performance?

Module 9.3

Social and Personality Development in Late Adulthood

Pottering About in the Sun

Simone Thomas, 81, sets up her easel and watercolors in the garden of her California home. "I've been illustrating children's books for 50 years," she says. Simone had once hoped to become a famous painter and after art school moved to Italy to pursue her dream. "I didn't become the next Michelangelo," she says, laughing, "but my life worked out just fine. I met my husband, Gabriel, over there, so how could things have gone better?"

Gabriel died 5 years ago. "It was really hard to get through that first year," Simone admits. "I went to Italy and remembered it all, our meeting and falling in love, and I cried a lot. But then I came home and started illustrating two new books. It's a lifeline, my work, and though I only take on about half as many jobs as I used to, it pays the

rent, and I get to spend time doing what I love. That's mainly playing the piano rather badly and walking the beach with my grandkids when they visit."

The newest thing in Simone's life? "My brother Dev lost his wife to cancer last year, so I've asked him to move in with me. We've always been close, and he's good about pulling his own weight with cooking and such. We'll be a happy pair of geriatrics, pottering about in the sun."

The desire to be productive and useful is not exclusive to any age group. For people in late adulthood such as Simone, talents honed over a lifetime and connections to family offer rich opportunities to stay active and connected with others.

In this module, we turn to the social and emotional aspects of late adulthood, which remain as central as in previous stages of the life span. We begin by considering how personality continues to develop, and we examine various ways people can age successfully. We also look at how culture governs the way we treat older people.

We then consider how various societal factors affect older adults. We discuss living arrangements and economic and financial issues. Next, we examine the influence of work and retirement on elderly individuals.

Finally, we consider relationships in late adulthood among married couples, relatives, and friends. We will see how social networks play an important—and sustaining—role in people's lives. We end with a discussion of elder abuse.

Santypan/Shutterstock

Personality Development and Successful Aging

> At age 82, Ella O'Leary still plays pickleball at her retirement community. And she often celebrates pickleball victories—and losses, as well—by drinking a celebratory Bloody Mary with her friends.
>
> If you asked, she'd tell you she's enjoying life as much as she did in her 20s. She says that she loves to socialize with her friends, adding, "at least the ones that are still alive!"

In many ways, Ella, with her wit, high spirits, and substantial activity level, is the same person she was in earlier years. Yet for other older adults, time and circumstances bring changes in their outlook on life, their views of themselves, and perhaps even their basic personalities. In fact, one of the fundamental questions asked by lifespan developmentalists concerns the degree to which personality remains stable or changes in later adulthood.

Continuity and Change in Personality During Late Adulthood

LO 9.10 Identify and describe the various theories of personality development in late adulthood.

Is personality relatively stable throughout adulthood, or does it vary significantly? The answer depends on which facets of personality we consider. According to developmental psychologists Paul Costa and Robert McCrae, whose work we discussed previously, the "Big Five" basic personality traits (neuroticism, extraversion, openness, agreeableness, and conscientiousness) are remarkably stable across adulthood. For instance, even-tempered people at 20 are still even-tempered at 75, and people who hold positive self-concepts early in adulthood still view themselves positively in late adulthood (Terracciano, McCrae, & Costa, 2010; Curtis, Windsor, & Soubelet, 2015; Kahlbaugh & Huffman, 2017).

Despite this continuity, change is still possible. Profound changes in people's social environments may produce personality changes. What is important to a person at 80 is not necessarily the same as what was important at 40.

To account for these changes, some theorists have focused on the discontinuities of development. As we'll see next, Erik Erikson, Robert Peck, Daniel Levinson, and Bernice Neugarten have examined personality changes that accompany new challenges in later adulthood.

EGO INTEGRITY VERSUS DESPAIR: ERIKSON'S FINAL STAGE Psychoanalyst Erik Erikson characterizes late adulthood as the time when people move into the last of life's eight stages of psychosocial development. Labeled the **ego-integrity-versus-despair stage**, this period is characterized by a process of looking back over one's life, evaluating it, and coming to terms with it.

People who are successful in this stage of development experience satisfaction and accomplishment, which Erikson terms "integrity." When people achieve integrity,

ego-integrity-versus-despair stage
Erikson's final stage of life, characterized by a process of looking back over one's life, evaluating it, and coming to terms with it

they feel they have fulfilled the possibilities that have come their way in life, and they have few regrets. Other people look back on their lives with dissatisfaction. They may feel that they have missed important opportunities and have not accomplished what they wished. Such individuals may be unhappy, depressed, angry, or despondent over what they have done, or failed to do, with their lives—in short, they despair.

PECK'S DEVELOPMENTAL TASKS   Although Erikson's approach provides a picture of the broad possibilities of later adulthood, other theorists offer a more differentiated view of the final stage of life. Psychologist Robert Peck (1968) suggests that personality development in elderly people is occupied by three major developmental tasks or challenges.

In Peck's view—part of a comprehensive description of change across adulthood—the first task in old age is to redefine oneself in ways that do not relate to work roles or occupations. He labels this stage **redefinition of self versus preoccupation with work role**. As we will see, the changes that occur when people stop working can trigger a difficult adjustment in the way people view themselves. Peck suggests that people must adjust their values to place less emphasis on themselves as workers or professionals and more on attributes that don't involve work, such as being a grandparent or a gardener.

The second major developmental task in late adulthood, according to Peck, is **body transcendence versus body preoccupation**. Elderly individuals can undergo significant changes in their physical abilities as a result of aging. In the body-transcendence-versus-body-preoccupation stage, people must learn to cope with and move beyond those physical changes (transcendence). If they don't, they become preoccupied with their physical deterioration, to the detriment of their personality development. Greta Roach, who gave up bowling only in her 90s, is an example of coping well with the physical changes of aging.

The third developmental task in old age is **ego transcendence versus ego preoccupation**, in which elderly people must come to grips with their coming death. They need to understand that although death is inevitable, and probably not too far off, they have made contributions to society. If they see these contributions, which can take the form of children or work and civic activities, as lasting beyond their own lives, they will experience ego transcendence. If not, they may become preoccupied with asking whether their lives had value and worth to society.

LEVINSON'S FINAL SEASON: THE WINTER OF LIFE   Daniel Levinson's theory of adult development does not focus as much on the challenges that aging adults must overcome. Instead, he looks at the processes that can lead to personality change as we grow old. According to Levinson, people enter late adulthood by passing through a transition stage that typically occurs around ages 60 to 65 (Levinson, 1986, 1992). During this stage, people come to view themselves as entering late adulthood—or, ultimately, as being "old." Knowing full well society's negative stereotypes about elderly individuals, they struggle with the notion that they are now in this category.

According to Levinson, people come to realize that they are no longer on the center stage, but are playing bit parts. This loss of power, respect, and authority may be difficult for individuals accustomed to having control in their lives.

On the other hand, people in late adulthood can serve as resources to younger individuals, and they may find that they are viewed as "venerated elders" whose advice is sought and relied upon. Furthermore, old age can bring a new freedom to do things simply for enjoyment and pleasure, rather than as obligations.

COPING WITH AGING: NEUGARTEN'S STUDY   Bernice Neugarten (Neugarten 1972, 1977)—in what became a classic study—examined the different ways that people cope with aging. Neugarten found four different personality types in her research on people in their 70s:

- **Disintegrated and disorganized personalities.**   Some people are unable to accept aging and experience despair as they get older. These people are often found in nursing homes or hospitals.
- **Passive-dependent personalities.**   Others become fearful—of falling ill, of the future, of their own inability to cope. They are so fearful that they may seek help from family and care providers, even when they don't need it.

redefinition of self versus preoccupation with work role
the theory that those in old age must redefine themselves in ways that do not relate to their work roles or occupations

body transcendence versus body preoccupation
a period in which people must learn to cope with and move beyond changes in physical capabilities as a result of aging

ego transcendence versus ego preoccupation
the period in which elderly people must come to grips with their coming death

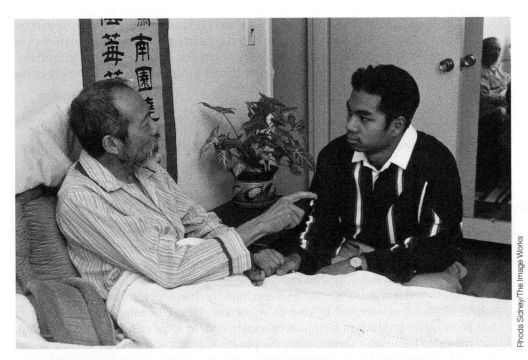

Older adults may become "venerated elders," whose advice is sought and relied upon.

- **Defended personalities.** Others respond to the fear of aging quite differently—by trying to stop it in its tracks. They may attempt to act young, exercising vigorously and engaging in youthful activities. Unfortunately, they may set unrealistic expectations and run the risk of disappointment as a result.
- **Integrated personalities.** The most successful individuals cope comfortably with aging. They accept it with a sense of self-dignity.

Neugarten found that the majority of the people she studied fell into the final category. They acknowledged aging and could look back at their lives and gaze into the future with acceptance.

LIFE REVIEW AND REMINISCENCE: THE COMMON THEME OF PERSONALITY DEVELOPMENT   **Life review**, in which people examine and evaluate their lives, is a major thread running through the work of Erikson, Peck, Neugarten, and Levinson, and a common theme among personality theorists who focus on late adulthood.

life review
the point in life in which people examine and evaluate their lives

According to gerontologist Robert Butler (2002), life review is triggered by the increasingly obvious prospect of death. People look back on their lives, remembering and reconsidering what has happened to them. Far from being a harmful process of reliving the past, wallowing in past problems, and reviving old wounds, life review usually leads to a better understanding of the past. People may resolve lingering problems and conflicts with others, such as an estrangement from a child, and they may feel they can face their current lives with greater serenity (Latorre et al., 2015; Bergström, 2017; Bademli et al., 2018).

Life review offers other benefits, including a sense of mutuality, a feeling of interconnectedness with others. Moreover, it can be a source of social interaction, as older adults share their experiences with others (Parks, Sanna, & Posey, 2003).

Reminiscence may even have cognitive benefits, improving memory. By reflecting on the past, people activate a variety of memories, which may trigger other memories and bring back sights, sounds, and even smells of the past (Brinker, 2013; Maruszewski et al., 2017).

On the other hand, life review can sometimes produce declines in psychological functioning. If people become obsessive about the past, reliving old insults and mistakes that cannot be rectified, they may end up feeling guilt, depression, and anger against acquaintances who may not even still be alive (Cappeliez, Guindon, & Robitaille, 2008).

Overall, though, the process of life review and reminiscence can play an important role by providing continuity between past and present, and increasing awareness of the contemporary world. It can also provide new insights into the past and into others, allowing people to continue personality growth and to function more effectively in the present (Coleman, 2005; Haber, 2006; Alwin, 2012).

Age Stratification Approaches to Late Adulthood

LO 9.11   **Explain how age relates to the distribution of resources, power, and privilege.**

age stratification theories

the view that an unequal distribution of economic resources, power, and privilege exists among people at different stages of life

Age, like race and gender, provides a way of ranking people within a society. **Age stratification theories** suggest that economic resources, power, and privilege are distributed unequally among people at different stages of life. Such inequality is particularly pronounced during late adulthood.

Even as medical advances have lengthened the life span, power and prestige for the elderly have eroded, at least in highly industrialized societies. The peak earning years are the 50s; later, earnings tend to decline. Further, younger people are often physically removed from their elders, and their increased independence may make older adults feel less important. In addition, rapidly changing technology makes older adults seem out of date and lacking in important skills. Ultimately, they are seen as not particularly productive members of society and, in some cases, simply irrelevant. According to Levinson's theory, older people are keenly aware of their decline in status, and adjusting to it is the major transition of late adulthood (Macionis, 2001).

Age stratification theories help explain why aging is viewed more positively in less industrialized societies. In predominantly agricultural societies, older people accumulate control over important resources such as animals and land. In such societies, the concept of retirement is unknown. Older individuals (especially males) are highly respected because they continue to be involved in daily activities central to the society. Furthermore, because the pace of change in agricultural societies is slower than in more technological societies, people in late adulthood have considerable relevant wisdom. Nor is respect for elders limited to agricultural countries; it is a characteristic of a variety of cultures, as discussed in the *Cultural Dimensions* box.

Cultural Dimensions

How Culture Shapes the Way We Treat People in Late Adulthood

Views of late adulthood are colored by culture. For example, compared to Western cultures, Asian societies generally hold elderly people, particularly family members, in higher esteem. Although this is changing in rapidly industrializing areas of Asia, the view of aging and the treatment of people in late adulthood still tend to be more positive than in Western cultures (Degnen, 2007; Smith & Hung, 2012; Gao & Bischoping, 2018).

What is it about Asian cultures that leads to esteem for old age? In general, cultures that value the elderly are relatively homogeneous in socioeconomic terms. In addition, the roles that people play in those societies entail greater responsibility with increasing age, and elderly people control resources to a relatively large extent.

Moreover, the roles of people in Asian societies display more continuity throughout the life span than in Western cultures, and older adults continue to engage in activities that are valued by society. Finally, Asian cultures are more organized around extended families in which the older generations are well integrated into the family structure (Fry, 1985; Sangree, 1989). In such an arrangement, younger family members tend to rely on older members to share their considerable accumulated wisdom.

What aspects of Asian cultures lead them to hold higher levels of esteem for old age?

Yet even societies that articulate strong ideals regarding older adults do not always live up to those standards. For instance, research in China, where admiration, respect, and even worship for individuals in late adulthood is strong, shows that people's actual behavior, in almost every segment of the society except for the most elite, fails to be as positive as their attitudes are. Furthermore, sons and their wives—but not daughters—are typically expected to care for elderly parents; parents with only daughters may find themselves with no one to care for them. In short, conduct toward elderly people in particular cultures is not uniform, and it is important not to make broad, global statements about how older adults are treated in a given society (Browne, 2010; Li, Ji, & Chen, 2014; Vauclair et al., 2017).

Asian cultures are not alone in esteeming the elderly. In many Latino cultures, the elderly are thought to have a special inner strength, and in many African cultures, reaching an old age is seen as a sign of divine intervention (Holmes & Holmes, 1995; Lehr, Seiler, & Thomae, 2000; Löckenhoff et al., 2009; Hess et al., 2017).

Does Age Bring Wisdom?

LO 9.12 Define wisdom, and describe how it is associated with age.

One of the benefits of age is supposed to be wisdom. But do people gain wisdom as they become older?

In fact, we don't know for sure, because the concept of **wisdom**—expert knowledge in the practical aspects of life—is only recently receiving attention from gerontologists and other researchers. This is partly because of the difficulty of defining and measuring the concept (Helmuth, 2003; Brugman, 2006). Wisdom can be seen as reflecting an accumulation of knowledge, experience, and contemplation, and by this definition, aging contributes to wisdom (Kunzmann & Baltes, 2005; Staudinger, 2008; Randall, 2012).

Distinguishing wisdom from intelligence is tricky. Some researchers have made suggestions: Whereas knowledge derived from intelligence is related to the here and now, wisdom is more timeless. While intelligence permits a person to think logically and systematically, wisdom provides an understanding of human behavior. According to psychologist Robert Sternberg, intelligence permits humans to invent the atom bomb, whereas wisdom prevents them from using it (Karelitz, Jarvin, & Sternberg, 2010; Wink & Staudinger, 2016).

Measuring wisdom is difficult. Paul Baltes and Ursula Staudinger (2000) designed a study showing that it is possible to assess people reliably on the concept. Pairs of people ranging in age from 20 to 70 discussed difficulties relating to life events. One problem involved someone who gets a phone call from a friend who is planning to commit suicide. Another involved a 14-year-old girl who wanted to move out of her family home immediately. Participants were asked what they should do and consider.

Although there were no absolute right or wrong answers, the responses were evaluated against several criteria, including how much factual knowledge they brought to bear; their knowledge of decision-making strategies; how well the participants considered the context of the central character's life span and values; and their recognition that there might not be a single, absolute solution. Using these criteria, the older participants' responses were wiser than those of younger participants.

The study also found that the older participants benefited more from an experimental condition designed to promote wise thinking, and other research suggests that the very wisest individuals may be older adults.

Other research has looked at wisdom in terms of the development of theory of mind—the ability to make inferences about others' thoughts, feelings, and intentions, their mental states. Although the research findings are mixed, some research finds that older adults, with their added years of experience to draw upon, use a more sophisticated theory of mind (Karelitz, Jarvin, & Sternberg, 2010; Rakoczy, Harder-Kasten, & Sturm, 2012; Booker & Dunsmore, 2016).

wisdom
expert knowledge in the practical aspects of life

Successful Aging: What Is the Secret?

LO 9.13 Differentiate the theories of aging, and explain how culture shapes the way older people are treated.

At age 77, Elinor Reynolds spends most of her time at home, leading a quiet, routine existence. Never married, Elinor receives visits from her two sisters every few weeks, and some of her nieces and nephews stop by on occasion. But for the most part, she keeps to herself. When asked, she says she is quite happy.

In contrast, Carrie Masterson, also 77, is involved in something different almost every day. If she is not visiting the senior center and participating in some activity, she is out shopping. Her daughter complains that Carrie is "never home" when she tries to reach her by phone, and Carrie replies that she has never been busier—or happier.

Clearly, there is no single way to age successfully. How people age depends on personality factors and people's circumstances. Some people become progressively less involved with day-to-day activities, whereas others maintain active ties to people and their personal interests. Three major approaches provide explanations: disengagement theory, activity theory, and continuity theory.

DISENGAGEMENT THEORY: GRADUAL RETREAT According to **disengagement theory**, late adulthood often involves a gradual withdrawal from the world on physical, psychological, and social levels (Cummings & Henry, 1961). On a physical level, elderly people have lower energy levels and slow down progressively. Psychologically, they begin to withdraw, showing less interest in the world around them and spending more time looking inward. Finally, on a social level, they engage in fewer interactions—both day-to-day, face-to-face encounters and participation in society as a whole. Older adults also become less involved and invested in the lives of others (Cashdollar et al., 2013).

Disengagement theory suggests that withdrawal is a mutual process. Because of norms and expectations about aging, society begins to disengage from those in late adulthood. For example, mandatory retirement ages compel elderly people to withdraw from work, which accelerates disengagement.

Although there is logic to disengagement theory, research support is limited. Furthermore, the theory has been criticized because it takes the failure of society to provide sufficient opportunities for meaningful engagement during late adulthood and then, in a sense, blames people in this age group for not being engaged.

Of course, some degree of disengagement is not necessarily all negative. For example, a gradual withdrawal in late adulthood may permit people to become more reflective about their own lives and less constrained by social roles. In addition, people can become more discerning in their social relationships, focusing on those who best meet their needs (Settersten, 2002; Wrosch, Bauer, & Scheier, 2005; Liang & Luo, 2012).

Today, most gerontologists reject disengagement theory, pointing out that disengagement is relatively uncommon. In most cases, people remain engaged, active, and busy throughout old age, and (especially in non-Western cultures) the expectation is that people will remain actively involved in everyday life. Clearly, disengagement is not an automatic, universal process (Bergstrom & Holmes, 2000; Crosnoe & Elder, 2002).

ACTIVITY THEORY: CONTINUED INVOLVEMENT The lack of support for disengagement theory led to an alternative. **Activity theory** suggests that successful aging occurs when people maintain the interests and activities of middle age and the amount and type of their social interactions. According to this perspective, happiness and satisfaction with life spring from involvement with the world (Hutchinson & Wexler, 2007; Rebok et al., 2014).

Activity theory suggests that continuation of activities is important. Even when continuation is no longer possible—such as continuing work after retirement—activity theory argues that successful aging occurs when replacement activities are found.

But activity theory, like disengagement theory, is not the full story. For one thing, activity theory makes little distinction among activities. Not every activity will have an equal impact on a person's satisfaction with life; in fact, the nature and quality of the activities are likely to be more critical than mere quantity or frequency (Adams, 2004).

A more significant concern is that for some people in late adulthood, the principle of "less is more" clearly holds: less activity brings greater enjoyment because they can slow down and do only the things that bring them the greatest satisfaction. In fact, some people view the ability to moderate their pace as one of the bounties of late adulthood. For them, a relatively inactive, and perhaps even solitary, existence is welcome (Kosma & Cardinal, 2016).

disengagement theory
The theory that late adulthood marks a gradual withdrawal from the world on physical, psychological, and social levels

activity theory
the theory suggesting that successful aging occurs when people maintain the interests, activities, and social interactions with which they were involved during middle age

From a social worker's perspective: How might cultural factors affect an older person's likelihood of pursuing either the disengagement theory or the activity theory?

CONTINUITY THEORY: A COMPROMISE POSITION   Neither disengagement theory nor activity theory provides a complete picture of successful aging. Consequently, a compromise view has emerged called continuity theory. **Continuity theory** suggests that people simply need to maintain their desired level of involvement in society to maximize their sense of well-being and self-esteem (Atchley, 2003; Ouwehand, de Ridder, & Bensing, 2007; Carmel, 2017).

According to continuity theory, those who were highly active and social will be happiest if they largely remain so. Those who enjoy solitude and solitary interests, such as reading or taking walks in the woods, will be happiest pursuing that level of sociability (Holahan & Chapman, 2002; Wang et al., 2014).

It is also clear that most older adults experience positive emotions as frequently as younger individuals. Furthermore, they become more skilled at regulating their emotions.

Other factors enhance happiness during late adulthood. The importance of physical and mental health cannot be overestimated, and having enough financial security to provide for basic needs is critical. In addition, a sense of autonomy, independence, and personal control over one's life is a significant advantage (Charles & Carstensen, 2010; Vacha-Haase, Hill, & Bermingham, 2012; Sutipan, Intarakamhang & Macaskill, 2017).

More specifically, developmental psychologist Laura Carstensen has suggested in her *socioemotional selectivity theory* that as the time horizon of older adults decreases, they become increasingly selective in the goals and activities in which they invest. Furthermore, as they become older and their time horizons are constrained, people in late adulthood become invested in present-oriented goals that provide emotional satisfaction and meaning, compared with longer-term goals (Charles & Carstensen, 2010, English & Carstensen, 2014; Carstensen, 2018).

Furthermore, socioemotional selectivity theory suggests that as they age, people develop a preference for seeking out positive information, compared with negative information. They are more likely to involve themselves with familiar individuals who provide positive experiences and who are more likely to fulfil their emotional needs. In short, they become more selective in their emotional engagements with others (Reed & Carstensen, 2012; English & Carstensen, 2014).

Finally, as we discussed previously, people's perceptions can influence their happiness and satisfaction. Those who view late adulthood favorably are apt to perceive themselves more positively than those who view old age in a more pessimistic way (Levy, Slade, & Kasl, 2002; Levy, 2003).

Ultimately, surveys find that as a group, people in late adulthood report being happier than younger people. And it's not that those older than 65 have always been happier. Instead, being older seems to bring a degree of contentment in the majority of people (Yang, 2008).

SELECTIVE OPTIMIZATION WITH COMPENSATION: A GENERAL MODEL OF SUCCESSFUL AGING   In considering the factors that lead to successful aging, developmental psychologists Paul Baltes and Margret Baltes focus on the "selective optimization with compensation" model. As we noted previously, the assumption underlying the model is that late adulthood brings with it changes and losses in underlying capabilities, which vary from one person to another. However, it is possible to overcome such shifts in capabilities through selective optimization.

Selective optimization is the process by which people concentrate on particular skill areas to compensate for losses in other areas. They do this to fortify their general motivational, cognitive, and physical resources. A person who has run marathons all her life may have to cut back or give up other activities entirely to increase her training. By giving up other activities, she may be able to maintain her running skills through concentration on them (Burnett-Wolle & Godbey, 2007; Scheibner & Leathem, 2012; Hahn & Lachman, 2015).

continuity theory
the theory suggesting that people need to maintain their desired level of involvement in society to maximize their sense of well-being and self-esteem

selective optimization
the process by which people concentrate on selected skill areas to compensate for losses in other areas

Similarly, elderly individuals engage in compensation for age-related losses. For instance, a person may compensate for a hearing loss by using a hearing aid. Piano virtuoso Arthur Rubinstein provides another example of selective optimization with compensation. In his later years, he maintained his concert career by reducing the number of pieces he played at concerts—an example of being selective—and by practicing those pieces more often—optimization. Finally, in an example of compensation, he slowed down the tempo of musical passages immediately preceding faster passages, thereby fostering the illusion that he was playing as fast as ever (Baltes & Baltes, 1990).

In short, the model of selective optimization with compensation illustrates the fundamentals of successful aging. Although late adulthood may bring changes in capabilities, people who focus on making the most of particular areas may be able to compensate for limitations and losses. The outcome is a life that is reduced in some areas, but transformed and modified and, ultimately, successful.

The Daily Life of Late Adulthood

> Before I retired 10 years ago, everyone told me I'd miss work, get lonely, and feel flat without the challenges of business. Baloney! This is the best time of my life! Miss work? No way. What's to miss? Meetings? Training sessions? Evaluations? Sure, there's less money and people, but I have all I need with my savings, my hobbies, and my traveling.

This positive view of life in late adulthood was expressed by a 75-year-old retired insurance worker. Although the story is certainly not the same for all retirees, many, if not most, find their post-work lives happy and involving. We will consider some of the ways in which people lead their lives in late adulthood, beginning with where they live.

Living Arrangements: The Places and Spaces of Their Lives

LO 9.14 Describe the living arrangements available to older adults, and explain how each affects the quality of their lives.

continuing-care community
a community that offers an environment in which all the residents are of retirement age or older

Think "old age," and your thoughts are likely to turn to nursing homes. But the reality is different. Only 5 percent of people finish their lives in nursing homes; most live out their entire lives in home environments, typically with at least one family member.

LIVING AT HOME   Many older adults live alone. People older than 65 represent a quarter of America's 9.6 million single-person households. Roughly two-thirds of people older than 65 live with other members of the family, mostly spouses. Some older adults live with their siblings, and others live in multigenerational settings with their children, grandchildren, and even great-grandchildren.

The setting in which an older adult lives has varied effects. For married couples, living with a spouse represents continuity. On the other hand, moving in with children represents an adjustment to a multigenerational setting that can be jarring. Not only is there a potential loss of independence and privacy, but older adults may feel uncomfortable with the way their children are raising their grandchildren. Unless there are household ground rules about people's roles, conflicts can arise (Navarro, 2006).

For some groups, living in extended families is more typical than for other groups. For instance, blacks are more likely than whites to live in multigenerational families. Furthermore, the amount of influence that family members have over one another and the interdependence of extended families are generally greater in African American, Asian American, and Hispanic families than in Caucasian families (Becker, Beyene, & Newsom, 2003; Easthope et al., 2017).

Living in a multigenerational setting with children and their families can be rewarding and helpful for those in late adulthood. Are there any disadvantages to this type of situation? What are some solutions?

SPECIALIZED LIVING ENVIRONMENTS   For some 10 percent of those in late adulthood, home is an institution. In fact, there are many types of specialized environments in which elderly people live.

One of the more recent innovations is the **continuing-care community**, typically an environment in which all the residents are of retirement age or older.

The community provides various levels of care, and residents sign contracts for the level they need. In many such communities, people start out in separate houses or apartments, living either independently or with occasional home care. As they age, they may move into *assisted living*, which involves independent housing supported by medical providers to the extent required. Continuing care ultimately extends all the way to full-time nursing care, which is often provided at an on-site nursing home.

Continuing-care communities tend to be fairly homogeneous in terms of religious, racial, and ethnic backgrounds, and they are often organized by private or religious organizations. Because joining may involve a substantial initial payment, members tend to be relatively well-off. Increasingly, though, continuing-care communities are making efforts to increase diversity and also to enhance intergenerational interaction by establishing day-care centers on the premises and developing programs that involve younger populations (Chaker, 2003; Berkman, 2006).

Several types of nursing institutions exist, ranging from those that provide part-time day care to homes that offer 24-hour-a-day, live-in care. In **adult day-care facilities**, elderly individuals receive care only during the day but spend nights and weekends in their own homes. During the time that they are at the facility, people receive nursing care, take their meals, and participate in scheduled activities. Sometimes adult facilities are combined with infant and child day-care programs, an arrangement that allows for interaction between the old and the young (Gitlin et al., 2006; Dabelko & Zimmerman, 2008; Teitelman et al., 2017).

adult day-care facilities
a facility in which elderly individuals receive care only during the day but spend nights and weekends in their own homes

Other institutional settings offer more extensive care. The most intensive are **skilled-nursing facilities**, which provide full-time nursing care for people who have chronic illnesses or are recovering from a temporary medical condition. Although only 4.5 percent of those age 65 and older live in nursing homes, the number increases dramatically with age. Around 3 percent of the population older than 65 lives in nursing homes, and around 10 percent of the population older than 85 lives in nursing homes (Administration on Aging, 2010; Nursing Home Data Compendium, 2013).

skilled-nursing facilities
a facility that provides full-time nursing care for people who have chronic illnesses or are recovering from a temporary medical condition

The more intensive the care, the greater the adjustment required of residents. Although some newcomers adjust relatively rapidly, the loss of independence may lead to difficulties. In addition, elderly people are as susceptible as other people to society's stereotypes about nursing homes, and their expectations may be negative. They may see themselves as just marking time until they die, forgotten and discarded by a society that venerates youth (Natan, 2008; Kostka & Jachimowicz, 2010).

INSTITUTIONALISM AND LEARNED HELPLESSNESS   Although the fears of those in nursing homes may be exaggerated, they can lead to **institutionalism**, a psychological state in which people develop apathy, indifference, and a lack of caring about themselves. Institutionalism is brought about, in part, by *learned helplessness*, a belief that one has no control over one's environment (Peterson & Park, 2007).

institutionalism
a psychological state in which people in nursing homes develop apathy, indifference, and a lack of caring about themselves

The sense of helplessness brought about by institutionalism can be literally deadly. When people enter nursing homes in late adulthood, they lose control over their most basic activities. They may be told when and what to eat, when to sleep, and even when to go to the bathroom (Iecovich & Biderman, 2012; de Oliveira Brito et al., 2014).

A classic experiment showed the consequences of such a loss of control. Psychologists Ellen Langer and Irving Janis (1979) divided elderly residents of a nursing home into two groups. One group was encouraged to make choices about their day-to-day activities. The other group was given no choices and was encouraged to let the nursing home staff care for them. The results were clear. The participants who had choices were not only happier, but they were also healthier. In fact, 18 months after the experiment began, only 15 percent of the choice group had died—compared to 30 percent of the comparison group.

In short, loss of control can have a profound effect on well-being. The best nursing homes go out of their way to permit residents to make basic life decisions and maintain a sense of control over their lives.

> **From the perspective of a health-care provider:** What policies might a nursing home institute to minimize the chances that its residents will develop institutionalism? Why are such policies relatively uncommon?

Finances, Work, and Retirement

LO 9.15   Discuss the financial security of older people and the social and economic ramifications of work and retirement in later adulthood.

We now turn to a discussion of the financial security of older people in the United States and the role of work and retirement.

THE ECONOMICS OF LATE ADULTHOOD   Like everyone, people in late adulthood range from one end of the socioeconomic spectrum to the other.

However, social inequities affecting various groups previously in life are magnified with increasing age. Even so, everyone who reaches late adulthood today may experience growing economic pressure because the increasing human life span means it is more likely that they will run through their savings.

Overall, 10 percent of people age 65 and older live in poverty—a proportion about equal to that for people younger than 65—and around 6 percent of the elderly live in near poverty (see Figure 9-11). However, there are significant gender and racial differences. Women are almost twice as likely as men to be living in poverty. About a quarter of elderly women living alone live on incomes below the poverty line. A married woman may also slip into poverty if she becomes widowed because she may have used up savings to pay for her husband's final illness, and the husband's pension may cease with his death (Administration on Aging, 2010; DeNavas-Walt & Proctor, 2015; Carr, 2019).

As for racial differences, 8 percent of whites in late adulthood live below the poverty line, contrasted with 19 percent of Hispanics and 24 percent of blacks. Minority women fare the worst of any category. For example, 47 percent of divorced black women aged 65 to 74 were below the poverty level (Federal Interagency Forum on Aging-Related Statistics, 2000; U.S. Bureau of the Census, 2013).

Figure 9-11 Poverty in Late Adulthood

Ten percent of those 65 years of age and older live in poverty.

SOURCE: U.S. Census Bureau, Current Population Survey, 2015 Annual Social and Economic Supplement.

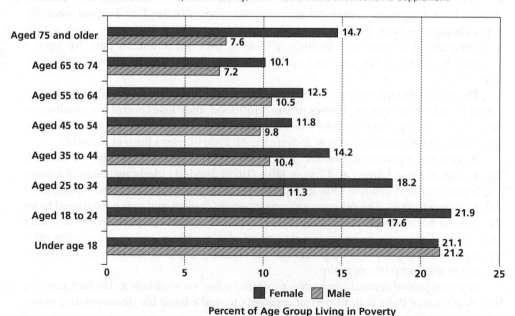

Percent of Age Group Living in Poverty

Age Group	Female	Male
Aged 75 and older	14.7	7.6
Aged 65 to 74	10.1	7.2
Aged 55 to 64	12.5	10.5
Aged 45 to 54	11.8	9.8
Aged 35 to 44	14.2	10.4
Aged 25 to 34	18.2	11.3
Aged 18 to 24	21.9	17.6
Under age 18	21.1	21.2

■ Female ▨ Male

During late adulthood, the range of socioeconomic well-being mirrors that of earlier years.

One source of financial vulnerability is the reliance on a fixed income. The income of an elderly person, which typically comes from a combination of Social Security, pensions, and savings, rarely keeps up with inflation. What may have been a reasonable income at age 65 is worth much less 20 years later, as the elderly person gradually slips into poverty.

The rising cost of health care is another source of financial vulnerability in older adults. The average older person spends close to 20 percent of his or her income for health-care costs. For those who require care in nursing home facilities, the financial costs can be staggering, running an average of more than $80,000 a year (U.S. Department of Health and Human Services, 2017).

Unless major changes are made in the way that Social Security and Medicare are financed, a larger proportion of younger people's pay will have to be taxed to fund benefits for the elderly. This is apt to lead to increasing friction and segregation between younger and older generations. Indeed, as we'll see, Social Security payments are one key factor in many people's decisions about how long to work.

WORK AND RETIREMENT IN LATE ADULTHOOD

When to retire is a major decision faced by the majority of individuals in late adulthood. Some wish to work as long as they can. Others retire the moment their financial circumstances permit it.

When they do retire, many people have some difficulty with the identity shift from "worker" to "retiree." They lack a professional title, they may no longer have people asking them for advice, and they can't say "I work for the Diamond Company."

For others, though, retirement offers the chance to lead, perhaps for the first time in adulthood, a life of leisure. Because a significant number of people retire as early as age 55 or 60, and because life spans are expanding, many people spend far more time in retirement than in previous generations. Moreover, because the number of people in late adulthood continues to increase, retirees are an increasingly significant and influential segment of the U.S. population.

Retirement is a different journey for each individual. Some are content with a more sedate lifestyle, whereas others continue to remain active and in some cases pursue new activities. Can you explain why many non-Western cultures do not follow the disengagement theory of retirement?

Older Workers: Combating Age Discrimination   Many people continue to work, either full- or part-time, for some part of late adulthood. That they can do so is largely because of age discrimination legislation that was passed in the late 1970s, in which mandatory retirement ages were made illegal in almost every profession (Lindemann & Kadue, 2003; Lain, 2012; Voss, Wolff, & Rothermund, 2017).

Whether older adults continue to work for intellectual and social reasons or financial reasons, many encounter age discrimination, which is a reality despite laws against it. Some employers encourage older workers to leave their jobs so they can replace them with younger employees with lower salaries. And some employers believe that older workers are not up to the demands of the job or are less willing to adapt to a changing workplace—enduring stereotypes that laws can't change (Bowen & Skirbekk, 2013; Marquet et al., 2018).

There is little evidence to support the idea that older workers lose their ability to perform their jobs. In many fields, such as art, literature, science, politics, and entertainment, it is easy to find examples of people who have made some of their greatest contributions during late adulthood. Even in those few professions that were specifically exempted from laws prohibiting mandatory retirement ages—those involving public safety—the evidence does not support the notion that workers should be retired early (Landy & Conte, 2004).

Although age discrimination remains a problem, market forces may help reduce its severity. As baby boomers retire and the workforce drastically shrinks, companies may begin to offer incentives to older adults to either remain in or return to the workforce. Still, for most older adults, retirement is the norm.

Retirement: Filling a Life of Leisure   Why do people retire? Although the basic reason seems apparent—to stop working—there are actually many factors. For instance, sometimes workers burn out after a lifetime of work and seek to ease the tension and frustration of their jobs and the sense that they have not accomplished as much as they wished. Others retire because their health has declined, and still others because they receive incentives from their employers. Finally, some people have planned for years to retire and intend to use their increased leisure to travel, study, or spend more time with their children and grandchildren (Nordenmark & Stattin, 2009; Petkoska & Earl, 2009; Müller et al., 2014).

Whatever the reason they retire, people often pass through a series of retirement stages. Retirement may begin with a *honeymoon* period, in which people engage in a variety of activities, such as travel, that were previously hindered by work. The next phase may be *disenchantment*, in which they conclude that retirement is not all they thought it would be because they miss the stimulation and companionship of work or find it hard to keep busy (Osborne, 2012; Schlosser, Zinni, & Armstrong-Stassen, 2012; Rafalski et al., 2017).

The next phase is *reorientation*, in which retirees reconsider their options and become engaged in new, more fulfilling activities. If successful, this leads to the *retirement routine* stage, in which they come to grips with the realities of retirement and feel fulfilled. Not all people reach this stage; some may feel disenchanted for years.

The last phase is *termination*. Although for some people this occurs when they go back to work, for most it follows major physical deterioration. In this case, health becomes so bad that the person can no longer function independently.

Obviously, not everyone passes through all stages, and the sequence is not universal. In large measure, a person's reactions to retirement stem from the reasons he or she retired in the first place. For example, a person forced to retire for health reasons will have a different experience from a person who eagerly chose to retire at a particular age. Similarly, the retirement of people who loved their jobs may differ from that of people who despised their work.

In short, the psychological consequences of retirement vary from one individual to the next. For many people, retirement is a continuation of a life well-lived. Moreover, as we see in the *Development in Your Life* box, there are ways to plan a good retirement.

Development in Your Life

Planning for—and Living—a Good Retirement

What makes for a good retirement? Gerontologists suggest several factors (Borchard & Donohoe, 2008; Noone, Stephens, & Alpass, 2009; Wöhrmann, Fasbender & Deller, 2016):

- **Plan ahead financially.** Because Social Security pensions are likely to be inadequate in the future, personal savings are critical, as is adequate health insurance.

- **Consider tapering off from work gradually.** Sometimes it is helpful to prepare for retirement by shifting from full-time to part-time work.

- **Explore your interests before you retire.** Assess what you like about your current job and think about how to translate those things into leisure activities.

- **If you are married or in a long-term partnership, spend some time discussing your views of the ideal**

retirement with your partner. You may find that you need to negotiate a vision that will suit you both.

- **Consider where you want to live.** Try out, temporarily, a community to which you are thinking of moving.

- **Don't live *too* close to your kids and grandkids.** Living in close proximity to your grandchildren may turn you into a full-time babysitter—something that may or may not fit with your vision of retirement.

- **Plan to volunteer your time.** People who retire have a wealth of skills that are often needed by nonprofit organizations and small businesses. Organizations such as the Retired Senior Volunteer Program or the Foster Grandparent Program can help match your skills with people who need them.

Relationships: Old and New

Leonard Timbola, 94, describes how he met his wife, Ellen, 90.

"I was 23 when Pearl Harbor happened and I enlisted right away. I was sent to Fort Bragg and I was lonely. I'd often go into Fayetteville and just poke around. One day I was in a bookstore reaching for a book. You remember what it was?"

"*Out of the Silent Planet*," Ellen says. "I happened to be reaching for it at the same time. Our hands met, and then our eyes."

"And that was the end of my bachelorhood," says Leonard. "Fate sent me to that bookstore."

Ellen continues. "We shared that book and everything else from then on. We were married 4 months later."

"Just before I shipped out," says Leonard.

This is the way they are: He starts a thought, she finishes it. Unless it's the other way around.

"She wrote every day. I got her letters in bunches, and that was the best reading I ever did." He places his hand on Ellen's knee. Her hand joins his there.

"You weren't nearly as frequent a writer," she reminds him gently. "But when I did get one from you, I read it every day."

"Well that's the same thing," he laughs.

The warmth and affection between Leonard and Ellen are unmistakable. Their relationship, spanning eight decades, continues to bring them quiet joy, and their life is the sort to which many couples aspire. Yet it is also rare for the last stage of life. For every older person who is part of a couple, many more are alone.

What is the social world of late adulthood? To answer the question, we will first consider marriage.

Marriage in the Later Years: Together, Then Alone

LO 9.16 Identify the issues couples face in late adulthood, and describe the challenges presented by the death of a spouse or partner.

When it comes to marriage after 65, men have more choices than women. The proportion of men who are married is far greater than that of women (see Figure 9-12). One reason

Figure 9-12 Living Patterns of Older Americans

SOURCE: Administration on Aging. (2006). Profiles of older Americans 2005: Research report. Washington, DC: U.S. Department of Health and Human Resources.

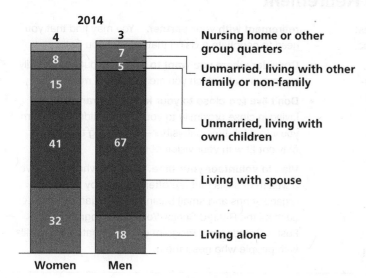

is that 70 percent of women outlive their husbands by at least a few years. Because there are fewer men available (many have died), these women are unlikely to remarry.

Furthermore, the marriage gradient that we discussed previously is still a powerful influence. Reflecting societal norms that women should marry older men, the marriage gradient keeps women single even in the later years of life. At the same time, it makes remarriage for men much easier, because the pool of eligible partners is much larger (Bookwala, 2012).

The vast majority of people who are still married in later life report that they are satisfied with their marriages. Their partners provide substantial companionship and emotional support. Because at this period in life they have typically been together for a long time, they have great insight into their partners (Jose & Alfons, 2007).

Still, not every aspect of marriage is satisfying, and marriages may undergo stress as spouses experience changes in their lives. For instance, the retirement of one or both people can shift the nature of a couple's relationship (Henry, Miller, & Giarrusso, 2005; Rauer & Jensen, 2016).

DIVORCE For some couples, the stress is so great that one spouse or the other seeks a divorce. Although the exact numbers are hard to come by, at least 12 percent of divorces in the United States involve women older than 66—an incidence that has tripled since the 1980s (Brown & Lin, 2012; Ellin, 2015).

The reasons for divorce so late in life are varied. Often, women divorce because their husbands are abusive or alcoholic. But in the more frequent case of a husband divorcing his wife, the reason is often that he has found a younger woman. Many times the divorce occurs soon after retirement, when men who have been highly involved in their careers are in psychological turmoil (Franz et al., 2015; Brown & Wright, 2017).

Divorce so late in life is particularly difficult for women. Between the marriage gradient and the limited pool of eligible men, it is unlikely that an older divorced woman will remarry. For many women, marriage has been their primary role and the center of their identity, and they may view divorce as a major failure. As a consequence, happiness and the quality of life for divorced women often plummet (Davies & Denton, 2002; Connidis, 2010).

Seeking a new relationship becomes a priority for many men and women who are divorced or whose spouses or partners have died. People seeking to develop relationships use the same strategies to meet potential partners as younger people, such as joining singles organizations or even using the Internet to find companionship (Durbin, 2003).

Of course, some people enter late adulthood having never married. For this group—about 5 percent of the population—late adulthood may bring fewer transitions, because living status does not change. In fact, never-married individuals report feeling less lonely than do most people their age, and they have a greater sense of independence (DePaulo, 2006).

DEALING WITH RETIREMENT: TOO MUCH TOGETHERNESS? When Morris Abercrombie finally stopped working full-time, his wife, Roxanne, found some aspects of his increased presence at home troubling. Although their marriage was strong, his intrusion into her daily routine and his constant questioning about whom she was on the phone with and where she was going were irksome. Finally, she began to wish he would spend less time around the house. This was ironic: She had passed much of Morris's preretirement years wishing that he would spend more time at home.

The situation in which Morris and Roxanne found themselves is not unique. For many couples, relationships need to be renegotiated because the couple will probably spend more time together than at any other point in their marriage. For others, retirement alters the longstanding distribution of household chores, with men taking on more responsibility than before for the everyday functioning of the household.

In fact, research suggests that an interesting role reversal often takes place. In contrast to the early years of marriage, in late adulthood husbands' companionship needs tend to be greater than their wives'. The power structure of marriage also changes: Men become more affiliative and less competitive following retirement. At the same time, women become more assertive and autonomous (Williams, Sawyer, & Allman, 2012; Lee & Cho, 2018).

CARING FOR AN AGING SPOUSE OR PARTNER The shifts in health that accompany late adulthood sometimes require women and men to care for their spouses or partners in ways that they never envisioned. Health issues may force them into nearly full-time caretaking, a role they may have never envisioned for themselves.

At the same time, some people view caring for an ailing and dying spouse or partner as a final opportunity to demonstrate love and devotion. In fact, some caregivers report feeling satisfied at fulfilling what they see as their responsibility to their partner. And some of those who experience emotional distress initially find that the distress declines as they successfully adapt (Kulik, 2002).

Yet there is no getting around the fact that giving care is arduous, made more difficult by the fact that the partners providing the care are probably not in the peak of health themselves. In fact, caregiving may be detrimental to the provider's own physical and psychological health. For instance, caregivers report lower levels of satisfaction with life than do noncaregivers (Percy, 2010; Mausbach et al., 2012; Davis et al., 2014; Glauber, 2017).

In almost three-quarters of the cases, it should be noted, the care provider is the wife. Part of the reason is demographic: Men tend to die earlier than women, and consequently to contract the diseases leading to death earlier than women. A second reason, though, relates to society's traditional gender roles, which view women as "natural" caregivers. As a consequence, health-care providers may be more likely to suggest that a wife care for her husband than that a husband care for his wife (Khalaila & Cohen, 2016).

THE DEATH OF A SPOUSE OR PARTNER Hardly any event is more painful and stressful than the death of one's spouse or long-term partner. Especially for those who married young, the death leads to profound feelings of loss and often brings drastic changes in economic and social circumstances. If the marriage was a good one, the death means the loss of a companion, a lover, a confidante, a helper.

Upon a partner's death, spouses suddenly assume a new and unfamiliar societal role: widowhood. At the same time, they lose the role with which they were most familiar: spouse. Suddenly, they are no longer part of a couple; instead, they are viewed by society, and themselves, as individuals. All this occurs as they are dealing with profound and sometimes overwhelming grief (which we discuss more in the next chapter).

Widowhood brings new demands and concerns. There is no longer a companion to share the day's events. If the deceased spouse primarily did the household chores, the surviving spouse must learn how to do these tasks every day. Although initially family and friends provide a great deal of support, this assistance quickly fades and newly widowed people are left to make the adjustment on their own (Hanson & Hayslip, 2000; Smith, 2012; Isherwood, King & Luszcz, 2017).

People's social lives often change drastically. Married couples tend to socialize with other married couples; widowed people may feel like "fifth wheels" as they seek to maintain the friendships they enjoyed as part of a couple. Eventually, such friendships may cease, although they may be replaced by friendships with other single people (Bookwala, 2016).

Economic issues are of major concern to many widowed people. Although many have insurance, savings, and pensions to provide economic security, some people, most often women, experience a decline in their economic well-being as the result of a spouse's death. This can force wrenching decisions, such as selling the house in which the couple spent their married lives (Meyer, Wolf, & Himes, 2006).

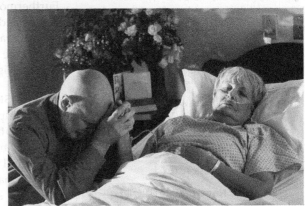

One of the most difficult responsibilities of later adulthood can be caring for one's ill spouse or partner.

Photodisc/Getty Images

The process of adjusting to widowhood encompasses three stages. In the first stage, *preparation*, spouses prepare, in some cases years and even decades ahead of time, for the eventual death of the partner. Consider, for instance, the purchase of life insurance, the preparation of a will, and the decision to have children who may eventually provide care in one's old age. Each of these actions helps prepare for the eventuality that one will be widowed and will require some degree of assistance (Roecke & Cherry, 2002).

The second stage of adjustment to widowhood, *grief and mourning*, is an immediate reaction to the death of a spouse. It starts with the shock and pain of loss, and continues as the survivor works through the emotions the loss brings up. The time a person spends in this period depends on the support received from others, as well as on personality factors. In some cases, grief and mourning may last for years, whereas in others it lasts a few months.

The last stage of adjustment to the death of a spouse is *adaptation*. In adaptation, the widowed individual starts a new life. The period begins with the acceptance of loss and continues with the reorganization of roles and the formation of new friendships. The adaptation stage also encompasses a period of reintegration in which a new identity—as an unmarried person—is developed.

It is important to keep in mind that this three-stage model of loss and change does not apply to everyone, and the timing of the stages varies considerably. Moreover, some people experience *complicated grief*, a form of unrelenting mourning that continues sometimes for months and even years. In complicated grief, people find it difficult to let go of a loved one, and they have intrusive memories of the deceased that impede normal functioning (Piper et al., 2009; Zisook & Shear, 2009; Hirsch, 2018).

For most people, though, life returns to normal and becomes enjoyable once again after the death of a spouse. Still, the death of a spouse is a profound event in any period of life. During late adulthood, its implications are particularly powerful, because it can be seen as a forewarning of one's own mortality.

> **From a social worker's perspective:** What are some factors that can combine to make older adulthood a more difficult time for women than for men?

Friends and Family in Late Adulthood

LO 9.17   Identify the relationships that are important to older adults, and explain why they matter.

Elderly people enjoy friends as much as younger people do, and friendships play an important role in their lives. In fact, time spent with friends is often valued more highly during late adulthood than time spent with family because friends are often seen as more important providers of support. Furthermore, around one-third of older people report that they made a new friend within the past year, and many older adults engage in significant interaction with others. In fact, more time for friends and family is one of the biggest benefits of growing older (Pew Research Center, 2009; also see Figure 9-13).

FRIENDSHIP: WHY FRIENDS MATTER IN LATE ADULTHOOD Friendships are characterized by a sense of control: In friendship relationships, unlike family relationships, we choose whom we like and whom we dislike. Because late adulthood often causes a gradual loss of control in other areas, such as in health, the ability to maintain friendships may take on more importance than in other stages of life (Demir, Orthel, & Andelin, 2013; Singh & Srivastava, 2014).

In addition, friendships—especially recent ones—may be more flexible than family relationships, because they lack the long history

Figure 9-13 Activity in Late Adulthood

During late adulthood, people view more time for family as one of the biggest benefits of the period.

SOURCE: Pew Research Center, 2009.

More time for hobbies/interests	65
More time with family	70
Volunteer work	52
More travel	52
More financial security	64
Less stress	59
Not working	66
More respect	59
Second carrer	14

of obligations and conflicts that often typify family ties and that can reduce the emotional sustenance they provide (McLaughlin et al., 2010; Lester et al., 2012; Lecce et al., 2017).

Friendships in late adulthood are also important because of the increasing likelihood, over time, that one will be without a marital partner. When a spouse dies, people typically seek out friends to help deal with their loss and for some of the companionship that was provided by the deceased spouse.

Of course, it isn't only spouses who die during old age; friends die, too. The way adults view friendship in late adulthood determines how vulnerable they are to the death of a friend. If they have defined the friendship as irreplaceable, the loss of the friend may be quite difficult. On the other hand, if the friendship is defined as one of many, the death of a friend may be less traumatic (Blieszner, 2006).

Friendships also provide one of the basic social needs: social support. **Social support** is assistance and comfort supplied by a network of caring, interested people. Such support plays a critical role in successful aging (Avlund, Lund, & Holstein, 2004; Gow et al., 2007; Evans, 2009).

social support
assistance and comfort supplied by another person or a network of caring, interested people

Social support brings considerable benefits. A social support network can offer emotional support by lending a sympathetic ear and providing a sounding board for concerns. Furthermore, people who are experiencing similar problems—such as the loss of a spouse—can provide an unmatched degree of understanding and a pool of helpful suggestions for coping strategies that would be less credible coming from others.

Finally, people can furnish material support, such as helping with rides or picking up groceries. They can provide help in solving problems, such as dealing with a difficult landlord or fixing a broken appliance.

The benefits of social support extend to the provider as well as the recipient. People who offer support experience feelings of usefulness and heightened self-esteem, knowing that they are making a contribution to someone else's welfare.

What kinds of social support are most effective and appropriate? Certainly preparing food, accompanying someone to a movie, or inviting someone to dinner is helpful. But the opportunity for reciprocity is important, too. Reciprocity is the expectation that if someone provides something positive to another person, eventually, the favor will be returned. In Western societies, older adults—like younger people—value relationships in which reciprocity is possible. However, with increasing age, it may be progressively more difficult to reciprocate the social support that one receives. As a consequence, relationships may become more asymmetrical, placing the recipient in a difficult psychological position (Becker, Beyenem, & Newsom, 2003).

FAMILY RELATIONSHIPS: THE TIES THAT BIND   Even after the death of a spouse, most older adults are part of a larger family unit. Connections with siblings, children, grandchildren, and even great-grandchildren continue and may be an important source of comfort to adults in the last years of their lives.

Siblings can provide unusually strong emotional support because they often share old, pleasant memories of childhood, and because they usually represent a person's oldest existing relationships. Although not every memory of childhood may be pleasant, continuing interaction with brothers and sisters can enhance late adulthood.

Children   Even more important than siblings are children and grandchildren. Even in an age in which geographic mobility is high, most parents and children remain fairly close, both geographically and psychologically. Some 75 percent of children live within a 30-minute drive of their parents, and parents and children visit and talk with one another frequently. Daughters tend to be in more frequent contact with their parents than sons, and mothers tend to be the recipients of communication more often than fathers (Ji-liang, Li-qing, & Yan, 2003; Diamond, Fagundes, & Butterworth, 2010; Byrd-Craven et al., 2012).

Because the great majority of older adults have at least one child who lives fairly close, family members still provide significant aid to one another. Moreover, parents and children tend to share similar views of how adult children should behave toward their parents. In particular, they expect that children should help their parents understand their resources, provide emotional support, and talk over such important matters as medical issues. Furthermore, it is most often children who end up caring for their aging parents when they require assistance (Dellmann-Jenkins & Brittain, 2003; Ron, 2006; Funk, 2010).

The bonds between parents and children are sometimes asymmetrical, with parents seeking a closer relationship and children a more distant one. Parents have a greater *developmental stake* in close ties, because they see their children as perpetuating their beliefs, values, and standards. On the other hand, children are motivated to maintain their autonomy and live independently from their parents. These divergent perspectives make parents more likely to minimize conflicts they experience with their children, and children more likely to maximize them.

Grandchildren and Great-Grandchildren As we discussed previously, not all grandparents are equally involved with their grandchildren. Even those grandparents who take great pride in their grandchildren may be relatively detached from them, avoiding any direct care role. On the other hand, many grandparents include their grandchildren as an integral part of their social networks. (Coall & Hertwig, 2011; Geurts, van Tilburg, & Poortman, 2012; Moore & Rosenthal, 2017).

Grandmothers tend to be more involved than grandfathers, and most young adult grandchildren feel closer to their grandmothers. In addition, most express a preference for their maternal grandmothers over their paternal grandmothers (Hayslip, Shore, & Henderson, 2000; Lavers-Preston & Sonuga-Barke, 2003; Bishop et al., 2009).

African American grandparents tend to be more involved with their grandchildren than Caucasian grandparents, and African American grandchildren often feel closer to their grandparents. Moreover, grandfathers seem to play a more central role in the lives of African American children than in the lives of Caucasian children. These racial differences probably stem in large measure from the higher proportion of multigenerational families among African Americans than among Caucasians. In such families, grandparents usually play a central role in childrearing (Crowther & Rodriguez, 2003; Stevenson, Henderson, & Baugh, 2007; Gelman, Tompkins, & Ihara, 2014).

Great-grandchildren play less of a role in the lives of both white and black great-grandparents. Most great-grandparents do not have close relationships with their great-grandchildren. Close relationships tend to occur only when the great-grandparents and great-grandchildren live relatively near one another (McConnell, 2012).

There are several explanations for this relative lack of involvement. One is that by the time they reach great-grandparenthood, people are so old that they do not have much physical or psychological energy to expend on relationships with their great-grandchildren. Another is that there may be so many great-grandchildren that great-grandparents do not feel strong emotional ties to them and may not even be able to keep track of them. When President John Kennedy's mother, Rose Kennedy (who had given birth to a total of nine children), died at the age of 104, she had 30 grandchildren and 41 great-grandchildren!

Still, great-grandparents profit emotionally from the mere fact that they have great-grandchildren. They may see their great-grandchildren as representing both their own and their family's continuation, as well as providing a concrete sign of their longevity. Furthermore, as health advances in late adulthood continue to increase, great-grandparents are physically able to contribute more to the lives of their great-grandchildren (McConnell, 2012).

Elder Abuse: Relationships Gone Wrong

LO 9.18   Discuss what causes elder abuse and how it can be prevented.

When Lorene Templeton was 74, her son Aaron moved in with her. "I was lonely and welcomed the company. When Aaron offered to take care of my finances, I gave him my power of attorney."

For the next 3 years, Aaron cashed Lorene's checks, withdrew her money, and used her credit card. "When I found out, Aaron apologized. He said he needed the money to get out of trouble. He promised to stop."

But he didn't. Aaron emptied Lorene's accounts and then demanded the key to her safe deposit box. When she refused, he beat her until she lost consciousness.

"His problem was drugs," Lorene says. "Finally, I called the police and they arrested him. Now I feel free for the first time in years."

It would be easy to assume that such cases are rare. The truth of the matter, however, is that they are considerably more common than we would like to believe. According to some estimates, **elder abuse**, the physical or psychological mistreatment or neglect of elderly individuals, may affect as many as 11 percent of the elderly each year. Even these estimates may be too low, because people who are abused are often too embarrassed or humiliated to report their plight. And as the number of elderly people increases, experts believe that the number of cases of elder abuse will also rise (Starr, 2010; Dow & Joosten, 2012; Jackson, 2018).

elder abuse
the physical or psychological mistreatment or neglect of elderly individuals

Elder abuse is most frequently directed at family members and particularly at parents. Those most at risk are likely to be less healthy and more isolated than average, and they are more likely to be living in a caregiver's home. Although there is no single cause for elder abuse, it often stems from economic, psychological, and social pressures on caregivers who must provide high levels of care 24 hours a day. Thus, people with Alzheimer's disease or other sorts of major neurocognitive disorder are particularly likely to be targets of abuse (Lee, 2008; Castle & Beach, 2013; Fang & Yan, 2018).

The best way to deal with elder abuse is to prevent it. Family members caring for an older adult should take breaks and should contact social support agencies for advice and concrete support. For instance, the National Family Caregivers Association (800-896-3650) maintains a caregivers' network and publishes a newsletter.

Anyone suspecting that an elderly person is being abused should contact local authorities, such as their state's Adult Protective Services or Elder Protective Services.

Review, Check, and Apply

Review

LO 9.10 Identify and describe the various theories of personality development in late adulthood.

Erikson calls older adulthood the ego-integrity-versus-despair stage; Peck focuses on three tasks that define the period; Levinson suggests that older people can experience liberation and self-regard; and Neugarten focuses on the ways people cope with aging.

LO 9.11 Explain how age relates to the distribution of resources, power, and privilege.

Age stratification theories suggest that the unequal distribution of economic resources, power, and privilege is particularly pronounced during late adulthood. In general, Western societies do not hold elderly people in as high esteem as many Asian societies.

LO 9.12 Define wisdom, and describe how it is associated with age.

Wisdom reflects the accumulation of knowledge related to human behavior. Because it is gathered through experience, it appears to be correlated with age.

LO 9.13 Differentiate the theories of aging, and explain how culture shapes the way older people are treated.

Disengagement theory suggests that older people gradually withdraw from the world, whereas activity theory suggests that the happiest people continue to be engaged with the world. A compromise theory—continuity theory—may be the most useful approach to successful aging, and the most successful model for aging may be selective optimization with compensation. Societies in which elderly people are respected are generally characterized by social homogeneity, extended families, responsible roles for older people, and control of significant resources by older people.

LO 9.14 Describe the living arrangements available to older adults, and explain how each affects the quality of their lives.

Elderly people live in a variety of settings, although most live at home with a family member. For others there are specialized living environments that range from continuing-care communities to skilled-nursing facilities. Living with a spouse or partner represents continuity for older adults, whereas moving in with children in a multigenerational setting can be challenging. Living in a nursing home or other institutional setting involves a loss of independence, which many older adults fear.

LO 9.15 Discuss the financial security of older people and the social and economic ramifications of work and retirement in later adulthood.

Financial issues can trouble older people, largely because their incomes are fixed, health-care costs are increasing, and the life span is lengthening. After retirement, many people pass through stages, including a honeymoon period, disenchantment, reorientation, retirement routine, and termination. There are ways to plan a good retirement, including tapering off from work gradually, exploring interests before retiring, and trying to plan ahead financially.

LO 9.16 Identify the issues couples face in late adulthood, and describe the challenges presented by the death of a spouse or partner.

Although couples in older adulthood are generally happy, the many changes of the period cause stresses that can result in divorce. The death of a spouse or partner has major psychological, social, and material effects on the survivor and makes the formation and continuation of friendships highly important.

LO 9.17 Identify the relationships that are important to older adults, and explain why they matter.

Friendships are highly valued in late adulthood and an important source of social support. Family relationships are a part of most older people's lives, especially relationships with siblings and children. They provide both emotional support and continuity.

LO 9.18 Discuss what causes elder abuse and how it can be prevented.

Parents who are socially isolated and in poor health may be abused by children who are forced to act as caregivers. The best defense against elder abuse is prevention by ensuring that caregivers receive time off and have access to social support.

Check Yourself

1. According to Erikson, individuals in late adulthood engage in looking back over their lives, evaluating their experiences and coming to terms with decisions. This is also known as _____.

   a. ego transcendence versus ego preoccupation
   b. acceptance versus disassociation
   c. generativity versus stagnation
   d. ego integrity versus despair

2. Models of successful aging include _____.

   a. compensation theory, disengagement theory, and maximization theory
   b. activity theory, continuity theory, and selective optimization
   c. capability theory, sociability theory, and withdrawal strategies
   d. social optimization, compensation theory, and life events theory

3. After retiring from work, people often pass through a series of stages, including _____.

   a. honeymoon, disenchantment, reorientation, and termination
   b. disorientation, dissatisfaction, reorientation, and acceptance
   c. increased activity, confusion, recommitment, and termination
   d. resentment, loneliness, reappraisal, and fulfillment

4. The first stage of adjustment to the death of a spouse or partner is _____.

   a. adaptation
   b. preparation
   c. anger
   d. bargaining

Applying Lifespan Development

What are some ways the retirement of a spouse or partner can bring stress to a marriage? Is retirement likely to be less stressful in households where both people work, or twice as stressful?

Chapter 9 Summary
Putting It All Together: Late Adulthood

PETER SARNOV AND ELLA MALONE may live together, but they have chosen two different ways to live out their late adulthood. Whereas Peter loves staying home, Ella enjoys a hectic retirement filled with activities, social engagements, and work. What the two retirees have in common is their commitment to maintaining their physical health, intellectual activity, and key relationships—even if they have chosen radically different ways to do these things. By paying attention to their needs in all three spheres, Peter and Ella have remained optimistic and cheerful.

MODULE 9.1
PHYSICAL DEVELOPMENT IN LATE ADULTHOOD

- Though both are chronologically among the "oldest old," Peter and Ella are "young old" in their functional ages. (pp. 397–398)
- Both defy ageist stereotypes in their health and attitudes. (pp. 398–399)
- Both appear to have avoided Alzheimer's and most of the other physical and psychological disorders associated with old age. (pp. 403–406)
- Peter and Ella have made healthy lifestyle choices—exercising, eating right, and avoiding bad habits. (pp. 406–407)

MODULE 9.2
COGNITIVE DEVELOPMENT IN LATE ADULTHOOD

- Both Peter and Ella are apparently rich in crystallized intelligence—their store of information, skills, and strategies. (pp. 412–414)
- They demonstrate plasticity by using stimulation, practice, and motivation to maintain their mental abilities. (pp. 413–414)
- Both may have slight memory problems, such as a decline in episodic or autobiographical memory. (pp. 414–416)

MODULE 9.3
SOCIAL AND PERSONALITY DEVELOPMENT IN LATE ADULTHOOD

- Peter and Ella are navigating Erikson's ego-integrity-versus-despair. (pp. 419–420)
- The two appear to be coping with aging differently, according to Neugarten's personality categories. (pp. 420–421)
- Both seem to have acquired wisdom with age, knowing who they are and how to deal with others. (p. 423)
- Both siblings have chosen to establish themselves together in a new home. (p. 426)
- Neither Peter nor Ella seems to have gone through the classic retirement stages. (pp. 428–430)

What would a RETIREMENT COUNSELOR do?

What advice would you give a person who wants to keep working forever, the way Ella seems to want to do? What advice would you give someone like Peter, who seems content with a relaxed retirement? What characteristics would you look for in these individuals that would help you give the right advice?

Steve Hix/Corbis/Getty Images

What would a HEALTHCARE PROVIDER do?

Why do you think Peter and Ella continue to be in good physical health? What strategies has Ella used that Peter may not have? What strategies has Peter used that Ella may not have? What strategies do they share?

Photodisc/Getty Images

What would YOU do?

If you were asked to do an oral history project involving Peter and Ella, how complete and accurate would you expect their recollections to be? Would they be more reliable about the 1960s or the 2000s? Which sibling do you think you would enjoy talking to more?

Odua Images/Shutterstock

What would an EDUCATOR do?

Would you recommend cognitive training for either Peter or Ella? What about college courses via Road Scholar or online? Why or why not?

Tom Baker/123RF

Chapter 10
Death and Dying

Maskot/Getty Images

Jackson LeRoi knew that he'd be dying soon—very soon. At the age of 71, he'd been diagnosed with a particularly aggressive form of brain cancer, and his doctors were clear that his time was limited.

LeRoi made a choice: rather than endure grueling rounds of chemotherapy, which would only extend his life for a few months at best, he chose to refuse treatment, except for drugs that would keep his final days pain-free.

"I've led a good life. I'm happy with what I've accomplished," he said. And he had a lot of friends, many of whom attended a party he threw when his doctor told him he had less than 2 weeks to live. People laughed, people cried, but, for LeRoi, it was what he wanted: a celebration of a life well lived.

Appropriately enough, in this last chapter we discuss the final chapter of life. We begin by considering how the moment of death is defined, and we examine how people view and react to death at different points in the life span. Then we look at how people confront their own deaths, covering a theory that people pass through stages as they come to grips with their approaching death. We also look at how people endeavor to exert control over the circumstances that surround death, using living wills and assisted suicide. Finally, we consider bereavement and grief. We distinguish normal from unhealthy grief, and we discuss the consequences of a loss. Finally, we look at mourning and funerals, discussing how people acknowledge the passing of a loved one.

Module 10.1 *Death and Dying* Across the Life Span

LO 10.1   Describe how the moment of death is defined.
LO 10.2   Analyze causes of and reactions to death across the life span.
LO 10.3   Describe the aims and benefits of death education.

Module 10.2 *Confronting Death*

LO 10.4   Analyze Kübler-Ross's theory on the process of dying.
LO 10.5   Explain ways in which people can exercise control over how they spend their last days.
LO 10.6   Describe alternatives for providing end-of-life care for the terminally ill.

Module 10.3 *Grief and Bereavement*

LO 10.7   Analyze the cultural meaning of funeral rites in Western and other cultures.
LO 10.8   Describe how survivors react to and cope with death.

Module 10.1

Death and Dying Across the Life Span

Feel Like a Dinosaur

When Jules Beckham turned 100 last October, his family threw him a big party. "My kids, grandkids, and great-grandkids all came," he recalls. "We were 40 in all, and two of my great-granddaughters are pregnant." Missing from the celebration were Jules's eldest son, who died of cancer 5 years ago, and a granddaughter who was killed in a car accident. Absent, too, were his former colleagues from the high school where he taught English for 40 years. They're all dead now. The same is true of the men he fought beside in the Pacific in World War II. Even the friends he played chess with after retirement are all gone. "I'm the last man standing," he says. "I love my family dearly, but they've heard my reminiscences a hundred times, and they don't get my references to anything that happened before 1960."

Jules has drawn up a living will and shared it with his eldest daughter and his doctors. "It's funny," he says. "When I was facing enemy fire in the war, I had to battle with the fear of dying every day, but now I'm calmer. I don't want to die, but I feel a bit like a dinosaur, and I don't want my life prolonged if I have severe brain damage or am paralyzed. If 100 years has taught me anything, it's that quality of life is much more valuable than quantity."

Even if we reach 100 years, death is an experience that will happen to all of us at some time, as universal to the human condition as birth. As such, it is a milestone of life that is central to an understanding of the life span.

Only recently have lifespan developmentalists given serious study to the developmental implications of dying. In this module we will discuss death and dying from several perspectives. We begin by considering how we define death—a determination that is more complex than it seems. We then examine how people view and react to death at different points in the life span. And we consider the different views of death held by various societies.

Lisa F. Young/Shutterstock

Understanding Death

> It took a major legal and political battle, but eventually Terri Schiavo's husband won the right to remove a feeding tube that had kept her alive for 15 years. Lying in a hospital bed all those years in what physicians called a "persistent vegetative state," Schiavo was never expected to regain consciousness after suffering brain damage as a result of respiratory and cardiac arrest. After a series of court battles, her husband—despite the wishes of her parents—was allowed to direct caretakers to remove the feeding tube; Schiavo died soon afterward.

Was Schiavo's husband right in seeking to remove her feeding tube? Was she already dead when it was removed? Were her constitutional rights ignored by her husband's action?

Such difficult questions illustrate the complexity of what are, literally, matters of life and death. Death is not only a biological event; it involves psychological aspects as well. We need to consider not only what defines death, but also how our conception of death changes across the life span.

Defining Death: When Does Life End?

LO 10.1   Describe how the moment of death is defined.

What is death? The question seems clear, but defining the point at which life ceases is surprisingly complex. Medicine has advanced to the point where some people who would have been considered dead a few years ago would now be considered alive.

functional death

the absence of a heartbeat and breathing

Functional death is defined by an absence of heartbeat and breathing. This definition, however, is more ambiguous than it seems. For example, a person whose heartbeat and breathing have ceased for as long as 5 minutes may be resuscitated and suffer little damage from the experience. Was the person who is now alive previously dead, as the functional definition would have it?

brain death

a diagnosis of death based on the cessation of all signs of brain activity, as measured by electrical brain waves

Because of this imprecision, brain functioning is now used to determine the moment of death rather than heartbeat or respiration. In **brain death**, all signs of brain activity, as measured by electrical brain waves, have ceased. When brain death occurs, it is impossible to restore functioning.

Some medical experts suggest that defining death only as a lack of brain waves is too restrictive. They argue that losing the ability to think, reason, feel, and experience the world may define death, as well. In this view, which considers the psychological ramifications, a person who suffers irreversible brain damage, who is in a coma, and who will never experience anything approaching a human life can be considered dead, even if some sort of primitive brain activity continues (Young & Teitelbaum, 2010; Burkle, Sharp, & Wijdicks, 2014; Wang et al., 2017).

This argument, which moves us from strictly medical criteria to moral and philosophical considerations, is controversial. As a result, death is legally defined in most localities in the United States as the absence of brain functioning, although some laws still include the absence of respiration and heartbeat in their definition. In reality, no matter where a death occurs, brain waves are seldom measured. Usually, they are closely monitored only in special circumstances—when the time of death is significant, when organs may be transplanted, or when criminal or legal issues are involved.

The difficulty in establishing legal and medical definitions of death may reflect changes in understanding and attitudes that occur over the course of people's lives.

Death Across the Life Span: Causes and Reactions

LO 10.2   Analyze causes of and reactions to death across the life span.

> Cheryl played flute in the school band. She had shoulder-length brown hair, brown eyes, and a smile that often gave way to a lopsided grin when her friends or older brother said something funny.
>
> Cheryl's family owned a small farm, and it was her job to feed the chickens and gather any eggs every morning before the school bus arrived. After she completed her chores, she gathered up whatever sewing project she was working on in Family and Consumer

Sciences—Cheryl loved designing and creating her own clothing—and waved good-bye to her parents. "Don't take any wooden nickels," her dad always called after her. Cheryl thought it was a really dumb joke, but she loved that her dad never forgot to say it.

One Friday night, Cheryl's dad suggested they hop in the truck and go get pizza. There were only two seat belts in the narrow cab, but Cheryl felt safe wedged in between her dad and her brother. They were riding down a two-lane highway, singing along with some silly song on the radio, when a car in the lane opposite lost control and crossed the center line, slamming into the truck. Without a seat belt, Cheryl flew through the windshield. Her father and brother survived, but for Cheryl, 13, life was over.

Death is something we associate with old age, but for many individuals, death comes earlier. Because it seems "unnatural" for a young person like Cheryl to die, the reactions to such a death are particularly extreme. In the United States, in fact, some people believe that children should be sheltered from the reality of death. Yet people of every age can experience the death of friends and family members, as well as their own death. How do our reactions to death evolve as we age? We will consider several age groups.

DEATH IN INFANCY AND CHILDHOOD   Despite its economic wealth, the United States has a relatively high infant mortality rate. Some 55 other countries have a smaller percentage of infants who die in the first year of life than the United States (*World Factbook*, 2017).

As these statistics indicate, the number of parents who lose an infant is substantial. The death of a child arouses all the typical reactions one would have to a timelier death, but family members may suffer severe effects as they struggle to deal with death at such an early age. One common reaction is extreme depression (Murphy, Johnson, & Wu, 2003; Cacciatore, 2010; Christiansen, 2017).

An exceptionally difficult death to confront is prenatal death, or *miscarriage*. Parents often form psychological bonds with their unborn child and may feel profound grief if it dies before birth. Moreover, friends and relatives often fail to understand the emotional impact of miscarriage, making parents feel their loss all the more keenly (Wheeler & Austin, 2001; Nikčević & Nicolaides, 2014).

Another form of death that produces extreme stress, in part because it is so unanticipated, is sudden infant death syndrome. With **sudden infant death syndrome (SIDS)**, which usually occurs between the ages of 2 and 4 months, a seemingly healthy baby stops breathing and dies inexplicably.

sudden infant death syndrome (SIDS)
the unexplained death of a seemingly healthy baby

In cases of SIDS, parents often feel intense guilt, and acquaintances may be suspicious of the "true" cause of death. However, there is no known cause for SIDS, which seems to strike randomly, and parents' guilt is unwarranted (Kinney & Thach, 2009; Mitchell, 2009; Horne, 2017; Gollenberg & Fendley, 2018).

During childhood, the most frequent cause of death is accidents, most of them as a result of motor vehicle crashes, fires, and drowning. However, a substantial number of children in the United States are victims of homicides, which have nearly tripled in number since 1960. Homicide is among the top four leading causes of death for children between the ages of 1 and 24, and is the leading cause of death for 15- to 24-year-old African Americans (National Vital Statistics Report, 2016).

For parents, the death of a child produces a profound sense of loss and grief. There is no worse death for most parents, including the loss of a spouse or of one's own parents. They may feel their trust in the natural order of the world—where children "should" outlive their parents—has been violated. Believing it is their primary responsibility to protect their children from harm, they may feel they have failed when a child dies (Granek et al., 2015; Jonas et al., 2018).

Parents are almost never prepared to deal with the death of a child, and they may obsessively ask themselves why the death occurred. Because the bond between children and parents is so strong, parents sometimes feel that a part of themselves has died as well. The stress is so profound that it significantly increases the risk of hospitalization for a mental disorder (Nikkola, Kaunonen, & Aho, 2013; Fox, Cacciatore, & Lacasse, 2014; Currie et al., 2018).

CHILDHOOD CONCEPTIONS OF DEATH   Children do not really begin to develop a concept of death until around age 5. Although they are already well aware of death, they tend to view it as a temporary, diminished state of living, rather than a cessation. A preschool-age child might say, "Dead people don't get hungry—well, maybe a little" (Kastenbaum, 1985, p. 629).

Some preschool children think of death as a sleep people may wake from, just as Sleeping Beauty awoke in the fairy tale. For these children, death is not particularly fearsome; rather, it is a curiosity. If people merely tried hard enough—by administering medicine, providing food, or using magic—dead people might "return" (Russell, 2017).

Children's misunderstanding of death can have devastating emotional consequences. Children may believe they are somehow responsible for a person's death. They may assume their bad behavior caused the death. They may also think that if the dead person really wanted to, she or he could return.

> **From an educator's perspective:** Given their developmental level and understanding of death, how do you think preschool children react to the death of a parent?

Around age 5, children better grasp the finality and irreversibility of death. They may personify death as a ghostlike or devilish figure. They do not regard death as universal, but as something that happens only to certain people. It is not until about age 9 that they accept the universality and finality of death. By middle childhood, there is an awareness of the customs around death, such as funerals, cremation, and cemeteries (Hunter & Smith, 2008; Corr, 2010; Panagiotaki et al., 2018).

DEATH IN ADOLESCENCE   We might expect the significant cognitive development that occurs in adolescence to bring about a sophisticated, thoughtful, and reasoned view of death. However, in many ways, adolescents' views of death are as unrealistic as those of younger children, although along different lines.

Adolescents understand the finality and irreversibility of death, yet they tend to think it can't happen to them, which can lead to risky behavior. As we discussed previously, adolescents develop a *personal fable*, a set of beliefs that makes them feel unique and special. Thus, they may believe that they are invulnerable and that the bad things that happen to other people won't happen to them (Elkind, 1985; Wenk, 2010).

Many times, the risky behavior that results from these beliefs causes death in adolescence. For instance, the most frequent cause of death among adolescents is accidents, most often involving motor vehicles. Other frequent causes include homicide, suicide, cancer, and AIDS (National Vital Statistics Report, 2016).

When adolescent feelings of invulnerability confront a fatal illness, the results can be shattering. Adolescents who learn they are terminally ill often feel angry and cheated—that life has been unjust to them. Because they feel—and act—so negatively, it may be difficult for medical personnel to treat them effectively.

In contrast, some adolescents who are terminally ill react with total denial. Feeling indestructible, they may not accept the seriousness of their illness. If it does not cause them to reject medical treatment, some degree of denial may be useful because it allows an adolescent to continue living a normal life as long as possible (Beale, Baile, & Aaron, 2005; Barrera et al., 2013; Cullen, 2017).

DEATH IN YOUNG ADULTHOOD   Young adults feel primed to begin their lives. Past the preparatory time of childhood and adolescence, they are ready to make their mark on the world. Because death at such a point seems close to unthinkable, its occurrence is particularly difficult. In active pursuit of life goals, they are angry and impatient with any illness that threatens their future.

For young adults, the leading cause of death continues to be accidents, followed by suicide, homicide, and cancer. By the end of early adulthood, however, death from disease becomes more prevalent.

Tracy Whiteside/Shutterstock

Adolescents' views of death may be highly romanticized and dramatic.

For young adults facing death, several concerns are acutely important. One is the desire to develop intimate relationships and express sexuality, each of which is inhibited, or completely prevented, by a terminal illness. For instance, people who test positive for the AIDS virus may find it difficult to start new relationships. Within evolving relationships, sexual activities present even more challenging issues (Balk, 2014).

Future planning is another concern of young adults. At a time when most people are mapping out careers and deciding when to start a family, young adults who are terminally ill face additional burdens. Should they marry, even though they may soon leave a partner widowed? Should a couple seek to conceive a child if it is likely to be raised by only one parent? How soon should one's employer be told about a terminal illness, when the revelation may cost the young adult his or her job? None of these questions is easily answered.

DEATH IN MIDDLE ADULTHOOD For middle-aged people, the shock of a life-threatening disease—the most common cause of death in this period—is not so great. By this point, people are well aware that they will die someday, and they may be able to accept this possibility in a realistic manner.

Their sense of realism, though, doesn't make the possibility of dying any easier. Fears about death are often greater in midlife than at any time previously—or even in later life. These fears may lead people to switch their focus to the number of years they have remaining rather than the number of years they have already lived (Akhtar, 2010).

The most frequent cause of death in midlife is heart attack or stroke. Dying so unexpectedly does not allow for preparation, but it may be easier than a slow and painful death from a disease such as cancer. It is the kind of death most people prefer: When asked, they say they would like an instant and painless death that does not involve loss of any body part (Taylor, 2014; Bernard et al., 2017).

DEATH IN LATE ADULTHOOD By late adulthood, people know that the end is approaching. They face an increasing number of deaths in their worlds: spouses, siblings, and friends may have already died, a constant reminder of their own mortality.

Interestingly, the prevalence of death in the lives of the elderly makes them less anxious about dying. However, this does not mean that people in late adulthood welcome death. Rather, they are more realistic and reflective about it. They think about death, and they may begin to prepare for it. Some begin to pull away from the world as physical and psychological energy diminishes (Akhtar, 2010).

Impending death is sometimes accompanied by rapid declines in cognitive functioning. In what is known as the *terminal decline*, a significant drop in memory and reading ability may foreshadow death within the next few years (Hülür et al., 2013; Gerstorf et al., 2016; Brandmaier et al., 2017).

Some elderly people actively seek out death, turning to suicide. In fact, the suicide rate for men climbs steadily during late adulthood, and no age group has a higher suicide rate than white men older than age 85. (Adolescents and young adults commit suicide in greater numbers, but their *rate* of suicide—the number of suicides as a proportion of the general adolescent population—is actually lower.) Suicide is often a consequence of severe depression or some form of dementia, or it may arise from the loss of a spouse (Kjølseth, Ekeberg, & Steihaug, 2010; Dombrovski et al., 2012; McCue & Balasubramaniam, 2017).

A critical issue for older adults who are terminally ill is whether their lives still have value. More than younger adults, elderly people who are dying worry that they are burdens to their family or to society. They may even be given the message, sometimes inadvertently, that society no longer values them and that they are viewed as "dying" rather than being "very sick" (Kastenbaum, 2000; Meagher & Balk, 2013).

In most cases, older people want to know if death is impending. Like younger patients, who usually prefer to know the truth about an illness, older people want the details. Ironically, caregivers usually wish to avoid telling patients that they are dying (Goold, Williams, & Arnold, 2000; Hagerty et al., 2004; Span, 2016).

Not all people, however, wish to know about their condition or that they are dying. Individuals react to death in substantially different ways, in part because of personality factors. For example, people who are generally anxious worry more about death. There are also significant cultural differences in how people view and react to death, as we consider in the *Cultural Dimensions* box.

Cultural Dimensions

Differing Conceptions of Death

In the midst of a tribal celebration, an older man waits for his oldest son to place a cord around his neck. The older man has been sick, and he is ready to relinquish his ties to this earthly world. He asks that his son lift him to his death, and the son complies.

To Hindus in India, death is not an ending, but rather part of a continual cycle. Because they believe in reincarnation, death is thought to be followed by rebirth into a new life. Death, then, is seen as a companion to life.

People's responses to death take many forms, particularly in different cultures. But even in Western societies, reactions to death and dying are quite diverse. For instance, is it better for a man to die after a full life in which he has raised a family and been successful in his job, or for a courageous and valiant young soldier to die defending his country in wartime? Has one person died a better death than the other?

The answer depends on one's values, which reflect cultural and subcultural teachings, often shared through religious beliefs. Some societies view death as a punishment or as a judgment about one's contributions to the world. Others see death as redemption from an earthly life of travail. Some view death as the start of an eternal life, while others believe that an earthly life is all there is (Bryant, 2003).

For members of some Native American tribes, death is seen as a continuation of life. Members of the Lakota tribe believe that in death, people move to a spirit land called Wanagi Makoce, which is inhabited by all people and animals. Death, then, is not viewed with anger or seen as unfair. Similarly, some religions, such as Buddhism and Hinduism, believe in *reincarnation*, the conviction that the soul or spirit comes back to life in a newborn body, continuing the cycle of life (Huang, 2004; Sharp et al., 2015; Tseng et al., 2018).

The age at which people learn about death varies among cultures. In cultures with high levels of violence and death, an awareness of death may come earlier in life. Research shows that children in Israel understand the finality, irreversibility, and inevitability of death at an earlier age than children in the United States and Britain (Atchley, 2000; Braun, Pietsch, & Blanchette, 2000; Panagiotaki et al., 2015).

Anne-Marie Palmer/Alamy Stock Photo

Differing conceptions of death lead to different rituals. For example, in India, bodies may be floated in the Ganges River following death.

Death Education: Preparing for the Inevitable?

LO 10.3   Describe the aims and benefits of death education.

"When will Mom come back from being dead?"
"Why did Barry have to die?"
"Did Grandpa die because I was bad?"

Children's questions such as these illustrate why many developmentalists, as well as **thanatologists**, people who study death and dying, have suggested that death education should be a component of everyone's schooling. Recently, such instruction has emerged. *Death education* encompasses programs designed to help people of all ages deal better with death, dying, and grief—both others' deaths and their own.

Death education arose as a response to the way we hide death, at least in most Western societies. We typically let hospitals deal with the dying, and we do not talk to children about death or allow them to go to funerals for fear of disturbing them. Even emergency workers and medical specialists are uncomfortable talking about it. Because it is seldom discussed and is so removed from everyday life, people may have little opportunity to confront their feelings about death or to gain a realistic sense of it (Waldrop & Kirkendall, 2009; Kellehear, 2015; Chapple et al., 2017).

thanatologists
people who study death and dying

Several types of death education programs exist. Among them are:

- **Crisis intervention education.** After the 2012 shooting at Sandy Hook Elementary School, surviving children received crisis intervention designed to deal with their anxieties. Younger children, whose conceptions of death were shaky at best, needed explanations of the loss of life that day geared to their levels of cognitive development. Crisis intervention education is used in less extreme times as well. For example, it is common for schools to make emergency counseling available if a student is killed or commits suicide (Sandoval, Scott, & Padilla, 2009; Markell, 2010; Reeves & Fernandez, 2017).

- **Routine death education.** Although relatively little curricular material on death exists for elementary students, coursework in high schools is becoming more common. Colleges and universities increasingly include courses about death in such departments as psychology, human development, sociology, and education (Eckerd, 2009; Bonoti, Leondari, & Mastora, 2013; Corr, 2015).

- **Death education for members of the helping professions.** Professionals who will deal with death, dying, and grief in their careers have a special need for death education. Almost all medical and nursing schools now offer some form of death education. The most successful programs not only offer providers ways to help patients deal with their own impending deaths or those of family members, but also allow students to explore their feelings about the topic (Haas-Thompson, Alston, & Holbert, 2008; Kehl & McCarty, 2012; Chapple et al., 2017).

Although death education will not completely demystify death, the programs just described may help people come to grips with what is, along with birth, the most universal—and certain—of all human experiences.

Review, Check, and Apply

Review

LO 10.1 Describe how the moment of death is defined.

Functional death is defined as the cessation of heartbeat and respiration; brain death is defined by the absence of electrical brain waves. The definition of death has changed as medical advances have allowed us to resuscitate people who would once have been considered dead. Some medical experts believe that death occurs when a person can no longer think, reason, or feel, and can never again live anything resembling a human life.

LO 10.2 Analyze causes of and reactions to death across the life span.

The death of an infant or young child can be particularly difficult for parents, and for an adolescent death appears to be unthinkable. Cultural differences in attitudes and beliefs about death strongly influence people's reactions to it.

LO 10.3 Describe the aims and benefits of death education.

Thanatologists recommend that death education become a normal part of learning to help people understand one of the most universal, and certain, of all human experiences.

Check Yourself

1. The cessation of the heartbeat and breathing is the definition of _____ death.
   a. functional
   b. biomedical
   c. brain
   d. legal

2. The concept of the personal fable, which can lead to feelings of invulnerability, makes death occurring during _____ particularly surprising and shattering.
   a. childhood
   b. adolescence
   c. young adulthood
   d. middle adulthood

3. _____ are people who study death and dying.
   a. Cytologists
   b. Thanatologists
   c. Neuropathologists
   d. Teratologists

4. Emergency counseling provided within schools to help students deal with school shootings is known as _____.
   a. routine death education
   b. thanatology training
   c. crisis intervention education
   d. demystification training

Applying Lifespan Development

Do you think schools should teach preteens and adolescents about suicide? Are there disadvantages to teaching this age group about suicide, or is it best to deal with the topic early?

Module 10.2

Confronting Death

Deciding to Say Good-Bye

Carol Reyes had been active all her life. When she broke her pelvis at 89, she was determined to walk again. With 6 months of intensive physical therapy, she did. At 93, she came down with pneumonia. After a month in the hospital, she returned home to the things she loved—her cats, her books, and taking an active part in local politics—a little weaker, but basically sound.

Three years later, Carol's doctor told her she had ALS, a disease in which the motor neurons in the brain and spinal cord slowly die. She could take a drug called Rilutek to slow its progress, but eventually her muscles would atrophy, making it hard to use her hands or walk. She'd have trouble speaking and swallowing. In the end, her lungs would be paralyzed.

Carol agreed to try the drug, but told her doctor she wanted a DNR—Do Not Resuscitate Order—for when her lungs began seizing up and breathing became difficult. "That's not a life I'd like to be living," she said.

Four months later, Carol Reyes found herself gasping for breath. She refused oxygen. She refused to go to the hospital. She died quickly, in her own bed. Like other deaths, Reyes's raises a myriad of difficult questions. Was her refusal to take oxygen equivalent to suicide? Should the ambulance medic have complied with the request? Was she coping with her impending death effectively? How do people come to terms with death, and how do they react and adapt to it? Lifespan developmentalists and other specialists in death and dying have struggled to find answers.

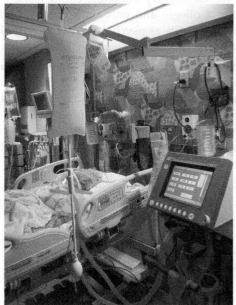

Mediscan/Alamy Stock Photo

In this module, we look at how people confront their own death. We discuss the theory that people move through stages as they come to grips with their approaching death. We also look at how people use living wills and assisted suicide.

Understanding the Process of Dying

No individual has influenced our understanding of the way people confront death more than Elisabeth Kübler-Ross. A psychiatrist, Kübler-Ross developed a theory of death and dying based on interviews with dying people and those caring for them. Although, as we shall see, subsequent research has called into question the universality of her findings, her work had an enormous influence, and it served as a catalyst for subsequent research into how people reacted to others' and their own impending deaths (Kübler-Ross, 1969, 1982).

Steps Toward Death: Kübler-Ross's Theory

LO 10.4   **Analyze Kübler-Ross's theory on the process of dying.**

Kübler-Ross initially suggested that people pass through five basic steps as they move toward death (summarized in Figure 10-1).

DENIAL   "No, I can't be dying. There must be some mistake." It is typical for people to protest on learning that they have a terminal disease. This is the first stage of dying, *denial*. In denial, people resist the idea that they are going to die. They may argue that their test results have been mixed up, an X-ray has been misread, or their physician is just wrong. They may flatly reject the diagnosis, simply refusing to believe the news. In extreme cases, memories of weeks in the hospital are forgotten. In other forms of denial, patients fluctuate between refusing to accept the news and confiding that they know they are going to die (Teutsch, 2003).

Figure 10-1 Moving Toward the End of Life

The steps toward death, according to Elisabeth Kübler-Ross (1975).

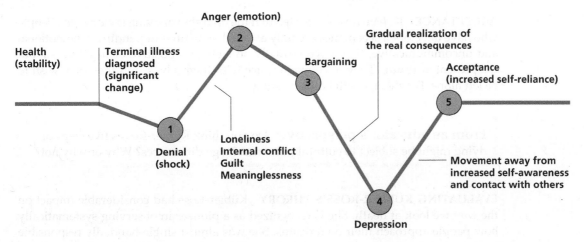

Far from a sign of a lost sense of reality and deteriorating mental health, denial is a defense mechanism that helps people absorb the news on their own terms and at their own pace. Then they can move on and come to grips with the reality of their death.

ANGER After denial, people may express *anger*. They may be angry at everyone: people in good health, spouses and family members, caregivers, children. They may lash out and wonder—sometimes aloud—why *they* are dying and not someone else. They may be furious at God, reasoning that they have led good lives and that far worse people in the world should be dying.

It is not easy to be around people in the anger stage. They may say and do things that are painful and sometimes unfathomable. Eventually, though, most move beyond anger to another development—bargaining.

BARGAINING "If you're good, you'll be rewarded." Many people try to apply this pearl of childhood wisdom to their impending death, promising to be better people if they are rewarded by staying alive.

In *bargaining*, dying people try to negotiate their way out of death. They may swear to dedicate their lives to the poor if God saves them. They may promise that if they can just live long enough to see a son married, they will willingly accept death later.

However, these promises are rarely kept. If one request appears to be granted, people typically seek another, and yet another. Furthermore, they may be unable to fulfill their promises because their illnesses keep progressing and prevent them from achieving what they said they would do.

In some ways, bargaining may have positive consequences. Although death cannot be postponed indefinitely, having a goal of attending a particular event or living until a certain time may in fact delay death until then. For instance, death rates of Jewish people fall just before Passover and rise just after. Similarly, the death rate among older Chinese women falls before and during important holidays and rises after (Meagher & Balk, 2013).

In the end, of course, no one can bargain away death. When people eventually realize this, they often move into the depression stage.

DEPRESSION Many dying people experience *depression*. Realizing that the issue is settled and can't be bargained away, they are overwhelmed with a deep sense of loss. They know that they are losing their loved ones and reaching the end of their lives.

Their depression may be reactive or preparatory. In *reactive depression*, the sadness is based on events that have already occurred: the loss of dignity with many medical procedures, the end of a job, or the knowledge that they will never return home. In *preparatory depression*, people feel sadness over future losses. They know that death will end their relationships and that they will never see future generations. The reality of death is inescapable in this stage, and it brings profound sadness over the unalterable conclusion of one's life.

ACCEPTANCE Kübler-Ross suggested that the final step of dying is *acceptance*. People who have developed acceptance are fully aware that death is impending. Unemotional and uncommunicative, they have virtually no feelings—positive or negative—about the present or future. They have made peace with themselves, and they may wish to be left alone. For them, death holds no sting.

> **From an educator's perspective:** Do you think Kübler-Ross's five steps of dying might be subject to cultural influences? Age differences? Why or why not?

EVALUATING KÜBLER-ROSS'S THEORY Kübler-Ross had considerable impact on the way we look at death. She is recognized as a pioneer in observing systematically how people approach their own deaths. She was almost single-handedly responsible for bringing death as a phenomenon into public awareness. Her contributions have been particularly influential among those who provide direct care to the dying.

On the other hand, there are some obvious limitations to her conception of dying. It is largely limited to those who are aware that they are dying and who die relatively slowly. It does not apply to people who suffer from diseases where the outcome and timing are uncertain.

The most important criticisms, however, concern the stage-like nature of Kübler-Ross's theory. Not every person passes through every step on the way to death, and some people move through the steps in a different sequence. Some people even go through the same steps several times. Depressed patients may show bursts of anger, and an angry patient may bargain for more time. In addition, Kübler-Ross's theory doesn't consider social or cultural factors, and it focuses almost solely on emotional responses to grief, ignoring thoughts (Corr, 2015; Jurecic, 2017; Stroebe, Schut, & Boerner, 2017).

In short, not everyone proceeds through the stages in the same way. For example, a study of more than 200 recently bereaved people were interviewed immediately and then several months later. If Kübler-Ross's theory was correct, the final stage of acceptance comes at the end of a lengthy grieving process. But most of the participants expressed acceptance of the passing of their loved one right from the beginning. Moreover, rather than feeling anger or depression, two of the other putative stages of grief, participants reported mostly feeling a yearning for the deceased person. Rather than a series of fixed stages, grief looks more like an assortment of symptoms that rise and fall and eventually dissipate (Maciejewski et al., 2007; Genevro & Miller, 2010; Gamino & Ritter, 2012).

The finding that people often follow their own, unique personal trajectories of grief has been especially important for medical and other caregivers who work with dying people. Because Kübler-Ross's stages have become so well known, well-meaning caregivers have sometimes tried to encourage patients to work through the steps in a prescribed order, without enough consideration for their individual needs (Wortman & Boerner, 2011).

Finally, people's reactions to impending death differ. The cause of death; the duration of the dying process; the person's age, sex, and personality; and the social support available from family and friends all influence the course of dying and one's responses to it (Carver & Scheier, 2002; Roos, 2013; Hendrickson et al., 2018).

ALTERNATIVES TO KÜBLER-ROSS'S THEORY In response to concerns about Kübler-Ross's account, other theorists have developed alternative ideas. Psychologist Edwin Shneidman, for example, suggests that "themes" in people's reactions to dying can occur—and recur—in any order. These include incredulity, a sense of unfairness, fear of pain or even general terror, and fantasies of being rescued (Shneidman, 2007).

Another theorist, Charles Corr, suggests that, as in other periods of life, people who are dying face a set of psychological tasks. These include minimizing physical stress and satisfying physical needs. Other tasks involve psychological requirements such as maintaining a sense of security and autonomy, as well maximizing the richness of life, continuing or deepening their relationships with other people, and fostering hope, often through spiritual searching (Corr, Nabe, & Corr, 2006, 2010; Corr, 2015).

One of the most important alternatives to Kübler-Ross is the *four component theory* developed by psychologist George Bonanno. Bonanno's theory suggests that there are four primary components to grieving. First, there is the context in which a loss occurs (whether it was expected or sudden, for example). The second component is the meanings given to the loss (whether the person experiencing the loss has a positive, negative, or ambivalent relationship with the person who died). The third component relates to how the deceased person continues to be represented in memory, and the fourth relates to coping and emotion regulation. In contrast to Kübler-Ross's theory, there is considerable research support for Bonanno's theory (Boerner, Mancini, & Bonanno, 2013; Boerner et al., 2015; Maccallum, Malgaroli, & Bonanno, 2017).

Choosing the Nature of Death

LO 10.5   Explain ways in which people can exercise control over how they spend their last days.

When Colin Rapasand was a first-year resident years ago, one of his first assignments was the geriatric ward. Cheerful and outgoing, Colin invariably addressed the patients as "Uncle" and "Auntie," reflecting his deep Southern roots.

He recalls one patient in particular. "When my crazy schedule allowed, I loved spending time with Auntie Jessica. Auntie J was 93 years old, rapidly failing, but with the sharpest mind. When I had late rounds, I would sometimes sit on the foot of her bed and chat with her. Great stories, huge spirit, lively intelligence.

"Auntie J's chart had her listed as a DNR, and I knew that she didn't want 'any of that mechanical nonsense' done to her, as she put it. But one night I was all alone on rounds and stopped in to see her. Her respiration was just about zero and her heart was beating fitfully. I watched as her numbers got worse. Instead of 'letting nature take its course,' I went to her side and leaned over her, calling her name. At the same time, I compressed her chest rapidly, 100 times a minute, performing CPR on her slight body. I got the respiration going fairly well, but her heart was still weak and fluttering.

"I grabbed the paddles and jolted her once, twice, then third time lucky. Her breathing became audible and her heartbeat returned to its usual level. Auntie J lived another 4 months.

"I claimed to the administrators that in the heat of the moment I had forgotten about the DNR. But I knew I hadn't. I had simply 'let nature take its course'—my nature, my human nature."

DNRS   The letters "DNR" on a patient's medical chart have a simple and clear meaning: Do Not Resuscitate. DNR means that no extraordinary means are to be taken to keep a patient alive. For terminally ill patients, having a DNR may mean the difference between dying immediately or living additional days, months, or even years, kept alive only by the most extreme, invasive, and even painful medical procedures.

The DNR decision entails several issues. One is differentiating "extreme" and "extraordinary" measures from routine ones. There are no hard-and-fast rules; people making the decision must consider the needs of the patient, his or her prior medical history, and factors such as age and even religion. For instance, different standards might apply to a 12-year-old and an 85-year-old with the same medical condition. Other questions concern quality of life. How can we determine an individual's current quality of life and whether it will be improved or diminished by a medical intervention? Who makes these decisions—the patient, a family member, or medical personnel?

One thing is clear: Like Colin Rapasand, medical personnel are reluctant to carry out the wishes of the terminally ill and their families to suspend aggressive treatment.

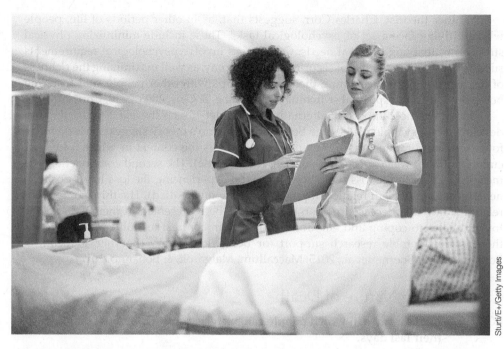

Sturti/E+/Getty Images

Many terminally ill patients choose DNR, or Do Not Resuscitate, as a way to avoid extraordinary medical interventions.

Even when it is certain that a patient is going to die, and the patient does not wish further treatment, physicians often claim to be unaware of their patients' wishes. Although one-third of patients ask not to be resuscitated, less than half of these people's physicians say they know their patients' preferences. In addition, only 49 percent of patients have their wishes entered on their medical charts. Physicians and other providers may be reluctant to act on DNR requests in part because they are trained to save patients, not permit them to die, and in part to avoid legal liability (McArdle, 2002; Goldman et al., 2013; Wan et al., 2017).

LIVING WILLS To gain more control over death decisions, people are increasingly signing living wills. A **living will** is a legal document that designates the medical treatments a person does or does not want if the person cannot express his or her wishes (see Figure 10-2).

living wills

legal documents designating what medical treatments people want or do not want if they cannot express their wishes

Some people designate a specific person, called a *health-care proxy*, to act as their representative for health-care decisions. Health-care proxies are authorized either in living wills or in a legal document known as a *durable power of attorney*. Health-care proxies may be authorized to deal with all medical care problems (such as a coma) or only with terminal illnesses.

As with DNR orders, living wills are ineffective unless people make sure their health-care proxies and doctors know their wishes. Although they may be reluctant to do this, people should have frank conversations with their health-care proxies.

EUTHANASIA AND ASSISTED SUICIDE Dr. Jack Kevorkian became well known in the 1990s for his invention and promotion of a "suicide machine," which allowed patients to push a button and release anesthesia and a drug that stops the heart. By supplying the machine and the drugs, which patients administered themselves, Kevorkian was participating in *assisted suicide*, providing the means for a terminally ill person to commit suicide. Kevorkian spent 8 years in prison for second-degree murder for his participation in an assisted suicide shown on the television show *60 Minutes*.

Assisted suicide continues to raise bitter conflict in the United States, and the practice is illegal in most states. Today, seven major jurisdictions (California, Colorado, Montana, Oregon, Vermont, Washington, and Washington, DC) have passed "right to die" laws, and Montana has legal physician-assisted suicide following a court order. In Oregon alone, more than 1,100 people have taken medication to end their own lives (Edwards, 2015; Oregon Death with Dignity Act, 2016).

In many countries, assisted suicide is widely accepted. For instance, in the Netherlands medical personnel may help end their patients' lives if they meet several conditions: At least two physicians must determine that the patient is terminally ill, there must be unbearable physical or mental suffering, the patient must give informed consent in writing, and relatives must be informed beforehand (Battin et al., 2007; Onwuteaka-Philipsen et al., 2010; Augestad et al., 2013; Nolen, 2016).

Assisted suicide is one form of **euthanasia**, the practice of assisting terminally ill people to die more quickly. Popularly known as "mercy killing," euthanasia has several forms. *Passive euthanasia* involves removing respirators or other medical equipment that may be sustaining a patient's life, to allow him or her to die naturally—such as when medical staff follow a DNR order. In *voluntary active euthanasia* caregivers or medical staff act to end a person's life before death would normally occur, perhaps by administering a lethal dose of pain medication. Assisted suicide, as we have seen, lies between passive and voluntary active euthanasia. For all the controversy surrounding the practice, euthanasia is surprisingly widespread. One survey of nurses in intensive care units found that 20 percent had deliberately hastened a patient's death at least once, and other experts assert that euthanasia is far from rare (Asch, 1996).

The controversy arises from the question of who should control life. Does the right to one's life belong to the individual, the person's physicians, his or her dependents, the government, or some deity? Because we claim to have the absolute right to create lives in the form of babies, some people argue that we should also have the absolute right to end our lives (Allen et al., 2006; Goldney, 2012; Monteverde et al., 2017).

Many opponents argue that the practice is morally wrong. In their view, prematurely ending the life of a person, no matter how willing the person is, is murder. Others point out that physicians are often inaccurate in predicting how long a person will live. For example, in some cases patients have lived for years after being given no more than a 50 percent chance of living 6 more months (Bishop, 2006; Peel & Harding, 2015).

Another argument against euthanasia focuses on the emotional state of the patient. Even if patients beg health-care providers to help them die, they may be suffering from a form of depression that may be treated with antidepressant drugs. Once the depression lifts, patients may change their minds about wanting to die (Gostin, 2006; McLachlan, 2008; Schildmann & Schildmann, 2013).

Where to Die: Easing the Final Passage

LO 10.6   Describe alternatives for providing end-of-life care for the terminally ill.

Dina Bianga loves her work. Dina is a registered nurse with the Hospice of Michigan; her job is to meet the physical and psychological needs of the terminally ill.

Figure 10-2 An Example of a Living Will

What steps can people take to make sure the wishes they write into their living wills are carried out?

I,_____,
being of sound mind, make this statement as a directive to be followed if I become permanently unable to participate in decisions regarding my medical care. These instructions reflect my firm and settled commitment to decline medical treatment under the circumstances indicated below:

I direct my attending physician to withhold or withdraw treatment that merely prolongs my dying, if I should be in **an incurable or irreversible mental or physical condition** with no reasonable expectation of recovery, including but not limited to: (a) a **terminal condition**; (b) a **permanently unconscious condition**; or (c) a **minimally conscious condition in which I am permanently unable to make decisions or express my wishes**.

I direct that treatment be limited to measures to keep me comfortable and to relieve pain, including any pain that might occur by withholding or withdrawing treatment.
While I understand that I am not legally required to be specific about future treatments, **if I am in the condition(s) described above I feel especially strongly about the following treatments:**

I do not want cardiac resuscitation.
I do not want mechanical respiration.
I do not want tube feeding.
I do not want antibiotics.

However, I **do want** maximum pain relief, even if it may hasten my death.

Other directions (insert personal instructions):

These directions express my legal right to refuse treatment under federal and state law. I intend my instructions to be carried out, unless I have revoked them in a new writing or by clearly indicating that I have changed my mind.

Signed:_____ Date:_____

Address:_____

- -

Statement by Witnesses
I declare that the person who signed this document appears to be at least eighteen (18) years of age, of sound mind, and under no constraint or undue influence. The person who signed this document appeared to do so willingly and free from duress. He or she signed (or asked another to sign for him or her) this document in my presence.

Witness:_____

Address:_____

- -

Witness:_____

Address:_____

- -

euthanasia
the practice of assisting people who are terminally ill to die more quickly

"You need compassion and a good clinical background," she says. "You also have to be flexible. You go into the home, hospital, nursing home, adult foster care—wherever the patient is."

Dina likes the interdisciplinary approach that hospice work requires. "You form a team with others who provide social work, spiritual care, home health aid, grief support, and administrative support."

Surprisingly, the patients are not the most challenging part of the job. Families and friends are.

"Families are frightened, and everything seems out of control. They're not always ready to accept that death is coming soon, so you have to be careful and sensitive how you word things. If they are well informed on what to expect, the transition is smoother and a more comfortable atmosphere is created for the patient."

About half the people in the United States who die do so in hospitals. Yet hospitals are among the least desirable places in which to face death. They are typically impersonal, with staff rotating through the day. Because visiting hours are limited, people frequently die alone, without the comfort of loved ones.

Hospitals are designed to make people better, not provide custodial care for the dying, which is extraordinarily expensive. Consequently, hospitals typically don't have the resources to deal adequately with the emotional requirements of terminally ill patients and their families.

home care
an alternative to hospitalization in which dying people stay in their homes and receive treatment from their families and visiting medical staff

Because of this, several alternatives to hospitalization have arisen. In **home care**, dying people stay in their homes and receive treatment from their families and visiting medical staff. Many dying patients prefer home care because they can spend their final days in a familiar environment, with people they love and a lifetime accumulation of treasures around them.

But home care can be quite difficult for family members. True, giving something precious to people they love offers family members substantial emotional solace, but being on call 24 hours a day is extraordinarily draining, both physically and emotionally. Furthermore, because most relatives are not trained in nursing, they may provide less than optimal medical care (Day, Anderson, & Davis, 2014; Woodman, Baillie, & Sivell, 2016).

hospice care
care provided for the dying in institutions devoted to those who are terminally ill

Another alternative to hospitalization that is becoming increasingly prevalent is hospice care. **Hospice care** is care for the dying provided in institutions devoted to the terminally ill. They are designed to provide a warm, supportive environment for the dying. They do not focus on extending people's lives, but on making their final days pleasant and meaningful. Typically, people who go to hospices no longer face painful treatments or extraordinary or invasive means to extend their lives. The emphasis is on making patients' lives as full as possible, not on squeezing out every possible moment of life at any cost (Hanson et al., 2010; York et al., 2012; Prochaska et al., 2017).

Although the research is far from conclusive, hospice patients appear to be more satisfied with the care they receive than those who receive treatment in more traditional settings. Hospice care, then, provides a clear alternative to traditional hospitalization for the terminally ill (Seymour et al., 2007; Rhodes et al., 2008; Clark, 2015).

Review, Check, and Apply

Review

LO 10.4 Analyze Kübler-Ross's theory on the process of dying.

Elisabeth Kübler-Ross identified five steps toward dying: denial, anger, bargaining, depression, and acceptance. Although Kübler-Ross has added to our understanding of the process of dying, the steps she identified are not universal. Recently, other theorists have developed alternative ideas.

LO 10.5 Explain ways in which people can exercise control over how they spend their last days.

Issues surrounding dying are highly controversial, including the measures that physicians should apply to keep dying patients alive and who should make the decisions about those measures. Assisted suicide and, more generally, euthanasia are highly controversial and are illegal in most of the United States, although many people believe they should be legalized if they are regulated.

Check Yourself

1. Kübler-Ross initially suggested that people pass through basic steps or stages as they approach death. The first stage is _____.
   a. grief
   b. acceptance
   c. anger
   d. denial

2. According to Kübler-Ross, dying people who promise to give their money to charity if only they can have another few months of life are in the _____ stage of dying.
   a. anger
   b. depression
   c. denial
   d. bargaining

LO 10.6 Describe alternatives for providing end-of-life care for the terminally ill.

Although most people in the United States die in hospitals, increasing numbers are choosing home care or hospice care for their final days.

3. In the medical community, DNR stands for _____.
   a. Do Not Renew
   b. Daily Notice of Revision
   c. Decision Not to Revive
   d. Do Not Resuscitate

4. Some people designate a specific person, called a _____, to act as their representative for health-care decisions.
   a. health associate
   b. health-care proxy
   c. legal aide
   d. personal care attendant

Applying Lifespan Development

Do you think it would be wise to suggest hospice care to a terminally ill family member who is in the bargaining stage of dying? Which of the stages identified by Kübler-Ross would be the most appropriate for making such a suggestion?

Module 10.3
Grief and Bereavement

Facing the Void

When they told me my husband, Jim, had died during surgery, I went mute. All I wanted was to go into a dark room, curl up in a ball, and sleep. Spooky, isn't it, because what I wanted to do was a lot like dying. But I couldn't stand words and I couldn't stand feeling—I didn't want to feel anything. Because, of course, the pain was so huge, I was afraid it would break me. I went home 2 days after he died and everything hurt. The sight of his clothing, his guitar, and all the photographs. It's been 2 months and I'm better now, but it still hurts.

—Kate S., 78, widow.

It is a universal experience, but most of us are surprisingly ill-prepared for the grief that follows the death of a loved one. Particularly in Western societies, where life expectancy is long and mortality rates are low, people view death as atypical rather than expected. This attitude makes grief all the more difficult to bear.

In this module, we consider bereavement and grief. We examine the difficulties in distinguishing normal from unhealthy grief and the consequences of loss. The module also looks at mourning and funerals, discussing how people can prepare themselves for the inevitability of death.

Death: Effects on Survivors

In our culture, only babies are buried; just about everyone else is cremated. When my father died, my elder brother took the lead and, with the other men observing, approached the pyre and lit it.

My father's body burned well. After the fire died down, my brother oversaw the gathering of the ashes and bone fragments, and we all took a bath to purify us. Despite this and subsequent baths, we in the close family were considered polluted for 13 days.

Finally, after the 13 days, we gathered for a big meal. The centerpiece was the preparation of rice balls (pinda), which we offered to the spirit of my father. At the end of the meal we dedicated gifts for distribution to the poor.

In Hindu culture, the idea behind these ceremonies is to honor the dead person's memory. More traditional people believe that it helps the soul pass to the realm of Yama, the god of death, rather than hanging on in this world as a ghost.

This ritual is specifically Hindu, and yet, in its carefully prescribed roles for survivors and its focus on honoring the dead, it shares key elements with Western rituals. The first step in grieving, for most survivors in Western countries, is some sort of funeral.

Saying Farewell: Final Rites and Mourning

LO 10.7   **Analyze the cultural meaning of funeral rites in Western and other cultures.**

Death is a big business in the United States. The average funeral and burial costs $7,000 to $10,000, including an ornate, polished coffin; limousine transportation; and preservation and viewing of the body (Bryant, 2003; American Association of Retired Persons [AARP], 2004; Sheridan, 2013; Beard & Burger, 2017).

Funerals are grandiose in part because of the vulnerability of the survivors who typically make the arrangements. Wishing to demonstrate love and affection, the survivors are susceptible to suggestions that they should "provide the best" for the deceased (Varga, 2014; McManus & Schafer, 2014; Dobscha, 2015).

But in large measure, social norms and customs determine the nature of funerals just as they do for weddings. In a sense, a funeral is not only a public acknowledgment that an individual has died, but a recognition of everyone's mortality and an acceptance of the cycle of life.

In Western societies, funeral rituals follow a typical pattern. The body is prepared in some way and dressed in special clothing. There is usually a religious rite, a eulogy, a procession of some sort, and some formal period, such as the wake for Irish Catholics and Shiva for Jews, in which relatives and friends visit the family and pay their respects. Military funerals typically include the firing of weapons and a flag draped over the coffin.

As we saw in the prologue, non-Western funerals are different. In some societies, mourners shave their heads as a sign of grief, and in others they allow the hair to grow and stop shaving for a time. In other cultures, mourners may be hired to wail and grieve. Sometimes noisy celebrations take place, whereas in other cultures silence is the norm. Culture determines even the nature of emotional displays, such as the amount and timing of crying (Peters, 2010; Hoy, 2013; Shohet, 2018).

Mourners in Balinese funerals in Indonesia attempt to show little emotion because they believe the gods will hear their prayers only if they are calm. In contrast, mourners at African American funerals show their grief, and funeral rituals allow attendees to display their feelings. Widows in Egypt are considered abnormal if they don't weep unconsolably, and Chinese mourners sometimes hire professional wailers (Collins & Doolittle, 2006; Walter, 2012; Carteret, 2017).

Historically, some cultures developed rather extreme funeral rites. For example, in *suttee*, a traditional Hindu practice in India that is now illegal, a widow was expected to throw herself into the fire that consumed her husband's body. In ancient China, servants were sometimes buried (alive) with their masters' bodies.

Ultimately, no matter the ritual, all funerals basically serve the same function: They mark the endpoint of the life of the person who has died—and provide a formal forum for the feelings of the survivors, a place where they can come together, share their grief, and comfort one another.

Stockbyte/Getty Images

Every society has its own ways of mourning.

Bereavement and Grief

LO 10.8 · Describe how survivors react to and cope with death.

> The news hit the world like a tidal wave: The musician Prince was dead at age 57. Prince, a pop phenomenon who had earned tens of millions of dollars from his recordings and performances, seemed too young to die.
>
> Prince's death set off an explosion of public grief. Tributes poured in from politicians and celebrities, and musical tributes were held in many locales. Sales of Prince's music reached unprecedented levels.

After the death of a loved one, a painful period of adjustment follows, involving bereavement and grief. **Bereavement** is acknowledgment of the objective fact that one has experienced a death, and **grief** is the emotional response to one's loss. (Also see the *From Research to Practice* box.)

The first stage of grief typically entails shock, numbness, disbelief, or outright denial. People try to avoid the reality of the situation and pursue their usual routines, although the pain may break through, causing anguish, fear, and deep sorrow and distress. In some ways, numbness may be beneficial because it permits the survivor to make funeral arrangements and carry out other psychologically difficult tasks. Typically, people pass through this stage in a few days or weeks.

bereavement
acknowledgment of the objective fact that one has experienced a death

grief
the emotional response to one's loss

From Research to Practice

Moving On: Surviving the Loss of a Long-Time Spouse

As you may well imagine, the death of a spouse is almost always a traumatic experience that is usually followed by intense grief and anguish. In the case of older couples who had been married for a very long time, losing a spouse can mean losing a lifelong companion and typically a partner's primary and sometimes sole source of emotional support. Intuition may therefore suggest that the period of grieving such a loss would be particularly prolonged for a surviving spouse who had enjoyed a close and happy marriage.

But a growing body of research suggests otherwise: It seems in fact that people who had a successful marriage are better able to work through their mourning of a lost spouse and get on with the rest of their lives than those with less successful marriages. In fact, research now suggests that around half of those who report having satisfying marriages are able to get past their grief within 6 months of the death of their spouses (Carr, Nesse, & Wortman, 2005; Carr, 2015, 2016).

One explanation for these findings is that people who enjoy close and happy marriages tend to have strong interpersonal skills on which to rely during their time of loss. They may be better equipped to call upon friends, family, and even a professional counselor if necessary to assist them through their grieving period. One way that others help the surviving spouse is by providing a diversion to keep him or her from dwelling on the loss and also by encouraging him or her to replace the void with new interests and activities. Strong interpersonal skills may also facilitate a positive approach to dating new people when the time is right (Carr, 2015; Collins, 2018).

Another reason for the resiliency of surviving spouses of close marriages is the knowledge that they and their departed partner had culminated what they set out to achieve: a successful and satisfying relationship. Surviving partners of strained marriages might feel more sadness over never having achieved a desired level of closeness, or they might regret not having an opportunity to resolve lingering conflicts, or they might feel guilty about not working harder to make their marriage better when they had the chance.

On the other hand, surviving spouses who enjoyed a close marriage are more likely to have settled lingering issues and to have talked through what would happen after either of them died; they therefore are more likely to feel secure in knowing what their departed would have wanted for them in widowhood. Finally, spouses who have a close and secure relationship may simply have a better opportunity to say their final goodbyes as one partner's health fails (Mancini, Sinan, & Bonanno, 2015).

Of course, having a secure marriage is no guarantee that life as a widow or widower will be lacking in pain. Even very resilient survivors grieve deeply in the immediate months following the death of their spouses. And indeed, it's possible to be too close to one's spouse, making the loss more difficult; men in particular may be hit hard by the loss of a wife who was their only emotional confidant. But in many cases, the final gift of a close and loving spouse is the security to move on with one's life within a reasonable time after his or her death (Boerner et al., 2005; Maccallum, Malgaroni, & Bonanno, 2017).

Shared Writing Prompt:

What other factors besides interpersonal closeness might affect the duration of grief after losing a long-time spouse?

In the next phase, people begin to confront the death and realize the extent of their loss. They fully experience their grief and begin to acknowledge that the separation from the dead person will be permanent. They may suffer deep unhappiness or even depression, a normal feeling in this situation. They may yearn for the dead individual. Emotions can range from impatient to lethargic. However, they also begin to view their past relationship with the deceased realistically, good and bad. In so doing, they begin to free themselves from some of the bonds that tied them to the loved one (Norton & Gino, 2014; Rosenblatt, 2015).

Finally, they reach the accommodation stage. They begin to pick up the pieces of their lives and to construct new identities. For instance, rather than seeing herself as a widowed spouse, a woman whose husband has died may come to regard herself as a single person. Still, there are moments when intense feelings of grief occur.

Ultimately, most people emerge from grieving and live new, independent lives. They form new relationships, and some even find that coping with the death has helped them to grow as individuals. They become more self-reliant and more appreciative of life.

It is important to keep in mind that not everyone passes through the stages of grief in the same manner and in the same order. People display vast individual differences, partly because of their personalities, the nature of the relationship with the deceased, and the opportunities that are available to them for continuing their lives after the loss.

In fact, most bereaved people are quite resilient, experiencing strong positive emotions such as joy even soon after the death of a loved one. According to psychologist George Bonanno, who has studied bereavement extensively, humans are prepared in an evolutionary sense to move on after the death of someone close. He rejects the notion that there are fixed stages of mourning and argues that most people move on with their lives quite effectively (Bonanno, 2009; Mancini & Bonanno, 2012; McCoyd & Walter, 2016).

DIFFERENTIATING UNHEALTHY GRIEF FROM NORMAL GRIEF Although ideas abound about what separates normal grief from unhealthy grief, careful research has shown that many of the assumptions that both laypersons and clinicians hold are wrong. There is no particular timetable for grieving, despite the common notion that grieving should be complete a year after a spouse has died.

For some people (but not all), grieving may take considerably longer than a year. And some individuals experience *complicated grief* (or sometimes *prolonged grief disorder*), a type of mourning that continues unceasingly for months and years (as we discussed in the previous chapter). An estimated 15 percent of those who are bereaved suffer from complicated grief (Maercker, Neimeyer & Simiola, 2017; Maccallum, Malgaroli, & Bonanno, 2017; Kokou-Kpolou, Megalakaki, & Nieuviarts, 2018).

Other people show *incomplete grief*, a lingering form of grief following a loss in which people are unable to grieve effectively. They may be unaware of how unhappy they truly are, or they may lack societal "permission" to grieve. For example, a gay teenager who has not told his parents about his homosexuality and who suffers the death of a lover may be forced to hide his grief. His inability to show his grief may make the process of grieving even more difficult.

Research also contradicts the assumption that depression inevitably follows a death. In fact, only 15 to 30 percent of people show relatively deep depression following the loss of a loved one (Bonanno et al., 2002; Hensley, 2006).

Similarly, it is often assumed that people who show little initial distress are not facing up to reality, and that they are likely to have problems later. In fact, those who show the most intense distress immediately after a death are the most apt to have adjustment difficulties and health problems later (Boerner, Wortman, & Bonanno, 2005).

After a death, people move through a painful period of bereavement and grief. These mourners in Syria grieve the loss of Kurdish fighters who died in clashes with the Islamic State.

Ahmad Halabisaz/Xinhua/Alamy Live News/Alamy Stock Photo

THE CONSEQUENCES OF GRIEF AND BEREAVEMENT   In a sense, death is catching. Evidence suggests that widowed people are particularly at risk of death. Some studies find that the risk of death can be seven times higher than normal in the first year after the death of a spouse, particularly for men and younger women. Remarriage seems to lower the risk of death, especially for widowed men, although the reasons are not clear (Aiken, 2000; Elwert & Christakis, 2008; Sullivan & Fenelon, 2013).

> **From a social worker's perspective:** Why do you think the risk of death is so high for people who have recently lost a spouse? Why might remarriage lower the risk?

Bereavement is more likely to produce depression or other negative consequences if the person is already insecure, anxious, or fearful and therefore is less able to cope effectively. Relationships marked by ambivalence before death are more apt to cause poor post-death outcomes than secure relationships. Highly dependent people are apt to suffer more after the death, as are those who spend a lot of time reflecting on the death and their own grief.

Bereaved people who lack social support from family, friends, or a connection to some other group, religious or otherwise, are more likely to experience feelings of loneliness, and therefore are more at risk. Finally, people who are unable to make sense of the death or find meaning in it (such as a new appreciation of life) show less overall adjustment (Nolen-Hoeksema & Davis, 2002; Torges, Stewart, & Nolen-Hoeksema, 2008; Howard Sharp et al., 2018).

The suddenness of the death also affects the course of grieving. People who unexpectedly lose their loved ones are less able to cope than those who could anticipate the death. In one study, people who experienced a sudden death had not fully recovered 4 years later. In part, this may be because sudden deaths are often the result of violence, which occurs more frequently among younger individuals (Burton, Haley, & Small, 2006; De Leo et al., 2014; Kõlves et al., 2019).

As we noted previously, children may need special help understanding and mourning the death of someone they love. (See the *Development in Your Life* box.)

Social networking sites like Facebook provide a means for public grieving.

Keith Morris/Alamy Stock Photo

Development in Your Life

Helping a Child Cope with Grief

Because of their limited understanding of death, younger children need special help in coping with grief. Among the strategies that can help are the following:

- **Be honest.** Don't say that the person is "sleeping" or "on a long trip." Use age-appropriate language to tell the truth. Gently but clearly point out that death is final and universal.

- **Encourage expressions of grief.** Don't tell children *not* to cry or show their feelings. Instead, tell them that it is understandable to feel terrible, and that they may always miss the deceased. Encourage them to draw a picture, write a letter, or express their feelings some other way.

- **Reassure children that they are not to blame.** Children sometimes attribute a loved one's death to their own behavior—if they had not misbehaved, they mistakenly reason, the person would not have died.

- **Understand that children's grief may surface in unanticipated ways.** Children may show little initial grief but later may become upset for no apparent reason or revert to behaviors like thumb sucking or wanting to sleep with their parents.

- **Children may respond to books for young people about death.** One especially effective book is *When Dinosaurs Die* by Laurie Krasny Brown and Marc Brown.

Review, Check, and Apply

Review

LO 10.7 Analyze the cultural meaning of funeral rites in Western and other cultures.

After a death, most cultures prescribe some sort of funeral ritual to honor the passing of a community member. Funeral rites play a significant role in helping people acknowledge the death of a loved one, recognize their own mortality, and proceed with their lives.

LO 10.8 Describe how survivors react to and cope with death.

Bereavement refers to the loss of a loved one; grief refers to the emotional response to that loss. For many people, grief passes through the denial, sorrow, and accommodation stages. Common assumptions about the nature and duration of "normal" grief have been shown to be erroneous. The length and intensity of the mourning period vary widely.

Check Yourself

1. Researchers who have studied grief have found that _____.
   a. grief follows a fixed, universal pattern that is similar for all people
   b. the larger and more expensive the funeral, the less grief experienced by survivors
   c. grief follows many paths, and there is no one "right" way to experience grief
   d. for most people, hiding their grief from others and acting like the death of a loved one isn't bothering them is the fastest way to recover and move on from the death

2. One of the main purposes of the funeral ritual across cultures is to _____.
   a. encourage survivors to look more favorably on the prospect of dying
   b. cheer the dying person with the prospect of a grand sendoff
   c. offer survivors an opportunity to share their grief
   d. enable the dying person to express final thoughts in writing or on tape

3. In the final stage of grief, people tend to _____.
   a. pick up the pieces of their lives and construct new identities
   b. cycle back to numbness if the pain is too severe
   c. avoid the reality of the situation through denial
   d. suffer deep unhappiness and even depression

4. Bereaved people who lack _____ are more likely to experience loneliness and are at greater risk for negative post-death outcomes.
   a. ambivalence
   b. rituals
   c. independence
   d. social support

Applying Lifespan Development

Why do so many people in the United States feel reluctant to think and talk about death? Why do people in other cultures feel less reluctant?

Chapter 10 Summary
Putting It All Together: Death and Dying

JACKSON LEROI, the 71-year-old man we met in the chapter opener, resigned to his impending death, was determined to go out the way he wanted—celebrating a life well lived with a gathering 2 weeks before his death. It was Jackson's last party, and it was a grand one!

Maskot/Getty Images

MODULE 10.1
DEATH AND DYING ACROSS THE LIFE SPAN

- Jackson has confronted the question of when life ends and prepared for it. (p. 441)
- Jackson, at age 71, clearly feels that he has had a life worth celebrating. (p. 463)
- He has tried to anticipate and deal in advance with the feelings of his family members. (p. 463)

MODULE 10.2
CONFRONTING DEATH

- Jackson appears to have passed successfully through the steps of dying. (pp. 449–452)
- He has decided to make his own life-or-death (e.g., DNR) decisions. (pp. 452–455)
- He does not seem to have even considered the idea of assisted suicide, preferring to die naturally with family and friends at his side. (pp. 453–454)

MODULE 10.3
GRIEF AND BEREAVEMENT

- Jackson understands the importance of funeral ceremonies and has undertaken the planning of a party to celebrate his life. (p. 457)
- He has evidently anticipated the grief that his family and friends will experience and has planned an event that emphasizes celebration of a life rather than mourning of a death. (pp. 458–460)

What would YOU do?

Given what you know about possible places to die, what would you recommend for your closest loved one, in the event it was needed: hospitalization, home care, or hospice care? Why? Would other choices be more appropriate for other loved ones you know?

Odua Images/Shutterstock

What would a POLICYMAKER do?

Should the government get involved in determining whether to permit individuals to make decisions about continuing their own lives in times of critical illness or extreme pain? Should this be a matter of law or of personal conscience?

Steve Hix/Corbis/ Getty Images

What would a HEALTH-CARE PROVIDER do?

Which criteria are most important in deciding whether or not to discontinue life-support systems? Do you think the criteria differ in different cultures?

Mark Andersen/ Rubberball/Getty Images

What would an EDUCATOR do?

What sorts of topics should be covered in depth in death education courses for health providers? For lay people?

Tom Baker/123RF

Glossary

abstract modeling   the process in which modeling paves the way for the development of more general rules and principles.

acceleration   special programs that allow gifted students to move ahead at their own pace, even if this means skipping to higher grade levels.

accommodation   changes in existing ways of thinking that occur in response to encounters with new stimuli or events.

achieving stage   the point reached by young adults in which intelligence is applied to specific situations involving the attainment of long-term goals regarding careers, family, and societal contributions.

acquisitive stage   according to Schaie, the first stage of cognitive development, encompassing all of childhood and adolescence.

activity theory   the theory suggesting that successful aging occurs when people maintain the interests, activities, and social interactions with which they were involved during middle age.

addictive drugs   drugs that produce a biological or psychological dependence in users, leading to increasingly powerful cravings for them.

adolescence   the developmental stage that lies between childhood and adulthood.

adolescent egocentrism   a state of self-absorption in which the world is viewed from one's own point of view.

adult day-care facilities   a facility in which elderly individuals receive care only during the day but spend nights and weekends in their own homes.

affordances   the action possibilities that a given situation or stimulus provides.

age stratification theories   the view that an unequal distribution of economic resources, power, and privilege exists among people at different stages of life.

ageism   prejudice and discrimination directed at older people.

agentic professions   occupations that are associated with getting things accomplished, such as carpentry.

aggression   intentional injury or harm to another person.

Ainsworth Strange Situation   a sequence of staged episodes that illustrate the strength of attachment between a child and (typically) his or her mother.

alcoholics   people with alcohol problems who have learned to depend on alcohol and are unable to control their drinking.

Alzheimer's disease   a progressive brain disorder that produces loss of memory and confusion.

ambivalent attachment pattern   a style of attachment in which children display a combination of positive and negative reactions to their mothers.

amniocentesis   the process of identifying genetic defects by examining a small sample of fetal cells drawn by a needle inserted into the amniotic fluid surrounding the unborn fetus.

androgynous   a state in which gender roles encompass characteristics thought typical of both sexes.

anorexia nervosa   a severe eating disorder in which individuals refuse to eat, while denying that their behavior and appearance, which may become skeletal, are out of the ordinary.

anoxia   a restriction of oxygen to the baby, lasting a few minutes during the birth process, which can produce cognitive defects.

Apgar scale   a standard measurement system that looks for a variety of indications of good health in newborns.

applied research   research meant to provide practical solutions to immediate problems.

artificial insemination   a process of fertilization in which a man's sperm is placed directly into a woman's reproductive tract by a physician.

assimilation   the process in which people understand an experience in terms of their current stage of cognitive development and way of thinking.

associative play   play in which two or more children actually interact with one another by sharing or borrowing toys or materials, although they do not do the same thing.

attachment   the positive emotional bond that develops between a child and a particular individual.

attention deficit hyperactivity disorder (ADHD)   a learning disorder marked by inattention, impulsiveness, a low tolerance for frustration, and generally a great deal of inappropriate activity.

auditory impairment   a special need that involves the loss of hearing or some aspect of hearing.

authoritarian parents   parents who are controlling, punitive, rigid, and cold, and whose word is law. They value strict, unquestioning obedience from their children and do not tolerate expressions of disagreement.

authoritative parents   parents who are firm, setting clear and consistent limits, but who try to reason with their children, giving explanations for why they should behave in a particular way.

autobiographical memory   memory of particular events from one's own life.

autonomy   having independence and a sense of control over one's life.

autonomy-versus-shame-and-doubt stage   the period during which, according to Erik Erikson, toddlers (age 18 months to 3 years) develop independence and autonomy if they are allowed the freedom to explore, or shame and self-doubt if they are restricted and overprotected.

avoidant attachment pattern   a style of attachment in which children do not seek proximity to the mother; after the mother has left, they seem to avoid her when she returns as if they are angered by her behavior.

babbling   making speechlike but meaningless sounds.

Bayley Scales of Infant Development   a measure that evaluates an infant's development from 2 to 42 months.

behavior modification   a formal technique for promoting the frequency of desirable behaviors and decreasing the incidence of unwanted ones.

behavioral genetics   the study of the effects of heredity on behavior.

behavioral perspective   the approach that suggests that the keys to understanding development are observable behavior and outside stimuli in the environment.

bereavement   acknowledgment of the objective fact that one has experienced a death.

bicultural identity   maintaining one's original cultural identity while integrating oneself into the dominant culture.

bilingualism   the use of more than one language.

bioecological approach   the perspective suggesting that levels of the environment simultaneously influence individuals.

blended families   remarried couples who have at least one stepchild living with them.

body transcendence versus body preoccupation   a period in which people must learn to cope with and move beyond changes in physical capabilities as a result of aging.

bonding   close physical and emotional contact between parent and child during the period immediately following birth.

boomerang children   young adults who return, after leaving home for some period, to live in the homes of their middle-aged parents.

brain death   a diagnosis of death based on the cessation of all signs of brain activity, as measured by electrical brain waves.

Brazelton Neonatal Behavioral Assessment Scale (NBAS)   a measure designed to determine infants' neurological and behavioral responses to their environment.

bulimia nervosa   an eating disorder characterized by binges on large quantities of food, followed by purges of the food through vomiting or the use of laxatives.

burnout   a situation that occurs when workers experience dissatisfaction, disillusionment, frustration, and weariness from their jobs.

career consolidation   according to Vaillant, a stage that is entered between the ages of 20 and 40, when young adults become centered on their careers.

case studies   studies that involve extensive, in-depth interviews with a particular individual or small group of individuals.

centration   the process of concentrating on one limited aspect of a stimulus and ignoring other aspects.

cephalocaudal principle   the principle that growth follows a pattern that begins with the head and upper body parts and then proceeds down to the rest of the body.

cerebral cortex   the upper layer of the brain.

cesarean delivery   a birth in which the baby is surgically removed from the uterus, rather than traveling through the birth canal.

childhood-onset fluency disorder (stuttering)   substantial disruption in the rhythm and fluency of speech; the most common speech impairment.

chorionic villus sampling (CVS)   a test used to find genetic defects that involves taking samples of hairlike material that surrounds the embryo.

chromosomes   rod-shaped portions of DNA that are organized in 23 pairs.

chronological (or physical) age   the actual age of the child taking the intelligence test.

classical conditioning   a type of learning in which an organism responds in a particular way to a neutral stimulus that normally does not bring about that type of response.

cliques   groups of from 2 to 12 people whose members have frequent social interactions with one another.

cognitive development   development involving the ways that growth and change in intellectual capabilities influence a person's behavior.

cognitive neuroscience approaches   approaches that examine cognitive development through the lens of brain processes.

cognitive perspective   the approach that focuses on the processes that allow people to know, understand, and think about the world.

cohabitation   couples living together without being married.

cohort   a group of people born at around the same time in the same place.

collectivistic orientation   a philosophy that promotes the notion of interdependence.

communal professions   occupations that are associated with relationships, such as nursing.

companionate love   the strong affection for those with whom our lives are deeply involved.

concrete operational stage   the period of cognitive development between 7 and 12 years of age, which is characterized by the active, and appropriate, use of logic.

conservation   the knowledge that quantity is unrelated to the arrangement and physical appearance of objects.

constructive play   play in which children manipulate objects to produce or build something.

contextual perspective   the theory that considers the relationship between individuals and their physical, cognitive, personality, and social worlds.

continuing-care community   a community that offers an environment in which all the residents are of retirement age or older.

continuity theory   the theory suggesting that people need to maintain their desired level of involvement in society to maximize their sense of well-being and self-esteem.

continuous change   gradual development in which achievements at one level build on those of previous levels.

controversial adolescents   children who are liked by some peers and disliked by others.

cooperative play   play in which children genuinely interact with one another, taking turns, playing games, or devising contests.

coping   the effort to control, reduce, or learn to tolerate the threats that lead to stress.

coregulation   a period in which parents and children jointly control children's behavior.

correlational research   research that seeks to identify whether an association or relationship between two factors exists.

creativity   the combination of responses or ideas in novel ways.

critical period   a specific time during development when a particular event has its greatest consequences and the presence of certain kinds of environmental stimuli are necessary for development to proceed normally.

cross-sectional research   research in which people of different ages are compared at the same point in time.

crowds   larger groups than cliques, composed of individuals who share particular characteristics but who may not interact with one another.

crystallized intelligence   the accumulation of information, skills, and strategies that people have learned through experience and that they can apply in problem-solving situations.

cultural assimilation model   the model in which the goal was to assimilate individual cultural identities into a unique, unified American culture.

cycle of violence hypothesis   the theory that the abuse and neglect that children suffer predispose them as adults to abuse and neglect their own children.

decentering   the ability to take multiple aspects of a situation into account.

decision/commitment component   according to Sternberg, the third aspect of love that embodies both the initial cognition that one loves another person and the longer-term determination to maintain that love.

defensive coping   coping that involves unconscious strategies that distort or deny the true nature of a situation.

dependent variable   the variable that researchers measure to see if it changes as a result of the experimental manipulation.

developmental quotient   an overall developmental score that relates to performance in four domains: motor skills, language use, adaptive behavior, and personal–social.

difficult babies   babies who have negative moods and are slow to adapt to new situations; when confronted with a new situation, they tend to withdraw.

discontinuous change   development that occurs in distinct steps or stages, with each stage bringing about behavior that is assumed to be qualitatively different from behavior at previous stages.

disengagement theory   the theory that late adulthood marks a gradual withdrawal from the world on physical, psychological, and social levels.

disorganized–disoriented attachment pattern   a style of attachment in which children show inconsistent, often contradictory behavior, such as approaching the mother when she returns but not looking at her.

dizygotic twins   twins who are produced when two separate ova are fertilized by two separate sperm at roughly the same time.

DNA (deoxyribonucleic acid) molecules   the substance that genes are composed of that determines the nature of every cell in the body and how it will function.

dominance hierarchy   rankings that represent the relative social power of those in a group.

dominant trait   the one trait that is expressed when two competing traits are present.

Down syndrome   a disorder produced by the presence of an extra chromosome on the 21st pair; once referred to as *mongolism*.

easy babies   babies who have a positive disposition; their body functions operate regularly, and they are adaptable.

ego transcendence versus ego preoccupation   the period in which elderly people must come to grips with their coming death.

egocentric thought   thinking that does not take into account the viewpoints of others.

ego-integrity-versus-despair stage   Erikson's final stage of life, characterized by a process of looking back over one's life, evaluating it, and coming to terms with it.

elder abuse   the physical or psychological mistreatment or neglect of elderly individuals.

embryonic stage   the period from 2 to 8 weeks following fertilization during which significant growth occurs in the major organs and body systems.

emerging adulthood   the period from the late teenage years extending to the mid-20s in which people are still sorting out their options for the future.

emotional intelligence   the set of skills that underlie the accurate assessment, evaluation, expression, and regulation of emotions.

emotional self-regulation   the capability to adjust emotions to a desired state and level of intensity.

empathy   an emotional response that corresponds to the feelings of another person.

empty nest syndrome   the experience that relates to parents' feelings of unhappiness, worry, loneliness, and depression resulting from their children's departure from home.

enrichment   an approach through which students are kept at grade level but are enrolled in special programs and given individual activities to allow greater depth of study on a given topic.

episiotomy   an incision sometimes made to increase the size of the opening of the vagina to allow the baby to pass.

Erikson's theory of psychosocial development   the theory that considers how individuals come to understand themselves and the meaning of others'—and their own—behavior.

euthanasia   the practice of assisting people who are terminally ill to die more quickly.

evolutionary perspective   the theory that seeks to identify behavior that is a result of our genetic inheritance from our ancestors.

executive stage   the period in middle adulthood when people take a broader perspective than previously, including concerns about the world.

experiment   a process in which an investigator, called an *experimenter*, devises two different experiences for participants and then studies and compares the outcomes.

experimental research   research designed to discover causal relationships between various factors.

expertise   the acquisition of skill or knowledge in a particular area.

expressive style   a style of language use in which language is used primarily to express feelings and needs about oneself and others.

extrinsic motivation   motivation that drives people to obtain tangible rewards, such as money and prestige.

fantasy period   according to Ginzberg, the period, lasting until about age 11, when career choices are made, and discarded, without regard to skills, abilities, or available job opportunities.

fast mapping   instances in which new words are associated with their meaning after only a brief encounter.

female climacteric   the period that marks the transition from being able to bear children to being unable to do so.

fertilization   the process by which a sperm and an ovum—the male and female gametes, respectively—join to form a single new cell.

fetal alcohol effects (FAE)   a condition in which children display some, but not all, of the problems of FASD as a result of the mother's consumption of alcohol during pregnancy.

fetal alcohol spectrum disorder (FASD)   a disorder caused by the pregnant mother consuming substantial quantities of alcohol during pregnancy, potentially resulting in mental retardation and delayed growth in the child.

fetal monitor   a device that measures the baby's heartbeat during labor.

fetal stage   the stage that begins at about 8 weeks after conception and continues until birth.

fetus   a developing child, from 8 weeks after conception until birth.

field study   a research investigation carried out in a naturally occurring setting.

first-year adjustment reaction   a cluster of psychological symptoms, including loneliness, anxiety, withdrawal, and depression, relating to the college experience suffered by first-year college students.

fluid intelligence   reflects the ability to solve and reason about novel problems.

formal operational stage   the period at which people develop the ability to think abstractly.

fragile X syndrome   a disorder produced by injury to a gene on the X chromosome, producing mild to moderate intellectual disability.

functional death   the absence of a heartbeat and breathing.

functional play   play that involves simple, repetitive activities typical of 3-year-olds.

gender   the sense of being male or female.

gender constancy   the belief that people are permanently males or females, depending on fixed, unchangeable biological factors.

gender identity   the perception of oneself as male or female.

gender schema a cognitive framework that organizes information relevant to gender.

generalized slowing hypothesis the theory that processing in all parts of the nervous system, including the brain, is less efficient as we age.

generation gap a divide between parents and adolescents in attitudes, values, aspirations, and worldviews.

generativity-versus-stagnation according to Erikson, the stage during middle adulthood in which people consider their contributions to family and society.

genes the basic unit of genetic information.

genetic counseling the discipline that focuses on helping people deal with issues relating to inherited disorders.

genetic programming theories of aging theories that suggest that our body's DNA genetic code contains a built-in time limit for the reproduction of human cells.

genotype the underlying combination of genetic material present (but not outwardly visible) in an organism.

germinal stage the first—and shortest—stage of the prenatal period, which takes place during the first 2 weeks following conception.

gerontologists specialists who study aging.

gifted and talented children who show evidence of high performance capability in areas such as intellectual, creative, artistic, leadership capacity, or specific academic fields.

glaucoma a condition in which pressure in the fluid of the eye increases, either because the fluid cannot drain properly or because too much fluid is produced.

goodness-of-fit the notion that development is dependent on the degree of match between children's temperament and the nature and demands of the environment in which they are being raised.

grammar the system of rules that determine how our thoughts can be expressed.

grief the emotional response to one's loss.

habituation the decrease in the response to a stimulus that occurs after repeated presentations of the same stimulus.

handedness the preference of using one hand over another.

heterozygous inheriting different forms of a gene for a given trait from each parent.

holophrases one-word utterances that stand for a whole phrase, the meaning of which depends on the particular context in which they are used.

home care an alternative to hospitalization in which dying people stay in their homes and receive treatment from their families and visiting medical staff.

homogamy the tendency to marry someone who is similar in age, race, education, religion, and other basic demographic characteristics.

homozygous inheriting similar genes for a given trait from both parents.

hospice care care provided for the dying in institutions devoted to those who are terminally ill.

humanistic perspective the theory that contends that people have a natural capacity to make decisions about their lives and control their behavior.

hypothesis a prediction stated in a way that permits it to be tested.

identity achievement the status of adolescents who commit to a particular identity following a period of crisis during which they consider various alternatives.

identity diffusion the status of adolescents who consider various identity alternatives, but never commit to one or never even consider identity options in any conscious way.

identity foreclosure the status of adolescents who prematurely commit to an identity without adequately exploring alternatives.

identity-versus-identity-confusion stage according to Erik Erikson, the period during which teenagers seek to determine what is unique and distinctive about themselves.

imaginary audience an adolescent's belief that his or her own behavior is a primary focus of others' attention and concerns.

in vitro fertilization (IVF) a procedure in which a woman's ova are removed from her ovaries, and a man's sperm are used to fertilize the ova in a laboratory.

independent variable the variable that researchers manipulate in an experiment.

individualistic orientation a philosophy that emphasizes personal identity and the uniqueness of the individual.

industry-versus-inferiority stage according to Erik Erikson, the period from age 6 to 12 characterized by a focus on efforts to attain competence in meeting the challenges presented by parents, peers, school, and the other complexities of the modern world.

infant mortality death within the first year of life.

infant-directed speech a type of speech directed toward infants, characterized by short, simple sentences.

infantile amnesia the lack of memory for experiences that occurred before 3 years of age.

infertility the inability to conceive after 12 to 18 months of trying to become pregnant.

information processing approaches the model that seeks to identify the ways individuals take in, use, and store information.

initiative-versus-guilt stage according to Erik Erikson, the period during which children age 3 to 6 years experience conflict between independence of action and the sometimes negative results of that action.

institutionalism a psychological state in which people in nursing homes develop apathy, indifference, and a lack of caring about themselves.

instrumental aggression aggression motivated by the desire to obtain a concrete goal.

intellectual disability a disability characterized by significant limitations both in intellectual functioning and in adaptive behavior, which covers many everyday social and practical skills.

intelligence quotient (IQ) a score that accounts for a student's mental *and* chronological age.

intelligence the capacity to understand the world, think with rationality, and use resources effectively when faced with challenges.

intimacy component according to Sternberg, the component of love that encompasses feelings of closeness, affection, and connectedness.

intimacy-versus-isolation stage according to Erikson, the period of postadolescence into the early 30s that focuses on developing close, intimate relationships with others.

intrinsic motivation motivation that causes people to work for their own enjoyment, for personal rewards.

intuitive thought thinking that reflects preschoolers' use of primitive reasoning and their avid acquisition of knowledge about the world.

Kaufman Assessment Battery for Children, Second Edition (KABC-II) an intelligence test that measures children's ability to integrate different stimuli simultaneously and to use sequential thinking.

Klinefelter's syndrome a disorder resulting from the presence of an extra X chromosome that produces underdeveloped genitals, extreme height, and enlarged breasts.

labeling theory of passionate love the theory that individuals experience romantic love when two events occur together: intense physiological arousal and situational cues suggesting that the arousal is a result of love.

laboratory study a research investigation conducted in a controlled setting explicitly designed to hold events constant.

language the systematic, meaningful arrangement of symbols, which provides the basis for communication.

language-acquisition device (LAD) a neural system of the brain hypothesized to permit understanding of language.

lateralization the process in which certain cognitive functions are located more in one hemisphere of the brain than in the other.

learning disabilities difficulties in the acquisition and use of listening, speaking, reading, writing, reasoning, or mathematical abilities.

learning theory approach the theory that language acquisition follows the basic laws of reinforcement and conditioning.

least restrictive environment the setting that is most similar to that of children without special needs.

life events theories the approach to personality development that is based on the timing of particular events in an adult's life rather than on age per se.

life expectancy the average age of death for members of a population.

life review the point in life in which people examine and evaluate their lives.

lifespan development the field of study that examines patterns of growth, change, and stability in behavior that occur throughout the entire life span.

living wills legal documents designating what medical treatments people want or do not want if they cannot express their wishes.

longitudinal research research in which the behavior of one or more participants in a study is measured as they age.

low-birthweight infants infants who weigh less than 2,500 grams (around 5.5 pounds) at birth.

major neurocognitive disorder the most common mental disorder of the elderly, it covers several diseases, each of which includes serious memory loss accompanied by declines in other mental functioning.

mainstreaming an educational approach in which exceptional children are integrated to the extent possible into the traditional educational system and are provided with a broad range of educational alternatives.

male climacteric the period of physical and psychological change relating to the male reproductive system that occurs during late middle age.

masturbation sexual self-stimulation.

maturation the predetermined unfolding of genetic information.

memory the process by which information is initially recorded, stored, and retrieved.

menarche the onset of menstruation.

menopause the cessation of menstruation.

mental age the typical intelligence level found for people at a given chronological age.

metacognition the knowledge that people have about their own thinking processes and their ability to monitor their cognition.

metalinguistic awareness an understanding of one's own use of language.

metamemory an understanding about the processes that underlie memory, which emerges and improves during middle childhood.

midlife crisis a stage of uncertainty and indecision brought about by the realization that life is finite.

mild intellectual disability intellectual disability in which IQ scores fall in the range of 50 or 55 to 70.

mnemonics formal strategies for organizing material in ways that make it more likely to be remembered.

moderate intellectual disability intellectual disability in which IQ scores range from 35 or 40 to 50 or 55.

monozygotic twins twins who are genetically identical.

moral development the changes in people's sense of justice and of what is right and wrong, and in their behavior related to moral issues.

moratorium the status of adolescents who may have explored various identity alternatives to some degree, but have not yet committed themselves.

multicultural education a form of education in which the goal is to help minority students develop confidence in the culture of the majority group while maintaining positive group identities that build on their original cultures.

multifactorial transmission the determination of traits by a combination of both genetic and environmental factors in which a genotype provides a range within which a phenotype may be expressed.

multimodal approach to perception the approach that considers how information that is collected by various individual sensory systems is integrated and coordinated.

myelin protective insulation that surrounds parts of neurons—which speeds the transmission of electrical impulses along brain cells but also adds to brain weight.

nativist approach the theory that a genetically determined, innate mechanism directs language development.

naturalistic observation a type of correlational study in which some naturally occurring behavior is observed without intervention in the situation.

neglected adolescents children who receive relatively little attention from their peers in the form of either positive or negative interactions.

neonates the term used for newborns.

neuron the basic nerve cell of the nervous system.

nonorganic failure to thrive a disorder in which infants stop growing due to a lack of stimulation and attention as the result of inadequate parenting.

normative-crisis theories the approach to personality development that is based on fairly universal stages tied to a sequence of age-related crises.

norms the average performance of a large sample of children of a given age.

obesity body weight more than 20 percent higher than the average weight for a person of a given age and height.

object permanence the realization that people and objects exist even when they cannot be seen.

onlooker play action in which children simply watch others at play, but do not actually participate themselves.

operant conditioning a form of learning in which a voluntary response is strengthened or weakened by its association with positive or negative consequences.

operations organized, formal, logical mental processes.

osteoporosis a condition in which the bones become brittle, fragile, and thin, often brought about by a lack of calcium in the diet.

overextension the overly broad use of words, overgeneralizing their meaning.

parallel play action in which children play with similar toys, in a similar manner, but do not interact with each other.

passion component according to Sternberg, the component of love that comprises the motivational drives relating to sex, physical closeness, and romance.

passionate (or romantic) love a state of powerful absorption in someone.

peer pressure the influence of one's peers to conform to their behavior and attitudes.

perception the sorting out, interpretation, analysis, and integration of stimuli involving the sense organs and brain.

peripheral slowing hypothesis the theory that suggests that overall processing speed declines in the peripheral nervous system with increasing age.

permissive parents parents who provide lax and inconsistent feedback and require little of their children.

personal fables the view held by some adolescents that what happens to them is unique, exceptional, and shared by no one else.

personality development development involving the ways that the enduring characteristics that differentiate one person from another change over the life span.

personality the sum total of the enduring characteristics that differentiate one individual from another.

phenotype an observable trait; the trait that is actually seen.

physical development development involving the body's physical makeup, including the brain, nervous system, muscles, and senses, and the need for food, drink, and sleep.

placenta a conduit between the mother and fetus, providing nourishment and oxygen via the umbilical cord.

plasticity the degree to which a developing structure or behavior is modifiable as a result of experience.

pluralistic society model the concept that American society is made up of diverse, coequal cultural groups that should preserve their individual cultural features.

polygenic inheritance inheritance in which a combination of multiple gene pairs is responsible for the production of a particular trait.

postformal thought thinking that acknowledges that adult predicaments must sometimes be solved in relativistic terms.

postmature infants infants still unborn 2 weeks after the mother's due date.

practical intelligence according to Sternberg, intelligence that is learned primarily by observing others and modeling their behavior.

pragmatics the aspect of language that is related to communicating effectively and appropriately with others.

preoperational stage according to Piaget, the stage from approximately age 2 to age 7 in which children's use of symbolic thinking grows, mental reasoning emerges, and the use of concepts increases.

presbycusis loss of the ability to hear sounds of high frequency.

presbyopia a nearly universal change in eyesight during middle adulthood that results in some loss of near vision.

preterm infants infants who are born prior to 38 weeks after conception (also known as *premature infants*).

primary aging aging that involves universal and irreversible changes that, because of genetic programming, occur as people get older.

primary appraisal the assessment of an event to determine whether its implications are positive, negative, or neutral.

primary sex characteristics characteristics associated with the development of the organs and structures of the body that directly relate to reproduction.

principle of hierarchical integration the principle that simple skills typically develop separately and independently but are later integrated into more complex skills.

principle of the independence of systems the principle that different body systems grow at different rates.

private speech speech by children that is spoken and directed to themselves.

profound intellectual disability intellectual disability in which IQ scores fall below 20 or 25.

prosocial behavior helping behavior that benefits others.

proximodistal principle the principle that development proceeds from the center of the body outward.

psychoanalytic theory the theory proposed by Freud that suggests that unconscious forces act to determine personality and behavior.

psychodynamic perspective the approach that states that behavior is motivated by inner forces, memories, and conflicts that are generally beyond people's awareness and control.

psychological maltreatment abuse that occurs when parents or other caregivers harm children's behavioral, cognitive, emotional, or physical functioning.

psychoneuroimmunology (PNI) the study of the relationship among the brain, the immune system, and psychological factors.

psychophysiological methods research that focuses on the relationship between physiological processes and behavior.

psychosexual development according to Freud, a series of stages that children pass through in which pleasure, or gratification, is focused on a particular biological function and body part.

psychosocial development according to Erik Erikson, development that encompasses changes in the understandings individuals have of themselves as members of society and in their comprehension of the meaning of others' behavior.

puberty the period during which the sexual organs mature.

race dissonance the phenomenon in which minority children indicate preferences for majority values or people.

rapid eye movement (REM) sleep the period of sleep that is found in older children and adults and is associated with dreaming.

realistic period the third stage of Ginzberg's theory, which occurs in early adulthood, when people begin to explore specific career options, either through actual experience on the job or through training for a profession, and then narrow their choices and make a commitment.

recessive trait a trait within an organism that is present but is not expressed.

redefinition of self versus preoccupation with work role the theory that those in old age must redefine themselves in ways that do not relate to their work roles or occupations.

reference groups groups of people with whom one compares oneself.

referential style a style of language use in which language is used primarily to label objects.

reflexes unlearned, organized involuntary responses that occur automatically in the presence of certain stimuli.

reintegrative stage the period of late adulthood during which the focus is on tasks that have personal meaning.

rejected adolescents children who are actively disliked, and whose peers may react to them in an obviously negative manner.

relational aggression nonphysical aggression that is intended to hurt another person's psychological well-being.

resilience the ability to overcome circumstances that place a child at high risk for psychological or physical damage.

responsible stage the stage where the major concerns of middle-aged adults relate to their personal situations, including protecting and nourishing their spouses, families, and careers.

rhythms repetitive, cyclical patterns of behavior.

sample the group of participants chosen for the experiment.

sandwich generation couples who in middle adulthood must fulfill the needs of both their children and their aging parents.

scaffolding the support for learning and problem solving that encourages independence and growth.

schemas organized bodies of information stored in memory.

schema organized patterns of functioning that adapt and change with mental functioning.

scientific method the process of posing and answering questions using careful, controlled techniques that include systematic, orderly observation and the collection of data.

scripts broad representations in memory of events and the order in which they occur.

secondary aging changes in physical and cognitive functioning that are as a result of illness, health habits, and other individual differences, but are not the result of increased age itself and are not inevitable.

secondary appraisal the assessment of whether one's coping abilities and resources are adequate to overcome the harm, threat, or challenge posed by the potential stressor.

secondary sex characteristics the visible signs of sexual maturity that do not directly involve the sex organs.

secular trend a pattern of change occurring over several generations.

secure attachment pattern a style of attachment in which children use the mother as a kind of home base and are at ease when she is present; when she leaves, they become upset and go to her as soon as she returns.

selective optimization the process by which people concentrate on selected skill areas to compensate for losses in other areas.

self-awareness knowledge of oneself.

self-care children children who let themselves into their homes after school and wait alone until their caretakers return from work; previously known as *latchkey children*.

self-concept a person's identity, or set of beliefs about what one is like as an individual.

self-esteem an individual's overall and specific positive and negative self-evaluation.

senescence the natural physical decline brought about by aging.

sensation the physical stimulation of the sense organs.

sensitive period a point in development when organisms are particularly susceptible to certain kinds of stimuli in their environments, but the absence of those stimuli does not always produce irreversible consequences.

sensorimotor stage (of cognitive development) Piaget's initial major stage of cognitive development, which can be broken down into six substages.

separation anxiety the distress displayed by infants when a customary care provider departs.

sequential studies research in which researchers examine a number of different age groups over several points in time.

severe intellectual disability intellectual disability in which IQ scores range from 20 or 25 to 35 or 40.

sex cleavage sex segregation in which boys interact primarily with boys and girls primarily with girls.

sexually transmitted infection (STI) an infection that is spread through sexual contact.

sickle-cell anemia a blood disorder that gets its name from the shape of the red blood cells.

skilled-nursing facilities a facility that provides full-time nursing care for people who have chronic illnesses or are recovering from a temporary medical condition.

slow-to-warm babies babies who are inactive, showing relatively calm reactions to their environment; their moods are generally negative, and they withdraw from new situations, adapting slowly.

small-for-gestational-age infants infants who, because of delayed fetal growth, weigh 90 percent (or less) of the average weight of infants of the same gestational age.

social competence the collection of social skills that permit individuals to perform successfully in social settings.

social development the way in which individuals' interactions with others and their social relationships grow, change, and remain stable over the course of life.

social problem-solving the use of strategies for solving social conflicts in ways that are satisfactory both to oneself and to others.

social referencing the intentional search for information about others' feelings to help explain the meaning of uncertain circumstances and events.

social speech speech directed toward another person and meant to be understood by that person.

social support assistance and comfort supplied by another person or a network of caring, interested people.

social-cognitive learning theory learning by observing the behavior of another person, called a model.

socialized delinquents adolescent delinquents who know and subscribe to the norms of society and who are fairly normal psychologically.

sociocultural theory the approach that emphasizes how cognitive development proceeds as a result of social interactions between members of a culture.

speech impairment speech that deviates so much from the speech of others that it calls attention to itself, interferes with communication, or produces maladjustment in the speaker.

Stanford-Binet Intelligence Scales, Fifth Edition (SB5) a test that consists of a series of items that vary according to the age of the person being tested.

state the degree of awareness an infant displays to both internal and external stimulation.

states of arousal different degrees of sleep and wakefulness through which newborns cycle, ranging from deep sleep to great agitation.

status the evaluation of a role or person by other relevant members of a group.

stereotype threat obstacles to performance that come from awareness of the stereotypes held by society about academic abilities.

stillbirth the delivery of a child who is not alive, occurring in fewer than 1 delivery in 100.

stranger anxiety the caution and wariness displayed by infants when encountering an unfamiliar person.

stress the physical and emotional response to events that threaten or challenge us.

sudden infant death syndrome (SIDS) the unexplained death of a seemingly healthy baby.

survey research a type of study where a group of people chosen to represent some larger population are asked questions about their attitudes, behavior, or thinking on a given topic.

synapse the gap at the connection between neurons, through which neurons chemically communicate with one another.

synaptic pruning the elimination of neurons as the result of nonuse or lack of stimulation.

syntax the way in which an individual combines words and phrases to form sentences.

Tay-Sachs disease a disorder that produces blindness and muscle degeneration before death; there is no treatment.

telegraphic speech speech in which words not critical to the message are left out.

temperament patterns of arousal and emotionality that represent consistent and enduring characteristics of an individual.

tentative period the second stage of Ginzberg's theory, which spans adolescence, when people begin to think more practically about the requirements of various jobs and how their own abilities might fit with them.

teratogen a factor that produces a birth defect.

thanatologists people who study death and dying.

theoretical research research designed specifically to test some developmental explanation and expand scientific knowledge.

theories broad explanations, and predictions about phenomena of interest.

theory of mind knowledge and beliefs about how the mind works and how it affects behavior.

transformation the process in which one state is changed into another.

triarchic theory of intelligence Sternberg's theory that intelligence is made up of three major components: componential, experiential, and contextual.

trust-versus-mistrust stage according to Erik Erikson, the period during which infants develop a sense of trust or mistrust, largely depending on how well their needs are met by their caregivers.

ultrasound sonography a process in which high-frequency sound waves scan the mother's womb to produce an image of the unborn baby, whose size and shape can then be assessed.

underextension the overly restrictive use of words, common among children just mastering spoken language.

undersocialized delinquents adolescent delinquents who are raised with little discipline or with harsh, uncaring parental supervision.

uninvolved parents parents who show almost no interest in their children and indifferent, rejecting behavior.

universal grammar Noam Chomsky's theory that all the world's languages share a similar underlying structure.

very-low-birthweight infants infants who weigh less than 1,250 grams (around 2.25 pounds) or, regardless of weight, have been in the womb less than 30 weeks.

visual impairment a difficulty in seeing that may include blindness or partial sightedness.

wear-and-tear theories of aging the theory that the mechanical functions of the body simply wear out with age.

Wechsler Intelligence Scale for Children, Fifth Edition (WISC-V) a test for children that provides separate measures of verbal and performance (or nonverbal) skills, as well as a total score.

wisdom expert knowledge in the practical aspects of life.

X-linked genes genes that are considered recessive and located only on the X chromosome.

zone of proximal development (ZPD) according to Vygotsky, the level at which a child can *almost*, but not fully, perform a task independently, but can do so with the assistance of someone more competent.

zygote the new cell formed by the process of fertilization.

References

AAP Council on Communications and the Media. (2016). Media and young minds. *Pediatrics, 138*(5).

Aazami, S., Shamsuddin, K., & Akmal, S. (n.d.). Assessment of work-family conflict among women of the sandwich generation. *Journal of Adult Development, 25*(2), 135–140.

Abbot-Smith, K., & Tomasello, M. (2010). The influence of frequency and semantic similarity on how children learn grammar. *First Language, 30*, 79–101.

Abe, J., Grills, C., Ghavami, N., Xiong, G., Davis, C., & Johnson, C. (2018). Making the invisible visible: Identifying and articulating culture in practice-based evidence. *American Journal of Community Psychology, 62*(1–2), 121–134.

Abrutyn, S., & Mueller, A. S. (2014). Are suicidal behaviors contagious in adolescence? Using longitudinal data to examine suicide suggestion. *American Sociological Review, 79*, 211–227.

Acevedo, B. P. (2018). The positive psychology of romantic love. In M. A. Warren & S. I. Donaldson (Eds.), *Toward a positive psychology of relationships: New directions in theory and research.* (pp. 55–75). Santa Barbara, CA: Praeger/ABC-CLIO.

Ackerman, B. P., & Izard, C. E. (2004). Emotion cognition in children and adolescents: Introduction to the special issue. [Special issue: Emotional cognition in children] *Journal of Experimental Child Psychology, 89*, 271–275.

Acocella, J. (2003, August 18 & 25). Little people. *The New Yorker*, pp. 138–143.

Adams, C., & Labouvie-Vief, G. (1986, November 20). *Modes of knowing and language processing. Symposium on developmental dimensions of adult adaptations. Perspectives in mind, self, and emotion.* Paper presented at the meeting of the Gerontological Association of America, Chicago, Illinois.

Adams, G. R., Montemayor, R., & Gullotta, T. P. (Eds.). (1996). *Psychosocial development during adolescence.* Thousand Oaks, CA: Sage Publications.

Adams, K. B. (2004). Changing investment in activities and interests in elders' lives: Theory and measurement. *International Journal of Aging and Human Development, 58*, 87–108.

Adams, P. (2010). Understanding the different realities, experience, and use of self-esteem between black and white adolescent girls. *Journal of Black Psychology, 36*, 255–276.

Adashi, E. Y., & Gutman, R. (2018). Delayed childbearing as a growing, previously unrecognized contributor to the national plural birth excess. *Obstetrics & Gynecology*, doi: 10.1097/AOG.0000000000002853

Adebayo, B. (2008). Gender gaps in college enrollment and degree attainment: An exploratory analysis. *College Student Journal, 42*, 232–237.

Adhya, D., Annuario, E., Lancaster, M. A., Price, J., Baron-Cohen, S., & Srivastava, D. P. (2018). Understanding the role of steroids in typical and atypical brain development: Advantages of using a "brain in a dish" approach. *Journal of Neuroendocrinology, 30*(2).

ADL. (2017). Myths and facts about immigrants and immigration. Accessed online, 11/29/17; https://www.adl.org/education/resources/fact-sheets/myths-and-facts-about-immigrants-and-immigration

Administration on Aging. (2010). *A statistical profile of older Americans aged 65+.* Washington, DC: Administration on Aging, U.S. Department of Health and Human Services.

Adolph, K. E., Kretch, K. S., & LoBue, V. (2014). Fear of heights in infants? *Current Directions in Psychological Science, 23*, 60–66.

Afifi, T., Brownridge, D., Cox, B., & Sareen, J. (2006, October). Physical punishment, childhood abuse and psychiatric disorders. *Child Abuse & Neglect, 30*, 1093–1103.

Afifi, T. O., Ford, D., Gershoff, E. T., Merrick, M., Grogan-Kaylor, A., Ports, K. A., … Bennett, R. P. (2017). Spanking and adult mental health impairment: The case for the designation of spanking as an adverse childhood experience. *Child Abuse & Neglect, 71*, 24–31

Agcaoglu, O., Miller, R., Mayer, A. R., Hugdahl, K., & Calhoun, V. D. (2015). Lateralization of resting state networks and relationship to age and gender. *NeuroImage, 104*, 310–325.

Ahmed, R. (2018, July 31). Honour killing: Woman tortured to death by husband in Peshawar. *The Express Tribune.* Accessed online, 3/26/19; https://tribune.com.pk/story/1770224/1-honour-killing-women-tortured-death-husband-peshawar/

Ahn, W., Gelman, S., & Amsterlaw, J. (2000). Causal status effect in children's categorization. *Cognition, 76*, B35–B43.

Aichele, S., Rabbitt, P., & Ghisletta, P. (2016). Think fast, feel fine, live long: A 29-year study of cognition, health, and survival in middle-aged and older adults. *Psychological Science, 27*, 518–529.

Aiken, L. R. (2000). *Dying, death, and bereavement* (4th ed.). Mahwah, NJ: Lawrence Erlbaum.

Ainsworth, M. D. S., Blehar, M. C., Waters, E., & Wall, S. (1978). *Patterns of attachment: A psychological study of the strange situation.* Hillsdale, NJ: Lawrence Erlbaum.

Akhtar, S. (2010). *The wound of mortality: Fear, denial, and acceptance of death.* Lanham, MD: Jason Aronson.

Albert, D., Chein, J., & Steinberg, L. (2013). The teenage brain: Peer influences on adolescent decision making. *Current Directions in Psychological Science, 22*, 114–120.

Alberts, A., Elkind, D., & Ginsberg, S. (2007). The personal fable and risk-taking in early adolescence. *Journal of Youth and Adolescence, 36*, 71–76.

Albrecht, G. L. (2005). *Encyclopedia of disability* (General ed.). Thousand Oaks, CA: Sage Publications.

Alderfer, C. (2003). The science and nonscience of psychologists' responses to *The Bell Curve. Professional Psychology: Research & Practice, 34*, 287–293.

Aldwin, C. M., & Igarashi, H. (2015). Successful, optimal, and resilient aging: A psychosocial perspective. In P. A. Lichtenberg, B. T. Mast, B. D. Carpenter, J. Loebach Wetherell (Eds.), *APA handbook of clinical geropsychology, Vol. 1: History and status of the field and perspectives on aging.* Washington, DC: American Psychological Association.

Alexander, B., Turnbull, D., & Cyna, A. (2009). The effect of pregnancy on hypnotizability. *American Journal of Clinical Hypnosis, 52*, 13–22.

Alexander, G. M., & Hines, M. (2002). Sex differences in response to children's toys in nonhuman primates. *Evolution and Human Behavior, 23*, 467–479.

Alexander, G. M., Wilcox, T., & Woods, R. (2009). Sex differences in infants' visual interest in toys. *Archives of Sexual Behavior, 38*, 427–433.

Alfred, M., & Chlup, D. (2010). Making the invisible, visible: Race matters in human resource development. *Advances in Developing Human Resources, 12*, 332–351.

Alisky, J. M. (2007). The coming problem of HIV-associated Alzheimer's disease. *Medical Hypotheses, 12*, 47–55.

Allam, M. D., Marlier, L., & Schall, B. (2006). Learning at the breast: Preference formation for an artificial scent and its attraction against the odor of maternal milk. *Infant Behavior & Development, 29*, 308–321.

Allen, B. (2008). An analysis of the impact of diverse forms of childhood psychological maltreatment on emotional adjustment in early adulthood. *Child Maltreatment, 13*, 307–312.

Allen, J., Chavez, S., DeSimone, S., Howard, D., Johnson, K., LaPierre, L., & … Sanders, J. (2006, June). Americans' attitudes toward euthanasia and physician-assisted suicide, 1936–2002. *Journal of Sociology & Social Welfare, 33*, 5–23.

Allison, B., & Schultz, J. (2001). Interpersonal identity formation during early adolescence. *Adolescence, 36*, 509–523.

Allison, C. M., & Hyde, J. (2013). Early menarche: Confluence of biological and contextual factors. *Sex Roles, 68*, 55–64.

Allison, S. J. (2018). High salt intake as a driver of obesity. *Nature Reviews Nephrology, 14*.

Al-Namlah, A. S., Meins, E., & Fernyhough, C. (2012). Self-regulatory private speech relates to children's recall and organization of autobiographical memories. *Early Childhood Research Quarterly.* Accessed online, 7/18/12; http://www.sciencedirect.com/science/article/pii/S0885200612000300

Al-Owidha, A., Green, K., & Kroger, J. (2009). On the question of an identity status category order: Rasch model step and scale statistics used to identify category order. *International Journal of Behavioral Development, 33*, 88–96.

Alshaarawy, O., & Anthony, J. C. (2014). Month-wise estimates of tobacco smoking during pregnancy for the United States, 2002–2009. *Maternal and Child Health Journal, 19*, 1010–1015. Accessed online, 3/14/15; http://www.ncbi.nlm.nih.gov/pubmed/25112459

Altermatt, E. R., & Broady, E. F. (2009). Coping with achievement-related failure: An examination of conversations between friends. *Merrill-Palmer Quarterly, 55*, 454–487.

Álvarez, M. J., Fernandez, D., Gomez-Salgado, J., Rodriguez-Gonzalez, D., Roson, M., & Lapena, S. (2017). The effects of massage therapy in hospitalized preterm neonates: A systematic review. *International Journal of Nursing Studies, 69*, 119–136.

Alwin, D. F. (2012). Integrating varieties of life course concepts. *The Journals of Gerontology: Series B: Psychological Sciences and Social Sciences, 67B*, 206–220.

Alzheimer's Association. (2004, May 28). *Standard prescriptions for Alzheimer's.* Accessed online; http://www.alz.org/AboutAD/Treatment/Standard.asp

Alzheimer's Association. (2017). 2017 Alzheimer's disease facts and figures. Accessed online, 12/11/17; https://www.alz.org/facts/overview.asp#prevalence

Alzheimer's Association. (2017a). FDA-approved treatments for Alzheimer's. Accessed online, 12/1/18; https://www.alz.org/media/Documents/fda-approved-treatments-alzheimers-ts.pdf

Alzheimer's Association, & Centers for Disease Control and Prevention. (2018). *Healthy Brain Initiative, state and local public health partnerships to address dementia: The 2018-2023 road map.* Chicago, IL: Alzheimer's Association.

Amato, P. R., & Afifi, T. D. (2006). Feeling caught between parents: Adult children's relations with parents and subjective well-being. *Journal of Marriage and Family, 68*, 222–235.

Ambrose, H. N., & Menna, R. (2013). Physical and relational aggression in young children: The role of mother-child interactional synchrony. *Early Child Development and Care, 183*, 207–222.

American Academy of Family Physicians. (2002). *Position paper on neonatal circumcision.* Leawood, KS: American Academy of Family Physicians.

American Academy of Pediatrics. (1999, August). Media education. *Pediatrics, 104*, 341–343.

American Academy of Pediatrics. (2004, June 3). *Sports programs.* Accessed online; http://www.medem.com/medlb/article_detaillb_for_printer.cfm?article_

American Academy of Pediatrics. (2008). Newborn screening fact sheets. *Pediatrics, 118*, 934–963.

American Academy of Pediatrics. (2009). *Toilet training.* Elk Grove Village, IL: Author.

American Academy of Pediatrics. (2012). Circumcision Policy Statement. *Pediatrics, 130*, 686.

American Academy of Pediatrics. (2012b, March 5). Discipline and your child. Accessed online, 7/23/12; http://www.healthychildren.org/english/family-life/family-dynamics/communication-discipline/pages/disciplining-your-child.aspx?nfstatus=401&nftoken

American Academy of Pediatrics. (2013). Prevalence and reasons for introducing infants early to solid foods: Variations by milk feeding type. *Pediatrics, 131.* Accessed online, 6/25/14; http://pediatrics.aappublications.org/content/131/4/e1108

American Academy of Pediatrics. (2016, October 21). American Academy of Pediatrics announces new recommendations for children's media use. Accessed online, 3/3/17; https://www.aap.org/en-us/about-the-aap/aap-press-room/pages/american-academy-of-pediatrics-announces-new-recommendations-forchildrens-media-use.aspx

American Academy of Pediatrics Healthychildren.org. (2015). *Choosing a child care center.* Accessed online, 10/31/17; https://www.healthychildren.org/English/family-life/work-play/Pages/Choosing-a-Childcare-Center.aspx

American Association of Community Colleges. (2018). Fast facts. Accessed online, 10/26/18; https://www.aacc.nche.edu/research-trends/fast-facts/

American Association of Retired Persons (AARP). (2004, May 25). *Funeral arrangements and memorial service.* Accessed online; http://www.aarp.org/griefandloss/articles/73_a.html

American Association of Retired Persons (AARP). (2005). A *profile of older Americans.* Washington, DC: Author.

American Association on Intellectual and Developmental Disabilities. (2012). *Definition of intellectual disability.* Accessed online, 7/23; www.aamr.org

American Cancer Society. (2017). American Cancer Society guidelines for the early detection of cancer. Accessed online, 11/28/17; https://www.cancer.org/healthy/find-cancer-early/cancer-screening-guidelines/american-cancersociety-guidelines-for-the-early-detection-of-cancer.html

American College Health Association. (2017). *American College Health Association–National College Health Assessment II: Reference Group Executive Summary Fall 2017.* Hanover, MD: American College Health Association, 2018.

American College of Medical Genetics. (2006). *Genetics in Medicine, 8*(5, Suppl.).

American College of Obstetricians and Gynecologists. (2017). Medications for pain relief during labor and delivery. Accessed online, 10/1/18; https://www.acog.org/Patients/FAQs/Medications-for-Pain-Relief-During-Labor-and-Delivery

American College of Sports Medicine (ACSM). (2011). *ACSM issues new recommendations on quantity of and quality of exercise.* Accessed online, 9/13/16; http://www.acsm.org/about-acsm/media-room/news-releases/2011/08/01/acsm-issues-new-recommendations-on-quantity-and-quality-of-exercise

American Heart Association (AHA). (2010). *Heart facts.* Dallas, TX: Author.

American Psychological Association (APA). (2002). *Ethical principles of psychologists and code of conduct. Updated.* Washington, DC: Author.

American Psychological Association (APA). (2014, October 8). *Childhood psychological abuse as harmful as sexual or physical abuse.* Accessed online, 8/24/16; http://www.apa.org/news/press/releases/2014/10/psychological-abuse.aspx

American Psychological Association. (2015, February 4). *Stress in America: Paying with our health.* Accessed online, 3/6/19; http://www.apa.org/news/press/releases/stress/2014/stress-report.pdf

American Psychological Association. (2017). Ethical principles of psychologists and code of conduct. Accessed online, 5/1/18; http://www.apa.org/ethics/code/

Amitai, Y., Haringman, M., Meiraz, H., Baram, N., & Leventhal, A. (2004). Increased awareness, knowledge and utilization of preconceptional folic acid in Israel following a national campaign. *Preventive Medicine: An International Journal Devoted to Practice and Theory, 39*, 731–737.

Ammerman, R. T., & Patz, R. J. (1996). Determinants of child abuse potential: Contribution of parent and child factors. *Journal of Clinical Child Psychology, 25*, 300–307.

Amsterlaw, J., & Wellman, H. (2006). Theories of mind in transition: A microgenetic study of the development of false belief understanding. *Journal of Cognition and Development, 7*, 139–172.

Anderson, J. (2016, March 2). The idea that Mozart makes your baby smarter is one of parenting's most persistent myths. Accessed online, 10/30/17; https://qz.com/628331/the-idea-that-mozart-makes-babies-smarter-isone-of-parentings-most-bizarre-myths/

Anderson, K. N., Rueter, M. A., Connor, J. J., Chen, M., & Damario, M. (2015). Conformity expectations: Differential effects on IVF twins and singletons' parent-child relationships and adjustment. *Journal of Family Psychology, 29*(4), 558–567.

Anderson, R. E., Edwards, L. J., Silver, K. E., & Johnson, D. M. (2018). Intergenerational transmission of child abuse: Predictors of child abuse potential among racially diverse women residing in domestic violence shelters. *Child Abuse & Neglect.* doi:10.1016/j.chiabu.2018.08.004

Anderson, M., & Perrin, A. (2017, May 17). *Tech adoption climbs among older adults.* Washington, DC: Pew Research Center.

Andersson, M. A., & Conley, C. S, (2013). Optimizing the perceived benefits and health outcomes of writing about traumatic life events. *Stress and Health: Journal of the International Society for the Investigation of Stress, 29*, 40–49.

Andreoni, J., & Petrie, R. (2008). Beauty, gender and stereotypes: Evidence from laboratory experiments. *Journal of Economic Psychology, 29*, 73–93.

Andreotti, C., Garrard, P., Venkatraman, S. L., & Compas, B. E. (2014). Stress-related changes in attentional bias to social threat in young adults: Psychobiological associations with the early family environment. *Cognitive Therapy and Research, 39*, 332–342.

Andrews, B., d'Avossa, G., & Sapir, A. (2017). Aging changes 3D perception: Evidence for hemispheric rebalancing of lateralized processes. *Neuropsychologia, 99*, 121–127.

Andruski, J. E., Casielles, E., & Nathan, G. (2014). Is bilingual babbling language-specific? Some evidence from a case study of Spanish–English dual acquisition. *Bilingualism: Language and Cognition, 17*, 660–672.

Ankrum, J. W., Genest, M. T., & Belcastro, E. G. (2013). The power of verbal scaffolding: "Showing" beginning readers how to use reading strategies. *Early Childhood Education Journal.* Accessed online, 6/5/13; http://link.springer.com/article/10.1007%2Fs10643-013-0586-5#page-1

Ansari, A., & Pianta, R. C. (2018). Variation in the long-term benefits of child care: The role of classroom quality in elementary school. *Developmental Psychology, 54*(10), 1854–1867.

Antovich, D. M., & Graf Estes, K. (2018). Learning across languages: Bilingual experience supports dual language statistical word segmentation. *Developmental Science, 21*(2), 1–11.

Antshel, K., & Antshel, K. (2002). Integrating culture as a means of improving treatment adherence in the Latino population. *Psychology, Health & Medicine, 7*, 435–449.

Anyan, F., & Hjemdal, O. (2016). Adolescent stress and symptoms of anxiety and depression: Resilience explains and differentiates the relationships. *Journal of Affective Disorders, 203*, 213–220.

Anzman-Frasca, S., Liu, S., Gates, K. M., Paul, I. M., Rovine, M. J., & Birch, L. L. (2013). Infants' transitions out of a fussing/crying state are modifiable and are related to weight status. *Infancy, 18*, 662–686.

Aoyagi, K., Santos, C. E., & Updegraff, K. A. (2017). Longitudinal associations between gender and ethnic-racial identity felt pressure from family and peers and self-esteem among African American and Latino youth. *Journal of Youth and Adolescence.* Accessed online, 11/29/17; https://www.ncbi.nlm.nih.gov/pubmed/28986744

APA Reproductive Choice Working Group. (2000). *Reproductive choice and abortion: A resource packet.* Washington, DC: American Psychological Association.

Apgar, V. (1953). A proposal for a new method of evaluation of the newborn infant. *Current Research in Anesthesthesia and Analgesia, 32*, 260–267.

Apperly, I., & Robinson, E. (2002). Five-year-olds' handling of reference and description in the domains of language and mental representation. *Journal of Experimental Child Psychology, 83*, 53–75.

Arai, J., Li, S., Hartley, D., and Feig, L. (2009). Transgenerational rescue of a genetic defect in long-term potentiation and memory formation by juvenile enrichment. *Journal of Neuroscience, 29*, 1496–1502.

Araujo, M. A., Mohr, B. A., & McKinlay, J. B. (2004). Changes in sexual function in middle-aged and older men: Longitudinal data from the Massachusetts male aging study. *Journal of the American Geriatrics Society, 52*, 1502–1509.

Aravind, A., de Villiers, J., Pace, A., Valentine, H., Golinkoff, R., Hirsh-Pasek, K.,... Wilson, M. S. (2018). Fast mapping word meanings across trials: Young children forget all but their first guess. *Cognition, 177*, 177–188.

Archer, J. (2009). The nature of human aggression. *International Journal of Law and Psychiatry, 32*, 202–208.

Archer, M., Steele, M., Lan, J., Jin, X., Herreros, F., & Steele, H. (2015). Attachment between infants and mothers in China: Strange situation procedure findings to date and a new sample. *International Journal of Behavioral Development, 39*(6), 485–491.

Archer-Banks, D. A. M., & Behar-Horenstein, L. S. (2012). Ogbu revisited: Unpacking high-achieving African American girls' high school experiences. *Urban Education, 47*(1), 198–223.

Archimi, A., & Kuntsche, E. (2014). Do offenders and victims drink for different reasons? Testing mediation of drinking motives in the link between bullying subgroups and alcohol use in adolescence. *Addictive Behaviors, 39*, 713–716.

Aries, P. (1962). *Centuries of childhood: A social history of family life.* New York, NY: Random House.

Arístegui, I., Castro Solano, A., & Buunk, A. P. (2018). Mate preferences in Argentinean transgender people: An evolutionary perspective. *Personal Relationships*, doi:10.1111/pere.12247

Armstrong, J., Hutchinson, I., Laing, D., & Jinks, A. (2007). Facial electromyography: Responses of children to odor and taste stimuli. *Chemical Senses, 32*, 611–621.

Armstrong, P., Rounds, J., & Hubert, L. (2008). Re-conceptualizing the past: Historical data in vocational interest research. *Journal of Vocational Behavior, 72*, 284–297.

Arnarson, E. Ö., Matos, A. P., Salvador, C., Ribeiro, C., Sousa, B., & Craighead, W. E. (2016). Longitudinal study of life events, well-being, emotional regulation and depressive symptomatology. *Journal of Psychopathology and Behavioral Assessment, 38*, 159–171.

Arnautovska, U., & Grad, O. (2010). Attitudes toward suicide in the adolescent population. *Crisis: The Journal of Crisis Intervention and Suicide Prevention, 31*, 22–29.

Arnett, J. (2010). Oh, grow up! Generational grumbling and the new life stage of emerging adulthood—Commentary on Trzesniewski & Donnellan (2010). *Perspectives on Psychological Science, 5*, 89–92.

Arnett, J. J. (2000). Emerging adulthood: A theory of development from the late teens through the twenties. *American Psychologist, 55*, 469–480.

Arnett, J. J. (2006). *Emerging adulthood: The winding road from the late teens through the twenties.* New York: Oxford University Press.

Arnett, J. J. (2011). Emerging adulthood(s): The cultural psychology of a new life stage. In L. Jensen (Ed.), *Bridging cultural and developmental approaches to psychology: New syntheses in theory, research, and policy.* New York: Oxford University Press.

Arnett, J. J. (2014a). *Emerging adulthood: The winding road from the late teens through the twenties* (2nd ed.). New York, NY: Oxford University Press.

Arnett, J. J. (2014b). Presidential address: The emergence of emerging adulthood: A personal history. *Emerging Adulthood, 2*, 155–162.

Arnett, J. J. (2015). *The Oxford Handbook of emerging adulthood.* New York, NY: Oxford University Press

Arnett, J. J. (2016). *The Oxford handbook of emerging adulthood.* New York, NY: Oxford University Press.

Arnett, J. J. (2017). Life stage concepts across history and cultures: Proposal for a new field on indigenous life stages. *Human Development, 59*(5), 290–316.

Arnsten, A., Berridge, C., & McCracken, J. (2009). The neurobiological basis of attention-deficit/hyperactivity disorder. *Primary Psychiatry, 16*, 47–54.

Aronson, M., & Bialostok, S. (2016). 'Do some wondering': Children and their self-understanding selves in early elementary classrooms. *Symbolic Interaction, 39*, 229–251.

Arsenault, L., Moffitt, T. E., Caspi, A., Taylor, A., Rijsdijk, F. V., Jaffee, S. R., &… Measelle, J. R. (2003). Strong genetic effects on cross-situational antisocial behaviour among 5-year-old children according to mothers, teachers, examiner-observers, and twins' self-reports. *Journal of Child Psychology and Psychiatry, 44*, 832–848.

Arts, J. A. R., Gijselaers, W. H., & Boshuizen, H. P. A. (2006). Understanding managerial problem-solving, knowledge use and information processing: Investigating stages from school to the workplace. *Contemporary Educational Psychology, 31*, 387–410.

Asadi, S., Amiri, S., & Molavi, H. (2014). Development of post-formal thinking from adolescence through adulthood. *Journal of Iranian Psychologists, 10*, 161–174.

Asch, D. A. (1996, May 23). The role of critical care nurses in euthanasia and assisted suicide. *New England Journal of Medicine, 334*, 1374–1379.

Aschbacher, K., O'Donovan, A., Wolkowitz, O. M., Dhabhar, F. S., Su, Y., & Epel, E. (2013). Good stress, bad stress and oxidative stress: Insights from anticipatory cortisol reactivity. *Psychoneuroendocrinology.* Accessed online, 6/7/13; http://www.sciencedirect.com/science/article/pii/S0306453013000425

Atchley, R. C. (2000). *Social forces and aging* (9th ed.). Belmont, CA: Wadsworth Thomson Learning.

Atchley, R. C. (2003). Why most people cope well with retirement. In J. Ronch & J. Goldfield (Eds.), *Mental wellness in aging: Strengths-based approaches* (pp. 123–138). Baltimore, MD: Health Professions Press.

Athanasiu, L., Giddaluru, S., Fernandes, C., Christoforou, A., Reinvang, I., Lundervold, A. J., &… Le Hellard, S. (2017). A genetic association study of CSMD1 and CSMD2 with cognitive function. *Brain, Behavior, and Immunity, 61*, 209–216.

Athanasopoulou, E., & Fox, J. E. (2014). Effects of kangaroo mother care on maternal mood and interaction patterns between parents and their preterm, low birth weight infants: A systematic review. *Infant Mental Health Journal, 35*, 245–262.

Atkins, D. C., & Furrow, J. (2008, November). *Infidelity is on the rise: But for whom and why?*

Paper presented at the annual meeting of the Association for Behavioral and Cognitive Therapies, Orlando, FL.

Atkins, S. M., Bunting, M. F., Bolger, D. J., & Dougherty, M. R. (2012). Training the adolescent brain: Neural plasticity and the acquisition of cognitive abilities. In V. F. Reyna, S. B. Chapman, M. R. Dougherty, & J. Confrey (Eds.), *The adolescent brain: Learning, reasoning, and decision making* (pp. 211–241). Washington, DC: American Psychological Association.

Augestad, K. M., Norum, J., Dehof, S., Aspevik, R., Ringber, U., Nestvold, T., &… Lindsetmo, R-O. (2013). Cost-effectiveness and quality of life in surgeon versus general practitioner-organised colon cancer surveillance: A randomised controlled trial. *British Medical Journal, 3*, 88–96.

Aujoulat, I., Luminet, O., & Deccache, A. (2007). The perspective of patients on their experience of powerlessness. *Qualitative Health Research, 17*, 772–785.

Austen, E., & Griffiths, S. (2018). Why do men stigmatize individuals with eating disorders more than women? Experimental evidence that sex differences in conformity to gender norms, not biological sex, drive eating disorders' stigmatization. *Eating Disorders: The Journal of Treatment & Prevention.* doi:10.1080/10640266.2018.1499337

Austin, J. (2016). 2020 vision: Genetic counselors as acknowledged leaders in integrating genetics and genomics into healthcare. *Journal of Genetic Counseling, 25*, 1–5.

Avinun, R., Israel, S., Shalev, I., Grtsenko, I., Bornstein, G., Ebstein, R. P., & Knafo, A. (2011). AVPRIA variant associated with preschoolers' lower altruistic behavior. *PLoS One, 6.* Accessed online, 7/5/12; http://www.sproutonline.com/kindnesscounts/dr-nancy-eisenberg/eight-tips-for-developing-caring-kids

Avlund, K., Lund, R., & Holstein, B. (2004). Social relations as determinant of onset of disability in aging. *Archives of Gerontology & Geriatrics, 38*, 85–99.

Ayalon, L., & Koren, C. (2015). Marriage, second couplehood, divorce, and singlehood in old age. In P. A. Lichtenberg, B. T. Mast, B. D. Carpenter, & J. Loebach Wetherell (Eds.), *APA handbook of clinical geropsychology, Vol. 2: Assessment, treatment, and issues of later life.* Washington, DC: American Psychological Association.

Ayalon, L., & Tesch-Römer, C. (2017). Taking a closer look at ageism: Self- and other-directed ageist attitudes and discrimination. *European Journal of Ageing, 14*, 1–4.

Aydiner, F., Yetkin, C. E., & Seli, E. (2010). Perspectives on emerging biomarkers for non-invasive assessment of embryo viability in assisted reproduction. *Current Molecular Medicine, 10*, 206–215.

Aylward, G. P., & Verhulst, S. J. (2000). Predictive utility of the Bayley Infant Neurodevelopmental Screener (BINS) risk status classifications: Clinical interpretation and application. *Developmental Medicine & Child Neurology, 42*, 25–31.

Ayoola, A., Nettleman, M., Stommel, M., & Canady, R. (2010). Time of pregnancy recognition and prenatal care use: A population-based study in the United States. *Birth: Issues in Perinatal Care, 37*, 37–43.

Ayoub, N. C. (2005, February 25). A pleasing birth: Midwives and maternity care in the Netherlands. *The Chronicle of Higher Education*, p. 9.

Ayres, M. M., & Leaper, C. (2013). Adolescent girls' experiences of discrimination: An examination of coping strategies, social support, and self-esteem. *Journal of Adolescent Research, 28*, 479–508.

Azagba, S. (2018). E-cigarette use, dual use of e-cigarettes and tobacco cigarettes, and frequency of cannabis use among high school students. *Addictive Behaviors, 79*, 166–170.

Babenko, O., Kovalchuk, I., & Metz, G. S. (2015). Stress-induced perinatal and transgenerational epigenetic programming of brain development and mental health. *Neuroscience and Biobehavioral Reviews, 48*, 70–91.

Bacchus, L., Mezey, G., & Bewley, S. (2006). A qualitative exploration of the nature of domestic violence in pregnancy. *Violence Against Women, 12*, 588–604.

Bademli, K., Lök, N., & Selçuk, T. A. (2018). The effect of reminiscence therapy on cognitive functions, depression, and quality of life in Alzheimer patients: Randomized controlled trial. *International Journal of Geriatric Psychiatry.* doi:10.1002/gps.4980

Badenhorst, W., Riches, S., Turton, P., & Hughes, P. (2006). The psychological effects of stillbirth and neonatal death on fathers: Systematic review. *Journal of Psychosomatic Obstetrics & Gynecology, 27*, 245–256.

Baer, J. S., Sampson, P. D., & Barr, H. M. (2003). A 21-year longitudinal analysis of the effects of prenatal alcohol exposure on young adult drinking. *Archives of General Psychiatry, 60*, 377–385.

Bagci, S. C., Kumashiro, M., Smith, P. K., Blumberg, H., & Rutland, A. (2014). Cross-ethnic friendships: Are they really rare? Evidence from secondary schools around London. *International Journal of Intercultural Relations, 41*, 125–137.

Bährer-Kohler, S. (2013). *Burnout for experts: Prevention in the context of living and working.* New York, NY: Springer Science + Business Media.

Bahrick, L. E., Todd, J. T., Castellanos, I., & Sorondo, B. M. (2016). Enhanced attention to speaking faces versus other event types emerges gradually across infancy. *Developmental Psychology, 52*, 1705–1720.

Bai, S., Repetti, R. L., & Sperling, J. B. (2016). Children's expressions of positive emotion are sustained by smiling, touching, and playing with parents and siblings: A naturalistic observational study of family life. *Developmental Psychology, 52*, 88–101.

Bailey-Davis, L., Poulsen, M. N., Hirsch, A. G., Pollak, J., Glass, T. A., & Schwartz, B. S. (2017). Home food rules in relation to youth eating behaviors, body mass index, waist circumference, and percent body fat. *Journal of Adolescent Health, 60*, 270–276.

Baillargeon, R., & DeJong, G. F. (2017). Explanation-based learning in infancy. *Psychonomic Bulletin & Review.* Accessed online, 10/29/17; https://www.ncbi.nlm.nih.gov/pubmed/28698990

Baillargeon, R., Scott, R. M., He, Z., Sloane, S., Setoh, P., Jin, K., &… Bian, L. (2015). Psychological and sociomoral reasoning in infancy. In M. Mikulincer, P. R. Shaver, E. Borgida, & J. A. Bargh (Eds.), *APA handbook of personality and social psychology, Volume 1: Attitudes and social cognition.* Washington, DC: American Psychological Association.

Bainbridge, K. E., & Wallhagen, M. I. (2014). Hearing loss in an aging American population: Extent, impact, and management. *Annual Review of Public Health, 35*, 139–152.

Baker, J., Maes, H., Lissner, L., Aggen, S., Lichtenstein, P., & Kendler, K. (2009). Genetic risk factors for disordered eating in adolescent males and females. *Journal of Abnormal Psychology, 118*, 576–586.

Baker, L. R., McNulty, J. K., & VanderDrift, L. E. (2017). Expectations for future relationship satisfaction: Unique sources and critical implications for commitment. *Journal of Experimental Psychology: General, 146*, 700–721.

Baker, P., & Sussman, D. (2012, May 15). Obama's switch on same-sex marriage stirs skepticism. *The New York Times*, p. A17.

Baker, T., Brandon, T., & Chassin, L. (2004). Motivational influences on cigarette smoking. *Annual Review of Psychology, 55*, 463–491.

Bakken, L., Brown, N., & Downing, B. (2017). Early childhood education: The long-term benefits. *Journal of Research in Childhood Education, 31*(2), 255–269.

Bakoyiannis, I., Gkioka, E., Pergialiotis, V., Mastroleon, I., Prodromidou, A., Vlachos, G. D., & Perrea, D. (2014). Fetal alcohol spectrum disorders and cognitive functions of young children. *Reviews in the Neurosciences, 25*, 631–639.

Bal, E., Harden, E., Lamb, D., Van Hecke, A., Denver, J., & Porges, S. (2010). Emotion recognition in children with autism spectrum disorders: Relations to eye gaze and autonomic state. *Journal of Autism and Developmental Disorders, 40,* 358–370.

Balin, B. J., Hammond, C. J., Little, C. S., Hingley, S. T., Al-Atrache, Z., Appelt, D. M.,… Hudson, A. P. (2018). Chlamydia pneumoniae: An etiologic agent for late-onset dementia. *Frontiers in Aging Neuroscience, 10.* doi:10.3389/fnagi.2018.00302

Balk, D. E. (2014). *Dealing with dying, death, and grief during adolescence.* New York: Routledge/Taylor & Francis Group.

Ball, H. L., & Volpe, L. E. (2013). Sudden Infant Death Syndrome (SIDS) risk reduction and infant sleep location—Moving the discussion forward. *Social Science & Medicine, 79,* 84–91.

Ball, M., & Orford, J. (2002). Meaningful patterns of activity amongst the long-term inner city unemployed: A qualitative study. *Journal of Community & Applied Social Psychology, 12,* 377–396.

Ballas, S. (2010). Neurocognitive complications of sickle cell anemia in adults. *JAMA: Journal of the American Medical Association, 303,* 1862–1863.

Ballesteros-Meseguer, C., Carrillo-Garcia, C., Meseguer-de-Pedro, M., Canteras-Jordana, M., & Martinez-Roche, M. E. (2016). Episiotomy and its relationship to various clinical variables that influence its performance. *Revista Latino-Americana De Enfermagem, 24,* 22–27.

Balsam, R. H. (2013). Appreciating difference: Roy Schafer on psychoanalysis and women. *The Psychoanalytic Quarterly, 82,* 23–38.

Balsam, R. H. (2018). 'Castration anxiety' revisited: Especially 'female castration anxiety.' *Psychoanalytic Inquiry, 38*(1), 11–22. doi:10.1080/07 351690.2018.1395613

Baltes, P. B. (2003). On the incomplete architecture of human ontogeny: Selection, optimization and compensation as foundation of developmental theory. In U. M. Staudinger & U. Lindenberger (Eds.), *Understanding human development: Dialogues with lifespan psychology* (pp. 17–43). Dordrecht, the Netherlands: Kluwer Academic Publishers.

Baltes, P. B., & Baltes, M. M. (1990). Psychological perspectives on successful aging: The model of selective optimization with compensation. In P. B. Baltes & M. M. Baltes (Eds.), *Successful aging: Perspectives from the behavioral sciences.* Cambridge, UK: Cambridge University Press.

Baltes, P. B., & Staudinger, U. M. (2000). Wisdom: A metaheuristic (pragmatic) to orchestrate mind and virtue toward excellence. *American Psychologist, 55,* 122–136.

Bandura, A. (2002). Social cognitive theory in cultural context [Special Issue]. *Applied Psychology: An International Review, 51,* 269–290.

Bandura, A. (2016). The power of observational learning through social modeling. In R. J. Sternberg, S. T. Fiske, & D. J. Foss (Eds.), *Scientists making a difference: One hundred eminent behavioral and brain scientists talk about their most important contributions* (pp. 235–239). New York, NY: Cambridge University Press.

Bandura, A. (2018). Toward a psychology of human agency: Pathways and reflections. *Perspectives on Psychological Science, 13*(2), 130–136.

Bandura, A., Grusec, J. E., & Menlove, F. L. (1967). Vicarious extinction of avoidance behavior. *Journal of Personality and Social Psychology, 5,* 16–23.

Bandura, A., Ross, D., & Ross, S. (1963). Vicarious extinction of avoidance behavior. *Journal of Personality and Social Psychology, 67,* 601–607.

Banks, M. E. (2016). Neuropsychological consequences of intimate partner violence among ethnic minority and cross-cultural populations. In F. R. Ferraro & F. R. Ferraro (Eds.), *Minority and cross-cultural aspects of neuropsychological assessment: Enduring and emerging trends* (2nd ed.). Philadelphia, PA: Taylor & Francis.

Baptista, T., Aldana, E., Angeles, F., & Beaulieu, S. (2008). Evolution theory: An overview of its applications in psychiatry. *Psychopathology, 41,* 17–27.

Barber, A. D., Srinivasan, P., Joel, S. E., Caffo, B. S., Pekar, J. J., & Mostofsky, S. H. (2012). Motor "dexterity"? Evidence that left hemisphere lateralization of motor circuit connectivity is associated with better motor performance in children. *Cerebral Cortex, 22,* 51–59.

Barber, S., & Gertler, P. (2009). Empowering women to obtain high quality care: Evidence from an evaluation of Mexico's conditional cash transfer programme. *Health Policy and Planning, 24,* 18–25.

Barberá, E. (2003). Gender schemas: Configuration and activation processes. *Canadian Journal of Behavioural Science, 35,* 176–180.

Barboza, G., Schiamberg, L., Oehmke, J., Korzeniewski, S., Post, L., & Heraux, C. (2009). Individual characteristics and the multiple contexts of adolescent bullying: An ecological perspective. *Journal of Youth and Adolescence, 38,* 101–121.

Barker, E. D., Cecil, C. A. M., Walton, E., & Meehan, A. J. (2018). Genetic and gene-environment influences on disruptive behavior disorders. In J. E. Lochman & W. Matthys (Eds.), *The Wiley handbook of disruptive and impulse-control disorders.* (pp. 127–141). Wiley-Blackwell.

Barlett, C., Chamberlin, K., & Witkower, Z. (2017). Predicting cyberbullying perpetration in emerging adults: A theoretical test of the Barlett Gentile Cyberbullying Model. *Aggressive Behavior, 43,* 147–154.

Barnes, J. C., & Jacobs, B. A. (2013). Genetic risk for violent behavior and environmental exposure to disadvantage and violent crime: The case for gene-environment interaction. *Journal of Interpersonal Violence, 28,* 92–120.

Barnett, R. C., & Hyde, J. S. (2001). Women, men, work, and family. *American Psychologist, 56,* 781–796.

Barrera, M., Alam, R., D'Agostino, N., Nicholas, D. B., & Schneiderman, G. (2013). Parental perceptions of siblings' grieving after a childhood cancer death: A longitudinal study. *Death Studies, 37,* 25–46.

Barrett, D. E., & Katsiyannis, A. (2017). The Clemson juvenile delinquency project: Major findings from a multi-agency study. *Journal of Child and Family Studies, 26,* 2050–2058.

Barrouillet, P. (2015). Theories of cognitive development: From Piaget to today. *Developmental Review, 38,* 1–12.

Barry, L. M., Hudley, C., Kelly, M., & Cho, S. (2009). Differences in self-reported disclosure of college experiences by first-generation college student status. *Adolescence, 44,* 55–68.

Barsade, S. G., & O'Neill, O. A. (2014). What's love got to do with it? A longitudinal study of the culture of companionate love and employee and client outcomes in a long-term care setting. *Administrative Science Quarterly, 59,* 551–598.

Bartlett, C. P., Prot, S., Anderson, C. A., & Gentile, D. A. (2017). An empirical examination of the strength differential hypothesis in cyberbullying behavior. *Psychology of Violence, 7,* 22–32.

Bass, S., Shields, M. K., & Behrman, R. E. (2004). Children, families, and foster care: Analysis and recommendations. *The Future of Children, 14,* 5–30.

Battin, M., van der Heide, A., Ganzini, L., van der Wal, G., & Onwuteaka-Philipsen, B. (2007). Legal physician-assisted dying in Oregon and the Netherlands: Evidence concerning the impact on patients in "vulnerable" groups. *Journal of Medical Ethics, 33,* 591–597.

Bauer, P. J. (2007). Recall in infancy: A neuro-developmental account. *Current Directions in Psychological Science, 16,* 142–146.

Baulac, S., Lu, H., Strahle, J., Yang, T., Goldberg, M., Shen, J., &… Xia, W. (2009). Increased DJ-1 expression under oxidative stress and in Alzheimer's disease brains. *Molecular Neurodegeneration, 4,* 27–37.

Bauld, R., & Brown, R. (2009). Stress, psychological distress, psychosocial factors, menopause symptoms and physical health in women. *Maturitas, 62,* 160–165.

Baum, A. (1994). Behavioral, biological, and environmental interactions in disease processes.

In S. Blumenthal, K. Matthews, & S. Weiss (Eds.), *New research frontiers in behavioral medicine: Proceedings of the National Conference* (pp. 61–70). Washington, DC: NIH Publications.

Baumrind, D. (1971). Current patterns of parental authority. *Developmental Psychology Monographs, 4*(1), 1–103.

Baumrind, D. (1980). New directions in socialization research. *Psychological Bulletin, 35,* 639–652.

Bayley, N. (1993). *Bayley scales of infant development. (BSID-II)* (2nd ed.). San Antonio, TX: The Psychological Corporation.

Bayley, N., & Oden, M. (1955). The maintenance of intellectual ability in gifted adults. *Journal of Gerontology, 10,* 91–107.

Beale, E. A., Baile, W. F., & Aaron, J. (2005). Silence is not golden: Communicating with children dying from cancer. *Journal of Clinical Oncology, 23,* 3629–3631.

Beals, K., Impett, E., & Peplau, L. (2002). Lesbians in love: Why some relationships endure and others end. *Journal of Lesbian Studies, 6,* 53–63.

Beard, V. R., & Burger, W. C. (2017). Change and innovation in the funeral industry: A typology of motivations. *Omega: Journal of Death and Dying, 75,* 47–68.

Bearman, P., & Bruckner, H. (2004). *Study on teenage virginity pledge.* Paper presented at meeting of the National STD Prevention Conference, Philadelphia, PA.

Beck, M. (2012, June 5). Hormone use benefits may trump risks; age matters. *Wall Street Journal,* pp. D1, D2.

Becker, B., & Luthar, S. (2007, March). Peer-perceived admiration and social preference: Contextual correlates of positive peer regard among suburban and urban adolescents. *Journal of Research on Adolescence, 17,* 117–144.

Becker, G., Beyene, Y., & Newsom, E. (2003). Creating continuity through mutual assistance: Intergenerational reciprocity in four ethnic groups. *Journals of Gerontology: Series B: Psychological Sciences & Social Sciences, 58B,* S151–S159.

Becker, T. E., Kernan, M. C., Clark, K. D., & Klein, H. J. (2018). Dual commitments to organizations and professions: Different motivational pathways to productivity. *Journal of Management, 44*(3), 1202–1225.

Beckman, M. (2004, July 30). Neuroscience: Crime, culpability, and the adolescent brain. *Science, 305,* 596–599.

Begley, D. (2018). Deliver, then depart. Accessed online, 10/1/18; http://www.sharonlbegley.com/deliver-then-depart

Beilby, J. M., Byrnes, M. L., & Young, K. N. (2012). The experiences of living with a sibling who stutters: A preliminary study. *Journal of Fluency Disorders, 37,* 135–148.

Beisert, M., Zmyj, N., Liepelt, R., Jung, F., Prinz, W., & Daum, M. M. (2012). Rethinking "rational imitation" in 14-month-old infants: A perceptual distraction approach. *Plos ONE, 7*(3), Accessed online, 7/9/12; http://www.plosone.org/article/info%3Adoi%2F10.1371%2Fjournal.pone.0032563

Beitel, M., Bogus, S., Hutz, A., Green, D., Cecero, J. J., & Barry, D. T. (2014). Stillness and motion: An empirical investigation of mindfulness and self-actualization. *Person-Centered and Experiential Psychotherapies, 13,* 187–202.

Bekendam, M. T., Kop, W. J., Barzilay, S., Widdershoven, J. W., Aarnoudse, W., Denollet, J., & Mommersteeg, P. M. C. (2018). The predictive value of positive affect and Type D personality for adverse cardiovascular clinical outcomes in patients with non-obstructive coronary artery disease. *Journal of Psychosomatic Research, 104,* 108–114.

Belcher, J. R. (2003). Stepparenting: Creating and recreating families in America today. *Journal of Nervous & Mental Disease, 191,* 837–838.

Belkin, L. (1999, July 25). Getting the girl. *The New York Times Magazine,* pp. 26–35.

Belkin, L. (2004, September 12). The lessons of Classroom 506: What happens when a boy with cerebral palsy goes to kindergarten like all the other kids. *The New York Times Magazine*, pp. 41–49.

Bell, A., & Weinberg, M. S. (1978). *Homosexuality: A study of diversities among men and women.* New York, NY: Simon & Schuster.

Bell, T., & Romano, E. (2012). Opinions about child corporal punishment and influencing factors. *Journal of Interpersonal Violence, 27*, 2208–2229.

Belsky, J. (2006). Early child care and early child development: Major findings from the NICHD Study of Early Child Care. *European Journal of Developmental Psychology, 3*, 95–110.

Belsky, J. (2009). Classroom composition, childcare history and social development: Are childcare effects disappearing or spreading? *Social Development, 18*, 230–238.

Belsky, J., Vandell, D. L., Burchinal, M., Clarke-Stewart, A. K., McCartney, K., & Owen, M. T. (2007). Are there long-term effects of early child care? *Child Development, 78*, 188–193.

Beltz, A. M., Corley, R. P., Bricker, J. B., Wadsworth, S. J., & Berenbaum, S. A. (2014). Modeling pubertal timing and tempo and examining links to behavior problems. *Developmental Psychology, 50*, 2715–2726.

Bem, S. (1987). Gender schema theory and its implications for child development: Raising gender-aschematic children in a gender-schematic society. In M. R. Walsh (Ed.), *The psychology of women: Ongoing debates.* New Haven, CT: Yale University Press.

Benelli, B., Belacchi, C., Gini, G., & Lucangeli, D. (2006, February). "To define means to say what you know about things": The development of definitional skills as metalinguistic acquisition. *Journal of Child Language, 33*, 71–97.

Benenson, J. F., & Apostoleris, N. H. (1993, March). *Gender differences in group interaction in early childhood.* Paper presented at the biennial meeting of the Society for Research in Child Development, New Orleans, LA.

Bengtson, V. L., Acock, A. C., Allen, K. R., & Dilworth-Anderson, P. (Eds.). (2004). *Sourcebook of family theory and research.* Thousand Oaks, CA: Sage Publications.

Benjuya, N., Melzer, I., & Kaplanski, J. (2004). Aging-induced shifts from a reliance on sensory input to muscle cocontraction during balanced standing. *Journal of Gerontology: Series A: Biological Sciences and Medical Sciences, 59*, 166–171.

Bennani, L., Allali, F., Rostom, S., Hmamouchi, I., Khazzani, H., El Mansouri, L., & … Hajjaj-Hassouni, N. (2009). Relationship between historical height loss and vertebral fractures in postmenopausal women. *Clinical Rheumatology, 28*, 1283–1289.

Benner, A. D., Wang, Y., Shen, Y., Boyle, A. E., Polk, R., & Cheng, Y.-P. (2018). Racial/ethnic discrimination and well-being during adolescence: A meta-analytic review. *American Psychologist, 73*(7), 855–883.

Benner, A. D., & Wang, Y. (2017). Racial/ethnic discrimination and adolescents' well-being: The role of cross-ethnic friendships and friends' experiences of discrimination. *Child Development, 88*, 493–504.

Bennett, J. (2008, September 15). It's not just white girls. *Newsweek*, p. 96.

Ben-Noam, S. (2018). Cracking the intrapsychic "glass ceiling" for women in leadership: Therapeutic interventions. *Psychoanalytic Inquiry, 38*(4), 299–311.

Benoit, A., Lacourse, E., & Claes, M. (2014). Pubertal timing and depressive symptoms in late adolescence: The moderating role of individual, peer, and parental factors. *Development and Psychopathology, 25*, 455–471.

Benson, E. (2003, March). Goo, gaa, grr? *Monitor on Psychology*, pp. 50–51.

Benson, H., and Scribner, W. P. (2011). *Relaxation revolution: The science and genetics of mind body healing.* New York: Simon & Schuster.

Benson, S., & Proctor, W. (2011). *Relaxation revolution: The science and genetics of mind body healing.* New York, NY: Scribner.

Benton, S. A., Robertson, J. M., Tseng, W.-C., Newton, F. B., & Benton, S. L. (2003). Changes in counseling center client problems across 13 years. *Professional Psychology: Research and Practice, 34*, 66–72.

Bentz, W. E. (2015). Hospital stay for healthy newborn infants. *Pediatrics.* Accessed online, 10/25/17; www.pediatrics.org/cgi/doi/10.1542/peds.2015-0699

Berenson, P. (2005). *Understand and treat alcoholism.* New York, NY: Basic Books.

Bergelson, E., & Swingley, D. (2012). At 6-9 months, human infants know the meanings of many common nouns. *PNAS Proceedings of the National Academy of Sciences of the United States of America, 109*, 3253–3258.

Berger, L. (2000, April 11). What children do when home and alone. *The New York Times*, p. F8.

Berger, L. M., Hill, J., & Waldfogel, J. (2005). Maternity leave, early maternal employment and child health and development in the US. *Economic Journal, 115*(501), F29–F47.

Berger, S. E., Chin, B., Basra, S., & Kim, H. (2015). Step by step: A microgenetic study of the development of strategy choice in infancy. *British Journal of Developmental Psychology, 33*, 106–122.

Bergman, A., Blom, I., & Polyak, D. (2012). Attachment and separation-individuation: Two ways of looking at the mother/infant relationship. In S. Akhtar (Ed.), *The mother and her child: Clinical aspects of attachment, separation, and loss* (pp. 55–68). Lanham, MD: Jason Aronson.

Bergman, A., Blom, I., Polyak, D., & Mayers, L. (2015). Attachment and separation–individuation: Two ways of looking at the mother–infant relationship. *International Forum of Psychoanalysis, 24*, 16–21.

Bergmann, R. L., Bergman, K. E., & Dudenhausen, J. W. (2008). Undernutrition and growth restriction in pregnancy. *Nestle Nutritional Workshop Series; Pediatrics Program, 61*, 103–121.

Bergstrom, M. (2017). 'I could've had a better life': Reflective life reviews told by late-middle-aged and older women and men with ongoing long-term alcohol problems. *NAT Nordisk Alkohol & Narkotikatidskrift, 34*, 6–17.

Bergstrom, M. J., & Holmes, M. E. (2000). Lay theories of successful aging after the death of a spouse: A network text analysis of bereavement advice. *Health Communication, 12*, 377–406.

Berkman, R. (Ed.). (2006). *Handbook of social work in health and aging.* New York, NY: Oxford University Press.

Berko, J. (1958). The child's learning of English morphology. *Word, 14*, 150–177.

Berlin, L., Cassidy, J., & Appleyard, K. (2008). The influence of early attachments on other relationships. In J. Cassidy & P. R. Shaver (Eds.), *Handbook of attachment: Theory, research, and clinical applications* (2nd ed., pp. 295–316). New York, NY: Guilford Press.

Bernard, J. (1982). *The future of marriage.* New Haven, CT: Yale University Press.

Bernard, M., Strasser, F., Gamondi, C., Braunschweig, G., Forster, M., Kaspers-Elekes, K., … Borasio, G. D. (2017). Relationship between spirituality, meaning in life, psychological distress, wish for hastened death, and their influence on quality of life in palliative care patients. *Journal of Pain and Symptom Management, 54*(4), 514–522.

Bernier, A., & Meins, E. (2008). A threshold approach to understanding the origins of attachment disorganization. *Developmental Psychology, 44*, 969–982.

Bernstein, D. M., Coolin, A., Fischer, A. L., Thornton, W. L., & Sommerville, J. A. (2017). False-belief reasoning from 3 to 92 years of age. *PLoS ONE, 12*(9).

Bernstein, E. (2010, April 20). Honey, do you have to … *Wall Street Journal*, pp. D1, D3.

Bernstein, N. (2004, March 7). Behind fall in pregnancy, a new teenage culture of restraint. *The New York Times*, pp. 1, 20.

Berry, G. L. (2003). Developing children and multicultural attitudes: The systemic psychosocial influences of television portrayals in a multimedia society. *Cultural Diversity and Ethnic Minority Psychology, 9*, 360–366.

Berscheid, E. (1985). Interpersonal attraction. In G. Lindzey & E. Aronson (Eds.), *Handbook of social psychology* (3rd ed., pp. 413–484). New York, NY: Random House.

Berscheid, E., & Walster, E. (1974). Physical attractiveness. In G. Lindzey & E. Aronson (Eds.), *Handbook of social psychology* (3rd ed.). New York, NY: Random House.

Bertera, E. M., & Crewe, S. (2013). Parenthood in the twenty-first century: African American grandparents as surrogate parents. *Journal of Human Behavior in the Social Environment, 23*, 178–192.

Besage, V. E. (2006). *Understanding girls' friendships, fights and feuds: A practical approach to girls' bullying.* Maidenhead, Berkshire: Open University Press/McGraw-Hill Education.

Bešić, E., Paleczek, L., Krammer, M., & Gasteiger-Klicpera, B. (2017). Inclusive practices at the teacher and class level: The experts' view. *European Journal of Special Needs Education, 32*, 329–345.

Best, P., Manktelow, R., & Taylor, B. (2014). Online communication, social media and adolescent well-being: A systematic narrative review. *Children and Youth Services Review, 41*, 27–36.

Bhagat, N., Laskar, A., & Sharma, N. (2012). Women's perception about sex selection in an urban slum in Delhi. *Journal of Reproductive and Infant Psychology, 30*, 92–104.

Bhargava, P. (2014). "I have a family, therefore I am": Children's understanding of self and others. In N. Chaudhary, S. Anandalakshmy, & J. Valsiner (Eds.), *Cultural realities of being: Abstract ideas within everyday lives.* New York, NY: Routledge/Taylor & Francis Group.

Bibace, R. (2013). Challenges in Piaget's legacy. *Integrative Psychological & Behavioral Science, 47*, 167–175.

Biblarz, T. J., & Stacey, J. (2010). How does the gender of parents matter? *Journal of Marriage and Family, 72*, 3–22.

Biddle, B. J. (2001). *Social class, poverty, and education.* London, UK: Falmer Press.

Bielak, A. M., Cherbuin, N., Bunce, D., & Anstey, K. J. (2013). Intraindividual variability is a fundamental phenomenon of aging: Evidence from an 8-year longitudinal study across young, middle, and older adulthood. *Developmental Psychology.* Accessed online, 6/11/12; http://www.ncbi.nlm.nih.gov/pubmed/23586940

Bierman, K. L. (2004). *Peer rejection: Developmental processes and intervention strategies.* New York, NY: Guilford Press.

Bigelow, A. E., & Power, M. (2012). The effect of mother-infant skin-to-skin contact on infants' response to the Still Face Task from newborn to three months of age. *Infant Behavior & Development, 35*, 240–251.

Bionna, R. (2006). *Coping with stress in a changing world.* New York, NY: McGraw-Hill.

Bird, C. M., & Burgess, N. (2008). The hippocampus and memory: Insights from spatial processing. *Nature Reviews Neuroscience, 9*, 182–194.

Birney, D. P., & Sternberg, R. J. (2006). Intelligence and cognitive abilities as competencies in development. In E. Bialystok, & F. M. Craik (Eds.), *Lifespan cognition: Mechanisms of change.* New York, NY: Oxford University Press.

Biro, F., Striegel-Moore, R., Franko, D., Padgett, J., & Bean, J. (2006, October). Self-esteem in adolescent females. *Journal of Adolescent Health, 39*, 501–507.

Bisagno, E., & Morra, S. (2018). How do we learn to 'kill' in volleyball? The role of working memory capacity and expertise in volleyball motor learning. *Journal of Experimental Child Psychology, 167*, 128–145.

Bischof-Köhler, D. (2012). Empathy and self-recognition in phylogenetic and ontogenetic perspective. *Emotion Review, 4*, 40–48.

Bishop, D. I., Meyer, B., Schmidt, T., & Gray, B. (2009). Differential investment behavior between grandparents and grandchildren: The role of paternity uncertainty. *Evolutionary Psychology, 7*, 66–77.

Bishop, D. V. M., & Leonard, L. B. (Eds.). (2001). *Speech and language impairments in children: Causes, characteristics, intervention and outcome*. Philadelphia, PA: Psychology Press.

Bishop, J. (2006, April). Euthanasia, efficiency, and the historical distinction between killing a patient and allowing a patient to die. *Journal of Medical Ethics, 32*, 220–224.

Bjorklund, D. (2006). Mother knows best: Epigenetic inheritance, maternal effects, and the evolution of human intelligence. *Developmental Review, 26*, 213–242.

Bjorklund, D. F. (2018). A metatheory for cognitive development (or "Piaget is dead" revisited). *Child Development*. Accessed online, 3/25/19; https://doi-org.silk.library.umass.edu/10.1111/cdev.13019

Black, K. (2002). Associations between adolescent–mother and adolescent–best friend interactions. *Adolescence, 37*, 235–253.

Blackburn, E., & Epel, E. (2017). *The telomere effect*. New York: Grand Central Publishing.

Blair, P., Sidebotham, P., Berry, P., Evans, M., & Fleming, P. (2006). Major epidemiological changes in sudden infant death syndrome: A 20-year population-based study in the UK. *Lancet, 367*, 314–319.

Blake, G., Velikonja, D., Pepper, V., Jilderda, I., & Georgiou, G. (2008). Evaluating an in-school injury prevention programme's effect on children's helmet wearing habits. *Brain Injury, 22*, 501–507.

Blakemore, J. (2003). Children's beliefs about violating gender norms: Boys shouldn't look like girls, and girls shouldn't act like boys. *Sex Roles, 48*, 411–419.

Blakemore, S. (2012). Imaging brain development: The adolescent brain. *Neuroimage, 61*, 397–406.

Bland, V. J., Lambie, I., & Best, C. (2018). Does childhood neglect contribute to violent behavior in adulthood? A review of possible links. *Clinical Psychology Review, 60*, 126–135.

Blankenstein, N. E., Schreuders, E., Peper, J. S., Crone, E. A., & van Duijvenvoorde, A. C. K. (2018). Individual differences in risk-taking tendencies modulate the neural processing of risky and ambiguous decision-making in adolescence. *NeuroImage, 172*, 663–673.

Blass, E. M., & Camp, C. A. (2015). The ontogeny of face recognition: Eye contact and sweet taste induce face preference in 9- and 12-week-old human infants. *Developmental Psychology, 37*, 762–774.

Blewitt, P., Rump, K., Shealy, S., & Cook, S. (2009). Shared book reading: When and how questions affect young children's word learning. *Journal of Educational Psychology, 101*, 294–304.

Blieszner, R. (2006). A lifetime of caring: Dimensions and dynamics in late-life close relationships. *Personal Relationships, 12*, 1–18.

Blom, E. H., Ho, T. C., Connolly, C. G., LeWinn, K. Z., Sacchet, M. D., Tymofiyeva, O., & … Yang, T. T. (2016). The neuroscience and context of adolescent depression. *Acta Paediatrica, 105*, 358–365.

Blomqvist, Y. T., Nyqvist, K. H., Rubertsson, C., & Funkquist, E. (2017). Parents need support to find ways to optimise their own sleep without seeing their preterm infant's sleeping patterns as a problem. *Acta Paediatrica, 106*, 223–228.

Bloom, C., & Lamkin, D. (2006). The Olympian struggle to remember the cranial nerves: Mnemonics and student success. *Teaching of Psychology, 33*, 128–129.

Blount, B. G. (1982). Culture and the language of socialization: Parental speech. In D. A. Wagner & H. W. Stevenson (Eds.), *Cultural perspectives on child development* (pp. 54–76). San Francisco, CA: Freeman.

Blumberg, M., Coleman, C., Gerth, A., & McMurray, B. (2013). Spatiotemporal structure of REM sleep twitching reveals developmental origins of motor synergies. *Current Biology, 232*, 100–109.

Blumenshine, P. M., Egerter, S. A., Libet, M. L., & Braveman, P. A. (2011). Father's education: An independent marker of risk for preterm birth. *Maternal and Child Health Journal, 15*, 60–67.

Blumenthal, S. (2000). Developmental aspects of violence and the institutional response. *Criminal Behaviour & Mental Health, 10*, 185–198.

Bober, S., Humphry, R., & Carswell, H. (2001). Toddlers' persistence in the emerging occupations of functional play and self-feeding. *American Journal of Occupational Therapy, 55*, 369–376.

Bodell, L. P., Joiner, T. E., & Ialongo, N. S. (2012). Longitudinal association between childhood impulsivity and bulimic symptoms in African American adolescent girls. *Journal of Consulting and Clinical Psychology, 80*, 313–316.

Bodell, L. P., Wildes, J. E., Cheng, Y., Goldschmidt, A. B., Keenan, K., Hipwell, A. E., & Stepp, S. D. (2018). Associations between race and eating disorder symptom trajectories in Black and White girls. *Journal of Abnormal Child Psychology, 46*(3), 625–638.

Bodner, E., Bergman, Y. S., & Cohen-Fridel, S. (2012). Different dimensions of ageist attitudes among men and women: A multigenerational perspective. *International Psychogeriatrics, 24*(6), 895–901. doi:10.1017/S1041610211002936

Boerner, K., Brennan, M., Horowitz, A., & Reinhardt, J. (2010). Tackling vision-related disability in old age: An application of the life-span theory of control to narrative data. *Journals of Gerontology: Series B: Psychological Sciences and Social Sciences, 65B*, 22–31.

Boerner, K., Mancini, A. D., & Bonanno, G. (2013). On the nature and prevalence of uncomplicated and complicated patterns of grief. In M. Stroebe, H. Schut, & J. van den Bout (Eds.), *Complicated grief: Scientific foundations for health care professionals*. (pp. 55–67). New York: Routledge/Taylor & Francis Group.

Boerner, K., Stroebe, M., Schut, H., & Wortman, C.B. (2015). *Theories of grief and bereavement. Encyclopedia of geronpsychology*. New York: Springer.

Boerner, K., Wortman, C. B., & Bonanno, G. A. (2005). Resilient or at risk? A 4-year study of older adults who initially showed high or low distress following conjugal loss. *Journals of Gerontology: Series B, Psychological Sciences and Social Sciences, 60*, P67–P73.

Bogar, S., Szabo, A., Woodruff, S., & Johnson, S. (2017). Urban youth knowledge and attitudes regarding lead poisoning. *Journal of Community Health: The Publication for Health Promotion and Disease Prevention, 42*(6), 1255–1266.

Bogle, K. A. (2008). "Hooking up": What educators need to know. *Chronicle of Higher Education*, p. A32.

Bolhuis, J. J., Tattersal, I., Chomsky, N., & Berwick, R. C. (2014). How could language have evolved? *Plos Biology, 12*, 88–95.

Bonanno, G. A. (2009). *The other side of sadness*. New York, NY: Basic Books.

Bonanno, G. A., Wortman, C. B., Lehman, D. R., Tweed, R. G., Haring, M., Sonnega, J., Nesse, R. M. (2002). Resilience to loss and chronic grief: A prospective study from preloss to 18-months postloss. *Journal of Personality and Social Psychology, 83*, 1150–1164.

Bonavita, S., & Tedeschi, G. (2017). Neural structure, connectivity, and cognition changes associated to physical exercise. In R. R. Watson (Ed.), *Physical activity and the aging brain: Effects of exercise on neurological function*. San Diego, CA: Elsevier Academic Press.

Bonifacci, P., Storti, M., Tobia, V., & Suardi, A. (2016). Specific learning disorders: A look inside children's and parents' psychological well-being and relationships. *Journal of Learning Disabilities, 49*, 532–545.

Bonoti, F., Leondari, A., & Mastora, A. (2013). Exploring children's understanding of death: Through drawings and the Death Concept Questionnaire. *Death Studies, 37*, 47–60.

Booker, J. A., & Dunsmore, J. C. (2016). Profiles of wisdom among emerging adults: Associations with empathy, gratitude, and forgiveness. *Journal of Positive Psychology, 11*, 315–325.

Bookheimer, S. Y., Strojwas, M. H., Cohen, M. S., Saunders, A. M., Pericak-Vance, M. A., Mazziotta, J. C., & Small, G. W. (2000). Patterns of brain activation in people at risk for Alzheimer's disease. *New England Journal of Medicine, 343*(7), 450–456. doi:10.1056/NEJM200008173430701

Bookwala, J. (2012). Marriage and other partnered relationships in middle and late adulthood. In R. Blieszner & V. H. Bedford (Eds.), *Handbook of families and aging* (2nd ed.) (pp. 91–123). Santa Barbara, CA: Praeger/ABC-CLIO.

Bookwala, J. (2016). *Couple relationships in the middle and later years: Their nature, complexity, and role in health and illness*. Washington, DC: American Psychological Association.

Booth, C., Kelly, J., & Spieker, S. (2003). Toddlers' attachment security to child-care providers: The Safe and Secure Scale. *Early Education & Development, 14*, 83–100.

Bor, W., & Bor, W. (2004). Prevention and treatment of childhood and adolescent aggression and antisocial behavior: A selective review. *Australian & New Zealand Journal of Psychiatry, 38*, 373–380.

Borchard, D. C., & Donohoe, P. A. (2008). *The joy of retirement: Finding happiness, freedom, and the life you've always wanted*. New York, NY: AMACOM.

Bornstein, M. H. (2012). Cultural approaches to parenting. *Parenting: Science and Practice, 12*(2–3), 212–221.

Bornstein, M. H., Cote, L., & Maital, S. (2004). Cross-linguistic analysis of vocabulary in young children: Spanish, Dutch, French, Hebrew, Italian, Korean, and American English. *Child Development, 75*, 1115–1139.

Bornstein, M. H., & Lamb, M. E. (1992). *Development in infancy: An introduction*. New York, NY: McGraw-Hill.

Bornstein, M. H., Suwalsky, J. D., & Breakstone, D. A. (2012). Emotional relationships between mothers and infants: Knowns, unknowns, and unknown unknowns. *Development and Psychopathology, 24*, 113–123.

Bornstein, M. H., Tamis-LeMonda, C. S., Hahn, C., & Haynes, O. M. (2008). Maternal responsiveness to young children at three ages: Longitudinal analysis of a multidimensional, modular, and specific parenting construct. *Developmental Psychology, 44*, 867–874.

Börsch-supan, A., Bristle, J., Brugiavini, A., & Jusot, F. (2019). *Health and socio-economic status over the life course: First results from Share Waves 6 and 7*. Berlin, Germany: De Gruyter Oldenbourg.

Borse, N. N., Gilchrist, J., Dellinger, A. M., Rudd, R. A., Ballesteros, M. F., & Sleet, D. A. (2008). *CDC childhood injury report: Patterns of unintentional injuries among 0–19 year olds in the United States, 2000–2006*. Atlanta, GA: Centers for Disease Control and Prevention, National Center for Injury Prevention and Control.

Bos, A. F. (2013). Bayley-II or Bayley-III: What do the scores tell us? *Developmental Medicine & Child Neurology, 55*, 978–979.

Bos, C. S., & Vaughn, S. S. (2005). *Strategies for teaching students with learning and behavior problems* (6th ed.). Boston, MA: Allyn & Bacon.

Bos, H. W., Knox, J. R., van Rijn-van Gelderen, L., & Gartrell, N. K. (2016). Same-sex and different-sex parent households and child health outcomes: Findings from the National Survey of Children's Health. *Journal of Developmental and Behavioral Pediatrics, 37*, 179–187.

Bosco, F. M., Angeleri, R., Colle, L., Sacco, K., & Bara, B. G. (2013). Communicative abilities in children: An assessment through different phenomena and expressive means. *Journal of Child Language, 40*, 741–778.

Bouchard, G., Lee, C. M., Asgary, V. & Pelletier, L. (2007). Fathers' motivation for involvement with their children: A self-determination theory perspective. *Fathering, 5*, 25–41.

Bouchard, T. J., Jr., Lykken, D. T., McGue, M., Segal, N. L., & Tellegen, A. (1990, October 12). Sources of human psychological differences: The Minnesota study of twins reared apart. *Science, 250*, 223–228.

Bouchard, T. J., Jr., & McGue, M. (1981). Familial studies of intelligence: A review. *Science, 212*, 1055–1059.

Bowen, C. E., & Skirbekk, V. (2013). National stereotypes of older people's competence are related to older adults' participation in paid and volunteer work. *Journals of Gerontology: Series B: Psychological Sciences and Social Sciences, 68B*, 974–983.

Bowen, F. (2013). Asthma education and health outcomes of children aged 8 to 12 years. *Clinical Nursing Research, 22*, 172–185.

Bowen, G. L., & Jensen, T. M. (2017). Late-life divorce and postdivorce adult subjective well-being. *Journal of Family Issues, 38*, 1363–1388.

Bower, T. G. R. (1977). *A primer of infant development.* San Francisco, CA: Freeman.

Bowers, A. J., Sprott, R., & Taff, S. A. (2013). Do we know who will drop out? A review of the predictors of dropping out of high school: Precision, sensitivity, and specificity. *The High School Journal, 96*, 77–100.

Bowlby, J. (1951). Maternal care and mental health. *Bulletin of the World Health Organization, 3*, 355–534.

Boyatzis, C. J. (2013). The nature and functions of religion and spirituality in children. In K. I. Pargament, J. J. Exline, & J. W. Jones (Eds.), *APA handbook of psychology, religion, and spirituality (Vol 1): Context, theory, and research.* Washington, DC: American Psychological Association.

Boyatzis, C. J., Mallis, M., & Leon, I. (1999). Effects of game type of children's gender-based peer preferences: A naturalistic observational study. *Sex Roles, 40*, 93–105.

Bracken, B., & Brown, E. (2006, June). Behavioral identification and assessment of gifted and talented students. *Journal of Psychoeducational Assessment, 24*, 112–122.

Bracken, B., & Lamprecht, M. (2003). Positive self-concept: An equal opportunity construct. *School Psychology Quarterly, 18*, 103–121.

Braden, B. B., Dassel, K. B., Bimonte-Nelson, H. A., O'Rourke, H. P., Connor, D. J., Moorhous, S., & ... Baxter, L. C. (2017). Sex and post-menopause hormone therapy effects on hippocampal volume and verbal memory. *Aging, Neuropsychology, and Cognition, 24*, 227–246.

Bradshaw, M., & Ellison, C. (2008). Do genetic factors influence religious life? Findings from a behavior genetic analysis of twin siblings. *Journal for the Scientific Study of Religion, 47*, 529–544.

Brady, S. A. (2011). Efficacy of phonics teaching for reading outcomes: Indications from post-NRP research. In S. A. Brady, D. Braze, & C. A. Fowler (Eds.), *Explaining individual differences in reading: Theory and evidence* (pp. 69–96). New York, NY: Psychology Press.

Brainerd, C. (2003). Jean Piaget, learning research, and American education. In B. Zimmerman (Ed.), *Educational psychology: A century of contributions* (pp. 251–287). Mahwah, NJ: Lawrence Erlbaum.

Brandmaier, A. M., Ram, N., Wagner, G. G., & Gerstorf, D. (2017). Terminal decline in well-being: The role of multi-indicator constellations of physical health and psychosocial correlates. *Developmental Psychology, 53*, 996–1012.

Brandone, A. C., Cimpian, A., Leslie, S., & Gelman, S. A. (2012). Do lions have manes? For children, generics are about kinds rather than quantities. *Child Development, 83*, 423–433.

Branje, S. (2018). Development of parent–adolescent relationships: Conflict interactions as a mechanism of change. *Child Development Perspectives, 12*(3).

Branum, A. (2006). Teen maternal age and very preterm birth of twins. *Maternal & Child Health Journal, 10*, 229–233.

Braun, K. L., Pietsch, J. H., & Blanchette, P. L. (Eds.). (2000). *Cultural issues in end-of-life decision making.* Thousand Oaks, CA: Sage Publications.

Braun, S. I., Kim, Y., Jetton, A. E., Kang, M., & Morgan, D. W. (2017). Sedentary behavior, physical activity, and bone health in postmenopausal women. *Journal of Aging and Physical Activity, 25*, 173–181.

Braun, S. S., & Davidson, A. J. (2016). Gender (non)conformity in middle childhood: A mixed methods approach to understanding gender-typed behavior, friendship, and peer preference. *Sex Roles.* Accessed online, 8/9/17; https://link.springer.com/article/10.1007/s11199-016-0693-z

Braun, S., & Kavšek, M. (2018). Infants perceive two-dimensional shape from horizontal disparity. *Infant Behavior & Development, 52*, 140–145.

Braungart-Rieker, J. M., Zentall, S., Lickenbrock, D. M., Ekas, N. V., Oshio, T., & Planalp, E. (2015). Attachment in the making: Mother and father sensitivity and infants' responses during the still-face paradigm. *Journal of Experimental Child Psychology, 125*, 63–84.

Bray, G. A. (2008). Is new hope on the horizon for obesity? *The Lancet, 372*, 1859–1860.

Brazelton, T. B., & Sparrow, J. D. (2003). *Discipline: The Brazelton way.* New York, NY: Perseus.

Bredesen, D. (2009). Neurodegeneration in Alzheimer's disease: Caspases and synaptic element interdependence. *Molecular Neurodegeneration, 4*, 52–59.

Breheny, M., & Stephens, C. (2003). Healthy living and keeping busy: A discourse analysis of mid-aged women's attributions for menopausal experience. *Journal of Language & Social Psychology, 22*, 169–189.

Bremner, G., & Fogel, A. (Eds.). (2004). *Blackwell handbook of infant development.* Malden, MA: Blackwell Publishers.

Bremner, J. G., Slater, A. M., & Johnson, S. P. (2015). Perception of object persistence: The origins of object permanence in infancy. *Child Development Perspectives, 9*, 7–13.

Briley, D. A., & Tucker-Drob, E. M. (2017). Comparing the developmental genetics of cognition and personality over the life span. *Journal of Personality, 85*, 51–64.

Brinker, J. K. (2013). Rumination and reminiscence in older adults: Implications for clinical practice. *European Journal of Ageing.* Accessed online, 6/13/13; http://link.springer.com/article/10.1007/s10433-013-0271-y#page-1

Brinkman, B. G., Rabenstein, K. L., Rosén, L. A., & Zimmerman, T. S. (2014). Children's gender identity development: The dynamic negotiation process between conformity and authenticity. *Youth & Society, 46*, 835–852.

Brito, N., & Barr, R. (2014). Flexible memory retrieval in bilingual 6-month-old infants. *Developmental Psychobiology, 56*, 1156–1163.

Broadbent, J., & Papadopoulos, T. (2013). Bridging the digital divide—An Australian story. *Behaviour & Information Technology, 32*, 4–13.

Broce, I. J., Tan, C. H., Fan, C. C., Jansen, I., Savage, J. E., Witoelar, A., ... Desikan, R. S. (2018). Dissecting the genetic relationship between cardiovascular risk factors and Alzheimer's disease. *Acta Neuropathologica.* doi:10.1007/s00401-018-1928-6

Broesch, T. L., & Bryant, G. A. (2015). Prosody in infant-directed speech is similar across Western and traditional cultures. *Journal of Cognition and Development, 16*, 31–43.

Bronfenbrenner, U. (2000). Ecological theory. In A. Kazdin (Ed.), *Encyclopedia of psychology* (pp. 129–133). Washington, DC: American Psychological Association/Oxford University Press.

Bronfenbrenner, U. (2002). Preparing a world for the infant in the twenty-first century: The research challenge. In J. Gomes-Pedro, J. Nugent, J. Young, & T. Brazelton (Eds.), *The infant and family in the twenty-first century* (pp. 45–52). New York, NY: Brunner-Routledge.

Brotanek, J., Gosz, J., Weitzman, M., & Flores, G. (2007). Iron deficiency in early childhood in the United States: Risk factors and racial/ethnic disparities. *Pediatrics, 120*, 568–575.

Brouwer, R. M., van Soelen, I. C., Swagerman, S. C., Schnack, H. G., Ehli, E. A., Kahn, R. S., & ... Boomsma, D. I. (2014). Genetic associations between intelligence and cortical thickness emerge at the start of puberty. *Human Brain Mapping, 35*, 88–97.

Brown, B. B., & Klute, C. (2003). Friendships, cliques, and crowds. In G. R. Adams & M. D. Berzonsky (Eds.), *Blackwell handbook of adolescence* (pp. 330–348). Malden, MA: Blackwell Publishing.

Brown, D. L., Jewell, J. D., Stevens, A. L., Crawford, J. D., & Thompson, R. (2012). Suicidal risk in adolescent residential treatment: Being female is more important than a depression diagnosis. *Journal of Child and Family Studies, 21*, 359–367.

Brown, E. L., & Bull, R. (2007). Can task modifications influence children's performance on false belief tasks? *European Journal of Developmental Psychology, 4*, 273–292.

Brown, R., & Fraser, C. (1963). The acquisition syntax. In C. N. Cofer & B. Musgrave (Eds.), *Verbal behavior and learning: Problems and processes* (pp. 158–201). New York, NY: McGraw-Hill.

Brown, S., & Lin, I-Fen. (2012, March). *The gray divorce revolution: Rising divorce among middle-aged and older adults, 1990–2009* (Working Paper Series WP-12-04). Bowling Green, OH: National Center for Family & Marriage Research, Bowling Green State University.

Brown, S. A. (2004). Measuring youth outcomes from alcohol and drug treatment. *Addiction, 99*, 38–46.

Brown, S. L. & Wright, M. R. (2017). Marriage, cohabitation, and divorce in later life. *Innovation in Aging, 1*(2).

Brown, W. M., Hines, M., & Fane, B. A. (2002). Masculinized finger length patterns in human males and females with congenital adrenal hyperplasia. *Hormones and Behavior, 42*, 380–386.

Browne, C. (2010). Review of "Asian American elders in the twenty-first century: Key indicators of well-being." *Journal of Women & Aging, 22*, 151–153.

Browne, K. (2006, March). Evolved sex differences and occupational segregation. *Journal of Organizational Behavior, 27*, 143–162.

Brownell, C. A. (2016). Prosocial behavior in infancy: The role of socialization. *Child Development Perspectives, 10*, 222–227.

Brownell, C., Nichols, S., Svetlova, M., Zerwas, S., & Ramani, G. (2010). The head bone's connected to the neck bone: When do toddlers represent their own body topography? *Child Development, 81*, 797–810.

Bruck, M., & Ceci, S. J. (2012). Forensic developmental psychology in the courtroom. In D. Faust (Ed.), *Coping with psychiatric and psychological testimony: Based on the original work by Jay Ziskin., 6th ed.* (pp. 723–736). New York, NY: Oxford University Press.

Bruckner, P. (2013). *Has marriage for love failed?* Cambridge, UK: Polity.

Brueggemann, A., & Gable, S. (2018). Preschoolers' selective sustained attention and numeracy skills and knowledge. *Journal of Experimental Child Psychology, 171*, 138–147.

Brugman, G. (2006). *Wisdom and aging.* Amsterdam, the Netherlands: Elsevier.

Bruskas, D. (2008). Children in foster care: A vulnerable population at risk. *Journal of Child and Adolescent Psychiatric Nursing, 21*, 70–77.

Bryant, C. D. (Ed.). (2003). *Handbook of death and dying.* Thousand Oaks, CA: Sage Publications.

Bucci, D., & Stanton, M. (2017). The ontogeny of learning and memory. *Neurobiology of Learning and Memory, 143*, 88–97.

Buchmann, C., & DiPrete, T. (2006, August). The growing female advantage in college completion: The role of family background and academic achievement. *American Sociological Review, 7*, 515–541.

Buckley, J., Letukas, L., & Wildavsky, B. (2018). *Measuring success: Testing, grades, and the future of college admissions*. Baltimore, MD: Johns Hopkins University Press.

Bukowski, W. M., Laursen, B., & Rubin, K. H. (Eds.). (2018). *Handbook of peer interactions, relationships, and groups* (2nd ed.). New York, NY: Guilford Press.

Bumpus, M. F., Crouter, A. C., & McHale, S. M. (2001). Parental autonomy granting during adolescence: Exploring gender differences in context. *Developmental Psychology, 37*, 163–173.

Buon, M., Habib, M., & Frey, D. (2017). Moral development: Conflicts and compromises. In J. A. Sommerville & J. Decety (Eds.), *Social cognition: Development across the life span*. New York: Routledge/Taylor & Francis Group.

Burakevych, N., Mckinlay, C. D., Alsweiler, J. M., Wouldes, T. A., & Harding, J. E. (2017). Bayley-III motor scale and neurological examination at 2 years do not predict motor skills at 4.5 years. *Developmental Medicine & Child Neurology, 59*, 216–223.

Burbach, J., & van der Zwaag, B. (2009). Contact in the genetics of autism and schizophrenia. *Trends in Neurosciences, 32*, 69–72. Available online at http://search.ebscohost.com

Bureau of Labor Statistics. (2018). American time use survey summary. Accessed online, 10/27/18; https://www.bls.gov/news.release/atus.nr0.htm

Bureau of Labor Statistics. (2018). Employment characteristics of families—2017. Accessed online, 3/25/19; https://www.bls.gov/news.release/pdf/famee.pdf

Burgaleta, M., Baus, C., Díaz, B., & Sebastián-Gallés, N. (2013). Brain structure is related to speech perception abilities in bilinguals. *Brain Structure & Function*. Accessed online, 6/6/13; http://www.ncbi.nlm.nih.gov/pubmed/23686398

Burgers, C. (2016). Conceptualizing change in communication through metaphor. *Journal of Communication, 66*, 250–265.

Burgess, R. L., & Huston, T. L. (Eds.). (1979). *Social exchanges in developing relationships*. New York, NY: Academic Press.

Burkle, C. M., Sharp, R. R., & Wijdicks, E. F. (2014). Why brain death is considered death and why there should be no confusion. *Neurology, 83*, 1464–1469.

Burnett-Wolle, S., & Godbey, G. (2007). Refining research on older adults' leisure: Implications of selection, optimization, and compensation and socioemotional selectivity theories. *Journal of Leisure Research, 39*, 498–513.

Burnham, M., Goodlin-Jones, B., & Gaylor, E. (2002). Nighttime sleep-wake patterns and self-soothing from birth to one year of age: A longitudinal intervention study. *Journal of Child Psychology & Psychiatry & Allied Disciplines, 43*, 713–725.

Burton, A., Haley, W., & Small, B. (2006, May). Bereavement after caregiving or unexpected death: Effects on elderly spouses. *Aging & Mental Health, 10*, 319–326.

Burton, L., Henninger, D., Hafetz, J., & Cofer, J. (2009). Aggression, gender-typical childhood play, and a prenatal hormonal index. *Social Behavior and Personality, 37*, 105–116.

Bushman, B. J., Gollwitzer, M., & Cruz, C. (2014). There is broad consensus: Media researchers agree that violent media increase aggression in children, and pediatricians and parents concur. *Psychology of Popular Media Culture*. Accessed online, 3/20/15; http://psycnet.apa.org/-psycinfo/2014-41977-001/

Buss, A. H. (2012). *Pathways to individuality: Evolution and development of personality traits*. Washington, DC: American Psychological Association.

Buss, D. M. (2003). *The evolution of desire: Strategies of human mating* (Rev. ed.). New York, NY: Basic Books.

Buss, D. M. (2006). The evolution of love. In R. J. Sternberg & K. Weis (Eds.), *The new psychology of love*. (pp. 65–86). New Haven, CT: Yale University Press.

Buss, D. M., Abbott, M., Angleitner, A., Asherian, A., Biaggio, A., Blanco-Villasenor, A., & … Yang, K-S. (1990). International preferences in selecting mates: A study of 37 cultures. *Journal of Cross-Cultural Psychology, 21*, 5–47.

Butler, R. J., Wilson, B. L., & Johnson, W. G. (2012). A modified measure of health care disparities applied to birth weight disparities and subsequent mortality. *Health Economics, 21*, 113–126.

Butler, R. N. (2002). The life review. *Journal of Geriatric Psychiatry, 35*, 7–10.

Butzer, B., & Campbell, L. (2008). Adult attachment, sexual satisfaction, and relationship satisfaction: A study of married couples. *Personal Relationships, 15*, 141–154.

Byrd, D., Katcher, M., Peppard, P., Durkin, M., & Remington, P. (2007). Infant mortality: Explaining black/white disparities in Wisconsin. *Maternal and Child Health Journal, 11*, 319–326.

Byrd-Craven, J., Auer, B. J., Granger, D. A., & Massey, A. R. (2012). The father-daughter dance: The relationship between father-daughter relationship quality and daughters' stress response. *Journal of Family Psychology, 26*, 87–94.

Byrne, A. (2000). Singular identities: Managing stigma, resisting voices. *Women's Studies Review, 7*, 13–24.

Byun, S., & Park, H. (2012). The academic success of East Asian American youth: The role of shadow education. *Sociology of Education, 85*, 40–60.

Cacciatore, J. (2010). The unique experiences of women and their families after the death of a baby. *Social Work in Health Care, 49*, 134–148.

Cacciatore, J., & Bushfield, S. (2007). Stillbirth: The mother's experience and implications for improving care. *Journal of Social Work in End-of-Life & Palliative Care, 3*, 59–79.

Caino, S., Kelmansky, D., Lejarraga, H., & Adamo, P. (2004). Short-term growth at adolescence in healthy girls. *Annals of Human Biology, 31*, 182–195.

Calhoun, F., & Warren, K. (2007). Fetal alcohol syndrome: Historical perspectives. *Neuroscience & Biobehavioral Reviews, 31*, 168–171.

Callaghan, B. L., Li, S., & Richardson, R. (2014). The elusive engram: What can infantile amnesia tell us about memory? *Trends in Neurosciences, 37*, 47–53.

Callahan, P. M., Hutchings, E. J., Kille, N. J., Chapman, J. M., & Terry, A. R. (2013). Positive allosteric modulator of alpha 7 nicotinic-acetylcholine receptors, PNU-120596 augments the effects of donepezil on learning and memory in aged rodents and non-human primates. *Neuropharmacology, 67*, 201–212.

Callister, L. C., Khalaf, I., Semenic, S., Kartchner, R., & Vehvilainen-Julkunen, K. (2003). The pain of childbirth: Perceptions of culturally diverse women. *Pain Management Nursing, 4*, 145–154.

Calvert, S. L., Kotler, J. A., Zehnder, S., & Shockey, E. (2003). Gender stereotyping in children's reports about educational and informational television programs. *Media Psychology, 5*, 139–162.

Calzada, E. J., Huang, K., Anicama, C., Fernandez, Y., & Brotman, L. (2012). Test of a cultural framework of parenting with Latino families of young children. *Cultural Diversity and Ethnic Minority Psychology, 18*, 285–296.

Camarota, S. A., & Zeigler, K. (2015, April 21). *Immigrant population to hit highest percentage ever in 8 years*. Washington, DC: Center for Immigration Studies

Campbell, A., Shirley, L., & Candy, J. (2004). A longitudinal study of gender-related cognition and behaviour. *Developmental Science, 7*, 1–9.

Campbell, O. M. R., Cegolon, L., Macleod, D., Benova, L. (2016). Length of stay after childbirth in 92 countries and associated factors in 30 low- and middle-income countries: Compilation of reported data and a cross-sectional analysis from nationally representative surveys. *PLOS Medicine 13*, 88–96.

Campione-Barr, N., Lindell, A. K., Short, S. D., Greer, K. B., & Drotar, S. D. (2015). First- and second-born adolescents' decision-making autonomy throughout adolescence. *Journal of Adolescence, 45*, 250–262.

Campos, J. J., Langer, A., & Krowitz, A. (1970). Cardiac responses on the visual cliff in prelocomotor human infants. *Science, 170*, 196–197.

Camras, L., Oster, H., Bakeman, R., Meng, Z., Ujiie, T., & Campos, J. (2007). Do infants show distinct negative facial expressions for fear and anger? Emotional expression in 11-month-old European American, Chinese, and Japanese Infants. *Infancy, 11*, 131–155.

Canals, J., Fernandez-Ballart, J., & Esparo, G. (2003). Evolution of Neonatal Behavior Assessment Scale scores in the first month of life. *Infant Behavior & Development, 26*, 227–237.

Canham, S. L., Mahmood, A., Stott, S., Sixsmith, J., & O'Rourke, N. (2014). 'Til divorce do us part: Marriage dissolution in later life. *Journal of Divorce & Remarriage, 55*, 591–612.

Cantin, V., Lavallière, M., Simoneau, M., & Teasdale, N. (2009). Mental workload when driving in a simulator: Effects of age and driving complexity. *Accident Analysis and Prevention, 41*, 763–771.

Cao, Z., Bennett, M., Orr, C., Icke, I., Banaschewski, T., Barker, G. J.,… Whelan, R. (2018). Mapping adolescent reward anticipation, receipt, and prediction error during the monetary incentive delay task. *Human Brain Mapping*. doi:10.1002/hbm.24370

Cappeliez, P., Guindon, M., & Robitaille, A. (2008). Functions of reminiscence and emotional regulation among older adults. *Journal of Aging Studies, 22*, 266–272.

Caputi, M., Lecce, S., Pagnin, A., & Banerjee, R. (2012). Longitudinal effects of theory of mind on later peer relations: The role of prosocial behavior. *Developmental Psychology, 48*, 257–270.

Carbone, I., Lazzarotto, T., Ianni, M., Porcellini, E., Forti, P., Masliah, E., & … Licastro, F. (2014). Herpes virus in Alzheimer's disease: Relation to progression of the disease. *Neurobiology of Aging, 35*, 122–129.

Cardman, M. (2004). Rising GPAs, course loads a mystery to researchers. *Education Daily, 37*, 1–3.

Carey, B. (2012, March 29). Diagnoses of autism on the rise, report says. *The New York Times*, p. A20.

Carleton, R. N., Duranceau, S., Freeston, M. H., Boelen, P. A., McCabe, R. E., & Antony, M. M. (2014). 'But it might be a heart attack': Intolerance of uncertainty and panic disorder symptoms. *Journal of Anxiety Disorders, 28*, 463–470.

Carmichael, O., Mungas, D., Beckett, L., Harvey, D., Farias, S., Reed, B., & … deCarli, C. (2012). MRI predictors of cognitive change in a diverse and carefully characterized elderly population. *Neurobiology of Aging, 33*, 83–95.

Carmel, S. (2017). The will-to-live scale: Development, validation, and significance for elderly people. *Aging & Mental Health, 21*, 289–296.

Carmody, K., Haskett, M. E., Loehman, J., & Rose, R. A. (2014). Physically abused children's adjustment at the transition to school: Child, parent, and family factors. *Journal of Child and Family Studies*. Accessed online, 2/13/14; http://link.springer.com/article/10.1007%2Fs10826-014-9906-7#page-1

Caron, A. (2009). Comprehension of the representational mind in infancy. *Developmental Review, 29*, 69–95.

Carr, D. (2015). Spousal/intimate partner loss and bereavement. In G. Christ, C. Messner, & L. Behar (Eds.), *Handbook of oncology social work: Psychosocial care for people with cancer*. New York: Oxford University Press.

Carr, D. (2016). Is death 'the great equalizer'? The social stratification of death quality in the United States. *Annals of the American Academy of Political and Social Science, 663*, 331–354.

Carr, D., Nesse, R. M., & Wortman, C. B. (2005). *Spousal bereavement in late life*. New York: Springer.

Carr, P. B., & Steele, C. M. (2009). Stereotype threat and inflexible perseverance in problem solving. *Journal of Experimental Social Psychology, 45*, 853–859.

Carrns, A. (2016, August 12). Multigenerational households: The benefits, and perils. *The New York Times.* Accessed online, 11/8/17; https://www.nytimes.com/2016/08/12/your-money/multigenerational-households-financialadvice.html?r=0

Carson, A., Chabot, C., Greyson, D., Shannon, K., Duff, P., & Shoveller, J. (2016). A narrative analysis of the birth stories of early-age mothers. *Sociology of Health & Illness,* doi: 10.1111/1467-9566.12518/abstract

Carson, R. G. (2006). Neural pathways mediating bilateral interactions between the upper limbs. *Brain Research Review, 49*, 641–662.

Carstensen, L. L. (2018). Integrating cognitive and emotion paradigms to address the paradox of aging. *Cognition and Emotion.* doi:10.1080/0269993 1.2018.1543181

Carteret, M. (2017). *Cultural aspects of death and dying.* Accessed online, 10/23/17; http://www.dimensionsofculture.com/2010/11/cultural-aspects-of-deathand-dying/

Carton, A., & Aiello, J. (2009). Control and anticipation of social interruptions: Reduced stress and improved task performance. *Journal of Applied Social Psychology, 39*, 169–185.

Carver, C., & Scheier, M. (2002). Coping processes and adjustment to chronic illness. In A. Christensen & M. Antoni (Eds.), *Chronic physical disorders: Behavioral medicine's perspective* (pp. 47–68). Malden, MA: Blackwell Publishers.

Casalin, S., Luyten, P., Vliegen, N., & Meurs, P. (2012). The structure and stability of temperament from infancy to toddlerhood: A one-year prospective study. *Infant Behavior & Development, 35*, 94–108.

Case, R. (1991). Stages in the development of the young child's first sense of self. *Developmental Review, 11*, 210–230.

Case, R. (1999). Conceptual development. In M. Bennett (Ed.), *Developmental psychology: Achievements and prospects* (pp. 36–54). Philadelphia, PA: Psychology Press.

Caserta, M., O'Connor, T., Wyman, P., Wang, H., Moynihan, J., Cross, W., &... Jin, X. (2008). The associations between psychosocial stress and the frequency of illness, and innate and adaptive immune function in children. *Brain, Behavior, and Immunity, 22*, 933–940.

Casey, B. J., Jones, R. M., & Somerville, L. H. (2011). Braking and accelerating of the adolescent brain. *Journal of Research on Adolescence, 21*, 21–33.

Cashdollar, N., Fukuda, K., Bocklage, A., Aurtenetxe, S., Vogel, E. K., & Gazzaley, A. (2013). Prolonged disengagement from attentional capture in normal aging. *Psychology and Aging, 28*, 77–86.

Caspi, A. (2000). The child is father of the man: Personality continuities from childhood to adulthood. *Journal of Personality and Social Psychology, 78*, 158–172.

Caspi, J. (2012). *Sibling aggression: Assessment and treatment.* New York, NY: Springer Publishing Co.

Cassidy, J., & Berlin, L. J. (1994). The insecure/ambivalent pattern of attachment: Theory and research. *Child Development, 65*, 971–991.

Castel, A., & Craik, F. (2003). The effects of aging and divided attention on memory for item and associative information. *Psychology & Aging, 18*, 873–885.

Castle, N., & Beach, S. (2013). Elder abuse in assisted living. *Journal of Applied Gerontology, 32*, 248–267.

Castles, A., Rastle, K., & Nation, K. (2018). Ending the reading wars: Reading acquisition from novice to expert. *Psychological Science in the Public Interest, 19*(1), 5.

Castro-Schilo, L., & Kee, D. (2010). Gender differences in the relationship between emotional intelligence and right hemisphere lateralization for facial processing. *Brain and Cognition, 73*, 62–67.

Casu, G., Ulivi, G., Zaia, V., Fernandes Martins, M. C., Parente Barbosa, C., & Gremigni, P. (2018). Spirituality, infertility-related stress, and quality of life in Brazilian infertile couples: Analysis using the actor-partner interdependence mediation model. *Research in Nursing & Health,* doi:10.1002/nur.21860

Catell, R. B. (1987). *Intelligence: Its structure, growth, and action.* Amsterdam, the Netherlands: North-Holland.

Cauce, A. (2008). Parenting, culture, and context: Reflections on excavating culture. *Applied Developmental Science, 12*, 227–229.

Cauce, A., & Domenech-Rodriguez, M. (2002). Latino families: Myths and realities. In J. M. Contreras, J. K. A. Kerns, & A. M. Neal-Barnett (Eds.), *Latino children and families in the United States* (pp. 3–26). Westport, CT: Praeger.

Cavallini, A., Fazzi, E., & Viviani, V. (2002). Visual acuity in the first two years of life in healthy term newborns: An experience with the Teller Acuity Cards. *Functional Neurology: New Trends in Adaptive & Behavioral Disorders, 17*, 87–92.

Cavallo, M. C., Gugiatti, A., Fattore, G., Gerzeli, S., Barbieri, D., & Zanini, R., on behalf of the Neonatal Adequate Care for Quality of Life (NEO-ACQUA) Study Group. (2015). Cost of care and social consequences of very low birth weight infants without premature-related morbidities in Italy. *Italian Journal of Pediatrics, 41*, 59.

Ceci, S. J., & Williams, W. M. (2010). *The mathematics of sex: How biology and society conspire to limit talented women and girls.* New York, NY: Oxford University Press.

Celano, M. P., Holsey, C., & Kobrynski, L. J. (2012). Home-based family intervention for low-income children with asthma: A randomized controlled pilot study. *Journal of Family Psychology, 26*, 171–178.

Centers for Disease Control and Prevention. (2005). Births: Final data for 2003. *National Vital Statistics Report, 54*, 1–116.

Centers for Disease Control and Prevention. (2011). HIV and male circumcision. Accessed online, 9/15/18; https://www.cdc.gov/healthcommunication/toolstemplates/entertainment/tips/HivCircumcision.html

Centers for Disease Control and Prevention. (2012). *National Action Plan for Child Injury Prevention.* Atlanta, GA: National Center for Injury Prevention and Control.

Centers for Disease Control and Prevention. (2017). Asthma. National Center for Health Statistics. Accessed online, 10/22/18; https://www.cdc.gov/nchs/fastats/asthma.htm

Centers for Disease Control and Prevention. (2017). Births—Method of delivery. National Center for Health Statistics. Accessed online, 9/15/18; https://www.cdc.gov/nchs/fastats/delivery.htm

Centers for Disease Control and Prevention. (2017). Pregnancy. Accessed online, 10/25/17; https://www.cdc.gov/pregnancy/during.html

Centers for Disease Control and Prevention. (2017a). Preventing abusive head trauma. Accessed online, 10/27/17; https://www.cdc.gov/violenceprevention/childmaltreatment/Abusive-Head-Trauma.html

Centers for Disease Control and Prevention. (2017). STDs in adolescents and young adults. Accessed online, 10/11/18; https://www.cdc.gov/std/stats16/adolescents.htm

Centers for Disease Control and Prevention. (2018). Information for providers to share with male patients and parents regarding male circumcision and the prevention of HIV infection, sexually transmitted infections, and other health outcomes. Accessed online, 10/2/18; https://stacks.cdc.gov/view/cdc/58456

Centers for Disease Control and Prevention. (2018). Sexual risk behaviors: HIV, STD, & teen pregnancy prevention. Accessed online, 10/11/18; https://www.cdc.gov/healthyyouth/sexualbehaviors/

Centers for Disease Control and Prevention. (2019, January 9). Sudden unexpected infant death and sudden infant death syndrome. Accessed online, 2/27/19; https://www.cdc.gov/sids/data.htm#

Central Intelligence Agency. (2018). *World Factbook.* Accessed online, 3/26/19; https://www.cia.gov/library/publications/resources/the-world-factbook/

Chaffin, M. (2006). The changing focus of child maltreatment research and practice within psychology. *Journal of Social Issues, 62*, 663–684.

Chahal, H. H., Fung, C. C., Kuhle, S. S., & Veugelers, P. J. (2013). Availability and night-time use of electronic entertainment and communication devices are associated with short sleep duration and obesity among Canadian children. *Pediatric Obesity, 8*, 42–51.

Chaker, A. M. (2003, September 23). Putting toddlers in a nursing home. *Wall Street Journal,* p. D1.

Chakraborty, R., & De, S. (2014). Body image and its relation with the concept of physical self among adolescents and young adults. *Psychological Studies, 59*, 419–426.

Chall, J. S. (1992). The new reading debates: Evidence from science, art, and ideology. *Teachers College Record, 94*, 315–328.

Chamberlain, P., Price, J., Reid, J., Landsverk, J., Fisher, P., & Stoolmiller, M. (2006, April). Who disrupts from placement in foster and kinship care? *Child Abuse & Neglect, 30*, 409–424.

Chan, D. W. (1997). Self-concept and global self-worth among Chinese adolescents in Hong Kong. *Personality & Individual Differences, 22*, 511–520.

Chan, S., & Chan, K. (2013). Adolescents' susceptibility to peer pressure: Relations to parent–adolescent relationship and adolescents' emotional autonomy from parents. *Youth & Society, 45*, 286–302.

Chandra, A., Mosher, W. D., Copen, C., & Sionean, C. (2011). Sexual behavior, sexual attraction, and sexual identity in the United States: Data from the 2006–2008 National Survey of Family Growth. *National health statistics reports; no 36.* Hyattsville, MD: National Center for Health Statistics.

Channell, M. M., Thurman, A. J., Kover, S. T., & Abbeduto, L. (2014). Patterns of change in nonverbal cognition in adolescents with Down syndrome. *Research in Developmental Disabilities, 35*, 2933–2941.

Chaplin, T., Gillham, J., & Seligman, M. (2009). Gender, anxiety, and depressive symptoms: A longitudinal study of early adolescents. *Journal of Early Adolescence, 29*, 307–327.

Chapman, R. (2016). A case study of gendered play in preschools: How early childhood educators' perceptions of gender influence children's play. *Early Child Development and Care, 186*, 1271–1284.

Chapple, H. S., Bouton, B. L., Chow, A. Y. M., Gilbert, K. R., Kosminsky, P., Moore, J., & Whiting, P. P. (2017). The body of knowledge in thanatology: An outline. *Death Studies, 41*(2), 118–125.

Chapuis-de-Andrade, S., de Araujo, R. M., & Lara, D. R. (2017). Association of weight control behaviors with body mass index and weight-based self-evaluation. *Revista Brasileira De Psiquiatria, 39*, 237–243.

Charles, S., & Carstensen, L. (2010). Social and emotional aging. *Annual Review of Psychology, 61*, 383–409.

Charness, N., & Boot, W. R. (2009). Aging and information technology use: Potential and barriers. *Current Directions in Psychological Science, 18*, 253–258.

Chassin, L., Macy, J., Seo, D., Presson, C., & Sherman, S. (2009). The association between membership in the sandwich generation and health behaviors: A longitudinal study. *Journal of Applied Developmental Psychology, 31*, 38–46.

Chasteen, A. L., Bhattacharyya, S., Horhota, M., Tam, R., & Hasher, L. (2005). How feelings of stereotype threat influence older adults' memory performance. *Experimental Aging Research, 31*, 235–260.

Cheah, C., Leung, C., Tahseen, M., & Schultz, D. (2009). Authoritative parenting among immigrant Chinese mothers of preschoolers. *Journal of Family Psychology, 23*, 311–320.

Chen, C., Mizuno, T., Elston, R., Kariuki, M., Hall, K., Unverzagt, F., &... Kalaria, R. N. (2010).

A comparative study to screen dementia and APOE genotypes in an ageing East African population. *Neurobiology of Aging, 31,* 732–740.

Chen, D., Yang, X., & Dale Aagard, S. (2012). The empty nest syndrome: Ways to enhance quality of life. *Educational Gerontology, 38,* 520–529.

Chen, J., Chen, T., & Zheng, X. (2012). Parenting styles and practices among Chinese immigrant mothers with young children. *Early Child Development and Care, 182,* 1–21.

Chen, J., & Gardner, H. (2005). Assessment based on multiple-intelligences theory. In D. P. Flanagan & P. L. Harrison (Eds.), *Contemporary intellectual assessment: Theories, tests, and issues* (pp. 77–102). New York, NY: Guilford Press.

Chen, J. J., Sun, P., & Yu, Z. (2017). A comparative study on parenting of preschool children between the Chinese in China and Chinese immigrants in the United States. *Journal of Family Issues, 38,* 1262–1287.

Cheng, H. G., & Anthony, J. C. (2018). Male-female differences in the onset of heavy drinking episode soon after first full drink in contemporary United States: From early adolescence to young adulthood. *Drug and Alcohol Dependence, 190,* 159–165.

Cheng, J. T., Tracy, J. L., Ho, S., & Henrich, J. (2016). Listen, follow me: Dynamic vocal signals of dominance predict emergent social rank in humans. *Journal of Experimental Psychology: General, 145,* 536–547.

Cherney, I., Kelly-Vance, L., & Glover, K. (2003). The effects of stereotyped toys and gender on play assessment in children aged 18 to 47 months. *Educational Psychology, 23,* 95–105.

Chetty, R., Stepner, M., Cutler, D., et al. (2016). The association between income and life expectancy in the United States, 2001–2014. *JAMA: Journal of the American Medical Association [serial online], 315,* 1750–1766.

Cheung, W., Maio, G. R., Rees, K. J., Kamble, S., & Mane, S. (2016). Cultural differences in values as self-guides. *Personality and Social Psychology Bulletin, 42,* 769–781.

Chien, S., Bronson-Castain, K., Palmer, J., & Teller, D. (2006). Lightness constancy in 4-month-old infants. *Vision Research, 46,* 2139–2148.

ChildStats.gov. (2017). America's children: Key national indicators of well-being, 2017. Accessed online, 11/8/17; https://www.childstats.gov/americaschildren/family1.asp#f1

Child Welfare Information Gateway. (2013). *Leaving your child home alone.* Washington, DC: Children's Bureau.

Child Welfare Information Gateway. (2017). *Foster care statistics 2015.* Washington, DC: Department of Health and Human Services, Children's Bureau.

Child Welfare Information Gateway. (2018). Child abuse and neglect fatalities 2016: Statistics and interventions. Accessed online, 3/25/19; https://www.childwelfare.gov/pubs/factsheets/fatality/

Chiodo, L. M., Bailey, B. A., Sokol, R. J., Janisse, J., Delaney-Black, V., & Hannigan, J. H. (2012). Recognized spontaneous abortion in mid-pregnancy and patterns of pregnancy alcohol use. *Alcohol, 46,* 261–267.

Chisolm, T., Willott, J., & Lister, J. (2003). The aging auditory system: Anatomic and physiologic changes and implications for rehabilitation. *International Journal of Audiology, 42,* 2S3–2S10.

Chiu, M. M., & McBride-Chang, C. (2006). Gender, context, and reading: A comparison of students in 43 countries. *Scientific Studies of Reading, 10,* 331–362.

Cho, S. B., Aliev, F., Clark, S. L., Adkins, A. E., Edenberg, H. J., Bucholz, K. K., & ... Dick, D. M. (2017). Using patterns of genetic association to elucidate shared genetic etiologies across psychiatric disorders. *Behavior Genetics, 47,* 405–415.

Choi, C. Q. (2017). Countries with most twins identified. *LiveScience.* Accessed online, 10/24/17; https://www.livescience.com/16469-twins-countries-twinning-rates.html

Choi, D., Conture, E. G., Walden, T. A., Lambert, W. E. & Tumanova, V. (2013). Behavioral inhibition and childhood stuttering. *Journal of Fluency Disorders, 38,* 171–183.

Chomsky, N. (1999). On the nature, use, and acquisition of language. In W. C. Ritchie & T. J. Bhatia (Eds.), *Handbook of child language acquisition* (pp. 33–54). San Diego: Academic Press.

Chomsky, N. (2005). Editorial: Universals of human nature [serial online]. *Psychotherapy and Psychosomatics, 74,* 263–268.

Chonody, J. M. (2016). Positive and negative ageism: The role of benevolent and hostile sexism. *Affilia: Journal of Women & Social Work, 31,* 207–218.

Choo, H., & Shek, D. (2013). Quality of parent-child relationship, family conflict, peer pressure, and drinking behaviors of adolescents in an Asian context: The case of Singapore. *Social Indicators Research, 110,* 1141–1157.

Chopik, W. J., Bremner, R. H., Defever, A. M., & Keller, V. N. (2018). How (and whether) to teach undergraduates about the replication crisis in psychological science. *Teaching of Psychology, 45*(2), 158–163.

Choy, C. M., Yeung, Q. S., Briton-Jones, C. M., Cheung, C. K., Lam, C. W., & Haines, C. J. (2002). Relationship between semen parameters and mercury concentrations in blood and in seminal fluid from subfertile males in Hong Kong. *Fertility and Sterility, 78,* 426–428.

Chrisler, J. C., & Johnston-Robledo, I. (2018). The aging body. In *Woman's embodied self: Feminist perspectives on identity and image* (pp. 141–163). Washington, DC: American Psychological Association.

Christakis, D., & Zimmerman, F. (2007). Violent television viewing during preschool is associated with antisocial behavior during school age. *Pediatrics, 120,* 993–999.

Christiansen, D. M. (2017). Posttraumatic stress disorder in parents following infant death: A systematic review. *Clinical Psychology Review, 51,* 60–74.

Christodoulou, J., Lac, A., & Moore, D. S. (2017). Babies and math: A meta-analysis of infants' simple arithmetic competence. *Developmental Psychology, 53*(8), 1405–1418.

Chronis, A., Jones, H., & Raggi, V. (2006, June). Evidence-based psychosocial treatments for children and adolescents with attention-deficit/hyperactivity disorder. *Clinical Psychology Review, 26,* 486–502.

Chuang, S. S., Glozman, J., Green, D. S., & Rasmi, S. (2018). Parenting and family relationships in Chinese families: A critical ecological approach. *Journal of Family Theory & Review.* doi:10.1111/jftr.12257

Chung, S. A., Wei, A. Q., Connor, D. E., Webb, G. C., Molloy, T., Pajic, M., Diwan, A. D. (2007). Nucleus pulposus cellular longevity by telomerase gene therapy. *Spine, 15,* 1188–1196.

Cicchetti, D., & Cohen, D. J. (2006). *Developmental psychopathology, Vol. 1: Theory and method* (2nd ed.). Hoboken, NJ: Wiley.

Cid-Fernández, S., Lindín, M., & Díaz, F. (2016). Information processing becomes slower and predominantly serial in aging: Characterization of response-related brain potentials in an auditory–visual distraction–attention task. *Biological Psychology, 113,* 12–23.

Cirulli, F., Berry, A., & Alleva, E. (2003). Early disruption of the mother-infant relationship: Effects on brain plasticity and implications for psychopathology. *Neuroscience & Biobehavioral Reviews, 27,* 73–82.

Clark, A., & Lappin, S. (2013). Complexity in language acquisition. *Topics in Cognitive Science, 5,* 89–110.

Clark, D. (2015). Hospice care of the dying. In J. M. Stillion, & T. Attig (Eds.), *Death, dying, and bereavement: Contemporary perspectives, institutions, and practices.* New York, NY: Springer Publishing Company.

Clark, J. E., & Humphrey, J. H. (Eds.). (1985). *Motor development: Current selected research.* Princeton, NJ: Princeton Book Company.

Clark, K. B., & Clark, M. P. (1947). Racial identification and preference in Negro children. In T. M. Newcomb & E. L. Hartley (Eds.), *Readings in social psychology* (pp. 169–178). New York, NY: Holt, Rinehart & Winston.

Clarke, A. R., Barry, R. J., McCarthy, R., Selikowitz, M., & Johnstone, S. J. (2008). Effects of imipramine hydrochloride on the EEG of children with attention-deficit/hyperactivity disorder who are non-responsive to stimulants. *International Journal of Psychophysiology, 68,* 186–192.

Clearfield, M., & Nelson, N. (2006, January). Sex differences in mothers' speech and play behavior with 6-, 9-, and 14-month-old infants. *Sex Roles, 54,* 127–137.

Cline, K. D., & Edwards, C. P. (2017). Parent–child book-reading styles, emotional quality, and changes in early head start children's cognitive scores. *Early Education and Development, 28,* 41–58.

Close, F. T., Suther, S., Foster, A., El-Amin, S., & Battle, A. M. (2013). Community perceptions of black infant mortality: A qualitative inquiry. *Journal of Health Care for the Poor and Underserved, 24,* 1089–1101.

Closson, L. (2009). Status and gender differences in early adolescents' descriptions of popularity. *Social Development, 18,* 412–426.

Closson, L. M., Hart, N. C., & Hogg, L. D. (2017). Does the desire to conform to peers moderate links between popularity and indirect victimization in early adolescence? *Social Development, 26*(3), 489–502.

Coall, D. A., & Hertwig, R. (2011). Grandparental investment: A relic of the past or a resource for the future? *Current Directions in Psychological Science, 20,* 93–98.

Coates, S. W. (2016). Can babies remember trauma? Symbolic forms of representation in traumatized infants. *Journal of the American Psychoanalytic Association, 64,* 751–776.

Cockrill, K., & Gould, H. (2012). Letter to the editor: Response to "What women want from abortion counseling in the United States: A qualitative study of abortion patients in 2008." *Social Work in Health Care, 51,* 191–194.

Coelho, V. A., Marchante, M., & Jimerson, S. R. (2016). Promoting a positive middle school transition: A randomized-controlled treatment study examining self-concept and self-esteem. *Journal of Youth and Adolescence.* Accessed online, 6/13/16; http://www.ncbi.nlm.nih.gov/pubmed/27230119

Coffman, J. L., Grammer, J. K., Hudson, K. N., Thomas, T. E., Villwock, D., & Ornstein, P. A. (2018). Relating children's early elementary classroom experiences to later skilled remembering and study skills. *Journal of Cognition and Development.* doi:10.1080/15248372.2018.1470976

Cogan, L. W., Josberger, R. E., Gesten, F. C., & Roohan, P. J. (2012). Can prenatal care impact future well-child visits? The experience of a low income population in New York State Medicaid managed care. *Maternal and Child Health Journal, 16,* 92–99.

Cohen, J. (1999, March 19). Nurture helps mold able minds. *Science, 283,* 1832–1833.

Cohen, L. B., & Cashon, C. H. (2003). Infant perception and cognition. In R. M. Lerner & M. A. Easterbrooks (Eds.), *Handbook of psychology: Developmental psychology, Vol. 6.* New York, NY: Wiley.

Cohen, R. A., Mather, N., Schneider, D. A., & White, J. M. (2016). A comparison of schools: Teacher knowledge of explicit code-based reading instruction. *Reading and Writing.* Accessed online, 3/16/17; http://link.springer.com/article/10.1007/s11145-016-9694-0

Cohen-Zion, M., Shabi, A., Levy, S., Glasner, L., & Wiener, A. (2016). Effects of partial sleep deprivation on information processing speed in adolescence. *Journal of the International Neuropsychological Society, 22*(4), 388–398.

Cohrs, J., Abele, A., & Dette, D. (2006, July). Integrating situational and dispositional determinants of job satisfaction: Findings from three samples of professionals. *Journal of Psychology: Interdisciplinary and Applied, 140,* 363–395.

Cokley, K. (2003). What do we know about the motivation of African American students? Challenging the "anti-intellectual" myth. *Harvard Educational Review, 73,* 524–558.

Colarusso, C. A. (2012). The central masturbation fantasy in heterosexual males across the life cycle: Masturbation fantasies across the normality-pathology spectrum. *Journal of the American Psychoanalytic Association, 60*(5), 917–948.

Colarusso, C. A., & Nemiroff, R. A. (1981). *Adult development: A new dimension in psychodynamic theory and practice.* New York: Plenum.

Colby, A., & Kohlberg, L. (1987). *The measurement of moral adjudgment* (Vols. 1–2). New York, NY: Cambridge University Press.

Colby, S. L. & Ortman, J. M. (2014). Projections of the size and composition of the U.S. population: 2014 to 2060. *Current Population Reports, P25-1143.* Washington, DC: U.S. Census Bureau.

Cole, M. (1992). Culture in development. In M. H. Bornstein & M. E. Lamb (Eds.), *Developmental psychology: An advanced textbook* (3rd ed.). Hillsdale, NJ: Lawrence Erlbaum.

Cole, S. A. (2005). Infants in foster care: Relational and environmental factors affecting attachment. *Journal of Reproductive & Infant Psychology, 23,* 43–61.

Coleman, J. (2014). *Why won't my teenager talk to me?* New York: Routledge/Francis Taylor Group.

Colella, A. J., & King, E. B. (Eds.). (2018). *The Oxford handbook of workplace discrimination.* New York, NY: Oxford University Press.

Coleman, M., Ganong, L., & Weaver, S. (2001). Relationship maintenance and enhancement in remarried families. In J. Harvey & A. Wenzel (Eds.), *Close romantic relationships: Maintenance and enhancement.* Mahwah, NJ: Lawrence Erlbaum.

Coleman, P. (2005, July). Editorial: Uses of reminiscence: Functions and benefits. *Aging & Mental Health, 9,* 291–294.

Coleman-Cowger, V. H., Oga, E. A., Peters, E. N., & Mark, K. (2018). Prevalence and associated birth outcomes of co-use of cannabis and tobacco cigarettes during pregnancy. *Neurotoxicology and Teratology, 68,* 84–90.

Colen, C., Geronimus, A., & Phipps, M. (2006, September). Getting a piece of the pie? The economic boom of the 1990s and declining teen birth rates in the United States. *Social Science & Medicine, 63,* 1531–1545.

College Board. (2005). *2001 college bound seniors are the largest, most diverse group in history.* New York, NY: College Board.

Collins, J. (2012). Growing up bicultural in the United States: The case of Japanese-Americans. In R. Josselson & M. Harway (Eds.), *Navigating multiple identities: Race, gender, culture, nationality, and roles.* New York, NY: Oxford University Press.

Collins, T. (2018). The personal communities of men experiencing later life widowhood. *Health Soc Care Community, 26*(3), e422–e430.

Collins, W. (2003). More than myth: The developmental significance of romantic relationships during adolescence. *Journal of Research on Adolescence, 13,* 1 24.

Collins, W., & Andrew, L. (2004). Changing relationships, changing youth: Interpersonal contexts of adolescent development. *Journal of Early Adolescence, 24,* 55–62.

Collins, W., & Doolittle, A. (2006, December). Personal reflections of funeral rituals and spirituality in a Kentucky African American family. *Death Studies, 30,* 957–969.

Collishaw, S., Pickles, A., Messer, J., Rutter, M., Shearer, C., & Maughan, B. (2007). Resilience to adult psychopathology following childhood maltreatment: Evidence from a community sample. *Child Abuse & Neglect, 31,* 211–229.

Colom, R., Lluis-Font, J. M., & André-Pueyo, A. (2005). The generational intelligence gains are caused by decreasing variance in the lower half of the distribution: Supporting evidence for the nutrition hypothesis. *Intelligence, 33,* 83–91.

Colpin, H., & Soenen, S. (2004). Bonding through an adoptive mother's eyes. *Midwifery Today: International Midwife, 70,* 30–31.

Coltrane, S., & Adams, M. (1997). Children and gender. In T. Arendell (Ed.), *Contemporary parenting: Challenges and issues. Understanding families* (Vol. 9, pp. 219–253). Thousand Oaks, CA: Sage Publications.

Commission on Ending Childhood Obesity. (2018). World Health Organization. Accessed online, 10/9/18; http://www.who.int/end-childhood-obesity/facts/en/

Commons, M. L., Galaz-Fontes, J. F., & Morse, S. J. (2006). Leadership, cross-cultural contact, socioeconomic status, and formal operational reasoning about moral dilemmas among Mexican non-literate adults and high school students. *Journal of Moral Education, 35,* 247–267.

Compton, R., & Weissman, D. (2002). Hemispheric asymmetries in global-local perception: Effects of individual differences in neuroticism. *Laterality, 7,* 333–350.

Condly, S. (2006, May). Resilience in children: A review of literature with implications for education. *Urban Education, 41,* 211–236.

Condon, J., Corkindale, C., Boyce, P., & Gamble, E. (2013). A longitudinal study of father-to-infant attachment: Antecedents and correlates. *Journal of Reproductive and Infant Psychology, 31,* 15–30.

Condry, J., & Condry, S. (1976). Sex differences: A study of the eye of the beholder. *Child Development, 47,* 812–819.

Conel, J. L. (1939, 1975). *The postnatal development of the human cerebral cortex* (Vols. I–VIII). Cambridge, MA: Harvard University Press.

Cong, Y.-Q., Junge, C., Aktar, E., Raijmakers, M., Franklin, A., & Sauter, D. (2018). Pre-verbal infants perceive emotional facial expressions categorically. *Cognition and Emotion.* doi:10.1080/02699931.2018.1455640

Congressional Budget Office. (2013). *A description of the immigrant population: 2013 update.* Washington, DC: Author.

Connally, E. L., Ward, D., Pilatsikas, C., Finnegan, S., Jenkinson, M., Boyles, R. & Watkins, K. E. (2018). Separation of trait and state in stuttering. *Human Brain Mapping, 39*(8), 3109–3126.

Connell-Carrick, K. (2006). Early child care and early child development: Major findings of the NICHD study of early child care. *Child Welfare Journal, 85,* 819–836.

Conner, K., & Goldston, D. (2007, March). Rates of suicide among males increase steadily from age 11 to 21: Developmental framework and outline for prevention. *Aggression and Violent Behavior, 12*(2), 193–207.

Connidis, I. (2010). *Family ties and aging* (2nd ed.). Thousand Oaks, CA: Pine Forge Press/Sage Publications.

Conry-Murray, C. (2013). Children's reasoning about gender-atypical preferences in different settings. *Journal of Experimental Child Psychology, 115,* 210–217.

Conway, J. R., Noë, N., Stulp, G., & Pollet, T. V. (2015). Finding your soulmate: Homosexual and hetcrosexual age preferences in online dating. *Personal Relationships, 22*(4), 666–678.

Cook, E., Buehler, C., & Henson, R. (2009). Parents and peers as social influences to deter antisocial behavior. *Journal of Youth and Adolescence, 38,* 1240–1252.

Corballis, P. (2003). Visuospatial processing and the right-hemisphere interpreter. *Brain & Cognition, 53,* 171–176.

Corcoran, J., & Pillai, V. (2007, January). Effectiveness of secondary pregnancy prevention programs: A meta-analysis. *Research on Social Work Practice, 17,* 5–18.

Cordova, J. V. (2014). *The marriage checkup practitioner's guide: Promoting lifelong relationship health.* Washington, DC: American Psychological Association.

Cornish, K., Turk, J., & Hagerman, R. (2008). The fragile X continuum: New advances and perspectives. *Journal of Intellectual Disability Research, 52,* 469–482.

Corr, C. (2010). Children's emerging awareness and understandings of loss and death. In C. A. Corr & D. E. Balk (Eds.), *Children's encounters with death, bereavement, and coping* (pp. 21–38). New York, NY: Springer Publishing Co.

Corr, C., Nabe, C., & Corr, D. (2006). *Death & dying, life & living* (6th ed.). Belmont, CA: Thomson Wadsworth.

Corr, C., Nabe, C., & Corr, D. (2010). *Death & dying, life & living* (8th ed.). Belmont, CA: Thomson Wadsworth.

Corr, C. A. (2015). Death education at the college and university level in North America. In J. M. Stillion & T. Attig (Eds.), *Death, dying, and bereavement: Contemporary perspectives, institutions, and practices.* New York, NY: Springer Publishing Co.

Corrow, S., Granrud, C. E., Mathison, J., & Yonas, A. (2012). Infants and adults use line junction information to perceive 3D shape. *Journal of Vision, 12,* 8.

Corry, M., While, A., Neenan, K., & Smith, V. (2014). A systematic review of intervention for caregivers of people with chronic conditions. Accessed online, 1/1/2015; doi:10.1111/jan.12523/abstract

Cortese, S., Holtmann, M., Banaschewski, T., Buitelaar, J., Coghill, D., Danckaerts, M., &… European ADHD Guidelines Group. (2013). Practitioner review: Current best practice in the management of adverse events during treatment with ADHD medications in children and adolescents. *Journal of Child Psychology and Psychiatry, 54,* 227–246.

Costa, L. V., & Veloso, A. I. (2016). Factors influencing the adoption of video games in late adulthood: A survey of older adult gamers. *International Journal of Technology and Human Interaction (IJTHI), 12,* 35–50.

Costa, P. T., & McCrae, R. R. (1992). *Revised NEO Personality Inventory (NEO-PI-R) and NEO Five-Factor Inventory (NEO-FFI) professional manual.* Odessa, FL: Psychological Assessment Resources.

Costa-Martins, J. M., Pereira, M., Martins, H., Moura-Ramos, M., Coelho, R., & Tavares, J. (2014). The role of maternal attachment in the experience of labor pain: A prospective study. *Psychosomatic Medicine, 76,* 221–228.

Cottini, M., Basso, D., & Palladino, P. (2018). The role of declarative and procedural metamemory in event-based prospective memory in school-aged children. *Journal of Experimental Child Psychology, 166,* 17–33.

Couperus, J., & Nelson, C. (2006). Early brain development and plasticity. In K.McCartney & D. Phillips (Eds.), *Blackwell handbook of early childhood development* (pp. 85–105). New York, NY: Blackwell Publishing.

Cousins, W. (2013). Maps for the midway journey. *PsycCRITIQUES, 58*(8), 88–94.

Couzin, J. (2002, June 21). Quirks of fetal environment felt decades later. *Science, 296,* 2167–2169.

Cox, C., & Miner, J. (2014). Grandchildren raised by grandparents: Comparing the experiences of African-American and Tanzanian grandchildren. *Journal of Intergenerational Relationships, 12,* 9–24.

Cox, C., Kotch, J., & Everson, M. (2003). A longitudinal study of modifying influences in the relationship between domestic violence and child maltreatment. *Journal of Family Violence, 18,* 5–17.

Cox, R., Skouteris, H., Rutherford, L., & Fuller-Tyszkiewicz, M. (2012). The association between television viewing and preschool child body mass index: A systematic review of English papers published from 1995 to 2010. *Journal of Children and Media, 6*(2), 198–220. doi:10.1080/17482798.2 011.587145

Coyne, S. M. (2016). Effects of viewing relational aggression on television on aggressive behavior in adolescents: A three-year longitudinal study. *Developmental Psychology, 52,* 284–295.

Craik, F., & Salthouse, T. A. (Eds.). (2008). *The hand-book of aging and cognition* (3rd ed.). New York, NY: Psychology Press.

Cramer, E. M., Song, H., & Drent, A. M. (2016). Social comparison on Facebook: Motivation, affective consequences, self-esteem, and Facebook fatigue. *Computers in Human Behavior, 64,* 39–746.

Crampton, A., & Hall, J. (2017). Unpacking socio-economic risks for reading and academic self-concept in primary school: Differential effects and the role of the preschool home learning environment. *British Journal of Educational Psychology, 87,* 365–382.

Cratty, B. (1979). *Perceptual and motor development in infants and children* (2nd ed.). Englewood Cliffs, NJ: Prentice-Hall.

Cratty, B. (1986). *Perceptual and motor development in infants and children* (3rd ed.). Englewood Cliffs, NJ: Prentice-Hall.

Crawford, M., & Unger, R. (2004). *Women and gender: A feminist psychology* (4th ed.). New York, NY: McGraw-Hill.

Credé, M., & Niehorster, S. (2012). Adjustment to college as measured by the Student Adaptation to College Questionnaire: A quantitative review of its structure and relationships with correlates and consequences. *Educational Psychology Review, 24,* 133–165.

Crews, D., Gillette, R., Scarpino, S. V., Manikkam, M., Savenkova, M. I., & Skinner, M. K. (2012). Epigenetic transgenerational inheritance of altered stress responses. *PNAS Proceedings of the National Academy of Sciences of the United States of America, 109,* 9143–9148.

Criss, D. (2017). A parent killing a child happens more than we think. CNN. Accessed online, 3/25/19; https://www.cnn.com/2017/07/07/health/filicide-parents-killing-kids-stats-trnd/index.html

Crocetti, E. (2017). Identity formation in adolescence: The dynamic of forming and consolidating identity commitments. *Child Development Perspectives.* Accessed online, 3/22/17; doi:10.1111/cdep.12226/abstract

Crosland, K., & Dunlap, G. (2012). Effective strategies for the inclusion of children with autism in general education classrooms. *Behavior Modification, 36,* 251–269.

Crosnoe, R., & Elder, G. H., Jr. (2002). Successful adaptation in the later years: A life course approach to aging. *Social Psychology Quarterly, 65,* 309–328.

Cross, J. R., Frazier, A. D., Kim, M., & Cross, T. L. (2018). A comparison of perceptions of barriers to academic success among high-ability students from high- and low-income groups: Exposing poverty of a different kind. *Gifted Child Quarterly, 62(1),* 111–129.

Cross, T., Cassady, J., Dixon, F., & Adams, C. (2008). The psychology of gifted adolescents as measured by the MMPI-A. *Gifted Child Quarterly, 52,* 326–339.

Crowe, C. (2016). Self-care and burnout in oncology professionals. In B. Lechner, R. Chow, N. Pulenzas, M. Popovic, N. Zhang, X. Zhang, &… J. Merrick (Eds.), *Cancer: Treatment, decision making and quality of life.* Hauppauge, NY: Nova Biomedical Books.

Crowley, B., Hayslip, B., & Hobdy, J. (2003). Psychological hardiness and adjustment to life events in adulthood. *Journal of Adult Development, 10,* 237–248.

Crowley, J. (2018). *Gray divorce.* Berkeley: University of California Press.

Crowne, K. (2013). An empirical analysis of three intelligences. *Canadian Journal of Behavioural Science/Revue Canadienne Des Sciences Du Comportement, 45,* 105–114.

Crowther, M., & Rodriguez, R. (2003). A stress and coping model of custodial grandparenting among African Americans. In B. Hayslip & J. Patrick (Eds.), *Working with custodial grandparents* (pp. 145–162). New York, NY: Springer Publishing Co.

Crozier, S., Robertson, N., & Dale, M. (2015). The psychological impact of predictive genetic testing for Huntington's disease: A systematic review

of the literature. *Journal of Genetic Counseling, 24,* 29–39.

Crupi, R., & Brondolo, E. (2017). Posttraumatic stress disorder post 9/11: A review of the evidence and implications for public health policy. *TPM—Testing, Psychometrics, Methodology in Applied Psychology, 24,* 363–378.

Cruz, N., & Bahna, S. (2006, October). Do foods or additives cause behavior disorders? *Psychiatric Annals, 36,* 724–732.

Cservenka, A., & Brumback, T. (2017). The burden of binge and heavy drinking on the brain: Effects on adolescent and young adult neural structure and function. *Frontiers in Psychology, 8,* 188–197.

Cuervo, A. (2008). Calorie restriction and aging: The ultimate "cleansing diet." *Journals of Gerontology: Series A: Biological Sciences and Medical Sciences, 63A,* 547–549.

Cullen, C. (2017). Difficult conversations: Children, adolescents, and death. In R. G. Stevenson & G. R. Cox (Eds.), *Children, adolescents and death: Questions and answers.* New York: Routledge/Taylor & Francis Group.

Cumming, G. P., Currie, H. D., Moncur, R., & Lee, A. J. (2009). Web-based survey on the effect of menopause on women's libido in a computer-literate population. *Menopause International, 15,* 8–12.

Cummings, E., & Henry, W. E. (1961). *Growing old.* New York, NY: Basic Books.

Cuperman, R., Robinson, R. L., & Ickes, W. (2014). On the malleability of self-image in individuals with a weak sense of self. *Self and Identity, 13,* 1–23.

Currie, E. R., Christian, B. J., Hinds, P. S., Perna, S. J., Robinson, C., Day, S.,… Meneses, K. (2018). Life after loss: Parent bereavement and coping experiences after infant death in the neonatal intensive care unit. *Death Studies.* doi:10.1080/07481187.2018.1474285

Curtis, R. G., Windsor, T. D., & Soubelet, A. (2015). The relationship between Big-5 personality traits and cognitive ability in older adults—A review. *Aging, Neuropsychology, and Cognition, 22,* 42–71.

Czerwińska-Jasiewicz, M. (2017). The creation of a concept of one's own life by adolescents as a manifestation of subjectivity and autonomy. *Polish Psychological Bulletin, 48,* 28–37.

Dabelko, H., & Zimmerman, J. (2008). Outcomes of adult day services for participants: A conceptual model. *Journal of Applied Gerontology, 27,* 78–92.

Dagan, O., & Sagi, S. A. (2018). Early attachment network with mother and father: An unsettled issue. *Child Development Perspectives, 12(2),* 115–121.

Dagys, N., McGlinchey, E. L., Talbot, L. S., Kaplan, K. A., Dahl, R. E., & Harvey, A. G. (2012). Double trouble? The effects of sleep deprivation and chronotype on adolescent affect. *Journal of Child Psychology and Psychiatry, 53,* 660–667.

Dahl, A., Satlof-Bedrick, E. S., Hammond, S. I., Drummond, J. K., Waugh, W. E., & Brownell, C. A. (2017). Explicit scaffolding increases simple helping in younger infants. *Developmental Psychology, 53,* 407–416.

Dai, D., Tan, X., Marathe, D., Valtcheva, A., Pruzek, R. M., & Shen, J. (2012). Influences of social and educational environments on creativity during adolescence: Does SES matter? *Creativity Research Journal, 24,* 191–199.

Dale, B. A., Finch, M. H. Á., Mcintosh, D. E., Rothlisberg, B. A., & Finch, W. H. (2014). Utility of the Stanford-Binet Intelligence Scales, Fifth Edition, with ethnically diverse preschoolers. *Psychology in the Schools, 51(6),* 581–590.

Daley, K. C. (2004). Update on sudden infant death syndrome. *Current Opinion in Pediatrics, 16,* 227–232.

Daley, M. F., & Glanz, J. M. (2011). Straight talk about vaccination. *Scientific American, 305, 32,* 34.

Dalton, T. C., & Bergenn, V. W. (2007). *Early experience, the brain, and consciousness: An historical and interdisciplinary synthesis.* Mahwah, NJ: Lawrence Erlbaum.

Damashek, A., Morgan, E. C., Corlis, M., & Richardson, H. (2018). Primary and secondary prevention of child maltreatment. In J. N. Butcher & P. C. Kendall (Eds.), *APA handbook of psychopathology: Child and adolescent psychopathology, Vol. 2.* (pp. 55–77). Washington, DC: American Psychological Association.

Damon, W. (1983). *Social and personality development.* New York, NY: Norton.

Damon, W., & Hart, D. (1988). *Self-understanding in childhood and adolescence.* New York, NY: Cambridge University Press.

Daniel, J. R., Santos, A. J., Antunes, M., Fernandes, M., & Vaughn, B. E. (2016). Co-evolution of friendships and antipathies: A longitudinal study of pre-school peer groups. *Frontiers in Psychology, 7.*

Daniel, S., & Goldston, D. (2009). Interventions for suicidal youth: A review of the literature and developmental considerations. *Suicide and Life-Threatening Behavior, 39,* 252–268.

Daniels, E. A., & Lavoi, N. M. (2013). Athletics as solution and problem: Sport participation for girls and the sexualization of female athletes. In E. L. Zurbriggen & T. Roberts (Eds.), *The sexualization of girls and girlhood: Causes, consequences, and resistance* (pp. 63–83). New York, NY: Oxford University Press.

Daniels, H. (2006, February). The 'social' in post-Vygotskian theory. *Theory & Psychology, 16,* 37–49.

Danielson, M. L., Bitsko, R. H., Ghandour, R. M., Holbrook, J. R., Kogan, M. D., & Blumberg, S. J. (2018). Prevalence of parent-reported ADHD diagnosis and associated treatment among U.S. children and adolescents, 2016. *Journal of Clinical Child & Adolescent Psychology, 47(2),* 199–212.

Dare, W. N., Noronha, C. C., Kusemiju, O. T., & Okanlawon, O. A. (2002). The effect of ethanol on spermatogenesis and fertility in male Sprague-Dawley rats pretreated with acetylsalicylic acid. *Nigeria Postgraduate Medical Journal, 9,* 194–198.

Das, A. (2007). Masturbation in the United States. *Journal of Sex & Marital Therapy, 33,* 301–317.

Darwin, Z., Green, J., McLeish, J., Willmot, H., & Spiby, H. (2017). Evaluation of trained volunteer doula services for disadvantaged women in five areas in England: Women's experiences. *Health & Social Care in the Community, 25,* 466–477.

Dasen, P. R. (2000). Rapid social change and the turmoil of adolescence: A cross-cultural perspective. *International Journal of Group Tensions, 29,* 17–49.

Dasen, P. R., & Mishra, R. C. (2002). Cross-cultural views on human development in the third millennium. In W. W. Hartup & R. K. Silbereisen (Eds.), *Growing points in developmental science: An introduction* (pp. 266–286). Philadelphia, PA: Psychology Press.

Dasen, P. R., Inhelder, B., Lavallee, M., & Retschitzki, J. (1978). *Naissance de l'intelligence chez l'enfant Baoule de Cote d'Ivoire.* Berne, Germany: Hans Huber.

Dasen, P. R., Ngini, L., & Lavallee, M. (1979). Cross-cultural training studies of concrete operations. In L. H. Eckenberger, W. J. Lonner, & Y. H. Poortinga (Eds.), *Cross-cultural contributions to psychology.* Amsterdam, the Netherlands: Swets & Zeilinger.

Davenport, B., & Bourgeois, N. (2008). Play, aggression, the preschool child, and the family: A review of literature to guide empirically informed play therapy with aggressive preschool children. *International Journal of Play Therapy, 17,* 2–23.

Davies, K., Tropp, L. R., Aron, A. P., Thomas, T., & Wright, S. C. (2011). Cross-group friendships and intergroup attitudes: A meta-analytic review. *Personality and Social Psychology Review, 15,* 332–351.

Davies, S., & Denton, M. (2002). The economic well-being of older women who become divorced or separated in mid- or later life. *Canadian Journal on Aging, 21,* 477–493.

Davis, A. (2003). *Your divorce, your dollars: Financial planning before, during, and after divorce.* Bellingham, WA: Self-Counsel Press.

Davis, B. L., Smith-Bynum, M. A., Saleem, F. T., Francois, T., & Lambert, S. F. (2017). Racial socialization, private regard, and behavior problems in African American youth: Global self-esteem as a mediator. *Journal of Child and Family Studies, 26,* 709–720.

Davis, L. L., Chestnutt, D., Molloy, M., Deshefy-Longhi, T., Shim, B., & Gilliss, C. L. (2014). Adapters, strugglers, and case managers: A typology of spouse caregivers. *Qualitative Health Research, 24,* 1492–1500.

Davis, N. L., & Voirin, J. (2016). Reciprocal writing as a creative technique. *Journal of Creativity in Mental Health, 11,* 66–77.

Davis, R. R., & Hofferth, S. L. (2012). The association between inadequate gestational weight gain and infant mortality among U.S. infants born in 2002. *Maternal and Child Health Journal, 16,* 119–124.

Davis, T. S., Saltzburg, S., & Locke, C. R. (2009). Supporting the emotional and psychological well being of sexual minority youth: Youth ideas for action. *Children and Youth Services Review, 31,* 1030–1041.

Daxinger L, Whitelaw E. (2012). Understanding transgenerational epigenetic inheritance via the gametes in mammals. *National Review of Genetics, 13,* 153–62.

Day, J. R., Anderson, R. A., & Davis, L. L. (2014). Compassion fatigue in adult daughter caregivers of a parent with dementia. *Issues in Mental Health Nursing, 35*(10), 796–804.

Debast, I., van Alphen, S., Rossi, G., Tummers, J. A., Bolwerk, N., Derksen, J. L., & Rosowsky, E. (2014). Personality traits and personality disorders in late middle and old age: Do they remain stable? A literature review. *Clinical Gerontologist: Journal of Aging and Mental Health, 37,* 253–271.

de Bruin, E. J., van Run, C., Staaks, J., & Meijer, A. M. (2017). Effects of sleep manipulation on cognitive functioning of adolescents: A systematic review. *Sleep Medicine Reviews, 32,* 45–57.

De Conto, C. (2017). Intimite et sexualite en geriatrie. (Intimacy and sexuality in geriatrics.) *NPG Neurologie—Psychiatrie—Gériatrie, 17,* 264–269.

de Dios, A. (2012). United States of America. In J. Arnett (Ed.), *Adolescent psychology around the world.* New York, NY: Psychology Press.

de Frias, C. M., & Whyne, E. (2015). Stress on health-related quality of life in older adults: The protective nature of mindfulness. *Aging & Mental Health, 19,* 201–206.

de Graag, J. A., Cox, R. A., Hasselman, F., Jansen, J., & de Weerth, C. (2012). Functioning within a relationship: Mother-infant synchrony and infant sleep. *Infant Behavior & Development, 35,* 252–263.

de Haan, A. M., Smit, M., Van der Stigchel, S., Keyner, S. A., & Dijkerman, H. C. (2018). Body representation does not lag behind in updating for the pubertal growth spurt. *Journal of Experimental Child Psychology, 175,* 48–66.

De Jesus-Zayas, S. R., Buigas, R., & Denney, R. L. (2012). Evaluation of culturally diverse populations. In D. Faust (Ed.), *Coping with psychiatric and psychological testimony: Based on the original work by Jay Ziskin* (6th ed., pp. 248–265). New York, NY: Oxford University Press.

de Lauzon-Guillain, B., Wijndaele, K., Clark, M., Acerini, C. L., Hughes, I. A., Dunger, D. B., & ... Ong, K. K. (2012). Breastfeeding and infant temperament at age three months. *PLoS One, 7,* 182–190.

de Onis, M., Garza, C., Onyango, A. W., & Borghi, E. (2007). Comparison of the WHO child growth standards and the CDC 2000 growth charts. *Journal of Nutrition, 137,* 144–148.

De Pauw, S. W., & Mervielde, I. (2011). The role of temperament and personality in problem behaviors of children with ADHD. *Journal of Abnormal Child Psychology: An Official Publication of the International Society for Research in Child and Adolescent Psychopathology, 39,* 277–291.

de Schipper, E. J., Riksen-Walraven, J. M., & Geurts, S. A. E. (2006). Effects of child-caregiver ratio on the interactions between caregivers and children in child-care centers: An experimental study. *Child Development, 77,* 861–874.

de St. Aubin, E., & McAdams, D. P. (Eds.). (2004). *The generative society: Caring for future generations.* Washington, DC: American Psychological Association.

Dean, D. I., O'Muircheartaigh, J., Dirks, H., Waskiewicz, N., Lehman, K., Walker, L., & ... Deoni, S. L. (2014). Modeling healthy white matter and myelin development: 3 through 60 months of age. *Neuroimage, 84,* 742–752.

Deal, J. J., & Levenson, A. (2016). *What millennials want from work: How to maximize engagement in today's workforce.* New York: McGraw-Hill Education.

Deaner, R. O., Balish, S. M., & Lombardo, M. P. (2016). Sex differences in sports interest and motivation: An evolutionary perspective. *Evolutionary Behavioral Sciences, 10,* 73–97.

Dearing, E., McCartney, K., & Taylor, B. (2009). Does higher quality early child care promote low-income children's math and reading achievement in middle childhood? *Child Development, 80,* 1329–1349.

Deary, I. (2010). Cognitive epidemiology: Its rise, its current issues, and its challenges. *Personality and Individual Differences, 49,* 337–343.

Deary, I. J. (2012). Intelligence. *Annual Review of Psychology, 63,* 453–482.

Deary, I. J. (2014). The stability of intelligence from childhood to old age. *Current Directions in Psychological Science, 23,* 239–245.

Deater-Deckard, K., & Cahill, K. (2006). Nature and nurture in early childhood. In K. McCartney & D. Phillips (Eds.), *Blackwell handbook of early childhood development* (pp. 3–21). New York, NY: Blackwell Publishing.

De Jesus Moreno, M. (2003). Cognitive improvement in mild to moderate Alzheimer's dementia after treatment with the acetylcholine precursor choline alfoscerate: A multicenter, double-blind, randomized, placebo-controlled trial. *Clinical Therapeutics, 25,* 178–193.

De Leo, D., Cimitan, A., Dyregrov, K., Grad, O., & Andriessen, K. (2014). *Bereavement after traumatic death: Helping the survivors.* Cambridge, MA: Hogrefe Publishing.

de Oliveira Brito, L. V., Maranhao Neto, G. A., Moraes, H., Emerick, R. S., & Deslandes, A. C. (2014). Relationship between level of independence in activities of daily living and estimated cardiovascular capacity in elderly women. *Archives of Gerontology and Geriatrics, 59,* 367–371.

Del Giudice, M. (2015). Self-regulation in an evolutionary perspective. In G. H. E. Gendolla, M. Tops, S. L. Koole, (Eds.), *Handbook of biobehavioral approaches to self-regulation* (pp. 25–41). New York, NY: Springer Science + Business Media.

Deb, S., & Adak, M. (2006, July). Corporal punishment of children: Attitude, practice and perception of parents. *Social Science International, 22,* 3–13.

DeBlois, J. P., & Lefferts, W. K. (2017). Maybe the fountain of youth was actually a treadmill: Role of exercise in reversing microvascular and diastolic dysfunction. *Journal of Physiology, 595,* 5755–5756.

DeCasper, A. J., & Fifer, W. P. (1980). Of human bonding: Newborns prefer their mothers' voices. *Science, 208,* 1174–1176.

DeCasper, A. J., & Spence, M. J. (1986). Prenatal maternal speech influences newborns' perception of speech sounds. *Infant Behavior and Development, 9,* 133–150.

DeFrancisco, B., & Rovee-Collier, C. (2008). The specificity of priming effects over the first year of life. *Developmental Psychobiology, 50,* 486–501.

Degnen, C. (2007). Minding the gap: The construction of old age and oldness amongst peers. *Journal of Aging Studies, 21,* 69–80.

Dehaene-Lambertz, G., Hertz-Pannier, L., & Dubois, J. (2006). Nature and nurture in language acquisition: Anatomical and functional brain-imaging studies in infants [Special issue: Nature and nurture in brain development and neurological disorders]. *Neurosciences, 29,* 367–373.

Delamater, J. (2012). Sexual expression in later life: A review and synthesis. *Journal of Sex Research, 49,* 125–141.

DeLisi, M. (2006). Zeroing in on early arrest onset: Results from a population of extreme career criminals. *Journal of Criminal Justice, 34,* 17–26.

Delle Fave, A., Wissing, M., Brdar, I., Vella-Brodrick, D., & Freire, T. (2013). Cross-cultural perceptions of meaning and goals in adulthood: Their roots and relations with happiness. In A. S. Waterman (Ed.), *The best within us: Positive psychology perspectives on eudaimonia.* Washington, DC: American Psychological Association.

Dellmann-Jenkins, M., & Brittain, L. (2003). Young adults' attitudes toward filial responsibility and actual assistance to elderly family members. *Journal of Applied Gerontology, 22,* 214–229.

DeLoache, J. S., Chiong, C., Sherman, K., Islam, N., Vanderborght, M., Troseth, G. L., Strouse, G. A., & O'Doherty, K. (2010). Do babies learn from baby media? *Psychological Science, 21,* 1570–1574.

Demir, M., Orthel, H., & Andelin, A. (2013). Friendship and happiness. In S. A. David, I. Boniwell, & A. Conley Ayers (Eds.), *The Oxford handbook of happiness.* New York, NY: Oxford University Press.

DeNavas-Walt, C. & Proctor, B. D. (2015). *U.S. Census Bureau, current population reports, P60-252, Income and poverty in the United States: 2014.* Washington, DC: U.S. Government Printing Office.

Deng, C., Armstrong, P., & Rounds, J. (2007). The fit of Holland's RIASEC model to US occupations. *Journal of Vocational Behavior, 71,* 1–22.

Denizet-Lewis, B. (2004, May 30). Friends, friends with benefits and the benefits of the local mall. *The New York Times Magazine,* pp. 30–35, 54–58.

Dennehy, T. C., Smith, J. S., Moore, C., & Dasgupta, N. (2018). Stereotype threat and stereotype inoculation for underrepresented students in the first year of college. In R. S. Feldman (Ed.), *The first year of college: Research, theory, and practice on improving the student experience and increasing retention* (pp. 309-344). New York: Cambridge University Press.

Dennis, T. A., Cole, P. M., Zahn-Wexler, C., & Mizuta, I. (2002). Self in context: Autonomy and relatedness in Japanese and U.S. mother-preschooler dyads. *Child Development, 73,* 1803–1817.

Dennis, W. (1966). Age and creative productivity. *Journal of Gerontology, 21,* 1–8.

Dentato, M. P., Argüello, T. M., & Smith, M. (2018). Dating, relationships, and family issues. In M. P. Dentato (Ed.), *Social work practice with the LGBTQ community: The intersection of history, health, mental health, and policy factors.* (pp. 159–196). New York, NY: Oxford University Press.

Deoni, S., Dean, D. I., Joelson, S., O'Regan, J., & Schneider, N. (2018). Early nutrition influences developmental myelination and cognition in infants and young children. *Neuroimage, 178,* 649–659.

DePaolis, R. A., Vihman, M. M., & Nakai, S. (2013). The influence of babbling patterns on the processing of speech. *Infant Behavior & Development, 36,* 642–649.

DeParle, J., & Tavernise, S. (2012, February 17). Unwed mothers now a majority before age of 30. *The New York Times,* p. A1.

DePaulo, B. (2006). *Singled out: How singles are stereotyped, stigmatized, and ignored, and still live happily ever after.* New York, NY: St Martin's Press.

DePaulo, B. (2018). Toward a positive psychology of single life. In D. S. Dunn (Ed.), *Positive psychology: Established and emerging issues.* (pp. 251–275). New York, NY: Routledge/Taylor & Francis Group.

DePaulo, B. M., & Morris, W. L. (2006). The unrecognized stereotyping and discrimination against singles. *Current Directions in Psychological Science, 15*, 251–254.

Der, G., & Deary, I. (2006, March). Age sex differences in reaction time in adulthood: Results from the United Kingdom health and lifestyle survey. *Psychology and Aging, 21*(1), 62–73.

Dereli-İman, E. (2013). Adaptation of social problem solving for children questionnaire in 6 age groups and its relationships with preschool behavior problems. *Kuram Ve Uygulamada Eğitim Bilimleri, 13*, 491–498.

Derevensky, J., Shek, D., & Merrick, J. (2010). Adolescent gambling. *International Journal of Adolescent Medicine and Health, 22*, 1–2.

Deruelle, F., Nourry, C., Mucci, P., Bart, F., Grosbois, J. M., Lensel, G. H., Fabre, C. (2008). Difference in breathing strategies during exercise between trained elderly men and women. *Scandinavian Journal of Medical Science in Sports, 18*, 213–220.

Dervic, K., Friedrich, E., Oquendo, M., Voracek, M., Friedrich, M., & Sonneck, G. (2006, October). Suicide in Austrian children and young adolescents aged 14 and younger. *European Child & Adolescent Psychiatry, 15*, 427–434.

Désiréa, L., Blondiaux, E., Carrière, J., Haddad, R., Sol, O., Fehlbaum-Beurdeley, P., &… Pando, M. P. (2013). Blood transcriptomic biomarkers of Alzheimer's disease patients treated with EHT 0202. *Journal of Alzheimer's Disease, 34*, 469–483.

Desilver, D. (2017). U.S. students' academic achievement still lags that of their peers in many other countries. Pew Research Center. Accessed online, 3/25/19; http://www.pewresearch.org/fact-tank/2017/02/15/u-s-students-internationally-math-science/

Destounis, S., Hanson, S., Morgan, R., Murphy, P., Somerville, P., Seifert, P., &… Logan-Young, W. (2009). Computer-aided detection of breast carcinoma in standard mammographic projections with digital mammography. *International Journal of Computer Assisted Radiological Surgery, 4*, 331–336.

Deurenberg, P., Deurenberg-Yap, M., Foo, L. F., Schmidt, G., & Wang, J. (2003). Differences in body composition between Singapore Chinese, Beijing Chinese and Dutch children. *European Journal of Clinical Nutrition, 57*, 405–409.

Deurenberg, P., Deurenberg-Yap, M., & Guricci, S. (2002). Asians are different from Caucasians and from each other in their body mass index/body fat percent relationship. *Obesity Review, 3*, 141–146.

Dev, D. A., Speirs, K. E., Williams, N. A., Ramsay, S., McBride, B. A., & Hatton-Bowers, H. (2017). Providers' perspectives on self-regulation impact their use of responsive feeding practices in child care. *Appetite, 118*, 66–74.

DeVader, S. R., Neeley, N. L., Myles, T. D., & Leet, T. L. (2007). Evaluation of gestational weight gain guidelines for women with normal prepregnancy body mass index. *Obstetrics and Gynecology, 110*, 745–751.

Deveny, K. (1994, December 5). Chart of kindergarten awards. *Wall Street Journal*, p. B1.

DeVries, R. (2005). *A pleasing birth*. Philadelphia, PA: Temple University Press.

DeWolf, M. (2017, March 1). *12 stats about working women*. Accessed online, 11/25/17; https://blog.dol.gov/2017/03/01/12-stats-about-working-women

Dey, A. N., & Bloom, B. (2005). Summary health statistics for U.S. Children: National Health Interview Survey, 2003. *Vital Health Statistics, 10*(223), 1–78.

Diambra, L., & Menna-Barreto, L. (2004). Infradian rhythmicity in sleep/wake ratio in developing infants. *Chronobiology International, 21*, 217–227.

Diamond, L. (2003a). Love matters: Romantic relationships among sexual-minority adolescents. In P. Florsheim (Ed.), *Adolescent romantic relations and sexual behavior: Theory, research, and practical implications*. Mahwah, NJ: Lawrence Erlbaum.

Diamond, L, Fagundes, C. P., & Butterworth, M. R. (2010). Intimate relationships across the life span. In M. E. Lamb & A. M. Freund (Eds.), *The handbook of life-span development* (pp. 379–433). New York, NY: Wiley.

Diamond, L. M., & Savin-Williams, R. (2003). The intimate relationships of sexual-minority youths. In G. Adams & M. Berzonsky (Eds.), *Blackwell handbook of adolescence* (pp. 393–412). Malden, MA: Blackwell Publishers.

Diamond, M. (2013). Transsexuality among twins: Identity concordance, transition, rearing, and orientation. *International Journal of Transgenderism, 14*, 24–38.

Dick, D., Rose, R., & Kaprio, J. (2006). The next challenge for psychiatric genetics: Characterizing the risk associated with identified genes. *Annals of Clinical Psychiatry, 18*, 223–231.

Dickinson, D., Golinkoff, R., & Hirsh-Pasek, K. (2010). Speaking out for language: Why language is central to reading development. *Educational Researcher, 39*, 305–310.

Diego, M., Field, T., Hernandez-Reif, M., Vera, Y., Gil, K., & Gonzalez-Garcia, A. (2007). Caffeine use affects pregnancy outcome. *Journal of Child & Adolescent Substance Abuse, 17*, 41–49.

Diener, E. (2000). Subjective well-being: The science of happiness and a proposal for a national index. *American Psychologist, 55*, 34–43.

Diener, E., Lucas, R. E., & Scollon, C. N. (2009). Beyond the hedonic treadmill: Revising the adaptation theory of well-being. In E. Diener (Ed.), *The science of well-being: The collected works of Ed Diener*. New York, NY: Springer Science + Business Media.

Diener, E., Seligman, M. E. P., Choi, H., & Oishi, S. (2018). Happiest people revisited. *Perspectives on Psychological Science, 13*(2), 176–184.

Dietrich, J. F., Huber, S., Dackermann, T., Moeller, K., & Fischer, U. (2016). Place-value understanding in number line estimation predicts future arithmetic performance. *British Journal of Developmental Psychology, 34*, 502–517.

Diez-Fairen, M., Benitez, B. A., Ortega-Cubero, S., Lorenzo-Betancor, O., Cruchaga, C., Lorenzo, E., &… Pastor, P. (2018). Pooled-DNA target sequencing of Parkinson genes reveals novel phenotypic associations in Spanish population. *Neurobiology of Aging, 70e1 e5*. doi:10.1016/j.neurobiolaging.2018.05.008

DiGiovanna, A. G. (1994). *Human aging: Biological perspectives*. New York, NY: McGraw-Hill.

DiNallo, J. M., Downs, D., & Le Masurier, G. (2012). Objectively assessing treadmill walking during the second and third pregnancy trimesters. *Journal of Physical Activity & Health, 9*, 21–28.

Dinella, L. M., Weisgram, E. S., & Fulcher, M. (2017). Children's gender-typed toy interests: Does propulsion matter? *Archives of Sexual Behavior, 46*, 1295–1305.

Dinero, R., Conger, R., Shaver, P., Widaman, K., & Larsen-Rife, D. (2008). Influence of family of origin and adult romantic partners on romantic attachment security. *Journal of Family Psychology, 22*, 622–632.

Dionísio, J., de Moraes, M. M., Tudella, E., de Carvalho, W. B., & Krebs, V. J. (2015). Palmar grasp behavior in full-term newborns in the first 72 hours of life. *Physiology & Behavior, 139*, 21–25.

Di Paolo, E. A., Buhrmann, T., & Barandiaran, X. E. (2017). *Sensorimotor life: An enactive proposal*. New York: Oxford University Press.

Dittman, M. (2005). Generational differences at work. *Monitor on Psychology, 36*, 54–55.

Diversity in Academe. (2018, September 28). Student diversity at more than 1,700 institutions. *The Chronicle of Higher Education*, p. B34.

Dixon, L., & Browne, K. (2003). The heterogeneity of spouse abuse: A review. *Aggression & Violent Behavior, 8*, 107–130.

Dixon, R. A., & Cohen, A. (2003). Cognitive development in adulthood. In R. M. Lerner, M. A. Easterbrooks, & J. Mistry (Eds.), *Handbook of psychology: Developmental psychology*, Vol. 6. Hoboken, NJ: John Wiley & Sons Inc.

Dixon, W. E., Jr. (2004). There's a long, long way to go. *PsycCRITIQUES*.

Djurdjinovic, L., & Peters, J. A. (2017). Special issue introduction: Dealing with psychological and social complexity in genetic counseling. *Journal of Genetic Counseling, 26*, 1–4.

Dmitrieva, J., Chen, C., & Greenberg, E. (2004). Family relationships and adolescent psychosocial outcomes: Converging findings from Eastern and Western cultures. *Journal of Research on Adolescence, 14*, 425–447.

Dobele, A. R., Rundle-Thiele, S., & Kopanidis, F. (2014). The cracked glass ceiling: Equal work but unequal status. *Higher Education Research & Development, 33*, 456–468.

Dobscha, S. (Ed.). (2015). *Death in a consumer culture*. London: Routledge

Dobson, V. (2000). The developing visual brain. *Perception, 29*, 1501–1503.

Dodge, K. A. (1985). A social information processing model of social competence in children. In M. Perlmutter (Ed.), *Minnesota Symposia on Child Psychology, 18*, 77–126.

Dodge, K. A., & Pettit, G. S. (2003). A biopsychosocial model of the development of chronic conduct problems in adolescence. *Developmental Psychology, 39*, 349–371.

Dodge, K. A., & Price, J. M. (1994). On the relation between social information processing and socially competent behavior in early school-aged children. *Child Development, 65*, 1385–1397.

Dodge, K. A., Lansford, J. E., & Burks, V. S. (2003). Peer rejection and social information-processing factors in the development of aggressive behavior problems in children. *Child Development, 74*, 374–393.

Dombrovski, A. Y., Siegle, G. J., Szanto, K. K., Clark, L. L., Reynolds, C., & Aizenstein, H. H. (2012). The temptation of suicide: Striatal gray matter, discounting of delayed rewards, and suicide attempts in late-life depression. *Psychological Medicine, 42*, 1203–1215.

Domeij, H., Fahlström, G., Bertilsson, G., Hultcrantz, M., Munthe-Kaas, H., Gordh, C. N., & Helgesson, G. (2018). Experiences of living with fetal alcohol spectrum disorders: A systematic review and synthesis of qualitative data. *Developmental Medicine & Child Neurology, 60*(8), 741–752.

Donaldson, P. J., Grey, A. C., Maceo Heilman, B., Lim, J. C., & Vaghefi, E. (2017). The physiological optics of the lens. *Progress in Retinal & Eye Research, 56*, e1–e24.

Donat, D. (2006, October). Reading their way: A balanced approach that increases achievement. *Reading & Writing Quarterly: Overcoming Learning Difficulties, 22*, 305–323.

Dondi, M., Simion, F., & Caltran, G. (1999). Can newborns discriminate between their own cry and the cry of another newborn infant? *Developmental Psychology, 35*, 418–426.

Donlan, C. (1998). *The development of mathematical skills*. Philadelphia, PA: Psychology Press.

Donleavy, G. (2008). No man's land: Exploring the space between Gilligan and Kohlberg. *Journal of Business Ethics, 80*, 807–822.

Donnerstein, E. (2005, January). *Media violence and children: What do we know, what do we do?* Paper presented at the annual National Teaching of Psychology meeting, St. Petersburg, Florida.

Dotti Sani, G. M., & Treas, J. (2016). Educational gradients in parents' childcare time across countries, 1965–2012. *Journal of Marriage and Family, 78*, 1083–1096.

Doub, A. E., Small, M., & Birch, L. L. (2016). A call for research exploring social media influences on mothers' child feeding practices and childhood obesity risk. *Appetite, 99*, 298–305.

Douglass, A., & Klerman, L. (2012). The strengthening families initiative and child care quality improvement: How strengthening families influenced change in child care programs in one state. *Early Education and Development, 23*, 373–392.

Douglass, R., & McGadney-Douglass, B. (2008). The role of grandmothers and older women in the survival of children with Kwashiorkor in urban Accra, Ghana. *Research in Human Development, 5,* 26–43.

Doull, M., Wolowic, J., Saewyc, E., Rosario, M., Prescot, T., & Ybarra, M. (2017). Why girls choose not to use barriers to prevent sexually transmitted infection during female-to-female sex. *Journal of Adolescent Health.* doi:10.1016/j.jadohealth.2017.10.005

Dow, B., & Joosten, M. (2012). Understanding elder abuse: A social rights perspective. *International Psychogeriatrics, 24,* 853–855.

Doyle, P. M., Byrne, C., Smyth, A., & Le Grange, D. (2014). Evidence-based interventions for eating disorders. In C. A. Alfano, & D. C. Beidel (Eds.), *Comprehensive evidence based interventions for children and adolescents.* Hoboken, NJ: John Wiley & Sons Inc.

Doyle, R. (2004a, January). Living together. *Scientific American,* p. 28.

Dozor, A. J., & Amler, R. W. (2013). Children's environmental health. *Journal of Pediatrics, 162,* 6–7.

Drane, C. F., Modecki, K. L., & Barber, B. L. (2017). Disentangling development of sensation seeking, risky peer affiliation, and binge drinking in adolescent sport. *Addictive Behaviors, 66,* 60–65.

Draper, T., Holman, T., Grandy, S., & Blake, W. (2008). Individual, demographic, and family correlates of romantic attachments in a group of American young adults. *Psychological Reports, 103,* 857–872.

Driscoll, A. K., Russell, S. T., & Crockett, L. J. (2008). Parenting styles and youth well-being across immigrant generations. *Journal of Family Issues, 29,* 185–209.

Driver, J., Tabares, A., & Shapiro, A. (2003). Interactional patterns in marital success and failure: Gottman laboratory studies. In F. Walsh (Ed.), *Normal family processes: Growing diversity and complexity* (3rd ed.). New York, NY: Guilford Press.

Drozdick, L. W., Singer, J. K., Lichtenberger, E. O., Kaufman, J. C., Kaufman, A. S., & Kaufman, N. L. (2018). The Kaufman Assessment Battery for Children—Second Edition and KABC-II Normative Update. In D. P. Flanagan & E. M. McDonough (Eds.), *Contemporary intellectual assessment: Theories, tests, and issues* (4th ed) (pp. 333–359). New York, NY: Guilford Press.

Ducharme, J. (2018, August 29). Why STD rates are higher than they've ever been. *Time.* Accessed online, 3/26/19; http://time.com/5381625/std-rates-funding/

Duenwald, M. (2004, May 11). For couples, stress without a promise of success. *The New York Times,* p. D3.

Duggan, K. A., & Friedman, H. S. (2014). Lifetime biopsychosocial trajectories of the Terman gifted children: Health, well-being, and longevity. In D. K. Simonton (Ed.), *The Wiley handbook of genius.* New York: Wiley-Blackwell.

Duijts, L., Jaddoe, V. W. V., Hofman, A., & Moll, H. A. (2010, June 21). Prolonged and exclusive breastfeeding reduces the risk of infectious diseases in infancy. *Pediatrics.* doi:10.1542/peds.2008-3256

Dumont, V., Bulla, J., Bessot, N., Gonidec, J., Zabalia, M., Guillois, B., & Roche-Labarbe, N. (2017). The manual orienting response habituation to repeated tactile stimuli in preterm neonates: Discrimination of stimulus locations and interstimulus intervals. *Developmental Psychobiology, 59,* 590–602.

Dunbar, M. S., Davis, J. P., Rodriguez, A., Tucker, J. S., Seelam, R., D'Amico, E. J. (2018). Disentangling within- and between-person effects of shared risk factors on e-cigarette and cigarette use trajectories from late adolescence to young adulthood. *Nicotine & Tobacco Research.* doi:10.1093/ntr/nty179

Duncan, G. J., & Brooks-Gunn, J. (2000). Family poverty, welfare reform, and child development. *Child Development, 71,* 188–196.

Duncan, G. J., Magnuson, K., & Votruba-Drzal, E. (2014). Boosting family income to promote child development. *The Future of Children, 24,* 99–120.

Duncan, G. J., Magnuson, K., & Votruba-Drzal, E. (2017). Moving beyond correlations in assessing the consequences of poverty. *Annual Review of Psychology, 68,* 413–434.

Duncan, J. R., Paterson, D. S., Hoffman, J. M., Mokler, D. J., Borenstein, N. S., Belliveau, R. A., & . . . Kinney, H. C. (2010). Brainstem serotonergic deficiency in sudden infant death syndrome. *Journal of the American Medical Association, 303,* 430–437.

Dundas, E. M., Plaut, D. C., & Behrmann, M. (2013). The joint development of hemispheric lateralization for words and faces. *Journal of Experimental Psychology: General, 142,* 348–358.

Dunford, B. B., Shipp, A. J., Boss, R., Angermeier, I., & Boss, A. D. (2012). Is burnout static or dynamic? A career transition perspective of employee burnout trajectories. *Journal of Applied Psychology, 97,* 637–650.

Dunn, M., Thomas, J. O., Swift, W., & Burns, L. (2012). Elite athletes' estimates of the prevalence of illicit drug use: Evidence for the false consensus effect. *Drug and Alcohol Review, 31,* 27–32.

DuPaul, G., & Weyandt, L. (2006, June). School-based intervention for children with attention deficit hyperactivity disorder: Effects on academic, social, and behavioural functioning. *International Journal of Disability, Development and Education, 53,* 161–176.

Dupper, D. R. (2013). *School bullying: New perspectives on a growing problem.* New York, NY: Oxford University Press.

Durbin, J. (2003, October 6). Internet sex unzipped. *McCleans,* p. 18.

Duriez, B., Luyckx, K., Soenens, B., & Berzonsky, M. (2012). A process-content approach to adolescent identity formation: Examining longitudinal associations between identity styles and goal pursuits. *Journal of Personality, 80,* 135–161.

Dwyer, A., Jones, C., Davis, C., Kitamura, C., & Ching, T. C. (2018). Maternal education influences Australian infants' language experience from six months. *Infancy,* doi:10.1111/infa.12262

Dyson, A. H. (2003). "Welcome to the jam": Popular culture, school literacy and making of childhoods. *Harvard Educational Review, 73,* 328–361.

Eagly, A. H., & Wood, W. (2003). The origins of sex differences in human behavior: Evolved dispositions versus social roles. In C. B. Travis (Ed.), *Evolution, gender, and rape.* Cambridge, MA: MIT Press.

Eaker, E. D., Sullivan, L. M., Kelly-Hayes, M., D'Agostino, R. B., Sr., & Benjamin, E. J. (2004). Anger and hostility predict the development of atrial fibrillation in men in the Framingham Offspring Study. *Circulation, 109,* 1267–1271.

Earle, J. R., Perricone, P. J., Davidson, J. K., Moore, N. B., Harris, C. T., & Cotton, S. R. (2007). Premarital sexual attitudes and behavior at a religiously-affiliated university: Two decades of change. *Sexuality & Culture: An Interdisciplinary Quarterly, 11,* 39–61.

Easterbrooks, M., Bartlett, J., Beeghly, M., & Thompson, R. A. (2013). Social and emotional development in infancy. In R. M. Lerner, M. Easterbrooks, J. Mistry, I. B. Weiner (Eds.), *Handbook of psychology, Vol. 6: Developmental psychology* (2nd ed.). Hoboken, NJ: John Wiley & Sons Inc.

Easthope, H., Liu, E., Burnley, I., & Judd, B. (2017). Changing perceptions of family: A study of multigenerational households in Australia. *Journal of Sociology, 53*(1), 182–200.

Easton, J., Schipper, L., & Shackelford, T. (2007). Morbid jealousy from an evolutionary psychological perspective. *Evolution and Human Behavior, 28,* 399–402.

Eaves, B. J., Feldman, N. H., Griffiths, T. L., & Shafto, P. (2016). Infant-directed speech is consistent with teaching. *Psychological Review, 123,* 758–771.

Eberling, J. L., Wu, C., Tong-Turnbeaugh, R., & Jagust, W. J. (2004). Estrogen- and tamoxifen-associated effects on brain structure and function. *NeuroImage, 21,* 364–371.

Eccles, J., Templeton, J., & Barber, B. (2003). Adolescence and emerging adulthood: The critical passage ways to adulthood. In M. Bornstein & L. Davidson (Eds.), *Well-being: Positive development across the life course* (pp. 383–406). Mahwah, NJ: Lawrence Erlbaum.

Eckerd, L. (2009). Death and dying course offerings in psychology: A survey of nine Midwestern states. *Death Studies, 33,* 762–770.

Eckerman, C. O., & Oehler, J. M. (1992). Very-low-birthweight newborns and parents as early social partners. In S. L. Friedman & M. D. Sigman (Eds.), *The psychological development of low-birthweight children* (pp. 91–124). Norwood, NJ: Ablex.

Eckerman, C. O., & Peterman, K. (2001). Peers and infant social/communicative development. In G. Bremner & A. Fogel (Eds.), *Blackwell handbook of infant development.* Malden, MA: Blackwell Publishers.

Edgerley, L., El-Sayed, Y., Druzin, M., Kiernan, M., & Daniels, K. (2007). Use of a community mobile health van to increase early access to prenatal care. *Maternal & Child Health Journal, 11,* 235–239.

Edwards, J. G. (2015). Assisted Dying Bill calls for stricter safeguards. *Lancet, 385,* 686–687

Edwards, L. A., Wagner, J. B., Simon, C. E., & Hyde, D. C. (2015). Functional brain organization for number processing in pre-verbal infants. *Developmental Science.* Accessed online, 5/25/16; http://onlinelibrary.wiley.com/doi/10.1111/desc.12333/abstract

Ehm, J., Lindberg, S., & Hasselhorn, M. (2013). Reading, writing, and math self-concept in elementary school children: Influence of dimensional comparison processes. *European Journal of Psychology of Education.* Accessed online, 2/18/14; http://link.springer.com/article/10.1007%2Fs10212-013-0198-x#page-1

Ehrensaft, M., Cohen, P., & Brown, J. (2003). Intergenerational transmission of partner violence: A 20-year prospective study. *Journal of Consulting & Clinical Psychology, 71,* 741–753.

Ehrensaft, M. K., Knous-Westfall, H. M., Cohen, P., & Chen, H. (2015). How does child abuse history influence parenting of the next generation? *Psychology of Violence, 5,* 16–25.

Eichelsheim, V., Buist, K., Dekovic, M., Wissink, I., Frijns, T., van Lier, P., & . . . Meeus, W. H. J. (2010). Associations among the parent-adolescent relationship, aggression and delinquency in different ethnic groups: A replication across two Dutch samples. *Social Psychiatry and Psychiatric Epidemiology, 45,* 293–300.

Eid, M., Riemann, R., Angleitner, A., & Borkenau, P. (2003). Sociability and positive emotionality: Genetic and environmental contributions to the covariation between different facets of extraversion. *Journal of Personality, 71,* 319–346.

Eisbach, A. O. (2004). Children's developing awareness of diversity in people's trains of thought. *Child Development, 75,* 1694–1707.

Eisenberg, N. (2012). *Eight tips to developing caring kids.* Accessed online, 7/15/12; http://www.csee.org/products/87

Eisenberg, N., & Valiente, C. (2002). Parenting and children's prosocial and moral development. In M. Bornstein (Ed.), *Handbook of parenting: Vol. 5: Practical issues in parenting* (pp. 111–142). Mahwah, NJ: Lawrence Erlbaum.

Eisenberg, N., Spinrad, T. L., & Morris, A. (2014). Empathy-related responding in children. In M. Killen, & J. G. Smetana (Eds.), *Handbook of moral development* (2nd ed.). New York, NY: Psychology Press.

Ekinci, B. (2014). The relationships among Sternberg's triarchic abilities, Gardner's multiple intelligences, and academic achievement. *Social Behavior and Personality, 42,* 625–633.

El Ayoubi, M., Patkai, J., Bordarier, C., Desfrere, L., Moriette, G., Jarreau, P., & Zeitlin, J. (2016). Impact of fetal growth restriction on neurodevelopmental outcome at 2 years for extremely preterm infants: A single institution study. *Developmental Medicine & Child Neurology, 58,* 1249–1256.

Eley, T., Liang, H., & Plomin, R. (2004). Parental familial vulnerability, family environment, and their interactions as predictors of depressive symptoms in adolescents. *Child & Adolescent Social Work Journal, 21,* 298–306.

Elkind, D. (1985). Egocentrism redux. *Developmental Review, 5,* 218–226.

Elkind, D. (1996). Inhelder and Piaget on adolescence and adulthood: A postmodern appraisal. *Psychological Science, 7,* 216–220.

Elkins, D. (2009). Why humanistic psychology lost its power and influence in American psychology: Implications for advancing humanistic psychology. *Journal of Humanistic Psychology, 49,* 267–291.

Ellin, A. (2015, October 30). After full lives together, more older couples are divorcing. *New York Times,* p. B4.

Elliott, K., & Urquiza, A. (2006). Ethnicity, culture, and child maltreatment. *Journal of Social Issues, 62,* 787–809.

Ellis, B. H., MacDonald, H. Z., Lincoln, A. K., & Cabral, H. J. (2008). Mental health of Somali adolescent refugees: The role of trauma, stress, and perceived discrimination. *Journal of Consulting and Clinical Psychology, 76,* 184–193.

Ellis, B. J. (2004). Timing of pubertal maturation in girls: An integrated life history approach. *Psychological Bulletin, 130,* 920–958.

Ellis, L. (2006, July). Gender differences in smiling: An evolutionary neuroandrogenic theory. *Physiology & Behavior, 88,* 303–308.

Elmore, J. G., Jackson, S. L., Abraham, L., Miglioretti, D. L., Carney, P. A., Geller, B. M., & … Buist, D. S. (2009). Variability in interpretive performance at screening mammography and radiologists' characteristics associated with accuracy. *Radiology, 253,* 641–651.

Elwert, F., & Christakis, N. A. (2008). The effect of widowhood on mortality by the causes of death of both spouses. *American Journal of Public Health, 98*(11), 2092–2098.

Emery, C. F., Anderson, D. R., & Goodwin, C. L. (2013). Coronary heart disease and hypertension. In A. M. Nezu, C. Nezu, P. A. Geller, & I. B. Weiner (Eds.), *Handbook of psychology, Vol. 9: Health psychology* (2nd ed.). Hoboken, NJ: John Wiley & Sons Inc.

Emilson, A., Folkesson, A., & Lindberg, I. M. (2016). Gender beliefs and embedded gendered values in preschool. *International Journal of Early Childhood, 48,* 225–240.

Emslie, C., & Hunt, K. (2008). The weaker sex? Exploring lay understandings of gender differences in life expectancy: A qualitative study. *Social Science & Medicine, 67,* 808–816.

Endo, S. (1992). Infant-infant play from 7 to 12 months of age: An analysis of games in infant-peer triads. *Japanese Journal of Child and Adolescent Psychiatry, 33,* 145–162.

Endrass, T., Schreiber, M., & Kathmann, N. (2012). Speeding up older adults: Age-effects on error processing in speed and accuracy conditions. *Biological Psychology, 89,* 426–432.

Engineer, N., Darwin, L., Nishigandh, D., Ngianga-Bakwin, K., Smith, S. C., & Grammatopoulos, D. K. (2013). Association of glucocorticoid and type 1 corticotropin-releasing hormone receptors gene variants and risk for depression during pregnancy and post-partum. *Journal of Psychiatric Research, 47,* 1166–1173.

Engler-Chiurazzi, E. B., Singh, M., & Simpkins, J. W. (2016). From the 90s to now: A brief historical perspective on more than two decades of estrogen neuroprotection. *Brain Research, 1633,* 96–100.

English, D., Lambert, S. F., & Ialongo, N. S. (2014). Longitudinal associations between experienced racial discrimination and depressive symptoms in African American adolescents. *Developmental Psychology, 50,* 1190–1196.

English, T., & Carstensen, L. L. (2014). Selective narrowing of social networks across adulthood is associated with improved emotional experience in daily life. *International Journal of Behavioral Development, 38,* 195–202.

Enright, E. (2004, July/August). A house divided. *AARP Magazine,* pp. 54, 57.

Epel, E. (2009). Telomeres in a life-span perspective: A new "psychobiomarker"? *Current Directions in Psychological Science, 18,* 6–10.

Erber, J. (2010). *Aging and older adulthood* (2nd ed.). New York, NY: Wiley-Blackwell.

Erdley, C. A., & Day, H. J. (2017). Friendship in childhood and adolescence. In M. Hojjat & A. Moyer (Eds.), *The psychology of friendship.* New York: Oxford University Press.

Erickson, J. J., Martinengo, G., & Hill, E. J. (2010). Putting work and family experiences in context: Differences by family life stage. *Human Relations, 63,* 955–979.

Erikson, E. H. (1963). *Childhood and society.* New York, NY: Norton.

Erickson, J., & Johnson, G. M. (2011). Internet use and psychological wellness during late adulthood. *Canadian Journal on Aging, 30,* 197–209.

Eriksson, L., & Mazerolle, P. (2015). A cycle of violence? Examining family-of-origin violence, attitudes, and intimate partner violence perpetration. *Journal of Interpersonal Violence, 30,* 945–964.

Erwin, P. (1993). *Friendship and peer relations in children.* Chichester, UK: Wiley.

Eshel, N., Nelson, E. E., Blair, R. J., Pine, D. S., & Ernst, M. (2007). Neural substrates of choice selection in adults and adolescents: Development of the ventrolateral prefrontal and anterior cingulated cortices. *Neuropsychologia, 45,* 1270–1279.

Espelage, D. L., & Colbert, C. L. (2016). School-based bullying: Definition, prevalence, etiology, outcomes, & preventive strategies. In M. K. Holt, & A. Grills (Eds.), *Critical issues in school mental health: Evidence-based research, practice, and interventions* (pp. 132–144). New York: Routledge.

Estell, D. B., Jones, M. H., Pearl, R., Van Acker, R., Farmer, T. W., & Rodkin, P. C. (2008). Peer groups, popularity, and social preference: Trajectories of social functioning among students with and without learning disabilities. *Journal of Learning Disabilities, 41,* 5–14.

Esteban-Guitart, M. (2018). The biosocial foundation of the early Vygotsky: Educational psychology before the zone of proximal development. *History of Psychology.* doi:10.1037/hop0000092

Estévez, E., Emler, N. P., Cava, M. J., & Inglés, C. J. (2014). Psychosocial adjustment in aggressive popular and aggressive rejected adolescents at school. *Psychosocial Intervention, 23,* 57–67.

Etaugh, C. (2018). Midlife transitions. In C. B. Travis, J. W. White, A. Rutherford, W. S. Williams, S. L. Cook, K. F. Wyche (Eds.), *APA handbook of the psychology of women: History, theory, and battlegrounds.* Washington, DC: American Psychological Association.

Ethier, L., Couture, G., & Lacharite, C. (2004). Risk factors associated with the chronicity of high potential for child abuse and neglect. *Journal of Family Violence, 19,* 13–24.

Evans, D. W., & Leckman, J. F. (2006). Origins of obsessive-compulsive disorder: Developmental and evolutionary perspectives. In D. Cicchetti & D. Cohen (Eds), *Developmental psychopathology.* (2nd ed.). New York: Wiley.

Evans, D. W., Leckman, J. F., Carter, A., Reznick, J. S., Henshaw, D., King, R. A., & Pauls, D. (1997). Ritual, habit, and perfectionism: The prevalence and development of compulsive-like behavior in normal young children. *Child Development, 68*(1), 58–68. doi:10.2307/1131925

Evans, G. W. (2004). The environment of childhood poverty. *American Psychologist, 59,* 77–92.

Evans, R. (2009). A comparison of rural and urban older adults in Iowa on specific markers of successful aging. *Journal of Gerontological Social Work, 52,* 423–438.

Evans, T., Whittingham, K., & Boyd, R. (2012). What helps the mother of a preterm infant become securely attached, responsive and well-adjusted? *Infant Behavior & Development, 35,* 1–11.

Ezzo, F., & Young, K. (2012). Child maltreatment risk inventory: Pilot data for the Cleveland child abuse potential scale. *Journal of Family Violence, 27,* 145–155.

Evenson, K. R. (2011). Towards an understanding of change in physical activity from pregnancy through postpartum. *Psychology of Sport and Exercise, 12,* 36–45.

Faber, A., & Wittenborn, A. (2010). The role of attachment in children's adjustment to divorce and remarriage. *Journal of Family Psychotherapy, 21,* 89–104.

Fagan, J., & Holland, C. (2007). Racial equality in intelligence: Predictions from a theory of intelligence as processing. *Intelligence, 35,* 319–334.

Fagan, J., & Ployhart, R. E. (2015). The information processing foundations of human capital resources: Leveraging insights from information processing approaches to intelligence. *Human Resource Management Review, 25,* 4–11.

Fagan, M. (2009). Mean length of utterance before words and grammar: Longitudinal trends and developmental implications of infant vocalizations. *Journal of Child Language, 36,* 495–527.

Fais, L., Kajikawa, S., Amano, S., & Werker, J. (2010). Now you hear it, now you don't: Vowel devoicing in Japanese infant-directed speech. *Journal of Child Language, 37,* 319–340.

Falbe, J., Willett, W. C., Rosner, B., & Field, A. E. (2017). Body mass index, new modes of TV viewing and active video games. *Pediatric Obesity, 12*(5), 406–413. doi:10.1111/ijpo.12158

Falck-Ytter, T., Gredeback, G., & von Hofsten, C. (2006). Infants predict other people's action goals. *Nature and Neuroscience, 9,* 878–879.

Falgares, G., Lo Gioco, A., Verrocchio, M. C., & Marchetti, D. (2018). Anxiety and depression among adult amputees: The role of attachment insecurity, coping strategies and social support. *Psychology, Health & Medicine.* doi:10.1080/13548506.2018.1529324

Fang, B., & Yan, E. (2018). Abuse of older persons with dementia: A review of the literature. *Trauma, Violence, & Abuse, 19*(2), 127–147.

Fanger, S., Frankel, L., & Hazen, N. (2012). Peer exclusion in preschool children's play: Naturalistic observations in a playground setting. *Merrill-Palmer Quarterly, 58,* 224–254.

Fantz, R. L. (1961). The origin of form perception. *Scientific American, 204,* 66–72.

Fantz, R. L. (1963). Pattern vision in newborn infants. *Science, 140,* 296–297.

Farr, R. H. (2017). Does parental sexual orientation matter? A longitudinal follow-up of adoptive families with school-age children. *Developmental Psychology, 53,* 252–264.

Farran, L. K., Lee, C.-C., Yoo, H., & Oller, D. K. (2016). Cross-cultural register differences in infant-directed speech: An initial study. *PLoS ONE, 11*(3).

Farrell, L. J., Ollendick, T. H., Muris, P. (Eds.) (2019). *Innovations in CBT for childhood anxiety, OCD, and PTSD: Improving access and outcomes.* Cambridge, UK: Cambridge University Press.

Farroni, T., Menon, E., Rigato, S., & Johnson, M. (2007). The perception of facial expressions in newborns. *European Journal of Developmental Psychology, 4,* 2–13.

Farzin, F., Charles, E., & Rivera, S. (2009). Development of multimodal processing in infancy. *Infancy, 14,* 563–578.

Fast, A. A., & Olson, K. R. (2017). Gender development in transgender preschool children. *Child Development.* Accessed online, 11/10/17; https://www.ncbi.nlm.nih.gov/pubmed/28439873

Fayers, T., Crowley, T., Jenkins, J. M., & Cahill, D. J. (2003). Medical student awareness of sexual health is poor. *International Journal STD/AIDS, 14,* 386–389.

Fedele, D. A., Tooley, E., Busch, A., McQuaid, E. L., Hammond, S. K., & Borrelli, B. (2016). Comparison of secondhand smoke exposure in minority and nonminority children with asthma. *Health Psychology, 35,* 115–122.

Federal Interagency Forum on Aging-Related Statistics. (2000). *Older Americans 2000: Key indicators of well-being.* Hyattsville, MD: Author.

Federal Interagency Forum on Aging-Related Statistics. (2010). *Older Americans 2010: Key indicators of well-being.* Washington, DC: Author.

Fedichev, P. O. (2018). Hacking aging: A strategy to use big data from medical studies to extend human life. *Frontiers in genetics, 9,* 483.

Fedewa, A. L., Black, W. W., & Ahn, S. (2015). Children and adolescents with same-gender parents: A meta-analytic approach in assessing outcomes. *Journal of GLBT Family Studies, 11*(1), 1–34.

Feldman, R., & Masalha, S. (2007). The role of culture in moderating the links between early ecological risk and young children's adaptation. *Development and Psychopathology, 19,* 1–21.

Feldman, D. C., & Ng, T. H. (2013). Theoretical approaches to the study of job transitions. In N. W. Schmitt, S. Highhouse, & I. B. Weiner (Eds.), *Handbook of psychology, Vol. 12: Industrial and organizational psychology* (2nd ed.). Hoboken, NJ: John Wiley & Sons Inc.

Feldman, R. S., Tomasian, J., & Coats, E. J. (1999). Adolescents' social competence and nonverbal deception abilities: Adolescents with higher social skills are better liars. *Journal of Nonverbal Behavior, 23,* 237–249.

Fell, J., & Williams, A. (2008). The effect of aging on skeletal-muscle recovery from exercise: Possible implications for aging athletes. *Journal of Aging and Physical Activity, 16,* 97–115.

Ferguson, C. J., & Donnellan, M. B. (2014). Is the association between children's baby video viewing and poor language development robust? A reanalysis of Zimmerman, Christakis, and Meltzoff (2007). *Developmental Psychology, 50,* 129–137.

Ferguson, R., & Brohaugh, B. (2010). The aging of Aquarius. *Journal of Consumer Marketing, 27,* 76–81.

Fergusson, D., Horwood, L., Boden, J., & Jenkin, G. (2007, March). Childhood social disadvantage and smoking in adulthood: Results of a 25-year longitudinal study. *Addiction, 102,* 475–482.

Fergusson, E., Maughan, B., & Golding, J. (2008). Which children receive grandparental care and what effect does it have? *Journal of Child Psychology and Psychiatry, 49,* 161–169.

Fernald, A. (2001). Hearing, listening, and understanding: Auditory development in infancy. In G. Bremner & A. Fogel (Eds.), *Blackwell handbook of infant development* (pp. 35–70). Malden, MA: Blackwell Publishers.

Fernald, A., & Morikawa, H. (1993). Common themes and cultural variations in Japanese and American mothers' speech to infants. *Child Development, 64,* 637–656.

Fernández, C. (2013). Mindful storytellers: Emerging pragmatics and theory of mind development. *First Language, 33,* 20–46.

Ferri, R., Novelli, L., & Bruni, O. (2017). Sleep structure and scoring from infancy to adolescence. In S. Nevšimalova & O. Bruni (Eds.), *Sleep disorders in children.* Cham, Switzerland: Springer International Publishing.

Feshbach, S., & Tangney, J. (2008). Television viewing and aggression: Some alternative perspectives. *Perspectives on Psychological Science, 3,* 387–389.

Field, M. J., & Behrman, R. E. (Eds.). (2003). *When children die.* Washington, DC: National Academies Press.

Field, T. (2014). *Touch* (2nd ed.). Cambridge, MA: MIT Press.

Field, T., Diego, M., & Hernandez-Reif, M. (2008). Prematurity and potential predictors. *International Journal of Neuroscience, 118,* 277–289.

Field, T., Diego, M., & Hernandez-Reif, M. (2009). Depressed mothers' infants are less responsive to faces and voices. *Infant Behavior & Development, 32,* 239–244.

Field, T., Diego, M., & Hernandez-Reif, M. (2010). Preterm infant massage therapy research: A review. *Infant Behavior & Development, 33,* 115–124.

Filippi, M., Valsasina, P., Misci, P., Falini, A., Comi, G., & Rocca, M. A. (2013). The organization of intrinsic brain activity differs between genders: A resting-state FMRI study in a large cohort of young healthy subjects. *Human Brain Mapping, 34,* 1330–1343.

Finer, L. B., & Philbin, J. M. (2013). Sexual initiation, contraceptive use, and pregnancy among young adolescents. *Pediatrics, 131*(5), 886–891.

Finkelhor, D., Ormrod, R., Turner, H. & Hamby, S. (2005). The victimization of children and youth: A comprehensive, national survey. *Child Maltreatment, 10,* 5–25.

Finley, G., & Schwartz, S. (2010). The divided world of the child: Divorce and long-term psychosocial adjustment. *Family Court Review, 48,* 516–527.

First, J. M., & Cardenas, J. (1986). A minority view on testing. *Educational Measurement Issues and Practice, 5,* 6–11.

Fischer, T. (2007). Parental divorce and children's socio-economic success: Conditional effects of parental resources prior to divorce, and gender of the child. *Sociology, 41,* 475–495.

Fischer, K. W., & Rose, S. P. (1995). Concurrent cycles in the dynamic development of brain and behavior. *Newsletter of the Society for Research in Child Development,* p. 16.

Fish, J. M. (Ed.). (2001). *Race and intelligence: Separating science from myth.* Mahwah, NJ: Lawrence Erlbaum.

Fisher, C., Hauck, Y., & Fenwick, J. (2006). How social context impacts on women's fears of childbirth: A Western Australian example. *Social Science & Medicine, 63,* 64–75.

Fisher, C. B. (2004). Informed consent and clinical research involving children and adolescents: Implications of the revised APA Ethics Code and HIPAA. *Journal of Clinical Child & Adolescent Psychology, 33,* 832–839.

Fisher-Thompson, D. (2017). Contributions of look duration and gaze shift patterns to infants' novelty preferences. *Infancy, 22,* 190–222.

Fiske, S. T., & Taylor, S. E. (1991). *Social cognition* (2nd ed.). New York, NY: McGraw-Hill.

Fitzgerald, D., & White, K. (2002). Linking children's social worlds: Perspective-taking in parent-child and peer contexts. *Social Behavior & Personality, 31,* 509–522.

Fitzgerald, P. (2008). A neurotransmitter system theory of sexual orientation. *Journal of Sexual Medicine, 5,* 746–748.

Fitzpatrick, E. M., Al-Essa, R. S., Whittingham, J., & Fitzpatrick, J. (2017). Characteristics of children with unilateral hearing loss. *International Journal of Audiology, 56,* 819–828.

Fitzpatrick, M. (2018, October 9). French press review. RFI. Accessed online, 10/19/18; http://en.rfi.fr/france/20181009-french-press-review-9-october-2018

Flanigan, J. (2005, July 3). Immigrants benefit U.S. economy now as ever. *Los Angeles Times.*

Fleer, M. (2017). Digital role-play: The changing conditions of children's play in preschool settings. *Mind, Culture, and Activity, 24,* 3–17.

Fleer, M., Gonzalez Rey, F., & Veresov, N. (2017). *Perezhivanie, emotions and subjectivity: Advancing Vygotsky's legacy.* New York: Springer Science + Business Media.

Fletcher, A. C., Darling, N. E., Steinberg, L., & Dornbusch, S. M. (1995). The company they keep: Relation of adolescents' adjustment and behavior to their friends' perceptions of authoritative parenting in the social network. *Developmental Psychology, 31,* 300–310.

Fletcher, G. J. O., Simpson, J. A., Campbell, L., & Overall, N. C. (2015). Pair-bonding, romantic love, and evolution: The curious case of Homo sapiens. *Perspectives on Psychological Science, 10*(1), 20–36.

Fling, B. W., Walsh, C. M., Bangert, A. S., Reuter-Lorenz, P. A., Welsh, R. C., & Seidler, R. D. (2011). Differential callosal contributions to bimanual control in young and older adults. *Journal of Cognitive Neuroscience, 23,* 2171–2185.

Flom, R., & Bahrick, L. (2007). The development of infant discrimination of affect in multimodal and unimodal stimulation: The role of intersensory redundancy. *Developmental Psychology, 43,* 238–252.

Florsheim, P. (2003). Adolescent romantic and sexual behavior: What we know and where we go from here. In P. Florsheim (Ed.), *Adolescent romantic relations and sexual behavior: Theory, research, and practical implications* (pp. 371–385). Mahwah, NJ: Lawrence Erlbaum.

Flouri, E. (2005). *Fathering and child outcomes.* New York, NY: Wiley.

Flouri, E., & Midouhas, E. (2017). Environmental adversity and children's early trajectories of problem behavior: The role of harsh parental discipline. *Journal of Family Psychology, 31,* 234–243.

Floyd, R. G. (2005). Information-processing approaches to interpretation of contemporary intellectual assessment instruments. In D. P. Flanagan & P. L. Harrison (Eds.), *Contemporary intellectual assessment: Theories, tests, and issues* (pp. 203–233). New York, NY: Guilford Press.

Fok, M. S. M., & Tsang, W. Y. W. (2006). 'Development of an instrument measuring Chinese adolescent beliefs and attitudes towards substance use': Response to commentary. *Journal of Clinical Nursing, 15,* 1062–1063.

Folbre, N. (2012, July 2). Price tags for parents. *Economix-The New York Times.* Accessed online, 7/7/12; http://economix.blogs.nytimes.com/2012//07/02/price-tags-for-parents

Folkman, S. (2010). Stress, coping, and hope. *Psycho-Oncology, 19,* 901–908.

Fontes, S., & Oliveira, A. (2013). Senescence with more time and better. *Arquivos De Neuro-Psiquiatria, 71*(2), 72–73.

Foote, W. E. (2013). Forensic evaluation in Americans with Disabilities Act cases. In R. K. Otto & I. B. Weiner (Eds.), *Handbook of psychology, Vol. 11: Forensic psychology* (2nd ed.). Hoboken, NJ: John Wiley & Sons Inc.

Ford, J. A. (2007). Alcohol use among college students: A comparison of athletes and nonathletes. *Substance Use & Misuse, 42,* 1367–1377.

Forhan, S. E., Gottlieb, S. L., Sternberg, M. R., Xu, F., Datta, S. D., McQuillan, G. M., & Markowitz, L. E. (2009). Prevalence of sexually transmitted infections among female adolescents aged 14 to 19 in the United States. *Pediatrics, 124,* 1505–1512.

Forni L. G., Darmon, M., & Schetz, M. (2017). Renal replacement in 2050: From renal support to renal replacement? *Intensive Care Medicine, 43*(7), 1044–1047.

Forno, E., and Celedon, J. C. (2009, April). Asthma and ethnic minorities: Socioeconomic status and beyond. *Current Opinion in Allergy and Clinical Immunology, 9*(2), 154–160.

Foroud, A., & Whishaw, I. Q. (2012). The consummatory origins of visually guided reaching in human infants: A dynamic integration of whole-body and upper-limb movements. *Behavioural Brain Research, 231,* 343–355.

Förster, F., Stein, J., Löbner, M., Pabst, A., Angermeyer, M. C., König, H.-H., & Riedel-Heller, S. G. (2018). Loss experiences in old age and their impact on the social network and depression–Results of the Leipzig Longitudinal Study of the Aged (LEILA 75+). *Journal of Affective Disorders, 241,* 94–102.

Fortenbaugh, F. C., DeGutis, J., Germine, L., Wilmer, J. B., Grosso, M., Russo, K., & Esterman, M. (2015).

Sustained attention across the life span in a sample of 10,000:Dissociating ability and strategy. *Psychological Science, 26*, 1497–1510. doi:10.1177/0956797615594896

Fousiani, K., Van Petegem, S., Soenens, B., Vansteenkiste, M., & Chen, B. (2014). Does parental autonomy support relate to adolescent autonomy? An in-depth examination of a seemingly simple question. *Journal of Adolescent Research, 29*(3), 299–330.

Fowers, B. J., & Davidov, B. J. (2006). The virtue of multiculturalism: Personal transformation, character, and openness to the other. *American Psychologist, 61*, 581–594.

Fowler, J. W., & Dell, M. L. (2006). Stages of faith from infancy through adolescence: Reflections on three decades of faith development theory. In E. C. Roehlkepartain, P. E. King, L. Wagener, & P. L. Benson (Eds.), *The handbook of spiritual development in childhood and adolescence*. Thousand Oaks, CA: Sage Publications.

Fowler, R. C. (2017). Reframing the debate about the relationship between learning and development: An effort to resolve dilemmas and reestablish dialogue in a fractured field. *Early Childhood Education Journal, 45*, 155–162.

Fox, M., Cacciatore, J., & Lacasse, J. R. (2014). Child death in the United States: Productivity and the economic burden of parental grief. *Death Studies, 38*, 597–602.

Fraenkel, P. (2003). Contemporary two-parent families: Navigating work and family challenges. In F. Walsh (Ed.), *Normal family processes: Growing diversity and complexity* (3rd ed.). New York, NY: Guilford Press.

Francis, A. N., Bhojraj, T. S., Prasad, K. M., Montrose, D., Eack, S. M., Rajarethinam, R., &... Keshavan, M. S. (2013). Alterations in the cerebral white matter of genetic high risk offspring of patients with schizophrenia spectrum disorder. *Progress in Neuro-Psychopharmacology & Biological Psychiatry, 40*, 187–192.

Franck, I., & Brownstone, D. (1991). *The parent's desk reference*. New York, NY: Prentice-Hall.

Franic, S., Middeldorp, C., Dolan, C., Ligthart, L., & Boomsma, D. (2010). Childhood and adolescent anxiety and depression: Beyond heritability. *Journal of the American Academy of Child & Adolescent Psychiatry, 49*, 820–829.

Frank, M. C., Tenenbaum, J. B., & Fernald, A. (2013). Social and discourse contributions to the determination of reference in cross-situational word learning. *Language Learning and Development, 9*, 1–24.

Frankenburg, W. K., Dodds, J., Archer, P., Shapiro, H., & Bresnick, B. (1992). The Denver II: A major revision and restandardization of the Denver Developmental Screening Test. *Pediatrics, 89*, 91–97.

Frankenhuis, W. E., Barrett, H., & Johnson, S. P. (2013). Developmental origins of biological motion perception. In K. L. Johnson & M. Shiffrar (Eds.), *People watching: Social, perceptual, and neurophysiological studies of body perception*. New York: Oxford University Press.

Fransson, M., Granqvist, P., Marciszko, C., Hagekull, B., & Bohlin, G. (2016). Is middle childhood attachment related to social functioning in young adulthood? *Scandinavian Journal of Psychology, 57*, 108–116.

Franz, C. E., McKenzie, R. M., Ramundo, A., Landrum, E., & Shahroudi, A. (2015). Interpersonal relationships in late adulthood. In B. N. Horwitz, J. M. Neiderhiser, B. N. Horwitz, & J. M. Neiderhiser (Eds.), *Gene-environment interplay in interpersonal relationships across the lifespan*. New York, NY: Springer Science + Business Media.

Frawley, T. (2008). Gender schema and prejudicial recall: How children misremember, fabricate, and distort gendered picture book information. *Journal of Research in Childhood Education, 22*, 291–303.

Frederickson, N., & Petrides, K. (2008). Ethnic, gender, and socio-economic group differences in academic performance and secondary school selection: A longitudinal analysis. *Learning and Individual Differences, 18*, 144–151.

Freedman, A. M., & Ellison, S. (2004, May 6). Testosterone patch for women shows promise. *Wall Street Journal*, pp. A1, B2.

Freedman, D. G. (1979, January). Ethnic differences in babies. *Human Nature*, 15–20.

Freeman, E., Sammel, M., & Liu, L. (2004). Hormones and menopausal status as predictors of depression in women in transition to menopause. *Archives of General Psychiatry, 61*, 62–70.

Freeman, H., Newland, L. A., & Coyl, D. D. (2010). New directions in father attachment. *Early Child Development and Care, 180*, 1–8.

Freeman, J. M. (2007). Beware: The misuse of technology and the law of unintended consequences. *Neurotherapeutics, 4*, 549–554.

Freud, S. (1920). *A general introduction to psychoanalysis*. New York, NY: Boni & Liveright.

Frewen, A. R., Chew, E., Carter, M., Chunn, J., & Jotanovic, D. (2015). A cross-cultural exploration of parental involvement and child-rearing beliefs in Asian cultures. *Early Years: An International Journal of Research and Development, 35*, 36–49.

Frey, T. K., & Tatum, N. T. (2016). Hoverboards and "hovermoms": Helicopter parents and their influence on millennial students' rapport with instructors. *Communication Education, 65*, 359–361.

Freyne, B., Hamilton, K., Mc Garvey, C., Shannon, B., Matthews, T. G., & Nicholson, A. J. (2014). Sudden unexpected death study underlines risks of infants sleeping in sitting devices. *Acta Paediatrica, 103*, e130–e132.

Frías, M. T., Shaver, P. R., & Mikulincer, M. (2015). Measures of adult attachment and related constructs. In G. J. Boyle, D. H. Saklofske, & G. Matthews (Eds.), *Measures of personality and social psychological constructs*. San Diego, CA: Elsevier Academic Press.

Frick, P. J., Cornell, A. H., Bodin, S. D., Dane, H. A., Barry, C. T., & Loney, B. R. (2003). Callous-unemotional traits and developmental pathways to severe conduct problems. *Developmental Psychology, 39*, 246–260.

Fridlund, A. J., Beck, H. P., Goldie, W. D., & Irons, G. (2012, July 9). Little Albert: A neurologically impaired child. *History of Psychology, 15*, 302–327.

Frie, R. (2014). What is cultural psychoanalysis? Psychoanalytic anthropology and the interpersonal tradition. *Contemporary Psychoanalysis, 50*, 371–394.

Friedlander, L. J., Connolly, J. A., Pepler, D. J., & Craig, W. M. (2007). Biological, familial, and peer influences on dating in early adolescence. *Archives of Sexual Behavior, 36*, 821–830.

Friedman, S., Heneghan, A., & Rosenthal, M. (2009). Characteristics of women who do not seek prenatal care and implications for prevention. *Journal of Obstetric, Gynecologic, & Neonatal Nursing: Clinical Scholarship for the Care of Women, Childbearing Families, & Newborns, 38*, 174–181.

Friedman, W., & Janssen, S. (2010). Aging and the speed of time. *Acta Psychologica, 134*, 130–141.

Friedrich, J. (2014). Vygotsky's idea of psychological tools. In A. Yasnitsky, R. van der Veer, & M. Ferrari (Eds.), *The Cambridge handbook of cultural-historical psychology*. New York, NY: Cambridge University Press.

Fritz, G., & Rockney, R. (2004). Summary of the practice parameter for the assessment and treatment of children and adolescents with enuresis. *Work Group on Quality Issues; Journal of the American Academy of Child & Adolescent Psychiatry, 43*, 123–125.

Frome, P., Alfeld, C., Eccles, J., & Barber, B. (2006, August). Why don't they want a male-dominated job? An investigation of young women who changed their occupational aspirations. *Educational Research and Evaluation, 12*, 359–372.

Frumkes, L. A. (2018, October 18). A second language for every student. *Language Magazine*. Accessed online, 10/16/18; https://www.languagemagazine.com/2018/10/15/a-second-language-for-every-student/

Fry, C. L. (1985). Culture, behavior, and aging in the comparative perspective. In J. E. Birren & K. W. Schaie (Eds.), *Handbook of the psychology of aging*. New York, NY: Van Nostrand Reinhold.

Fu, G., Xu, F., Cameron, C., Heyman, G., & Lee, K. (2007, March). Cross-cultural differences in children's choices, categorizations, and evaluations of truths and lies. *Developmental Psychology, 43*(2), 278–293.

Fu, X., & Heaton, T. (2008). Racial and educational homogamy: 1980 to 2000. *Sociological Perspectives, 51*, 735–758.

Fujisawa, T. X., & Shinohara, K. (2011). Sex differences in the recognition of emotional prosody in late childhood and adolescence. *Journal of Physiological Science, 61*, 429–435.

Fujitsuka, N., Asakawa, A., Morinaga, A., Amitani, M. S., Amitani, H., Katsuura, G., &... Inui, A. (2016). Increased ghrelin signaling prolongs survival in mouse models of human aging through activation of sirtuin1. *Molecular Psychiatry, 21*, 1613–1623.

Fulcher, M., Sutfin, E. L., & Patterson, C. J. (2008). Individual differences in gender development: Associations with parental sexual orientation, attitudes, and division of labor. *Sex Roles: A Journal of Research, 58*, 330–341.

Fulcher, M., Sutfin, E., Chan, R., Scheib, J., & Patterson, C. (2006). Lesbian mothers and their children: Findings from the Contemporary Families Study. In A. M. Omoto & H. S. Kurtzman (Eds.), *Sexual orientation and mental health: Examining identity and development in lesbian, gay, and bisexual people*. Washington, DC: American Psychological Association.

Fuligni, A. J. (2012). The intersection of aspirations and resources in the development of children from immigrant families. In C. Coll & A. Marks (Eds.), *The immigrant paradox in children and adolescents: Is becoming American a developmental risk?* Washington, DC: American Psychological Association.

Fuligni, A. J., & Fuligni, A. S. (2008). Immigrant families and the educational development of their children. In J. E. Lansford et al. (Eds.), *Immigrant families in contemporary society*. New York, NY: Guilford Press.

Fuligni, A. J., & Yoshikawa, H. (2003). Socioeconomic resources, parenting, and child development among immigrant families. In M. Bornstein & R. Bradley (Eds.), *Socioeconomic status, parenting, and child development* (pp. 107–124). Mahwah, NJ: Lawrence Erlbaum.

Funk, L. (2010). Prioritizing parental autonomy: Adult children's accounts of feeling responsible and supporting aging parents. *Journal of Aging Studies, 24*, 57–64.

Furman, W., & Shaffer, L. (2003). The role of romantic relationships in adolescent development. In P. Florsheim (Ed.), *Adolescent romantic relations and sexual behavior: Theory, research, and practical implications*. Mahwah, NJ: Lawrence Erlbaum.

Furnham, A., & Weir, C. (1996). Lay theories of child development. *Journal of Genetic Psychology, 157*, 211–226.

Fuso, A., Nicolia, V., Ricceri, L., Cavallaro, R. A., Isopi, E., Mangia, F., &... Scarpa, S. (2012). S-adenosylmethionine reduces the progress of the Alzheimer-like features induced by B-vitamin deficiency in mice. *Neurobiology of Aging, 33*, e1–e16.

Gagneux, P. (2016). Assisted reproductive technologies: Evolution of human niche construction? Paper presented at the annual meeting of the American Association for the Advancement of Science. Washington, DC.

Galambos, N., Leadbeater, B., & Barker, E. (2004). Gender differences in and risk factors for depression in adolescence: A 4-year longitudinal study. *International Journal of Behavioral Development, 28*, 16–25.

Galéra, C., Bernard, J. Y., van der Waerden, J., Bouvard, M., Lioret, S., Forhan, A., &... Heude, B.

(2016). Prenatal caffeine exposure and child IQ at age 55 years: The EDEN mother-child cohort. *Biological Psychiatry, 80*(9), 720–726.

Galler, J., Bryce, C., Waber, D., Hock, R., Exner, N., Eaglesfield, D., Fitzmaurice, G. (2010). Early childhood malnutrition predicts depressive symptoms at ages 11–17. *Journal of Child Psychology and Psychiatry, 51*, 789–798.

Gallup Poll. (2004). How many children? *The Gallup Poll Monthly.*

Galst, J. P. (2018). The elusive connection between stress and infertility: A research review with clinical implications. *Journal of Psychotherapy Integration, 28*(1), 1–13. doi:10.1037/int0000081

Galvao, T. F., Silva, M. T., Zimmermann, I. R., Souza, K. M., Martins, S. S., & Pereira, M. G. (2013). Pubertal timing in girls and depression: A systematic review. *Journal of Affective Disorders, 155*, 13–19.

Gamino, L. A., & Ritter, R. R. (2012). Death competence: An ethical imperative. *Death Studies, 36*, 23–40.

Gandhi, P. K., Schwartz, C. E., Reeve, B. B., DeWalt, D. A., Gross, H. E., & Huang, I. (2016). An item-level response shift study on the change of health state with the rating of asthma-specific quality of life: A report from the PROMIS® pediatric asthma study. *Quality of Life Research: An International Journal of Quality Of Life Aspects of Treatment, Care & Rehabilitation, 25*, 1349–1359.

Ganley, C. M., Mingle, L. A., Ryan, A. M., Ryan, K., Vasilyeva, M., & Perry, M. (2013). An examination of stereotype threat effects on girls' mathematics performance. *Developmental Psychology, 49*, 1886–1897.

Gansen, H. M. (2018). Push-ups versus clean-up: Preschool teachers' gendered beliefs, expectations for behavior, and disciplinary practices. *Sex Roles.* doi:10.1007/s11199-018-0944-2

Gao, Z., & Bischoping, K. (2018). The emergence of an elder-blaming discourse in twenty-first century China. *Journal of Cross Cultural Gerontology, 33*(2), 197–215.

Garbarino, J. (2013). The emotionally battered child. In R. D. Krugman, J. E. Korbin (Eds.), *C. Henry Kempe: A 50-year legacy to the field of child abuse and neglect.* New York, NY: Springer Science + Business Media.

Garcia, J. M., & Teixeira, L. A. (2017). Modulating children's manual preference through spontaneous nondominant hand use. *Perceptual and Motor Skills, 124*(5), 932–945.

Garcia-Moreno, C., Heise, L., Jansen, H. A. F. M., Ellsberg, M., & Watts, C. (2005, November 25). Violence against women. *Science, 310*, 1282–1283.

Garcia-Portilla, M. (2009). Depression and perimenopause: A review. *Actas Esp Psiquiatr, 37*, 231–321.

García-Ruiz, M., Rodrigo, M., Hernández-Cabrera, J. A., & Máiquez, M. (2013). Contribution of parents' adult attachment and separation attitudes to parent-adolescent conflict resolution. *Scandinavian Journal of Psychology, 54*, 459–467.

Gardner, H., & Moran, S. (2006). The science of multiple intelligences theory: A response to Lynn Waterhouse. *Educational Psychologist, 41*, 227–232.

Gardner, P. (2007). *Parent involvement in the college recruiting process: To what extent?* (Research Brief 2-2007). Collegiate Employment Research Institute, Michigan State University.

Garlick, D. (2003). Integrating brain science research with intelligence research. *Current Directions in Psychological Science, 12*, 185–189.

Gartrell, N., & Bos, H. (2010). US National Longitudinal Lesbian Family Study: Psychological adjustment of 17-year-old adolescents. *Pediatrics, 126*, 28–36.

Gartstein, M. A., Prokasky, A., Bell, M. A., Calkins, S., Bridgett, D. J., Braungart-Rieker, J., & ... Seamon, E. (2017). Latent profile and cluster analysis of infant temperament: Comparisons across person-centered approaches. *Developmental Psychology, 53*, 1811–1825.

Gates, G. J. (2013, February). *LBGT parenting in the United States.* Los Angeles: Williams Institute.

Gattringer, T., Enzinger, C., Ropele, S., Gorani, F., Petrovic, K., Schmidt, R., & Fazekas, F. (2012). Vascular risk factors, white matter hyperintensities and hippocampal volume in normal elderly individuals. *Dementia and Geriatric Cognitive Disorders, 33*(1), 29–34.

Gaugler, J. E., Yu, F., Davila, H. W., & Shippee, T. (2014). Alzheimer's disease and nursing homes. *Health Affairs (Project Hope), 33*(4), 650–657.

Gaulden, M. E. (1992). Maternal age effect: The enigma of Down syndrome and other trisomic conditions. *Mutation Research, 296*, 69–88.

Gauthier, S., & Scheltens, P. (2009). Can we do better in developing new drugs for Alzheimer's disease? *Alzheimer's & Dementia, 5*, 489–491.

Gauvain, M. (1998). Cognitive development in social and cultural context. *Current Directions in Psychological Science, 7*, 188–194.

Gavin, T., & Myers, A. (2003). Characteristics, enrollment, attendance, and dropout patterns of older adults in beginner Tai-Chi and line-dancing programs. *Journal of Aging & Physical Activity, 11*, 123–141.

Gawande, A. (2007, April 30). The way we age now. *The New Yorker,* pp. 49–59.

Geary, D. C., & Berch, D. B. (2016). *Evolutionary perspectives on child development and education.* Cham, Switzerland: Springer International Publishing.

Gebuza, G., Kaźmierczak, M., Gdaniec, A., Mieczkowska, E., Gierszewska, M., Dombrowska-Pali, A., & ... Maleńczyk, M. (2018). Episiotomy and perineal tear risk factors in a group of 4493 women. *Health Care for Women International,* doi:10.1080/07399332.2018.1464004

Geller, P. A., Nelson, A. R., & Bonacquisti, A. (2013). Women's health psychology. In A. M. Nezu, C. Nezu, P. A. Geller, & I. B. Weiner (Eds.), *Handbook of psychology, Vol. 9: Health psychology* (2nd ed.). Hoboken, NJ: John Wiley & Sons Inc.

Gelman, C. R., Tompkins, C. J., & Ihara, E. S. (2014). The complexities of caregiving for minority older adults: Rewards and challenges. In K. E. Whitfield, T. A. Baker, C. M. Abdou, J. L. Angel, L. A. Chadiha, K. Gerst-Emerson, & ... R. J. Thorpe (Eds.), *Handbook of minority aging.* New York, NY: Springer Publishing Co.

Gelman, R. (2015). Learning in core and non-core number domains. *Developmental Review, 38*, 185–200.

Gelman, R., & Baillargeon, R. (1983). A review of some Piagetian concepts. In P. H. Mussen (Ed.), *Handbook of child psychology: Vol 3. Cognitive development* (4th ed.). New York, NY: Wiley.

Gelman, S. A., Taylor, M. G., & Nguyen, S. (2004). Mother-child conversations about gender. *Monographs of the Society for Research in Child Development, 69.*

Genetics Home Reference. (2017). *Your guide to understanding genetic conditions.* Washington, DC: U.S. National Library of Medicine. Accessed online, 10/25/17; https://ghr.nlm.nih.gov/

Genevro, J. L., & Miller, T. L. (2010). The emotional and economic costs of bereavement in health care settings. *Psychologica Belgica, 50*, 69–88.

Gentier, I., D'Hondt, E., Shultz, S., Deforche, B., Augustijn, M., Hoorne, S., ... Lenoir, M. (2013). Fine and gross motor skills differ between healthy-weight and obese children. *Research in Developmental Disabilities, 34*(11), 4043–4051.

Gerard, C. M., Harris, K. A., & Thach, B. T. (2002). Spontaneous arousals in supine infants while swaddled and unswaddled during rapid eye movement and quiet sleep. *Pediatrics, 110*, 70.

Gerressu, M., Mercer, C., Graham, C., Wellings, K., & Johnson, A. (2008). Prevalence of masturbation and associated factors in a British national probability survey. *Archives of Sexual Behavior, 37*, 266–278.

Gershoff, E. T. (2002). Parental corporal punishment and associated child behaviors and experiences: A meta-analytic and theoretical review. *Pychological Bulletin, 128*, 539–579.

Gershoff, E. T., Goodman, G. S., Miller-Perrin, C. L., Holden, G. W., Jackson, Y., & Kazdin, A. E. (2018). The strength of the causal evidence against physical punishment of children and its implications for parents, psychologists, and policymakers. *American Psychologist, 73*(5), 626–638.

Gershoff, E. T., Lansford, J. E., Sexton, H. R., Davis-Kean, P., & Sameroff, A. J. (2012). Longitudinal links between spanking and children's externalizing behaviors in a national sample of White, Black, Hispanic, and Asian American families. *Clinical Psychology Review, 23*, 197–224.

Gerstorf, D., Hoppmann, C. A., Löckenhoff, C. E., Infurna, F. J., Schupp, J., Wagner, G. G., & Ram, N. (2016). Terminal decline in well-being: The role of social orientation. *Psychology and Aging, 31*, 149–165.

Gesell, A. L. (1946). The ontogenesis of infant behavior. In L. Carmichael (Ed.), *Manual of child psychology.* New York, NY: Harper.

Geurts, T., van Tilburg, T. G., & Poortman, A. (2012). The grandparent-grandchild relationship in childhood and adulthood: A matter of continuation? *Personal Relationships, 19*, 267–278.

Ghaemi, S., Vohringer, P. A., & Whitham, E. A. (2013). Antidepressants from a public health perspective: Re-examining effectiveness, suicide, and carcinogenicity. *Acta Psychiatrica Scandinavica, 127*, 89–93.

Gharaei, N., Thijs, J., & Verkuyten, M. (2018). Ethnic identity in diverse schools: Preadolescents' private regard and introjection in relation to classroom norms and composition. *Journal of Youth and Adolescence.* doi:10.1007/s10964-018-0881-y

Ghazi, A., Henis-Korenblit, S., & Kenyon, C. (2009). A transcription elongation factor that links signals from the reproductive system to lifespan extension in Caenorhabditis elegans. *PLoS Genetics, 5*, 71–77.

Ghetti, S., & Angelini, L. (2008). The development of recollection and familiarity in childhood and adolescence: Evidence from the dual-process signal detection model. *Child Development, 79*, 339–358.

Ghisletta, P., Kennedy, K., Rodrigue, K., Lindenberger, U., & Raz, N. (2010). Adult age differences and the role of cognitive resources in perceptual-motor skill acquisition: Application of a multilevel negative exponential model. *The Journals of Gerontology: Series B: Psychological Sciences and Social Sciences, 65B*, 163–173.

Ghisletta, P., Rabbitt, P., Lunn, M., & Lindenberger, U. (2012). Two thirds of the age-based changes in fluid and crystallized intelligence, perceptual speed, and memory in adulthood are shared. *Intelligence, 40*, 260–268.

Ghule, M., Balaiah, D., & Joshi, B. (2007). Attitude towards premarital sex among rural college youth in Maharashtra, India. *Sexuality & Culture, 11*, 1–17.

Giacalone, D., Wendin, K., Kremer, S., Frøst, M. B., Bredie, W. P., Olsson, V., & ... Risvik, E. (2016). Health and quality of life in an aging population—Food and beyond. *Food Quality and Preference, 47*(PartB), 166–170.

Gibbs, N. (2002, April 15). Making time for a baby. *Time,* pp. 48–54.

Gibson, E. J., & Walk, R. D. (1960). The "visual cliff." *Scientific American, 202*, 64–71.

Giedd, J. N. (2012). The digital revolution and adolescent brain evolution. *Journal of Adolescent Health, 51*, 101–105.

Gifford-Smith, M., & Brownell, C. (2003). Childhood peer relationships: Social acceptance, friendships, and peer networks. *Journal of School Psychology, 41*, 235–284.

Gilbert, S. (2004, March 16). New clues to women veiled in black. *The New York Times,* p. D1.

Gillham, A., Law, A., & Hickey, L. (2010). A psychodynamic perspective. In C. Cupitt (Eds.), *Reaching out: The psychology of assertive outreach.* New York, NY: Routledge/Taylor & Francis Group.

Gillies, R. M. (2014). Developments in cooperative learning: Review of research. *Anales De Psicología, 30*, 792–801.

Gilligan, C. (1982). *In a different voice: Psychological theory and women's development.* Cambridge, MA: Harvard University Press.

Gilligan, C. (2004). Recovering psyche: Reflections on life-history and history. *Annual of Psychoanalysis, 32*, 131–147.

Gilligan, C. (2015). In a different voice: Women's conceptions of self and morality. In V. Burr (Ed.), *Gender and psychology., Vol. II.* (pp. 33–74). New York, NY: Routledge/Taylor & Francis Group.

Gilligan, C., Brown, L. M., & Rogers, A. G. (1990). Psyche embedded: A place for body, relationships, and culture in personality theory. In A. I. Rabin & R. A. Zucker (Eds.), *Studying persons and lives.* New York, NY: Springer.

Gillmore, M., Gilchrist, L., Lee, J., & Oxford, M. (2006, August). Women who gave birth as unmarried adolescents: Trends in substance use from adolescence to adulthood. *Journal of Adolescent Health, 39*, 237–243.

Gilmore, C. K., & Spelke, E. S. (2008). Children's understanding of the relationship between addition and subtraction. *Cognition, 107*, 932–945.

Ginzberg, E. (1972). Toward a theory of occupational choice: A restatement. *Vocational Guidance Quarterly, 12*, 10–14.

Giralt, S., Müller, K. W., Beutel, M. E., Dreier, M., Duven, E., & Wölfling, K. (2018). Prevalence, risk factors, and psychosocial adjustment of problematic gambling in adolescents: Results from two representative German samples. *Journal of Behavioral Addictions, 7*(2), 339–347.

Gitlin, L., Reever, K., Dennis, M., Mathieu, E., & Hauck, W. (2006, October). Enhancing quality of life of families who use adult day services: Short- and long-term effects of the Adult Day Services Plus Program. *The Gerontologist, 46*, 630–639.

Glaser, D. (2012). Effects of child maltreatment on the developing brain. In M. Garralda & J. Raynaud (Eds.), *Brain, mind, and developmental psychopathology in childhood.* Lanham, MD: Jason Aronson.

Glasson, E. J., Jacques, A., Wong, K., Bourke, J., & Leonard, H. (2016). Improved survival in Down syndrome over the last 60 years and the impact of perinatal factors in recent decades. *Journal of Pediatrics, 169*, 214–220.

Glatt, S., Chayavichitsilp, P., Depp, C., Schork, N., & Jeste, D. (2007). Successful aging: From phenotype to genotype. *Biological Psychiatry, 62*, 282–293.

Glauber, R. (2017). Gender differences in spousal care across the later life course. *Research on Aging, 39*, 934–959.

Glick, P., & Fiske, S. T. (2012). An ambivalent alliance: Hostile and benevolent sexism as complementary justifications for gender inequality. In J. Dixon & M. Levine (Eds.), *Beyond prejudice: Extending the social psychology of conflict, inequality and social change.* New York, NY: Cambridge University Press.

Gliga, T., Elsabbagh, M., Andravizou, A., & Johnson, M. (2009). Faces attract infants' attention in complex displays. *Infancy, 14*, 550–562.

Glina, S., Cohen, D. J., & Vieira, M. (2014). Diagnosis of erectile dysfunction. *Current Opinion in Psychiatry, 27*, 394–399.

Glover, C. P., Jenkins, T. S., & Troutman, S. (2019). Culture, community, and educational success: Reimagining the invisible knapsack (race and education in the twenty-first century). Lanham, MD: Lexington Books.

Glynn, L. M., & Sandman, C. A. (2014). Evaluation of the association between placental corticotrophin-releasing hormone and postpartum depressive symptoms. *Psychosomatic Medicine, 76*, 355–362.

Godard, O., Baudouin, J., Schaal, B., & Durand, K. (2016). Affective matching of odors and facial expressions in infants: Shifting patterns between 3 and 7 months. *Developmental Science, 19*(1), 155–163.

Godefroy, O., Roussel, M., Despretz, P., Quaglino, V., & Boucart, M. (2010). Age-related slowing: Perceptuomotor, decision, or attention decline? *Experimental Aging Research, 36*, 169–189.

Goede, I., Branje, S., & Meeus, W. (2009). Developmental changes in adolescents' perceptions of relationships with their parents. *Journal of Youth and Adolescence, 38*, 75–88.

Goetz, A., & Shackelford, T. (2006). Modern application of evolutionary theory to psychology: Key concepts and clarifications. *American Journal of Psychology, 119*, 567–584.

Gogtay, N., Sporn, A., Clasen, L. S., Nugent, T. I., Greenstein, D., Nicolson, R., & ... Rapoport, J. L. (2004). Comparison of progressive cortical gray matter loss in childhood-onset schizophrenia with that in childhood-onset atypical psychoses. *Archives of General Psychiatry, 61*(1), 17–22. doi:10.1001/archpsyc.61.1.17

Gökçe, M. İ., & Yaman, Ö. (2017). Erectile dysfunction in the elderly male. *Turkish Journal of Urology, 43*, 247–251.

Goldberg, A. E. (2004). But do we need universal grammar? Comment on Lidz et al. *Cognition, 94*, 77–84.

Goldberg, A. E. (2010a). Children of lesbian and gay parents: Adjustment and experiences. In A. E. Goldberg, *Lesbian and gay parents and their children: Research on the family life cycle.* Washington, DC: American Psychological Association.

Goldberg, A. E. (2010b). *Lesbian and gay parents and their children: Research on the family life cycle.* Washington, DC: American Psychological Association.

Goldberg, L. R., & Gould, T. J. (2018). Multigenerational and transgenerational effects of paternal exposure to drugs of abuse on behavioral and neural function. *European Journal of Neuroscience*, doi:10.1111/ejn.14060

Goldfield, G. S., Harvey, A., Grattan, K., & Adamo, K. B. (2012). Physical activity promotion in the preschool years: A critical period to intervene. *International Journal of Environmental Research and Public Health, 9*, 1326–1342.

Goldman, D., & Domschke, K. (2014). Making sense of deep sequencing. *International Journal of Neuropsychopharmacology, 17*, 1717–1725.

Goldman, L., Chu, P. W., Osmond, D., & Bindman, A. (2013). Accuracy of do not resuscitate (DNR) in administrative data. *Medical Care Research and Review, 70*, 98–112.

Goldman, R. (2004). Circumcision policy: A psychosocial perspective. *Pediatrics and Child Health, 9*, 630–633.

Goldney, R. D. (2012). Neither euthanasia nor suicide, but rather assisted death. *Australian and New Zealand Journal of Psychiatry, 46*, 185–187.

Goldschmidt, L., Richardson, G., Willford, J., & Day, N. (2008). Prenatal marijuana exposure and intelligence test performance at age 6. *Journal of the American Academy of Child & Adolescent Psychiatry, 47*, 254–263.

Goldstein, S., & Brooks, R. B. (2013). *Handbook of resilience in children* (2nd ed.). New York, NY: Springer Science + Business Media.

Gollenberg, A., & Fendley, K. (2018). Is it time for a Sudden Infant Death Syndrome (SIDS) awareness campaign? Community stakeholders' perceptions of SIDS. *Child Care in Practice, 24*(1), 53–64.

Golombok, S., Golding, J., Perry, B., Burston, A., Murray, C., Mooney-Somers, J., & Stevens, M. (2003). Children with lesbian parents: A community study. *Developmental Psychology, 39*, 20–33.

Golombok, S., & Tasker, F. (1996). Do parents influence the sexual orientation of their children? Findings from a longitudinal study of lesbian families. *Developmental Psychology, 32*, 3–11.

Gomes, A. I., Barros, L., & Pereira, A. I. (2017). Predictors of parental concerns about child weight in parents of healthy-weight and overweight 2–6 year olds. *Appetite, 108*, 491–497.

Gondolf, E. W. (1985). Fighting for control: A clinical assessment of men who batter. *Social Casework, 66*, 48–54.

Gonzales, A. (2016). The contemporary US digital divide: From initial access to technology maintenance. *Information, Communication & Society, 19*, 234–248.

Goodman, G. S. (2006). Children's eyewitness memory: A modern history and contemporary commentary. *Journal of Social Issues, 62*, 811–832.

Goodnough, A., & Atkinson, S. (2016, April 30). A potent side effect to the Flint water crisis: Mental health problems. *The New York Times*, p. A16.

Goodwin, M. H. (1990). Tactical uses of stories: Participation frameworks within girls' and boys' disputes. *Discourse Processes, 13*, 33–71.

Goold, S. D., Williams, B., & Arnold, R. M. (2000). Conflicts regarding decisions to limit treatment: A differential diagnosis. *JAMA: The Journal of the American Medical Association, 283*, 909–914.

Goorabi, K., Hoseinabadi, R., & Share, H. (2008). Hearing aid effect on elderly depression in nursing home patients. *Asia Pacific Journal of Speech, Language, and Hearing, 11*, 119–124.

Gopinath, B., Schneider, J., Hickson, L., McMahon, C. M., Burlutsky, G., Leeder, S. R., & Mitchell, P. (2012). Hearing handicap, rather than measured hearing impairment, predicts poorer quality of life over 10 years in older adults. *Maturitas, 72*, 146–151.

Gopnik, A. (2010, July). How babies think. *Scientific American*, pp. 76–81.

Gopnik, A. (2012, January 28). What's wrong with the teenage mind? *Wall Street Journal*, pp. C1–C2.

Gopnik, A. I., O'Grady, S., Lucas, C. G., Griffiths, T. L., Wente, A., et al. (2017). Changes in cognitive flexibility and hypothesis search across human life history from childhood to adolescence to adulthood. *PNAS, 114*, 892–899.

Gordon, I., Pratt, M., Bergunde, K., Zagoory-Sharon, O., & Feldman, R. (2017). Testosterone, oxytocin, and the development of human parental care. *Hormones and Behavior, 93*, 184–192.

Gordon, I., Voos, A. C., Bennett, R. H., Bolling, D. Z., Pelphrey, K. A., & Kaiser, M. D. (2013). Brain mechanisms for processing affective touch. *Human Brain Mapping, 34*, 914–922.

Gordon, N. (2007). The cerebellum and cognition. *European Journal of Paediatric Neurology, 30*, 214–220.

Gören, J. L. (2008). Antidepressants use in pediatric populations. *Expert Opinions on Drug Safety, 7*, 223–225.

Gorman, A. (2010, January 7). UCLA study says legalizing undocumented immigrants would help the economy. *Los Angeles Times*.

Gormley, W. T., Jr., Gayer, T., Phillips, D., & Dawson, B. (2005). The effects of universal pre-K on cognitive development. *Developmental Psychology, 41*, 872–884.

Gostin, L. (2006, April). Physician-assisted suicide a legitimate medical practice? *Journal of the American Medical Association, 295*, 1941–1943.

Gottesman, I. I. (1991). *Schizophrenia genesis: The origins of madness.* New York, NY: Freeman.

Gottman J. M., & Gottman, J. S. (2018). *The science of couples and family therapy: Behind the scenes at the "Love Lab."* New York: W. W. Norton & Co.

Gould, R. L. (1978). *Transformations: Growth and change in adult life.* New York, NY: Simon & Schuster.

Gow, A., Pattie, A., Whiteman, M., Whalley, L., & Deary, I. (2007). Social support and successful aging: Investigating the relationships between lifetime cognitive change and life satisfaction. *Journal of Individual Differences, 28*, 103–115.

Gowey, M. A., Reiter-Purtill, J., Becnel, J., Peugh, J., Mitchell, J. E., & Zeller, M. H. (2016). Weight-related correlates of psychological dysregulation in adolescent and young adult (AYA) females with severe obesity. *Appetite, 99*, 211–218.

Goyette-Ewing, M. (2000). Children's after-school arrangements: A study of self-care and developmental outcomes. *Journal of Prevention & Intervention in the Community, 20*, 55–67.

Grabner, R. H., Neubauer, A. C., & Stern, E. (2006). Superior performance and neural efficiency: The impact of intelligence and expertise. *Brain Research Bulletin, 69*, 422–439.

Graddol, D. (2004, February 27). The future of language. *Science, 303*, 1329–1331.

Grady, D. (2009, November 3). Quandary with mammograms: Get a screening or just skip it? *The New York Times*, p. D2.

Graf Estes, K. (2014). Learning builds on learning: Infants' use of native language sound patterns to learn words. *Journal of Experimental Child Psychology, 126*, 313–327.

Graham, S. A., Nilsen, E., Mah, J. T., Morison, S., MacLean, K., Fisher, L., &… Ames, E. (2014). An examination of communicative interactions of children from Romanian orphanages and their adoptive mothers. *Canadian Journal of Behavioural Science/Revue Canadienne Des Sciences Du Comportement, 46*, 9–19.

Grall, T. S. (2009). *Custodial mothers and fathers and their child support: 2007*. Washington, DC: U.W. Department of Commerce.

Granek, L., Barrera, M., Scheinemann, K., & Bartels, U. (2015). When a child dies: Pediatric oncologists' follow-up practices with families after the death of their child. *Psychooncology, 24*, 1626–1631.

Granic, I., Hollenstein, T., & Dishion, T. (2003). Longitudinal analysis of flexibility and reorganization in early adolescence: A dynamic systems study of family interactions. *Developmental Psychology, 39*, 606–617.

Granié, M. (2010). Gender stereotype conformity and age as determinants of preschoolers' injury-risk behaviors. *Accident Analysis and Prevention, 42*, 726–733.

Grant, C., Wall, C., Brewster, D., Nicholson, R., Whitehall, J., Super, L., & Pitcher, L. (2007). Policy statement on iron deficiency in pre-school-aged children. *Journal of Paediatrics and Child Health, 43*, 513–521.

Grant, R. J. (2017). *Play-based intervention for autism spectrum disorder and other developmental disabilities*. New York: Routledge/Taylor & Francis Group.

Graves, T. A., Tabri, N., Thompson-Brenner, H., Franko, D. L., Eddy, K. T., Bourion-Bedes, S., &… Thomas, J. J. (2017). A meta-analysis of the relation between therapeutic alliance and treatment outcome in eating disorders. *International Journal of Eating Disorders, 50*, 323–340.

Gray, S., & Rarick, S. (2018). Exploring gender and racial/ethnic differences in the effects of child sexual abuse. *Journal of Child Sexual Abuse: Research, Treatment, & Program Innovations for Victims, Survivors, & Offenders*. doi:10.1080/10538712.2018.1484403

Gredler, M. E. (2012). Understanding Vygotsky for the classroom: Is it too late? *Educational Psychology Review, 24*, 113–131.

Gredler, M. E., & Shields, C. C. (2008). *Vygotsky's legacy: A foundation for research and practice*. New York, NY: Guilford Press.

Green, C. S., & Bavelier, D. (2012). Learning, attentional control, and action video games. *Current Biology, 22*, 197–206.

Green, M., DeCourville, N., & Sadava, S. (2012). Positive affect, negative affect, stress, and social support as mediators of the forgiveness-health relationship. *Journal of Social Psychology, 152*, 288–307.

Greenberg, J. (2012). Psychoanalysis in North America after Freud. In G. O. Gabbard, B. E. Litowitz, & P. Williams (Eds.), *Textbook of psychoanalysis* (2nd ed.). Arlington, VA: American Psychiatric Publishing, Inc.

Greenberg, L., Cwikel, J., & Mirsky, J. (2007, January). Cultural correlates of eating attitudes: A comparison between native-born and immigrant university students in Israel. *International Journal of Eating Disorders, 40*, 51–58.

Greene, K., Krcmar, M., Walters, L. H., Rubin, D. L., & Hale, J. L. (2000). Targeting adolescent risk-taking behaviors: The contribution of egocentrism and sensation-seeking. *Journal of Adolescence, 23*, 439–461.

Greene, M. M., Patra, K., Silvestri, J. M., & Nelson, M. N. (2013). Re-evaluating preterm infants with the Bayley-III: Patterns and predictors of change. *Research in Developmental Disabilities, 34*(7), 2107–2117.

Greene, S., Anderson, E., & Hetherington, E. (2003). Risk and resilience after divorce. In F. Walsh (Ed.), *Normal family processes: Growing diversity and complexity*. New York, NY: Guilford Press.

Greenstein, A. (2016). *Radical inclusive education: Disability, teaching and struggles for liberation*. New York, NY: Routledge/Taylor & Francis Group.

Greenwood, D. N., & Pietromonaco, P. R. (2004). The interplay among attachment orientation, idealized media images of women, and body dissatisfaction: A social psychological analysis. In L. J. Shrum (Ed.), *Psychology of entertainment media: Blurring the lines between entertainment and persuasion*. Mahwah, NJ: Lawrence Erlbaum.

Greer, B. D., Neidert, P. L., & Dozier, C. L. (2016). A component analysis of toilet-training procedures recommended for young children. *Journal of Applied Behavior Analysis, 49*, 69–84.

Greitemeyer, T. (2018). The spreading impact of playing violent video games on aggression. *Computers in Human Behavior, 80*, 216–219.

Gremigni, P., Casu, G., Mantoani Zaia, V., Viana Heleno, M. G., Conversano, C., & Barbosa, C. P. (2018). Sexual satisfaction among involuntarily childless women: A cross-cultural study in Italy and Brazil. *Women & Health, 58*(1), 1-15.

Greydanus, D. E., & Pratt, H. D. (2016). Human sexuality. *International Journal of Child and Adolescent Health, 9*, 291–312.

Griffin, L. K., Adams, N., & Little, T. D. (2017). Self-determination theory, identity development, and adolescence. In M. L. Wehmeyer, K. A. Shogren, T. D. Little, & S. J. Lopez (Eds.), *Development of self-determination through the lifecourse*. New York: Springer Science + Business Media.

Griffith, D. R., Azuma, S. D., & Chasnoff, I. J. (1994). Three-year outcome of children exposed prenatally to drugs. *Journal of the American Academy of Child and Adolescent Psychiatry, 33*, 20–27.

Griffith, S. F., & Grolnick, W. S. (2014). Parenting in Caribbean families: A look at parental control, structure, and autonomy support. *Journal of Black Psychology, 40*(2), 166–190.

Grigorenko, E., Jarvin, L., Diffley, R., Goodyear, J., Shanahan, E., & Sternberg, R. (2009). Are SSATS and GPA enough? A theory-based approach to predicting academic success in secondary school. *Journal of Educational Psychology, 101*, 964–981.

Grinkevičiūtė, D., Jankauskaitė, L., Kėvalas, R., & Gurskis, V. (2016). Shaken baby syndrome and consciousness. In G. Leisman & J. Merrick (Eds.), *Considering consciousness clinically* (pp. 193–200). Hauppauge, NY: Nova Biomedical Books.

Grønhøj, A., & Thøgersen, J. (2012). Action speaks louder than words: The effect of personal attitudes and family norms on adolescents' pro-environmental behaviour. *Journal of Economic Psychology, 33*, 292–302.

Grosse, S. D, Waitzman, N. J., Yang, N., Abe, K., & Barfield, W. D. (2017). Employer-sponsored plan expenditures for infants born preterm. *Pediatrics, 140*(4).

Grunbaum, J. A., Lowry, R., & Kann, L. (2001). Prevalence of health-related behaviors among alternative high school students as compared with students attending regular high schools. *Journal of Adolescent Health, 29*, 337–343.

Grundy, E., & Henretta, J. (2006, September). Between elderly parents and adult children: A new look at the intergenerational care provided by the "sandwich generation." *Ageing & Society, 26*, 707–722.

Gruszczyńska, E. (2013). State affect and emotion-focused coping: Examining correlated change and causality. *Anxiety, Stress & Coping: An International Journal, 26*, 103–119.

Gruttadaro, D., & Croudo, D. (2012). *College students speak: A survey report on mental health*. Arlington, VA: National Alliance on Mental Illness.

Guadalupe, K. L., & Welkley, D. L. (2012). *Diversity in family constellations: Implications for practice*. Chicago, IL: Lyceum Books.

Guasti, M. T. (2002). *Language acquisition: The growth of grammar*. Cambridge, MA: MIT Press.

Guérin, E., Goldfield, G., & Prud'homme, D. (2017). Trajectories of mood and stress and relationships with protective factors during the transition to menopause: Results using latent class growth modeling in a Canadian cohort. *Archives of Women's Mental Health*. doi:10.1007/s00737-017-0755-4

Guerrero, A., Hishinuma, E., Andrade, N., Nishimura, S., & Cunanan, V. (2006, July). Correlations among socioeconomic and family factors and academic, behavioral, and emotional difficulties in Filipino adolescents in Hawaii. *International Journal of Social Psychiatry, 52*, 343–359.

Guerrero, S., Enesco, I., Lago, O., & Rodríguez, P. (2010). Preschool children's understanding of racial cues in drawings and photographs. *Cognitive Development, 25*, 79–89.

Guerrini, I., Thomson, A., & Gurling, H. (2007). The importance of alcohol misuse, malnutrition and genetic susceptibility on brain growth and plasticity. *Neuroscience & Biobehavioral Reviews, 31*, 212–220.

Guilamo-Ramos, V., Lee, J. J., Kantor, L. M., Levine, D. S., Baum, S., & Johnsen, J. (2015). Potential for using online and mobile education with parents and adolescents to impact sexual and reproductive health. *Prevention Science, 16*, 53–60.

Gumz, A., Kästner, D., Geyer, M., Wutzler, U., Villmann, T., & Brähler, E. (2010). Instability and discontinuous change in the experience of therapeutic interaction: An extended single-case study of psychodynamic therapy processes. *Psychotherapy Research, 20*, 398–412.

Guo, S., Wu, Q., Smokowski, P. R., Bacallao, M., Evans, C. R., & Cotter, K. L. (2015). A longitudinal evaluation of the Positive Action program in a low-income, racially diverse, rural county: Effects on self-esteem, school hassles, aggression, and internalizing symptoms. *Journal of Youth and Adolescence, 44*, 2337–2358.

Güre, A., Uçanok, Z., & Sayil, M. (2006). The associations among perceived pubertal timing, parental relations and self-perception in Turkish adolescents. *Journal of Youth and Adolescence, 35*, 541–550.

Gurung, R. (2010). *Health psychology: A cultural approach* (2nd ed.). Belmont, CA: Wadsworth/Cengage Learning.

Gutek, G. L. (2003). Maria Montessori: Contributions to educational psychology. In B. J. Zimmerman (Ed.), *Educational psychology: A century of contributions*. Mahwah, NJ: Lawrence Erlbaum.

Gutnick, A. L., Robb, M., Takeuchi, L., & Kotler, J. (2010, March 10). *Always connected: The new digital media habits of young children*. New York: Joan Ganz Cooney Center.

Guttmacher Institute. (2012, February). *Facts on American teens' sexual and reproductive health*. New York, NY: Guttmacher Institute.

Guttmacher Institute. (2017, September.) *Induced abortion worldwide*. New York: Guttmacher Institute.

Guttmann, J., & Rosenberg, M. (2003). Emotional intimacy and children's adjustment: A comparison between single-parent divorced and intact families. *Educational Psychology, 23*, 457–472.

Guttmannova, K., Hill, K. G., Bailey, J. A., Hartigan, L. A., Small, C. M., & Hawkins, J. D. (2016). Parental alcohol use, parenting, and child on-time development. *Infant and Child Development*, doi:10.1002/icd.2013/abstract

Guzzetta, A., & Cion, G. (2016). Impact of infantile massage on brain development. In A. Sale (Ed.), *Environmental experience and plasticity of the developing brain*. (pp. 215–223). Hoboken, NJ: Wiley-Blackwell.

Guzzetta, A., Fiori, S., Scelfo, D., Conti, E., & Bancale, A. (2013). Reorganization of visual fields after periventricular hemorrhagic infarction: Potentials and limitations. *Developmental Medicine & Child Neurology, 55* (Suppl 4), 23–26.

Haabrekke, K., Siqveland, T., Nygaaard, E., Bjornebekk, A., Slinning, K., Wentzel-Larsen, T., &... Moe, V. (2018). Cognitive and socioemotional functioning at 4½ years in children born to mothers who have received treatment for substance-abuse problems while pregnant. *Infant Mental Health Journal*, doi:10.1002/imhj.21733

Haas-Thompson, T., Alston, P., & Holbert, D. (2008). The impact of education and death-related experiences on rehabilitation counselor attitudes toward death and dying. *Journal of Applied Rehabilitation Counseling, 39*, 20–27.

Haber, D. (2006). Life review: Implementation, theory, research, and therapy. *International Journal of Aging & Human Development, 63*, 153–171.

Hagan-Burke, S., Coyne, M. D., Kwok, O. M., Simmons, D. C., Kim, M., Simmons, L. E., &... McSparran, R. M. (2013). The effects and interactions of student, teacher, and setting variables on reading outcomes for kindergartners receiving supplemental reading intervention. *Journal of Learning Disabilities, 46*, 260–277.

Hagmann-von Arx, P., Lemola, S., & Grob, A. (2018). Does IQ = IQ? Comparability of intelligence test scores in typically developing children. *Assessment, 25*, 691–701.

Hagerty, R. G., Butow, P. N., Ellis, P. A., Lobb, E. A., Pendlebury, S., Leighl, N., &... Tattersall, M. H. (2004). Cancer patient preferences for communication of prognosis in the metastatic setting. *Journal of Clinical Oncology, 22*, 1721–1730.

Hahn, E., Gottschling, J., & Spinath, F. M. (2012). Short measurements of personality—Validity and reliability of the GSOEP Big Five Inventory (BFI-S). *Journal of Research in Personality, 46*, 355–359.

Hahn, E. A., & Lachman, M. E. (2015). Everyday experiences of memory problems and control: The adaptive role of selective optimization with compensation in the context of memory decline. *Aging, Neuropsychology, and Cognition, 22*, 25–41.

Hale, A. J., Ricotta, D. N., Freed, J., Smith, C. C., & Huang, G. C. (2018). Adapting Maslow's hierarchy of needs as a framework for resident wellness. *Teaching and Learning in Medicine*, doi:10.1080/10401334.2018.1456928

Hales, C. M., Carroll, M. D., Fryar, C. D., & Ogden, C. L. (2017). Prevalence of obesity among adults and youth: United States, 2015–2016. NCHS Data Brief. No. 288.

Haleem, M., Barton, K., Borges, G., Crozier, A., & Anderson, A. (2008). Increasing antioxidant intake from fruits and vegetables: Practical strategies for the Scottish population. *Journal of Human Nutrition and Dietetics, 21*, 539–546.

Haley, D., Grunau, R., Weinberg, J., Keidar, A., & Oberlander, T. (2010). Physiological correlates of memory recall in infancy: Vagal tone, cortisol, and imitation in preterm and full-term infants at 6 months. *Infant Behavior & Development, 33*, 219–234.

Halgunseth, L. C., Ispa, J. M., & Rudy, D. (2006). Parental control in Latino families: An integrated review of the literature. *Child Development, 77*, 1282–1297.

Halim, M. L., Ruble, D. N., Tamis-LeMonda, C. S., Zosuls, K. M., Lurye, L. E., & Greulich, F. K. (2014). Pink frilly dresses and the avoidance of all things 'girly': Children's appearance rigidity and cognitive theories of gender development. *Developmental Psychology, 50*, 1091–1101.

Halim, M. L. D., Walsh, A. S., Tamis-LeMonda, C. S., Zosuls, K. M., & Ruble, D. N. (2018). The roles of self-socialization and parent socialization in toddlers' gender-typed appearance. *Archives of Sexual Behavior*. doi:10.1007/s10508-018-1263-y

Halkier, B. (2013). Review of the case study as research method: A practical handbook and how to do your case study: A guide for students & researchers. *Qualitative Research, 13*(1), 107–110.

Hall, J. J., Neal, T., & Dean, R. S. (2008). Lateralization of cerebral functions. In A. M. McNeil & D. Wedding (Eds.), *The neuropsychology handbook* (3rd ed.). New York, NY: Springer Publishing.

Halpern, D. F. (2014). It's complicated—in fact, it's complex: Explaining the gender gap in academic achievement in science and mathematics. *Psychological Science in the Public Interest, 15*, 72–74.

Hamasaki, A., Akazawa, N., Yoshikawa, T., Myoenzono, K., Tagawa, K., & Maeda, S. (2018). Age-related declines in executive function and cerebral oxygenation hemodynamics. *The Tohoku Journal of Experimental Medicine, 245*(4), 245–250.

Hamel, L. M., & Robbins, L. B. (2013). Computer- and web-based interventions to promote healthy eating among children and adolescents: A systematic review. *Journal of Advanced Nursing, 69*, 16–30.

Hamer, R., & van Rossum, E. J. (2016). Six languages in education—looking for postformal thinking. *Behavioral Development Bulletin*. Accessed online, 3/21/17; http://psycnet.apa.org/psycinfo/2016-59293-001/

Hamer, R., & van Rossum, E. J. (2017). Six languages in education—Looking for postformal thinking. *Behavioral Development Bulletin, 22*(2), 377–393.

Hamilton, B. E., Martin, J. A., & Ventura, S. J. (2009). *National vital statistics reports*. Hyattsville, MD: National Center for Health Statistics.

Hamilton, B. E., Martin, J. A., & Ventura, S. J. (2011). Births: Preliminary data for 2010. *National Vital Statistics Reports. 60*(2). Hyattsville, MD: National Center for Health Statistics.

Hamilton B.E., Rossen, L., Lu, L., and Chong Y. (2018). *U.S. and state trends on teen births, 1990–2016*. Washington, DC: National Center for Health Statistics.

Hamilton, B. S., & Ventura, J. A. (2012, April) *Birth rates for U.S. teenagers reach historic lows for all age and ethnic groups* (NCHS Data Brief, No. 89). Washington, DC: National Center for Health Statistics.

Hamlet, H. S., & Herrick, M. (2014). Career challenges in midlife and beyond. In G. T. Eliason, T. Eliason, J. L. Samide, & J. Patrick, (Eds.), *Career development across the lifespan: Counseling for community, schools, higher education, and beyond*. Charlotte, NC: IAP Information Age Publishing.

Hamm, J. V., Brown, B. B., and Heck, D. J. (2005). Bridging the ethnic divide: Student and school characteristics in African American, Asian-descent, Latino, and white adolescents' cross-ethnic friend nominations. *Journal of Research on Adolescence, 15*(1), 21–46.

Hanafin, S. (2018). Sleep patterns and problems in infants and young children in Ireland. *Child: Care, Health and Development, 44*(3), 470–475.

Hanawa, S., Sugiura, M., Nozawa, T., Kotozaki, Y., Yomogida, Y., Ihara, M., &... Kawashima, R. (2016). The neural basis of the imitation drive. *Social Cognitive and Affective Neuroscience, 11*, 66–77.

Hane, A., Feldstein, S., & Dernetz, V. (2003). The relation between coordinated interpersonal timing and maternal sensitivity in four-month-old infants. *Journal of Psycholinguistic Research, 32*, 525–539.

Hanna, G. P. (2016). Arts, health, and aging. In P. D. Lambert (Ed.), *Managing arts programs in healthcare*. New York, NY: Routledge/Taylor & Francis Group.

Hannon, K. (2015). Over 50 and back in college, preparing for a new career. *New York Times*. Accessed online, 12/1/18; https://www.nytimes.com/2015/04/04/your-money/over-50-and-back-in-college-preparing-for-a-new-career.html

Hannover, B., Morf, C. C., Neuhaus, J., Rau, M., Wolfgramm, C., & Zander-Music, L. (2013). How immigrant adolescents' self-views in school and family context relate to academic success in Germany. *Journal of Applied Social Psychology, 43*, 175–189.

Hansen, C., Konradsen, H., Abrahamsen, B., & Pedersen, B. D. (2014). Women's experiences of their osteoporosis diagnosis at the time of diagnosis and 6 months later: A phenomenological hermeneutic study. *International Journal of Qualitative Studies on Health and Well-Being, 9*, 22438.

Hanson, J. D. (2012). Understanding prenatal health care for American Indian women in a Northern Plains Tribe. *Journal of Transcultural Nursing, 23*, 29–37.

Hanson, L., Schenck, A., Rokoske, F., Abernethy, A., Kutner, J., Spence, C., & Pearson, J. L. (2010). Hospices' preparation and practices for quality measurement. *Journal of Pain and Symptom Management, 39*, 1–8.

Hanson, R., & Hayslip, B. (2000). Widowhood in later life. In J. Harvey & E. Miller (Eds.), *Loss and trauma: General and close relationship perspectives*. New York, NY: Brunner-Routledge.

Harada, C. N, Natelson Love, M. C., & Triebold, K. (2013). Normal cognitive aging. *Clinical and Geriatric Medicine, 29*, 737–752.

Harden, K., Turkheimer, E., & Loehlin, J. (2007). Genotype by environment interaction in adolescents' cognitive aptitude. *Behavior Genetics, 37*, 273–283.

Hare, A. L., Szwedo, D. E., Schad, M. M., & Allen, J. P. (2015). Undermining adolescent autonomy with parents and peers: The enduring implications of psychologically controlling parenting. *Journal of Research on Adolescence, 25*(4), 739–752.

Hare, T. A., Tottenham, N., Galvan, A., & Voss, H. U. (2008). Biological substrates of emotional reactivity and regulation in adolescence during an emotional go-nogo task. *Biological Psychiatry, 63*, 927–934.

Harris, J., Vernon, P., & Jang, K. (2007). Rated personality and measured intelligence in young twin children. *Personality and Individual Differences, 42*, 75–86.

Harris, J. L., & Kalnova, S. S. (2018). Food and beverage TV advertising to young children: Measuring exposure and potential impact. *Appetite, 123*, 49–55.

Harris, M., Prior, J., & Koehoorn, M. (2008). Age at menarche in the Canadian population: Secular trends and relationship to adulthood BMI. *Journal of Adolescent Health, 43*, 548–554.

Harris, M. A., Gruenenfelder-Steiger, A. E., Ferrer, E., Donnellan, M. B., Allemand, M., Fend, H., &... Trzesniewski, K. H. (2015). Do parents foster self-esteem? Testing the prospective impact of parent closeness on adolescent self-esteem. *Child Development*. doi: 10.1111/cdev.12356

Hartley, C. A., & Lee, F. S. (2015). Sensitive periods in affective development: Nonlinear maturation of fear learning. *Neuropsychopharmacology, 40*, 50–60.

Hartman, K. M., Ratner, N. B., & Newman, R. S. (2017). Infant-directed speech (IDS) vowel clarity and child language outcomes. *Journal of Child Language, 44*, 1140–1162.

Harvey, J. H., & Fine, M. A. (2004). *Children of divorce: Stories of loss and growth*. Mahwah, NJ: Lawrence Erlbaum.

Hasan, Y., Bègue, L., Scharkow, M., & Bushman, B. J. (2013). The more you play, the more aggressive you become: A long-term experimental study of cumulative violent video game effects on hostile expectations and aggressive behavior. *Experimental Social Psychology, 49*, 224–227.

Haslett, A. (2004, May 31). Love supreme. *The New Yorker*, pp. 76–80.

Hastings, P. D., McShane, K. E., Parker, R., & Ladha, F. (2007). Ready to make nice: Parental socialization of young sons' and daughters' prosocial behaviors with peers. *Journal of Genetic Psychology, 168*, 177–200.

Hatton, C. (2002). People with intellectual disabilities from ethnic minority communities in the United States and the United Kingdom. In L. M. Glidden (Ed.), *International review of research in mental retardation, Vol. 25.* San Diego: Academic Press.

Haugaard, J. J. (2000). The challenge of defining child sexual abuse. *American Psychologist, 55,* 1036–1039.

Hauser, S. R., Wilden, J. A., Batra, V., & Rodd, Z. A. (2017). Deep brain stimulation: A possible therapeutic technique for treating refractory alcohol and drug addiction behaviors. In R. R. Watson & S. Zibadi (Eds.), *Addictive substances and neurological disease: Alcohol, tobacco, caffeine, and drugs of abuse in everyday lifestyles.* (pp. 239–248). San Diego, CA: Elsevier

Hawkins, A. J., Willoughby, B. J., & Doherty, W. J. (2012). Reasons for divorce and openness to marital reconciliation. *Journal of Divorce & Remarriage, 53,* 453–463.

Hawkins-Rodgers, Y. (2007). Adolescents adjusting to a group home environment: A residential care model of reorganizing attachment behavior and building resiliency. *Children and Youth Services Review, 29,* 1131–1141.

Hayes, S. W., & Endale, E. (2018). "Sometimes my mind, it has to analyze two things": Identity development and adaptation for refugee and newcomer adolescents. *Peace and Conflict: Journal of Peace Psychology, 24*(3), 283–290.

Hayden, T. (1998, September 21). The brave new world of sex selection. *Newsweek,* p. 93.

Hayflick, L. (2007). Biological aging is no longer an unsolved problem. *Annals of the New York Academy of Sciences,* pp. 1–13.

Hayslip, B., Jr., Shore, R. J., & Henderson, C. E. (2000). Perceptions of grandparents' influence in the lives of their grandchildren. In B. Hayslip, Jr., & R. S. Goldberg-Glen (Eds.), *Grandparents raising grandchildren: Theoretical, empirical, and clinical perspectives.* New York, NY: Springer.

Healthychildren.org. (2016, October 18). Teen suicide statistics. Accessed online, 11/13/17; https://www.healthychildren.org/English/health-issues/conditions/emotional-problems/Pages/Teen-Suicide-Statistics.aspx

Heard, E., & Martienssen, R. A. (2014). Transgenerational epigenetic inheritance: myths and mechanisms. *Cell, 157,* 95–109.

Hebe, H. N. (2017). Towards a theory–driven integration of environmental education: The application of Piaget and Vygotsky in Grade R. *International Journal of Environmental and Science Education, 12*(6), 1525–1545.

Hebscher, M., & Gilboa, A. (2016). A boost of confidence: The role of the ventromedial prefrontal cortex in memory, decision-making, and schemas. *Neuropsychologia, 90,* 46–58.

Hedegaard, M., & Fleer, M. (2013). *Play, learning, and children's development: Everyday life in families and transition to school.* New York, NY: Cambridge University Press.

Heilbronner, N. N. (2013). The STEM pathway for women: What has changed? *Gifted Child Quarterly, 57,* 39–55.

Heimann, M. (Ed.). (2003). *Regression periods in human infancy.* Mahwah, NJ: Lawrence Erlbaum.

Helmsen, J., Koglin, U., & Petermann, F. (2012). Emotion regulation and aggressive behavior in preschoolers: The mediating role of social information processing. *Child Psychiatry and Human Development, 43,* 87–101.

Helmuth, L. (2003, February 28). The wisdom of the wizened. *Science, 299,* 1300–1302.

Hendren, S., Humiston, S., & Fiscella, K. (2012). Partnering with safety-net primary care clinics: A model to enhance screening in low-income populations—Principles, challenges, and key lessons. In R. Elk & H. Landrine (Eds.), *Cancer disparities: Causes and evidence-based solutions.* New York, NY: Springer Publishing Co.

Hendrick, C., & Hendrick, S. (2003). Romantic love: Measuring cupid's arrow. In S. Lopez & C. Snyder (Eds.), *Positive psychological assessment: A handbook of models and measures.* Washington, DC: American Psychological Association.

Hendrickson, Z. M., Kim, J., Tol, W. A., Shrestha, A., Kafle, H. M., Luitel, N. P., & … Surkan, P. J. (2018). Resilience among Nepali widows after the death of a spouse: "That was my past and now I have to see my present." *Qualitative Health Research, 28*(3), 466–478.

Hendrie, H. C., Ogunniyi, A., Hall, K. S., Baiyewu, O., Unverzagt, F. W., Gureje, O., & … Hui, S. L. (2001). Incidence of dementia and Alzheimer disease in 2 communities: Yoruba residing in Ibadan, Nigeria, and African Americans residing in Indianapolis, Indiana. *JAMA: The Journal of the American Medical Association, 285,* 739–747.

Henry J. Kaiser Family Foundation. (2014, August 20). *Sexual health of adolescents and young adults in the United States.* Menlo Park, CA: Author.

Henry, R., Miller, R., & Giarrusso, R. (2005). Difficulties, disagreements, and disappointments in late-life marriages. *International Journal of Aging & Human Development, 61,* 243–264.

Henschel, S., de Bruin, M., & Möhler, E. (2014). Self-control and child abuse potential in mothers with an abuse history and their preschool children. *Journal of Child and Family Studies, 23,* 824.

Hensley, P. (2006, July). Treatment of bereavement-related depression and traumatic grief. *Journal of Affective Disorders, 92,* 117–124.

Hentschel, S., Eid, M., & Kutscher, T. (2017). The influence of major life events and personality traits on the stability of affective well-being. *Journal of Happiness Studies, 18,* 719–741.

Hepach, R., & Westermann, G. (2013). Infants' sensitivity to the congruence of others' emotions and actions. *Journal of Experimental Child Psychology, 115,* 16–29.

Herbenick, D., Reece, M., Schick, V., Sanders, S., Dodge, B., & Fortenberry, J. D. (2010). Sexual behavior in the United States: Results from a national probability sample of men and women ages 14 to 94. *Journal of Sexual Medicine, 7*(Suppl. 5), 255–265.

Herberman Mash, H. B., Fullerton, C. S., Shear, M. K., & Ursano, R. J. (2014). Complicated grief and depression in young adults: Personality and relationship quality. *Journal of Nervous and Mental Disease, 202,* 539–543.

Herbert, J. S., Eckerman, C. O., Goldstein, R. F., Stanton, M. E. (2004). Contrasts in infant classical eyeblink conditioning as a function of premature birth. *Infancy, 5,* 367–383.

Herendeen, L. A., & MacDonald, A. (2014). Planning for healthy homes. In I. L. Rubin & J. Merrick (Eds.), *Environmental health: Home, school and community.* Hauppauge, NY: Nova Biomedical Books.

Herman-Kinney, N. J., & Kinney, D. A. (2013). Sober as deviant: The stigma of sobriety and how some college students "stay dry" on a "wet" campus. *Journal of Contemporary Ethnography, 42,* 64–103.

Hermanto, N., Moreno, S., & Bialystok, E. (2012). Linguistic and metalinguistic outcomes of intense immersion education: How bilingual? *International Journal of Bilingual Education, 15,* 131–145.

Hermida, R. C., Ayala, D. E., Crespo, J. J., Mojón, A., Chayán, L., Fontao, M. J., & Fernandez, J. R. (2013). Influence of age and hypertension treatment-time on ambulatory blood pressure in hypertensive patients. *Chronobiology International, 30,* 176–191

Hernandez, D. J., Denton, N. A., & McCartney, S. E. (2008). Children in immigrant families: Looking to America's Future. *Social Policy Report, 22,* 3–24.

Hernandez-Reif, M., Field, T., Diego, M., Vera, Y., & Pickens, J. (2006, January). Brief report: Happy faces are habituated more slowly by infants of depressed mothers. *Infant Behavior & Development, 29,* 131–135.

Herpertz-Dahlmann, B. (2015). Adolescent eating disorders: Update on definitions, symptomatology, epidemiology, and comorbidity. *Child and Adolescent Psychiatric Clinics of North America, 24,* 1771–196.

Herrnstein, R. J., & Murray, C. (1994). *The bell curve: Intelligence and class structure in American life.* New York, NY: Free Press.

Hertz, R., & Nelson, M. K. (2015). Introduction. *Journal of Family Issues, 36,* 447–460.

Hertzberg, V. S., Hinton, C. F., Therrell, B. L., & Shapira, S. K. (2011). Birth prevalence rates of newborn screening disorders in relation to screening practices in the United States. *Journal of Pediatrics, 159,* 555–560.

Hespos, S. J., & vanMarle, K. (2012). *Everyday physics: How infants learn about objects and entities in their environment.* Invited manuscript for Wiley Interdisciplinary Reviews, Cognitive Science.

Hess, T., Auman, C., & Colcombe, S. (2003). The impact of stereotype threat on age differences in memory performance. *The Journals of Gerontology: Series B, 58*(1), p3–p11.

Hess, T. M., O'Brien, E. L., Voss, P., Kornadt, A. E., Rothermund, K., Fung, H. H., & Popham, L. E. (2017). Context influences on the relationship between views of aging and subjective age: The moderating role of culture and domain of functioning. *Psychology and Aging, 32*(5), 419–431.

Hess, T. M., Hinson, J. T., & Hodges, E. A. (2009). Moderators of and mechanisms underlying stereotype threat effects on older adults' memory performance. *Experimental Aging Research, 31,* 153–177.

Hetherington, E., & Elmore, A. (2003). Risk and resilience in children coping with their parents' divorce and remarriage. In S. Luthar (Ed.), *Resilience and vulnerability: Adaptation in the context of childhood adversities.* New York, NY: Cambridge University Press.

Hetrick, S. E., Parker, A. G., Robinson, J., Hall, N., & Vance, A. (2012). Predicting suicidal risk in a cohort of depressed children and adolescents. *Crisis: Journal of Crisis Intervention and Suicide Prevention, 33,* 13–20.

Hewstone, M. (2003). Intergroup contact: Panacea for prejudice? *Psychologist, 16,* 352–355.

Heyman, R., & Slep, A. M. (2002). Do child abuse and interparental violence lead to adulthood family violence? *Journal of Marriage & Family, 64,* 864–870.

Hietala, J., Cannon, T. D., & van Erp, T. G. M. (2003). Regional brain morphology and duration of illness in never-medicated first-episode patients with schizophrenia. *Schizophrenia, 64,* 79–81.

Higgins, D., & McCabe, M. (2003). Maltreatment and family dysfunction in childhood and the subsequent adjustment of children and adults. *Journal of Family Violence, 18,* 107–120.

Hill, B. D., Foster, J. D., Elliott, E. M., Shelton, J., McCain, J., & Gouvier, W. (2013). Need for cognition is related to higher general intelligence, fluid intelligence, and crystallized intelligence, but not working memory. *Journal of Research in Personality, 47,* 22–25.

Hillman, J. (2012). *Sexuality and aging: Clinical perspectives.* New York, NY: Springer Science + Business Media.

Hilton, J., & Anderson, T. (2009). Characteristics of women with children who divorce in midlife compared to those who remain married. *Journal of Divorce & Remarriage, 50,* 309–329.

Hipke, K. N., Wolchik, S. A., & Sandler, I. N. (2010). Divorce, children of. In G. Fink (Ed.), *Stress consequences: Mental, neuropsychological and socioeconomic.* San Diego, CA: Elsevier Academic Press.

Hirsch, M., & Morlière, C. (2017). Health psychology: Understanding culture's role in health and illness. In G. J. Rich, U. P. Gielen, & H. Takooshian (Eds.), *Internationalizing the teaching of psychology.* Charlotte, NC: IAP Information Age Publishing.

Hirsch, P. (2018). Mind and mourning: The primacy of 'we' in complicated grief. *Death Studies.* doi: 10.1080/07481187.2018.1504835

Hirsh-Pasek, K., & Michnick-Golinkoff, R. (1995). *The origins of grammar: Evidence from early language comprehension.* Cambridge, MA: MIT Press.

Hirschtritt, M. E., Pagano, M. E., Christian, K. M., McNamara, N. K., Stansbrey, R. J., Lingler, J., & Findling, R. L. (2012). Moderators of fluoxetine treatment response for children and adolescents with comorbid depression and substance use disorders. *Journal of Substance Abuse Treatment, 42,* 366–372.

Hitlin, S., Brown, J. S., & Elder, G. H., Jr. (2006). Racial self-categorization in adolescence: Multiracial development and social pathways. *Child Development, 77,* 1298–1308.

Hjelmstedt, A., Widström, A., & Collins, A. (2006). Psychological correlates of prenatal attachment in women who conceived after in vitro fertilization and women who conceived naturally. *Birth: Issues in Perinatal Care, 33,* 303–310.

Hocking, D. R., Kogan, C. S., & Cornish, K. M. (2012). Selective spatial processing deficits in an at-risk subgroup of the fragile X premutation. *Brain and Cognition, 79,* 39–44.

Hoehl, S., Wahl, S., Michel, C., & Striano, T. (2012). Effects of eye gaze cues provided by the caregiver compared to a stranger on infants' object processing. *Developmental Cognitive Neuroscience, 2,* 81–89.

Hoelter, L. F., Axinn, W. G., & Ghimire, D. J. (2004). Social change, premarital nonfamily experiences, and marital dynamics. *Journal of Marriage & Family, 66,* 1131–1151.

Hoessler, C., & Chasteen, A. L. (2008). Does aging affect the use of shifting standards? *Experimental Aging Research, 34,* 1–12.

Hoeve, M., Blokland, A., Dubas, J., Loeber, R., Gerris, J., & van der Laan, P. (2008). Trajectories of delinquency and parenting styles. *Journal of Abnormal Child Psychology: An Official Publication of the International Society for Research in Child and Adolescent Psychopathology, 36,* 223–235.

Hoff, E. (2012). Interpreting the early language trajectories of children from low-SES and language minority homes: Implications for closing achievement gaps. *Developmental Psychology, 49,* 4–14.

Hoff, E., & Core, C. (2013). Input and language development in bilingually developing children. *Seminars in Speech and Language, 34,* 215–226.

Hofferth, S., & Sandberg, J. F. (2001). How American children spend their time. *Journal of Marriage and the Family, 63,* 295–308.

Hoffman, L. (2003). Why high schools don't change: What students and their yearbooks tell us. *High School Journal, 86,* 22–37.

Hofmeier, S. M., Runfola, C. D., Sala, M., Gagne, D. A., Brownley, K. A., & Bulik, C. M. (2017). Body image, aging, and identity in women over 50: The Gender and Body Image (GABI) study. *Journal of Women & Aging, 29,* 3–14.

Holahan, C., & Chapman, J. (2002). Longitudinal predictors of proactive goals and activity participation at age 80. *The Journals of Gerontology: Series B, 57(1),* p418–p425.

Holl, K., He, H., Wedemeyer, M., Clopton, L., Wert, S., Meckes, J. K., &… Solberg Woods, L. C. (2018). Heterogeneous stock rats: A model to study the genetics of despair-like behavior in adolescence. *Genes, Brain & Behavior, 17(2),* 139–148.

Holland, A. S., & McElwain, N. L. (2013). Maternal and paternal perceptions of coparenting as a link between marital quality and the parent-toddler relationship. *Journal of Family Psychology, 27,* 117–126.

Holland, J. L. (1997). *Making vocational choices: A theory of vocational personalities and environments* (3rd ed.). Odessa, FL: Psychological Assessment Resources.

Holland, N. (1994, August). *Race dissonance—Implications for African American children.* Paper presented at the annual meeting of the American Psychological Association, Los Angeles, CA.

Holliday, E., & Gould, T. J. (2016). Nicotine, adolescence, and stress: A review of how stress can modulate the negative consequences of adolescent nicotine abuse. *Neuroscience and Biobehavioral Reviews, 65,* 173–184.

Holly, L. E., Little, M., Pina, A. A., & Caterino, L. C. (2015). Assessment of anxiety symptoms in school children: A cross-sex and ethnic examination. *Journal of Abnormal Child Psychology, 43,* 297–309.

Holman, M. A., Quillin, J., York, T. P., Testa, C. M., Rosen, A. R., & Norris, V. W. (2018). The changing age of individuals seeking presymptomatic genetic testing for Huntington disease. *Journal Of Genetic Counseling, 27(5)* 1157–1166.

Holmes, E. R., & Holmes, L. D. (1995). *Other cultures, elder years.* Thousand Oaks, CA: Sage Publications.

Holowaka, S., & Petitto, L. A. (2002). Left hemisphere cerebral specialization for babies while babbling. *Science, 287,* 1515.

Homae, F., Watanabe, H., Nakano, T., & Taga, G. (2012). Functional development in the infant brain for auditory pitch processing. *Human Brain Mapping, 33,* 596–608.

Hong, D. S., Hoeft, F., Marzelli, M. J., Lepage, J., Roeltgen, D., Ross, J., & Reiss, A. L. (2014). Influence of the X-chromosome on neuroanatomy: Evidence from Turner and Klinefelter syndromes. *Journal of Neuroscience, 34,* 3509–3516.

Hong, S. B., & Trepanier-Street, M. (2004). Technology: A tool for knowledge construction in a Reggio Emilia inspired teacher education program. *Early Childhood Education Journal, 32,* 87–94.

Hood, M., & Duffy, A. L. (2018). Understanding the relationship between cyber-victimisation and cyber-bullying on social network sites: The role of moderating factors. *Personality and Individual Differences, 133,* 103–108.

Hooks, B., & Chen, C. (2008). Vision triggers an experience-dependent sensitive period at the retinogeniculate synapse. *Journal of Neuroscience, 28,* 4807–4817.

Hopkins, B., & Westra, T. (1990). Motor development, maternal expectation, and the role of handling. *Infant Behavior and Development, 13,* 117–122.

Horiuchi, S., Finch, C., & Mesle, F. (2003). Differential patterns of age-related mortality increase in middle age and old age. *Journals of Gerontology: Series A: Biological Sciences & Medical Sciences, 58A,* 495–507.

Horne, R. C. (2017). Sleep disorders in newborns and infants. In S. Nevšimalova & O. Bruni (Eds.), *Sleep disorders in children.* Cham, Switzerland: Springer International Publishing.

Horning, M. L., Olsen, J. M., Lell, S., Thorson, D. R., & Monsen, K. A. (2018). Description of public health nursing nutrition assessment and interventions for home-visited women. *Public Health Nursing.* doi:10.1111/phn.12410

Hornor, G. (2008). Reactive attachment disorder. *Journal of Pediatric Health Care, 22,* 234–239.

Horwitz, B. N., Luong, G., & Charles, G. T. (2008). Neuroticism and extraversion share genetic and environmental effects with negative and positive mood spillover in a nationally representative sample. *Personality and Individual Differences, 45,* 636–642.

Horwitz, B. N., Reynolds, C. A., Walum, H., Ganiban, J., Spotts, E. L., Reiss, D., &… Neiderhiser, J. M. (2016). Understanding the role of mate selection processes in couples' pair-bonding behavior. *Behavior Genetics, 46,* 143–149.

Hosokawa, R., & Katsura, T. (2018). Socioeconomic status, emotional/behavioral difficulties, and social competence among preschool children in Japan. *Journal of Child and Family Studies,* doi:10.1007/s10826-018-1231-0

Hou, Y., Kim, S. Y., & Wang, Y. (2016). Parental acculturative stressors and adolescent adjustment through interparental and parent–child relationships in Chinese American families. *Journal of Youth and Adolescence, 45,* 1466–1481.

House, S. H. (2007). Nurturing the brain nutritionally and emotionally from before conception to late adolescence. *Nutritional Health, 19,* 143–161.

Howard, J. S., Stanislaw, H., Green, G., Sparkman, C. R., & Cohen, H. G. (2014). Comparison of behavior analytic and eclectic early interventions for young children with autism after three years. *Research in Developmental Disabilities, 35,* 3326–3344.

Howard Sharp, K. M., Russell, C., Keim, M., Barrera, M., Gilmer, M. J., Foster Akard, T., &… Gerhardt, C. A. (2018). Grief and growth in bereaved siblings: Interactions between different sources of social support. *School Psychology Quarterly, 33(3),* 363–371

Howe, M. J. (1997). *IQ in question: The truth about intelligence.* London, UK: Sage Publications.

Howe, M. L. (2003). Memories from the cradle. *Current Directions in Psychological Science, 12,* 62–65.

Howe, M. L., Courage, M. L., & Edison, S. C. (2004). When autobiographical memory begins. In S. Algarabel, A. Pitarque, T. Bajo, S. E. Gathercole, & M. A. Conway (Eds.), *Theories of memory: Vol. 3.* New York, NY: Psychology Press.

Howell, P., Bailey, E., & Kothari, N. (2010). Changes in the pattern of stuttering over development for children who recover or persist. *Clinical Linguistics & Phonetics, 24,* 556–575.

Howes, O., & Kapur, S. (2009). The dopamine hypothesis of schizophrenia: Version III—The final common pathway. *Schizophrenia Bulletin, 35,* 549–562.

Howlader, N., Noone, A. M., Krapcho, M., Miller, D., Bishop, K., Kosary, C. L., Yu, M., Ruhl, J., Tatalovich, Z., Mariotto, A., Lewis, D. R., Chen, H.S., Feuer, E. J., Cronin, K. A. (Eds.). *SEER cancer statistics review, 1975–2014.* Accessed online, 4/25/17; https://seer.cancer.gov/csr/1975_2014/

Hoy, W. G. (2013). *Do funerals matter? The purposes and practices of death rituals in global perspective.* New York, NY: Routledge/Taylor & Francis Group.

Hsin, L., & Snow, C. (2017). Social perspective taking: A benefit of bilingualism in academic writing. *Reading and Writing.* Accessed online, 3/16/17; http://link.springer.com/article/10.1007/s11145-016-9718-9

Hu, Y., Xu, Y., & Tornello, S. L. (2016). Stability of self-reported same-sex and both-sex attraction from adolescence to young adulthood. *Archives of Sexual Behavior, 45,* 651–659.

Huang, A., Subak, L., Thom, D., Van Den Eeden, S., Ragins, A., Kuppermann, M., &… Brown, J. S. (2009). Sexual function and aging in racially and ethnically diverse women. *Journal of the American Geriatrics Society, 57,* 1362–1368.

Huang, C. T. (2012). Outcome-based observational learning in human infants. *Journal of Comparative Psychology, 126,* 139–149.

Huang, D. C., Lanza, H., Wright-Volel, K., & Anglin, M. (2013). Developmental trajectories of childhood obesity and risk behaviors in adolescence. *Journal of Adolescence, 36,* 139–148.

Huang, J. (2004). Death: Cultural traditions. *From On Our Own Terms: Moyers on Dying.* Available online, www.pbs.org

Hubel, D. H., & Wiesel, T. N. (2004). *Brain and visual perception: The story of a 25-year collaboration.* New York: Oxford University Press.

Hubley, A. M., & Arim, R. G. (2012). Subjective age in early adolescence: Relationships with chronological age, pubertal timing, desired age, and problem behaviors. *Journal of Adolescence, 35,* 357–366.

Hudley, C. (2016). Achievement and expectations of immigrant, second generation, and non-immigrant Black students in US higher education. In C. Hudley (Ed.), *Adolescent identity and schooling: Diverse perspectives.* (pp. 123–137). New York, NY: Routledge/Taylor & Francis Group.

Hueston, W., Geesey, M., & Diaz, V. (2008). Prenatal care initiation among pregnant teens in the

United States: An analysis over 25 years. *Journal of Adolescent Health, 42*, 243–248.

Hugdahl, K., & Westerhausen, R. (2010). *The two halves of the brain: Information processing in the cerebral hemispheres.* Cambridge, MA: MIT Press.

Hughett, K., Kohler, F. W., & Raschke, D. (2013). The effects of a buddy skills package on preschool children's social interactions and play. *Topics in Early Childhood Special Education, 32*, 246–254.

Huh, S. Y., Rifas-Shiman, S. L., Zera, C. A., Rich Edwards, J. W., Oken, E., Weiss, S. T., & Gillman, M. W. (2011). Delivery by caesarean section and risk of obesity in preschool age children: A prospective cohort study. *Archives of Disabled Children, 34*, 66–79.

Huijbregts, S., Tavecchio, L., Leseman, P., & Hoffenaar, P. (2009). Child rearing in a group setting: Beliefs of Dutch, Caribbean Dutch, and Mediterranean Dutch caregivers in center-based child care. *Journal of Cross-Cultural Psychology, 40*, 797–815.

Hülür, G., Gasimova, F., Robitzsch, A., & Wilhelm, O. (2017). Change in fluid and crystallized intelligence and student achievement: The role of intellectual engagement. *Child Development.* Accessed online 11/16/17; https://www.ncbi.nlm.nih.gov/pubmed/28369877

Hülür, G., Infurna, F. J., Ram, N., & Gerstorf, D. (2013). Cohorts based on decade of death: No evidence for secular trends favoring later cohorts in cognitive aging and terminal decline in the AHEAD study. *Psychology and Aging, 28*, 115–127

Hülür, G., Willis, S. L., Hertzog, C., Schaie, K. W., & Gerstorf, D. (2018). Is subjective memory specific for memory performance or general across cognitive domains? Findings from the Seattle Longitudinal Study. *Psychology and Aging, 33*(3), 448–460.

Humphries, M. L., & Korfmacher, J. (2012). The good, the bad, and the ambivalent: Quality of alliance in a support program for young mothers. *Infant Mental Health Journal, 33*, 22–33.

Hunt, M. (1993). *The story of psychology.* New York, NY: Doubleday.

Hunter, J., & Mallon, G. P. (2000). Lesbian, gay, and bisexual adolescent development: Dancing with your feet tied together. In B. Greene & G. L. Croom (Eds.), *Education, research, and practice in lesbian, gay, bisexual, and transgendered psychology: A resource manual, Vol. 5.* Thousand Oaks, CA: Sage Publications.

Hunter, S., & Smith, D. (2008). Predictors of children's understandings of death: Age, cognitive ability, death experience and maternal communicative competence. *Omega: Journal of Death and Dying, 57*, 143–162.

Huntley, J. D., Hampshire, A., Bor, D., Owen, A. M., & Howard, R. J. (2017). The importance of sustained attention in early Alzheimer's disease. *International Journal of Geriatric Psychiatry, 32*(8), 860–867.

Huntsinger, C. S., Jose, P. E., Liaw, F., & Ching, W.-D. (1997). Cultural differences in early mathematics learning: A comparison of Euro-American, Chinese-American, and Taiwan-Chinese families. *International Journal of Behavioral Development, 21*, 371–388.

Huppert, E., Cowell, J. M., Cheng, Y., Contreras, I. C., Gomez, S. N., Gonzalez, G. L. M., & … Decety, J. (2018). The development of children's preferences for equality and equity across 13 individualistic and collectivist cultures. *Developmental Science.* doi:10.1111/desc.12729

Hur, K., Choi, J. S., Zheng, M., Shen, J., & Wrobel, B. (2018). Association of alterations in smell and taste with depression in older adults. *Laryngoscope investigative otolaryngology, 3*(2), 94–99.

Huston, T. L., Caughlin, J. P., Houts, R. M., & Smith, S. E. (2001). The connubial crucible: Newlywed years as predictors of marital delight, distress, and divorce. *Journal of Personality and Social Psychology, 80*, 237–252.

Hutchinson, A., Whitman, R., & Abeare, C. (2003). The unification of mind: Integration of hemispheric semantic processing. *Brain & Language, 87*, 361–368.

Hutchinson, D., & Rapee, R. (2007). Do friends share similar body image and eating problems? The role of social networks and peer influences in early adolescence. *Behaviour Research and Therapy, 45*, 1557–1577.

Hutchinson, S., & Wexler, B. (2007, January). Is "raging" good for health? Older women's participation in the Raging Grannies. *Health Care for Women International, 28*, 88–118.

Hutton, P. H. (2004). *Phillippe Arie and the politics of French cultural history.* Amherst, MA: University of Massachusetts Press.

Hvolgaard Mikkelsen, S., Obel, C., Olsen, J., Niclasen, J., & Bech, B. H. (2017). Maternal caffeine consumption during pregnancy and behavioral disorders in 11-year-old offspring: A Danish national birth cohort study. *The Journal of Pediatrics, 189*, 120–127.

Hyde, J. S., & DeLamater, J. D. (2004). *Understanding human sexuality* (9th ed.). Boston, MA: McGraw-Hill.

Hyde, J. S., & DeLamater, J. D. (2008). *Understanding human sexuality* (10th ed.). New York, NY: McGraw-Hill.

Hyde, J., & DeLamater, J. (2013). *Understanding human sexuality.* New York: McGraw-Hill.

Hyde, J. S., & DeLamater, J. D. (2017). *Understanding human sexuality* (13th ed.). New York: McGraw-Hill.

Hyde, J. S., Mezulis, A., & Abramson, L. (2008). The ABCs of depression: Integrating affective, biological, and cognitive models to explain the emergence of the gender difference in depression. *Psychological Review, 115*, 291–313.

Hynes, S. M., Fish, J., & Manly, T. (2014). Intensive working memory training: A single case experimental design in a patient following hypoxic brain damage. *Brain Injury, 28*, 1766–1775.

Iavarone, A., Ziello, A. R., Pastore, F., Fasanaro, A. M., & Poderico, C. (2014). Caregiver burden and coping strategies in caregivers of patients with Alzheimer's disease. *Neuropsychiatric Disease and Treatment, 10*, 37–44.

Ibbotson, P., & Tomasello, M. (2016). Language in a new key. *Scientific American*, pp. 71–75.

IDEA. (2018). Individuals with Disabilities Education Act. Accessed online, 10/17/18; https://sites.ed.gov/idea/about-idea/

Iecovich, E., & Biderman, A. (2012). Attendance in adult day care centers and its relation to loneliness among frail older adults. *International Psychogeriatrics, 24*, 439–448.

Ige, T. J., DeLeon, P., & Nabors, L. (2017). Motivational interviewing in an obesity prevention program for children. *Health Promotion Practice, 18*, 263–274.

Ilmarinen, V., Lönnqvist, J., & Paunonen, S. (2016). Similarity-attraction effects in friendship formation: Honest platoon-mates prefer each other but dishonest do not. *Personality and Individual Differences, 92*, 153–158.

Inagaki, M. (2013). Developmental transformation of narcissistic amae in early, middle, and late adolescents: Relation to ego identity. *Japanese Journal of Educational Psychology, 61*, 56–66.

Ingram, D. K., Young, J., & Mattison, J. A. (2007). Calorie restriction in nonhuman primates: Assessing effects on brain and behavioral aging. *Neuroscience, 14*, 1359–1364.

Inguaggiato, E., Sgandurra, G., & Cioni, G. (2017). Brain plasticity and early development: Implications for early intervention in neurodevelopmental disorders. *Neuropsychiatrie De L'enfance Et De L'adolescence, 65*, 299–306.

Inguglia, C., Ingoglia, S., Liga, F., Lo Coco, A., & Lo Cricchio, M. G. (2014). Autonomy and relatedness in adolescence and emerging adulthood: Relationships with parental support and psychological distress. *Journal of Adult Development, 22*, 1–15

Inoue, K., Tanii, H., Abe, S., Kaiya, H., Nata, M., & Fukunaga, T. (2006, December). The correlation between rates of unemployment and suicide rates in Japan between 1985 and 2002. *International Medical Journal, 13*, 261–263.

International Committee for Monitoring Assisted Reproductive Technologies (ICMART). (2012, July.) The world's number of IVF and ICSI babies has now reached a calculated total of 5 million. Paper presented at the annual meeting of the European Society of Human Reproduction and Embryology, Istanbul, Turkey.

International Human Genome Sequencing Consortium. (2001). Initial sequencing and analysis of the human genome. *Nature, 409*, 860–921.

Inzlicht, M., & Ben-Zeev, T. (2000). A threatening intellectual environment: Why females are susceptible to experiencing problem-solving deficits in the presence of males. *Psychological Science, 11*, 365–371.

Irland, J. M. (2010). Childbirth. In F. A. Barabasz & K. Olness (Eds.), *Medical hypnosis primer: Clinical and research evidence.* New York, NY: Routledge/Taylor & Francis Group.

Irwin, M. R. (2015). Why sleep is important for health: A psychoneuroimmunology perspective. *Annual Review of Psychology, 66*, 143–172.

Isaacs, K. L., Barr, W. B., Nelson, P. K., & Devinsky, O. (2006). Degree of handedness and cerebral dominance. *Neurology, 66*, 1855–1858.

Isay, R. A. (1990). *Being homosexual: Gay men and their development.* New York, NY: Avon.

Isherwood, L. M., King, D. S., & Luszcz, M. A. (2017). Widowhood in the fourth age: Support exchange, relationships and social participation. *Ageing & Society, 37*, 188–212.

Ishi-Kuntz, M. (2000). Diversity within Asian-American families. In D. H. Demo, K. R. Allen, & M. A. Fine (Eds.), *Handbook of family diversity.* New York, NY: Oxford.

Ishizuka, B., Kudo, Y., & Tango, T. (2008). Cross-sectional community survey of menopause symptoms among Japanese women. *Maturitas, 61*, 260–267.

Ising, M., Mather, K. A., Zimmermann, P., Brückl, T., Höhne, N., Heck, A., & … Reppermund, S. (2014). Genetic effects on information processing speed are moderated by age—converging results from three samples. *Genes, Brain & Behavior.* Accessed online, 3/31/15; http://onlinelibrary.wiley.com/doi/10.1111/gbb.12132/abstract

Izard, C. E., Woodburn, E., & Finlon, K. (2010). Extending emotion science to the study of discrete emotions in infants. *Emotion Review, 2*, 134–136.

Jack, F., Simcock, G., & Hayne, H. (2012). Magic memories: Young children's verbal recall after a 6-year delay. *Child Development, 83*, 159–172.

Jackson, M. I. (2015). Early childhood WIC participation, cognitive development and academic achievement. *Social Science & Medicine, 126*, 145–153.

Jackson, S. L. (2018). Introduction and overview of elder abuse. In *Understanding elder abuse: A clinician's guide.* (pp. 3–22). Washington, DC: American Psychological Association.

Jacob, K. S. (2014). DSM-5 and culture: The need to move towards a shared model of care within a more equal patient-physician partnership. *Asian Journal of Psychiatry, 7*, 89–91.

Jacobson, C., Batejan, K., Kleinman, M., & Gould, M. (2013). Reasons for attempting suicide among a community sample of adolescents. *Suicide and Life-Threatening Behavior, 43*, 646–662.

Jager, R., Mieler, W., & Miller, J. (2008). Age-related macular degeneration. *New England Journal of Medicine, 358*, 2606–2617.

Jahoda, G. (1983). European "lag" in the development of an economic concept: A study in Zimbabwe. *British Journal of Developmental Psychology, 1*, 113–120.

Jalonick, M. C. (2011, January 13). New guidelines would make school lunches healthier. *The Washington Post.*

James, J., Ellis, B. J., Schlomer, G. L., & Garber, J. (2012). Sex-specific pathways to early puberty, sexual debut, and sexual risk taking: Tests of an integrated evolutionary-developmental model. *Developmental Psychology, 48,* 687–702.

James, W. (1890/1950). *The principles of psychology.* New York, NY: Holt.

Jäncke, L., Mérillat, S., Liem, F., & Hänggi, J. (2015). Brain size, sex, and the aging brain. *Human Brain Mapping, 36,* 150–169.

Janda, L. H., & Klenke-Hamel, K. E. (1980). *Human sexuality.* New York, NY: Van Nostrand.

Janevic, T. T., Loftfield, E. E., Savitz, D. A., Bradley, E. E., Illuzzi, J. J., & Lipkind, H. H. (2014). Disparities in cesarean delivery by ethnicity and nativity in New York City. *Maternal and Child Health Journal, 18,* 250–257.

Janicke, D. M. (2013). Treatment of pediatric obesity using a parent-only approach: A case example. *Health Psychology, 32,* 345–350.

Jansen, P. W., Mieloo, C. L., Dommisse-van Berkel, A., Verlinden, M., van der Ende, J., Stevens, G., &... Tiemeier, H. (2016). Bullying and victimization among young elementary school children: The role of child ethnicity and ethnic school composition. *Race and Social Problems, 8,* 271–280.

Janssen, D. F. (2007). First stirrings: Cultural notes on orgasm, ejaculation, and wet dreams. *Journal of Sex Research, 44*(2), 122–134.

Janusek, L., Cooper, D., & Mathews, H. L. (2012). Stress, immunity, and health outcomes. In V. Rice (Ed.), *Handbook of stress, coping, and health: Implications for nursing research, theory, and practice* (2nd ed.). Thousand Oaks, CA: Sage Publications, Inc.

Jarrold, C., & Hall, D. (2013). The development of rehearsal in verbal short-term memory. *Child Development Perspectives, 7,* 182–186.

Jaswal, V., & Dodson, C. (2009). Metamemory development: Understanding the role of similarity in false memories. *Child Development, 80,* 629–635.

Jaworski, M., & Accardo, P. (2010). Behavioral phenotypes: Nature versus nurture revisited. In B. K. Shapiro & P. J. Accardo (Eds.), *Neurogenetic syndromes: Behavioral issues and their treatment.* Baltimore, MD: Paul H. Brookes Publishing.

Jay, M. (2012, April 14). The downside of cohabiting before marriage. *The New York Times,* p. SR4.

Jenkins, L. N., & Demaray, M. K. (2015). Indirect effects in the peer victimization-academic achievement relation: The role of academic self-concept and gender. *Psychology in the Schools, 52,* 235–247.

Jensen, A. (2003). Do age-group differences on mental tests imitate racial differences? *Intelligence, 31,* 107–121.

Jensen, L. A. (2008). Coming of age in a multicultural world: Globalization and adolescent cultural identity formation. In D. L. Browning (Ed.), *Adolescent identities: A collection of readings.* New York, NY: Analytic Press/Taylor & Francis Group.

Jensen, L. A., & Dost-Gözkan, A. (2014). Adolescent–parent relations in Asian Indian and Salvadoran immigrant families: A cultural–developmental analysis of autonomy, authority, conflict, and cohesion. *Journal of Research on Adolescence.* DOI: 10.1111/jora.1211

Jesmin, S. S. (2014). Review of agewise: Fighting the new ageism in America. *Journal of Women & Aging, 26,* 369–371.

Jeynes, W. (2007). The impact of parental remarriage on children: A meta-analysis. *Marriage & Family Review, 40,* 75–102.

Jia, R., Lang, S. N., & Schoppe-Sullivan, S. J. (2016). A developmental examination of the psychometric properties and predictive utility of a revised psychological self-concept measure for preschool-age children. *Psychological Assessment, 28,* 226–238.

Jiang, Y., Granja, M. R., & Koball, H. (2017). *Basic facts about low-income children.* New York: National Center for Children in Poverty.

Ji-liang, S., Li-qing, Z., & Yan, T. (2003). The impact of intergenerational social support and filial expectation on the loneliness of elder parents. *Chinese Journal of Clinical Psychology, 11,* 167–169.

Jindal, V. (2013). Glaucoma: An extension of various chronic neurodegenerative disorders. *Molecular Neurobiology.* doi: 10.1007/s12035-013-8416-8

Johnson, D. J., Jaeger, E., Randolph, S. M., Cauce, A. M., Ward, J., & National Institute of Child Health and Human Development: Early Child Care Research Network. (2003). Studying the effects of early child care experiences on the development of children of color in the United States: Toward a more inclusive research agenda. *Child Development, 74,* 1227–1244.

Johnson, H. J., Barnard-Brak, L. S., Terrill, F., & Johnson, M. K. (2012). An experimental study of the effects of stereotype threat and stereotype lift on men and women's performance in mathematics. *Journal of Experimental Education, 80,* 137–149.

Johnson, J. (2011, May 5). Jumping the broom or jumping to conclusions? 4 myths about Black marriage. Accessed online, 9/13/16; https://drjasonjohnson.com/2011/05/05/jumping-the-broom-or-jumping-to-conclusions-4-myths-about-black-marriage/

Johnston, L. D., Bachman, J. G., & O'Malley, P. M. (2016). *Monitoring the future study.* Lansing, MI: University of Michigan.

Johnston, L. D., O'Malley, P. M., Bachman, J. G., & Schulenberg, J. E. (2007). *Monitoring the future national results on adolescent drug use: Overview of key findings, 2006* (NIH Publication No. 07-6202). Bethesda, MD: National Institute on Drug Abuse.

Johnston, L. D., O'Malley, P. M., Miech, R.A., Bachman, J. G., & Schulenberg, J. E. (2018). *Monitoring the Future national results on adolescent drug use: Overview of key findings, 2017.* Ann Arbor, MI: Institute for Social Research.

Johnson, S. L., Moding, K. J., Maloney, K., & Bellows, L. L. (2018). Development of the Trying New Foods Scale: A preschooler self-assessment of willingness to try new foods. *Appetite, 128,* 21–31.

Joireman, J., & Van Lange, P. M. (2015). Ethical guidelines for data collection and analysis: A cornerstone for conducting high-quality research. In *How to publish high-quality research.* Washington, DC: American Psychological Association.

Jonas, D., Scanlon, C., Rusch, R., Ito, J., & Joselow, M. (2018). Bereavement after a child's death. *Child and Adolescent Psychiatric Clinics of North America.* doi:10.1016/j.chc.2018.05.010

Jonas, M. (2016). Child health advice and parental obligation: The case of safe sleep recommendations and sudden unexpected death in infancy. *Bioethics, 30,* 129–138.

Jones, D. E., Carson, K. A., Bleich, S. N., & Cooper, L. A. (2012). Patient trust in physicians and adoption of lifestyle behaviors to control high blood pressure. *Patient Education and Counseling, 89,* 57–62.

Jones, H. (2006). Drug addiction during pregnancy: Advances in maternal treatment and understanding child outcomes. *Current Directions in Psychological Science, 15,* 126–130.

Jones, N. A., & Mize, K. D. (2016). Introduction to the special issue: Psychophysiology and psychobiology in emotion development. *Journal of Experimental Child Psychology, 142,* 239–244.

Jones, S. (2007). Imitation in infancy: The development of mimicry. *Psychological Science, 18,* 593–599.

Jones-Harden, B. (2004). Safety and stability for foster children: A developmental perspective. *The Future of Children, 14,* 31–48.

Jopp, D. S., & Hertzog, C. (2010). Assessing adult leisure activities: An extension of a self-report activity questionnaire. *Psychological Assessment, 22,* 108–120.

Jordan, A. B., & Robinson, T. N. (2008). Children's television viewing, and weight status: Summary and recommendations from an expert panel meeting. *Annals of the American Academy of Political and Social Science, 615,* 119–132.

Jordan-Young, R. M. (2012). Hormones, context, and "brain gender": A review of evidence from congenital adrenal hyperplasia. *Social Science & Medicine, 74,* 1738–1744.

Jose, O., & Alfons, V. (2007). Do demographics affect marital satisfaction? *Journal of Sex and Marital Therapy, 33,* 73–85.

Judge, T. A., Ilies, R., & Zhang, Z. (2012). Genetic influences on core self-evaluations, job satisfaction, and work stress: A behavioral genetics mediated model. *Organizational Behavior and Human Decision Processes, 117,* 208–220.

Julvez, J., Guxens, M., Carsin, A., Forns, J., Mendez, M., Turner, M. C., & Sunyer, J. (2014). A cohort study on full breastfeeding and child neuropsychological development: The role of maternal social, psychological, and nutritional factors. *Developmental Medicine & Child Neurology, 56,* 148–156.

Jung, E., & Zhang, Y. (2016). Parental involvement, children's aspirations, and achievement in new immigrant families. *Journal of Educational Research, 109,* 333–350.

Jung, M., & Brawley, L. (2010). Concurrent management of exercise with other valued life goals: Comparison of frequent and less frequent exercisers. *Psychology of Sport and Exercise, 11,* 372–377.

Jurecic, A. (2017). Cautioning health-care professionals: Bereaved persons are misguided through the stages of grief. *Omega: Journal of Death and Dying, 75*(1), 92–93. doi:10.1177/0030222817701499

Jurimae, T., & Saar, M. (2003). Self-perceived and actual indicators of motor abilities in children and adolescents. *Perception and Motor Skills, 97,* 862–866.

Juvonen, J., Schacter, H. L., Sainio, M., & Salmivalli, C. (2016). Can a school-wide bullying prevention program improve the plight of victims? Evidence for risk × intervention effects. *Journal of Consulting and Clinical Psychology, 84,* 334–344.

Kaarre, O., Kallioniemi, E., Könönen, M., Tolmunen, T., Kekkonen, V., Kivimäki, P., &... Määttä, S. (2018). Heavy alcohol use in adolescence is associated with altered cortical activity: A combined TMS–EEG study. *Addiction Biology, 23*(1), 268–280. doi:10.1111/adb.12486

Kadam, G. (2014). Psychological health of parents whose children are away from them. *Indian Journal of Community Psychology, 10,* 358–363.

Kaffashi, F., Scher, M. S., Ludington-Hoe, S. M., & Loparo, K. A. (2013). An analysis of the kangaroo care intervention using neonatal EEG complexity: A preliminary study. *Clinical Neurophysiology, 124,* 238–246.

Kagan, J. (2000, October). Adult personality and early experience. *Harvard Mental Health Letter,* pp. 4–5.

Kagan, J. (2003). An unwilling rebel. In R. J. Sternberg (Ed.), *Psychologists defying the crowd: Stories of those who battled the establishment and won.* Washington, DC: American Psychological Association.

Kagan, J. (2008). In defense of qualitative changes in development. *Child Development, 79,* 1606–1624.

Kagan, J. (2010). *The temperamental thread: How genes, culture, time, and luck make us who we are.* Washington, DC: Dana Press.

Kagan, J., Kearsley, R., & Zelazo, P. R. (1978). *Infancy: Its place in human development.* Cambridge, MA: Harvard University Press.

Kahlbaugh, P., & Huffman, L. (2017). Personality, emotional qualities of leisure, and subjective well-being in the elderly. *International Journal of Aging & Human Development, 85,* 164–184.

Kahlenberg, S. G. & Hein, M. M. (2010). Progression on Nickelodeon? Gender role stereotypes in toy commercials. *Sex Roles, 62,* 830–847.

Kahn, J. P. (2004). Hostility, coronary risk, and alpha-adrenergic to beta-adrenergic receptor density ratio. *Psychosomatic Medicine, 66,* 289–297.

Kahn, R. L., & Rowe, J. W. (1999). *Successful aging.* New York, NY: Dell.

Kahneman, D., Krueger, A., Schkade, D., Schwarz, N., & Stone, A. (2006, June). Would you be happier if you were richer? A focusing illusion. *Science, 312,* 1908–1910.

Kail, R. (2003). Information processing and memory. In M. Bornstein & L. Davidson (Eds.), *Well-being: Positive development across the life course.* Mahwah, NJ: Lawrence Erlbaum Associates.

Kail, R. V. (2004). Cognitive development includes global and domain-specific processes [Special issue: 50th anniversary issue: Part II, the maturing of the human development sciences: Appraising past, present, and prospective agendas]. *Merrill-Palmer Quarterly, 50*, 445–455.

Kail, R. V., & Miller, C. A. (2006). Developmental change in processing speed: Domain specificity and stability during childhood and adolescence. *Journal of Cognition and Development, 7*, 119–137.

Kalashnikova, M., & Burnham, D. (2018). Infant-directed speech from 7 to 19 months has similar acoustic properties but different functions. *Journal of Child Language, 45*(5), 1035–1053.

Kalb, C. (1997, Spring/Summer). The top 10 health worries. *Newsweek Special Issue*, pp. 42–43.

Kalb, C. (2004, January 26). Brave new babies. *Newsweek*, pp. 45–53.

Kalb, C. (2006, February 5). In our blood. *Newsweek*. Accessed online, 5/2/18; http://www.newsweek.com/our-blood-113321

Kalb, C. (2012, February). Fetal armor. *Scientific American*, p. 73.

Kaltiala-Heino, R., Kosunen, E., & Rimpela, M. (2003). Pubertal timing, sexual behaviour and self-reported depression in middle adolescence. *Journal of Adolescence, 26*, 531–545.

Kalynchuk, L. (2010). Behavioral and neurobiological consequences of stress. *Progress in Neuro-Psychopharmacology & Biological Psychiatry, 34*, 731–732.

Kam, J. A., Pérez Torres, D., & Steuber Fazio, K. (2018). Identifying individual- and family-level coping strategies as sources of resilience and thriving for undocumented youth of Mexican origin. *Journal of Applied Communication Research*. doi: 10.1080/00909882.2018.1528373

Kaminaga, M. (2007). Pubertal development and depression in adolescent boys and girls. *Japanese Journal of Educational Psychology, 55*, 21–33.

Kanat-Maymon, Y., Almog, L., Cohen, R., & Amichai-Hamburger, Y. (2018). Contingent self-worth and Facebook addiction. *Computers in Human Behavior, 88*, 227–235.

Kandler, C., Bleidorn, W., & Riemann, R. (2012). Left or right? Sources of political orientation: The roles of genetic factors, cultural transmission, assortative mating, and personality. *Journal of Personality and Social Psychology, 102*, 633–645.

Kandler, C., Bleidorn, W., Riemann, R., Angleitner, A., & Spinath, F. M. (2012). Life events as environmental states and genetic traits and the role of personality: A longitudinal twin study. *Behavior Genetics, 42*, 57–72.

Kann, L., McManus, T., Harris, W. A., et al. (2018). Youth risk behavior surveillance—United States, 2017. *MMWR Surveillance Summaries 67*(SS-8), 1–114. doi:10.15585/mmwr.ss6708a1

Kantor, J. (2015, June 27). Historic day for gay rights, but a twinge of loss for gay culture. *The New York Times*, A1.

Kantrowitz, E. J., & Evans, G. W. (2004). The relation between the ratio of children per activity area and off-task behavior and type of play in day care centers. *Environment & Behavior, 36*, 541–557.

Kao, G. (2000). Psychological well-being and educational achievement among immigrant youth. In D. J. Hernandez (Ed.), *Children of immigrants: Health, adjustment, and public assistance*. Washington, DC: National Academy Press.

Kapke, T. L., Gerdes, A. C., & Lawton, K. E. (2017). Global self-worth in Latino youth: The role of acculturation and acculturation risk factors. *Child & Youth Care Forum, 46*, 307–333.

Kaplan, H., & Dove, H. (1987). Infant development among the Ache of Eastern Paraguay. *Developmental Psychology, 23*, 190–198.

Karagianni, P., Kyriakidou, M., Mitsiakos, G., Chatzioanidis, H., Koumbaras, E., Evangeliou, A., & Nikolaides, N. (2010). Neurological outcome in preterm small for gestational age infants compared to appropriate for gestational age preterm

at the age of 18 months: A prospective study. *Journal of Child Neurology, 25*, 165–170.

Karandashev, V. (2017). *Romantic love in cultural contexts*. Cham, Switzerland: Springer International Publishing.

Karatzias, T., Yan, E., & Jowett, S. (2015). Adverse life events and health: A population study in Hong Kong. *Journal of Psychosomatic Research, 78*, 173–177.

Karelitz, T. M., Jarvin, L., & Sternberg, R. J. (2010). The meaning of wisdom and its development throughout life. In W. F. Overton & R. M. Lerner (Eds.), *The handbook of life-span development, Vol. 1: Cognition, biology, and methods*. Hoboken, NJ: John Wiley & Sons.

Karl, J. M., Wilson, A. M. Bertoli, M. E., Shubear, N. S. (2018). Touch the table before the target: Contact with an underlying surface may assist the development of precise visually controlled reach and grasp movements in human infants. *Experimental Brain Research, 236*(8), 2185–2208.

Karmiloff-Smith, A., Aschersleben, G., de Schonen, S., Elsabbagh, M., Hohenberger, A., & Serres, J. (2010). Constraints on the timing of infant cognitive change: Domain-specific or domain-general? *European Journal of Developmental Science, 4*, 31–45.

Karney, B. R., & Bradbury, T. N. (2005). Contextual influences on marriage. *Current Directions in Psychological Science, 14*, 171–174.

Karniol, R. (2009). Israeli kindergarten children's gender constancy for others' counter-stereotypic toy play and appearance: The role of sibling gender and relative age. *Infant and Child Development, 18*, 73–94.

Karoly, L. A. (2018). The economic returns to early childhood education. Accessed online, 10/9/18; https://files.eric.ed.gov/fulltext/EJ1118537.pdf

Karraker, A., DeLamater, J., & Schwartz, C. R. (2011). Sexual frequency decline from midlife to later life. *Journals of Gerontology, Series B, Psychological Sciences, 66B*, 502–512.

Kaslow, F. W. (2001). Families and family psychology at the millennium: Intersecting crossroads. *American Psychologist, 56*, 37–44.

Kastenbaum, R. (1985). Dying and death: A life-span approach. In J. E. Birren & K. W. Schaie (Eds.), *Handbook of the psychology of aging*. New York, NY: Van Nostrand Reinhold.

Kastenbaum, R. (2000). *The psychology of death* (3rd ed.). New York, NY: Springer.

Katsimpardi, L., Litterman, N. K., Schein, P. A., Miller, C. M., Loffredo, F. S., Wojtkiewicz, G. R., &... Rubin, L. L. (2014). Vascular and neurogenic rejuvenation of the aging mouse brain by young systemic factors. *Science, 344*, 630–634.

Katz, J. (2017, June 15). Drug deaths in America are rising faster than ever. *New York Times*. Accessed online, 11/9/17; https://www.nytimes.com/interactive/2017/06/05/upshot/opioid-epidemicdrug-overdose-deaths-are-rising-faster-than-ever.html

Katz, S., & Marshall, B. (2003). New sex for old: Lifestyle, consumerism, and the ethics of aging well. *Journal of Aging Studies, 17*, 3–16.

Katz, S. & Marshall, B. L. (2018). Tracked and fit: FitBits, brain games, and the quantified aging body. *Journal of Aging Studies, 45*, 63–68.

Katzer, C., Fetchenhauer, D., & Belschak, F. (2009). Cyberbullying: Who are the victims? A comparison of victimization in Internet chatrooms and victimization in school. *Journal of Media Psychology: Theories, Methods, and Applications, 21*, 25–36.

Kaufman, J. C., Kaufman, A. S., Kaufman-Singer, J., & Kaufman, N. L. (2005). The Kaufman assessment battery for children—second edition and the Kaufman adolescent and adult Intelligence test. In D. P. Flanagan & P. L. Harrison (Eds.), *Contemporary intellectual assessment: Theories, tests, and issues*. New York, NY: Guilford Press.

Kawakami, K. (2014). The early sociability of toddlers: The origins of teaching. *Infant Behavior & Development, 37*, 174–177.

Kayton, A. (2007). Newborn screening: A literature review. *Neonatal Network, 26*, 85–95.

Keating, D. P. (2004). Cognitive and brain development. In R. M. Lerner & L. Steinberg (Eds.), *Handbook of adolescent psychology* (2nd ed.). Hoboken, NJ: John Wiley & Sons.

Kecskes, I., & Papp, T. (2000). *Foreign language and mother tongue*. Mahwah, NJ: Lawrence Erlbaum.

Keel, P. K., Gravener, J. A., Joiner, T. E., Jr., & Haedt, A. (2010). Twenty-year follow-up of bulimia nervosa and related eating disorders not otherwise specified. *International Journal of Eating Disorders, 43*, 492–497.

Keene, J. R., Prokos, A. H., & Held, B. (2012). Grandfather caregivers: Race and ethnic differences in poverty. *Sociological Inquiry, 82*, 49–77.

Kehl, K. A., & McCarty, K. N. (2012). Readability of hospice materials to prepare families for caregiving at the time of death. *Research in Nursing & Health, 35*, 242–249.

Kelch-Oliver, K. (2008). African American grandparent caregivers: Stresses and implications for counselors. *The Family Journal, 16*, 43–50.

Kellehear, A. (2015). Death education as a public health issue. In J. M. Stillion, T. Attig, J. M. Stillion, T. Attig (Eds.), *Death, dying, and bereavement: Contemporary perspectives, institutions, and practices*. New York, NY: Springer Publishing Co.

Keller, H., Otto, H., Lamm, B., Yovsi, R. D., & Kartner, J. (2008). The timing of verbal/vocal communications between mothers and their infants: A longitudinal cross-cultural comparison. *Infant Behavior & Development, 31*, 217–226.

Kelloway, E., & Francis, L. (2013). Longitudinal research and data analysis. In R. R. Sinclair, M. Wang, & L. E. Tetrick (Eds.), *Research methods in occupational health psychology: Measurement, design, and data analysis*. New York: Routledge/Taylor & Francis Group.

Kelley, G., Kelley, K., Hootman, J., & Jones, D. (2009). Exercise and health-related quality of life in older community-dwelling adults: A meta-analysis of randomized controlled trials. *Journal of Applied Gerontology, 28*, 369–394.

Kelly, G. (2001). *Sexuality today: A human perspective* (7th ed.). New York, NY: McGraw-Hill.

Kelly-Weeder, S., & Cox, C. (2007). The impact of lifestyle risk factors on female infertility. *Women & Health, 44*, 1–23.

Kemker, D. (2017, January 9). Ameen Abdulrasool. My Hero Stories Scientists. Accessed online, 11/13/17; https://myhero.com/Abdulrasool_06

Kemper, S. (2012). The interaction of linguistic constraints, working memory, and aging on language production and comprehension. In M. Naveh-Benjamin & N. Ohta (Eds.), *Memory and aging: Current issues and future directions*. New York, NY: Psychology Press.

Kendler, K. S., Ohlsson, H., Sundquist, J., & Sundquist, K. (2018). Transmission of alcohol use disorder across three generations: A Swedish national study. *Psychological Medicine, 48*(1), 33–42.

Kenett, Y. N., Beaty, R. E., Silvia, P. J., Anaki, D., & Faust, M. (2016). Structure and flexibility: Investigating the relation between the structure of the mental lexicon, fluid intelligence, and creative achievement. *Psychology of Aesthetics, Creativity, and the Arts*. doi: 10.1037/aca0000056

Kennedy-Hendricks, A., Barry, C. L., Gollust, S. E., Ensminger, M. E., Chisolm, M. S., & McGinty, E. E. (2017). Social stigma toward persons with prescription opioid use disorder: Associations with public support for punitive and public health–oriented policies. *Psychiatric Services, 68*, 462–469.

Kennell, J. H. (2002). On becoming a family: Bonding and the changing patterns in baby and family behavior. In J. Gomes-Pedro & J. K. Nugent (Eds.), *The infant and family in the twenty-first century*. New York, NY: Brunner-Routledge.

Keski-Rahkonen, A., Raevuori, A., Bulik, C. M., Hoek, H. W., Sihvola, E., Kaprio, J., & Rissanen, A. (2013). Depression and drive for thinness are associated with persistent bulimia nervosa in the community. *European Eating Disorders Review, 21*, 121–129.

Khader, Y. S., Al-Akour, N., AlZubi, I. M., & Lataifeh, I. (2011). The association between secondhand smoke and low birth weight and preterm delivery. *Maternal and Child Health Journal, 15*(4), 453–459.

Khodarahimi, S., & Fathi, R. (2017). Mate selection, meaning of marriage and positive cognitive constructs on younger and older married individuals. *Contemporary Family Therapy: An International Journal, 39*, 132–139.

Khalaila, R., & Cohen, M. (2016). Emotional suppression, caregiving burden, mastery, coping strategies and mental health in spousal caregivers. *Aging & Mental Health, 20*(9), 908–917.

Kiang, L., & Bhattacharjee, K. (2018). Developmental change and correlates of autonomy in Asian American adolescents. *Journal of Youth and Adolescence.* doi:10.1007/s10964-018-0909-3

Kieffer, C. C. (2012). Secure connections, the extended family system, and the socio-cultural construction of attachment theory. In S. Akhtar (Ed.), *The mother and her child: Clinical aspects of attachment, separation, and loss.* Lanham, MD: Jason Aronson.

Kiilo, T., Kasearu, K., & Kutsar, D. (2016). Intergenerational family solidarity: Study of older migrants in Estonia. *Geropsych: Journal of Gerontopsychology And Geriatric Psychiatry, 29*, 71–80.

Kilmann, P., & Vendemia, J. C. (2013). Partner discrepancies in distressed marriages. *Journal of Social Psychology, 153*, 196–211.

Kim, B., Chow, S., Bray, B., & Teti, D. M. (2017). Trajectories of mothers' emotional availability: Relations with infant temperament in predicting attachment security. *Attachment & Human Development, 19*, 38–57.

Kim, H. I., & Johnson, S. P. (2013). Do young infants prefer an infant-directed face or a happy face? *International Journal of Behavioral Development, 37*, 125–130.

Kim, J., Bushway, S., & Tsao, H. (2016). Identifying classes of explanations for crime drop: Period and cohort effects for New York State. *Journal of Quantitative Criminology, 32*, 357–375.

Kim, J.-S., & Lee, E.-H. (2003). Cultural and noncultural predictors of health outcomes in Korean daughter and daughter in-law caregivers. *Public Health Nursing, 20*, 111–119.

Kim, Y. G. (2016) Direct and mediated effects of language and cognitive skills on comprehension of oral narrative texts (listening comprehension) for children. *Journal of Experimental Child Psychology, 141*, 101–120.

Kimm, S., Glynn, N. W., Kriska, A., Barton, B. A., Kronsberg, S. S., Daniels, S. R., et al. (2003). Decline in physical activity in Black girls and White girls during adolescence. *New England Journal of Medicine, 347*, 709–715.

Kimmel, D. C. (2015). Theories of aging applied to LGBT older adults and their families. In N. A. Orel & C. A. Fruhauf (Eds.), *The lives of LGBT older adults: Understanding challenges and resilience* (pp. 73–90). Washington, DC: American Psychological Association.

Kimura, K., Yasunaga, A., & Wang, L. (2013). Correlation between moderate daily physical activity and neurocognitive variability in healthy elderly people. *Archives of Gerontology and Geriatrics, 56*, 109–117.

King, D., Delfabbro, P., & Griffiths, M. (2010). The convergence of gambling and digital media: Implications for gambling in young people. *Journal of Gambling Studies, 26*, 175–187.

Kingston, D., Heaman, M., Urquia, M., O'Campo, P., Janssen, P., Thiessen, K., & Smylie, J. (2016). Correlates of abuse around the time of pregnancy: Results from a national survey of Canadian women. *Maternal and Child Health Journal, 20*(4), 778–789.

Kinney, H. C., Randall, L. L., Sleeper, L. A., Willinger, M., Beliveau, R. A., Zec, N., & ... Welty, T. K. (2003). Serotonergic brainstem abnormalities in Northern Plains Indians with the sudden infant death syndrome. *Journal of Neuropathology and Experimental Neurology, 62*, 1178–1191.

Kinney, H. C., & Thach, B. (2009). Medical progress: The sudden infant death syndrome. *New England Journal of Medicine, 361*, 795–805.

Kinsey, A. C., Pomeroy, W. B., & Martin, C. E. (1948). *Sexual behavior in the human male.* Philadelphia, PA: Saunders.

Kirby, J. (2006, May). From single-parent families to stepfamilies: Is the transition associated with adolescent alcohol initiation? *Journal of Family Issues, 27*, 685–711.

Kirchengast, S., & Hartmann, B. (2003). Impact of maternal age and maternal-somatic characteristics on newborn size. *American Journal of Human Biology, 15*, 220–228.

Kirkorian, H. L., Lavigne, H. J., Hanson, K. G., Troseth, G. L., Demers, L. B., & Anderson, D. R. (2016). Video deficit in toddlers' object retrieval: What eye movements reveal about online cognition. *Infancy, 21*, 37–64.

Kirsh, S. J. (2012). *Children, adolescents, and media violence: A critical look at the research* (2nd ed.). Thousand Oaks, CA: Sage Publications, Inc.

Kitamura, C., & Lam, C. (2009). Age-specific preferences for infant-directed affective intent. *Infancy, 14*, 77–100.

Kiuru, N., Nurmi, J., Aunola, K., & Salmela-Aro, K. (2009). Peer group homogeneity in adolescents' school adjustment varies according to peer group type and gender. *International Journal of Behavioral Development, 33*, 65–76.

Kjerulff, K. H., & Brubaker, L. H. (2017). New mothers' feelings of disappointment and failure after cesarean delivery. *Birth: Issues in Perinatal Care.* Accessed online, 10/29/17; https://www.ncbi.nlm.nih.gov/pubmed/?term=New+mothers%E2%80%99+feelings+of+disappointment+and+failure+after+cesarean+delivery.+Birth%3A+Issues+In+Perinatal+Care

Kjølseth, I., Ekeberg, Ø., & Steihaug, S. (2010). Why suicide? Elderly people who committed suicide and their experience of life in the period before their death. *International Psychogeriatrics, 22*, 209–218.

Klaming, R., Annese, J., Veltman, D. J., & Comijs, H. C. (2017). Episodic memory function is affected by lifestyle factors: A 14-year follow-up study in an elderly population. *Aging, Neuropsychology, and Cognition, 24*, 528–542.

Kläning, U., Trumbetta, S. L., Gottesman, I. I., Skytthe, A., Kyvik, K. O., & Bertelsen, A. (2016). A Danish twin study of schizophrenia liability: Investigation from interviewed twins for genetic links to affective psychoses and for cross-cohort comparisons. *Behavior Genetics, 46*, 193–204.

Klein, A. (2017, August 29). On parenting: When is it safe to start leaving kids home alone? *Washington Post.* Accessed online, 11/20/17; https://www.washingtonpost.com/lifestyle/on-parenting/when-is-it-safe-to-start-leavingkids-home-alone/2017/08/28/a86390c0-7891-11e7-8839-ec48ec4cae25_story.html?utm_term=.dbd0f2e774a8

Klein, M. C. (2012). The tyranny of meta-analysis and the misuse of randomized controlled trials in maternity care. *Birth: Issues in Perinatal Care, 39*, 80–82.

Klimstra, T. A., Luyckx, K., Germeijs, V., Meeus, W. J., & Goossens, L. (2012). Personality traits and educational identity formation in late adolescents: Longitudinal associations and academic progress. *Journal of Youth and Adolescence, 41*, 346–361.

Klingberg, T., & Betteridge, N. (2013). *The learning brain: Memory and brain development in children.* New York, NY: Oxford University Press.

Klitzman, R. L. (2012). *Am I my genes? Confronting fate and family secrets in the age of genetic testing.* New York, NY: Oxford University Press.

Kloep, M., Güney, N., Çok, F., & Simsek, Ö. (2009). Motives for risk-taking in adolescence: A cross-cultural study. *Journal of Adolescence, 32*, 135–151.

Kluger, J. (2010, November 1). Keeping young minds healthy. *Time*, pp. 40–50.

Knafo, A., & Schwartz, S. H. (2003). Parenting and accuracy of perception of parental values by adolescents. *Child Development, 73*, 595–611.

Knežević, M., & Marinković, K. (2017). Neurodynamic correlates of response inhibition from emerging to mid adulthood. *Cognitive Development, 43*, 106–118.

Knickmeyer, R., & Baron-Cohen, S. (2006, December). Fetal testosterone and sex differences. *Early Human Development, 82*, 755–760.

Knifsend, C. A., & Juvonen, J. (2014). Social identity complexity, cross-ethnic friendships, and intergroup attitudes in urban middle schools. *Child Development, 85*, 709–721.

Knight, G. P., Safa, M. D., & White, R. M. B. (2018). Advancing the assessment of cultural orientation: A developmental and contextual framework of multiple psychological dimensions and social identities. *Development and Psychopathology.* doi:10.1017/S095457941800113X

Knight, J., Wigham, C., & Nigam, Y. (2017). Anatomy and physiology of aging 6: the eyes and ears. *Nursing Times* [online]; *113*(7), 39-42.

Knight, Z. G. (2017). A proposed model of psychodynamic psychotherapy linked to Erik Erikson's eight stages of psychosocial development. *Clinical Psychology & Psychotherapy.* Accessed online, 3/2/17; https://www.ncbi.nlm.nih.gov/pubmed/28124459

Knoll, L. J., Fuhrmann, D., Sakhardande, A. L., Stamp, F., Speekenbrink, M., & Blakemore, S. (2016). A window of opportunity for cognitive training in adolescence. *Psychological Science, 27*, 1620–1631.

Knorth, E. J., Harder, A. T., Zandberg, T., & Kendrick, A. J. (2008). Under one roof: A review and selective meta-analysis on the outcomes of residential child and youth care. *Children and Youth Services Review, 30*, 123–140.

Koball, H. & Jiang, Y. (2018). Basic facts about low-income children: Children under 18 years, 2016. National Center for Children in Poverty. Accessed online, 9/22/18; http://www.nccp.org/publications/pub_1194.html

Kochanska, G., & Aksan, N. (2004). Development of mutual responsiveness between parents and their young children. *Child Development, 75*, 1657–1676.

Koenig, L. B., McGue, M., Krueger, R. F., & Bouchard, T. J., Jr. (2005). Genetic and environmental influences on religiousness: Findings for retrospective and current religiousness ratings. *Journal of Personality, 73*, 471–488.

Kogan, S. M., Yu, T., Allen, K. A., & Brody, G. H. (2014). Racial microstressors, racial self-concept, and depressive symptoms among male African Americans during the transition to adulthood. *Journal of Youth and Adolescence, 44*, 898–909.

Koh, S., & Sewell, D. D. (2015). Sexual functions in older adults. *American Journal of Geriatric Psychiatry, 23*, 223–226.

Kohlberg, L. (1966). A cognitive-developmental anaylsis of children's sex-role concepts and attitudes. In E. E. Maccoby (Ed.), *The development of sex differences.* Stanford, CA: Stanford University Press.

Kohlberg, L. (1969). Stages and sequences: The cognitive development approach to socialization. In D. A. Goslin, Ed., *Handbook of Socialization Theory of Research.* Chicago, IL: Rand McNally.

Kohut, S. A., & Riddell, R. P. (2009). Does the Neonatal Facial Coding System differentiate between infants experiencing pain-related and non-pain-related distress? *Journal of Pain, 10*, 214–220.

Koike, K. J. (2014). *Everyday audiology: A practical guide for health care professionals* (2nd ed.). San Diego, CA: Plural Publishing.

Kokou-Kpolou, K., Megalakaki, O., & Nieuviarts, N. (2018). Persistent depressive and grief symptoms for up to 10 years following perinatal loss: Involvement of negative cognitions. *Journal of Affective Disorders, 241*, 360–366.

Kolling, T., & Knopf, M. (2014). Late life human development: Boosting or buffering universal biological aging. *Geropsych: Journal of*

Gerontopsychology and Geriatric Psychiatry, 27, 103–108.

Kõlves, K., Zhao, Q., Ross, V., Hawgood, J., Spence, S. H., & de Leo, D. (2019). Suicide and other sudden death bereavement of immediate family members: An analysis of grief reactions six-months after death. *Journal of Affective Disorders, 243,* 96–102.

Kolyada, A. K., Vaiserman, A. M., Krasnenkov, D. S., & Karaban, I. N. (2016). Studies of telomere length in patients with Parkinson's disease. *Neuroscience and Behavioral Physiology, 46,* 344–347.

Kong, A., Thorleifsson, G., Frigge, M. L., Vilhjalmsson, B. J., Young, A. I., Thorgeirsson, T. E., & ... Stefansson, K. (2018). The nature of nurture: Effects of parental genotypes. *Science, 359*(6374), 424–428.

Konigsberg R. D. (2011). Chore Wars. *Time, 178,* pp. 44–49.

Koopmans, S., & Kooijman, A. (2006, November). Presbyopia correction and accommodative intra-ocular lenses. *Gerontechnology, 5,* 222–230.

Kopans, D. B. (2017). The facts about mammography screening: A conversation with your physician. American College of Radiology. Accessed online, 11/28/17; https://www.sbi-online.org/Portals/0/downloads/documents/pdfs/THE%20FACTS%20ABOUT%20MAMMOGRAPHY%20SCREENINGKopans.pdf

Kornides, M. L., Rimm, E. B., Chavarro, J. E., Gillman, M. W., Rosner, B., & Field, A. E. (2018). Seasonal variations in meeting physical activity recommendations and development of overweight during adolescence. *Childhood Obesity, 14*(1), 33–40.

Korol, L., Fietzer, A. W., & Ponterotto, J. G. (2018). The relationship between multicultural personality, intergroup contact, and positive outgroup attitudes toward Asian Americans. *Asian American Journal of Psychology, 9*(3), 200–210. doi:10.1037/aap0000107

Korotchikova, I., Stevenson, N. J., Livingstone, V., Ryan, C. A., & Boylan, G. B. (2016). Sleep–wake cycle of the healthy term newborn infant in the immediate postnatal period. *Clinical Neurophysiology, 127,* 2095–2101.

Kosma, M., & Cardinal, B. J. (2016). Theory-based physical activity beliefs by race and activity levels among older adults. *Ethnicity & Health, 21*(2), 181–195.

Koska, J., Ksinantova, L., Sebokova, E., Kvetnansky, R., Klimes, I., Chrousos, G., & Pacak, K. (2002). Endocrine regulation of subcutaneous fat metabolism during cold exposure in humans. *Annals of the New York Academy of Science, 967,* 500–505.

Koss, M. P., Goodman, L. A., Browne, A., Fitzgerald, L. F., Keita, G. P., & Russo, N. F. (1993). *No safe haven: Violence against women, at home, at work, and in the community.* Final report of the American Psychological Association Women's Programs Office Task Force on Violence Against Women. Washington, DC: American Psychological Association.

Kostka, T., & Jachimowicz, V. (2010). Relationship of quality of life to dispositional optimism, health locus of control and self-efficacy in older subjects living in different environments. *Quality of Life Research, 19,* 351–361.

Kotre, J., & Hall, E. (1990). *Seasons of life.* Boston: Little, Brown.

Kottak, C. (2019). *Anthropology: Appreciating human diversity* (17th ed.). New York: McGraw-Hill.

Kottak, C. (2019). *Cultural anthropology* (18th ed.). New York: McGraw-Hill.

Kowal, M., Toth, A. J., Exton, C., & Campbell, M. J. (2018). Different cognitive abilities displayed by action video gamers and non-gamers. *Computers in Human Behavior, 88,* 255–262.

Kramer, M. S., Aboud, F., Mironova, E., Vanilovich, I., Platt, R. W., Lutush, L., & ... PROBIT Study Group. (2008). Breastfeeding and child cognitive development: New evidence for a large randomized trial. *Archives of General Psychiatry, 65*(5), 378–384.

Krause, M. S. (2018). Mathematical expression and sampling issues of treatment contrasts: Beyond significance testing and meta-analysis to clinically useful research synthesis. *Psychotherapy Research, 28*(1), 58–75.

Kreager, D. A., Molloy, L. E., Moody, J., & Feinberg, M. E. (2016). Friends first? The peer network origins of adolescent dating. *Journal of Research on Adolescence, 26,* 257–269.

Krekula, C. (2016). Contextualizing older women's body images: Time dimensions, multiple reference groups, and age codings of appearance. *Journal of Women & Aging, 28,* 58–67.

Kretch, K. S., & Adolph, K. E. (2013). Cliff or step? Posture-specific learning at the edge of a drop-off. *Child Development, 84,* 226–240.

Kretsch, N., Mendle, J., Cance, J. D., & Harden, K. P. (2016). Peer group similarity in perceptions of pubertal timing. *Journal of Youth and Adolescence, 45,* 1696–1710.

Krishna, A. (2018). Poison or prevention? Understanding the linkages between vaccine-negative individuals' knowledge deficiency, motivations, and active communication behaviors. *Health Communication, 33*(9), 1088–1096.

Kroger, J. (2006). *Identity development: Adolescence through adulthood.* Thousand Oaks, CA: Sage Publications.

Kross, E., & Grossmann, I. (2012). Boosting wisdom: Distance from the self enhances wise reasoning, attitudes, and behavior. *Journal of Experimental Psychology: General, 141,* 43–48.

Kross, E., Verduyn, P., Demiralp, E., Park, J., Lee, D. S., Lin, N., & ... Ybarra, O. (2013). Facebook use predicts declines in subjective well-being in young adults. *Plos ONE, 8,* 22–29.

Krüger, O., Korsten, P., & Hoffman, J. I. (2017). The rise of behavioral genetics and the transition to behavioral genomics and beyond. In J. Call, G. M. Burghardt, I. M. Pepperberg, C. T. Snowdon, & T. Zentall (Eds.), *APA handbook of comparative psychology: Basic concepts, methods, neural substrate, and behavior.* Washington, DC: American Psychological Association.

Kruschke, J. K., & Liddell, T. M. (2018). The Bayesian New Statistics: Hypothesis testing, estimation, meta-analysis, and power analysis from a Bayesian perspective. *Psychonomic Bulletin & Review, 25*(1), 178–206.

Kübler-Ross, E. (1969). *On death and dying.* New York, NY: Macmillan.

Kübler-Ross, E. (Ed.). (1975). *Death: The final stage of growth.* Englewood Cliffs, NJ: Prentice-Hall.

Kübler-Ross, E. (1982). *Working it through.* New York, NY: Macmillan.

Kuhl, P. K., Andruski, J. E., Chistovich, I. A., Chistovich, L. A., Kozhevnikova, E. V., Ryskina, V. L., & ... Lacerda, F. (1997, August 1). Cross-language analysis of phonetic units in language addressed to infants. *Science, 277,* 684–686.

Kuhn, D. (2008). Formal operations from a twenty-first century perspective. *Human Development, 51,* 48–55.

Kuhn, D., Garcia-Mila, M., Zohar, A., & Andersen, C. (1995). Strategies of knowledge acquisition. With commentary by S. H. White, D. Klahr, & S. M. Carver, and a reply by D. Kuhn. *Monographs of the Society for Research in Child Development, 60,* 122–137.

Kulik, L. (2002). "His" and "Her" marriage: Differences in spousal perceptions of marital life in late adulthood. In S. P. Serge (Ed.), *Advances in psychology research, Vol. 17.* Hauppauge, NY: Nova Science Publishers.

Kulkarni, V., Khadilkar, R. J., Srivathsa, M. S., & Inamdar, M. S. (2011). Asrij maintains the stem cell niche and controls differentiation during drosophila lymph gland hematopoiesis. *PLoS ONE, 6,* 22–29.

Kung, F. H., Chao, M. M., Yao, D. J., Adair, W. L., Fu, J. H., & Tasa, K. (2018). Bridging racial divides: Social constructionist (vs essentialist) beliefs facilitate trust in intergroup contexts. *Journal of Experimental Social Psychology, 74,* 121–134.

Kunzmann, U., & Baltes, P. (2005). *The psychology of wisdom: Theoretical and empirical challenges.* New York, NY: Cambridge University Press.

Kupersmidt, J. B., & Dodge, K. A. (Eds.). (2004). *Children's peer relations: From development to intervention.* Washington, DC: American Psychological Association.

Kuppens, S., & Ceulemans, E. (2018). Parenting styles: A closer look at a well-known concept. *Journal of Child and Family Studies.* doi:10.1007/s10826-018-1242-x

Kurdek, L. A. (2003). Negative representations of the self/spouse and marital distress. *Personal Relationships, 10,* 511–534.

Kurdek, L. A. (2006, May). Differences between partners from heterosexual, gay, and lesbian cohabiting couples. *Journal of Marriage and Family, 68,* 509–528.

Kurdek, L. A. (2008). Change in relationship quality for partners from lesbian, gay male, and heterosexual couples. *Journal of Family Psychology, 22,* 701–711.

Kuron, L. J., Lyons, S. T., Schweitzer, L., & Ng, E. W. (2015). Millennials' work values: Differences across the school to work transition. *Personnel Review, 44,* 991–1009.

Kurtines, W. M., & Gewirtz, J. L. (1987). *Moral development through social interaction.* New York, NY: Wiley.

Kurtz-Costes, B., Swinton, A. D., & Skinner, O. D. (2014). Racial and ethnic gaps in the school performance of Latino, African American, and White students. In F. L. Leong, L. Comas-Díaz, G. C. Nagayama Hall, V. C. McLoyd, J. E. Trimble, F. L. Leong, & ... J. E. Trimble (Eds.), *APA handbook of multicultural psychology, Vol. 1: Theory and research.* Washington, DC: American Psychological Association.

Kusangi, E., Nakano, S., & Kondo-Ikemura, K. (2014). The development of infant temperament and its relationship with maternal temperament. *Psychologia: An International Journal of Psychological Sciences, 57,* 31–38.

Kwant, P. B., Finocchiaro, T., Forster, F., Reul, H., Rau, G., Morshuis, M., & ... Steinseifer, U. (2007). The MiniACcor: Constructive redesign of an implantable total artificial heart, initial laboratory testing and further steps. *International Journal of Artificial Organs, 30,* 345–51.

Kyweluk, M. A., Georgiev, A. V., Borja, J. B., Gettler, L. T., & Kuzawa, C. W. (2018). Menarcheal timing is accelerated by favorable nutrition but unrelated to developmental cues of mortality or familial instability in Cebu, Philippines. *Evolution and Human Behavior, 39*(1), 76–81.

Labouvie-Vief, G. (2006). Emerging structures of adult thought. In J. J. Arnett & J. L. Tanner (Eds.), *Emerging adults in America: Coming of age in the 21st century.* Washington, DC: American Psychological Association.

Labouvie-Vief, G. (2009). Cognition and equilibrium regulation in development and aging. *Restorative Neurology and Neuroscience, 27,* 551–565.

Lacerda, F., von Hofsten, C., & Heimann, M. (2001). *Emerging cognitive abilities in early infancy.* Mahwah, NJ: Lawrence Erlbaum.

Lachapelle, U., Noland, R. B., & Von Hagen, L. (2013). Teaching children about bicycle safety: An evaluation of the New Jersey Bike School program. *Accident Analysis and Prevention, 52,* 237–249.

Lachmann, T., Berti, S., Kujala, T., & Schroger, E. (2005). Diagnostic subgroups of developmental dyslexia have different deficits in neural processing of tones and phonemes. *International Journal of Psychophysiology, 56,* 105–120.

Lackey, C. (2003). Violent family heritage, the transition to adulthood, and later partner violence. *Journal of Family Issues, 24,* 74–98.

LaCoursiere, D., Hirst, K. P., & Barrett-Connor, E. (2012). Depression and pregnancy stressors affect the association between abuse and postpartum depression. *Maternal and Child Health Journal, 16,* 929–935.

LaCroix, A. Z., Chlebowski, R. T., Manson, J. E., Aragaki, A. K., Johnson, K. C., Martin, L.,… Wactawski-Wende, J. (2011). Health outcomes after stopping conjugated equine estrogens among postmenopausal women with prior hysterectomy: A randomized controlled trial. *JAMA: Journal of the American Medical Association, 305*(13), 1305–1314.

Laflamme, D., Pomerleau, A., & Malcuit, G. (2002). A comparison of fathers' and mothers' involvement in childcare and stimulation behaviors during free-play with their infants at 9 and 15 months. *Sex Roles, 47*, 507–518.

Laghi, F., Baiocco, R., Di Norcia, A., Cannoni, E., Baumgartner, E., & Bombi, A. S. (2014). Emotion understanding, pictorial representations of friendship and reciprocity in school-aged children. *Cognition and Emotion, 28*, 1338–1346.

Lahat, A., Walker, O. L., Lamm, C., Degnan, K. A., Henderson, H. A., & Fox, N. A. (2014). Cognitive conflict links behavioural inhibition and social problem solving during social exclusion in childhood. *Infant and Child Development, 23*, 273–282.

Lai, C. (2006). How much of human height is genetic and how much is due to nutrition? *Scientific American.* Accessed online, 10/21/18; https://www.scientificamerican.com/article/how-much-of-human-height/

Lain, D. (2012). Working past 65 in the UK and the USA: Segregation into "Lopaq" occupations? *Work, Employment and Society, 26*, 78–94.

Lakhani, B., Borich, M. R., Jackson, J. N., Wadden, K. P., Peters, S., Villamayor, A., &… Boyd, L. A. (2016). Motor skill acquisition promotes human brain myelin plasticity. *Neural Plasticity, 2016*.

Lamaze, F. (1970). *Painless childbirth: The Lamaze method.* Chicago: Regnery.

Lamb, M. E., Sternberg, K. J., Hwang, C. P., & Broberg, A. G. (Eds.). (1992). *Child care in context: Cross-cultural perspectives.* Hillsdale, NJ: Erlbaum.

Lambiase, A., Aloe, L., Centofanti, M., Parisi, V., Mantelli, F., Colafrancesco, V., &… Levi-Montalcini, R. (2009). Experimental and clinical evidence of neuroprotection by nerve growth factor eye drops: Implications for glaucoma. *Proceedings of the National Academy of Sciences of the United States of America, 106*, 13469–13474.

Lambrick, D., Westrupp, N., Kaufmann, S., Stoner, L., & Faulkner, J. (2016). The effectiveness of a high-intensity games intervention on improving indices of health in young children. *Journal of Sports Sciences, 34*, 190–198.

Lambrinoudaki, I., & Pérez-López, F. R. (2013). Hormone therapy and the prevention of cardiovascular disease and cognitive decline: Where do we stand? *Maturitas, 74*, 107–108.

Lamidi, E., & Cruz, J. (2014). *Remarriage rate in the U.S., 2012. (FP-14-10).* National Center for Family & Marriage Research. Accessed online, 11/29/17; http://www.bgsu.edu/content/dam/BGSU/college-ofarts-and-sciences/NCFMR/documents/FP/FP-14-10-remarriage-rate-2012.pdf

Lamm, B., & Keller, H. (2007). Understanding cultural models of parenting: The role of intracultural variation and response style. *Journal of Cross-Cultural Psychology, 38*, 50–57.

Landis, M., Peter-Wight, M., Martin, M., & Bodenmann, G. (2013). Dyadic coping and marital satisfaction of older spouses in long-term marriage. *Geropsych: The Journal of Gerontopsychology and Geriatric Psychiatry, 26*, 39–47.

Landrine, H., & Klonoff, E. A. (1994). Cultural diversity in causal attributions for illness: The role of the supernatural. *Journal of Behavior Medicine, 17*, 181–193.

Landy, F., & Conte, J. M. (2004). *Work in the 21st century.* New York, NY: McGraw-Hill.

Lane, J. D., Wellman, H. M., Olson, S. L., Miller, A. L., Wang, L., & Tardif, T. (2013). Relations between temperament and theory of mind development in the United States and China: Biological and behavioral correlates of preschoolers' false-belief understanding. *Developmental Psychology, 49*, 825–836.

Lane, K. A., Goh, J. X., & Driver-Linn, E. (2012). Implicit science stereotypes mediate the relationship between gender and academic participation. *Sex Roles, 66*, 220–234.

Langer, E., & Janis, I. (1979). *The psychology of control.* Beverly Hills, CA: Sage Publications.

Langille, D. (2007). Teenage pregnancy: Trends, contributing factors and the physician's role. *Canadian Medical Association Journal, 176*, 1601–1602.

Langlais, M. R., Anderson, E. R., & Greene, S. M. (2017). Divorced young adult mothers' experiences of breakup: Benefits and drawbacks. *Emerging Adulthood, 5*(4), 280–292.

Lansford, J. (2009). Parental divorce and children's adjustment. *Perspectives on Psychological Science, 4*, 140–152.

Lansford, J. E., Chang, L., Dodge, K. A., Malone, P. S., Oburu, P., Palmérus, K., &… Quinn, N. (2005). Physical discipline and children's adjustment: Cultural normativeness as a moderator. *Child Development, 76*, 1234–1246.

Lansford, J. E., Yu, T., Pettit, G. S., Bates, J. E., & Dodge, K. A. (2014). Pathways of peer relationships from childhood to young adulthood. *Journal of Applied Developmental Psychology, 35*, 111–117.

Lanza, S. T., Russell, M. A., & Braymiller, J. L. (2017). Emergence of electronic cigarette use in US adolescents and the link to traditional cigarette use. *Addictive Behaviors, 67*, 38–43.

Lapidot-Lefler, N., & Dolev-Cohen, M. (2014). Comparing cyberbullying and school bullying among school students: Prevalence, gender, and grade level differences. *Social Psychology of Education.* Accessed online, 3/22/15; http://link.springer.com/article/10.1007%2Fs11218-014-9280-8#close

Lapsley, D. (2016). Teaching moral development. In M. C. Smith & N. DeFrates-Densch (Eds.), *Challenges and innovations in educational psychology teaching and learning* (pp. 287–302). Charlotte, NC: IAP Information Age Publishing.

Largo, R. H., Fischer, J. E., & Rousson, V. (2003). Neuromotor development from kindergarten age to adolescence: Developmental course and variability. *Swedish Medical Weekly, 133*, 193–199.

Larsen, K. E., O'Hara, M. W., & Brewer, K. K. (2001). A prospective study of self-efficacy expectancies and labor pain. *Journal of Reproductive and Infant Psychology, 19*, 203–214.

Laska, M. N., Murray, D. M., Lytle, L. A., & Harnack, L. J. (2012). Longitudinal associations between key dietary behaviors and weight gain over time: Transitions through the adolescent years. *Obesity, 20*, 118–125.

Latorre, J. M., Serrano, J. P., Ricarte, J., Bonete, B., Ros, L., & Sitges, E. (2015). Life review based on remembering specific positive events in active aging. *Journal of Aging and Health, 27*, 140–157.

Lathrop, A., Bonsack, C. F., & Haas, D. M. (2018). Women's experiences with water birth: A matched groups prospective study. *Birth: Issues in Perinatal Care,* doi:10.1111/birt.12362

Lau, M., Markham, C., Lin, H., Flores, G., & Chacko, M. (2009). Dating and sexual attitudes in Asian-American adolescents. *Journal of Adolescent Research, 24*, 91–113.

Lauer, R., & Lauer, J. (2019). *Marriage and family: The quest for intimacy* (9th ed.). New York: McGraw-Hill.

Laugharne, J., Janca, A., & Widiger, T. (2007). Posttraumatic stress disorder and terrorism: 5 years after 9/11. *Current Opinion in Psychiatry, 20*, 36–41.

Lavers-Preston, C., & Sonuga-Barke, E. (2003). An intergenerational perspective on parent-child relationships: The reciprocal effects of tri-generational grandparent–parent–child relationships. In R. Gupta & D. Parry-Gupta (Eds.), *Children and parents: Clinical issues for psychologists and psychiatrists.* London, UK: Whurr Publishers, Ltd.

Lavezzi, A. M., Corna, M. F., & Matturri, L. (2013). Neuronal nuclear antigen (NeuN): A useful marker of neuronal immaturity in sudden unexplained perinatal death. *Journal of the Neurological Sciences, 329*, 45–50.

Lavner, J. A., Weiss, B., Miller, J. D., & Karney, B. R. (2018). Personality change among newlyweds: Patterns, predictors, and associations with marital satisfaction over time. *Developmental Psychology, 54*(6), 1172–1185.

Law, D. M., Shapka, J. D., Hymel, S., Olson, B. F., & Waterhouse, T. (2012). The changing face of bullying: An empirical comparison between traditional and internet bullying and victimization. *Computers in Human Behavior, 28*, 226–232.

Lawrence, E., Rothman, A., Cobb, R., Rothman, M., & Bradbury, T. (2008). Marital satisfaction across the transition to parenthood. *Journal of Family Psychology, 22*, 41–50.

Lawrence, H. R., Nangle, D. W., Schwartz-Mette, R. A., & Erdley, C. A. (2017). Medication for child and adolescent depression: Questions, answers, clarifications, and caveats. *Practice Innovations, 2*, 39–53.

Lazarus, R. S. (1991). *Emotion and adaptation.* New York, NY: Oxford University Press.

Le, H., Oh, I., Shaffer, J., & Schmidt, F. (2010). Implications of methodological advances for the practice of personnel selection: How practitioners benefit from meta-analysis. In *Readings in organizational behavior.* New York, NY: Routledge/Taylor & Francis.

Leach, P., Barnes, J., Malmberg, L., Sylva, K., & Stein, A. (2008). The quality of different types of child care at 10 and 18 months: A comparison between types and factors related to quality. *Early Child Development and Care, 178*, 177–209.

Leaper, C. (2002). Parenting girls and boys. In M. Bornstein (Ed.), *Handbook of parenting: Vol. 1: Children and parenting.* Mahwah, NJ: Lawrence Erlbaum.

Leat, S. J., Yadav, N.K., & Irving, E.L. (2009). Development of visual acuity and contrast sensitivity in children. *Journal of Optometry, 2*, 19–26.

Leathers, S., & Kelley, M. (2000). Unintended pregnancy and depressive symptoms among first-time mothers and fathers. *American Journal of Orthopsychiatry, 70*, 523–531.

Leavitt, L. A., & Goldson, E. (1996). Introduction to special section: Biomedicine and developmental psychology: New areas of common ground. *Developmental Psychology, 32*, 387–389.

Lecce, S., Bianco, F., Demicheli, P., & Cavallini, E. (2014). Training preschoolers on first-order false belief understanding: Transfer on advanced ToM skills and metamemory. *Child Development, 85*, 2404–2418.

Lecce, S., Ceccato, I., Bianco, F., Rosi, A., Bottiroli, S., & Cavallini, E. (2017). Theory of mind and social relationships in older adults: The role of social motivation. *Aging & Mental Health, 21*, 253–258.

Lee, A., & Cho, J. (2018). Effects of working couple's retirement sequence on satisfaction in patriarchal culture country: Probing on gender difference. *The International Journal of Aging and Human Development, 87*(3), 244–267.

Lee, C., Yong, H.-H., Borland, R., McNeill, A., & Hitchman, S. C. (2018). Acceptance and patterns of personal vaporizer use in Australia and the United Kingdom: Results from the International Tobacco Control survey. *Drug and Alcohol Dependence, 185*, 142–148.

Lee, C.C., Jhang, Y., Relyea, G., Chen, L., & Oller, D. K. (2018). Babbling development as seen in canonical babbling ratios: A naturalistic evaluation of all-day recordings. *Infant Behavior & Development, 50*, 140–153.

Lee, G. Y., & Kisilevsky, B. S. (2014). Fetuses respond to father's voice but prefer mother's voice after birth. *Developmental Psychobiology, 56*, 1–11.

Lee, M. (2008). Caregiver stress and elder abuse among Korean family caregivers of older adults with disabilities. *Journal of Family Violence, 23,* 707–712.

Lee, P. C. (2017). Maternal behavior. In J. Call, G. M. Burghardt, I. M. Pepperberg, C. T. Snowdon, & T. Zentall (Eds.), *APA handbook of comparative psychology: Basic concepts, methods, neural substrate, and behavior.* Washington, DC: American Psychological Association.

Lee, R. M. (2005). Resilience against discrimination: Ethnic identity and other-group orientation as protective factors for Korean Americans. *Journal of Counseling Psychology, 52,* 36–44.

Lee, S., Olszewski-Kubilius, P., & Thomson, D. (2012). Academically gifted students' perceived interpersonal competence and peer relationships. *Gifted Child Quarterly, 56,* 90–104.

Leen-Feldmer, E. W., Reardon, L. E., Hayward, C., & Smith, R. C. (2008). The relation between puberty and adolescent anxiety: Theory and evidence. In M. J. Zvolensky & J. A. Smits (Eds). *Anxiety in health behaviors and physical illness.* New York, NY: Springer Science + Business Media.

LeFevre, J. (2016). Numerical cognition: Adding it up. *Canadian Journal of Experimental Psychology/Revue Canadienne De Psychologie Expérimentale, 70,* 3–11.

Legerstee, M. (2014). The developing social brain: Social connections and social bonds, social loss, and jealousy in infancy. In M. Legerstee, D. W. Haley, M. H. Bornstein (Eds.), *The infant mind: Origins of the social brain.* New York, NY: Guilford Press.

Legerstee, M., & Markova, G. (2008). Variations in 10-month-old infant imitation of people and things. *Infant Behavior & Development, 31,* 81–91.

Lehman, D., Chiu, C., & Schaller, M. (2004). Psychology and culture. *Annual Review of Psychology, 55,* 689–714.

Lehr, U., Seiler, E., & Thomae, H. (2000). Aging in a cross-cultural perspective. In A. L. Comunian & U. P. Gielen (Eds.), *International perspectives on human development.* Lengerich, Germany: Pabst Science Publishers.

Leloux-Opmeer, H., Kuiper, C., Swaab, H., & Scholte, E. (2016). Characteristics of children in foster care, family-style group care, and residential care: A scoping review. *Journal of Child and Family Studies, 25,* 2357–2371.

Lemaire, P. (Ed.) (2018). *Cognitive development from a strategy perspective: A festschrift for Robert S. Siegler.* New York, NY: Routledge.

Lemieux, A. (2013). Post-formal thought in gerontagogy or beyond Piaget. *Psychologie Française, 58*(3), 241–253.

LeMoine, S., Mayoral, M.V., & Dean, A. (2015). *Zero to three critical competencies for infant-toddler educators.* Washington, D.C.: Zero to Three.

Lemonick, M. D. (2000, October 30). Teens before their time. *Time,* pp. 68–74.

Lenhart, A. (2010, April 20). *Teens, cell phones, and texting.* Washington, DC: Pew Research Center.

Lenhart, A., Smith, A., & Anderson, M. (2015, October). *Teens, technology and romantic relationships.* Washington, DC: Pew Research Center.

Leonard, J., & Higson, H. (2014). A strategic activity model of enterprise system implementation and use: Scaffolding fluidity. *Journal of Strategic Information Systems, 23,* 62–86.

Lerner, R. M., Fisher, C. B., & Weinberg, R. A. (2000). Toward a science for and of the people: Promoting civil society through the application of developmental science. *Child Development, 71,* 11–20.

Lerner, R. M., Theokas, C., & Jelicic, H. (2005). Youth as active agents in their own positive development: A developmental systems perspective. In W. Greve, K. Rothermund, & D. Wentura (Eds.), *Adaptive self: Personal continuity and intentional self-development.* Ashland, OH: Hogrefe & Huber.

Lesner, S. (2003). Candidacy and management of assistive listening devices: Special needs of the elderly. *International Journal of Audiology, 42,* 2S68–2S76.

Lester, H., Mead, N., Graham, C., Gask, L., & Reilly, S. (2012). An exploration of the value and mechanisms of befriending for older adults in England. *Ageing & Society, 32,* 307–328.

Lester, P., Paley, B., Saltzman, W., & Klosinski, L. E. (2013). Military service, war, and families: Considerations for child development, prevention and intervention, and public health policy—Part 2. *Clinical Child and Family Psychology Review, 16,* 345–347.

Leung, C., Pe-Pua, R., & Karnilowicz, W. (2006, January). Psychological adaptation and autonomy among adolescents in Australia: A comparison of Anglo-Celtic and three Asian groups. *International Journal of Intercultural Relations, 30,* 99–118.

Levant, R. F., McDermott, R. C., Hewitt, A. A., Alto, K. M., & Harris, K. T. (2016). Confirmatory factor analytic investigation of variance composition, gender invariance, and validity of the Male Role Norms Inventory-Adolescent-revised (MRNI-A-r). *Journal of Counseling Psychology, 63,* 543–556.

LeVay, S., & Valente, S. M. (2003). *Human sexuality.* Sunderland, MA: Sinauer Associates.

Levenson, M. R., Aldwin, C. M., & Igarashi, H. (2013). Religious development from adolescence to middle adulthood. In R. F. Paloutzian, C. L. Park (Eds.), *Handbook of the psychology of religion and spirituality* (2nd ed.). New York, NY: Guilford Press.

Leverone, D., & Epstein, B. (2010). Nonpharmacological interventions for the treatment of rheumatoid arthritis: A focus on mind-body medicine. *Journal of Pharmacy Practice, 23,* 101–109.

Leversen, J. R., Hopkins, B., & Sigmundsson, H. (2013). Ageing and driving: Examining the effects of visual processing demands. *Transportation Research Part F: Traffic Psychology and Behaviour, 17,* 1–4.

Levin, R. J. (2007). Sexual activity, health and well-being—the beneficial roles of coitus and masturbation. *Sexual and Relationship Therapy, 22,* 135–148.

Levin, S., Matthews, M., Guimond, S., Sidanius, J., Pratto, F., Kteily, N., & . . . Dover, T. (2012). Assimilation, multiculturalism, and colorblindness: Mediated and moderated relationships between social dominance orientation and prejudice. *Journal of Experimental Social Psychology, 48,* 207–212.

Levine, R. V. (1993, February). Is love a luxury? *American Demographics,* 29–37.

Levinson, D. (1992). *The seasons of a woman's life.* New York, NY: Knopf.

Levinson, D. J. (1986). A conception of adult development. *American Psychologist, 41,* 3–13.

Levy, B. L., & Langer, E. (1994). Aging free from negative stereotypes: Successful memory in China and among the American deaf. *Journal of Personality and Social Psychology, 66,* 989–997.

Levy, B. R. (2003). Mind matters: Cognitive and physical effects of aging self-stereotypes. *Journal of Gerontology: Series B: Psychological Sciences and Social Sciences, 58B,* P203–P211.

Levy, B. R., Slade, M. D., & Kasl, S. V. (2002). Longitudinal benefit of positive self-perceptions of aging on functioning health. *Journal of Gerontology: Psychological Sciences, 57,* 166–195.

Lewis, B. A., Minnes, S., Min, M. O., Short, E. J., Wu, M., Lang, A., & . . . Singer, L. T. (2018). Blood lead levels and longitudinal language outcomes in children from 4 to 12 years. *Journal of Communication Disorders, 71,* 85–96.

Lewis, V. (2009). Undertreatment of menopausal symptoms and novel options for comprehensive management. *Current Medical Research Opinion, 25,* 2689–2698.

Lewis, Y. D., Gilon Mann, T., Enoch, L. A., Dubnov, R. G., Gothelf, D., Weizman, A., & Stein, D. (2018). Obsessive–compulsive symptomatology in female adolescent inpatients with restrictive compared with binge–purge eating disorders. *European Eating Disorders Review.* doi:10.1002/erv.2638

Lewkowicz, D. (2002). Heterogeneity and heterochrony in the development of intersensory perception. *Cognitive Brain Research, 14,* 41–63.

Leyens, J. P., Camino, L., Parke, R. D., & Berkowitz, L. (1975). Effects of movie violence on aggression in a field setting as a function of group dominance and cohesion. *Journal of Personality and Social Psychology, 32,* 346–360.

Li, G. R., & Zhu, X. D. (2007). Development of the functionally total artificial heart using an artery pump. *ASAIO Journal, 53,* 288–291.

Li, H., Ji, Y., & Chen, T. (2014). The roles of different sources of social support on emotional well-being among Chinese elderly. *Plos ONE, 9*(3), 88–97.

Li, N. P., Bailey, J. M., Kenrick, D. T., & Linsenmeier, J. A. W. (2002). The necessities and luxuries of mate preferences: Testing the tradeoffs. *Journal of Personality and Social Psychology, 82,* 947–955.

Li, S. (2012). Neuromodulation of behavioral and cognitive development across the life span. *Developmental Psychology, 48,* 810–814.

Li, T. C., & Darius, K. S. (2012). How anxious and avoidant attachment affect romantic relationship quality differently: A meta-analytic review. *European Journal of Social Psychology, 42,* 406–419.

Li, Y., Allen, J., & Casillas, A. (2017). Relating psychological and social factors to academic performance: A longitudinal investigation of high-poverty middle school students. *Journal of Adolescence, 56,* 179–189.

Li, Y., & Wright, M. F. (2013). Adolescents' social status goals: Relationships to social status insecurity, aggression, and prosocial behavior. *Journal of Youth and Adolescence, 43,* 146–160.

Liang, J., & Luo, B. (2012). Toward a discourse shift in social gerontology: From successful aging to harmonious aging. *Journal of Aging Studies, 26,* 327–334.

Liang Y., & Wang Z. (2018). Which is the most reasonable anti-aging strategy: Meta-analysis. *Advances in Experimental Medicine and Biology, 1086,* 267–282.

Libert, S., Zwiener, J., Chu, X., Vanvoorhies, W., Roman, G., & Pletcher, S. D. (2007, February 23). Regulation of Drosophila life span by olfaction and food-derived odors. *Science, 315,* 1133–1137.

Libertus, K., Joh, A. S., & Needham, A. W. (2016). Motor training at 3 months affects object exploration 12 months later. *Developmental Science, 19,* 1058–1066.

Lickliter, R., & Bahrick, L. E. (2000). The development of infant intersensory perception: Advantages of a comparative convergent-operations approach. *Psychological Bulletin, 126,* 260–280.

Liechty, J. (2010). Body image distortion and three types of weight loss behaviors among non-overweight girls in the United States. *Journal of Adolescent Health, 47,* 176–182.

Lin, C., Chiu, H., & Yeh, C. (2012). Impact of socio-economic backgrounds, experiences of being disciplined in early childhood, and parenting value on parenting styles of preschool children's parents. *Chinese Journal of Guidance and Counseling, 32,* 123–149.

Lin, F., Heffner, K., Mapstone, M., Chen, D., & Porsteisson, A. (2014). Frequency of mentally stimulating activities modifies the relationship between cardiovascular reactivity and executive function in old age. *American Journal of Geriatric Psychiatry, 22,* 1210–1221.

Lin, I., Wang, S., Chu, I., Lu, Y., Lee, C., Lin, T., & Fan, S. (2017). The association of Type D personality with heart rate variability and lipid profiles among patients with coronary artery disease. *International Journal of Behavioral Medicine, 24,* 101–109.

Lin, P. (2016). Risky behaviors: Integrating adolescent egocentrism with the theory of planned behavior. *Review of General Psychology, 20,* 392–398.

Lindau, S., Schumm, L., Laumann, E., Levinson, W., O'Muircheartaigh, C., & Waite, L. (2007). A study of sexuality and health among older adults in the United States. *New England Journal of Medicine, 357,* 762–775.

Lindemann, B. T., & Kadue, D. D. (2003). *Age discrimination in employment law*. Washington, DC: BNA Books.

Lindsey, E., & Colwell, M. (2003). Preschoolers' emotional competence: Links to pretend and physical play. *Child Study Journal, 33*, 39–52.

Lindstrom, H., Fritsch, T., Petot, G., Smyth, K., Chen, C., Debanne, S., &... Friedland, R. P. (2005, July). The relationships between television viewing in midlife and the development of Alzheimer's disease in a case-control study. *Brain and Cognition, 58*, 157–165.

Link, B. G., Susser, E. S., Factor-Litvak, P., March, D., Kezios, K. L., Lovasi, G. S., &... Cohn, B. A. (2017). Disparities in self-rated health across generations and through the life course. *Social Science & Medicine, 174*, 17–25.

Lino, M., Kuczynski, K., Rodriguez, N., and Schap, T. (2017). *Expenditures on children by families, 2015*. Miscellaneous Publication No. 1528-2015. Washington, DC: U.S. Department of Agriculture, Center for Nutrition Policy and Promotion.

Lipperman-Kreda, S., & Grube, J. W. (2018). Impacts of marijuana commercialization on adolescents' marijuana beliefs, use, and co-use with other substances. *Journal of Adolescent Health, 63*(1), 5–6.

Lipsitt, L. P. (1986). Toward understanding the hedonic nature of infancy. In L. P. Lipsitt & J. H. Cantor (Eds.), *Experimental child psychologist: Essays and experiments in honor of Charles C. Spiker*. Hillsdale, NJ: Lawrence Erlbaum.

Lipsitt, L. (2003). Crib death: A biobehavioral phenomenon? *Current Directions in Psychological Science, 12*, 164–170.

Lipsitt, L. P., & Rovee-Collier, C. (2012). The psychophysics of olfaction in the human newborn: Habituation and cross-adaptation. In G. M. Zucco, R. S. Herz, & B. Schaal (Eds.), *Olfactory cognition: From perception and memory to environmental odours and neuroscience*. Amsterdam, Netherlands: John Benjamins Publishing Company.

Lisabeth, L., & Bushnell, C. (2012). Stroke risk in women: The role of menopause and hormone therapy. *Lancet Neurology, 11*, 82–91.

Litzinger, S., & Gordon, K. (2005, October). Exploring relationships among communication, sexual satisfaction, and marital satisfaction. *Journal of Sex & Marital Therapy, 31*, 409–444.

Liu, D., Wellman, H., Tardif, T., & Sabbagh, M. (2008, March). Theory of mind development in Chinese children: A meta-analysis of false-belief understanding across cultures and languages. *Developmental Psychology, 44*, 523–531.

Liu, H., Elliott, S., & Umberson, D. J. (2010). Marriage in young adulthood. In Jon E. Grant & Marc N. Potenza (Eds.), *Young adult mental heath*. New York, NY: Oxford University Press.

Liu, K. A., & Dipietro Mager, N. A. (2016). Women's involvement in clinical trials: historical perspective and future implications. *Pharmacy Practice, 14*(1), 708.

Liu, N., Chen, Y., Yang, X., & Hu, Y. (2017). Do demographic characteristics make differences? Demographic characteristics as moderators in the associations between only child status and cognitive/non-cognitive outcomes in China. *Frontiers in Psychology, 8*, 221–232.

Liu, N., Liang, Z., Li, Z., Yan, J., & Guo, W. (2012). Chronic stress on IL-2, IL-4, IL-18 content in SD rats. *Chinese Journal of Clinical Psychology, 20*, 35–36.

Livingston, G. (2014). *Four-in-ten couples are saying "I do," again: The demographics of remarriage*. Washington, DC: Pew Research Center.

Lloyd, K. K. (2012). Health-related quality of life and children's happiness with their childcare. *Child: Care, Health and Development, 38*, 244–250.

Lloyd, P. (2018, April 5). *Perinatal health and infant mortality rate*. Washington, DC: District of Columbia Department of Health.

Lobo, R. A. (2009). The risk of stroke in postmenopausal women receiving hormonal therapy. *Climacteric, 12*(Suppl. 1), 81–85.

Locke, K. D. & Heller, S. (2017). Communal and agentic interpersonal and intergroup motives predict preferences for status versus power. *Personality and Social Psychology Bulletin, 43*(1), 71–86. doi:10.1177/0146167216675333

Löckenhoff, C. E., De Fruyt, F., Terracciano, A., McCrae, R. R., De Bolle, M., Costa, P. T.,... Yik, M. (2009). Perceptions of aging across 26 cultures and their culture-level associates. *Psychology and Aging, 24*(4), 941–954.

Loeb, S., Fuller, B., Kagan, S. L., & Carrol, B. (2004). Child care in poor communities: Early learning effects of type, quality and stability. *Child Development, 75*, 47–65.

Loewen, S. (2006). Exceptional intellectual performance: A neo-Piagetian perspective. *High Ability Studies, 17*, 159–181.

Loftus, E. F. (2004). Memories of things unseen. *Current Directions in Psychological Science, 13*, 145–147.

Loggins, S., & Andrade, F. D. (2014). Despite an overall decline in U.S. infant mortality rates, the Black/White disparity persists: Recent trends and future projections. *Journal of Community Health: The Publication for Health Promotion and Disease Prevention, 39*, 118–123.

Logsdon, R., McCurry, S., Pike, K., & Teri, L. (2009). Making physical activity accessible to older adults with memory loss: A feasibility study. *The Gerontologist, 49*(Suppl. 1), S94–S99.

Lohbeck, A., Tietjens, M., & Bund, A. (2016). Physical self-concept and physical activity enjoyment in elementary school children. *Early Child Development and Care, 186*, 1792–1801.

Lohman, D. (2005). Reasoning abilities. In R. J. Sternberg & J. E. Pretz (Eds.), *Cognition and intelligence: Identifying the mechanisms of the mind*. New York, NY: Cambridge University Press.

Longo, G. S., Bray, B. C., & Kim-Spoon, J. (2017). Profiles of adolescent religiousness using latent profile analysis: Implications for psychopathology. *British Journal of Developmental Psychology, 35*, 91–105.

Lopez, M. H., & Gonzalez-Barrera, A. (2014, March 6). *Women's college enrolment gains leave men behind*. Washington, DC: Pew Research Center.

Lorenz, K. (1974). *Civilized man's eight deadly sins*. New York, NY: Harcourt Brace Jovanovich.

Lorenz, K. Z. (1965). *Evolution and the modification of behavior*. Chicago, IL: University of Chicago Press.

Losonczy-Marshall, M. (2008). Gender differences in latency and duration of emotional expression in 7- through 13-month-old infants. *Social Behavior and Personality, 36*, 267–274.

Lourie, M. (2016). Bicultural education policy in New Zealand. *Journal of Education Policy, 31*(5), 637–650.

Love, A., & Burns, M. S. (2006). "It's a hurricane! it's a hurricane!": Can music facilitate social constructive and sociodramatic play in a preschool classroom? *Journal of Genetic Psychology, 167*, 383–391.

Low, J., & Perner, J. (2012). Implicit and explicit theory of mind: State of the art. *British Journal of Developmental Psychology, 30*, 1–13.

Lowe, M. R., Doshi, S. D., Katterman, S. N., & Feig, E. H. (2013). Dieting and restrained eating as prospective predictors of weight gain. *Frontiers in Psychology, 4*, 577–586.

Lowenstein, J., Blank, H., & Sauer, J. (2010). Uniforms affect the accuracy of children's eyewitness identification decisions. *Journal of Investigative Psychology and Offender Profiling, 7*, 59–73.

Lu, L. (2006). The transition to parenthood: Stress, resources, and gender differences in a Chinese society. *Journal of Community Psychology, 34*, 471–488.

Lubinski, D. (2004). Introduction to the special section on cognitive abilities: 100 years after Spearman's (1904) "'General intelligence,' objectively determined and measured." *Journal of Personality and Social Psychology, 86*, 96–111.

Luby, J. L., Belden, A. C., Whalen, D., Harms, M. P., & Barch, D. M. (2016). Breastfeeding and childhood IQ: The mediating role of gray matter volume. *Journal of the American Academy of Child & Adolescent Psychiatry, 55*, 367–375.

Lucas, R. E. (2005). Time does not heal all wounds: A longitudinal study of reaction and adaptation to divorce. *Psychological Science, 16*, 945–951.

Lucas, R. E. (2007). Adaptation and the set-point model of subjective well-being: Does happiness change after major life events? *Current Directions in Psychological Science, 16*, 75–79.

Lucas, S. R., & Berends, M. (2002). Sociodemographic diversity, correlated achievement, and de facto tracking. *Sociology of Education, 75*, 328–349.

Lucassen, A. (2012). Ethical implications of new genetic technologies. *Developmental Medicine & Child Neurology, 54*, 124–130.

Ludden, J. (2012, February 6). Helicopter parents hover in the workplace. *All things considered*. National Public Radio.

Ludlow, V., Newhook, L., Newhook, J., Bonia, K., Goodridge, J., & Twells, L. (2012). How formula feeding mothers balance risks and define themselves as "good mothers." *Health, Risk & Society, 14*, 291–306.

Ludwig, M., & Field, T. (2014). Touch in parent-infant mental health: Arousal, regulation, and relationships. In K. Brandt, B. D. Perry, S. Seligman, & E. Tronick (Eds.), *Infant and early childhood mental health: Core concepts and clinical practice*. Arlington, VA: American Psychiatric Publishing, Inc.

Luhmann, M., Lucas, R. E., Eid, M., & Diener, E. (2013). The prospective effect of life satisfaction on life events. *Social Psychological and Personality Science, 4*, 39–45.

Lui, P. P., & Rollock, D. (2013). Tiger mother: Popular and psychological scientific perspectives on Asian culture and parenting. *American Journal of Orthopsychiatry, 83*, 450–456.

Luke, B., & Brown, M. B. (2008). Maternal morbidity and infant death in twin vs triplet and quadruplet pregnancies. *American Journal of Obstetrics and Gynecology, 198*, 1–10.

Luke, M. A., Sedikides, C., & Carmelley, K. (2012). Your love lifts me higher! The energizing quality of secure relationships. *Personality and Social Psychology Bulletin, 38*, 721–735.

Luna, B., & Wright, C. (2016). Adolescent brain development: Implications for the juvenile criminal justice system. In K. Heilbrun, D. DeMatteo, & N. S. Goldstein (Eds.), *APA handbook of psychology and juvenile justice*. Washington, DC: American Psychological Association.

Lundberg, I., & Reichenberg, M. (2013). Developing reading comprehension among students with mild intellectual disabilities: An intervention study. *Scandinavian Journal of Educational Research, 57*, 89–100.

Lundblad, B., Hellström, A., & Berg, M. (2010). Children's experiences of attitudes and rules for going to the toilet in school. *Scandinavian Journal of Caring Sciences, 24*, 219–223.

Lundby, E. (2013) "You can't buy friends, but..." children's perception of consumption and friendship. *Young Consumers, 14*, 360–374.

Luo, C., Zhang, J., & Pan, J. (2013). One-year course and effects of insomnia in rural Chinese adolescents. *Sleep: Journal of Sleep and Sleep Disorders Research, 36*, 377–384.

Luo, J., Derringer, J., Briley, D. A., & Roberts, B. W. (2017). Genetic and environmental pathways underlying personality traits and perceived stress: Concurrent and longitudinal twin studies. *European Journal of Personality*. Accessed online, 10/27/17; http://onlinelibrary.wiley.com/doi/10.1002/per.2127/abstract

Luo, L., & Craik, F. (2009). Age differences in recollection: Specificity effects at retrieval. *Journal of Memory and Language, 60*, 421–436.

Lustgarten, M., Muller, F. L., & Van Remmen, H. (2011). An objective appraisal of the free radical theory of aging. In E. J. Masoro & S. N. Austad (Eds.), *Handbook of the biology of aging* (7th ed.) (pp. 177–202). San Diego, CA: Elsevier Academic Press.

Lyall, S. (2004, February 15). In Europe, lovers now propose: Marry me, a little. *The New York Times*, p. D2.

Lye, T. C., Piguet, O., Grayson, D. A., Creasey, H., Ridley, L. J., Bennett, H. P., & Broe, G. A. (2004). Hippocampal size and memory function in the ninth and tenth decades of life: The Sydney Older Persons Study. *Journal of Neurology, Neurosurgery, and Psychiatry, 75*, 548–554.

Lynne, S., Graber, J., Nichols, T., Brooks-Gunn, J., & Botvin, G. (2007, February). Links between pubertal timing, peer influences, and externalizing behaviors among urban students followed through middle school. *Journal of Adolescent Health, 40*, 35–44.

Mabbott, D. J., Noseworthy, M., Bouffet, E., Laughlin, S., & Rockel, C. (2006). White matter growth as a mechanism of cognitive development in children. *Neuroimaging, 15*, 936–946.

Maccallum, F., Malgaroli, M., & Bonanno, G. A. (2017). Networks of loss: Relationships among symptoms of prolonged grief following spousal and parental loss. *Journal of Abnormal Psychology, 126*(5), 652–662.

Macchi Cassia, V., Picozzi, M., Girelli, L., & de Hevia, M. (2012). Increasing magnitude counts more: Asymmetrical processing of ordinality in 4-month-old infants. *Cognition, 124*, 183–193.

Macchione, A. F., Anunziata, F., Haymal, B. O., Abate, P., & Molina, J. C. (2018). Brief ethanol exposure and stress-related factors disorganize neonatal breathing plasticity during the brain growth spurt period in the rat. *Psychopharmacology, 235*(4), 983–998.

Maccoby, E. E., & Lewis, C. C. (2003). Less day care or different day care? *Child Development, 74*, 1069–1075.

Maccoby, E. E., & Martin, J. A. (1983). Socialization in the context of the family: Parent-child interaction. In P. H. Mussen (Ed.) & E. M. Hetherington (Vol. Ed.), *Handbook of child psychology: Vol. 4. Socialization, personality, and social development* (4th ed.). New York, NY: Wiley.

MacDonald, H., Beeghly, M., Grant-Knight, W., Augustyn, M., Woods, R., Cabral, H., & ... Frank, D. A. (2008). Longitudinal association between infant disorganized attachment and childhood posttraumatic stress symptoms. *Development and Psychopathology, 20*, 493–508.

MacDonald, W. (2003). The impact of job demands and workload stress and fatigue. *Australian Psychologist, 38*, 102–117.

MacDorman, M. F., & Matthews, T. J. (2009). Behind international rankings of infant mortality: How the United States compares with Europe. *NCHS Data Brief, # 23*.

MacDorman, M. F., Martin, J. A., Mathews, T. J., Hoyert, D. L., & Ventura, S. J. (2005). Explaining the 2001-02 infant mortality increase: Data from the linked birth/infant death data set. *National Vital Statistics Report, 53*, 1–22.

Maciejewski, P. K., Zhang, B., Block, S. D., & Prigerson, H. G. (2007). An empirical examination of the stage theory of grief. *Journal of the American Medical Association, 297*, 716–723.

Macionis, J. J. (2001). *Sociology*. Upper Saddle River, NJ: Prentice Hall.

MacLean, P. C., Rynes, K. N., Aragón, C., Caprihan, A., Phillips, J. P., & Lowe, J. R. (2014). Mother–infant mutual eye gaze supports emotion regulation in infancy during the Still-Face paradigm. *Infant Behavior & Development, 37*, 512–522.

Madigan, S., Plamondon, A., & Jenkins, J. M. (2017). Marital conflict trajectories and associations with children's disruptive behavior. *Journal of Marriage and Family, 79*, 437–450.

Madison, G., Mosing, M. A., Verweij, K. H., Pedersen, N. L., & Ullen, F. (2016). Common genetic influences on intelligence and auditory simple reaction time in a large Swedish sample. *Intelligence, 59*, 157–162.

Madlensky, L., Trepanier, A. M., Cragun, D., Lerner, B., Shannon, K. M., & Zierhut, H. (2017). A rapid systematic review of outcomes studies in genetic counseling. *Journal of Genetic Counseling, 26*, 361–378.

Madsen, H. B., & Kim, J. H. (2016). Ontogeny of memory: An update on 40 years of work on infantile amnesia. *Behavioural Brain Research, 298* (Part A), 4–14.

Madsen, P. B., & Green, R. (2012). Gay adolescent males' effective coping with discrimination: A qualitative study. *Journal of LGBT Issues in Counseling, 6*, 139–155.

Maercker, A., Neimeyer, R. A., & Simiola, V. (2017). Depression and complicated grief. In S. N. Gold (Ed.), *APA handbook of trauma psychology: Foundations in knowledge*. Washington, DC: American Psychological Association.

Maes, S. J., De Mol, J., & Buysse, A. (2012). Children's experiences and meaning construction on parental divorce: A focus group study. *Childhood: A Global Journal of Child Research, 19*, 266–279.

Magee, C. A., Gordon, R., & Caputi, P. (2014). Distinct developmental trends in sleep duration during early childhood. *Pediatrics, 133*, e1561-e1567.

Maggi, S., Busetto, L., Noale, M., Limongi, F., & Crepaldi, G. (2015). Obesity: Definition and epidemiology. In A. Lenzi, S. Migliaccio, & L. M. Donini (Eds.), *Multidisciplinary approach to obesity: From assessment to treatment*. Cham, Switzerland: Springer International Publishing.

Mahalel, A. T. (2018). Memory, mourning, and writing: Abram Kardiner's memoir of Freud. *Psychoanalytic Review, 105*(4), 397–424.

Mahn, H., & John-Steiner, V. (2013). Vygotsky and sociocultural approaches to teaching and learning. In W. M. Reynolds, G. E. Miller, & I. B. Weiner (Eds.), *Handbook of psychology, Vol. 7: Educational psychology* (2nd ed.). Hoboken, NJ: John Wiley & Sons Inc.

Mahrer, N. E., & Wolchik, S. A. (2017). Moody child: Depression in the context of parental divorce. In C. A. Galanter & P. S. Jensen (Eds.), *DSM-5® casebook and treatment guide for child mental health*. Arlington, VA: American Psychiatric Publishing, Inc.

Maimari, I. (2017). Stress hormones. In S. Wadhwa (Ed.), *Stress in the modern world: Understanding science and society*. Santa Barbara, CA: Greenwood Press/ABC-CLIO.

Majors, K. (2012). Friendships: The power of positive alliance. In S. Roffey (Ed.), *Positive relationships: Evidence based practice across the world*. New York, NY: Springer Science + Business Media.

Mäkinen, M., Puukko-Viertomies, L., Lindberg, N., Siimes, M. A., & Aalberg, V. (2012). Body dissatisfaction and body mass in girls and boys transitioning from early to mid-adolescence: Additional role of self-esteem and eating habits. *BMC Psychiatry, 12*, 123–131.

Malchiodi, C. A. (2012). Humanistic approaches. In C. A. Malchiodi (Ed.), *Handbook of art therapy* (2nd ed.). New York, NY: Guilford Press.

Malhotra R., Chan A., Alay S., Ma S., Saito Y. (2016). Variation in the gender gap in inactive and active life expectancy by the definition of inactivity among older adults. *Journal of Aging & Health, 28*(7), 1279–1298.

Mallan, K. M., Sullivan, S. E., de Jersey, S. J., & Daniels, L. A. (2016). The relationship between maternal feeding beliefs and practices and perceptions of infant eating behaviours at 4 months. *Appetite, 105*, 1–7.

Maller, S. (2003). Best practices in detecting bias in nonverbal tests. In R. McCallum (Ed.), *Handbook of nonverbal assessment*. New York, NY: Kluwer Academic/Plenum Publishers.

Malone, J. C., Liu, S. R., Vaillant, G. E., Rentz, D. M., & Waldinger, R. J. (2016). Midlife Eriksonian psychosocial development: Setting the stage for late-life cognitive and emotional health. *Developmental Psychology, 52*, 496–508.

Manard, M., Carabin, D., Jaspar, M., & Collette, F. (2015). Age-related decline in cognitive control: The role of fluid intelligence and processing speed. *BMC Neuroscience, 15*, 88–97.

Mancini, A. D., & Bonanno, G. A. (2012). Differential pathways to resilience after loss and trauma. In R. A. McMackin, E. Newman, J. M. Fogler, & T. M. Keane (Eds.), *Trauma therapy in context: The science and craft of evidence-based practice*. Washington, DC: American Psychological Association.

Mancini, A. D., Sinan, B., & Bonanno, G. A. (2015). Predictors of prolonged grief, resilience, and recovery among bereaved spouses. *Journal of Clinical Psychology, 71*, 1245–1258.

Mandal, B. (2018). The effect of paid leave on maternal mental health. *Maternal and Child Health Journal*, doi:10.1007/s10995-018-2542-x

Mangiatordi, A. (2012). Inclusion of mobility-impaired children in the one-to-one computing era: A case study. *Mind, Brain, and Education, 6*, 54–62.

Mangweth, B., Hausmann, A., & Walch, T. (2004). Body fat perception in eating-disordered men. *International Journal of Eating Disorders, 35*, 102–108.

Manning, M., & Hoyme, H. (2007). Fetal alcohol spectrum disorders: A practical clinical approach to diagnosis. *Neuroscience & Biobehavioral Reviews, 31*, 230–238.

Manning, R. C., Dickson, J. M., Palmier-Claus, J., Cunliffe, A., & Taylor, P. J. (2017). A systematic review of adult attachment and social anxiety. *Journal of Affective Disorders, 211*, 44–59.

Manning, W., Giordano, P., & Longmore, M. (2006, September). Hooking up: The relationship contexts of "nonrelationship" sex. *Journal of Adolescent Research, 21*, 459–483.

Manning, W. D., Longmore, M. A., Copp, J., & Giordano, P. C. (2014). The complexities of adolescent dating and sexual relationships: Fluidity, meaning(s), and implications for young adults' well-being. *New Directions for Child and Adolescent Development, 144*, 53–69.

Mansson, D. (2013). The grandchildren received affection scale: Examining affectual solidarity factors. *Southern Communication Journal, 78*, 70–90.

Manzanares, S., Cobo, D., Moreno-Martinez, M., Sanchez-Gila, M., & Pineda, A. (2013). Risk of episiotomy and perineal lacerations recurring after first delivery. *Birth: Issues in Perinatal Care, 40*, 307–311.

Mao, A., Burnham, M. M., Goodlin-Jones, B. L., Gaylor, E. E., & Anders, T. F. (2004). A comparison of the sleep-wake patterns of cosleeping and solitary-sleeping infants. *Child Psychiatry and Human Development, 35*, 95–105.

Marcia, J. E. (1980). Identity in adolescence. In J. Adelson (Ed.), *Handbook of adolescent psychology*. New York, NY: Wiley.

Marcia, J. E. (2007). Theory and measure: The identity status interview. In M. Watzlawik & A. Born (Eds.), *Capturing identity: Quantitative and qualitative methods*. Lanham, MD: University Press of America.

Marcus, A. D. (2004, February 3). The new math on when to have kids. *Wall Street Journal*, pp. D1, D4.

Marcus, D., Fulton, J., & Clarke, E. (2010). Lead and conduct problems: A meta-analysis. *Journal of Clinical Child and Adolescent Psychology, 39*, 234–241.

Marin, T., Chen, E., Munch, J., & Miller, G. (2009). Double-exposure to acute stress and chronic family stress is associated with immune changes in children with asthma. *Psychosomatic Medicine, 71*, 378–384.

Marinellie, S. A., & Kneile, L. A. (2012). Acquiring knowledge of derived nominals and derived adjectives in context. *Language, Speech, and Hearing Services in Schools, 43*, 53–65.

Marino, C., Gini, G., Vieno, A., & Spada, M. M. (2018). The associations between problematic Facebook use, psychological distress and well-being among adolescents and young adults: A systematic review and meta-analysis. *Journal of Affective Disorders, 226*, 274–281.

Markell, K. (2010). Educating children about death-related issues. In C. A. Corr & D. E. Balk (Eds.), *Children's encounters with death, bereavement, and coping*. New York, NY: Springer Publishing.

Marques, A. H., Bjørke-Monsen, A., Teixeira, A. L., & Silverman, M. N. (2014). Maternal stress, nutrition and physical activity: Impact on immune function, CNS development and psychopathology. *Brain Research, 1617*, 28–46.

Marquet, M., Chasteen, A. L., Plaks, J. E., & Balasubramaniam, L. (2018). Understanding the mechanisms underlying the effects of negative age stereotypes and perceived age discrimination on older adults' well-being. *Aging & Mental Health*. doi:10.1080/13607863.2018.1514487

Marschik, P., Einspieler, C., Strohmeier, A., Plienegger, J., Garzarolli, B., & Prechtl, H. (2008). From the reaching behavior at 5 months of age to hand preference at preschool age. *Developmental Psychobiology, 50*, 512–518.

Marsh, H. W., Ellis, L., & Craven, R. (2002). How do preschool children feel about themselves? Unraveling measurement and multidimensional self-concept structure. *Developmental Psychology, 38*, 376–393.

Marsh, H. W., & Hau, K. T. (2003). Big-fish-little-pond effect on academic self-concept. *American Psychologist, 58*, 364–376.

Martin, A., Onishi, K. H., & Vouloumanos, A. (2012). Understanding the abstract role of speech in communication at 12 months. *Cognition, 123*, 50–60.

Martin, C., & Dinella, L. M. (2012). Congruence between gender stereotypes and activity preference in self-identified tomboys and non-tomboys. *Archives of Sexual Behavior, 41*, 599–610.

Martin, C. L., & Fabes, R. (2001). The stability and consequences of young children's same-sex peer interactions. *Developmental Psychology, 37*, 431–446.

Martin, C. L., Kornienko, O., Schaefer, D. R., Hanish, L. D., Fabes, R. A., & Goble, P. (2013). The role of sex of peers and gender-typed activities in young children's peer affiliative networks: A longitudinal analysis of selection and influence. *Child Development, 84*(3), 921–937.

Martin, C. L., & Ruble, D. (2004). Children's search for gender cues: Cognitive perspectives on gender development. *Current Directions in Psychological Science, 13*, 67–70.

Martin, J. A., Hamilton, B. E., Osterman, M. J. K., Driscoll, A. K, & Drake, P. (2018). Births: Final data for 2017. *National Vital Statistics Reports, 67*(8).

Martin, K. A., & Barbieri, R. L. (2018). Treatment of menopausal symptoms with hormone therapy. UpToDate. Accessed online, 3/26/19; https://www.uptodate.com/contents/treatment-of-menopausal-symptoms-with-hormone-therapy

Martin, L., McNamara, M., Milot, A., Halle, T., & Hair, E. (2007). The effects of father involvement during pregnancy on receipt of prenatal care and maternal smoking. *Maternal and Child Health Journal, 11*, 595–602.

Martin, S., Li, Y., Casanueva, C., Harris-Britt, A., Kupper, L., & Cloutier, S. (2006). Intimate partner violence and women's depression before and during pregnancy. *Violence Against Women, 12*, 221–239.

Martin-Prudent, A., Lartz, M., Borders, C., & Meehan, T. (2016). Early intervention practices for children with hearing loss: Impact of professional development. *Communication Disorders Quarterly, 38*, 13–23.

Martinelli, P., Anssens, A., Sperduti, M., & Piolino, P. (2013). The influence of normal aging and Alzheimer's disease in autobiographical memory highly related to the self. *Neuropsychology, 27*, 69–78.

Martinez, G., Copen, C. E., & Abma, J. C. (2011). Teenagers in the United States: Sexual activity, contraceptive use, and childbearing, 2006–2010 National Survey of Family Growth. *National Center for Health Statistics. Vital Health Stat, 23*(31).

Martinez-Torteya, C., Bogat, G., von Eye, A., & Levendosky, A. (2009). Resilience among children exposed to domestic violence: The role of risk and protective factors. *Child Development, 80*, 562–577.

Maruszewski, T., Bonk, E., Karcz, B., & Retowski, S. (2017). Elderly people's preferences regarding reminiscence material. *Educational Gerontology, 43*(11), 531–539.

Masapollo, M., Polka, L., & Ménard, L. (2015). When infants talk, infants listen: Pre-babbling infants prefer listening to speech with infant vocal properties. *Developmental Science, 19*, 318–328.

Masataka, N. (2000). The role of modality and input in the earliest stage of language acquisition: Studies of Japanese sign language. In C. Chamerlain & J. P. Morford (Eds.), *Language acquisition by eye*. Mahwah, NJ: Lawrence Erlbaum.

Masataka, N. (2003). *The onset of language*. Cambridge, UK: Cambridge University Press.

Mash, C., Bornstein, M. H., & Arterberry, M. E. (2013). Brain dynamics in young infants' recognition of faces: EEG oscillatory activity in response to mother and stranger. *Neuroreport: For Rapid Communication of Neuroscience Research, 24*, 359–363.

Maslow, A. H. (1970). *Motivation and personality* (2nd ed.). New York, NY: Harper & Row.

Massey, S. H., Mroczek, D. K., Reiss, D., Miller, E. S., Jakubowski, J. A., Graham, E. K., & … Neiderhiser, J. M. (2018). Additive drug-specific and sex-specific risks associated with co-use of marijuana and tobacco during pregnancy: Evidence from 3 recent developmental cohorts (2003–2015). *Neurotoxicology and Teratology, 68*, 97–106.

Master, S., Amodio, D., Stanton, A., Yee, C., Hilmert, C., & Taylor, S. (2009). Neurobiological correlates of coping through emotional approach. *Brain, Behavior, and Immunity, 23*, 27–35.

Mathews, G., Fane, B., Conway, G., Brook, C., & Hines, M. (2009). Personality and congenital adrenal hyperplasia: Possible effects of prenatal androgen exposure. *Hormones and Behavior, 55*, 285–291.

Matias, M., Ferreira, T., Vieira, J., Cadima, J., Leal, T., & Mena Matos, P. (2017). Workplace family support, parental satisfaction, and work–family conflict: Individual and crossover effects among dual-earner couples. *Applied Psychology: An International Review, 66*, 628–652.

Mather, M., Jacobsen, L. A., & Pollard, K. M. (2016). Aging in the United States. *Population Bulletin, 70*, 2.

Mathiesen, K. S., Sanson, A. V., & Karevold, E. B. (2018). Methodology: Measures and analytical approaches. In K. S. Mathiesen, A. V. Sanson, & E. B. Karevold (Eds.), *Tracking opportunities and problems from infancy to adulthood: 20 years with the TOPP study* (pp. 235–260). Boston, MA: Hogrefe Publishing.

Matlin, M. (2003). From menarche to menopause: Misconceptions about women's reproductive lives. *Psychology Science, 45*, 106–122.

Matlung, S. E., Bilo, R. A. C., Kubat, B., & van Rijn, R. R. (2011). Multicysticencephalomalacia as an end-stage finding in abusive head trauma. *Forensic Scientific Medicine and Pathology, 7*, 355–363.

Maton, K. I., Schellenbach, C. J., Leadbeater, B. J., & Solarz, A. L. (Eds.). (2004). *Investing in children, youth, families and communities*. Washington, DC: American Psychological Association.

Matriano, E., & Swee-Hin, T. (2013). Multicultural education, global education: Synergies for a peaceful world. In R. L. Lowman (Ed.), *Internationalizing multiculturalism: Expanding professional competencies in a globalized world*. Washington, DC: American Psychological Association.

Matsuda, Y., Ueno, K., Waggoner, R., Erickson, D., Shimura, Y., Tanaka, K., & … Mazuka, R. (2011). Processing of infant-directed speech by adults. *NeuroImage, 54*, 611–621.

Matsumoto, D., & Yoo, S. H. (2006). Toward a new generation of cross-cultural research. *Perspectives on Psychological Science, 1*, 234–250.

Matthes, J., Prieler, M., & Adam, K. (2016). Gender-role portrayals in television advertising across the globe. *Sex Roles, 75*, 314–327.

Mauas, V., Kopala-Sibley, D. C., & Zuroff, D. C. (2014). Depressive symptoms in the transition to menopause: The roles of irritability, personality vulnerability, and self-regulation. *Archives of Women's Mental Health, 17*, 279–289.

Mausbach, B. T., Roepke, S. K., Chattillion, E. A., Harmell, A. L., Moore, R., Romero-Moreno, R., & Grant, I. (2012). Multiple mediators of the relations between caregiving stress and depressive symptoms. *Aging & Mental Health, 16*, 27–38.

Maxmen, A. (2012, February). Harnessing the wisdom of the ages. *Monitor on Psychology*, pp. 50–53.

Maxson, S. C. (2013). Behavioral genetics. In R. J. Nelson, S. Y. Mizumori, & I. B. Weiner (Eds.), *Handbook of psychology, Vol. 3: Behavioral neuroscience* (2nd ed.). New York, NY: John Wiley & Sons Ltd.

Maynard, A. (2008). What we thought we knew and how we came to know it: Four decades of cross-cultural research from a Piagetian point of view. *Human Development, 51*, 56–65.

Mazoyer, B., Houdé, O., Joliot, M., Mellet, E., & Tzourio-Mazoyer, N. (2009). Regional cerebral blood flow increases during wakeful rest following cognitive training. *Brain Research Bulletin, 80*, 133–138.

McArdle, E. F. (2002). New York's Do-Not-Resuscitate law: Groundbreaking protection of patient autonomy or a physician's right to make medical futility determinations? *DePaul Journal of Health Care Law, 8*, 55–82.

McCabe, P., & Shaw, S. (2010). *Genetic and acquired disorders*. Thousand Oaks, CA: Corwin Press.

McCall, R. B., Groark, C. J., Hawk, B. N., Julian, M. M., Merz, E. C., Rosas, J. M.,… Nikiforova, N. V. (2018). Early caregiver–child interaction and children's development: Lessons from the St Petersburg-USA orphanage intervention research project. *Clinical Child and Family Psychology Review*. doi:10.1007/s10567-018-0270-9

McCardle, P., & Hoff, E. (Eds.). (2006). *Childhood bilingualism: Research on infancy through school age*. Clevedon, Avon, UK: Multilingual Matters.

McCarthy, B., & Pierpaoli, C. (2015). Sexual challenges with aging: Integrating the GES approach in an elderly couple. *Journal of Sex & Marital Therapy, 41*, 72–82.

McClain, S., & Cokley, K. (2017). Academic disidentification in black college students: The role of teacher trust and gender. *Cultural Diversity and Ethnic Minority Psychology, 23*, 125–133.

McClelland, D. C. (1993). Intelligence is not the best predictor of job performance. *Current Directions in Psychological Research, 2*, 5–8.

McConnell, V. (2012, February 16). Great granny to the rescue! *Mail Online*. Accessed online, 7/13/12; http://www.dailymail.co.uk/femail/article-2101720/As-live-work-longer-great-grandparents-filling-childcare-gap.html

McCormick, C. B., & Scherer, D. G. (2018). *Child and adolescent development for educators* (2nd ed.). New York, NY: Guilford Press.

McCowan, L. M. E., Dekker, G. A., Chan, E., Stewart, A., Chappell, L. C., Hunger, M., & … North, R. A. (2009). Spontaneous preterm birth and small for gestational age infants in women who stop smoking early in pregnancy: Prospective cohort study. *British Medical Journal, 338*(7710).

McCoyd, J. M., & Walter, C. A. (2016). *Grief and loss across the lifespan: A biopsychosocial perspective* (2nd ed.). New York, NY: Springer Publishing Co.

McCrink, K., & Wynn, K. (2009). Operational momentum in large-number addition and subtraction by 9-month-olds. *Journal of Experimental Child Psychology, 103*, 400–408.

McCue, R. E., & Balasubramaniam, M. (2017). *Rational suicide in the elderly: Clinical, ethical, and sociocultural aspects*. Cham, Switzerland: Springer International Publishing.

McCullough, M. E., Tsang, J., & Brion, S. (2003). Personality traits in adolescence as predictors of religiousness in early maturity: Findings from the Terman longitudinal study. *Personality & Social Psychology Bulletin, 29*, 980–991.

McDonnell, C. G., Valentino, K., Comas, M., & Nuttall, A. K. (2016). Mother–child reminiscing at risk: Maternal attachment, elaboration, and child autobiographical memory specificity. *Journal of Experimental Child Psychology, 143*, 65–84.

McDonnell, L. M. (2004). *Politics, persuasion, and educational testing.* Cambridge, MA: Harvard University Press.

McDonough, L. (2002). Basic-level nouns: First learned but misunderstood. *Journal of Child Language, 29*, 357–377.

McElhaney, K., Antonishak, J., & Allen, J. (2008). "They like me, they like me not": Popularity and adolescents' perceptions of acceptance predicting social functioning over time. *Child Development, 79*, 720–731.

McElwain, N., & Booth-LaForce, C. (2006, June). Maternal sensitivity to infant distress and nondistress as predictors of infant-mother attachment security. *Journal of Family Psychology, 20*, 247–255.

McFarland, J., Hussar, B., Wang, X., Zhang, J., Wang, K., Rathbun, A., Barmer, A., Forrest Cataldi, E., & Bullock Mann, F. (2018). *The Condition of Education 2018.* Washington, DC: National Center for Education Statistics.

McGlothlin, H., & Killen, M. (2005). Children's perceptions of intergroup and intragroup similarity and the role of social experience. *Journal of Applied Developmental Psychology, 26*, 680–698.

McGonigle-Chalmers, M., Slater, H., & Smith, A. (2014). Rethinking private speech in preschoolers: The effects of social presence. *Developmental Psychology, 50*, 829–836.

McGough, R. (2003, May 20). MRIs take a look at reading minds. *Wall Street Journal*, p. D8.

McGue, M. (2010). The end of behavioral genetics? *Behavior Genetics, 40*, 284–296.

McGuffin, P., Riley, B., & Plomin, R. (2001, February 16). Toward behavioral genomics. *Science, 291*, 1232–1233.

McGugin, R., & Tanaka, J. (2010). Transfer and interference in perceptual expertise: When expertise helps and when it hurts. In M. T. Banich & D. Caccamise (Eds.), *Generalization of knowledge: Multidisciplinary perspectives.* New York, NY: Psychology Press.

McGuinness, D. (1972). Hearing: Individual differences in perceiving. *Perception, 1*, 465–473.

McGuire, S., & Shanahan, L. (2010). Sibling experiences in diverse family contexts. *Child Development Perspectives, 4*, 72–79.

McHale, J. P., & Rotman, T. (2007). Is seeing believing? Expectant parents' outlooks on coparenting and later coparenting solidarity. *Infant Behavior & Development, 30*, 63–81.

McHale, S. M., Kim, J.-Y., & Whiteman, S. D. (2006). Sibling relationships in childhood and adolescence. In P. Noller & J. A. Feeney (Eds.), *Close relationships: Functions, forms and processes.* Hove, UK: Psychology Press/Taylor & Francis.

McHale, S. M., Updegraff, K. A., Shanahna, L., Crouter, A. C., & Killoren, S. E. (2005). Gender, culture, and family dynamics: Differential treatment of siblings in Mexican American families. *Journal of Marriage and the Family, 67*, 1259–1274.

McLachlan, H. (2008). The ethics of killing and letting die: Active and passive euthanasia. *Journal of Medical Ethics, 34*, 636–638.

McLaughlin, H., Vagenas, D., Pachana, N. A., Begum, N., & Dobson, A. (2010). Gender differences in social network size and satisfaction in adults in their 70s. *Journal of Health Psychology, 15*(5), 671–679.

McLean, K. C. & Syed, M. (2015). *The Oxford handbook of identity development.* New York, NY: Oxford University Press.

McManus, R., & Schafer, C. (2014). Final arrangements: Examining debt and distress. *Mortality, 19*(4), 379–397.

McMurray, B., Aslin, R. N., & Toscano, J. C. (2009). Statistical learning of phonetic categories: Insights from a computational approach. *Developmental Science, 12*, 369–378.

McNulty, J. K., & Karney, B. R. (2004). Positive expectations in the early years of marriage: Should couples expect the best or brace for the worst? *Journal of Personality and Social Psychology, 86*, 729–743.

McNulty, J. K., Olson, M. A., Meltzer, A. L., & Shaffer, M. J. (2013). Though they may be unaware newlyweds implicitly know whether their marriage will be satisfying. *Science, 342*(6162), 1119–1120.

McPake, J., Plowman, L., & Stephen, C. (2013). Preschool children creating and communicating with digital technologies in the home. *British Journal of Educational Technology, 44*, 421–431.

McQuade, J., Achufusi, A., Shoulberg, E., & Murray-Close, D. (2014). Biased self-perceptions of social competence and engagement in physical and relational aggression: The moderating role of peer status and sex. *Aggressive Behavior [serial online], 40*, 512–525.

McQuade, J. D., Breaux, R. P., Gómez, A. F., Zakarian, R. J., & Weatherly, J. (2016). Biased self-perceived social competence and engagement in subtypes of aggression: Examination of peer rejection, social dominance goals, and sex of the child as moderators. *Aggressive Behavior, 42*, 498–509.

Mead, M. (1942). *Environment and education, a symposium held in connection with the fiftieth anniversary celebration of the University of Chicago.* Chicago, IL: University of Chicago.

Meade, C., Kershaw, T., & Ickovics, J. (2008). The intergenerational cycle of teenage motherhood: An ecological approach. *Health Psychology, 27*, 419–429.

Meador, K. J., Boyd, A., & Loring, D. W. (2017). Relationship of reaction time to perception of a stimulus and volitionally delayed response. *Cognitive and Behavioral Neurology, 30*, 57–61.

Meagher, D. K., & Balk, D. E. (Eds.). (2013). *Handbook of thanatology: The essential body of knowledge for the study of death, dying, and bereavement* (2nd ed.). New York: Routledge/Taylor & Francis Group

Mealey, L. (2000). *Sex differences: Developmental and evolutionary strategies.* Orlando, FL: Academic Press.

Medeiros, R., Prediger, R. D., Passos, G. F., Pandolfo, P., Duarte, F. S., Franco, J. L., & ... Calixto, J. B. (2007). Connecting TNF-alpha signaling pathways to iNOS expression in a mouse model of Alzheimer's disease: Relevance for the behavioral and synaptic deficits induced by amyloid beta protein. *Journal of Neuroscience, 16*, 5394–5404.

Medina, A., Lederhos, C., & Lillis, T. (2009). Sleep disruption and decline in marital satisfaction across the transition to parenthood. *Families, Systems, & Health, 27*, 153–160.

Meece, J. L., & Kurtz-Costes, B. (2001). Introduction: The schooling of ethnic minority children and youth. *Educational Psychologist, 36*, 1–7.

Mehlenbeck, R. S., Farmer, A. S., & Ward, W. L. (2014). Obesity in children and adolescents. In L. Grossman & S. Walfish (Eds.), *Translating psychological research into practice.* New York, NY: Springer Publishing Co.

Meijer, A. M., & van den Wittenboer, G. L. H. (2007). Contribution of infants' sleep and crying to marital relationship of first-time parent couples in the first year after childbirth. *Journal of Family Psychology, 21*, 49–57.

Meins, E. (2016). Attachment: Theory and classification. In A. Wenzel (Ed.), *The Oxford handbook of perinatal psychology* (pp. 87–107). New York, NY: Oxford University Press.

Meinzen-Derr, J., Wiley, S., Grether, S., Phillips, J., Choo, D., Hibner, J., & Barnard, H. (2014). Functional communication of children who are deaf or hard-of-hearing. *Journal of Developmental and Behavioral Pediatrics, 35*, 197–206.

Meister, H., & von Wedel, H. (2003). Demands on hearing aid features—special signal processing for elderly users? *International Journal of Audiology, 42*, 2S58–2S62.

Melancia, F., & Trezza, V. (2018). Modelling fragile X syndrome in the laboratory setting: A behavioral perspective. *Behavioural Brain Research, 350*, 149–163.

Meland, A., Ishimatsu, K., Pensgaard, A. M., Wagstaff, A., Fonne, V., Garde, A. H., & Harris, A. (2015). Impact of mindfulness training on physiological measures of stress and objective measures of attention control in a military helicopter unit. *International Journal of Aviation Psychology, 25*, 191–208.

Meldrum, R. C., Miller, H. V., & Flexon, J. L. (2013). Susceptibility to peer influence, self-control, and delinquency. *Sociological Inquiry, 83*, 106–129.

Mella, N., Fagot, D., & de Ribaupierre, A. (2016). Dispersion in cognitive functioning: Age differences over the lifespan. *Journal of Clinical and Experimental Neuropsychology, 38*, 111–126.

Meltzoff, A. N. (1981). Imitation, intermodal coordination and representation in early infancy. In G. Butterworth (Ed.), *Infancy and epistemology.* Brighton, UK: Harvester Press.

Meltzoff, A. N., & Moore, M. K. (1977). Imitation of facial and manual gestures by human neonates. *Science, 198*, 75–78.

Meltzoff, A. N., & Moore, M. (2002). Imitation, memory, and the representation of persons. *Infant Behavior & Development, 25*, 39–61.

Melzer, D., Hurst, A., & Frayling, T. (2007). Genetic variation and human aging: Progress and prospects. *Journals of Gerontology: Series A: Biological Sciences and Medical Sciences, 62*, 301–307.

Ménard, C., Pfau, M. L., Hodes, G. E., & Russo, S. J. (2017). Immune and neuroendocrine mechanisms of stress vulnerability and resilience. *Neuropsychopharmacology, 42*, 62–80.

Mendle, J., Turkheimer, E., & Emery, R. E. (2007). Detrimental psychological outcomes associated with early pubertal timing in adolescent girls. *Developmental Review, 27*, 151–171.

Mendonça, B., Sargent, B., & Fetters, L. (2016). Cross-cultural validity of standardized motor development screening and assessment tools: A systematic review. *Developmental Medicine & Child Neurology, 58*, 1213–1222.

Mendoza, C. (2006, September). Inside today's classrooms: Teacher voices on No Child Left Behind and the education of gifted children. *Roeper Review, 29*, 28–31.

Mendoza, M. M., Dmitrieva, J., Perreira, K. M., Hurwich-Reiss, E., & Watamura, S. E. (2017). The effects of economic and sociocultural stressors on the well-being of children of Latino immigrants living in poverty. *Cultural Diversity and Ethnic Minority Psychology, 23*, 15–26.

Menolascino, N., & Jenkins, L. N. (2018). Predicting bystander intervention among middle school students. *School Psychology Quarterly, 33*(2), 305–313. doi:10.1037/spq0000262

Mensah, F. K., Bayer, J. K., Wake, M., Carlin, J. B., Allen, N. B., & Patton, G. C. (2013). Early puberty and childhood social and behavioral adjustment. *Journal of Adolescent Health, 53*, 118–124.

Mercer, J. R. (1973). *Labeling the mentally retarded.* Berkeley, CA: University of California Press.

Merikangas, K. R., Nakamura, E. F. & Kessler, R. C. (2009). Epidemiology of mental disorders in children and adolescents. *Dialogues Clinical Neuroscience, 11*, 7–20.

Merlo, L., Bowman, M., & Barnett, D. (2007). Parental nurturance promotes reading acquisition in low socioeconomic status children. *Early Education and Development, 18*, 51–69.

Merritt, A., LaQuea, R., Cromwell, R., & Ferguson, C. J. (2016). Media managing mood: A look at the possible effects of violent media on affect. *Child & Youth Care Forum, 45*, 241–258.

Merrow, J. (2012, January 11). In education, back to basics. *Huffington Post*. Accessed online, 11/7/17; https://www.huffingtonpost.com/john-merrow/ineducation-back-to-basi_b_1199924.html

Merwin, S. M., Smith, V. C., Kushner, M., Lemay, E. J., & Dougherty, L. R. (2017). Parent-child adrenocortical concordance in early childhood: The moderating role of parental depression and child temperament. *Biological Psychology, 124*, 100–110.

Meyer, M., Wolf, D., & Himes, C. (2006, March). Declining eligibility for social security spouse and widow benefits in the United States? *Research on Aging, 28*, 240–260.

Miao, X., & Wang, W. (2003). A century of Chinese developmental psychology. *International Journal of Psychology, 38*, 258–273.

Michaels, M. (2006). Factors that contribute to stepfamily success: A qualitative analysis. *Journal of Divorce & Remarriage, 44*, 53–66.

Miche, M., Elsässer, V. C., Schilling, O. K., & Wahl, H. (2014). Attitude toward own aging in midlife and early old age over a 12-year period: Examination of measurement equivalence and developmental trajectories. *Psychology and Aging, 29*, 588–600.

Mickelson, K. D., Biehle, S., Chong, A., & Gordon, A. E. (2017). Perceived stigma of postpartum depression in first-time parents: A dual-pathway model. *Sex Roles, 76*, 306–318.

Miesnik, S., & Reale, B. (2007). A review of issues surrounding medically elective cesarean delivery. *Journal of Obstetric, Gynecologic, & Neonatal Nursing: Clinical Scholarship for the Care of Women, Childbearing Families, & Newborns, 36*, 605–615.

Migliaccio, S., Marocco, C., Mocini, E., Lenzi, A., & Greco, E. A. (2018). Role of Mediterranean diet in bone health. *Clinical Cases in Mineral & Bone Metabolism, 15*(1), 16–18.

Mikkola, T. M., Portegijs, E., Rantakokko, M., Gagné, J., Rantanen, T., & Viljanen, A. (2015). Association of self-reported hearing difficulty to objective and perceived participation outside the home in older community-dwelling adults. *Journal of Aging and Health, 27*, 103–122.

Mikulincer, M., & Shaver, P. R. (2009). An attachment and behavioral systems perspective on social support. *Journal of Social and Personal Relationships, 26*, 7–19.

Mikulincer, M., Shaver, P. R., Simpson, J. A., & Dovidio, J. F. (2015). *APA handbook of personality and social psychology, Volume 3: Interpersonal relations*. Washington, DC: American Psychological Association.

Mikulovic, J., Marcellini, A., Compte, R., et al. (2011). Prevalence of overweight in adolescents with intellectual deficiency. Differences in socioeducative context, physical activity, and dietary habits. *Appetite, 56*, 403–407.

Milburn, T. F., Lonigan, C. J., DeFlorio, L., & Klein, A. (2018). Dimensionality of preschoolers' informal mathematical abilities. *Early Childhood Research Quarterly*. doi:10.1016/j.ecresq.2018.07.006

Miles, R., Cowan, F., Glover, V., Stevenson, J., & Modi, N. (2006). A controlled trial of skin-to-skin contact in extremely preterm infants. *Early Human Development, 2*(7), 447–455.

Milkie, M. A., Nomaguchi, K. M., & Denny, K. E. (2015). Does the amount of time mothers spend with children or adolescents matter? *Journal of Marriage and Family, 77*, 355–372.

Miller, A. J., Sassler, S., & Kus-Appough. (2011). The specter of divorce: Views from work- and middle-class cohabitors. *Family Relations, 60*, 602–616.

Miller, B. G., Kors, S., & Macfie, J. (2017). No differences? Meta-analytic comparisons of psychological adjustment in children of gay fathers and heterosexual parents. *Psychology of Sexual Orientation and Gender Diversity, 4*(1), 14–22.

Miller, D. P., & Brooks-Gunn, J. (2015). Obesity. In T. P. Gullotta, R. W. Plant, & M. A. Evans (Eds.), *Handbook of adolescent behavioral problems:*

Evidence-based approaches to prevention and treatment (2nd ed.). New York: Springer Science + Business Media.

Miller, E. M. (1998). Evidence from opposite-sex twins for the effects of prenatal sex hormones. In L. Ellis & L. Ebertz (Eds.), *Males, females, and behavior: Toward biological understanding*. Westport, CT: Praeger Publishers/Greenwood Publishing Group.

Miller, S. A. (2012). *Theory of mind: Beyond the preschool years*. New York, NY: Psychology Press.

Miller, S. A., Church, E. B., & Poole, C. (2018). Ages and stages: How children develop motor skills. Accessed online, 9/23/18; https://www.scholastic.com/teachers/articles/teaching-content/ages-stages-how-children-develop-motor-skills/

Milner, A., Too, L. S., & Spittal, M. J. (2018). Cluster suicides among unemployed persons in Australia over the period 2001–2013. *Social Indicators Research, 137*(1), 189–201.

Miltenberger, R. G. (2016). *Behavior modification: Principles and procedures* (6th ed.). Boston: Cengage Learning.

Mindell, J. A., Leichman, E. S., & Walters, R. M. (2017). Sleep location and parent-perceived sleep outcomes in older infants. *Sleep Medicine*. doi:10.1016/j.sleep.2017.08.003

Mindell, J. A., Sadeh, A., Kwon, R., & Goh, D. Y. T. (2013). Cross-cultural comparison of maternal sleep. *Sleep: Journal of Sleep and Sleep Disorders Research, 36*(11), 1699–1706.

Mireault, G. C., Crockenberg, S. C., Sparrow, J. E., Pettinato, C. A., Woodard, K. C., & Malzac, K. (2014). Social looking, social referencing and humor perception in 6- and 12-month-old infants. *Infant Behavior & Development, 37*, 536–545.

Mirecki, R. M., Chou, J. L., Elliott, M., & Schneider, C. M. (2013). What factors influence marital satisfaction? Differences between first and second marriages. *Journal of Divorce & Remarriage, 54*, 78–93.

Mishna, F., Saini, M., & Solomon, S. (2009). Ongoing and online: Children and youth's perceptions of cyber bullying. *Children and Youth Services Review, 31*, 1222–1228.

Mishra, R. C., & Dasen, P. R. (2013). Culture and cognitive development: The development of geocentric language and cognition. In B. Kar (Ed.), *Cognition and brain development: Converging evidence from various methodologies*. Washington, DC: American Psychological Association.

Misri, S. (2007). Suffering in silence: The burden of perinatal depression. *The Canadian Journal of Psychiatry/La Revue canadienne de psychiatrie, 52*, 477–478.

Missana, M., Altvater-Mackensen, N., & Grossmann, T. (2017). Neural correlates of infants' sensitivity to vocal expressions of peers. *Developmental Cognitive Neuroscience, 26*, 39–44.

Mistry, J., & Saraswathi, T. (2003). The cultural context of child development. In R. Lerner & M. Easterbrooks (Eds.), *Handbook of psychology: Developmental psychology* (Vol. 6). New York, NY: Wiley.

Mitchell, E. (2009). What is the mechanism of SIDS? Clues from epidemiology. *Developmental Psychobiology, 51*, 215–222.

Mitchell, K., Wolak, J., & Finkelhor, D. (2007, February). Trends in youth reports of sexual solicitations, harassment and unwanted exposure to pornography on the Internet. *Journal of Adolescent Health, 40*, 116–126.

Mitchell, K. J., Ybarra, M. L., & Korchmaros, J. D. (2014). Sexual harassment among adolescents of different sexual orientations and gender identities. *Child Abuse & Neglect, 38*, 280–295.

Mitchell, S. (2002). *American generations: Who they are, how they live, what they think*. Ithaca, NY: New Strategists Publications.

Mitra, S., Kavoor, A. R., & Mahintamani, T. (2018). The butterflies in the brain—What would it take to understand the genetic basis of psychiatric disorders? *Asian Journal of Psychiatry, 31*, 13–14.

Mittendorf, R., Williams, M. A., Berkey, C. S., & Cotter, R. F. (1990). The length of uncomplicated human gestation. *Obstetrics and Gynecology, 75*, 73–78.

Miyasaki, J. M., Rheaume, C., Gulya, L., Ellenstein, A., Schwarz, H. B., Vidic, T. R., & Busis, N. A. (2017). Qualitative study of burnout, career satisfaction, and well-being among US neurologists in 2016. *Neurology, 89*, 1730–1738.

Miyata, K., Yoshikawa, T., Morikawa, M., Mine, M., Okamoto, N., Kurumatani, N., & Ogata, N. (2018). Effect of cataract surgery on cognitive function in elderly: Results of Fujiwara-kyo Eye Study. *PLoS ONE, 13*(2).

Mohajeri, M., & Leuba, G. (2009). Prevention of age-associated dementia. *Brain Research Bulletin, 80*, 315–325.

Mohan, J., & Singh, S. (2016). A study of Type A behavior in relation to hostility, stress and optimism among rural and urban male coronary heart disease patients. *Journal of Psychosocial Research, 11*(2), 447–458.

Mok, A., & Morris, M. W. (2012). Managing two cultural identities: The malleability of bicultural identity integration as a function of induced global or local processing. *Personality and Social Psychology Bulletin, 38*, 233–246.

Mølgaard-Nielsen, D., Pasternak, B., & Hviid, A. (2013). Use of oral fluconazole during pregnancy and the risk of birth defects. *New England Journal of Medicine, 369*, 830–839.

Molero, F., Shaver, P. R., Fernández, I., Alonso-Arbiol, I., & Recio, P. (2016). Long-term partners' relationship satisfaction and their perceptions of each other's attachment insecurities. *Personal Relationships, 23*, 159–171.

Molina, J. C., Spear, N. E., Spear, L. P., Mennella, J. A., & Lewis, M. J. (2007). The International Society for Developmental Psychobiology 39th annual meeting symposium: Alcohol and development: Beyond fetal alcohol syndrome. *Developmental Psychobiology, 49*, 227–242.

Monahan, C. I., Beeber, L. S., & Harden, B. (2012). Finding family strengths in the midst of adversity: Using risk and resilience models to promote mental health. In S. Summers & R. Chazan-Cohen (Eds.), *Understanding early childhood mental health: A practical guide for professionals*. Baltimore, MD: Paul H. Brookes Publishing.

Monahan, K., Steinberg, L., & Cauffman, E. (2009). Affiliation with antisocial peers, susceptibility to peer influence, and antisocial behavior during the transition to adulthood. *Developmental Psychology, 45*, 1520–1530.

Monastra, V. (2008). The etiology of ADHD: A neurological perspective. In V. J. Monastra (Ed.), *Unlocking the potential of patients with ADHD: A model for clinical practice*. Washington, DC: American Psychological Association.

Monk, C., Georgieff, M. K., & Osterholm, E. A. (2013). Research review: Maternal prenatal distress and poor nutrition—mutually influencing risk factors affecting infant neurocognitive development. *Journal of Child Psychology and Psychiatry, 54*, 115–130.

Montemurro, B. (2014). Review of "Celebrating debutantes and quinceañeras: Coming of age in American ethnic communities." *Gender & Society, 28*(1), 163–165.

Monteverde, S., Terkamo-Moisio, A., Kvist, T., Kangasniemi, M., Laitila, T., Ryynanen, O., & Pietila, A. (2017). Nurses' attitudes towards euthanasia in conflict with professional ethical guidelines. *Nursing Ethics, 24*, 70–86.

Moon, C. (2002). Learning in early infancy. *Advances in Neonatal Care, 2*, 81–83.

Moon, R. Y. (2016). SIDS and other sleep-related infant deaths: Evidence base for 2016 Updated Recommendations for a Safe Infant Sleeping Environment. *Pediatrics, 138*(5).

Moor, N., & Graaf, P. (2016). Temporary and long-term consequences of bereavement on happiness. *Journal of Happiness Studies, 17*(3), 913–936.

Moore, K. L. (1974). *Before we are born: Basic embryology and birth defects*. Philadelphia, PA: Saunders.

Moore, K. L., & Persaud, T. V. N. (2003). *Before we were born* (6th ed.). Philadelphia, PA: Saunders.

Moore, M. C. & de Costa, C. M. (2006). *Pregnancy and parenting after thirty-five: Mid-life, new life*. Baltimore, MD: Johns Hopkins University Press.

Moore, R. L., & Wei, L. (2012). Modern love in China. In M. A. Paludi (Ed.), *The psychology of love* (Vols. 1–4). Santa Barbara, CA: Praeger/ABC-CLIO.

Moore, S., & Rosenthal, D. (2017). *Grandparenting: Contemporary perspectives*. New York: Routledge/Taylor & Francis Group.

Moraes, L. J., Miranda, M. B., Loures, L. F., Mainieri, A. G., & Mármora, C. H. C. (2018). A systematic review of psychoneuroimmunology-based interventions. *Psychology, Health & Medicine*, 23(6), 635–652.

Morales, J. R., & Guerra, N. F. (2006). Effects of multiple context and cumulative stress on urban children's adjustment in elementary school. *Child Development*, 77, 907–923.

Morange-Majoux, F. F., Lemoine, C. C., & Dellatolas, G. G. (2013). Early manifestations of manual specialisation in infants: A longitudinal study from 20 to 30 weeks. *Laterality: Asymmetries of Body, Brain and Cognition*, 18, 231–250.

Morbidity and Mortality Weekly Report (MMWR). (2008, August 1). Trends in HIV- and STD-related risk behaviors among high school students—United States, 1991–2007. *Morbidity and Mortality Weekly Report*, 57, 817–822.

Morbidity and Mortality Weekly Report. (2017). QuickStats: Suicide rates for teens aged 15–19 years, by sex—United States, 1975–2015. *Morbidity and Mortality Weekly Report 66*, 816. doi:10.15585/mmwr.mm6630a6

Morfei, M. Z., Hooker, K., Carpenter, J., Blakeley, E., & Mix, C. (2004). Agentic and communal generative behavior in four areas of adult life: Implications for psychological well-being. *Journal of Adult Development*, 11, 55–58.

Morin, R. T., & Midlarsky, E. (2017). Predictors of WAIS–R vocabulary in late life: Differences by race. *Journal of Clinical and Experimental Neuropsychology*, 39(9), 833–841.

Morita, J., Miwa, K., Kitasaka, T., Mori, K., Suenaga, Y., Iwano, S., &… Ishigaki, T. (2008). Interactions of perceptual and conceptual processing: Expertise in medical image diagnosis. *International Journal of Human-Computer Studies*, 66, 370–390.

Morley, J. E. (2012). Sarcopenia in the elderly. *Family Practice*, 29(Suppl. 1), I44–I48

Morris, B. J., Bailis, S. A., Wiswell, T. E. (2014). Circumcision rates in the United States: Rising or falling? What effect might the new affirmative pediatric policy statement have? *Mayo Clinic Proceedings*, 89, 677–686.

Morris, B. J., Krieger, J. N., & Klausner, J. D. (2017). CDC's male circumcision recommendations represent a key public health measure. *Global Health: Science and Practice*, 5(1), 15–27.

Morris, P., & Fritz, C. (2006, October). How to improve your memory. *The Psychologist*, 19, 608–611.

Morrison, K. M., Shin, S., Tarnopolsky, M., & Taylor, V. H. (2015). Association of depression & health related quality of life with body composition in children and youth with obesity. *Journal of Affective Disorders*, 172, 18–23.

Morrongiello, B., Corbett, M., & Bellissimo, A. (2008). "Do as I say, not as I do": Family influences on children's safety and risk behaviors. *Health Psychology*, 27, 498–503.

Morrongiello, B., Klemencic, N., & Corbett, M. (2008). Interactions between child behavior patterns and parent supervision: Implications for children's risk of unintentional injury. *Child Development*, 79, 627–638.

Morrongiello, B., Zdzieborski, D., Sandomierski, M., & Lasenby-Lessard, J. (2009). Video messaging: What works to persuade mothers to supervise young children more closely in order to reduce injury risk? *Social Science & Medicine*, 68, 1030–1037.

Mortensen, C., & Cialdini, R. (2010). Full-cycle social psychology for theory and application. *Social and Personality Psychology Compass*, 4, 53–63.

Moser, S., Luxenberger, W., & Freidl, W. (2017). The influence of social support and coping on quality of life among elderly with age-related hearing loss. *American Journal of Audiology*, 26, 170–179.

Mõttus, R., Kandler, C., Bleidorn, W., Riemann, R., & McCrae, R. R. (2017). Personality traits below facets: The consensual validity, longitudinal stability, heritability, and utility of personality nuances. *Journal of Personality and Social Psychology*, 112, 474–490.

Moura-Ramos, M., & Canavarro, M. C. (2018). Was it worth it? Infertile couples' experience of assisted reproductive treatment and psychosocial adjustment one year after treatment. *Psychologica*, 61(1), 107–123.

Mrazek, A. J., Harada, T., & Chiao, J. Y. (2015). Cultural neuroscience of identity development. In K. C. McLean & M. Syed (Eds.), *The Oxford handbook of identity development*. New York, NY: Oxford University Press.

Mrug, S., Elliott, M. N., Davies, S., Tortolero, S. R., Cuccaro, P., & Schuster, M. A. (2014). Early puberty, negative peer influence, and problem behaviors in adolescent girls. *Pediatrics*, 133, 7–14.

Mruk, C. J. (2013). *Self-esteem and positive psychology: Research, theory, and practice* (4th ed.). New York, NY: Springer Publishing Co.

Mu, Z., & Xie, Y. (2014). Marital age homogamy in China: A reversal of trend in the reform era? *Social Science Research*, 44, 141–157.

Muda, R., Kicia, M., Michalak-Wojnowska, M., Ginszt, M., Filip, A., Gawda, P., & Majcher, P. (2018). The Dopamine Receptor D4 gene (DRD4) and financial risk-taking: Stimulating and instrumental risk-taking propensity and motivation to engage in investment activity. *Frontiers in Behavioral Neuroscience*, 12.

Mueller, M., Wilhelm, B., & Elder, G. (2002). Variations in grandparenting. *Research on Aging*, 24, 360–388.

Muenchow, S., & Marsland, K. W. (2007). Beyond baby steps: Promoting the growth and development of U.S. child-care policy. In L. J. Aber et al. (Eds.), *Child development and social policy: Knowledge for action*. Washington, DC: American Psychological Association.

Muiños, M., & Ballesteros, S. (2014). Peripheral vision and perceptual asymmetries in young and older martial arts athletes and non-athletes. *Attention, Perception, & Psychophysics*, 76, 2465–2476.

Müller, D., Ziegelmann, J. P., Simonson, J., Tesch-Römer, C., & Huxhold, O. (2014). Volunteering and subjective well-being in later adulthood: Is self-efficacy the key? *International Journal of Developmental Science*, 8, 125–135.

Müller, U., Burman, J., & Hutchison, S. (2013). The developmental psychology of Jean Piaget: A quinquagenary retrospective. *Journal of Applied Developmental Psychology*, 34, 52–55.

Müller, U., Ten Eycke, K., & Baker, L. (2015). Piaget's theory of intelligence. In S. Goldstein, D. Princiotta, & J. A. Naglieri (Eds.), *Handbook of intelligence: Evolutionary theory, historical perspective, and current concepts*. New York, NY: Springer Science + Business Media.

Multon, K. D. (2000). Career: Career development. In A. E. Kazdin (Ed.), *Encyclopedia of psychology, Vol. 2* (pp. 25–29). Washington, DC; New York, NY: American Psychological Association.

Mundy, B., & Wofsy, M. (2017). Diverse couple and family forms and universal family processes. In S. Kelly (Ed.), *Diversity in couple and family therapy: Ethnicities, sexualities, and socioeconomics*. Santa Barbara, CA: Praeger/ABC-CLIO.

Munniksma, A., Scheepers, P., Stark, T. H., & Tolsma, J. (2017). The impact of adolescents' classroom and neighborhood ethnic diversity on same- and cross-ethnic friendships within classrooms. *Journal of Research on Adolescence*, 27, 20–33.

Munro, B. A., Weyandt, L. L., Marraccini, M. E., & Oster, D. R. (2017). The relationship between nonmedical use of prescription stimulants, executive functioning and academic outcomes. *Addictive Behaviors*, 65, 250–257.

Munro, C., Randall, L. & Lawrie, S. M. (2017). An integrative bio-psycho-social theory of anorexia nervosa. *Clinical Psychology and Psychotherapy*, 24, 1–24.

Munsey, C. (2012, February). Anti-bullying efforts ramp up. *Monitor on Psychology*, pp. 54–57.

Munthali, R. J., Kagura, J., Lombard, Z., & Norris, S. A. (2017). Early life growth predictors of childhood adiposity trajectories and future risk for obesity: Birth to 20 cohort. *Childhood Obesity*, 13(5), 384–391.

Murasko, J. E. (2015). Overweight/obesity and human capital formation from infancy to adolescence: Evidence from two large US cohorts. *Journal of Biosocial Science*, 47, 220–237.

Murdock, K. W., Zilioli, S., Ziauddin, K., Heijnen, C. J., & Fagundes, C. P. (2017). Attachment and telomere length: More evidence for psychobiological connections between close relationships, health, and aging. *Journal of Behavioral Medicine*. Accessed online, 12/12/17; https://www.ncbi.nlm.nih.gov/pubmed/29067540

Murguia, A., Peterson, R. A., & Zea, M. C. (1997, August). *Cultural health beliefs*. Paper presented at the annual meeting of the American Psychological Association, Toronto, Canada.

Murphy, B., & Eisenberg, N. (2002). An integrative examination of peer conflict: Children's reported goals, emotions, and behaviors. *Social Development*, 11, 534–557.

Murphy, C. (2008). The chemical senses and nutrition in older adults. *Journal of Nutrition for the Elderly*, 27, 247–265.

Murphy, F. A., Lipp, A., & Powles, D. L. (2012, March 14). Follow-up for improving psychological well being for women after a miscarriage. *Cochrane Database System Reviews*.

Murphy, P., Buehl, M., Zeruth, J., Edwards, M., Long, J., & Monoi, S. (2010). Examining the influence of epistemic beliefs and goal orientations on the academic performance of adolescent students enrolled in high-poverty, high-minority schools. In L. D. Bendixen & F. C. Feucht (Eds.), *Personal epistemology in the classroom: Theory, research, and implications for practice*. New York, NY: Cambridge University Press.

Murphy, S., Johnson, L., & Wu, L. (2003). Bereaved parents' outcomes 4 to 60 months after their children's death by accident, suicide, or homicide: A comparative study demonstrating differences. *Death Studies*, 27, 39–61.

Murray, L., Cooper, P., Creswell, C., Schofield, E., & Sack, C. (2007, January). The effects of maternal social phobia on mother-infant interactions and infant social responsiveness. *Journal of Child Psychology and Psychiatry*, 48, 45–52.

Murray, S., Bellavia, G., & Rose, P. (2003). Once hurt, twice hurtful: How perceived regard regulates daily marital interactions. *Journal of Personality & Social Psychology*, 84, 126–147.

Murray, T., & Lewis, V. (2014). Gender-role conflict and men's body satisfaction: The moderating role of age. *Psychology of Men & Masculinity*, 15, 40–48.

Murray-Close, D., Ostrov, J., & Crick, N. (2007, December). A short-term longitudinal study of growth of relational aggression during middle childhood: Associations with gender, friendship intimacy, and internalizing problems. *Development and Psychopathology*, 19, 187–203.

Mustanski, B., Kuper, L., & Greene, G. J. (2014). Development of sexual orientation and identity. In D. L. Tolman, L. M. Diamond, J. A. Bauermeister, W. H. George, J. G. Pfaus, & L. M. Ward (Eds.), *APA handbook of sexuality and psychology, Vol. 1:*

Person-based approaches. Washington, DC: American Psychological Association.

Mutiso, S. K., Murage, A., & Mukaindo, A. M. (2018). Prevalence of positive depression screen among post miscarriage women—a cross-sectional study. *BMC Psychiatry, 18.*

Mychasiuk, R., & Metz, G. S. (2016). Epigenetic and gene expression changes in the adolescent brain: What have we learned from animal models? *Neuroscience and Biobehavioral Reviews, 70*, 189–197.

Myers, D. (2000). *A quiet world: Living with hearing loss.* New Haven, CT: Yale University Press.

Myers, R. H. (2004). Huntington's disease genetics. *NeuroRx, 1*, 255–262.

Myrtek, M. (2007). *Type A behavior and hostility as independent risk factors for coronary heart disease.* Washington, DC: American Psychological Association.

Naglieri, J., Goldstein, S., & LeBuffe, P. (2010). Resilience and impairment: An exploratory study of resilience factors and situational impairment. *Journal of Psychoeducational Assessment, 28*, 349–356.

Nagy, E. (2006). From imitation to conversation: The first dialogues with human neonates. *Infant and Child Development, 15*, 223–232.

Nakajima, N., Hasan, A., Jung, H., Brinkman, S. A., Pradhan, M. P. Kinnell, A. (2016). *Investing in school readiness: An analysis of the cost-effectiveness of early childhood education pathways in rural Indonesia (English).* Policy Research working paper; no. WPS 7832; WDR 2018 background paper. Washington, DC: World Bank Group. Accessed online, 3/25/18; http://documents.worldbank.org/curated/en/656521474904442550/Investing-in-school-readiness-an-analysis-of-the-cost-effectiveness-of-early-childhood-education-pathways-in-rural-Indonesia

Nappi, R., & Polatti, F. (2009). The use of estrogen therapy in women's sexual functioning. *Journal of Sexual Medicine, 6*, 603–616.

Narang, S., & Clarke, J. (2014). Abusive head trauma: Past, present, and future. *Journal of Child Neurology, 29*, 1747–1756.

Nash, A., Pine, K., & Messer, D. (2009). Television alcohol advertising: Do children really mean what they say? *British Journal of Developmental Psychology, 27*, 85–104.

Nassif, A., & Gunter, B. (2008). Gender representation in television advertisements in Britain and Saudi Arabia. *Sex Roles, 58*, 752–760.

Natan, B. M. (2008). Perceptions of nurses, families, and residents in nursing homes concerning residents' needs. *International Journal of Nursing Practice, 14*, 195–199.

Nation, M., & Heflinger, C. (2006). Risk factors for serious alcohol and drug use: The role of psychosocial variables in predicting the frequency of substance use among adolescents. *American Journal of Drug and Alcohol Abuse, 32*, 415–433.

National Association for the Education of Young Children. (2005). Position statements of the NAEYC. Accessed online, 3/25/19; http://www.naeyc.org/about/positions.asp#where

National Cancer Center. (2012). NIH study finds leisure-time physical activity extends life expectancy as much as 4.5 years. Accessed online, 11/16/12; http://www.nih.gov/news/health/nov2012/nci-06.htm

National Center for Children in Poverty. (2013). *Basic facts about low-income children in the United States.* New York, NY: National Center for Children in Poverty.

National Center for Education Statistics (2016a). Percentage of high school dropouts among persons 16 to 24 years old (status dropout rate), by sex and race/ethnicity: Selected years, 1960 through 2016. Accessed online, 10/11/18; https://nces.ed.gov/programs/digest/d17/tables/dt17_219.70.asp

National Center for Education Statistics (2016b). Percentage of high school dropouts among persons 16 to 24 years old (status dropout rate), by income level, and percentage distribution of status dropouts, by labor force status and years of school completed: Selected years, 1970 through 2016. Accessed online, 10/11/18; https://nces.ed.gov/programs/digest/d17/tables/dt17_219.75.asp

National Center for Health Statistics. (2016). Life expectancy. Accessed online, 9/15/16; http://www.cdc.gov/nchs/fastats/life-expectancy.htm

National Center for Health Statistics. (2017, November 25.) National marriage and divorce trends. Accessed online, 11/25/17; https://www.cdc.gov/nchs/nvss/marriage_divorce_tables.htm

National Center for Health Statistics (NCHS). (2017). Older persons' health. Accessed online, 12/1/18; https://www.cdc.gov/nchs/fastats/older-american-health.htm

National Center for Health Statistics. (2018). Clinical growth charts. Accessed online, 10/9/18; https://www.cdc.gov/growthcharts/clinical_charts.htm

National Center for Learning Disabilities (2017). The state of learning disabilities: Understanding the 1 in 5. Accessed online, 10/16/18; https://www.ncld.org/the-state-of-learning-disabilities-understanding-the-1-in-5

National Clearinghouse on Child Abuse and Neglect Information. (2004). *Child maltreatment 2002: Summary of key findings/National Clearinghouse on Child Abuse and Neglect Information.* Washington, DC: Author.

National Council on Aging. (2015). USA15 national fact sheet. Accessed online, 12/11/17; https://www.ncoa.org/resources/usa15-national-fact-sheet-pdf/

National Council on Aging. (2016). Chronic disease self-management. Arlington, VA: Author.

National Health and Nutrition Examination Survey (NHANES). (2014). *NHANES 2013-2014.* Atlanta, GA: Centers for Disease Control and Prevention.

National Health Interview Survey. (2015). Health status of children. Accessed online, 11/1/17; https://ftp.cdc.gov/pub/Health_Statistics/NCHS/NHIS/SHS/2015_SHS_Table_C-5.pdf

National Institute on Aging. (2004, May 31). *Sexuality in later life.* Available online at http://www.niapublications.org/engagepages/sexuality.asp

National Institute on Aging. (2017). What happens to the brain in Alzheimer's disease? Accessed online, 3/26/19; https://www.nia.nih.gov/health/what-happens-brain-alzheimers-disease

National Institute on Alcohol Abuse and Alcoholism. (2018). College drinking. Accessed online, 10/12/18; https://pubs.niaaa.nih.gov/publications/CollegeFactSheet/Collegefactsheet.pdf

National Institute on Deafness and Other Communication Disorders (NIDCD). (2016). Quick statistics about voice, speech, language. Accessed online, 10/22/18; https://www.nidcd.nih.gov/health/statistics/quick-statistics-voice-speech-language

National Institute on Deafness and Other Communication Disorders (NIDCD). (2018). Age-related hearing loss. Accessed online, 11/3/18; https://www.nidcd.nih.gov/health/age-related-hearing-loss

National Safety Council. (2013). *Accident facts: 2013 edition.* Chicago, IL: National Safety Council.

National Science Foundation (NSF), Division of Science Resources Statistics. (2002). *Women, minorities, and persons with disabilities in science and engineering: 2002.* Arlington, VA: Author.

National Vital Statistics Report. (2016). *Deaths: Final data for 2013.* Hyattsville, MD: National Center for Health Statistics.

Navarro, M. (2006, May 25). Families add 3rd generation to households. *The New York Times*, pp. A1, A22.

Nazzi, T., & Bertoncini, J. (2003). Before and after the vocabulary spurt: Two modes of word acquisition? *Developmental Science, 6*, 136–142.

NCD Risk Factor Collaboration. (2017). Worldwide trends in body mass index, underweight, overweight, and obesity from 1975 to 2016: a pooled analysis of 2416 population-based measurement studies in 128.9 million children, adolescents, and adults. doi:10.1016/S0140-6736(17)32129-3

Neal Kimball, C., & Turner, S. (2018). Nurturing the apprentice: An immersion training in qualitative research. *Qualitative Psychology, 5*(2), 290–299.

Neiderberger, C., Pellicer, A., Cohen, J., Gardner, D. K., Palermo, G. D., O'Neill, C. L. & … LaBarbera, A. R. (2018). Forty years of IVF. *Fertility and Sterility, 110*(2), 185–324.

Nelson, C. A., & Bosquet, M. (2000). Neurobiology of fetal and infant development: Implications for infant mental health. In C. H. Zeanah, Jr. (Ed.), *Handbook of infant mental health* (2nd ed.). New York, NY: Guilford Press.

Nelson, T. D. (2016). Ageism. In T. D. Nelson (Ed.), *Handbook of prejudice, stereotyping, and discrimination* (2nd ed.). New York, NY: Psychology Press.

Németh, R., Háden G. P., Török, M., Winkler, I. (2016). Processing of horizontal sound localization cues in newborn infants. *Ear and Hearing, 36* (5), 550–556.

Nesheim, S., Henderson, S., Lindsay, M., Zuberi, J., Grimes, V., Buehler, J., &… Bulterys, M. (2004). *Prenatal HIV testing and antiretroviral prophylaxis at an urban hospital—Atlanta, Georgia, 1997-2000.* Atlanta, GA: Centers for Disease Control and Prevention.

Nestler, E. J. (2011, December). Hidden switches in the mind. *Scientific American*, pp. 77–83.

Nestler, E. J. (2016). Transgenerational epigenetic contributions to stress responses: Fact or fiction? *Plos Biology, 14*, 22–26.

Neugarten, B. L. (1972). Personality and the aging process. *The Gerontologist, 12*, 9–15.

Neugarten, B. L. (1977). Personality and aging. In J. E. Birren & K. W. Schaie (Eds.), *Handbook for the psychology of aging.* New York, NY: Van Nostrand Reinhold.

Newland, L. A. (2014). Supportive family contexts: Promoting child well-being and resilience. *Early Child Development and Care, 184*(9-10), 1336–1346.

Newman, S. (2018). Vygotsky, Wittgenstein, and sociocultural theory. *Journal for the Theory of Social Behaviour*, doi:10.1111/jtsb.12174

Newmeyer, F. J. (2016). Form and function in the evolution of grammar. *Cognitive Science.* doi: 10.1111/cogs.12333

Neyro, V., Elie, V., Thiele, N., & Jacqz-Aigrain, E. (2018). Clinical trials in neonates: How to optimise informed consent and decision making? A European Delphi survey of parent representatives and clinicians. *PLoS ONE, 13*(6).

Ng, W., & Nicholas, H. (2010). A progressive pedagogy for online learning with high-ability secondary school students: A case study. *Gifted Child Quarterly, 54*, 239–251.

Ngo, B. (2010). Doing "diversity" at dynamic high: Problems and possibilities of multicultural education in practice. *Education and Urban Society, 42*, 473–495.

NICHD Early Child Care Research Network. (2003a). Does quality of child care affect child outcomes at age 4 1/2? *Developmental Psychology, 39*, 451–469.

NICHD Early Child Care Research Network. (2005). *Child care and child development: Results from the NICHD study of early child care and youth development.* New York, NY: Guilford Press.

NICHD Early Child Care Research Network. (2006). *The NICHD study of early child care and youth development: Findings for children up to age 4 1/2 years* (Figure 5, p. 20). Washington, DC: Author.

Nicholson, J. M., D'Esposito, F., Lucas, N., & Westrupp, E. M. (2014). Raising children in single-parent families. In A. Abela & J. Walker (Eds.), *Contemporary issues in family studies: Global perspectives on partnerships, parenting and support in a changing world.* New York, NY: Wiley-Blackwell.

Nicholson, L. M., & Browning, C. R. (2012). Racial and ethnic disparities in obesity during the transition to adulthood: The contingent and nonlinear impact of neighborhood disadvantage. *Journal of Youth and Adolescence, 41*, 53–66.

Nicklas, T. A., Goh, E. T., Goodell, L. S., Acuff, D. S., Reiher, R., Buday, R.,& Ottenbacher, A. (2011). Impact of commercials on food preferences of low-income, minority preschoolers. *Journal of Nutrition Education and Behavior*, 43(1), 35-41. doi:10.1016/j.jneb.2009.11.007

Nieto, S. (2005). Public education in the twentieth century and beyond: High hopes, broken promises, and an uncertain future. *Harvard Educational Review*, 75, 43–65.

Nigg, J. T., Knottnerus, G., Martel, M., Nikolas, M., Cavanagh, K., Karmaus, W., & Rapperly, M. D. (2008). Low blood lead levels associated with clinically diagnosed attention-deficit/hyperactivity disorder and mediated by weak cognitive control. *Biological Psychiatry*, 63, 325–331.

Nihart, M. A. (1993). Growth and development of the brain. *Journal of Child and Adolescent Psychiatric and Mental Health Nursing*, 6, 39–40.

Nikčević, A. V., & Nicolaides, K. H. (2014). Search for meaning, finding meaning and adjustment in women following miscarriage: A longitudinal study. *Psychology & Health*, 29, 50–63.

Nikkola, I., Kaunonen, M., & Aho, A. (2013). Mother's experience of the support from a bereavement follow-up intervention after the death of a child. *Journal of Clinical Nursing*, 22, 1151–1162.

Nikolaidis, A., & Barbey, A. K. (2018). Network dynamics theory of human intelligence. In R. E. Jung & O. Vartanian (Eds.), *The Cambridge handbook of the neuroscience of creativity* (pp. 382–404). New York, NY: Cambridge University Press.

Nikolas, M., Klump, K. L., & Burt, S. (2012). Youth appraisals of inter-parental conflict and genetic and environmental contributions to attention-deficit hyperactivity disorder: Examination of GxE effects in a twin sample. *Journal of Abnormal Child Psychology*, 40, 543–554.

Nilsson, I. (2003). Memory function in normal aging. *Acta Neurologica Scandinavica*, 107, 7–13.

Ninety-Seventh U.S. Congress. (1981, August 13). *Omnibus Budget Reconciliation Act of 1981. Public Law 97-35, Section 582.* Washington, DC.

Nisbett, R. E. (2005). Heredity, environment, and race differences in IQ: A commentary on Rushton and Jensen (2005). *Psychology, Public Policy, and Law*, 11(2), 302–310.

Nisbett, R. E., Aronson, J., Blair, C., Dickens, W., Flynn, J., Halpern, D. F., & Turkheimer, E. (2012). Intelligence: New findings and theoretical developments. *American Psychologist*, 67, 130–159.

Njoroge, W. M., Elenbaas, L. M., Myaing, M. T., Garrison, M. M., & Christakis, D. A. (2016). What are young children watching? Disparities in concordant TV viewing. *Howard Journal of Communications*, 27, 203–217.

Noakes, M. A., & Rinaldi, C. M. (2006). Age and gender differences in peer conflict. *Journal of Youth and Adolescence*, 35, 881–891.

Nobre, R. G., de Azevedo, D. V., de Almeida, P. C., de Almeida, N. S., & de Lucena Feitosa, F. E. (2017). Weight-gain velocity in newborn infants managed with the kangaroo method and associated variables. *Maternal and Child Health Journal*, 21, 128–135.

Nockels, R., & Oakeshott, P. (1999). Awareness among young women of sexually transmitted chlamydia infection. *Family Practice*, 16, 94.

Nolen, W. (2016). Physician assisted suicide in psychiatry; is there something to be learned from the Dutch law and practice? *Bipolar Disorders*, 18(Suppl 1), 38–39.

Nolen-Hoeksema, S., & Davis, C. (2002). Positive responses to loss: Perceiving benefits and growth. In C. Snyder & S. Lopez (Eds.), *Handbook of positive psychology*. London, UK: Oxford University Press.

Noonan, C. W., & Ward, T. J. (2007). Environmental tobacco smoke, woodstove heating and risk of asthma symptoms. *Journal of Asthma*, 44, 735–738.

Noonan, D. (2003, September 22). When safety is the name of the game. *Newsweek*, pp. 64–66.

Noone, J., Stephens, C., & Alpass, F. (2009). Preretirement planning and well-being in later life: A prospective study. *Research on Aging*, 31, 295–317.

Nordenmark, M., & Stattin, M. (2009). Psychosocial wellbeing and reasons for retirement in Sweden. *Ageing & Society*, 29, 413–430.

Nordin, S., Razani, L., & Markison, S. (2003). Age-associated increases in intensity discrimination for taste. *Experimental Aging Research*, 29, 371–381.

Nordt, C., Warnke, I., Seifritz, E., & Kawohl, W. (2015). Modelling suicide and unemployment: a longitudinal analysis covering 63 countries, 2000–11. *The Lancet Psychiatry*, 2(3), 239–245.

Normand, M. T., Moreno-Torres, I. I., Parisse, C. C., & Dellatolas, G. G. (2013). How do children acquire early grammar and build multiword utterances? A corpus study of French children aged 2 to 4. *Child Development*, 84, 647–661.

Norton, A., & D'Ambrosio, B. (2008). ZPC and ZPD: Zones of teaching and learning. *Journal for Research in Mathematics Education*, 39, 220–246.

Norton, M. I., & Gino, F. (2014). Rituals alleviate grieving for loved ones, lovers, and lotteries. *Journal of Experimental Psychology: General*, 143, 266–272.

Nosarti, C., Reichenberg, A., Murray, R. M., Cnattingius, S., Lambe, M. P., Yin, L., & … Hultman, C. M. (2012). Preterm birth and psychiatric disorders in young adult life preterm birth and psychiatric disorders. *Archives of General Psychiatry*, 69(6).

Novotney, A. (2014). Students under pressure. *Monitor on Psychology*, 45(8), 36.

Nursing Home Data Compendium. (2013). *Nursing Home Data Compendium, 2013 Edition.* Baltimore, MD: Centers for Medicare and Medicaid Services.

Nygaard, E., Slinning, K., Moe, V., & Walhovd, K. B. (2017). Cognitive function of youths born to mothers with opioid and poly-substance abuse problems during pregnancy. *Child Neuropsychology*, 23, 159–187.

Oakhill, J., Cain, K., & Elbro, C. (2014). *Understanding and teaching reading comprehension: A handbook* (1st ed.) New York: Routledge.

Oberlander, S. E., Black, M., & Starr, R. H. (2007). African American adolescent mothers and grandmothers: A multigenerational approach to parenting. *American Journal of Community Psychology*, 39, 37–46.

O'Brien, E. (2018, April 19). Here's how much the average couple will spend on health care costs in retirement. *Time*. Accessed online, 3/26/19; http://time.com/money/5246882/heres-how-much-the-average-couple-will-spend-on-health-care-costs-in-retirement/

Ockerman, E. (2017, August 15). Pregnant women addicted to opioids face tough choices. *Washington Post*. Accessed online, 10/25/17; https://www.washingtonpost.com/national/pregnant-women-addicted-to-opioids-facetough-choices-fear-treatment-can-lead-to-separation-andharm/2017/08/13/8844e51a-6d78-11e7-b9e2-2056e768a7e5_story.html?utm_term=.8e1a5948eb1d

O'Connor, A. M., & Evans, A. D. (2018). The relation between having siblings and children's cheating and lie-telling behaviors. *Journal of Experimental Child Psychology*, 168, 49–60. doi:10.1016/j.jecp.2017.12.006

O'Connor, M., & Whaley, S. (2006). Health care provider advice and risk factors associated with alcohol consumption following pregnancy recognition. *Journal of Studies on Alcohol*, 67, 22–31.

Ocorr, K., Reeves, N. L., Wessells, R. J., Fink, M., Chen, H. S., Akasaka, T., & … Bodmer, R. (2007). KCNQ potassium channel mutations cause cardiac arrhythmias in Drosophila that mimic the effects of aging. *Proceedings of the National Academy of Sciences of the United States of America*, 104, 3943–3948.

O'Doherty, K. (2014). Review of Telling genes: The story of genetic counseling in America. *Journal of the History of the Behavioral Sciences*, 50, 115–117.

OECD (2017). *Starting strong 2017: Key OECD indicators on early childhood education and care.* Paris: OECD Publishing. doi:10.1787/9789264276116-en

Office of Adolescent Health. (2016, February). *Teens' social media use: How they connect and what it means for health.* Washington, DC: U.S. Department of Health & Human Services. Accessed online, 11/9/17; https://www.hhs.gov/ash/oah/news/e-updates/february-2016-teens-social-media-use/index.html

Ogbu, J. U. (1992). Understanding cultural diversity and learning. *Educational Researcher*, 21, 5–14.

Ogden, C. L., Carroll, M. D., Fryar, C. D., & Flegal, K .M. (2015). Prevalence of obesity among adults and youth: United States, 2011–2014. *NCHS data brief, no 219.* Hyattsville, MD: National Center for Health Statistics.

Ogolsky, B. G., Dennison, R. P., & Monk, J. K. (2014). The role of couple discrepancies in cognitive and behavioral egalitarianism in marital quality. *Sex Roles*, 70, 329–342.

O'Grady, W., & Aitchison, J. (2005). *How children learn language.* New York, NY: Cambridge University Press.

Ogunyemi, B. (2017). Cultural–ecological theory of academic disengagement used to explain a story of race, culture and education. *Journal of the National Medical Association*, 109(1), 21–22.

O'Hara, R., Gibbons, F., Weng, C., Gerrard, M., & Simons, R. (2012). Perceived racial discrimination as a barrier to college enrollment for African Americans. *Personality and Social Psychology Bulletin*, 38, 77–89.

Ohta, H., & Ohgi, S. (2013). Review of 'The Neonatal Behavioral Assessment Scale.' *Brain & Development*, 35, 79–80.

Ojala, H., Pietilä, I., & Nikander, P. (2016). Immune to ageism? Men's perceptions of age-based discrimination in everyday contexts. *Journal of Aging Studies*, 39, 44–53.

Okie, S. (2005). *Winning the war against childhood obesity.* Washington, DC: Joseph Henry Publications.

Oksenberg, J., & Hauser, S. (2010). Mapping the human genome with newfound precision. *Annals of Neurology*, 67, A8–A10.

O'Leary, S. G. (1995). Parental discipline mistakes. *Current Directions in Psychological Science*, 4, 11–13.

Oliveira, E. T., de Menezes, T. N., & de Olinda, R. A. (2017). High blood pressure and self-reported systemic hypertension in elderly enrolled in the family health strategy program. *Journal of Aging and Health*, 29, 708–728.

Olness, K. (2003). Effects on brain development leading to cognitive impairment: A worldwide epidemic. *Journal of Developmental & Behavioral Pediatrics*, 24, 120–130.

Olsen, S. (2009, October 30). Will the digital divide close by itself? *The New York Times.* Available online at http://bits.blogs.nytimes.com/2009/10/30/will-the-digital-divide-close-by-itself

Olson, D., DeFrain, J., & Skogrand, L. (2019). *Marriages and families: Intimacy, diversity, and strengths* (9th ed.). New York: McGraw-Hill.

Olszewski-Kubilius, P., & Thomson, D. (2013). Gifted education programs and procedures. In W. M. Reynolds, G. E. Miller, & I. B. Weiner (Eds.), *Handbook of psychology, Vol. 7: Educational psychology* (2nd ed.). Hoboken, NJ: John Wiley & Sons Inc.

O'Neil, J. M., & Denke, R. (2016). An empirical review of gender role conflict research: New conceptual models and research paradigms. In Y. J. Wong & S. R. Wester (Eds.), *APA handbook of men and masculinities.* Washington, DC: American Psychological Association.

Onnis, L., Truzzi, A., & Ma, X. (2018). Language development and disorders: Possible genes and environment interactions. *Research in Developmental Disabilities.* doi:10.1016/j.ridd.2018.06.015

Onwuteaka-Philipsen, B., Rurup, M., Pasman, H., & van der Heide, A. (2010). The last phase of life: Who requests and who receives euthanasia or physician-assisted suicide? *Medical Care*, 48, 596–603.

Oostermeijer, M., Boonen, A. H., & Jolles, J. (2014). The relation between children's constructive play activities, spatial ability, and mathematical word problem-solving performance: A mediation analysis in sixth-grade students. *Frontiers in Psychology, 5*, 782.

Orbuch, T. (2009). *Five simple steps to take your marriage from good to great*. Oakland, CA: Oakland Press.

Oregon Death with Dignity Act. (2016). *Oregon Death with Dignity Act: Annual report for 2016*. Portland, OR: Death with Dignity National Center.

Oretti, R. G., Harris, B., & Lazarus, J. H. (2003). Is there an association between life events, postnatal depression and thyroid dysfunction in thyroid antibody positive women? *International Journal of Social Psychiatry, 49*, 70–76.

Organization for Economic Cooperation and Development (OECD). (1998). *Education at a glance: OECD indicators, 1998*. Paris, France: Author.

Organization for Economic Cooperation and Development (OECD). (2001). *Education at a glance: OECD indicators, 2001*. Paris, France: Author.

Organization for Economic Cooperation and Development (OECD). (2014). *PISA 2012 results in focus: What 15-year-olds know and what they can do with what they know*. Paris, France: Author.

Organization for Economic Cooperation and Development (OECD). (2015). OECD Health Statistics 2015. Available online; http://dx.doi.org/10.1787/health-data-en

Ornaghi, V., Pepe, A., & Grazzani, I. (2016). False-belief understanding and language ability mediate the relationship between emotion comprehension and prosocial orientation in preschoolers. *Frontiers in Psychology, 7*, 212–222.

Orr, E. (2018). Beyond the pre-communicative medium: A cross-behavioral prospective study on the role of gesture in language and play development. *Infant Behavior & Development, 52*, 66–75.

Ortiz, S. O., & Dynda, A. M. (2005). Use of intelligence tests with culturally and linguistically diverse populations. In D. P. Flanagan & P. L. Harrison (Eds.), *Contemporary intellectual assessment: Theories, tests, and issues*. New York, NY: Guilford Press.

Osanloo, A. F., Reed, C. J., & Schwartz, J. P. (2017). *Creating and negotiating collaborative spaces for socially just anti-bullying interventions for K-12 schools*. Information Age.

Osborne, J. W. (2012). Psychological effects of the transition to retirement. *Canadian Journal of Counselling and Psychotherapy, 46*, 45–58.

Osofsky, J. (2003). Prevalence of children's exposure to domestic violence and child maltreatment: Implications for prevention and intervention. *Clinical Child & Family Psychology Review, 6*, 161–170.

Osorio-Valencia, E., Torres-Sánchez, L., López-Carrillo, L., Rothenberg, S. J., & Schnaas, L. (2018). Early motor development and cognitive abilities among Mexican preschoolers. *Child Neuropsychology, 24*(8),1015–1025.

Osterman, M. J. K. & Martin, J. A. (2011). Epidural and spinal anesthesia use during labor: 27-state reporting area, 2008. *National vital statistics reports; vol. 59, no 5*. Hyattsville, MD: National Center for Health Statistics.

Otgaar, H., Chan, J. C. K., Calado, B., & La Rooy, D. (2018). Immediate interviewing increases children's suggestibility in the short term, but not in the long term. *Legal and Criminological Psychology*. doi:10.1111/lcrp.12137

Otsuka, Y., Hill, H. H., Kanazawa, S., Yamaguchi, M. K., & Spehar, B. (2012). Perception of Mooney faces by young infants: The role of local feature visibility, contrast polarity, and motion. *Journal of Experimental Child Psychology, 111*, 164–179.

Otsuka, Y., Ichikawa, H., Kanazawa, S., Yamaguchi, M. K., & Spehar, B. (2014). Temporal dynamics of spatial frequency processing in infants. *Journal of Experimental Psychology: Human Perception and Performance, 40*, 995–1008.

Otto, K., Dette-Hagenmeyer, D. E., & Dalbert, C. (2010). Occupational mobility in members of the labor force: Explaining the willingness to change occupations. *Journal of Career Development, 36*, 262–288.

Oudeyer, P., & Smith, L. B. (2016). How evolution may work through curiosity-driven developmental process. *Topics in Cognitive Science, 8*, 492–502.

Oura, K. (2014). The validity of pragmatic reasoning schemas theory for children's conditional evaluation. *Japanese Journal of Developmental Psychology, 25*(3), 207–220.

Ouwehand, C., de Ridder, D. T., & Bensing, J. M. (2007). A review of successful aging models: Proposing proactive coping as an important additional strategy. *Clinical Psychology Review, 43*, 101–116.

Owens, R. (2016). *Language development* (9th ed.) Hoboken, NJ: Pearson.

Owings, M., Uddin, S., & Williams, S. (2013). Trends in circumcision for male newborns in U.S. hospitals: 1979–2010. National Center for Health Statistics. Centers for Disease Control and Prevention. Accessed online, 9/15/18; https://www.cdc.gov/nchs/data/hestat/circumcision_2013/Circumcision_2013.htm

Owsley, C., Ghate, D., & Kedar, S. (2018). Vision and aging. In M. Rizzo, S. Anderson, & B. Fritzsch (Eds.), *The Wiley handbook on the aging mind and brain*. (pp. 296–314). New York: Wiley-Blackwell.

Owsley, C., Stalvey, B., & Phillips, J. (2003). The efficacy of an educational intervention in promoting self-regulation among high-risk older drivers. *Accident Analysis & Prevention, 35*, 393–400.

Oxford, M., Gilchrist, L., Gillmore, M., & Lohr, M. (2006, July). Predicting variation in the life course of adolescent mothers as they enter adulthood. *Journal of Adolescent Health, 39*, 20–26.

Oyefiade, A. A., Ameis, S., Lerch, J. P., Rockel, C., Szulc, K. U., Scantlebury, N., &... Mabbott, D. J. (2018). Development of short-range white matter in healthy children and adolescents. *Human Brain Mapping, 39*(1), 204–217. doi:10.1002/hbm.23836

Oyserman, D., Kemmelmeier, M., Fryberg, S., Brosh, H., & Hart-Johnson, T. (2003). Racial ethnic self-schemas. *Social Psychology Quarterly, 66*, 333–347.

Ozawa, M., & Yoon, H. (2003). Economic impact of marital disruption on children. *Children & Youth Services Review, 25*, 611–632.

Ozmen, C. B., Brelsford, G. M., & Danieu, C. R. (2017). Political affiliation, spirituality, and religiosity: Links to emerging adults' life satisfaction and optimism. *Journal of Religion and Health*. Accessed online, 12/3/17; https://www.ncbi.nlm.nih.gov/pubmed/28803368

Ozmeral, E. J., Eddins, A. C., Frisina, D. S., & Eddins, D. A. (2016). Large cross-sectional study of presbycusis reveals rapid progressive decline in auditory temporal acuity. *Neurobiology of Aging, 43*, 72–78.

Paans, N. P. G., Bot, M., Brouwer, I. A., Visser, M., Roca, M., Kohls, E., &... Penninx, B. W. J. H. (2018). The association between depression and eating styles in four European countries: The MooDFOOD prevention study. *Journal of Psychosomatic Research, 108*, 85–92.

Pacala, J. T., & Yueh, B. (2012). Hearing deficits in the older patient: "I didn't notice anything." *Journal of the American Medical Association, 307*(11), 1185–1194.

Paine, E. A., Umberson, D., & Reczek, C. (2018). Sex in midlife: Women's sexual experiences in lesbian and straight marriages. *Journal of Marriage and Family*. doi:10.1111/jomf.12508

Pajkrt, E., Weisz, B., Firth, H. V., & Chitty, L. S. (2004). Fetal cardiac anomalies and genetic syndromes. *Prenatal Diagnosis, 24*, 1104–1115.

Pajulo, M., Helenius, H., & MaYes, L. (2006, May). Prenatal views of baby and parenthood: Association with sociodemographic and pregnancy factors. *Infant Mental Health Journal, 27*, 229–250.

Palanca-Maresca, I., Ruiz-Antoran, B., Centeno-Soto, G. A., Forti-Buratti, M. A., Siles, A., Usano, A., & Avendano-Sola, C. (2017). Prevalence and risk factors of prolonged corrected QT interval among children and adolescents treated with antipsychotic medications: A long-term follow-up in a real-world population. *Journal of Clinical Psychopharmacology, 37*, 78–83.

Palfai, T., Halperin, S., & Hoyer, W. (2003). Age inequalities in recognition memory: Effects of stimulus presentation time and list repetitions. *Aging, Neuropsychology, & Cognition, 10*, 134–140.

Palm, G. (2014). Attachment theory and fathers: Moving from "being there" to "being with." *Journal of Family Theory & Review, 6*(4), 282–297.

Palmore, E. B. (1992). Knowledge about aging: What we know and need to know. *Gerontologist, 32*, 149–150.

Palmore, E. B. (2017). Auto-gerontology: A personal odyssey. *Journal of Applied Gerontology, 36*, 1295–1305.

Paludi, M. A. (2012). *The psychology of love* (Vols. 1–4). Santa Barbara, CA: Praeger/ABC-CLIO.

Paludi, M. A., Paludi, C. A., Jr., & DeSouza, E. R. (Eds.). (2011). *Praeger handbook on understanding and preventing workplace discrimination, Vols 1 & 2*. Santa Barbara, CA: Praeger/ABC-CLIO.

Panagiotaki, G., Hopkins, M., Nobes, G., Ward, E., & Griffiths, D. (2018). Children's and adults' understanding of death: Cognitive, parental, and experiential influences. *Journal of Experimental Child Psychology, 166*, 96–115.

Panagiotaki, G., Nobes, G., Ashraf, A., & Aubby, H. (2015). British and Pakistani children's understanding of death: Cultural and developmental influences. *British Journal of Developmental Psychology, 33*(1), 31–44.

Palusci, V. J., & Ondersma, S. J. (2012). Services and recurrence after psychological maltreatment confirmed by child protective services. *Child Maltreatment, 17*, 153–163.

Pandina, R., Johnson, V., & White, H. (2010). Peer influences on substance use during adolescence and emerging adulthood. In L. M. Scheier (Ed.), *Handbook of drug use etiology: Theory, methods, and empirical findings*. Washington, DC: American Psychological Association.

Pankalla, A., & Kośnik, K. (2018). Religion as an invaluable source of psychological knowledge: Indigenous Slavic psychology of religion. *Journal of Theoretical and Philosophical Psychology, 38*(3), 154–164.

Paolella, F. (2013). La pedagogia di Loris Malaguzzi. Per una storia del Reggio Emiliaapproach. *Rivista Sperimentale Di Freniatria: La Rivista Della Salute Mentale, 137*, 95–112.

Parazzini, F., Cipriani, S., Bianchi, S., Bulfoni, C., Bortolus, R., & Somigliana, E. (2016). Risk of monozygotic twins after assisted reproduction: A population-based approach. *Twin Research and Human Genetics, 19*, 72–76.

Pargman, D., & Dobersek, U. (2018). Exercise and aging. In S. Razon & M. L. Sachs (Eds.), *Applied exercise psychology: The challenging journey from motivation to adherence* (pp. 258–274). New York: Routledge/Taylor & Francis Group.

Parisi, J. M., Gross, A. L., Marsiske, M., Willis, S. L., & Rebok, G. W. (2017). Control beliefs and cognition over a 10-year period: Findings from the ACTIVE trial. *Psychology and Aging, 32*, 69–75.

Park, A. (2008, June 23). Living large. *Time*, pp. 90–92.

Park, C. L., Riley, K. E., & Snyder, L. B. (2012). Meaning making coping, making sense, and post-traumatic growth following the 9/11 terrorist attacks. *Journal of Positive Psychology, 7*, 198–207.

Park, J. E., Lee, J., Suh, G., Kim, B., & Cho, M. J. (2014). Mortality rates and predictors in community-dwelling elderly individuals with cognitive impairment: An eight-year follow-up after initial assessment. *International Psychogeriatrics, 26*, 1295–1304.

Parke, R., Simpkins, S., & McDowell, D. (2002). Relative contributions of families and peers to children's social development. In P. Smith & C. Hart (Eds.), *Blackwell handbook of childhood social development*. Malden, MA: Blackwell Publishers.

Parke, R. D. (2004). Development in the family. *Annual Review of Psychology, 55*, 365–399.

Parker, K. (2012). *The boomerang generation*. Washington, DC: Pew Research Center.

Parks, C. D., Sanna, L., & Posey, D. (2003). Retrospection in social dilemmas: How thinking about the past affects future cooperation. *Journal of Personality & Social Psychology, 84*, 988–996.

Parsons, A., & Howe, N. (2013). "This is Spiderman's mask." "No, it's Green Goblin's": Shared meanings during boys' pretend play with superhero and generic toys. *Journal of Research in Childhood Education, 27*, 190–207.

Parten, M. B. (1932). Social participation among preschool children. *Journal of Abnormal and Social Psychology, 27*, 243–269.

Paterno, M. T., McElroy, K., & Regan, M. (2016). Electronic fetal monitoring and cesarean birth: A scoping review. *Birth: Issues in Perinatal Care, 43*, 277–284.

Patterson, C. J. (2007). Lesbian and gay family issues in the context of changing legal and social policy environments. In K. J. Bieschke, R. M. Perez, & K. A. DeBord (Eds.), *Handbook of counseling and psychotherapy with lesbian, gay, bisexual, and transgender clients* (2nd ed.). Washington, DC: American Psychological Association.

Patterson, C. J. (2009). Children of lesbian and gay parents: Psychology, law, and policy. *American Psychologist, 64*, 727–736.

Patterson, C. J. (2013). Children of lesbian and gay parents: Psychology, law, and policy. *Psychology of Sexual Orientation and Gender Diversity, 1*(S), 27–34.

Patterson, C. J. (2018). Sexual orientation and gender diversity in the family lives of girls and women. In C. B. Travis, J. W. White, A. Rutherford, W. S. Williams, S. L. Cook, & K. F. Wyche (Eds.), *APA handbook of the psychology of women: Perspectives on women's private and public lives., Vol. 2*. (pp. 133–149). Washington, DC: American Psychological Association.

Patton, G.C., & Viner, R. (2007). Pubertal transitions in health. *Lancet, 369*, 1130–1139.

Paul, K., & Moser, K. (2009). Unemployment impairs mental health: Meta-analyses. *Journal of Vocational Behavior, 74*, 264–282.

Pauletti, R. E., Menon, M., Cooper, P. J., Aults, C. D., & Perry, D. G. (2017). Psychological androgyny and children's mental health: A new look with new measures. *Sex Roles, 76*(11–12), 705–718.

Paulino, M. (2016). *Forensic psychology of spousal violence*. London, UK: Academic Press.

Paulus, M. (2014). How and why do infants imitate? An ideomotor approach to social and imitative learning in infancy (and beyond). *Psychonomic Bulletin & Review, 21*, 1139–1156.

Paulus, M. (2016). Friendship trumps neediness: The impact of social relations and others' wealth on preschool children's sharing. *Journal of Experimental Child Psychology, 146*, 106–120.

Paulus, M., & Moore, C. (2014). The development of recipient-dependent sharing behavior and sharing expectations in preschool children. *Developmental Psychology, 50*, 914–921.

Pavlov, I. P. (1927). *Conditioned reflexes*. London, UK: Oxford University Press.

Pawluski, J. L., Lonstein, J. S., & Fleming, A. S. (2017). The neurobiology of postpartum anxiety and depression. *Trends in Neurosciences, 40*(2), 106–120.

Payá-González, B., López-Gil, J., Noval-Aldaco, E., & Ruiz-Torres, M. (2015). Gender and first psychotic episodes in adolescence. In M. Sáenz-Herrero (Ed.), *Psychopathology in women: Incorporating gender perspective into descriptive*

psychopathology. Cham, Switzerland: Springer International Publishing.

Paz-Albo Prieto, J., Cvencek, D., Llácer, C. V. H., Escobar, A. H., & Meltzoff, A. N. (2017). Preschoolers' mathematical play and colour preferences: A new window into the development of gendered beliefs about math. *Early Child Development and Care, 187*(8), 1273–1283. doi:10.10 80/03004430.2017.1295234

Peach, H. D., & Gaultney, J. F. (2013). Sleep, impulse control, and sensation-seeking predict delinquent behavior in adolescents, emerging adults, and adults. *Journal of Adolescent Health, 53*, 293–299.

Pearson, C., Combs, J., & Smith, G. (2010). A risk model for disordered eating in late elementary school boys. *Psychology of Addictive Behaviors, 22*, 88–97.

Peck, R. C. (1968). Psychological developments in the second half of life. In B. L. Neugarten (Ed.), *Middle age and aging*. Chicago, IL: University of Chicago Press.

Pedersen, S., Vitaro, F., Barker, E. D., & Borge, A. I. H. (2007). The timing of middle-childhood peer rejection and friendship: Linking early behavior to early-adolescent adjustment. *Child Development, 78*, 1037–1051.

Peel, E., & Harding, R. (2015). A right to "dying well" with dementia? Capacity, "choice" and relationality. *Feminism & Psychology, 25*, 137–142.

Peeters, M., Cillessen, A., & Scholte, R. (2010). Clueless or powerful? Identifying subtypes of bullies in adolescence. *Journal of Youth and Adolescence, 39*, 1041–1052.

Pelaez, M., Borroto, A. R., & Carrow, J. (2018). Infant vocalizations and imitation as a result of adult contingent imitation. *Behavioral Development, 23*(1), 81–88.

Pelham, W. J., Fabiano, G. A., Waxmonsky, J. G., Greiner, A. R., Gnagy, E. M., Pelham, W. I., &… Murphy, S. A. (2016). Treatment sequencing for childhood ADHD: A multiple-randomization study of adaptive medication and behavioral interventions. *Journal of Clinical Child and Adolescent Psychology, 45*, 396–415.

Peltola, M. J., Yrttiaho, S., & Leppänen, J. M. (2018). Infants' attention bias to faces as an early marker of social development. *Developmental Science.* doi:10.1111/desc.12687

Pelzer, B., Schaffrath, S., & Vernaleken, I. (2014). Coping with unemployment: The impact of unemployment on mental health, personality, and social interaction skills. *Work: Journal of Prevention, Assessment & Rehabilitation, 48*, 289–295.

Peng, W., Li, G., Guan, Y., Wang, D., & Huang, S. (2016). A study of cognitive functions in female elderly patients with osteoporosis: A multi-center cross-sectional study. *Aging & Mental Health, 20*, 647–654.

Penido, A., de Souza Rezende, G., Abreu, R., de Oliveira, A., Guidine, P., Pereira, G., &… Moraes, M. F. (2012). Malnutrition during central nervous system growth and development impairs permanently the subcortical auditory pathway. *Nutritional Neuroscience, 15*, 31–36.

Peralta, O., Salsa, A., del Rosario Maita, M., & Mareovich, F. (2013). Scaffolding young children's understanding of symbolic objects. *Early Years: An International Journal of Research and Development, 33*, 266–274.

Percy, K. (2010). *Working with aging families: Therapeutic solutions for caregivers, spouses, & adult children*. New York, NY: Norton.

Perelli-Harris, B., Berrington, A., Gassen, N. S., Galezewska, P., & Holland, J. A. (2017). The rise in divorce and cohabitation: Is there a link? *Population Development Review, 43*(2), 303–329.

Perelli-Harris, B., & Styrc, M. (2017). Mental well-being differences in cohabitation and marriage: The role of childhood selection. *Journal of Marriage and Family.* Accessed online, 12/3/17; doi:10.1111/jomf.12431/full

Perez-Brena, N. J., Updegraff, K. A., & Umaña-Taylor, A. J. (2012). Father- and mother-adolescent

decision-making in Mexican-origin families. *Journal of Youth and Adolescence, 41*, 460–473.

Perreira, K. M., & Ornelas, I. J. (2011, Spring). The physical and psychological well-being of immigrant children. *The Future of Children, 21*, 195–218.

Perrine, N. E., & Aloise-Young, P. A. (2004). The role of self-monitoring in adolescents' susceptibility to passive peer pressure. *Personality & Individual Differences, 37*, 1701–1716.

Perry, W. G. (1981). Cognitive and ethical growth: The making of meaning. In A. W. Chickering & Associates (Eds.), *The modern American college*. San Francisco, CA: Jossey-Bass.

Persson, A., & Musher-Eizenman, D. R. (2003). The impact of a prejudice-prevention television program on young children's ideas about race. *Early Childhood Research Quarterly, 18*, 530–546.

Persson, G. E. B. (2005). Developmental perspectives on prosocial and aggressive motives in preschoolers' peer interactions. *International Journal of Behavioral Development, 29*, 80–91.

Petanjek, Z., Judas, M., Kostovic, I., & Uylings, H. B. M. (2008). Lifespan alterations of basal dendritic trees of pyramidal neurons in the human prefrontal cortex: A layer-specific pattern. *Cerebral Cortex, 18*, 915–929.

Peters, B. (2010). Under threat from HIV/AIDS: Burial societies in Limpopo Province, South Africa. In A. Kalayjian & D. Eugene (Eds.), *Mass trauma and emotional healing around the world: Rituals and practices for resilience and meaning-making, Vol. 2: Human-made disasters*. Santa Barbara, CA: Praeger/ABC-CLIO.

Peters, E., Hess, T. M., Vastfjall, D., & Auman, C. (2007). Adult age differences in dual information processes: Implications for the role of affective and deliberative processes in older adults' decision making. *Perspectives on Psychological Science, 2*, 1–23.

Petersen, A. (2000). A longitudinal investigation of adolescents' changing perceptions of pubertal timing. *Developmental Psychology, 36*, 37–43.

Peterson, C. (2014). Theory of mind understanding and empathic behavior in children with autism spectrum disorders. *International Journal of Developmental Neuroscience, 39*, 16–21.

Peterson, C., & Park, N. (2007). Explanatory style and emotion regulation. In J. J. Gross (Ed.), *Handbook of emotion regulation*. New York, NY: Guilford Press.

Peterson, D. M., Marcia, J. E., & Carpendale, J. I. (2004). Identity: Does thinking make it so? In C. Lightfood, C. Lalonde, & M. Chandler (Eds.), *Changing conceptions of psychological life*. Mahwah, NJ: Lawrence Erlbaum.

Peterson, M., & Wilson, J. F. (2004). Work stress in America. *International Journal of Stress Management, 11*, 91–113.

Petkoska, J., & Earl, J. (2009). Understanding the influence of demographic and psychological variables on retirement planning. *Psychology and Aging, 24*, 245–251.

Petrou, S. (2006). Preterm birth—What are the relevant economic issues? *Early Human Development, 82*(2), 75–76.

Petrou, S., & Kupek, E. (2010). Poverty and childhood undernutrition in developing countries: A multi-national cohort study. *Social Science & Medicine, 71*, 1366–1373.

Pew Research Center. (2009). *Growing old in America: Expectations versus reality*. Washington, DC: Pew Research Center.

Pew Research Center. (2012). *The Boomerang Generation*. Washington, DC: Pew Research Center.

Pew Research Center. (2014a). *Four in ten couples are saying "I do" again*. Accessed online; http://www.pewsocialtrends.org/2014/11/14/four-in-ten-couples-are-saying-i-do-again/

Pew Research Center. (2014b). *What today's Supreme Court decision means for gay marriage*. Washington, DC: PEW Research Center.

Pew Research Center. (2015). Parenting in America: Outlook, worries, aspirations are strongly linked to financial situation. Pew Research

Center. Accessed online, 10/21/18; http://www.pewresearch.org/wp-content/uploads/sites/3/2015/12/2015-12-17_parenting-in-america_FINAL.pdf

Pfeifer, J., & Hamann, S. (2018). The nature and nurture of congenital amusia: A twin case study. *Frontiers in Behavioral Neuroscience, 12,* doi:10.3389/fnbeh.2018.00120

Philippot, P., & Feldman, R. S. (Eds.). (2005). *The regulation of emotion.* Mahwah, NJ: Lawrence Erlbaum.

Phillips, D., Gormley, W., & Anderson, S. (2016). The effects of Tulsa's CAP Head Start program on middle-school academic outcomes and progress. *Developmental Psychology, 52,* 1247–1261.

Phillips, M. L. (2011, April). The mind at midlife. *Monitor on Psychology,* pp. 39–41.

Phinney, J. S. (2005). Ethnic identity in late modern times: A response to Rattansi and Phoenix. *Identity, 5,* 187–194.

Phinney, J. S. (2008). Ethnic identity exploration in emerging adulthood. In D. L. Browning (Ed.), *Adolescent identities: A collection of readings.* New York, NY: Analytic Press/Taylor & Francis Group.

Phinney, J. S., Ferguson, D. L., & Tate, J. D. (1997). Intergroup attitudes among ethnic minority adolescents: A causal model. *Child Development, 68,* 955–969.

Phung, J. N., Milojevich, H. M., & Lukowski, A. F. (2014). Adult language use and infant comprehension of English: Associations with encoding and generalization across cues at 20 months. *Infant Behavior & Development, 37,* 465–479.

Piaget, J. (1932). *The moral judgment of the child.* New York, NY: Harcourt, Brace & World.

Piaget, J. (1952). *The origins of intelligence in children.* New York, NY: International Universities Press.

Piaget, J. (1962). *Play, dreams and imitation in childhood.* New York, NY: Norton.

Piaget, J. (1983). Piaget's theory. In W. Kessen (Ed.), & P. H. Mussen (Series Ed.), *Handbook of child psychology: Vol. 1. History, theory, and methods.* New York, NY: Wiley.

Piaget, J., & Inhelder, B. (1958). *The growth of logical thinking from childhood to adolescence* (A. Parsons & S. Seagrin, Trans.). New York, NY: Basic Books.

Pianta, R. C., Barnett, W. S., Burchinal, M., & Thornburg, K. R. (2009, August). The effects of preschool education: What we know, how public policy is or is not aligned with the evidence base, and what we need to know. *Psychological Science in the Public Interest, 10,* 49–88.

Pickles, A., Hill, J., Breen, G., Quinn, J., Abbott, K., Jones, H., & Sharp, H. (2013). Evidence for interplay between genes and parenting on infant temperament in the first year of life: Monoamine oxidase, a polymorphism, moderates effects of maternal sensitivity on infant anger proneness. *Journal of Child Psychology and Psychiatry, 54,* 1308–1317.

Piekarski, D. J., Johnson, C. M., Boivin, J. R., et al. (2017). Does puberty mark a transition in sensitive periods for plasticity in the associative neocortex? *Brain Research, 1654*(Part B), 123–144.

Pietri, E. S., Hennes, E. P., Dovidio, J. F., Brescoll, V. L., Bailey, A. H., Moss-Racusin, C. A., & Handelsman, J. (2018). Addressing unintended consequences of gender diversity interventions on women's sense of belonging in stem. *Sex Roles: A Journal of Research.* doi:10.1007/s11199-018-0952-2

Piller, I. (2010). Review of "The bilingual edge: Why, when, and how to teach your child a second language." *International Journal of Bilingual Education and Bilingualism, 13,* 115–118.

Ping, R., & Goldin-Meadow, S. (2008). Hands in the air: Using ungrounded iconic gestures to teach children conservation of quantity. *Developmental Psychology, 44,* 1277–1287.

Piper, W. E., Ogrodniczuk, J. S., Joyce, A. S., & Weidman, R. (2009). Follow-up outcome in short-term group therapy for complicated grief. *Group Dynamics: Theory, Research, and Practice, 13,* 46–58.

Pirog, M. A., Jung, H., & Lee, D. (2018). The changing face of teenage parenthood in the United States: Evidence from NLSY79 and NLSY97. *Child & Youth Care Forum, 47*(3), 317–342.

Pittman, L. D., & Boswell, M. K. (2007). The role of grandmothers in the lives of preschoolers growing up in urban poverty. *Applied Developmental Science, 11,* 20–42.

Platt, I., Green, H. J., Jayasinghe, R., & Morrissey, S. A. (2014). Understanding adherence in patients with coronary heart disease: Illness representations and readiness to engage in healthy behaviours. *Australian Psychologist, 49,* 127–137.

Platt, L. F., Wolf, J. K., & Scheitle, C. P. (2018). Patterns of mental health care utilization among sexual orientation minority groups. *Journal of Homosexuality, 65*(2), 135–153.

Plomin, R. (2005). Finding genes in child psychology and psychiatry: When are we going to be there? *Journal of Child Psychology and Psychiatry, 46,* 1030–1038.

Plomin, R., DeFries, J. C., Knopik, V. S., & Neiderhiser, J. M. (2016). Top 10 replicated findings from behavioral genetics. *Perspectives on Psychological Science, 11,* 3–23.

Polkinghorne, D. E. (2005). Language and meaning: Data collection in qualitative research [Special issue: Knowledge in context: Qualitative methods in counseling psychology research]. *Journal of Counseling Psychology, 52,* 137–145.

Pölkki, T., Korhonen, A., Axelin, A., Saarela, T., & Laukkala, H. (2015). Development and preliminary validation of the Neonatal Infant Acute Pain Assessment Scale (NIAPAS). *International Journal of Nursing Studies, 51,* 1585–1594.

Pollack, W., Shuster, T., & Trelease, J. (2001). *Real boys' voices.* New York, NY: Penguin.

Pollak, S., Holt, L., & Wismer Fries, A. (2004). Hemispheric asymmetries in children's perception of nonlinguistic human affective sounds. *Developmental Science, 7,* 10–18.

Pomares, C. G., Schirrer, J., & Abadie, V. (2002). Analysis of the olfactory capacity of healthy children before language acquisition. *Journal of Developmental Behavior and Pediatrics, 23,* 203–207.

Pomerantz, E. M., Qin, L., Wang, Q., & Chen, H. (2011). Changes in early adolescents' sense of responsibility to their parents in the United States and China: Implications for academic functioning. *Child Development, 82,* 1136–1151.

Pomatto L. C. D. & Davies K. J. A. (2018). Adaptive homeostasis and the free radical theory of ageing. *Free Radical Biology and Medicine, 124,* 420–430.

Pompili, M., Masocco, M., Vichi, M., Lester, D., Innamorati, M., Tatarelli, R., & Vanacore, N. (2009). Suicide among Italian adolescents: 1970-2002. *European Child & Adolescent Psychiatry, 18,* 525–533.

Ponton, L. E. (2001). *The sex lives of teenagers: Revealing the secret world of adolescent boys and girls.* New York, NY: Penguin Putnam.

Poorthuis, A. G., Thomaes, S., Aken, M. G., Denissen, J. A., & de Castro, B. O. (2014). Dashed hopes, dashed selves? A sociometer perspective on self-esteem change across the transition to secondary school. *Social Development, 23,* 770–783.

Pope, A. L., & Cashwell, C. S. (2013). Moral commitment in intimate committed relationships: A conceptualization from cohabiting same-sex and opposite-sex partners. *The Family Journal, 21,* 5–14.

Population Council Report. (2009). *Divorce rates around the world.* New York, NY: Population Council.

Porac, C. (2016). *Laterality: Exploring the enigma of left-handedness.* San Diego, CA: Elsevier Academic Press.

Posid, T., & Cordes, S. (2015). The small-large divide: A case of incompatible numerical representations in infancy. In D. C. Geary, D. B. Berch, & K. M. Koepke (Eds.), *Evolutionary origins and early development of number processing.* San Diego, CA: Elsevier Academic Press.

Posthuma, D., & de Geus, E. (2006, August). Progress in the molecular-genetic study of intelligence. *Current Directions in Psychological Science, 15,* 151–155.

Poulin-Dubois, D., Serbin, L., & Eichstedt, J. (2002). Men don't put on make-up: Toddlers' knowledge of the gender stereotyping of household activities. *Social Development, 11,* 166–181.

Poulton, R., & Caspi, A. (2005). Commentary: How does socioeconomic disadvantage during childhood damage health in adulthood? Testing psychosocial pathways. *International Journal of Epidemiology, 23,* 51–55.

Pow, A. M., & Cashwell, C. S. (2017). Posttraumatic stress disorder and emotion-focused coping among disaster mental health counselors. *Journal of Counseling & Development, 95,* 322–331.

Powell, R. (2004, June 19). Colleges construct housing for elderly: Retiree students move to campus. *Washington Post,* p. F13.

Power, M., & Green, A. (2010). The Attitudes to Disability Scale (ADS): Development and psychometric properties. *Journal of Intellectual Disability Research, 54,* 860–874.

Preciado, P., Snijders, T. B., Burk, W. J., Stattin, H., & Kerr, M. (2012). Does proximity matter? Distance dependence of adolescent friendships. *Social Networks, 34,* 18–31.

Preckel, F., Niepel, C., Schneider, M., & Brunner, M. (2013). Self-concept in adolescence: A longitudinal study on reciprocal effects of self-perceptions in academic and social domains. *Journal of Adolescence, 36,* 1165–1175.

Presseau, C., Contractor, A. A., Reddy, M. K., & Shea, M. T. (2017). Childhood maltreatment and post-deployment psychological distress: The indirect role of emotional numbing. *Psychological Trauma: Theory, Research, Practice, and Policy.* Accessed online, 11/13/17; https://www.ncbi.nlm.nih.gov/pubmed/2898131

Pressley, M., & Schneider, W. (1997). *Introduction to memory development during childhood and adolescence.* Mahwah, NJ: Lawrence Erlbaum.

Price, C. S., Thompson, W. W., Goodson, B., Weintraub, E. S., Croen, L. A., Hinrichsen, V. L., &... DeStefano, F. (2010). Prenatal and infant exposure to thimerosal from vaccines and immunoglobulins and risk of autism. *Pediatrics, 126,* 656–664.

Priddis, L., & Howieson, N. (2009). The vicissitudes of mother-infant relationships between birth and six years. *Early Child Development and Care, 179,* 43–53.

Prieler, M., Kohlbacher, F., Hagiwara, S., & Arima, A. (2011). Gender representation of older people in Japanese television advertisements. *Sex Roles, 64,* 405–415.

Prigerson, H. (2003). Costs to society of family caregiving for patients with end-stage Alzheimer's disease. *New England Journal of Medicine, 349,* 1891–1892.

Prince, C. B., Young, M. B., Sappenfield, W., & Parrish, J. W. (2016). Investigating the decline of fetal and infant mortality rates in Alaska during 2010 and 2011. *Maternal and Child Health Journal, 20,* 754–759.

Prince, M. (2000, November 13). How technology has changed the way we have babies. *Wall Street Journal,* pp. R4, R13.

Prince-Embury, S., & Saklofske, D. H. (2014). *Resilience interventions for youth in diverse populations.* New York: Springer Science + Business Media.

Prochaska, M. T., Putman, M. S., Tak, H. J., Yoon, J. D., & Curlin, F. A. (2017). US physicians overwhelmingly endorse hospice as the better option for most patients at the end of life. *American Journal of Hospice & Palliative Medicine, 34,* 556–558.

Proctor, C., Barnett, J., & Muilenburg, J. (2012). Investigating race, gender, and access to cigarettes in an adolescent population. *American Journal of Health Behavior, 36*, 513–521.

Prohaska, V. (2012). Strategies for encouraging ethical student behavior. In R. Landrum & M. A. McCarthy (Eds.), *Teaching ethically: Challenges and opportunities*. Washington, DC: American Psychological Association.

Proulx, M., & Poulin, F. (2013). Stability and change in kindergartners' friendships: Examination of links with social functioning. *Social Development, 22*, 111–125.

Pruis, T., & Janowsky, J. (2010). Assessment of body image in younger and older women. *Journal of General Psychology, 137*, 225–238.

Puchalski, M., & Hummel, P. (2002). The reality of neonatal pain. *Advances in Neonatal Care, 2*, 245–247.

Puckering, C., Connolly, B., Werner, C., et al. (2011). Rebuilding relationships: A pilot study of the effectiveness of the Mellow Parenting Programme for children with reactive attachment disorder. *Clinical Child Psychology and Psychiatry, 16*, 73–87.

Pudelewicz, A., Talarska, D., & Bączyk, G. (2018). Burden of caregivers of patients with Alzheimer's disease. *Scandinavian Journal of Caring Sciences*. doi:10.1111/scs.12626

Pun, A., Birch, S. A., & Baron, A. S. (2017). Foundations of reasoning about social dominance. *Child Development Perspectives*. Accessed online, 11/17/17; http://onlinelibrary.wiley.com/doi/10.1111/cdep.12235/full

Pundir, A., Hameed, L., Dikshit, P. C., Kumar, P., Mohan, S., Radotra, B., & Iyengar, S. (2012). Expression of medium and heavy chain neurofilaments in the developing human auditory cortex. *Brain Structure & Function, 217*, 303–321.

Puntambekar, S., & Hübscher, R. (2005). Tools for scaffolding students in a complex learning environment: What have we gained and what have we missed? *Educational Psychologist, 40*, 1–12.

Purdy, S. C., Sharma, M. M., Munro, K. J., & Morgan, C. A. (2013). Stimulus level effects on speech-evoked obligatory cortical auditory evoked potentials in infants with normal hearing. *Clinical Neurophysiology, 124*, 474–480.

Puterman, E., Prather, A. A., Epel, E. S., Loharuka, S., Adler, N. E., Laraia, B., & Tomiyama, A. J. (2016). Exercise mitigates cumulative associations between stress and BMI in girls age 10 to 19. *Health Psychology, 35*(2), 191–194.

Putney, N. M., & Bengtson, V. L. (2001). Families, intergenerational relationships and kinkeeping in midlife. In M. E. Lachman (Ed.), *Handbook of midlife development*. Hoboken, NJ: Wiley.

Pyke, K., & Adams, M. (2010). What's age got to do with it? A case study analysis of power and gender in husband-older marriages. *Journal of Family Issues, 31*, 748–777.

Qian, Z., Zhang, D., & Wang, L. (2013). Is aggressive trait responsible for violence? Priming effects of aggressive words and violent movies. *Psychology, 4*, 96–100.

Quinn, M. (1990, January 29). Don't aim that pack at us. *Time*, p. 60.

Quinn, P. (2008). In defense of core competencies, quantitative change, and continuity. *Child Development, 79*, 1633–1638.

Quinn, P., Uttley, L., Lee, K., Gibson, A., Smith, M., Slater, A., et al. (2008). Infant preference for female faces occurs for same- but not other-race faces. *Journal of Neuropsychology, 2*, 15–26.

Quintana, S. M. (2007). Racial and ethnic identity: Developmental perspectives and research. *Journal of Counseling Psychology, 54*, 259–270.

Quintana, S. M., & McKown, C. (2008). *Handbook of race, racism, and the developing child*. Hoboken, NJ: John Wiley & Sons Inc.

Quintana, S. M., McKown, C., Cross, W. E., & Cross, T. B. (2008). In S. M. Quintana & C. McKown (Eds.), *Handbook of race, racism, and the developing child*. Hoboken, NJ: John Wiley.

Ra, J. S., & Cho, Y. H. (2017). Depression moderates the relationship between body image and health-related quality of life in adolescent girls. *Journal of Child and Family Studies, 26*, 1799–1807.

Raag, T. (2003). Racism, gender identities and young children: Social relations in a multi-ethnic, inner-city primary school. *Archives of Sexual Behavior, 32*, 392–393.

Raboteg-Saric, Z., & Sakic, M. (2013). Relations of parenting styles and friendship quality to self-esteem, life satisfaction and happiness in adolescents. *Applied Research in Quality of Life, 9*, 749–765.

Raeburn, P. (2004, October 1). Too immature for the death penalty? *The New York Times Magazine*, 26–29.

Rafalski, J. C., Noone, J. H., O'Loughlin, K., & de Andrade, A. L. (2017). Assessing the process of retirement: A cross-cultural review of available measures. *Journal of Cross-Cultural Gerontology, 32*, 255–279.

Rahko, J. S., Vuontela, V. A., Carlson, S., Nikkinen, J., Hurtig, T. M., Kuusikko-Gauffin, S., &... Kiviniemi, V. J. (2016). Attention and working memory in adolescents with autism spectrum disorder: A functional MRI study. *Child Psychiatry and Human Development, 47*, 503–517.

Rai, P., Ganguli, A., Balachandran, S., Gupta, R., & Neogi, S. B. (2018). Global sex selection techniques for family planning: A narrative review. *Journal of Reproductive and Infant Psychology*. doi:10.1080/02646838.2018.1508871

Rai, R., Mitchell, P., Kadar, T., & Mackenzie, L. (2016). Adolescent egocentrism and the illusion of transparency: Are adolescents as egocentric as we might think? *Current Psychology: A Journal for Diverse Perspectives on Diverse Psychological Issues, 35*, 285–294.

Raikes, H. H., Roggman, L. A., Peterson, C. A., Brooks-Gunn, J., Chazan-Cohen, R., Zhang, X., & Schiffman, R. F. (2014). Theories of change and outcomes in home-based Early Head Start programs. *Early Childhood Research Quarterly, 29*, 574–585.

Rajhans, P., Jessen, S., Missana, M., & Grossmann, T. (2016). Putting the face in context: Body expressions impact facial emotion processing in human infants. *Developmental Cognitive Neuroscience, 19*, 115–121.

Rakison, D. H., & Krogh, L. (2012). Does causal action facilitate causal perception in infants younger than 6 months of age? *Developmental Science, 15*, 43–53.

Rakison, D. H., & Oakes, L. (2003). *Early category and concept development: Making sense of the blooming, buzzing confusion*. London, UK: Oxford University Press.

Rakoczy, H., Harder-Kasten, A., & Sturm, L. (2012). The decline of theory of mind in old age is (partly) mediated by developmental changes in domain-general abilities. *British Journal of Psychology, 103*, 58–72.

Ramasubramanian, S. (2017). Mindfulness, stress coping and everyday resilience among emerging youth in a university setting: A mixed methods approach. *International Journal of Adolescence and Youth, 22*, 308–321.

Ramaswamy, V., & Bergin, C. (2009). Do reinforcement and induction increase prosocial behavior? Results of a teacher-based intervention in preschools. *Journal of Research in Childhood Education, 23*, 527–538.

Ramsay, J. R. (2010). Relationships and social functioning. In J. R. Ramsay (Ed.), *Nonmedication treatments for adult ADHD: Evaluating impact on daily functioning and well-being*. Washington, DC: American Psychological Association.

Rancourt, D., Conway, C. C., Burk, W. J., & Prinstein, M. J. (2013). Gender composition of preadolescents' friendship groups moderates peer socialization of body change behaviors. *Health Psychology, 32*, 283–292.

Randall, W. L. (2012). Positive aging through reading our lives: On the poetics of growing old. *Psychological Studies, 57*, 172–178.

Ranganath, C., Minzenberg, M., & Ragland, J. (2008). The cognitive neuroscience of memory function and dysfunction in schizophrenia. *Biological Psychiatry, 64*, 18–25.

Rankin, B. (2004). The importance of intentional socialization among children in small groups: A conversation with Loris Malaguzzi. *Early Childhood Education Journal, 32*, 81–85.

Ransjö-Arvidson, A. B., Matthiesen, A. S., Lilja, G., Nissen, E., Widström, A. M., & Unvä-Moberg, K. (2001). Maternal analgesia during labor disturbs newborn behavior: Effects on breastfeeding, temperature, and crying. *Birth, 28*, 5–12.

Rantanen, J., Kinnunen, U., Pulkkinen, L., & Kokko, K. (2012). Developmental trajectories of work-family conflict for Finnish workers in midlife. *Journal of Occupational Health Psychology, 17*, 290–303.

Ratanachu-Ek, S. (2003). Effects of multivitamin and folic acid supplementation in malnourished children. *Journal of the Medical Association of Thailand, 4*, 86–91.

Rattan, S. I. S., Kristensen, P., & Clark, B. F. C. (Eds.). (2006). *Understanding and modulating aging*. Malden, MA: Blackwell Publishing on behalf of the New York Academy of Sciences.

Rauer, A., & Jensen, J. F. (2016). These happy golden years? The role of retirement in marital quality. In J. Bookwala (Ed.), *Couple relationships in the middle and later years: Their nature, complexity, and role in health and illness*. (pp. 157–176). Washington, DC: American Psychological Association.

Ravanipour, M., Gharibi, T., & Gharibi, T. (2013). Elderly women's views about sexual desire during old age: A qualitative study. *Sexuality and Disability, 31*, 179–188.

Ray, E., & Heyes, C. (2011). Imitation in infancy: The wealth of the stimulus. *Developmental Science, 14*, 92–105.

Ray, L., Bryan, A., MacKillop, J., McGeary, J., Hesterberg, K., & Hutchison, K. (2009). The dopamine D receptor (DRD4) gene exon III polymorphism, problematic alcohol use and novelty seeking: Direct and mediated genetic effects. *Addiction Biology, 14*, 238–244.

Razani, J., Murcia, G., Tabares, J., & Wong, J. (2007). The effects of culture on WASI test performance in ethnically diverse individuals. *The Clinical Neuropsychologist, 21*, 776–788.

Raznahan, A., Shaw, P., Lalonde, F., Stockman, M., Wallace, G. L., Greenstein, D., Clasen, L., Gogtay, N., & Giedd, J. N. (2011). How does your cortex grow? *Journal of Neuroscience, 31*, 7174–7177.

Read, S. L., & Spar, J. E. (2018). Capacity, informed consent, and guardianship. In J. C. Holzer, R. Kohn, J. M. Ellison & P. R. Recupero (Eds.), *Geriatric forensic psychiatry: Principles and practice*. (pp. 75–81). New York, NY: Oxford University Press.

Rebok, G. W., Ball, K., Guey, L. T., Jones, R. N., Kim, H., King, J. W., &... Willis, S. L. (2014). Ten-year effects of the advanced cognitive training for independent and vital elderly cognitive training trial on cognition and everyday functioning in older adults. *Journal of the American Geriatrics Society, 62*, 16–24.

Rebok, G. W., Langbaum, J. S., Jones, R. N., Gross, A. L., Parisi, J. M., Spira, A. P., &... Brandt, J. (2013). Memory training in the ACTIVE study: How much is needed and who benefits? *Journal of Aging and Health, 25*, 21S–42S.

Reddy, B. M., Ganguly, E., & Sharma, P. K. (2018). Hypertension and its correlates in the oldest old population aged 80 years and above in urban South India. *Journal of Gerontology & Geriatric Research, 7*(3), 472.

Reddy, V. (1999). Prelinguistic communication. In M. Barrett (Ed.), *The development of language*. Philadelphia, PA: Psychology Press.

Reed, R. K. (2005). *Birthing fathers: The transformation of men in American rites of birth*. New Brunswick, NJ: Rutgers University Press.

Reeves, M. L., & Fernandez, B. S. (2017). Evidence-based interventions for comprehensive school crises. In L. A. Theodore (Ed.),

Handbook of evidence-based interventions for children and adolescents. New York: Springer Publishing Co.

Reich, S. M. (2017). Connecting offline social competence to online peer interactions. *Psychology of Popular Media Culture, 6,* 291–310.

Reifman, A. (2000). Revisiting *The Bell Curve. Psycoloquy,* 11.

Reijman, S., Foster, S., & Duschinsky, R. (2018). The infant disorganised attachment classification: "Patterning within the disturbance of coherence." *Social Science & Medicine, 200,* 52–58.

Reio, T. J., & Ortega, C. L. (2016). Cyberbullying and its emotional consequences: What we know and what we can do. In S. Y. Tettegah & D. L. Espelage (Eds.), *Emotions, technology, and behaviors.* San Diego, CA: Elsevier Academic Press.

Reis, S., & Renzulli, J. (2004). Current research on the social and emotional development of gifted and talented students: Good news and future possibilities. *Psychology in the Schools, 41,* 119–130.

Reissland, N., & Cohen, D. (2012). *The development of emotional intelligence: A case study.* New York, NY: Routledge/Taylor & Francis Group.

Rembis, M. (2009). (Re)defining disability in the "genetic age": Behavioral genetics, "new" eugenics and the future of impairment. *Disability & Society, 24,* 585–597.

Renner, L., & Slack, K. (2006, June). Intimate partner violence and child maltreatment: Understanding intra- and intergenerational connections. *Child Abuse & Neglect, 30,* 599–617.

Rentmeester, S. T., Pringle, J., & Hogue, C. R. (2017). An evaluation of the addition of critical congenital heart defect screening in Georgia newborn screening procedures. *Maternal and Child Health Journal.* Accessed online, 10/29/17; https://www.ncbi.nlm.nih.gov/pubmed/28730329

Rentner, T. L., Dixon, L., & Lengel, L. (2012). Critiquing fetal alcohol syndrome health communication campaigns targeted to American Indians. *Journal of Health Communication, 17,* 6–21.

Rentz, D. M., Locascio, J. J., Becker, J. A., Moran, E. K., Eng, E., Buckner, R. L., & … Johnson, K. A. (2010). Cognition, reserve, and amyloid deposition in normal aging. *Annals of Neurology, 67*(3), 353–364.

Reproductive Medicine Associates of New Jersey. (2002). *Age and rate of infertility in women.* Basking Ridge, NJ: RMANJ.

Resing, W. M., Bakker, M., Pronk, C. E., & Elliott, J. G. (2017). Progression paths in children's problem solving: The influence of dynamic testing, initial variability, and working memory. *Journal of Experimental Child Psychology, 153,* 83–109.

Reuter, E., Voelcker-Rehage, C., Vieluf, S., & Godde, B. (2012). Touch perception throughout working life: Effects of age and expertise. *Experimental Brain Research, 216,* 287–297.

Reuter, E., Voelcker-Rehage, C., Vieluf, S., & Godde, B. (2014). Effects of age and expertise on tactile learning in humans. *European Journal of Neuroscience, 40,* 2589–2599.

Reuters Health eLine. (2002, June 26). Baby's injuring points to danger of kids imitating television. *Reuters Health eLine.*

Reyna, V. F., & Farley, F. (2006). Risk and rationality in adolescent decision making. *Psychological Science in the Public Interest, 7,* 1–44.

Reynolds, C. I. (2016). Telomere attrition: A window into common mental disorders and cellular aging. *American Journal of Psychiatry, 173,* 556–558.

Rhoades, G., Stanley, S., & Markman, H. (2009). The pre-engagement cohabitation effect: A replication and extension of previous findings. *Journal of Family Psychology, 23,* 107–111.

Rhodes, R., Mitchell, S., Miller, S., Connor, S., & Teno, J. (2008). Bereaved family members' evaluation of hospice care: What factors influence overall satisfaction with services? *Journal of Pain and Symptom Management, 35,* 365–371.

Rice, T. M., McGill, J., & Adler-Baeder, F. (2017). Relationship education for youth in high school: Preliminary evidence from a non-controlled study on dating behavior and parent–adolescent relationships. *Child & Youth Care Forum, 46,* 51–68.

Rice, W. S., Goldfarb, S. S., Brisendine, A. E., Burrows, S., & Wingate, M. S. (2017). Disparities in infant mortality by race among Hispanic and non-Hispanic infants. *Maternal and Child Health Journal.* Accessed online, 10/29/17; https://www.ncbi.nlm.nih.gov/pubmed/28197819

Richards, T. L., Grabowskia, T. J., Boorda, P., Yaglea, K., Askrena, M., Mestrea, Z., Robinsona, P., Welkera, O., Gulliforda, D., Nagy, W., & Berninger V. (2015). Contrasting brain patterns of writing-related DTI parameters, fMRI connectivity, and DTI–fMRI connectivity correlations in children with and without dysgraphia or dyslexia. *NeuroImage: Clinical, 8,* 408-421.

Richardson, K. A., Hester, A. K., & McLemore, G. L. (2016). Prenatal cannabis exposure—The 'first hit' to the endocannabinoid system. *Neurotoxicology and Teratology, 58,* 5–14.

Richert, R. A., & Schlesinger, M. A. (2017). The role of fantasy–reality distinctions in preschoolers' learning from educational video. *Infant and Child Development, 26*(4).

Richmond-Rakerd, L. S. (2013). Modern advances in genetic testing: Ethical challenges and training implications for current and future psychologists. *Ethics & Behavior, 23,* 31–43.

Richtel, M. (2010, November 21). Growing up digital, wired for distraction. *The New York Times,* pp. A1, A20.

Rideout, V., Foehr, U., & Roberts, D. (2010). *Generation M2: Media in the lives of 8-to-18-year-olds.* Menlo Park, CA: The Henry J. Kaiser Family Foundation.

Rideout, V., and Robb, M. B. (2018). *Social media, social life: Teens reveal their experiences.* San Francisco, CA: Common Sense Media.

Rideout, V., Vandewater, E., & Wartella, E. (2003). *Zero to Six: Electronic media in the lives of infants, toddlers, and preschoolers.* Menlo Park, CA: Kaiser Family Foundation.

Ridgway, V. (2018). Social work students' perceptions of ageing. *Practice: Social Work in Action.* doi: 10.1080/09503153.2018.1473356

Rieffe, C., Ketelaar, L., & Wiefferink, C. (2010). Assessing empathy in young children: Construction and validation of an Empathy Questionnaire (EmQue). *Personality and Individual Differences, 49,* 362–367.

Riesch, S., Anderson, L., Pridham, K., Lutz, K., & Becker, P. (2010). Furthering the understanding of parent-child relationships: A nursing scholarship review series. Part 5: Parent-adolescent and teen parent-child relationships. *Journal for Specialists in Pediatric Nursing, 15,* 182–201.

Riley, T. A. (2014). Boys are like puppies, girls aim to please: How teachers' gender stereotypes may influence student placement decisions and classroom teaching. *Alberta Journal of Educational Research, 60*(1), 1–21.

Rinaldi, C. (2002). Social conflict abilities of children identified as sociable, aggressive, and isolated: Developmental implications for children at-risk for impaired peer relations. *Developmental Disabilities Bulletin, 30,* 77–94.

Rippon, R., Isla, J., & Steptoe, A. (2015). Feeling old vs being old: Associations between self-perceived age and mortality. *JAMA Intern Medicine, 175,* 307–309.

Ritzen, E. M. (2003). Early puberty: What is normal and when is treatment indicated? *Hormone Research, 60*(Suppl. 3), 31–34.

Riyani, I., & Parker, L. (2018). Women exercising sexual agency in Indonesia. *Women's Studies International Forum, 69,* 92–99.

Rizzoli, R., Abraham, C., & Brandi, M. (2014). Nutrition and bone health: Turning knowledge and beliefs into healthy behaviour. *Current Medical Research and Opinion, 30,* 131–141.

Robb, M., Richert, R., & Wartella, E. (2009). Just a talking book? Word learning from watching baby videos. *British Journal of Developmental Psychology, 27,* 27–45.

Robbins, M. W. (1990, December 10). Sparing the child: How to intervene when you suspect abuse. *The New York Times Magazine,* pp. 42–53.

Robbins, R. (2016, September 6). The Federal Trade Commission will be sending out rebates to thousands of Lumosity customers misled by company ads. *Scientific American.* Accessed online, 12/11/17; https://www.scientificamerican.com/article/u-s-cracking-down-on-brain-training-games/

Roberts, B. W., Walton, K. E., & Viechtbauer, W. (2006). Patterns of mean-level change in personality traits across the life course: A meta-analysis of longitudinal studies. *Psychological Bulletin, 132,* 1–25.

Roberts, R. D., & Lipnevich, A. A. (2012). From general intelligence to multiple intelligences: Meanings, models, and measures. In K. R. Harris, S. Graham, T. Urdan, S. Graham, J. M. Royer, & M. Zeidner (Eds.), *APA educational psychology handbook, Vol. 2: Individual differences and cultural and contextual factors.* Washington, DC: American Psychological Association.

Roberts, R. E., Roberts, C., & Duong, H. (2009). Sleepless in adolescence: Prospective data on sleep deprivation, health and functioning. *Journal of Adolescence, 32,* 1045–1057.

Roberts, S. (2006, October 15). It's official: To be married means to be outnumbered. *The New York Times,* p. 22.

Roberts, S. (2009, November 24). Economy is forcing young adults back home in big numbers, survey finds. *The New York Times,* p. A16.

Robins, R. W., & Trzesniewski, K. H. (2005). Self-esteem development across the lifespan. *Current Directions in Psychological Science, 14,* 158–162.

Robinson, A. J., & Pascalis, O. (2005). Development of flexible visual recognition memory in human infants. *Developmental Science, 7,* 527–533.

Robinson, O. C., Demetre, J. D., & Litman, J. A. (2017). Adult life stage and crisis as predictors of curiosity and authenticity: Testing inferences from Erikson's lifespan theory. *International Journal of Behavioral Development, 41,* 426–431.

Rocha-Ferreira, E., & Hristova, M. (2016). Plasticity in the neonatal brain following hypoxic-ischaemic injury. *Neural Plasticity.* Accessed online, 10/29/17; https://www.hindawi.com/journals/np/2016/4901014/

Rochat, P. (2004). Emerging co-awareness. In G. Bremner & A. Slater (Eds.), *Theories of infant development.* Malden, MA: Blackwell Publishers.

Rochat, P., Broesch, T., & Jayne, K. (2012). Social awareness and early self-recognition. *Consciousness and Cognition: An International Journal, 21,* 1491–1497.

Rocheleau, M. (2016, March 28). On campus, women outnumber men more than ever. *Boston Globe.* Accessed online, 11/16/17; https://www.bostonglobe.com/metro/2016/03/28/look-how-women-outnumber-men-college-campusesnationwide/YROqwfCPSlKPtSMAzpWloK/story.html#comments

Rodkey, E. N., & Riddell, R. P. (2013). The infancy of infant pain research: The experimental origins of infant pain denial. *Journal of Pain, 14,* 338–350.

Rodkin, P. C., & Ryan, A. M. (2012). Child and adolescent peer relations in educational context. In K. R. Harris, S. Graham, T. Urdan, S. Graham, J. M. Royer, & M. Zeidner (Eds.), *APA educational psychology handbook, Vol. 2: Individual differences and cultural and contextual factors.* Washington, DC: American Psychological Association.

Rodnitzky, R. L. (2012). Upcoming treatments in Parkinson's disease, including gene therapy. *Parkinsonism & Related Disorders, 18*(Suppl. 1), S37–S40.

Roecke, C., & Cherry, K. (2002). Death at the end of the 20th century: Individual processes and developmental tasks in old age. *International Journal of Aging & Human Development, 54,* 315–333.

Roelofs, J., Meesters, C., Ter Huurne, M., Bamelis, L., & Muris, P. (2006, June). On the links between attachment style, parental rearing behaviors, and internalizing and externalizing problems in non-clinical children. *Journal of Child and Family Studies, 15,* 331–344.

Roffwarg, H. P., Muzio, J. N., & Dement, W. C. (1966). Ontogenic development of the human sleep-dream cycle. *Science, 152,* 604–619.

Rogan, J. (2007). How much curriculum change is appropriate? Defining a zone of feasible innovation. *Science Education, 91,* 439–460.

Rogers, C. R. (1971). A theory of personality. In S. Maddi (Ed.), *Perspectives on personality.* Boston, MA: Little, Brown.

Rogers, K. (2018). Nine bizarre myths about pregnancy. Britannica. Accessed online, 10/2/18; https://www.britannica.com/list/9-bizarre-myths-about-pregnancy

Rogers, S. L., & Blissett, J. (2017). Breastfeeding duration and its relation to weight gain, eating behaviours and positive maternal feeding practices in infancy. *Appetite, 108,* 399–406.

Roggeveen, A. B., Prime, D. J., & Ward, L. M. (2007). Lateralized readiness potentials reveal motor slowing in the aging brain. *Journals of Gerontology: Series B: Psychological Science and Social Science, 62,* P78–P84.

Rohleder, N. (2012). Acute and chronic stress induced changes in sensitivity of peripheral inflammatory pathways to the signals of multiple stress systems-2011 Curt Richter Award Winner. *Psychoneuroendocrinology, 37,* 307–316.

Rolle, L., Giardina, G., Caldarera, A. M., Gerino, E., & Brustia, P. (2018). When intimate partner violence meets same sex couples: A review of same sex intimate partner violence. *Frontiers in Psychology, 9,* 1506.

Rolls, E. (2000). Memory systems in the brain. *Annual Review of Psychology, 51,* 599–630.

Romero, S. T., Coulson, C. C., & Galvin, S. L. (2012). Cesarean delivery on maternal request: A western North Carolina perspective. *Maternal and Child Health Journal, 16,* 725–734.

Ron, P. (2006). Care giving offspring to aging parents: How it affects their marital relations, parenthood, and mental health. *Illness, Crisis, & Loss, 14,* 1–21.

Ron, P. (2014). Attitudes towards filial responsibility in a traditional vs modern culture: A comparison between three generations of Arabs in the Israeli society. *Gerontechnology, 13,* 31–38.

Roos, S. (2013). The Kubler-Ross Model: An esteemed relic. *Gestalt Review, 17*(3), 312–315.

Ropars, S., Tessier, R., Charpak, N., & Uriza, L. F. (2018). The long-term effects of the Kangaroo Mother Care intervention on cognitive functioning: Results from a longitudinal study. *Developmental Neuropsychology, 43*(1), 82–91.

Rosburg, T., Weigl, M., & Sörös, P. (2014). Habituation in the absence of a response decrease? *Clinical Neurophysiology, 125,* 210–211.

Rose, A. J., & Asher, S. R. (1999). Children's goals and strategies in response to conflicts within a friendship. *Developmental Psychology, 35,* 69–79.

Rose, C. A., Richman, D. M., Fettig, K., Hayner, A., Slavin, C., & Preast, J. L. (2016). Peer reactions to early childhood aggression in a preschool setting: Defenders, encouragers, or neutral bystander. *Developmental Neurorehabilitation, 19,* 246–254.

Rose, R. J., Viken, R. J., Dick, D. M., Bates, J. E., Pulkkinen, L., & Kaprio, J. (2003). It does take a village: Nonfamilial environments and children's behavior. *Psychological Science, 14,* 273–278.

Rose, S. (2008, January 21). Drugging unruly children is a method of social control. *Nature, 451,* 521.

Rose, S. A., Feldman, J. F., & Jankowski, J. J. (2009). Information processing in toddlers: Continuity from infancy and persistence of preterm deficits. *Intelligence, 37,* 311–320.

Rosenblatt, P. C. (2015). Death and bereavement in later adulthood: Cultural beliefs, behaviors,

and emotions. In L.A. Jensen (Ed.), *The Oxford handbook of human development and culture: An interdisciplinary perspective* (pp. 697–709). New York: Oxford University Press.

Ross, K. R., Storfer-Isser, A., Hart, M. A., Kibler, A. V., Rueschman, M., Rosen, C. L., & Redline, S. (2012). Sleep-disordered breathing is associated with asthma severity in children. *Journal of Pediatrics, 160,* 736–742.

Rossi, S., Telkemeyer, S., Wartenburger, I., & Obrig, H. (2012). Shedding light on words and sentences: Near-infrared spectroscopy in language research. *Brain and Language, 121,* 152–163.

Rössler, W., Hengartner, M. P., Ajdacic-Gross, V., & Angst, J. (2015). Predictors of burnout: Results from a prospective community study. *European Archives of Psychiatry and Clinical Neuroscience, 265,* 19–25.

Rote, W. M., Smetana, J. G., Campione-Barr, N., Villalobos, M., & Tasopoulos-Chan, M. (2012). Associations between observed mother-adolescent interactions and adolescent information management. *Journal of Research on Adolescence, 22,* 206–214.

Roth, M. S. (2016). Psychoanalysis and history. *Psychoanalytic Psychology, 33*(Suppl 1), S19–S33.

Rothbart, M. (2007). Temperament, development, and personality. *Current Directions in Psychological Science, 16,* 207–212.

Rothbaum, F., Weisz, J., Pott, M., Miyake, K., & Morelli, G. (2000). Attachment and culture: Security in the United States and Japan. *American Psychologist, 55,* 1093–1104.

Rothenberger, A., & Rothenberger, L. G. (2013). Psychopharmacological treatment in children: Always keeping an eye on adherence and ethics. *European Child & Adolescent Psychiatry, 22,* 453–455.

Rotigel, J. V. (2003). Understanding the young gifted child: Guidelines for parents, families, and educators. *Early Childhood Education Journal, 30,* 209–214.

Rouse, M. L., Fishbein, L. B., Minshawi, N. F., & Fodstad, J. C. (2017). Historical development of toilet training. In J. L. Matson (Ed.), *Clinical guide to toilet training children* (pp. 1–18). Cham, Switzerland: Springer International Publishing.

Rousseau, P. V., Matton, F., Lecuyer, R., & Lahaye, W. (2017). The Moro reaction: More than a reflex, a ritualized behavior of nonverbal communication. *Infant Behavior & Development, 46,* 169–177.

Roussotte, F. F., Gutman, B. A., Madsen, S. K., Colby, J. B., & Thompson, P. M. (2014). Combined effects of Alzheimer risk variants in the CLU and ApoE genes on ventricular expansion patterns in the elderly. *Journal of Neuroscience, 34,* 6537–6545.

Rovee-Collier, C. (1999). The development of infant memory. *Current Directions in Psychological Science, 8,* 80–85.

Rowe-Finkbeiner, K., Martin, R., Abrams, B., Zuccaro, A., & Dardari, J. (2016). Why paid family and medical leave matters for the future of America's families, businesses and economy. *Maternal and Child Health Journal, 20*(Suppl 1), 8–12.

Rowley, S., Burchinal, M., Roberts, J., & Zeisel, S. (2008). Racial identity, social context, and race-related social cognition in African Americans during middle childhood. *Developmental Psychology, 44,* 1537–1546.

Roy, A. L., & Raver, C. C. (2014). Are all risks equal? Early experiences of poverty-related risk and children's functioning. *Journal of Family Psychology, 28,* 391–400.

Rozalski, M., Stewart, A., & Miller, J. (2010). How to determine the least restrictive environment for students with disabilities. *Exceptionality, 18,* 151–163.

Rozance, P. J., & Rosenberg, A. A. (2012). The neonate. In S. G. Gabbe, J. R. Niebyl, J. L. Simpson, et al. (Eds.), *Obstetrics: Normal and problem pregnancies* (6th ed.). Philadelphia, PA: Elsevier Saunders.

Rubin, D. C. (1986). *Autobiographical memory.* Cambridge, UK: Cambridge University Press.

Rubin, D. C. (2000). Autobiographical memory and aging. In C. D. Park & N. Schwarz et al.

(Eds.), *Cognitive aging: A primer.* Philadelphia, PA: Psychology Press/Taylor & Francis.

Rubin, K. H., & Chung, O. B. (Eds.). (2006). *Parenting beliefs, behaviors, and parent-child relations: A cross-cultural perspective.* New York, NY: Psychology Press.

Ruble, D. N., Taylor, L. J., Cyphers, L., Greulich, F. K., Lurye, L. E., & Shrout, P. E. (2007). The role of gender constancy in early gender development. *Child Development, 78,* 1121–1136.

Rudd, L. C., Cain, D. W., & Saxon, T. F. (2008). Does improving joint attention in low-quality childcare enhance language development? *Early Child Development and Care, 178,* 315–338.

Rudman, L. A., & Fetterolf, J. C. (2014). How accurate are metaperceptions of sexism? Evidence for the illusion of antagonism between hostile and benevolent sexism. *Group Processes & Intergroup Relations, 17,* 275–285.

Ruff, H. A. (1989). The infant's use of visual and haptic information in the perception and recognition of objects. *Canadian Journal of Psychology, 43,* 302–319.

Ruffman, T. (2014). To belief or not belief: Children's theory of mind. *Developmental Review, 34,* 265–293.

Ruffman, T., Lorimer, B., & Scarf, D. (2017). Do infants really experience emotional contagion? *Child Development Perspectives.* Accessed online, 11/13/17; doi:10.1111/cdep.12244/full

Ruiz-Casares, M., & Heymann, J. (2009). Children home alone unsupervised: Modeling parental decisions and associated factors in Botswana, Mexico, and Vietnam. *Child Abuse & Neglect, 33*(5), 312–323.

Russ, S. W. (2014). Pretend play and creativity: An overview. In *Pretend play in childhood: Foundation of adult creativity.* Washington, DC: American Psychological Association.

Russell, J. (2017). 'Everything has to die one day.' Children's explorations of the meanings of death in human-animal-nature relationships. *Environmental Education Research, 23*(1), 75–90.

Russell, S. T., & Consolacion, T. (2003). Adolescent romance and emotional health in the United States: Beyond binaries. *Journal of Clinical Child & Adolescent Psychology, 32,* 499–508.

Russell, S. T., Crockett, L. J., & Chao, R. K. (2010). Conclusions: The role of Asian American culture in parenting and parent-adolescent relationships. In S. T. Russell, L. J. Crockett, & R. K. Chao (Eds.), *Asian American parenting and parent–adolescent relationships* (pp. 117–128). New York, NY: Springer Science + Business Media.

Rust, J., Golombok, S., Hines, M., Johnston, K., & Golding, J., & ALSPAC Study Team. (2000). The role of brothers and sisters in the gender development of preschool children. *Journal of Experimental Child Psychology, 77,* 292–303.

Rutter, M. (2003). Commentary: Causal processes leading to antisocial behavior. *Developmental Psychology, 39,* 372–378.

Rutter, M. (2006). *Genes and behavior: Nature-nurture interplay explained.* New York, NY: Blackwell Publishing.

Ruzek, E., Burchinal, M., Farkas, G., & Duncan, G. J. (2014). The quality of toddler child care and cognitive skills at 24 months: Propensity score analysis results from the ECLS-B. *Early Childhood Research Quarterly, 29,* 12–21.

Ryan, B. P. (2001). *Programmed therapy for stuttering in children and adults* (2nd ed.). Springfield, IL: Charles C. Thomas.

Ryding, E. L., Lukasse, M., Van Parys, A., Wangel, A., Karro, H., Kristjansdottir, H., & ... Schei, B. (2015). Fear of childbirth and risk of cesarean delivery: A cohort study in six European countries. *Birth: Issues in Perinatal Care, 42,* 48–55.

Saad, L. (2011, June 30). *Americans' preference for smaller families edges higher.* Princeton, NJ: Gallup Poll.

Sabbagh, M. (2009). Drug development for Alzheimer's disease: Where are we now and where are we headed? *American Journal of Geriatric Pharmacotherapy (AJGP), 7,* 167–185.

Sadeghi, N., Prastawa, M., Fletcher, P., Wolff, J., Gilmore, J. H., & Gerig, G. (2013). Regional characterization of longitudinal DT-MRI to study white matter maturation of the early developing brain. *NeuroImage, 68*, 236–247.

Sadker, D., & Silber, E. S. (Eds.). (2007). *Gender in the classroom: Foundations, skills, methods, and strategies across the curriculum.* Mahwah, NJ: Lawrence Erlbaum Associates Publishers.

Sadker, M., & Sadker, D. (1994). *Failing at fairness: How America's schools cheat girls.* New York, NY: Scribner's.

Saiegh-Haddad, E. (2007). Linguistic constraints on children's ability to isolate phonemes in Arabic. *Applied Psycholinguistics, 28*, 607–625.

Salahuddin, M., Mandell, D. J., Lakey, D. L., Eppes, C. S., & Patel, D. A. (2018). Maternal risk factor index and cesarean delivery among women with nulliparous, term, singleton, vertex deliveries, Texas, 2015. *Birth: Issues in Perinatal Care.* doi:10.1111/birt.12392

Salley, B., Miller, A., & Bell, M. (2013). Associations between temperament and social responsiveness in young children. *Infant and Child Development, 22*, 270–288.

Sallis, J., & Glanz, K. (2006, March). The role of built environments in physical activity, eating, and obesity in childhood. *The Future of Children, 16*, 89–108.

Salthouse, T. A. (1994). The aging of working memory. *Neuropsychology, 8*, 535–543.

Salthouse, T. A. (2006). Mental exercise and mental aging: Evaluating the validity of the "Use it or lose it" hypothesis. *Perspectives on Psychological Science, 1*, 68–87.

Salthouse, T. A. (2009). When does age-related cognitive decline begin? *Neurobiology of Aging, 30*, 507–514.

Salthouse, T. A. (2010). *Major issues in cognitive aging.* New York, NY: Oxford University Press.

Salthouse, T. A. (2012a). Consequences of age-related cognitive declines. *Annual Review of Psychology, 63*, 201–226.

Salthouse, T. A. (2012b). Does the level at which cognitive change occurs change with age? *Psychological Science, 23*, 18–23.

Salthouse, T. A. (2014). Relations between running memory and fluid intelligence. *Intelligence, 43*, 1–7.

Salthouse, T. A. (2017). Why is cognitive change more negative with increased age? *Neuropsychology.* Accessed online, 12/11/17; http://psycnet.apa.org/record/2017-43357-001

Salthouse, T. A., Atkinson, T. M., & Berish, D. E. (2003). Executive functioning as a potential mediator of age-related cognitive decline in normal adults. *Journal of Experimental Psychology: General, 132*, 566–594.

Sammons, M. (2009). Writing a wrong: Factors influencing the overprescription of antidepressants to youth. *Professional Psychology: Research and Practice, 40*, 327–329.

Sánchez-Castañeda, C., Squitieri, F., Di Paola, M., Dayan, M., Petrollini, M., & Sabatini, U. (2015). The role of iron in gray matter degeneration in Huntington's disease: A magnetic resonance imaging study. *Human Brain Mapping, 36*, 50–66.

Sanchez-Garrido, M. A., & Tena-Sempere, M. (2013). Metabolic control of puberty: Roles of leptin and kisspeptins. *Hormones and Behavior, 64*, 187–194.

Sandall, J. (2014). The 30th International Confederation of Midwives Triennial Congress: Improving women's health globally. *Birth: Issues in Perinatal Care, 41*, 303–305.

Sanders, S., Ott, C., Kelber, S., & Noonan, P. (2008). The experience of high levels of grief in caregivers of persons with Alzheimer's disease and related dementia. *Death Studies, 32*, 495–523.

Sandis, E. (2000). The aging and their families: A cross-national review. In A. L. Comunian & U. P. Gielen (Eds.), *International perspectives on human development.* Lengerich, Germany: Pabst Science Publishers.

Sandoval, J., Scott, A., & Padilla, I. (2009). Crisis counseling: An overview. *Psychology in the Schools, 46*, 246–256.

Sandrini, M., Manenti, R., Brambilla, M., Cobelli, C., Cohen, L. G., & Cotelli, M. (2016). Older adults get episodic memory boosting from noninvasive stimulation of prefrontal cortex during learning. *Neurobiology of Aging, 39*, 210–216.

Sang, B., Miao, X., & Deng, C. (2002). The development of gifted and nongifted young children in metamemory knowledge. *Psychological Science (China), 25*, 406–409, 424.

Sangree, W. H. (1989). Age and power: Life-course trajectories and age structuring of power relations in East and West Africa. In D. I. Kertzer & K. W. Schaie (Eds.), *Age structuring in comparative perspective.* Hillsdale, NJ: Lawrence Erlbaum.

Santos, R. X., Correia, S. C., Cardoso, S., Carvalho, C., Santos, M. S., & Moreira, P. I. (2011). Effects of rapamycin and TOR on aging and memory: Implications for Alzheimer's disease. *Journal of Neurochemistry, 117*, 927–936.

Santtila, P., Sandnabba, N., Harlaar, N., Varjonen, M., Alanko, K., & von der Pahlen, B. (2008, January). Potential for homosexual response is prevalent and genetic. *Biological Psychology, 77*(1), 102–105.

Sapyla, J. J., & March, J. S. (2012). Integrating medical and psychological therapies in child mental health: An evidence-based medicine approach. In M. Garralda & J. Raynaud (Eds.), *Brain, mind, and developmental psychopathology in childhood.* Lanham, MD: Jason Aronson.

Sargent-Cox, K. A., Anstey, K. J., & Luszcz, M. A. (2012). The relationship between change in self-perceptions of aging and physical functioning in older adults. *Psychology and Aging.* doi:10.1037/a0027578

Sasisekaran, J. (2014). Exploring the link between stuttering and phonology: A review and implications for treatment. *Seminars in Speech and Language, 35*, 95–113.

Saunders, J., Davis, L., & Williams, T. (2004). Gender differences in self-perceptions and academic outcomes: A study of African American high school students. *Journal of Youth & Adolescence, 33*, 81–90.

Sauvet, F., Gomez-Merino, D., Dorey, R., Ciret, S., Gallopin, T., Drogou, C., Arnal, P. J., Chennaoui, M. (2018). Lengthening of the photoperiod influences sleep characteristics before and during total sleep deprivation in rat. *Journal of Sleep Research.* doi:10.1111/jsr.12709

Savin-Williams, R. C. (2003). Lesbian, gay, and bisexual youths' relationships with their parents. In L. Garnets & D. Kimmel (Eds.), *Psychological perspectives on lesbian, gay, and bisexual experiences* (2nd ed.). New York, NY: Columbia University Press.

Savin-Williams, R. C. (2006). *The new gay teenager.* Cambridge, MA: Harvard University Press.

Savin-Williams, R. C. (2016). *Becoming who I am: Young men on being gay.* Cambridge, MA: Harvard University Press.

Sawatzky, J., & Naimark, B. (2002). Physical activity and cardiovascular health in aging women: A health-promotion perspective. *Journal of Aging & Physical Activity, 10*, 396–412.

Sawicka, M. (2016). Searching for a narrative of loss. Interactional ordering of ambiguous grief. *Symbolic Interaction.* Accessed online, 10/24/17; http://onlinelibrary.wiley.com/doi/10.1002/symb.270/full

Sawyer, J. (2017). I think I can: Preschoolers' private speech and motivation in playful versus non-playful contexts. *Early Childhood Research Quarterly, 38*, 84–96.

Sawyer, R. (2012). *Explaining creativity: The science of human innovation* (2nd ed.). New York, NY: Oxford University Press.

Sayal, K., Heron, J., Maughan, B., Rowe, R., & Ramchandani, P. (2014). Infant temperament and childhood psychiatric disorder: Longitudinal study. *Child: Care, Health And Development, 40*, 292–297.

Scarborough, P., Nnoaham, K. E., Clarke, D., Capewell, S., & Rayner, M. (2012). Modelling the impact of a healthy diet on cardiovascular disease and cancer mortality. *Journal of Epidemiology and Community Health, 66*, 420–426.

Scarr, S. (1998). American child care today. *American Psychologist, 53*, 95–108.

Schaan, V. K., & Vogele, C. (2016). Resilience and rejection sensitivity mediate long-term outcomes of parental divorce. *European Child & Adolescent Psychiatry, 25*, 1267–1269.

Schachner, D., Shaver, P., & Gillath, O. (2008). Attachment style and long-term singlehood. *Personal Relationships, 15*, 479–491.

Schaefer, M. K., & Salafia, E. B. (2014). The connection of teasing by parents, siblings, and peers with girls' body dissatisfaction and boys' drive for muscularity: The role of social comparison as a mediator. *Eating Behaviors, 15*, 599–608.

Schaeffer, C., Petras, H., & Ialongo, N. (2003). Modeling growth in boys' aggressive behavior across elementary school: Links to later criminal involvement, conduct disorder, and antisocial personality disorder. *Developmental Psychology, 39*, 1020–1035.

Schafer, D. P., & Stevens, B. (2013). Phagocytic glial cells: Sculpting synaptic circuits in the developing nervous system. *Current Opinion in Neurobiology, 23*, 1034–1040.

Schaie, K. W. (1977–1978). Toward a stage of adult theory of adult cognitive development. *Journal of Aging and Human Development, 8*, 129–138.

Schaie, K. W. (1985). *Longitudinal studies of adult psychological development.* New York, NY: Guilford Press.

Schaie, K. W. (1993). The Seattle longitudinal studies of adult intelligence. *Current Directions in Psychological Science, 2*, 171–175.

Schaie, K. W. (1994). The course of adult intellectual development. *American Psychologist, 49*, 304–313.

Schaie, K. W. (2016). The longitudinal study of adult cognitive development. In R. J. Sternberg, S. T. Fiske, & D. J. Foss (Eds.), *Scientists making a difference: One hundred eminent behavioral and brain scientists talk about their most important contributions.* New York: Cambridge University Press.

Schaie, K. W., & Willis, S. I. (1993). Age difference patterns of psychometric intelligence in adulthood: Generalizability within and across ability domains. *Psychology and Aging, 8*, 44–55.

Schaie, K. W., & Willis, S. L. (2011). *Handbook of the psychology of aging.* (7th ed.) San Diego, CA: Elsevier Academic Press.

Schaie, K. W., & Zanjani, F. A. K. (2006). Intellectual development across adulthood. In C. Hoare (Ed.), *Handbook of adult development and learning.* New York, NY: Oxford University Press.

Schaie, W. K., Willis, S. L., & Pennak, S. (2005). An historical framework for cohort differences in intelligence. *Research in Human Development, 2*, 43–67.

Scharf, M. (2014). Children's social competence within close friendship: The role of self-perception and attachment orientations. *School Psychology International, 35*, 206–220.

Schatz, M. (1994). *A toddler's life.* New York, NY: Oxford University Press.

Schechter, D., & Willheim, E. (2009). Disturbances of attachment and parental psychopathology in early childhood. *Child and Adolescent Psychiatric Clinics of North America, 18*, 665–686.

Schecklmann, M., Pfannstiel, C., Fallgatter, A. J., Warnke, A., Gerlach, M., & Romanos, M. (2012). Olfaction in child and adolescent anorexia nervosa. *Journal of Neural Transmission, 119*, 721–728.

Schecter, T., Finkelstein, Y., & Koren, G. (2005). Pregnant "DES daughters" and their offspring. *Canadian Family Physician, 51*, 493–494.

Scheibner, G., & Leathem, J. (2012). Memory control beliefs and everyday forgetfulness in adulthood: The effects of selection, optimization, and compensation strategies. *Aging, Neuropsychology, and Cognition, 19*, 362–379.

Schemo, D. J. (2001, December 5). U.S. students prove middling on 32-nation test. *The New York Times*, p. A21.

Schemo, D. J. (2004, March 2). Schools, facing tight budgets, leave gifted programs behind. *The New York Times*, pp. A1, A18.

Scherf, K. S., Sweeney, J. A., & Luna, B. (2006). Brain basis of developmental change in visuospatial working memory. *Journal of Cognitive Neuroscience, 18*, 1045–1058.

Schieman, S., McBrier, D. B., & van Gundy, K. (2003). Home-to-work conflict, work qualities, and emotional distress. *Sociological Forum, 18*, 137–164.

Schildmann, J., & Schildmann, E. (2013). There is more to end-life practices than euthanasia. *Lancet, 381*, 202.

Schiller, J. S., & Bernadel, L. (2004). Summary health statistics for the U.S. population: National Health Interview Survey, 2002. *Vital Health Statistics, 10*, 1–110.

Schlosser, F., Zinni, D., & Armstrong-Stassen, M. (2012). Intention to unretire: HR and the boomerang effect. *The Career Development International, 17*, 149–167.

Schmiedek, F. (2017). Development of cognition and intelligence. In J. Specht (Ed.), *Personality development across the lifespan*. San Diego, CA: Elsevier Academic Press.

Schmitt, M., Kliegel, M., & Shapiro, A. (2007). Marital interaction in middle and old age: A predictor of marital satisfaction? *International Journal of Aging & Human Development, 65*, 283–300.

Shneidman, E. (2007). Criteria for a good death. *Suicide and Life-Threatening Behavior, 37*, 245–247.

Schnitzer, P. G. (2006). Prevention of unintentional childhood injuries. *American Family Physician, 11*, 1864–1869.

Schoenfeld, E. A., Loving, T. J., Pope, M. T., Huston, T. L., & Štulhofer, A. (2017). Does sex really matter? Examining the connections between spouses' nonsexual behaviors, sexual frequency, sexual satisfaction, and marital satisfaction. *Archives of Sexual Behavior, 46*, 489–501.

Schoklitsch, A., & Baumann, U. (2012). Generativity and aging: A promising future research topic? *Journal of Aging Studies, 26*, 262–272.

Schonert-Reichl, K. A., Smith, V., Zaidman-Zait, A., & Hertzman, C. (2012). Promoting children's prosocial behaviors in school: Impact of the "Roots of Empathy" program on the social and emotional competence of school-aged children. *School Mental Health, 4*, 1–21.

Schoppe-Sullivan, S., Diener, M., Mangelsdorf, S., Brown, G., McHale, J., & Frosch, C. (2006, July). Attachment and sensitivity in family context: The roles of parent and infant gender. *Infant and Child Development, 15*, 367–385.

Schoppe-Sullivan, S., Mangelsdorf, S., Brown, G., & Sokolowski, M. (2007, February). Goodness-of-fit in family context: Infant temperament, marital quality, and early coparenting behavior. *Infant Behavior & Development, 30*, 82–96.

Schulenberg, J. E., Johnston, L. D., O'Malley P. M., Bachman, J. G., Miech, R. A., & Patrick, M. E. (2017). Monitoring the future: National survey results on drug use 1975-2017. National Institute on Drug Abuse, National Institutes of Health. Accessed online, 3/25/19; http://www.monitoringthefuture. org//pubs/monographs/mtf-vol2_2017.pdf

Schultz, R., & Curnow, C. (1988). Peak performance and age among superathletes: Track and field, swimming, baseball, tennis, and golf. *Journal of Gerontology, 43*, P113–P120.

Schulz, K., Rudolph, A., Tscharaktschiew, N., & Rudolph, U. (2013). Daniel has fallen into a muddy puddle—Schadenfreude or sympathy? *British Journal of Developmental Psychology, 31*, 363–378.

Schutt, R. K. (2001). *Investigating the social world: The process and practice of research*. Thousand Oaks, CA: Sage Publications.

Schvey, N. A., Eddy, K. T., & Tanofsky-Kraff, M. (2016). Diagnosis of feeding and eating disorders in children and adolescents. In B. T. Walsh, E. Attia, D. R. Glasofer, & R. Sysko (Eds.), *Handbook of assessment and treatment of eating disorders*. Arlington, VA: American Psychiatric Publishing, Inc.

Schwartz, I. M. (1999). Sexual activity prior to coital interaction: A comparison between males and females. *Archives of Sexual Behavior, 28*, 63–69.

Schwartz, P., Maynard, A., & Uzelac, S. (2008). Adolescent egocentrism: A contemporary view. *Adolescence, 43*, 441–448.

Schwarz, A. (2012, Oct 9). Attention disorder or not, pills to help in school. *The New York Times*, A1.

Schwarz, J. M., & Bilbo, S. D. (2014). Microglia and neurodevelopment: Programming of cognition throughout the lifespan. In A. W. Kusnecov & H. Anisman (Eds.), *The Wiley-Blackwell handbook of psychoneuroimmunology*. New York, NY: Wiley-Blackwell.

Schwarz, T. F., Huang, L., Medina, D., Valencia, A., Lin, T., Behre, U., &... Descamps, D. (2012). Four-year follow-up of the immunogenicity and safety of the HPV-16/18 AS04-adjuvanted vaccine when administered to adolescent girls aged 10-14 years. *Journal of Adolescent Health, 50*, 187–194.

Schwenkhagen, A. (2007). Hormonal changes in menopause and implications on sexual health. *Journal of Sexual Medicine, 4*(Suppl. 3), 220–226.

Sciaraffa, M. A., Zeanah, P. D., & Zeanah, C. H. (2017). Understanding and promoting resilience in the context of adverse childhood experiences. *Early Childhood Education Journal*. doi:10.1007/s10643-017-0869-3

Sciberras, E., Efron, D., Schilpzand, E. J., Anderson, V., Jongeling, B., Hazell, P., &... Nicholson, J. M. (2013). The Children's Attention Project: A community-based longitudinal study of children with ADHD and non-ADHD controls. *BMC Psychiatry, 18*, 13–18

Scientific American. (2002, March 1). Scars that won't heal: The neurobiology of child abuse. *Scientific American*, p. 71.

Scott, R. M., & Baillargeon, R (2013). Do infants really expect others to act efficiently? A critical test of the rationality principle. *Psychological Science, 24*, 466–474.

Seaton, S. E., King, S., Manktelow, B. N., Draper, E. S., & Field, D. J. (2012). Babies born at the threshold of viability: Changes in survival and workload over 20 years. *Archives of Disable Children and Neonatal Education, 9*, 22–35.

Seçkin, G. (2013). Satisfaction with health status among cyber patients: Testing a mediation model of electronic coping support. *Behaviour & Information Technology, 32*, 91–101.

Sedgh, G., Finer, L. B., Bankole, A., Eilers, M. A., & Singh, S. (2015). Adolescent pregnancy, birth, and abortion rates across countries: Levels and recent trends. *Journal of Adolescent Health, 56*(2), 223–230.

Sedgh, G., Singh, S., Shah, I. H., Ahman, E., Henshaw, S. K., & Kankole, A. (2012). Induced abortion: Incidence and trends worldwide from 1995 to 2008. *Lancet, 379*, 625–632.

Sedlak, A. J., Mettenburg, J., Basena, M., Petta, I., McPherson, K., Greene, A., & Li, S. (2010). Fourth national incidence study of child abuse and neglect (NIS-4): Report to congress. Washington, DC: U.S. Department of Health and Human Services, Administration for Children and Families.

Seedat, S. (2014). Controversies in the use of antidepressants in children and adolescents: A decade since the storm and where do we stand now? *Journal of Child and Adolescent Mental Health, 26*, iii.

Segal, J., & Gollan, T. H. (2018). What's left for balanced bilinguals? Language proficiency and item familiarity affect left-hemisphere specialization in metaphor processing. *Neuropsychology*. doi:10.1037/neu0000467

Segal, N. L. (2000). Virtual twins: New findings on within-family environmental influences on intelligence. *Journal of Educational Psychology, 92*, 188–194.

Segal, N. L., Cortez, F. A., Zettel-Watson, L., Cherry, B. J., Mechanic, M., Munson, J. E., &... Reed, B. (2015). Genetic and experiential influences on behavior: Twins reunited at seventy-eight years. *Personality and Individual Differences, 73*, 110–117.

Segall, M. H., Dasen, P. R., Berry, J. W., & Poortinga, Y. H. (1990). *Human behavior in global perspective*. Boston, MA: Allyn & Bacon.

Seibert, A., & Kerns, K. (2009). Attachment figures in middle childhood. *International Journal of Behavioral Development, 33*, 347–355.

Seidman, S. (2003). The aging male: Androgens, erectile dysfunction, and depression. *Journal of Clinical Psychiatry, 64*, 31–37.

Seijo, D., Fariña, F., Corras, T., Novo, M., & Arce, R. (2016). Estimating the epidemiology and quantifying the damages of parental separation in children and adolescents. *Frontiers in Psychology, 7*.

Selig, J., & Lopez, A. (2016). Social psychology. In R. Bargdill & R. Broomé (Eds.), *Humanistic contributions for psychology 101: Growth, choice, and responsibility*. New York, NY: University Professors Press.

Seligman, M. E. P. (2007). Coaching and positive psychology. *Australian Psychologist, 42*, 266–267.

Semerci, Ç. (2006). The opinions of medicine faculty students regarding cheating in relation to Kohlberg's moral development concept. *Social Behavior and Personality, 34*, 41–50.

Sengoelge, M., Hasselberg, M., Ormandy, D., & Laflamme, L. (2014). Housing, income inequality and child injury mortality in Europe: A cross-sectional study. *Child: Care, Health and Development, 40*(2), 283–291.

Senín-Calderon, C., Rodriguez-Testal, J. F., Perona-Garcelan, S., & Perpina, C. (2017). Body image and adolescence: A behavioral impairment model. *Psychiatry Research, 248*, 121–126.

Senju, A., Southgate, V., Snape, C., Leonard, M., & Csibra, G. (2011). Do 18 month olds really attribute mental states to others? A critical test. *Science, 331*, 477–480.

Senna, I., Addabbo, M., Bolognini, N., Longhi, E., Macchi Cassia, V., & Turati, C. (2017). Infants' visual recognition of pincer grip emerges between 9 and 12 months of age. *Infancy, 22*, 389–402.

Sentis, V., Nguyen, G., Soler, V., & Cassagne, M. (2016). Patients âgés et glaucome. Elderly patients and glaucoma. *NPG Neurologie-Psychiatrie-Gériatrie, 16*, 73–82.

Serbin, L., Poulin-Dubois, D., & Colburne, K. (2001). Gender stereotyping in infancy: Visual preferences for and knowledge of gender-stereotyped toys in the second year. *International Journal of Behavioral Development, 25*, 7–15.

Serrat, R., Villar, F., Pratt, M. W., & Stukas, A. A. (2017). On the quality of adjustment to retirement: The longitudinal role of personality traits and generativity. *Journal of Personality*. Accessed online, 12/12/17; https://www.ncbi.nlm.nih.gov/pubmed/28509366

Serretti, A., & Fabbri, C. (2013). Shared genetics among major psychiatric disorders. *Lancet, 381*, 1339–1341.

Servin, A., Nordenström, A., Larsson, A., & Bohlin, G. (2003). Prenatal androgens and gender-typed behavior: A study of girls with mild and severe forms of congenital adrenal hyperplasia. *Developmental Psychology, 39*, 440–450.

Setoh, P., Lee, K. J., Zhang, L., Qian, M. K., Quinn, P. C., Heyman, G. D., & Lee, K. (2017). Racial categorization predicts implicit racial bias in preschool children. *Child Development*. Accessed online, 11/13/17; https://www.ncbi.nlm.nih.gov/pubmed/28605007

Settersten, R. (2002). Social sources of meaning in later life. In R. Weiss & S. Bass (Eds.), *Challenges of the third age: Meaning and purpose in later life*. London, UK: Oxford University Press.

Sexton, M., Byrd, M., & von Kluge, S. (2010). Measuring resilience in women experiencing infertility using the CD-RISC: Examining infertility-related stress, general distress, and coping styles. *Journal of Psychiatric Research, 44,* 236–241.

Seyfarth, R. M., & Cheney, D. L. (2013). The evolution of concepts about agents. In M. R. Banaji & S. A. Gelman (Eds.), *Navigating the social world: What infants, children, and other species can teach us.* New York: Oxford University Press.

Seymour, J., Payne, S., Chapman, A., & Holloway, M. (2007). Hospice or home? Expectations of end-of-life care among white and Chinese older people in the UK. *Sociology of Health & Illness, 29,* 872–890.

Shah, R., Chauhan, N., Gupta, A. K., & Sen, M. S. (2016). Adolescent-parent conflict in the age of social media: Case reports from India. *Asian Journal of Psychiatry, 23,* 24–26.

Shamloul, R., & Ghanem, H. (2013). Erectile dysfunction. *Lancet, 381,* 153–165.

Shangguan, F., & Shi, J. (2009). Puberty timing and fluid intelligence: A study of correlations between testosterone and intelligence in 8- to 12-year-old Chinese boys. *Psychoneuroendocrinology, 34,* 983–988.

Shapiro, A. F., Gottman, J. M., & Carrè, S. (2000). The baby and the marriage: Identifying factors that buffer against decline in marital satisfaction after the first baby arrives. *Journal of Family Psychology, 14,* 124–130.

Shapiro, J., Aronson, J., & McGlone, M. S. (2016). Stereotype threat. In T. D. Nelson (Ed.), *Handbook of prejudice, stereotyping, and discrimination* (2nd ed.). New York, NY: Psychology Press.

Sharp, C., Beckstein, A., Limb, G., & Bullock, Z. (2015). Completing the circle of life: Death and grief among Native Americans. In J. Cacciatore & J. DeFrain (Eds.), *The world of bereavement: Cultural perspectives on death in families.* (pp. 221–239). Cham, Switzerland: Springer International Publishing.

Shaunessy, E., Suldo, S., Hardesty, R., & Shaffer, E. (2006, December). School functioning and psychological well-being of international baccalaureate and general education students: A preliminary examination. *Journal of Secondary Gifted Education, 17,* 76–89.

Shaver, P. R., Hazan, C., & Bradshaw, D. (1988). Love as attachment: The integration of three behavioral systems. In R. J. Sternberg & M. L. Barnes (Eds.), *The psychology of love.* New Haven, CT: Yale University Press.

Shaver, P. R., Mikulincer, M., Sahdra, B. K., & Gross, J. T. (2017). Attachment security as a foundation for kindness toward self and others. In K. W. Brown & M. R. Leary (Eds.), *The Oxford handbook of hypo-egoic phenomena.* (pp. 223–242). New York, NY: Oxford University Press.

Shaw, P., Eckstrand, K., Sharp, W., Blumenthal, J., Lerch, J. P., Greenstein, D., &... Rapport, J. L. (2007). Attention-deficit/hyperactivity disorder is characterized by a delay in cortical maturation. *Proceedings of the National Academy of Sciences of the United States of America, 104,* 19649–19654.

Shaywitz, S. (2004). *Overcoming dyslexia: A new and complete science-based program for reading problems at any level.* New York, NY: Vintage.

Shea, J. (2006, September). Cross-cultural comparison of women's midlife symptom-reporting: A China study. *Culture, Medicine and Psychiatry, 30,* 331–362.

Sheldon, K. M., Joiner, T. E., Jr., & Pettit, J. W. (2003). Reconciling humanistic ideals and scientific clinical practice. *Clinical Psychology, 10,* 302–315.

Shellenbarger, S. (2003, January 9). Yes, that weird day-care center could scar your child, researchers say. *Wall Street Journal,* p. D1.

Shen, Y., Hu, H., Taylor, B., Kan, H., & Xu, X. (2016). Early menarche and gestational diabetes mellitus at first live birth. *Maternal and Child Health Journal, 21,* 593–598.

Shenhav, S., Campos, B., & Goldberg, W. A. (2017). Dating out is intercultural: Experience and perceived parent disapproval by ethnicity and immigrant generation. *Journal of Social and Personal Relationships, 34,* 397–422.

Sheridan, T. (2013, April 11). 10 facts funeral directors won't tell you. Fox Business. Accessed online, 5/1/13; http://www.foxbusiness.com/personalfinance/2013/04/11/10-facts-funeral-directors-may-not-tell/

Shelton, A. L., Cornish, K., Clough, M., Gajamange, S., Kolbe, S., & Fielding, J. (2017). Disassociation between brain activation and executive function in Fragile X premutation females. *Human Brain Mapping, 38,* 1056–1067.

Shernoff, D., & Schmidt, J. (2008). Further evidence of an engagement-achievement paradox among U.S. high school students. *Journal of Youth and Adolescence, 37,* 564–580.

Shi, X., & Lu, X. (2007). Bilingual and bicultural development of Chinese American adolescents and young adults: A comparative study. *Howard Journal of Communications, 18,* 313–333.

Shimizu, M., & Pelham, B. (2004). The unconscious cost of good fortune: Implicit and explicit self-esteem, positive life events, and health. *Health Psychology, 23,* 101–105.

Shin, H. B., & Bruno, R. (2003). *Language use and English speaking ability: 2000.* Washington, DC: U.S. Census Bureau.

Shin, N., Kim, M., Goetz, S., & Vaughn, B. E. (2014). Dyadic analyses of preschool-aged children's friendships: Convergence and differences between friendship classifications from peer sociometric data and teacher's reports. *Social Development, 23*(1), 178–195.

Shiner, R., Masten, A., & Roberts, J. (2003). Childhood personality foreshadows adult personality and life outcomes two decades later. *Journal of Personality, 71,* 1145–1170.

Shohet, M. (2018). Two deaths and a funeral: Ritual inscriptions' affordances for mourning and moral personhood in Vietnam. *American Ethnologist, 45*(1), 60–73.

Shor, R. (2006, May). Physical punishment as perceived by parents in Russia: Implications for professionals involved in the care of children. *Early Child Development and Care, 176,* 429–439.

Shrout, P. E., & Rodgers, J. L. (2018). Psychology, science, and knowledge construction: Broadening perspectives from the replication crisis. *Annual Review of Psychology, 69,* 487–510.

Shuster, L., Rhodes, D., Gostout, B., Grossardt, B., & Rocca, W. (2010). Premature menopause or early menopause: Long-term health consequences. *Maturitas, 65,* 161–166.

Shute, R. H. (2018). Schools, mindfulness, and metacognition: A view from developmental psychology. *International Journal of School & Educational Psychology.* doi:10.1080/21683603.2018.1435322

Shutts, K. (2015). Young children's preferences: Gender, race, and social status. *Child Development Perspectives, 9,* 262–266.

Shweder, R. A. (2003). *Why do men barbecue? Recipes for cultural psychology.* Cambridge, MA: Harvard University Press.

Sieber, J. E. (2000). Planning research: Basic ethical decision-making. In B. D. Sales & S. Folkman (Eds.), *Ethics in research with human participants.* Washington, DC: American Psychological Association.

Siegal, M. (1997). *Knowing children: Experiments in conversation and cognition* (2nd ed.). Hove, UK: Psychology Press/Lawrence Erlbaum, Taylor & Francis.

Siegel, S., Dittrich, R., & Vollmann, J. (2008). Ethical opinions and personal attitudes of young adults conceived by in vitro fertilisation. *Journal of Medical Ethics, 34,* 236–240.

Siegler, R. S. (1994). Cognitive variability: A key to understanding cognitive development. *Current Directions in Psychological Science, 3,* 1–5.

Siegler, R. S. (1998). *Children's thinking* (3rd ed.). Upper Saddle River, NJ: Prentice Hall.

Siegler, R. S. (2007). Cognitive variability. *Developmental Science, 10,* 104–109.

Siegler, R. S. (2012). From theory to application and back: Following in the giant footsteps of David Klahr. In J. Shrager & S. Carver (Eds.), *The journey from child to scientist: Integrating cognitive development and the education sciences.* Washington, DC: American Psychological Association.

Siegler, R. S. (2016). Continuity and change in the field of cognitive development and in the perspectives of one cognitive developmentalist. *Child Development Perspectives, 10,* 128–133.

Siegler, R. S., & Lin, X. (2010). Self-explanations promote children's learning. In H. S. Waters, W. Schneider, & J. G. Borkowski (Eds.), *Metacognition, strategy use, and instruction.* New York, NY: Guilford Press.

Siegler, R. S., & Lortie-Forgues, H. (2014). An integrative theory of numerical development. *Child Development Perspectives, 8,* 144-150.

Sierpowska, J., Fernandez-Coello, A., Gomez-Andres, A., Camins, À., Castañer, S., Juncadella, M., &... Rodríguez-Fornells, A. (2018). Involvement of the middle frontal gyrus in language switching as revealed by electrical stimulation mapping and functional magnetic resonance imaging in bilingual brain tumor patients. *Cortex: A Journal Devoted to the Study of the Nervous System and Behavior, 99,* 78–92.

Sierra, F. (2006, June). Is (your cellular response to) stress killing you? *Journals of Gerontology: Series A: Biological Sciences and Medical Sciences, 61,* 557–561.

Signorella, M., & Frieze, I. (2008). Interrelations of gender schemas in children and adolescents: Attitudes, preferences, and self-perceptions. *Social Behavior and Personality, 36,* 941–954.

Silton, N. R., & Ferris, A. (2017). I want to know what love is: The ingredients of liking, attraction, dating, and successful marital relationships. In N. R. Silton (Ed.), *Family dynamics and romantic relationships in a changing society.* Hershey, PA: Information Science Reference/IGI Global.

Silventoinen, K., Iacono, W. G., Krueger, R., & McGue, M. (2012). Genetic and environmental contributions to the association between anthropometric measures and IQ: A study of Minnesota twins at age 11 and 17. *Behavior Genetics, 42,* 393–401.

Silverthorn, P., & Frick, P. J. (1999). Developmental pathways to antisocial behavior: The delayed-onset pathway in girls. *Developmental & Psychopathology, 11,* 101–126.

Sim, Z. L., & Xu, F. (2017). Infants preferentially approach and explore the unexpected. *British Journal of Developmental Psychology, 35,* 596–608.

Simkin, P. (2014). Preventing primary cesareans: Implications for laboring women, their partners, nurses, educators, and doulas. *Birth: Issues in Perinatal Care, 41,* 220–222.

Simmons, S. W., Cyna, A. M., Dennis, A. T., & Hughes, D. (2007). Combined spinal-epidural versus epidural analgesia in labour. *Cochrane Database and Systematic Review, 18,* CD003401.

Simonton, D. K. (2009). Varieties of (scientific) creativity: A hierarchical model of domain-specific disposition, development, and achievement. *Perspectives on Psychological Science, 4,* 441–452.

Simonton, D. K. (2017). Creative productivity across the life span. In J. A. Plucker (Ed.), *Creativity and innovation: Theory, research, and practice.* Waco, TX: Prufrock Press.

Simpson, E. (2017, March 3). America's 1st test-tube baby, a Norfolk native, set to meet world's 1st test-tube baby. *Virginian-Pilot.*

Simpson, J. A., Collins, W., Tran, S., & Haydon, K. (2007, February). Attachment and the experience and expression of emotions in romantic relationships: A developmental perspective. *Journal of Personality and Social Psychology, 92,* 355–367.

Simpson, J. A., & Rholes, W. S. (Eds.) (2015). *Attachment theory and research: New directions and emerging themes.* New York, NY: Guilford Press.

Simson, S. P., Wilson, L. B., & Harlow-Rosentraub, K. (2006). Civic engagement and lifelong learning institutes: Current status and future directions. In L. Wilson & S. P. Simson (Eds.), *Civic engagement and the baby boomer generation: Research, policy, and practice perspectives.* New York, NY: Haworth Press.

Sinclair, D. A., & Guarente, L. (2006). Unlocking the secrets of longevity genes. *Scientific American, 294,* 48–51, 54–57.

Singh, K., & Srivastava, S. K. (2014). Loneliness and quality of life among elderly people. *Journal of Psychosocial Research, 9,* 11–18.

Singh, S., & Darroch, J. E. (2000). Adolescent pregnancy and childbearing: Levels and trends in developed countries. *The Canadian Journal of Human Sexuality, 9,* 67–72.

Siniatchkin, M., Jonas, A., Baki, H., van Baalen, A., Gerber, W., & Stephani, U. (2010). Developmental changes of the contingent negative variation in migraine and healthy children. *Journal of Headache and Pain, 11,* 105–113.

Siu, A., & Shek, D. (2010). Social problem solving as a predictor of well-being in adolescents and young adults. *Social Indicators Research, 95,* 393–406.

Skinner, B. F. (1957). *Verbal behavior.* New York, NY: Appleton-Century-Crofts.

Skinner, B. F. (1975). The steep and thorny road to a science of behavior. *American Psychologist, 30,* 42–49.

Skinner, J. D., Ziegler, P., Pac, S., & Devaney, B. (2004). Meal and snack patterns of infants and toddlers. *Journal of the American Dietary Association, 104,* S65–S70.

Skinner, M. (2010). Metabolic disorders: Fathers' nutritional legacy. *Nature, 467,* 922–923.

Skledar, M., Nikolac, M., Dodig-Curkovic, K., Curkovic, M., Borovecki, F., & Pivac, N. (2012). Association between brain-derived neurotrophic factor Val66Met and obesity in children and adolescents. *Progress in Neuro-Psychopharmacology & Biological Psychiatry, 36,* 136–140.

Sklenarova, H., Schulz, A., Schuhmann, P., Osterheider, M., & Neutze, J. (2018). Online sexual solicitation by adults and peers—Results from a population-based German sample. *Child Abuse & Neglect, 76,* 225–236.

Skoog, T. (2013). Adolescent and adult implications of girls' pubertal timing. In A. Andershed (Ed.), *Girls at risk: Swedish longitudinal research on adjustment.* New York, NY: Springer Science + Business Media.

Skoog, T., & Özdemir, S. B. (2016). Explaining why early-maturing girls are more exposed to sexual harassment in early adolescence. *Journal of Early Adolescence, 36,* 490–509.

Skowronski, J., Walker, W., & Betz, A. (2003). Ordering our world: An examination of time in autobiographical memory. *Memory, 11,* 247–260.

Skrzypek, S., Maciejewska-Sobczak, B., & Stadnicka-Dmitriew, Z. (2014). *Siblings: Envy and rivalry, coexistence and concern.* London, UK: Karnac Books.

Slaughter, V., & Peterson, C. C. (2012). How conversational input shapes theory of mind development in infancy and early childhood. In M. Siegal, L. Surian (Eds.), *Access to language and cognitive development.* New York, NY: Oxford University Press.

Slavin, R. E. (2013). Cooperative learning and achievement: Theory and research. In W. M. Reynolds, G. E. Miller, I. B. Weiner (Eds.), *Handbook of psychology, Vol. 7: Educational psychology* (2nd ed.). Hoboken, NJ: John Wiley & Sons Inc.

Sleeboom-Faulkner, M. (2010). Reproductive technologies and the quality of offspring in Asia: Reproductive pioneering and moral pragmatism? *Culture, Health & Sexuality, 12,* 139–152.

Sloan, S., Stewart, M., & Dunne, L. (2010). The effect of breastfeeding and stimulation in the home on cognitive development in one-year-old infants. *Child Care in Practice, 16,* 101–110.

Sloane, S., Baillargeon, R., & Premack, D. (2012). Do infants have a sense of fairness? *Psychological Science, 23,* 196–207.

Slugocki, C., & Trainor, L. J. (2014). Cortical indices of sound localization mature monotonically in early infancy. *European Journal of Neuroscience, 40,* 3608–3619.

Slusser, E., Ditta, A., & Sarnecka, B. (2013). Connecting numbers to discrete quantification: A step in the child's construction of integer concepts. *Cognition, 129,* 31–41.

Smedley, A., & Smedley, B. D. (2005). Race as biology is fiction, racism as a social problem is real: Anthropological and historical perspectives on the social construction of race. *American Psychologist, 60,* 16–26.

Smetana, J. G. (2005). Adolescent-parent conflict: Resistance and subversion as developmental process. In L. Nucci (Ed.), *Conflict, contradiction, and contrarian elements in moral development and education.* Mahwah, NJ: Lawrence Erlbaum.

Smetana, J. G., Daddis, C., & Chuang, S. (2003). "Clean your room!" A longitudinal investigation of adolescent-parent conflict and conflict resolution in middle-class African American families. *Journal of Adolescent Research, 18,* 631–650.

Smiley, P. A., Tan, S. J., Goldstein, A., & Sweda, J. (2016). Mother emotion, child temperament, and young children's helpless responses to failure. *Social Development, 25,* 285–303.

Smith, A. R., Chein, J., & Steinberg, L. (2013). Impact of socio-emotional context, brain development, and pubertal maturation on adolescent risk-taking. *Hormones and Behavior, 64*(2), 323–332.

Smith, C., & Hung, L. (2012). The influence of Eastern philosophy on elder care by Chinese Americans: Attitudes toward long-term care. *Journal of Transcultural Nursing, 23,* 100–105.

Smith, C. G., & Weiss, A. (2017). Evolutionary aspects of personality development: Evidence from nonhuman animals. In J. Specht (Ed.), *Personality development across the lifespan.* San Diego, CA: Elsevier Academic Press.

Smith, J. M. (2012). Toward a better understanding of loneliness in community-dwelling older adults. *Journal of Psychology: Interdisciplinary and Applied, 146,* 293–311.

Smith, K. (2018). How culture and biology interact to shape language and the language faculty. *Topics in Cognitive Science.* doi:10.1111/tops.12377

Smith, N. A., & Trainor, L. J. (2008). Infant-directed speech is modulated by infant feedback. *Infancy, 13,* 410–420.

Smith, P. K., & Drew, L. M. (2002). Grandparenthood. In M. Bornstein (Ed.), *Handbook of parenting* (2nd ed). Mahwah, NJ: Lawrence Erlbaum.

Smith, R. J., Bale, J. F., Jr., & White, K. R. (2005, March 2). Sensorineural hearing loss in children. *Lancet, 365,* 879–890.

Smith, S., Quandt, S., Arcury, T., Wetmore, L., Bell, R., & Vitolins, M. (2006, January). Aging and eating in the rural, southern United States: Beliefs about salt and its effect on health. *Social Science & Medicine, 62,* 189–198.

Smith, S. G., Chen, J., Basile, K.C., Gilbert, L. K., Merrick, M.T., Patel, N., Walling, M., & Jain, A. (2017). *The National Intimate Partner and Sexual Violence Survey (NISVS): 2010-2012 State Report.* Atlanta, GA: National Center for Injury Prevention and Control, Centers for Disease Control and Prevention.

Smulevich, A. B., Germanova, K. N., Chitlova, V. V., & Voronova, E. I. (2018). Stress-induced depression and reactive schizophrenia. *International Journal of Culture and Mental Health, 11*(1), 27–41.

Snyder, T. D. (2018). *Mobile digest of education statistics, 2017* (NCES 2018-138). U.S. Department of Education. Washington, DC: National Center for Education Statistics.

So, H., Chau, K., Ao, F., Mo, C., & Sham, P. (2018). Exploring shared genetic bases and causal relationships of schizophrenia and bipolar disorder with 28 cardiovascular and metabolic traits. *Psychological Medicine.* doi:10.1017/S0033291718001812

Soares, C., & Frey, B. (2010). Challenges and opportunities to manage depression during the menopausal transition and beyond. *Psychiatric Clinics of North America, 33,* 295–308.

Social Security Administration. (2018). Actuarial life table. Accessed online, 10/24/18; https://www.ssa.gov/oact/STATS/table4c6.html

Soderstrom, M. (2007). Beyond babytalk: Reevaluating the nature and content of speech input to preverbal infants. *Developmental Review, 27,* 501–532.

Soderstrom, M., Blossom, M., Foygel, R., & Morgan, J. (2008). Acoustical cues and grammatical units in speech to two preverbal infants. *Journal of Child Language, 35,* 869–902.

Solberg, P. A., Kvamme, N., Raastad, T., Ommundsen, Y., Tomten, S., Halvari, H., & … Hallèn, J. (2013). Effects of different types of exercise on muscle mass, strength, function and well-being in elderly. *European Journal of Sport Science, 13,* 112–125.

Somerset, W., Newport, D., Ragan, K., & Stowe, Z. (2006). Depressive disorders in women: From menarche to beyond the menopause. In L. M. Keyes & S. H. Goodman (Eds.), *Women and depression: A handbook for the social, behavioral, and biomedical sciences.* New York, NY: Cambridge University Press.

Sonne, J. L. (2012). Psychological assessment measures. In *PsycEssentials: A pocket resource for mental health practitioners.* Washington, DC: American Psychological Association.

Sonnen, J., Larson, E., Gray, S., Wilson, A., Kohama, S., Crane, P., & … Montine, T. J. (2009). Free radical damage to cerebral cortex in Alzheimer's disease, microvascular brain injury, and smoking. *Annals of Neurology, 65,* 226–229.

Sorrenti, L., Filippello, P., Buzzai, C., Buttò, C., & Costa, S. (2018). Learned helplessness and mastery orientation: The contribution of personality traits and academic beliefs. *Nordic Psychology, 70*(1), 71–84. doi:10.1080/19012276.2017.1339625

Sosinsky, L., & Kim, S. (2013). A profile approach to child care quality, quantity, and type of setting: Parent selection of infant child care arrangements. *Applied Developmental Science, 17,* 39–56.

Soska, K., Adolph, K., & Johnson, S. (2010). Systems in development: Motor skill acquisition facilitates three-dimensional object completion. *Developmental Psychology, 46,* 129–138.

Sousa, D. L. (2005). *How the brain learns to read.* Thousand Oaks, CA: Corwin Press.

South, A. (2013). Perceptions of romantic relationships in adult children of divorce. *Journal of Divorce & Remarriage, 54,* 126–141.

South, S. C., Reichborn-Kjennerud, T., Eaton, N. R., & Krueger, R. F. (2015). Genetics of personality. In M. Mikulincer, P. R. Shaver, M. L. Cooper, & R. J. Larsen (Eds.), *APA handbook of personality and social psychology, Volume 4: Personality processes and individual differences.* Washington, DC: American Psychological Association.

Sowell, E. R., Peterson, B. S., Thompson, P. M., Welcome, S. E., Henkenius, A. L., & Toga, A. W. (2003). Mapping cortical change across the human life span. *Nature Neuroscience, 6,* 309–315.

Span, P. (2016, July 5). The prognosis is upsetting, for the doctor. *New York Times,* p. D5.

Sparks, M. B. (2008). Inpatient care for persons with Alzheimer's disease. *Alzheimer's Care Today, 9,* 204–210.

Sparrow, J. (2016). Culture, community, and context in child development: Implications for family programs and policies. In D. Narvaez, J. M. Braungart-Rieker, L. E. Miller-Graff, L. T. Gettler, & P. D. Hastings (Eds.), *Contexts for young child flourishing: Evolution, family, and society.* New York: Oxford University Press.

Spear, C. F., Strickland-Cohen, M. K., Romer, N., & Albin, R. W. (2013). An examination of social validity within single-case research with students with emotional and behavioral disorders. *Remedial and Special Education, 34,* 357–370.

Spatz Widom, C., Czaja, S. J., & DuMont, K. A., (2015). Intergenerational transmission of child abuse and neglect: Real or detection bias? *Science, 347*(6229), 1480–1485.

Spear, L. (2010). *The behavioral neuroscience of adolescence.* New York, NY: Norton.

Spearman, C. (1927). *The abilities of man.* London, UK: Macmillan.

Spessato, B., Gabbard, C., Valentini, N., & Rudisill, M. (2013). Gender differences in Brazilian children's fundamental movement skill performance. *Early Child Development and Care, 183,* 916–923.

Spiers, P. (2012). *Master class: Living longer, stronger, and happier.* New York: Center Street/Hatchette Book Group.

Spiess, M., Bernardi, G., Kurth, S., Ringli, M., Wehrle, F. M., Jenni, O. G., Huber, R., Siclari, F. (2018). How do children fall asleep? A high-density EEG study of slow waves in the transition from wake to sleep. *NeuroImage, 178,* 23–36.

Spinelli, L. (2015, September 14). Fighting for every child. *Northern Virginia.* Accessed online, 10/24/17; https://www.northernvirginiamag.com/family/family-features/2015/09/14/fighting-for-every-child

Spörer, N., Brunstein, J., & Kieschke, U. (2009). Improving students' reading comprehension skills: Effects of strategy instruction and reciprocal teaching. *Learning and Instruction, 19,* 272–286.

Sprecher, S., Brooks, J. E., & Avogo, W. (2013). Self-esteem among young adults: Differences and similarities based on gender, race, and cohort (1990–2012). *Sex Roles, 69,* 264–275.

Sprecher, S., Sullivan, Q., & Hatfield, E. (1994). Mate selection preferences: Gender differences examined in a national sample. *Journal of Personality and Social Psychology, 66,* 1074–1080.

Spring, L. (2015). Older women and sexuality—Are we still just talking lube? *Sexual and Relationship Therapy, 30,* 4–9.

Squeglia, L. M., Sorg, S. F., Schweinsburg, A., Dager, W., Reagan, R., & Tapert, S. F. (2012). Binge drinking differentially affects adolescent male and female brain morphometry. *Psychopharmacology, 220,* 529–539.

Srivastava, P. (2017). Supernatural and religious beliefs among rural and urban older adults. *Journal of Psychosocial Research, 12*(1), 11–19.

St. Mary, J., Calhoun, M., Tejada, J., & Jenson, J. M. (2018). Perceptions of academic achievement and educational opportunities among black and African American youth. *Child & Adolescent Social Work Journal,* doi:10.1007/s10560-018-0538-4

Stahl, A. E., & Feigenson, L. (2018). Infants use linguistic group distinctions to chunk items in memory. *Journal of Experimental Child Psychology, 172,* 149–167.

Starr, L. (2010). Preparing those caring for older adults to report elder abuse. *Journal of Continuing Education in Nursing, 41,* 231–235.

Staudinger, U. (2008). A psychology of wisdom: History and recent developments. *Research in Human Development, 5,* 107–120.

Staunton, H. (2005). Mammalian sleep. *Naturwissenschaften, 92,* 203–220.

Stedman, L. C. (1997). International achievement differences: An assessment of a new perspective. *Educational Researcher, 26,* 4–15.

Steel, A., Adams, J., Sibbritt, D., Broom, A., Frawley, J., & Gallois, C. (2014). The influence of complementary and alternative medicine use in pregnancy on labor pain management choices: Results from a nationally representative sample of 1,835 women. *Journal of Alternative and Complementary Medicine, 20,* 87–97.

Steele, C. J., Bailey, J. A., Zatorre, R. J., & Penhune, V. B. (2013). Early musical training and white-matter plasticity in the corpus callosum: Evidence for a sensitive period. *The Journal of Neuroscience, 33,* 1282–1290.

Steele, C. M. (2012). Conclusion: Extending and applying stereotype threat research: A brief essay. In M. Inzlicht & T. Schmader (Eds.), *Stereotype threat: Theory, process, and application.* New York, NY: Oxford University Press.

Stein, D., Latzer, Y., & Merick, J. (2009). Eating disorders: From etiology to treatment. *International Journal of Child and Adolescent Health, 2,* 139–151.

Stein, Z., Susser, M., Saenger, G., & Marolla, F. (1975). *Famine and human development: The Dutch hunger winter of 1944–1945.* New York, NY: Oxford University Press.

Steinbach, R., Green, J., Kenward, M. G., & Edwards, P. (2016). Is ethnic density associated with risk of child pedestrian injury? A comparison of inter-census changes in ethnic populations and injury rates. *Ethnicity & Health, 21,* 1–19.

Steinberg, L. (2014). *Age of opportunity: Lessons from the new science of adolescence.* Boston, MA: Houghton Mifflin Harcourt.

Steinberg, L., & Scott, S. S. (2003). Less guilty by reason of adolescence: Developmental immaturity, diminished responsibility, and the juvenile death penalty. *American Psychologist, 58,* 1009–1018.

Steiner, A. M., & Fletcher, P. C. (2017). Sandwich generation caregiving: A complex and dynamic role. *Journal of Adult Development, 24,* 133–143.

Steiner, L. M., Durand, S., Groves, D., & Rozzell, C. (2015). Effect of infidelity, initiator status, and spiritual well-being on men's divorce adjustment. *Journal of Divorce & Remarriage, 56,* 95–108.

Steinmetz, J., Bosak, J., Sczesny, S., & Eagly, A. H. (2014). Social role effects on gender stereotyping in Germany and Japan. *Asian Journal of Social Psychology, 17*(1), 52–60. doi:10.1111/ajsp.12044

Stephenson, J., Heslehurst, N., Hall, J., Schoenaker, D. M., Hutchinson, J., Cade, J. E., & … Mishra, G. D. (2018). Before the beginning: Nutrition and lifestyle in the preconception period and its importance for future health. *Lancet, 391*(10132), 1830–1841.

Stepler, R. (2017). Number of U.S. adults cohabiting with a partner continues to rise, especially among those 50 and older. Pew Research Center. Accessed online, 10/26/18; http://www.pewresearch.org/fact-tank/2017/04/06/number-of-u-s-adults-cohabiting-with-a-partner-continues-to-rise-especially-among-those-50-and-older/

Steri, A. O., & Spelke, E. S. (1988). Haptic perception of objects in infancy. *Cognitive Psychology, 20,* 1–23.

Stern, J. A., Fraley, R. C., Jones, J. D., Gross, J. T., Shaver, P. R., & Cassidy, J. (2018). Developmental processes across the first two years of parenthood: Stability and change in adult attachment style. *Developmental Psychology, 54*(5), 975–988.

Sternberg K. (2014). *Psychology of love 101.* New York, NY: Springer Publishing Co.

Sternberg, R. J. (2003a). A broad view of intelligence: The theory of successful intelligence. *Consulting Psychology Journal: Practice & Research, 55,* 139–154.

Sternberg, R. J. (2003b). Our research program validating the triarchic theory of successful intelligence: Reply to Gottfredson. *Intelligence, 31,* 399–413.

Sternberg, R. J. (2005). The triarchic theory of successful intelligence. In D. P. Flanagan & P. L. Harrison (Eds.), *Contemporary intellectual assessment: Theories, tests, and issues.* New York, NY: Guilford Press.

Sternberg, R. J. (2006). A duplex theory of love. In R. J. Sternberg & K. Sternberg (Eds.), *The new psychology of love.* New Haven, CT: Yale University Press.

Sternberg, R. J. (2008). Schools should nurture wisdom. In B. Z. Presseisen (Ed.), *Teaching for intelligence* (2nd ed.). Thousand Oaks, CA: Corwin Press.

Sternberg, R. J. (2009). The nature of creativity. In R. J. Sternberg, J. C. Kaufman, & E. L. Grigorenko (Eds), *The essential Sternberg: Essays on intelligence, psychology, and education.* New York, NY: Springer Publishing Co.

Sternberg, R. J. (2015). Successful intelligence: A model for testing intelligence beyond IQ tests. *European Journal of Education and Psychology, 8,* 76–84.

Sternberg, R. J. (2016). A triangular theory of creativity. *Psychology of Aesthetics, Creativity, and the Arts.* Accessed online, 3/16/17; http://dx.doi.org/10.1037/aca0000095

Sternberg, R. J., Conway, B. E., Ketron, J. L., & Bernstein, M. (1981). Peoples' conceptions of intelligence. *Journal of Personality and Social Psychology, 41,* 37–55.

Sternberg, R. J., & Grigorenko, E. L. (Eds.). (2002). *The general factor of intelligence: How general is it?* Mahwah, NJ: Lawrence Erlbaum.

Sternberg, R. J., Kaufman, J. C., & Pretez, J. E. (2002). *The creativity conundrum: A propulsion model of creative contributions.* Philadelphia, PA: Psychology Press.

Stevens, W., Hasher, L., Chiew, K., & Grady, C. (2008). A neural mechanism underlying memory failure in older adults. *The Journal of Neuroscience, 28,* 12820–12824.

Stevenson, J. (2006). Dietary influences on cognitive development and behaviour in children. *Proceedings of the Nutrition Society, 65,* 361–365.

Stevenson, M., Henderson, T., & Baugh, E. (2007, February). Vital defenses: Social support appraisals of black grandmothers parenting grandchildren. *Journal of Family Issues, 28,* 182–211.

Stiles, J., & Jernigan, T. L. (2010). The basics of brain development. *Neuropsychology Review, 20,* 327–348.

Stikes, R., & Barbier, D. (2013). Applying the plan-do-study-act model to increase the use of kangaroo care. *Journal of Nursing Management, 21,* 70–78.

Stiles, J. (2012). The effects of injury to dynamic neural networks in the mature and developing brain. *Developmental Psychobiology, 54,* 343–349.

Stipp, S. (2012, January). A new path to longevity. *Scientific American,* pp. 33–39.

Stolzenberg, S., & Pezdek, K. (2013). Interviewing child witnesses: The effect of forced confabulation on event memory. *Journal of Experimental Child Psychology, 114,* 77–88.

Stone, A. A., Schwartz, J. E., Broderick, J. E., & Deaton, A. (2010). A snapshot of the age distribution of psychological well-being in the United States. *PNAS Proceedings of the National Academy of Sciences of the United States of America, 107,* 9985–9990.

Stopa, L., Denton, R , Wingfield, M., & Taylor, K. (2013). The fear of others: A qualitative analysis of interpersonal threat in social phobia and paranoia. *Behavioural and Cognitive Psychotherapy, 41,* 188–209.

Storey, K., Slaby, R., Adler, M., Minotti, J., & Katz, R. (2008). *Eyes on bullying … What can you do?* Boston, MA: Education Development Center.

Story, M., Nanney, M., & Schwartz, M. (2009). Schools and obesity prevention: Creating school environments and policies to promote healthy eating and physical activity. *Milbank Quarterly, 87,* 71–100.

Strachan, E., Duncan, G., Horn, E., & Turkheimer, E. (2017). Neighborhood deprivation and depression in adult twins: Genetics and gene × environment interaction. *Psychological Medicine, 47,* 627–638.

Strasburger, V. (2009). Media and children: What needs to happen now? *JAMA: Journal of the American Medical Association, 301,* 2265–2266.

Straus, M. A., & Gelles, R. J. (Eds.). (1990). *Physical violence in American families.* New Brunswick, NJ: Transaction.

Straus, M. A., & McCord, J. (1998). Do physically punished children become violent adults? In S. Nolen-Hoeksema (Ed.), *Clashing views on abnormal psychology: A Taking Sides custom reader.* Guilford, CT: Dushkin/McGraw-Hill.

Strauss, J. R. (2011). Contextual influences on women's health concerns and attitudes toward menopause. *Health & Social Work, 36,* 121–127.

Strauss, J. R. (2013). The baby boomers meet menopause: Fertility, attractiveness, and affective response to the menopausal transition. *Sex Roles, 68,* 77–90.

Streissguth, A. (2007). Offspring effects of prenatal alcohol exposure from birth to 25 years:

The Seattle Prospective Longitudinal Study. *Journal of Clinical Psychology in Medical Settings, 14,* 81–101.

Striano, T., & Vaish, A. (2006, November). Seven- to 9-month-old infants use facial expressions to interpret others' actions. *British Journal of Developmental Psychology, 24,* 753–760.

Strobel, A., Dreisbach, G., Müller, J., Goschke, T., Brocke, B., & Lesch, K. (2007, December). Genetic variation of serotonin function and cognitive control. *Journal of Cognitive Neuroscience, 19,* 1923–1931.

Stroebe, M., Schut, H., & Boerner, K. (2017). Cautioning health-care professionals: Bereaved persons are misguided through the stages of grief. *Omega: Journal of Death and Dying, 74,* 455–473.

Strohl, M., Bednar, C., & Longley, C. (2012). Residents' perceptions of food and nutrition services at assisted living facilities. *Family and Consumer Sciences Research Journal, 40,* 241–254.

Strong, B. & Cohen, T. F. (2013). *The marriage and family experience: Intimate relationships in a changing society.* New York, NY: Wadsworth.

Stroope, S., McFarland, M. J., & Uecker, J. E. (2015). Marital characteristics and the sexual relationships of U.S. older adults: An analysis of National Social Life, Health, and Aging Project data. *Archives of Sexual Behavior, 44,* 233–247.

Struempler, B. J., Parmer, S. M., Mastropietro, L. M., Arsiwalla, D., & Bubb, R. R. (2014). Changes in fruit and vegetable consumption of third-grade students in body quest: Food of the warrior, a 17-class childhood obesity prevention program. *Journal of Nutrition Education and Behavior, 46,* 286–292.

Stutzer, A., & Frey, B. (2006, April). Does marriage make people happy, or do happy people get married? *The Journal of Socio-Economics, 35,* 326–347.

Su, Q., Chen, Z., Li, R., Elgar, F. J., Liu, Z., & Lian, Q. (2018). Association between early menarche and school bullying. *Journal of Adolescent Health.* doi:10.1016/j.jadohealth.2018.02.008

Suárez-Orozco, C., Suárez-Orozco, M., & Todorova, I. (2008). *Learning a new land: Immigrant students in American society.* Cambridge, MA: Belknap Press/ Harvard University Press.

Subotnik, R. (2006). Longitudinal studies: Answering our most important questions of prediction and effectiveness. *Journal for the Education of the Gifted, 29,* 379–383.

Sudharsanan, N., Behrman, J. R., & Kohler, H. (2016). Limited common origins of multiple adult health-related behaviors: Evidence from U.S. twins. *Social Science & Medicine, 171,* 67–83.

Sudia-Robinson, T. (2011, March 14). Ethical implications of newborn screening, life-limiting conditions, and palliative care. *MCN, American Journal of Maternal Child Nursing.* Accessed online, 4/3/11; http://journals.lww.com/mcnjournal/Abstract/publishahead/Ethical_Implications_of_Newborn_Screening,.99982.aspx

Suetta, C., & Kjaer, M. (2010). What are the mechanisms behind disuse and age-related skeletal muscle atrophy? *Scandinavian Journal of Medicine & Science in Sports, 20,* 167–168.

Sugarman, S. (1988). *Piaget's construction of the child's reality.* Cambridge, UK: Cambridge University Press.

Suitor, J. J., Minyard, S. A., & Carter, R. S. (2001). Did you see what I saw? Gender differences in perceptions of avenues to prestige among adolescents. *Sociological Inquiry, 71,* 437–454.

Sullivan, A. R., & Fenelon, A. (2013). Patterns of widowhood mortality. *The Journals of Gerontology. Series B, Psychological Sciences and Social Sciences, 69*(1), 53–62.

Sumner, E., Connelly, V., & Barnett, A. L. (2014). The influence of spelling ability on handwriting production: Children with and without dyslexia. *Journal of Experimental Psychology: Learning, Memory, and Cognition, 40,* 1441–1447.

Sumner, R., Burrow, A. L., & Hill, P. L. (2015). Identity and purpose as predictors of subjective well-being in emerging adulthood. *Emerging Adulthood, 3,* 46–54.

Sun, Y., Liu, Y., Yan, S., Hu, J., Xu, G., Liu, J., & Tao, F. (2016). Longitudinal pattern of early maturation on morning cortisol and depressive symptoms: Sex-specific effects. *Psychoneuroendocrinology, 71,* 58–63.

Sundnes, A., & Andenaes, A. (2016). Parental regulation of infant sleep: Round-the-clock efforts for social synchronization. *Infant Mental Health Journal, 37*(3), 247–258.

Super, C. M. (1976). Environmental effects on motor development: A case of African infant precocity. *Developmental Medicine and Child Neurology, 18,* 561–576.

Super, C. M., & Harkness, S. (1982). The infant's niche in rural Kenya and metropolitan America. In L. Adler (Ed.), *Issues in cross-cultural research.* New York, NY: Academic Press.

Supple, A., Ghazarian, S., Peterson, G., & Bush, K. (2009). Assessing the cross-cultural validity of a parental autonomy granting measure: Comparing adolescents in the United States, China, Mexico, and India. *Journal of Cross-Cultural Psychology, 40,* 816–833.

Sutherland, R., Pipe, M., & Schick, K. (2003). Knowing in advance: The impact of prior event information on memory and event knowledge. *Journal of Experimental Child Psychology, 84,* 244–263.

Sutipan, P., Intarakamhang, U., & Macaskill, A. (2017). The impact of positive psychological interventions on well-being in healthy elderly people. *Journal of Happiness Studies, 18,* 269–291.

Swanson, L. A., Leonard, L. B., & Gandour, J. (1992). Vowel duration in mothers' speech to young children. *Journal of Speech and Hearing Research, 35,* 617–625.

Swiatek, M. (2002). Social coping among gifted elementary school students. *Journal for the Education of the Gifted, 26,* 65–86.

Swift, H. J., Abrams, D., Lamont, R. A., & Drury, L. (2017). The risks of ageism model: How ageism and negative attitudes toward age can be a barrier to active aging. *Social Issues and Policy Review, 11,* 195–231.

Swingley, D. (2017). The infant's developmental path in phonological acquisition. *British Journal of Psychology, 108,* 28–30.

Syed, M., & Seiffge-Krenke, I. (2013). Personality development from adolescence to emerging adulthood: Linking trajectories of ego development to the family context and identity formation. *Journal of Personality and Social Psychology, 104,* 371–384.

Szaflarski, J. P., Rajagopal, A., Altaye, M., Byars, A. W., Jacola, L., Schmithorst, V., & Holland, S. K. (2012). Left-handedness and language lateralization in children. *Brain Research, 1433,* 85–97.

Szczygieł, D., & Mikolajczak, M. (2017). Why are people high in emotional intelligence happier? They make the most of their positive emotions. *Personality and Individual Differences, 117,* 177–181.

Tajfel, H., & Turner, J. C. (2004). The social identity theory of intergroup behavior. In J. T. Jost & J. Sidanius (Eds.), *Political psychology: Key readings.* New York, NY: Psychology Press.

Tamis-LeMonda, C. S., Song, L., Leavell, A., Kahana-Kalman, R., & Yoshikawa, H. (2012). Ethnic differences in mother-infant language and gestural communications are associated with specific skills in infants. *Developmental Science, 15,* 384–397.

Tan, H., Wen, S. W., Mark, W., Fung, K. F., Demissie, K., & Rhoads, G. G. (2004). The association between fetal sex and preterm birth in twin pregnancies. *Obstetrics and Gynecology, 103,* 327–332.

Tang, C., Curran, M., & Arroyo, A. (2014). Cohabitors' reasons for living together, satisfaction with sacrifices, and relationship quality. *Marriage & Family Review, 50,* 598–620.

Tandon, P. S., Zhou, C., Lozano, P., & Christakis, D. A. (2011). Preschoolers' total daily screen time at home and by type of child care. *The Journal of Pediatrics, 158,* 297–300. doi:10.1016/j.jpeds.2010.08.005

Tang, C., Wu, M., Liu, J., Lin, H., & Hsu, C. (2006). Delayed parenthood and the risk of cesarean delivery—Is paternal age an independent risk factor? *Birth: Issues in Perinatal Care, 33,* 18–26.

Tangri, S., Thomas, V., & Mednick, M. (2003). Predictors of satisfaction among college-educated African American women in midlife. *Journal of Adult Development, 10,* 113–125.

Tanner, J. (1972). Sequence, tempo, and individual variation in growth and development of boys and girls aged twelve to sixteen. In J. Kagan & R. Coles (Eds.), *Twelve to sixteen: Early adolescence.* New York, NY: Norton.

Tanner, J. L., Arnett, J., & Leis, J. (2009). Emerging adulthood: Learning and development during the first stage of adulthood. In M. C. Smith & N. DeFrates-Densch (Eds.), *Handbook of research on adult learning and development.* New York, NY: Routledge/Taylor & Francis Group.

Tappan, M. B. (2006, March). Moral functioning as mediated action. *Journal of Moral Education, 35,* 1–18.

Tardif, T. (1996). Nouns are not always learned before verbs: Evidence from Mandarin speakers' early vocabularies. *Developmental Psychology, 32,* 492–504.

Tardif, T., Wellman, H. M., & Cheung, K. M. (2004). False belief understanding in Cantonese-speaking children. *Journal of Child Language, 31,* 779–800.

Task Force on Sudden Infant Death Syndrome. (2011). SIDS and other sleep-related infant deaths: Expansion of Recommendations for a Safe Infant Sleeping Environment. American Academy of Pediatrics. Accessed online, 9/22/18; http://pediatrics.aappublications.org/content/pediatrics/early/2011/10/12/peds.2011-2284.full.pdf

Tattersall, M., Cordeaux, Y., Charnock-Jones, D., & Smith, G. S. (2012). Expression of gastrin-releasing peptide is increased by prolonged stretch of human myometrium, and antagonists of its receptor inhibit contractility. *The Journal of Physiology, 590,* 2081–2093.

Tatum, B. (2017). *Why are all the Black kids sitting together in the cafeteria?: And other conversations about race.* (20th anniversary ed.) New York: Basic Books.

Tavernise, S. (2014). Obesity rate for young children plummets 43% in a decade. *New York Times,* p 1.

Taylor, A., Wilson, C., Slater, A., & Mohr, P. (2012). Self-esteem and body dissatisfaction in young children: Associations with weight and perceived parenting style. *Clinical Psychologist, 16,* 25–35.

Taylor, D. M. (2002). *The quest for identity: From minority groups to Generation Xers.* Westport, CT: Praeger Publishers/Greenwood Publishing.

Taylor, J. S. (2014). Death, posthumous harm, and bioethics. *Journal of Medical Ethics, 40,* 636–637.

Taylor, R. L., & Rosenbach, W. E. (Eds.). (2005). *Military leadership: In pursuit of excellence* (5th ed.). Boulder, CO: Westview Press.

Taylor, W. D. (2014). Depression in the elderly. *New England Journal of Medicine, 371,* 1228–1235.

Taynieoeaym, M., & Ruffman, T. (2008). Stepping stones to others' minds: Maternal talk relates to child mental state language and emotion understanding at 15, 24, and 33 months. *Child Development, 79,* 284–302.

Tazopoulou, E., Miljkovitch, R., Truelle, J., Schnitzler, A., Onillon, M., Zucco, T., &… Montreuil, M. (2016). Rehabilitation following cerebral anoxia: An assessment of 27 patients. *Brain Injury, 30,* 95–103.

Tefft, B. C. (2012). *Motor vehicle crashes, injuries, and deaths in relation to driver age: United States 1995–2010.* Washington, DC: AAA Foundation for Traffic Safety.

Teitelman, J., Hartman, G., Moossa, J., Uhl, K., & Vizzier, E. (2017). Assessing wellness outcomes for participants in adult day services: Options for activity professionals. *Activities, Adaptation & Aging, 41,* 258–267.

Tellegen, A., Lykken, D. T., Bouchard, T. J., Jr., Wilcox, K. J., Segal, N. L., & Rich, S. (1988).

Personality similarity in twins reared apart and together. *Journal of Personality and Social Psychology, 54,* 1031–1039.

Teoli, D. A., Zullig, K. J., & Hendryx, M. S. (2015). Maternal fair/poor self-rated health and adverse infant birth outcomes. *Health Care for Women International, 36,* 108–120.

Terracciano, A., McCrae, R., & Costa, P. (2010). Intra-individual change in personality stability and age. *Journal of Research in Personality, 44,* 31–37.

Terzidou, V. (2007). Preterm labour. Biochemical and endocrinological preparation for parturition. *Best Practices of Research in Clinical Obstetrics and Gynecology, 21,* 729–756.

Teutsch, C. (2003). Patient-doctor communication. *Medical Clinics of North America, 87,* 1115–1147.

Thapar, A., Collishaw, S., Pine, D. S., & Thapar, A. (2012). Depression in adolescence. *Lancet, 379*(9820), 1056–1067.

Thapar, A., & Cooper, M. (2016). Attention deficit hyperactivity disorder. *Lancet, 387,* 1240-1250.

Tharp, R. G. (1989). Psychocultural variables and constants: Effects on teaching and learning in schools [Special issue: Children and their development: Knowledge base, research agenda, and social policy application]. *American Psychologist, 44,* 349–359.

Thelen, E., & Bates, E. (2003). Connectionism and dynamic systems: Are they really different? *Developmental Science, 6,* 378–391.

Theodosiou-Zipiti, G., & Lamprianou, I. (2016). Linguistic and cultural effects on the attainment of ethnic minority students: Some methodological considerations. *British Journal of Sociology of Education, 37,* 1229–1250.

Thibodeau, R. B., Gilpin, A. T., Brown, M. M., & Meyer, B. A. (2016). The effects of fantastical pretend-play on the development of executive functions: An intervention study. *Journal of Experimental Child Psychology, 145,* 120–138.

Thielen, F. W., Have, M., Graaf, R., Cuijpers, P., Beekman, A., Evers, S., & Smit, F. (2016). Longterm economic consequences of child maltreatment: A population-based study. *European Child & Adolescent Psychiatry.* doi:10.1007/s00787-016-0850-5

Thijs, J., & Verkuyten, M. (2013). Multiculturalism in the classroom: Ethnic attitudes and classmates' beliefs. *International Journal of Intercultural Relations, 37,* 176–187.

Thivel, D., Isacco, L., Rousset, S., Boirie, Y., Morio, B., & Duché, P. (2011). Intensive exercise: A remedy for childhood obesity? *Physiology & Behavior, 102*(2), 132–136.

Thoermer, C., Woodward, A., Sodian, B., Perst, H., & Kristen, S. (2013). To get the grasp: Seven-month-olds encode and selectively reproduce goal-directed grasping. *Journal of Experimental Child Psychology, 116,* 499–509.

Thomaes, S., Brummelman, E., & Sedikides, C. (2017). Why most children think well of themselves. *Child Development, 88,* 1873–1884.

Thoman, E. B., & Whitney, M. P. (1990). Sleep states of infants monitored in the home: Individual differences, developmental trends, and origins of diurnal cyclicity. *Infant Behavior and Development, 12,* 59–75.

Thomas, A., & Chess, S. (1980). *The dynamics of psychological development.* New York, NY: Brunner-Mazel.

Thomas, A., Chess, S., & Birch, H. G. (1968). *Temperament and behavior disorders in children.* New York, NY: New York University Press.

Thomas, R. L., Misra, R., Akkunt, E., Ho, C., Spence, C., & Bremner, A. J. (2018). Sensitivity to auditory-tactile colocation in early infancy. *Developmental Science, 21*(4).

Thomas, R. M. (2001). *Recent human development theories.* Thousand Oaks, CA: Sage Publications.

Thompson, C., & Prottas, D. (2006, January). Relationships among organizational family support, job autonomy, perceived control, and employee well-being. *Journal of Occupational Health Psychology, 11,* 100–118.

Thompson, R., Briggs-King, E. C., & LaTouche-Howard, S. A. (2012). Psychology of African American children: Strengths and challenges. In E. C. Chang & C. A. Downey (Eds.), *Handbook of race and development in mental health.* New York, NY: Springer Science + Business Media.

Thoms, K. M., Kuschal, C., & Emmert, S. (2007). Lessons learned from DNA repair defective syndromes. *Experimental Dermatology, 16,* 532–544.

Thöni, A., Mussner, K., & Ploner, F. (2010). Water birthing: Retrospective review of 2625 water births. Contamination of birth pool water and risk of microbial cross-infection. *Minerva Ginecologia, 62,* 203–211.

Thornberry, T. P., & Krohn, M. D. (1997). Peers, drug use, and delinquency. In D. M. Stoff, J. Breiling, & J. D. Maser (Eds.), *Handbook of antisocial behavior.* New York, NY: Wiley.

Thornton, R. (2010). Verb phrase ellipsis in children's answers to questions. *Language Learning and Development, 6,* 1–31.

Thorpe, A. M., Pearson, J. F., Schluter, P. J., Spittlehouse, J. K., & Joyce, P. R. (2014). Attitudes to aging in midlife are related to health conditions and mood. *International Psychogeriatrics, 26,* 2061–2071.

Thorsen, C., Gustafsson, J., & Cliffordson, C. (2014). The influence of fluid and crystallized intelligence on the development of knowledge and skills. *British Journal of Educational Psychology, 84,* 556–570.

Tian, L., Yu, T., & Huebner, E. S. (2017). Achievement goal orientations and adolescents' subjective well-being in school: The mediating roles of academic social comparison directions. *Frontiers in Psychology, 8,* 27–37.

Tibben, A. (2007). Predictive testing for Huntington's disease. *Brain Research Bulletin, 72,* 165–171.

Tiesler, C. T., & Heinrich, J. (2014). Prenatal nicotine exposure and child behavioural problems. *European Child & Adolescent Psychiatry, 23,* 913–929.

Tighe, E. L., Little, C. W., Arrastia-Chisholm, M. C., Schatschneider, C., Diehm, E., Quinn, J. M., & Edwards, A. A. (2018). Assessing the direct and indirect effects of metalinguistic awareness to the reading comprehension skills of struggling adult readers. *Reading and Writing.* doi:10.1007/s11145-018-9881-2

Tikotzky, L., & Sadeh, A. (2009). Maternal sleep-related cognitions and infant sleep: A longitudinal study from pregnancy through the 1st year. *Child Development, 80,* 860–874.

Time. (1980, September 8). People section.

Timmermans, S., & Buchbinder, M. (2012). Expanded newborn screening: Articulating the ontology of diseases with bridging work in the clinic. *Sociology of Health & Illness, 34,* 208–220.

Tine, M. (2014). Working memory differences between children living in rural and urban poverty. *Journal of Cognition and Development, 15*(4), 599–613.

Tissaw, M. (2007). Making sense of neonatal imitation. *Theory & Psychology, 17,* 217–242.

Titi, N., van Niekerk, A., & Ahmed, R. (2018). Child understandings of the causation of childhood burn injuries: Child activity, parental domestic demands, and impoverished settings. *Child: Care, Health and Development, 44*(3), 494–500.

Toga, A. W., & Thompson, P. M. (2003). Temporal dynamics of brain anatomy. *Annual Review of Biomedical Engineering, 5,* 119–145.

Toldson, I. A., & Lemmons, B. P. (2013). Social demographics, the school environment, and parenting practices associated with parents' participation in schools and academic success among Black, Hispanic, and White students. *Journal of Human Behavior in the Social Environment, 23,* 237–255.

Tomasello, M. (2011). Human culture in evolutionary perspective. In M. J. Gelfand, C. Chiu, & Y. Hong (Eds.), *Advances in culture and psychology* (Vol. 1). New York: Oxford University Press.

Tomlinson, M., Murray, L., & Cooper, P. (2010). Attachment theory, culture, and Africa: Past, present, and future. In P. Erdman & K.-M. Ng (Eds.), *Attachment: Expanding the cultural connections.* New York, NY: Routledge/Taylor & Francis Group.

Tongsong, T., Iamthongin, A., Wanapirak, C., Piyamongkol, W., Sirichotiyakul, S., Boonyanurak, P., &... Neelasri, C. (2005). Accuracy of fetal heart-rate variability interpretation by obstetricians using the criteria of the National Institute of Child Health and Human Development compared with computer-aided interpretation. *Journal of Obstetric and Gynaecological Research, 31,* 68–71.

Tooley, U. A., Makhoul, Z., & Fisher, P. A. (2016). Nutritional status of foster children in the U.S.: Implications for cognitive and behavioral development. *Children and Youth Services Review, 70,* 369–374.

Toomey, R. B., Ryan, C. D., Rafael, M., Card, N. A., & Russell, S. T. (2010). Gender-nonconforming lesbian, gay, bisexual, and transgender youth: School victimization and young adult psychosocial adjustment. *Developmental Psychology, 46,* 1580–1589.

Toporek, R. L., Kwan, K., & Williams, R. A. (2012). Ethics and social justice in counseling psychology. In N. A. Fouad, J. A. Carter, & L. M. Subich (Eds.), *APA handbook of counseling psychology, Vol. 2: Practice, interventions, and applications.* Washington, DC US: American Psychological Association.

Torges, C., Stewart, A., & Nolen-Hoeksema, S. (2008). Regret resolution, aging, and adapting to loss. *Psychology and Aging, 23,* 169–180.

Torvaldsen, S., Roberts, C. L., Simpson, J. M., Thompson, J. F., & Ellwood, D. A. (2006). Intrapartum epidural analgesia and breastfeeding: A prospective cohort study. *International Breastfeeding Journal, 24,* 1–24.

Tosi, M., & Grundy, E. (2018). Returns home by children and changes in parents' well-being in Europe. *Social Science & Medicine, 200,* 99–106.

Tracy, M., Zimmerman, F., Galea, S., McCauley, E., & Vander Stoep, A. (2008). What explains the relation between family poverty and childhood depressive symptoms? *Journal of Psychiatric Research, 42,* 1163–1175.

Trainor, L. J. (2012). Predictive information processing is a fundamental learning mechanism present in early development: Evidence from infants. *International Journal of Psychophysiology, 83,* 256–258.

Trapnell, P. D., & Paulhus, D. L. (2012). Agentic and communal values: Their scope and measurement. *Journal of Personality Assessment, 94,* 39–52.

Treat-Jacobson, D., Bronäs, U. G., & Salisbury, D. (2014). Exercise. In R. Lindquist, M. Snyder, & M. F. Tracy, (Eds.), *Complementary and alternative therapies in nursing* (7th ed.). New York, NY: Springer Publishing Co.

Trehub, S. E. (2003). The developmental origins of musicality. *Nature Neuroscience, 6,* 669–673.

Triche, E. W., & Hossain, N. (2007). Environmental factors implicated in the causation of adverse pregnancy outcome. *Seminars in Perinatology, 31,* 240–242.

Tronick, E. Z. (1995). Touch in mother-infant interactions. In T. M. Field (Ed.), *Touch in early development.* Hillsdale, NJ: Lawrence Erlbaum.

Tropp, L. (2003). The psychological impact of prejudice: Implications for intergroup contact. *Group Processes & Intergroup Relations, 6,* 131–149.

Trotter, A. (2004, December 1). Web searches often overwhelm young researchers. *Education Week, 24,* 8.

Truman, J. L., & Morgan, R. E. (2014). *Nonfatal domestic violence, 2003-1012.* Washington, DC: U.S. Department of Justice.

Trzesniewski, K. H., Donnellan, M. B., & Robins, R. W. (2003). Stability of self-esteem across the life span. *Journal of Personality and Social Psychology, 84,* 205–220.

Tsapelas, I., Aron, A., & Orbuch, T. (2009). Marital boredom now predicts less satisfaction 9 years later. *Psychological Science, 20,* 543–545.

Tse, C., & Altarriba, J. (2007). Testing the associative-link hypothesis in immediate serial recall: Evidence from word frequency and word imageability effects. *Memory, 15*, 675–690.

Tseng, Y., Hsu, M., Hsieh, Y., & Cheng, H. (2018). The meaning of rituals after a stillbirth: A qualitative study of mothers with a stillborn baby. *Journal of Clinical Nursing*. doi:10.1111/jocn.14142

Tucker-Drob, E. M., & Briley, D. A. (2014). Continuity of genetic and environmental influences on cognition across the life span: A meta-analysis of longitudinal twin and adoption studies. *Psychological Bulletin, 140*, 949–979.

Tucker-Drob, E. M., & Harden, K. (2012). Intellectual interest mediates gene × socioeconomic status interaction on adolescent academic achievement. *Child Development, 83*, 743–757.

Tudge, J., & Scrimsher, S. (2003). Lev S. Vygotsky on education: A cultural-historical, interpersonal, and individual approach to development. In B. Zimmerman (Ed.), *Educational psychology: A century of contributions*. Mahwah, NJ: Lawrence Erlbaum.

Tuggle, F. J., Kerpelman, J. L., & Pittman, J. F. (2014). Parental support, psychological control, and early adolescents' relationships with friends and dating partners. *Family Relations: An Interdisciplinary Journal of Applied Family Studies, 63*, 496–512.

Tulving, E. (2016). Episodic memory. In R. J. Sternberg, S. T. Fiske, & D. J. Foss (Eds.), *Scientists making a difference: One hundred eminent behavioral and brain scientists talk about their most important contributions*. (pp. 152–155). New York, NY: Cambridge University Press.

Turiel, E. (2010). Domain specificity in social interactions, social thought, and social development. *Child Development, 81*, 720–726.

Turkheimer, E., Beam, C. R., Sundet, J. M., & Tambs, K. (2017). Interaction between parental education and twin correlations for cognitive ability in a Norwegian conscript sample. *Behavior Genetics, 47*, 507–515.

Turney, K., & Kao, G. (2009). Barriers to school involvement: Are immigrant parents disadvantaged? *Journal of Educational Research, 102*, 257–271.

Turriff, A., Macnamara, E., Levy, H. P., & Biesecker, B. (2016). The impact of living with Klinefelter syndrome: A qualitative exploration of adolescents and adults. *Journal of Genetic Counseling*. Accessed online, 10/25/17; https://www.ncbi.nlm.nih.gov/pubmed/27832510

Turton, P., Evans, C., & Hughes, P. (2009). Long-term psychosocial sequelae of stillbirth: Phase II of a nested case-control cohort study. *Archives of Women's Mental Health, 12*, 35–41.

Twardosz, S., & Lutzker, J. (2009). Child maltreatment and the developing brain: A review of neuroscience perspectives. *Aggression and Violent Behavior, 15*, 59–68.

Twenge, J. M., Gentile, B., & Campbell, W. K. (2015). Birth cohort differences in personality. In M. Mikulincer, P. R. Shaver, M. L. Cooper, & R. J. Larsen (Eds.), *APA handbook of personality and social psychology, Volume 4: Personality processes and individual differences* (pp. 535–551). Washington, DC: American Psychological Association.

Twenge, J. M., Martin, G. N., & Spitzberg, B. H. (2018). Trends in US adolescents' media use, 1976–2016: The rise of digital media, the decline of TV, and the (near) demise of print. *Psychology of Popular Media Culture*. doi:10.1037/ppm0000203

Tyler, S., Corvin, J., McNab, P., Fishleder, S., Blunt, H., & VandeWeerd, C. (2014). "You can't get a side of willpower": Nutritional supports and barriers in The Villages, Florida. *Journal of Nutrition in Gerontology and Geriatrics, 33*, 108–125.

Tyre, P., & McGinn, D. (2003, May 12). She works, he doesn't. *Newsweek*, pp. 45–52.

Tyre, P., & Scelfo, J. (2003, September 22). Helping kids get fit. *Newsweek*, pp. 60–62.

Uchikoshi, Y. (2006). Early reading in bilingual kindergartners: Can educational television help? *Scientific Studies of Reading, 10*, 89–120.

Umaña-Taylor, A. J., Quintana, S. M., Lee, R. M., Cross, W. E., Rivas-Drake, D., Schwartz, S. J., & …

Seaton, E. (2014). Ethnic and racial identity during adolescence and into young adulthood: An integrated conceptualization. *Child Development, 85*, 21–39.

Umberson, D., Williams, K., Powers, D. A., Liu, H., & Needham, B. (2006). You make me sick: Marital quality and health over the life course. *Journal of Health and Social Behavior, 47*, 1–16.

UNAIDS. (2018). The global HIV/AIDS epidemic. HIV.gov. Accessed online, 10/11/18; https://www.hiv.gov/hiv-basics/overview/data-and-trends/global-statistics

Underwood, M. (2005). Introduction to the special section: Deception and observation. *Ethics & Behavior, 15*, 233–234.

United Nations Children's Fund, World Health Organization, & World Bank Group (2018). Levels and trends in child malnutrition: Key findings of the 2018 Edition of the Joint Child Malnutrition Estimates.

United Nations, Department of Economic and Social Affairs, Population Division. (2013). *World Population Ageing 2013*. ST/ESA/SER.A/348. New York, NY: United Nations.

United Nations Statistics Division. (2012). *Statistical Annex Table 2.A Health*. Accessed online, 7/18/12; unstats.un.org/unsd/demographic/products/.%20pdf/Table2A.pdf

United Nations World Population Prospects (2006). Accessed online, 7/12/12; http://www.un.org/esa/population/publications/wpp2006/WPP2006_Highlights_rev.pdf

Updegraff, K. A., McHale, S. M., Whiteman, S. D., Thayer, S. M., & Crouter, A. C. (2006). The nature and correlates of Mexican-American adolescents' time with parents and peers. *Child Development, 77*, 1470–1486.

Uphold-Carrier, H., & Utz, R. (2012). Parental divorce among young and adult children: A long-term quantitative analysis of mental health and family solidarity. *Journal of Divorce & Remarriage, 53*, 247–266. doi:10.1080/10502556.2012.663272

U.S. Bureau of Labor Statistics. (2012, March 1). *Labor force statistics from the Current Population Survey*. Downloaded July 10, 2012, from http://www.bls.gov/cps/cpsaat37.htm

U.S. Bureau of the Census. (2001). *Living arrangements of children*. Washington, DC: Author.

U.S. Bureau of the Census. (2010a). *Current population survey*. Washington, DC: Author. U.S. Department of Agriculture, Center for Nutrition Policy and Promotion.

U.S. Bureau of the Census. (2011). *Current population survey and annual social and economic supplements*. Washington, DC: Author.

U.S. Bureau of the Census. (2012). Current population survey and annual social and economic supplements. Washington, DC: Author.

U.S. Bureau of the Census. (2013). *Income, Poverty, and Health Insurance Coverage in the United States: 2012*, Washington, DC: U.S. Government Printing Office.

U.S. Bureau of the Census. (2017). *American community survey*. Washington, DC: Author. Accessed online, 3/9/19; https://www.census.gov/newsroom/press-releases/2017/acs-single-year.html?CID=CBSM+ACS16.

U.S. Bureau of the Census. (2017). America's families and living arrangements: 2016. Accessed online, 9/22/18; https://www.census.gov/data/tables/2016/demo/families/cps-2016.html

U.S. Bureau of the Census (2017). Average number of people per family household, by race and Hispanic origin, marital status, age, and education of householder: 2016. Accessed online, 10/21/18; https://www.census.gov/data/tables/2016/demo/families/cps-2016.html

U.S. Bureau of the Census. (2017). *Decennial censuses, 1890–1940, and current population survey, annual social and economic supplements, 1947 to 2017*. Washington, DC: Author.

U.S. Bureau of the Census. (2017). Historical living arrangements of children. Accessed online,

9/27/18; https://www.census.gov/data/tables/time-series/demo/families/children.html

U.S. Bureau of Labor Statistics. (2013). *Current Population Survey*. Washington, DC: Author.

U.S. Bureau of Labor Statistics. (2014). *Highlights of women's earnings in 2013*. Washington, DC: Author.

U.S. Bureau of Labor Statistics, U.S. Department of Labor. (2017, March 8). Women's median earnings 82 percent of men's in 2016. *The Economics Daily*. Accessed online, 11/28/17; https://www.bls.gov/opub/ted/2017/womens-median-earnings-82-percent-ofmens-in-2016.htm

U.S. Department of Agriculture. (2006). *Dietary Guidelines for Americans 2005*. Washington, DC: Author.

U.S. Department of Education. (2015). *The condition of education, 2014*. Washington, DC: Author.

U.S. Department of Education. (2016). *38th annual report to Congress on the implementation of the Individuals with Disabilities Education Act, 2016*. Washington, DC: U.S. Department of Education.

U.S. Department of Education. (2016). Integrated postsecondary education data system. Washington, DC: Author.

U.S. Department of Education, National Center for Education Statistics. (2017). Indicator 21: Postsecondary graduation rates. Accessed online, 10/26/18; https://nces.ed.gov/programs/raceindicators/indicator_red.asp

U.S. Department of Health and Human Services, Administration on Children Youth and Families. (2007). *Child Maltreatment 2005*. Washington, DC: U.S. Government Printing Office.

U.S. Department of Health and Human Services, Health Resources and Services Administration, Maternal and Child Health Bureau. (2009). *Child Health USA 2008-2009*. Rockville, MD: U.S. Department of Health and Human Services.

U.S. Department of Health and Human Services. (2017). Costs of care. Accessed online, 11/20/18; https://longtermcare.acl.gov/costs-how-to-pay/costs-of-care.html

U.S. Department of Health and Human Services, National Institutes of Health, Eunice Kennedy Shriver Institute of Child Health and Human Development. (2017). What are the risk factors for preterm labor and birth? Accessed online, 10/26/17; https://www.nichd.nih.gov/health/topics/preterm/conditioninfo/Pages/who_risk.aspx

U.S. Preventive Services Task Force. (2017) Screening for obesity in children and adolescents: U.S. Preventive Services Task Force recommendation statement. *JAMA: Journal of the American Medical Association, 317*, 2417–2426.

Uttal, D. H., Meadow, N. G., Tipton, E., Hand, L. L., Alden, A. R., Warren, C., & Newcombe, N. S. (2013). The malleability of spatial skills: A meta-analysis of training studies. *Psychological Bulletin, 139*, 352–402.

Uylings, H. (2006). Development of the human cortex and the concept of "critical" or "sensitive" periods. *Language Learning, 56*, 59–90.

Vacha-Haase, T., Hill, R. D., & Bermingham, D. W. (2012). Aging theory and research. In N. A. Fouad, J. A. Carter, & L. M. Subich (Eds.), *APA handbook of counseling psychology, Vol. 1: Theories, research, and methods*. Washington, DC: American Psychological Association.

Vaillant, G. E. (2003). Mental health. *The American Journal of Psychiatry, 160*(8), 1373–1384.

Vaillant, G. E., & Vaillant, C. O. (1981). Natural history of male psychological health, X: Work as a predictor of positive mental health. *The American Journal of Psychiatry, 138*, 1433–1440.

Vaillant, G. E., & Vaillant, C. O. (1990). Natural history of male psychological health, XII: A 45-year study of predictors of successful aging. *American Journal of Psychiatry, 147*(1), 31–37.

Vaish, V. (2014). Whole language versus code-based skills and interactional patterns in Singapore's early literacy program. *Cambridge Journal of Education, 44*, 199–215.

Valentino, K., McDonnell, C. G., Comas, M., & Nuttall, A. K. (2018). Preschoolers' autobiographical memory specificity relates to their emotional adjustment. *Journal of Cognition and Development, 19*(1), 47–64.

Valentino, K., Nuttall, A. K., Comas, M., McDonnell, C. G., Piper, B., Thomas, T. E. & Fanuele, S. (2014). Mother-child reminiscing and autobiographical memory specificity among preschool-age children. *Developmental Psychology, 50*, 1197–1207.

Valeri, B. O., Holsti, L., & Linhares, M. M. (2015). Neonatal pain and developmental outcomes in children born preterm: A systematic review. *Clinical Journal of Pain, 31*, 355–362.

Vallejo-Sánchez, B., & Pérez-García, A. M. (2015). The role of personality and coping in adjustment disorder. *Clinical Psychologist.* doi: 10.1111/cp.12064

Valles, N., & Knutson, J. (2008). Contingent responses of mothers and peers to indirect and direct aggression in preschool and school-aged children. *Aggressive Behavior, 34*, 497–510.

Van Balen, F. (2005). The choice for sons or daughters. *Journal of Psychosomatic Obstetrics & Gynecology, 26*, 229–320.

van den Berg, Y. M., Deutz, M. F., Smeekens, S., & Cillessen, A. N. (2017). Developmental pathways to preference and popularity in middle childhood. *Child Development, 88*, 1629–1641

van den Herik, J. C. (2017). Linguistic know-how and the orders of language. *Language Sciences, 61*, 17–27.

van den Tooren, M., & Rutte, C. (2016). Explaining emotional exhaustion and work engagement: The role of job demands-resources and Type D personality. *International Journal of Stress Management, 23*, 147–166.

Vandermaas-Peeler, A., Cox, D., Fisch-Friedman, M., Griffin, R., & Jones, R. P. (2018). *Emerging consensus on LGBT issues: Findings from the 2017 American Values Atlas.* PRRI. Accessed online, 3/26/19; https://www.prri.org/research/emerging-consensus-on-lgbt-issues-findings-from-the-2017-american-values-atlas/

van der Veer, R., & Yasnitsky, A. (2016). Vygotsky the published: Who wrote Vygotsky and what Vygotsky actually wrote. In A. Yasnitsky & R. van der Veer (Eds.), *Revisionist revolution in Vygotsky studies.* New York: Routledge/Taylor & Francis Group.

van Ditzhuijzen, J., ten Have, M., de Graaf, R., van Nijnatten, C. J., & Vollebergh, W. M. (2013). Psychiatric history of women who have had an abortion. *Journal of Psychiatric Research, 47*, 1737–1743.

van Haren, N. M., Rijsdijk, F., Schnack, H. G., Picchioni, M. M., Toulopoulou, T., Weisbrod, M., & ... Kahn, R. S. (2012). The genetic and environmental determinants of the association between brain abnormalities and schizophrenia: The schizophrenia twins and relatives consortium. *Biological Psychiatry, 71*, 915–921.

van Heugten, M., & Johnson, E. (2010). Linking infants' distributional learning abilities to natural language acquisition. *Journal of Memory and Language, 63*, 197–209.

VanLaningham, J., Johnson, D. R., & Amato, P. (2001). Marital happiness, marital duration, and the U-shaped curve: Evidence from a five-wave panel study. *Social Forces, 79*(4), 1313–1341.

van Marle, K., & Wynn, K. (2009). Infants' auditory enumeration: Evidence for analog magnitudes in the small number range. *Cognition, 111*, 302–316.

Van Neste, J., Hayden, A., Lorch, E. P., & Milich, R. (2015). Inference generation and story comprehension among children with ADHD. *Journal of Abnormal Child Psychology, 43*, 259–270.

van Nunen, K., Kaerts, N., Wyndaele, J.-J., Vermandel, A., & Van Hal, G. (2015). Parents' views on toilet training (TT): A quantitative study to identify the beliefs and attitudes of parents concerning TT. *Journal of Child Health Care, 19*(2), 265–274.

Vandell, D. L., Burchinal, M. R., Belsky, J., Owen, M. T., Friedman, S. L., Clarke-Stewart, A., et al. (2005). *Early child care and children's development in the primary grades: Follow-up results from the NICHD Study of Early Child Care.* Paper presented at the biennial meeting of the Society for Research in Child Development, Atlanta, GA.

Vandello, J., & Cohen, D. (2003). Male honor and female fidelity: Implicit cultural scripts that perpetuate domestic violence. *Journal of Personality & Social Psychology, 84*, 997–1010.

Vandenberghe-Descamps, M., Laboure, H., Septier, C., Feron, G., & Sulmont-Rosse, C. (2017). Oral comfort: A new concept to understand elderly people's expectations in terms of food sensory characteristics. *Food Quality and Preference.* Accessed online, 12/12/17; http://www.sciencedirect.com/science/article/pii/S095032931730188X

van Reenen, S. L., & van Rensburg, E. (2013). The influence of an unplanned Caesarean section on initial mother-infant bonding: Mothers' subjective experiences. *Journal of Psychology in Africa, 23*, 269–274.

van Schooten, K.S., Duran, L., Visschedijk, M., Pijnappels, M., Lord, S., Richardson, J., & Delbaere, K. (2018). Catch the ruler: concurrent validity and test-retest reliability of the ReacStick measures of reaction time and inhibitory executive function in older people. *Aging Clin Exp Res.* doi:10.1007/s40520-018-1050-6

VanWeelden, K. (2016). Understanding the individualized education program model within the United States. In D. V. Blair & K. A. McCord (Eds.), *Exceptional music pedagogy for children with exceptionalities: International perspectives.* (pp. 278–295). New York, NY: Oxford University Press.

Varga, M. A. (2014). Why funerals matter: Death rituals across cultures. *Death Studies, 38*, 546–547.

Vartanian, L. R. (2000). Revisiting the imaginary audience and personal fable constructs of adolescent egocentrism: A conceptual review. *Adolescence, 35*, 639–646.

Vauclair, C., Hanke, K., Huang, L., & Abrams, D. (2017). Are Asian cultures really less ageist than Western ones? It depends on the questions asked. *International Journal of Psychology, 52*(2), 136–144.

Vedantam, S. (2006, December 20). Short mental workouts may slow decline of aging minds, study finds. *Washington Post*, p. A1.

Venker, C. E., Kover, S. T., & Weismer, S. E. (2016). Brief report: Fast mapping predicts differences in concurrent and later language abilities among children with ASD. *Journal of Autism and Developmental Disorders, 46*, 1118–1123.

Veraksa, N., Shiyan, O., Shiyan, I., Pramling, N., & Pramling-Samuelsson, I. (2016). Communication between teacher and child in early child education: Vygotskian theory and educational practice. *Infancia Y Aprendizaje/Journal for the Study of Education and Development, 39*, 221–243.

Veras, R. P., & Mattos, L. C. (2007). Audiology and aging: Literature review and current horizons. *Revista Brasileira de Otorrinolaringologia (English Edition), 73*, 122–128.

Verdoux, H., Devouche, E., Tournaire, M., & Levadou, A. (2017). Impact of prenatal exposure to diethylstilbestrol (DES) on psychological outcome: A national survey of DES daughters and unexposed controls. *Archives of Women's Mental Health, 20*(3), 389–395.

Vereijken, C. M., Riksen-Walraven, J. M., & Kondo-Ikemura, K. (1997). Maternal sensitivity and infant attachment security in Japan: A longitudinal study. *International Journal of Behavioral Development, 21*, 35–49.

Verhoeven, M., Sawyer, M. G., & Spence, S. H. (2013). The factorial invariance of the CES-D during adolescence: Are symptom profiles for depression stable across gender and time? *Journal of Adolescence, 36*, 181–190.

Verkuyten, M. (2008). Life satisfaction among ethnic minorities: The role of discrimination and group identification. *Social Indicators Research, 89*(3), 391–404.

Verschueren, K., Doumen, S., & Buyse, E. (2012). Relationships with mother, teacher, and peers: Unique and joint effects on young children's self-concept. *Attachment & Human Development, 14*, 233–248.

Verschueren, M., Rassart, J., Claes, L., Moons, P., & Luyckx, K. (2017). Identity statuses throughout adolescence and emerging adulthood: A large-scale study into gender, age, and contextual differences. *Psychologica Belgica, 57*, 32–42.

Veselka, L., Just, C., Jang, K. L., Johnson, A. M., & Vernon, P. A. (2012). The general factor of personality: A critical test. *Personality and Individual Differences, 52*, 261–264.

Vidaver, R. M., Lafleur, B., Tong, C., Bradshaw, R., & Marts, S. A. (2000). Women subjects in NIH-funded clinical research literature: Lack of progress in both representation and analysis by sex. *Journal of Women's Health, Gender-Based Medicine, 9*, 495–504.

Villarosa, L. (2003, December 23). More teenagers say no to sex, and experts are sure why. *The New York Times*, p. D6.

Vincent, J. A., Phillipson, C. R., & Downs, M. (2006). *The futures of old age.* Thousand Oaks, CA: Sage Publications.

Vingolo, E. M., Salvatore, S., & Limoli, P. G. (2013). MP-1 biofeedback: Luminous pattern stimulus versus acoustic biofeedback in age related macular degeneration (AMD). *Applied Psychophysiology and Biofeedback, 38*, 11–16.

Vink, D., Aartsen, M., Comijs, H., Heymans, M., Penninx, B., Stek, M., et al. (2009). Onset of anxiety and depression in the aging population: Comparison of risk factors in a 9-year prospective study. *The American Journal of Geriatric Psychiatry, 17*, 642–652.

Visser, S. S., Hutter, I., & Haisma, H. (2016). Building a framework for theory-based ethnographies for studying intergenerational family food practices. *Appetite, 97*, 49–57.

Vivanti, G., Paynter, J., Duncan, E., Fothergill, H., Dissanayake, C., & Rogers, S. J. (2014). Effectiveness and feasibility of the Early Start Denver Model implemented in a group-based community childcare setting. *Journal of Autism and Developmental Disorders, 44*, 3140–3153.

Vogel, E. A., Rose, J. P., Roberts, L. R., & Eckles, K. (2014). Social comparison, social media, and self-esteem. *Psychology of Popular Media Culture, 3*(4), 206.

Volker, S. (2007). Infants' vocal engagement oriented towards mother versus stranger at 3 months and avoidant attachment behavior at 12 months. *International Journal of Behavioral Development, 31*, 88–95.

von Hofsten, C., & Rosander, K. (2015). On the development of the mirror neuron system. In P. F. Ferrari & G. Rizzolatti (Eds.), *New frontiers in mirror neurons research.* New York: Oxford University Press.

Voss, P., Wolff, J. K., & Rothermund, K. (2017). Relations between views on ageing and perceived age discrimination: A domain-specific perspective. *European Journal of Ageing, 14*, 5–15.

Vota, N. (2017). Keeping the free-range parent immune from child neglect: You cannot tell me how to raise my children. *Family Court Review, 55*(1), 152–167.

Vreeswijk, C. M., Maas, A. M., Rijk, C. M., & van Bakel, H. A. (2013). Fathers' experiences during pregnancy: Paternal prenatal attachment and representations of the fetus. *Psychology of Men & Masculinity.* Accessed online, 10/25/17; http://psycnet.apa.org/psycinfo/2013-27681-001/

Vu, J. A. (2015). Children's representations of relationships with mothers, teachers, and friends, and associations with social competence. *Early Child Development and Care, 185*(10), 1695–1713.

Vyas, S. (2004). Exploring bicultural identities of Asian high school students through the analytic window of a literature club. *Journal of Adolescent & Adult Literacy, 48,* 12–18.

Vygotsky, L. S. (1926/1997). *Educational psychology.* Delray Beach, FL: St. Lucie Press.

Waber, D. P., Bryce, C. P., Fitzmaurice, G. M., Zichlin, M. L., McGaughy, J., Girard, J. M., & Galler, J. R. (2014). Neuropsychological outcomes at midlife following moderate to severe malnutrition in infancy. *Neuropsychology, 28,* 530–540.

Wada, A., Kunii, Y., Ikemoto, K., Yang, Q., Hino, M., Matsumoto, J., & Niwa, S. (2012). Increased ratio of calcineurin immunoreactive neurons in the caudate nucleus of patients with schizophrenia. *Progress in Neuro-Psychopharmacology & Biological Psychiatry, 37,* 8–14.

Wade, T. D., & Watson, H. J. (2012). Psychotherapies in eating disorders. In J. Alexander & J. Treasure (Eds.), *A collaborative approach to eating disorders.* New York, NY: Routledge/Taylor & Francis Group.

Wahlin, T. (2007). To know or not to know: A review of behaviour and suicidal ideation in preclinical Huntington's disease. *Patient Education and Counseling, 65,* 279–287.

Wahlstrom, D., Raiford, S. E., Breaux, K. C., Zhu, J., & Weiss, L. G. (2018). The Wechsler Preschool and Primary Scale of Intelligence—Fourth Edition, Wechsler Intelligence Scale for Children—Fifth Edition, and Wechsler Individual Achievement Test—Third Edition. In D. P. Flanagan & E. M. McDonough (Eds.), *Contemporary intellectual assessment: Theories, tests, and issues* (4th ed.) (pp. 245–282). New York, NY: Guilford Press.

Wainright, J. L., & Patterson, C. J. (2008). Peer relations among adolescents with female same-sex parents. *Developmental Psychology, 44,* 117–126.

Wainwright, J. L., Russell, S. T., & Patterson, C. J. (2004). Psychosocial adjustment, school outcomes, and romantic relationships of adolescents with same-sex parents. *Child Development, 75,* 1886–1898.

Waisbren, S. E., & Antshel, K. M. (2013). Phenylketonuria. In I. Baron & C. Rey-Casserly (Eds.), *Pediatric neuropsychology: Medical advances and lifespan outcomes.* New York, NY: Oxford University Press.

Wałaszewska, E. (2011). Broadening and narrowing in lexical development: How relevance theory can account for children's overextensions and underextensions. *Journal of Pragmatics, 43,* 314–326.

Walder, D. J., Faraone, S. V., Glatt, S. J., Tsuang, M. T., & Seidman, L. J. (2014). Genetic liability, prenatal health, stress and family environment: Risk factors in the Harvard Adolescent Family High Risk for Schizophrenia Study. *Schizophrenia Research, 157,* 142–148.

Waldfogel, J. (2001). International policies toward parental leave and child care. *Caring for Infants and Toddlers, 11,* 99–111.

Waldrop, D. P., & Kirkendall, A. M. (2009). Comfort measures: A qualitative study of nursing home-based end-of-life care. *Journal of Palliative Medicine, 12,* 718–724.

Walker, J., Anstey, K., & Lord, S. (2006, May). Psychological distress and visual functioning in relation to vision-related disability in older individuals with cataracts. *British Journal of Health Psychology, 11,* 303–317.

Walker, L. E. (1979). Behind the closed doors of the middle-class wifebeater's family. *Contemporary Psychology, 24,* 404–405.

Walker, L. E. (1999). Psychology and domestic violence around the world. *American Psychologist, 54,* 21–29.

Walker, W. A., & Humphries, C. (2005). *The Harvard Medical School guide to healthy eating during pregnancy.* New York, NY: McGraw-Hill.

Walker, W. A., & Humphries, C. (2007, September 17). Starting the good life in the womb. *Newsweek,* pp. 56–57.

Walker-Andrews, A., Krogh-Jespersen, S., Mayhew, E., & Coffield, C. (2013). The situated infant: Learning in context. In M. Legerstee, D. W. Haley, & M. H. Bornstein (Eds.), *The infant mind: Origins of the social brain.* New York, NY: Guilford Press.

Walle, E. A., Reschke, P. J., & Knothe, J. M. (2017). Social referencing: Defining and delineating a basic process of emotion. *Emotion Review, 9,* 245–252.

Walpole, S. C. (18 June 2012). The weight of nations: an estimation of adult human biomass. *BMC Public Health, 12,* 439.

Walter, T. (2012). Why different countries manage death differently: A comparative analysis of modern urban societies. *British Journal of Sociology, 63,* 123–145.

Walters, E., & Gardner, H. (1986). The theory of multiple intelligences: Some issues and answers. In R. J. Sternberg & R. K. Wagner (Eds.), *Practical intelligence.* New York, NY: Cambridge University Press.

Wamba, N. G. (2010). Poverty and literacy: An introduction. *Reading & Writing Quarterly: Overcoming Difficulties, 26,* 109–114.

Wan, B. A., Jiang, C., Agarwal, A., Lam, M., Chow, E., & Henry, B. (2017). Impact of 'do-not-resuscitate' orders on mortality and quality of care. In B. Henry, A. Agarwal, E. Chow, & J. Merrick (Eds.), *Palliative care: Psychosocial and ethical considerations.* Hauppauge, NY: Nova Biomedical Books.

Wang, H. H., Varelas, P. N., Henderson, G. V., Wijdicks, E. M., & Greer, D. M. (2017). Improving uniformity in brain death determination policies over time. *Neurology, 88,* 562–568.

Wang, J., Tan., L., Wang, H. F., Tan, C. C., Meng, X. F., Wang, C., Tang, S. W., & Yu, J. T. (2015). Anti-inflammatory drugs and risk of Alzheimer's disease: an updated systematic review and meta-analysis. *Journal of Alzheimer's Disease, 44*(2), 385–396.

Wang, L., Tracy, C., Moineddin, R., & Upshur, R. G. (2013). Osteoporosis prescribing trends in primary care: A population-based retrospective cohort study. *Primary Health Care Research and Development, 14,* 1–6.

Wang, Q. (2006). Culture and the development of self-knowledge. *Current Directions in Psychological Science, 15,* 182–187.

Wang, Y., Douglass, S., & Yip, T. (2017). Longitudinal relations between ethnic/racial identity process and content: Exploration, commitment, and salience among diverse adolescents. *Developmental Psychology, 53,* 2154–2169.

Wang, Z., Deater-Deckard, K., Cutting, L., Thompson, L. A., & Petrill, S. A. (2012). Working memory and parent-rated components of attention in middle childhood: A behavioral genetic study. *Behavior Genetics, 42,* 199–208.

Wang, Z., Devine, R. T., Wong, K. K., & Hughes, C. (2016). Theory of mind and executive function during middle childhood across cultures. *Journal of Experimental Child Psychology, 149,* 6–22.

Wardle, J., Guthrie, C., & Sanderson, S. (2001). Food and activity preferences in children of lean and obese parents. *International Journal of Obesity & Related Metabolic Disorders, 25,* 971–977.

Warford, M. K. (2011). The zone of proximal teacher development. *Teaching and Teacher Education, 27,* 252–258.

Warne, R. T., & Liu, J. K. (2017). Income differences among grade skippers and non-grade skippers across genders in the Terman sample, 1936–1976. *Learning and Instruction, 47,* 1–12.

Wasserman, J. D., & Tulsky, D. S. (2005). The history of intelligence assessment. In D. P. Flanagan & P. L. Harrison (Eds.), *Contemporary intellectual assessment: Theories, tests, and issues.* New York, NY: Guilford Press.

Waterhouse, J. M., & DeCoursey, P. J. (2004). Human circadian organization. In J. C. Dunlap & J. J. Loros (Eds.), *Chronobiology: Biological timekeeping.* Sunderland, MA: Sinauer Associates.

Waterland, R. A., & Jirtle, R. L. (2004). Early nutrition, epigenetic changes at transposons and imprinted genes, and enhanced susceptibility to adult chronic diseases. *Nutrition, 20,* 63–68.

Waters, L., & Moore, K. (2002). Predicting self-esteem during unemployment: The effect of gender financial deprivation, alternate roles and social support. *Journal of Employment Counseling, 39,* 171–189.

Watling, D., & Bourne, V. J. (2007). Linking children's neuropsychological processing of emotion with their knowledge of emotion expression regulation. *Laterality: Asymmetries of Body, Brain and Cognition, 12,* 381–396.

Waters, S. F., West, T. V., Karnilowicz, H. R., & Mendes, W. B. (2017). Affect contagion between mothers and infants: Examining valence and touch. *Journal of Experimental Psychology: General, 146,* 1043–1051.

Watson, J. B. (1925). *Behaviorism.* New York, NY: Norton.

Watson, J. B., & Rayner, R. (1920). Conditioned, emotional reactions. *Journal of Experimental Psychology, 3,* 1–14.

Weaver, J. M., & Schofield, T. J. (2015). Mediation and moderation of divorce effects on children's behavior problems. *Journal of Family Psychology, 29,* 39–48.

Webb, R., Ayers, S., & Endress, A. (2018). The City Infant Faces Database: A validated set of infant facial expressions. *Behavior Research Methods, 50*(1), 151–159. doi:10.3758/s13428-017-0859-9

Wechsler, D. (1975). Intelligence defined and undefined. *American Psychologist, 30,* 135–139.

Weinberger, D. R. (2001, March 10). A brain too young for good judgment. *The New York Times,* p. D1.

Weiner, B. A., & Zinner, L. (2015). Attitudes toward straight, gay male, and transsexual parenting. *Journal of Homosexuality, 62,* 327–339.

Weinstein, B. E. (2018). The cost of age related hearing loss: To treat or not to treat? *Speech, Language and Hearing.* doi:10.1080/20505 71X.2018.1533622

Weiss, R. (2003, September 2). Genes' sway over IQ may vary with class. *Washington Post,* p. A1.

Weiss, R., & Raz, I. (2006, July). Focus on childhood fitness, not just fatness. *Lancet, 368,* 261–262.

Weissman, A. S., Chu, B. C., Reddy, L. A., & Mohlman, J. (2012). Attention mechanisms in children with anxiety disorders and in children with attention deficit hyperactivity disorder: Implications for research and practice. *Journal of Clinical Child and Adolescent Psychology, 41,* 117–126.

Welch, M. G. (2016). Calming cycle theory: The role of visceral/autonomic learning in early mother and infant/child behaviour and development. *Acta Paediatrica, 105,* 1266–1274.

Welch, M. G., & Ludwig, R. J. (2017). Calming cycle theory and the co-regulation of oxytocin. *Psychodynamic Psychiatry, 45*(4), 519-541.

Weller, C. (2017). Americans work less than ever before but still feel like there's no free time — and there's a simple explanation. *Business Insider.* Accessed online, 10/24/18; https://www.businessinsider.com/why-it-feels-like-you-have-no-free-time-anymore-2017-11

Wellings, K., Collumbien, M., Slaymaker, E., Singh, S., Hodges, Z., Patel, D., & Bajos, N. (2006). Sexual behaviour in context: A global perspective. *Lancet, 368,* 1706–1738.

Wellman, H., Fang, F., Liu, D., Zhu, L., & Liu, G. (2006, December). Scaling of theory-of-mind understandings in Chinese children. *Psychological Science, 17,* 1075–1081.

Wellman, H., Lopez-Duran, S., LaBounty, J., & Hamilton, B. (2008). Infant attention to intentional action predicts preschool theory of mind. *Developmental Psychology, 44,* 618–623.

Wellman, H. M. (2012). Theory of mind: Better methods, clearer findings, more development. *European Journal of Developmental Psychology, 9,* 313–330.

Wells, B., Peppé, S., & Goulandris, N. (2004). Intonation development from five to thirteen. *Journal of Child Language, 31,* 749–778.

Wells, R., Lohman, D., & Marron, M. (2009). What factors are associated with grade acceleration? An analysis and comparison of two U.S. databases. *Journal of Advanced Academics, 20,* 248–273.

Welsh, T., Ray, M., Weeks, D., Dewey, D., & Elliott, D. (2009). Does Joe influence Fred's action? Not if Fred has autism spectrum disorder. *Brain Research, 1248,* 141–148.

Wenk, G. L. (2010). Why do teenagers feel immortal? *Psychology Today.* Accessed online, 11/17/18; https://www.psychologytoday.com/us/blog/your-brain-food/201008/why-do-teenagers-feel-immortal

Wentzell, E. (2017). How did erectile dysfunction become 'natural'? A review of the critical social scientific literature on medical treatment for male sexual dysfunction. *Journal of Sex Research, 54,* 486–506.

Werker, J. F., Pons, F., Dietrich, C., Kajikawa, S., Fais, L., & Amano, S. (2007). Infant-directed speech supports phonetic category learning in English and Japanese. *Cognition, 103,* 147–162.

Werner, E. E., Myers, M., Fifer, W., Cheng, B., Fang, Y., Allen, R., & Monk, C. (2007). Prenatal predictors of infant temperament. *Developmental Psychobiology, 49,* 474–484.

Westermann, G., Mareschal, D., Johnson, M. H., Sirois, S., Spratling, M. W., & Thomas, M. S. (2007). Neuroconstructivism. *Developmental Science, 10,* 75–83.

Wettstein, M., Tauber, B., Kuźma, E., & Wahl, H. (2017). The interplay between personality and cognitive ability across 12 years in middle and late adulthood: Evidence for reciprocal associations. *Psychology and Aging, 32,* 259–277.

Wexler, B. (2006). *Brain and culture: Neurobiology, ideology, and social change.* Cambridge, MA: MIT Press.

Whalen, C. K., Jamner, L. D., Henker, B., Delfino, R. J., & Lozano, J. M. (2002). The ADHD spectrum and everyday life: Experience sampling of adolescent moods, activities, smoking, and drinking. *Child Development, 73,* 209–227.

Wheaton, B., & Montazer, S. (2010). Stressors, stress, and distress. In T. L. Scheid & T. N. Brown (Eds.), *A handbook for the study of mental health: Social contexts, theories, and systems* (2nd ed.). New York, NY: Cambridge University Press.

Wheeler, S., & Austin, J. (2001). The impact of early pregnancy loss. *American Journal of Maternal/Child Nursing, 26,* 154–159.

Whitbourne, S. K. (2007, October). *Crossing over the bridges of adulthood: Multiple pathways through midlife.* Presidential keynote presented at the 4th Biannual Meeting of the Society for the Study of Human Development, Pennsylvania State University, University Park, PA.

Whitbourne, S. K., Sneed, J., & Sayer, A. (2009). Psychosocial development from college through midlife: A 34-year sequential study. *Developmental Psychology, 45,* 1328–1340.

White, K. (2007). Hypnobirthing: The Mongan method. *Australian Journal of Clinical Hypnotherapy and Hypnosis, 28,* 12–24.

White, M. G. (2017). *Which professionals are prone to burnout?* Accessed online, 11/29/17; http://stress.lovetoknow.com/Which_Professionals_are_Prone_to_Burnout

Whiting, E., Chenery, H. J., & Copland, D. A. (2011). Effect of aging on learning new names and descriptions for objects. *Aging, Neuropsychology and Cognition, 18,* 594–619.

Whiting, J., Simmons, L., Havens, J., Smith, D., & Oka, M. (2009). Intergenerational transmission of violence: The influence of self-appraisals, mental disorders and substance abuse. *Journal of Family Violence, 24,* 639–648.

Whittaker, A. (2015). Media debates and 'ethical publicity' on social sex selection through preimplantation genetic diagnosis (PGD) technology in Australia. *Culture, Health & Sexuality, 17(8),* 962–976.

Whittaker, A. C. (2018). Stress, the immune system, and healthy aging. In E. Peel, C. Holland, & M. Murray (Eds.), *Psychologies of Aging.* Cham, Switzerland: Palgrave Macmillan.

Wickrama, K., O'Neal, C. W., & Lorenz, F. O. (2018). The decade-long effect of work insecurity on husbands' and wives' midlife health mediated by anxiety: A dyadic analysis. *Journal of Occupational Health Psychology, 23(3),* 350–360.

Widman, L., Nesi, J., Choukas-Bradley, S., & Prinstein, M. J. (2014). Safe sext: Adolescents' use of technology to communicate about sexual health with dating partners. *Journal of Adolescent Health, 54,* 612–614.

Wiederhold, B. K. (2014). Cyberbullying and LGBTQ youth: A deadly combination. *Cyberpsychology, Behavior, and Social Networking, 17(9),* 569–570.

Wielgosz, A. T., & Nolan, R. P. (2000). Biobehavioral factors in the context of ischemic cardiovascular disease. *Journal of Psychosomatic Research, 48,* 339–345.

Wiggins, J. L., Bedoyan, J. K., Carrasco, M., Swartz, J. R., Martin, D. M., & Monk, C. S. (2014). Age-related effect of serotonin transporter genotype on amygdala and prefrontal cortex function in adolescence. *Human Brain Mapping, 35,* 646–658.

Wilcox, H. C., Conner, K. R., & Caine, E. D. (2004). Association of alcohol and drug use disorders and completed suicide: An empirical review of cohort studies [Special issue: Drug abuse and suicidal behavior]. *Drug & Alcohol Dependence, 76,* S11–S19.

Wild, B., Heider, D., Maatouk, I., Slaets, J., König, H., Niehoff, D., & ... Herzog, W. (2014). Significance and costs of complex biopsychosocial health care needs in elderly people: Results of a population-based study. *Psychosomatic Medicine, 76,* 497–502.

Wiley, T. L., Nondahl, D. M., Cruickshanks, K. J., & Tweed, T. S. (2005). Five-year changes in middle ear function for older adults. *Journal of the American Academy of Audiology, 16,* 129–139.

Wilfond, B., & Ross, L. (2009). From genetics to genomics: Ethics, policy, and parental decision-making. *Journal of Pediatric Psychology, 34,* 639–647.

Wilhoit, L. F., Scott, D. A., & Simecka, B. A. (2017). Fetal alcohol spectrum disorders: Characteristics, complications, and treatment. *Community Mental Health Journal.* Accessed online, 10/27/17; https://www.ncbi.nlm.nih.gov/pubmed/28168434

Wilkes, S., Chinn, D., Murdoch, A., & Rubin, G. (2009). Epidemiology and management of infertility: A population-based study in UK primary care. *Family Practice, 26,* 269–274.

Wilkinson, C. B., Infantolino, Z. P., & Wacha-Montes, A. (2017). Evidence-based practice as a potential solution to burnout in university counseling center clinicians. *Psychological Services, 14,* 543–548.

Wilkinson, N., Paikan, A., Gredeback, G., Rea, F., & Metta, G. (2014). Staring us in the face? An embodied theory of innate face preference. *Developmental Science, 17,* 809–825.

Willford, J. A., Richardson, G. A., & Day, N. L. (2012). Sex-specific effects of prenatal marijuana exposure on neurodevelopment and behavior. In M. Lewis, & L. Kestler (Eds.), *Gender differences in prenatal substance exposure.* Washington, DC: American Psychological Association.

Williams, B. R., Sawyer, P., & Allman, R. M. (2012). Wearing the garment of widowhood: Variations in time since spousal loss among community-dwelling older adults. *Journal of Women & Aging, 24,* 126–139.

Williams, K., & Dunne-Bryant, A. (2006, December). Divorce and adult psychological well-being: Clarifying the role of gender and child age. *Journal of Marriage and Family, 68,* 1178–1196.

Williams, L. (2016). FOCCUS and REFOCCUS: Preparing and sustaining couples for marriage. In J. J. Ponzetti (Ed.), *Evidence-based approaches to relationship and marriage education.* New York, NY: Routledge/Taylor & Francis Group.

Willie, C., & Reddick, R. (2003). *A new look at black families* (5th ed.). Walnut Creek, CA: AltaMira Press.

Willis, S. L., Martin, M., & Rocke, C. (2010). Longitudinal perspectives on midlife development and change. *European Journal of Ageing, 7,* 131–134.

Willis, S., Tennstedt, S., Marsiske, M., Ball, K., Elias, J., Koepke, K., Morris, J., Rebok, G., Unverzagt, F., Stoddard, A., & Wright, E. (2006). Long-term effects of cognitive training on everyday functional outcomes in older adults. *JAMA: Journal of the American Medical Association, 296,* 2805–2814.

Wills, T., Sargent, J., Stoolmiller, M., Gibbons, F., & Gerrard, M. (2008). Movie smoking exposure and smoking onset: A longitudinal study of mediation processes in a representative sample of U.S. adolescents. *Psychology of Addictive Behaviors, 22,* 269–277.

Wilson, B. J., Smith, S. L., Potter, W. J., Kunkel, D., Linz, D., Colvin, C. M., & Donnerstein, E. (2002). Violence in children's television programming: Assessing the risks. *Journal of Communication, 52,* 5–35.

Wilson, C., & Hutchison, B. (2014). The foundations of career theory: Holland and super theories. In G. T. Eliason, T. Eliason, J. L. Samide, & J. Patrick (Eds.), *Career development across the lifespan: Counseling for community, schools, higher education, and beyond.* (pp. 17–43). Charlotte, NC: IAP Information Age Publishing.

Wilson, K. L., Smith, M. L., Rosen, B. L., Pulczinski, J. C., & Ory, M. G. (2017). HPV vaccination status and mandate support for school-aged adolescents among college females: A descriptive study. *Journal of School Nursing, 33,* 232–245.

Wilson, S. L. (2003). Post-Institutionalization: The effects of early deprivation on development of Romanian adoptees. *Child & Adolescent Social Work Journal, 20,* 473–483.

Wines, M. (2006, August 24). Africa adds to miserable ranks for child workers. *The New York Times,* p. D1.

Winger, G., & Woods, J. H. (2004). *A handbook on drug and alcohol abuse: The biomedical aspects.* Oxford, UK: Oxford University Press.

Wingfield, A., Tun, P. A., & McCoy, S. L. (2005). Hearing loss in older adulthood: What it is and how it interacts with cognitive performance. *Current Directions in Psychological Science, 14,* 144–147.

Winiarski, D. A., Hendrix, C. L., Smearman, E. L., & Brennan, J. (2018). Prenatal and perinatal risk factors. In J. E. Lochman & W. Matthys (Eds.), *The Wiley handbook of disruptive and impulse-control disorders* (pp. 189–204). Hoboken, NJ: Wiley-Blackwell.

Wink, P., & Staudinger, U. M. (2016). Wisdom and psychosocial functioning in later life. *Journal of Personality, 84,* 306–318.

Winsler, A., Feder, M., Way, E., & Manfra, L. (2006, July). Maternal beliefs concerning young children's private speech. *Infant and Child Development, 15,* 403–420.

Winterich, J. (2003). Sex, menopause, and culture: Sexual orientation and the meaning of menopause for women's sex lives. *Gender & Society, 17,* 627–642.

Winters, S., Martin, C., Murphy, D., & Shokar, N. K. (2017). Breast cancer epidemiology, prevention and screening. *Progress in Molecular Biology and Translational Science, 151,* 1–32.

Wirth, A., Wabitsch, M., & Hauner, H. (2014). The prevention and treatment of obesity. *Deutsches Ärzteblatt International, 111,* 705–713.

Wisse, B., & Sleebos, E. (2016). When change causes stress: Effects of self-construal and change consequences. *Journal of Business and Psychology, 31,* 249–264.

Witt, E. A., Donnellan, M., & Trzesniewski, K. H. (2011). Self-esteem, narcissism, and Machiavellianism: Implications for understanding antisocial behavior in adolescents and young adults. In C. T. Barry, P. K. Kerig, K. K. Stellwagen, & T. D. Barry (Eds.), *Narcissism and Machiavellianism in youth: Implications for the development of adaptive and maladaptive behavior*. Washington, DC: American Psychological Association.

Witvliet, M., van Lier, P., Cuijpers, P., & Koot, H. (2010). Change and stability in childhood clique membership, isolation from cliques, and associated child characteristics. *Journal of Clinical Child and Adolescent Psychology, 39*, 12–24.

Wöhrmann, A. M., Fasbender, U., & Deller, J. (2016). Using work values to predict post-retirement work intentions. *The Career Development Quarterly, 64*, 98–113.

Wolfson, A. R., & Richards, M. (2011). Young adolescents: Struggles with insufficient sleep. In M. El-Sheikh (Ed.), *Sleep and development: Familial and socio-cultural considerations*. New York, NY: Oxford University Press.

Wong, C. (2016). *Emotional intelligence at work: 18-year journey of a researcher*. New York, NY: Routledge/Taylor & Francis Group.

Wood, W., & Eagly, A. (2010). Gender. In S. T. Fiske, D. T. Gilbert, & G. Lindzey (Eds.), *Handbook of social psychology, Vol. 1* (5th ed.). Hoboken, NJ: Wiley.

Wood, W., & Eagly, A. H. (2015). Two traditions of research on gender identity. *Sex Roles: A Journal of Research, 73*(11–12), 461–473.

Woodhouse, S. S., Dykas, M. J., & Cassidy, J. (2012). Loneliness and peer relations in adolescence. *Social Development, 21*, 273–293.

Woodman, C., Baillie, J., & Sivell, S. (2016) The preferences and perspectives of family caregivers towards place of care for their relatives at the end-of-life. A systematic review and thematic synthesis of the qualitative evidence. *BMJ Supportive Palliative Care, 6*, 418–429.

Woods, R. (2009). The use of aggression in primary school boys' decisions about inclusion in and exclusion from playground football games. *British Journal of Educational Psychology, 79*, 223–238.

World Bank. (2017). *Fertility rate, total (births per woman)*. Washington, DC: Author.

World Factbook. (2017). Life expectancy at birth. Accessed online, 12/11/17; https://www.cia.gov/library/publications/the-world-factbook/rankorder/2102rank.html

World Factbook. (2018). Life expectancy at birth. Accessed online 12/26/18; https://www.cdc.gov/nchs/data/nvsr/nvsr66/nvsr66_04.pdf

World Factbook (2018). North America: United States. Accessed online, 9/15/18; https://www.cia.gov/library/publications/the-world-factbook/geos/us.html

World Food Programme. (2016). *Hunger statistics*. Rome: World Food Programme. Accessed online, 5/21/16; https://www.wfp.org/hunger/stats

Wörmann, V., Holodynski, M., Kärtner, J., & Keller, H. (2014). The emergence of social smiling: The interplay of maternal and infant imitation during the first three months in cross-cultural comparison. *Journal of Cross-Cultural Psychology, 45*, 339–361.

Worrell, F., Szarko, J., & Gabelko, N. (2001). Multi-year persistence of nontraditional students in an academic talent development program. *Journal of Secondary Gifted Education, 12*, 80–89.

Wortman, C. B., & Boerner, K. (2011). Beyond the myths of coping with loss: Prevailing assumptions versus scientific evidence. In H. S. Friedman (Ed.), *The Oxford handbook of health psychology*. (pp. 438–476). New York, NY: Oxford University Press.

Wright, C., & Geraghty, S. (2017). Mind over matter: Inside hypnobirthing. *Sleep and Hypnosis, 19*(3), 54–60.

Wright, R. (1995, March 13). The biology of violence. *New Yorker*, pp. 68–77.

Wroolie, T., & Holcomb, M. (2010). Menopause. In B. L. Levin & M. A. Becker (Eds.), *A public health*

perspective of women's mental health. New York, NY: Springer Science + Business Media.

Wrosch, C., Bauer, I., & Scheier, M. (2005, December). Regret and quality of life across the adult life span: The influence of disengagement and available future goals. *Psychology and Aging, 20*, 657–670.

Wrzus, C., Zimmermann, J., Mund, M., & Neyer, F. J. (2017). Friendships in young and middle adulthood: Normative patterns and personality differences. In M. Hojjat & A. Moyer (Eds.), *The psychology of friendship* (pp. 21–38). New York, NY: Oxford University Press.

Wu, C., Honarmand, A. R., Schnell, S., Kuhn, R., Schoeneman, S. E., Ansari, S. A., Carr, J., Markl, M., & Shaibani, A. (2016). Age-related changes of normal cerebral and cardiac blood flow in children and adults aged 7 months to 61 years. *Journal of the American Heart Association, 5*(1), e002657.

Wu, P., & Liu, H. (2014). Association between moral reasoning and moral behavior: A systematic review and meta-analysis. *Acta Psychologica Sinica, 46*, 1192–1207.

Wu, P., Hoven, C. W., Okezie, N., Fuller, C. J., & Cohen, P. (2007). Alcohol abuse and depression in children and adolescents. *Journal of Child & Adolescent Substance Abuse, 17*, 51–69.

Wu, T., Treiber, F. A., & Snieder, H. (2013). Genetic influence on blood pressure and underlying hemodynamics measured at rest and during stress. *Psychosomatic Medicine, 75*, 404–412.

Wu, Y., Tsou, K., Hsu, C., Fang, L., Yao, G., & Jeng, S. (2008). Brief report: Taiwanese infants' mental and motor development—6–24 months. *Journal of Pediatric Psychology, 33*, 102–108.

Wu, Z., & Su, Y. (2014). How do preschoolers' sharing behaviors relate to their theory of mind understanding? *Journal of Experimental Child Psychology, 120*, 73–86.

Wupperman, P., Marlatt, G., Cunningham, A., Bowen, S., Berking, M., Mulvihill-Rivera, N., & Easton, C. (2012). Mindfulness and modification therapy for behavioral dysregulation: Results from a pilot study targeting alcohol use and aggression in women. *Journal of Clinical Psychology, 68*, 50–66.

Wyer, R. (2004). The cognitive organization and use of general knowledge. In J. Jost & M. Banaji (Eds.), *Perspectivism in social psychology: The yin and yang of scientific progress*. Washington, DC: American Psychological Association.

Wyra, M., Lawson, M. J., & Hungi, N. (2007). The mnemonic keyword method: The effects of bidirectional retrieval training and of ability to image on foreign language vocabulary recall. *Learning and Instruction, 17*, 360–371.

Xie, R., Gaudet, L., Krewski, D., Graham, I. D., Walker, M. C., & Wen, S. W. (2015). Higher cesarean delivery rates are associated with higher infant mortality rates in industrialized countries. *Birth: Issues in Perinatal Care, 42*, 62–69.

Xing, X., Tao, F., Wan, Y., Xing, C., Qi, X., Hao, J., &… Huang, L. (2010). Family factors associated with suicide attempts among Chinese adolescent students: A national cross-sectional survey. *Journal of Adolescent Health, 46*, 592–599.

Xu, C., & LeFevre, J. (2016). Training young children on sequential relations among numbers and spatial decomposition: Differential transfer to number line and mental transformation tasks. *Developmental Psychology, 52*, 854–866.

Xu, J., Harper, J. A., Van Enkevort, E. A., Latimer, K., Kelley, U., & McAdams, C. J. (2017). Neural activations are related to body shape, anxiety, and outcomes in adolescent anorexia nervosa. *Journal of Psychiatric Research, 87*, 1–7.

Xu, J., Murphy, S. L., Kochanek, K. D., Bastian, B., Arias, E. (2018). Deaths: Final data for 2016. *National Vital Statistics Reports, 67*(6).

Xu, J., Saether, L., & Sommerville, J. A. (2016). Experience facilitates the emergence of

sharing behavior among 7.5-month-old infants. *Developmental Psychology, 52*, 1732–1743.

Xue, B., Cadar, D., Fleischmann, M., Stansfeld, S., Carr, E., Kivimäki, M., McMunn, A., & Head, J. (2018). Effect of retirement on cognitive function: The Whitehall II cohort study. *European Journal of Epidemiology, 33*(10), 989–1001.

Yagmurlu, B., & Sanson, A. (2009). Parenting and temperament as predictors of prosocial behaviour in Australian and Turkish Australian children. *Australian Journal of Psychology, 61*, 77–88.

Yamamoto, H. W., & Haryu, E. (2018). The role of pitch pattern in Japanese 24-month-olds' word recognition. *Journal of Memory and Language, 99*, 90–98.

Yaman, A., Mesman, J., van IJzendoorn, M., Bakermans-Kranenburg, M., & Linting, M. (2010). Parenting in an individualistic culture with a collectivistic cultural background: The case of Turkish immigrant families with toddlers in the Netherlands. *Journal of Child and Family Studies, 19*, 617–628.

Yan, J., Li, H., & Liao, Y. (2010). Developmental motor function plays a key role in visual search. *Developmental Psychobiology, 52*, 505–512.

Yang, C., & Brown, B. B. (2015). Factors involved in associations between Facebook use and college adjustment: Social competence, perceived usefulness, and use patterns. *Computers in Human Behavior, 46*, 245–253.

Yang, C., Crain, S., Berwick, R. C., Chomsky, N., & Bolhuis, J. J. (2017). The growth of language: Universal grammar, experience, and principles of computation. *Neuroscience and Biobehavioral Reviews*. Accessed online, 10/29/17; http://www.sciencedirect.com/science/article/pii/S0149763416305656

Yang, C. D. (2006). *The infinite gift: How children learn and unlearn the languages of the world*. New York, NY: Scribner.

Yang, H., Hartanto, A., & Yang, S. (2016). The importance of bilingual experience in assessing bilingual advantages in executive functions. *Cortex: A Journal Devoted to the Study of the Nervous System and Behavior, 75*, 237–240.

Yang, Q., Liu, S., Sullivan, D., & Pan, S. (2016). Interpreting suffering from illness: The role of culture and repressive suffering construal. *Social Science & Medicine, 160*, 67–74.

Yang, R., & Blodgett, B. (2000). Effects of race and adolescent decision-making on status attainment and self-esteem. *Journal of Ethnic & Cultural Diversity in Social Work, 9*, 135–153.

Yang, Y. (2008). Social inequalities in happiness in the U.S. 1972–2004: An age-period-cohort analysis. *American Sociological Review, 73*, 204–226.

Yanaoka, K., & Saito, S. (2017). Developing control over the execution of scripts: The role of maintained hierarchical goal representations. *Journal of Experimental Child Psychology, 163*, 87–106.

Yarber, W., & Sayad, B. (2019). *Human sexuality: Diversity in contemporary society*. New York: McGraw-Hill.

Yardley, J. (2001, July 2). Child-death case in Texas raises penalty questions. *The New York Times*, p. A1.

Yasnitsky, A., & van der Veer, R. (2016). *Revisionist revolution in Vygotsky studies*. New York, NY: Routledge/Taylor & Francis Group.

Ybarra, M. L., & Thompson, R. E. (2017). Predicting the emergence of sexual violence in adolescence. *Prevention Science*. Accessed online, 12/12/17; https://www.ncbi.nlm.nih.gov/pubmed/28685211

Yell, M. L. (2019). *The law and special education*. New York: Pearson.

Yeniasir, M., Gökbulut, B., & Yaraşir, Ö. (2017). Knowledge and opinions of families regarding games—Toy selection for 6- to 12-year-old children (the case of Northern Cyprus). *Journal of Human Behavior in the Social Environment, 27*(6), 546–558.

Yildiz, O. (2007). Vascular smooth muscle and endothelial functions in aging. *Annals of the New York Academy of Sciences, 1100*, 353–360.

Yim, I., Glynn, L., Schetter, C., Hobel, C., Chicz-DeMet, A., & Sandman, C. (2009). Risk of postpartum depressive symptoms with elevated corticotropin-releasing hormone in human pregnancy. *Archives of General Psychiatry, 66*, 162–169.

Yip, T., Sellers, R. M., & Seaton, E. K. (2006). African American racial identity across the lifespan: Identity status, identity content, and depressive symptoms. *Child Development, 77*, 1504–1517.

Yonker, J. E., Schnabelrauch, C. A., & DeHaan, L. G. (2012). The relationship between spirituality and religiosity on psychological outcomes in adolescents and emerging adults: A meta-analytic review. *Journal of Adolescence, 35*, 299–314.

Yoon, E., Adams, K., Clawson, A., Chang, H., Surya, S., & Jeremie-Brink, G. (2017). East Asian adolescents' ethnic identity development and cultural integration: A qualitative investigation. *Journal of Counseling Psychology, 64*, 65–79.

York, E. (2008). Gender differences in the college and career aspirations of high school valedictorians. *Journal of Advanced Academics, 19*, 578–600.

York, G. S., Churchman, R., Woodard, B., Wainright, C., & Rau-Foster, M. (2012). Free-text comments: Understanding the value in family member descriptions of hospice caregiver relationships. *American Journal of Hospice & Palliative Medicine, 29*, 98–105.

Yoshikawa, K., Wang, H., Jaen, C., Haneoka, M., Saito, N., Nakamura, J., Adappa, N. D., Cohen, N. A.,… Dalton, P. (2018). The human olfactory cleft mucus proteome and its age-related changes. *Scientific Reports, 8*(1), 17170.

Yoshinaga-Itano, C. (2003). From screening to early identification and intervention: Discovering predictors to successful outcomes for children with significant hearing loss. *Journal of Deaf Studies & Deaf Education, 8*, 11–30.

Yott, J., & Poulin-Dubois, D. (2016). Are infants' theory-of-mind abilities well integrated? Implicit understanding of intentions, desires, and beliefs. *Journal of Cognition and Development, 17*, 683–698.

You, J.-I., & Bellmore, A. (2012). Relational peer victimization and psychosocial adjustment: The mediating role of best friendship qualities. *Personal Relationships, 19*, 340–353.

Young, A. M., Elliston, A., & Ruble, L. A. (2016). Children with autism and vaccinations. In J. Merrick (Ed.), *Children and childhood: Some international aspects.* Hauppauge, NY: Nova Biomedical Books.

Young, G., & Teitelbaum, J. (2010). Brain drain: Using the deep venous system to declare brain death. *Canadian Journal of Neurological Sciences/ Le Journal Canadien Des Sciences Neurologiques, 37*, 429–430.

Young, S., Rhee, S., Stallings, M., Corley, R., & Hewitt, J. (2006, July). Genetic and environmental vulnerabilities underlying adolescent substance use and problem use: General or specific? *Behavior Genetics, 36*, 603–615.

Yousafzai, A. K., Yakoob, M. Y., & Bhutta, Z. A. (2013). Nutrition-based approaches to early childhood development. In P. Britto, P. L. Engle, & C. M. Super (Eds.), *Handbook of early childhood development research and its impact on global policy.* New York, NY: Oxford University Press.

Yu, C., Hung, C., Chan, T., Yeh, C., & Lai, C. (2012). Prenatal predictors for father-infant attachment after childbirth. *Journal of Clinical Nursing, 21*, 1577–1583.

Yu, M., & Stiffman, A. (2007). Culture and environment as predictors of alcohol abuse/dependence symptoms in American Indian youths. *Addictive Behaviors, 32*, 2253–2259.

Yuan, A. (2012). Perceived breast development and adolescent girls' psychological well-being. *Sex Roles, 66*, 790–806.

Zafeiriou, D. I. (2004). Primitive reflexes and postural reactions in the neurodevelopmental examination. *Pediatric Neurology, 31*, 1–8.

Zajac, L., Bookhout, M. K., Hubbard, J. A., Carlson, E. A., & Dozier, M. (2018). Attachment disorganization in infancy: A developmental precursor to maladaptive social information processing at age 8. *Child Development.* doi:10.1111/cdev.13140

Zakrzewski, A. C., Johnson, J. M., & Smith, J. D. (2017). The comparative psychology of metacognition. In J. Call, G. M. Burghardt, I. M. Pepperberg, C. T. Snowdon, & T. Zentall (Eds.), *APA handbook of comparative psychology: Perception, learning, and cognition.* Washington, DC: American Psychological Association.

Zalsman, G., Oquendo, M., Greenhill, L., Goldberg, P., Kamali, M., Martin, A., & Mann, J. J. (2006, October). Neurobiology of depression in children and adolescents. *Child and Adolescent Psychiatric Clinics of North America, 15*, 843–868.

Zampi, C., Fagioli, I., & Salzarulo, P. (2002). Time course of EEG background activity level before spontaneous awakening in infants. *Journal of Sleep Research, 11*, 283–287.

Zeanah, C. (2009). The importance of early experiences: Clinical, research and policy perspectives. *Journal of Loss and Trauma, 14*, 266–279.

Zeedyk, M., & Heimann, M. (2006). Imitation and socio-emotional processes: Implications for communicative development and interventions. *Infant and Child Development, 15*, 219–222.

Zeiders, K. H., Umaña-Taylor, A. J., & Derlan, C. L. (2013). Trajectories of depressive symptoms and self-esteem in Latino youths: Examining the role of gender and perceived discrimination. *Developmental Psychology, 49*, 951–963.

Zelazo, P. D., Muller, U., Frye, D., & Marcovitch, S. (2003). The development of executive function in early childhood. *Monographs of the Society for Research in Child Development, 68*, 103–122.

Zemach, I., Chang, S., & Teller, D. (2007). Infant color vision: Prediction of infants' spontaneous color preferences. *Vision Research, 47*, 1368–1381.

Zhang, J., Xiaonan Yu, N., Zhang, J., & Zhou, M. (2018). Age stereotypes, flexible goal adjustment, and well-being among Chinese older adults. *Psychology, Health & Medicine, 23*(2), 210–215.

Zhang, Q., Li, H., Zheng, A., Dong, X., & Tu, W. (2017). Evaluation of auditory perception development in neonates by event-related potential technique. *Brain & Development, 39*(7), 564–572.

Zhang, Y., Bokov, A., Gelfond, J., Soto, V., Ikeno, Y., Hubbard, G., &… Fischer, K. (2014). Rapamycin extends life and health in C57BL/6 mice. *Journals of Gerontology: Series A: Biological Sciences and Medical Sciences, 69A*, 119–130.

Zhang, Y., Zhou, X., Pu, J., Zhang, H., Yang, L., Liu, L., &… Xie, P. (2018). Antidepressants for depressive disorder in children and adolescents: A database of randomised controlled trials. *BMC Psychiatry, 18.*

Zhao, S., Wang, C., Huang, T., Chen, Y., Hsiao, C., Tseng, C., &… Chen, L. (2018). A qualitative study exploring the attitudes toward prenatal genetic testing for autism spectrum disorders among parents of affected children in Taiwan. *Research in Autism Spectrum Disorders, 48*, 36–43.

Zhe, C., & Siegler, R. S. (2000). Across the great divide: Bridging the gap between understanding of toddlers' and older children's thinking. *Monographs of the Society for Research in Child Development, 65*(2, Serial No. 261).

Zhu, J., & Weiss, L. (2005). The Wechsler Scales. In D. P. Flanagan & P. L. Harrison (Eds.), *Contemporary intellectual assessment: Theories, tests, and issues.* New York, NY: Guilford Press.

Ziegler, M., Danay, E., Heene, M., Asendorpf, J., & Bühner, M. (2012). Openness, fluid intelligence, and crystallized intelligence: Toward an integrative model. *Journal of Research in Personality, 46*, 173–183.

Zimmer-Gembeck, M. J., & Collins, W. A. (2003). Autonomy development during adolescence. In G. R. Adams, & M. D. Berzonsky (Eds.), *Blackwell handbook of adolescence.* Malden, MA: Blackwell Publishing.

Zimmerman, F. J., Christakis, D. A., & Meltzoff, A. N. (2007). Associations between media viewing and language development in children under age 2 years. *Journal of Pediatrics, 151*, 364–368.

Zisook, S., & Shear, K. (2009). Grief and bereavement: What psychiatrists need to know. *World Psychiatry, 8*, 67–74.

Zolotor, A., Theodore, A., Chang, J., Berkoff, M., & Runyan, D. (2008). Speak softly—and forget the stick: Corporal punishment and child physical abuse. *American Journal of Preventive Medicine, 35*, 364–369.

Zong, N., Nam, S., Eom, J., Ahn, J., Joe, H., & Kim, H. (2015). Aligning ontologies with subsumption and equivalence relations in Linked Data. *Knowledge-Based Systems, 76*, 30–41.

Zosuls, K. M., Field, R. D., Martin, C. L., Andrews, N. Z., & England, D. E. (2014). Gender-based relationship efficacy: Children's self-perceptions in intergroup contexts. *Child Development, 85*, 1663–1676.

Zosuls, K. M., Ruble, D. N., & Tamis-LeMonda, C. S. (2014). Self-socialization of gender in African American, Dominican immigrant, and Mexican immigrant toddlers. *Child Development, 85*, 2202–2217.

Zuccarini, M., Sansavini, A., Iverson, J. M., Savini, S., Guarini, A., Alessandroni, R., &… Aureli, T. (2016). Object engagement and manipulation in extremely preterm and full term infants at 6 months of age. *Research in Developmental Disabilities, 55*, 173–184.

Zuckerman, G., & Shenfield, S. D. (2007). Child-adult interaction that creates a zone of proximal development. *Journal of Russian & East European Psychology, 45*, 43–69.

Zuelke, A. E., Luck, T., Schroeter, M. L., Witte, A. V., Hinz, A., Engel, C.,… Riedel-Heller, S. G. (2018). The association between unemployment and depression–Results from the population-based LIFE-adult-study. *Journal of Affective Disorders, 235*, 399–406.

Zwelling, E. (2006). A challenging time in the history of Lamaze international: An interview with Francine Nichols. *Journal of Perinatal Education, 15*, 10–17.

Zyphur, M. J., Zhang, Z., Barsky, A. P., & Li, W. (2013). An ACE in the hole: Twin family models for applied behavioral genetics research. *Leadership Quarterly, 24*, 572–594.

Name Index

A

AAP Council on Communications and the Media, 128
Aaron, J., 445
AARP (American Association of Retired Persons), 402, 457
Aazami, S., 384
Abbot-Smith, K., 175
Abe, J., 314
Abele, A., 388
Abreu, R., 4
Abrutyn, S., 292
Accardo, P., 53
Acevedo, B.P., 334
Ackerman, B.P., 137
Acocella, J., 11
Adair, W.L., 7
Adak, M., 192
Adams, G.R., 285
Adams, K.B., 424
Adams, M., 337
Adams, P., 286
Adashi, E.Y., 43
Adebayo, B., 325
Adhya, D., 62
ADL 17, 391
Administration on Aging, 427, 428
Adolph, K.E., 112, 112
Afifi, T., 190, 192
Afifi, T.D., 253
Agcaoglu, O., 161
Ahmed, R., 387
Ahn, W., 141
Aichele, S., 411
Aiello, J., 347
Aiken L.R., 460
Aitchison, J., 130, 131, 132, 175, 175
Akamal, S., 384
Akhtar, S., 446
Aksan, N., 146
Al-Namlah, A.S., 175
Al-Owidha, A., 289
Albert, D., 267
Alberts, A., 76, 276, 278
Albrecht, G.L., 312
Aldana, E., 22
Alderfer, C., 231
Aldwin, C.M., 409
Alexander, B., 75
Alexander, G.M., 87, 148
Alfons, V., 432
Alfred, M., 7
Alisky, J.M., 405
Allam, M.D., 113
Allen J., 454
Allen, B., 193
Alleva, E., 100
Allison, B., 286
Allison, C.M., 261
Allison, S.J., 313
Almong, L., 19
Aloise-Young, P.A., 300
Alshaarawy, O., 68
Altarriba, J., 372
Altermatt, E.R., 245
Álvarez, M.J., 74
Alwin, D.F., 422
Alzheimer's Association, 405
Alzheimer's Association & Centers for Disease Control and Prevention, 404
Amato, P.R., 253
Ambrose, H.N., 144, 196
American Academy of Family Physicians, 88
American Academy of Pediatrics, 74, 88, 111, 163, 176, 190, 208
American Academy of Pediatrics HealthyChildren.org, 151

American Association of Community Colleges, 326
American Association on Intellectual and Developmental Disabilities, 232
American Cancer Society, 366
American College Health Association, 292
American College of Medical Genetics, 73
American College of Obstetricians and Gynecologists, 76
American College of Radiology, 366
American College of Sports Medicine, 313
American Psychological Association, 35, 191, 361
American SIDS Institute, 104
Ames, E., 28
Amichai-Hamburger, Y., 19
Amiri, S., 276
Amitai, Y., 69
Amler, R.W., 159
Ammerman, R.T., 191
Amsterlaw, J., 141, 187
Andelin, A., 434
Andenaes, A., 103
Anderson, J., 128
Anderson, K.N., 64
Anderson, M., 416
Anderson, R.A., 455
Anderson, R.E., 192
Anderson, S., 32
Andersson, M.A., 322
Andrade, F.D., 83
André-Pueyo, A., 26
Andreoni, J., 355
Andreotti, C., 316
Andrew, L., 296
Andrews B., 356
Andruski, J.E., 131
Angeles, F., 22
Ankrum, J.W., 173
Ansari, A., 178
Anthony, J.C., 68, 269
Antovich, D.M., 131
Antshel, K., 314
Antshel, K.M., 45
Anyan, F., 291
Anzman-Frasca, S., 101
Aoyagi, K., 286
APA Reproductive Choice Working Group, 64
Apgar, V., 73
Apostoleris, N.H., 248
Apperly, I., 220
Appleyard, K., 339
Arai, J., 52
Araujo, M.A., 407
Aravind, A., 174
Archer-Banks, D.A.M., 280
Archer, J., 196
Archer, M., 144
Archimi, A., 270
Argüello, T.M., 302
Aries, P., 11
Arístegui, I., 21
Armstrong, J., 87
Armstrong, P., 348
Arnarson, E.Ö., 375
Arnautovska, U., 292
Arnett, J.J., 5, 7, 295, 310, 332
Arnsten, A., 213
Aronson, M., 236
Arsenault, L., 58
Arts, J.A.R., 371
Asadi, S., 276
Asch, D.A., 454
Asher, S.R., 245
Atchley, R.C., 425, 447
Athanasiu, L., 99

Athanasopoulou, E., 79
Atkins, D.C., 381
Atkins, S.M., 277
Augestad, K.M., 454
Aujoulat, I., 245
Austen, E., 266
Austin, J., 48, 444
Avinun, R., 195
Avlund, K., 435
Ayalon, L., 382, 398
Aydiner, F., 63
Aylward, G.P., 127
Ayoola, A., 84
Ayoub, N.C., 76
Ayres, M.M., 285
Azagba, S., 271

B

Babenko, O., 51
Bacchus, L., 69
Bademli K., 421
Badenhorst, W., 83
Baer, J.S., 68
Bagci, S.C., 248
Bahna, S., 213
Bährer-Kohler, S., 389
Bahrick, L.E., 112, 114
Bai, S., 139
Baile, W.F., 445
Bailey-Davis, L., 265
Baillargeon, R., 122
Bainbridge, K.E., 402
Baker, J., 266
Baker, L.R., 380
Baker, P., 305
Baker, T., 271
Bakken, L., 178
Bakoyiannis, I., 68
Bal, E., 18
Balasubramaniam, M., 446
Balin, B.J., 405
Balish, S.M., 208
Balk, D.E., 446, 446, 450
Ball, H.L., 103
Ball, M., 390
Ballas, S., 47
Ballesteros-Meseguer, C., 72
Ballesteros, S., 4
Balsam, R.H., 13
Baltes, M.M., 370, 425, 426
Baltes, P., 423
Baltes, P.B., 9, 370, 423, 425, 426
Bandura, A., 15, 194, 195, 197
Banks M.E., 387
Baptista, T., 22
Barandiaran, X.E., 118
Barber, A.D., 161
Barber, B., 260
Barber, B.L., 270
Barber, S., 85
Barberá, E., 185
Barbieri, R.L., 360
Barboza, G., 247
Barker, E.D., 58
Barlett, C., 32, 246
Barnes, J.C., 47, 375
Barnett, R.C., 343
Baron-Cohen, S., 184
Barr, H.M., 68
Barr, R., 125
Barrera, M., 445
Barrett, D.E., 301
Barry, C.I., 32
Barry, D.T., 19
Barry, L.M., 328
Barsade, S.G., 334
Bartlett, C.P., 282
Bass, S., 254
Bates, J.E., 7
Battin, M., 454

Bauer, P.J., 125
Baulac, S., 405
Bauld, R., 360
Baum, A., 364
Baumann, U., 375
Baumrind D., 189
Bayley, N., 126, 368
Beach, S., 437
Beale, E.A., 445
Beals, K., 338
Beard, V.R., 457
Bearman, P., 306
Beaulieu, S., 22
Beck, M., 320, 360
Becker, B., 299
Becker, G., 346, 426
Begley, D., 76
Behar-Horenstein, L.S., 280
Behrman, J.R., 10
Behrman, R.E., 254
Behrmann, M., 161
Beilby, J.M., 212
Beisert, M., 90
Beitel, M., 19
Bekendam, M.T., 365
Belcastro, E.G., 173
Belcher, J.R., 250
Belkin, L., 44, 232
Bell, A., 304
Bell, T., 190
Bellmore, A., 333
Belsky, J., 152, 152, 152, 261
Beltz, A.M., 263
Ben-Noam, S., 349
Ben-Zeev, T., 328
Benelli, B., 220
Benenson, J.F., 248
Bengtson, V.L., 250, 384
Benjuya, N., 401
Bennani, L., 355
Benner, A.D., 286, 298
Bennett, J., 266
Benoit, A., 264
Benson, E., 138
Benson, S., 317
Benton S.A., 329
Bentz, W.E., 77
Berch, D.B., 21
Berends, M., 298
Berenson, P., 270
Bergelson, E., 135
Bergenn, V.W., 160
Berger, L., 252
Berger, S.E., 128
Bergin, C., 194
Bergman, A., 142, 143
Bergman, Y.S., 399
Bergmann, K.E., 79
Bergmann, R.L., 79
Bergström, M., 421, 424
Bergstrom, M.J., 424
Berking, M., 15
Berkman, R., 427
Berko, J., 175
Berkowitz, L., 29
Berlin, L., 339
Berlin, L.J., 143
Bernard, J., 337
Bernard, M., 446
Bernier, A., 143
Bernstein, D.M., 171
Bernstein, E., 380
Bernstein, N., 306
Berridge, C., 213
Berry, A., 100
Berry, G.L., 176
Berscheid, E, 334
Berscheid, E., 334
Bertera, E.M., 385
Bertoncini, J., 131

Subject Index

Answers to Check Yourself Questions

Chapter 1

Module 1.1
(1) a
(2) b
(3) c
(4) a

Module 1.2
(1) d
(2) c
(3) c
(4) a

Module 1.3
(1) b
(2) b
(3) a
(4) c

Chapter 2

Module 2.1
(1) b
(2) d
(3) d
(4) b

Module 2.2
(1) a
(2) c
(3) a—fetal, b—embryonic, c—germinal
(4) b

Module 2.3
(1) a
(2) d
(3) d
(4) d

Chapter 3

Module 3.1
(1) d
(2) b
(3) a
(4) d

Module 3.2
(1) d
(2) b
(3) b
(4) a

Module 3.3
(1) c
(2) c
(3) b
(4) d

Chapter 4

Module 4.1
(1) c
(2) d
(3) a
(4) b

Module 4.2
(1) a
(2) c
(3) b
(4) d

Module 4.3
(1) c
(2) b
(3) a
(4) b

Chapter 5

Module 5.1
(1) b
(2) a
(3) d
(4) b

Module 5.2
(1) b
(2) c
(3) d
(4) c

Module 5.3
(1) b
(2) c
(3) d
(4) b

Chapter 6

Module 6.1
(1) c
(2) d
(3) d
(4) b

Module 6.2
(1) b
(2) a
(3) b
(4) d

Module 6.3
(1) b
(2) d
(3) a
(4) c

Chapter 7

Module 7.1
(1) c
(2) b
(3) d
(4) a

Module 7.2
(1) c
(2) a
(3) c
(4) b

Module 7.3
(1) d
(2) d
(3) b
(4) a

Chapter 8

Module 8.1
(1) b
(2) c
(3) d
(4) a

Module 8.2
(1) c
(2) b
(3) a
(4) a

Module 8.3
(1) c
(2) c
(3) d
(4) a

Chapter 9

Module 9.1
(1) d
(2) a
(3) c
(4) c

Module 9.2
(1) c
(2) a
(3) c
(4) b

Module 9.3
(1) d
(2) b
(3) a
(4) b

Chapter 10

Module 10.1
(1) a
(2) b
(3) b
(4) c

Module 10.2
(1) d
(2) d
(3) d
(4) b

Module 10.3
(1) c
(2) c
(3) a
(4) d